CLYMER®

VOLVO PENTA

STERN DRIVE SHOP MANUAL

1994-2000

The world's finest publisher of mechanical how-to manuals

PRIMEDIA
Business Directories & Books

P.O. Box 12901, Overland Park, KS 66282-2901

FIRST EDITION
First Printing November, 1997
SECOND EDITION
First Printing October, 2000
Second Printing February, 2002
Third Printing January, 2003
Fourth Printing December, 2003

Printed in U.S.A.
CLYMER and colophon are registered trademarks of PRIMEDIA Business Magazines and Media Inc.
This book was printed at Von Hoffmann an ISO certified company.
ISBN: 0-89287-753-7
Library of Congress: 00-107262

Tools shown in Chapter Two courtesy of Thorsen Tool, Dallas, Texas. Test equipment shown in Chapter Two courtesy of Dixson, Inc., Grand Junction, Colorado.

Technical illustrations by Micheal St. Clair, Robert Caldwell and Steve Amos.

Technical assistance provided by Mike Burleson, Burleson Marine, Garland, Texas.

COVER: Courtesy of Cobalt Boat Company, Neodeska, Kansas.

PRODUCTION: Veronica Bollin.

CLYMER PUBLICATIONS

PRIMEDIA Business Magazines & Media

Chief Executive Officer Martin Maleska
Senior Vice President, Sales Operation John French
Vice President, PRIMEDIA Business Directories & Books Bob Moraczewski

EDITORIAL

Managing Editor
James Grooms

Associate Editor
Jason Beaver

Technical Writers
Ron Wright
Ed Scott
George Parise
Mark Rolling
Michael Morlan
Jay Bogart

Editorial Production Manager
Dylan Goodwin

Senior Production Editors
Greg Araujo
Shirley Renicker

Production Editors
Holly Messinger
Shara Pierceall
Darin Watson

Associate Production Editor
Susan Hartington

Technical Illustrators
Steve Amos
Errol McCarthy
Mitzi McCarthy
Bob Meyer
Mike Rose

MARKETING/SALES AND ADMINISTRATION

Publisher
Shawn Etheridge

Marketing Manager
Elda Starke

Advertising & Promotions Coordinators
Melissa Abbott
Wendy Stringfellow

Art Directors
Chris Paxton

Sales Managers
Ted Metzger, Manuals
Dutch Sadler, Marine
Matt Tusken, Motorcycles

Sales Coordinator
Marcia Jungles

Operations Manager
Patricia Kowalczewski

Customer Service Manager
Terri Cannon

Customer Service Supervisor
Ed McCarty

Customer Service Representatives
Susan Kohlmeyer
April LeBlond
Courtney Hollars
Jennifer Lassiter
Ernesto Suarez
Shawna Davis

Warehouse & Inventory Manager
Leah Hicks

The following product lines are published by PRIMEDIA Business Directories & Books.

The Electronics Source Book®

More information available at *primediabooks.com*

Contents

CHAPTER FOUR
LUBRICATION, MAINTENANCE AND TUNE-UP 75

CHAPTER FIVE
LAY-UP, COOLING SYSTEM SERVICE AND FITTING OUT 112

CHAPTER SIX
3.0 LITER 4-CYLINDER ENGINES 120

CHAPTER SEVEN
4.3 LITER V6, 5.0, 5.7, 7.4 AND 8.2 LITER V8 ENGINES 165

CHAPTER EIGHT
5.0 LITER AND 5.8 LITER V8 ENGINES 228

CHAPTER NINE
FUEL DELIVERY SYSTEMS 283

CHAPTER TEN
COOLING SYSTEM 369

CHAPTER ELEVEN
ELECTRICAL SYSTEMS 385

CHAPTER TWELVE
DRIVE UNIT AND UPPER GEARCASE 416

Quick Reference Data

IGNITION SYSTEM APPLICATION

Model	Fuel system	Ignition type	Firing order
3.0	Carburetor	Delco EST[1]	1-3-4-2
4.3	Carburetor	Delco EST[1]	1-6-5-4-3-2
4.3	Fuel injection	Delco EST[1] and Di[4]	1-6-5-4-3-2
5.0	Carburetor	Prestolite BID[2]	1-3-7-2-6-5-4-8
5.0	Fuel injection	TFI-IV[3]	1-3-7-2-6-5-4-8
5.0	Carburetor	Prestolite BID	1-8-4-3-6-5-7-2
5.0	Fuel injection	Delco EST[1] and Di[4]	1-8-4-3-6-5-7-2
5.7	Carburetor	Prestolite BID[2]	1-8-4-3-6-5-7-2
5.7	Fuel injection	Delco EST[1] and Di[4]	1-8-4-3-6-5-7-2
5.8	Carburetor	Prestolite BID[2]	1-3-7-2-6-5-4-8
5.8	Fuel injection	TFI-IV[3]	1-3-7-2-6-5-4-8
7.4	Carburetor	Prestolite BID[2]	1-8-4-3-6-5-7-2
7.4	Fuel injection	Delco EST[1] and Di[4]	1-8-4-3-6-5-7-2
8.2	Carburetor	Prestolite BID[2]	1-8-4-3-6-5-7-2
8.2	Fuel injection	Delco EST[1] and Di[4]	1-8-4-3-6-5-7-2

1. (EST) Delco electronic spark timing system.
2. (BID) Prestolite breakerless inductive distributor.
3. (TFI-IV) Thick film integrated ignition system.
4. (Di) Distributor ignition system.

IGNITION SYSTEM SPECIFICATIONS

EST and Di coil	
Primary resistance	1.35-1.45 ohms
Secondary resistance	7,500-9,000 ohms
Pickup coil resistance	700-900 ohms
Operating amperage @ 75° F (24° C)	1.0 amp maximum*
BID coil	
Primary resistance	1.43-1.58 ohms
Secondary resistance	7,500-6,700 ohms
Operating amperage @ 75° F (24° C)	1.0 maximum*
BID sensor air gap	0.203 mm (0.008 in.)

*Coil must be able to sustain 25-30 kilovolts for 30 seconds.

ENGINE OIL VISCOSITY/TEMPERATURE

Above 32° F (0° C)	SAE 30
0 to 32 ° F (-18 to 0° C)	SAE 20W-20
Below 0° F (-18° C)	SAE 10W

APPROXIMATE ENGINE OIL CAPACITIES

Model	Hp	Displacement Liters (cid)	Cyls.	Capacity* qt (L) with filter	without filter
3.0 GL	120	3.0 (181)	4	4.0 (3.8)	3.5 (3.3)
3.0 GS	135	3.0 (181)	4	4.0 (3.8)	3.5 (3.3)

APPROXIMATE ENGINE OIL CAPACITIES (continued)

Model	Hp	Displacement Liters (cid)	Cyls.	Capacity* qt (L) with filter	Capacity* qt (L) without filter
4.3 GL	160	4.3 (262)	V6	4.5 (4.3)	4.0 (3.8)
4.3 GS	185	4.3 (262)	V6	4.5 (4.3)	4.0 (3.8)
4.3 Gi	180	4.3 (262)	V6	4.5 (4.3)	4.0 (3.8)
5.0 FL	190	5.0 (302)	V8	6.0 (5.7)	5.0 (4.7)
5.0 Fi	220	5.0 (302)	V8	6.0 (5.7)	5.0 (4.7)
5.0 GL	220	5.0 (305)	V8	6.0 (5.68)	5.0 (4.73)
5.0 Gi	250	5.0 (305)	V8	6.0 (5.68)	5.0 (4.73)
5.7 GL	225	5.7 (350)	V8	5.0 (4.7)	4.0 (3.8)
5.7 Gi	250	5.7 (350)	V8	6.0 (5.7)	5.0 (4.7)
5.7 GS	250	5.7 (350)	V8	6.0 (5.68)	5.0 (4.73)
5.7 GSi	280	5.7 (350)	V8	6.0 (5.68)	5.0 (4.73)
5.8 FL	230-235	5.8 (351)	V8	6.0 (5.7)	5.0 (4.7)
5.8 Fi	255	5.8 (351)	V8	5.0 (4.7)	4.0 (3.8)
5.8 FSi	265	5.8 (351)	V8	5.0 (4.7)	4.0 (3.8)
7.4 GL	300	7.4 (454)	V8	7.0 (6.6)	6.0 (5.7)
7.4 Gi	330	7.4 (454)	V8	9.0 (8.5)	8.0 (7.5)
7.4 GSi	385	7.4 (454)	V8	9.0 (8.5)	8.0 (7.5)
8.2 GL/DPX	390	8.2 (502)	V8	7.0 (6.6)	6.0 (5.7)

* All capacaties in this table are approximate. To ensure correct oil level and prevent overfilling the engine, always use the dipstick as recommended in the text.

RECOMMENDED STERN DRIVE LUBRICANTS

Model	Lubricant
SX	
Driveshaft splines	Molybdenum grease
Gear unit	Volvo Penta DuraPlus synthetic GL5 gear oil
Gimbal bearing	Wheel bearing grease
Universal joints	Wheel bearing grease
DP	
Driveshaft splines	Molybdenum grease
Gear unit	Mineral GL5 API gear oil
Steering shaft bearings	
Upper and lower	Water resistant grease
Universal joints	Wheel bearing grease
DPX	
Driveshaft splines	Molybdenum grease
Gear unit	Volvo Penta DuraPlus synthetic GL5 gear oil
Steering shaft bearings	
Upper & lower	Water resistant grease
Universal joints	Wheel bearing grease

APPROXIMATE STERN DRIVE CAPACITIES

Model	Capacity
SX	71 oz (2.1 L)
DP	
Standard and 1 in. (25.4 mm) extension	2 3/4 qt (2.6 L)
With 4 in. (101.6 mm) extension	3 qt (2.8 L)

SPARK PLUG APPLICATION

Engine model	Ignition	Spark plugs Make	Type	Gap mm (in.)	Torque N.m (ft.-lb.)
3.0	EST	AC	MR43LTS	1.143 (0.045)	27 (20)
4.3 GL & GS 1994-1997	EST	AC	MR43T	1.143 (0.045)	30 (22)
4.3 Gi 1994-1997	EST	AC	R43TS	1.143 (0.045)	30 (22)
4.3 GL, GS, & Gi 1998-on	EST & Di	AC	MR43LTS	1.143 (0.045)	30 (22)
5.0 FL	BID	MC[1]	ASF32C	0.889 (0.035)	6.7-13.5 (5-10)
5.0 Fi	TFI-IV	MC[1]	AWSF32C	1.143 (0.045)	6.7-13.5(5-10)
5.0 GL & GS 1998-on	BID	AC	MR43LTS	0.89 (0.035)	27 (20)
5.0 Gi 1998-on	Di	CHP[2]	RS12YC	1.143 (0.045)	27 (20)
5.7 GL 1994-1997	BID	AC	MR43T	1.143 (0.045)	30 (22)
5.7 Gi 1994-1997	EST	AC	R43TS	1.143 (0.045)	30 (22)
5.7 GS 1998-on	EST	AC	MR43LTS	0.89 (0.035)	27 (20)
5.7 GSi 1998-on	Di	AC	MR43LTS	1.143 (0.045)	27 (20)
5.8 FL	BID	MC[1]	ASF32C	0.889 (0.035)	6.7-13.5 (5-10)
5.8 Fi & FSi	TFI-IV	MC[1]	AWSF22C	0.889 (0.035)	6.7-13.5 (5-10)
7.4 GL 1994-1997	BID	AC	MR43T	1.143 (0.045)	30 (22)
7.4 Gi 1994-1997	EST	AC	R43TS	1.143 (0.045)	30 (22)
7.4 Gi 1998-on	Di	AC	MR43LTS	1.143 (0.045)	27 (20)
7.4 GSi	EST & Di	AC	MR43T	1.143 (0.045)	27 (20)
8.2 GL 1994-1997	BID	AC	MR43T	1.143 (0.045)	30 (22)
8.2 GSi 1998-on	Di	AC	MR43T	1.143 (0.045)	27 (20)

1. MC – Motorcraft
2. CHP – Champion

RECOMMENDED THERMOSTAT

	Starts opening °F (C)	Fully open °F (C)
3.0 L	157-163 (69.5-72.8)	182 (83.4)
4.3 L	157-163 (69.5-72.8)	182 (83.4)
5.0/5.8 L (Ford)	157-163 (69.5-72.8)	182 (83.4)
5.0/5.7 L	157-163 (69.5-72.8)	182 (83.4)
7.4/8.2 L	138-142 (58.9-61.1)	162 (72.3)

VOLVO PENTA MODELS

Model	Hp	Displacement Liters (cid)
3.0 GL[1]	120	3.0 (181)
3.0 GS[1]	135	3.0 (181)
4.3 GL[1]	160	4.3 (262)
4.3 GS[1]	185	4.3 (262)
4.3 Gi[1]	180	4.3 (262)
5.0 FL[2]	190	5.0 (302)
5.0 Fi[2]	220	5.0 (302)
5.0 GL[1]	220	5.0 (305)
5.0 Gi[1]	250	5.0 (305)
5.7 GL[1]	225	5.7 (350)
5.7 Gi[1]	250	5.7 (350)
5.7 GS[1]	250	5.7 (350)
5.7 GSI[1]	280	5.7 (350)
5.8 FL[2]	235	5.8 (351)
5.8 Fi[2]	255	5.8 (351)
5.8 FSi[2]	265	5.8 (351)
7.4 GL[1]	300	7.4 (454)
7.4 Gi[1]	330	7.4 (454)
7.4 GSi[1]	385	7.4 (454)
8.2 GL[1]	390	8.2 (502)
8.2 GSi[1]	415	8.2 (502)

1. GM Product
2. Ford Product

CLYMER®

VOLVO PENTA

STERN DRIVE SHOP MANUAL

1994-2000

Introduction

This Clymer shop manual covers the engine and stern drive of all Volvo Penta models from 1994-on. Step-by-step instructions and hundreds of illustrations guide you through jobs ranging from simple maintenance to a complete overhaul.

This manual can be used by anyone from a first-time do-it-yourselfer to a professional mechanic. Easy-to-read type, detailed drawings and clear photographs give you all the information you need to do the work right.

Having a well-maintained engine and stern drive unit will increase your enjoyment of your boat as well as ensure your safety when offshore. Keep this shop manual handy and use it often. It can save you hundreds of dollars in maintenance and repair bills and make yours a reliable, top-performing boat.

Chapter One

General Information

This detailed, comprehensive manual contains complete information covering maintenance, repair and overhaul. Hundreds of photos and drawings guide the reader through every procedure.

Troubleshooting, tune-up, maintenance and repair are not difficult if you know what tools and equipment to use and what to do. Anyone not afraid to get their hands dirty, of average intelligence and with some mechanical ability can perform most of the procedures in this manual. See Chapter Two for more information on tools and techniques.

A shop manual is a reference. You want to be able to find information quickly. Clymer books are designed with you in mind. All chapters are thumb tabbed and important items are indexed at the end of the manual. All procedures, tables, photos and instructions in this manual assume the reader may be working on the machine or using the manual for the first time.

Keep the manual in a handy place in your toolbox or boat. It will help you to better understand how your boat runs, lower repair and maintenance costs and generally increase your enjoyment of your boat.

MANUAL ORGANIZATION

This chapter provides general information useful to boat owners and marine mechanics.

Chapter Two discusses the tools and techniques for preventative maintenance, troubleshooting and repair.

Chapter Three provides troubleshooting and testing procedures for all systems and individual components.

Following chapters describe specific systems, providing disassembly, inspection, assembly and adjustment procedures in simple step-by-step form. Specifications concerning a specific system are included at the end of the appropriate chapter.

NOTES, CAUTIONS AND WARNINGS

The terms NOTE, CAUTION and WARNING have specific meanings in this manual. A NOTE provides additional information to make a step or procedure easier or more clear. Disregarding a NOTE could cause inconvenience, but would not cause damage or personal injury.

A CAUTION emphasizes areas where equipment damage could cause permanent mechanical damage; however, personal injury is unlikely.

A WARNING emphasizes areas where personal injury or even death could result from negligence. Mechanical damage may also occur. WARNINGS *must* be taken seriously. In some cases, serious injury or death has resulted from disregarding similar warnings.

TORQUE SPECIFICATIONS

Torque specifications throughout this manual are given in foot-pounds (ft.-lb.), inch-pounds (in.-lb.) and newton meters (N•m.). Newton meters are being adopted in place of meter-kilograms (mkg) in accordance with the International Modernized Metric System. Existing torque wrenches calibrated in meter-kilograms can be used by performing a simple conversion: move the decimal point one place to the right. For example, 4.7 mkg = 47 N•m. This conversion is accurate enough for most mechanical operations even though the exact mathematical conversion is 3.5 mkg = 34.3 N•m.

ENGINE OPERATION

All marine engines, whether two or four-stroke, gasoline or diesel, operate on the Otto cycle of intake, compression, power and exhaust phases.

Two-Stroke Cycle

A two-stroke engine requires one crankshaft revolution (two strokes of the piston) to complete the Otto cycle. All engines covered in this manual are a two-stroke design. **Figure 1** shows gasoline two-stroke engine operation.

Four-Stroke Cycle

A four-stroke engine requires two crankshaft revolutions (four strokes of the piston) to complete the Otto cycle. **Figure 2** shows gasoline four-stroke engine operation.

FASTENERS

The material and design of the various fasteners used on marine equipment are carefully thought out and designed. Fastener design determines the type of tool required to work with the fastener. Fastener material is carefully selected to decrease the possibility of physical failure or corrosion. See *Galvanic Corrosion* in this chapter for information on marine materials.

Nuts, bolts and screws are manufactured in a wide range of thread patterns. To join a nut and bolt, the diameter of the bolt and the diameter of the hole in the nut must be the same. It is just as important that the threads are compatible.

The easiest way to determine if fastener threads are compatible is to turn the nut on the bolt, or bolt into its threaded opening, using fingers only. Be sure both pieces are clean. If much force is required, check the thread condition on each fastener. If the thread condition is good but the fasteners jam, the threads are not compatible.

Four important specifications describe the thread:

1. Diameter.
2. Threads per inch.
3. Thread pattern.

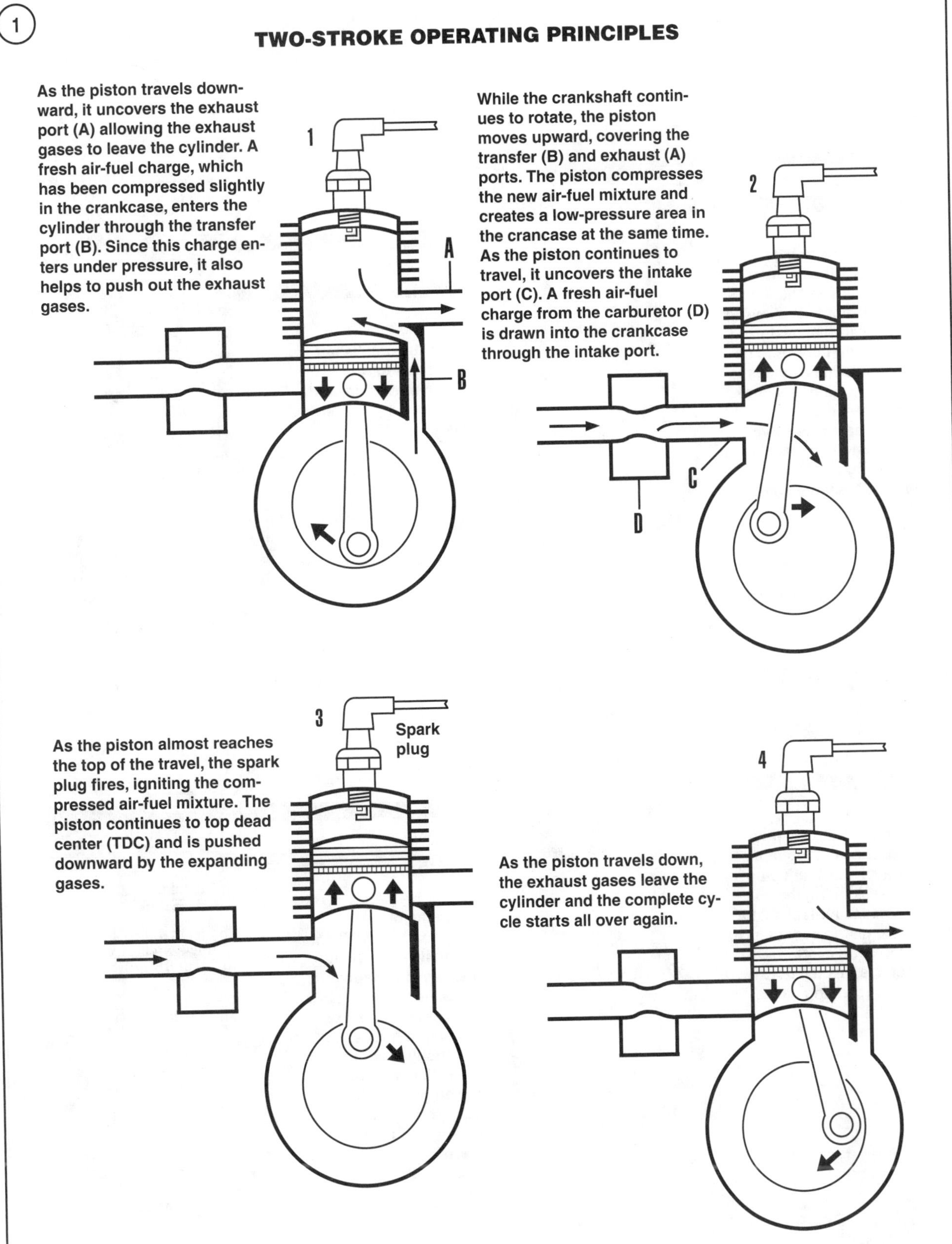
1
TWO-STROKE OPERATING PRINCIPLES
As the piston travels downward, it uncovers the exhaust port (A) allowing the exhaust gases to leave the cylinder. A fresh air-fuel charge, which has been compressed slightly in the crankcase, enters the cylinder through the transfer port (B). Since this charge enters under pressure, it also helps to push out the exhaust gases.
1
A
B
While the crankshaft continues to rotate, the piston moves upward, covering the transfer (B) and exhaust (A) ports. The piston compresses the new air-fuel mixture and creates a low-pressure area in the crancase at the same time. As the piston continues to travel, it uncovers the intake port (C). A fresh air-fuel charge from the carburetor (D) is drawn into the crankcase through the intake port.
2
C
D
As the piston almost reaches the top of the travel, the spark plug fires, igniting the compressed air-fuel mixture. The piston continues to top dead center (TDC) and is pushed downward by the expanding gases.
3
Spark plug
4
As the piston travels down, the exhaust gases leave the cylinder and the complete cycle starts all over again.

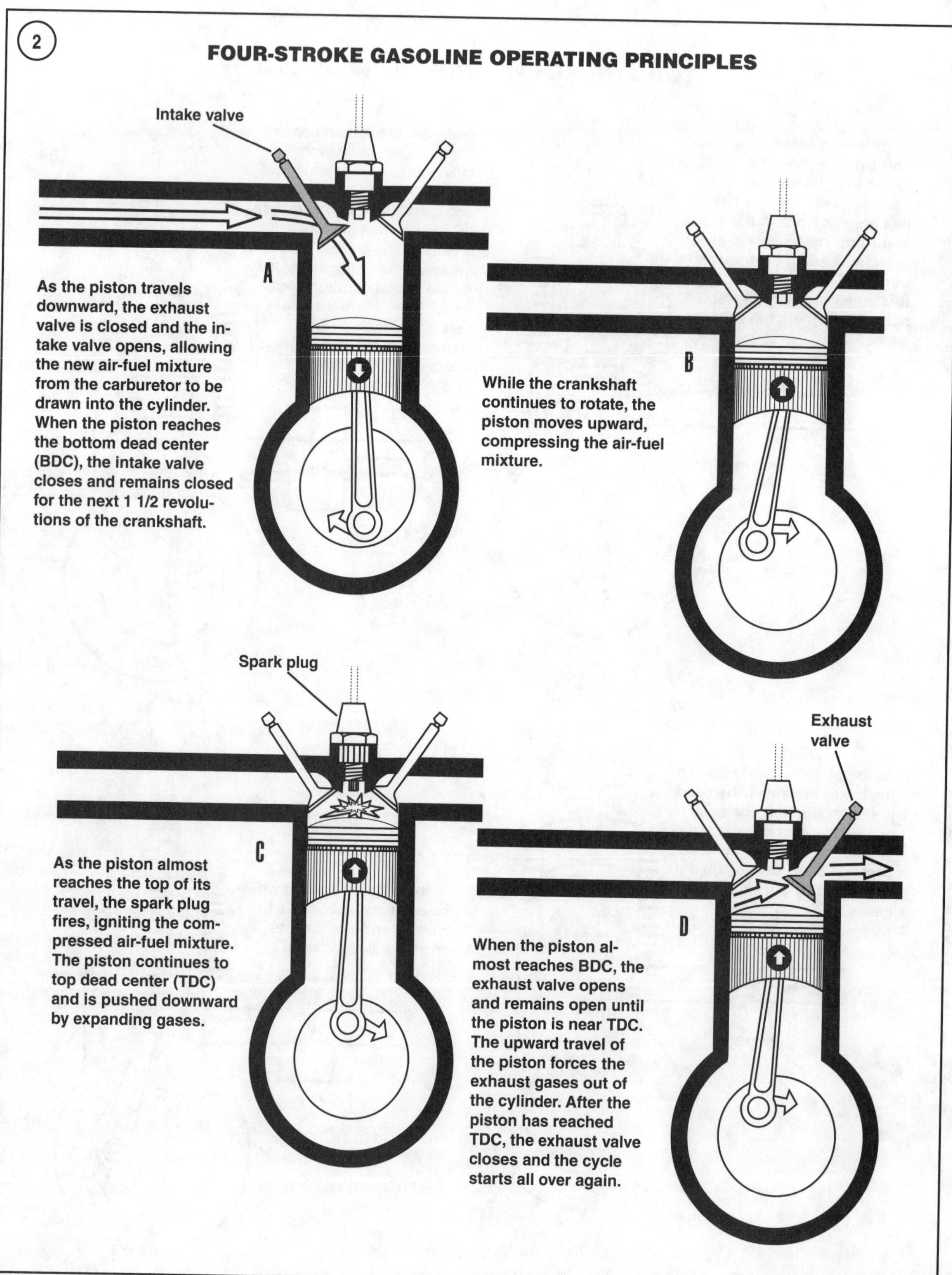
2
FOUR-STROKE GASOLINE OPERATING PRINCIPLES
Intake valve
A
As the piston travels downward, the exhaust valve is closed and the intake valve opens, allowing the new air-fuel mixture from the carburetor to be drawn into the cylinder. When the piston reaches the bottom dead center (BDC), the intake valve closes and remains closed for the next 1 1/2 revolutions of the crankshaft.
B
While the crankshaft continues to rotate, the piston moves upward, compressing the air-fuel mixture.
Spark plug
C
As the piston almost reaches the top of its travel, the spark plug fires, igniting the compressed air-fuel mixture. The piston continues to top dead center (TDC) and is pushed downward by expanding gases.
Exhaust valve
D
When the piston almost reaches BDC, the exhaust valve opens and remains open until the piston is near TDC. The upward travel of the piston forces the exhaust gases out of the cylinder. After the piston has reached TDC, the exhaust valve closes and the cycle starts all over again.

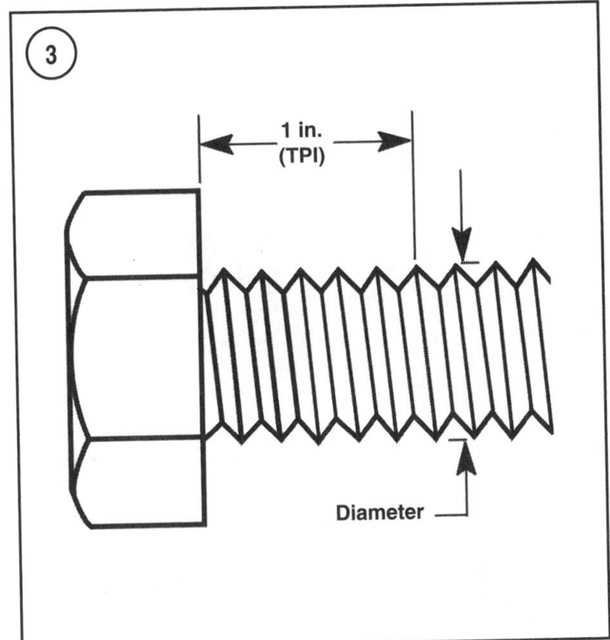

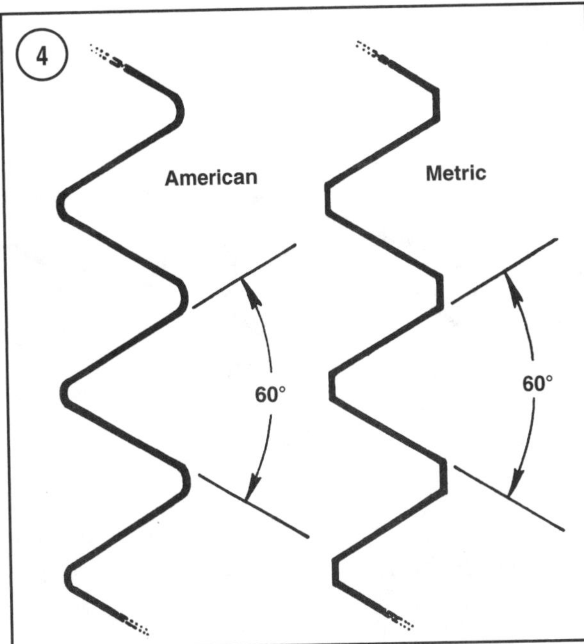

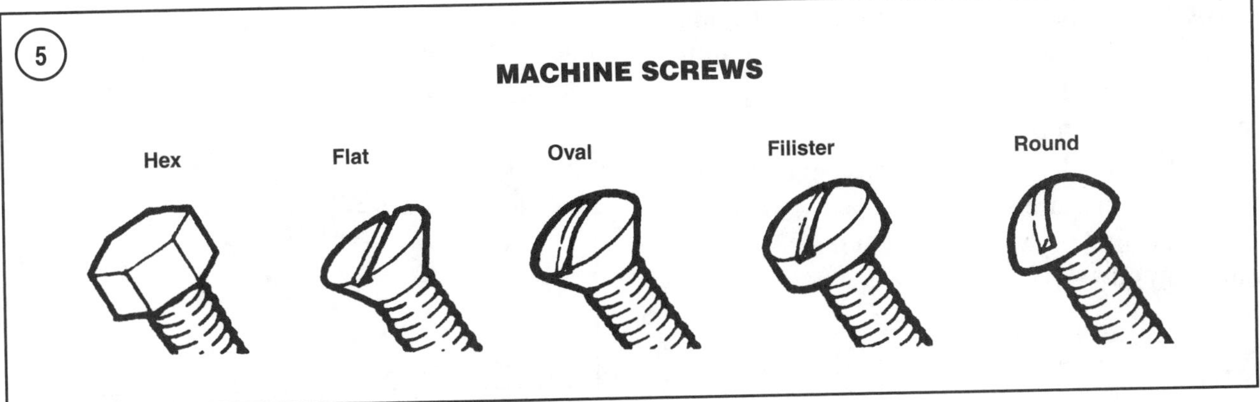

4. Thread direction

Figure 3 shows the first two specifications. Thread pattern is more subtle. Italian and British standards exist, but the most commonly used by marine equipment manufactures are American standard and metric standard. The root and top of the thread are cut differently as shown in **Figure 4**.

Most threads are cut so the fastener must be turned clockwise to tighten it. These are called right-hand threads. Some fasteners have left-hand threads; they must be turned counterclockwise to tighten. Left-hand threads are used in locations where normal rotation of the equipment would tend to loosen a right-hand threaded fastener. Assume all fasteners use right-hand threads unless the instructions specify otherwise.

Machine Screws

There are many different types of machine screws (**Figure 5**). Most are designed to protrude above the secured surface (rounded head) or be slightly recessed below the surface (flat head). In some applications the screw head is recessed well below the fastened sur-

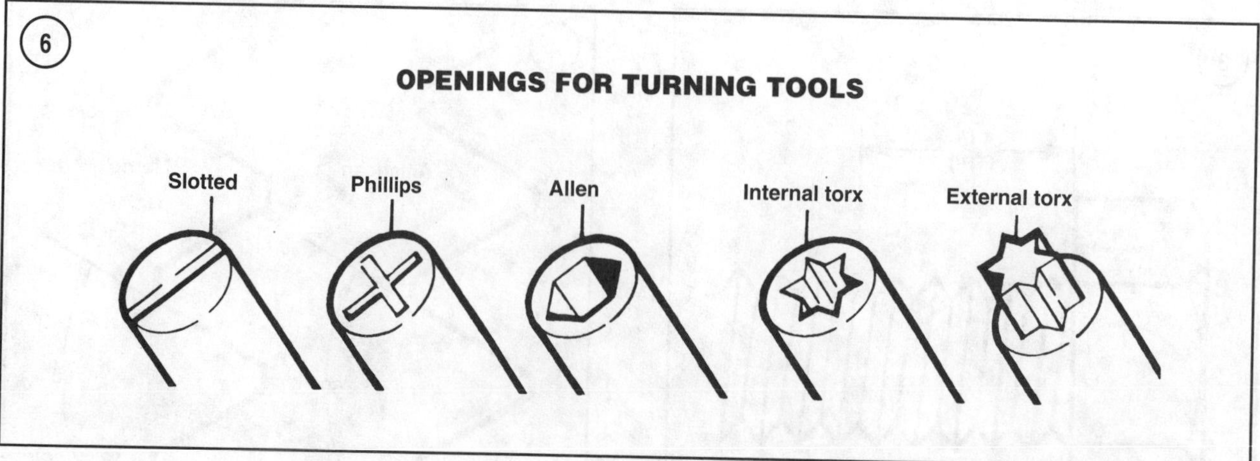

face. **Figure 6** shows a number of screw heads requiring different types of turning tools.

Bolts

Commonly called bolts, the technical name for this fastener is cap screw. They are normally described by diameter, threads per inch and length. For example, 1/4-20 × 1 indicates a bolt 1/4 in. in diameter with 20 threads per inch, 1 in. long. The measurement across two flats of the bolt head indicates the proper wrench size required to turn the bolt.

Nuts

Nuts are manufactured in a variety of types and sizes. Most are hexagonal (six-sides) and fit on bolts, screws and studs with the same diameter and threads per inch.

Figure 7 shows several types of nuts. The common nut is usually used with some type of lockwasher. Self-locking nuts have a nylon insert that helps prevent the nut from loosening; no lockwasher is required. Wing nuts are designed for fast removal by hand. Wing nuts are used for convenience in non-critical locations.

To indicate the size of a nut, manufactures specify the diameter of the opening and the threads per inch. This is similar to a bolt specification, but without the length dimension. The measurement across two flats of the nut indicates the wrench size required to turn the nut.

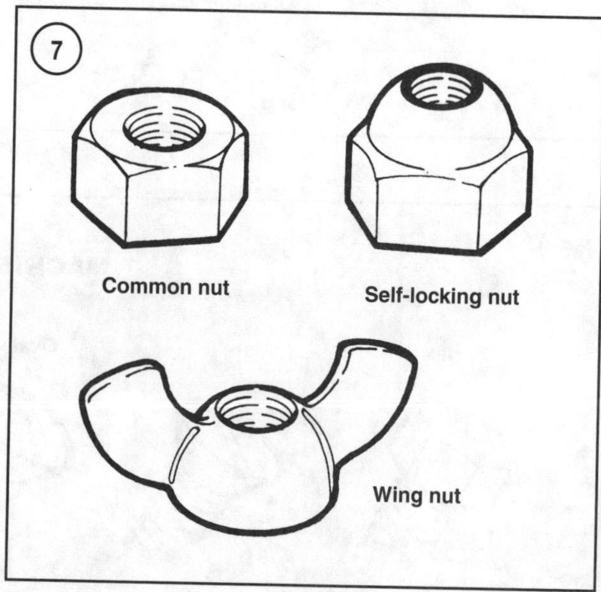

Washers

There are two basic types of washers: flat washers and lockwashers. A flat washer is a simple disc with a hole that fits the screw or bolt. Lockwashers are designed to prevent a fastener from working loose due to vibration, expansion and contraction. **Figure 8** shows several types of lockwashers. Note that flat washers are often

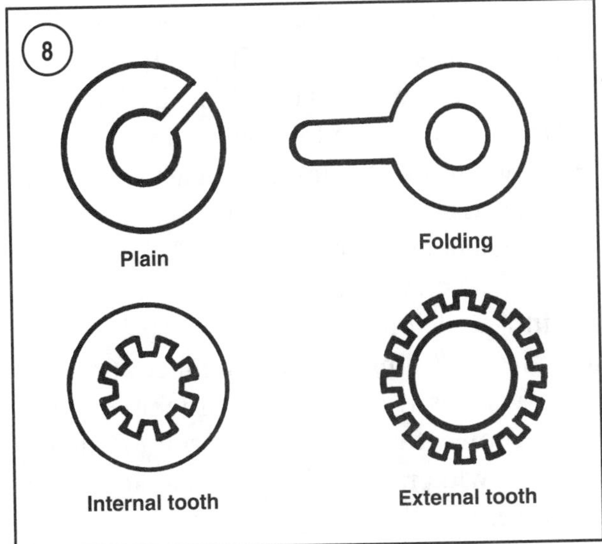

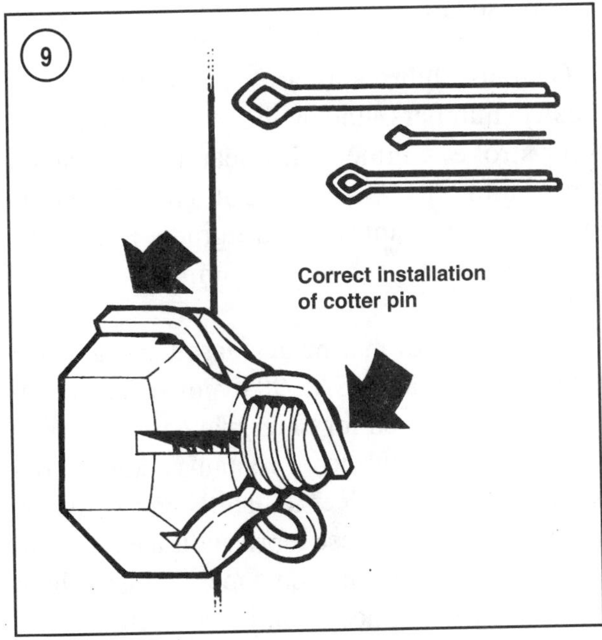

used between a lockwasher and a fastener to provide a smooth bearing surface. This allows the fastener to be turned easily with a tool.

Cotter Pins

In certain applications, a fastener must be secured so it cannot possibly loosen. The propeller nut on some marine drive systems is one such application. For this purpose, a cotter pin (**Figure 9**) and slotted or castellated nut is often used. To use a cotter pin, first make sure the pin fits snugly, but not too tight. Then, align a slot in the fastener with the hole in the bolt or axle. Insert the cotter pin through the nut and bolt or propeller shaft and bend the ends over to secure the cotter pin tightly. If the holes do not align, tighten the nut just enough to obtain the proper alignment. Unless specifically instructed to do so, never loosen the fastener to align the slot and hole. Because the cotter pin is weakened after installation and removal, never reuse a cotter pin. Cotter pins are available in several styles, lengths and diameters. Measure cotter pin length from the bottom of its head to the tip of its shortest prong.

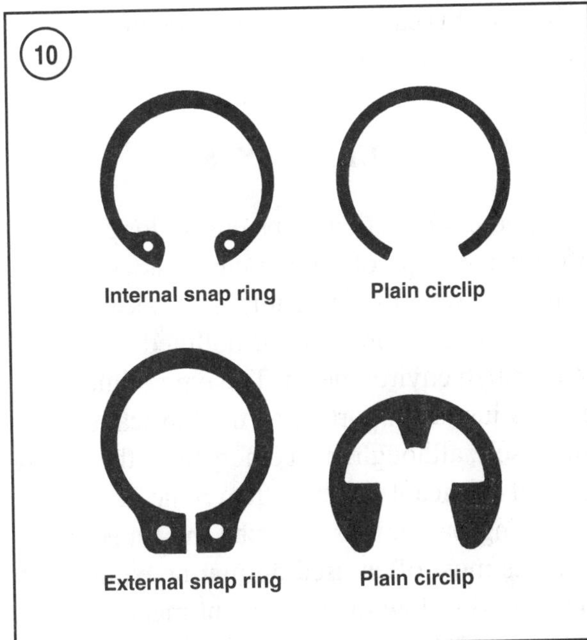

Snap Rings

Snap rings (**Figure 10**) can be an internal or external design. They are used to retain components on shafts (external type) or inside openings (internal type). Snap rings can be reused if they are not distorted during removal. In some applications, snap rings of varying thickness (selective fit) can be selected to position or control end play of parts assemblies.

LUBRICANTS

Periodic lubrication helps ensure long service life for any type of equipment. It is especially important with marine equipment because it is exposed to salt, brackish or polluted water and other harsh environments. The type of lubricant used is just as important as the lubrication service itself, although in an emergency, the wrong type of lubricant is better than none at all. The following paragraphs describe the types of lubricants most often used on marine equipment. Be sure to follow the equipment manufacture's recommendations for the lubricant types.

Generally, all liquid lubricants are called *oil.* They may be mineral-based (including petroleum bases), natural-based (vegetable and animal bases), synthetic-based or emulsions (mixtures).

Grease is lubricating oil that has had a thickening compound added. The resulting material is then usually enhanced with anticorrosion, antioxidant and extreme pressure (EP) additives. Grease is often classified by the type of thickener added; lithium and calcium soap are the most commonly used.

Four-Stroke Engine Oil

Oil for four-stroke engines is classified by the American Petroleum Institute (API) and the Society of Automotive Engineers (SAE) in several categories. Oil containers display these ratings on the top or label (**Figure 11**).

API oil grade is indicated by letters. Oils for gasoline engines are identified by an "S" and oils for diesel engines are identified by a "C". Most modern gasoline engines require SF or SG graded oil. Automotive and marine diesel engines use CC or CD graded oil.

Viscosity is an indication of the oil's thickness, or resistance to flow. The SAE uses numbers to indicate viscosity; thin oils have low numbers and thick oils have high numbers. A "W" after the number indicates that the viscosity testing was done at low temperatures to simulate cold weather operation. Engine oils fall into the 5W-20W and 20-50 range.

Multi-grade oils (for example, 10W-40) are less viscous (thinner) at low temperatures and more viscous (thicker) at high temperatures. This allows the oil to perform efficiently across a wide range of engine operating temperatures.

Gearcase Oil

Gearcase lubricants are assigned SAE viscosity numbers under the same system as four-stroke engine oil. Gearcase lubricant falls into the SAE 72-250 range. Some gearcase lubricants are multigrade. For example, SAE 80-90 is a common multigrade gear lubricant.

Three types of marine gearcase lubricants are generally available; SAE 90 hypoid gearcase lubricant is designed for older manual-shift units; type C gearcase lubricant contains additives designed for the electric shift mechanisms; high-viscosity gearcase lubricant is a heavier oil designed to withstand the shock loads of high performance engines or units subjected to severe duty use. Always use the gearcase lubricant specified by the manufacturer.

Grease

Greases are graded by the National Lubricating Grease Institute (NLGI). Greases are graded by number according to the consistency of the grease. These ratings range from No. 000 to No. 6, with No. 6 being the most solid. A typical multipurpose grease is NLGI No. 2. For specific applications, equipment manufacturers may require grease with an additive such as molybdenum disulfide (MOS^2).

GASKET SEALANT

Gasket sealant is used instead of preformed gaskets on some applications, or as a gasket dressing on others. Three types of gasket sealant are commonly used: gasket sealing compound, room temperature vulcanizing (RTV) and anaerobic. Because these materials have different sealing properties, they cannot be used interchangeably.

Gasket Sealing Compound

This nonhardening liquid is used primarily as a gasket dressing. Gasket sealing compound is available in tubes or brush top containers. When exposed to air or heat it forms a rubber-like coating. The coating fills in small imperfections in gasket and sealing surfaces. Do not use gasket sealing compound that is old, has began to solidify or has darkened in color.

Applying Gasket Sealing Compound

Carefully scrape residual gasket material, corrosion deposits or paint from the mating surfaces. Use a blunt scraper and work carefully to avoid damaging the mating surfaces. Use quick drying solvent and a clean shop towel and wipe oil or other contaminants from the surfaces. Wipe or blow loose material or contaminants from the gasket.

Brush a light coat of gasket sealing compound on the mating surfaces and both sides of the gasket. Do not apply more compound than needed. Excess compound will be squeezed out as the surfaces mate and may contaminate other components. Do not allow compound into bolt or alignment pin holes

A hydraulic lock can occur as the bolt or pin compresses the compound, resulting in incorrect bolt torque.

RTV Sealant

This is a silicone gel supplied in tubes. Moisture in the air causes RTV to cure. Always place the cap on the tube as soon as possible if using RTV. RTV has a shelf life of approximately one year and will not cure properly after the shelf life expires. Check the expiration date on the tube and keep partially used tubes tightly sealed. RTV can generally fill gaps up to 1/4 in. (6.3 mm) and works well on slightly flexible surfaces.

Applying RTV Sealant

Carefully scrape all residual sealant and paint from the mating surfaces. Use a blunt scraper and work carefully to avoid damaging the mating surfaces. The mating surfaces must be absolutely free of gasket material, sealant, dirt, oil grease or other contamination. Lacquer thinner, acetone, isopropyl alcohol or similar solvents work well to clean the surfaces. Do not use solvents with an oil, wax or petroleum base as they are not compatible with RTV compounds. Remove all sealant from bolt or alignment pin holes.

Apply RTV sealant in a continuous bead 0.08-0.12 in. (2-3 mm) thick. Circle all mounting bolt or alignment pin holes unless otherwise specified. Do not allow RTV sealant into bolt holes or other openings. A hydraulic lock can occur as the bolt or pin compresses the sealant, resulting in incorrect bolt torque. Tighten the mounting fasteners within 10 minutes after application.

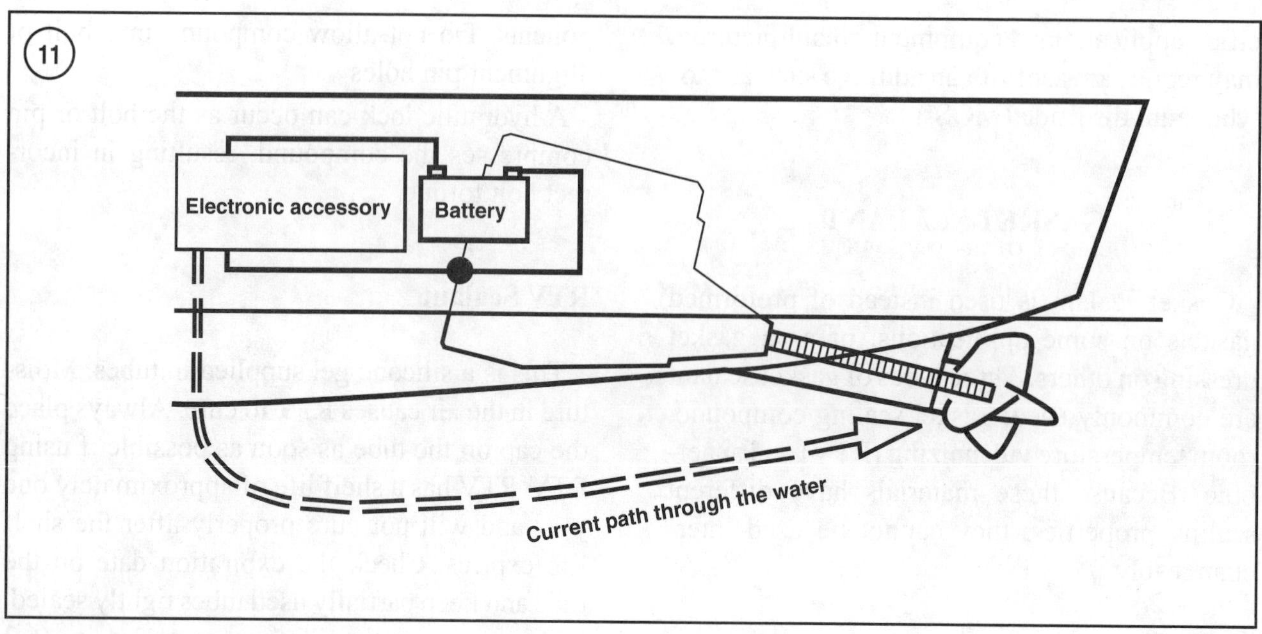

Anaerobic Sealant

This is a gel supplied in tubes. It cures only in the absence of air, as when squeezed tightly between two machined mating surfaces. For this reason, it will not spoil if the cap is left off the tube. Do not use anaerobic sealant if one of the surfaces is flexible. Anaerobic sealant is able to fill gaps up to 0.030 in. (0.8 mm) and generally works best on rigid, machined flanges or surfaces.

Applying Anaerobic Sealant

Carefully scrape all residual sealant from the mating surfaces. Use a blunt scraper and work carefully to avoid damaging the mating surfaces. The mating surfaces must be absolutely free of gasket material, sealant, dirt, oil grease or other contamination. Lacquer thinner, acetone, isopropyl alcohol or similar solvents work well to clean the surfaces. Avoid using solvents with an oil, wax or petroleum base as they are not compatible with anaerobic compounds.

Clean old sealant from the bolt or alignment pin holes. Apply anaerobic sealant in a 0.04 in. (1 mm) thick continuous bead onto one of the surfaces. Circle all bolt and alignment pin opening. Do not apply sealant into bolt holes or other openings. A hydraulic lock can occur as the bolt or pin compresses the sealant, resulting in incorrect bolt torque. Tighten the mounting fasteners within 10 minutes after application.

GALVANIC CORROSION

A chemical reaction occurs whenever two different types of metal are joined by an electrical conductor and immersed in an electrolytic solution such as water. Electrons transfer from one metal to the other through the electrolyte and return through the conductor.

The hardware on a boat is made of many different types of metal. The boat hull acts as a conductor between the metals. Even if the hull is wooden or fiberglass, the slightest film of water (electrolyte) on the hull provides conductivity. This combination creates a good environment for electron flow (**Figure 11**).

Unfortunately, this electron flow results in galvanic corrosion of the metal involved, causing one of the metals to be corroded or eroded away. The amount of electron flow, and therefore the amount of corrosion, depends on several factors:

1. The types of metal involved.
2. The efficiency of the conductor.
3. The strength of the electrolyte.

Metals

The chemical composition of the metal used in marine equipment has a significant effect on the amount and speed of galvanic corrosion. Certain metals are more resistant to corrosion than others. These electrically negative metals are commonly called *noble*; they act as the cathode in any reaction. Metals that are more subject to corrosion are electrically positive; they act as the anode in a reaction. The more *noble* metals include titanium, 18-8 stainless steel and nickel. Less *noble* metals include zinc, aluminum and magnesium. Galvanic corrosion becomes more severe as the difference in electrical potential between the two metals increases.

In some cases, galvanic corrosion can occur within a single piece of metal. For example, brass is a mixture of zinc and copper, and, when immersed in an electrolyte, the zinc portion of the mixture will corrode away as a galvanic reaction occurs between the zinc and copper particles.

Conductors

The hull of the boat often acts as the conductor between different types of metal. Marine equipment, such as the drive unit can act as the conductor. Large masses of metal, firmly connected together, are more efficient conductors than water. Rubber mountings and vinyl-based paint can act as insulators between pieces of metal.

Electrolyte

The water in which a boat operates acts as the electrolyte for the corrosion process. The more efficient a conductor is, the more severe and rapid the corrosion will be.

Cold, clean freshwater is the poorest electrolyte. Pollutants increase conductivity; therefore, brackish or saltwater is an efficient electrolyte. This is one of the reasons that most manufacturers recommend a freshwater flush after operating in polluted, brackish or saltwater.

Protection From Galvanic Corrosion

Because of the environment in which marine equipment must operate, it is practically impossible to totally prevent galvanic corrosion. However, there are several ways in which the process can be slowed. After taking these precautions, the next step is to *fool* the process into occurring only where you want it to occur. This is the role of sacrificial anodes and impressed current systems.

Slowing Corrosion

Some simple precautions can help reduce the amount of corrosion taking place outside the hull. These precautions are not substitutes for the corrosion protection methods discussed under *Sacrificial Anodes* and *Impressed Current Systems* in this chapter, but they can help these methods reduce corrosion.

Use fasteners made of metal more noble than the parts they secure. If corrosion occurs, the parts they secure may suffer but the fasteners are protected. The larger secured parts are more able to withstand the loss of material. Also major problems could arise if the fasteners corrode to the point of failure.

Keep all painted surfaces in good condition. If paint is scraped off and bare metal exposed, corrosion rapidly increases. Use a vinyl- or plastic-based paint, which acts as an electrical insulator.

Be careful when applying metal-based antifouling paint to the boat. Do not apply antifouling paint to metal parts of the boat or the drive unit. If applied to metal surfaces, this type of paint reacts with the metal and results in corrosion between the metal and the layer of paint. Maintain a minimum 1 in. (25 mm) border between the painted surface and any metal parts. Organic-based paints are available for use on metal surfaces.

Where a corrosion protection device is used, remember that it must be immersed in the electrolyte along with the boat to provide any protection. If you raise the gearcase out of the water with the boat docked, any anodes on the gearcase may be removed from the corrosion process rendering them ineffective. Never paint or apply any coating to anodes or other protection devices. Paint or other coatings insulate them from the corrosion process.

Any change in the boat's equipment, such as the installation of a new stainless steel propeller, changes the electrical potential and may cause increased corrosion. Always consider this when adding equipment or changing exposed materials. Install additional anodes or other protection equipment as required ensuring the corrosion protection system is up to the task. The expense to repair corrosion damage usually far exceeds that of additional corrosion protection.

Sacrificial Anodes

Sacrificial anodes are specially designed to do nothing but corrode. Properly fastening such pieces to the boat causes them to act as the anode in any galvanic reaction that occurs; any other metal in the reaction acts as the cathode and is not damaged.

Anodes are usually made or zinc, a far from a noble material. Some anodes are manufactured of an aluminum and indium alloy. This alloy is less noble than the aluminum alloy in drive system components, providing the desired sacrificial properties. The aluminum and indium alloy is more resistant to oxide coating than zinc anodes. Oxide coating occurs as the anode material reacts with oxygen in the water. An oxide coating will insulate the anode, dramatically reducing corrosion protection.

Anodes must be used properly to be effective. Simply fastening anodes to the boat in random locations will not do the job.

First determine how much anode surface is required to adequately protect the equipment's surface area. A good starting point is provided by the Military Specification MIL-A-818001, which states that one square inch of new anode protects either:

1. 800 square inches of freshly painted steel.
2. 250 square inches of bare steel or bare aluminum alloy.
3. 100 square inches of copper or copper alloy.

This rule is valid for a boat at rest. If underway, additional anode area is required to protect the same surface area.

The anode must be in good electrical contact with the metal that it protects. If possible, attach an anode to all metal surfaces requiring protection.

Good quality anodes have inserts around the fastener holes that are made of a more noble material. Otherwise, the anode could erode away around the fastener hole, allowing the anode to loosen or possibly fall off, thereby loosing needed protection.

Impressed Current System

An impressed current system can be added to any boat. The system generally consists of the anode, controller and reference electrode. The anode in this system is coated with a very noble

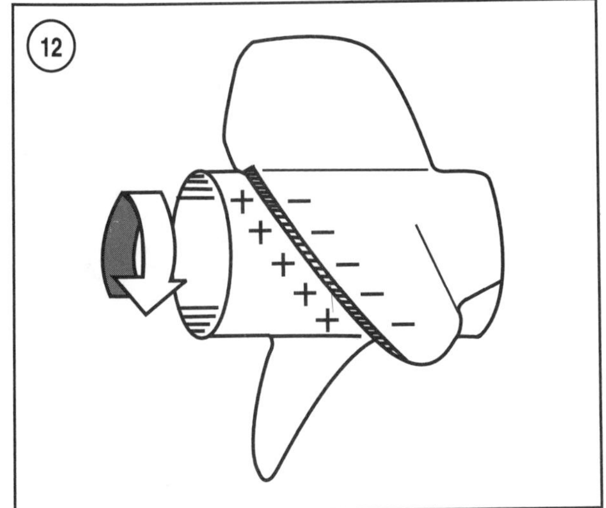

metal, such as platinum, so that it is almost corrosion-free and can last almost indefinitely. The reference electrode, under the boat's waterline, allows the control module to monitor the potential for corrosion. If the module senses that corrosion is occurring, it applies positive battery voltage to the anode. Current then flows from the anode to all other metal component, regardless of how noble or non-noble these components may be. Essentially, the electrical current from the battery counteracts the galvanic reaction to dramatically reduce corrosion damage.

Only a small amount of current is needed to counteract corrosion. Using input from the sensor, the control module provides only the amount of current needed to suppress galvanic corrosion. Most systems consume a maximum of 0.2 Ah at full demand. Under normal conditions, these systems can provide protection for 8-12 weeks without recharging the battery. Remember that this system must have constant connection to the battery. Often the battery supply to the system is connected to a battery switching device causing the operator to inadvertently shut off the system while docked.

An impressed current system is more expensive to install than sacrificial anodes but, considering its low maintenance requirements and the superior protection it provides, the long term cost may be lower.

PROPELLERS

The propeller is the final link between the boat's drive system and the water. A perfectly maintained engine and hull are useless if the propeller is the wrong type, is damaged or is deteriorated. Although propeller selection for a specific application is beyond the scope of this manual, the following provides the basic information needed to make an informed decision. The professional at a reputable marine dealership is the best source for a propeller recommendation.

How a Propeller Works

As the curved blades of a propeller rotate through the water, a high-pressure area forms on one side of the blade and a low-pressure area forms on the other side of the blade (**Figure 12**). The propeller moves toward the low-pressure area, carrying the boat with it.

Propeller Parts

Although a propeller is usually a one-piece unit, it is made of several different parts (**Figure 13**). Variations in the design of these parts make different propellers suitable for different applications.

The blade tip is the point of the blade furthest from the center of the propeller hub or propeller shaft bore. The blade tip separates the leading edge from the trailing edge.

The leading edge is the edge of the blade nearest the boat. During forward operation, this is the area of the blade that first cuts through the water.

The trailing edge is the surface of the blade furthest from the boat. During reverse operation,

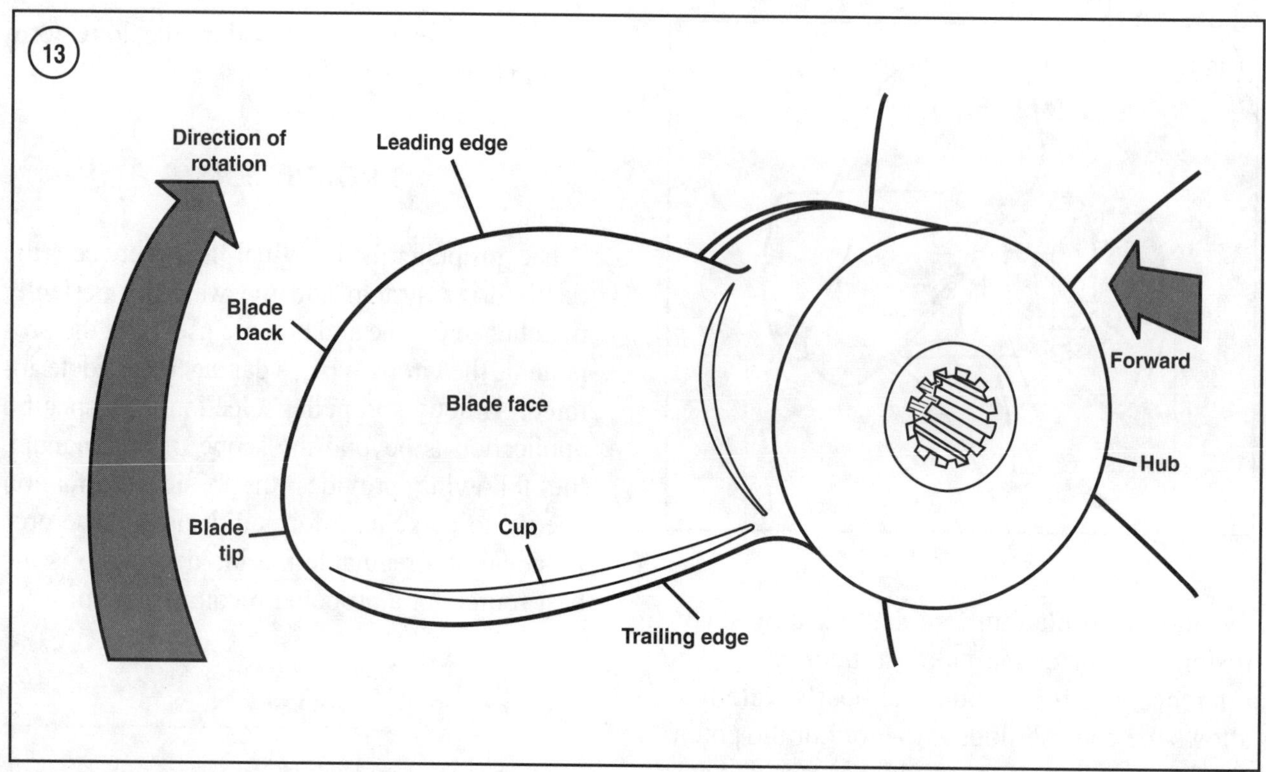

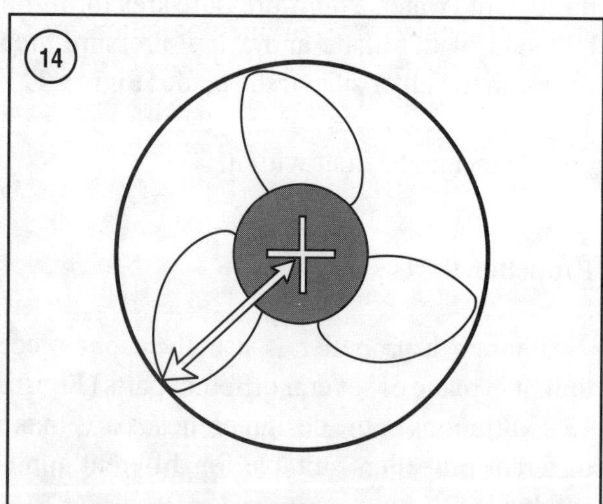

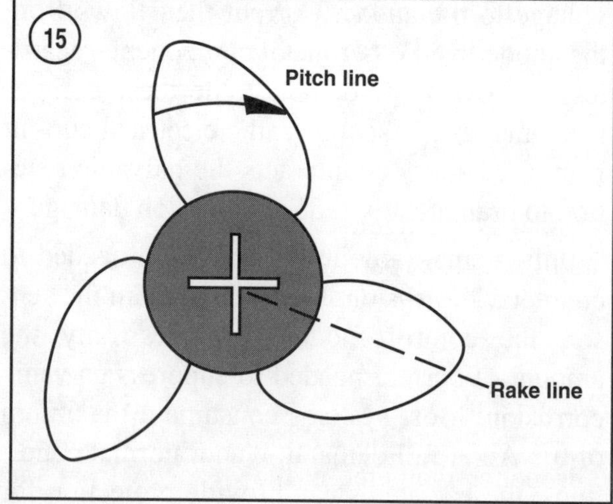

this is the area of the blade that first cuts through the water.

The blade face is the surface of the blade that faces away from the boat. During forward operation, high-pressure forms on this side of the blade.

The blade back is the surface of the blade that faces toward the boat. During forward gear operation, low-pressure forms on this side of the blade.

The cup is a small curve or lip on the trailing edge of the blade. Cupped propeller blades generally perform better than non-cupped propeller blades.

The hub is the center portion of the propeller. It connects the blades to the propeller shaft. On most drive systems, engine exhaust is routed through the hub; in this case, the hub is made up of an outer and inner portion, connected by ribs.

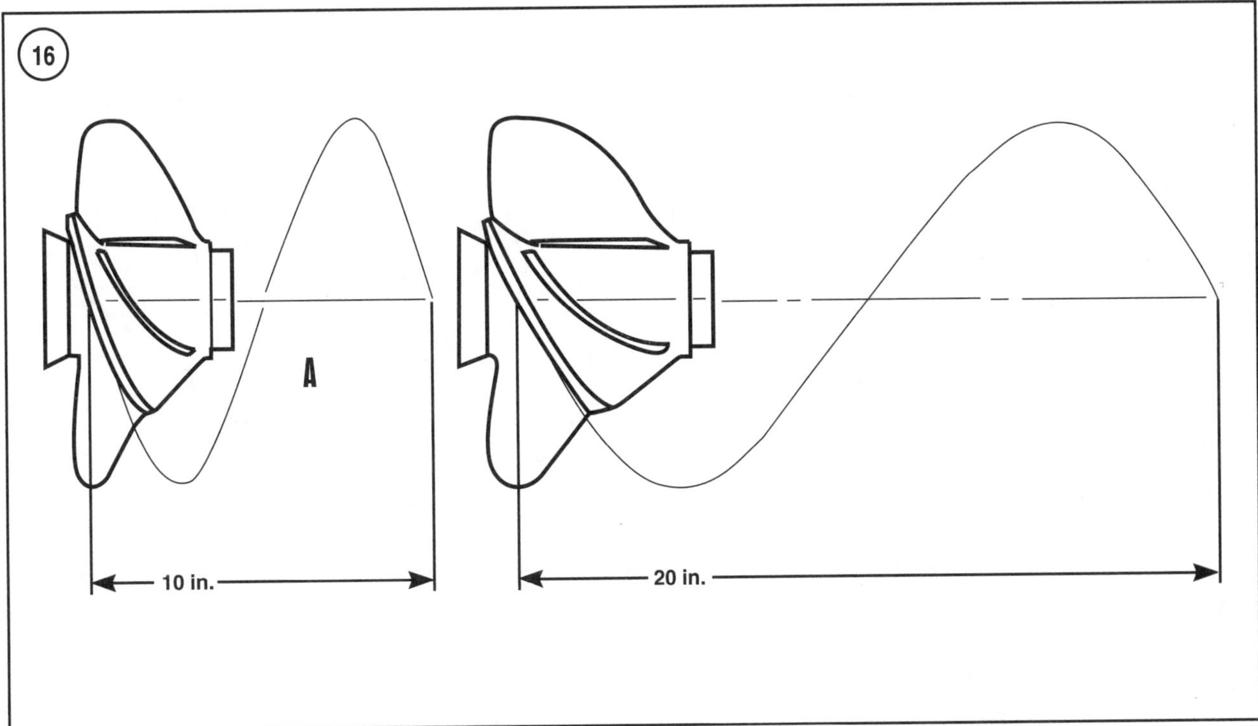

The diffuser ring is used on though- hub exhaust models to prevent exhaust gasses from entering the blade area.

Propeller Design

Changes in length, angle, thickness and material of propeller parts make different propellers suitable for different applications.

Diameter

Propeller diameter is the distance from the center of the hub to the blade tip, multiplied by two. Essentially it is the diameter of the circle formed by the blade tips during propeller rotation (**Figure 14**).

Pitch and rake

Propeller pitch and rake describe the placement of the blades in relation to the hub (**Figure 15**).

Pitch describes the theoretical distance the propeller would travel in one revolution. In A, **Figure 16**, the propeller would travel 10 inches in one revolution. In B, **Figure 16**, the propeller would travel 20 inches in one revolution. This distance is only theoretical; during operation, the propeller achieves only 75-85% of its pitch. Slip rate describes the difference in actual travel relative to the pitch. Lighter, faster boats typically achieve a lower slip rate than heavier, slower boats.

Propeller blades can be constructed with constant pitch (**Figure 17**) or progressive pitch (**Figure 18**). On a progressive propeller, the pitch starts low at the leading edge and increases toward the trailing edge. The propeller pitch specification is the average of the pitch across the entire blade. Propellers with progressive pitch usually provide better overall performance than constant pitch propellers.

Blade rake is specified in degrees and is measured along a line from the center of the hub to the blade tip. A blade that is perpendicular to the

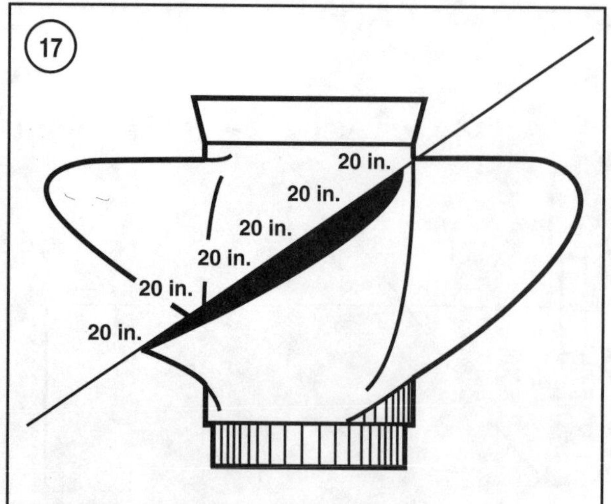

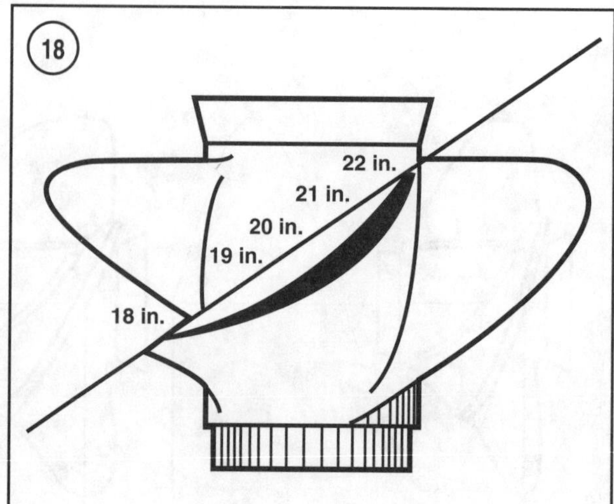

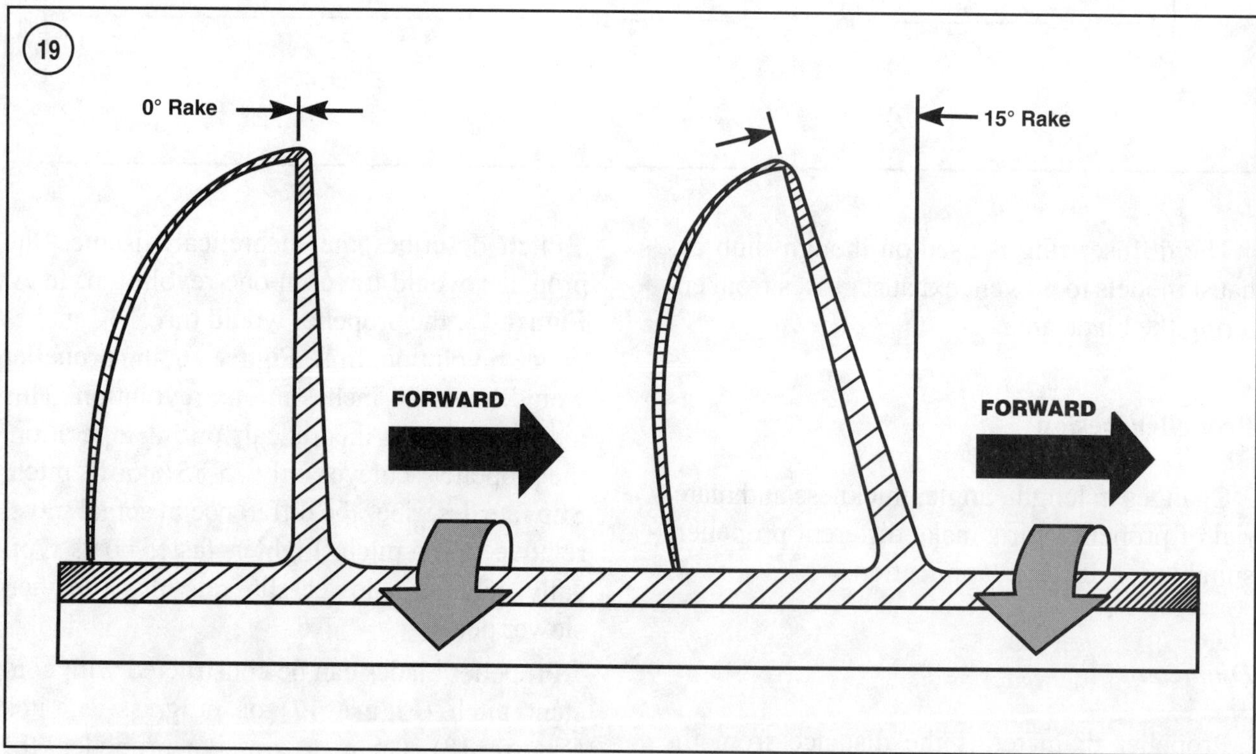

hub (**Figure 19**) has 0° rake. A blade that is angled from perpendicular (**Figure 19**) has a rake expressed by its difference from perpendicular. Most propellers have rakes ranging from 0-20°. Lighter faster boats generally perform better with propeller with a greater amount of rake. Heavier, slower boats generally perform better using a propeller with less rake.

Blade thickness

Blade thickness in not uniform at all points along the blade. For efficiency, blades are as thin a possible at all points while retaining enough strength to move the boat. Blades are thicker where they meet the hub and thinner at the blade tips (**Figure 20**). This is necessary to support the

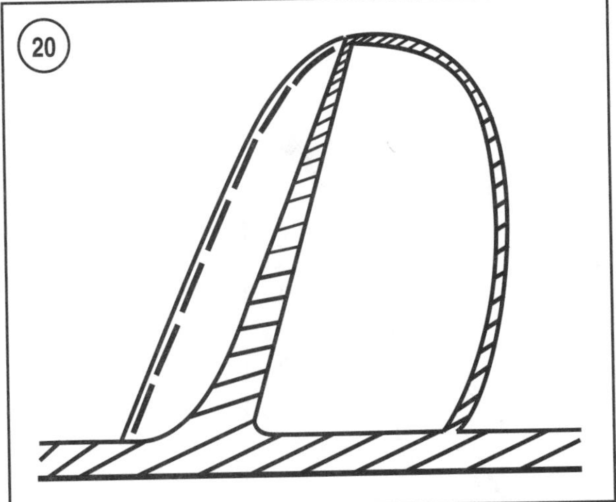

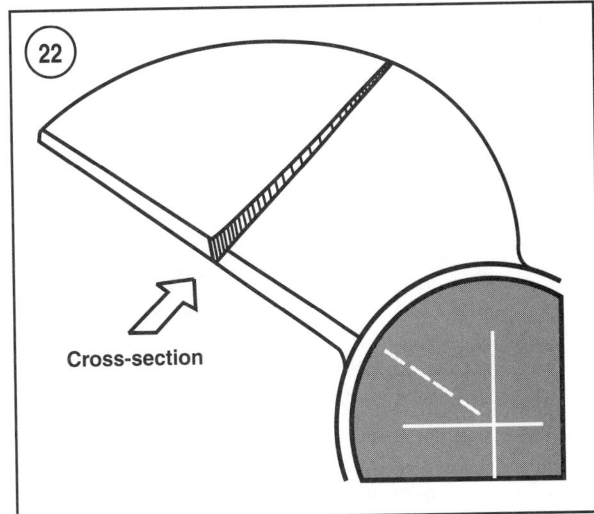

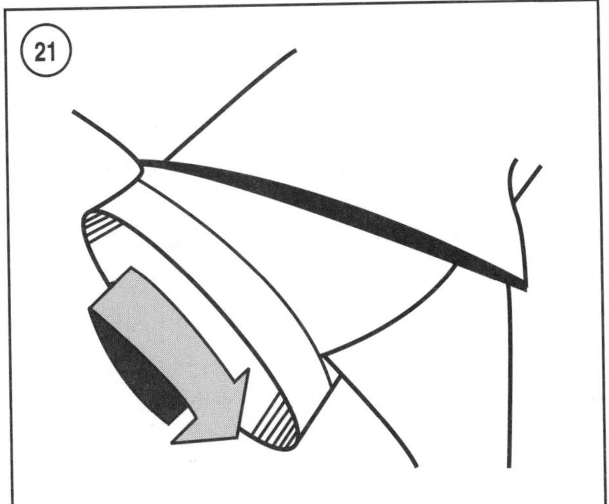

heavier loads at the hub section of the blade. Overall blade thickness is dependent on the strength of the material used.

When cut along a line from the leading edge to the trailing edge in the central portion of the blade (**Figure 21**), the propeller blade resembles and airplane wing. The blade face, where high-pressure exists during forward rotation, is almost flat. The blade back, where low-pressure exists during forward rotation, is curved, with the thinnest portions at the edges and the thickest portion at the center.

Propellers that run only partially submerged, as in racing applications, may have a wedge shaped cross-section (**Figure 22**). The leading edge is very thin and the blade thickness increases toward the trailing edge, where it is thickest. If a propeller such as this is run totally submerged, it is very inefficient.

Number of blades

The number of blades used on a propeller is a compromise between efficiency and vibration. A one-bladed propeller would the most efficient, but it would create an unacceptable amount of vibration. As blades are added, efficiency decreases, but so does vibration. Most propellers have three or four blades, representing the most practical trade-off between efficiency and vibration.

Material

Propeller materials are chosen for strength, corrosion resistance and economy. Stainless steel, aluminum, plastic and bronze are the most commonly used materials. Bronze is quite strong but rather expensive. Stainless steel is more common than bronze because of its combination of strength and lower cost. Aluminum alloy and plastic materials are the least expensive

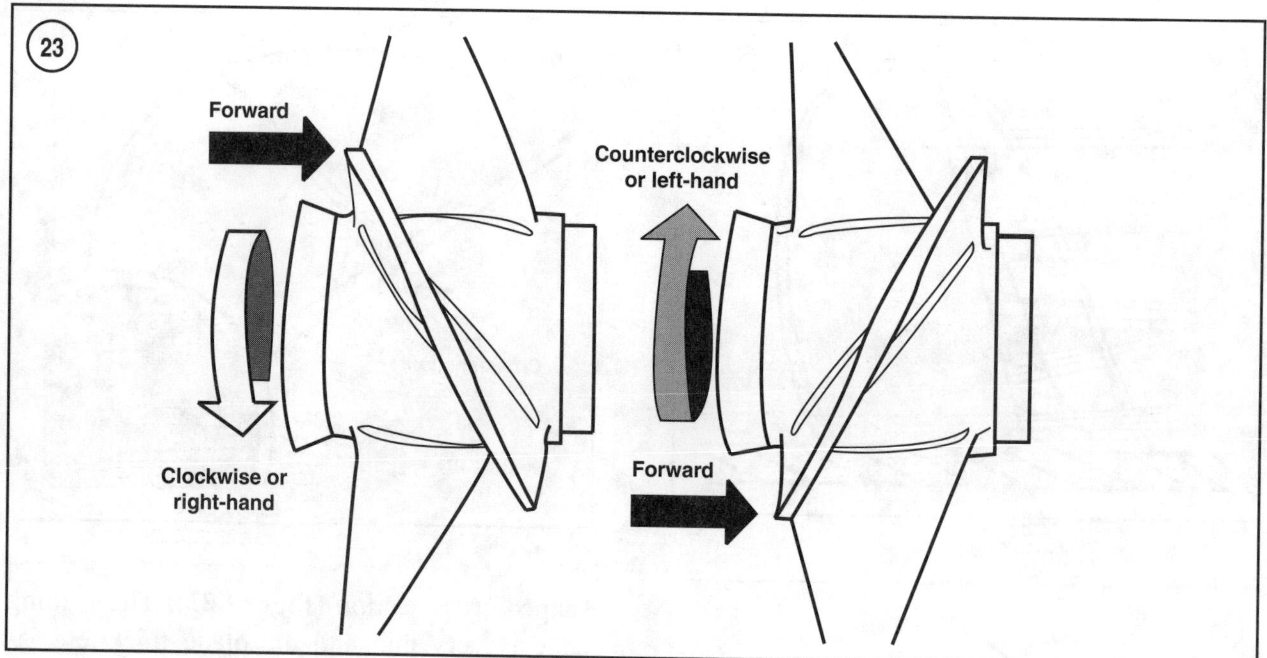

but usually lack the strength of stainless steel. Plastic propellers are more suited for lower horsepower applications.

Direction of rotation

Propellers are made for both right-hand and left hand rotations although right-hand is the most commonly used. As viewed from the rear of the boat while in forward gear, a right-hand propeller turns clockwise and a left-hand propeller turns counterclockwise. Off the boat, the direction of rotation is determined by observing the angle of the blades (**Figure 23**). A right-hand propeller's blade slant from the upper left to the lower right; a left-hand propeller's blades are opposite.

Cavitation and Ventilation

Cavitation and ventilation are *not* interchangeable terms; they refer to two distinct problems encountered during propeller operation.

To help understand cavitation, consider the relationship between pressure and the boiling point of water. At sea level, water boils at 212° F (100° C). As pressure increases, such as within an engine cooling system, the boiling point of the water increases—it boils at a temperature higher than 212° F (100° C). The opposite is also true. As pressure decreases, water boils at a temperature lower than 212° F (100° C). It the pressure drops low enough, water will boil at normal room temperature.

During normal propeller operation, low pressure forms on the blade back. Normally the pressure does not drop low enough for boiling to occur. However, poor propeller design, damaged blades or using the wrong propeller can cause unusually low pressure on the blade surface (**Figure 24**). If the pressure drops low enough, boiling occurs and bubbles form on the blade surfaces. As the boiling water moves to a higher pressure area of the blade, the boiling ceases and the bubbles collapse. The collapsing bubbles release energy that erodes the surface of the propeller blade.

Corroded surfaces, physical damage or even marine growth combined with high-speed operation can cause low pressure and cavitation on gearcase surfaces. In such cases, low pressure

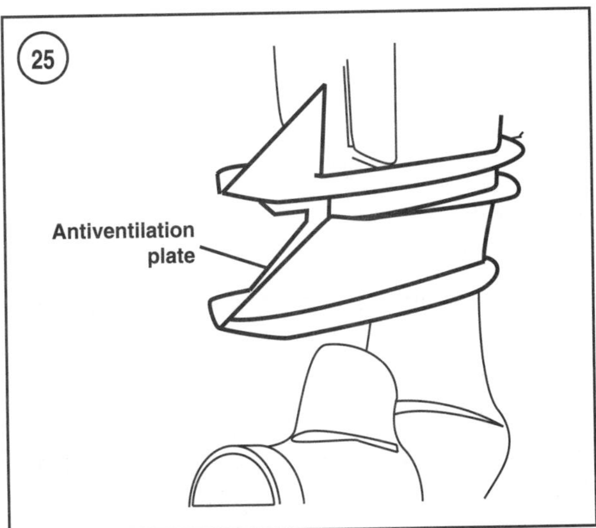

forms as water flows over a protrusion or rough surface. The boiling water forms bubbles that collapse as they move to a higher pressure area toward the rear of the surface imperfection.

This entire process of pressure drop, boiling and bubble collapse is called *cavitation*. The ensuing damage is called *cavitation burn*. Cavitation is caused by a decrease in pressure, not an increase in temperature.

Ventilation is not as complex a process as cavitation. Ventilation refers to air entering the blade area, either from above the water surface or from a though-hub exhaust system. As the blades meet the air, the propeller momentarily looses it bite with the water and subsequently loses most of its thrust. An added complication is that the propeller and engine over-rev, causing very low pressure on the blade back and massive cavitation.

Most marine drive systems have a plate (**Figure 25**) above the propeller designed to prevent surface air from entering the blade area. This plate is correctly called an *anti-ventilation plate*, although it is often incorrectly called an *anticavitation plate*.

Most propellers have a flared section at the rear of the propeller called a diffuser ring. This feature forms a barrier, and extends the exhaust passage far enough aft to prevent the exhaust gases from ventilating the propeller.

A close fit of the propeller to the gearcase is necessary to keep exhaust gasses from exiting and ventilating the propeller. Using the wrong propeller attaching hardware can position the propeller too far aft, preventing a close fit. The wrong hardware can also allow the propeller to rub heavily against the gearcase, causing rapid wear to both components. Wear or damage to these surfaces will allow the propeller to ventilate.

Chapter Two

Tools and Techniques

This chapter describes the common tools required for marine engine repair and troubleshooting. Techniques that make the work easier and more effective are also described. Some of the procedures in this book require special skills or expertise; in some cases it is better to entrust the job to a specialist or qualified dealership.

SAFETY FIRST

Professional mechanics can work for years and never suffer a serious injury. Avoiding injury is as simple as following a few rules and using common sense. Ignoring the rules can and often does lead to physical injury and/or damaged equipment.

1. Never use gasoline as a cleaning solvent.
2. Never smoke or use a torch near flammable liquids, such as cleaning solvent. Dirty or solvent soaked shop towels are extremely flammable. If working in a garage, remember that most home gas appliances have pilot lights.
3. Never smoke or use a torch in an area where a battery is being charged. Highly explosive hydrogen gas is formed during the charging process.
4. Use the proper size wrench to avoid damaged fasteners and bodily injury.
5. If loosening a tight or stuck fastener, consider what could happen if the wrench slips. Protect yourself accordingly.
6. Keep the work area clean, uncluttered and well lighted.
7. Wear safety goggles while using any type of tool. This is especially important when drilling, grinding or using a cold chisel.
8. Never use worn or damaged tools.
9. Keep a Coast Guard approved fire extinguisher handy. Ensure it is rated for gasoline (Class B) and electrical (Class C) fires.

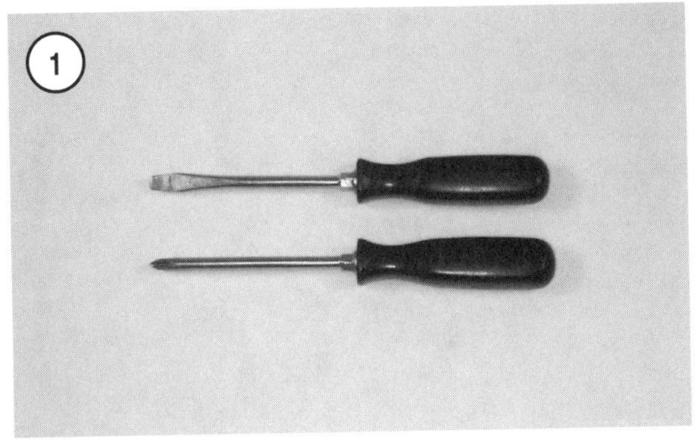

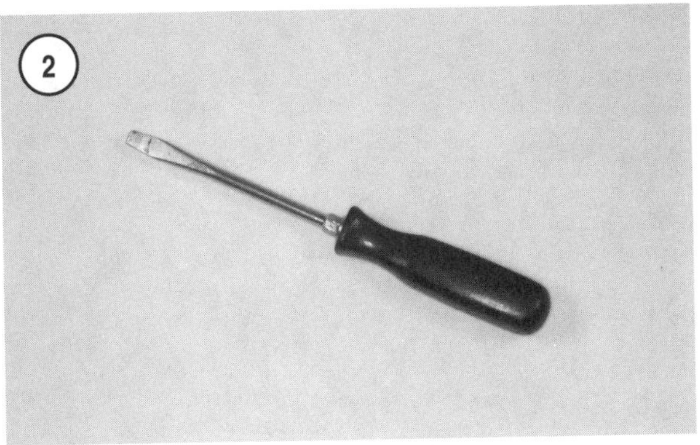

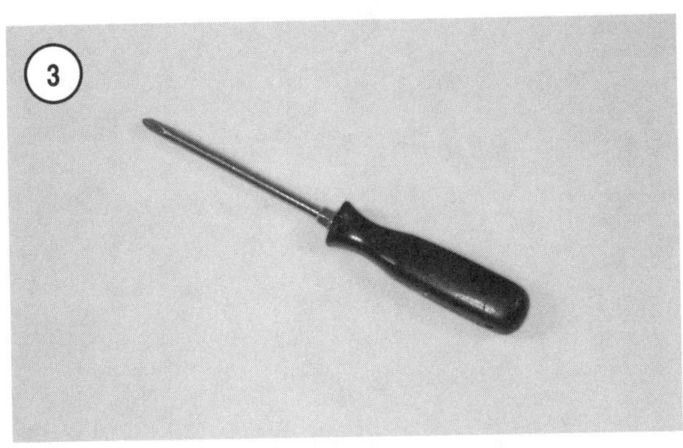

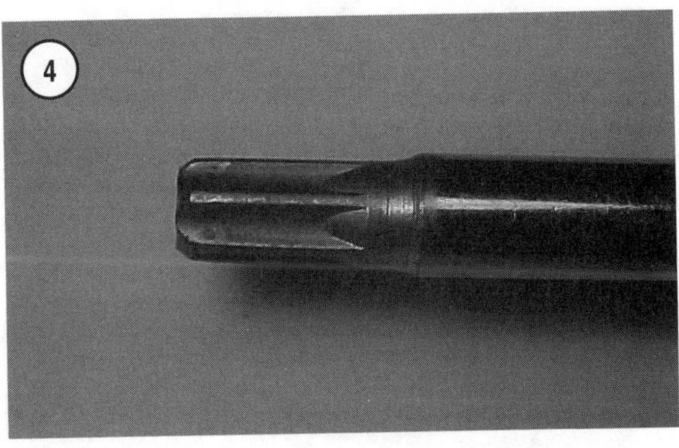

BASIC HAND TOOLS

A number of tools are required to maintain and repair a marine engine. Most of these tools are also used for home and automobile repair. Some tools are made especially for working on marine engines; these tools can be purchased from a marine dealership. Having the required tools always makes the job easier and more effective.

Keep the tools clean and in a suitable box. Keep them organized with related tools stored together. After using a tool, wipe it clean using a shop towel.

The following tools are required to perform virtually any repair job. Each tool is described and the recommended size given for starting a tool collection. Additional tools and some duplication may be added as you become more familiar with the equipment. You may need all U.S. standard tools, all metric size tools or a mixture of both.

Screwdrivers

A screwdriver (**Figure 1**) is a very basic tool, but if used improperly can do more damage than good. The slot on a screw has a definite dimension and shape. Always select a screwdriver that conforms to the shape of the screw. Use a small screwdriver for small screws and a large one for large screws or the screw head are damaged.

Three types of screwdrivers are commonly required: a slotted (flat-blade) screwdriver (**Figure 2**), Phillips screwdriver (**Figure 3**) and Torx screwdriver (**Figure 4**).

Screwdrivers are available in sets, which often include an assortment of slotted Phillips and Torx blades. If you buy them individually, buy at least the following:

a. Slotted screwdriver—5/16 × 6 in. blade.
b. Slotted screwdriver—3/8 × 12 in. blade.
c. Phillips screwdriver—No. 2 tip, 6 in. blade.

d. Phillips screwdriver—No. 3 tip, 6 in. blade.
e. Torx screwdriver—T15 tip, 6 in. blade.
f. Torx screwdriver—T20 tip, 6 in. blade.
g. Torx screwdriver—T25 tip, 6 in. blade.

Use screwdrivers only for driving screws. Never use a screwdriver for prying or chiseling. Do not attempt to remove a Phillips, Torx or Allen head screw with a slotted screwdriver; you can damage the screw head so that even the proper tool is unable to remove it.

Keep the tip of a slotted screwdriver in good condition. Carefully grind the tip to the proper size and taper if it is worn or damaged. The sides of the blade must be parallel and the blade tip must be flat. Replace a Phillips or Torx screwdriver if its tip is worn or damaged.

Pliers

Pliers come in a wide range of types and sizes. Pliers are useful for cutting, gripping, bending and crimping. Never use pliers to cut hardened objects or turn bolts or nuts. **Figure 5** shows several types of pliers.

Each type of pliers has a specialized function. General-purpose pliers are mainly used for gripping and bending. Locking pliers are used for gripping objects very tightly, like a vise. Use needlenose pliers to grip or bend small objects. Adjustable or slip-joint pliers (**Figure 6**) can be adjusted to grip various sized objects; the jaws remain parallel for gripping objects such as pipe or tubing. There are many more types of pliers. The ones described here are the most common.

Box-end and Open-end Wrenches

Box-end and open-end wrenches (**Figure 7**) are available in sets in a variety of sizes. The number stamped near the end of the wrench refers to the distance between two parallel flats on the hex head bolt or nut.

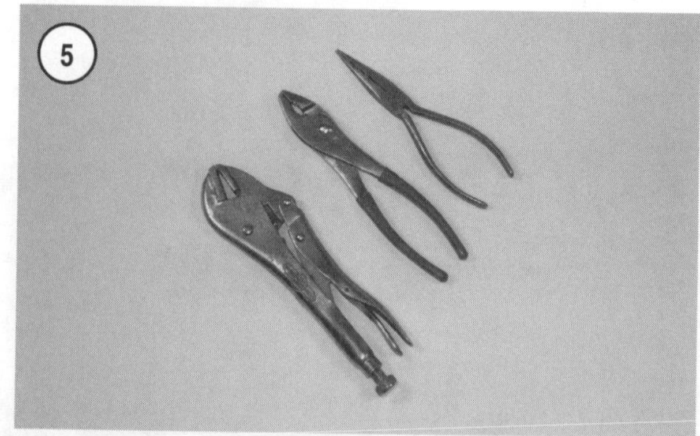
5

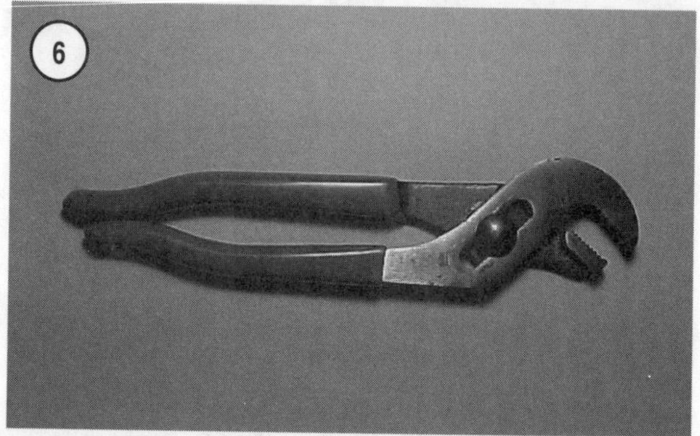
6

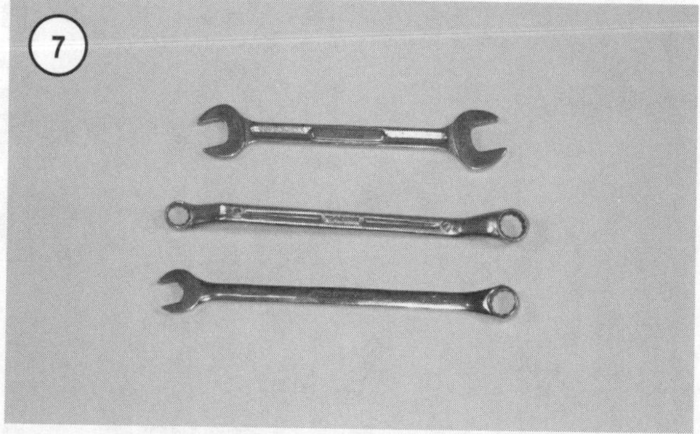
7

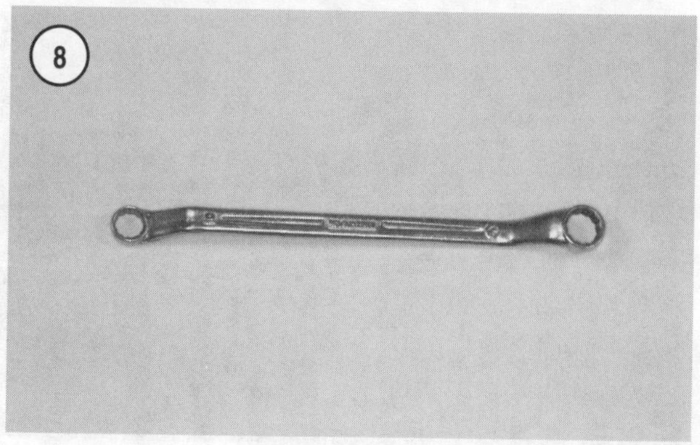
8

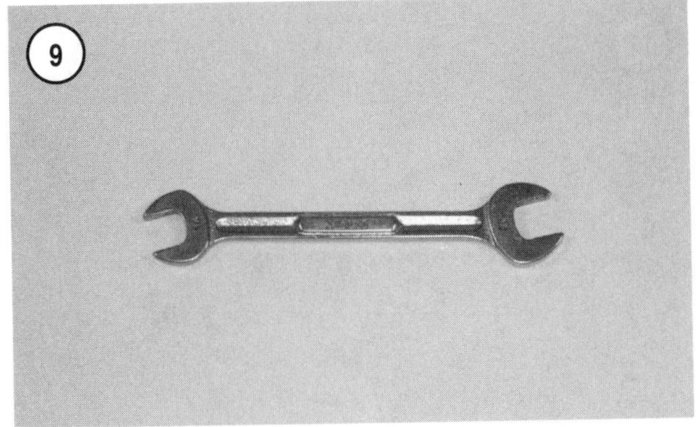
9

10

11

Box-end wrenches (**Figure 8**) provide a better grip on the nut and are stronger than open end wrenches. An open-end wrench (**Figure 9**) grips the nut on only two flats. Unless it fits well, it may slip and round off the points on the nut. A box-end wrench grips all six flats. Box-end wrenches are available with six-point or 12 point openings. The six-point opening provides superior holding power; the 12-point allow a shorter swing if working in tight quarters.

Use an open-end wrench if a box-end wrench cannot be positioned over the nut or bolt. To prevent damage to the fastener, avoid using and open-end wrench if a large amount of tightening or loosening toque is required.

A combination wrench has both a box-end and open- end. Both ends are the same size.

Adjustable Wrenches

An adjustable wrench (**Figure 10**) can be adjusted to fit virtually any nut or bolt head. However, it can loosen and slip from the nut or bolt, causing damage to the nut and possible physical injury. Use an adjustable wrench only if a proper size open-end or box-end wrench in not available. Avoid using an adjustable wrench if a large amount of tightening or loosening torque is required.

Adjustable wrenches come in sized ranging from 4-18 in. overall length. A 6 or 8 in. size is recommended as an all-purpose wrench.

Socket Wrenches

A socket wrench (**Figure 11**) is generally faster, safer and more convenient to use than a common wrench. Sockets, which attach to a suitable handle, are available with six-point or 12-point openings and use 1/4, 3/8, and 1/2 in. drive sizes. The drive size corresponds to the square hole that mates with the ratchet or flex handle.

Torque Wrench

A torque wrench (**Figure 12**) is used with a socket to measure how tight a nut or bolt is installed. They come in a wide price range and in 1/4, 3/8, and 1/2 in. drive sizes. The drive size corresponds to the square hole that mates with the socket.

A typical 1/4 in. drive torque wrench measures in in.-lb. increments, and has a range of 20-150 in.-lb. (2.2-17 N•m). A typical 3/8 or 1/2 in. torque measures in ft.-lb. increments, and has a range of 10-150 ft.-lb. (14-203 N•m).

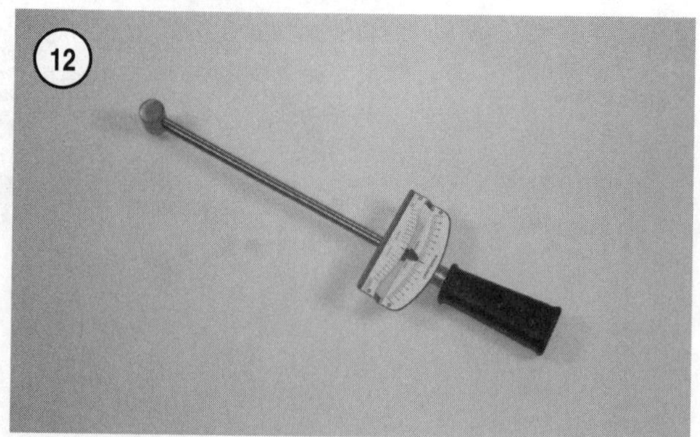
12

Impact Driver

An impact driver (**Figure 13**) makes removal of tight fasteners easy and reduces damage to bolts and screws. Interchangeable bits allow use on a variety of fasteners.

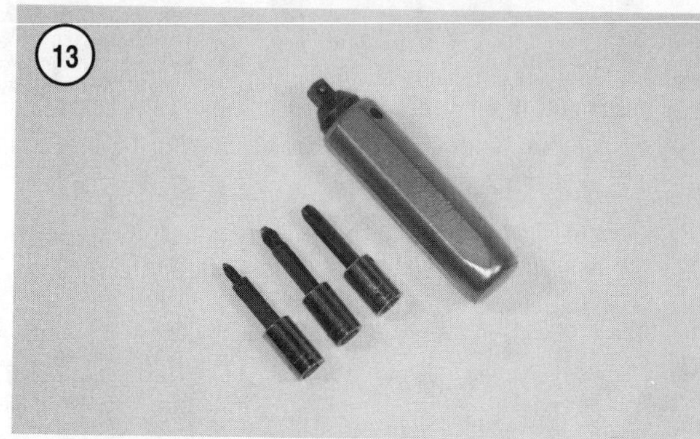
13

Snap Ring Pliers

Snap ring pliers are required to remove snap rings. Snap ring pliers (**Figure 14**) usually come with different size tips; many designs can be switched to handle internal or external type snap ring.

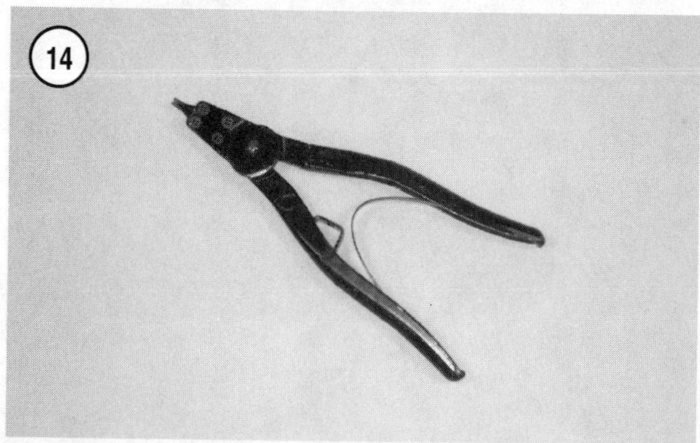
14

Hammers

Various types of hammers (**Figure 15**) are available to accommodate a number of applications. Use a ball-peen hammer to strike another tool, such as a punch or chisel. Use a soft-face hammer to strike a metal object without damaging it.

Never use a metal-faced hammer on engine and drive system components as severe damage will occur. You can always produce the same amount of force with a soft-faced hammer.

Always wear eye protection when using hammers. Make sure the hammer is in good condition and that the handle is not cracked. Select the correct hammer for the job and always strike the object squarely. Do not use the handle or the side of the hammer head to stroke an object.

15

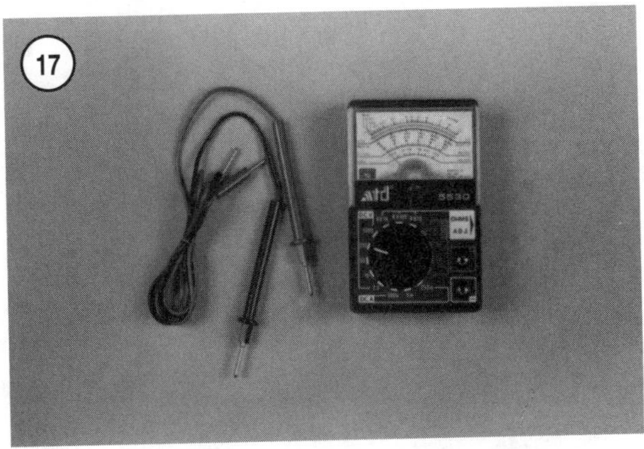

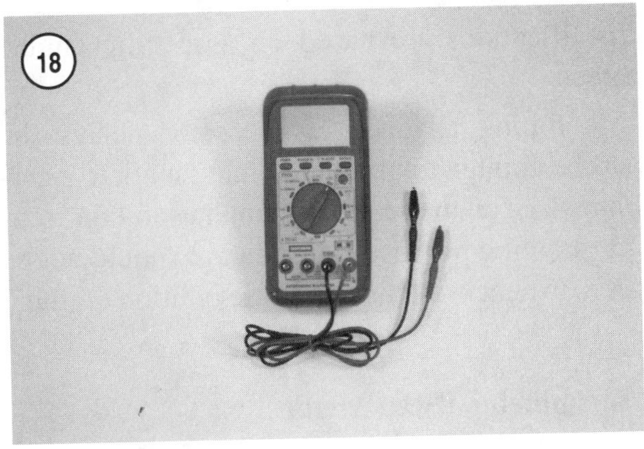

Feeler Gauges

This tool has either flat or wire measuring gauges (**Figure 16**). Use wire gauges to measure spark plug gap; use flat gauges for other measurements. A nonmagnetic (brass) gauge may be specified if working around magnetized components.

Other Special Tools

Many of the maintenance and repair procedures require special tools. Most of the necessary tools are available from a marine dealership or from tool suppliers. Instructions for their use and the manufacture's part number are included in the appropriate chapter.

Purchase the required tools from a local marine dealership or tool supplier. A qualified machinist, often at a lower price, can make some tools locally. Many marine dealerships and rental outlets will rent some of the required tools. Avoid using makeshift tools. Their use may result in damaged parts that cost far more than the recommended tool.

TEST EQUIPMENT

This section describes equipment used to perform testing, adjustments and measurements on marine engines. Most of these tools are available from a local marine dealership or automotive parts store.

Multimeter

This instrument is invaluable for electrical troubleshooting and service. It combines a voltmeter, ohmmeter and an ammeter in one unit. It is often called a VOM.

Two types of mutimeter are available, analog and digital. Analog meters (**Figure 17**) have a moving needle with marked bands on the meter face indicating the volt, ohm and amperage scales. An analog meter must be calibrated each time the scale is changed.

A digital meter (**Figure 18**) is ideally suited for electrical troubleshooting because it is easy to read and more accurate than an analog meter. Most models are auto-ranging, have automatic polarity compensation and internal overload protection circuits.

Either type of meter is suitable for most electrical testing described in this manual. An analog meter is better suited for testing pulsing voltage signals such as those produced by the ignition system. A digital meter is better suited for testing very low resistance or voltage reading (less than 1 volt or 1 ohm). The test procedure will indicate if a specific type of meter is required.

The ignition system produces electrical pulses that are too short in duration for accurate measurement with a using a conventional multimeter. Use a meter with peak-volt reading ca pability to test the ignition system. This type of meter captures the peak voltage reached during an electrical pulse.

Scale selection, meter specifications and test connections vary by the manufacturer and model of the meter. Thoroughly read the instructions supplied with the meter before performing any test. The meter and certain electrical components on the engine can be damaged if tested incorrectly. Have the test performed by a qualified professional if you are unfamiliar with the testing or general meter usage. The expense to replace damaged equipment can far exceed the cost of having the test performed by a professional.

Strobe Timing Light

This instrument is necessary for dynamic tuning (setting ignition timing while the engine is running). By flashing a light at the precise instant the spark plug fires, the position of the timing mark can be seen. The flashing light makes a moving mark appear to stand still next to a stationary mark.

Timing lights (**Figure 19**) range from inexpensive models with a neon bulb to expensive models with a xenon bulb, built in tachometer and timing advance compensator. A built in tachometer is very useful as most ignition timing

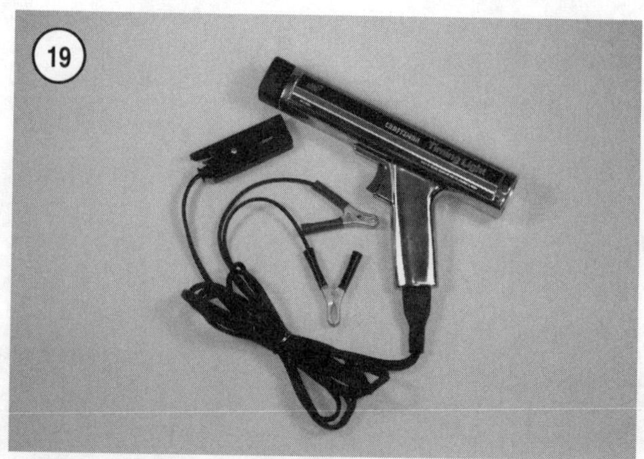
19

20

specifications are based on a specific engine speed.

A timing advance compensator delays the strobe enough to bring the timing mark to a certain place on the scale. Although useful for troubleshooting purposes, this feature should not be used to check or adjust the base ignition timing.

Tachometer/Dwell Meter

A portable tachometer (**Figure 20**) is needed to tune and test most marine engines. Ignition timing and carburetor adjustments must be performed at a specified engine speed. Tachometers are available with either an analog or digital display.

The fuel/air mixture must be adjusted with the engine running at idle speed. If using an analog

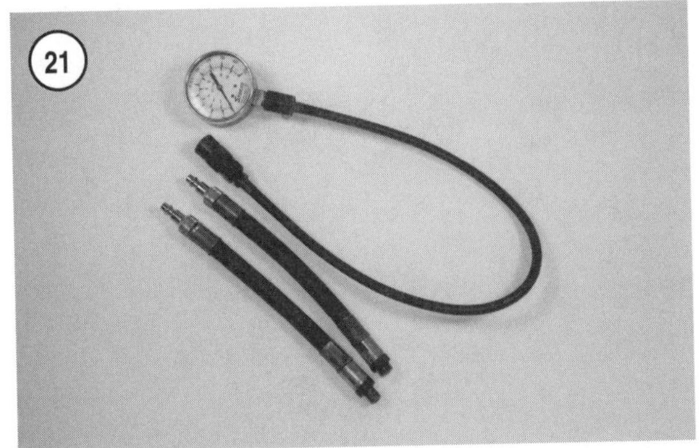

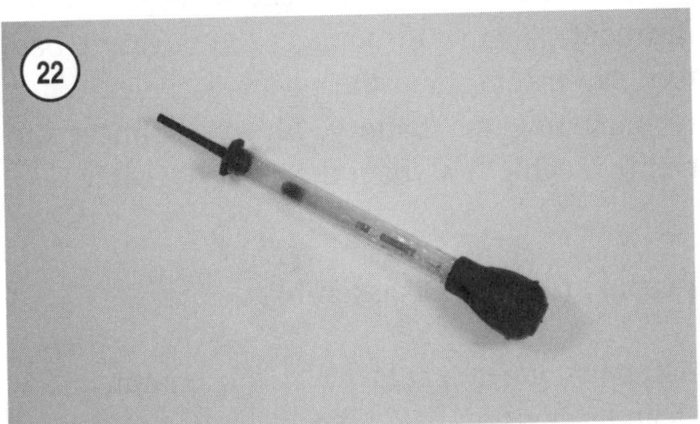

tachometer, choose one with a low range of 0-1000 rpm or 0-2000 rpm range and a high range of 0-6000 rpm. The high range setting is needed for testing purposes but lacks the accuracy needed at lower speeds. At lower speeds the meter must be capable of detecting changes of 25 rpm or less.

Digital tachometers are generally easier to use than most analog type tachometers. They provide accurate measurement at all speeds without the need to change the range or scale. Many of these use an inductive pickup to receive the signal from the ignition system.

A dwell meter is often incorporated into the tachometer to allow testing and/or adjustments to engines with a breaker point ignition system.

Compression Gauge

This tool (**Figure 21**) measures the amount of pressure created in the combustion chamber during the compression stroke. Compression indicates the general engine condition making it one of the most useful troubleshooting tools.

The easiest type to use has screw-in adapters that fit the spark plug holes. Rubber tipped, press-in type gauges are also available. This type must be held firmly in the spark plug hole to prevent leakage and inaccurate test results..

Hydrometer

Use a hydrometer to measure specific gravity in the battery. Specific gravity is the density of the battery electrolyte as compared to pure water and indicates the battery's state of charge. Choose a hydrometer (**Figure 22**) with automatic temperature compensation; otherwise the electrolyte temperature must be measured during charging to determine the actual specific gravity.

Precision Measuring Tools

Various tools are required to make precision measurements. A dial indicator (**Figure 23**), for example, is used to determine piston position in the cylinder, runout and end play of shafts and assemblies. It is also used to measure free movement between the gear teeth (backlash) in the drive unit.

Venier calipers (**Figure 24**), micrometers (**Figure 25**) and other precision tools are used to measure the size of parts, such as the piston.

Precision measuring equipment must be stored, handled and used carefully or it will not remain accurate.

SERVICE HINTS

Most of the service procedures in this manual are straightforward and can be performed by anyone reasonably handy with tools. It is suggested, however, that you consider your skills and available tools and equipment before attempting a repair involving major disassembly of the engine or drive unit.

Some operations, for example, require the use of a press. Other operations require precision measurement. Have the procedure or measurements performed by a professional if you do not have access to the correct equipment or are unfamiliar with its use.

Special Battery Precautions

Disconnecting or connecting the battery can create a spike or surge of current throughout the electrical system. This spike or surge can damage certain components of the charging system. Always verify the ignition switch is in the OFF position before connecting or disconnecting the battery or changing the selection on a battery switch.

Always disconnect both battery cables and remove the battery from the boat for charging. If the battery cables are connected, the charger may induce a damaging spike or surge of current into the electrical system. During charging, batteries produce explosive and corrosive gasses. These gases can cause corrosion in the battery compartment and creates an extremely hazardous condition.

Disconnect the cables from the battery prior to testing, adjusting or repairing many of the systems or components on the engine. This is nec-

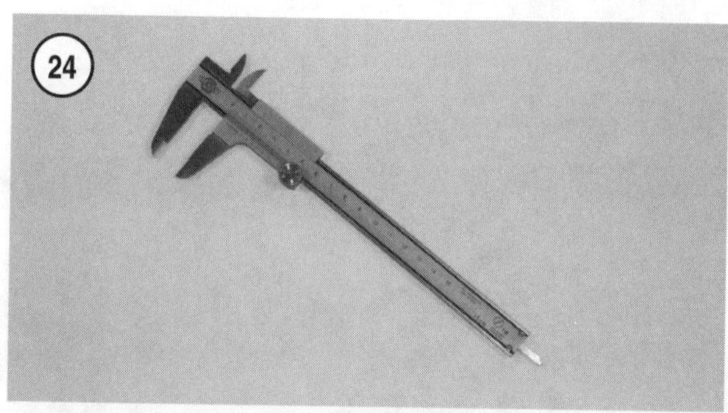
24

essary for safety, to prevent damage to test equipment and to ensure accurate testing or adjustment. Always disconnect the negative battery cable first, then the positive cable. When reconnecting the battery, always connect the positive cable first, then the negative cable.

Preparation for Disassembly

Repairs go much faster if the equipment is clean before you begin work. There are special cleaners such as Gunk or Bel-Ray Degreaser, for cleaning the engine and related components. Just spray or brush on the cleaning solution, let it stand, then rinse with a garden hose.

Use pressurized water to remove marine growth and corrosion or mineral deposits from external components such as the gearcase, drive shaft housing and clamp brackets. Avoid directing pressurized water directly as seals or gaskets; pressurized water can flow past seal and gasket surfaces and contaminate lubricating fluids.

WARNING

Never use gasoline as a cleaning agent. It presents an extreme fire hazard. Always work in a well-ventilated area if using cleaning solvent. Keep a Coast Guard approved fire extinguisher, rated for gasoline fires, readily accessible in the work area.

Much of the labor charged for a job performed at a dealership is usually for removal and disas-

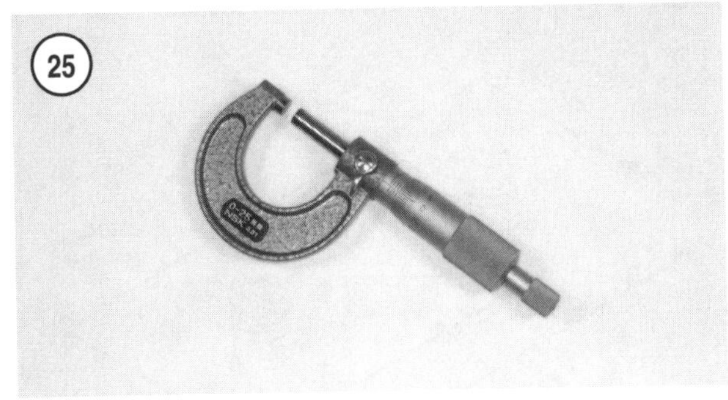
25

sembly of other parts to access defective parts or assemblies. It is frequently possible to perform most of the disassembly then take the defective part or assembly to the dealership for repair.

If you decide to perform the job yourself, read the appropriate section in this manual, in its entirety. Study the illustrations and text until you fully understand what is involved to complete the job. Make arrangements to purchase or rent all required special tools and equipment before starting.

Disassembly Precautions

During disassembly, keep a few general precautions in mind. Force is rarely needed to get things apart. If parts fit tightly, such as a bearing on a shaft, there is usually a tool designed to separate them. Never use a screwdriver to separate parts with a machined mating surface, such as the cylinder head or manifold. The surfaces will be damaged and leak.

Make diagrams or take instant photographs wherever similar-appearing parts are found. Often, disassembled parts are left for several days or longer before resuming work. You may not remember where everything came from, or carefully arranged parts may become disturbed.

Cover all openings after removing parts to keep contamination or other parts from entering.

Tag all similar internal parts for location and mounting direction. Reinstall all internal components in the same location and mounting direction as removed. Record the thickness and mounting location of any shims as they are removed. Place small bolts and parts in plastic sandwich bags. Seal and label the bags with masking tape.

Tag all wires, hoses and connections and make a sketch of the routing. Never rely on memory alone; it may be several days or longer before you resume work.

Protect all painted surfaces from physical damage. Never allow gasoline or cleaning solvent on these surfaces.

Assembly Precautions

No parts, except those assembled with a press fit, require unusual force during assembly. If a part is hard to remove or install, find out why before proceeding.

When assembling parts, start all fasteners, then tighten evenly in an alternating or crossing pattern unless a specific tightening sequence or procedure is given.

When assembling parts, be sure all shims, spacers and washers are installed in the same position and location as removed.

Whenever a rotating part butts against a stationary part, look for a shim or washer. Use new gaskets, seals and O-rings if there is any doubt about the conditions of the used ones. Unless otherwise specified, a thin coating of oil on gaskets may help them seal more effectively. Use heavy grease to hold small parts in place if they tend to fall out during assembly.

Use emery cloth and oil to remove high spots from piston surfaces. Use a dull screwdriver to remove carbon deposits from the cylinder head, ports and piston crown. *Do not* scratch or gouge these surfaces. Wipe the surfaces clean with a *clean* shop towel when finished.

If the carburetor must be repaired, completely disassemble it and soak all metal parts in a commercial carburetor cleaner. Never soak gaskets and rubber or plastic parts in these cleaners.

Clean rubber or plastic parts in warm soapy water. Never use a wire to clean jets and small passages because they are easily damaged. Use compressed air to blow debris from all passages in the carburetor body.

Take your time and do the job right. Break-in procedure for a newly rebuilt engine or drive is the same as for a new one. Use the recommended break-in oil and follow the instructions provided in the appropriate chapter.

SPECIAL TIPS

Because of the extreme demands placed on marine equipment, several points must be kept in mind when performing service and repair. The following are general suggestions that may improve the overall life of the machine and help avoid costly failure.

1. Unless otherwise specified, apply a threadlocking compound, such as Loctite Threadlocker, to all bolts and nuts, even if secured with a lockwasher. Use only the specified grade of threadlocking compound. A screw or bolt lost from an engine cover or bearing retainer could easily cause serious and expensive damage before the loss is noticed. When applying threadlocking compound, use only enough to lightly coat the threads. If too much is used, it can work its way down the threads and contaminate seals or bearings.
2. If self-locking fasteners are used, replace them with new ones. Do not install standard fasteners in place of self-locking ones.
3. Use caution when using air tools to remove stainless steel nuts or bolts. The heat generated during rapid spinning easily damages the threads of stainless steel fasteners. To prevent thread damage, apply penetrating oil as a cooling agent and loosen or tighten them slowly.
4. Use a wide chisel to straighten the tab of a fold-over type lockwasher. Such a tool provides a better contact surface than a screwdriver or pry bar, making straightening easier. During installation, use a new fold-over type lockwasher. If a new lockwasher is not available, fold over a tab on the washer that has not been previously used. Reusing the same tab may cause the washer to break, resulting in a loss of locking ability and a loose piece of metal adrift in the engine. When folding the tab into position, carefully pry it toward the flat on the bolt or nut. Use a pair or plies to bend the tab against the fastener. Do not use a punch and hammer to drive the tab into position. The resulting fold may be too sharp, weakening the washer and increasing its chance of failure.

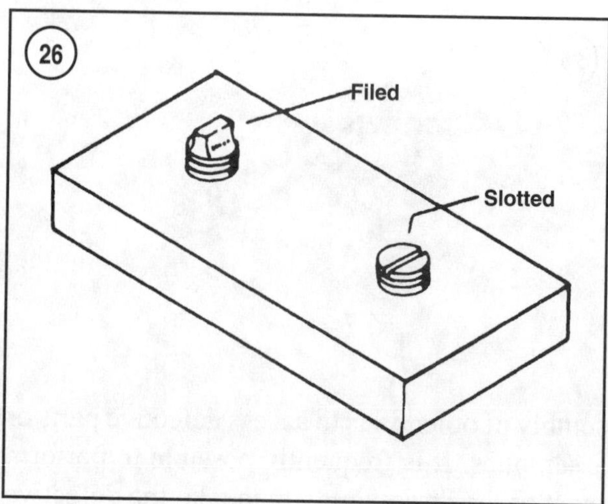

5. Use only the specified replacement parts if replacing a missing or damaged bolt, screw or nut. Many fasteners are specially hardened for the application.
6. Install only the specified gaskets. Unless specified otherwise, install them without sealant. Many gaskets are made with a material that swells when it contacts oil. Gasket sealer prevents them from swelling as intended and can result in oil leakage. Most gaskets must be a specific thickness. Installing a gasket that is too thin or too thick in a critical area could cause expensive damage.
7. Make sure all shims and washers are reinstalled in the same location and position. Whenever a rotating part contacts a stationary part, look for a shim or washer.

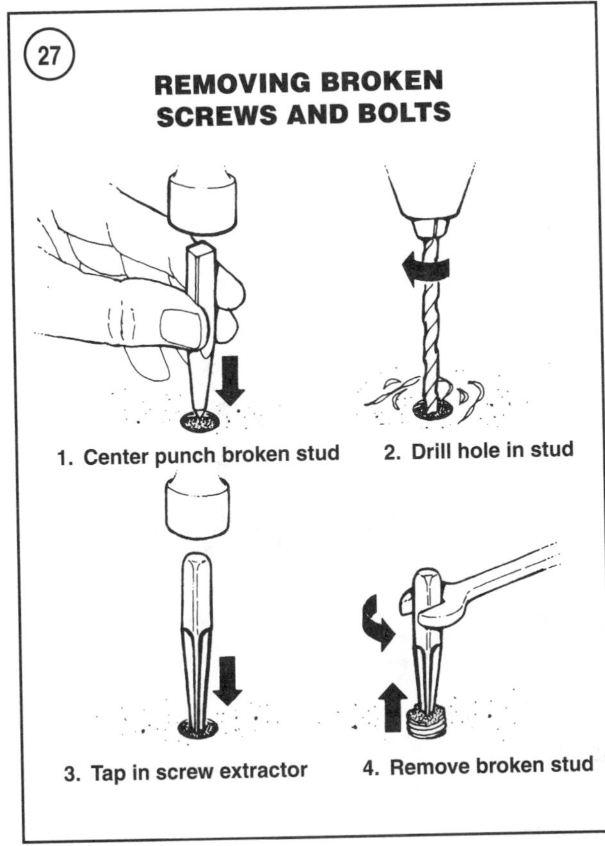
27
REMOVING BROKEN SCREWS AND BOLTS
1. Center punch broken stud
2. Drill hole in stud
3. Tap in screw extractor
4. Remove broken stud

MECHANICS TECHNIQUES

Marine engines are subjected to conditions very different from most engines. They are repeatedly subjected to a corrosive environment followed by periods of non-use for weeks or longer. Such use invites corrosion damage to fasteners, causing difficulty or breakage during removal. This section provides information that is useful for removing stuck or broken fasteners and repairing damaged threads.

Removing Stuck Fasteners

When a nut or bolt corrodes and cannot be removed, several methods may be used to loosen it. First, apply penetrating oil, such as Liquid Wrench or WD-40. Apply it liberally to the threads and allow it to penetrate for 10-15 minutes. Tap the fastener several times with a small hammer; however, do not hit it hard enough to cause damage. Reapply the penetrating oil if necessary.

For stuck screws, apply penetrating oil as described, then insert a screwdriver in the slot. Tap the top of the screwdriver with a hammer. This looses the corrosion in the threads allowing it to turn. If the screw head is too damaged to use a screwdriver, grip the head with locking pliers and twist the screw from the assembly.

A Phillips, Allen or Torx screwdriver may start to slip in the screw during removal. If slippage occurs, stop immediately and apply a dab of course valve lapping compound onto the tip of the screwdriver. Valve lapping compound or a special screw removal compound is available from most hardware and automotive parts stores. Insert the driver into the screw and apply downward pressure while turning. The gritty material in the compound improves the grip on the screw, allowing more rotational force before slippage occurs. Keep the compound away from any other engine components. It is very abrasive and can cause rapid wear if applied onto moving or sliding surfaces.

Avoid applying heat unless specifically instructed because it may melt, warp or remove the temper from parts.

Removing Broken Bolts or Screws

The head of bolt or screw may unexpectedly twist off during removal. Several methods are available for removing the remaining portion of the bolt or screw.

If a large portion of the bolt or screw projects out, try gripping it with locking pliers. If the projecting portion is too small, file it to fit a wrench or cut a slot in it to fit a screwdriver (**Figure 26**). If the head breaks off flush or cannot be turned with a screwdriver or wrench, use a screw extractor (**Figure 27**). To do this, center punch the remaining portion of the screw or bolt. Select the proper size of extractor for the size of the fastener. Using the drill size specified on the extractor, drill a hole into the fastener. Do not drill deeper than the remaining fastener. Carefully tap the extractor into the hole and back the remnant out using a wrench on the extractor.

Remedying Stripped Threads

Occasionally, threads are stripped through carelessness or impact damage. Often the threads can be repaired by running a tap (for internal threads on nuts) or die (for external threads on bolts) through threads (**Figure 28**).

To clean or repair spark plug threads, use a spark plug tap. If an internal thread is damaged, it may be necessary to install a Helicoil or some other type of thread insert. Follow the manufacturer's instructions when installing their insert.

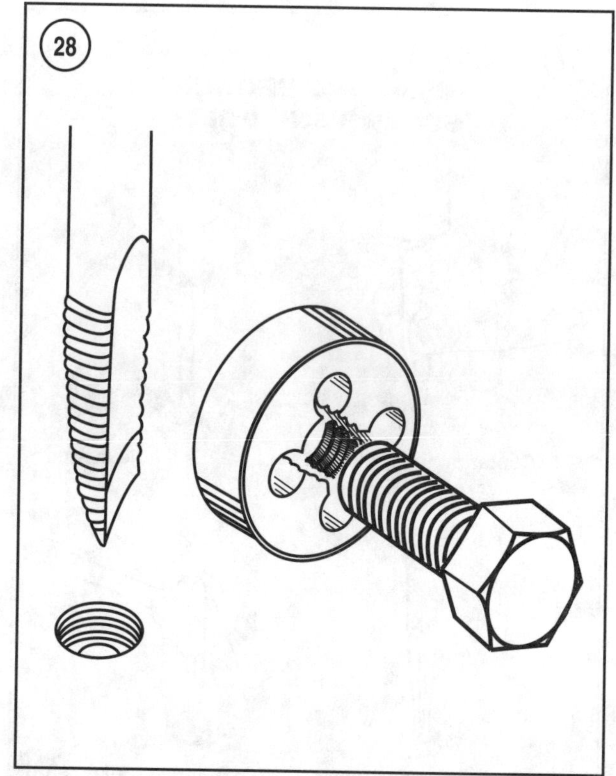

Chapter Three

3

Troubleshooting

Every internal combustion engine requires proper ignition, adequate compression and an uninterrupted supply of fuel and air. If any of these are lacking, the engine will not run.

Troubleshooting is a relatively simple matter when it is done logically. The first step in any troubleshooting procedure is to define the symptoms as fully as possible and then localize the problem. Subsequent steps involve testing and analyzing those areas which could cause the symptoms. A haphazard approach may eventually solve the problem, but it can be costly in terms of wasted time and unnecessary parts replacement.

Here are some axioms to remember about troubleshooting:

a. Never assume anything. Perform tests and inspections that are designed to locate problems and identify parts and systems that are operating properly.
b. Do not overlook the obvious. A dead battery or fuel tank that is empty will certainly provide problems with starting.
c. Do not skip the basics. Simple solutions often solve problems that appear to be complex.

If the engine suddenly stops running or refuses to start, check the easiest and most accessible areas first. Make sure there is fuel in the tank, and that the spark plugs and all wiring harnesses are properly connected. Something as simple as a loose terminal connection on the ignition coil can cause the engine to stop, especially if the craft is in turbulent water. It is embarrassing and sometimes costly to be towed back to shore in such a case. You should be familiar enough with your boat's engine compartment to know which wires go where. If a quick visual check does not turn up the cause of the problem, take a closer look.

Learning to recognize and describe symptoms accurately will make repairs easier for you or a technician at the shop. Saying that *it will not run* is not the same as saying *it quit at high speed and would not restart.* Identifying as many related symptoms as possible often aids in diagnosis. Note whether the engine lost power gradually or all at once, what color of smoke (if any) came from the exhaust and so on. After the symptoms are defined, continue to test and analyze those areas which are most likely to cause the problem(s). Often, you do not need complicated test equipment to determine if the repairs can be performed at home.

The electrical system is the weakest link in the chain. More problems result from electrical malfunctions than from any other source. Corrosion, loose connections, broken wires and other problems that break electrical contact are constant problems to marine equipment. Keep this in mind before you blame the fuel system and start making unnecessary carburetor adjustments. A few simple checks can keep a small problem from turning into a large one.

On the other hand, be realistic and do not attempt repairs beyond your abilities or with makeshift tools. Stripping the threads on a carburetor fuel inlet while trying to change the fuel filter will cost you several hundred dollars for a new carburetor. Also, marine service departments tend to charge heavily for putting together a disassembled engine or other component that may have been abused. Some will not even take on such a job. Use common sense and do not get in over your head or attempt a job without the proper tools.

Proper lubrication, maintenance and periodic tune-ups as described in Chapter Four will reduce the necessity for troubleshooting. However, even with the best of care, every marine engine is prone to problems which will eventually need troubleshooting.

If replacement components are to be installed, **do not** use automotive parts. Components, such as carburetors, starters and alternators specified for marine use may appear to be the same as automotive components, but they are different. Marine components have been designed or modified to withstand the unique requirements of marine service. Many components are changed to provide a measure of safety that is not required of automotive service. For example, a marine starter is flash-proofed to prevent possible ignition of fuel vapor in the bilge. The use of an automotive starter as a replacement can result in an explosion or fire. The cost of serious injury or loss of boat and life easily exceeds that of the correct component.

This chapter contains brief descriptions of each major operating system and troubleshooting procedures to be used. The troubleshooting procedures analyze common symptoms and provide logical methods of isolation. Always use a logical, systematic approach when troubleshooting.

Troubleshooting diagrams for individual systems are provided in this chapter. Master troubleshooting charts (**Table 1** and **Table 2**) are at the end of the chapter. Refer to *Quick Reference Data* for model coverage. Tables 1-10 are at the end of this chapter.

STARTING SYSTEM

The starting system consists of the battery, starter motor, starter solenoid, assist solenoid (relay), ignition switch, neutral start switch, 50/60 amp circuit breaker, 20 amp fuse and related circuitry. See the appropriate wiring diagram at the end of the manual. The neutral switch is located inside the remote control assembly and allows starter operation only if the shift selector lever is in NEUTRAL.

All 1994 models except the Ford based 5.0 L and 5.8 L engines are equipped with a conventional field-wound starter motor. The 1994 5.0 L and 5.8 L models and all 1995-on General Motors based engines are equipped with a permanent magnet, gear reduction type starter motor.

Field-Wound Starter Motor

On-boat testing

Two of these procedures require a fully charged 12-volt battery, to be used as a booster, and a pair of jumper cables. Use the jumper cables as outlined in *Jump Starting*, in Chapter Twelve. Disconnect the wiring harness and leads from the rear of the alternator before connecting a booster battery for these tests. This will protect the alternator diodes from possible damage.

Slow cranking starter

1. Connect the 12-volt booster battery to the engine's battery with jumper cables. Listen to the starter cranking speed as the engine is cranked. If the cranking speed sounds normal, check the battery for loose or corroded connections or a low charge. Clean and tighten the connections as required. Recharge the battery if necessary.
2. If cranking speed does not sound normal, clean and tighten all starter solenoid connections and the battery ground on the engine.
3. Repeat Step 1. If the cranking speed is still too slow, replace the starter.

Starter solenoid clicks, starter does not crank

1. Clean and tighten all starter and solenoid connections. Make sure the terminal eyelets are securely fastened to the wire strands and are not corroded.
2. Remove the battery terminal clamps. Clean the clamps and battery posts. Reinstall the clamps and tighten securely.
3. If the starter still does not crank, connect the 12-volt booster battery to the engine's battery with the jumper cables. If the starter still does not crank, replace the starter.

Starter solenoid does not click, starter does not crank

1. Make sure the shift control is in neutral. Current must pass through the neutral start safety switch in the shift control.
2. Detach the wire from the S terminal at the starter solenoid (at the starter motor). Connect a temporary jumper wire between this terminal and the positive battery post.
   a. If the engine starter engages, check the starter control circuit from the S terminal of the ignition switch to the assist solenoid, then to the S terminal of the starter solenoid. Clean and tighten all connections if necessary.
   b. If the starter does not engage properly, replace the starter solenoid.

Starter spins but does not crank

1. Remove the starter. See Chapter Eleven.
2. Check the starter pinion gear. If the teeth are chipped or worn, inspect the flywheel ring gear for damage. Replace the starter and/or ring gear as required.
3. If the pinion gear is in good condition, disassemble the starter and check the armature shaft for corrosion. See *Brush Replacement* in Chapter Eleven for disassembly procedure. If no corrosion is found, the starter drive mechanism is slipping. Replace the starter with a new or rebuilt marine unit.

Starter will not disengage when ignition switch is released

This problem is usually caused by a sticking switch or solenoid.

NOTE

A low battery or loose or corroded battery connections can also cause the starter to remain engaged with the flywheel ring gear. Low voltage at the

3

starter can cause the contacts inside the solenoid to chatter and weld together, resulting in the solenoid sticking in the ON position.

On models with an electric fuel pump, the orange diode for the fuel pump may be defective.

Loud grinding noises when starter runs

This can be caused by improper meshing of the starter pinion and flywheel ring gear or by a broken overrunning clutch mechanism.

1. Remove the starter. See Chapter Eleven.
2. Check the starter pinion gear. If the teeth are chipped or worn, inspect the flywheel ring gear for damage. Replace the starter and/or ring gear as required.
3. If the pinion gear is in good condition, disassemble and check the starter. See Chapter Eleven for disassembly procedure.

Starter resistance test

The following test will determine the amount of voltage reaching the starter motor during cranking and will also indicate if excessive resistance is present in the circuit.

Starter Solenoid Test (Field-Wound Starter Motor)

Refer to **Figure 1** for this procedure.

1. Check the battery and cable condition. Clean the terminals, replace suspect cables or recharge the battery as required.
2. Start the engine and warm to normal operating temperature.
3. Shut the engine off. Disconnect the distributor primary lead from the coil negative terminal to prevent the engine from starting.
4. Connect the positive lead of a voltmeter to the bottom terminal on the solenoid, then ground the negative lead to the starter frame. See **Figure 2**.

CAUTION
Do not crank the engine for more than 10 seconds in Step 5. Wait for at least 2 minutes before cranking the engine again or it may overheat and damage the starter motor.

5. Crank the engine for a few seconds while noting the voltmeter reading. If it reads less than 9 volts, connect the voltmeter as shown in **Figure 3**.
6. While cranking the engine, switch the voltmeter from its high to low scale, take the reading, then switch the meter back to its high scale and stop cranking the engine. If the voltmeter reading is more than 1/10 volt, replace the solenoid.
7. If the voltmeter reads less than 1/10 volt in Step 6, check the current draw of the solenoid windings:
   a. Remove the solenoid terminal screw (**Figure 1**) and bend the field leads enough so they will not touch the terminal. Ground the solenoid M terminal to the starter motor frame with a jumper wire.
   b. Connect a battery, a carbon pile and an ammeter with a 0-100 amp scale in series with the solenoid S terminal as shown in **Figure 1**. Ground the starter frame to the negative battery terminal.
   c. Connect the voltmeter between the solenoid frame and S terminal.
   d. Adjust the carbon pile slowly until the voltmeter shows 10 volts, then note the ammeter scale. The current draw of both windings in parallel should be 47-55 amps at 10 volts (room temperature).
   e. Remove the jumper wire installed between the M terminal and starter frame. Readjust the carbon pile until the voltmeter shows 10 volts, then note the ammeter scale. The current draw of the hold-in winding should be 14.5-16.5 amps at 10 volts (room temperature).
   f. If the solenoid windings do not perform as specified, replace the solenoid.

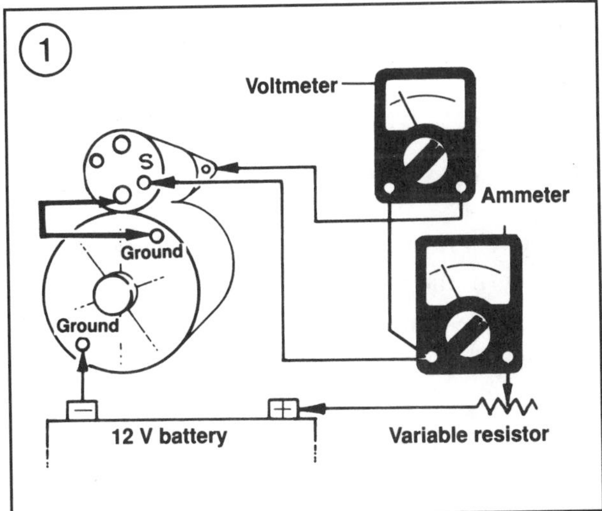

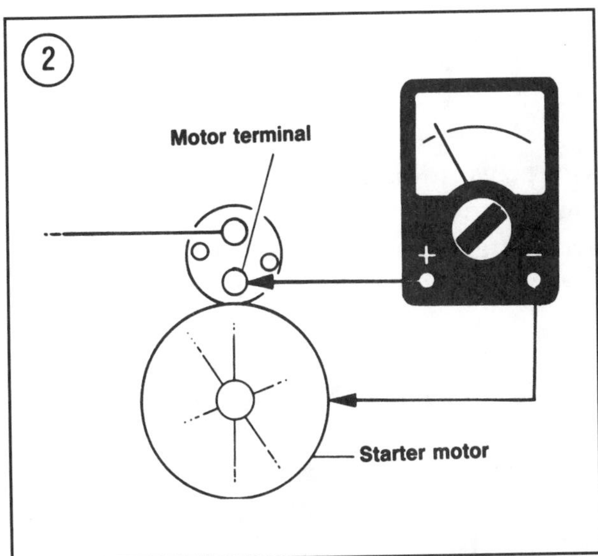

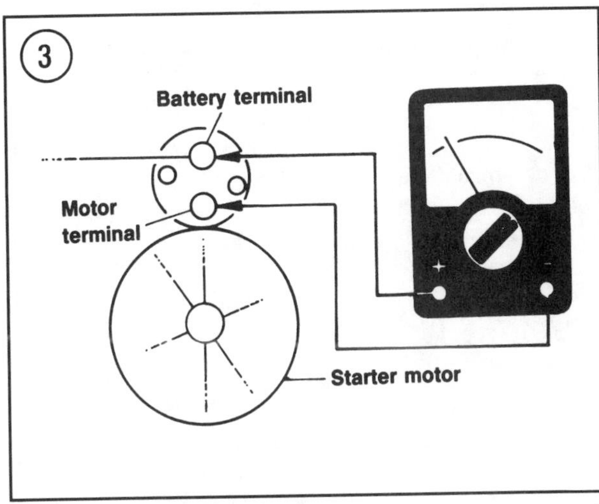

Permanent Magnet Gear Reduction Starter Motor

The permanent magnet starter motor contains no field coils or pole shoes. The magnetic field is provided by a series of small permanent magnets. As a result, there is no motor field circuit and thus no potential field wire-to-frame shorts or other electrical problems related to the field circuit. The motor uses only an armature circuit. Refer to Chapter Eleven for a full description of the motor.

The permanent magnet starter motor requires special handling during service. The permanent magnets are quite brittle, and the magnetic field can be destroyed by a sharp impact or by dropping the starter motor.

Use the following test procedures if a starting system malfunction occurs.

WARNING
Battery voltage is present at the starter motor cable at all times. Always disconnect the negative battery cable from the battery before servicing the starter motor or working in the area near the starter motor.

Starter motor inspection

Periodic inspection or lubrication of the starter motor is not required. If the starter motor cranks the engine at the normal speed, the motor and starting circuit can be considered to be in acceptable condition.

The ground path for the starter motor and solenoid is provided by their respective mounting and fasteners. Make sure the solenoid and motor mounting fasteners are tightened securely and that their mounting surfaces are clean (not painted). Resistance between the starter motor or solenoid and engine block should be approximately zero ohm.

Inspect the battery and battery cables for clean and tight connections. The battery must be fully charged and in acceptable condition for the starting system to operate correctly. Check the battery's state of charge as described in Chapter Eleven.

Starter motor test

CAUTION
Do not crank the engine for more than 10 seconds or the motor will overheat. Wait at least 2 minutes before cranking the engine again.

1. Disable the ignition system to prevent the engine from starting during this procedure.
   a. *Prestolite BID ignition*—Make sure the ignition switch is in the OFF position. Disconnect both primary ignition wires from the ignition coil.
   b. *EST ignition*—Make sure the ignition switch is in the OFF position. Disconnect the pink and brown wire connector from the E-coil (ignition coil).
   c. *TFI-IV ignition*—Make sure the ignition switch is in the OFF position. Disconnect the 3-pin connector from the E-coil (ignition coil).
2. Connect a voltmeter between the battery terminal (**Figure 4**) and the starter motor housing. Battery voltage should be present. If not, inspect the battery cable between the battery and starter solenoid loose or corroded connections. Also, make sure the starter motor is securely mounted and the starter-to-engine mounting surfaces are clean.
3. If battery voltage is noted in Step 2, connect a remote starter switch between the battery terminal and the S terminal on the solenoid. See **Figure 4**. Activate the remote starter switch. The starter should crank the engine normally. If not, replace the starter motor as described in Chapter Eleven. If the starter cranks the engine normally, inspect the wire between the assist solenoid and starter solenoid for an open circuit or loose or corroded connections. Repair or replace the wire as necessary.

Starter assist solenoid (relay) test

1. Connect a voltmeter between the assist solenoid S terminal and a good engine ground.
2. Turn the ignition switch to the ON position and note the voltmeter. Battery voltage should be noted.
3. If battery voltage is noted, connect the voltmeter to the solenoid output terminal and ground. Turn the ignition switch to ON and note the voltmeter. Replace the assist solenoid if less than battery voltage is noted.
4. If less than battery voltage is noted, first make sure the solenoid is securely grounded. If the solenoid ground is in good condition, check the wire between the solenoid S terminal and the engine wiring harness. Also, check for a defective neutral switch, ignition switch, blow 20 amp fuse or 50 amp circuit breaker.

CHARGING SYSTEM

The charging system consists of the alternator, voltage regulator, battery, ignition switch, instrument panel ammeter or voltmeter, the necessary connecting wiring and circuit breakers or fuses.

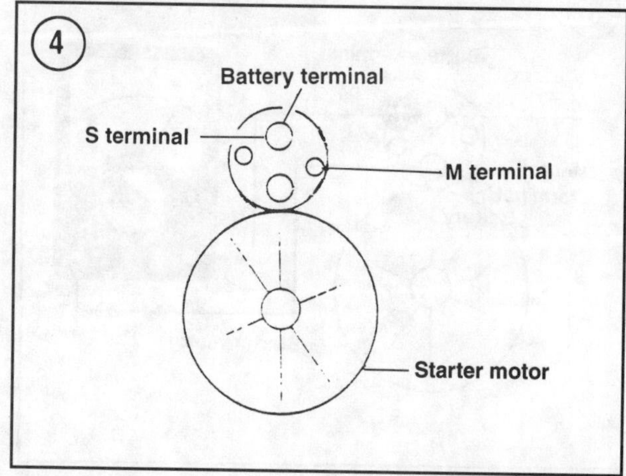

The alternator pulley is turned by a drive belt that is driven by the engine crankshaft pulley. As engine speed varies, the electrical output from the alternator can vary, so a voltage regulator is necessary to control the voltage output within a safe range. An ammeter or voltmeter on the boat's instrument panel indicates whether charging or discharging is taking place.

All models are equipped with either a 51 or 65 amp alternator with a transistorized voltage regulator attached to the rear of the alternator housing. The output rating is stamped on the alternator frame.

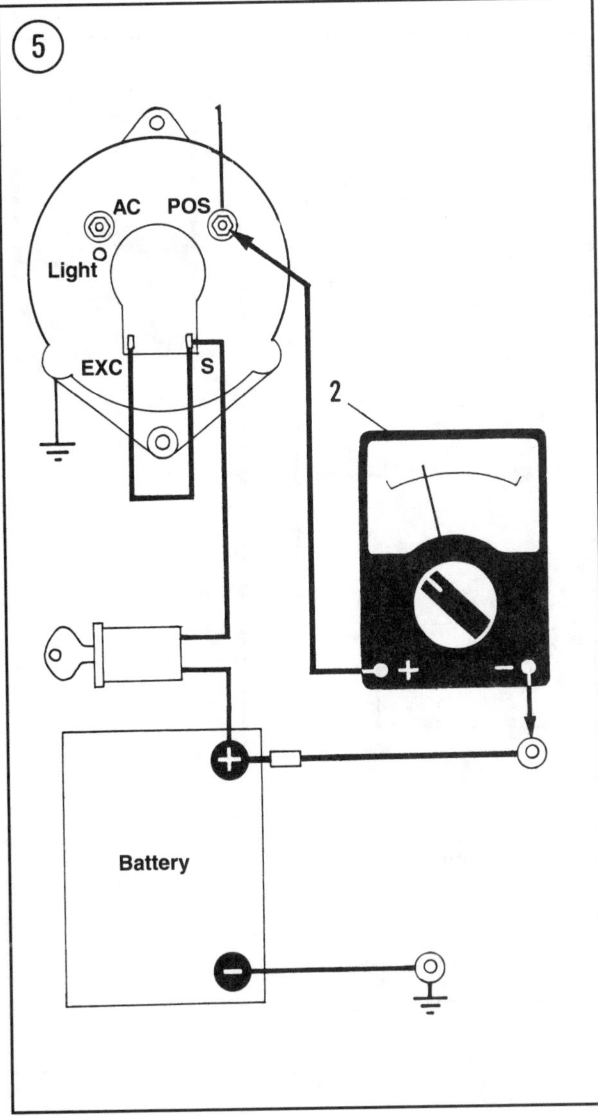

Initial Tests

Charging system troubles are generally caused by a defective alternator, voltage regulator, battery or a blown fuse. They may also be caused by something as simple as incorrect drive belt tension.

Output Test

1. Detach the Orange lead from the POS (+) stud (1, **Figure 5**) on the back of the alternator.
2. Attach a voltmeter in series between the POS (+) terminal and the detached orange wire. See 2, **Figure 5**.
3. Attach a calibrated test load to the battery terminals. A Stevens LB-85 Load Bank or other carbon pile set load should be used.
4. Start the engine and run the engine at the test speeds listed in **Table 4**.
5. Observe the maximum output amps at each of the test engine speeds. Adjust the test load as necessary for maximum output.
6. Unplug the red/purple wire from the EXC terminal on the rear of the alternator.
7. Connect a voltmeter (1, **Figure 6**) between the red/purple lead (2, **Figure 6**) and the engine ground (3).
8. Battery voltage (or nearly battery voltage) should be indicated when the ignition switch is ON.
9. If the voltmeter does not indicate voltage within 1 volt of battery voltage, check the red/purple wire for poor connections or damaged wiring. Correct as necessary.
10. Connect a voltmeter between the red/purple lead and the S terminal on the rear of the alternator. See **Figure 7**.
11. The indicated voltage should be the same as (or nearly the same as battery voltage) when the ignition switch is ON.

Excitation/Sensing Circuitry Test

The transistorized regulator attached to the rear of the alternator, includes excitation and sensing circuits. The excitation circuit, which is connected to the ignition switch, sends a small amount of current to the alternator rotor field winding, initiating output during starting. This initial voltage allows the alternator to generate voltage more quickly during startup than just relying on residual magnetism. The sensing circuit allows the regulator to sense resistance inside the alternator (internally) and outside the alternator (externally).

NOTE
Do not start the engine during this test.

1. Remove the protective cap from the stud marked LIGHT located on the rear of the alternator.
2. Attach the positive lead of a voltmeter to the LIGHT terminal. See **Figure 8**.
3. Attach the negative lead of a voltmeter to the battery ground (–) terminal.
4. Turn the key switch ON and observe the voltage at the terminal marked LIGHT.
5. If the indicated voltage is not within 1.5-3.0 volts, install a new voltage regulator assembly.

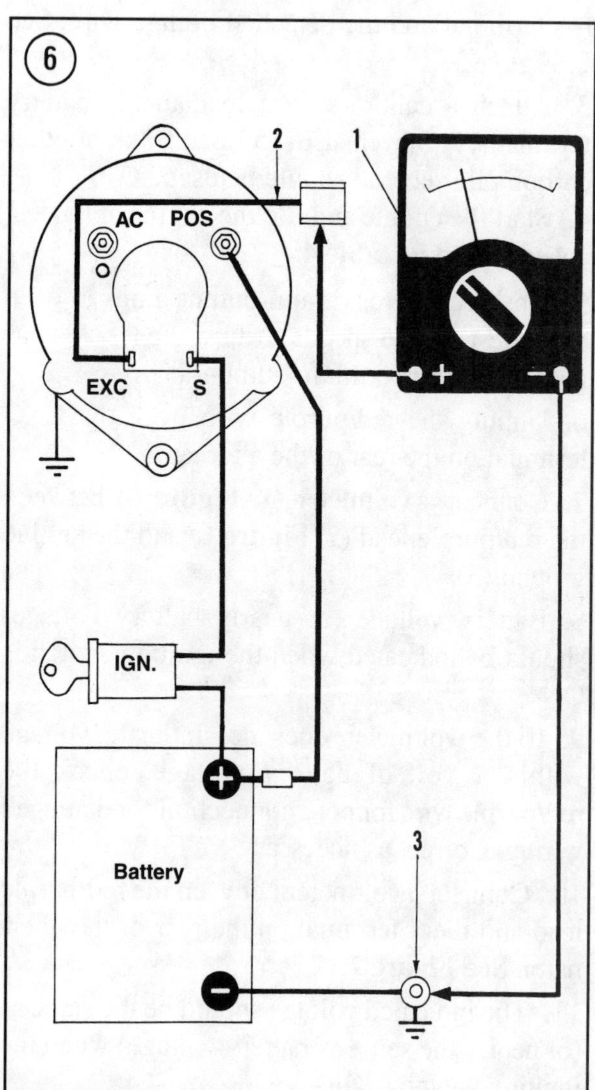

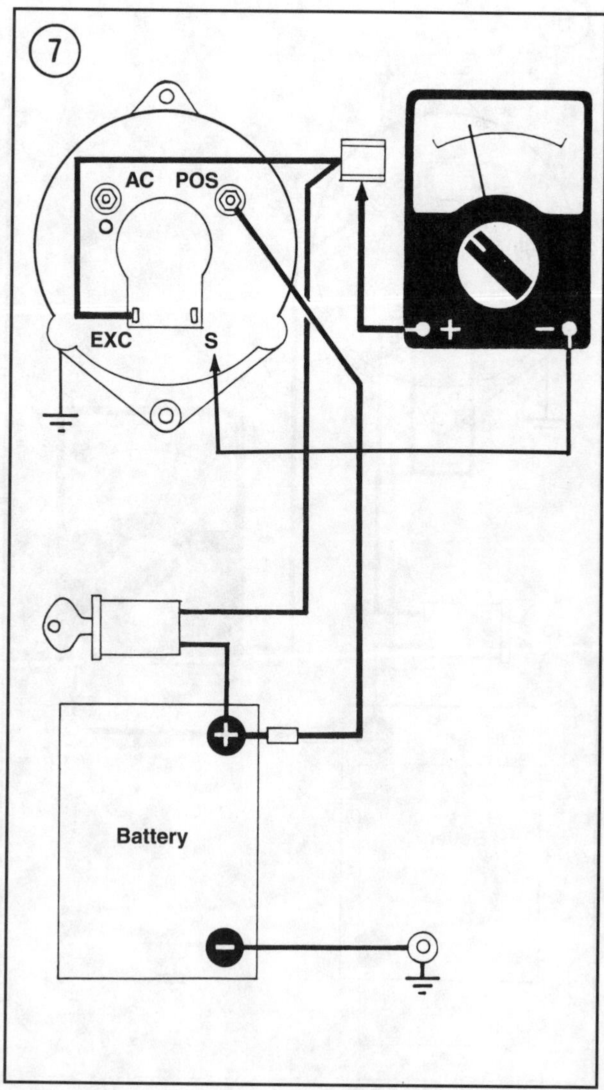

6. If the alternator output was not correct when tested in the *Output Test*, but the tests in Steps 1-5 are within specification, perform the *Diode Trio Test* as described in this chapter.

Diode Trio Test

1. Connect a jumper wire between the POS + and the LIGHT terminal. Both terminals are on the rear of the alternator.
2. Attach the positive lead of a voltmeter to the POS + terminal. See **Figure 9**.
3. Attach the negative lead of the voltmeter to the battery ground (–) point on the engine.
4. Start the engine and let it run at idle speed.
5. If voltage is present at the POS (+) terminal, the diode trio inside the alternator is damaged. Install a new or rebuilt alternator.

IGNITION SYSTEM

The Volvo-Penta models covered in this manual are equipped with the following ignition systems:

a. *EST (Electronic Spark Timing)*—3.0GL/GS, 4.3GL/GS/Gi, 5.0 Gi, 5.7Gi and 7.4Gi/GSi.

b. *Prestolite BID (Breakerless Inductive Distributor)*—5.0GL, 5.7GL, 7.4GL, 8.2GL, 5.0FL and 5.8FL.

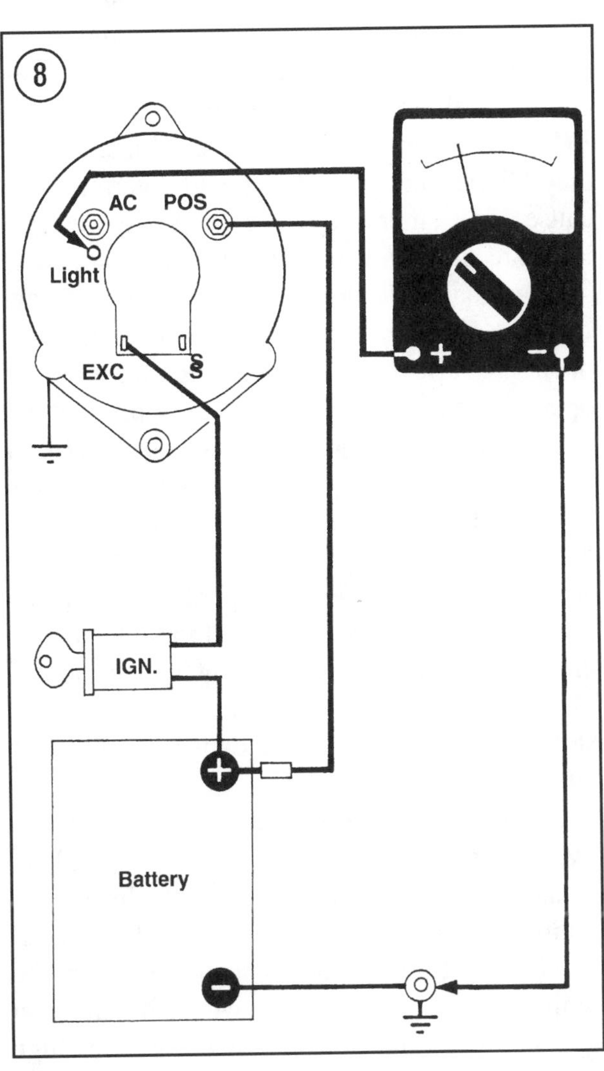

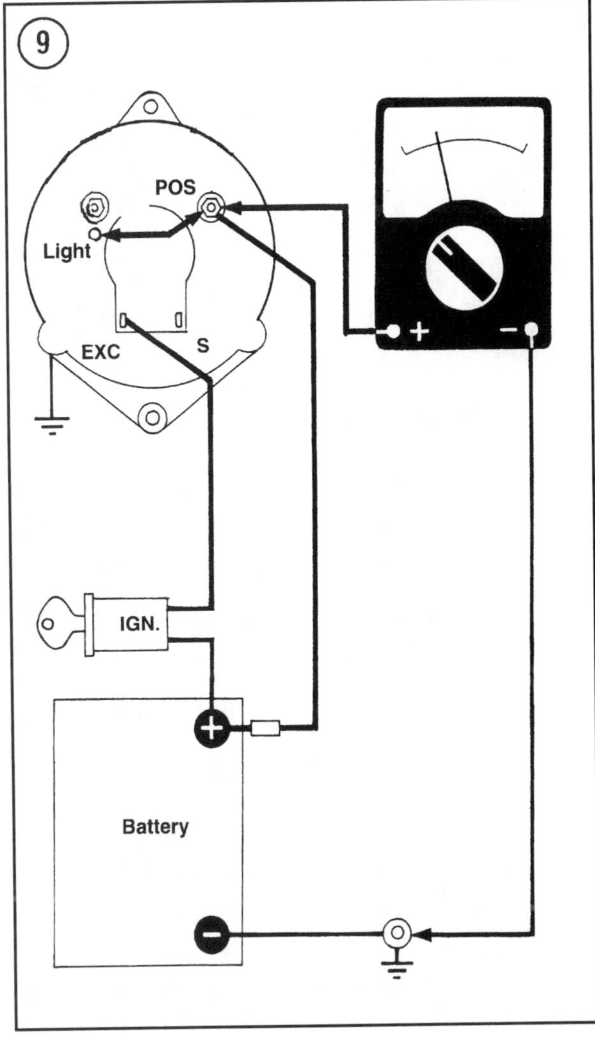

c. *TFI-IV (Thick Film Ignition, fouth generation)*—5.0Fi and 5.8Fi.

d. Di (Distributor ignition) 4.3Gi, 5.0Gi, 5.7, 7.4, and 8.2Gsi.

e. Di ignition replaced EST in 1999 on all EFI engines.

Refer to Table 5 for ignition system application.

Disable Ignition System

For some tests and service, such as a compression test, it is necessary to disable the ignition system to prevent the engine from starting. Using an improper method to disable can result in ignition system damage. Therefore, always use an approved method to disable the ignition system.

On models equipped with EST and Di ignition, remove the connector containing the pink and brown wires from the E-coil.

On models equipped with BID ignition, remove both primary ignition wires from the ignition coil.

On models equipped with TFI-IV ignition, remove the 3-pin primary ignition connector from the E-coil.

General Ignition Troubleshooting

Many problems involving failure to start, poor performance or rough running stem from trouble in the ignition system. Novice troubleshooters often assume that these symptoms point to the fuel system instead of the ignition system. Then, they become frustrated when changes to the fuel system are ineffective or make the problems worse.

Note the following performance symptoms:

a. Engine misfires.

b. Hesitates on acceleration (misfiring).

c. Loss of power at high speed (misfiring).

d. Hard starting (or not starting).

e. Rough idle.

These symptoms may be caused by one or more of the following ignition components:

a. Spark plug(s).

b. Secondary (spark plug) wire(s).

c. Distributor cap and rotor.

d. Ignition coil.

e. Ignition module (Delco EST, Di and TFI-IV ignition).

f. Knock sensor (TFI-IV ignition).

g. S.L.O.W. (speed limiting operational warning) switches (TFI-IV ignition).

h. Pickup coil (Delco EST and Di ignition).

i. Sensor coil (Prestolite ignition).

j. Breaker points (breaker-point ignition).

Most of the previously listed symptoms can also be caused by a carburetor or fuel injection system that is damaged, worn or improperly adjusted, or a fuel pump that is beginning to fail.

Ignition system troubles may be roughly divided between those affecting only one cylinder and those affecting all cylinders.

If the problem affects only one cylinder, locate the cylinder that is misfiring and determine the cause. Ignition problems affecting only one cylinder are almost always caused by the spark plug, high tension (spark plug) wire or the distributor cap.

Spark plug condition is an important indicator of engine performance. Spark plugs in a properly operating engine will have slightly pitted electrodes and a light tan insulator tip. **Figure 10** shows a normal plug and a number of others which indicate trouble in their respective cylinders. All of the spark plugs should be nearly alike. If one (or two) of the spark plugs appears different than the rest, it is an important clue that the cylinder is somehow different than the others. The difference could be a faulty plug, high tension wire or internal engine damage that affects only that cylinder.

If the problem affects all of the cylinders (weak or no spark), then the trouble is most likely located in the ignition coil, rotor, distributor, ignition sensor or associated wiring. Do not fail to check wiring connectors and fuses in the ignition circuit. Refer to the wiring diagrams at the end of the manual. Also, make sure the high

(10)

SPARK PLUG CONDITION

NORMAL

- Identified by light tan or gray deposits on the firing tip.
- Can be cleaned.

GAP BRIDGED

- Identified by deposit buildup closing gap between electrodes.
- Caused by oil or carbon fouling. If deposits are not excessive, the plug can be cleaned.

OIL FOULED

- Identified by wet black deposits on the insulator shell bore and electrodes.
- Caused by excessive oil entering combustion chamber through worn rings and pistons, excessive clearance between valve guides and stems or worn or loose bearings. Can be cleaned. If engine is not repaired, use a hotter plug.

CARBON FOULED

- Identified by black, dry fluffy carbon deposits on insulator tips, exposed shell surfaces and electrodes.
- Caused by too cold a plug, weak ignition, dirty air cleaner, too rich a fuel mixture or excessive idling. Can be cleaned.

LEAD FOULED

- Identified by dark gray, black, yellow or tan deposits or a fused glazed coating on the insulator tip.
- Caused by highly leaded gasoline. Can be cleaned.

WORN

- Identified by severely eroded or worn electrodes.
- Caused by normal wear. Should be replaced.

FUSED SPOT DEPOSIT

- Identified by melted or spotty deposits resembling bubbles or blisters.
- Caused by sudden acceleration. Can be cleaned.

OVERHEATING

- Identified by a white or light gray insulator with small black or gray brown spots and with bluish-burnt appearance of electrodes.
- Caused by engine overheating, wrong type of fuel, loose spark plugs, too hot a plug or incorrect ignition timing. Replace the plug.

PREIGNITION

- Identified by melted electrodes and possibly blistered insulator. Metallic deposits on insulator indicate engine damage.
- Caused by wrong type of fuel, incorrect ignition timing or advance, too hot a plug, burned valves or engine overheating. Replace the plug.

tension wires are attached to the correct spark plugs. The firing order is listed in **Table 5**.

Some tests of the ignition system require running the engine with one spark plug or the ignition coil wire unplugged. The safest way to do this is to disconnect the wire(s) with the engine stopped, then hold its end next to a metal surface with insulated pliers as shown in **Figure 11**, typical.

WARNING
Never disconnect a spark plug or ignition coil wire when the engine is running. The high voltage in the ignition system could cause serious injury or even death.

WARNING
Be certain the engine compartment is well ventilated and that no gasoline vapor is present during ignition system troubleshooting.

The overall condition of the ignition system can be determined as follows.

1. Detach the ignition coil wire from the distributor cap.
2. Position the end of the wire approximately 1/4 in. (6.3 mm) from a good engine ground (**Figure 11**). It may be necessary to insert an adapter into the end of the coil wire to extend the conductor to the end of the boot.
3. Crank the engine and check for spark.
4. If regular, sufficient spark is present at the coil wire in Step 3, the spark producing are in good condition. Further tests may be necessary to determine if the spark is occurring at the correct time (timing) or if some other problem is occurring.

Troubleshooting Electronic Spark Timing (EST) System

EST (electronic spark timing) ignition is used on 3.0GL/GS, 4.3GL/GS/Gi, 5.0Gi, 5.7Gi and 7.4Gi/GSi models. The system includes a distributor, pickup coil, electronic ignition module, ignition coil, battery, ignition switch and related circuitry. The ignition module and pickup coil are located inside the distributor assembly. Spark advance and dwell are controlled electronically by the ignition module, so there is no centrifugal spark advance mechanism. **Figure 12** shows an exploded view of a typical distributor's components.

Refer to the following procedure to help isolate ignition malfunctions in the EST ignition systems. This procedure assumes the battery and starting system are in acceptable condition.

NOTE
Models equipped with the EST and Di ignition and electronic fuel injection will have additional wires attached to the distributor for control of the fuel injection. Ignition troubleshooting procedures are the same as for models without fuel injection.

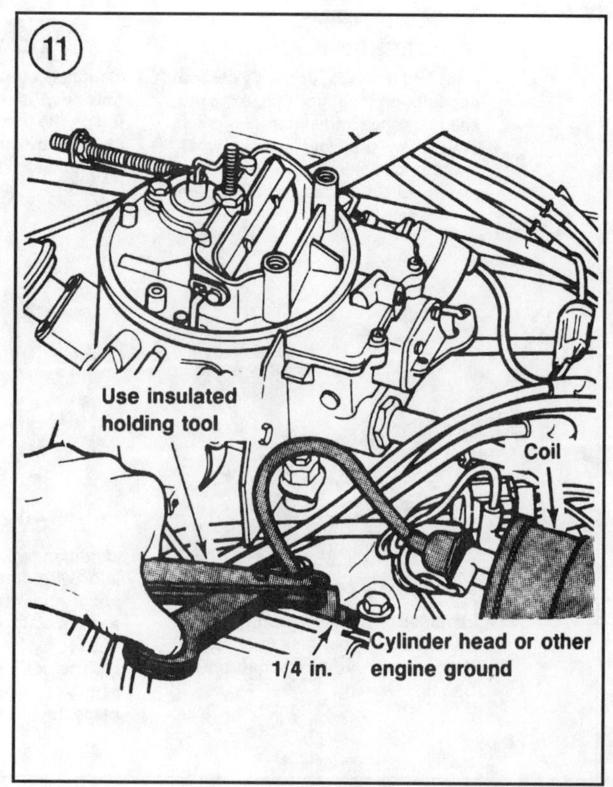

(12)

ELECTRONIC SPARK TIMING (EST) IGNITION

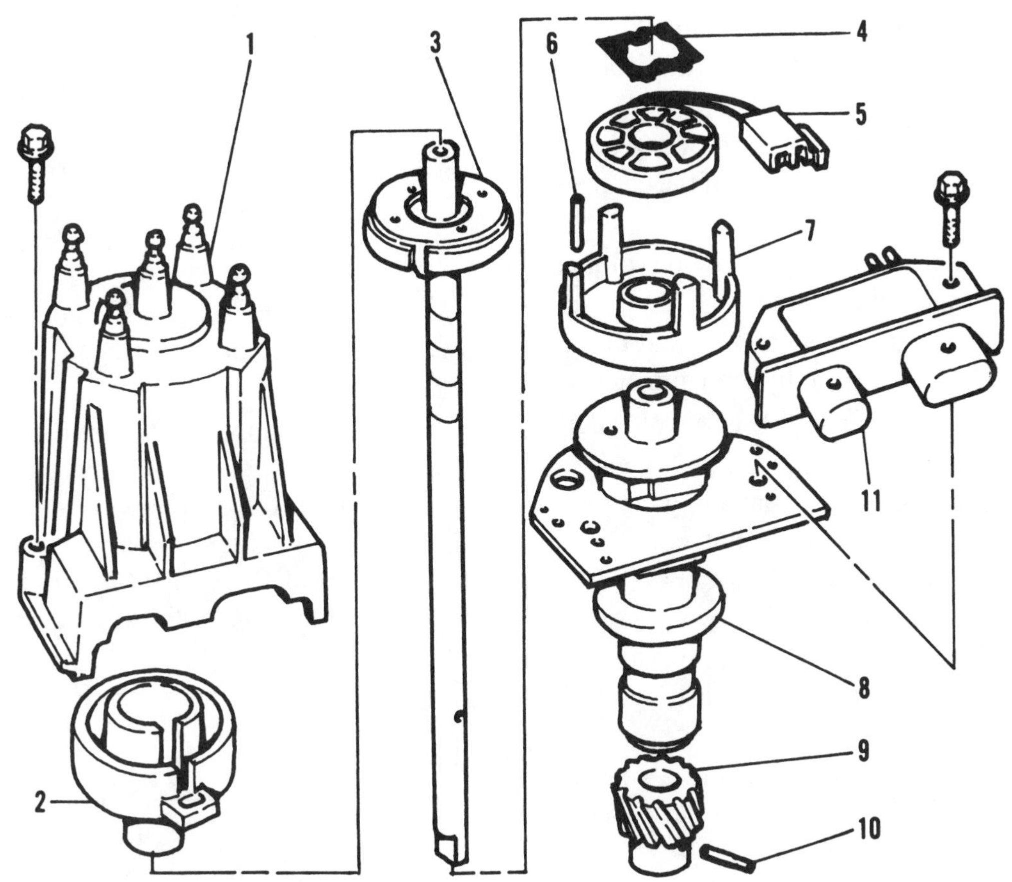

1. Distributor cap
2. Rotor
3. Shaft and magnet assembly
4. Retainer
5. Pickup coil
6. Locating pin
7. Pole piece
8. Housing
9. Driven gear
10. Roll pin
11. Ignition module

1. Make sure all terminal connections at the distributor, ignition module and ignition coil are clean and tight. Make sure the battery is in acceptable condition and fully charged. Make sure the distributor clamp screw is securely tightened.
2. Use a voltmeter and check for correct voltage delivery to the ignition coil as follows:
   a. Detach the connector containing the purple and gray wires from the ignition coil. See **Figure 13**.
   b. Attach the positive (+) lead of a voltmeter to the purple wire terminal of the connector detached in substep 2a.
   c. Attach the negative (–) lead of the voltmeter to a good engine ground.
   d. Turn the ignition switch ON and observe the voltage indicated by the voltmeter.
   e. If the voltage is not at least 8 volts, determine the cause.
   f. Attach the connector containing the purple and gray wires to the ignition coil.
3. Use a voltmeter and check for correct voltage delivery to the distributor as follows:
   a. Detach the connector containing the pink and brown wires from the distributor. See **Figure 14**.
   b. Attach the positive (+) lead of a voltmeter to the pink wire terminal of the connector detached in substep 3a.
   c. Attach the negative (–) lead of the voltmeter to a good engine ground.
   d. Turn the ignition switch ON and observe the voltage indicated by the voltmeter.
   e. If the voltage is not at least 8 volts, determine the cause.
   f. Attach the connector containing the pink and brown wires to the distributor.
4. Use an ohmmeter and check the ignition coil as follows. Coil temperature should be approximately 75° F (24° C) when testing.
   a. Detach both 2-wire connectors and the high tension (spark plug) wire from the ignition coil. One of the two wire connectors contains a purple and gray wire and the other connector contains a pink and brown wire.
   b. Use an ohmmeter to check the primary circuit for shorts to the frame. Connect the test leads between the purple wire terminal (**Figure 13**) and the coil frame. The reading should be no continuity. Any continuity indicates a short and a new coil should be installed.
   c. Use an ohmmeter to test resistance of the primary circuit. Connect the test leads between the purple wire terminal and the gray wire terminal. See **Figure 13**. Refer to **Table 6** for the resistance specifications of the primary circuit.
   d. Use an ohmmeter to test resistance of the secondary circuit. Connect the test leads between the purple wire terminal (**Figure 13**) and the terminal for the coil high tension lead. Refer to **Table 6** for the resistance specifications of the secondary circuit.

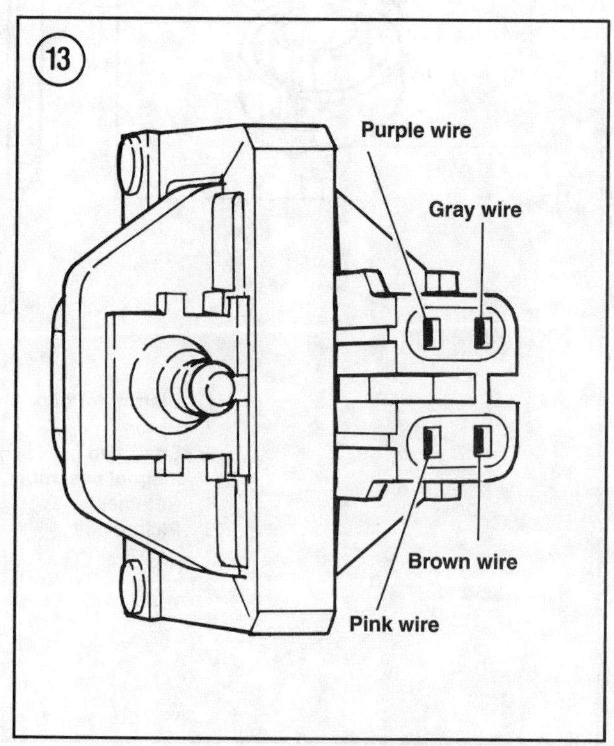

5. If coil resistance is correct, check the resistance of the high tension lead. If coil lead is good, reattach the connectors and coil lead to the coil.

6. Use an ohmmeter and check the pickup coil as follows:

a. Remove the distributor cap and rotor. It may be necessary to remove the flame arrestor cover from some models before the distributor cap can be removed.

b. Release the locking tab and unplug the connector from the pickup coil.

c. Use an ohmmeter to check the pickup coil for shorts to the frame. Connect one test lead to either of the wires from the pickup coil and the other to the distributor body. The reading should be no continuity. Any continuity indicates a short, and a new pickup coil should be installed.

d. Use an ohmmeter to test the resistance of the pickup coil. Connect the test leads to the 2 terminals of the connector detached in substep 6b. Refer to **Table 6** for pickup coil resistance specifications.

7. If pickup coil resistance is correct, reattach the connector to the pickup coil.

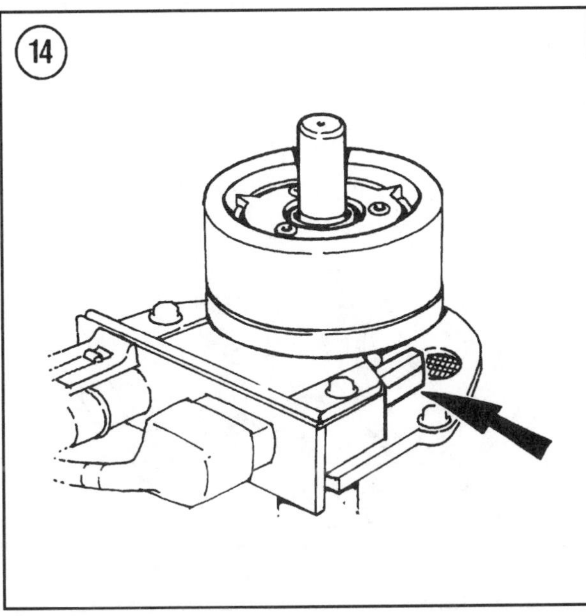

8. Failure of the ignition module in the distributor will either prevent spark or prevent any ignition advance. If the preceding test indicates that other parts are good, but the system will not cause a spark or will not advance the timing, install a new ignition module.

Troubleshooting Breakerless Inductive Distributor (BID) System

Prestolite BID (breakerless inductive distributor) ignition is used on 5.0GL, 5.7GL/GS, 7.4GL, 8.2GL, 5.0FL and 5.8FL models.

Refer to the following procedure to help isolate ignition malfunctions in the BID ignition system. This procedure assumes the battery and starting system are in acceptable condition.

1. Make sure all terminal connections at the distributor, ignition module and ignition coil are clean and tight. Make sure the battery is in acceptable condition and fully charged. Make sure the distributor clamp screw is securely tightened.

2. Use a voltmeter and check the primary control circuit (sensor coil and ignition module) as follows:

WARNING
It is important to ground the high tension wire during tests to prevent accidental electrical shock. Turning the ignition switch ON or OFF can produce a spark even though the trigger wheel in the distributor is not moved.

a. Detach the high tension wire from the center of the distributor and connect the detached end of the wire to a good engine ground.

b. Remove the distributor cap and turn the engine until 2 adjacent points of the trigger wheel are located equal distance from the small sensor coil. See **Figure 15**.

c. Turn the ignition switch ON.

d. Connect the positive (+) lead of a voltmeter to the positive (+) terminal of the battery and the negative (–) lead of the voltmeter to the negative (–) terminal of the battery. Measure and record the battery voltage, then detach the voltmeter leads from the battery. Recharge the battery if the measured voltage is not within 12-13 volts.

e. Connect the positive (+) lead of a voltmeter to the positive (+) terminal of the *high tension coil* and the negative (–) lead of the voltmeter to the negative (–) terminal of the battery or a good engine ground. The indicated voltage should be within 1 volt of the battery voltage indicated in substep 2d.
f. Connect the voltmeter leads between the negative (–) terminal of the battery (or engine ground) and the negative (–) terminal of the high tension coil. The voltmeter should indicate 4-8 volts.
g. If the voltage is correct when tested in substep 2f, place a screwdriver next to the face of the sensor coil. This should discharge the coil (which is grounded to the engine frame), and the voltmeter should indicate the voltage as 12-13 volts.
h. If the voltage tested in substep 2g is incorrect, test the ignition coil as described in Step 3. If the ignition high tension coil is found to be good, the problem is with the sensor coil/module circuit.
i. If the tests in substep 2f and substep 2g are okay, but the spark is erratic, check and reset the gap between the sensor (A, **Figure 16**) and the trigger wheel (B, **Figure 16**). **Table 6** lists the desired air gap. Chapter Four describes the procedure for setting the gap.
j. If the voltage in substep 2f is less than 4 volts, detach the primary wire from the negative (–) terminal of the coil. Attach the voltmeter to this terminal and observe the voltage.
k. If the voltage indicated in substep 2j is 12-13 volts, the sensor coil/module is shorted and a new assembly should be installed.
l. If the voltage indicated in substep 2j is 0, the coil primary circuit is open.
m. If the voltage in substep 2f is more than 8 volts, check for an open ground circuit on the distributor or a shorted coil primary circuit. If the distributor ground and the coil primary circuit are both good, the sensor coil/module circuit is faulty and should be replaced.

3. Use a voltmeter and check for correct voltage delivery to the ignition coil as follows:

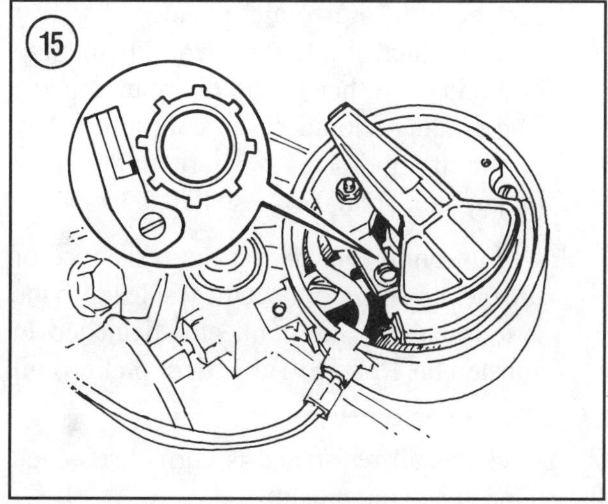

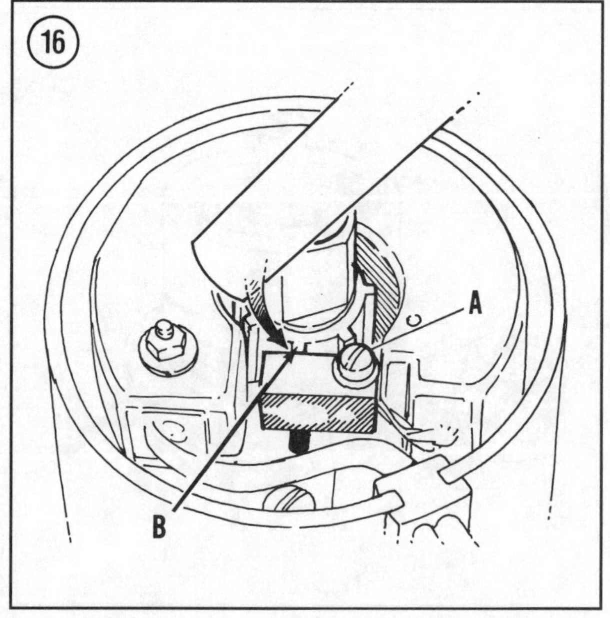

a. Attach the positive (+) lead of a voltmeter to the positive (+) terminal of the coil. This is the terminal that the purple wire is attached to.

b. Attach the negative (–) lead of the voltmeter to a good engine ground.

c. Turn the ignition switch ON and observe the voltage indicated by the voltmeter.

d. If the voltage is not at least 8 volts, determine the cause.

4. Use an ohmmeter and check the ignition coil as follows. Coil temperature should be approximately 75° F (24° C) when testing.

a. Detach the purple and gray wires from the coil's primary terminals. Detach the high tension lead from the coil.

b. Use an ohmmeter to check the primary circuit for shorts to the frame. Connect the test leads between the positive terminal of the coil and the coil's frame. The reading should be no continuity. Any continuity indicates a short and a new coil should be installed.

c. Use an ohmmeter to test resistance of the primary circuit. Connect the test leads between the coil's positive terminal and the negative terminal. Refer to **Table 6** for resistance specification.

d. Use an ohmmeter to test resistance of the secondary circuit in the coil. Connect the test leads between the purple wire terminal and the terminal for the high tension lead. Refer to **Table 6** for the resistance specification of the secondary circuit.

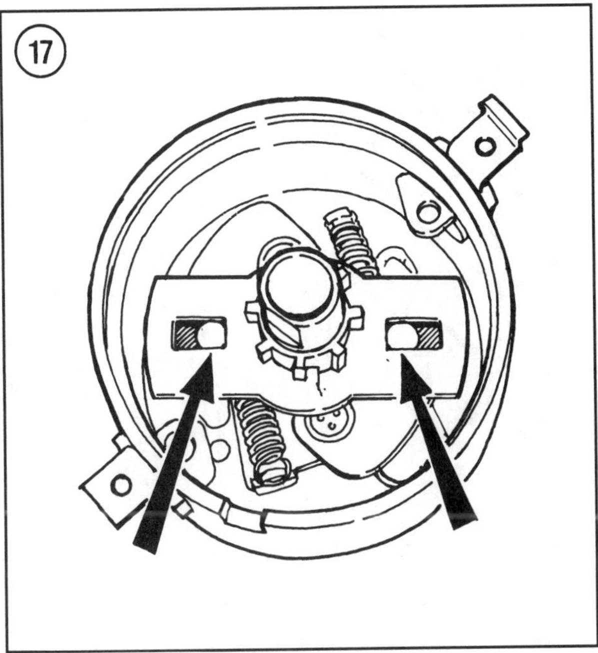

5. If coil resistance is correct, check the resistance of the high tension lead. The high tension lead should have 3,000-7,000 ohms of resistance per foot.

6. Reattach the high tension lead to the coil. Reattach the purple and gray wires to the ignition coil primary terminals.

7. The distributor uses conventional advance weights to control the ignition by changing the location of the trigger wheel. Broken advance springs or stuck advance weights will result in improper (sometimes erratic) ignition timing. A mechanical problem affecting the advance weights often results in difficult starting, low power, low speed, excessive fuel consumption or other problems not immediately apparent as an ignition problem. See **Figure 17**.

8. If an ignition malfunction is still evident, check the following possible causes.

a. Check the primary wire connections to the ignition coil. The purple wires should be attached to the positive (+) terminal and the grey and black wires should be attached to the negative terminal (–). All of the primary connections should be clean and tight.

b. Check the ignition high tension wires for clean, tight connections and proper sealing. Loose, moist and/or dirty connections will allow the spark to flash over. Once the path has been found and the ignition has flashed over, the wire, seals and distributor cap (or coil) must be replaced. High tension flash over can prevent the engine from starting even when dry.

3

c. Check the coil tower, distributor cap and rotor for visible carbon tracks. If tracks are found, install a new part. Cleaning is rarely successful. Tracking on a spark plug can also cause that cylinder to misfire.

Troubleshooting Thick Film Integrated Ignition (TFI-IV) System

The Thick Film Integrated Ignition (TFI-IV) system is installed on 5.0 L and 5.8 L engines which are also equipped with multipoint electronic fuel injection. Troubleshooting and servicing the integrated ignition/fuel control system requires special training and test equipment. Consult your Volvo Penta dealer for diagnosing problems associated with either the ignition or fuel injection.

As with other ignition systems, make sure the battery and starting system are in acceptable condition. It is also important that all electrical connections are clean, tight and waterproof.

FUEL SYSTEM (CARBURETOR MODELS)

On models equipped with a carburetor, fuel system problems should be isolated to the fuel tank, fuel pump, fuel lines, fuel filter or carburetor. Make sure that the fuel tank has a sufficient quantity of fresh fuel. Old or contaminated fuel is a leading cause of fuel system problems.

The following procedures assume that the ignition system is working properly and is correctly adjusted.

1. *Engine will not start*—Make sure there is fuel in the tank and that it is being delivered to the carburetor. Remove the flame arrestor, look into the carburetor throat and operate the throttle linkage several times. There should be a stream of fuel from the accelerator pump discharge tube each time the linkage is moved (**Figure 18**). If not, check the fuel pump pressure as described in Chapter Nine. Also, check the float condition and adjustment. If the engine will not start, check

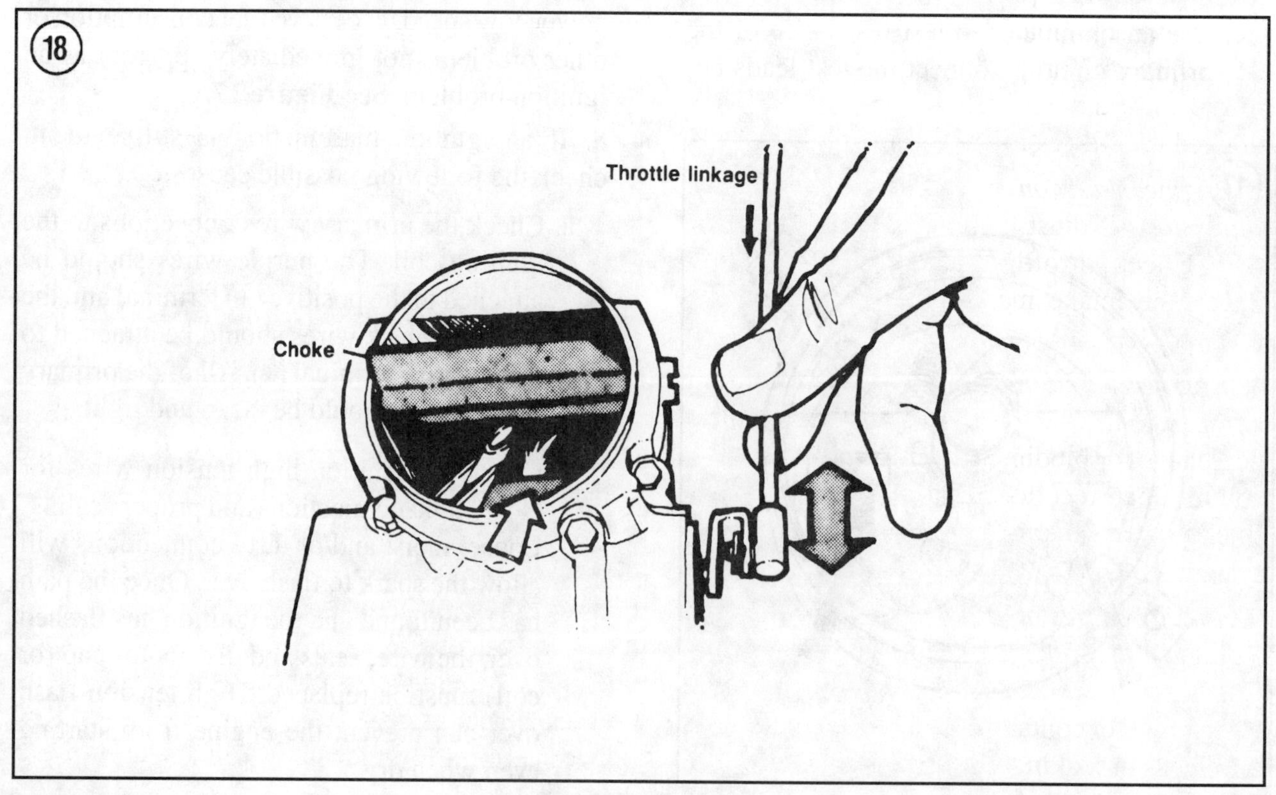

the automatic choke parts for sticking or damage. If necessary, rebuild or replace the carburetor as described in Chapter Nine.

2. *Engine runs at fast idle*—Check the choke setting, idle speed and mixture adjustments.

3. *Rough idle or engine misfire with frequent stalling*—Check choke linkage for proper adjustment. Check throttle stop screw adjustment. Check for sticking throttle plates. Set idle speed to specifications. Check float adjustment.

4. *Engine continues to run when ignition is switched off*—Check ignition timing and idle speed (probably too fast). Check linkage to make sure the fast idle cam is not hanging up. Check for engine overheating.

5. *Stumbling when accelerating from idle*—Check accelerator pump action (Step 1). Check for a clogged fuel filter, low fuel pump volume, plugged bowl vents or a power valve that is stuck closed.

6. *Engine misfires at high speed or lacks power*—This indicates possible fuel starvation. Check accelerator pump action as described in Step 1. Check float setting and needle valve action. Check for a plugged pump discharge nozzle or leaking nozzle gasket. Check for a clogged fuel filter or dirty flame arrestor.

7. *Engine stalls on deceleration or during a quick stop*—Adjust the idle speed to specification. Check throttle positioner functioning. Check the intake manifold or carburetor gasket(s) for leaks.

8. *Engine will not reach wide-open throttle and top speed and power are reduced*—Check throttle linkage for binding. Check for low fuel pump volume, incorrect float drop, a clogged fuel filter, stuck power valve or an inoperative secondary system.

9. *Engine surges at cruising speed*—Check for a plugged fuel filter. Adjust float level and drop. Check for low fuel pump volume or pressure. Check fuel for contamination. Check for blocked air bleeds or leaking plugs/lead seals.

10. *Black exhaust smoke*—Check for an excessively rich mixture. Check idle speed adjustment and choke setting. Check for excessive fuel pump pressure, leaky float or worn needle valve.

11. *Excessive fuel consumption*—Check for an excessively rich mixture or improperly blended gasohol. Check choke operation. Check the idle speed and mixture adjustments. Check for excessive fuel pump pressure, leaky float or worn needle valve.

CLYMER QUICK TIP

The composition material used in floats does gradually absorb fuel over a time. Such fuel absorption increases the weight of the float and prevents it from operating properly when set to correct specification. The best way to determine if fuel absorption has affected float performance is to weigh it with an inexpensive float scale available in most auto supply stores. The scale comes with weight specifications for most floats and can immediately pinpoint a fuel system problem that is often overlooked. If the correct weight is not known, weigh the float immediately after removing it, then weigh it again after it has been removed long enough for the absorbed fuel to evaporate. Install a new float if the weight is lighter at the later weighing.

FUEL SYSTEM (FUEL INJECTED 4.3 L 5.0 L AND 5.7 L ENGINES)

The Marine Electronic Fuel Injection (MEFI) system monitors the needs of the engine, then controls the amount of fuel injected to meet the need. The Throttle Body Injection (TBI) systems used on 4.3Gi, 5.0Gi and 5.7Gi models inject fuel into a common 2 barrel throttle body that is mounted to the intake manifold.

As with all fuel systems, old or contaminated fuel is a leading cause of problems. Before any mechanical or electrical component is serviced in an effort to correct a problem, make sure that

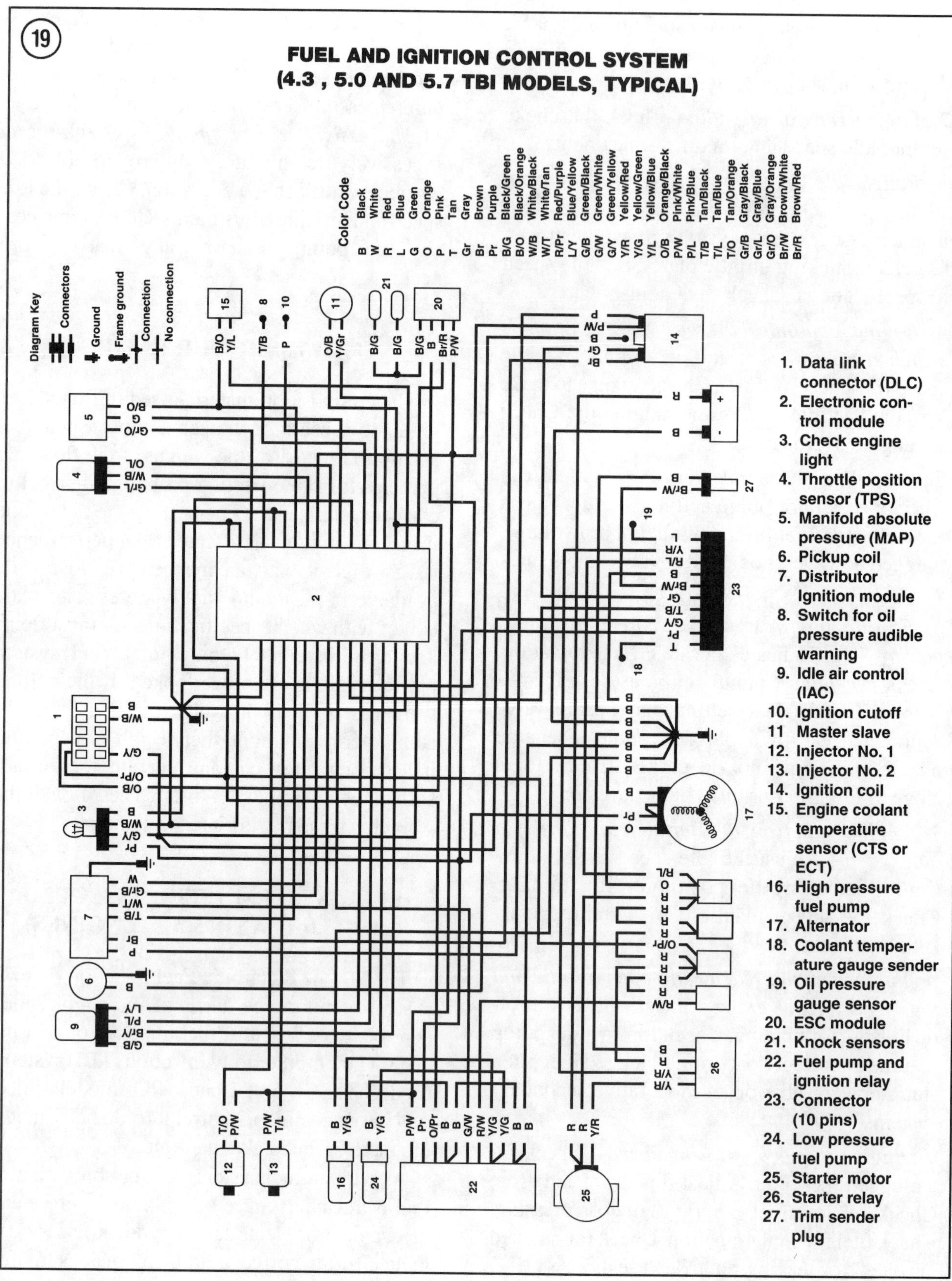
19
FUEL AND IGNITION CONTROL SYSTEM
(4.3 , 5.0 AND 5.7 TBI MODELS, TYPICAL)
Diagram Key
Connectors
Ground
Frame ground
Connection
No connection
Color Code
B Black
W White
R Red
L Blue
G Green
O Orange
P Pink
T Tan
Gr Gray
Br Brown
Pr Purple
B/G Black/Green
B/O Black/Orange
W/B White/Black
W/T White/Tan
R/Pr Red/Purple
L/Y Blue/Yellow
G/B Green/Black
G/W Green/White
G/Y Green/Yellow
Y/R Yellow/Red
Y/G Yellow/Green
Y/L Yellow/Blue
O/B Orange/Black
P/W Pink/White
P/L Pink/Blue
T/B Tan/Black
T/L Tan/Blue
T/O Tan/Orange
Gr/B Gray/Black
Gr/L Gray/Blue
Gr/O Gray/Orange
Br/W Brown/White
Br/R Brown/Red
1. Data link connector (DLC)
2. Electronic control module
3. Check engine light
4. Throttle position sensor (TPS)
5. Manifold absolute pressure (MAP)
6. Pickup coil
7. Distributor Ignition module
8. Switch for oil pressure audible warning
9. Idle air control (IAC)
10. Ignition cutoff
11 Master slave
12. Injector No. 1
13. Injector No. 2
14. Ignition coil
15. Engine coolant temperature sensor (CTS or ECT)
16. High pressure fuel pump
17. Alternator
18. Coolant temperature gauge sender
19. Oil pressure gauge sensor
20. ESC module
21. Knock sensors
22. Fuel pump and ignition relay
23. Connector (10 pins)
24. Low pressure fuel pump
25. Starter motor
26. Starter relay
27. Trim sender plug

the fuel tank has a sufficient quantity of fuel and that the fuel is fresh. It is important for the operator to use only quality fuel, and properly maintain the fuel system filters.

The system uses electrical current to monitor and control the fuel system, so it is important that the battery is fully charged and in acceptable condition. The starting system must also be able to crank the engine at its normal speed. All electrical connections must be clean, tight and waterproof.

Troubleshooting and servicing the fuel control system requires special training and test equipment. Diagnosing fuel injection problems that result in reductions in power or intermittent failure is especially difficult. The cost of the system's components makes it impractical to replace parts until the problem is corrected. Consult your Volvo Penta dealer for diagnosing problems associated with the fuel injection system.

An understanding of how the fuel is injected and controlled will often help locate the source of a problem. Refer to **Figure 19**. Refer to Chapter Eight for a description and additional troubleshooting procedures.

1. If the engine will not start, first make sure the ignition is operating properly and the starter is cranking the engine at a sufficient. If the battery and starter operate properly, the problem is probably insufficient fuel delivery.
   a. Make sure both electric fuel pumps are running by listening or feeling the pumps (16 and 24, **Figure 19**). The pump should operate for 2 seconds when the ignition switch is first turned ON, then should automatically turn OFF. The pumps should also run when the engine is being cranked with the electric starter. The electronic control module (ECM) signals the pump relay to deliver current to the electric fuel pump. If the pump is good, but does not operate as described, first check the pump relay (22, **Figure 19**).
   b. If the fuel pumps operate, but the engine will not start, determine if fuel is being sprayed into the throttle body. If fuel is being delivered, the electronic control module (ECM) is probably operating properly. A diaphragm type pressure regulator is located in the throttle body to maintain the correct fuel pressure. If the fuel pressure is low, it may not be delivering a sufficient volume of fuel to start the engine. With the ignition ON and the engine *not running*, fuel pressure should be 9-13 psi (62-89 kPa). Low fuel pressure may be caused by a clogged fuel filter, faulty pump or a faulty regulator.

2. If the engine is slow to start or if the engine continues to run after turning the ignition OFF, the injector assembly may be held partially open. Pressure in the fuel manifold will bleed off and it will necessary to crank the engine for a long time before pressure will be high enough for the engine to start. The leaking injector will also continue to deliver (leak) fuel after the engine is turned OFF.

3. A rough or erratic (too slow or too fast) idle condition or stalling at idle speed can be caused by a faulty idle air control (IAC) valve. The IAC valve is located in the throttle body and is operated by the electronic control module (ECM). The IAC valve has a tapered pintle valve which is positioned in an air passage in the throttle body. The ECM signals the IAC to extend or retract the tapered pintle valve as necessary to maintain the correct idle speed under all idle load conditions automatically. Retracting the pintle valve opens the throttle valve air passage, allowing additional air to bypass the throttle valve which increases idle speed. The opposite occurs when the pintle valve is extended, which closes the throttle valve air passage. The throttle stop screw on the throttle body is set at the factory and should not be readjusted unless the IAC valve is replaced.

Diagnostic Trouble Codes (DTC's)

Troubleshooting and servicing the integrated ignition/fuel control system is greatly facilitated by special training and test equipment available from Volvo Penta.

The electronic control module (ECM) constantly monitors the major sensors and compares the values obtained from the sensors with standard readings. If the values are not within normal limits, the ECM may store the code of the sensor in memory to help determine the possible cause of a problem.

If special tools and training are not readily available, it is often less expensive to consult your Volvo Penta dealer for diagnosing problems associated with either the ignition or fuel injection.

Tools, such as the marine diagnostic trouble code (MDTC) tool or one of the other diagnostic tools may be available from your tool supplier. Specific instruction (training) for the use of these special tools may also be available locally. Proceed as follows to access trouble codes using the marine diagnostic trouble code tool.

1. Turn the ignition switch OFF.
2. Remove the protective cover from the data link connector (DLC).
3. Make sure the switch on the tool is turned OFF, then plug the tool into the DLC (1, **Figure 19**).
4. Turn the ignition switch ON, but do not start the engine. The light on the MDTC tool should be ON and steady.

NOTE
Diagnostic Trouble Code 12 is displayed in Step 5 because the ECM is not receiving an ignition reference signal from the distributor indicating that the engine is not running.

5. Push the switch of the MDTC tool to the ON position. The light should flash code 12, then flash any other stored diagnostic code. For code 12, the light will flash one time, pause, then flash twice with only a very short interval between the 2 flashes. Each diagnostic code is repeated 3 times.
6. Refer to **Table 7** for a description of DTC's and indicated circuits.
7. To clear the trouble codes, proceed as follows:
   a. Attach the MDTC tool as described in Steps 1-4 if not already in place.
   b. Turn the switch on the tool ON.

NOTE
The engine must not be running while performing substep 7c.

   c. Move the throttle slowly from idle to fast (full throttle) position, then back to idle position.
   d. Turn the switch of the MDTC tool OFF.

NOTE
If the switch is not turned OFF in substep 7d, the engine may not start in substep 7e.

   e. Start the engine and run for at least 20 seconds, then turn the ignition switch OFF to stop the engine.
   f. Turn the switch of the MDTC tool ON and observe the DTC indicated by the flashing light. The MDTC tool should indicate only code 12, because the engine is not running.

NOTE
If other codes are present, check the condition of the battery. The battery must be fully charged and the engine cranking speed must be faster than 160 rpm to clear the stored codes. If code(s) remain stored and the battery is in good condition, it may indicate that a problem is still present in that system.

8. Turn the switch of the MDTC tool OFF and remove the tool from the data link connector (DLC).
9. Install the cover over the DLC to prevent the entrance of dirt.

FUEL SYSTEM (FUEL INJECTED 5.0 L AND 5.8 L ENGINES)

Multipoint fuel injection (MFI) and thick film ignition (TFI-IV) systems are used on these models. The electronic control system monitors and controls both ignition timing and the amount of fuel injected. The multipoint fuel injection (MFI) system used on 5.0 Fi, 5.8 Fi and 5.8 FSi (Ford engines) injects fuel into each cylinder's intake passage separately.

As with all fuel systems, old or contaminated fuel is a leading cause of problems. Before any mechanical or electrical component is serviced, make sure that the fuel tank has a sufficient quantity of fresh fuel and that fuel system filters are properly serviced.

The system uses electrical current to monitor and control the fuel system, so it is important that the battery is in acceptable condition and fully charged. The starting system must also be able to crank the engine at its normal speed and all electrical connections must be clean, tight and waterproof.

Troubleshooting and servicing the integrated ignition/fuel control system is greatly facilitated by special training and test equipment available from Volvo Penta. Refer to **Table 8** for reference values if an EEC-IV Monitor or EEC-IV Breakout Box is available. A MFI Tester is also available from Volvo Penta for conducting tests, including timing control tests and self-tests. Follow the instructions provided by the manufacturer of the specific tool.

Diagnosing fuel injection problems that result in reductions in power or intermittent failure may be especially difficult. The cost of most of the system's components makes it impractical to replace parts until the problem is corrected.

Some problems may be isolated without using the electronic diagnostic tools, but if special tools and training are not readily available, it is often less expensive to consult your Volvo Penta dealer for diagnosing problems associated with either the ignition or fuel injection. An understanding of how the fuel is injected and controlled will often help locate the source of a problem. Refer to **Figure 20**.

3

FUEL SYSTEM (FUEL INJECTED 7.4 L ENGINES)

The electronic control system monitors and controls both ignition timing and the amount of fuel injected. The multipoint fuel injection (MFI) system used on 7.4 Gi and 7.4 GSi (engines) injects fuel into each cylinder's intake passage separately.

Troubleshooting and servicing the integrated ignition/fuel control system is greatly facilitated by special training and test equipment available from Volvo Penta. If special tools and training are not readily available, it is often less expensive to consult your Volvo Penta dealer for diagnosing problems associated with either the ignition or fuel injection.

Some problems can be isolated without using the electronic diagnostic tools. An understanding of how the fuel is injected and controlled will often help locate the source of a problem. Refer to **Figure 21**. Refer to Chapter Eight for a description of the fuel system and additional troubleshooting procedures.

Low-Pressure System

The first step in diagnosing a fuel system problem is to make sure the boat's low-pressure fuel delivery is sufficient. Check to make sure the low-pressure electric pump (24, **Figure 22**) is operating, by either listening or feeling the pump. The low-pressure pump will only receive current to run for about 2 seconds, then will stop if the key is turned ON (engine not running). The low-pressure pump will continue to receive current to run if the electronic control module (ECM) receives a reference signal from the ignition system indicating that the engine is cranking

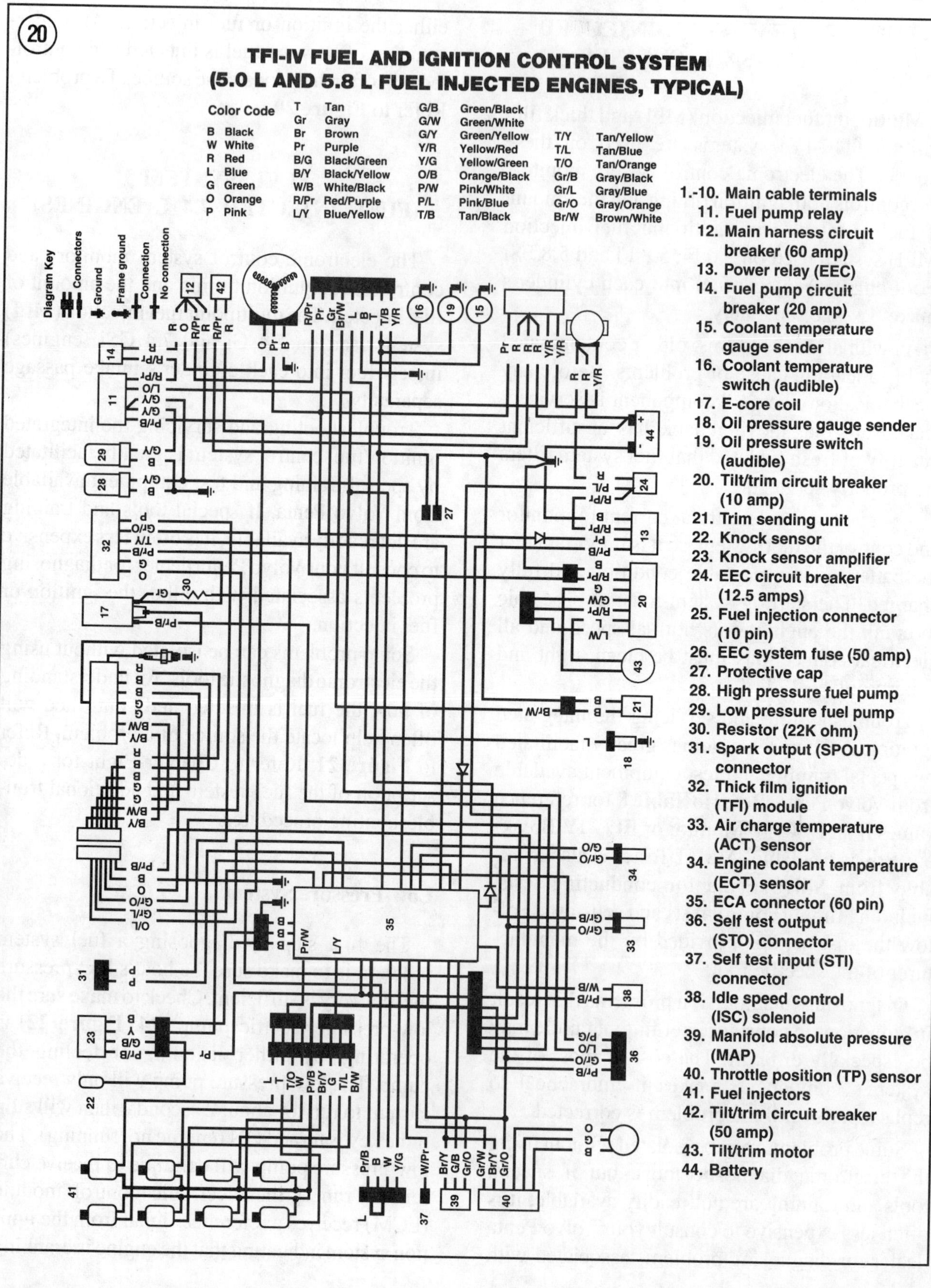
20
TFI-IV FUEL AND IGNITION CONTROL SYSTEM
(5.0 L AND 5.8 L FUEL INJECTED ENGINES, TYPICAL)
Color Code
B Black
W White
R Red
L Blue
G Green
O Orange
P Pink
T Tan
Gr Gray
Br Brown
Pr Purple
B/G Black/Green
B/Y Black/Yellow
W/B White/Black
R/Pr Red/Purple
L/Y Blue/Yellow
G/B Green/Black
G/W Green/White
G/Y Green/Yellow
Y/R Yellow/Red
Y/G Yellow/Green
O/B Orange/Black
P/W Pink/White
P/L Pink/Blue
T/B Tan/Black
T/Y Tan/Yellow
T/L Tan/Blue
T/O Tan/Orange
Gr/B Gray/Black
Gr/L Gray/Blue
Gr/O Gray/Orange
Br/W Brown/White
Diagram Key
Connectors
Ground
Frame ground
Connection
No connection
1.-10. Main cable terminals
11. Fuel pump relay
12. Main harness circuit breaker (60 amp)
13. Power relay (EEC)
14. Fuel pump circuit breaker (20 amp)
15. Coolant temperature gauge sender
16. Coolant temperature switch (audible)
17. E-core coil
18. Oil pressure gauge sender
19. Oil pressure switch (audible)
20. Tilt/trim circuit breaker (10 amp)
21. Trim sending unit
22. Knock sensor
23. Knock sensor amplifier
24. EEC circuit breaker (12.5 amps)
25. Fuel injection connector (10 pin)
26. EEC system fuse (50 amp)
27. Protective cap
28. High pressure fuel pump
29. Low pressure fuel pump
30. Resistor (22K ohm)
31. Spark output (SPOUT) connector
32. Thick film ignition (TFI) module
33. Air charge temperature (ACT) sensor
34. Engine coolant temperature (ECT) sensor
35. ECA connector (60 pin)
36. Self test output (STO) connector
37. Self test input (STI) connector
38. Idle speed control (ISC) solenoid
39. Manifold absolute pressure (MAP)
40. Throttle position (TP) sensor
41. Fuel injectors
42. Tilt/trim circuit breaker (50 amp)
43. Tilt/trim motor
44. Battery

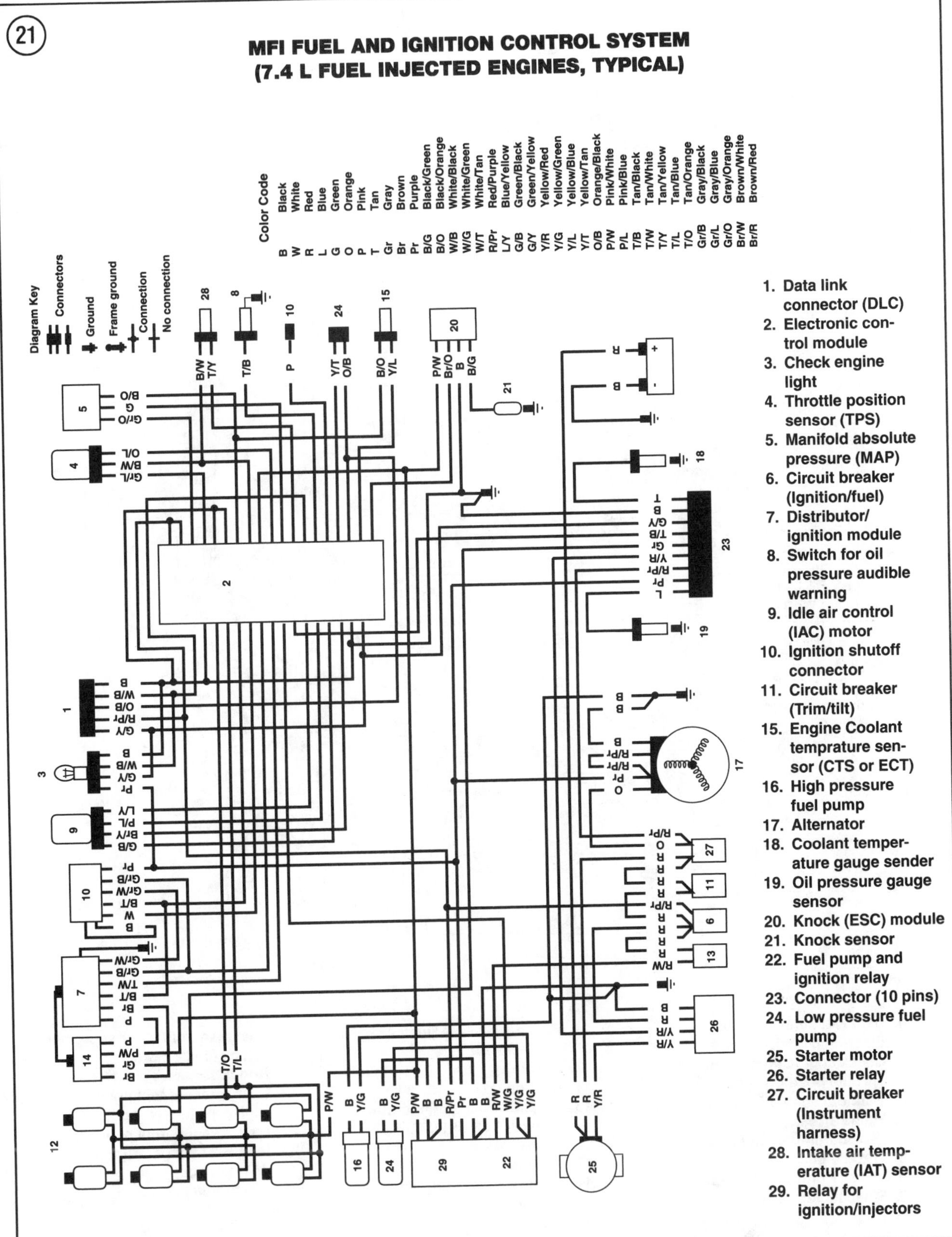
21
MFI FUEL AND IGNITION CONTROL SYSTEM
(7.4 L FUEL INJECTED ENGINES, TYPICAL)
Color Code
B Black
W White
R Red
L Blue
G Green
O Orange
P Pink
T Tan
Gr Gray
Br Brown
Pr Purple
B/G Black/Green
B/O Black/Orange
W/B White/Black
W/G White/Green
W/T White/Tan
R/Pr Red/Purple
L/Y Blue/Yellow
G/B Green/Black
G/Y Green/Yellow
Y/R Yellow/Red
Y/G Yellow/Green
Y/L Yellow/Blue
Y/T Yellow/Tan
O/B Orange/Black
P/W Pink/White
P/L Pink/Blue
T/B Tan/Black
T/W Tan/White
T/Y Tan/Yellow
T/L Tan/Blue
T/O Tan/Orange
Gr/B Gray/Black
Gr/L Gray/Blue
Gr/O Gray/Orange
Br/W Brown/White
Br/R Brown/Red
Diagram Key
Connectors
Ground
Frame ground
Connection
No connection
1. Data link connector (DLC)
2. Electronic control module
3. Check engine light
4. Throttle position sensor (TPS)
5. Manifold absolute pressure (MAP)
6. Circuit breaker (Ignition/fuel)
7. Distributor/ ignition module
8. Switch for oil pressure audible warning
9. Idle air control (IAC) motor
10. Ignition shutoff connector
11. Circuit breaker (Trim/tilt)
15. Engine Coolant temprature sensor (CTS or ECT)
16. High pressure fuel pump
17. Alternator
18. Coolant temperature gauge sender
19. Oil pressure gauge sensor
20. Knock (ESC) module
21. Knock sensor
22. Fuel pump and ignition relay
23. Connector (10 pins)
24. Low pressure fuel pump
25. Starter motor
26. Starter relay
27. Circuit breaker (Instrument harness)
28. Intake air temperature (IAT) sensor
29. Relay for ignition/injectors

or running. If the pump operates, shut off the ignition and attach a pressure gauge to the test point (22, **Figure 22**). Turn the ignition ON and observe the pressure indicated on the gauge. Refer to **Table 9** for recommended pressures. If the measured static pressure is too low, check for restrictions in the fuel tank or inlet screens before replacing the pump. The filter will not pass water and will plug quickly if the tank contains any water.

A low-pressure pump (24, **Figure 22**) is used to transfer fuel from the boat's storage tank(s) to

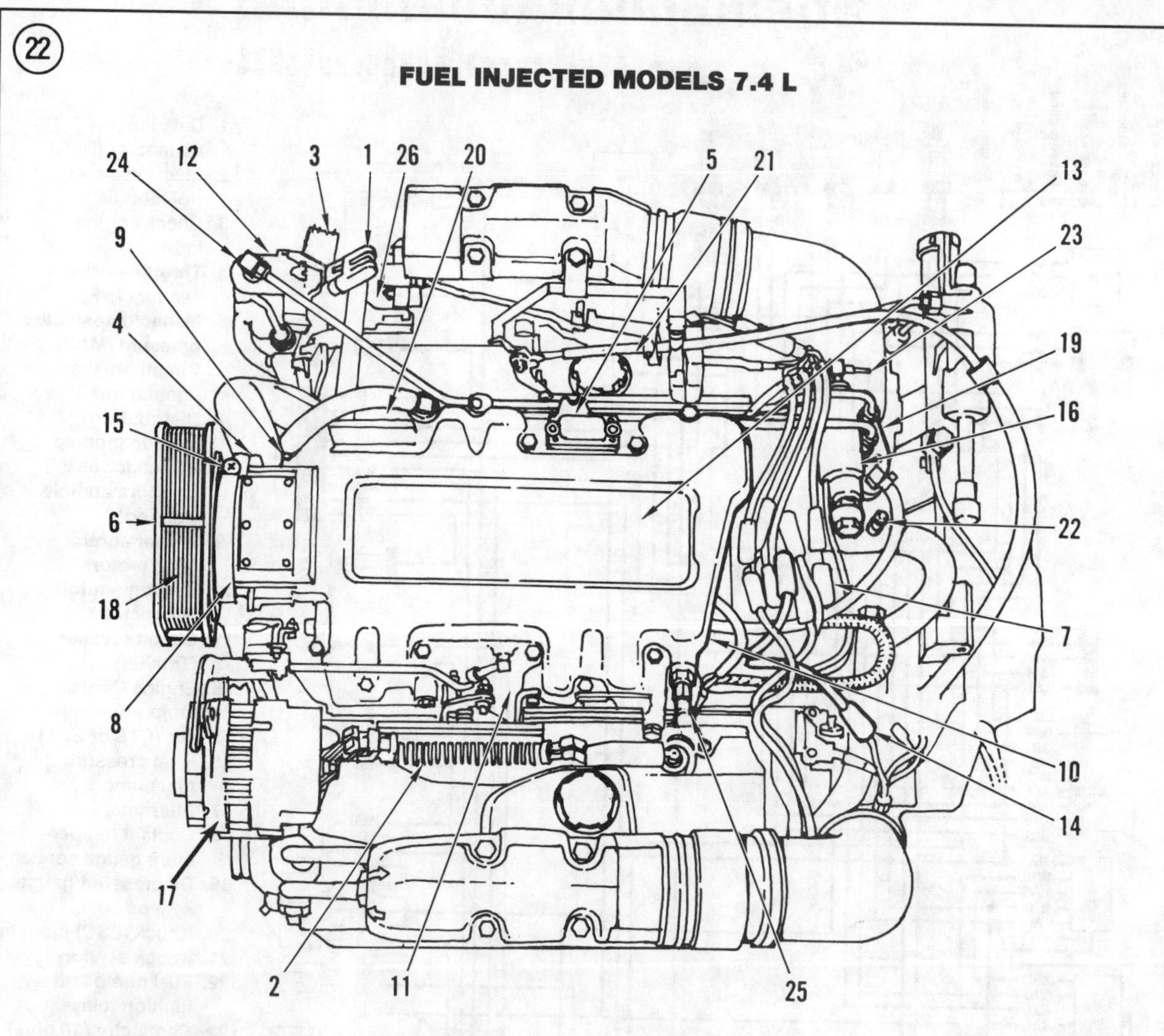

1. Data link connector (DLC)
2. Electronic control module
3. Check engine light connector
4. Throttle position sensor (TPS)
5. Manifold absolute pressure (MAP)
6. Flame arrestor
7. Distributor/ignition module
8. Throttle body
9. Idle air control (IAC) motor
10. Pulse limiter
11. Fuel pressure regulator
12. Fuel injectors
13. Fuel rail
14. Ignition coil
15. Engine coolant temperature sensor (CTS or ECT)
16. High pressure fuel pump
17. Alternator
18. Coolant temperature gauge sensor
19. Fuel reservoir/vapor separator
20. Knock (ESC) module
21. Knock sensor
22. Low pressure test point
23. High pressure test point
24. Low pressure fuel pump
25. Intake air temperature (IAT) sensor
26. Starter relay

the engine's reservoir system. The low-pressure system includes:

1. The boat's storage tank(s), fuel pickup screen, fuel lines, fittings, vents and antisiphon valve (if so equipped).
2. Valves, lines (hoses) and filters located between the tank and the low-pressure pump.
3. The low-pressure fuel pump (24, **Figure 22**). An electric low-pressure pump is used and tests must include electrical supply to the pump.
4. Fuel filter, water separator and lines (hoses) located between the low-pressure pump and the reservoir. The reservoir (19, **Figure 22**) is located below the high-pressure pump (16, **Figure 22**).

High-Pressure System

A high-pressure pump is used to pressurize the fuel delivered to the engine's injection nozzles. The high-pressure system includes.

1. The high-pressure fuel pump (16, **Figure 22** or 1, **Figure 23**).
2. Fuel rail (13, **Figure 22** or 2, **Figure 23**).
3. Fuel injectors (12, **Figure 22**).
4. Fuel pressure regulator (11, **Figure 22**).

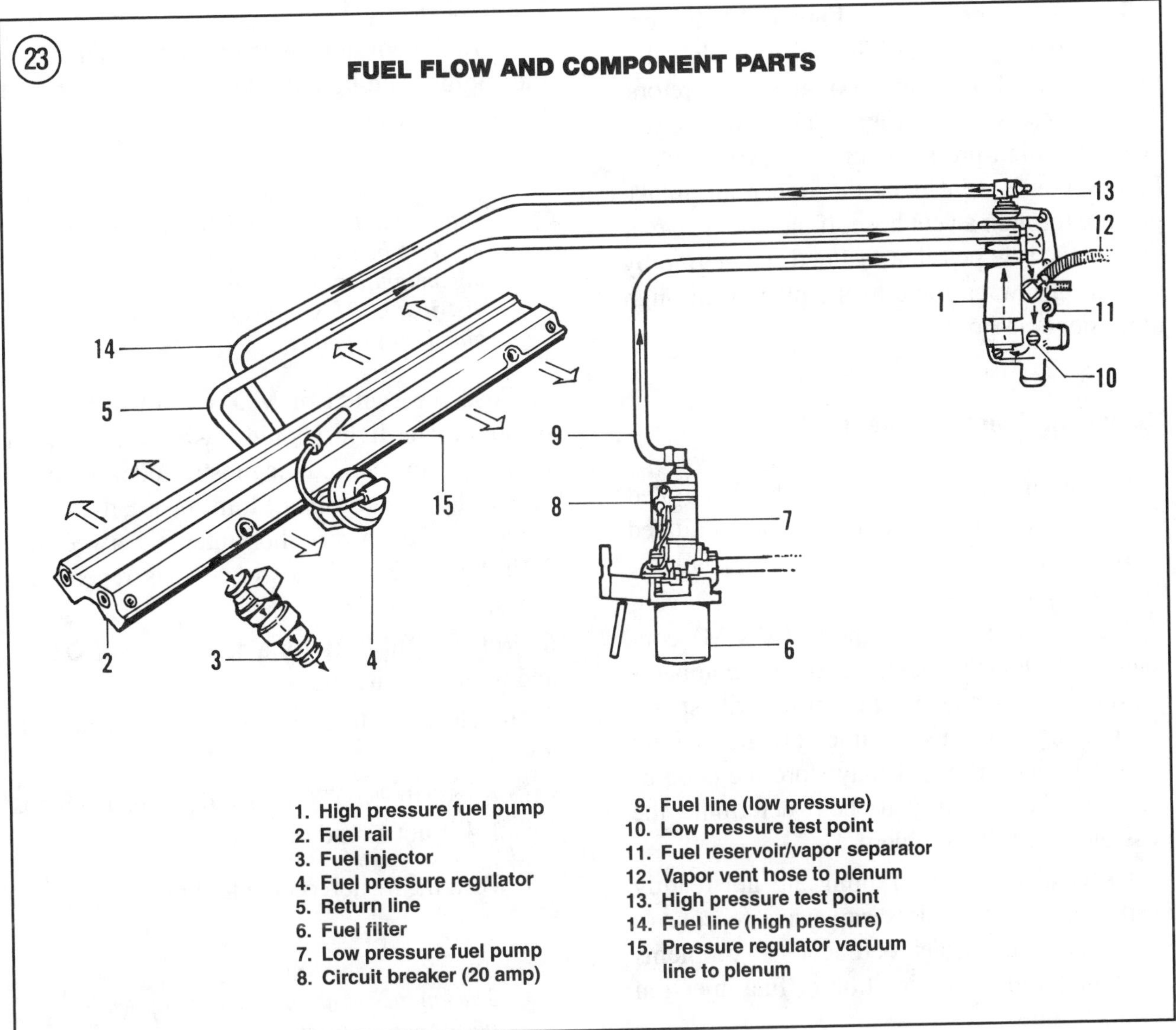

1. High pressure fuel pump
2. Fuel rail
3. Fuel injector
4. Fuel pressure regulator
5. Return line
6. Fuel filter
7. Low pressure fuel pump
8. Circuit breaker (20 amp)
9. Fuel line (low pressure)
10. Low pressure test point
11. Fuel reservoir/vapor separator
12. Vapor vent hose to plenum
13. High pressure test point
14. Fuel line (high pressure)
15. Pressure regulator vacuum line to plenum

5. Fuel return line (to reservoir).

Start (or crank) the engine and check to make sure the electric high-pressure pump is operating, by either listening or feeling the pump. If the pump is operating, attach a pressure gauge to the outlet line, start (or crank) the engine and observe the pump outlet pressure. Refer to **Table 9** for the recommended pressure. If the pressure is too low, check the reservoir assembly and the fuel pressure regulator assembly before installing a new high-pressure pump.

Fuel Reservoir/Vapor Separator Assembly

The fuel reservoir (11, **Figure 22**) is constructed with a float and fuel inlet needle valve much like the float chamber of most carburetors. The fuel reservoir (19, **Figure 22**) is located just below the high-pressure pump (16, **Figure 22**). Fuel vapor is vented to the upper air intake plenum through a vent hose. If the inlet valve or seat leaks, it is possible to flood the engine by delivering raw gasoline to the plenum through the vapor vent hose.

Diagnostic Trouble Codes (DTC's)

Troubleshooting and servicing the integrated ignition/fuel control system is greatly facilitated by special training and test equipment available from Volvo Penta.

The electronic control module (ECM) constantly monitors the major sensors and compares the values obtained from the sensors with standard readings. If sensor values are not within normal limits, the ECM may store the code of the sensor in memory to help determine the possible cause of a problem.

If special tools and training are not readily available, it is often less expensive to consult your Volvo Penta dealer for diagnosing problems associated with either ignition or fuel injection system.

Tools, such as the marine diagnostic trouble code (MDTC) tool or one of the other diagnostic tools may be available from your tool supplier. Specific instruction (training) for the use of these special tools may also be available locally. Check with your tool supplier for availability. Perform the following to access trouble codes using the marine diagnostic trouble code tool.

1. Turn the ignition switch OFF.
2. Remove the protective cover from the data link connector (DLC). The connector is located at 1, **Figure 22**.
3. Make sure the switch on the MDTC tool is turned OFF, then plug the tool into the DLC (1, **Figure 22**).
4. Turn the ignition switch ON, but do not start the engine. The light on the MDTC tool should be ON and steady.

NOTE

Diagnostic Trouble Code 12 is displayed in Step 5 because the ECM is not receiving an ignition reference signal from the distributor. This indicates that the engine is not running.

5. Push the switch of MDTC tool to the ON position. The light should flash code 12, then flash any other stored diagnostic code. For code 12, the light will flash one time, pause, then flash twice with only a very short interval between the 2 flashes. Each diagnostic code is repeated 3 times.
6. Refer to **Table 10** for a description of DTC's and indicated circuits.
7. To clear the trouble codes, proceed as follows:
   a. Attach the MDTC tool as described in Steps 1-4 if not already in place.
   b. Turn the switch on the tool ON.

NOTE

The engine should not be running while performing substep 7c.

c. Move the throttle slowly from idle to fast (full throttle) position, then back to idle position.
d. Turn the switch of the MDTC tool OFF.

NOTE
If the switch is not turned OFF in substep 7d, the engine may not start in substep 7e.

e. Start the engine and run it for at least 20 seconds, then turn the ignition switch OFF to stop the engine.
f. Turn the switch of the MDTC tool ON and observe the DTC. The MDTC tool should indicate only code 12, because the engine is not running.

NOTE
If other codes are present, check the condition of the battery. The battery must be fully charged and the engine cranking speed must be faster than 160 RPM to clear the stored codes. If codes remain stored and the battery is in good condition, it may indicate that a trouble code is still stored in that system.

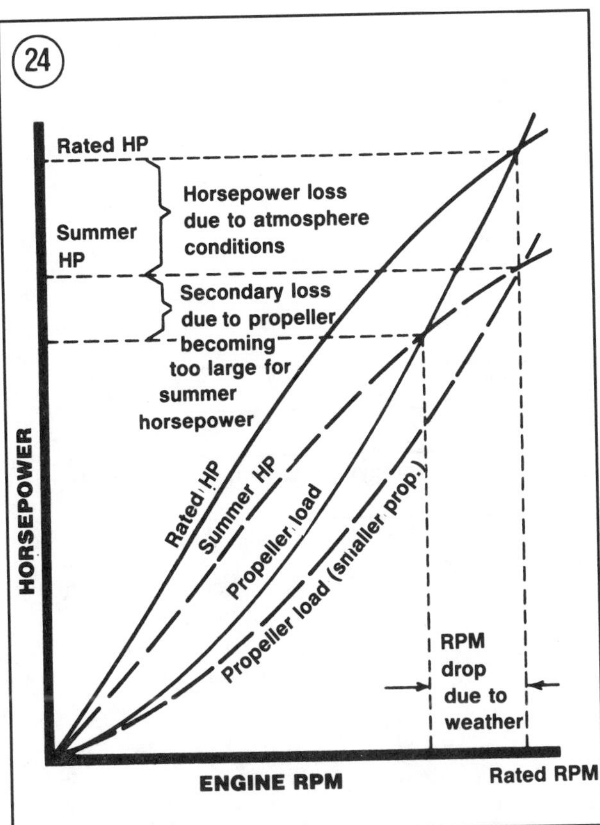

8. Turn the switch of the MDTC tool OFF and remove the tool from the data link connector (DLC).
9. Install the cover over the DLC to prevent the entrance of dirt.

3

ENGINE PERFORMANCE

Elevation and weather affect the maximum (wide-open throttle) power of any internal combustion engine. Air is thinner at higher elevation (altitude), resulting in a richer fuel/air mixture unless the mixture is adjusted. Installation of a lower pitch propeller can help by matching the load with the reduced performance, but the basic problem remains. Your Volvo Penta dealer can calculate the correct propeller diameter and pitch to provide optimum performance at high elevations.

Heat and humidity affect the density of the air and can similarly lower performance. Changes in the air density may be particularly noticeable during hot, humid days especially if the propeller was selected on a cool, dry day. The engine will noticeably lose its pep and may not be able to get the boat on plane. Loss of up to 14% of the available horsepower can easily result in a noticeable reduction in speed. **Figure 24** shows the relationship between horsepower and weather conditions.

A number of factors can make the engine difficult or impossible to start or cause rough running and poor performance. The majority of novice troubleshooters immediately suspect the fuel system (carburetor) as the cause of the problem, but the problem is just as frequently caused by another system.

The troubleshooting procedures outlined in **Figures 25-28** and **Table 1** will help you solve most engine performance problems in a systematic manner.

ENGINE OVERHEATING

There are a number of causes for engine overheating, some of which are often overlooked during troubleshooting.

a. A plugged or restricted inlet screen on the stern drive lower unit.
b. Water tube guide, seal or grommet inside the stern drive unit is plugged, improperly sealed or deteriorated.
c. Debris or freeze damage blocking the coolant passage in the upper gear unit housing.
d. Pivot housing seal is damaged or out of position.
e. Water passage transom nipple is blocked by debris or freeze damaged.
f. Transom shield water tube is blocked by debris.
g. Failed raw water pump, circulating (engine) pump or connecting hoses.
h. Thermostat or thermostat housing damaged or improperly assembled.
i. A loose drive belt (alternator or steering pump) may prevent the engine circulating water pump or raw water pump from operating at the proper speed.
j. Excessively advanced or retarded ignition timing.
k. Plugged or restricted water passage in the stern drive, engine block or cylinder head, due to operation while the drive unit was submerged in sand or silt.
l. Engine manifold or gasket improperly installed, damaged or plugged.

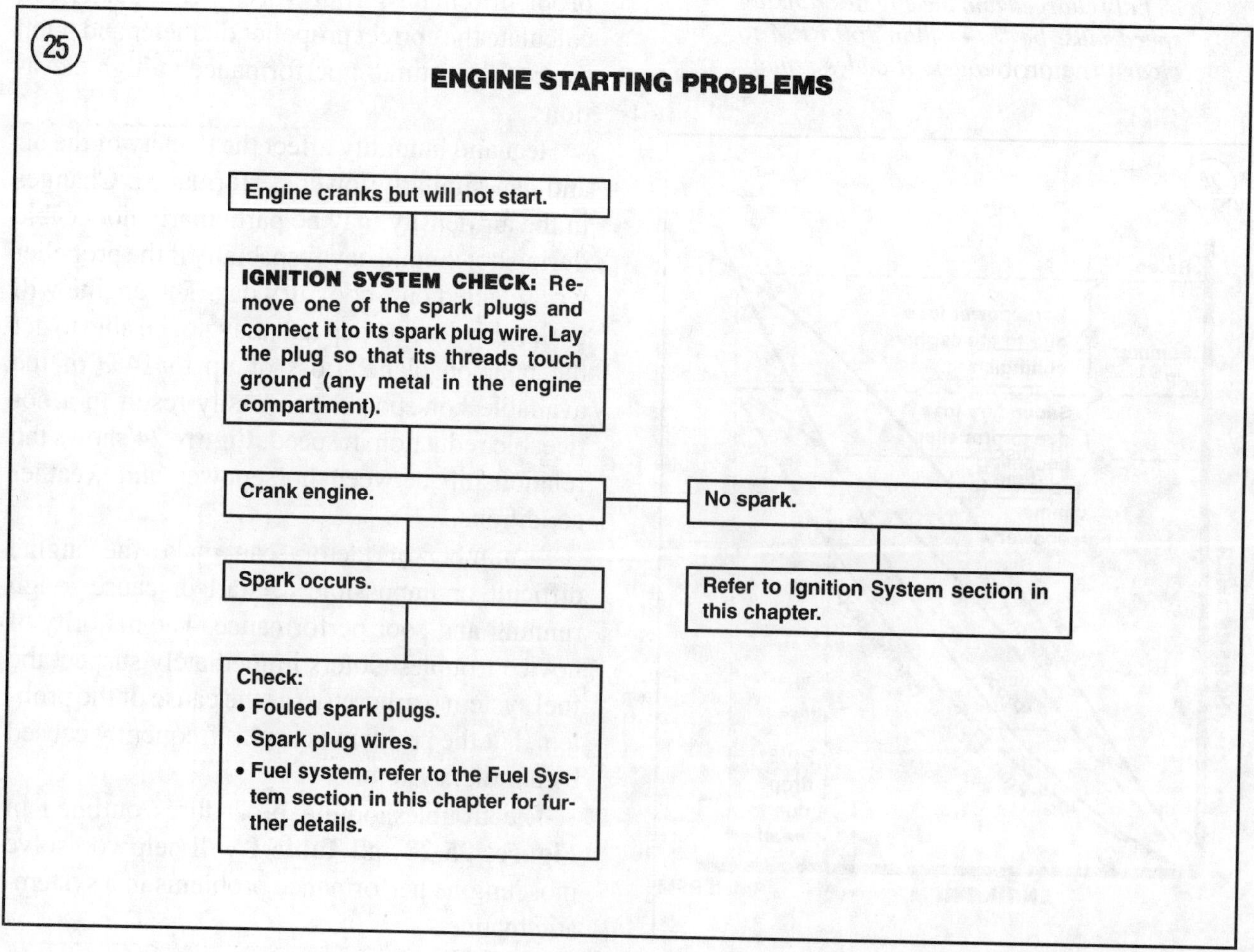

25
ENGINE STARTING PROBLEMS
Engine cranks but will not start.
IGNITION SYSTEM CHECK: Remove one of the spark plugs and connect it to its spark plug wire. Lay the plug so that its threads touch ground (any metal in the engine compartment).
Crank engine.
No spark.
Refer to Ignition System section in this chapter.
Spark occurs.
Check:
• Fouled spark plugs.
• Spark plug wires.
• Fuel system, refer to the Fuel System section in this chapter for further details.

ENGINE OIL PRESSURE

Proper oil pressure is vital to the engine. If oil pressure is insufficient, the engine can destroy itself in a short time. The oil pressure warning circuit monitors oil pressure constantly and if pressure drops below a predetermined level, the warning light will come on. Obviously, it is important for the warning circuit to be in working order to signal low oil pressure. Each time you turn on the ignition, but before starting the engine, the warning light should come on. If it does not, the problem is in the warning circuit, not the oil pressure system.

Once the engine is running, the warning light should remain off. If the warning light comes on or acts erratically while the engine is running, there is trouble with the engine oil pressure system. Stop the engine immediately and determine the cause of the problem.

ENGINE OIL LEAKS

Like automotive engines, Volvo Penta marine engines are subject to oil leaks. Boat installation, however, may make it difficult to determine exactly where the leak is. Many owners of new boats discover oil in the bilge. It is important to wipe up leaking or spilled oil so the source of any leaks can be located quickly.

A leaking oil pan, cam cover or rocker arm cover gasket will allow oil to drip down the outside of the engine when the engine is running. The most common cause of this type of leaking gasket is overtightening of the attaching screws. If a leak is traced to the oil pan or cover gasket, replace the gasket and make sure the gasket surface is clean. Also, check the pan or cover for possible warpage or other damage.

Other oil leaks may be found as hours are put on the engine. A leaking rear main oil seal will

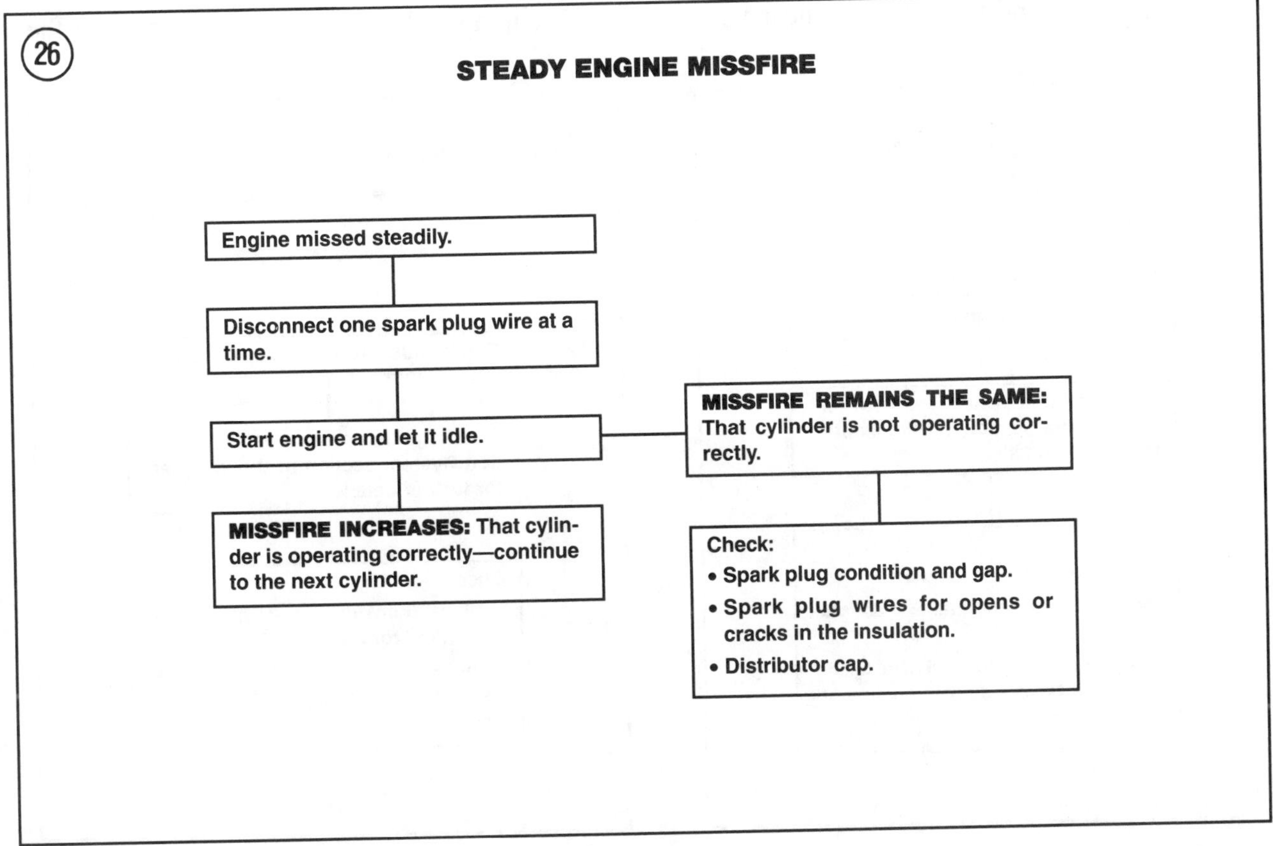

allow oil to run down the outside of the flywheel housing when the engine is running. Replacing the seal will stop the leak.

ENGINE NOISES

Often the first evidence of an internal engine problem is a strange noise. That knocking, clicking or tapping sound which you never heard before may be warning you of impending trouble.

While engine noises can indicate problems, they are difficult to interpret correctly, and an inexperienced mechanic can be seriously misled by them.

Professional mechanics often use a special stethoscope to isolate engine noises. You can do nearly as well with a *sounding stick* which can be an ordinary piece of doweling, a length of broom handle or a section of small hose. By placing one end in contact with the area to which you want to listen and the other end near your ear, you can hear sounds emanating from that area. The first time you do this, you may be horrified at the strange sounds coming from even a normal engine. If you can, have an experienced friend or mechanic help you sort out the noises.

Clicking or Tapping Noises

Clicking or tapping noises usually come from the valve train and indicate excessive valve clearance. A sticking valve may also sound like a valve with excessive clearance. In addition, excessive wear in valve train components can cause similar engine noises.

Knocking Noises

A heavy, dull knocking is usually caused by a worn main bearing. The noise is loudest when the engine is working hard, such as accelerating at low speed. You may be able to isolate the trouble to a single bearing by disconnecting the

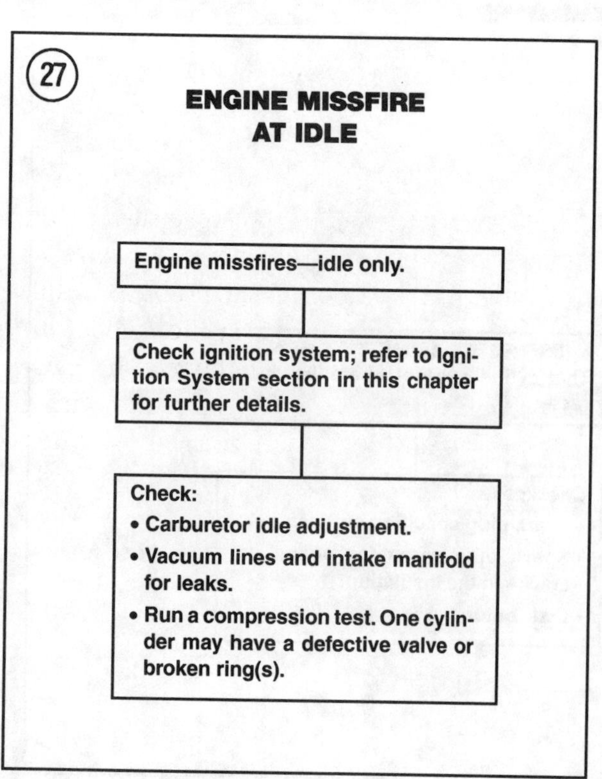

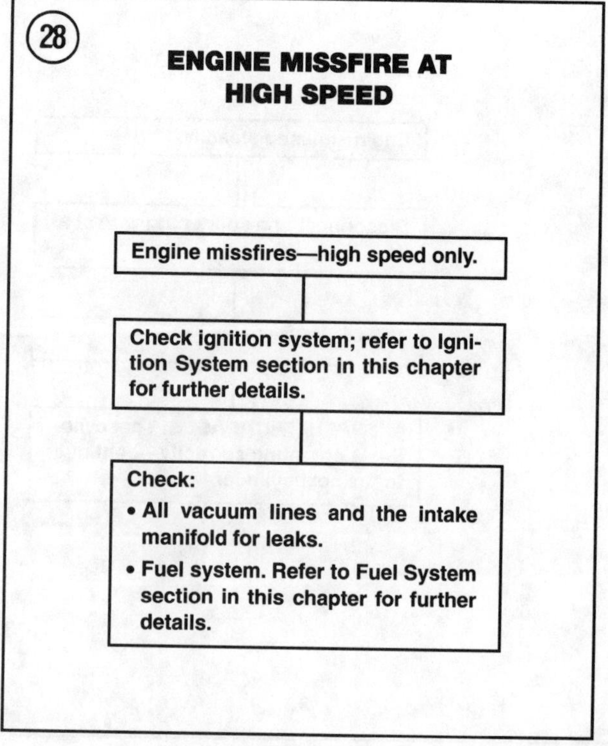

spark plugs one at a time. When you reach the spark plug nearest the bearing, the knock will be reduced or disappear.

Worn connecting rod bearings may also produce a knock, but the sound is usually more metallic. As with a main bearing, the noise is worse during acceleration. It may increase just as you go from acceleration to coasting. Disconnecting the spark plugs will help isolate this knock as well.

A double knock or clicking usually indicates a worn piston pin. Disconnecting spark plugs will isolate this to a particular piston; however, the noise will increase when you reach the affected piston.

A loose flywheel and excessive crankshaft end play also produces knocking noises. While similar to main bearing noises, they are usually intermittent, not constant, and they do not change when spark plugs are disconnected. When caused by a loose flywheel or coupling, the noise is generally heard at idle or during rapid deceleration. It is a good idea to recheck flywheel/coupler nut torque whenever the engine is removed from the boat.

Some mechanics confuse piston pin noise with piston slap (excessive piston clearance). The double knock will distinguish piston pin noise. In addition, piston slap is always be louder when the engine is cold.

STERN DRIVE UNIT

In normal straight-ahead operation, a stern drive makes very little noise. Changing direction to port or starboard will increase the noise level from the universal joints, but it should not be objectionable.

If universal joint noise is suspected, attach a flush-test device and run the engine at idle. Have an assistant turn the stern drive first to port then to starboard while you listen for noise at the universal joint housing. Any unusual noise during this test indicates either universal joint wear.

Propeller damage may occur without being obvious. If the propeller has hit many underwater objects, it may slip on its hub.

If water leaks into the boat, inspect the transom housing seal, universal joint bellows or shift cable bellows.

A shift handle that is difficult to move may be caused by a problem in the stern drive, transom shift cable, shift box or remote control cable. To isolate the problem, disconnect the remote control cable from the transom plate. If shifting is still difficult, the shift cable or control box is at fault. If shifting is normal, the problem is in the stern drive. Have an assistant turn the propeller by hand while you move the shift cable back and forth between the stern drive and transom plate. If the cable does not move freely, replace it.

Tilt/trim system problems may be mechanical, electrical or hydraulic. Any of these can prevent the stern drive from moving to a full up or full down position. First, make sure that the stern drive is in forward gear. If it is in reverse, the shift interlock switch will prevent the power trim system from operating. Mechanical problems result from frozen universal joints, lack of proper lubrication or nonuse over a lengthy period. Electrical problems involve the pump motor wiring circuit. Hydraulic problems are most often caused by low or contaminated hydraulic fluid.

Table 1 ENGINE TROUBLESHOOTING

Trouble	Probable cause	Correction
Starter will not start engine	Corroded battery terminals	Clean terminals
	Discharged battery	Charge or replace battery
	Loose connection in starting circuit	Clean and tighten all connections
	Defective starting switch	Replace switch
	Starting motor brushes worn	Replace brushes
	Faulty starter motor	Repair or replace motor
Starter turns but does not crank engine	Partially discharged battery	Charge or replace battery
	Faulty starter motor drive	Repair or replace starter
	Defective wiring or wiring capacity too low	Locate and replace defective wiring
Engine will not start (Fuel system)	Empty fuel tank	Fill tank with proper fuel
	Flooded engine	Remove spark plugs, crank engine several times, then install dry spark plugs
	Water in fuel system	Clean fuel tank, filters, lines and carburetor (or injection system), then refill with proper fuel
	Inoperative or sticking choke valve	Adjust choke, linkage and choke rod/cable for proper operation
	Improperly adjusted carburetor/injection	Adjust mixture
	Clogged fuel lines or filters	Replace filters or fuel lines
	Defective fuel pump or control circuit	Repair or replace fuel pump or electrical circuit
Engine will not start (Ignition system)	Fouled or broken spark plugs	Replace spark plugs
	Wet, cracked or broken distributor cap	Clean, dry and inspect cap; replace if necessary
	Damaged or improperly routed spark plug wires	Install good wires to the correct cylinders
	Ignition switch defective	Replace switch
	Damaged ignition system component	Locate and replace faulty component
	Ignition timing not correct	Set timing to correct specification
Engine will not start (Mechanical or other cause)	Air leak in intake system	Check for leaking or detached vacuum lines; also, check for leak around the intake manifold
	Valves leaking	Repair or replace leaking valves
	Loose spark plugs	Check all plugs for condition and tightness.
	Damaged cylinder head gasket	Check for leaks and replace gasket if leak is found
	Worn or broken piston rings	Replace rings and check cylinders for wear or damage

(continued)

Table 1 ENGINE TROUBLESHOOTING (continued)

Trouble	Probable cause	Correction
Hard to start when cold	Choke out of adjustment	Check and adjust for proper operation
	Stale or contaminated fuel	Drain and clean fuel tank and lines; refill with fresh fuel
	Improper ignition timing	Set timing to correct specification
	Fouled spark plugs	Remove and clean or replace spark plugs
	Leaking injector (models with TBI)	Repair or replace injector
	Low fuel pressure	Clean or replace fuel filter or repair pump as required
Hard starting when hot	Choke out of adjustment	Check and adjust for proper operation
	Improper ignition timing	Set timing to correct specification
	Incorrect or fouled spark plugs	Replace spark plugs with correct type
Coolant temperature too hot	No coolant circulation	Check for proper operation of the raw water pump and the engine coolant pump; repair or replace as necessary
	Defective thermostat	Replace thermostat
	Improper ignition timing	Set timing to correct specification
Low oil pressure	No oil in engine	Fill to correct level
	Defective oil pump or drive	Repair or replace oil pump or drive as necessary
	Worn or damaged engine bearings	Replace bearings
	Weak or damaged relief valve spring	Replace damaged parts
Oil pressure too high	Improper oil for temperature	Drain oil and replace with correct viscosity
	Pressure relief valve stuck	Clean and reset valve
Low engine speed	Damaged or improper propeller	Repair or replace propeller
	Bottom of boat dirty or damaged	Clean and inspect boat
	Engine not developing full power	Determine why engine is not running properly; could be caused by ignition system, fuel system or mechanical failure
Vibration	Damaged propeller	Replace propeller
	Misfiring	Check ignition system for proper operation
	Preignition	Check *Preignition* portion of this table
	Loose engine mounting	Check condition of mounts and bolts for tightness

(continued)

Table 1 ENGINE TROUBLESHOOTING (continued)

Trouble	Probable cause	Correction
Vibration (continued)	Loose or damaged crankshaft dampener	Inspect and tighten or replace
Loose or damaged flywheel	–	Inspect and tighten or replace
	Loose alternator or other driven accessory	Tighten mounting bolts
	Bent propeller shaft	Repair lower unit and replace shaft
	Damaged universal joints	Inspect and replace universal joints as necessary
Preignition/Detonation	Improper or damaged spark plugs	Install new spark plugs of the correct type
	Engine carbon	Remove cylinder head and clean carbon
	Improper timing	Set timing to correct specification
	Engine overheating	See *Coolant temperature too hot* portion of this table
Backfiring	Insufficient fuel reaching engine	See *Engine will not start (Fuel system)* portion of this table
	Faulty ignition or timing	See *Engine will not start (Ignition system)* portion of this table
Sludge in the oil	Infrequent oil changes	Drain and refill with proper oil at suggested intervals
	Water in the oil	Drain and refill with the proper oil; if trouble persists, check for cracked head, cracked block or defective cylinder head gasket
	Dirty oil filter	Change oil and install new oil filter

Table 2 STERN DRIVE TROUBLESHOOTING

Trouble	Probable cause	Correction
Gear housing noise	Contaminated lubricant or damaged parts	Disassemble, clean, inspect and reassemble; fill with clean lubricant
	Propeller installed incorrectly	Remove propeller, check for damage and reinstall properly
	Damaged propeller	Replace propeller
	Incorrect gear alignment/shimming	Check and correct alignment/shimming as required
	Worn, loose or damaged parts	Disassemble unit and replace parts as required
Drive shaft housing noise	Low lubricant level	Add lubricant
	Worn universal joint	Replace universal joint
	Contaminated lubricant or damaged parts	Disassemble, clean, inspect and reassemble; fill with clean lubricant

(continued)

Table 2 STERN DRIVE TROUBLESHOOTING (continued)

Trouble	Probable cause	Correction
Drive shaft housing noise (continued)	Incorrect gear alignment/shimming	Check and correct alignment/shimming as required
	Misaligned engine	Use proper tools and align
	Damaged coupling splines or shaft	Replace shaft or coupling
Hard steering (power steering)	Loose drive belt	Adjust belt tension
	Fluid level low	Fill reservoir to proper level
	Leaking hoses or air in system	Tighten or replace hoses
	Defective pump	Replace pump
	Faulty control valve	Clean, adjust or replace as required
	Defective cylinder	Replace cylinder
	Mounting screws improperly tightened	Screws may be too loose or too tight; tighten properly
Hard steering (manual steering)	Damaged cable	Replace cable
	Cable pinched or kinked	Align cable properly
	Incorrect length or wrong cable	Install correct cable
	Linkage fittings too tight	Tighten properly
	Insufficient lubrication	Disassemble and lubricate

Table 3 ALTERNATOR SPECIFICATIONS

Alternator model	Output @ engine speed
51 Amp	20 amps @ 650 rpm 47 amps @ 1,500 rpm 51 amps @ 2,000 rpm
65 Amp	20 amps @ 650 rpm 53 amps @ 1,500 rpm 56 amps @ 2,000 rpm
Regulated voltage range	13.5-14.8 volts (all models)

(continued)

Table 4 IGNITION SYSTEM APPLICATION

Model	Fuel system	Ignition type	Firing order
3.0	Carburetor	Delco EST[1] & Di[4]	1-3-4-2
4.3	Carburetor	Delco EST[1] & Di4	1-6-5-4-3-2
4.3	Fuel injection	Delco EST[1] & Di[4]	1-6-5-4-3-2
5.0	Carburetor	Prestolite BID[2]	1-3-7-2-6-5-4-8
5.0	Fuel injection	TFI-IV[3]	1-3-7-2-6-5-4-8
5.0	Fuel injection	Delco EST[1] & Di[4]	1-8-4-3-6-5-7-2
5.7	Carburetor	Prestolite BID[2]	1-8-4-3-6-5-7-2
5.7	Fuel injection	Delco EST[1]	1-8-4-3-6-5-7-2
5.8	Carburetor	Prestolite BID[2]	1-3-7-2-6-5-4-8
5.8	Fuel injection	TFI-IV[3]	1-3-7-2-6-5-4-8
7.4	Carburetor	Prestolite BID[2]	1-8-4-3-6-5-7-2
7.4	Fuel injection	Delco EST[1]& Di[4]	1-8-4-3-6-5-7-2
8.2	Carburetor	Prestolite BID[2]	1-8-4-3-6-5-7-2
8.2	Fuel injection	Delco EST[1] & Di[4]	1-8-4-3-6-5-7-2

1. (EST) Delco electronic spark timing system.
2. (BID) Prestolite integral breakerless inductive distributor.
3. (TFI-IV) Thick film integrated ignition system.
4. (Di) Distributor ignition system.

Table 5 IGNITION SYSTEM SPECIFICATIONS

EST coil	
Primary resistance	1.35-1.45 ohms
Secondary resistance	7,500-9,000 ohms
Pickup coil resistance	700-900 ohms
Operating amperage @ 75° F (24° C)	1.0 maximum*
BID coil	
Primary resistance	1.43-1.58 ohms
Secondary resistance	7,500-6,700 ohms
Operating amperage @ 75° F (24° C)	1.0 maximum*
BID sensor air gap	0.203 mm (0.008 in.)

*Coil must be able to sustain 25-30 kilovolts for 30 seconds.

Table 6 DIAGNOSTIC TROUBLE CODES (4.3 Gi, 5.0 Gi AND 5.7 Gi)

Code	Indicates
12	No ignition reference signal from distributor. This DTC is normal if the engine is not running.

(continued)

Table 6 DIAGNOSTIC TROUBLE CODES (4.3 Gi, 5.0 Gi AND 5.7 Gi) (continued)

Code	Indicates
14	Engine coolant temperature (ECT) sensor indicates that temperature is too high or too low. This code will also be set if the signal for the circuit is grounded or if the wires are open for 3 seconds or longer.
21	Throttle position (TP) sensor. Signal either too low or too high. This code will be stored if the TP is inconsistent with the MAP signals or if the signal circuit is grounded or open.
23	Intake air temperature (IAT) sensor indicates that temperature is too high or too low. This code will also be set if the signal for the circuit is open or if the wires are grounded for 3 seconds or longer.
33	Manifold absolute pressure (MAP) sensor. This code will be set if the signal voltage for the circuit is too high for 3 seconds or if the circuit is open. The code will also be set if the signal output is too low (or no output) with the engine running. Code will be stored if MAP output is inconsistent with throttle position (TP) signals.
42	Ignition control (IC) system is not receiving the correct voltage. The ECM has responded to an open or grounded IC or bypass circuit.
43	Knock sensor (KS) circuit. Voltage signal is either too high or too low. This code can also be stored as a result of an open or grounded circuit longer than 58 seconds.
51	Electronic erasable programmable read only memory (EEPROM) or Electronic control module (ECM) faulty.

Table 7 FUEL SYSTEM VOLTAGE REFERENCE VALUES (5.0 Fi, 5.8 Fi AND 5.8 FSi)

Sensor	Breakout box Black lead	Red lead	Test value
VREF	Pin 46	Pin 26	4.74-5.25 VDC
TP	Pin 46	Pin 47	Closed throttle – 0.9-1.15 VDC Wide-open throttle – 4.65 VDC
ECT	Pin 46	Pin 7	0.87-1.17 VDC
ACT	Pin 46	Pin 25	1.13-1.53 VDC
MAP	Pin 46	Pin 45	147 Hz @ 30.0 in. Hg[1]
PIP	Pin 46	Pin 56	0-0.3 VDC – opening aligned[2] Battery VDC – vane aligned[3]
KS	Pin 46	Pin 2	0.3 VDC

(continued)

Table 7 FUEL SYSTEM VOLTAGE REFERENCE VALUES (5.0 Fi, 5.8 Fi AND 5.8 FSi) (continued)

Sensor	Breakout box Black lead	Red lead	Test value
INJ			
Bank No. 1	Pin 40	Pin 58	Battery VDC
Bank No. 2	Pin 40	Pin 59	Battery VDC
ISC-BPA	Pin 40	Pin 21	Battery VDC
FP	Pin 40	Pin 52	Battery VDC
KAPWR	Pin 40/60	Pin 1	Battery VDC – Key ON & OFF
VPWR	Pin 40/60	Pin 37/57	Battery VDC – Key ON only
IGN GND	Pin 40/60	Pin 16	0
CSE GND	Pin 40/60	Pin 20	0
PWR GND	Pin 40/60	Pin 20	0

1. Hertz signal will increase as barometric pressure increases.
2. Opening in the distributor cup is aligned with the hall effect device.
3. Vane of the distributor cup is aligned with the hall effect device.

Table 8 FUEL SYSTEM SPECIFICATIONS (7.4 Gi AND 7.4 GSi)

7.4L Gi & GSi models	
Fuel system pressure	
Low pressure pump	
Static (not running)	4.5-7 psi (31-48 kPa)
Cranking/idle speed	5.9-8.4 psi (40.68-57.93 kPa)
Wide-open throttle	4.0 psi (27.5 kPa)
High pressure pump	
Static (not running)	36-42 psi (248-290 kPa)

Table 9 DIAGNOSTIC TROUBLE CODES (7.4 Gi AND 7.4 GSi)

Code	Indicates
12	No ignition reference signal from distributor. This DTC is normal if the engine is not running.
14	Engine coolant temperature (ECT) sensor indicates that temperature is too high or too low. This code will also be set if the signal for the circuit is grounded or if the wires are open for 3 seconds or longer.

(continued)

Table 9 DIAGNOSTIC TROUBLE CODES (7.4 Gi AND 7.4 GSi) (continued)

Code	Indicates
21	Throttle position (TP) sensor. Signal either too low or too high. This code will be stored if the TP is inconsistent with the rpm and MAP signals or if the signal circuit is grounded or open.
23	Intake air temperature (IAT) sensor indicates that temperature is too high or too low. This code will also be set if the signal for the circuit is open or if the wires are grounded for 3 seconds or longer.
33	Manifold absolute pressure (MAP) sensor. This code will be set if the signal voltage for the circuit is too high for 3 seconds (or longer) or if the circuit is open. The code will also be set if the signal output is too low (or no output) with the engine is running. Code will be stored if MAP output is inconsistent with rpm and throttle position (TP) signals.
42	Ignition control (IC) system is not receiving the correct voltage. The ECM has responded to an open or grounded IC or bypass circuit.
43	Knock sensor (KS) circuit. Voltage signal is either too high or too low. This code can also be stored as a result of an open or grounded circuit longer than 58 seconds.
51	Electronic erasable programmable read only memory (EEPROM) or Electronic control module (ECM) faulty.

Table 10 ACRONYMS AND TERMS

ACT	Air charge temperature sensor.
BASE	Initial or not changed, such as the BASE ignition timing that occurs when the SPOUT signal is interupted.
BPA	Bypass air valve. A valve attached to the ISC solenoid.
CEL	Check engine light.
CKP	Crankshaft postiton sensor.
DTC	Diagnostic Trouble Code.
DLC	Diagnostic link connector. The electrical connector provided for attaching test equipment to the system.
E-Core or E-Coil	The high-tension coil used to generate voltage sufficient to provide the spark at the spark plugs.
ECA	Electronic control assembly.
ECT	Engine coolant temperature sensor.
EEC-IV	Electronic engine control, fourth generation.
FPM	Fuel pump monitor.
IAC	Idle air control.
IAT	Intake air temperature sensor.
IDM	Ignition diagnositics monitor. A system that continuously monitors the ignition.
ISC	Idle speed control, such as ISC solenoid or ISC circuit. The ISC solenoid may attach to the throttle body assembly.
KAM	Keep alive memory is a series of battery powered memory locations that allow the microprocessor to store input about failures that are identified during operation.
KAPWR	Keep alive power is the battery current supplied to KAM.

(continued)

Table 10 ACRONYMS AND TERMS (continued)

KS	Knock sensor. The KS is a device that generates a signal current when it senses a specific frequency of vibration to identify knocking.
KOEO	Key on engine off, such as the KOEO self test.
LCD	Liquid crystal display.
MAP	Manifold absolute pressure. May be used when referring to the MAP sensor or circuit.
MDTC	Marine diagnostic trouble code.
MEFI	Marine electronic fuel injection.
MFI	Multipoint fuel injection.
OBD	On board diagnostics.
PIP	Profile ignition pickup. A switch such as that housed in the distributor provides crankshaft position information to the ECA.
Plenum	The upper part of the engine's intake manifold.
Relay	A switching device operated by low current to control the opening and closing of another (higher capacity) circuit.
Sensor	A monitoring device that transmits information, such as the coolant temperature sensor that provides temperature information to the ECA.
S.L.O.W. (or SLOW)	Speed limiting operational warning system. The system incorporates sensors to monitor coolant temperature and oil pressure as well as other operating conditions.
SPOUT	Spark output, such as the SPOUT connector. The SPOUT signal from the EEC-IV controls operation of the ignition module and loss of the signal puts the engine in BASE timing mode.
STI	Self test input. May be used to refer to the STI connector.
STO	Self test output, such as the circuit transmits service codes. May be used to identify the STO connector.
TBI	Throttle body injection.
TFI	Thick film integrated ignition system. TFI-IV is the fourth generation of the TFI system.
TP	Throttle position. May be used in reference to the TP sensor.
VREF	Voltage reference, such as the regulated VREF signal supplied to some sensors.

Chapter Four

Lubrication, Maintenance and Tune-up

All gasoline engines used with Volvo Penta drives are based on automotive engines; however, the average pleasure boat engine is subjected to operating conditions different from those encountered by the average automobile engine. Regular preventive maintenance and proper lubrication will pay dividends in longer engine and stern drive life, as well as safer boat operation.

This chapter provides the basis for such a program. The lubrication and maintenance intervals provided in **Table 1** are those recommended by Volvo Penta for normal operation. When the boat is used for continuous heavy-duty, high speed operation or under other severe operating conditions, all maintenance operations, including lubrication procedures, should be performed more frequently. If the boat is not used regularly, moisture and dirt will collect in and on the engine and stern drive. This eventually leads to rust, corrosion and other damage.

It is a good idea to keep the engine and accessory units clean and free of dirt, grime and grease buildup. Such a buildup may eventually reduce the engine's capacity for cooling by preventing heat from radiating from the metal. Frequent cleaning will allow you to locate leaks almost immediately, because you will notice them as you clean and they will be far more apparent on a clean engine than on one that has been allowed to accumulate a coating or buildup of contamination.

Tables 1-9 are at the end of the chapter.

PREOPERATIONAL CHECKS

Before starting the engine for the first time each day, perform the following checks.

1. Remove the engine compartment cover or hatch and check for the presence of raw gasoline fumes. If the boat is equipped with a bilge

blower, turn it on for a few minutes. If strong fumes can be smelled, determine their source and correct the problem before proceeding with any other service.

WARNING
Always have a Coast Guard-approved fire extinguisher close at hand when working around the engine.

2. Check the engine oil level with the dipstick as described in this chapter. Add oil if the level is low.
3. Check the electrolyte level in each battery cell as described in this chapter. Add distilled water if necessary.
4. Check the power steering pump fluid level, if so equipped.
5. Check the condition of all drive belts. If a belt is in poor condition, replace it. Spare belts are difficult to obtain offshore.
6. Check all water hoses for leaks, loose connections and general condition. Repair or replace as required.
7. Visually check the fuel filter sediment bowl, if so equipped. Clean the bowl and replace the element if dirty.
8. Check the oil level in the stern drive unit as described in this chapter. Add lubricant if necessary.
9. Check the fluid level in the trim/tilt reservoir, if so equipped. Add fluid if required.
10. Check the bilge for excessive water. If present, drain or pump water from the bilge until it is dry.
11. Check the propeller for nicks, dents and missing metal. Repair or replace the propeller if damaged.
12. Turn the fuel tank valve(s) ON.
13. Connect the battery cables to the battery (if disconnected).
14. Reinstall the engine compartment cover or hatch.

STARTING CHECKLIST

After performing the pre-operation checks, observe the following starting checklist:
1. Operate the bilge blower for at least 5 minutes before starting the engine.
2. Make sure the stern drive unit is in the water and fully lowered to its operating position. If the engine is run with the lower unit out of the water, make sure that a flushing kit is attached to supply the unit with cooling water.
3. If the engine is cold, prime it by operating the throttle. If equipped with a manual choke, set it to the closed position.
4. Make sure the gearshift lever is in NEUTRAL.

WARNING
Always have a fully charged fire extinguisher at hand before attempting to start the engine.

5. Start the engine and let it run at idle speed for a few minutes.

CAUTION
Prolonged operation of the engine with the gearshift lever in NEUTRAL can cause damage to gears in the stern drive unit due to improper circulation of the lubricant.

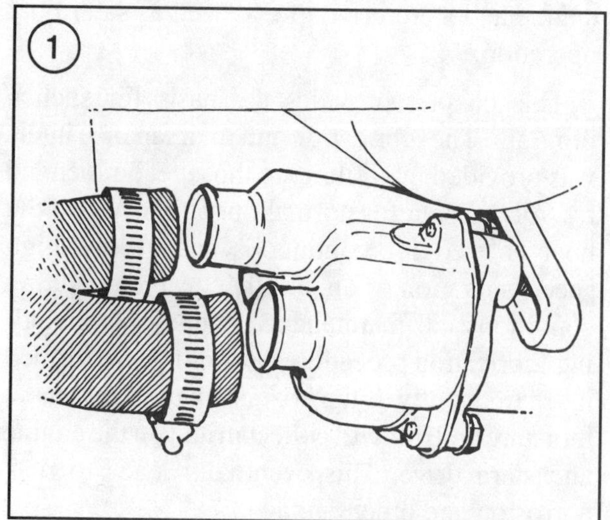

6. Check the gauges and warning lights to make sure that the engine is not overheating, that proper oil pressure is present and that the battery is not discharging. If any of these conditions occur, shut the engine down at once. Determine the cause and correct the problem before proceeding.

POST-OPERATIONAL CHECKS

Perform the following maintenance after each use.

1. If the boat was used in silty, muddy or salty water, flush the cooling system with freshwater as described in this chapter. This will minimize corrosion and buildup of deposits in the cooling system.
2. Disconnect the battery cables from the battery (negative cable first).
3. Shut off the fuel tank valve(s).
4. Top off the fuel tank(s), if possible, to minimize the possibility of moisture condensation in the tank(s).
5. Wash the interior and exterior surfaces of the boat with freshwater.
6. Check the bilge and drain or pump all water from the bilge.

COOLING SYSTEM FLUSHING

Flushing procedures differ slightly depending upon the type of cooling system and location of the water pump.

The standard cooling system includes a raw-water pump that delivers water from outside the boat to the circulating pump, any oil coolers and to the exhaust manifold cooling jacket. A second engine-driven circulating pump moves water through the engine's water passages to cool the engine.

Some models may be equipped with a closed cooling system which is divided into 2 separate subsystems. The raw-water system uses water from around the boat and the closed system uses only coolant contained in separate passages. The circulating pump moves coolant through the engine passages to cool the engine. Excessive heat is then transferred from the closed system coolant to the raw-water system in a heat exchanger.

A belt-driven, rubber vane type external raw-water pump is mounted on the engine on all models. See **Figure 1**, typical. The raw-water pump draws cooling water through the water intake and delivers it to an oil cooler (if so equipped), then to the distribution housing and exhaust manifold.

An engine-driven circulating pump (**Figure 2**) is also used to circulate cooling water through the engine. All models are equipped with a thermostat to regulate engine operating temperature.

Cooling water must *always* circulate through the stern drive and the raw-water pump whenever the engine is running to prevent damage.

WARNING
When the cooling system is flushed, make sure there is sufficient space to the side and behind the propeller and that no one is standing in the vicinity of the propeller. If possible, remove the propeller to prevent the possibility of serious personal injury.

Raw-Water Cooling System

A flush-test device must be used with this procedure to provide cooling water. **Figure 3** shows a typical unit in use.

1. Attach the flush-test device directly over the intake holes in the stern drive gear housing. Connect a hose between the device and the water tap.

CAUTION
Do not use full water tap pressure in Step 2.

2. Partially open the water tap to allow a low-pressure flow of water into the device. Let the water flow for several minutes before continuing.

CAUTION
Do not run the engine above idle speed while flushing the system in Step 3.

3. Place the gearshift lever in NEUTRAL. Start the engine and run at idle speed until the engine reaches normal operating temperature, as indicated by the temperature gauge.
4. Watch the water being flushed from the cooling system. When the flow is clear, shut the engine off.
5. Shut the water tap off. Disconnect and remove the flush-test device from the gear housing.

Closed Cooling System

Follow the procedure described in this chapter to flush the raw-water subsystem on models equipped with a closed cooling system. Since the closed cooling subsystem should be filled only with a mixture of ethylene glycol antifreeze and water, it should not be necessary to flush the system. If necessary to fluse the closed subsystem, use a series of fill and drain procedures described in this chapter.

COOLING SYSTEM DRAINING

1. Raise or lower the bow of the boat as necessary to make sure the engine is level. Water can be trapped in the engine block, exhaust manifold or other passage if the engine is not properly leveled.

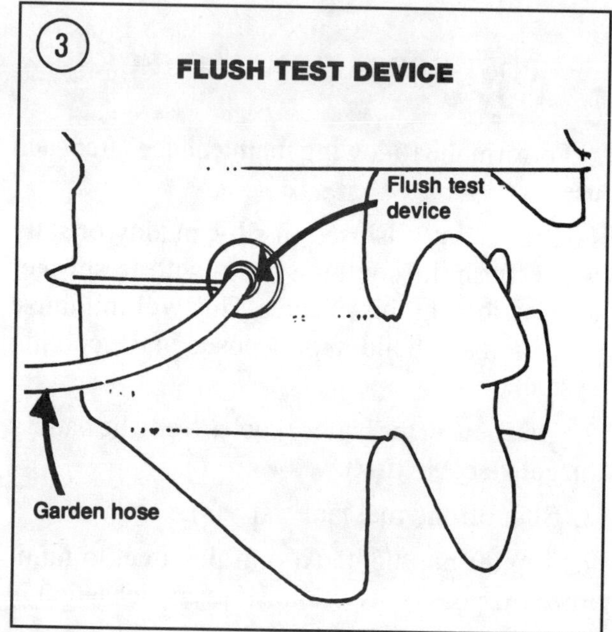

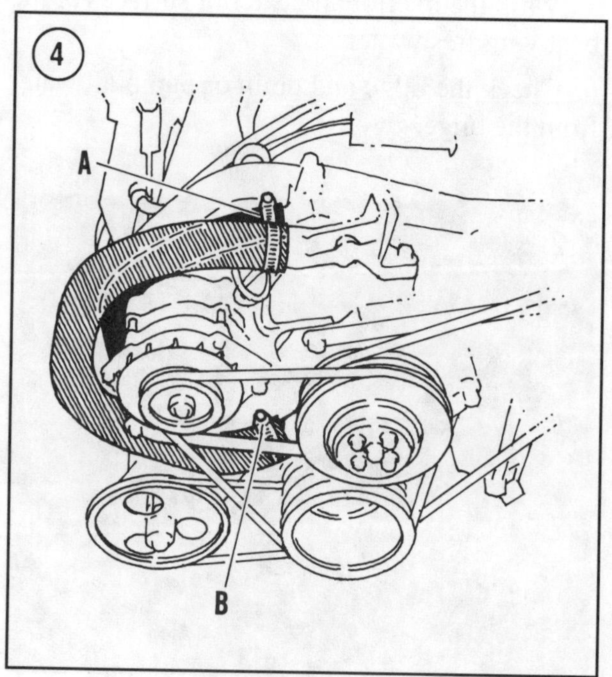

2. On models with a closed cooling system, remove the cap from the reservoir and heat exchanger.

3. Loosen the clamp on the upper hose attached to the distribution (or thermostat) housing, then detach the hose (A, **Figure 4**, typical).

4. Loosen the clamp on the lower end of the large hose attached to the circulation pump, then detach the hose (B, **Figure 4**, typical).

5. Drain the exhaust manifold(s). A drain plug or drain cock (A, **Figure 5**) is located in the bottom of the manifold on some models. If not equipped with a drain plug or drain cock, loosen the hose clamp, then detach the lower hose (A, **Figure 6**) from each exhaust manifold.

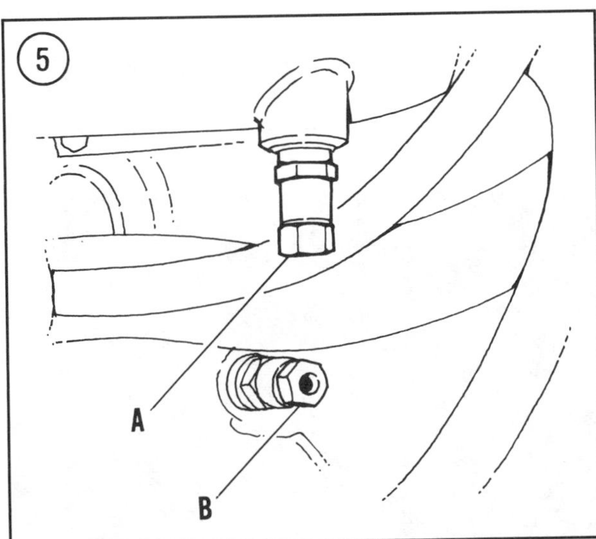

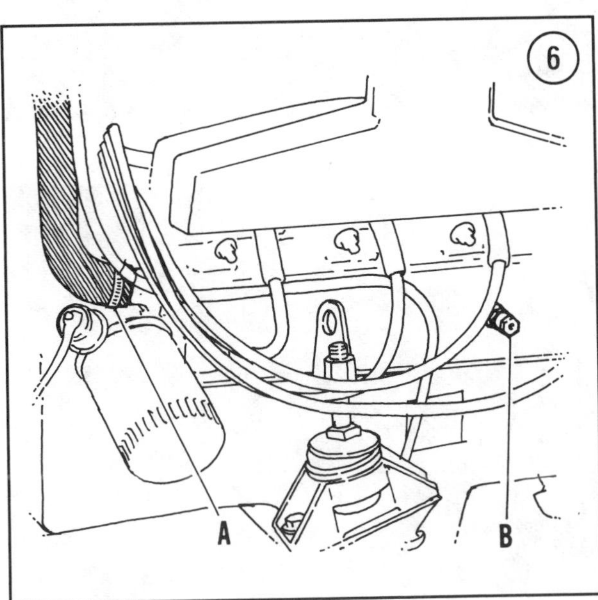

CAUTION
Insert a wire into the drains opened in Step 5 to make sure the passage is open and completely drained. The drain plugs or drain cocks are located at the lowest part of the coolant passages and may be plugged with sediment.

6. Drain the cylinder block. On 4 cylinder models, a drain plug or drain cock is located low on the port (left) side of the block. On 6- and 8-cylinder models, a drain plug or drain cock is located low on each side of the block. See B, **Figure 5** and **Figure 6**. It is important to drain both sides of 6- and 8-cylinder models.

7. If equipped with an oil cooler, loosen the clamps and detach the hoses from the cooler (**Figure 7**). Tip the cooler up so the opened hose connections are down and allow the cooler to drain completely.

8. Loosen the hose clamps on the raw-water pump, detach both hoses, then allow all water to drain from the pump. See **Figure 2**.

9. Drain water from the cavity in the pivot housing on SX models as follows:

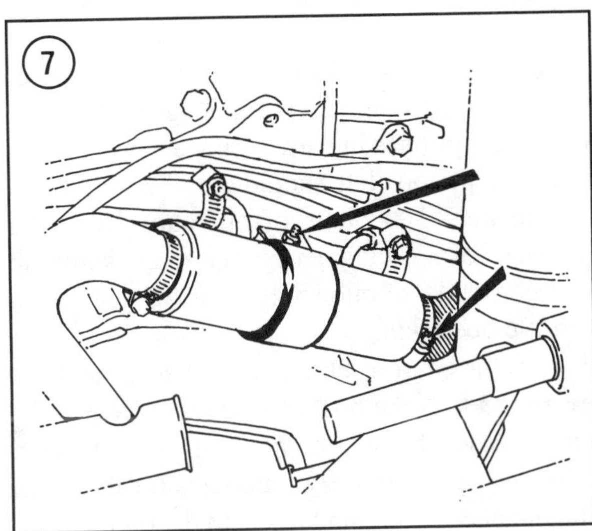

4

a. Tilt the drive unit UP to the completely raised position.
b. Remove the plug (**Figure 8**) from the port (left) side of the pivot housing.
c. Lower the drive unit and allow the cavity to drain.

10. If the system is drained for storage, make sure all water is drained, before closing the system.

CAUTION
Do not leave any part of the cooling system open while in storage. Replace hoses, clamps or plugs as needed.

11. Close drain cocks, reinstall drain plugs, reattach hoses and tighten hose clamps when finished.

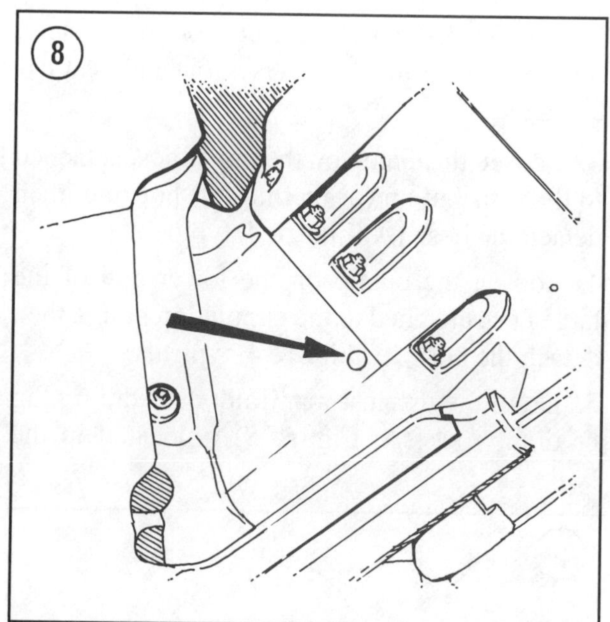

ENGINE MAINTENANCE AND LUBRICATION

Perform the maintenance tasks discussed in this section at the intervals indicated in **Table 1**. These intervals are only guidelines, so consider the frequency and extent of boat use when establishing the actual intervals. Perform the tasks more frequently if the boat is used under severe service conditions.

Engine Oil Level Check

All engines will consume a certain amount of oil as a lubricating and cooling agent. The rate of consumption is highest during a new engine's break-in period, but should stabilize after approximately 100 hours of operation. It is not unusual for a 4-cylinder engine to consume up to 1 qt. (0.9 L) of oil in 5-10 hours of wide-open throttle operation.

For this reason, check the oil level at least every week. If the boat is used more frequently, check the level each time the engine is shut down, allowing approximately 5 minutes for the oil in the upper end to drain back into the oil pan.

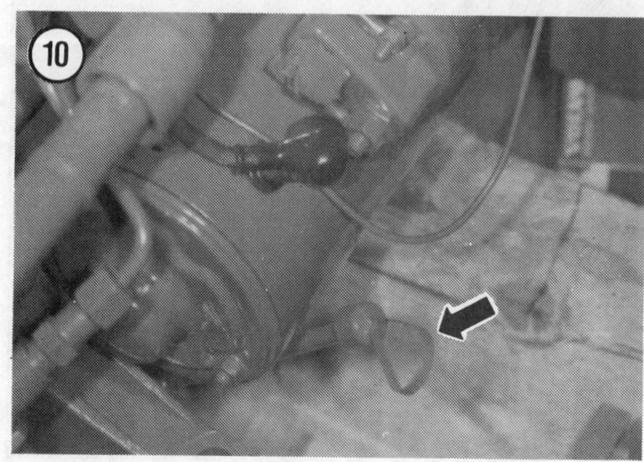

1. With the boat at rest in the water and the engine stopped, withdraw the dipstick. See **Figure 9** or **Figure 10** for typical locations. Wipe oil from the dipstick with a clean cloth or paper towel, reinsert it, then pull it out again. Note the oil level on the dipstick.

NOTE
Some dipsticks have ADD and FULL lines. Others read ADD 1 QT. and OPERATING RANGE. In either case, keep the oil level between the 2 lines.

2. Top up to the FULL or OPERATING RANGE mark on the dipstick if necessary. Use oil with API classification SG/CD and viscosity rating consistent with the air temperature as listed in **Table 2**.

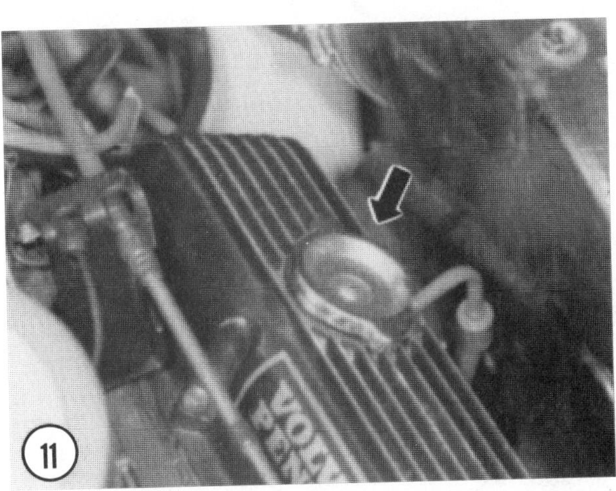

11

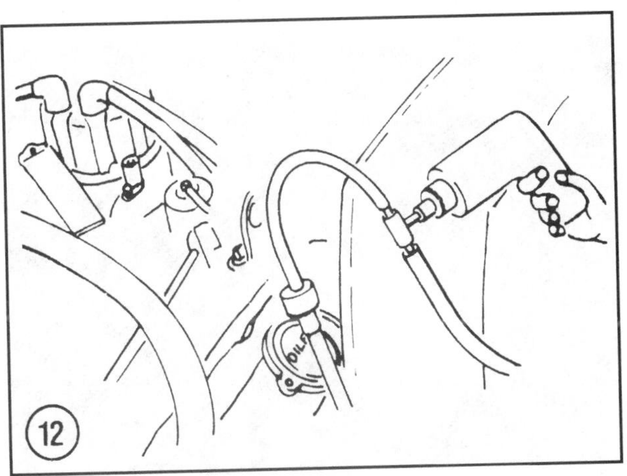

12

NOTE
Only single viscosity oil is recommended for marine applications. Disregard any decals on the engine that recommend multiviscosity oil. On models with 3.0 L, 4.3 L, 5.0 L, 5.7 L, 7.4 L and 8.2 L GM engines, use oil which meets General Motors Standard GM-6094-M. On models with 5.0 L and 5.8 L Ford engines, use oil which meets Ford Specification ESE-M2C153-E. Volvo Penta DuraPlus Motor Oils are recommended.

3. Remove the oil filler cap and add oil through the hole in the valve cover. See **Figure 11**, typical.

4

Engine Oil and Filter Change

Change the engine oil and filter at the end of the initial 20 hour break-in period, then as specified in **Table 1**. Change the oil and filter at least once per season even if the engine has minimal usage.

Use oil with API classification SG/CD and viscosity rating consistent with the air temperature as listed in **Table 2**. Only single viscosity oils are recommended for marine application. Disregard any decals on the engine that recommend multiviscosity oil. On models with 3.0 L, 4.3 L, 5.0 L, 5.7 L, 7.4 L and 8.2 L GM engines, use oil which meets General Motors Standard GM-6094-M. On models with 5.0 L and 5.8 L Ford engines, use oil which meets Ford Specification ESE-M2C153-E. Volvo Penta DuraPlus Motor Oil is recommended for use in all models.

Most installations do not leave enough space to permit the use of the oil pan drain plug. For this reason, an oil drain suction pump is the most common device used to drain the crankcase oil. The pump has a long, flexible hose which is inserted into the oil dipstick tube and fed into the crankcase. Several makes of pumps are available from marine supply dealers. Some are hand-operated, some are motorized and others are designed to be operated with an electric drill (**Figure 12**).

Pour the used oil into a sealable container for proper (and legal) disposal. There are several ways to discard the old oil safely. Many auto supply stores sell an oil disposal kit. The oil can then be taken to a service station for recycling.

NOTE
Check local regulations before disposing of oil. Never dump used oil overboard or on the ground.

Oil filters are the disposable spin-on type. An inexpensive oil filter wrench can be obtained from any auto parts or marine supply store. This wrench is handy in removing oil filters, but should *not* be used to install the new filter. A firm fit is all that is required. Overtightening the filter can damage it and/or cause an oil leak.

Some models may be equipped with a remote oil filter assembly. See your Volvo Penta dealer for availability and installation.

The installed angle of the engine effects oil level in the crankcase. To ensure that the oil is drained and replaced properly, perform the following procedure with the boat at rest in the water.

1. Start the engine and warm to normal operating temperature under load, then shut it off.
2. Remove the dipstick, wipe it clean with a lint-free cloth or paper towel and place it to one side out of the way.
3. Insert the oil drain pump hose into the dipstick tube as far as it will go.
4. Insert the other pump hose into a sealable container large enough to hold the oil from the crankcase. Most engine crankcases will contain 4-7 qt. (3.8-6.6 L) of oil. Refer to **Table 3** to determine the capacity of your engine crankcase.
5. Operate the pump until it has removed all of the oil possible, then withdraw the pump hose from the dipstick tube.
6. Place a drain pan or other suitable container under the filter to catch any oil spillage when the filter is removed. See **Figure 13**, typical.
7. Unscrew the filter counterclockwise. Use the filter wrench if the filter is too tight or too hot to remove by hand.
8. Wipe the gasket surface of the engine block clean with a paper towel.
9. Coat the neoprene gasket on the new filter with a thin coat of clean engine oil.
10. Screw the new filter onto the engine *by hand* until the gasket just touches the engine block. At this point, there will be a very slight resistance when turning the filter.

CAUTION
If the filter wrench is used to tighten the filter in Step 11, the filter will probably be overtightened, damaging the filter and causing an oil leak.

11. Tighten the filter another 1/2-3/4 turn *by hand.*
12. Remove the oil filler cap from the valve cover. See **Figure 14**, typical.
13. Reinstall the dipstick in the dipstick tube.
14. Refer to **Table 3** to determine the approximate capacity of the crankcase for your engine. Pour the specified amount of oil into the valve cover opening and install the oil filler cap. Wipe up any spills with a clean cloth as they occur.

NOTE
Check the area under and around the oil filter for leaks while the engine is running in Step 15.

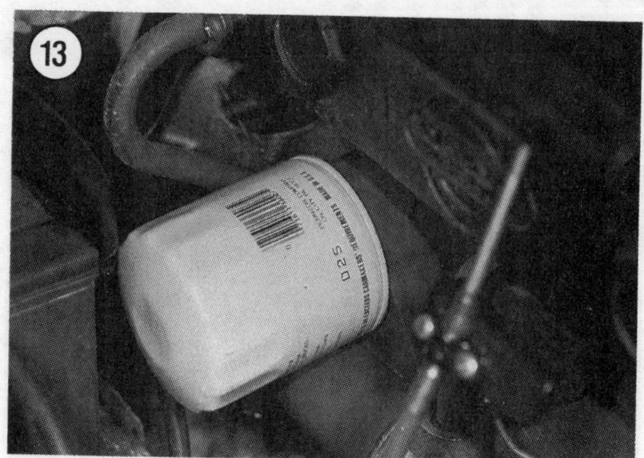
13

15. Start the engine and let it idle for 5 minutes, then shut the engine off.
16. Wait approximately 5 minutes to allow the oil to drain back to the oil pan, then remove the dipstick. Wipe the dipstick clean with a lint-free cloth or paper towel and reinsert it in the dipstick tube. Remove the dipstick a second time and check the oil level. Add oil, if necessary, to bring the level up to the FULL or OPERATING RANGE mark, but do not *overfill.*

CAUTION
If all of the oil was not removed while draining, filling with the amount of oil specified in ***Table 3*** *may result in overfilling. Overfilling may cause high operating temperature and foaming oil (mixing air with the oil), resulting in engine damage. Drain excess oil if overfilled.*

Fuel System Service

This service is particularly important, especially if the boat is equipped with a fiberglass fuel tank(s). Some types of fiberglass tanks contain a residue of particles which will prematurely clog the filter. Others contain a wax used during their manufacture which dissolves in gasoline. This wax is trapped by the filter, but since it cannot be seen, the filter appears to be clean. The resulting lean-out condition can only be cured by installing a new filter.

CAUTION
Be especially careful of using fuels containing alcohol. The 2 commonly used alcohol additives are ethanol (ethyl alcohol) and methanol (methyl alcohol). ***Do not use fuel containing methanol (methyl alcohol).*** *Check with your boat manufacturer to see if the fuel system components used will tolerate ethanol (ethyl alcohol). The engine will operate leaner with fuels containing alcohol and this lean condition may result in vapor lock, low speed stalling, or hard starting. Alcohol will attract and retain moisture (water) that increases the probability of fuel system problems. Alcohol blended fuels may cause metallic parts in the fuel system to rust or corrode and may cause nonmetallic parts to harden, stiffen or deteriorate. If using alcohol extended fuel, check for leaks frequently and repair immediately.*

Check all fuel lines for deterioration or loose connections at the intervals specified in **Table 1**. Replace lines, fittings, clamps or other parts as necessary and tighten any loose fittings or clamps. Repair leaks as soon as possible. Be sure to clean all spilled fuel and ventilate the bilge before starting the engine.

Remove and clean the fuel filter sediment bowl (if used) whenever moisture or contamination can be seen.

Replace the fuel filter at least once per year or more often if contaminated fuel is encountered.

NOTE
In areas where only poor quality fuel is available or where moisture tends to condense in the fuel tanks, it is advisable to install an inline fuel filter to remove moisture and other contaminants. These may already be installed and must be replaced frequently.

Fuel Filter Service

All models (except 1995-on 3.0L) are equipped with a spin-on cannister type fuel filter

(**Figure 15**). A fuel pump mounted filter is used on 1995-on 3.0 L models. See **Figure 16**. Some carburetted models are also equipped with a filter or screen behind the carburetor inlet nut (**Figure 17**). Replace the fuel filter once per year or after 100 hours of operation, whichever occurs first. If poor quality fuel is used, change the filter more frequently.

15

Canister-type filter replacement

This type of fuel filter may look much like a canister-type oil filter (**Figure 15**) and is replaced using a procedure similar to that for oil filter replacement. Unscrew the filter canister from the filter adapter (using a filter wrench, if necessary) and discard. Wipe the neoprene gasket of the new filter with a thin film of clean engine oil, then screw the filter onto the adapter until it is snug. *Do not overtighten*. Start the engine and check for leaks.

Fuel pump mounted filter replacement

Refer to **Figure 16** for this procedure.

1. Loosen the wire bail nut. Slide the wire bail aside and remove the filter bowl.
2. Remove the filter element and spring from the filter bowl. Discard the filter element.
3. Remove and discard the filter gasket.
4. Wipe out the bowl with a clean shop towel.
5. Place the spring into the filter bowl. Install a new filter element and gasket.
6. Install the bowl on the fuel pump and secure with the wire bail.

Carburetor fuel inlet filter replacement

Refer to **Figure 17** for this procedure.

1. Remove the flame arrestor (**Figure 18**) or carburetor cover if necessary to provide adequate working clearance.
2. Place one wrench on the carburetor inlet nut. Place a second wrench on the fuel line connector nut. Hold the fuel inlet nut from moving and loosen the connector nut.

16

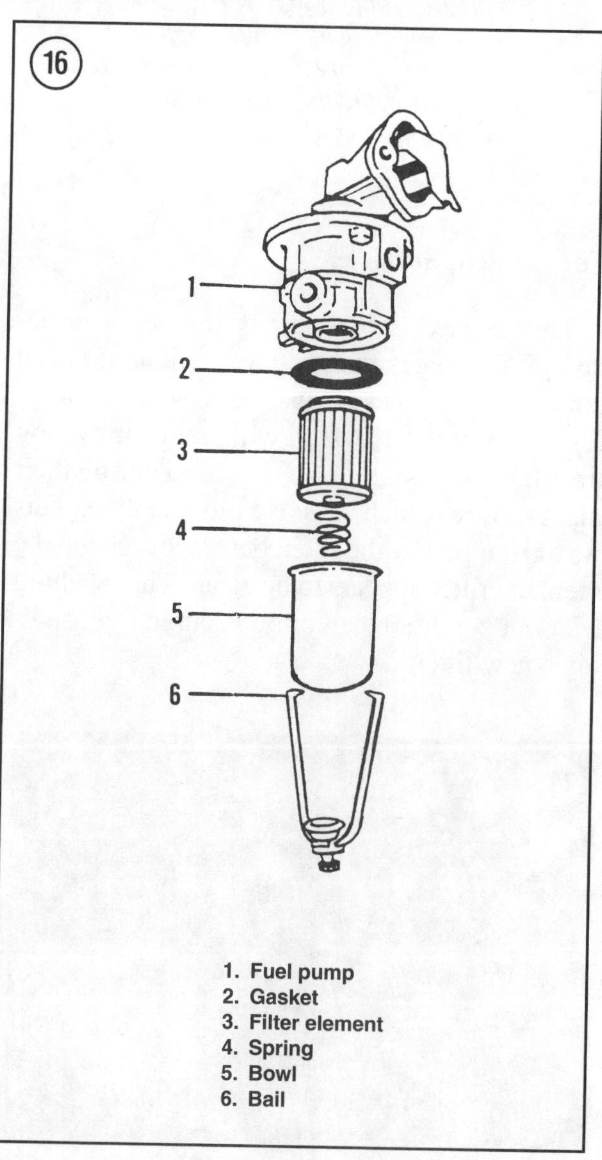

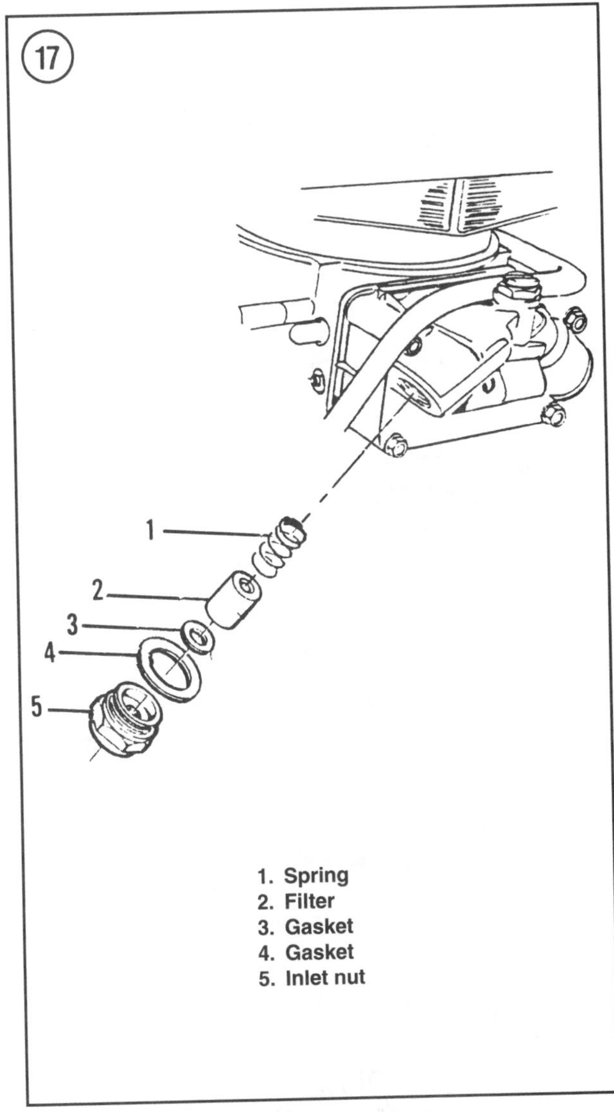

1. Spring
2. Filter
3. Gasket
4. Gasket
5. Inlet nut

3. Detach the fuel line from the inlet nut fitting, then remove the inlet nut from the carburetor.
4. Remove the filter element and spring from the carburetor fuel inlet.
5. Installation is the reverse of removal. Make sure the end of the filter with the hole faces the inlet nut. Use a new gasket if necessary. Tighten the inlet nut and connector nut snugly.
6. Install the flame arrestor, if removed. Start the engine and check for leaks. Correct any fuel leaks immediately.

Fuel Quality

Gasoline blended with alcohol is widely available and sold for marine use. Using blends of gasoline and alcohol is not recommended unless you can determine the nature of the blend and if the blend is approved by Volvo Penta and the boat manufacturer.

Two commonly used alcohol additives are ethanol (ethyl alcohol) and methanol (methyl alcohol). *Do not use fuel containing methanol (methyl alcohol).* Check with your boat manufacturer to see if the fuel system components used will tolerate ethanol (ethyl alcohol). Volvo Penta also recommends that no more than 10 percent ethanol be mixed with 90% unleaded gasoline.

Alcohol will attract and retain moisture (water) from the air. Any moisture in the fuel increases the probability of fuel system problems. When the moisture content of the fuel reaches approximately one half of one percent, it combines with the alcohol and separates from the fuel. This separation does not normally occur when gasohol is used in an automobile, as the tank is generally emptied within a few days after filling it.

The problem does occur more frequently in marine use, because boats often remain idle for days or even weeks. This length of time permits separation to take place. The water-alcohol mixture settles at the bottom of the tank where the fuel pickup carries it into the fuel line. Since the engine will not run on this mixture, it is necessary to drain the fuel tank, flush out the fuel system with clean gasoline then remove and clean the spark plugs before the engine can be started. If it is necessary to operate an engine on gasohol, do not store such fuel in the tank(s) for more than a few days, especially in climates with high humidity.

Alcohol blended fuels may cause metallic parts in the fuel system to rust or corrode and may cause nonmetallic parts (O-ring seals, inlet needle tips, accelerator pump cups and gaskets) to harden, stiffen or deteriorate. If using alcohol extended gasoline, check for leaks frequently and repair immediately.

Some methods of blending alcohol with gasoline now make use of cosolvents as suspension agents to prevent the water-alcohol from separating from the gasoline. Regardless of the method used to blend the alcohol with gasoline, the engine will operate leaner and this lean condition may result in vapor lock, low-speed stalling, or hard starting.

The following is an accepted and widely used field procedure to detect alcohol in gasoline. Use any small transparent bottle or tube that can be capped and provided with graduations or a mark at approximately 1/3 full. A pencil mark on a piece of adhesive tape is sufficient.

1. Fill the container with water to the 1/3 full mark.
2. Add gasoline until the container is almost full. Leave a small air space at the top.
3. Shake the container vigorously, then allow it to set for 3-5 minutes. If the volume of water appears to have increased, alcohol is present. If the dividing line between the water and gasoline becomes cloudy, reference the center of the cloudy band.

The detection procedure is performed with water as a reacting agent. However, if cosolvents have been used as suspension agents in alcohol blending, the test will not show the presence of alcohol unless ethylene glycol (automotive antifreeze) is used instead of water as a reacting agent. It is suggested that a gasoline sample be tested twice using the detection kit: first with water then with ethylene glycol (automotive antifreeze).

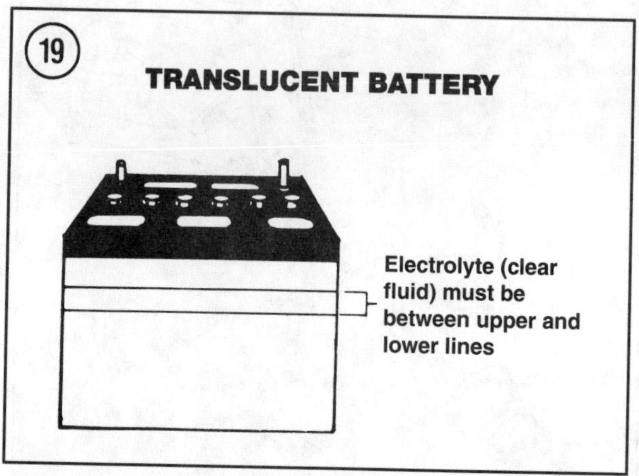

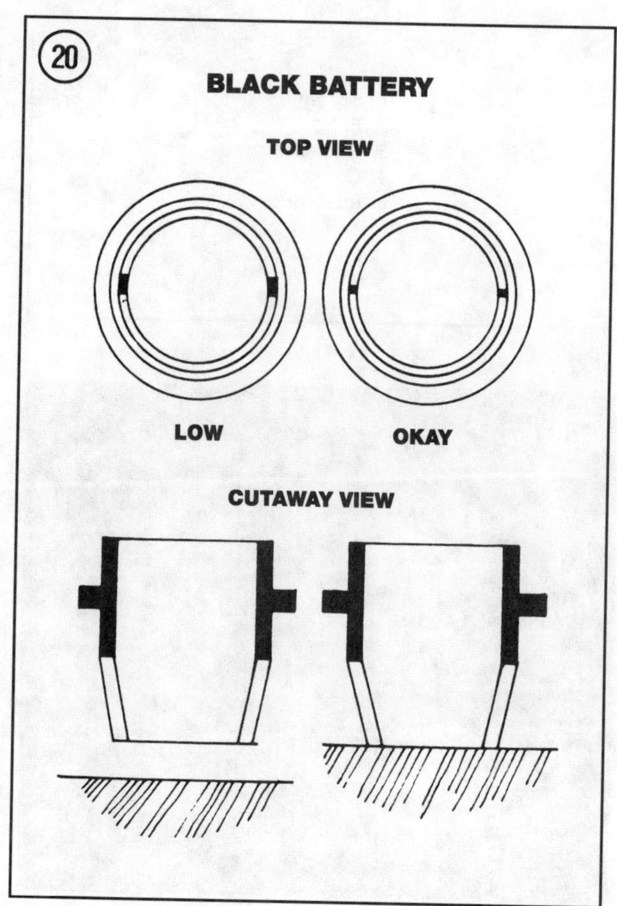

The procedure cannot differentiate between types of alcohol (ethanol or methanol) nor is it considered to be absolutely accurate from a scientific standpoint, but it is accurate enough to determine whether or not there is sufficient alcohol in the fuel to cause the user to take precautions. Maintaining a close watch on the quality of fuel used can save hundreds of dollars in marine engine and fuel system repairs.

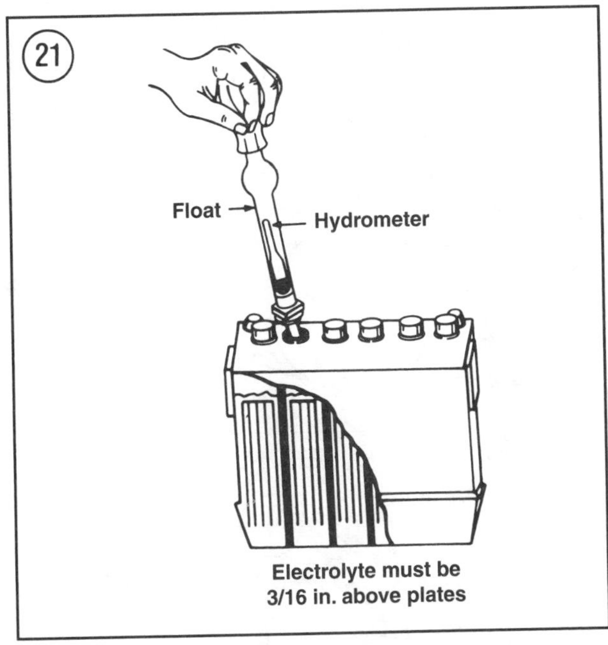

Flame Arrestor

The flame arrestor (**Figure 18**, typical) serves as an air filter and as a safety precaution against engine backfiring that might cause a dangerous explosion in the engine compartment. Remove and service the flame arrestor every 100 hours of operation or once per season. Wash in solvent and air dry thoroughly. Make sure the air inlet screen is not deformed and reinstall the flame arrestor.

Battery

Remove the battery vent caps and check the electrolyte level. On translucent batteries, it should be between the marks on the battery case (**Figure 19**). On black batteries, it should be about 4.8 mm (3/16 in.) above the plates or even with the bottom of the filler wells. See **Figure 20**. Test the battery condition with a hydrometer (**Figure 21**). See Chapter Eleven.

Drive Belt Condition and Tension

Refer to **Figure 22** for belt installation.

The alternator, power steering pump (on models so equipped), raw-water pump and circulating pump are belt driven by the crankshaft pulley. It is important that all belts are correctly tightened for proper operation. Check and adjust the tension of a new belt after the initial 10 hours of operation. Afterward, check belt tension at least every 50 hours of operation. Belts should have 1/4-1/2 in. (6-13 mm) deflection when pressed with your finger midway between the pulleys. Belts that are too tight can overload and damage the driven components. Belts that are too loose can slip, resulting in poor performance, accelerated belt wear and damaged pulleys.

Be sure to loosen all of the mounting bolts before attempting to tighten a drive belt.

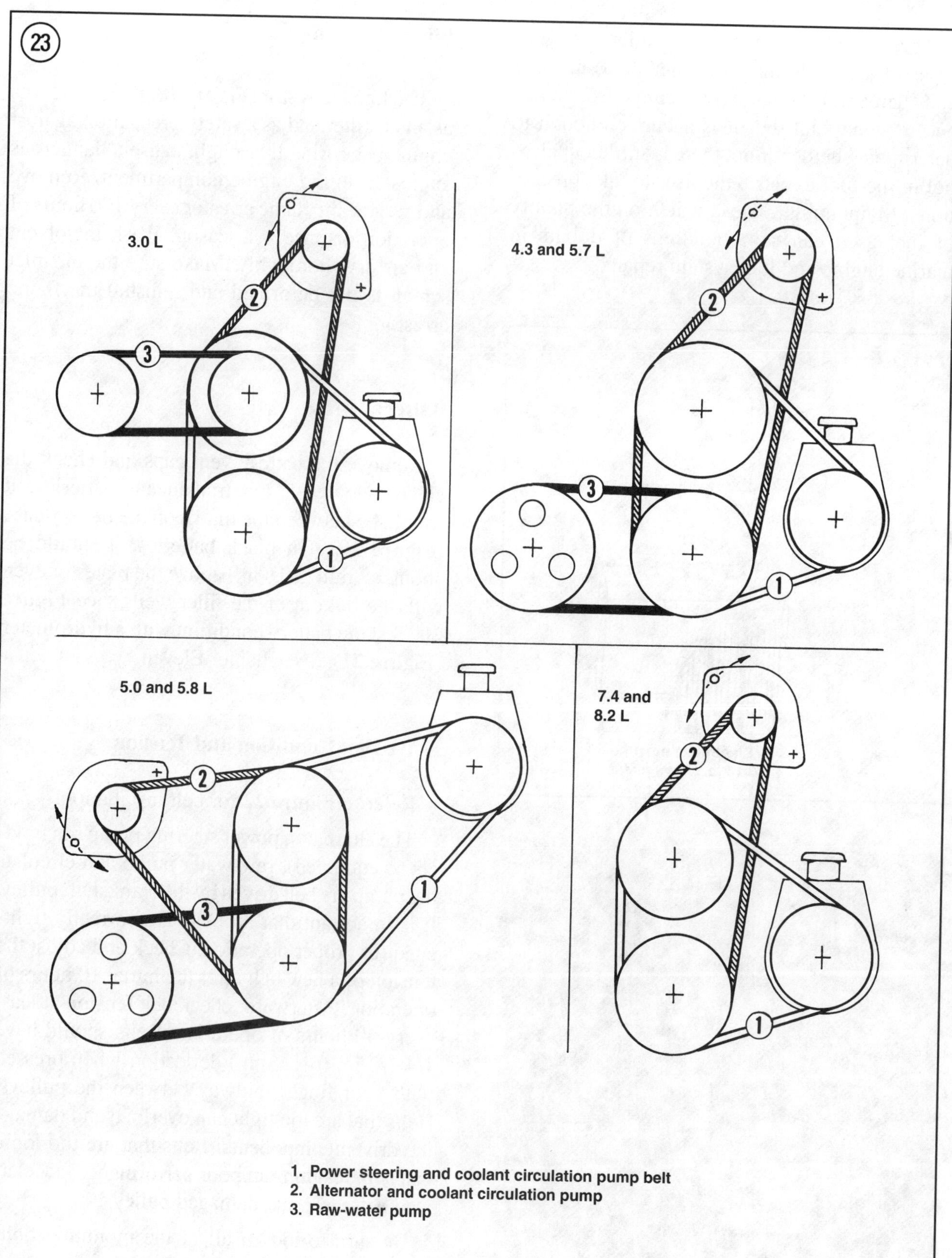

1. Power steering and coolant circulation pump belt
2. Alternator and coolant circulation pump
3. Raw-water pump

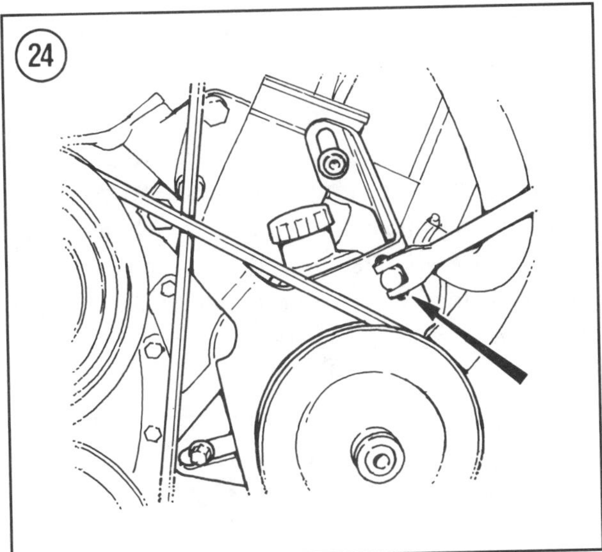

CAUTION
Do not pry against the pump reservoir or pull on the filler neck when tightening the power steering belt (1, ***Figure 23****). Also, be careful not to damage other parts by prying against the pulleys, stamped covers or other parts that could be damaged.*

The mounting bracket for the power steering pump used on most models is equipped with a 1/2 in. square hole so a breaker bar can be inserted to tighten the belt. See **Figure 24**. Tighten all of the mounting bolts when the tension is correct.

STEERING SERVICE

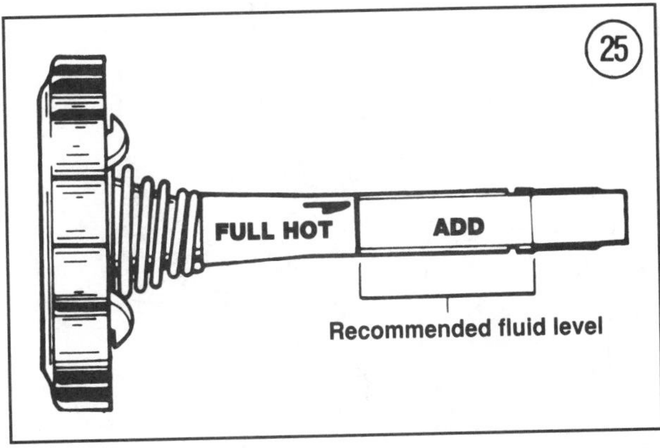

Coat the steering ram with grease at least every 60 days. If equipped with power steering, check the fluid level in the pump reservoir after the first 20 hours of operation, then at 100 hour intervals or at least once a year.

The dipstick for checking the level of power steering fluid is attached to the filler cap. See **Figure 25**. Maintain the fluid level between the FULL HOT and the ADD marks on the dipstick. Fill the reservoir with Volvo Penta Power Trim/Tilt and Steering Fluid or Dextron II automatic transmission fluid.

POWER TRIM/TILT SERVICE (SX MODELS)

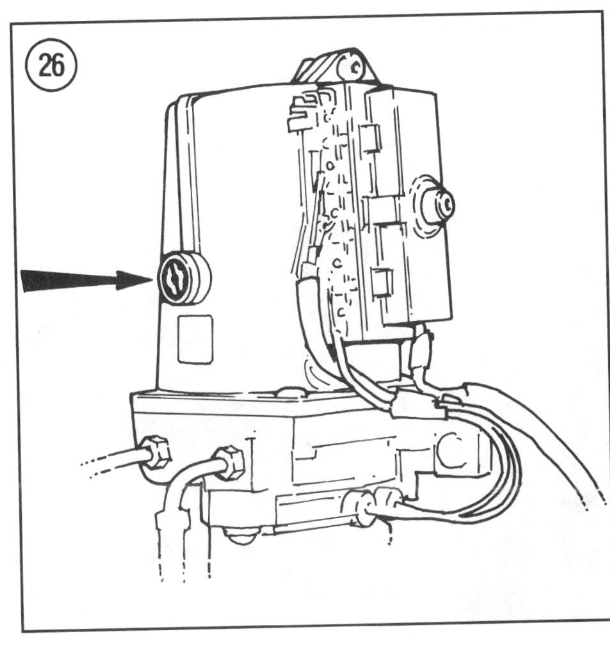

CAUTION
The stern drive unit must be tilted UP to relieve hydraulic pressure. Loosening the level/fill plug with the stern drive in the lowered position will result in a hazardous spray of hydraulic fluid.

Check the fluid level at the beginning of each season or if leaks are suspected.

1. Tilt the stern drive unit up.
2. Loosen, then remove the level/fill plug (**Figure 26**).

3. The fluid level should be at the bottom of the plug opening.
4. If necessary, add Volvo Penta Power Trim/Tilt and Steering Fluid to the reservoir.
5. Install and tighten the level/fill plug. Make sure the plug is tight.
6. Cycle the unit to the lowered, then raised position several times and check for leaks.

POWER TRIM/TILT SERVICE (DP AND DPX MODELS)

The trim/tilt on early DP models is different from later models. Refer to **Figure 27**.

To check the fluid level in the reservoir on early models, remove the level/fill plug (A, **Figure 27**). The fluid should be at the lower surface of the plug opening.

The reservoir on later models, is marked with MIN and MAX marks and the fluid level should remain between the 2 marks.

Volvo Penta Power Trim/Tilt and Steering Fluid, Dextron II automatic transmission fluid or the same oil as used in the engine may be used in the reservoir. It is important, however, that only one type of the fluid is in the system. If the type of oil is not known, it is suggested that all of the oil be drained and the system filled with Volvo Penta Power Trim/Tilt and Steering Fluid.

On later models, the reservoir is attached by a center screw to the valve assembly. Remove the reservoir by removing this screw. To reduce the chance of contamination, clean the reservoir, valve assembly and adjacent area before removing the reservoir. Filter rings located on the valve can be removed by clamping the filters with pliers and withdrawing in a twisting motion. Use a 5/8 in. socket wrench over the new filter rings and gently bump the filters into position with a hammer. Make sure the seals on the center (retaining) screw and between the reservoir and valve are in place and in good condition. Fill the system, then cycle the unit several times and check for leaks.

STERN DRIVE LUBRICATION

Perform the lubrication tasks described in this section at the intervals indicated in **Table 1**. These intervals are only guidelines, so consider the frequency and extent of boat use when setting actual intervals. Perform the tasks more frequently if the boat is used under severe service conditions.

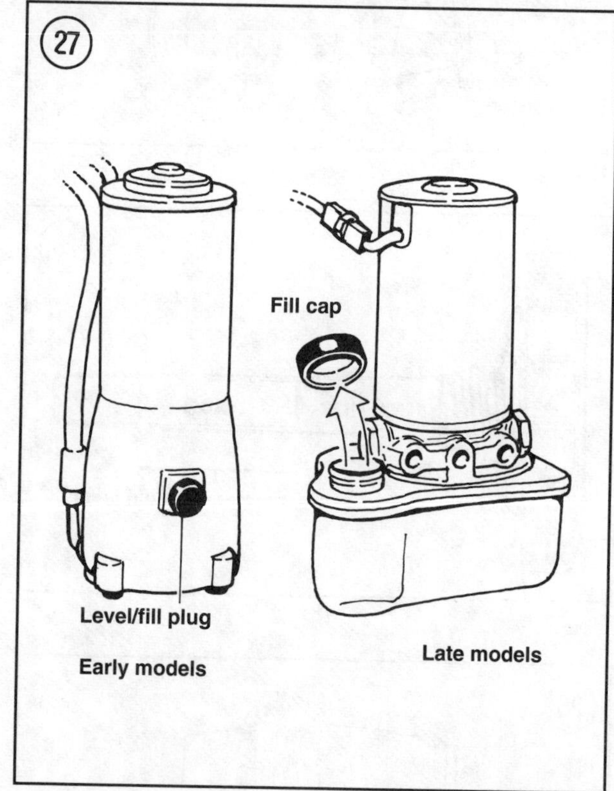

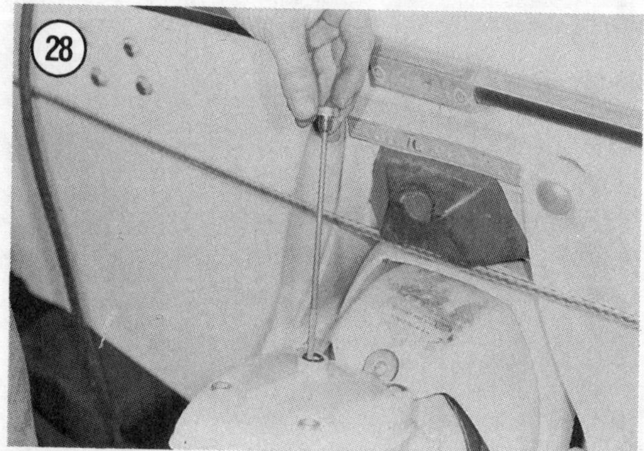

Recommended lubricants are listed in **Table 4** and capacity is listed in **Table 5**.

Stern Drive Lubricant Level Check

Maintain the stern drive oil level at the full mark on the dipstick (**Figure 28**). Also, periodically check the lubricant in the stern drive should also be periodically checked for water contamination. Water contamination is indicated by the oil becoming a milky brown color. Refer to **Table 4** to determine the correct type of oil for the unit.

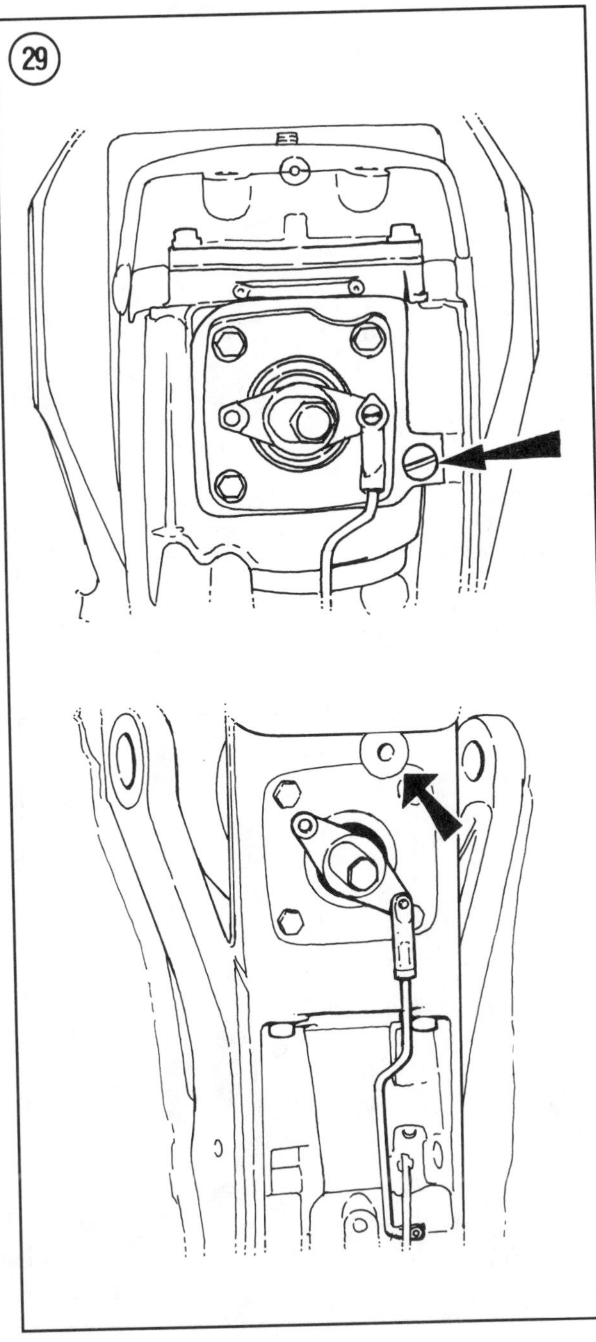

1. Lower the stern drive fully and remove the dipstick.
2. Wipe the dipstick with a clean cloth or paper towel.
3. Reinstall the dipstick and screw it fully into place, then remove the dipstick and check the oil level.
4. Add oil if the level is below the full mark. Oil can be added through the dipstick hole, but should be allowed to drain down before rechecking the level. Approximately 2.24 oz. (65.6 mL) of oil can be added between the add and full marks. If the unit requires more than about 2 oz. (58 mL) of lubricant, an oil leak is probable. A fill plug (**Figure 29**) is accessible after removing the rear cover for adding larger quantities of oil.
5. When the oil level is correct, reinstall the dipstick and tighten to the torque specification listed in **Table 6**.

4

Stern Drive Lubricant Change

Refer to **Table 4** to determine the correct type of oil for the unit.

1. Lower the stern drive fully and place a suitable container under the drive unit to catch the fluid.
2. Remove the dipstick (**Figure 28**).

CAUTION

When the drain plug is removed in Step 3, let a small quantity of fluid drain on your fingers. If the lubricant is milky brown or if water drains while removing the plug, the drive unit has a leak which must be corrected before it is returned to service.

3. Remove the drain plug (3, **Figure 30**) and allow the lubricant to drain *completely.* Clean the drain plug.

NOTE
On some models, a magnet is attached to the drain plug. On these models, inspect the fragments clinging to the magnet. Large fragments indicate severe damage that must be identified and repaired.

4. Remove the screw(s) attaching the rear cover (5, **Figure 30**), then remove the cover to access the level plug (**Figure 29**).
5. Remove the level plug.
6. Insert a lubricant pump into the drain hole (3, **Figure 30**). Inject lubricant from the pump up through the drain hole until it begins to flow from the level plug hole. Refer to **Table 5** for approximate capacity.

NOTE
To reduce spillage, reinstall the oil level plug and dipstick before removing the lubricant pump hose from oil drain plug hole.

7. Reinstall the oil level plug and washer to the torque specification listed in **Table 6**.
8. Reinstall the dipstick and sealing washer to the torque listed in **Table 6**.
9. Remove the lubricant pump and quickly reinstall the drain plug and washer to the torque specification listed in **Table 6**.
10. Wipe any excess lubricant from the drive housing and gearcase.
11. After the oil has had time to settle, recheck the fluid level as described in this chapter.
12. Reinstall the rear cover.

Gimbal Bearing, Driveshaft Splines and Universal Joints (SX Models)

The stern drive unit must be removed to lubricate the gimbal bearing, drive shaft splines and drive shaft universal joints. It is usually more convenient to remove the unit and service these parts at the close of the season while preparing the craft for off-season storage. If these parts are not serviced, early failure is likely.

1. Refer to Chapter Twelve for stern drive unit removal instructions.

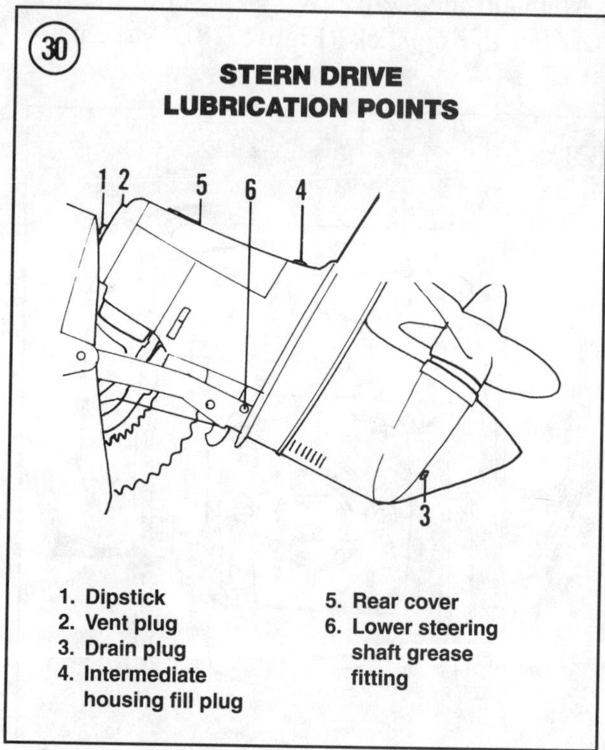

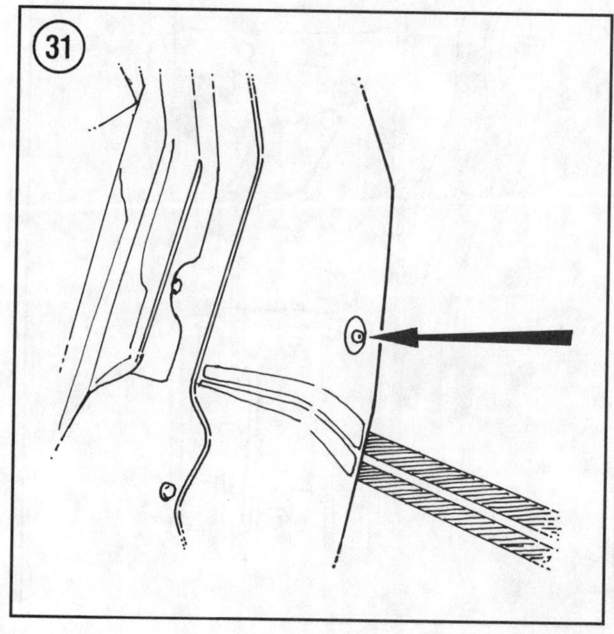

NOTE
The grease fitting for the gimbal bearing is accessible with the unit installed, but the manufacturer recommends that the stern drive be removed for gimbal bearing lubrication.

2. Lubricate the gimbal bearing through the fitting (**Figure 31**) located on the starboard side of the gimbal housing. Refer to **Table 4** for the recommended lubricant.
3. Lubricate the 2 fittings for the universal joints. Refer to **Table 4** for the recommended lubricant. Check the universal joints for tightness and freedom of movement.
4. Apply grease to the splines of the drive shaft. Make sure the O-rings are in good condition and oil the O-rings before assembling.
5. Check the condition of the bellows and hoses. Install new parts as necessary.
6. Reinstall the stern drive unit as described in Chapter Twelve.

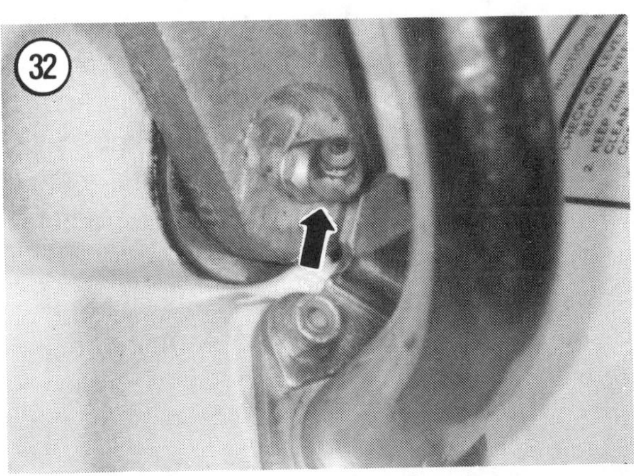
32

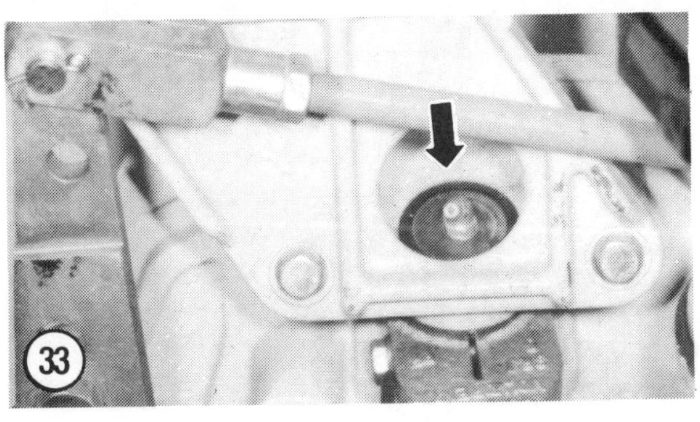
33

Steering and Tilt Bearings, Drive Shaft and Universal Joints (DP and DPX)

The stern drive unit must be removed to lubricate the drive shaft splines and drive shaft universal joints. It is usually more convenient to remove the unit and service these parts at the close of the season while preparing the craft for off-season storage. Failure to service these parts will lead to early failure.

1. Refer to Chapter Twelve for stern drive unit removal instructions.
2. Lubricate the fittings for the universal joints. Refer to **Table 4** for the recommended lubricant. Check the universal joints for tightness and freedom of movement.
3. Apply grease to the splines of the drive shaft. Make sure O-rings are in good condition and oil the O-rings before assembling.
4. Check the condition of bellows and hoses. Install new parts as necessary. The manufacturer recommends installing a new drive shaft bellows every other year.
5. Grease the fitting (6, **Figure 30**) that lubricates the lower steering shaft bearing until grease is forced from around the washer located between the yoke and the intermediate housing. Refer to **Table 4** for the recommended lubricant.
6. Lubricate the fittings (**Figure 32** and **Figure 33**) that lubricate the upper steering shaft bearing until grease is forced out of the bearings. Refer to **Table 4** for the recommended lubricant.
7. Reinstall the stern drive unit as described in Chapter Twelve.

Zinc Anode Check and Replacement

Every 14 days, check the zinc anode(s) to determine their condition. When corroded to less than 50 percent of their original size, install new anodes.

1. Remove the propeller(s) as described in Chapter Twelve.

2. Remove the 2 screws holding the zinc cover ring, then remove the cover ring (**Figure 34**).
3. Clean the contact surface on the mounting collar and/or propeller housing with a scraper and sandpaper to provide a bare metal surface for good contact.
4. Install the new cover ring.
5. Install the propeller(s) as described in Chapter Twelve.
6. If so equipped, remove the 2 screws attaching the anode under the mounting collar.
7. Scrape the contacting surface of the mounting collar to provide a bare metal surface for good contact with the anode.
8. Install a new anode under the mounting collar and tighten the screws securely.

ENGINE TUNE-UP

A smooth running, dependable marine engine is more than a convenience. At sea, it might save your life. To keep your engine running right, you must follow a regular program of preventive maintenance.

Part of any preventive maintenance program is a thorough engine tune-up. A tune-up includes a series of tests, accurate adjustments and replacement of parts to restore maximum power and performance.

Engine tune-ups are generally recommended at 100-hour intervals. If the engine is used infrequently, perform a tune-up at least once per season. Tune-up specifications are provided in tables at the end of the chapter. If the specifications on a decal attached to the engine conflict with the specifications given in a table, check with a Volvo Penta dealer. Specifications are subject to change, and generally it is best to follow those given on the decal.

A tune-up consists of the following:

a. Compression check.
b. Ignition system work.
c. Fuel system (carburetor or fuel injection system) inspection and adjustment.

Careful and accurate adjustment is crucial to a successful engine tune-up. Perform each procedure in this section exactly as described and in the order presented.

WARNING
Marine components are more expensive than comparable automotive parts (such as distributors, carburetors, alternators and starter motors). However, never substitute an automotive part for a part designed for use on marine equipment. Marine replacement parts are designed to withstand the harsh marine environment and are also flash-proofed to prevent an onboard fire or explosion.

Compression Check

Check the compression of each cylinder before attempting a tune-up. A compression test measures the compression pressure created in each cylinder. The results can be used to assess the general condition of the cylinder, piston, rings and valves. In addition, it can warn you that problems are developing inside the engine. If more than a 20 psi (138 kPa) difference exists between the highest and lowest reading cylinders, a problem exists which will prevent a tune-up from restoring the engine's performance.

1. If the boat is not in the water, attach a flush-test device to provide water before operating the engine.

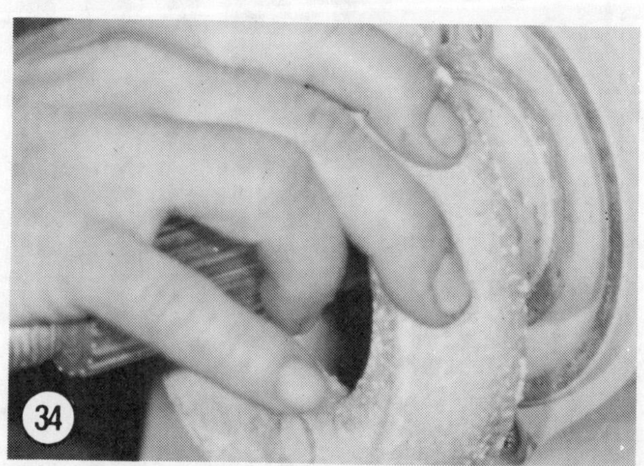
34

2. Warm the engine to normal operating temperature, then shut it off.
3. Remove the flame arrestor (**Figure 18**, typical) and make sure the choke and throttle valves are completely open.

NOTE
*During compression testing, the ignition system must be disabled to prevent sparking and possible ignition system damage while cranking the engine. Refer to **Prevent Ignition Sparking** in Chapter Three for the correct and safe way to disable the ignition.*

4A. To disable the ignition on models with *EST* ignition system, detach the connector containing the pink and brown wires from the distributor.
4B. To disable the ignition on models with *BID* ignition system, detach both primary wires from the ignition coil and tape the end terminals to prevent accidental grounding.
4C. To disable the ignition on 5.0L and 5.8L models with *TFI-IV* ignition system, detach the primary wire connector from the E-coil. Press the 2 side clips of the connector in to release the connector body from the coil.
5. Remove the spark plugs as described in this chapter.
6. Connect a remote start switch to the starter solenoid or assist solenoid according to the manufacturer's instructions. Leave the ignition switch in the OFF position.

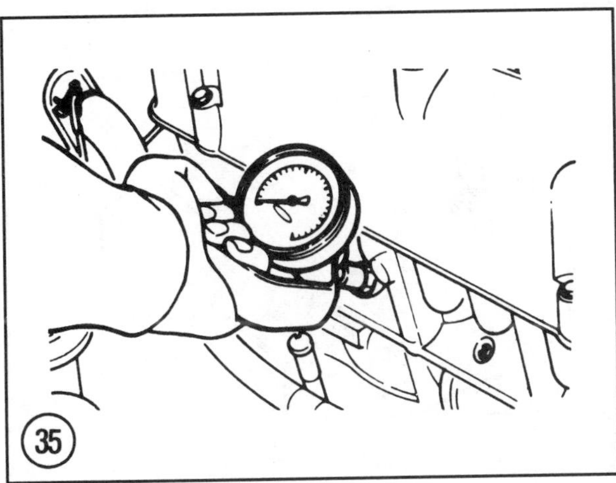
35

NOTE
The No. 1 cylinder is the front cylinder on all inline engines. The No. 1 cylinder is the front cylinder on the port (left) side on GM V6 and V8 engines. All odd number cylinders (1, 3, 5 and 7) are on the port (left) side on GM V6 and V8 engines. On Ford 5.0L and 5.8L V8 engines, the No. 1 cylinder is the front cylinder on the starboard (right) side. Cylinders on the starboard side are numbered consecutively (1, 2, 3 and 4) on Ford 5.0L and 5.8L V8 engines. The cylinders are numbered 5, 6, 7 and 8 front to rear on the port side of Ford V8 engines.

7. Attach a compression gauge to the No. 1 cylinder according to its manufacturer's instructions (**Figure 35**).
8. Hold the throttle wide open and crank the engine several revolutions (at least 5 turns) until the gauge indicates the highest reading.
9. Record the cylinder's compression.
10. Press the pressure release button on the gauge and remove the gauge.
11. Repeat Steps 7-10 for the remaining cylinders.
12. The difference in the compression between the cylinder with the highest pressure and the cylinder with the lowest pressure should not exceed 10%.
   a. If the compression of one cylinder is very low, a valve may be leaking or a ring may be stuck or broken. It is also possible that the piston is seriously damaged. To check further, pour about 1 tablespoon of engine oil into the low cylinder, then test compression a second time. If the pressure increases considerably, the piston rings are at fault. If the pressure does not improve significantly, a valve is probably burned.

b. If 2 adjacent cylinders have low compression, the cylinder head gasket may have failed between the 2 cylinders. There may also be coolant in the cylinders.

NOTE
Since the manufacturer does not list engine compression test specifications, it is important to compare the results of the current compression test with previous tests. If the pressure has changed enough to notice a difference, the cause should be investigated further.

13. Inspect, clean, regap and install spark plugs. Install new spark plugs if necessary.

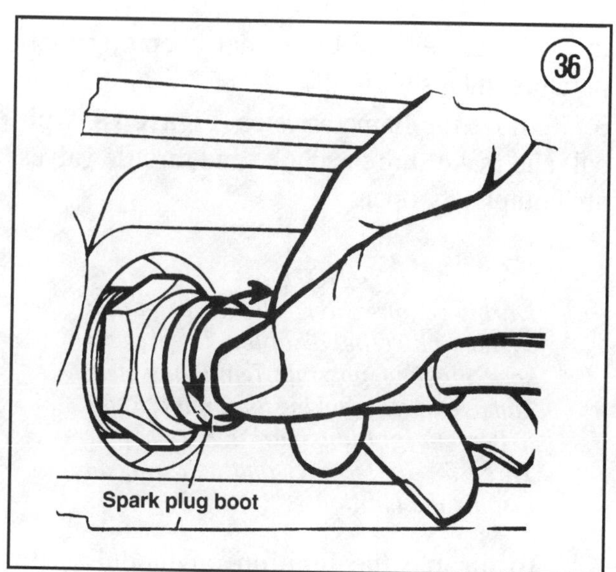

Valve Clearance

All models are equipped with zero-lash hydraulic lifters. Initial adjustment is part of the engine assembly. Refer to the appropriate engine chapter for assembly and for correcting noise or other problems associated with valve clearance.

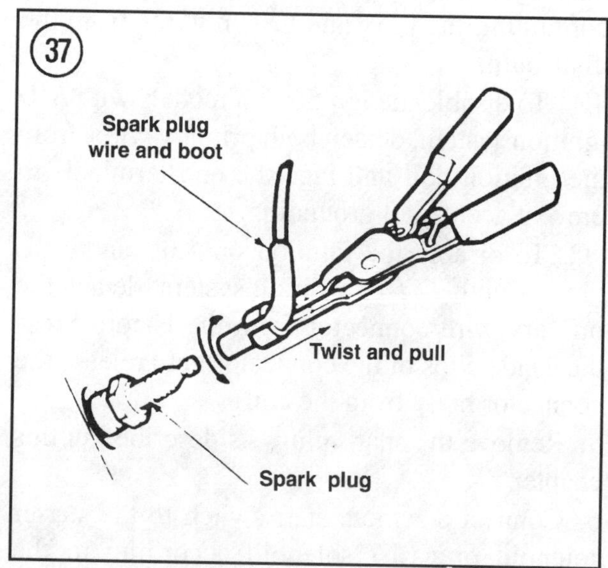

Ignition System

All models are equipped with a breakerless ignition system. Refer to **Table 7** for ignition system application.

The Delco Electronic Spark Timing (EST) System is used on some 3.0 L, 4.3 L, 5.0 L, 5.7 L and 7.4 L models. The Prestolite Integral Breakerless Inductive Distributor (BID) is used on some 5.0 L and 5.7 L models.

The Prestolite Thick Film Integrated Ignition (TFI-IV) system is used on some 5.0 L and 5.8 L models.

Total ignition service is covered for all mechanical breaker point systems, but tune-up service for other ignition systems is limited to the replacement of spark plugs, inspection and repair of wiring and checking/adjusting ignition timing.

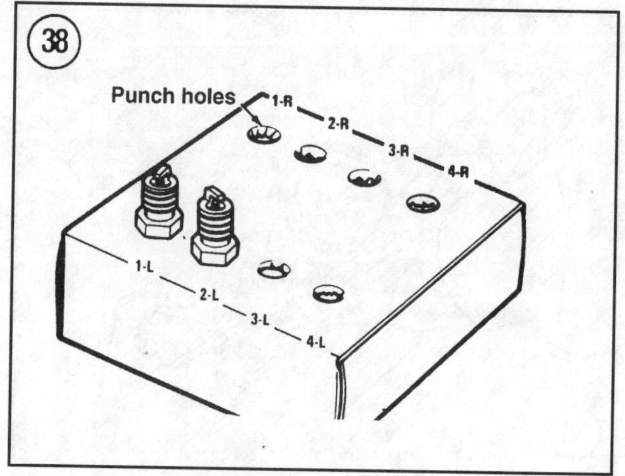

Spark plug removal

CAUTION
Whenever the spark plugs are removed, dirt from around them can fall into the spark plug holes. This can cause expensive engine damage.

1. Blow out any foreign material from around the spark plugs with compressed air.
2. Disconnect the spark plug wires by twisting the wire boot back and forth on the plug insulator while pulling upward (**Figure 36**). Pulling on the wire instead of the boot may break it. In some cases, you may find spark plug wire removal pliers (**Figure 37**) useful, especially when working around a warm or hot engine.
3. Remove the plugs using an appropriate size spark plug socket. Keep the plugs in order so you know which cylinder each came from. See **Figure 38**.
4. Examine each spark plug and compare its appearance with the illustrations in Chapter Three. Electrode appearance is a good indicator of performance in each cylinder and permits early recognition of trouble.
5. Discard the plugs. Although they could be cleaned, regapped and reused if in good condition, the cleaned plugs seldom last very long. New plugs are inexpensive and far more reliable.

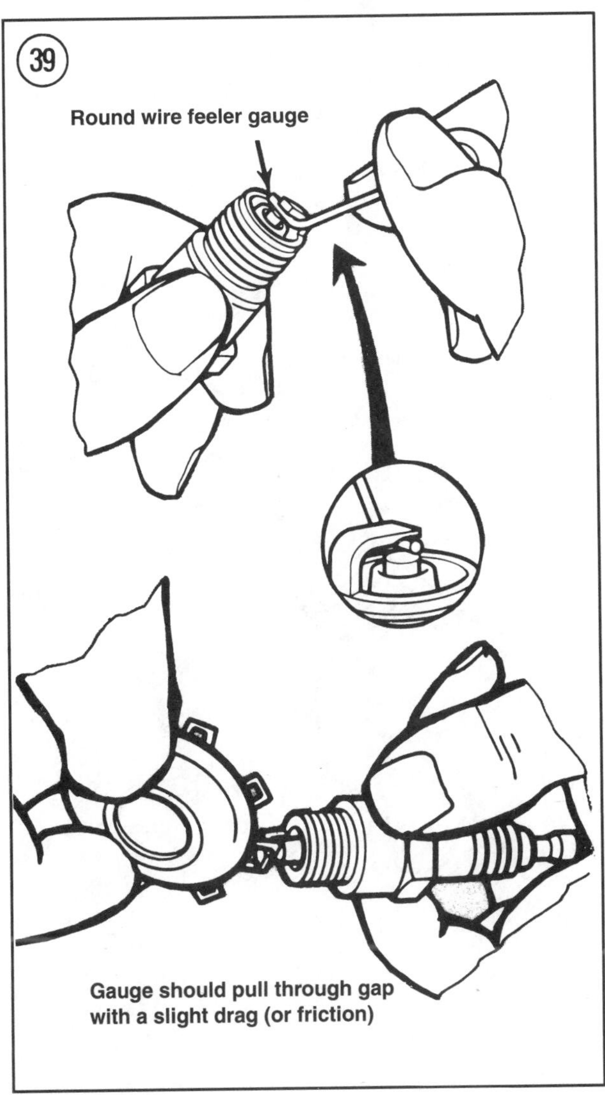

4

Spark plug gapping and installation

Carefully adjust the electrode gap on new plugs to ensure a reliable, consistent spark. Use a special spark plug tool with a wire gauge. See **Figure 39** for 2 common types.

1. Spark plugs with tapered seats do not use gaskets. Some plug brands have small terminal ends that must be screwed on before the plugs can be used.
2. Determine the correct gap setting from **Table 8**. Insert the appropriate size wire gauge between the electrodes. If the gap is correct, there will be a slight drag as the wire is pulled through. If there is no drag or if the wire will not pull through, bend the side electrode with the gapping tool (**Figure 40**) to change the gap. Make sure the side electrode is not twisted, then remeasure the gap.

CAUTION
Never try to close the electrode gap by tapping the spark plug on a solid surface. This can damage the plug internally. Always use the gap adjusting tool to open or close the gap.

3. Apply a drop of engine oil or antiseize compound to the threads of each spark plug. Screw

each plug in by hand until it seats. Very little effort is required. If force is necessary, the plug may be cross-threaded. Unscrew it and try again.

4. Tighten the spark plugs to the torque listed in **Table 8**.

NOTE
If a torque wrench is not available, tighten the plugs with your fingers until tight against the tapered seat or gasket, then tighten an additional 1/16 turn (tapered seat plug) or 1/4 turn (gasket-type plug) using a wrench.

5. Reinstall the wires to their correct cylinder location. Refer to **Figure 41**.
6. The distributor on some models is equipped with a mechanical (centrifugal) advance mechanism. Inspect and lubricate the mechanical advance as follows:
   a. Turn the distributor rotor, in its normal direction of rotation, then release it. The rotor should turn against the spring pressure of the advance mechanism, then snap back to its static position when released
   b. If the rotor does not return quickly and smoothly, the mechanical spark advance mechanism requires service. Determine the cause of the sticking and repair as required.
   c. Lightly lubricate the advance mechanism with clean engine oil.
7. Reinstall the rotor and distributor cap by reversing the removal procedure.

Sensor air gap (BID models)

Ignition timing is determined by detecting when the trigger wheel is near the sensor coil. The ignition system is sensitive to the gap between the trigger wheel and the sensor coil, so it is important that the gap be correctly set before attempting to troubleshoot or set the ignition timing.

1. Remove the distributor cap and rotor as described in this chapter.
2. Lift the rotor from the distributor shaft.
3. Inspect the trigger wheel and sensor coil for signs of contact or other damage. The sensor coil is available only as a unit with the ignition module.

NOTE
A convenient way to turn the engine crankshaft is to use a remote starter switch (button) available from most tool suppliers. Attach the remote switch to the starter solenoid or assist solenoid according to its manufacturer's instructions. Crank the engine using the electric starter by pressing, then releasing the starter button.

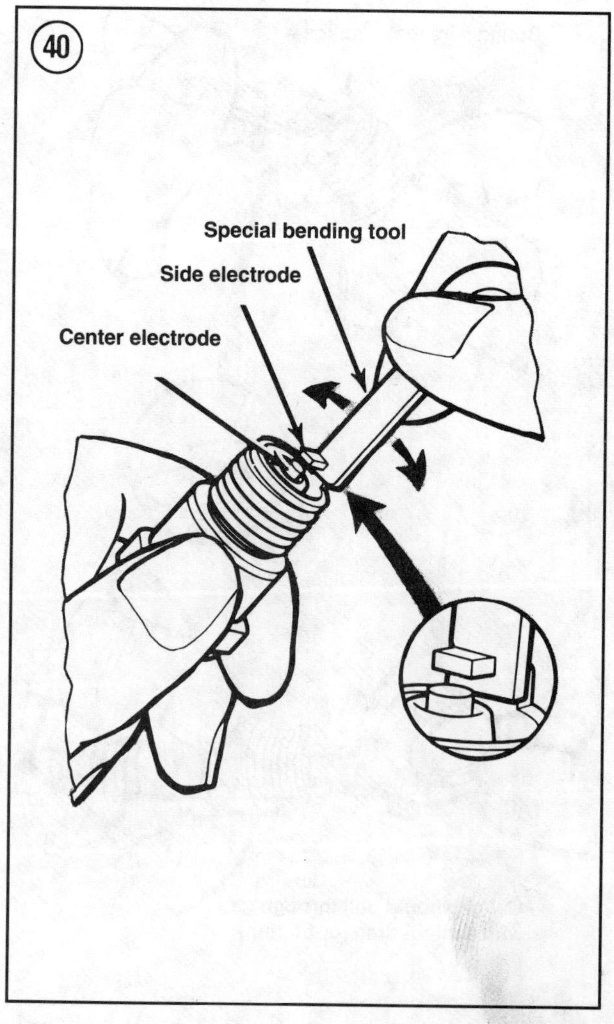

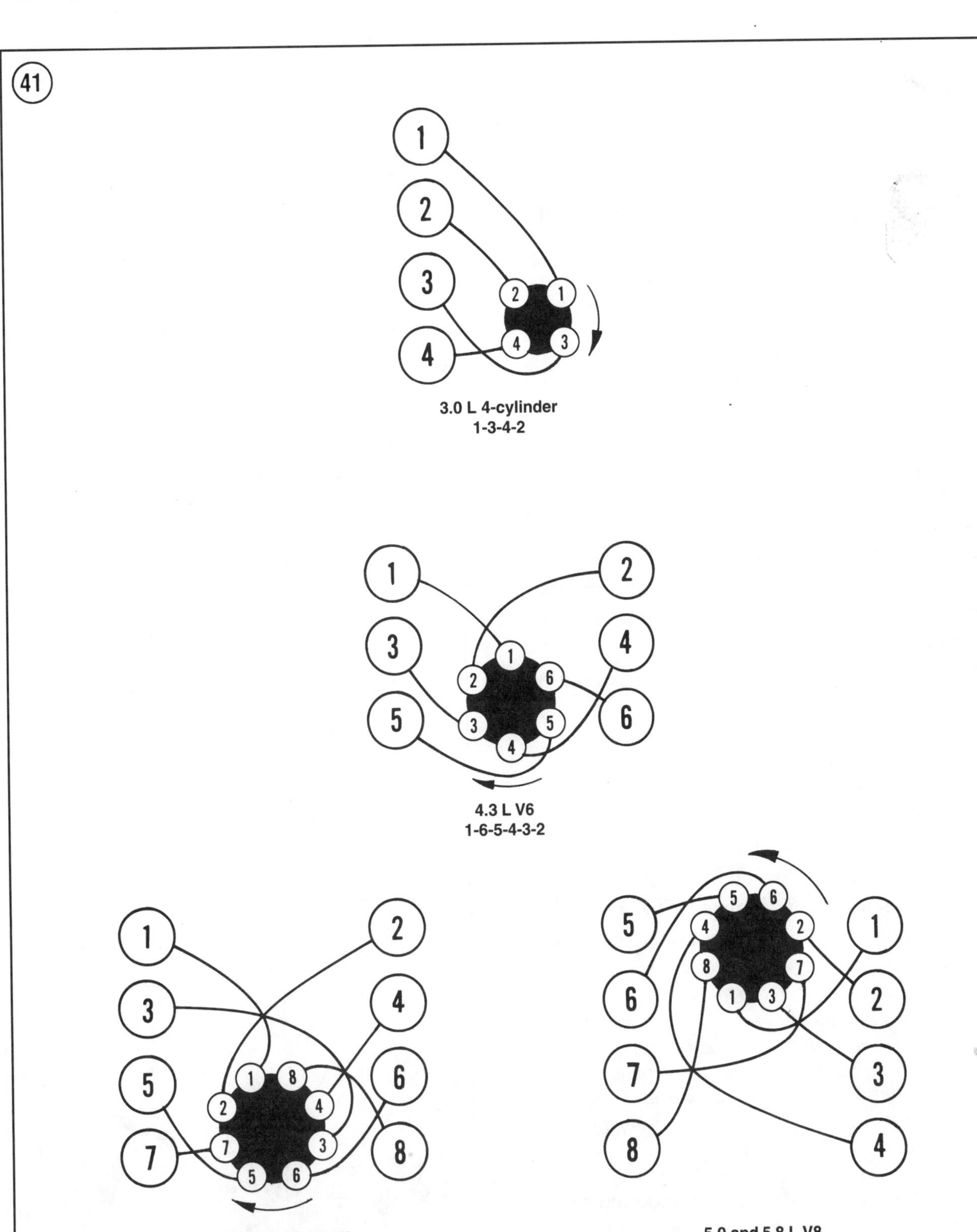

3.0 L 4-cylinder
1-3-4-2

4.3 L V6
1-6-5-4-3-2

5.7, 7.4 and 8.2 L V8
1-8-4-3-6-5-7-2

5.0 and 5.8 L V8
1-3-7-2-6-5-4-8

4. Turn the engine crankshaft until the tooth of the trigger wheel is aligned with the sensor as shown at A, **Figure 42**.

5. Measure the gap between the tooth of the trigger wheel and the sensor coil.

6. If gap is not 0.008 in. (0.20 mm), set the clearance as follows:

   a. Insert a nonmetallic feeler gauge of the correct thickness between the tooth of the trigger wheel and the sensor coil.

   b. Loosen the screw (**Figure 43**) that attaches the sensor coil.

   c. Move the sensor coil toward the trigger wheel trapping the feeler gauge.

   d. Tighten the screw retaining the sensor coil and withdraw the feeler gauge.

7. Align the rotor with the notch in the distributor shaft and push the rotor fully onto the distributor shaft.

8. Install the distributor cap, then check ignition timing as described in this chapter.

Ignition Timing

Improper (under-advanced or over-advanced) ignition timing will result in a loss of power and/or major engine damage. Check ignition timing frequently to ensure peak performance.

CAUTION
Never operate the engine without water circulating through the gear housing to the engine. Running the engine without cooling water will quickly damage the water pump and may result in engine damage.

Some form of cooling water is required whenever the engine is running. The use of a test tank is recommended; however, the timing procedure may also be performed with the boat in the water or with a flushing device connected to the gear housing.

3.0 and 4.3 L engines with EST ignition

1. Connect a suitable timing light to the spark plug lead for the No. 1 cylinder according to the light manufacturer's instructions.

2. Connect a shop tachometer to the engine according to its manufacturer's instructions. Do not rely on the boat tachometer.

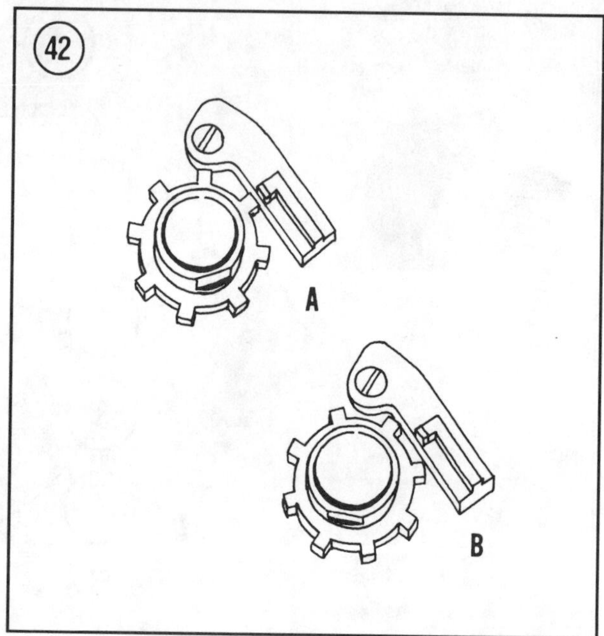

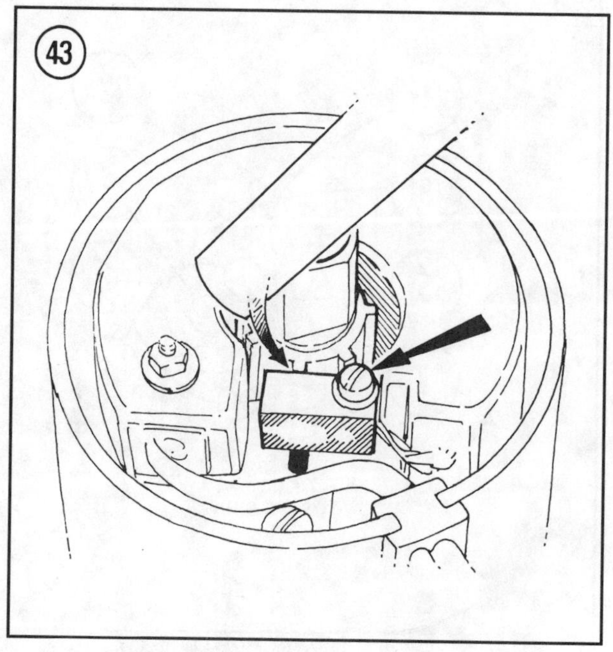

NOTE

The electronic timing advance system must be disabled (Step 3) to check or adjust ignition timing. An adapter plug (Volvo Penta part No. 885163-6) is necessary to check and adjust the timing.

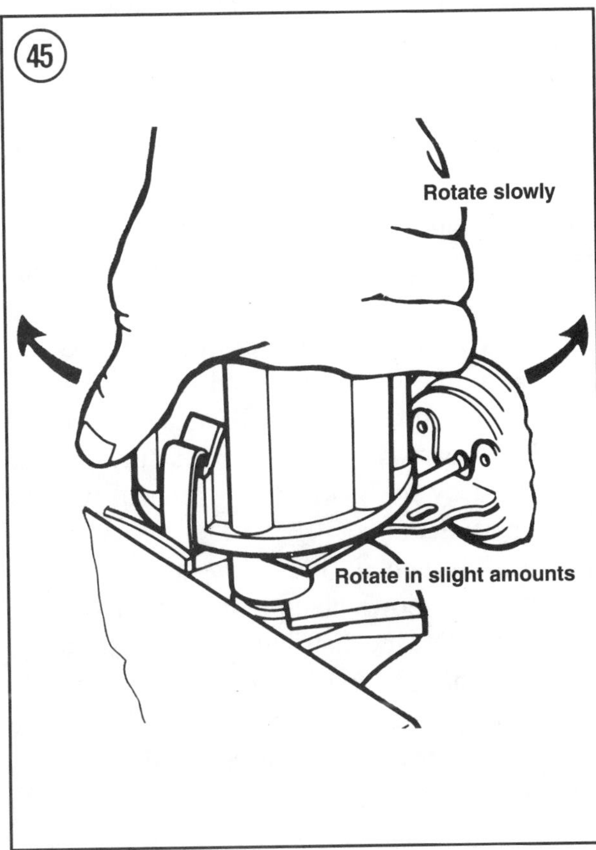

3. Disable the electronic ignition advance as follows:

   a. Detach the 4-wire connector from the distributor. Some models may not have a connector attached.

   b. Attach adapter (part No. 885163-6, or equivalent) plug to the distributor.

   c. Connect the bare wire from the adapter to a 12-volt engine power source.

4. Locate the timing marks on the engine timing cover and crankshaft pulley. If necessary, clean the timing marks. Apply white paint or chalk to the marks to make them more visible.

5. Start the engine and allow it to run until it reaches normal operating temperature. Make sure sufficient cooling water is flowing through the gear housing to the engine.

6. Run the engine at idle speed.

7. Point the timing light at the timing marks. The correct initial timing is listed in **Table 9**. The flash of the timing light will make the moving marks appear to be stopped. The actual timing is indicated by the mark that is aligned with the stationary mark.

8. If adjustment is necessary, loosen the distributor hold-down clamp bolt (**Figure 44**, typical) and rotate the distributor as necessary. See **Figure 45**.

9. After the timing is properly adjusted, tighten the distributor hold-down clamp bolt, then recheck the timing. Repeat Step 8 if necessary.

10. Stop the engine, disconnect the power (12-volts) from the test adapter, then remove the adapter from the distributor. Reattach the connector if so equipped.

11. With the timing light still connected, restart the engine and verify that the timing is advanced after removing the test adapter.

12. Increase the engine speed and check the full advanced timing. If the advanced timing is not correct, the ignition module is defective and must be replaced.

5.0 L, 5.7 L, 7.4 L and 8.2 L engines with breakerless inductive distributor (BID) ignition

Refer to the appropriate section to service 7.4 Gi and 7.4 GSi models with fuel injection.

Changing the sensor air gap will also change ignition timing. If the tests indicate improper timing, remove the distributor cap and check the sensor air gap before changing the distributor position.

1. Connect a suitable timing light to the spark plug lead for the No. 1 cylinder (**Figure 41**) according to the light manufacturer's instructions. The front cylinder on the port (left) side is No. 1.
2. Connect a shop tachometer to the engine according to its manufacturer's instructions. Do not rely on the boat tachometer.
3. Locate the timing marks on the engine timing cover and crankshaft pulley. If necessary, clean the timing marks. Application of white paint or chalk to the marks will make the marks more visible.
4. Start the engine and allow it to run until it reaches normal operating temperature. Make sure sufficient cooling water is flowing through the gear housing to the engine.
5. Run the engine at idle speed.
6. Point the timing light at the timing marks. The correct initial timing is listed in **Table 9**. The flash of the timing light will make the moving marks appear to be stopped. The actual timing is indicated by the mark that is aligned with the stationary mark.
7. If adjustment is necessary, loosen the distributor hold-down clamp bolt (**Figure 44**, typical) and rotate the distributor as necessary.
8. After the timing is properly adjusted, tighten the distributor hold-down clamp bolt, then recheck the timing. Repeat Step 7 if necessary.
9. Increase the engine speed and check the full advanced timing. If the advanced timing is not correct, the ignition module is defective and must be replaced.

5.0 FL and 5.8 FL models with breakerless inductive distributor (BID) ignition

Refer to the appropriate section to service 5.0 Fi, 5.8 Fi and 5.8 FSi fuel injected models with TFI-IV ignition.

On models with breakerless inductive distributor (BID) ignition, changing the sensor air gap will also change ignition timing. If the tests indicate improper timing, remove the distributor cap and check the sensor air gap before changing the distributor position.

1. Connect a suitable timing light to the spark plug lead for the No. 1 cylinder (**Figure 41**) according to the light manufacturer's instructions. The front cylinder on the starboard (right) side is No. 1.
2. Connect a shop tachometer to the engine according to its manufacturer's instructions. Do not rely on the boat tachometer.
3. Locate the timing marks on the engine timing cover and crankshaft pulley. If necessary, clean the timing marks. Application of white paint or chalk to the marks will make the marks more visible.
4. Start the engine and allow it to run until it reaches normal operating temperature. Make sure sufficient cooling water is flowing through the gear housing to the engine.
5. Slow the engine until it is running at idle speed.
6. Point the timing light at the timing marks. The correct initial timing is listed in **Table 9**. The flash of the timing light will make the moving marks appear to be stopped. The actual timing is indicated by the mark that is aligned with the stationary mark.
7. If adjustment is necessary, loosen the distributor hold-down clamp bolt (**Figure 44**, typical) and rotate the distributor as necessary.
8. After the timing is properly adjusted, tighten the distributor hold-down clamp bolt, then recheck the timing. Repeat Step 7 if necessary.
9. Increase the engine speed and check the full advanced timing. If the advanced timing is not

correct, the ignition module is defective and must be replaced.

5.0 Fi, 5.8 Fi and 5.8 FSi models with TFI-IV ignition

1. Connect an inductive timing light that has a variable advance to the spark plug lead for the No. 1 cylinder (**Figure 41**) according to the light manufacturer's instructions. The front cylinder on the starboard (right) side is No. 1.
2. Connect a shop tachometer to the engine according to its manufacturer's instructions. Do not rely on the boat tachometer.
3. Locate the timing marks on the engine timing cover and crankshaft pulley. If necessary, clean the timing marks. Application of white paint or chalk to the marks will make the marks more visible.
4. Start the engine and allow it to run until it reaches normal operating temperature. Make sure sufficient cooling water is flowing through the gear housing to the engine.
5. Slow the engine until it is running at idle speed.

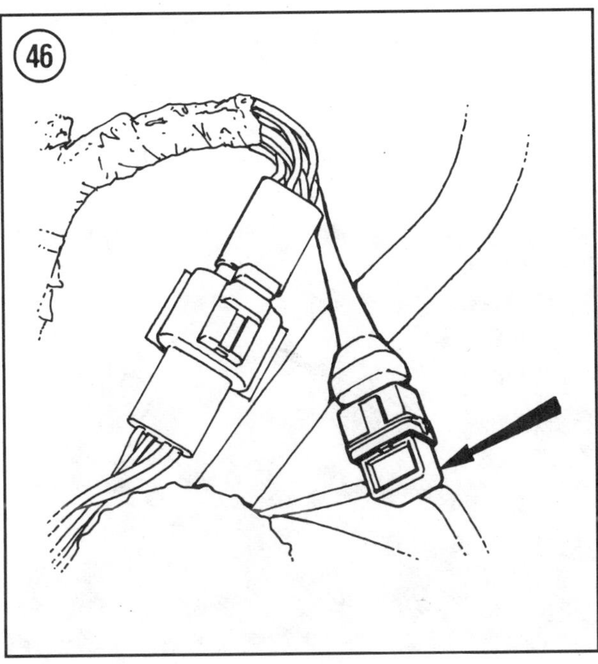

6. Remove the shorting bar (**Figure 46**) from the double wire SPOUT connector.

NOTE

It is important to follow the manufacturer's instruction for using the timing light. It is important to use a light with variable advance when checking the timing in Step 7.

7. Point the timing light at the timing marks and determine the exact timing. The correct initial timing is listed in **Table 9**.
8. If adjustment is necessary, loosen the distributor hold-down clamp bolt (**Figure 44**, typical) and rotate the distributor as necessary.
9. After the timing is properly adjusted, tighten the distributor hold-down clamp bolt, then recheck the timing. Repeat Step 8 if necessary.
10. Reinstall the shorting bar (**Figure 46**) in the double wire SPOUT connector. With the timing light still connected, restart the engine and verify that the timing advances after installing the shorting bar.

7.4 Gi and 7.4 GSi models with EST ignition and fuel injection

1. Connect an inductive timing light to the spark plug lead for the No. 1 cylinder (**Figure 41**) according to the light manufacturer's instructions. The front cylinder on the port (left) side is No. 1.
2. Connect a shop tachometer to the engine according to its manufacturer's instructions. Do not rely on the boat tachometer.
3. Locate the timing marks on the engine timing cover and crankshaft pulley. If necessary, clean the timing marks. Application of white paint or chalk to the marks will make the marks more visible.
4. Start the engine and allow it to run until it reaches normal operating temperature. Make sure sufficient cooling water is flowing through the gear housing to the engine.

5. Slow the engine until it is running at idle speed, then increase engine speed to 1,000 rpm.

6A. If the marine diagnostic trouble code (MDTC) tool is available, attach the tool to the 10-way data link connector (DLC). See **Figure 47**.

6B. If the special MDTC is not available, locate the 10-way data link connector (DLC), then attach a jumper wire between the terminals for the white/black and the black wires.

7. Point the timing light at the timing marks. The correct initial (base) timing is listed in **Table 9**.

8. If adjustment is necessary, loosen the distributor hold-down clamp bolt (**Figure 44**) and rotate the distributor as necessary.

9. After the timing is properly adjusted, tighten the distributor hold-down clamp bolt, then recheck the timing. Repeat Step 8 if necessary.

10. Remove the MDTC tool or jumper attached in Step Six.

CARBURETOR SERVICE

Idle Speed and Mixture

Refer to **Table 9** for recommended idle speed. Notice that the idle speed is not adjustable on models with fuel injection. Do not remove the flame arrestor when adjusting the idle speed or mixture.

1. Connect a shop tachometer to the engine according to its manufacturer's instructions. Do not rely on the boat tachometer.

2. Locate the mixture screw(s) on the carburetor. See **Figure 48** for typical mixture screw location.

3. Locate the idle speed stop screw on the carburetor or linkage. See **Figure 49**.

4. Start the engine and allow it to run until it reaches normal operating temperature. Make sure sufficient cooling water is flowing through the gear housing to the engine.

NOTE

It may be necessary to disconnect the throttle cable from the carburetor linkage so the speed control linkage will remain at idle when the shift linkage is in forward gear.

5. Slow the engine until it is running at slow idle speed, then shift to the FORWARD gear, while maintaining the idle setting.

NOTE

When checking the engine speed in Step Six, also notice any variance between the shop tachometer and the tachometer installed in the boat. The tachometer in the boat's dash is not intended to be as accurate as one used for service, but it should fairly represent the engine's speed.

6. Observe the engine speed indicated by the shop tachometer.

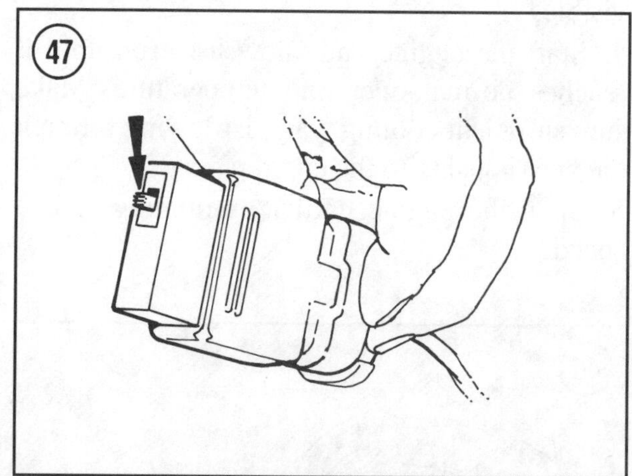

7. Turn the idle mixture screw slowly *clockwise* until the engine speed begins to drop *(mixture too lean)*. If the carburetor has 2 mixture screws, repeat the procedure with the second screw.

8. Record how far the idle mixture screw is moved while turning the idle mixture *counter-clockwise* until the engine speed begins to drop *(mixture too rich)*. If the carburetor has 2 mixture screws, repeat the procedure with the second screw.

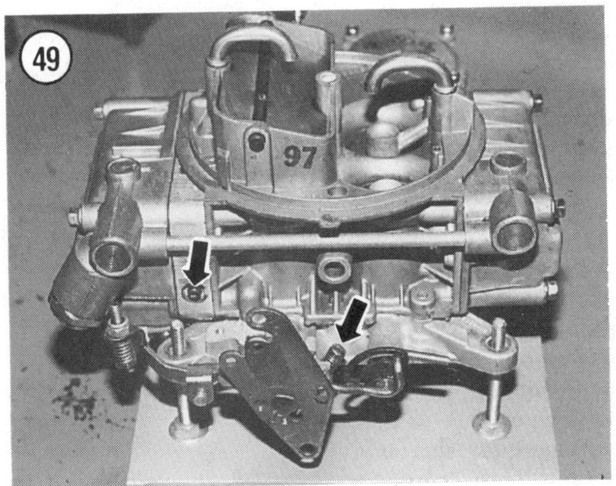

9. Turn the screw to the midpoint between the setting in Step 7 (which was too lean) and the setting in Step 8 (which was too rich). The engine should now run smoothly.

10. Recheck the idle speed.

11. Compare the idle speed with the speed recommended in **Table 9**. Adjust the idle speed (in forward gear) by turning the stop screw located on the linkage.

12. Shut the engine OFF and remove the tachometer. Reattach any linkage that was detached.

13. With the engine stopped, make sure the throttle valves open fully when the speed control is moved to the fast position. Adjust the speed control if necessary.

Table 1 MAINTENANCE SCHEDULE

Initial 20 hours	Change engine oil and filter Check level in power steering reservoir Check and adjust tension of all drive belts Check and adjust idle mixture and rpm (carbureted models) Check engine timing (except fuel injected 5.0L and 5.8L models) Check exhaust systems Check all hose clamps Check engine mount screws Change fuel filter and service fuel/water separator Lubricate grease fittings on transom shield Lubricate both U-joint fittings on drive unit (SX models) Drain and fill stern drive unit Check level in trim /tilt reservoir Coat the steering ram with grease Visually check for damage or problems
Daily	Check engine oil Check coolant level in expansion tank if so equipped Check quantity of fuel Check fuel system for leakage Check all electrical components
Every 14 days	Check cooling system and condition of hoses Check and adjust tension of all drive belts Check level in power steering reservoir Check battery condition Check stern drive lubricant level Check level in trim /tilt reservoir Check propeller condition
Every 60 days	Coat the steering ram with grease
Every 50 hours of operation or at least twice each season	Check tension of all drive belts
Every 100 hours of operation or at least once each season	Change engine oil and filter Clean flame arrestor Check and adjust idle mixture and rpm (carbureted models) Check and adjust tension of all drive belts Check engine timing (except fuel injected 5.0L and 5.8L models) Check distributor cap, rotor and wires Check electrical system connections and insulation Check battery condition Check cooling system and condition of hoses Check condition of raw-water pump impeller (replace every 2 years) Check level in power steering reservoir Check level in trim /tilt reservoir Coat the steering ram with grease On SX models, remove the stern drive and lubricate the U-joints and gimbal bearings Check condition of universal joint bellows. The manufacturer recommends that bellows be replaced every other year. Change lubricant in stern drive Check propeller condition Check sacrificial anode condition Visually check for damage or problems

Table 2 ENGINE OIL VISCOSITY/TEMPERATURE

Above 32° F (0° C)	SAE 30
0 to 32 ° F (-18 to 0° C)	SAE 20W-20
Below 0° F (-18° C)	SAE 10W

Table 3 APPROXIMATE ENGINE OIL CAPACITIES

Model	Hp	Displacement Liters (cid)	Cyls.	Capacity* qt. (L) with filter	without filter
3.0 GL	120	3.0 (181)	4	4.0 (3.8)	3.5 (3.3)
3.0 GS	135	3.0 (181)	4	4.0 (3.8)	3.5 (3.3)
4.3 GL	160	4.3 (262)	V6	4.5 (4.3)	4.0 (3.8)
4.3 GS	185	4.3 (262)	V6	4.5 (4.3)	4.0 (3.8)
4.3 Gi	180	4.3 (262)	V6	4.5 (4.3)	4.0 (3.8)
5.0 FL	190	5.0 (302)	V8	6.0 (5.7)	5.0 (4.7)
5.0 Fi	220	5.0 (302)	V8	6.0 (5.7)	5.0 (4.7)
5.0 GL	220	5.0 (305)	V8	6.0 (5.7)	5.0 (4.7)
5.0 Gi	250	5.0 (305)	V8	6.0 (5.7)	5.0 (4.7)
5.7 GL	225	5.7 (350)	V8	5.0 (4.7)	4.0 (3.8)
5.7 Gi	250	5.7 (350)	V8	6.0 (5.7)	5.0 (4.7)
5.7 Gsi	280	5.7 (350)	V8	6.0 (5.7)	5.0 (4.7)
5.8 FL	230-235	5.8 (351)	V8	6.0 (5.7)	5.0 (4.7)
5.8 Fi	255	5.8 (351)	V8	5.0 (4.7)	4.0 (3.8)
5.8 FSi	265	5.8 (351)	V8	5.0 (4.7)	4.0 (3.8)
7.4 GL	300	7.4 (454)	V8	7.0 (6.6)	6.0 (5.7)
7.4 Gi	330	7.4 (454)	V8	9.0 (8.5)	8.0 (7.5)
7.4 GSi	385	7.4 (454)	V8	9.0 (8.5)	8.0 (7.5)
8.2 GL/DPX	390	8.2 (502)	V8	7.0 (6.6)	6.0 (5.7)

* All capacaties in this table are approximate. To ensure correct oil level and prevent overfilling the engine, always use the dipstick as recommended in the text.

Table 4 RECOMMENDED STERN DRIVE LUBRICANTS

Model	Lubricant
SX	
Driveshaft splines	Molybdenum grease
Gear unit	Volvo Penta DuraPlus synthetic GL5 gear oil
Gimbal bearing	Wheel bearing grease
Universal joints	Wheel bearing grease
DP	
Driveshaft splines	Molybdenum grease
Gear unit	Mineral GL5 API gear oil
Steering shaft bearings	
Upper and lower	Water resistant grease
Universal joints	Wheel bearing grease
DPX	
Driveshaft splines	Molybdenum grease
Gear unit	Volvo Penta DuraPlus synthetic GL5 gear oil
Steering shaft bearings	
Upper & lower	Water resistant grease
Universal joints	Wheel bearing grease

Table 5 APPROXIMATE STERN DRIVE CAPACITIES

Model	Capacity
SX	71 oz (2.1 L)
DP	
Standard and 1 in. (25.4 mm) extension	2 3/4 qt (2.6 L)
With 4 in. (101.6 mm) extension	3 qt (2.8 L)
DPX	1.9 qt (2.0 L)

Table 6 TIGHTENING TORQUES

Model	Torque
SX	
Stern drive dipstick	5.4-8.1 N•m (48-72 in.-lb.)
Stern drive drain plug	6-7 N•m (50-60 in.-lb.)
Stern drive fill plug	6.8-9.5 N•m (60-84 in.-lb.)
DP	
Stern drive drain plug	10 N•m (88 in.-lb.)
Stern drive fill plug	35 N•m (25 ft.-lb.)
DPX	
Drain plug	17 N•m (12.5 ft.-lb.)
Fill plug	35 N•m (25.8 ft.-lb.)

Table 7 IGNITION SYSTEM APPLICATION

Model	Fuel system	Ignition type	Firing order
3.0	Carburetor	Delco EST[1]	1-3-4-2
431	Carburetor	Prestolite BID[2]	1-6-5-4-3-2
432	Carburetor	Prestolite BID[2]	1-6-5-4-3-2
4.3	Carburetor	Delco EST[1]	1-6-5-4-3-2
4.3	Fuel injection	Delco EST[1]	1-6-5-4-3-2
5.0	Carburetor	Prestolite BID[2]	1-3-7-2-6-5-4-8
5.0	Fuel injection	TFI-IV[3]	1-3-7-2-6-5-4-8
5.0	Carburetor	Prestolite BID	1-8-4-3-6-5-7-2
5.0	Fuel injection	Delco EST[1] & Di[4]	1-8-4-3-6-5-7-2
5.7	Carburetor	Prestolite BID[2]	1-8-4-3-6-5-7-2
5.7	Fuel injection	Delco EST[1]	1-8-4-3-6-5-7-2
5.8	Carburetor	Prestolite BID[2]	1-3-7-2-6-5-4-8
5.8	Fuel injection	TFI-IV[3]	1-3-7-2-6-5-4-8
7.4	Carburetor	Prestolite BID[2]	1-8-4-3-6-5-7-2
7.4	Fuel injection	Delco EST[1]	1-8-4-3-6-5-7-2
8.2	Carburetor	Prestolite BID[2]	1-8-4-3-6-5-7-2
8.2	Fuel injection	Delco EST[1] & Di[4]	1-8-4-3-6-5-7-2

1. (EST) Delco electronic spark timing system.
2. (BID) Prestolite integral breakerless inductive distributor.
3. (TFI-IV) Thick film integrated ignition system.
4. (Di) Distributor ignition system.

Table 8 SPARK PLUG APPLICATION

Engine model	Ignition	Spark plugs Make	Type	Gap mm (in.)	Torque N.m (ft.-lb.)
3.0	EST	AC	MR43LTS	1.143 (0.045)	27 (20)
4.3 GL & GS 1994-1997	EST	AC	MR43T	1.143 (0.045)	30 (22)
4.3 Gi 1994-1997	EST	AC	R43TS	1.143 (0.045)	30 (22)
4.3 GL, GS, & Gi 1998-on	EST & Di	AC	MR43LTS	1.143 (0.045)	30 (22)
5.0 FL	BID	MC[1]	ASF32C	0.889 (0.035)	6.7-13.5 (5-10)
5.0 Fi	TFI-IV	MC[1]	AWSF32C	1.143 (0.045)	6.7-13.5 (5-10)
5.0 GL & GS 1998-on	BID	AC	MR43LTS	0.89 (0.035)	27 (20)
5.0 Gi 1998-on	Di	CHP[2]	RS12YC	1.143 (0.045)	27 (20)
5.7 GL 1994-1997	BID	AC	MR43T	1.143 (0.045)	30 (22)
5.7 Gi 1994-1997	EST	AC	R43TS	1.143 (0.045)	30 (22)
5.7 GS 1998-on	EST	AC	MR43LTS	0.89 (0.035)	27 (20)
5.7 GSi 1998-on	Di	AC	MR43LTS	1.143 (0.045)	27 (20)
5.8 FL	BID	MC[1]	ASF32C	0.889 (0.035)	6.7-13.5 (5-10)
5.8 Fi & FSi	TFI-IV	MC[1]	AWSF22C	0.889 (0.035)	6.7-13.5 (5-10)
7.4 GL 1994-1997	BID	AC	MR43T	1.143 (0.045)	30 (22)
7.4 Gi 1994-1997	EST	AC	R43TS	1.143 (0.045)	30 (22)
1998-on	Di	AC	MR43LTS	1.143 (0.045)	27 (20)
7.4 GSi	EST & Di	AC	MR43T	1.143 (0.045)	27 (20)
8.2 GL 1994-1997	BID	AC	MR43T	1.143 (0.045)	30 (22)
8.2 GSi 1998-on	Di	AC	MR43T	1.143 (0.045)	27 (20)

1. MC – Motorcraft
2. CHP – Champion

TABLE 9 IGNITION TIMING AND ENGINE SPEED

	1994-1996	1997-on
3.0 GL, GS		
Idle speed	650-750 rpm	650-750 rpm
Wide open throttle range	4,200-4,600 rpm	4,200-4,600 rpm
Min. fuel requirement	AKI 87	AKI 86
Base timing	0° TDC	2° ATDC
Timing @ 600 rpm	10° BTDC	8° BTDC
Timing @ 2,500 rpm	20° BTDC	18° BTDC
Timing @ 4,600 rpm	23° BTDC	21° BTDC

(continued)

TABLE 9 IGNITION TIMING AND ENGINE SPEED (continued)

	1994-1996	1997-on
4.3 GL, GS		
Idle speed	550-650 rpm	550-650 rpm
Wide-open throttle range	4,200-4,600 rpm	4,200-4,600 rpm (GL) 4,200-4,800 rpm (GS)
Min. fuel requirement	AKI 87	AKI 86
Base timing	5° ATDC	1° BTDC
Timing @ 600 rpm	6° BTDC	18° BTDC
Timing @ 2,500 rpm	15° BTDC	25° BTDC
Timing @ 4,600 rpm	18° BTDC	25° BTDC
4.3 Gi		
Idle speed	600 rpm (not adjustable)	600 rpm (not adjustable)
Wide open throttle range	4,400-4,800 rpm	4,400-4,800 rpm
Min. fuel requirement		AKI 86
Timing @ idle	8° BTDC	8° BTDC
Timing @ 1,600 rpm		20° BTDC
5.0 FL		
Idle speed	550 rpm	
Wide open throttle range	4,200-4,600 rpm	
Min. fuel requirement	AKI 86	
Timing @ 950 rpm	10° BTDC	
Timing @ 2,050 rpm	20° BTDC	
Timing @ 4,400 rpm	28° BTDC	
5.0 Fi		
Idle speed	600 rpm (not adjustable)	
Wide open throttle range	4,200-4,600 rpm	
Min. fuel requirement	AKI 86	
Base timing	5° BTDC	
5.0 GL		
Idle speed		550-650 rpm
Wide open throttle range		4,400-4,800 rpm
Min. fuel requirement		AKI 86
Base timing		5° BTDC
Timing @ 600 rpm		3° BTDC
Timing @ 2,400 rpm		18° BTDC
Timing @ 4,600 rpm		26° BTDC
5.0 Gi		
Idle speed		600 rpm (not adjustable)
Wide open throttle range		4,600-5,000 rpm
Min. fuel requirement		AKI 86
Timing @ idle		8° BTDC
Timing @ 1,600 rpm		19° BTDC
5.7 GL, GS		
Idle speed	600-650 rpm	550-650 rpm
Wide open throttle range	4,200-4,600 rpm (GL)	4,400-4,800 rpm (GS)
Min. fuel requirement	AKI 87	AKI 86
Timing @ 600 rpm	3° BTDC	3° BTDC
Timing @ 2,800 rpm	22° BTDC	22° BTDC
Timing @ 4,600 rpm	26° BTDC	26° BTDC
5.7 Gi, GSi		
Idle speed	600 rpm (not adjustable)	600 rpm (not adjustable)
Wide open throttle range	4,200-4,600 rpm (Gi)	4,600-5,000 rpm (GSi)
Min. fuel requirement	AKI 87	AKI 86
Idle timing	8° BTDC	8° BTDC
Timing @ 1,600 rpm		19° BTDC (GSi)

(continued)

TABLE 9 IGNITION TIMING AND ENGINE SPEED (continued)

	1994-1996	1997-on
5.8 FL		
Idle speed	550-650 rpm	
Wide open throttle range	4,000-4,400 rpm	
Min. fuel requirement	AKI 86	
Timing @ 950 rpm	10° BTDC	
Timing @ 2,050 rpm	20° BTDC	
Timing @ 4,400	28° BTDC	
5.8 Fi		
Idle speed	600 rpm (not adjustable)	
Wide open throttle range	4,200-4,600 rpm	
Min. fuel requirement	AKI 86	
Base timing	5° BTDC	
5.8 FSi		
Idle speed	600 rpm (not adjustable)	
Wide open throttle range	4,600-5,000 rpm	
Min. fuel requirement	AKI 86	
Base timing	5° BTDC	
7.4 GL		
Idle speed	550-650 rpm	
Wide open throttle range	4,200-4,600 rpm	
Min. fuel requirement	AKI 87	
Timing @ 600 rpm	3° BTDC	
Timing @ 2,800 rpm	22° BTDC	
Timing @ 4,600 rpm	26° BTDC	
7.4 Gi, GSi		
Idle speed	600 rpm (not adjustable)	600 rpm (not adjustable)
Wide open throttle range	4,200-4,600 rpm (Gi)	4,800-5,200 rpm (GSi)
Min. fuel requirement	AKI 87 (Gi), 89 (GSi)	AKI 86
Base timing	10° BTDC	10° BTDC
8.2 GL, GSi		
Idle speed	550-650 rpm	600 rpm (not adjustable)
Wide open throttle range	4,400-4,800 rpm (GL)	4,600-5,000 rpm (GSi)
Min. fuel requirement	AKI 87	AKI 86
Base timing	3° BTDC	10° BTDC

Chapter Five

Lay-up, Cooling System Service and Fitting Out

LAY-UP

Boats that are to be stored for more than 4 or 5 weeks should be carefully prepared. This is necessary to prevent damage to the engine and the stern drive unit from freezing, corrosion or fuel system contamination. Begin preparation for lay-up, if possible, before removing the boat from the water.

If the boat is removed from the water, a supply of cooling water must be available to the engine. The stern drive unit can be submerged in a test tank or a flush/test device available from your Volvo Penta dealer can be used to supply freshwater through a garden hose as described in Chapter Four. If a flush/test device is used, remove the propeller to prevent any possible interference and always start the water flow before starting the engine.

The suggestions for lay-up preparation which follow are based on recommendations made by Volvo Penta. See Chapter Four for recommended lubricants.

In-the-water Preparation

NOTE

If the boat has already been removed from the water, attach a flushing/test device to the stern drive. See Cooling System Flushing in Chapter Four.

1. Make sure the fuel contains a marine fuel treatment and stabilizer. Follow recommendations on the container for the amount to add according to the size of your tank and *the amount of fuel* inside. This additive prevents gum and varnish from forming in the fuel system.

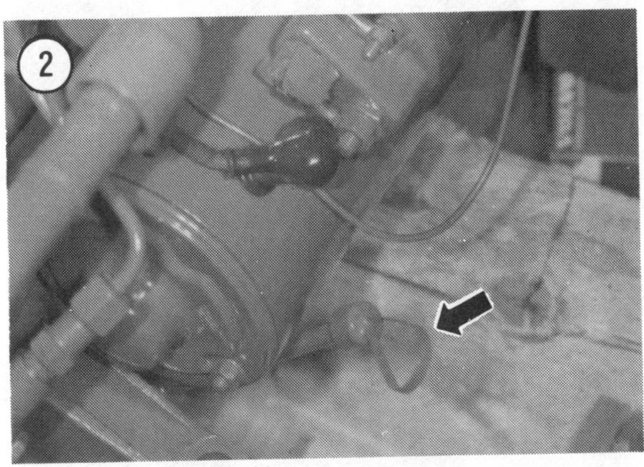

2A. If the boat is in the water, start the engine and run under load until it reaches normal operating temperature, then shut the engine off.

2B. If the boat is out of the water, attach a flushing adapter. Then, start the engine and run it at idle it reaches normal operating temperature, then shut the engine off.

3. Drain the engine oil and install a new oil filter (**Figure 1**, typical). See Chapter Four.

4. Refill the crankcase with the proper amount of fresh engine oil. Refer to Chapter Four for the recommended type, viscosity and amount of oil.

5. Make sure the stern drive is in its fully-down position. Restart the engine and run at fast idle (about 1,000-1,500 rpm) for several minutes to circulate the fresh oil throughout the engine. Check for leaks, especially around the new filter while the engine is running.

6. Shut the engine off and wait approximately 5 minutes, then check the oil level on the dipstick (**Figure 2**, typical location). Add oil, if necessary, to bring the level up to the FULL mark on the dipstick.

7. Remove the flame arrestor and its cover, if so equipped, (**Figure 3**) from the carburetor air horn.

8. Clean the flame arrestor with solvent, blow dry with compressed air, if available, and reinstall on the carburetor.

9. Service the fuel filter as described in Chapter Four.

10. Remove the boat from the water, keeping the bow higher than the stern, if possible, to assist in draining the exhaust system.

Out-of-water Preparation

1. Adjust the trailer or cradle so the engine is level.

2. Lower the stern drive unit to its fully-down position.

WARNING

Be sure to have a Coast Guard-approved fire extinguisher at hand before perform-

5

ing Step 3. Because of the extreme fire hazard, it is suggested that the boat be located away from other boats and structures while draining the fuel tank. It is also important to store the drained fuel in a sealed metal container away from heat, sparks and flame.

3. If possible completely drain the fuel tank of all gasoline.
4. Loosen all of the drive belts and inspect their condition. Replace belts as required. Tighten the adjusting bolts without placing tension on drive belts.
5. Drain the cooling system as described in this chapter.
6. Check all hoses for deterioration, cracks or other defects. Replace hoses as required.
7. Refill the closed cooling system, if so equipped, as described in this chapter.
8. Remove the battery (**Figure 4**) from the boat. Tape the vent holes closed and clean the battery case with a water and baking soda solution to remove any traces of corrosion and acid, then rinse with cold water. Check electrolyte level in each cell and top up with distilled water as required. Cover terminals with a light coat of petroleum jelly. Store the battery in a cool, dry place.

NOTE
Remove the battery from storage every 30-45 days. Check electrolyte level and slow-charge for 5-6 hours at 6 amperes.

9. Refer to Chapter Four to see if any routine maintenance is required. Some maintenance, such as removal of the stern drive and lubrication of the U-joints should be done when the boat is removed from the water, before storage.
10. Clean the engine exterior thoroughly and retouch any blemishes with engine touch-up paint. Wipe the engine and stern drive with a soft lint free towel and SAE 30 engine oil to leave a light coating on exterior surfaces.

Stern Drive Unit

Refer to Chapter Four for the location of lubrication points listed below and type of lubricant to be used.

1. Insert a length of wire into the drive shaft and gear housing water drain holes to make sure they are open.
2. Lubricate the following components with the appropriate lubricant.
   a. Steering cable grease fitting.
   b. Extended portion of steering cable.
   c. Steering system pivot points.
   d. Power steering control valve.

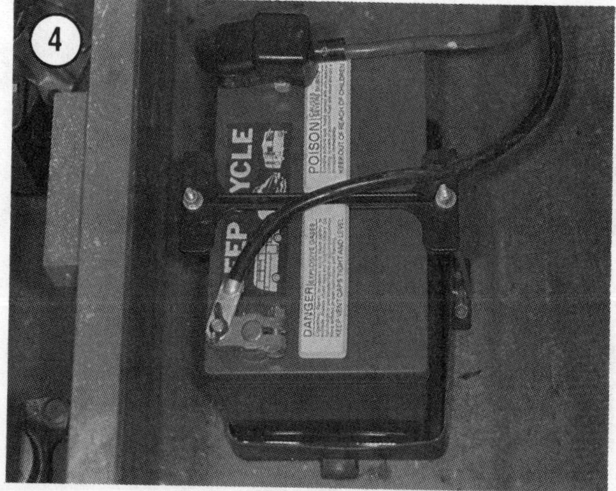

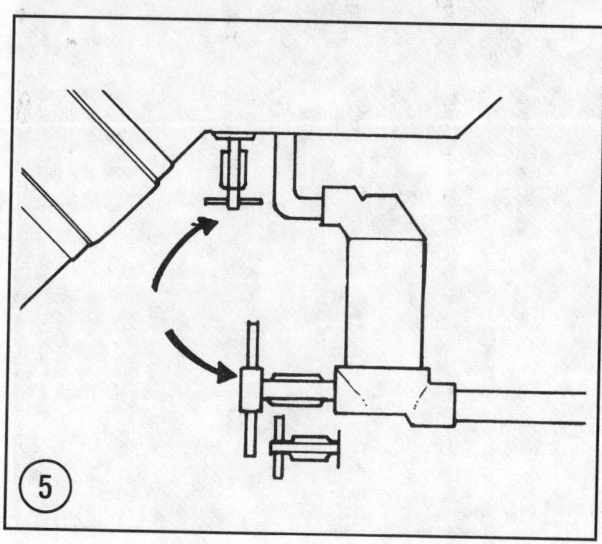

e. Gimbal housing swivel shaft, swivel pin, hinge pins and gimbal bearing.

f. U-joint bearings, shaft and engine coupling splines.

3. Remove the propeller(s) and wipe the propeller shaft(s) with a rust-inhibiting oil. Reinstall the propeller(s).

4. Check the condition of the bellows and clamps. Replace the bellows or tighten the clamps as required. Suggested replacement/maintenance is described in Chapter Four.

CAUTION
Do not paint sacrificial zinc rings, plugs or bars, if present. These must be left unpainted to prevent damage from galvanic corrosion.

5. Remove all marine growth and deposits from the stern drive unit. Clean and repaint scratched or nicked metal surfaces with touch-up paint.

6. Store the boat with the stern drive in its normal fully-down position. If the unit is stored in a tilted-up position, the universal joint bellows may develop a set that will lead to premature bellows failure once the unit is returned to service.

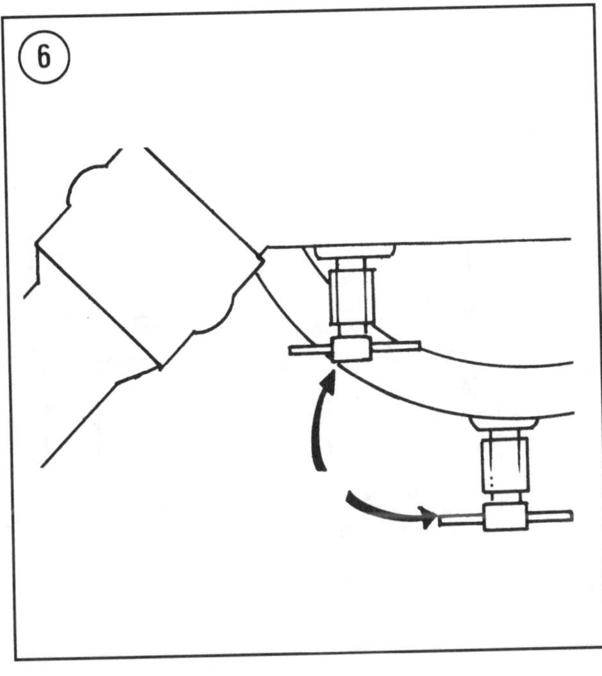

COOLING SYSTEM DRAINING

All water must be drained from the engine cooling system on boats stored in areas where the temperature may fall below 32° F (0° C). If all water is not drained, the engine block and other components can be cracked or damaged by expansion of frozen water.

The engine coolant section of a closed cooling system should always be filled with a 50:50 solution of pure water and ethylene glycol antifreeze. The antifreeze mixture should not require draining during winter months. However, the raw water system on these models must be drained and the closed system must be drained when replacing the antifreeze or when servicing components.

When subjected to freezing, inline engines tend to crack horizontally just below the core plugs or along the upper edge below the cylinder head. A V-block will usually crack near the hydraulic lifters or in the valley of the block below the intake manifold.

The following procedures are designed to prevent unnecessary engine damage during winter storage.

To ensure that the cooling system is completely drained, adjust the trailer or cradle so the forward end of inline engines is higher than the aft end. With V6 and V8 engines, adjust the trailer or cradle so the engine is level. With the engine level, the bow of the boat will be higher than the stern.

Raw Water Cooling System

Refer to **Figures 5-9** for typical drain valve locations.

1. Drain the raw water system as described in Chapter Four.

NOTE
Be sure to drain the exhaust manifold, power steering cooler, all hoses and any other location where water can accumu-

5

late, as well as both sides of V-6 and V-8 engine blocks.

2A. On models with a closed cooling system, loosen the clamps and detach the lower end of the cooling system hoses from the raw water pump, heat exchanger and exhaust manifold. Lower the hoses and allow them to drain.

2B. On models with a raw water cooling system, loosen the clamps and detach the lower end of all cooling system hoses from the engine, circulating pump, raw water pump, power steering cooler and exhaust manifold. Lower the hoses and allow the system to drain.

3. Remove the screws attaching the rear cover to the raw water pump and remove the cover.

4. Inspect the raw water pump impeller. Install a new impeller if the blades are hard, cracked, nicked or damaged in any way.

5. Reinstall the cover on the raw water pump and reconnect the hoses. Tighten the clamp on each hose securely.

6. Allow the cooling system to drain *completely,* then coat the drain plug threads with sealer and reinstall. Close any opened drain valves.

Closed Cooling System

The engine coolant section of a closed cooling system should always be filled with a 50:50 solution of pure water and ethylene glycol antifreeze. The antifreeze mixture should not require draining during winter months. The raw water section, however, *must* be drained *completely* to prevent freezing.

Drain the cylinder block on 4 cylinder models by removing a drain plug or drain cock located low on the port (left) side of the block. On 6- and 8-cylinder models, a drain plug or drain cock is located low on *each side* of the block. It is important to drain both sides of 6- and 8-cylinder engine blocks.

Raw water section

Refer to **Figure 5-9** for typical drain valve locations.

1. Drain the cooling system as described in Chapter Four.

NOTE

Be sure to drain the exhaust manifold, power steering cooler, all hoses and any other location where water can accumulate, as well as both sides of V-6 and V-8 engine blocks.

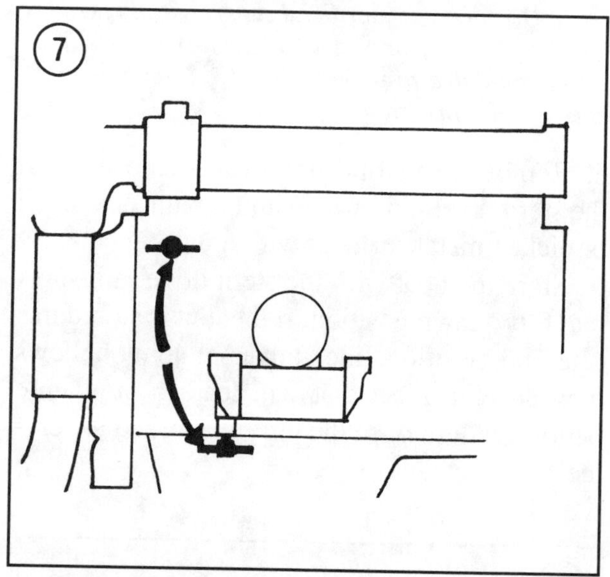

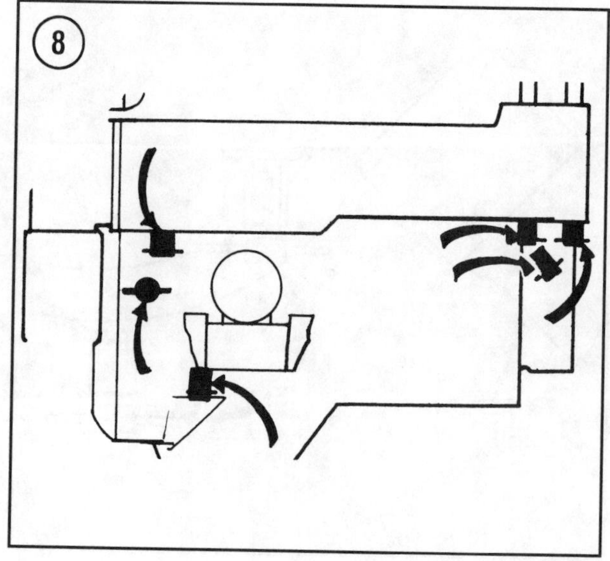

2. Loosen the clamps and detach the lower end of all cooling system hoses from the engine, circulating pump and exhaust manifold. Lower the hoses and allow them to completely drain.
3. Remove the screws attaching the rear cover to the raw water pump and remove the cover.
4. Inspect the raw water pump impeller. Install a new impeller if the blades are hard, cracked, nicked or damaged in any way.
5. Reinstall the cover on the raw water pump and reconnect the hoses. Tighten the clamp on each hose securely.
6. Examine the sacrificial anode (if so equipped) for erosion. If it is more than 25% eroded, install a new anode.
7. Allow the cooling system to drain *completely*, then coat the drain plug threads with sealer and reinstall. Close any opened drain valves.

FILLING CLOSED COOLING SYSTEM

Preparing the Engine For Storage

On models with a closed cooling system, the engine cooling passages should always be filled with an antifreeze and water mixture as described in Chapter Four. However, the raw water system on these models must be drained as described in the following paragraphs. If the antifreeze mixture is sufficient to protect from freezing, it may be left in the engine until just before the boat is to be returned to service following winter storage.

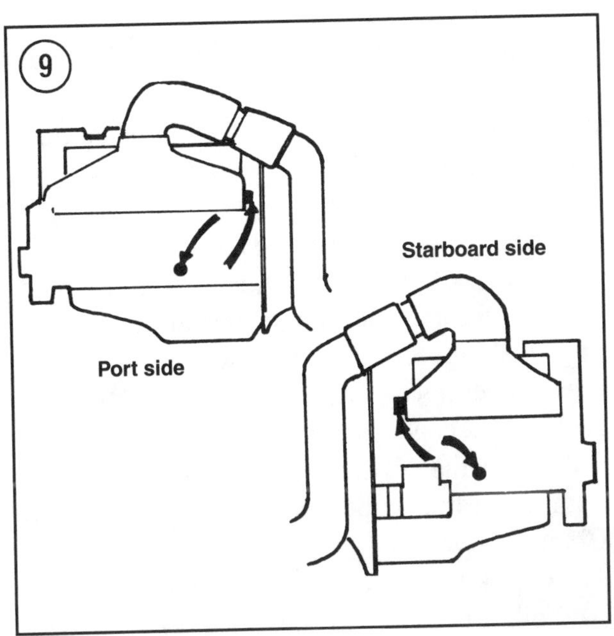

CAUTION

Do not run the engine after performing the storage service procedure that follows. Before returning the boat to service, drain the coolant as described in this chapter and tighten all fasteners and clamps to specification.

1. Close all drain valves and replace any hoses, caps, plugs or clamps that show deterioration.
2. Pour a 50:50 mixture of pure water and ethylene glycol antifreeze into the water distribution block until the cylinder head, block and manifold are full.
3. Reinstall the cap on the heat exchanger.

Returning the Engine to Service

Most ethylene glycol antifreeze solutions used in closed cooling systems tend to become corrosive after approximately 3 years of use or if a blown head gasket allows exhaust gases to enter the cooling system. While such corrosive tendencies will not cause significant damage to the engine, they do produce loose particles that can plug the coolant side of the heat exchanger.

The increased usage of aluminum components in engines, water pumps, manifolds and recovery tanks has led to the development of an antifreeze formulation recommended for use with aluminum engines. This type antifreeze formula should be used in the closed cooling systems of all Volvo Penta marine engines. Check the antifreeze container and make sure it meets one of the major automakers' specifications, such as Ford specification ESE-M97B44-A or GM specification 1825M.

5

1. Remove the pressure fill cap from the reservoir or heat exchanger.
2. Fill the closed section with a 50:50 mixture of pure water and ethylene glycol antifreeze until the fluid level is approximately 1 in. (25.4 mm) below the top of the filler neck.

CAUTION
Water must flow through the raw water pump in Step 3 or the pump and engine may be damaged. If the boat is not in the water, connect a flushing device and adjust water flow.

3. Start the engine and run at about 1,000 rpm, add coolant to the heat exchanger as necessary to maintain the level at approximately 1 in. (25.4 mm) below the top of the filler neck. When the engine reaches normal operating temperature and the coolant level remains constant, reinstall the pressure cap.
4. If equipped with a coolant recovery system, remove the cap from the recovery reservoir and fill with 50:50 mix of antifreeze to the FULL mark.
5. Check for leaks while the engine is running and note the position of the engine temperature gauge; it should be normal.

WARNING
Do not remove the pressure fill cap when the engine is warm or hot. You may be seriously scalded by coolant escaping under pressure.

6. Shut the engine off and allow it to cool for 30 minutes. Turn the pressure fill cap to the first detent and allow any pressure to escape. Remove the cap when the system is cooled.
7. Recheck the coolant level. Add coolant if required to raise the level to a point between the ADD and FULL marks.

FITTING OUT

Preparing the boat for use after storage is relatively easy if the engine and stern drive unit were properly prepared before storage. Depending upon the condition of the antifreeze installed in closed systems, it may be time to drain and fill the system with a new antifreeze mixture.

1. Clean the engine and stern drive unit with solvent to remove any accumulated dirt and preservative oil. Retouch any paint blemishes.

NOTE
*If the boat is to be left in the water for an extended period of time, it may be advisable to cover the underwater surfaces (including the stern drive unit) with an antifouling paint. Do **not** use a paint containing copper or mercury, as these elements may increase galvanic corrosion.*

2. Remove any protective covers installed on the flame arrestor, carburetor, exhaust outlets or fuel tank ventilators.
3. Drain antifreeze from the raw water cooling passages, if it was installed for storage.
4. Make sure all drain valves and plugs are tightly closed and all cooling system hoses are securely clamped in place.
5. Inspect all hoses for cracks, weak walls and leaks. Replace any that appear questionable.
6. Check all through-hull fittings for leaks and proper valve operation.
7. Remove, clean and reinstall the flame arrestor.
8. Check the fuel system. Refill the drained tanks. Turn the fuel valve(s) ON and check all fuel lines for leaks.
9. Check battery electrolyte level and fill if necessary. Make certain the battery is fully charged. Clean the battery terminals and install the battery, making certain the cables are connected with proper polarity. Cover the battery terminals with a light coat of petroleum jelly.
10. Drain the oil from stern drive unit. Refill with oil of the proper viscosity and grade. See Chapter Four.
11. Check the oil level in the engine crankcase. Add oil, if necessary. If the oil was not changed

at time of lay-up or if the engine has been in storage for an extended period of time, change the oil and oil filter.

12. Check the power steering and power trim hydraulic pump oil levels, if so equipped. Refer to Chapter Four and top up if low.

13. Check and adjust drive belt tension as described in Chapter Four.

14. Make a thorough check of the boat, engine and stern drive for loose or missing fasteners. Pay particular attention to the stern drive transom connection.

15. Examine sacrificial zinc elements and replace if more than 25% eroded.

16. Remove the distributor cap and examine the cap, rotor and distributor contact breaker points (if so equipped). Replace the point set if any wear is evident. Do not attempt to clean old points, rotor or distributor cap. If old parts are dirty enough to require cleaning, it is usually more effective to install new components. Refer to Chapter Four.

WARNING

If the boat is not equipped with a bilge blower, make sure the engine cover or hatch is open, properly supported and the bilge thoroughly ventilated before performing Step 17. This will prevent the buildup of any fumes that might result in an explosion if there is a fuel leak.

17. Provide a source of water for engine cooling. Make certain a Coast Guard-approved fire extinguisher is nearby, then start the engine. While the engine is warming up, watch the instrument panel gauges to make certain that all systems are operating as they should. Also check for any signs of fuel, oil or water leaks.

18. Proceed with engine tune-up. See Chapter Four for instructions and specifications.

Chapter Six

3.0 Liter 4-Cylinder Engines

This chapter covers 3.0 L 4-cylinder inline engines used with Volvo Penta stern drives. The cylinders are numbered 1-2-3-4 from front to rear and the firing order is 1-3-4-2.

The 4 intake and 4 exhaust valves are operated via pushrods and rocker arms by a camshaft located in the engine block. Camshaft motion is transferred through hydraulic lifters to the rocker arms by pushrods. The rocker arms move on ball-pivots located on individual threaded shoulder studs.

The camshaft is gear-driven and is supported by 4 bearings. The oil pump mounted at the bottom front of the engine block on the starboard side is driven by the distributor shaft. The distributor is driven by a gear on the camshaft.

The crankshaft is supported by 5 main bearings, with the rear bearing providing thrust surfaces to limit the crankshaft end play. The crankshaft rotates counterclockwise as viewed from the rear (drive unit end) of the engine, facing the normal direction of travel. If viewed from the front (looking toward the rear), the crankshaft turns clockwise.

The cylinder block is cast iron with water jackets around each cylinder.

Engine specifications (**Table 1**) and tightening torques (**Table 2**) are at the end of the chapter.

ENGINE SERIAL NUMBER AND CODE

The engine serial number and model designation are stamped on a plate attached to the rocker arm cover (**Figure 1**). If the plate or decal is missing, you can determine the model designation by checking the number stamped on the starboard side near the distributor. Ask your

Volvo Penta dealer for assistance if you have difficulty identifying your engine. This information identifies the engine and indicates if there are any unique parts or if internal changes have been made during the model year. The specific model number and serial number are important when ordering replacement parts for the engine. Be prepared to give these numbers to the parts department when obtaining or ordering parts.

SPECIAL TOOLS

Where special tools are required or recommended for engine overhaul, the tool numbers are provided. Special tools can also be purchased from a Volvo Penta dealership.

GASKET SEALANT

Gasket sealant is used instead of preformed gaskets between some mating surfaces on the engines covered in this chapter. Two types of gasket sealant are commonly used: room temperature vulcanizing (RTV) and anaerobic. Since these 2 materials have different sealing properties, they cannot be interchanged.

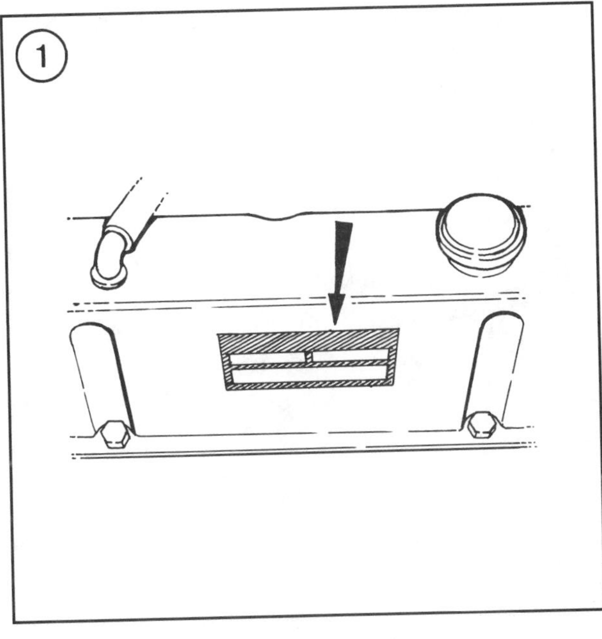

Room Temperature Vulcanizing (RTV) Sealant

This silicone gel is available in tubes that are available from most parts suppliers and Volvo Penta dealerships. Moisture in the air causes RTV to cure. Always place the cap on the tube as soon as possible when using RTV. RTV has a shelf life of approximately 1 year and will not cure properly when the shelf life has expired. Check the expiration date on RTV tubes before using and keep partially used tubes tightly sealed.

6

Applying RTV Sealant

Clean all gasket residue from the mating surfaces. The surfaces must be clean and free of oil or grease. Remove all RTV gasket material from blind attaching holes, as it can cause a hydraulic lock and affect bolt torque.

Unless otherwise specified, apply RTV sealant in a continuous bead 3-5 mm (1/8-3/16 in.) thick. Apply the sealant on the inner side of all mounting bolts. Torque mating parts within 10-15 minutes after application or the sealant will have started to cure. If this happens, the old sealant must be removed and new sealant applied.

Anaerobic Sealant

This is also a gel that is supplied in tubes. It cures only in the absence of air, as when squeezed tightly between 2 machined mating surfaces. For this reason, it will not spoil if the cap is left off the tube. It should not be used if 1 mating surface is flexible.

Applying Anaerobic Sealant

Clean all gasket residue from the mating surfaces. The surfaces must be clean and free of oil or grease. Remove all gasket material from blind attaching holes, as it can cause a hydraulic lock and affect bolt torque.

Unless otherwise specified, apply anaerobic sealant in a 1 mm (0.04 in.) or less continuous bead to 1 sealing surface. Apply the sealant on the inner side of all mounting holes.

REPLACEMENT PARTS

Various changes are made to automotive engines before they are used for marine applications. Numerous part changes are required due to operation in fresh and saltwater. For example, the cylinder head gasket must be corrosion resistant. Marine engines may use head gaskets of copper or stainless steel instead of the standard steel used in automotive applications. Brass expansion or core plugs must be used instead of the steel plugs found in automotive blocks.

Since marine engines are run at or near maximum speed most of the time, the use of special valve lifters, springs, pistons, bearings, camshafts and other heavy-duty components is necessary for maximum life and performance.

For these reasons, automotive-type parts must never be substituted for marine components. In addition, Volvo Penta recommends that only parts available through authorized Volvo Penta dealers be used. Parts offered by other manufacturers may look similar, but may not be manufactured to Volvo Penta's specifications. Any damage resulting from the use of incorrect parts will be the sole responsibility of the installer.

PRECAUTIONS

WARNING
The engine is heavy, awkward to handle and has sharp edges. It may shift or drop suddenly during removal. To prevent serious injury, always observe the following precautions.

1. Never place any part of your body where a moving or falling engine may trap, cut or crush you.
2. If you must push the engine during removal, use a board or similar tool to keep your hands out of danger.
3. Be sure the hoist is designed to lift engines and has enough load capacity for your engine.
4. Be sure the hoist is securely attached to safe lifting points on the engine.
5. The engine should not be difficult to lift with a proper hoist. If it is, stop lifting, lower the engine back onto its mounts and make sure the engine has been completely separated from the vessel.

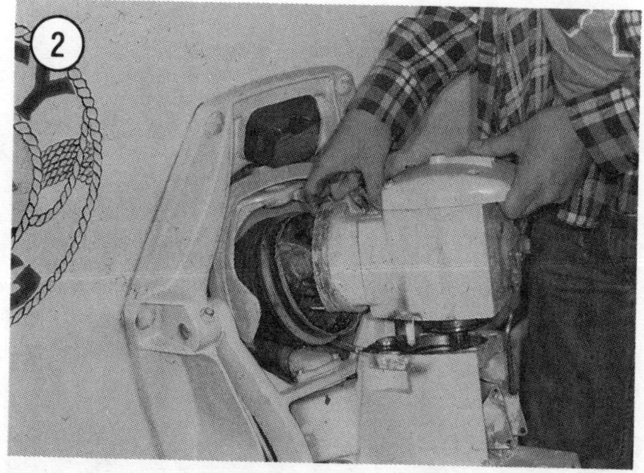

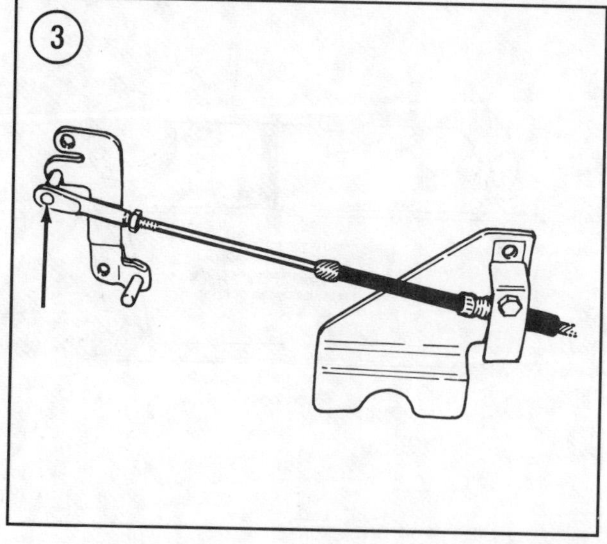

ENGINE REMOVAL

Some service procedures can be performed with the engine in the boat; others require removal. The boat design and service procedure to be performed determines whether the engine must be removed.

1. Remove the engine cover and all panels that interfere with engine removal. Move the cover and other parts out of the way.
2. Disconnect the negative battery cable, then the positive battery cable. As a precaution, remove the battery from the boat.
3. Remove the stern drive upper gear housing (**Figure 2**). Refer to Chapter Twelve.
4. Disconnect the throttle cable from the carburetor linkage (**Figure 3**, typical). Remove the cable from the anchor plates attached to the engine.
5. Detach the electrical cables from the engine. Separate the cables at the connectors.
6. Disconnect the fuel delivery line from the fuel pump. Plug the line and fitting to prevent leakage and the entry of contamination.
7. Loosen the hose clamp and detach the raw water hose from the raw water pump.

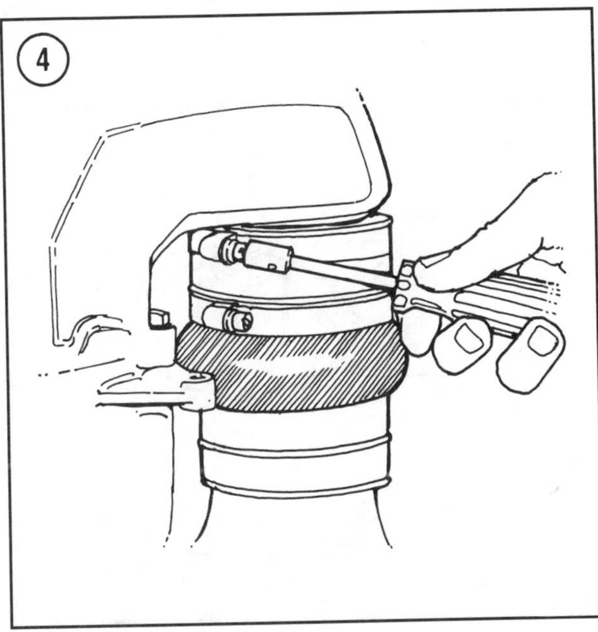

8. Open the engine drain cocks or remove the drain plugs and drain all coolant and water from the engine.
9. Loosen the clamp on the exhaust manifold bellows, then pull the bellows free from the manifold. See **Figure 4**.
10. Remove the shift mechanism cover from the stern drive and disconnect the shift cable from the lever. Remove the cable lock plate from the front of the stern drive intermediate housing.
11. If equipped with power steering, use a flare nut wrench to loosen and disconnect both power steering hydraulic lines from the control valve. Cap the lines and plug the control valve fittings to prevent leakage and the entry of contamination. Secure the lines at a point higher than the engine power steering pump during the remainder of this procedure to prevent damage or the loss of fluid.
12. Detach any wires, hoses or accessories connected to the engine that would interfere with removal.

NOTE
At this point, there should be no hoses, wires or linkage connecting the engine to the boat or stern drive unit. Recheck to make sure that nothing remains that will interfere with removal of the engine.

13. Attach a suitable hoist to the engine lifting brackets. The hoist must have a minimum lift capacity of 1,500 lb. (680 kg). Raise the hoist enough to remove all slack.

NOTE
Do not loosen or move the mounts at the engine attaching points or a complete realignment will be required when the engine is reinstalled. Engine alignment should not be disturbed if mounts are detached as described in Step 14.

14. Remove the lag screws (**Figure 5**) from the front engine mount, then remove the locknuts

6

(A, **Figure 6**) and washers (B) from the rear engine mounts.
15. Remove the mounting bolts (**Figure 7**) from the clamp ring at the rear.
16. Slide the engine forward until the flywheel cover is clear, then lift the engine from the boat.

ENGINE INSTALLATION

Engine installation is the reverse of removal, in addition to the following:
1. Clean the engine coupling splines and lubricate lightly with oil.
2. Reinstall any shims or adapters used with the engine mounts.
3. Inspect all self-locking nuts, hoses, bellows and other parts for wear or deterioration. The manufacturer suggests that the exhaust bellows be replaced every 2 years and elastic stop nuts should never be installed more than twice. It is a good idea to replace these parts anytime the engine is removed.
4. Guide bolts may be used to align the engine at the rear.
5. Tighten all fasteners to the specifications listed in **Table 2**.
6. If equipped with power steering, tighten both power steering fittings to the torque listed in **Table 2**. Bleed the power steering system as described in Chapter Sixteen.
7. Fill the engine with the quantity, type and viscosity of oil recommended in Chapter Four.
8. If equipped with a closed cooling system, fill the system with a 50:50 mixture of antifreeze and pure water. See Chapter Four.
9. Adjust the accessory drive belts. See Chapter Four.
10. Make sure all hoses, wires and linkage are reattached before starting the engine.

DISASSEMBLY CHECKLISTS

To use the checklists, remove and inspect each part in the order mentioned. To reassemble, go through the checklists backward, installing the parts in order. Each major part is covered in its own section in this chapter, unless otherwise noted.

Decarbonizing or Valve Service

1. Remove the rocker arm cover.
2. Remove the intake and exhaust manifolds.
3. Remove the rocker arms and pushrods.
4. Remove the cylinder head.
5. Remove and inspect the valves. Inspect the valve guides and seats, repairing or replacing as required.
6. Assemble by reversing Steps 1-5.

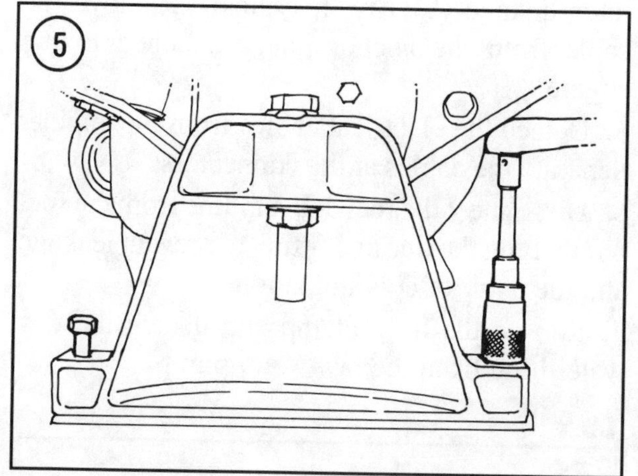

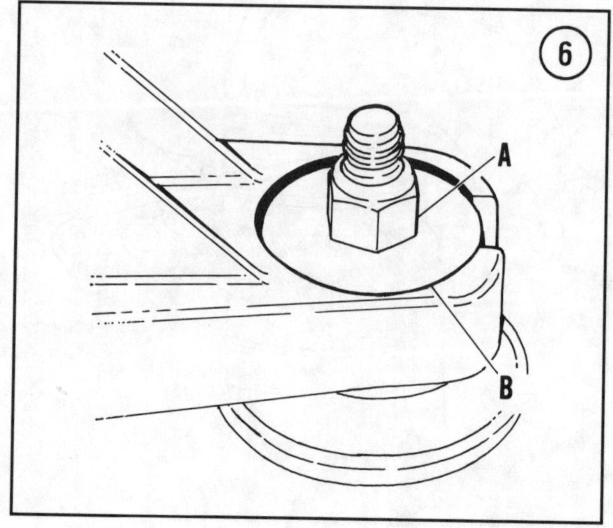

Valve and Ring Service

1. Perform Steps 1-5 of *Decarbonizing or Valve Service.*
2. Remove the oil pan and oil pump.
3. Remove the pistons and connecting rods.
4. Remove the piston rings. It is not necessary to separate the pistons from the connecting rods unless a piston, connecting rod or piston pin needs repair or replacement.
5. Assemble by reversing Steps 1-4.

General Overhaul

1. Remove the engine from the boat.
2. Remove the flywheel cover and flywheel.
3. Remove the mount brackets and oil pressure sending unit from the engine.
4. If available, mount the engine on an engine stand. These can be rented from equipment rental dealers. The stand is not absolutely necessary, but it will make the job much easier.
5. Check the engine for signs of coolant or oil leaks.
6. Clean the outside of the engine.
7. Remove the distributor. See Chapter Eleven.
8. If they are present remove the following accessories or components from the engine.
   a. Alternator and mounting bracket.
   b. Power steering pump and mounting bracket.
   c. Carburetor and fuel lines.
   d. Oil dipstick and tube.
   e. Raw water pump.
9. Detach all hoses and tubes connected to the engine.
10. Remove the fuel pump. See Chapter Nine.
11. Remove the intake and exhaust manifolds.
12. Remove the thermostat. See Chapter Ten.
13. Remove the rocker arm cover and rocker arms, then lift out the pushrods.
14. Remove the water circulation pump, crankshaft pulley and vibration damper.
15. Remove the timing case cover, then remove the timing chain and sprockets.
16. Remove the camshaft.
17. Remove the cylinder head.
18. Remove the oil pan and oil pump.
19. Remove the pistons and connecting rods.
20. Remove the crankshaft.
21. Inspect the cylinder block.
22. Assemble by reversing Steps 1-20.

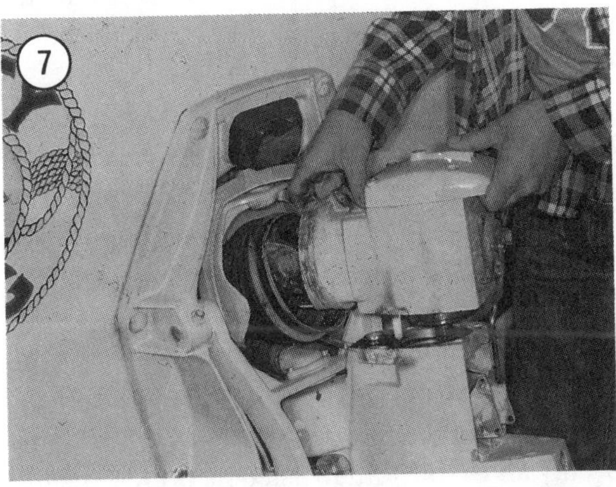

ROCKER ARM COVER

Removal/Installation

1. Disconnect the crankcase ventilation hose from the rocker arm cover.
2. Detach or remove any accessory unit that might interfere with removing the rocker arm cover.

NOTE
Be careful not to lose any of the cover retaining screws or load spreaders, especially those attaching the clamp for the trim and tilt cable.

3. Remove the cover fasteners and load spreaders.
4. Bump the rocker arm cover with a soft-faced mallet to break the gasket seal. Lift the rocker

arm cover from the engine and discard the gasket.
5. Clean any gasket or sealer residue from the cylinder head and rocker arm cover.
6. Coat 1 side of a new gasket with an oil-resistant sealer, then install the gasket onto the rocker arm cover with the sealer-side against the rocker arm cover. Gasket tabs must engage the notches in the cover and all of the holes for the retaining screws must be aligned and open.
7. Position the rocker arm cover on the cylinder head.
8. Make sure the load spreaders are on each screw, then install the screws. Tighten to the torque listed in **Table 2**.
9. Attach the crankcase ventilation hose to the rocker arm cover.

INTAKE/EXHAUST MANIFOLDS

The intake and exhaust manifolds are combined in 1 unit. **Figure 8** shows a typical manifold assembly and related components.

Removal/Installation

Refer to **Figure 8**, typical, as required for this procedure.
1. Detach the ground cable from the negative battery terminal.
2. Open (or remove) the drain cocks (A and B, **Figure 9**) located in the manifold and on the side of the cylinder block. Allow all of the water to drain. It may be necessary to insert a wire through the open drain to dislodge sediment.
3. Detach the throttle cable from the carburetor. See **Figure 3**. Remove the cable from the anchor plate attached to the exhaust manifold.
4. Detach both ends of the fuel line between the carburetor and fuel pump. Then remove the line from between the carburetor and fuel pump. It is usually better to remove the carburetor from the manifold at this point than risk damage by leaving the carburetor attached to the manifold.
5. Disconnect the water hoses from the manifold. It is often easier to remove the hoses than detach just 1 end.
6. On models with power steering, remove the alternator and detach the oil cooler mounting plate from the manifold.
7. Loosen the clamps (A, **Figure 10**) that attach the bellows to the exhaust elbow. Loosen the bellows after the clamps are loose.
8. Remove the fasteners (B, **Figure 10**) attaching the exhaust elbow to the manifold, then lift the elbow from the manifold and studs.

CAUTION
Be careful not to break the studs or bolts that attach the manifold to the cylinder head. If the fasteners are difficult to remove, consider grinding the heads off the bolts or the nuts from the studs, then lifting the manifold off the head. After the manifold is removed, apply a suitable penetrating fluid to the fastener threads in the cylinder head and remove the fastener.

9. Loosen the 4 screws and 2 nuts attaching the manifold to the cylinder head. Support the manifold, remove the attaching fittings, then lift the manifold from the cylinder head.
10. Remove and discard the manifold gasket, then clean all gasket residue from the cylinder head and manifold assembly. Make sure the gasket surfaces are completely clean and flat. Inspect the gasket surfaces of the manifold as described in this chapter.
11. Coat both sides of new gasket with sealer, then position the gasket on the cylinder head. The gasket should be supported by the 2 studs.
12. Position the manifold on the studs. Make sure gasket is properly aligned and slide the manifold against the cylinder head. Install the 2 special manifold nuts finger-tight.
13. Install the 4 manifold attaching screws. Tighten all of the fasteners (4 screws and 2 nuts) evenly and to the torque listed in **Table 2**, begin-

(8)

MANIFOLD AND EXHAUST
(3.0 L ENGINE)

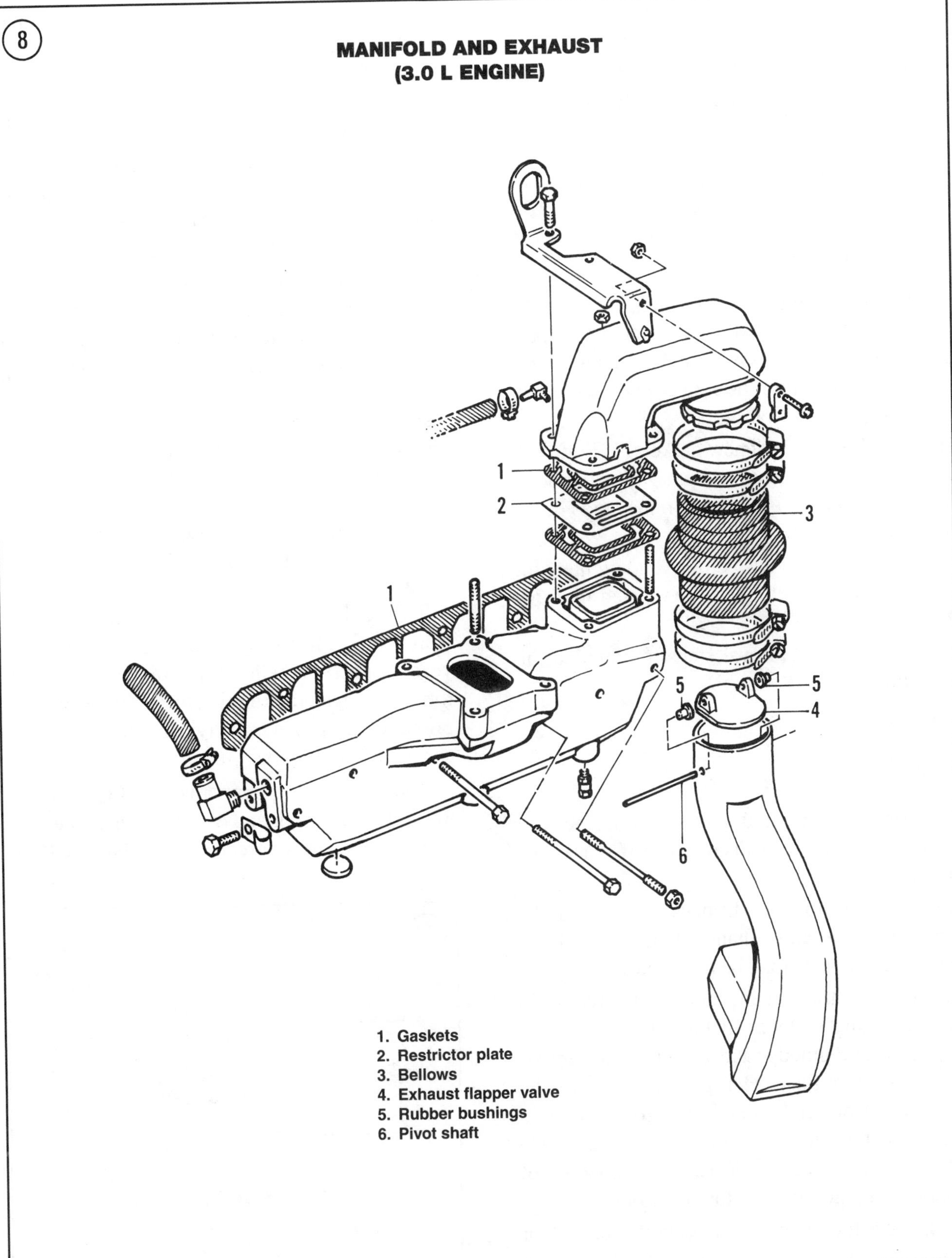

1. Gaskets
2. Restrictor plate
3. Bellows
4. Exhaust flapper valve
5. Rubber bushings
6. Pivot shaft

ning with the screws in the center and progressing to the ends.

14. Inspect the exhaust bellows and the exhaust flapper valve as described in this chapter.

NOTE
*Inspect the condition of the exhaust bellows (C, **Figure 10**). The manufacturer recommends that a new bellows be installed every other year.*

15. If a new bellows is installed, position the bellows and clamps on the exhaust collector, but do not tighten the clamps until the exhaust elbow is installed. Position the longer end of the bellows with 2 ribs toward top.

16. Coat both sides of new gaskets (1, **Figure 8**) with sealer, then position both gaskets and the restrictor plate (2, **Figure 8**) on the studs of the manifold.

17. Install the exhaust elbow and tighten the retaining fasteners to the torque listed in **Table 2**.

18. Reverse the removal steps to complete installation.

Inspection

1. Check the manifold assembly for cracks or distortion. Replace if distorted or if cracks are found.

2. Check the mating surfaces of the cylinder head, manifold and exhaust elbow for nicks or burrs. Small burrs may be removed with a file.

3. Place a straightedge across the manifold flange/mating surfaces. If there is any gap between the straightedge and gasket surface, measure it with a flat feeler gauge. Measure the manifold from end to end and from corner to corner. If the surface is not flat to within 0.006 in. (0.15 mm) per each 12 in. (30.5 cm) of manifold length, replace the manifold.

4. Inspect the engine exhaust ports for rust or corrosion.

5. Check water passages in the manifold and exhaust elbow for clogging. Check for sand, silt or other foreign material. Remove the plugs from manifold and exhaust elbow to facilitate inspection and cleaning.

6. Inspect the condition of the exhaust bellows (C, **Figure 10**). If damaged, replace the bellows. Position the clamps and the new bellows on the exhaust collector, but do not tighten the clamps until the exhaust elbow is installed.

7. Inspect the condition of the exhaust flapper valve located in the upper end of the exhaust pipe. The valve should move freely and the long side of the valve should be down. If damaged or installed improperly, exhaust can be restricted and water can back up into the exhaust.

EXHAUST BELLOWS AND FLAPPER VALVE

The manufacturer suggests that new exhaust bellows (3, **Figure 8**) be installed every other year. Inspect the bellows and replace it if hard, torn or damaged. Running the engine without proper cooling will quickly damage the bellows as well as other parts.

The exhaust flapper valve (4, **Figure 8**) is located in the upper end of the exhaust pipe. The valve should move freely. The exhaust can be

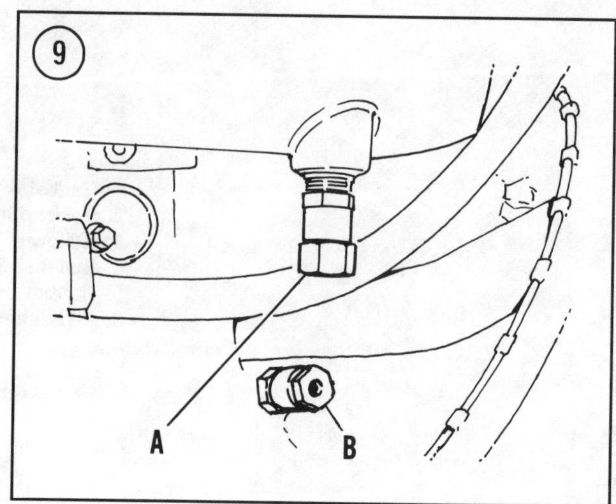

restricted and water can back up into the exhaust if the valve is damaged or installed improperly. New rubber bushings (5, **Figure 8**) must be installed when the valve is removed.

Removal/Installation

1. Loosen the upper clamps (A, **Figure 10**) that attach the bellows to the exhaust elbow. Loosen the bellows after the clamps are loose.
2. Remove the fasteners (B, **Figure 10**) attaching the exhaust elbow to the manifold, then lift the elbow from the manifold and studs. The bellows will probably be damaged if hardened or otherwise damaged.
3. Loosen the lower clamps and remove the bellows from the exhaust collector.

NOTE

If the exhaust flapper valve is stuck, damaged or installed improperly, exhaust can be restricted and water can back up into the exhaust causing engine damage.

4. Check the exhaust flapper valve (5, **Figure 8**) for freedom of movement.
5. If it is necessary to remove the flapper valve, proceed as follows:

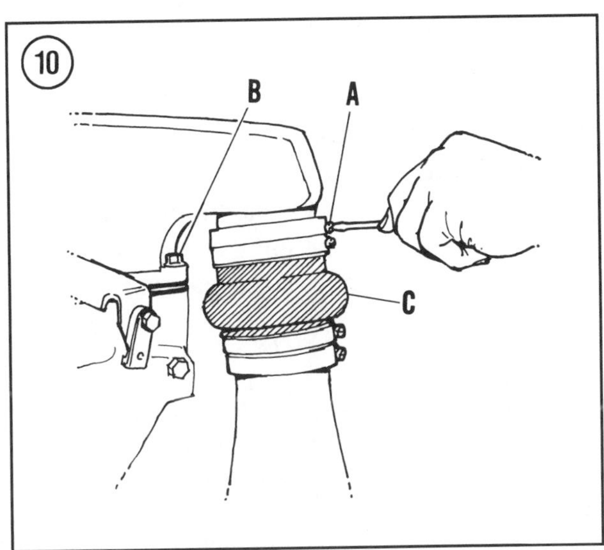

a. Drive the pivot shaft (6, **Figure 8**) from the valve and bushings using a small diameter punch.
b. Lift the flapper valve from the exhaust pipe.

NOTE

Use care to keep the bushings from falling into the exhaust pipe during flapper valve removal. The bushing flanges face toward the inside of the pipe.

c. Push (or drive) the rubber bushings from the exhaust pipe.
d. Apply Scotch Grip Rubber Adhesive to new the bushings and insert them into the bores of the exhaust pipe. The flanged side of the bushings must face toward the inside of the pipe.
e. Position the exhaust flapper valve in the pipe, between the bushings with the holes in flanges aligned with the rubber bushings. The long side of the valve must face down.
f. Insert the pin through 1 rubber bushing and the valve flanges, then align the pin with the second bushing and push the pin through the second rubber bushing.
g. Check the valve for freedom of movement. The ends of the pin should be flush with the exhaust pipe on both sides. It is important to have the valve correctly installed before completing the reassemby of the exhaust.

NOTE

Lubricate the inside of the bellows with soapy water to ease installation onto the exhaust pipe and elbow.

6. Place the bellows and clamps on the exhaust collector. Position the end of the bellows with 1 rib (short end) downward on the exhaust collector pipe. The end of the bellows with 2 ribs (long end) must be positioned toward the top.
7. Place 2 clamps around the top of the bellows. The clamps must be very loose, permitting installation of the exhaust elbow into the bellows.
8. Coat both sides of the new gaskets (1, **Figure 8**) with sealer, then position both gaskets and

restrictor plate (2, **Figure 8**) on the studs of the manifold.

9. Install the exhaust elbow and tighten the retaining fasteners to the torque listed in **Table 2**.

10. Make sure the bellows is on completely and not twisted, then tighten the clamp screws securely.

ROCKER ARM ASSEMBLIES

Removal/Installation

Each rocker arm moves against its own pivot ball (1, **Figure 11**). The rocker arm and pivot ball are retained by a nut. It is not necessary to remove the rocker arm for pushrod replacement. Loosen the nut and move the arm away from the pushrod. To remove the entire assembly, refer to **Figure 11**, typical, and proceed as follows.

1. Remove the rocker arm cover as described in this chapter.
2. Remove each rocker arm nut, ball, rocker arm and pushrod.

NOTE
The contact surface of the valves, rocker arms, pivot balls, pushrods and cam followers all develop a unique wear pattern and become matched to each other. Therefore, do not mix these parts with similar parts from another location. Mark all components to indicate their original location and direction in the engine.

3. Place each set (pivot ball, rocker arm and pushrod) in a separate container to keep them separated for reinstallation in the same position from which they were removed.
4. When assembling, observe the following.
   a. Clean all parts completely before assembling. This applies to new parts as well as the original parts.
   b. Lubricate the pushrods, rocker arms and pivot balls liberally with clean engine oil immediately before assembling.
5. Install the pushrods, making sure that each fits into its lifter socket.
6. Install the rocker arms, pivot balls and nuts. If new rocker arms or pivot balls are being installed, coat contact surfaces with Molykote.
7. Tighten the retaining nuts as described for *Valve Clearance Adjustment* in this chapter.
8. Install the rocker arm cover as described in this chapter.

Inspection

1. Clean all parts with solvent and use compressed air to blow out the oil passages in the pushrods.
2. Check each rocker arm, pivot ball, nut and pushrod for scuffing, pitting or excessive wear and replace as required. If 1 component is worn, replace all that operates that valve as a set.
3. Check pushrods for straightness by rolling them across a flat, even surface such as a pane of glass. Replace any pushrods that do not roll smoothly.
4. If a pushrod is worn from lack of lubrication, replace the corresponding lifter (cam follower) and rocker arm as well.
5. Make sure that all parts are completely clean and properly lubricated when assembling.

Valve Clearance Adjustment

Valve adjustment is required only if the valve train has been disassembled. The engine is equipped with hydraulic lifters that adjust to compensate for normal wear automatically. Adjust the valves with the engine stopped and the lifter on the base circle of the camshaft lobe.

NOTE
Adjusting used lifters can be especially difficult since the described adjustment may position internal parts of the lifter in a previously unused area of travel, causing the lifter to stick. If 1 valve requires adjustment after a period of nor-

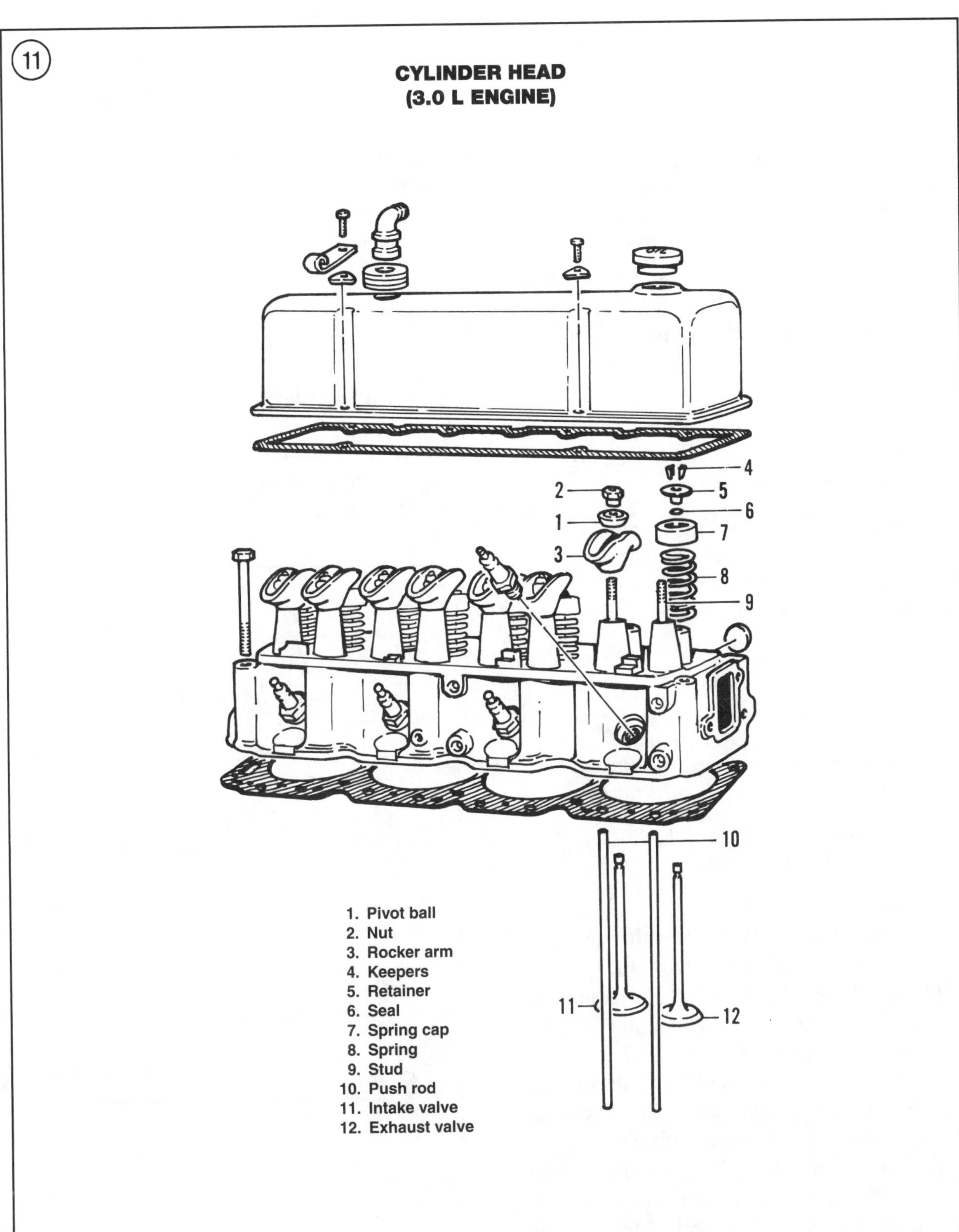
11
CYLINDER HEAD
(3.0 L ENGINE)
1
2
3
4
5
6
7
8
9
10
11
12
1. Pivot ball
2. Nut
3. Rocker arm
4. Keepers
5. Retainer
6. Seal
7. Spring cap
8. Spring
9. Stud
10. Push rod
11. Intake valve
12. Exhaust valve

mal operation, check the condition of the lifter and the cam lobe that operates that valve, as described in this chapter.

1. Rotate the crankshaft until the pulley notch aligns with the zero mark on the timing tab. See **Figure 12**. This positions the No. 1 cylinder at TDC. This position can be verified by placing a finger on the No. 1 cylinder rocker arms as the pulley notch nears the zero mark. If the valves are moving, the engine is in the No. 4 firing position. Rotate the crankshaft pulley 1 full turn to reach the No. 1 firing position.

NOTE

The intake valves are those closer to the intake ports. The exhaust valves are closer to the exhaust ports.

2. With the engine in the No. 1 firing position, refer to **Figure 13** and adjust both valves for the No. 1 (front) cylinder, the intake valve for No. 2 cylinder and the exhaust valve for the No. 3 cylinder.

CAUTION

Improper adjustment can prevent the engine from starting and may result in bent pushrods or other damage to the valve train. If the lifters are not full of oil, only the light pressure of the spring inside the lifter may be confused with clearance when performing Step 3.

3. To adjust each valve,
   a. Loosen (back off) the adjusting nut until some lash (clearance) is felt at the pushrod.
   b. Turn the nut clockwise (tighten) until all lash is just removed. This point is determined by turning the push rod with your fingers while slowly tightening the nut. See **Figure 14**. When lash is removed, the pushrod will not rotate freely.
   c. Turn the nut 1 additional complete turn (360°) to center the plunger inside the lifter.
4. Rotate the crankshaft exactly 1 full turn and realign the pulley notch and the timing tab zero mark (**Figure 12**). Turning the crankshaft 1 turn will position the No. 4 (rear) cylinder at Top Dead Center of its compression stroke. Refer to **Figure 13** and adjust the exhaust valve for the No. 2 cylinder, the intake valve for the No. 3 cylinder and both valves for the No. 4 (rear) cylinder.
5. Install the rocker arm cover as described in this chapter.

CRANKSHAFT PULLEY, HARMONIC BALANCER AND HUB

Removal/Installation

If engine is being serviced in the boat, attach a suitable hoist to support the front of the engine and remove the front mount bracket.

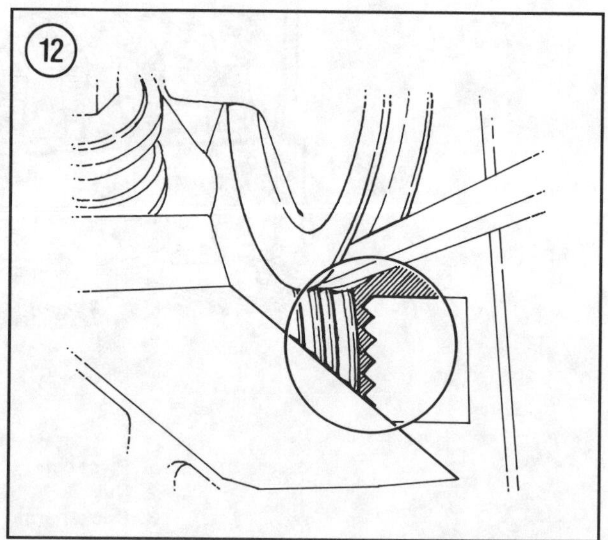

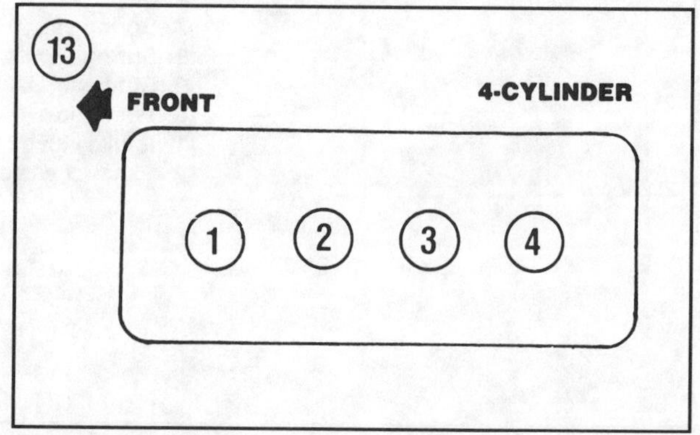

NOTE
To remove the alternator and the power steering pump drive belts, it is first necessary to remove the drive belt for the raw water pump. If the belts are in good condition, they do not need to be completely removed, but can be loosened and moved away from the crankshaft pulley.

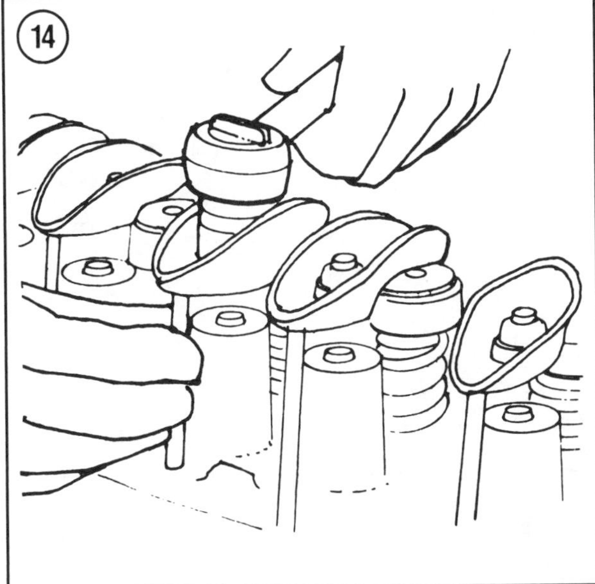

14

CRANKSHAFT PULLEY HUB REMOVAL

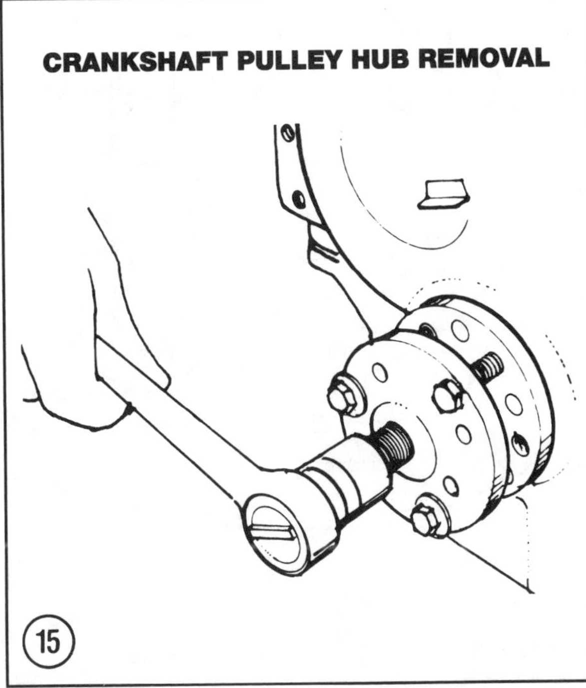

15

1. Loosen the alternator drive belt and the power steering pump drive belt (if so equipped). Remove the belts from around the crankshaft pulley.
2. Remove the screws attaching the pulley and harmonic balancer to the hub, then remove the pulley and balancer.

NOTE
Attach the puller to the hub in Step 3 using 3 3/8–24 × 2 in. screws.

3. Attach puller part No. J-6978-E, or equivalent, to the pulley hub and pull the hub from the crankshaft. See **Figure 15**.
4. Before installing the crankshaft pulley hub:
   a. Lubricate the lip of the seal in the front cover with clean engine oil.
   b. Clean the seal surface of the pulley hub.
   c. Lubricate the seal surface of the pulley hub with clean engine oil.
   d. Lubricate the crankshaft and inner bore of the pulley hub with clean engine oil.
5. Attach the installing tool part No. J-5590 to the pulley hub.
6. Position the pulley hub and tool against the crankshaft with the keyway aligned with the key.
7. Drive the pulley and balancer hub onto the crankshaft until fully seated. See **Figure 16**, typical.
8. Remove the installing tool and attach the balancer and pulley. The 2 3/8 in. holes and the 5/16 in. holes in the balancer and pulley must be aligned for the timing mark to be correctly located.
9. Reinstall and adjust the drive belts.
10. If the front mounting bracket was removed, reinstall it and detach the hoist.

TIMING GEAR COVER AND SEAL

Cover Removal/Installation

1. If engine is being serviced in the boat, attach a suitable hoist to support the front of the engine and remove the front mount bracket.

2. Remove the crankshaft pulley, balancer and pulley hub as described in this chapter.
3. Unbolt and remove the circulating pump pulley.
4. Drain the oil from the engine, detach the drain tube from the oil pan, then unbolt and remove the oil pan from the engine.
5. Unbolt and remove the front cover from the engine block. Remove and discard the gasket.
6. Remove the old seal from the cover and install a new seal using seal driver part No. J-23042. See **Figure 17**.
7. Install the cover using a new front cover gasket. Coat both sides of the gasket with light grease and stick the gasket to the front of the engine.
8. Center the cover over the crankshaft using centering tool part No. J-23042.
9. Tighten the cover retaining screws to the torque listed in **Table 2**.
10. Tighten the oil pan retaining screws to the torque listed in **Table 2**.
11. Install the crankshaft pulley, balancer and pulley hub as described in this chapter.
12. Refer to Chapter Three to service the engine with oil.

Seal Replacement

The seal can be replaced without removing the front cover. If the cover is removed and seal replacement is necessary, support the cover on a clean workbench and perform Steps 2-4.

1. Remove the crankshaft pulley, harmonic balancer and hub as described in this chapter.
2. Pry the old seal from the cover using a large screwdriver. Work carefully to prevent damage to the cover seal surface.
3. Clean the seal recess in the cover with solvent and blow dry with compressed air.
4. Position a new seal in the cover recess with its open end facing the inside of the cover. Drive the seal into place using installer part No. J-23042. See **Figure 17**.

TENSIONER DAMPER INSTALLATION

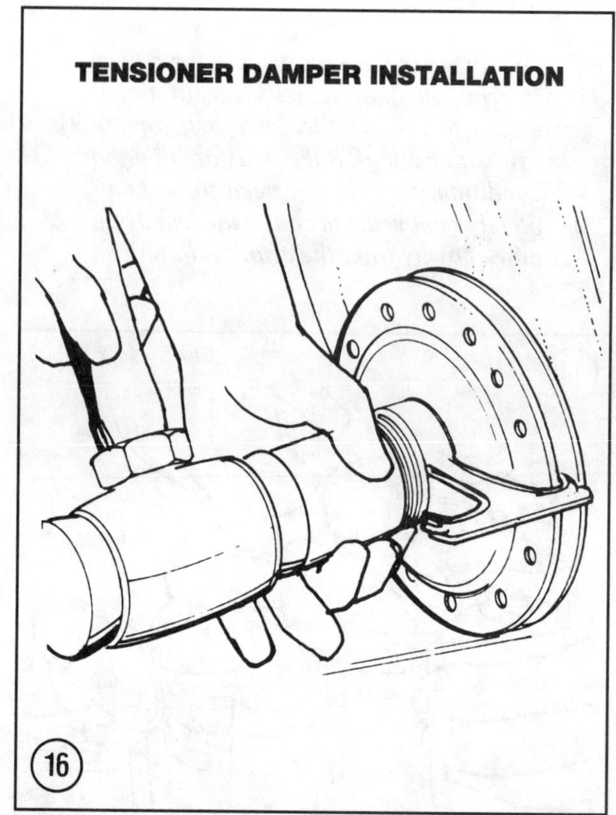

16

17

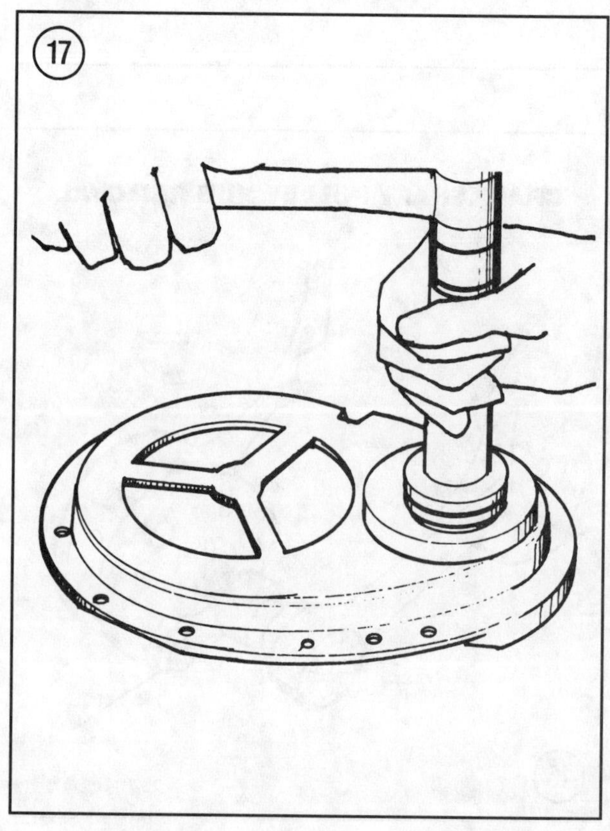

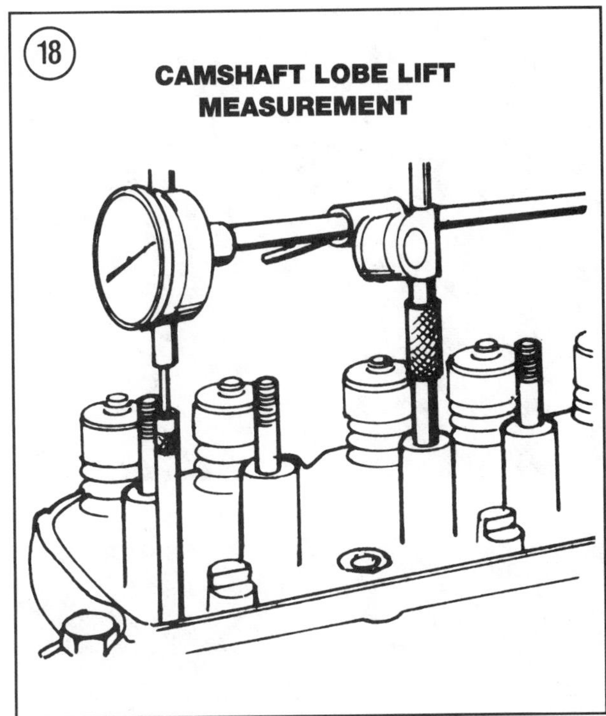

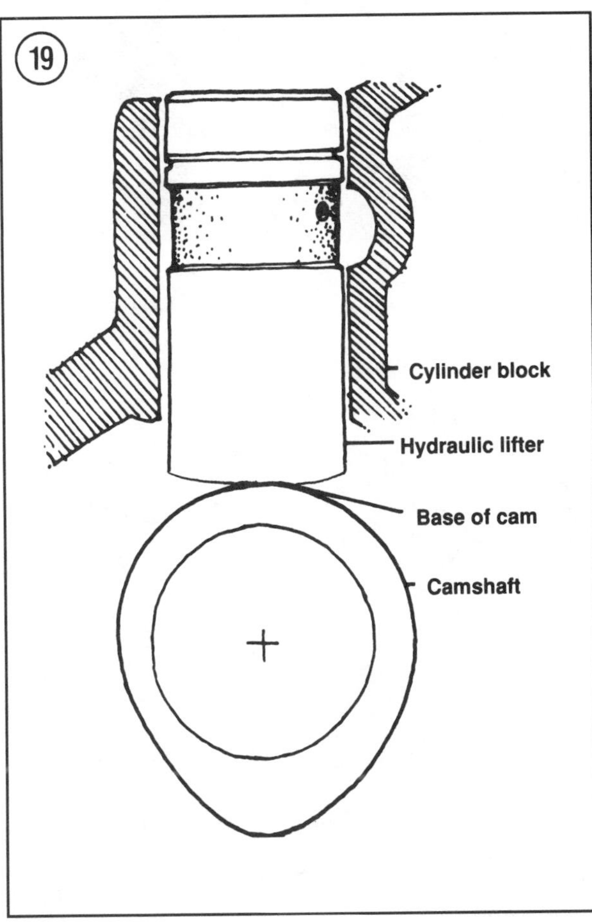

5. Reinstall the crankshaft pulley, balancer and hub as described in this chapter.

CAMSHAFT

Lobe Lift Measurement

Camshaft lobe lift can be measured with the camshaft in the cylinder block and the cylinder head in place.

1. Remove the rocker arm cover as described in this chapter.
2. Remove the rocker arm assemblies as described in this chapter.
3. Remove the spark plugs. See Chapter Four.
4. Attach a dial indicator to the cylinder head with its plunger contacting the end of 1 pushrod. Use a piece of rubber tubing to hold the dial indicator plunger in place against the center of the pushrod. See **Figure 18**, typical.
5. Rotate the crankshaft in the normal direction of rotation until the valve lifter seats against the heel or base circle of the cam (**Figure 19**). This positions the pushrod at its lowest point.
6. Set the dial indicator at zero, slowly rotate the crankshaft until the pushrod reaches its maximum travel and note the movement measured by the dial indicator.
7. Compare the measured movement of the pushrod with the specification listed in **Table 1**. Movement less than specified indicates the cam lobe is worn.
8. Repeat Steps 4-6 for each pushrod. If all lobes are within specifications in Step 6, reinstall the rocker arm assemblies and adjust the valves as described in this chapter.
9. If 1 or more lobes are worn beyond specification, replace the camshaft as described in this chapter.
10. Remove the dial indicator and reverse Steps 1-3.

Removal/Installation

1. Remove the rocker arm cover as described in this chapter.
2. Crank the engine until the No. 1 piston is at the top of its compression stroke. The timing mark on the pulley/balancer will align with the TDC mark on the timing gear cover (**Figure 12**) and the distributor rotor will point to the No. 1 spark plug terminal in the distributor cap.
3. Remove the distributor as described in Chapter Eleven.
4. Remove the timing gear cover as described in this chapter.
5. Remove the fuel pump. See Chapter Nine.
6. Loosen the rocker arm adjusting nut, twist the arm away from the pushrod, then withdraw the pushrod. Identify each pushrod so that it can be reinstalled in its original location with the same end toward the top.

NOTE
A rack can be made or purchased to hold the pushrods in the same order and with the same end down as originally installed. Marks on the rack will identify the front of the engine.

7. Repeat Step 6 to remove the remaining pushrods. Separate and identify each pushrod so they can be reinstalled correctly.
8. Remove the engine side cover (**Figure 20**) and discard the gasket.

NOTE
A rack can be made or purchased to hold the lifters in the same order as originally installed. Marks on the rack will identify the front of the engine.

9. Remove the valve lifters with a pencil-type magnet or lifter removing tool. Identify each lifter so it can be reinstalled in its original location. **Figure 21** shows 1 lifter removed.
10. Rotate the camshaft to align the timing gear marks (**Figure 22**).

20

21

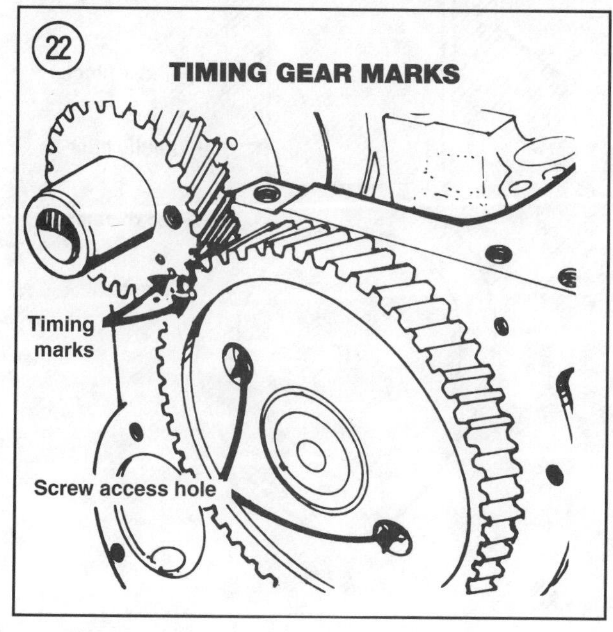

11. Work through the screw access holes in the camshaft gear (**Figure 22**) and remove the 2 camshaft thrust plate screws.

CAUTION
Do not cock, tip or drop the camshaft while withdrawing it from the cylinder block bores in Step 12. The camshaft or its bearing surfaces can be damaged by not withdrawing the camshaft straight out.

12. Carefully pull the camshaft straight from the front of the engine with a rotating motion while supporting the shaft to avoid damage to the camshaft bearings.
13. Installation is the reverse of removal. Observe the following:

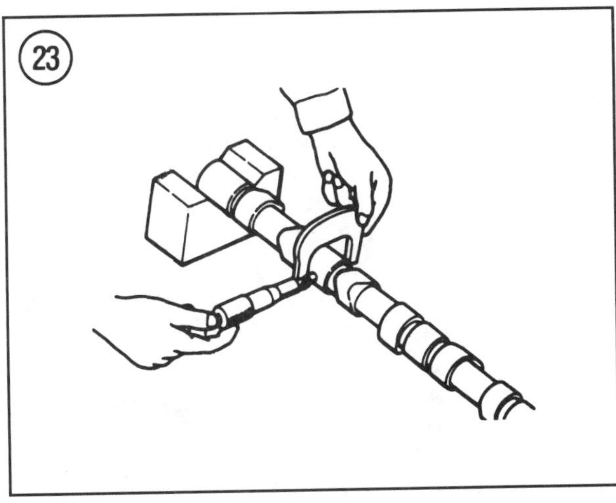

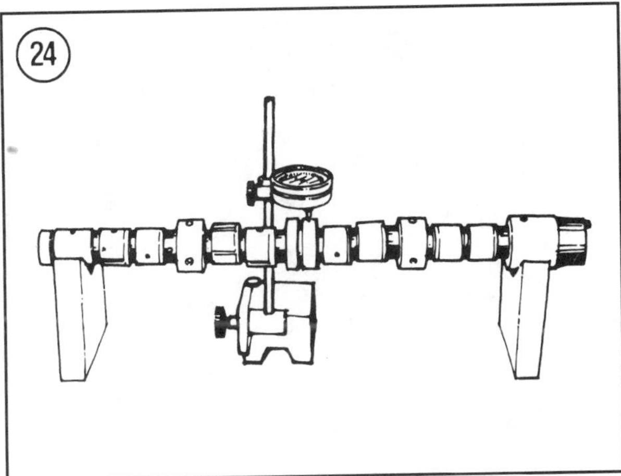

a. Coat the camshaft lobes with GM Super Engine Oil Supplement (part No. 1051858 or equivalent).
b. Lubricate the cam journals with clean engine oil before reinstalling in the block.
c. Check gear runout and backlash as described in this chapter.
d. Coat the bottom of each lifter with Molykote or equivalent before installing.
e. If a new camshaft or any new lifters have been installed, GM Super Engine Oil Supplement lubricant (part No. 1051858 or equivalent) should be added to the oil when refilling.

6

Inspection

1. Inspect the bottom (cam contact surface) of each lifter. The surface should be smooth, polished and slightly convex (curved out). The entire surface should be shiny, indicating the lifter has been rotating freely. If any lifter is galled, chipped, worn, or otherwise damaged by normal operation, the camshaft should also be replaced.
2. Inspect the camshaft journals and lobes for wear or scoring.

NOTE
If you do not have precision measuring equipment, a properly equipped machine shop should perform Steps 3 and 4.

3. Measure the camshaft journal diameters using a micrometer (**Figure 23**). Compare measurements with the specification listed in **Table 1**.
4. Suspend the camshaft between V-blocks and check for runout using a dial indicator (**Figure 24**). Compare any measured runout with the maximum specification listed in **Table 1**.
5. Check the distributor drive gear for excessive wear or damage.
6. Replace the camshaft if:
   a. Any wear is evident while inspecting the camshaft in Step 2.

b. One or more journals do not meet the specification measured in Step 3.

c. Runout measured in Step 4 exceeds the limit listed in **Table 1**.

d. The distributor drive gear is damaged.

7. Check the camshaft gear and thrust plate for wear or damage. Insert a flat feeler gauge between the thrust plate and camshaft to measure end play. See **Figure 25**. If end play exceeds the specification listed in **Table 1**, press the gear from the camshaft as described in this chapter and replace the thrust plate.

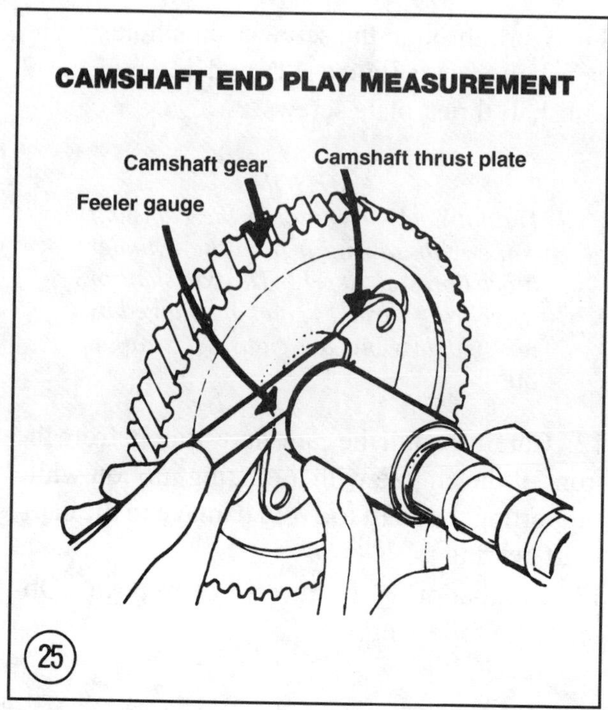

Camshaft/Crankshaft Gear Runout and Backlash

1. Attach a dial indicator to the cylinder block as shown in **Figure 26** with the plunger contacting the face of the gear. Rotate the camshaft (and gear) 360° to check gear runout.
2. Check runout of the crankshaft gear with the same procedure used for the camshaft gear in Step 1.
3. Attach a dial indicator as shown in **Figure 27** with the plunger contacting a gear tooth, then rock the camshaft gear back and forth to check gear backlash.
4. Compare the measurements with the specifications listed in **Table 2**.
   a. Replace the camshaft gear if the runout measured in Step 1 exceeds the specification listed in **Table 2**.
   b. Replace the crankshaft gear if the runout measured in Step 2 exceeds the specification listed in **Table 2**.
   c. Replace both gears if the backlash between gear teeth measured in Step 3 exceeds the specification listed in **Table 2**.

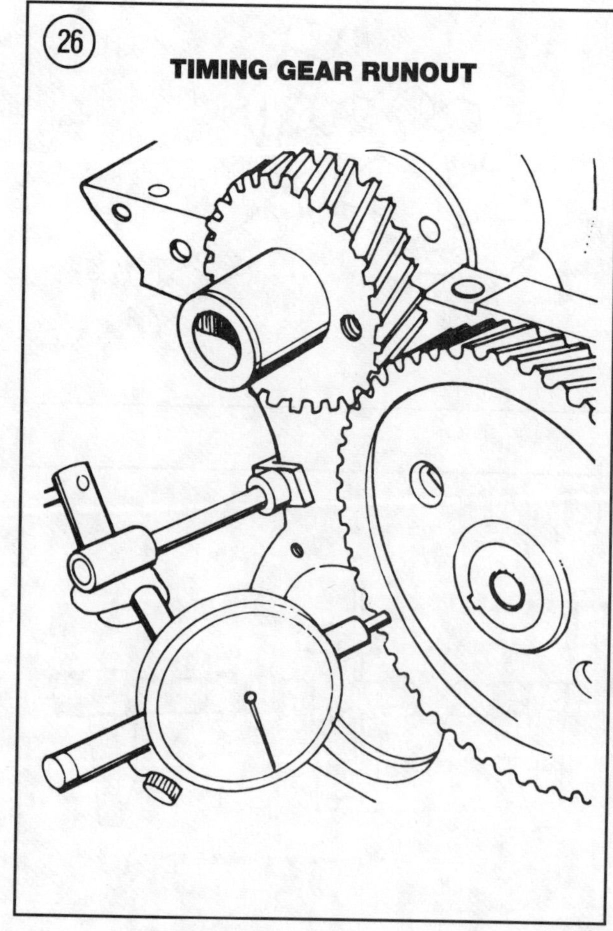

Bearing Replacement

Camshaft bearings can be replaced without complete engine disassembly. Replace bearings in complete sets. Camshaft bearings should only be removed and installed using a piloted driver.

1. Remove the camshaft as described in this chapter.

2. Remove the crankshaft as described in this chapter. The pistons can remain in the cylinder bores, but the connecting rods must be secured to the side of the engine to keep them out of the way while replacing the cam bearings.

3. Drive the camshaft welch plug from the rear of the cylinder block.

4. Use a piloted driver to remove the center bearing. The front and rear bearings can be removed by driving them toward the inside.

   a. Index the tool pilot in the front cam bearing. Install the puller screw through the pilot.
   b. Install the tool pilot with its shoulder facing the front intermediate bearing and the threads engaging the bearing.
   c. Hold the puller screw with 1 wrench. Turn the nut with a second wrench until the bearing is pulled from its bore. See **Figure 28**, typical.
   d. When the bearing is removed from the bore, remove the tool and bearing from puller screw.

NOTE
The outer diameter of the rear bearing may be larger than the front and center bearings. The center bearing should be installed first to reduce the chance of damage to the front or rear bearings by the installing tool.

CAUTION
Improper alignment of the rear bearing can cause a restriction and reduce the flow of oil to the valve train components. The oil holes in the bearings must align with the holes in the cylinder block. Since the oil holes are in the top of the bearing bore in the cylinder block, align the bearing oil hole with the hole in the bearing bore, then mark the opposite side of the bearing and bearing bore to assist in oil hole alignment.

5. Pull the new center bearing into position using the removal/installation tool. Make certain the bearing and cylinder block oil holes are aligned.

CAUTION
Make sure the front camshaft bearing does not block the timing gear oil nozzle.

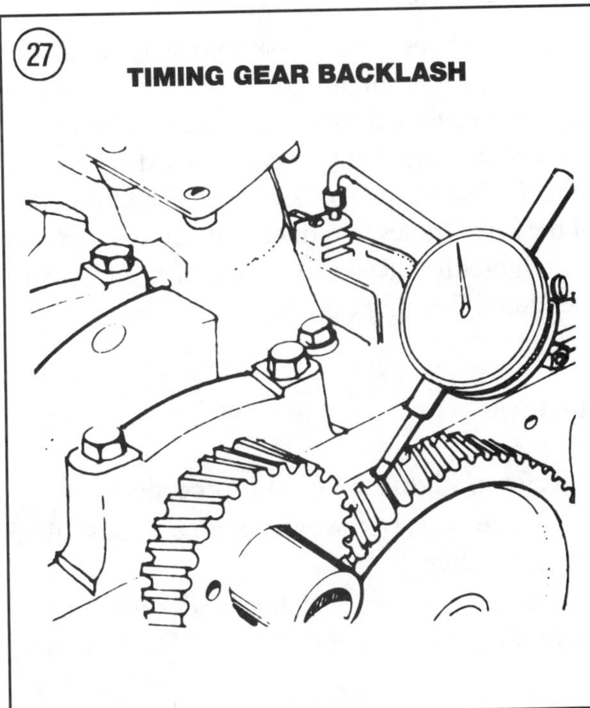

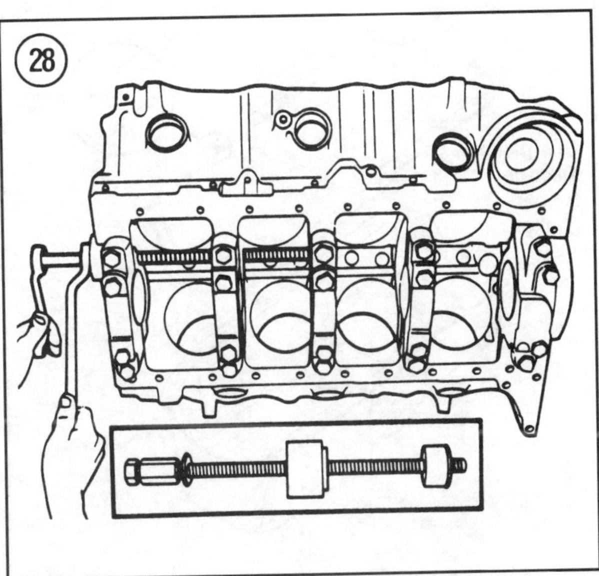

6

The bearing must be recessed approximately 1/8 in. (3.2 mm) from the face of the cylinder block. Note that late models do not use the timing gear oil nozzle and a plug is used to seal the nozzle hole.

6. Use a pilot to drive the front bearing into the bore from the front. Align the hole in the bearing with the oil hole in the block.
7. Use a pilot to drive the rear bearing into the bore from the rear. Align the hole in the bearing with the oil hole in the block. Drive the bearing into the bore until the forward edge of the bearing is flush with the forward edge of the block bore.
8. Wipe a new camshaft welch plug with sealer and install it flush to 1/32 in. (0.8 mm) deep to maintain a level surface on the rear of the block.

Timing Gear Replacement

If inspection indicates that the camshaft, gear or thrust plate should be replaced, press the gear from the camshaft using a press and appropriate size support sleeve. Position the thrust plate so it will not be damaged by the Woodruff key in the shaft when it separates from the gear. If the gear is to be reused, support its hub before applying pressure or it will be ruined. Install the camshaft gear by pressing it onto the shaft, then check end play as described in *Inspection* in this chapter.

OIL PAN

Ease of oil pan removal will depend on the installation within a given boat. In some cases, the oil pan can be removed without removing the engine. In others, engine removal is required to provide sufficient working space and clearance for oil pan removal.

Oil Leaks

Constant oil leakage around the oil pan may be caused by any of several factors:

a. Excessive torquing of the oil pan screws (squeezing the 2-piece gasket out and causing the end seals to split).
b. Gaskets with insufficient crush (contact) in certain areas to make a good seal.
c. Defective or improperly installed seals.
d. Improper machining of the crankshaft and/or block.

A soft rubber 1 piece gasket is used, which fills small gaps that might leak, but RTV sealer can also be used to seal the front and rear of the block. Do not use the 4 piece gasket used on earlier models. Metal spacers are located around each of the screw holes to reduce damage from excessive tightening. Refer to **Table 2** for the recommended tightening torque.

Removal

Refer to **Figure 29** for this procedure.

1. If necessary, remove the engine as described in this chapter.
2. Place a suitable container under the oil pan drain plug. Remove the plug and let the crank-

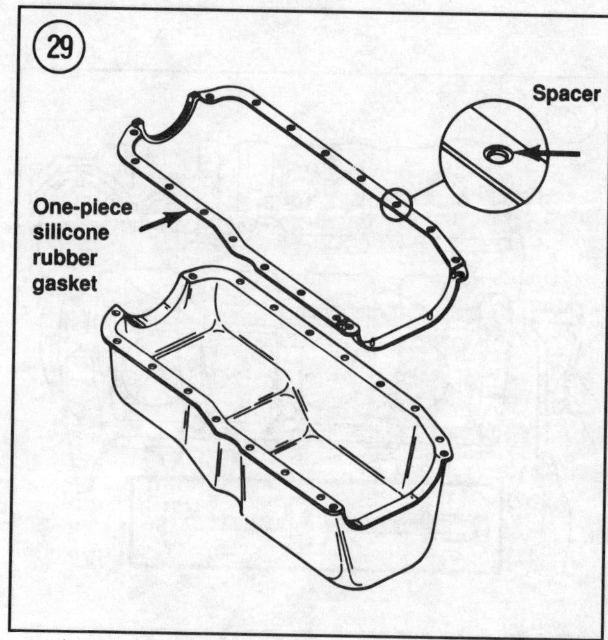

case drain completely, then reinstall the drain plug.

NOTE

If the engine is removed and attached to an engine stand, rotate the engine 180° to place the oil pan in an upright position.

3. Remove the starter motor. See Chapter Eleven.
4. Remove the screws attaching the oil pan, then carefully separate the oil pan from the cylinder block.
5. Remove and discard the gasket.

Inspection and Cleaning

1. Clean any gasket residue from the engine block, rear main bearing cap, front cover and the oil pan sealing flange.
2. Clean the pan thoroughly in solvent and check for dents or warped sealing surfaces. Straighten or replace the pan as required.

Installation

Refer to **Figure 29** for this procedure.

1. Install a new gasket on the pan flanges. Insert a screw on each side and at each end of the pan to position the gasket.
2. Carefully position the oil pan against the engine block, make sure the gasket is not misaligned and tighten the screws inserted in Step 1 finger-tight.
3. Install the remaining screws and tighten all of them to the torque specification listed in **Table 2**. Work from the center outward in each direction.
4. Reinstall the starter motor. See Chapter Eleven.
5. Install the engine in the boat as described in this chapter and fill the crankcase with oil (Chapter Four).

OIL PUMP

Removal/Installation

1. Remove the oil pan as described in this chapter.

NOTE

The oil pump pickup tube and screen are a press fit in the pump housing and should not be removed unless replacement is required.

2. Loosen the bolt and remove the attaching nut retaining the oil pickup tube bracket.
3. Remove the 2 screws attaching the oil pump to the bottom of the block. Remove the oil pump, gasket and pickup tube/screen as an assembly.
4. Position the pump against the block with the slot in the pump shaft aligned with the drive tang of the distributor shaft.
5. Tighten the screws attaching the pump and pickup tube bracket fasteners to the specifications listed in **Table 2**.
6. Install the oil pan as described in this chapter.

6

Disassembly/Assembly

Refer to **Figure 30** for this procedure.

1. Remove the cover screws, cover and gasket. Discard the gasket.
2. Mark the gear teeth to ensure reassembly with identical gear indexing then remove the idler and drive gear and shaft from the body.
3. Remove the pressure regulator valve pin, regulator, spring and valve.

CAUTION

Do not remove the pickup tube/screen assembly unless it needs replacement. Secure the pump body in a soft-jawed vise and separate the tube from the cover. Do not twist, shear or collapse the tube when installing it. If the pickup tube/screen assembly was removed, install a new 1. Secure the pump body in a soft-jawed vise, apply sealer to the new tube and gently tap it in place using a soft-faced mallet.

4. Lubricate all parts thoroughly with clean engine oil before reassembly.
5. Assembly is the reverse of disassembly. Index the previously affixed marks on the gears, then install the gasket and cover.
6. Rotate the pump drive shaft by hand to check for smooth operation. Tighten the cover bolts to the torque specified in **Table 2**.

Inspection

NOTE
The pump assembly and gears are serviced as an assembly. If either one is worn or damaged, replace the entire pump. No wear specifications are provided by the manufacturer.

1. Clean all parts thoroughly in solvent. Brush the inside of the body and the pressure regulator chamber to remove all dirt and metal particles. Dry with compressed air, if available.
2. Check the pump body and cover for cracks or excessive wear.
3. Check the pump gears for damage or excessive wear.
4. Check the drive gear shaft-to-body fit for excessive looseness.
5. Check the inside of the pump cover for wear that could allow oil to leak around the ends of the gears.
6. Check the pressure regulator valve for a proper fit.

CYLINDER HEAD

Removal

Perform Steps 1-7 if the engine is in the boat. If engine has been removed from the boat, begin with Step 8.

1. Open the engine block drain valves and drain all water from the block.
2. Remove the manifold assembly as described in this chapter.
3. Detach the fuel line support clamps from the cylinder head and remove the fuel line.
4. Disconnect the cooling hoses from the thermostat housing (**Figure 31**).
5. Detach the wire from the temperature sender, then unbolt and remove the thermostat housing.
6. Unbolt and remove the ignition coil and its bracket.

NOTE
It is not necessary to remove the spark plugs to remove the cylinder head, but the plugs are easier to remove before the head is removed. Also, the plugs

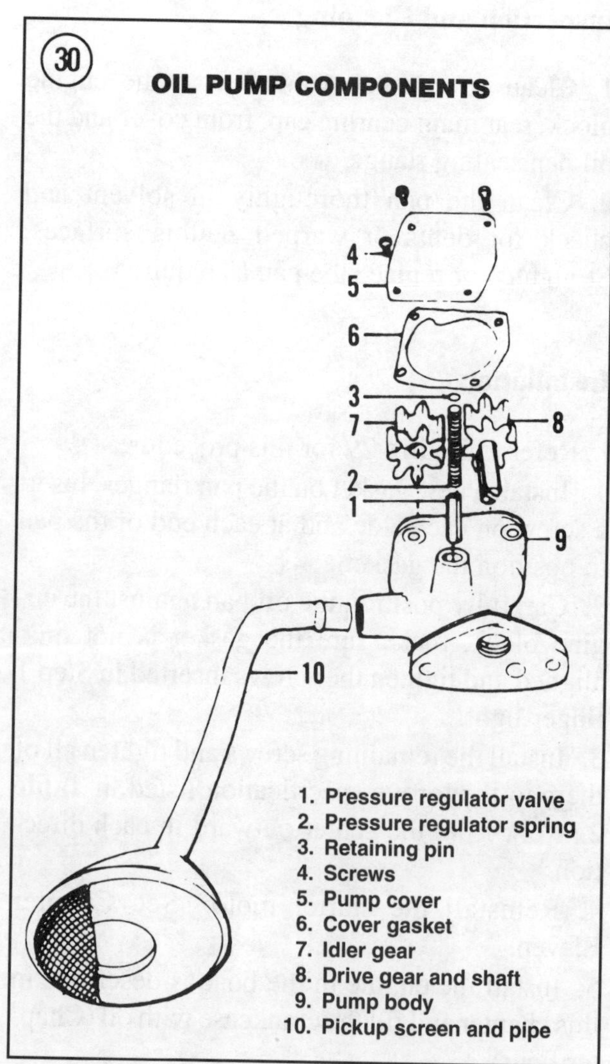

can be easily broken during cylinder headremoval.

7. Detach the spark plug cables and remove the spark plugs.
8. Unbolt and remove the rocker arm cover as described in this chapter.
9. Loosen the rocker arm adjusting nuts, twist the arms away from the pushrods, then withdraw the pushrods. Identify each pushrod so they can be reinstalled in their original location with the same end toward the top.

NOTE
A rack can be made or purchased to hold the pushrods in the same order and with the same end down as originally installed. Marks on the rack will identify the front of the engine.

10. Loosen the cylinder head bolts, beginning with those in the center and working toward the ends.
11. Remove the bolts, then carefully lift the head from the engine block and move it to a workbench.

NOTE
It may be necessary to bump the head with a soft-faced hammer to break the gasket seal.

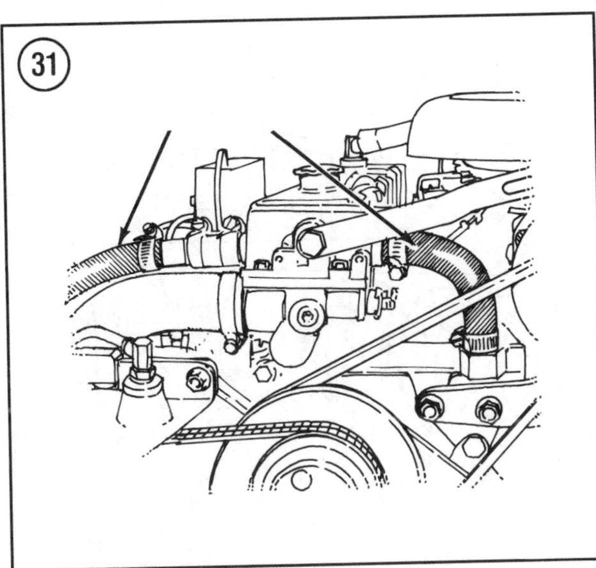

CAUTION
Be careful to place the head in a safe location and in a safe position to prevent damage to the valves or gasket surfaces.

12. Remove and discard the head gasket. Clean all gasket residue from the thermostat housing, rocker arm cover, cylinder head and block.

Decarbonizing

Check for any sign of oil or water leaks before cleaning the cylinder head.

1. Before removing the valves, clean all deposits from the combustion chambers, intake ports and exhaust ports. Use a fine wire brush dipped in solvent or make a scraper from hardwood. Be careful not to scratch or gouge the combustion chambers.
2. After all carbon is removed from the combustion chambers and ports, clean the entire head with solvent.
3. Clean carbon from the tops of the pistons.
4. Clean the pushrod guides, valve guide bores and all bolt holes. Use a cleaning solvent to remove dirt and grease.
5. Remove the valves as described in this chapter.
6. Clean the valves with a fine wire brush or buffing wheel.

Inspection

1. Check the cylinder head for any sign of oil or water leaks before cleaning.
2. Clean the cylinder head thoroughly in solvent. While cleaning, look for cracks or other visible signs of damage. Look for corrosion or foreign material in the oil and water passages. Clean the passages with a stiff spiral brush, then blow them out with compressed air.
3. Check the cylinder head studs for damage and replace if necessary.

4. Check the threaded rocker arm studs for damaged threads. Replace if necessary.
5. Check for warpage of the cylinder head-to-block gasket surface with a straightedge and feeler gauge (**Figure 32**). Measure diagonally, as well as end to end. If the gap exceeds 0.003 in. (0.08 mm) over any 6 in. (15 cm) span, or 0.007 in. (0.18 mm) overall, have the head resurfaced by a machine shop. If head resurfacing is necessary, do not remove more than 0.010 in. (0.25 mm). Replace the head if it is necessary to remove a greater amount to true the gasket surface.

Installation

1. Make sure the gasket surfaces (on the cylinder head and block) and bolt holes are clean. Dirt in the bolt holes or on the bolt threads will affect bolt torque.
2. Recheck all visible oil and water passages for cleanliness.

> CAUTION
> *Use only the marine cylinder head gasket available from Volvo Penta. Damage may result from installing an automotive head gasket.*

3. Fit a new head gasket over the dowels in the block.
4. Carefully position the head onto the cylinder block, engaging the dowel pins. Do not damage the gasket by sliding the cylinder head into position. Do not crush the gasket by dropping the head on 1 side or 1 corner.
5. Wipe all head bolt threads with Permatex or equivalent sealer. Install and tighten the head bolts finger-tight.
6. Tighten the cylinder head retaining screws evenly using a 3-step procedure as follows:
   a. Tighten the head bolts in the sequence shown in **Figure 33** until the Step 1 torque specified in **Table 2** is reached. Make sure that all screws are tightened evenly before continuing to the next step.

32

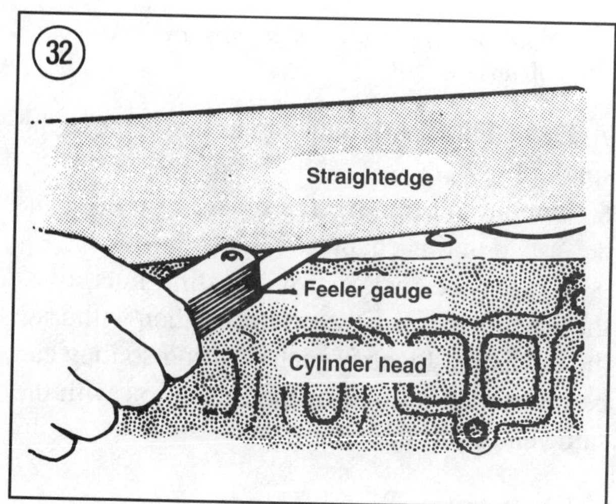

33

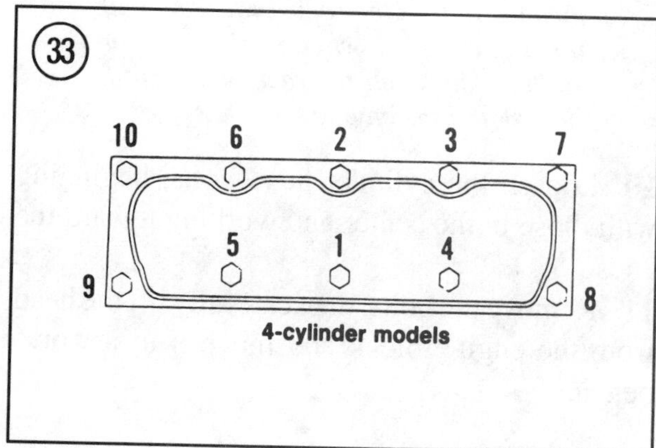

34

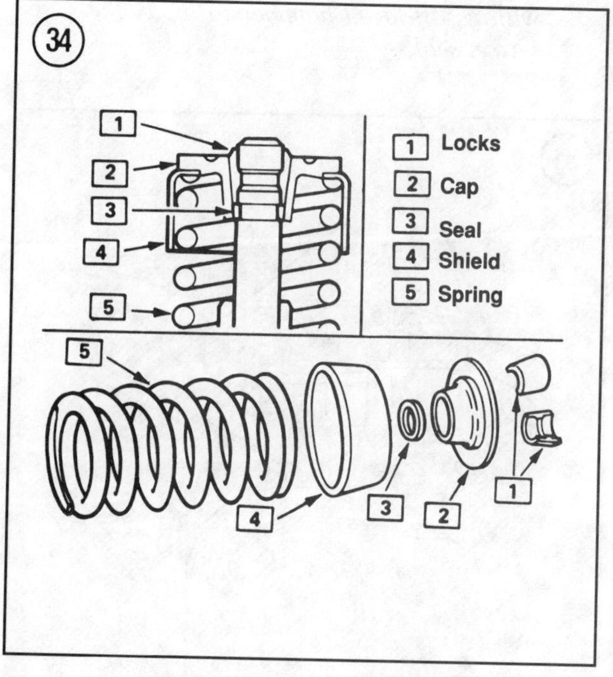

b. Tighten the head bolts to the torque specified in **Table 2**, Step 2, in the sequence shown in **Figure 33**.

c. Tighten the head bolts to the torque specified in **Table 2**, Step 3, in the sequence shown in **Figure 33**.

7. If the engine is in the boat, reverse Steps 1-9 of *Removal* in this chapter to complete installation. If engine is out of the boat, reverse Step 8 and Step 9 of *Removal* in this chapter. Adjust the rocker arms as described under *Valve Clearance Adjustment* in this chapter. Check and adjust ignition timing as described in Chapter Four.

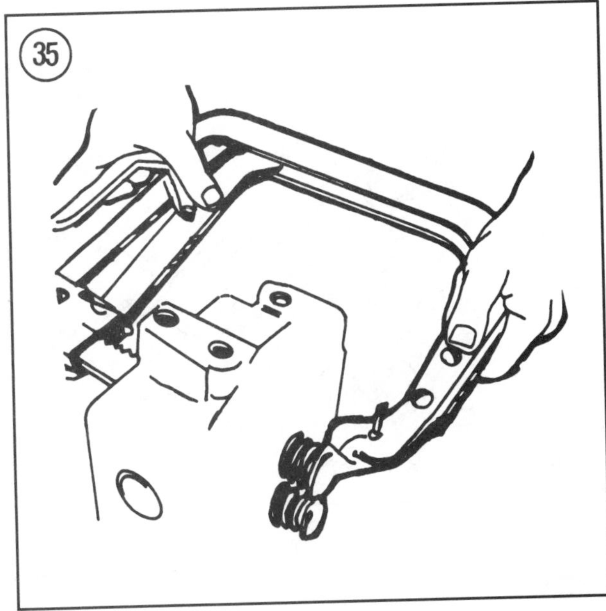

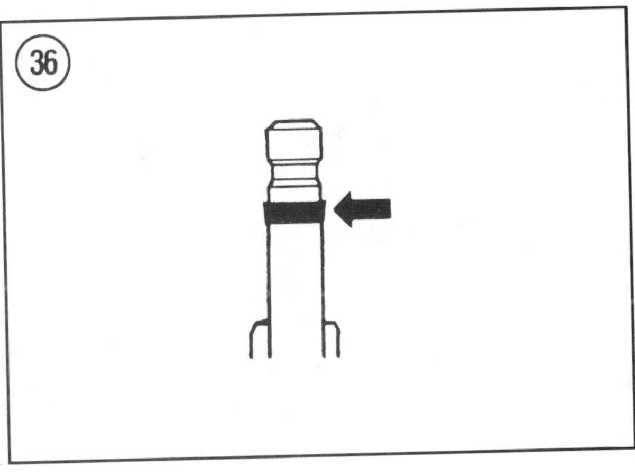

VALVES AND VALVE SEATS

Servicing the valves, guides and valve seats must be done by a dealer or machine shop, with trained technicians and the proper machine tools. A general practice for many who do their own service is to remove the cylinder head, perform all disassembly except valve removal and take the head to a dealership or machine shop for inspection and service. Since the cost is low relative to the required effort and equipment, this is usually the best approach, even for experienced mechanics.

Valve Removal

Refer to **Figure 34** for this procedure.

1. Remove the cylinder head as described in this chapter.
2. Remove the rocker arm assemblies as described in this chapter.

NOTE

Clean and inspect the cylinder head as described in this chapter before removing the valves.

3. Compress the valve spring with a compressor like the one shown in **Figure 35**. Remove the valve keys, then release the spring tension.
4. Remove the valve spring cap, shield and spring assembly.
5. Remove and discard the valve stem seal. See **Figure 36**. Check the cylinder head and remove the shim or spacer located under the spring, if used.

CAUTION

Remove any burrs from the valve stem lock grooves before removing the valve or the valve guide will be damaged. The valve stem will develop a small burr as a result of the locks pounding against the groove.

6. Remove the valve and repeat Steps 3-5 on each remaining valve.

7. Arrange the parts in order so they can be returned to their original positions when reassembled.

Inspection

1. Clean the valves with special tool part No. J-8101 or equivalent. Discard any cracked, warped or burned valves.
2. Measure the valve stems at the top, center and bottom for wear. A machine shop can do this when the valves are ground. Also measure the length of each valve and the diameter of each valve head.

> NOTE
>
> *Check the thickness of the valve edge or margin after the valves have been ground. See **Figure 37**. Discard any valve with a margin of less than 1/32 in. (0.8 mm).*

3. Remove all carbon and varnish from the valve guides using a stiff spiral wire brush.

> NOTE
>
> *The next step assumes that all valve stems have been measured and are within specification. Replace valves with worn stems before performing this step.*

4. Insert each valve into the guide from which it was removed. Holding the valve just slightly off its seat, rock it back and forth in a direction parallel to the rocker arms. This is the direction in which the greatest wear normally occurs. If the valve stem rocks more than slightly, the valve guide is probably worn.
5. If there is any doubt about valve guide condition after performing Step 4, have the valve guide and valve stem measured and compare the results with clearance listed in **Table 1**. Worn guides must be reamed (**Figure 38**) for the next oversize valve stem.
6. Test the valve springs under load on a spring tester (**Figure 39**). Replace any springs that test below the minimum limit listed in **Table 1**.

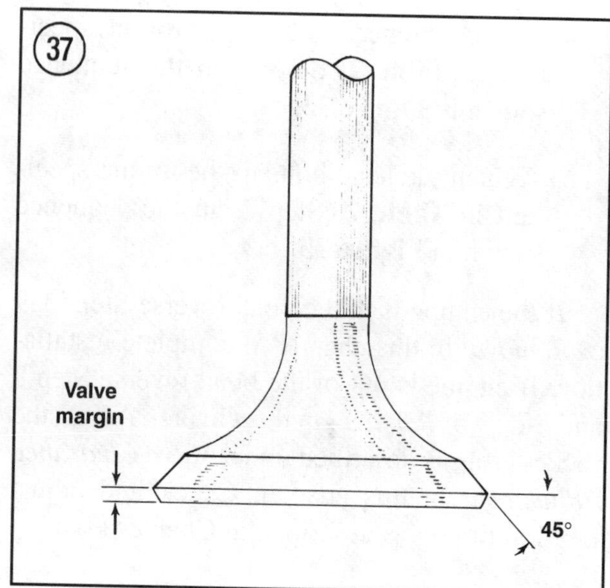

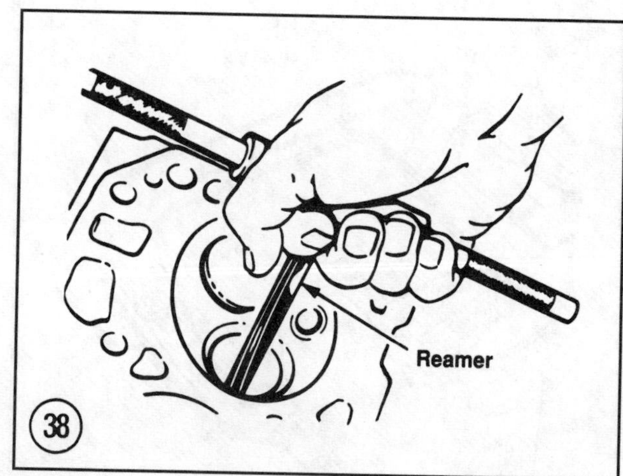

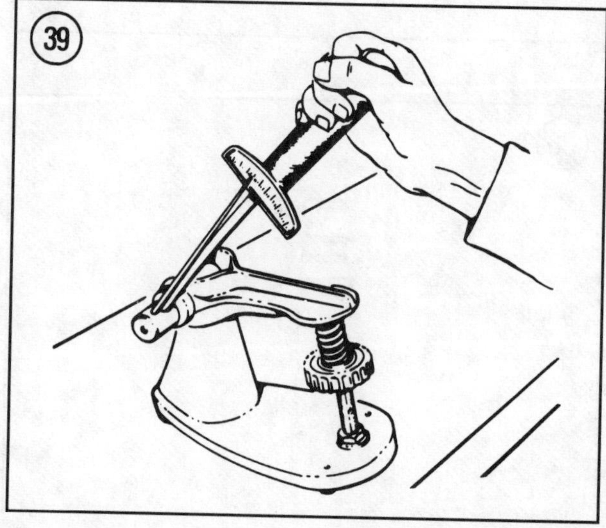

7. Inspect the valve seat inserts. If worn or burned, they must be reconditioned by a dealer or machine shop. The procedure is, however, described in this chapter.

8. Check each spring on a flat surface with a steel square. See **Figure 40**. Slowly turn the spring 360° and note the space between the top of the coil and the square. Replace the spring if it is not straight.

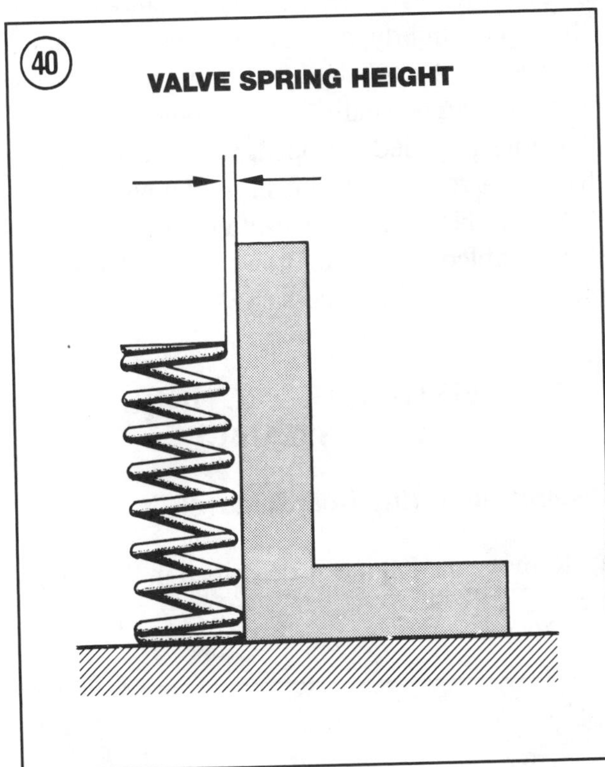

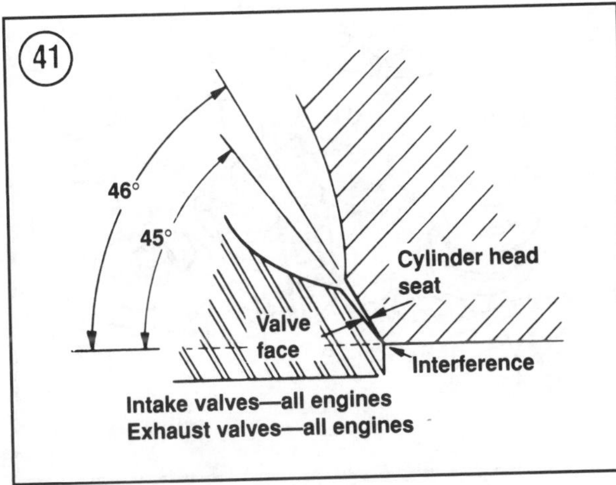

9. Check each valve lifter to make sure it fits freely in the block and that the end that contacts the camshaft lobe is smooth and not worn excessively.

Valve Guide Reaming

Worn valve guides must be reamed to accept a valve with an oversize stem. Valves are available in 3 oversizes for both intake and exhaust valves. Reaming must be done by hand (**Figure 38**) and is a job best left to an experienced machine shop. The valve seat must be refaced after the guide has been reamed.

Valve Seat Reconditioning

1. Cut the valve seats to the specified angle (**Table 1**) with a dressing stone. See **Figure 41**. Remove only enough metal to obtain a good finish.
2. Use stones of larger or smaller angles to obtain the specified seat width as necessary.
3. Coat the corresponding valve face with Prussian blue dye.
4. Insert the valve into the valve guide.
5. Apply light pressure to the valve and rotate it approximately 1/4 turn.
6. Lift the valve out. If it seats properly, the dye will transfer evenly to the valve face.
7. If the dye transfers to the top of the valve face, lower the seat. If it transfers to the bottom of the valve face, raise the seat.

Valve Installation

NOTE
Install all parts in the same positions from which they were removed.

1. Coat the valves with engine oil and install them in the cylinder head.

2. Install new oil seals on each valve. The seal must be flat and not twisted in the valve stem groove. See **Figure 36**.
3. Position the valve spring and damper around the valve guide boss, then install the spring retainer.
4. Compress the spring (**Figure 35**) and install the locks. Make sure both locks seat properly in the upper groove of the valve stem. See **Figure 34**.
5. Measure the installed spring height between the top of the valve seat and the underside of the spring retainer, as shown in **Figure 42**. If height is greater than specification, install a spring seat shim between the spring and the cylinder head, then remeasure the height.

VALVE LIFTERS

Removal/Installation

1. Remove the rocker arm assemblies, pushrods and engine side cover as described in this chapter.

NOTE
A rack can be made or purchased to hold the pushrods and lifters in the same order as originally installed. Marks on the rack will identify the front of the engine.

2. Remove the valve lifters. This can usually be done without special tools, although puller part No. J-3049 will help remove stuck lifters. Identify each lifter so it can be reinstalled in its original location.
3. Installation is the reverse of removal:
   a. Coat the bottom of each lifter with Molykote or equivalent before installing.
   b. Follow the assembly procedures described in this chapter when assembling.
   c. If a new camshaft or any new lifter is installed, add GM Super Engine Oil Supplement lubricant (part No. 1051858 or equivalent) to the oil when refilling.

Inspection

Keep the lifters in proper sequence for installation in their original position in the cylinder block. Clean lifters in solvent and wipe dry with a clean, lint-free cloth. Inspect and test the lifters separately to prevent intermixing of their internal parts. If any part requires replacement, replace the entire lifter.

Inspect the bottom (camshaft contact surface) of each lifter. The surface must be smooth, polished and slightly convex. The entire contact surface must be polished, indicating the lifter has been rotating normally. If the contact surface of any lifter is galled, chipped, worn or damaged, the lifter's respective camshaft lobe will also be damaged. Normally, valve lifters should not be disassembled. They can, however, be disassembled for cleaning if necessary.

PISTON/CONNECTING ROD ASSEMBLY

Piston/Connecting Rod Removal

1. Remove the engine as described in this chapter.

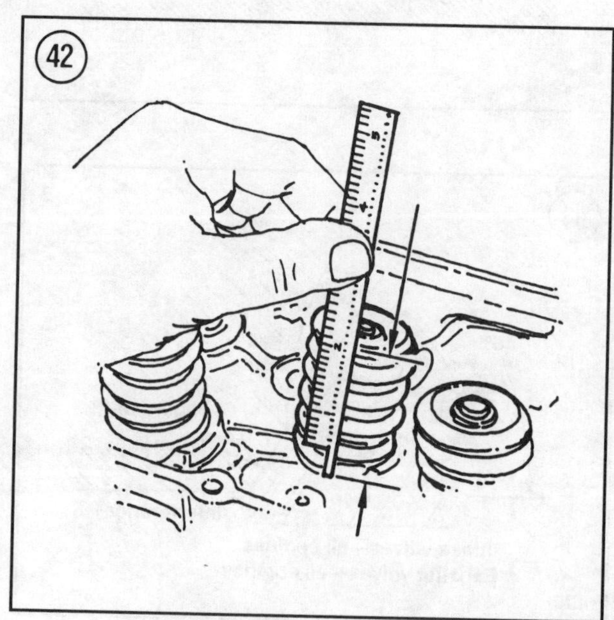

2. Place a suitable container under the oil pan and remove the drain plug. Let the crankcase oil drain, then reinstall the drain plug.
3. Remove the manifold assembly as described in this chapter.
4. Remove the cylinder head as described in this chapter.
5. Remove the oil pan and oil pump as described in this chapter.

CAUTION

Be careful to remove the carbon and cuttings left by the ridge reamer in Step 6 before turning the crankshaft and moving the piston up in the cylinder.

6. Turn the crankshaft until 2 pistons are at bottom dead center. Use a ridge reamer to remove the carbon ridge at the top of the cylinder bores. A ridge reamer can be rented from most tool rental agencies. Clean all shavings from the cylinder bore.
7. Repeat Step 6 for the remaining 2 cylinders and remove the ridge from those cylinders.
8. Turn the crankshaft until 2 of the connecting rods are near the bottom. Measure the side clearance between the connecting rod and the crankshaft journal flange with a flat feeler gauge (**Figure 43**, typical). If the clearance exceeds that listed in **Table 1**, replace the connecting rod during reassembly.
9. Repeat Step 8 for the remaining connecting rods.

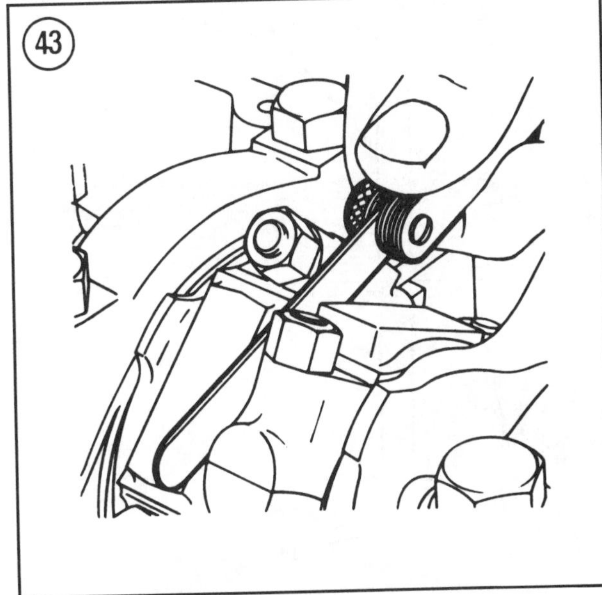

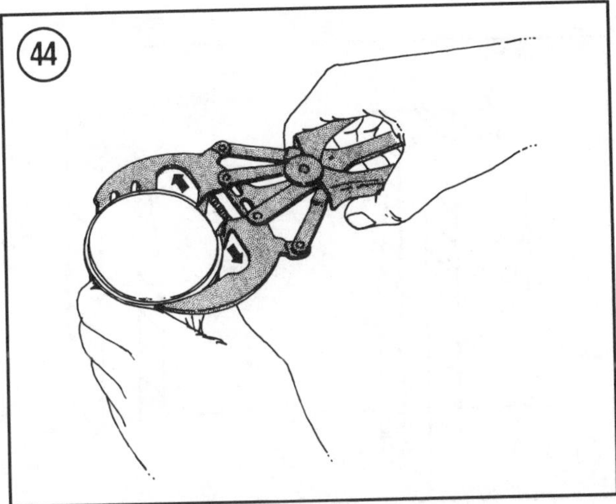

NOTE

Clean the tops of the pistons before removing them from the cylinders and check for cylinder numbers or identifying marks. Also check for cylinder identifying marks on the connecting rod and cap. If marks are not located on each part, use a suitable scribe or marker and mark the cylinder number on the piston, connecting rod and rod cap. The depression on the top of the piston must face toward the front of the engine.

10. Remove the nuts holding the connecting rod cap. Lift off the cap, together with the lower bearing insert.

NOTE

If the connecting rod caps are difficult to remove, tap the studs with a handle of a hammer or similar tool.

11. Use the handle of a hammer to push the piston and connecting rod from the cylinder bore. Be sure to remove the bearing insert.
12. Remove the piston rings with a ring remover (**Figure 44**).

13. Repeat Steps 10-12 for all remaining piston/connecting rods.

Piston Pin Removal/Installation

The piston pins are a press fit in the bores of the connecting rods and a light hand fit in the pistons. Do not press the piston pin from the connecting rod unless removal is required. Removal requires the use of a special support stand, removal/installer tool and an arbor press. This is a job for trained and properly equipped dealership technician or machinist. The piston pin is matched to the piston and the piston and pin are available only as an assembly. The pin should support its own weight in either pin boss when coated with light engine oil with all parts at 60° F (15.6 C). Differences in temperature will give a false indication of clearance.

Piston Clearance Check

Precision measuring equipment and training in its use is required to check this clearance. If you are not properly equipped and trained, have this procedure done at a machine shop.

1. Measure the piston diameter with a micrometer (**Figure 45**) just below the rings at a right angle to the piston pin bore.

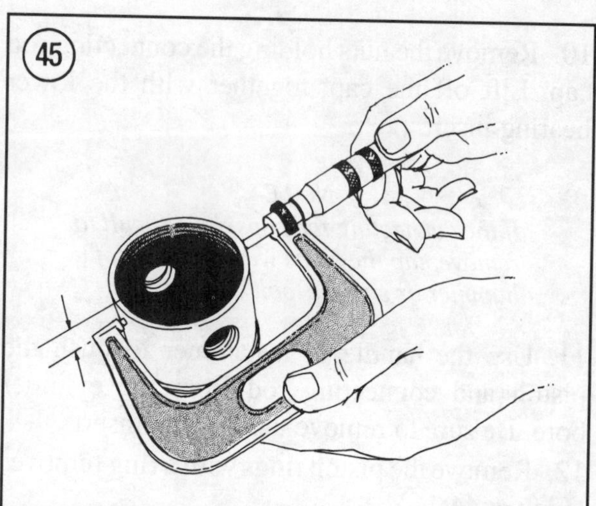

2. Measure the cylinder bore diameter with a bore gauge (**Figure 46**). **Figure 47** shows the points of normal cylinder wear. If the diameter at the top of the ring travel (A, **Figure 47**) exceeds the diameter at the bottom unused part of the cylinder (B, **Figure 47**) by more than

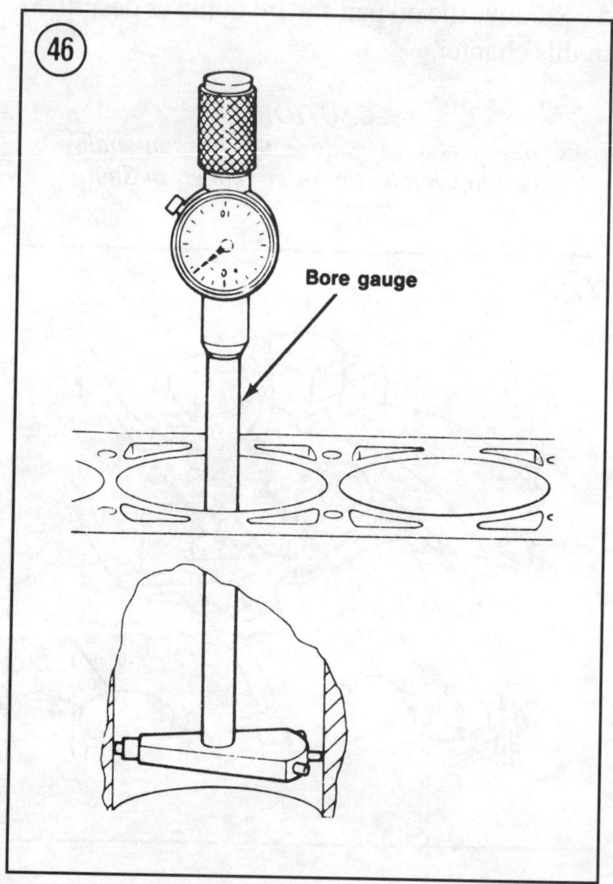

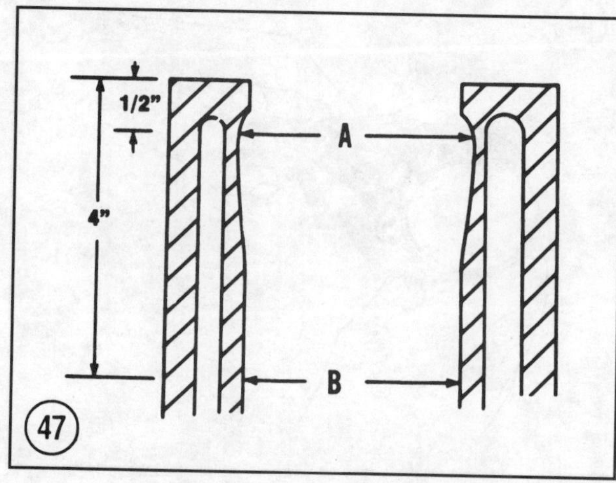

0.003 in. (0.08 mm), the cylinder must be rebored and a new piston/ring assembly installed.

3. Subtract the piston diameter from the largest cylinder bore reading. If it exceeds the specification in **Table 1**, the cylinder must be rebored and an oversized piston installed.

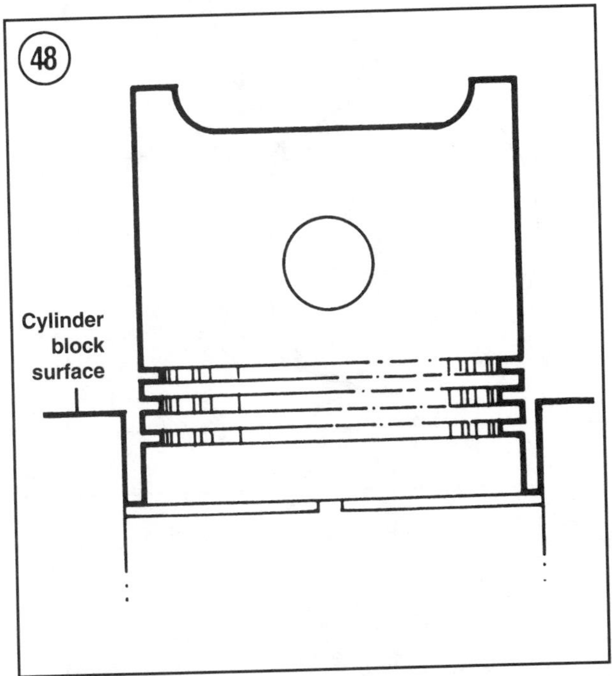

NOTE

Obtain the new piston and measure it to determine the correct cylinder bore oversize diameter.

Piston Ring Fit/Installation

Check the ring gap of each piston ring including new rings.

1. Position the ring at the bottom of the ring travel area and square it by moving it gently with an inverted piston. See **Figure 48**.

NOTE

If the cylinders have not been rebored, check the gap at the bottom of the ring travel, where the cylinder is least worn.

2. Measure the end gap of each ring in the cylinder with a feeler gauge as shown in **Figure 49**. Compare the gap with the specifications listed in **Table 1**. Gaps should never be more than 1/32 in. (0.8 mm).

3. If the measured gap is less than the minimum specification, first check to make sure the rings are correct for the size of the cylinder bore. The ends of new rings can be filed to increase the gap slightly. See **Figure 50**.

6

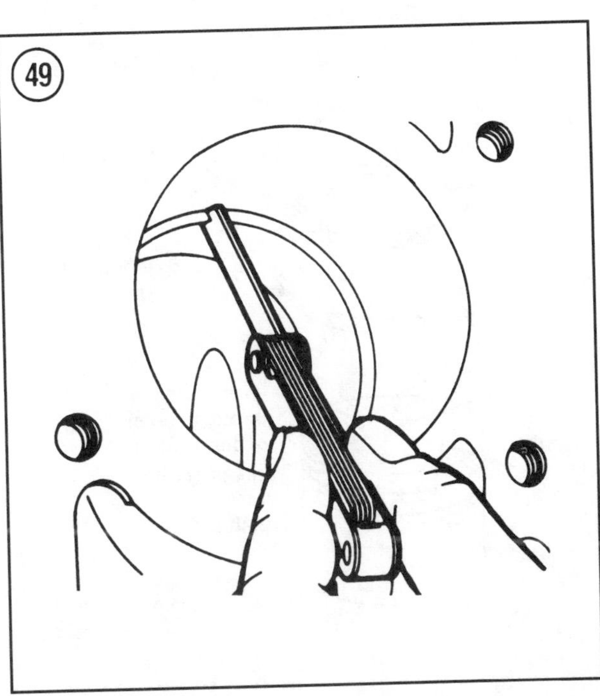

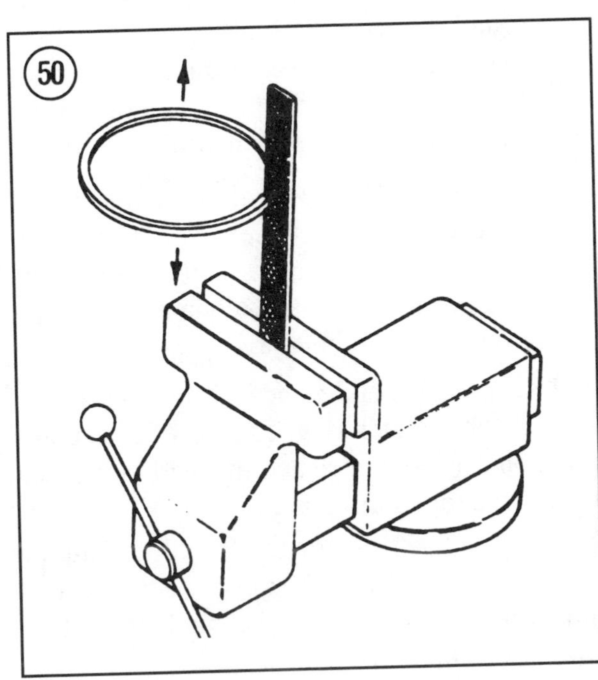

4. If the end gap is too wide, the wrong rings may be installed or the ends of the rings may have been filed too much. If the gap is within limits at the bottom but is too wide at the top of the ring travel, the cylinder is worn (tapered) to the point that it should be rebored and fitted with the next oversize piston and rings.
5. Check the side clearance of the rings in the grooves as shown in **Figure 51**. Place the feeler gauge alongside the ring all the way into the groove. If the measurement is not within specification (**Table 1**), either the rings or the ring grooves are worn. Inspect and replace as required.
6. Install the oil ring in the lowest groove of the piston before installing compression rings. Oil rings consist of 3 segments. The wavy segment is a spacer for the 2 rails. See **Figure 52**.
   a. Install the oil ring expander in the lower groove and engage the tang (that keeps the spacer from turning) with the oil hole.
   b. Hold the spacer with the ends butted (*not overlapped*) and install 1 of the rails at the top of the spacer. The end of the rail must be at least 1 in. (25.4 mm) from the gap in the spacer.
   c. Install the second rail at the bottom of the spacer. The end of the rail should be at least 1 in. (25.4 mm) from the gap in the spacer on the opposite side from the first (top) rail.
   d. Check to make sure the oil ring is assembled correctly and moves freely. The antirotation tang should keep the assembly from turning, but it should also compress into the groove without binding.
7. Use a ring expander and carefully install the second compression ring. The top of each compression ring is marked and the mark must face toward the top of the piston.
8. Use a ring expander and carefully install the top compression ring. The top of each compression ring is marked and the mark must face toward the top of the piston.

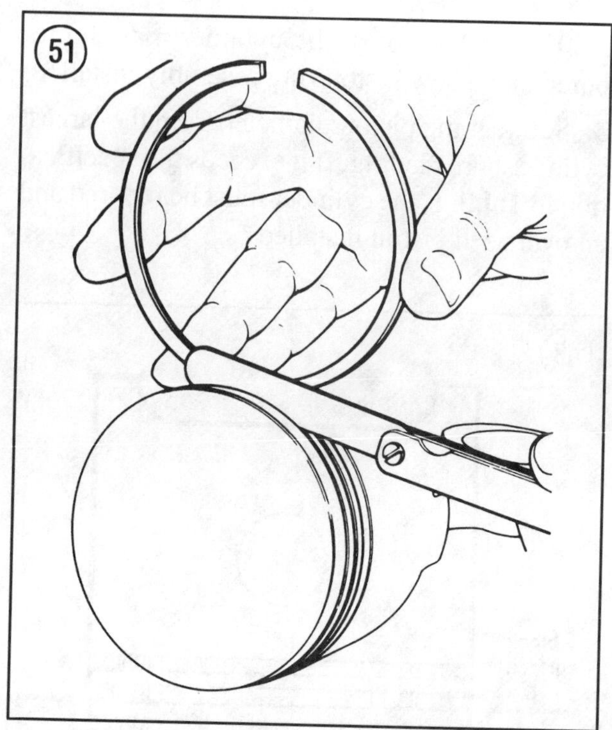

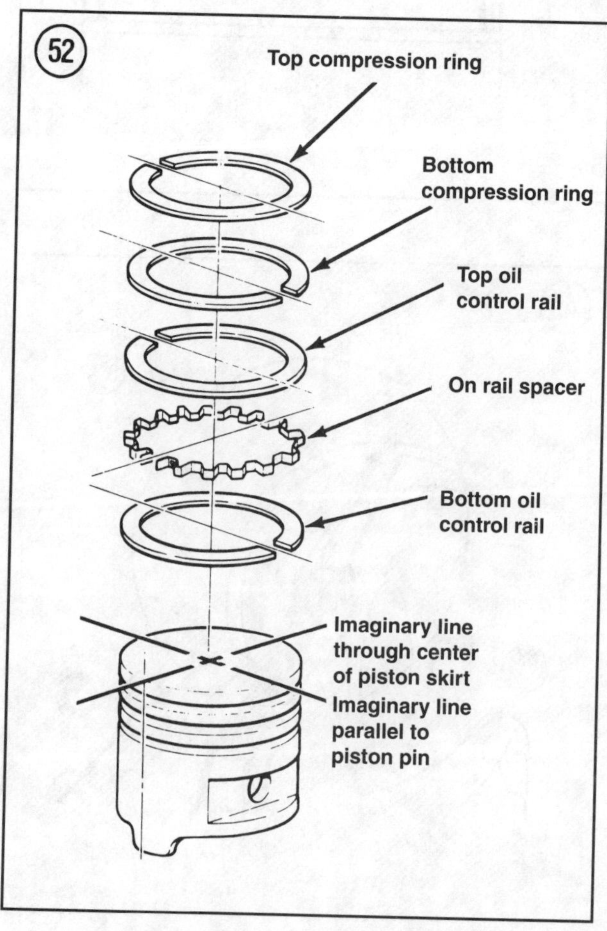

9. Stagger the piston ring end gaps 180° from each other. See **Figure 53**.

Connecting Rod Inspection

Have the connecting rods checked for straightness at a dealership or machine shop. When installing new connecting rods, have them checked for misalignment before installing the piston and piston pin. Connecting rods can spring out of alignment during shipping or handling.

Connecting Rod Bearing Clearance Measurement

CAUTION
Make sure the bearing bore and bearing insert are both clean. If even the smallest piece of dirt is between the bearing insert and the bearing bore, the clearance will be affected.

1. Install the upper half of the bearing insert in the connecting rod.
2. Install the lower half of the bearing insert in the connecting rod cap.
3. Cut a piece of Plastigage the width of the bearing (**Figure 54**) and place the piece *across* the crankpin journal.

NOTE
In Steps 4-6, be careful not to turn (move) the connecting rod or crankshaft until the rod cap has been installed, tightened, then removed. Turning will smear the Plastigage and make accurate measurement impossible. Also, the Plastigage should be placed on a flat surface of the crankpin, not across the oil hole.

4. Position the connecting rod and bearing against the connecting rod journal and install the cap assembly. Make sure the rod is assembled correctly and installed on the correct journal. position the numbers stamped on the side of the cap and connecting rod on the starboard side of the crankshaft.
5. Tighten the connecting rod retaining screws to the torque specified in **Table 2**. Do not rotate the crankshaft while the Plastigage is in place.
6. Remove the nuts retaining the connecting rod cap, then lift the cap off. The flattened Plastigage may either stick to the crankpin journal or the bearing insert.
7. Determine the bearing clearance by comparing the width of the flattened Plastigage with the markings on the envelope. See **Figure 55**.
8. Compare the measured bearing clearance with the specifications listed in **Table 1**.
9. If the clearance is excessive, the crankshaft must be machined to a smaller size and undersize bearings fitted. Consult with your dealer or machinist.
10. Measure the clearance for the remaining connecting rod bearings.

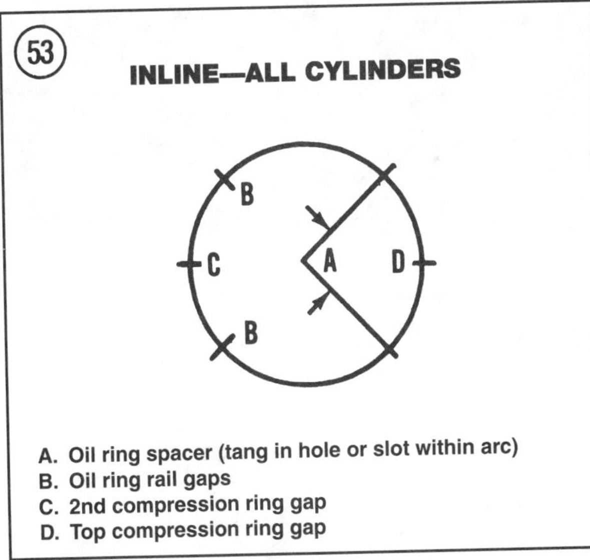

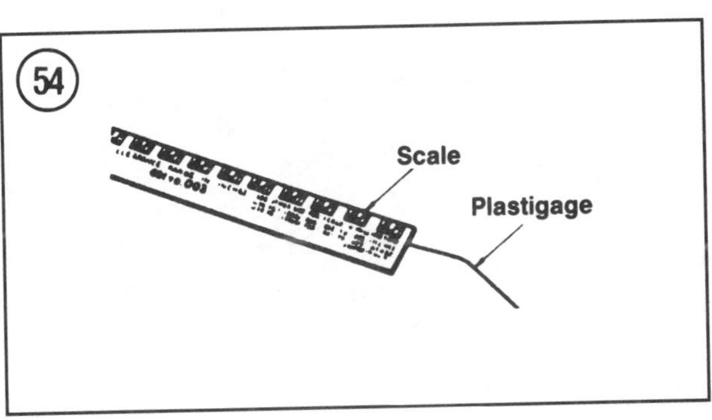

6

Piston/Connecting Rod Installation

1. Make sure the pistons are correctly installed on the connecting rods, if they were separated. The flange (heavy) side of the connecting rod should be on the same side (front) as the notch in the piston crown. See **Figure 56**.
2. Make sure the ring gaps are positioned as shown in **Figure 53**.

NOTE
If the special protector tubes are not available, short sections of hose can be fitted to the rod bolts in a similar way.

3. Slip special rod protector tubes (available from parts and tool suppliers) over the connecting rod bolts to help guide them into position and keep them from damaging the crankpin journals.
4. Coat the cylinder bore, rings and piston liberally in clean engine oil. The entire piston can be immersed in oil to ensure adequate lubrication.
5. Compress the piston rings using a suitable ring compressor. Be sure to space the ring end gaps evenly around the piston.

CAUTION
Be careful not to damage the piston rings while installing the connecting rod and piston assembly. It is sometimes difficult to buy a single ring. The crankpin can also be easily damaged by hitting 1 of the bolts against a polished bearing journal.

6. Insert the piston and connecting rod assembly into the correct cylinder bore. Make sure the notch (**Figure 56**) on the top of the piston faces toward the front, and align the lower end of the connecting rod with the crankshaft crankpin.

NOTE
Some mechanics protect the crankshaft journal by wrapping before installing the connecting rod and piston assembly. Special protector wraps made of plastic that curl around the journal are available from some tool and parts suppliers. Similar protection is possible by wrapping a piece of thin plastic or card stock

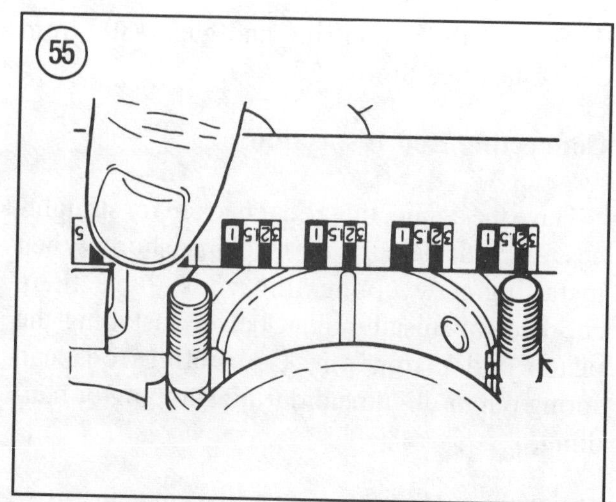

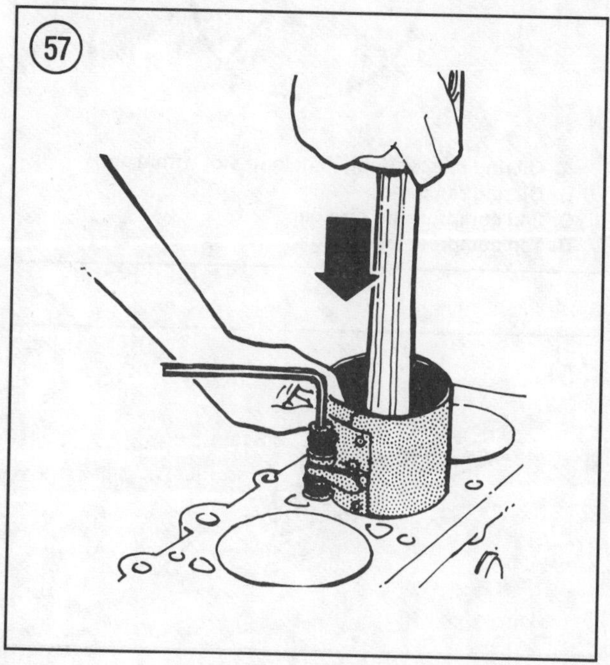

(paper) around the journal, then holding this in place with a short piece of tape while assembling. Do not allow any adhesive to stick to the journal.

CAUTION
Do not let any part of the connecting rod or the bolts hit the crankpin when installing the piston and rod assemblies. The polished surface of the crankpin can be damaged by the connecting rod.

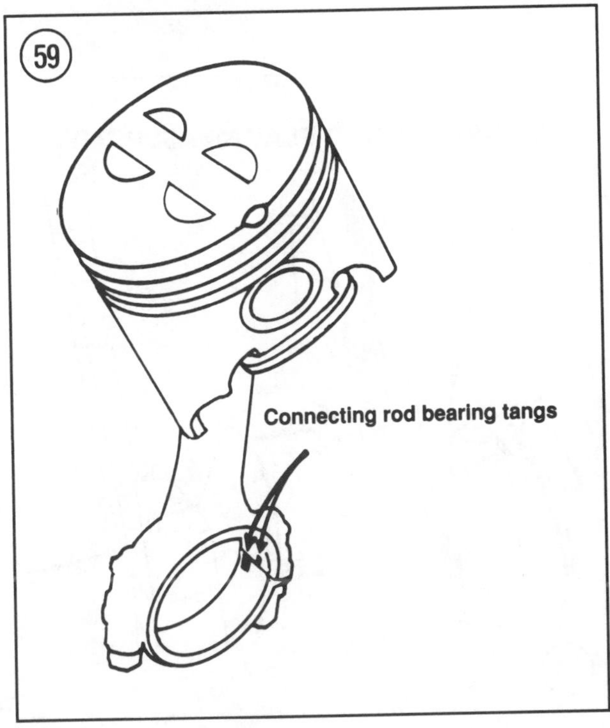

7. Push the piston and rings into the cylinder. Use the handle of a hammer to push the piston into the cylinder in 1 quick motion. See **Figure 57**.
8. Remove the hoses or protector tubes from the connecting rod bolts and make sure the threads are clean.
9. Clean the bearing inserts, connecting rod and rod cap, then install the bearing insert halves. Make sure the inserts are properly seated.
10. Lubricate the crankpin and connecting rod bearings liberally with clean engine oil.
11. Seat the crankpin firmly against the connecting rod bearing and insert. Check to make sure the insert is still correctly positioned in the connecting rod.
12. Install the connecting rod cap and install the retaining nuts. See **Figure 58**.

NOTE
*Make sure the bearing tangs (**Figure 59**) on the rod and cap are both on the same side. Also, make sure the pistons are installed correctly.*

13. Tighten the cap retaining nuts to torque specification in **Table 2**.
14. Check the connecting rod big-end play as described under *Piston/Connecting Rod Removal* in this chapter.
15. Repeat the preceding steps for each of the remaining rod and piston assemblies.

6

REAR MAIN OIL SEAL

A 1-piece rear main seal is used, and the seal is contained in a retainer attached to the rear of the engine block. The retainer and seal can be removed and replaced without removing the oil pan or the rear main bearing cap. Replace the seal as follows.

1. Remove the engine from the boat as described in this chapter.
2. Remove the engine coupler and flywheel from the engine.

CAUTION
Be extremely careful not to damage the seal surface of the crankshaft when removing the seal in Step 3.

3. Use a screwdriver inserted into the 3 slots around the seal retainer to carefully pry the rear main seal from the retainer. See **Figure 60**.
4. Thoroughly clean the seal bore in the retainer and the sealing surface of the crankshaft.
5. Lubricate the seal lip with engine oil or grease.
6. Place the seal into its bore in the retainer. Use a seal installer (part No. J-35621) to push the seal into its bore until it is fully seated.
7. Install the flywheel, engine coupler and install the engine into the boat as described in this chapter.

CRANKSHAFT

End Play Measurement

1. Pry the crankshaft to the front of the engine with a large screwdriver.
2. Measure the crankshaft end play at the front of the rear main bearing with a flat feeler gauge. See **Figure 61**. Compare to the specification in **Table 1**.
3. If the end play is excessive, replace the rear main bearing. If it is less than specified, check the bearing faces for damage.

Removal

1. Remove the engine from the boat as described in this chapter.
2. Remove the engine coupler and flywheel as described in this chapter.
3. Mount the engine on an engine stand, if available.
4. Remove the starter motor. See Chapter Eleven.
5. If the engine is mounted in an engine stand, invert the engine to bring the oil pan to an upright position.
6. Remove the oil pan and oil pump as described in this chapter.
7. Remove the timing gear cover as described in this chapter.
8. Remove the rear main oil seal as described in this chapter.

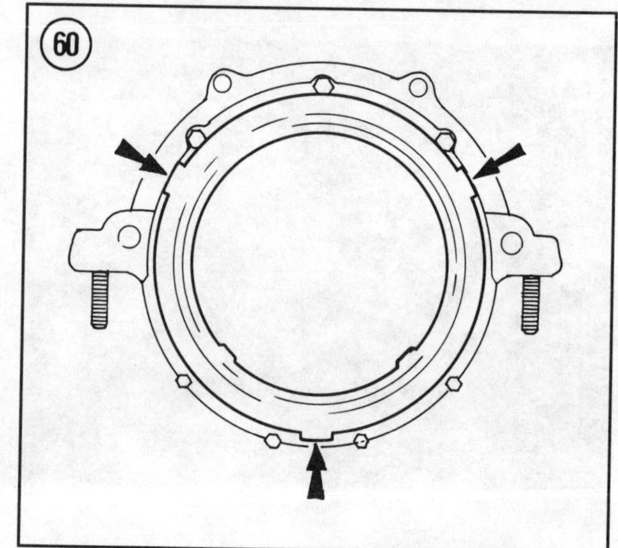

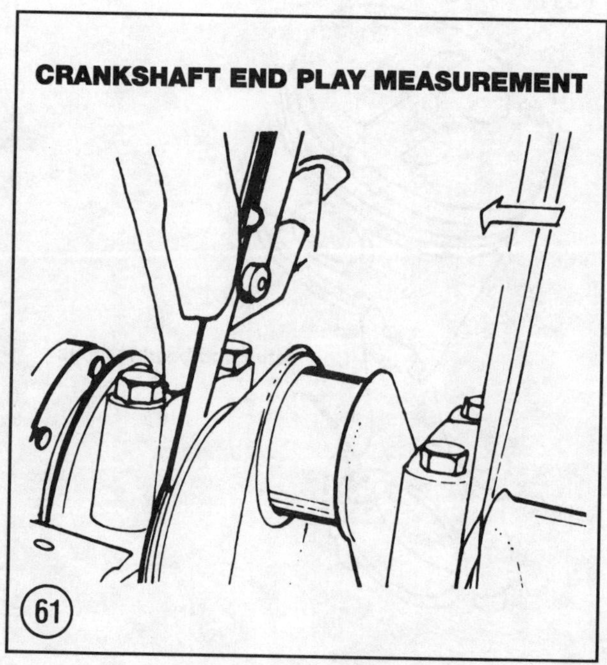

9. Remove the spark plugs to permit easy rotation of the crankshaft.

10. Measure crankshaft end play as described in this chapter.

11. Rotate the crankshaft to position 2 of the connecting rods at the bottom of their stroke.

12. Check the connecting rods and caps for identification numbers or marks. If the marks are not visible, clean the side of the rod and cap, then make your own mark. It is important that the connecting rod and cap be assembled exactly as removed.

NOTE

The bearing insert in the connecting rod should be removed when the cap is off so that it will not fall into the engine. If the same inserts are to be reinstalled, they should be marked so they can be installed in the same location. It is suggested that new bearing inserts be installed upon assembly.

13. Remove the connecting rod bearing cap and bearing (**Figure 58**). Move the piston/rod assembly up in the cylinder, away from the crankshaft.

14. Repeat Steps 11-13 for each of the remaining piston/rod assemblies.

15. Clean the main bearing caps with a wire brush and check for identification numbers or marks. If marks are not visible, mark each with numbers 1 through 5 beginning at the front bearing cap.

NOTE

*The arrow cast into the main bearing cap points to the front of the engine. See **Figure 62**.*

16. Unbolt and remove the main bearing caps and bearing inserts.

NOTE

If the caps are difficult to remove, lift the bolts partway out, then use the bolts to lever the caps from side to side.

6

17. Carefully lift the crankshaft from the engine block and place it on a clean workbench.

18. Remove the bearing inserts from the block. Place the bearing caps and inserts in order on a clean workbench. It is important to inspect the old bearings even if they will be replaced.

19. Remove the rear main oil seal from the cylinder block and rear bearing cap.

Inspection

1. Clean the crankshaft thoroughly with solvent. Blow out the oil passages with compressed air.

2. Check the main and connecting rod journals for wear, scratches, grooves, scoring or cracks. Check the oil seal surface for burrs, nicks or other sharp edges which might damage the seal during installation.

NOTE

Unless you have precision measuring equipment and training in its use, have a machine shop perform Step 3.

3. Check all journals for out-of-roundness and taper. See **Figure 63**. Compare the measurements with the specification listed in **Table 1**. Have the crankshaft reground and install undersize bearings, if necessary.

Main Bearing Clearance Measurement

Main bearing clearance is measured with Plastigage in the same way as the connecting rod bearing clearance, described in this chapter. If clearance is excessive, replace the bearings. If the crankshaft is worn it should be reground or a new crankshaft installed. If the crankshaft is reground to an undersize, the proper undersized bearings must be installed.

Installation

1. Install the main bearing inserts in the cylinder block. Oil holes in the bearing inserts must align with oil passages in the block and the tabs on the inserts must seat in the slots machined in the block.

NOTE
Check the main cap bolts for thread damage before reuse. If damaged, replace the bolts.

2. Lubricate the bolt threads with SAE 30 engine oil.
3. Install the bearing inserts in each cap and lubricate the bearings liberally with clean engine oil.
4. Carefully lower the crankshaft into position in the block.
5. Install the bearing caps in their marked positions with the arrows pointing toward the front of the engine (**Figure 62**).
6. Use the following procedure to align the crankshaft thrust surfaces of the rear main bearing.
   a. Install all screws attaching the main bearing caps and tighten finger-tight.
   b. Tighten screws retaining the front 4 main bearing caps (all except the rear cap) to the torque specified in **Table 2**.
   c. Tighten the screws retaining the rear main bearing cap to 10-12 ft.-lb. (13.5-16.3N.m).
   d. Use a heavy soft-faced (lead) hammer to bump the front of crankshaft and move the crankshaft to the rear.
   e. Bump the rear of the crankshaft to drive it forward.
   f. Tighten the screws attaching the rear main bearing cap to the torque listed in **Table 2**.
7. Retighten all main bearing caps to the torque listed in **Table 2**.
8. Rotate the crankshaft to make sure it turns smoothly. If not, remove the bearing caps and crankshaft and check that the bearings are clean and properly installed.
9. Reverse Steps 1-13 of *Removal* in this chapter. Refer to **Table 2** for tightening torques.
10. Install a new rear main bearing oil seal as described in this chapter.

DRIVE COUPLER AND FLYWHEEL

Removal/Installation

1. Remove the engine from the boat as described in this chapter.
2. Unbolt and remove the flywheel housing. Identify the location where electrical grounds are attached.
3. Remove the nuts retaining the coupler and flywheel to the crankshaft.
4. Pull the coupler from the studs, then remove the flywheel.

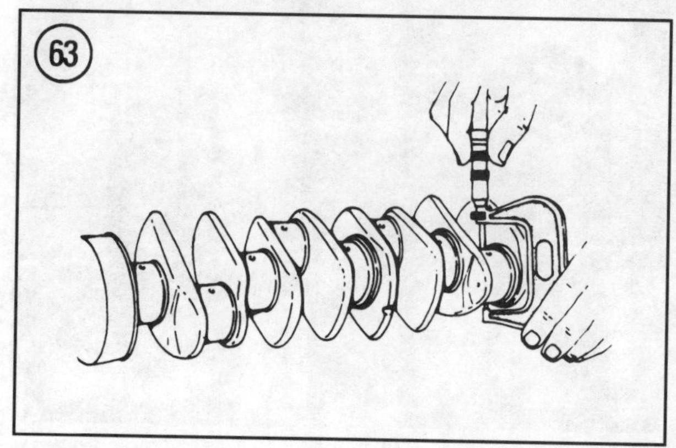

5. To install, first install the flywheel onto the studs, then fit the coupler on the studs.
6. Install the retaining nuts and tighten to the specification listed in **Table 2**. It may be necessary to use a crowfoot or similar attachment to tighten the nuts.
7. Attach a dial indicator to the engine and position the plunger against the machined surface of the flywheel and check runout. Remove the flywheel and check for burrs if runout is excessive.
8. Perform a runout check of the coupler similar to that described in Step 7.
9. Install the flywheel housing and tighten the retaining fasteners to the torque listed in **Table 2**. Electrical grounds are attached to some of the fasteners.
10. Lubricate coupler splines and reinstall the engine in the boat as described in this chapter.

Inspection

1. Visually check the flywheel for cracks or other damage.
2. Check the condition of the splines and cushion hub of the coupling.
3. Inspect the ring gear for cracks, broken teeth or excessive wear. If the ring gear teeth are damaged, check the starter motor drive gear teeth for similar wear or damage. If the flywheel ring gear is damaged, it can be removed and replaced at a machine shop.

64

CYLINDER BLOCK

Cleaning and Inspection

1. Check the cylinder block before cleaning for evidence of any fluid leakage. Identify possible sources of problems such as leaking plugs, gaskets or cracks. Examine these areas further while cleaning and after cleaning.
2. Clean the block thoroughly. Some cleaning procedures are facilitated by removing plugs from passages.
   a. Clean all gasket or RTV sealant residue from the machined surfaces.
   b. Check all core plugs (**Figure 64**, typical) for leaks and replace any that are suspect. See *Core Plug Replacement* in this chapter.
   c. Check coolant passages for sludge, dirt and corrosion while cleaning. If the passages are very dirty, have the block boiled out at a machine shop. Blow out all passages with compressed air.
   d. Remove the plugs from the oil passages to permit a more thorough cleaning. Check oil passages for sludge, dirt and corrosion while cleaning. If the passages are very dirty, have the block boiled out at a machine shop. Blow out all passages with compressed air.
   e. Check the threads in the head bolt holes to be sure they are clean. If dirty, use a tap to true up the threads and remove any deposits.
3. Examine the block for cracks. If cracked, the block must be repaired or replaced. A machine shop will be able to confirm suspicions about possible cracks. Another method is as follows:
   a. Mix 1 part of kerosene with 2 parts engine oil.
   b. Dissolve zinc oxide in wood alcohol.
   c. Coat the suspected area with the mixture of kerosene and oil, then wipe the area dry.

6

d. Immediately apply the solution of zinc oxide and wood alcohol.

e. A crack will appear as discoloration in the zinc oxide treated area.

4. Check the cylinder block deck (top surface) for flatness. Place an accurate straightedge on the block. If there is any gap between the block and straightedge, measure it with a flat feeler gauge (**Figure 65**). Measure from end to end and from corner to corner. Have the block resurfaced if it is warped more than 0.004 in. (0.102 mm).

5. Measure cylinder bores with a bore gauge (**Figure 66**) for out-of-roundness or excessive wear as described in *Piston Clearance Check* in this chapter. If the cylinders exceed maximum tolerance, they must be rebored. Reboring is also necessary if the cylinder walls are badly scuffed or scored.

NOTE

*Before boring, install all main bearing caps and tighten the cap bolts to specification in **Table 2**.*

CORE PLUG REPLACEMENT

Check the condition of all core plugs in the block (**Figure 67**) and cylinder head anytime the engine is out of the boat for service. If any signs of leakage or corrosion are found around 1 core plug, replace them all.

NOTE

Core plugs can be replaced inexpensively at a machine shop. If you are having machine work done on the en-

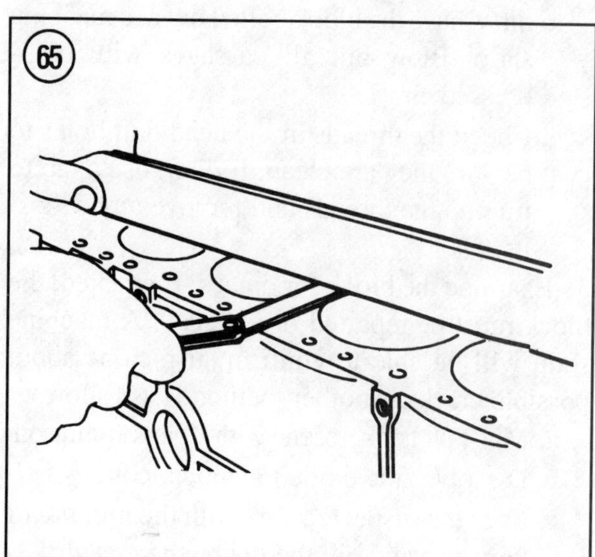

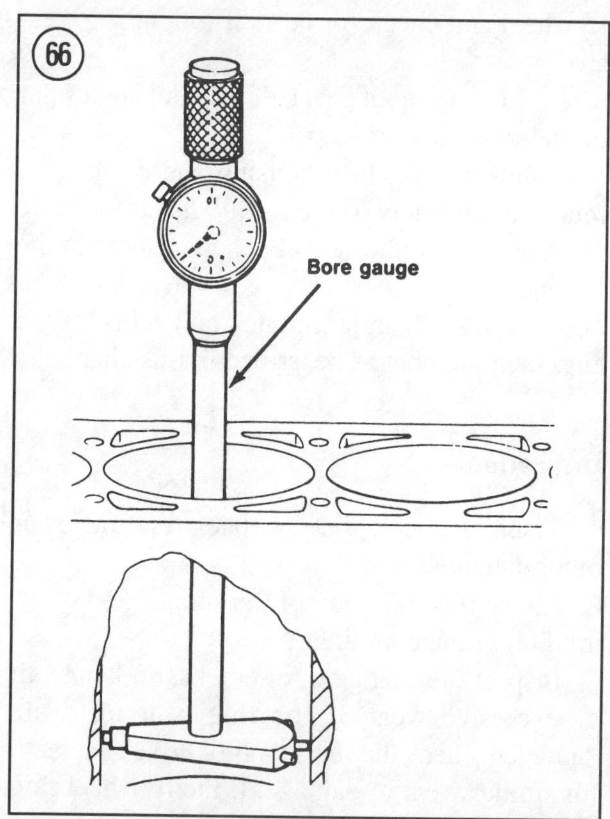

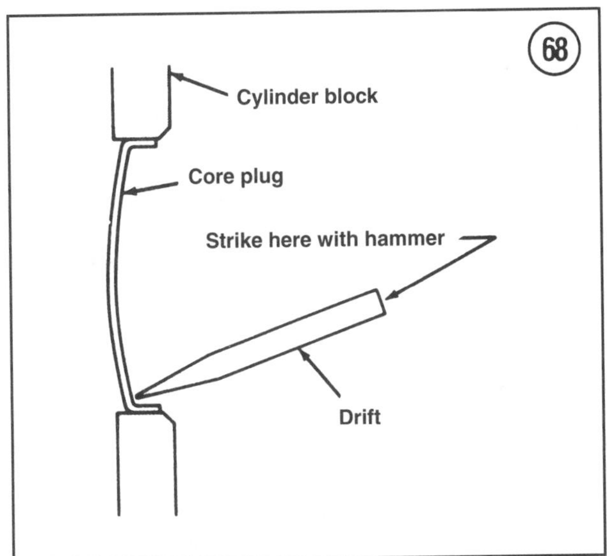

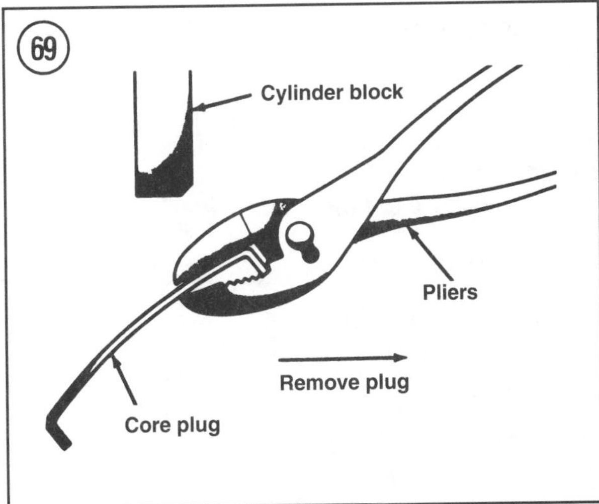

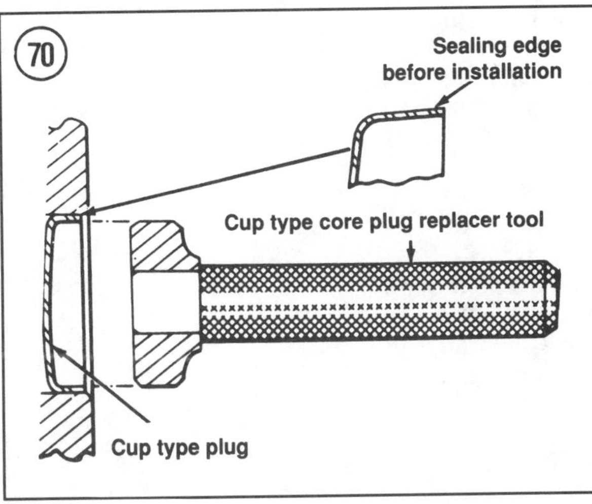

gine, have the core plugs replaced at the same time.

Removal/Installation

CAUTION

Do not drive core plugs into the engine casting. It will be impossible to retrieve them and they can restrict coolant circulation, resulting in serious engine damage.

1. Tap the bottom edge of the core plug with a hammer and drift. Use several sharp blows to push the bottom of the plug inward, tilting the top out (**Figure 68**).
2. Grip the top of the plug firmly with pliers. Pull the plug from its bore (**Figure 69**) and discard.

NOTE

Core plugs can also be removed by drilling a hole in the center of the plug and prying them out with an appropriate size drift or pin punch. On large core plugs, the use of a universal impact slide hammer is recommended.

3. Clean the plug bore thoroughly to remove all traces of the old sealer. Inspect the bore for any damage that might interfere with proper sealing of the new plug. If damage is evident, true the surface by boring for the next oversize plug.

NOTE

Oversize plugs can be identified by an OS stamped in the flat on the cup side of the plug.

4. Coat the inside diameter of the plug bore and the outer diameter of the new plug with sealer. Use an oil-resistant sealer if the plug is to be installed in an oil gallery or a water-resistant sealer for plugs installed in the water jacket.
5. Install the new core plug with an appropriate size core plug replacer tool (**Figure 70**), driver or socket. The sharp edge of the plug should be at least 0.02 in. (0.5 mm) inside the lead-in chamfer.
6. Repeat Steps 1-5 to replace each remaining core plug.

Table 1 ENGINE SPECIFICATIONS (3.0 L, 4-CYLINDER)

Type	Inline 4-cylinder
Displacement	181 cid (3.0 L)
Bore	4.0 in. (101.6 mm)
Stroke	3.60 in. (91.4 mm)
Cylinder numbering (front to rear)	1-2-3-4
Firing order	1-3-4-2
Piston clearance in cylinder bore	
At top land	0.0255-0.0345 in. (0.648-0.876 mm)
At bottom of skirt	0.0025-0.0035 in. (0.063-0.089 mm)
Piston rings	
End gap	
Top compression	0.010-0.020 in. (0.25-0.51 mm)
Second compression	0.013-0.025 in. (0.33-0.63 mm)
Oil ring	0.015-0.055 in. (0.38-1.40 mm)
Side clearance	
Compression rings	0.0020-0.0035 in. (0.051-0.089 mm)
Piston pin	
Diameter	0.9270-0.9273 in. (23.546-23.553 mm)
Fit in connecting rod	0.0008-0.0021 in. (0.020-0.053 mm)
Fit in Piston	
Desired	0.0003-0.0004 in. (0.008-0.010 mm)
Service limit	0.001 in. (0.025 mm)
Crankshaft	
Bearings	
Main bearing clearance	0.0003-0.0029 in. (0.008-0.074 mm)
End play (axial)	0.002-0.006 in. (0.05-0.15 mm)
Crankpin clearance	0.00085-0.00135 in. (0.022-0.034 mm)
Crankpins	
Diameter, new	2.099-2.100 in. (53.31-53.34 mm)
Main journals	
Diameter, new	2.2983-2.2993 in. (58.377-58.402 mm)
End play	0.008-0.015 in. (0.20-0.31 mm)
Gear runout	0.003 in. maximum (0.08 mm)
Connecting rod	
Length (center-center)	5.700 in. (144.78 mm)
Side play on crankpin	0.008-0.015 in. (0.20-0.38 mm)
Camshaft	
End play (axial)	0.001-0.005 in. (0.13 mm)
Gear backlash	0.004-0.006 in. (0.10-0.15 mm)
Gear runout	0.004 in. maximum (0.10 mm)
Journal diameter	1.8682-1.8692 in. (47.452-47.478 mm)
Out-of-round	0.001 in. maximum (0.025 mm)
Lobe lift	0.248-0.058 in. (6.30-6.68 mm)
Warpage, between V-blocks	0.002 in. maximum (0.05 mm)
Valves	
Face angle	45°
Seat angle	46°
Seat width	
Intake (1994-1996)	1/16 to 7/32 in. (1.59-5.56 mm)
Intake (1997-on)	0.050-0.070 in. (1.27-1.778 mm)
Exhaust (1994-1996)	1/16 to 3/32 in. (1.59-2.38 mm)
Exhaust (1997-on)	0.060-0.080 in (1.524-2.032 mm)
Valve stem clearance	
Inlet and exhaust	
Desired	0.0010-0.0027 in. (0.025-0.068 mm)

(continued)

Table 1 ENGINE SPECIFICATIONS (3.0 L, 4-CYLINDER) (continued)

Type	Inline 4-cylinder
Outer valve springs	
Free length	2.08 in. (52.8 mm)
Installed height	1 21/32 - 1 23/32 in. (42.06-43.66 mm)
Pressure	
1994-1996	78-86 lb. @ 1.66 in. (347-382 N @ 42.2 mm)
1997-on	100-110 lb @ 1.61 in. (444-490 N @48.89 mm)
Oil pump	
Pressure	40-60 psi @ 2,000 rpm (276-414 kPa @ 2,000 rpm)

Table 2 TIGHTENING TORQUES

	N·m	in.-lb.	ft.-lb.
Camshaft thrust plate	8-10	72-90	–
Cylinder head*			
First step	47	–	35
Second step	88	–	65
Third step			
1994-1996	129	–	95
1997-on	122	–	90
Connecting rod	47	–	35
Engine mounts			
Front			
Adjustment nuts	156-190	–	115-140
Rear			
Screw to square nut	60-71	–	44-52
Lock nuts	38-40	–	28-30
Exhaust elbow to manifold	16-19	–	12-14
Exhaust pipe to transom shield	27-34	–	20-25
Flywheel and coupler	54-61	–	40-45
Flywheel housing	47-54	–	35-40
Main bearing caps			
All except rear	81-95	–	60-70
Rear*			
Step 1	14-16	–	10-12
Step 2	81-95	–	60-70
Manifold to cylinder head	27-34	–	20-25
Oil pan			
1/4 × 20	9	80	–
5/16 × 18	18.6	165	–
Oil pump			
Attachment	12-14	110-120	10
Cover and suction pipe	7-8	65-75	–
Withdrawl tube flare	20-24	–	15-18
Power steering			
Pressure (small) hose	14-16	–	10-12
Return (large) hose	20-23	–	15-17

(continued)

Table 2 TIGHTENING TORQUES (continued)

	N·m	in.-lb.	ft.-lb.
Rear main seal retainer	15.3	135	11
Spark plugs (not oiled)	27	–	20
Timing gear cover	9	80	–
Valve cover screws	7.3	65	–

* Refer to the text for tightening instructions.

Chapter Seven

4.3 Liter V6; 5.0, 5.7, 7.4 and 8.2 Liter V8 Engines

GM

7

Volvo Penta installations may use one of several marine V6 and V8 engines. These include engines of the following displacements: 262 cid (4.3 L) V6, 305 cid (5.0 L) V8, 350 cid (5.7 L) V8, 454 cid (7.4 L) and 502 cid (8.2 L) V8. These are all similar in design and construction. Most of the repair and service procedures described in this chapter are typical and will apply to all of these engines. Exceptions are specifically noted.

The cylinders on V6 engines are numbered from front to rear (1-3-5 on the port side and 2-4-6 on the starboard side). The firing order is 1-6-5-4-3-2.

The cylinders on V8 engines are also numbered from front to rear (1-3-5-7 on the port side and 2-4-6-8 on the starboard side). The firing order is 1-8-4-3-6-5-7-2.

The cast iron cylinder head contains intake and exhaust valves with integral valve guides. Rocker arms are retained on individual threaded shoulder studs or shoulder bolts. Camshaft motion opens the valves via hydraulic lifters, pushrods and the rocker arms.

The chain-driven camshaft is located above the crankshaft between the 2 cylinder banks and supported by 4 (V6) or 5 (V8) bearings. The oil pump, mounted at the bottom of the engine block, is driven by the camshaft via the distributor.

A gear driven balance shaft is located above the camshaft on V6 models. The balance shaft dampens much of the vibration in the 1,700-2,000 rpm range.

The crankshaft is supported by 4 (V6) or 5 (V8) main bearings, with the rear bearing providing the crankshaft thrust control. Crankshaft rotation is counterclockwise when seen from the drive unit end of the engine.

Engine specifications (**Tables 1-3**) and tightening torques (**Table 4** and **Table 5**) are at the end of the chapter.

ENGINE MODEL AND SERIAL NUMBERS

The engine serial number and model designation is located on a plate or decal (**Figure 1**) attached to the valve (rocker arm) cover on the port side of the engine.

This information identifies the engine and indicates if there are any unique parts or if internal changes have been made during its manufacture. The specific model number and serial number are important when ordering replacement parts for the engine. You provide these numbers to the parts department when obtaining or ordering parts.

SPECIAL TOOLS

Where special tools are required or recommended for engine service, the tool numbers are provided. GM tool part numbers have a J- prefix and can often be rented from rental dealers. They can also be purchased from a Volvo Penta dealership.

GASKET SEALANT

Gasket sealant is used instead of preformed gaskets between some mating surfaces on the engines covered in this chapter. Two types of gasket sealant are commonly used: room temperature vulcanizing (RTV) and anaerobic. Since these 2 materials have different sealing properties, they cannot be interchanged.

Room Temperature Vulcanizing (RTV) Sealant

This silicone gel is available in tubes that are available from most parts suppliers and Volvo Penta dealers. Moisture in the air causes RTV to cure. Always place the cap on the tube as soon as possible when using RTV. RTV has a shelf life of approximately 1 year and will not cure properly when the shelf life has expired. Check the expiration date on RTV tubes before using and keep partially used tubes tightly sealed.

Applying RTV Sealant

Clean all gasket residue from mating surfaces. They must be clean and free of oil and grease. Remove all RTV gasket material from blind attaching holes, as it can cause a hydraulic lock and affect bolt torque.

Unless otherwise specified, apply RTV sealant in a continuous bead 3-5 mm (1/8-3/16 in.) thick. Apply the sealant on the inner side of all mounting bolts. Torque mating parts within 10-15 minutes after application or the sealant will have started to cure. If this happens, the old sealant must be removed and new sealant applied.

Anaerobic Sealant

This is also a gel that is supplied in tubes. It cures only in the absence of air, as when squeezed tightly between 2 machined mating surfaces. For this reason, it will not spoil if the cap is left off the tube. Do not use anaerobic sealant if 1 mating surface is flexible.

Applying Anaerobic Sealant

Clean all gasket residue from mating surfaces. They must be clean and free of oil and grease.

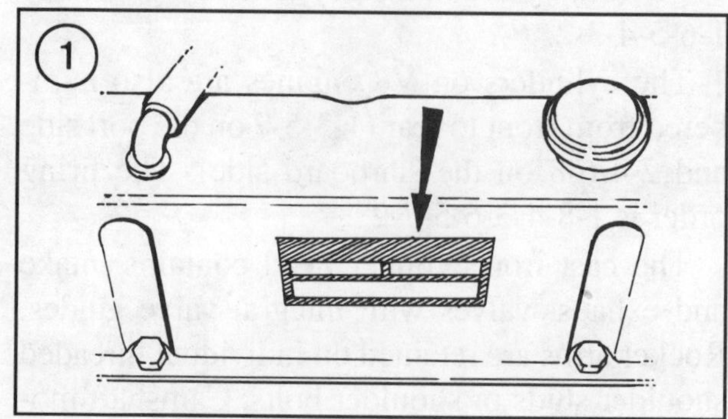

Remove all gasket material from blind attaching holes, as it can cause a hydraulic lock and affect bolt torque.

Unless otherwise specified, apply anaerobic sealant in a 1 mm (0.04 in.) or less continuous bead to 1 sealing surface. Apply the sealant on the inner side of all mounting holes.

REPLACEMENT PARTS

Various changes are made to automotive engines before they are used for marine applications. Numerous part changes are required due to operation in fresh and saltwater. For example, the cylinder head gasket must be corrosion resistant. Marine engines may use head gaskets of copper or stainless steel instead of the standard steel used in automotive applications. Expansion or core plugs may be made from different material than used in automotive applications.

Since marine engines are run at or near maximum speed most of the time, the use of special valve lifters, springs, pistons, bearings, camshafts and other heavy-duty components is necessary for maximum life and performance.

For these reasons, never substitute automotive-type parts for marine components. In addition, Volvo Penta recommends that only parts available through authorized Volvo Penta dealers be used. Parts offered by other manufacturers may look similar, but may not be manufactured to Volvo Penta's specifications. Any damage resulting from the use of incorrect parts will be the sole responsibility of the installer.

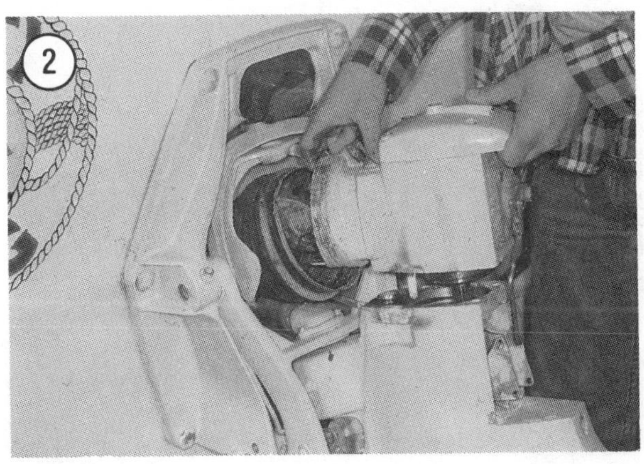

PRECAUTIONS

WARNING

The engine is heavy, awkward to handle and has sharp edges. It may shift or drop suddenly during removal. To prevent serious injury, always observe the following precautions.

1. Never place any part of your body where a moving or falling engine may trap, cut or crush you.
2. If you must push the engine during removal, use a board or similar tool to keep your hands out of danger.
3. Be sure the hoist is designed to lift engines and has enough load capacity for your engine.
4. Be sure the hoist is securely attached to safe lifting points on the engine.
5. The engine should not be difficult to lift with a proper hoist. If it is, stop lifting, lower the engine back onto its mounts and make sure the engine has been completely separated from the vessel.

ENGINE REMOVAL

Some service procedures can be performed with the engine in the boat; others require removal. The boat design and service procedure to be performed will determine whether the engine must be removed.

1. Remove the engine cover and all panels that interfere with engine removal. Move the cover and other parts out of the way.
2. Disconnect the negative battery cable, then the positive battery cable. As a precaution, remove the battery from the boat.
3. Remove the stern drive upper gear housing (**Figure 2**). Refer to ChapterTwelve.

4. Disconnect the throttle cable from the carburetor or fuel control linkage (**Figure 3**, typical). Remove the cable from the anchor plates attached to the engine.
5. Detach the electrical cables from the engine. Separate the cables at the connectors.
6. Disconnect the fuel line from the fuel filter. Plug the line and fitting to prevent leakage and the entry of contamination. See **Figure 4**, typical.
7. Loosen the hose clamp and detach the raw water line from the transom shield water tube. See **Figure 5**, typical.
8. Open the engine drain cocks or remove the drain plugs and drain all coolant and water from the engine.
9. Loosen the clamps on the exhaust manifold bellows, then pull the bellows free from the manifolds. See **Figure 6**.
10. Remove the shift mechanism cover from the stern drive and disconnect the shift cable from the lever. Remove the cable lock plate from the front of the stern drive intermediate housing.
11. If equipped with power steering, disconnect both power steering hydraulic lines from the control valve. See **Figure 7**. Cap the lines and plug the control valve fittings to prevent leakage and the entry of contamination. Secure the lines at a point higher than the engine power steering pump during the remainder of this procedure to prevent damage or the loss of fluid.
12. Detach any wires, hoses or accessories that will interfere with engine removal.

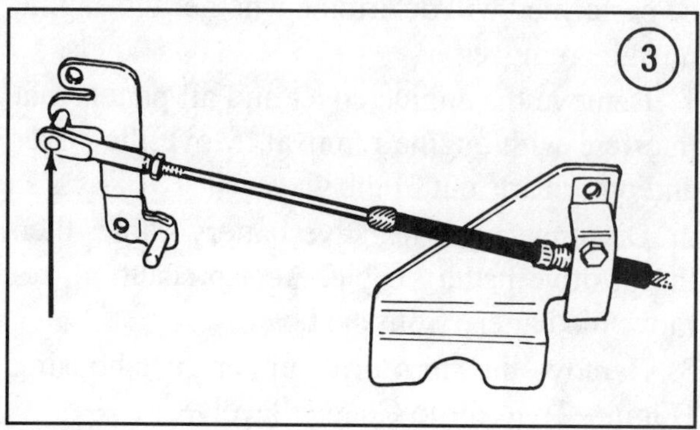

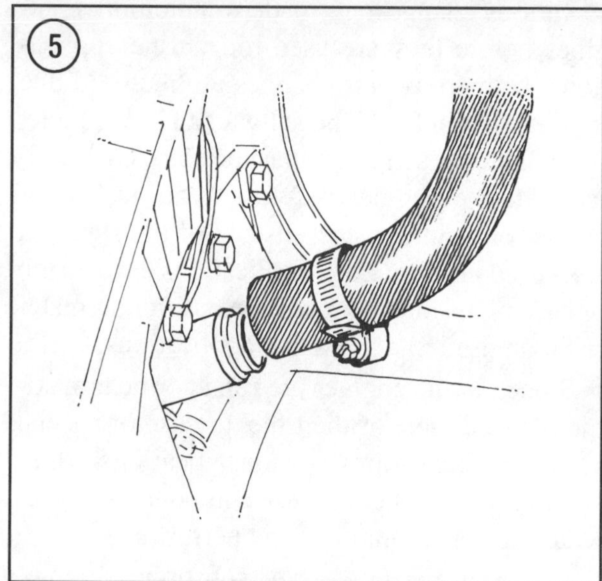

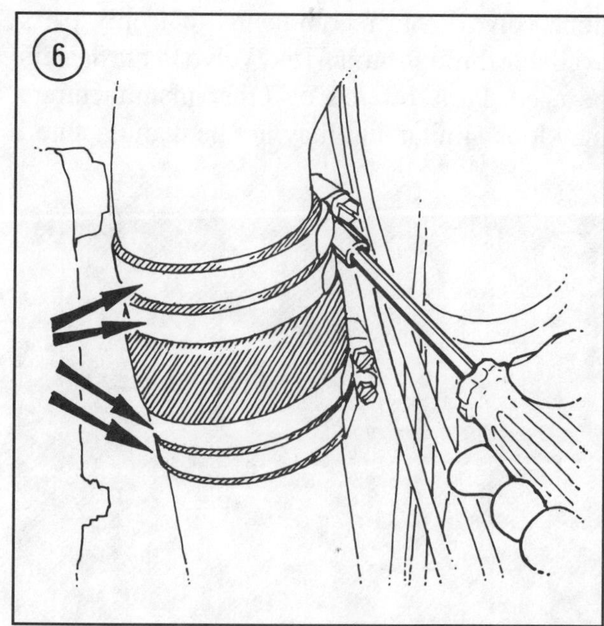

NOTE
At this point, there should be no hoses, wires or linkage connecting the engine to the boat or stern drive unit. Make sure nothing remains to interfere with engine removal.

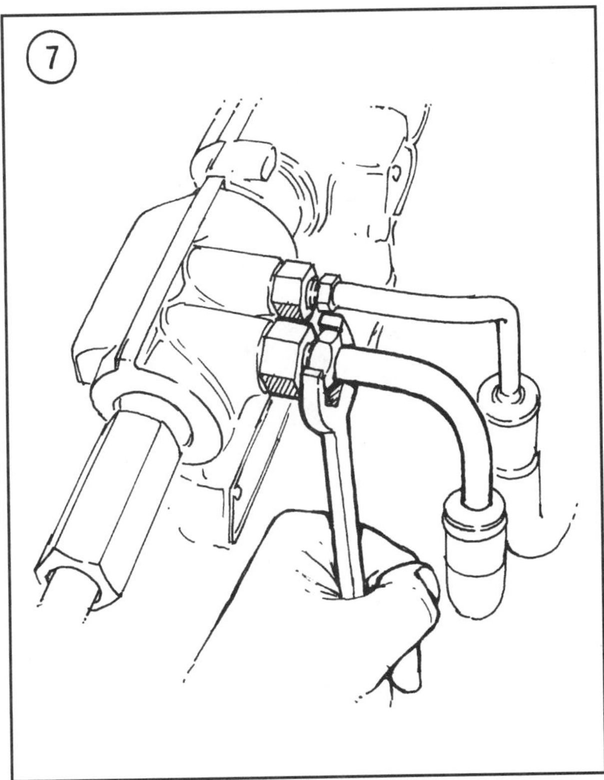

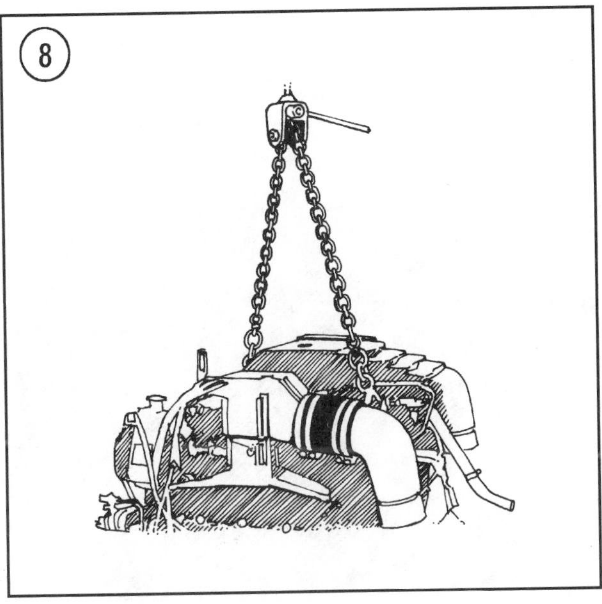

13. Attach a suitable hoist to the engine lifting brackets. The hoist must have a minimum lift capacity of 1,500 lb. (680 kg). Raise the hoist enough to remove all slack. See **Figure 8**.

NOTE
Do not loosen or move the mounts at the engine attaching points or a complete realignment will be required when the engine is reinstalled. Engine alignment should not be disturbed if mounts are detached as described in Step 14.

14. Remove the lag screws (**Figure 9**) from the front engine mount, then remove the locknuts (A, **Figure 10**) and washers (B) from the rear engine mounts.
15. Remove the mounting bolts (**Figure 11**) from the clamp ring at the rear.
16. Slide the engine forward until the flywheel cover is clear, then lift the engine from the boat.

ENGINE INSTALLATION

Engine installation is the reverse of removal, in addition to the following:

1. Clean the engine coupling splines and lubricate lightly.

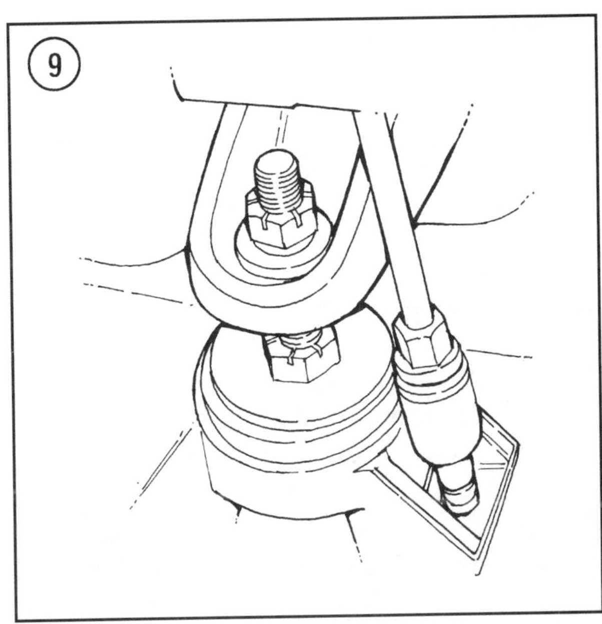

2. Reinstall any shims or adapters used with the engine mounts.
3. Inspect all self-locking nuts, hoses, bellows and other parts for wear or deterioration. The manufacturer suggests that the exhaust bellows should be replaced every 2 years and elastic stop nuts should never be installed more than twice. It is a good idea to replace these parts each time the engine is removed.
4. Guide bolts may be used to align the engine at the rear.
5. Tighten all fasteners to the specifications listed in **Table 4** or **Table 5**.
6. If equipped with power steering, tighten hose fittings and bleed the power steering system as described in Chapter Sixteen.
7. Fill the engine with the quantity, type and viscosity of oil recommended in Chapter Four.
8. If equipped with a closed cooling system, fill the system with a 50:50 mixture of antifreeze and pure water. See Chapter Four.
9. Adjust the accessory drive belts. See Chapter Four.
10. Make sure all hoses, wires and linkage are reattached before starting the engine.

DISASSEMBLY CHECKLISTS

To use the checklists, remove and inspect each part in the order mentioned. To reassemble, go through the checklists backward, installing the parts in order. Each major part is covered in its own section in this chapter, unless otherwise noted.

Decarbonizing or Valve Service

1. Remove the valve covers.
2. Remove the intake and exhaust manifolds.
3. Remove the rocker arms.
4. Remove the cylinder heads.
5. Remove and inspect the valves. Inspect the valve guides and seats, repairing or replacing as required.
6. Assemble by reversing Steps 1-5.

Valve and Ring Service

1. Perform Steps 1-5 of *Decarbonizing* or *Valve Service*.
2. Remove the oil pan and oil pump.
3. Remove the pistons and connecting rods.
4. Remove the piston rings.

NOTE
It is not necessary to separate the pistons from the connecting rods unless a piston, connecting rod or piston pin needs repair or replacement.

5. Assemble by reversing Steps 1-4.

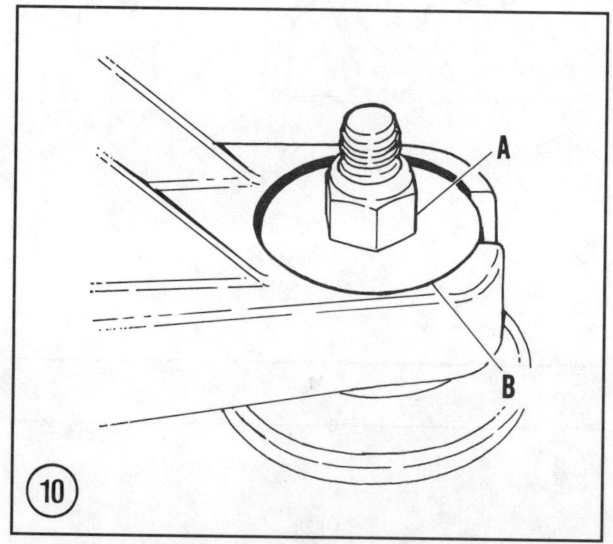

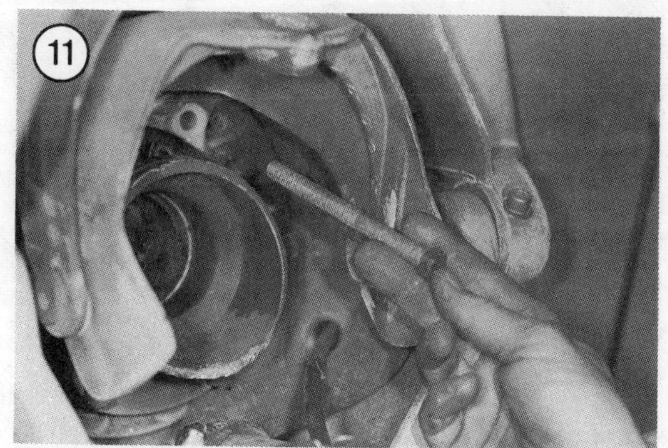

General Overhaul

1. Remove the engine from the boat.
2. Remove the flywheel.
3. Remove the mount brackets and oil pressure sending unit from the engine.
4. If available, mount the engine on an engine stand. These can be rented from equipment rental dealers. The stand is not absolutely necessary, but it will make the job much easier.
5. Remove the following accessories or components from the engine.
   a. Alternator and mounting bracket.
   b. Power steering pump and mounting bracket.
   c. Spark plug wires and distributor cap.
   d. Carburetor and fuel lines.
   e. Oil dipstick and tube.
   f. Raw water pump, if so equipped.

NOTE
Coolant or oil leaks indicate the possibility of a crack, leaking gasket, warped sealing surface or damaged part and should be inspected further when the engine is disassembled.

6. Check the engine for signs of leakage. Record the location of any possible leaks for further inspection or repair.
7. Clean the outside of the engine.
8. Remove the distributor. See Chapter Eleven.
9. Remove all hoses and tubes connected to the engine that need to be replaced. Also, remove any hoses or tubes that will interfere with disassembly.
10. Remove the mechanical fuel pump, if so equipped. See Chapter Nine.
11. Remove the intake and exhaust manifolds.
12. Unbolt and remove the valve covers and rocker arms.
13. Remove the crankshaft pulley, harmonic balancer, timing case cover and water pump. Remove the timing chain and sprockets.
14A. On V6 models, remove the camshaft and balance shaft.
14B. On V8 models, remove the camshaft.
15. Remove the cylinder heads.
16. Remove the oil pan and oil pump.
17. Remove the pistons and connecting rods.
18. Remove the flywheel and coupler.
19. Remove the crankshaft.
20. Inspect the cylinder block.
21. Assemble by reversing Steps 1-19.

VALVE COVERS

Removal/Installation

It may be necessary to remove other parts which interfere with removal of the valve (rocker arm) covers.

1. Detach the crankcase ventilation hose from the valve cover.
2. Remove the exhaust manifold(s) as described in this chapter.
3. Remove any other accessory unit that might interfere with valve cover removal.
4. Remove the cover attaching fasteners.
5. Tap 1 end of the valve cover with a soft-faced hammer to break the gasket or RTV seal. Remove the valve cover.
6. Remove all of the gasket or RTV sealant from the cylinder head and valve cover. Use a cleaning solvent and a putty knife to remove any residue remaining on the sealing surfaces.
7A. If a valve cover gasket is used, position the new gasket in the valve cover.
7B. If the valve cover uses RTV sealant (no gasket), first make sure the sealing surface of the valve cover and the mating rail on the cylinder head are clean and dry. Apply a 3/16 in. (4.8 mm) bead of RTV sealant along the sealing rail of the cylinder head. Run the bead of sealer to the inside of any fastener holes.
8. Position the valve cover on the cylinder head.

NOTE
Make sure that seals (if so equipped) around the fasteners are new or in good condition before installing the fasteners in Step 9. Liquid sealer should not be

used around the fasteners in an attempt to stop leakage.

9. Install the valve cover attaching fasteners and tighten to the specification in **Table 4** or **Table 5**.
10. Attach the spark plug cable retainers to the valve cover brackets and connect the wires to the appropriate spark plugs. See Chapter Four.
11. Attach the crankcase ventilation hose to the valve cover.

INTAKE MANIFOLD

The intake manifold used on fuel injected V6 and small block V8 models with throttle body injection (TBI) is similar to the one used for carbureted models. However, some of the following procedures may be different. See Chapter Nine.

The intake manifold of 7.4 Gi and 7.4 GSi big block engines with multipoint fuel injection (MFI) is located below the upper plenum which must be removed first. The fuel rail and fuel injectors are attached to the intake manifold and can be removed with the manifold. See Chapter Nine.

Removal/Installation

Figure 12 is typical of all models equipped with a carburetor. Refer to Chapter Nine for removal of upper plenum on fuel injected 7.4 Gi and 7.4 GSi models.

1. Disconnect the cable from the negative terminal of the battery.
2. Detach the hoses from both valve covers.
3. Remove the flame arrestor.
4. Open or remove the cylinder block water drains and allow all the water to drain. It may be necessary to remove sediment from the drain by inserting a wire into the opening.
5. Disconnect the water hoses from the manifold, thermostat housing and water pump.
6. Disconnect the throttle cable linkage from the carburetor.
7. Disconnect the wire from the coolant temperature sending unit. On some engines, it may be necessary to remove the sending unit to provide sufficient access for manifold fastener removal.
8. Remove the fuel line between the carburetor (or fuel rail) and fuel pump.
9. Disconnect wires from the spark plugs and detach the cable retainers from the valve covers.
10. Remove the distributor cap and place it (with plug wires attached) out of the way.

NOTE

If you mark the position of the distributor rotor in relation to the intake manifold before removing the distributor it will be easier to install the distributor, but only if the crankshaft is not moved. If, however, the engine crankshaft is turned while the distributor is removed, refer to Chapter Eleven for initial installation of the distributor.

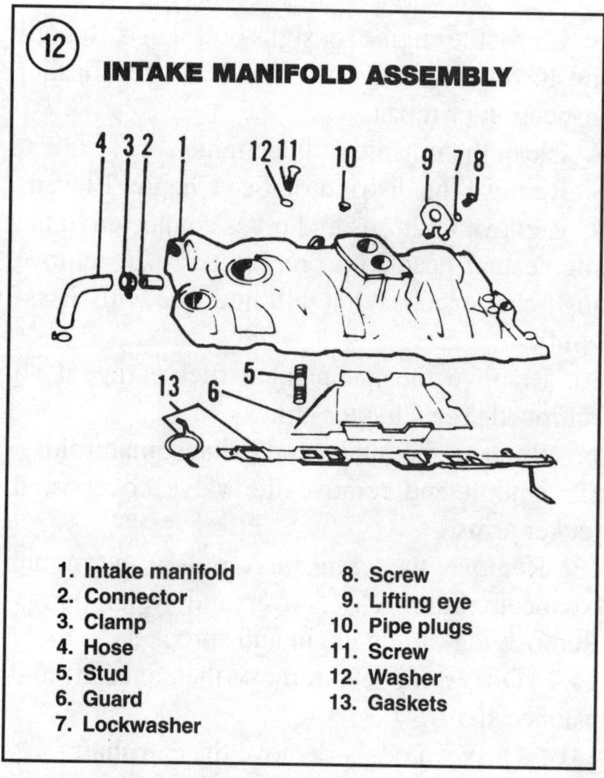

11. Mark the position of the distributor rotor on the intake manifold, remove the screw attaching the distributor hold-down clamp and the clamp, then withdraw the distributor.

NOTE
When withdrawing the distributor, the rotor will turn as the drive gears separate. Observe the direction that the rotor turns and its final location when the distributor is free. Knowing this angle will help you install the distributor in its original position.

12. Disconnect the wire from the oil pressure sender. On some engines, it may be necessary to remove the sender in order to remove the screws that attach the manifold.

13. Disconnect the wire from the electric choke and any other wires that will interfere with manifold removal.

NOTE
On V6 and small block V8 engines, the manifold is attached with 12 screws. On big block V8 engines, the manifold is attached with 16 screws. Make sure that all of the screws are removed before attempting to remove the manifold.

14. Loosen all of the screws attaching the intake manifold, then remove the fasteners. Pry the manifold loose, then lift it from the engine block.

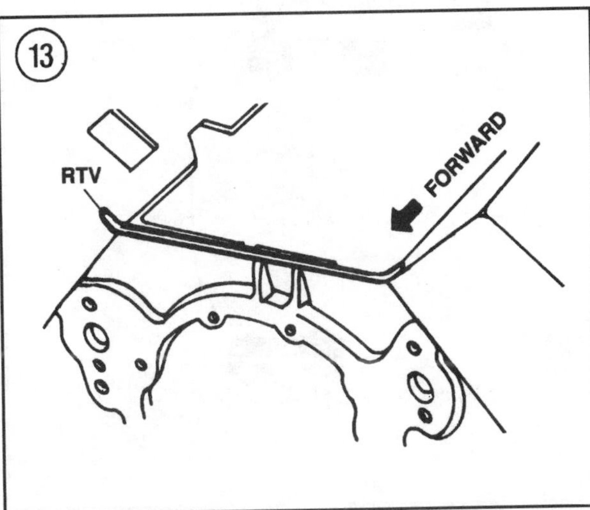

15. Remove and discard the intake manifold gaskets and end seals.

16. Clean all gasket and sealer residue from the block, cylinder heads and intake manifold with degreaser and a scraper.

17. If the intake manifold is being replaced, transfer the carburetor (or fuel rail and injectors), thermostat and housing, throttle cable anchor block unit, temperature sending unit and any other hardware from the old to the new manifold.

CAUTION
Make sure to use the correct gaskets between the intake manifold and the cylinder heads. It is important to remove the metal insert from the starboard gasket to provide sufficient clearance for the intake manifold heat pipe on some engines. It is important that metal inserts cover the center passage on other models. Purchase the correct gaskets for your engine and follow the manufacturer's instruction to be sure the automatic choke will function properly.

18. Coat the gaskets with sealer at the water passages. Position the gaskets against the cylinder head(s).

NOTE
Clearance between the manifold and the block is closer for models which do not use a gasket seal at the ends. Be sure to use the correct gaskets and method of sealing the ends for your engine.

19A. *On models without gaskets at the front and rear of the manifold,* apply a 3/16 in. (4.8 mm) bead of RTV sealant on the front and rear rails of the cylinder block (between the cylinder heads). Extend the sealant 1/2 in. (12.7 mm) up each end of the manifold side gaskets. See **Figure 13**.

19B. *On models with gaskets at the front and rear of the manifold,* use an approved adhesive to glue the rubber gaskets to the cylinder block (between the cylinder heads). Follow the instructions on the adhesive container. Then, apply a

small amount of RTV sealant to each end of the gaskets to provide a good seal between the side and end gaskets.
20. Lower the intake manifold straight down into position against the cylinder heads and block. Check the seal area to make sure the seals are in their proper positions. If not, remove the manifold, correct the seal position and reinstall the manifold.
21. Install the manifold attaching screws. Tighten the screws to specification (**Table 4** or **Table 5**) in the sequence shown in **Figure 14** (V6 and small block V8) or **Figure 15** (big block V8).
22. Refer to Chapter Eleven to install and time the ignition distributor.
23. Reverse Steps 1-13 to complete installation.

Inspection

1. Check the intake manifold for cracks or distortion. Replace the manifold if it is distorted or if cracks are found.
2. Check the mating surfaces for nicks or burrs. Remove small burrs may be removed with a file.
3. Place a straightedge across the manifold flange/mating surfaces. If there is any gap between the straightedge and surface, measure it with a flat feeler gauge. Measure the manifold from end to end and from corner to corner. If the mating surface is not flat within 0.006 in. (0.15 mm) per foot of manifold length, replace the manifold.

EXHAUST MANIFOLDS

Figures 16-18 show typical exhaust manifolds used on Volvo Penta models. Exhaust elbow high-rise kits are available for installations where the stern of the boat rests low in the water,

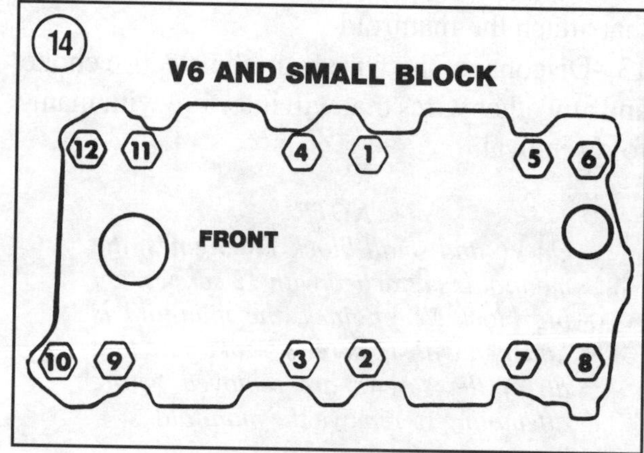

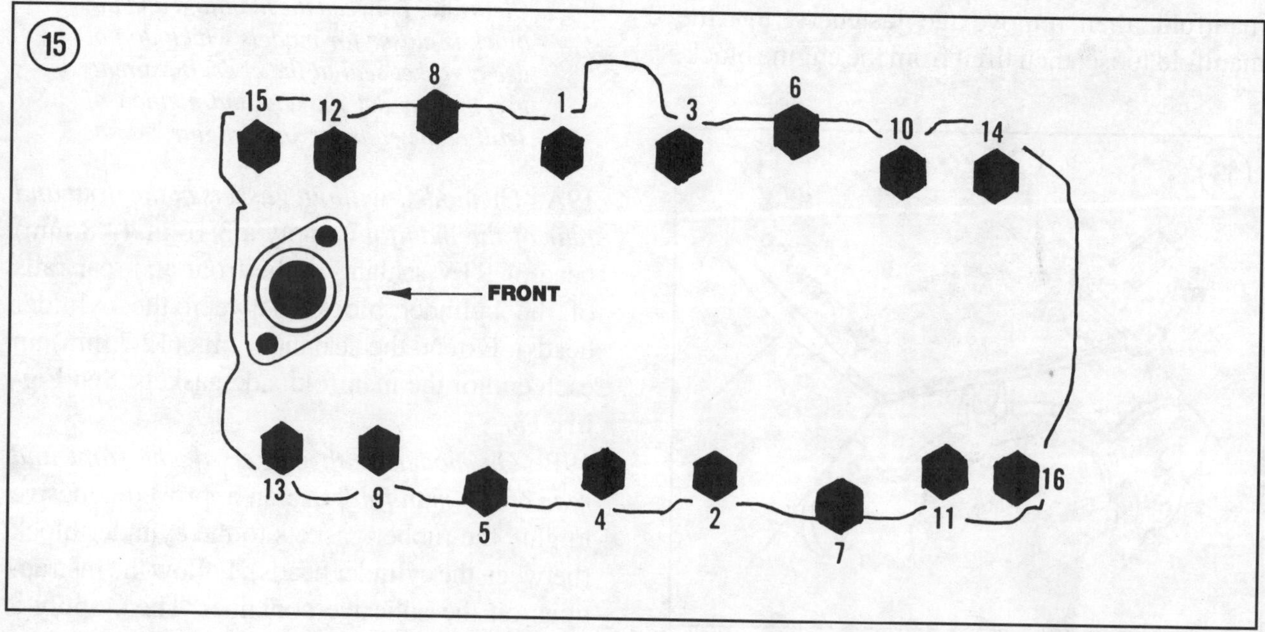

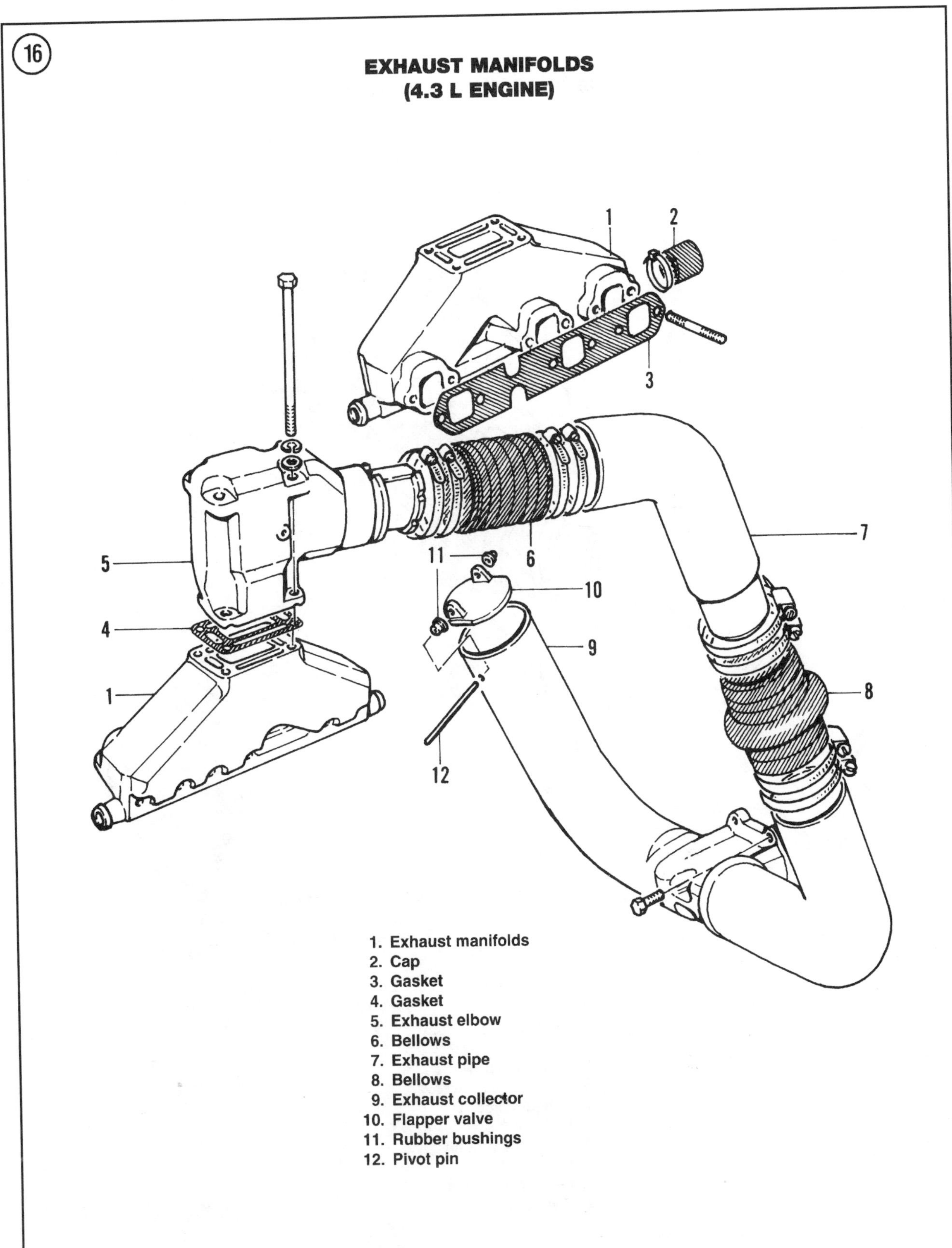
16
EXHAUST MANIFOLDS
(4.3 L ENGINE)
1
2
3
5
6
7
11
10
4
9
1
8
12
1. Exhaust manifolds
2. Cap
3. Gasket
4. Gasket
5. Exhaust elbow
6. Bellows
7. Exhaust pipe
8. Bellows
9. Exhaust collector
10. Flapper valve
11. Rubber bushings
12. Pivot pin

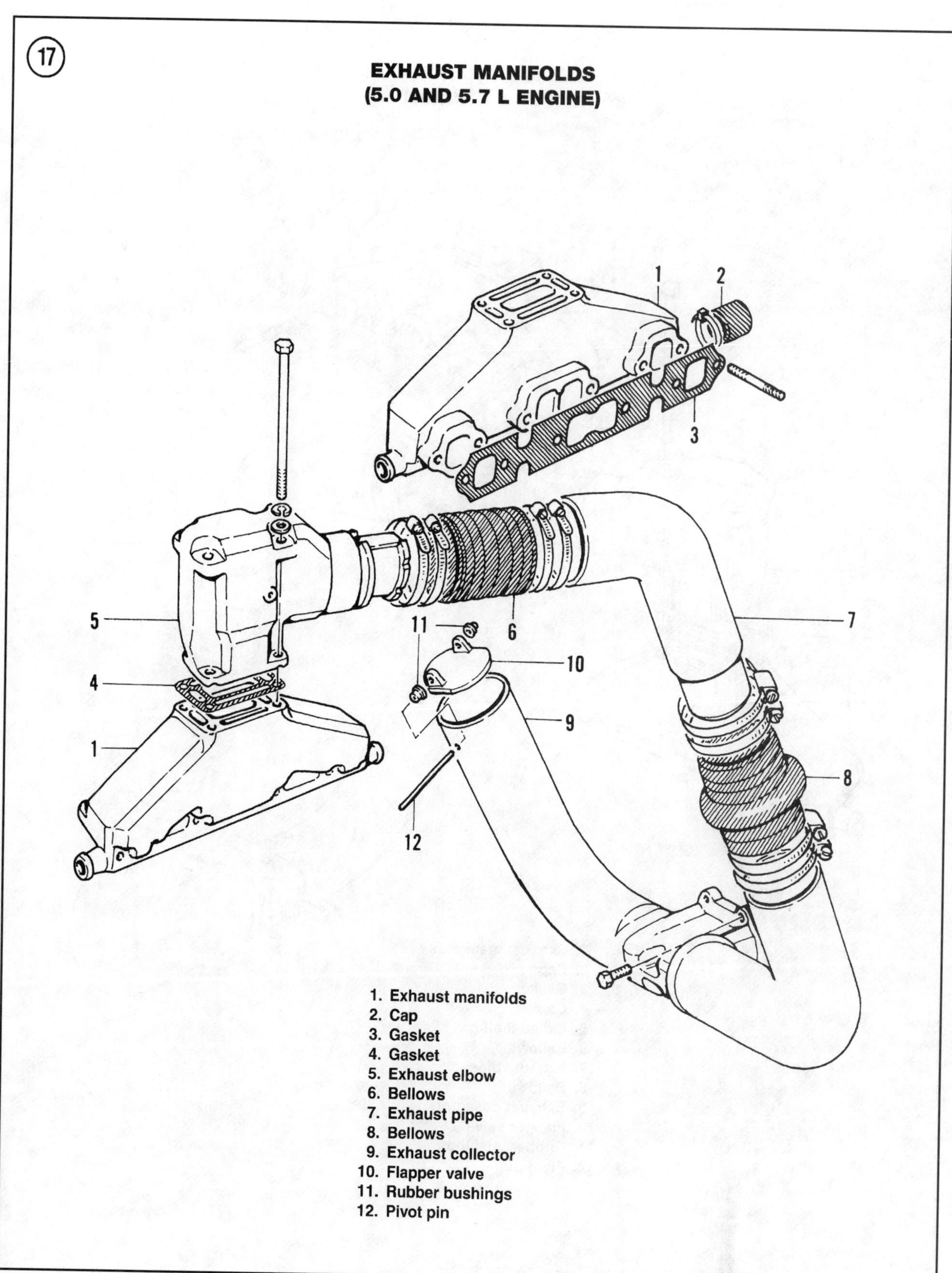
17
EXHAUST MANIFOLDS
(5.0 AND 5.7 L ENGINE)
1
2
3
5
4
1
11
6
10
9
7
8
12
1. Exhaust manifolds
2. Cap
3. Gasket
4. Gasket
5. Exhaust elbow
6. Bellows
7. Exhaust pipe
8. Bellows
9. Exhaust collector
10. Flapper valve
11. Rubber bushings
12. Pivot pin

or if the distance between the waterline and the top of the elbows is less than the recommended minimum. The minimum height is 13 in. (33 cm) for V6 models and 14 in. (35.6 mm) for V8 models. The boat manufacturer or installing dealer will usually determine if a high-rise kit is required. See your Volvo Penta dealer for further information.

Removal/Installation

Refer to **Figure 16**, **Figure 17** or **Figure 18** for this procedure.

1. Disconnect the battery cable from the negative terminal.
2. Open the cylinder block water drains and allow all water to drain. It may be necessary to remove the sediment from the open drain by inserting a wire into the opening.
3. Loosen the clamps on the exhaust manifold bellows, then pull the bellows free from the manifolds. See **Figure 19**.
4. Loosen hose clamps, then detach all coolant hoses from the manifolds.
5. Remove or detach any clamps or accessories that are attached to the manifolds, if necessary.

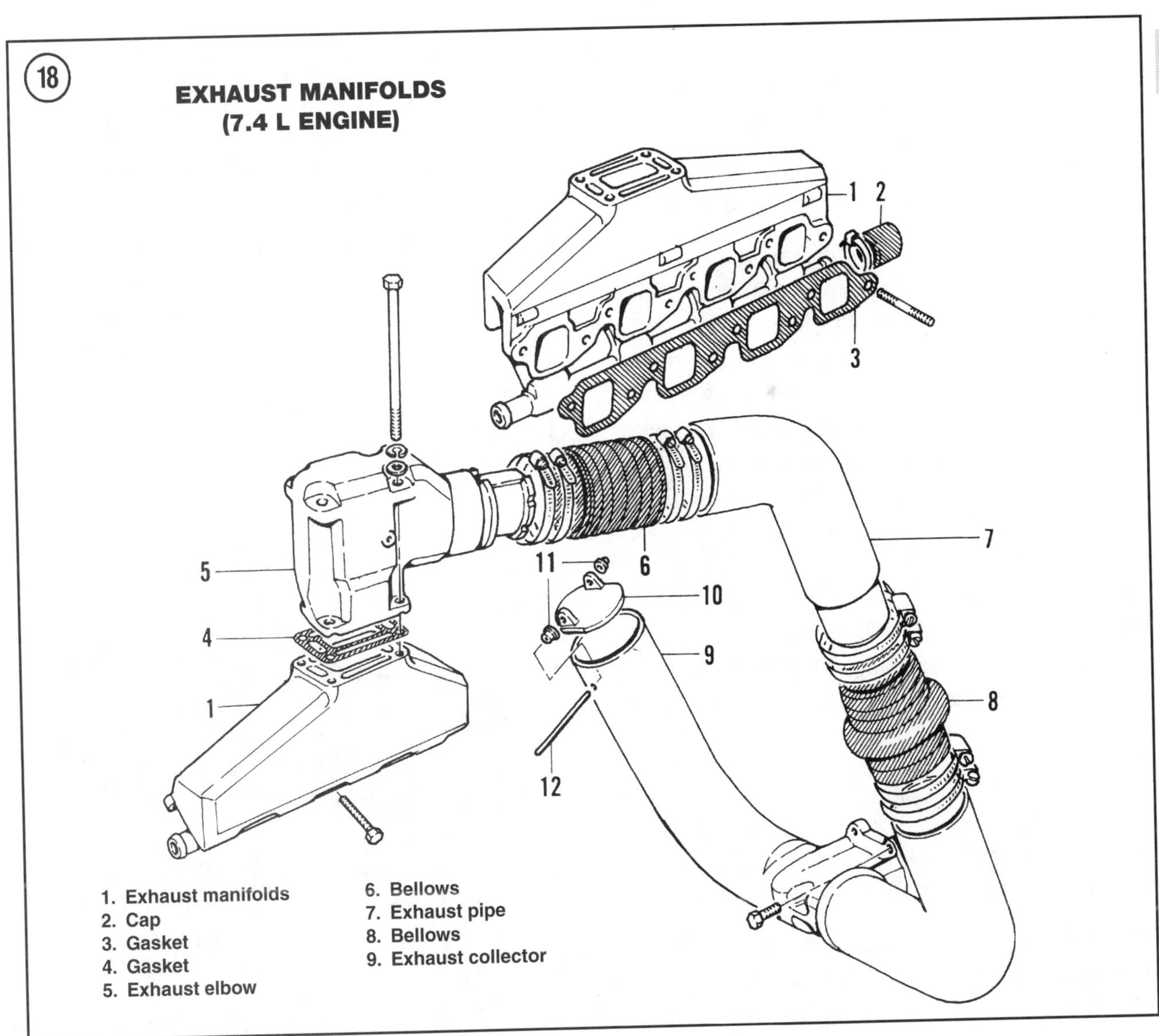

1. Exhaust manifolds
2. Cap
3. Gasket
4. Gasket
5. Exhaust elbow
6. Bellows
7. Exhaust pipe
8. Bellows
9. Exhaust collector

NOTE
The exhaust elbow can be unbolted from the manifold either before or after removing the manifold, but it is often easier to remove the attaching fasteners while the manifold is still attached to the engine. If fasteners are broken, remove the broken part and repair the threads as required before completing the assembly.

6. Remove the manifold attaching nuts or bolts and washers. Remove the manifold and discard the gasket(s).
7. Clean all gasket residue from the cylinder head, manifold and the riser mating surfaces.

NOTE
The manufacturer recommends replacing the exhaust bellows every 2 years. Also, do not use elastic stop nuts more than twice. It is a good idea to replace these parts each time they are removed.

8. Install the exhaust bellows and all of its clamps on the exhaust pipe. Make sure all of the clamps are in place, but not tightened, then slide the bellows down on the pipe to facilitate installation of the exhaust manifold and elbow.
9. Install the manifold on the cylinder head with a new gasket. Install all of the fasteners attaching the manifold to the cylinder head finger-tight. Tighten the fasteners to the torque specification in **Table 4** or **Table 5**, beginning with those at the center and working toward the ends.
10. Install the exhaust elbow if not already attached to the exhaust manifold. Tighten the fasteners to the torque specified in **Table 4** or **Table 5**.

NOTE
Lubricate the inside of the bellows with soapy water to ease installation onto the exhaust pipe and elbow.

11. Slide the exhaust bellows up onto the elbow, then tighten the attaching clamps.
12. Reverse Steps 1-5 to complete installation.

Inspection/Cleaning

1. Inspect the engine exhaust passages in the manifolds and exhaust risers for excessive corrosion or deposits. Replace the manifold if excessive corrosion is found.
2. Check water passages for clogging.
3. Remove pipe plugs and drains from the manifold and exhaust elbow, if so equipped. Check for sand, silt or other foreign matter.

EXHAUST BELLOWS AND FLAPPER VALVE

The manufacturer suggests that new exhaust bellows (6 and 8, **Figures 16-18**) be installed every other year. Inspect the bellows and replace if hard, torn or damaged. Running the engine without proper cooling will quickly damage the bellows as well as other parts.

An exhaust flapper valve (10, **Figures 16-18**) is located in the upper end of the exhaust pipe on some models. Flapper valves are installed to keep water from backing up into the engine. The

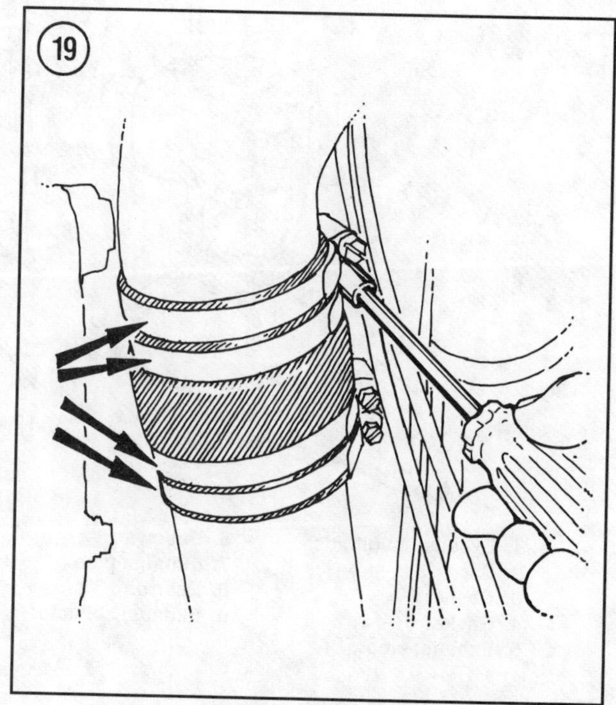

valves should move freely. If the valve(s) are stuck, damaged or installed improperly, the exhaust can be restricted or water can back up into the engine. New rubber bushings (11, **Figures 16-18**) must be installed whenever the valve is removed.

Removal/Installation

1. Loosen the clamps that attach the upper bellows (**Figure 19**) to the exhaust collector and the exhaust elbow. Loosen the bellows after the clamps are loose. Slide the bellows up, onto the exhaust elbow.
2. Loosen the clamps that attach the bellows (**Figure 19**) to the exhaust riser and the exhaust elbow.
3. Loosen the bellows after the clamps are loose, then remove the exhaust elbow and both bellows.
4. Loosen the lower clamps and remove the bellows from the exhaust collector.

NOTE
If the exhaust flapper valve is stuck, damaged or installed improperly, exhaust can be restricted and water can back up into the exhaust causing engine damage.

5. Check the exhaust flapper valve (10, **Figures 16-18**) for freedom of movement.
6. If it is necessary to remove the flapper valve, proceed as follows:
   a. Drive the pivot shaft (12, **Figures 16-18**) from the valve and bushings using a small diameter punch.
   b. Lift the flapper valve from the exhaust collector pipe.

   NOTE
   Use care to keep the bushings from falling into the exhaust collector when removing them. The bushing flanges are positioned toward the inside of the pipe.

   c. Push (or drive) the rubber bushings from the exhaust collector.
   d. Apply Scotch Grip Rubber Adhesive to new bushings and insert them into their bores in the exhaust collector. The flanged side of the bushings must face toward the inside.
   e. Position the exhaust flapper valve in the collector, between the bushings with the holes in flanges aligned with the rubber bushings. The long side of the valve must be down.
   f. Insert the pin through 1 rubber bushing and the valve flanges, then align the pin with the second bushing and push the pin through the second rubber bushing.
   g. Check the valve for freedom of movement. The ends of the pin must be flush with the exhaust collector on both sides. It is important to have the valve correctly installed before completing the reassembly of the exhaust system.

7

NOTE
Lubricate the inside of the bellows with soapy water to ease installation onto the exhaust pipe and elbow.

7. Position the upper and lower bellows and all of the clamps on the exhaust elbow, then install the exhaust elbow. All of the clamps should be very loose until both bellows are correctly attached to the exhaust riser, exhaust elbow and exhaust collector.
8. Make sure the bellows are on completely and not twisted, then tighten the clamp screws securely.

ROCKER ARMS

Removal

Each rocker arm moves on its own pivot ball, which is retained by a nut or a shoulder bolt. It is not necessary to remove the rocker arm to remove the pushrod, simply loosen the nut or bolt and move the arm away from the pushrod.

To remove the entire assembly, proceed as follows.

1. Remove the valve cover(s) as described in this chapter.

2A. On models with a nut and stud (**Figure 20**):

   a. Turn the crankshaft until the lifter is on the camshaft's base circle (valve closed).
   b. Remove the rocker arm nut and pivot ball.
   c. Remove the rocker arm.
   d. Remove the pushrod from the cylinder block if necessary.

2B. On models with a shoulder bolt (**Figure 21**):

   a. Remove the shoulder bolt, then lift the rocker arm and pivot ball from the cylinder head.
   b. Remove the pushrod from the cylinder block if necessary.

CAUTION

The rocker arm, pivot ball, pushrod and lifter establish a wear pattern to each other and to the valve which it opens. Therefore, always reinstall in their original location. Also, install the pushrod with the same end up as when originally assembled. When removing, identify the parts for correct assembly.

3. Repeat Step 2A or 2B for each remaining rocker arm. Place each rocker arm and pushrod assembly in a separate container or use a rack to keep them separated for reinstallation in the same position from which they were removed.

Installation

1. Lubricate the rocker arms and pivot balls with engine oil.
2. Install the pushrods, making sure that each fits into its lifter socket.
3. Install the rocker arms, pivot balls and nuts or shoulder bolts. If new rocker arms or pivot balls are being installed, coat the contact surfaces with engine oil or Molykote.

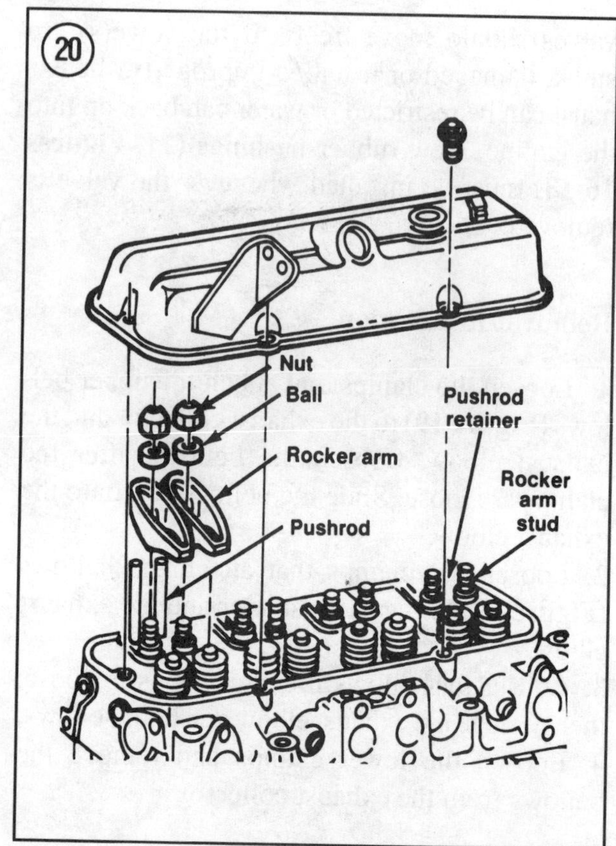

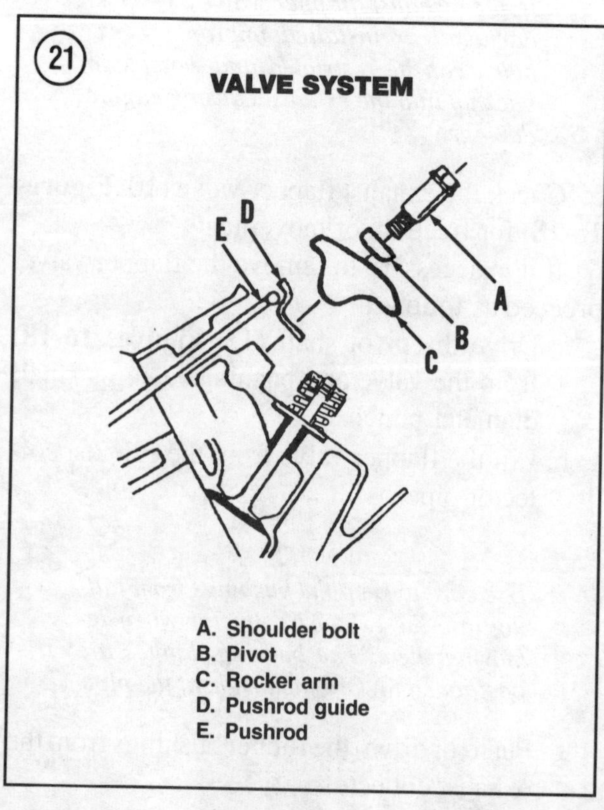

VALVE SYSTEM

A. Shoulder bolt
B. Pivot
C. Rocker arm
D. Pushrod guide
E. Pushrod

4A. If the rocker arm is attached with a nut and stud (**Figure 20**), adjust the valve clearance as described in this chapter.

4B. If the rocker arm is attached with a shoulder bolt (**Figure 21**), tighten the rocker arm shoulder bolts to the torque listed in **Table 4** or **Table 5**.

5. Install the valve cover(s) as described in this chapter.

Valve Clearance Adjustment

Valve adjustment is possible only on models with rocker arms retained by nuts and is not adjustable for models with shoulder bolts.

Adjustment should *not be required* unless the valve train has been disassembled. These engines are equipped with hydraulic lifters that automatically adjust to compensate for normal wear. Adjust the valves with the engine stopped and the lifter on the base circle of the camshaft lobe.

NOTE
Adjusting used lifters can be especially difficult since the described adjustment may position internal parts of the lifter in a previously unused area of travel, causing the lifter to stick. If 1 valve requires adjustment after a period of normal operation, the condition of the lifter and the cam lobe that operates that valve should be checked as described in this chapter.

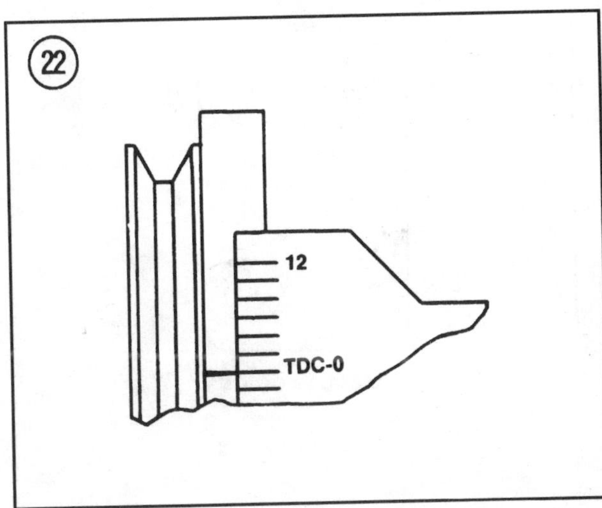

1. Rotate the crankshaft until the pulley notch aligns with the zero mark on the timing tab. See **Figure 22**, typical. This positions the No. 1 cylinder at TDC. This position can be verified by placing a finger on the No. 1 cylinder rocker arms as the pulley notch nears the zero mark. If the valves are moving, the engine is in the No. 4 (V6) or No. 6 (V8) firing position. Rotate the crankshaft pulley 1 full turn to reach the No. 1 firing position.

NOTE
The intake valves are those closer to the intake ports. The exhaust valves are closer to the exhaust ports.

2. With the engine in the No. 1 firing position, refer to **Figure 23** and adjust the following valves:
   a. Intake: 1, 2, 3 (V6) or 1, 2, 5, 7 (V8).
   b. Exhaust: 1, 5, 6 (V6) or 1, 3, 4, 8 (V8).

CAUTION
Improper adjustment can prevent the engine from starting and may result in bent push rods or other damage to the valve train. If the lifters are not full of oil, only the light pressure of the spring inside the lifter may be confused with clearance when performing Step 3.

3. To adjust each valve,
   a. Loosen (back off) the adjusting nut until some lash (clearance) is felt at the pushrod.
   b. Turn the nut clockwise (tighten) to just remove all lash. Determine this point by turning the pushrod with your fingers while slowly tightening the nut. See **Figure 24**. When lash has been removed, the pushrod will not rotate freely.
   c. Turn the nut 1 complete turn (360°) to center the plunger inside the lifter.

4. Rotate the crankshaft exactly 1 full turn and realign the pulley notch with the timing tab zero mark (**Figure 22**). Turning the crankshaft 1 turn

will position the No. 4 (V6) or No. 6 (V8) cylinder in the firing position. Refer to **Figure 23** and adjust the following valves:

a. Intake: 4, 5, 6 (V6) or 3, 4, 6, 8 (V8).

b. Exhaust: 2, 3, 4 (V6) or 2, 5, 6, 7 (V8).

5. Install the valve (rocker arm) cover as described in this chapter.

CRANKSHAFT PULLEY AND HARMONIC BALANCER

The crankshaft pulley and the harmonic balancer are located on the front of the crankshaft. The crankshaft pulley drives the raw water pump, coolant circulating pump, power steering pump and alternator. The pulley is attached to the harmonic balancer with screws. The harmonic balancer is keyed and is a press fit on the front of the crankshaft. The balancer is usually fitted with a large center retaining screw. The harmonic balancer is sometimes called a torsional damper or vibration damper and serves several critical functions.

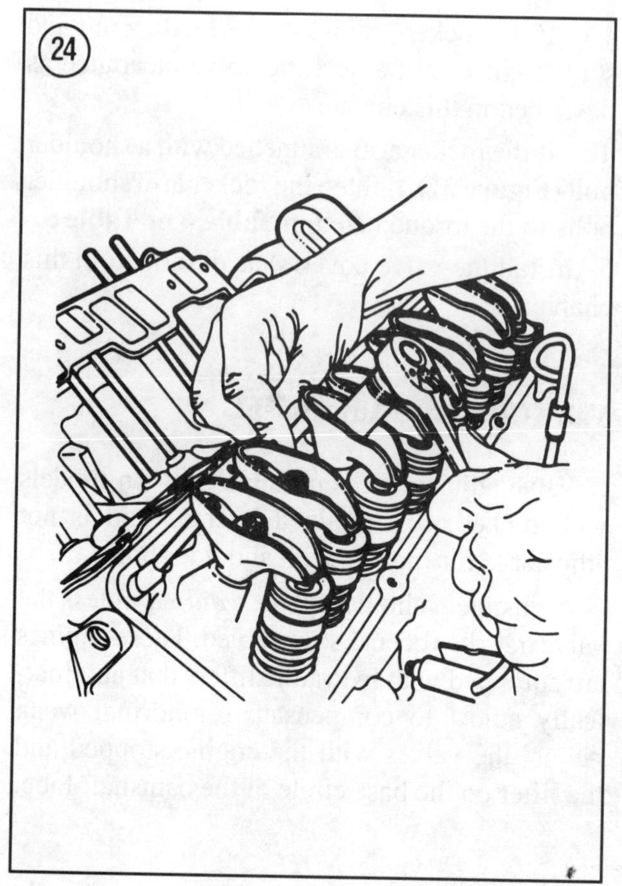

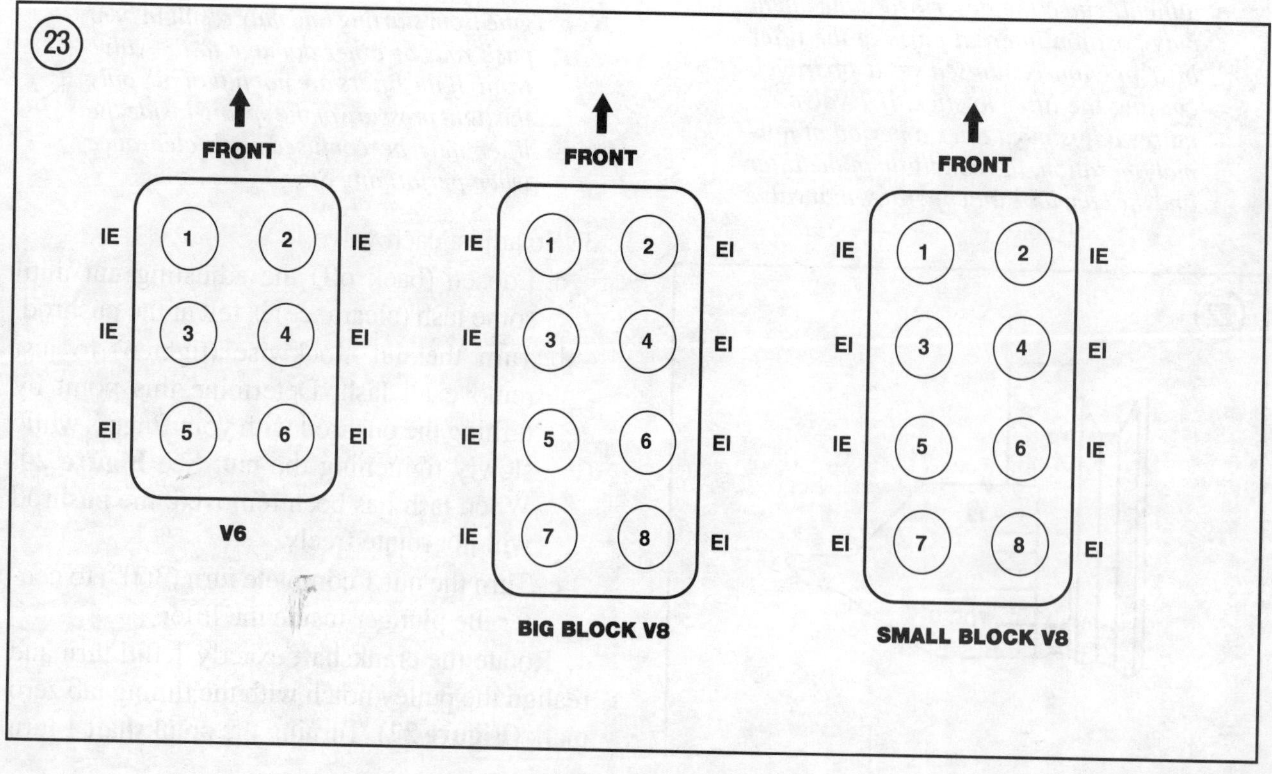

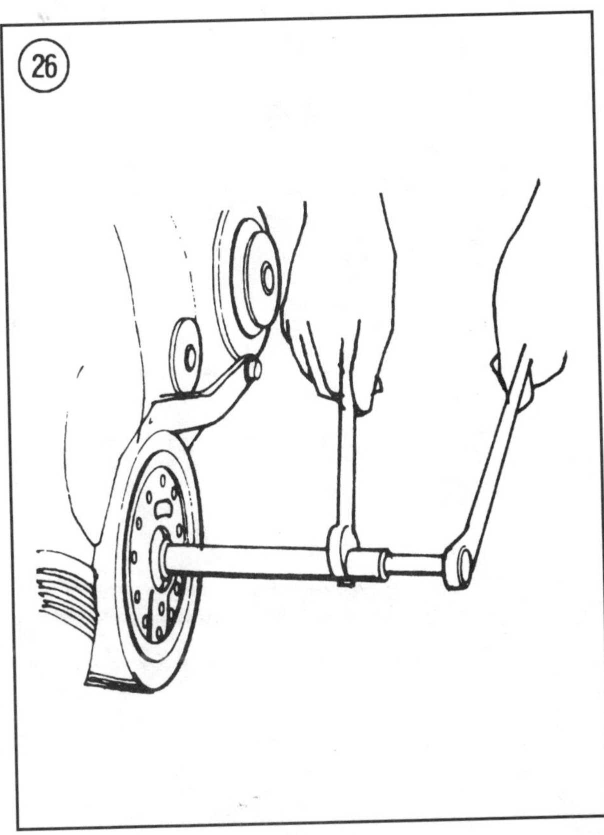

Removal/Installation

1. Remove the alternator drive belt. See Chapter Eleven.
2. Remove the screws attaching the pulley, then remove the pulley from the crankshaft and harmonic balancer.
3. Remove the large screw from the center of the harmonic balancer.
4. Attach a suitable puller (part No. J-39046 for V6 and small block V8 engines, part No. J-23523-E for big block engines) to the balancer and withdraw the harmonic balancer from the crankshaft. See **Figure 25**, typical.

NOTE
It is important to install the correct harmonic balancer for the specific engine. Timing marks on the balancer are used for ignition timing and other purposes. If the outside ring is loose, the mark will be allowed to move and will invalidate the mark. It may also cause other damage, so replace the balancer if its outer ring is loose. The balancer and the flywheel may also be used to balance the engine crankshaft.

5. Use clean engine oil to lubricate the lip of the seal located in the front cover, the seal contact surface on the harmonic balancer and the end of the crankshaft.

NOTE
If the appropriate special tool (listed in Step 4) is not available for use in Step 6, use a thick flat washer, a full-threaded 7/16-20 × 4 in. bolt and 7/16-20 nut to pull the balancer onto the crankshaft.

6. Position the harmonic balancer over the crankshaft key and install the threaded tool in the end of the crankshaft so that at least 1/2 in. (12.7 mm) of the tool threads are engaged. Install the plate, thrust bearing and nut to complete the tool installation.
7. Pull the balancer into position as shown in **Figure 26**, typical.

8. Remove the tool and install the large retaining bolt and washer. Tighten to specification listed in **Table 4** or **Table 5**.
9. Install the pulley and tighten the attaching bolts.
10. Install and adjust the alternator drive belt. See Chapter Eleven.

TIMING CHAIN FRONT COVER AND OIL SEAL

Front Cover Removal/Installation

The oil pan is sealed against the lower surface of the front cover and the lower oil pan gasket is usually damaged during front cover removal. The preferred method of front cover removal is to first remove the oil pan. However, the front cover can be removed without oil pan removal as follows.

1. Open the engine drain valve(s) and drain all the water (or coolant) from the block.
2. Drain the crankcase oil. See Chapter Four.
3. If the oil pan is to be removed, follow the procedure in this chapter.
4. Loosen, then remove the belts from the alternator, raw water pump, power steering pump and crankshaft pulleys.
5. Unbolt and remove the pulley from the engine coolant circulating pump.
6. Remove any accessory brackets attached to the engine coolant circulating pump.
7. Remove the engine coolant circulating pump. See Chapter Ten.
8. Unbolt and remove the crankshaft pulley, then pull the harmonic balancer from the crankshaft as described in this chapter.

9A. If the oil pan is not removed, proceed as follows:

a. Remove the 2 screws holding the front of the oil pan to the front cover.
b. Unbolt the front cover from the engine, pull the cover away from the block slightly, then use a sharp knife to cut the oil pan gasket flush with the front face of the cylinder block. See **Figure 27**.

9B. If the oil pan is removed, remove the screws attaching the front cover to the engine.

10. Lift the front cover away from the block and discard the gasket.
11. Clean oil, grease and gasket residue from the block and front cover sealing surfaces.

12A. If the oil pan is not removed, proceed as follows:

a. Cut a portion of the front of a new oil pan gasket to match the section that was removed with the front cover. See **Figure 28**.
b. Coat the exposed surface of the oil pan flange with sealer and install the portion of the gasket cut in substep a. Make sure it fits properly.

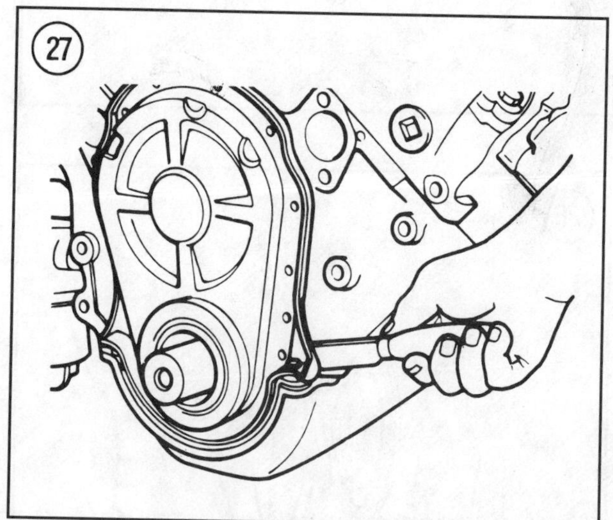

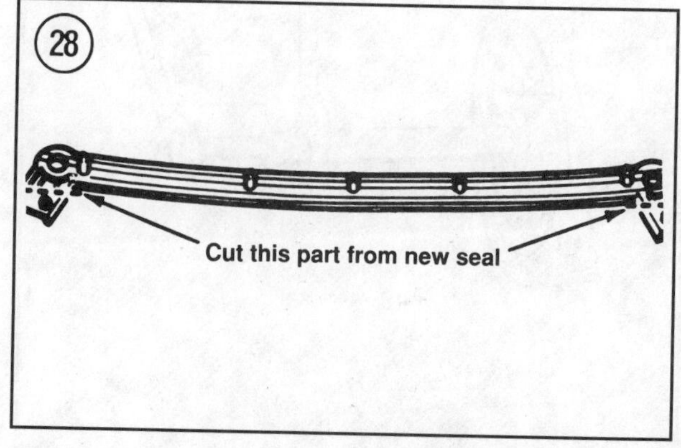

c. Apply a 1/8 in. (3.2 mm) bead of RTV sealant along the joint on each side where the oil pan, front cover and block meet. See **Figure 29**.
d. Coat the gasket surfaces of the block and front cover with sealer and install a new gasket over the dowel pins on the engine block.
e. Position the front cover on the engine block. Work carefully to prevent damage to the crankshaft seal or movement of the gaskets.
f. Apply downward pressure on the front cover and install the oil pan attaching screws finger-tight. Make sure the cover is correctly installed over the dowel pins.

12B. If the oil pan is removed, proceed as follows:

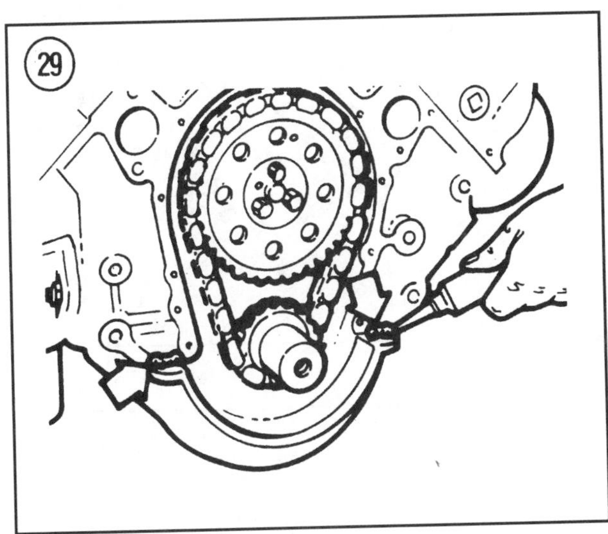

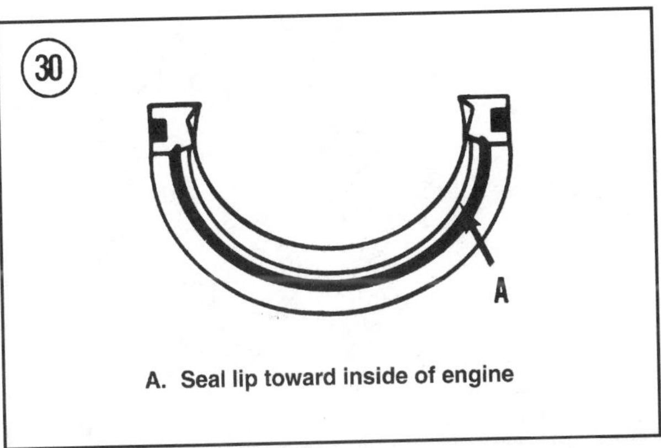

A. Seal lip toward inside of engine

a. Coat the gasket surfaces of the block and front cover with sealer and install a new gasket over the dowel pins on the engine block.
b. Position the front cover on the engine block.

13. Install and tighten the screws attaching the front cover. Install the oil pan as described in this chapter.
14. Reverse Steps 1-8 to complete installation. Be sure to lubricate the lip of the seal, harmonic balancer bore and the end of the crankshaft with oil before installing the balancer.

Front Cover Seal Replacement

The seal can be replaced without removing the front cover. If the cover has been removed and seal replacement is necessary, support the cover on a clean workbench and perform Steps 2-4.

1. Remove the harmonic balancer as described in this chapter.
2. Pry the oil seal from the cover with a large screwdriver or seal puller tool. Work carefully to prevent damage to the cover seal surface.
3. Clean the seal recess in the cover with solvent and blow dry with compressed air.
4. Position a new seal in the cover recess with its lip facing the inside of the engine (**Figure 30**). Drive seal into place with installer part No. J-35468 or equivalent tool. See **Figure 31**.
5. Install the harmonic balancer as described in this chapter.

7

TIMING CHAIN AND SPROCKETS

Removal

1. Remove the spark plugs. See Chapter Four.
2. Remove the harmonic balancer as described in this chapter.
3. Remove the front cover as described in this chapter.
4. Temporarily reinstall the large bolt and washer that retains the harmonic balancer in the

end of the crankshaft. Place a wrench on the bolt and rotate the crankshaft to position the camshaft and crankshaft sprocket marks as shown in **Figure 32**. Remove the bolt and washer.

NOTE
*With the marks on the camshaft and crankshaft sprockets together as shown in **Figure 32**, the engine's No. 1 cylinder is at TDC of its exhaust stroke. On V6 engines, the No. 4 cylinder is at TDC of compression (near ignition firing position) and on V8 engines, the No 6 cylinder is at TDC of compression.*

5. Remove the fasteners attaching the sprocket to the camshaft. Screws are used to attach the sprocket to the camshaft on V8 models. A special stud is also used to attach the balance shaft drive gear to the camshaft on V6 engines On this stud, the camshaft is retained by a nut.
6. Remove the camshaft sprocket and timing chain as an assembly.

NOTE
The sprocket is a snug fit, but should come off easily. If it does not, tap the lower edge of the sprocket lightly with a

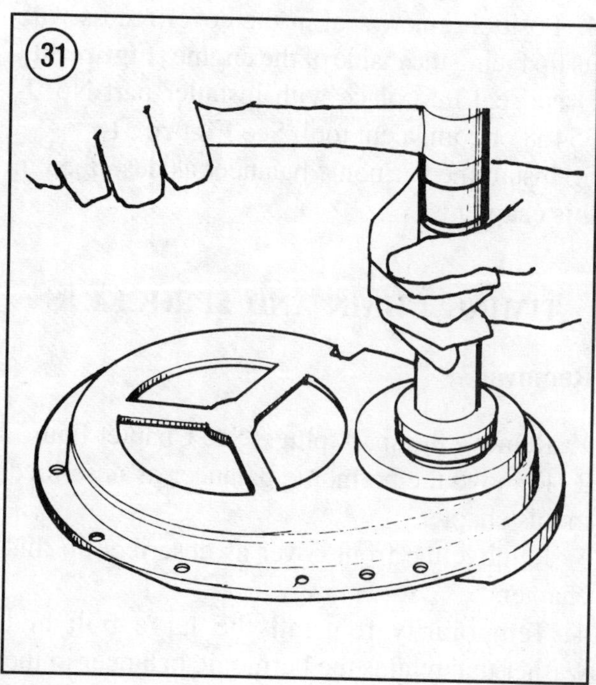

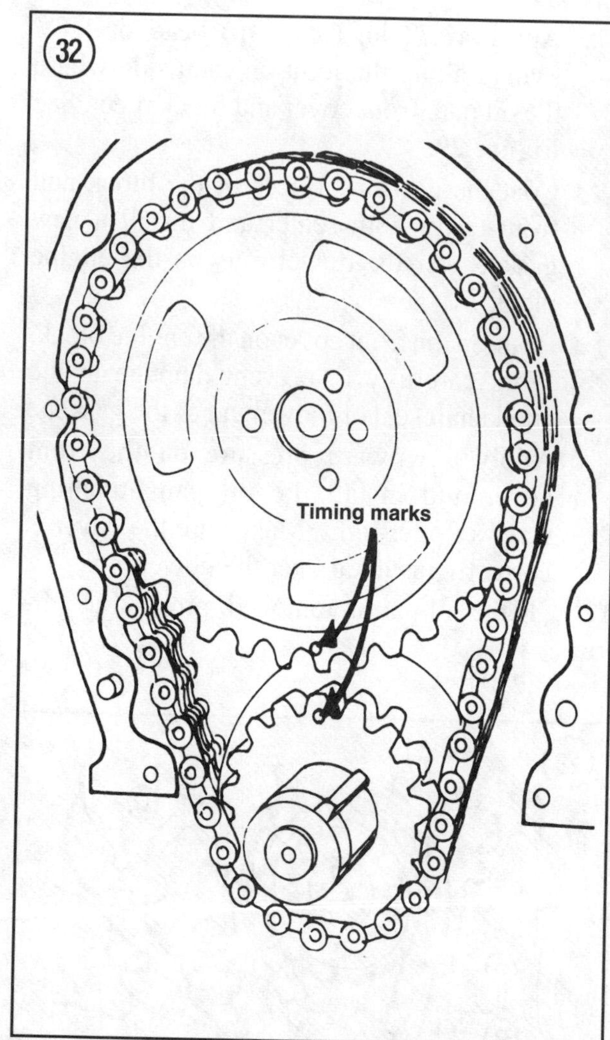

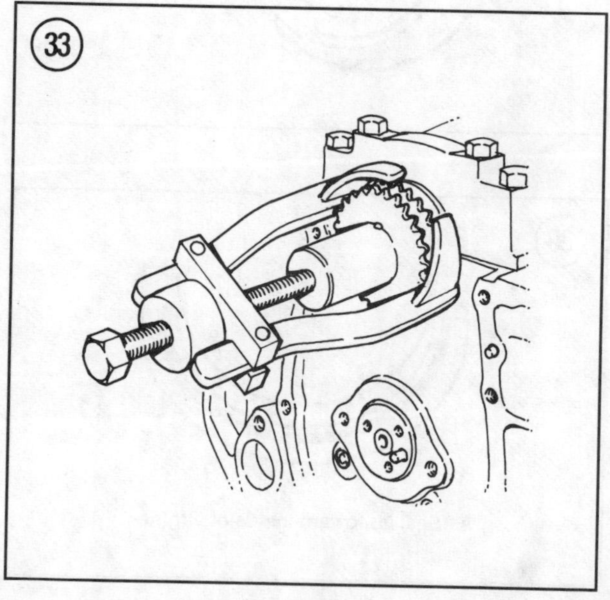

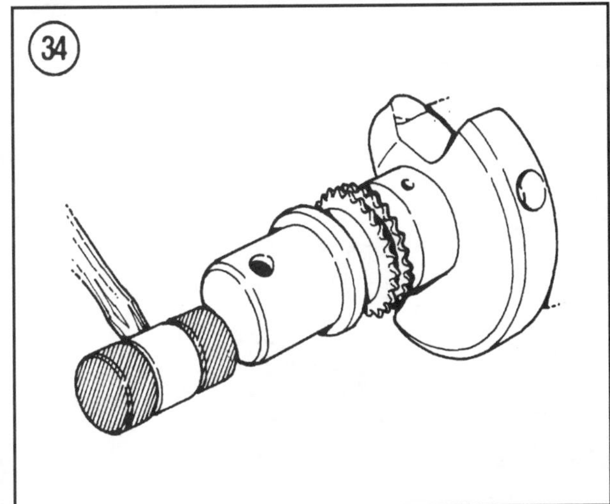
34

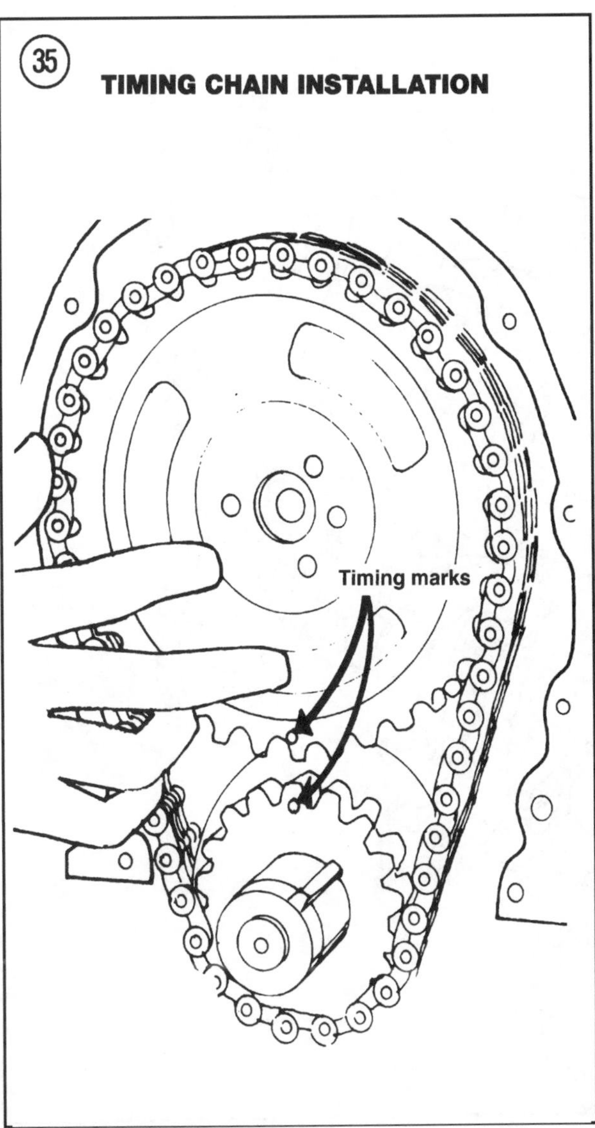

35 TIMING CHAIN INSTALLATION

soft faced hammer to dislodge it from the camshaft.

7. If the crankshaft sprocket requires removal, it may be necessary to use a suitable puller to remove it. See **Figure 33**.

Installation

Some engines are equipped with a link-type timing chain and aluminum/nylon camshaft sprocket, while other models are equipped with roller chain. The chain must be matched to the sprocket type. Make sure the correct parts are installed for your engine application.

1. Install the crankshaft sprocket, if removed. On some models, it is necessary to drive the sprocket into place with a special driver part No. J-22102, or equivalent. See **Figure 34**.
2. Turn the crankshaft until the sprocket timing mark is toward the top and in the center as shown in **Figure 32**.
3. Lubricate the timing chain with clean engine oil before installing.
4. Install the timing chain over the camshaft sprocket and allow the chain to hang freely from the sprocket.
5. Align the timing mark on the camshaft sprocket with the crankshaft sprocket timing mark and fit the lower section of the chain over the crankshaft sprocket. See **Figure 35**.

NOTE
Do not drive the camshaft sprocket into place in Step 6 or you may dislodge the core plug behind the camshaft in the rear of the block. The sprocket may be a tight fit, but should not bind.

6. If necessary, turn the camshaft to align the dowel in the camshaft with the dowel hole in the camshaft sprocket and install the attaching fasteners. Keep the timing marks aligned and do not disengage the chain from either sprocket.

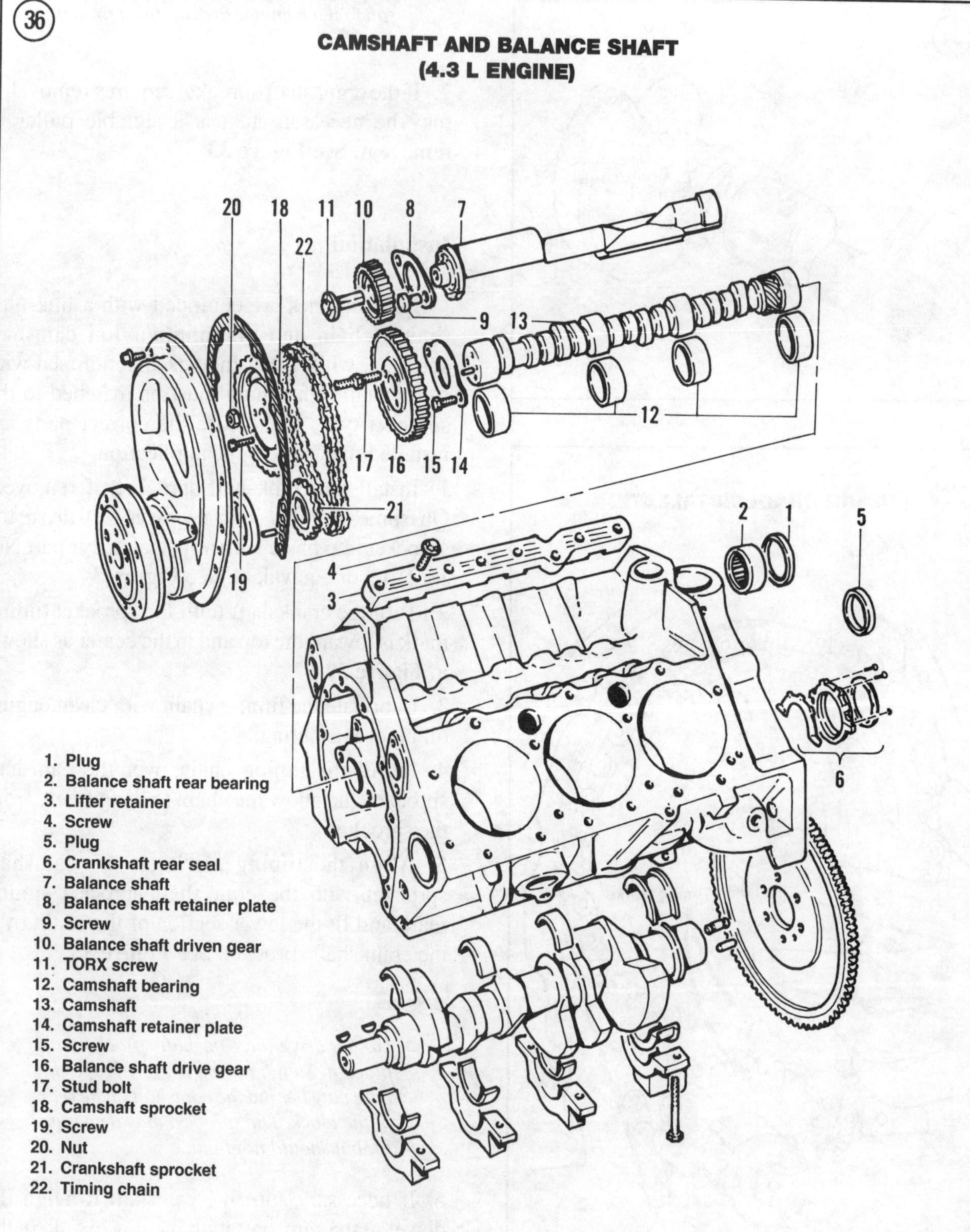
36
CAMSHAFT AND BALANCE SHAFT
(4.3 L ENGINE)
20
18
11
10
8
7
22
9
13
12
17
16
15
14
21
2
1
5
4
3
19
6
1. Plug
2. Balance shaft rear bearing
3. Lifter retainer
4. Screw
5. Plug
6. Crankshaft rear seal
7. Balance shaft
8. Balance shaft retainer plate
9. Screw
10. Balance shaft driven gear
11. TORX screw
12. Camshaft bearing
13. Camshaft
14. Camshaft retainer plate
15. Screw
16. Balance shaft drive gear
17. Stud bolt
18. Camshaft sprocket
19. Screw
20. Nut
21. Crankshaft sprocket
22. Timing chain

7. Tighten the camshaft sprocket mounting screws or nuts to the specification in **Table 4** or **Table 5**.

8. Make sure the camshaft sprocket timing mark is still exactly aligned with the crankshaft sprocket timing mark. Both marks must be on a straight line between the shafts. See **Figure 35**.

9. Install the front cover and harmonic balancer as described in this chapter.

10. Reinstall the spark plugs. See Chapter Four.

BALANCE SHAFT (V6 MODELS)

V6 models are equipped with a balance shaft designed to dampen much of the dynamic vibration in the 1,700-2,000 rpm range. The balance shaft is located in the engine block valley area, directly above the camshaft. The balance shaft is driven by a gear located behind the camshaft sprocket. See **Figure 36**. The balance shaft is supported by a roller bearing at the front and an insert type bearing at the rear.

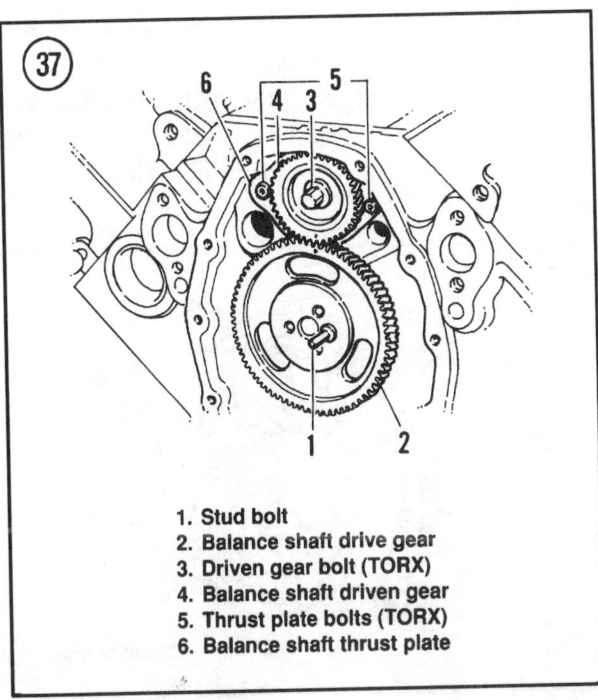

1. Stud bolt
2. Balance shaft drive gear
3. Driven gear bolt (TORX)
4. Balance shaft driven gear
5. Thrust plate bolts (TORX)
6. Balance shaft thrust plate

Removal/Inspection/Installation

1. Remove the intake manifold as described in this chapter.
2. Remove the crankcase front cover as described in this chapter.
3. Remove the camshaft sprocket and timing chain as described in this chapter.
4. Place a hardwood wedge between the balance shaft drive and driven gears to prevent the camshaft and balance shaft from turning.
5. Use the appropriate size Torx socket to remove the center bolt (3, **Figure 37**) retaining the driven gear, then remove the driven gear (4, **Figure 37**).
6. Remove the stud bolt (1, **Figure 37**), then remove the drive gear (2, **Figure 37**) from the camshaft.
7. Next, remove the 2 Torx bolts securing the balance shaft thrust plate.

CAUTION
Use caution when prying out the balance shaft in Step 7 to prevent damage to the shaft or cylinder block.

8. Place a suitable pry bar between the rear of the balance shaft counter weight and cylinder block. Carefully, pry the balance shaft straight forward to dislodge the shaft front bearing from its bore in the block. Slide the shaft and front bearing out of the cylinder block.
9. Clean the balance shaft and front bearing thoroughly, then dry with compressed air.
10. Inspect the balance shaft rear bearing for excessive wear or damage.
11. Inspect the front bearing for scoring, roughness or excessive wear. The front bearing is not available separately from the balance shaft. If the bearing requires replacement, replace the balance shaft assembly.
12. Inspect the balance shaft front bearing bore in the cylinder block for wear or evidence of the bearing spinning in the bore.

7

13. Inspect the balance shaft driven gear for chipped teeth or excessive wear. Replace the gear as necessary.
14. Lubricate the front and rear bearings with clean engine oil before installing the balance shaft.
15. Install the balance shaft in the cylinder block. Make sure the front bearing correctly enters its bore. Use a soft-face mallet to tap the balance shaft in until the snap ring around the front bearing is firmly seated against the cylinder block.
16. Install the balance shaft thrust plate and 2 Torx bolts. Tighten the bolts to the torque listed in **Table 4**.
17. Align the keyway in the driven gear with the key in the balance shaft and slide the gear onto the shaft.
18. Tighten the retaining Torx bolt until the driven (top) gear is snug, then rotate the balance shaft until the timing mark on the gear is facing DOWN (**Figure 38**).
19. Install the balance shaft drive gear on the camshaft, with the timing marks on both gears aligned as shown in **Figure 38**. Rotate the camshaft and balance shaft as necessary to align the marks. Install the stud bolt (1, **Figure 37**) and tighten to the torque listed in **Table 4**.
20. Install the camshaft sprocket and timing chain as described in this chapter.
21. Use the following procedure to tighten the Torx bolt attaching the gear to the balance shaft.

  a. Remove the center Torx bolt (3, **Figure 37**).
  b. Apply Loctite 271 to the threads of the Torx bolt.
  c. Reinstall the Torx bolt.
  d. Place a hardwood wedge between the balance shaft drive and driven gears to prevent the camshaft and balance shaft from turning.
  e. Then tighten the driven gear Torx bolt to the stage 1 torque listed in **Table 4**.
  f. Turn the driven gear Torx bolt an additional amount equalling the number of degrees listed as Step 2 in **Table 4**.

22. Install the crankcase front cover and intake manifold as described in this chapter.

Balance Shaft Bearing Replacement

The front of the balance shaft is supported with a roller bearing pressed on the shaft. The rear of the shaft is supported in an insert-type bearing. The front balance shaft bearing is not available separately from the shaft. Should the front bearing require replacement, install a new balance shaft and bearing assembly. Remove and install the rear bearing as follows.

1. Remove the engine as described in this chapter.
2. Remove the balance shaft as described in this chapter.

NOTE
Cover the lifters and valley area of the cylinder block to prevent debris from entering the crankcase.

3. Use a suitable punch to drive the core plug (1, **Figure 36**) from its bore at the rear of the cylinder block.
4. Assemble the bearing remover tool into the cylinder block and rear bearing. See **Figure 39**. Pull the bearing from its bore by tightening the nut at the front of the tool.
5. Install the rear bearing using bearing remover/installer tool (part No. J-38834). Coat the bearing with engine oil before installing.

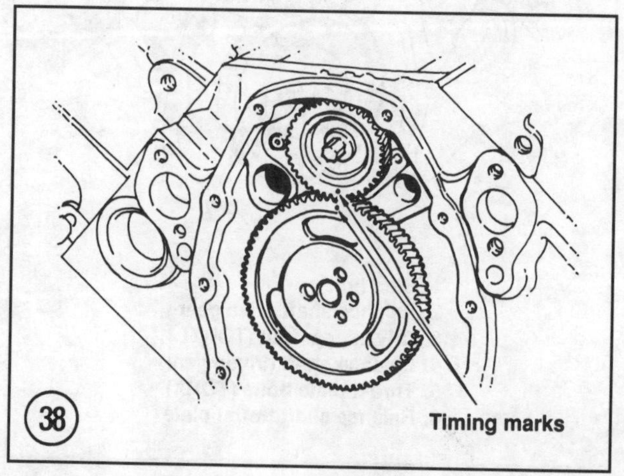

38

6. Install a new core plug (1, **Figure 36**). See Core Plug Replacement in this chapter. Coat the outer diameter of the core plug with Loctite 271 prior to installation.
7. Install the balance shaft as described in this chapter.

CAMSHAFT

Removal/Installation

CAUTION
The rocker arm, pivot ball, pushrod and lifter establish a wear pattern to each other and to the valve which it opens. Therefore, always reinstall these parts in their original location. Install the pushrods with the same end up as when originally assembled.

1. Remove the valve covers as described in this chapter.
2. Remove the intake manifold as described in this chapter.
3. Loosen the rocker arm adjusting nuts, swivel the arms away from the pushrods, then remove the pushrods. Identify each pushrod for reinstallation in its original location.

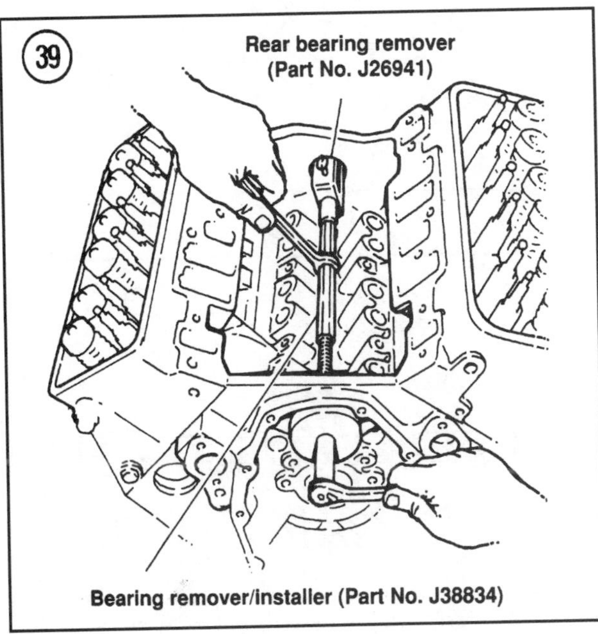

NOTE
A rack can be made or purchased to hold the pushrods in the same order and with the same end down as originally installed. Marks on the rack identify the front of the engine.

4. Remove the valve lifters as described in this chapter. Mark roller lifters before removing, so that they can be installed in the same direction. Place each lifter in a rack in the order of removal so they can be reinstalled in the original locations.

NOTE
A rack can be made or purchased to hold the lifters in the same order as originally installed. Marks on the rack identify the front of the engine.

5. If the engine is equipped with a mechanical fuel pump, remove the pump and its pushrod.
6. Remove the front cover, timing chain, camshaft sprocket and balance shaft drive gear as described in this chapter. Install 2 5/16-18 × 4 in. bolts in the camshaft bolt holes at the end of the camshaft.

CAUTION
Do not cock the camshaft during removal. This can damage the camshaft or its bearing surfaces.

7. Carefully withdraw the camshaft from the front of the engine with a rotating motion to avoid damage to the bearings.
8. Installation is the reverse of removal. Coat the bottom of any new lifters with Molykote.
9. Add an additive containing EP lubricant such as GM Engine Oil Supplement to the oil.
10. Check and adjust the ignition timing (Chapter Four).

Inspection

1. Inspect the bottom (cam contact surface) of each lifter. Refer to *Valve Lifter Inspection* in this chapter.

a. On models with roller type lifters, the roller must turn easily with no roughness.
b. On models with flat lifters, the contact surface must be smooth, polished and slightly convex (curved out). The entire surface should be shiny indicating the lifter has been rotating freely.
c. If any lifter is galled, chipped, worn, or damaged, replace the lifters and camshaft.

2. Inspect the camshaft journals and lobes for signs of wear or scoring.

NOTE

If you do not have precision measuring equipment, a properly equipped machine shop should perform Steps 3 and 4.

3. Measure the camshaft journal diameters with a micrometer (**Figure 40**). Compare the measurements with the specifications listed in **Tables 1-3**.
4. Suspend the camshaft between V-blocks and check for runout with a dial indicator (**Figure 41**). Compare measured runout with the maximum specification listed in **Tables 1-3**.
5. Check the distributor drive gear for excessive wear or damage.
6. Replace the camshaft if:
   a. Any wear is evident while inspecting the camshaft in Step 2.
   b. One or more journals do not meet specification measured in Step 3.
   c. Runout measured in Step 4 exceeds the limit listed in **Tables 1-3**.
   d. The distributor drive gear is damaged.

Lobe Lift Measurement

Camshaft lobe lift can be measured with the camshaft in the block and the cylinder head in place.

1. Remove the rocker arm cover as described in this chapter.
2. Remove the rocker arm assemblies as described in this chapter.
3. Remove the spark plugs. See Chapter Four.
4. Attach a dial indicator to the cylinder head with its plunger contacting the end of 1 pushrod. A piece of rubber tubing can be used to hold the dial indicator plunger in place against the center of the pushrod. See **Figure 42**, typical.
5. Rotate the crankshaft in the normal direction of rotation until the valve lifter seats against the heel or base circle of the cam (**Figure 43**). This positions the pushrod at its lowest point.
6. Set the dial indicator at zero, slowly rotate the crankshaft until the pushrod reaches its maximum travel and note the dial indicator.
7. Compare the measured movement of the pushrod with the specification listed in **Tables 1-3**. Movement that is less than specified indicates the lobe is worn.

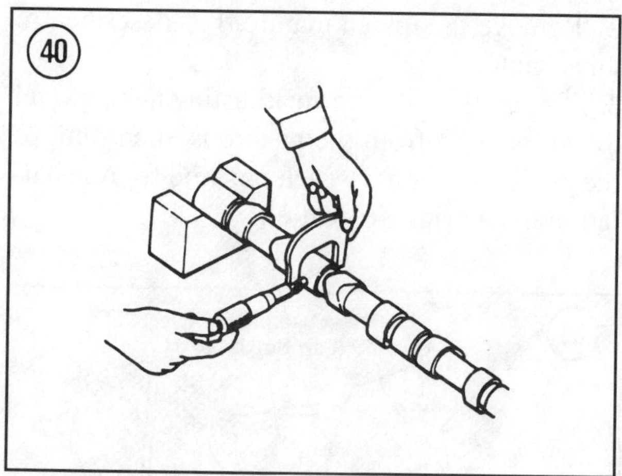

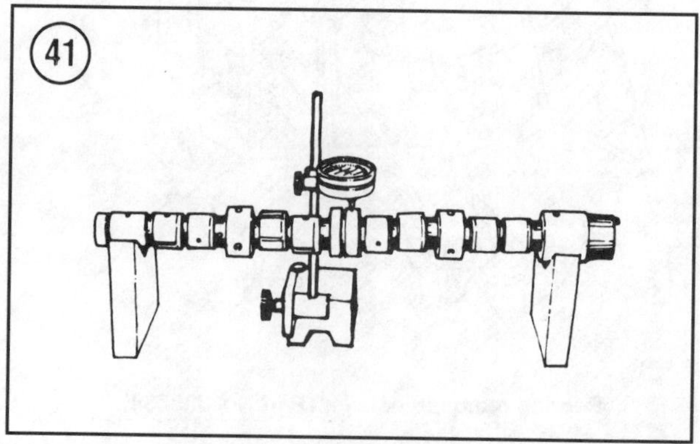

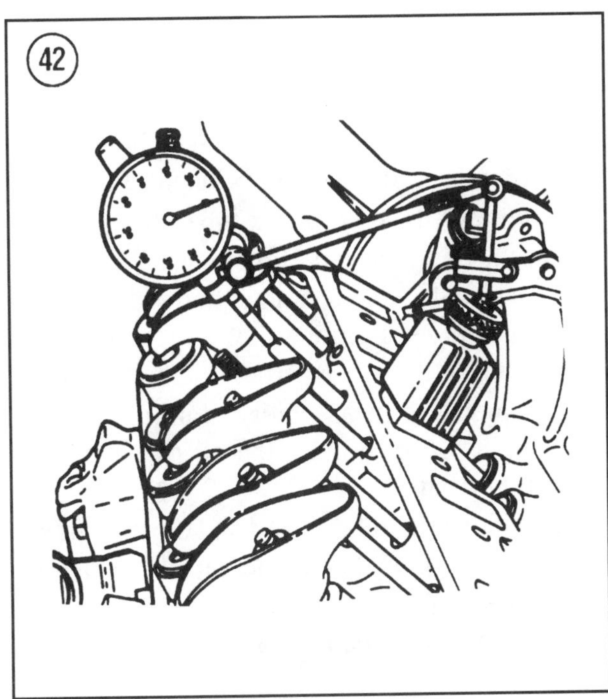

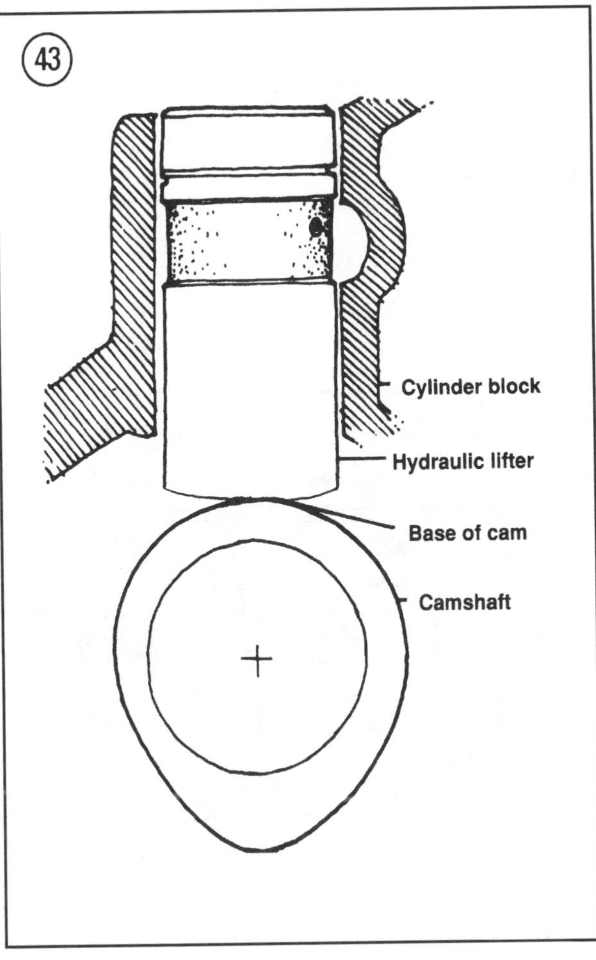

8. Repeat Steps 4-7 for each pushrod. If all lobes are within specification, reinstall the rocker arm assemblies. On models with nuts retaining the rocker arms, adjust the valves as described in this chapter.
9. If 1 or more lobes are excessively worn, replace the camshaft as described in this chapter.
10. Remove the dial indicator and reverse Steps 1-3.

Bearing Replacement

Camshaft bearings can be replaced without complete engine disassembly; however, replacement is often part of a complete overhaul. Replace bearings only in complete sets. Special camshaft bearing removal and installation tools are required.

1. Remove the camshaft as described in this chapter.
2. Remove the crankshaft as described in this chapter. The pistons can remain in cylinder bores.
3. Drive the camshaft core plug from the rear of the cylinder block.
4. If the connecting rods are not removed, secure them to the sides of the engine to keep them out of the way while replacing the cam bearings.
5. Use the special camshaft bearing removal and installation tool to remove the old bearings and to install the new bearings. The following procedure describes using special tool part No. J-6098.
   a. Install the nut and thrust washer on the tool.
   b. Index the tool pilot in the front cam bearing.
   c. Install the puller screw through the pilot.
   d. Install the tool with its shoulder facing the front intermediate bearing and the threads engaging the bearing.
   e. Hold the puller screw with 1 wrench and turn the nut with a second wrench until the bearing has been pulled from its bore. See **Figure 44**, typical.

f. When the bearing has been removed from the bore, remove the tool and bearing from puller screw.
g. Repeat substeps a-f to remove the center bearing.
h. Remove the tool and index it to the rear bearing to remove the rear intermediate bearing from the block.
i. Remove the front and rear bearings by driving them toward the center of the block.

CAUTION
Improper alignment of the rear bearing during Step 12 will restrict oil pressure reaching the valve train.

6. Installation of new bearings is the reverse of removal. Use the same tool to pull the new bearings into their bores. *Bearing oil holes must align with those in the block.* Since the oil hole is on the top of the bearings, and cannot be seen during installation, align the bearing oil hole with the hole in the bore and mark opposite side of the bearing and block at the bore to assist in positioning the oil hole during installation.
7. Wipe a new camshaft core plug with sealer and install it flush to 1/32 in. (0.8 mm) deep to maintain a level surface on the rear of the block.

OIL PAN

Ease of oil pan removal depends upon the installation within a given boat. In some cases, the oil pan can be removed without removing the engine. In others, engine removal is required to provide sufficient working space and clearance for oil pan removal.

A kit is attached to the pan on most engines to assist in draining the oil when the engine is in the boat. If it is not already installed, this kit can be installed on any engine oil pan when the engine is removed for service.

The 1-piece silicone rubber gasket has a spacer around each oil pan screw hole to prevent gasket damage from excessive torque.

Removal

1A. If the engine is in the boat:
a. Remove the oil dipstick and siphon the oil from the crankcase. See Chapter Four.
b. Remove the oil dipstick tube.

1B. If the engine is out of the boat:
a. Place a suitable container under the oil pan drain plug. Remove the plug and let the crankcase drain. Reinstall the drain plug.
b. If mounted in an engine stand, rotate the engine 180° to place the oil pan in an upright position.
c. Remove the oil dipstick and dipstick tube.

2. Remove all of the screws attaching the oil pan. Remove the oil pan.
3. Remove and discard the gasket.

Inspection and Cleaning

1. Clean any gasket residue from the oil pan rail on the engine block, rear main bearing cap, front cover and the oil pan sealing flange with degreaser and a scraper.

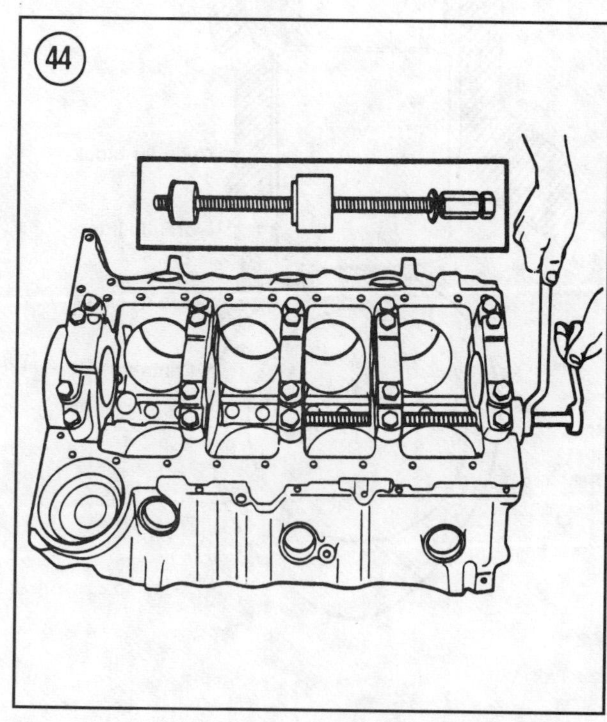

2. Clean the pan thoroughly in solvent and check for dents or warped gasket surfaces. Straighten or replace the pan as required.

Installation

1. Position the gasket on the rails of the oil pan and insert a screw at each corner of the pan to hold the gasket in place.
2. Carefully position the oil pan and gasket in place. Make sure the gasket is not misaligned, then install the attaching screws with lockwashers. Tighten screws to the specification listed in **Table 4** or **Table 5**, working from the center outward in each direction.
3. Reinstall the dipstick and guide tube.
4. Install the engine in the boat as described in this chapter and fill the crankcase with an oil recommended in Chapter Four.

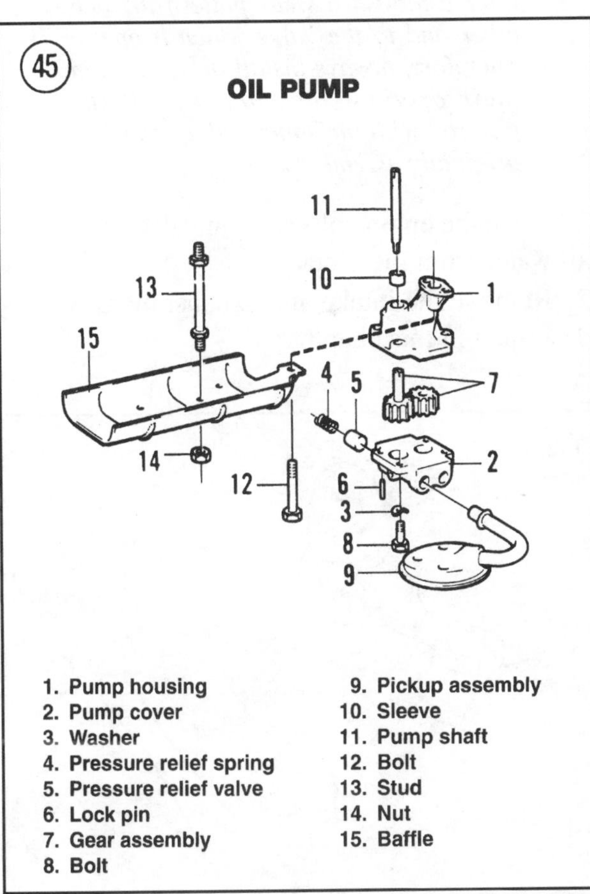

1. Pump housing
2. Pump cover
3. Washer
4. Pressure relief spring
5. Pressure relief valve
6. Lock pin
7. Gear assembly
8. Bolt
9. Pickup assembly
10. Sleeve
11. Pump shaft
12. Bolt
13. Stud
14. Nut
15. Baffle

OIL PUMP

Removal/Installation

1. Remove the oil pan as described in this chapter.

NOTE
The oil pump pickup tube and screen are a press fit in the pump housing and should not be removed from the pump.

2. Remove the screw(s) holding the pump to the rear main bearing cap.
3. Remove the pump and extension drive shaft.
4. To install, align the tang in the collar of the extension shaft with the drive slot in the top end of the pump drive shaft.

NOTE
The bottom edge of the oil pump pickup screen should be parallel to the oil pan rails when the pump is installed in Step 5.

5. Install the pump and extension shaft to the rear main bearing cap, aligning the slot at the top of the extension shaft with the tang on the lower end of the distributor shaft.
6. Tighten the pump retaining screw(s) to the torque specification in **Table 4** or **Table 5**.
7. Reinstall the oil pan as described in this chapter.

Disassembly/Assembly

Refer to **Figure 45** for this procedure.
1. Remove the screws that attach the cover and carefully remove the cover.
2. Remove the inner rotor and shaft assembly.
3. Remove the outer rotor.
4. Remove the pressure relief valve retaining pin, relief spring and valve.

NOTE
Do not remove the pickup tube and screen from the pump unless the pump or pickup tube requires replacement.

5. If a new pickup tube is being installed, proceed as follows:
   a. Secure the pump in a vise that has soft jaws.
   b. Apply sealer to the new tube.
   c. Align the tube with the pickup screen flat (parallel with the bottom of the oil pan).
   d. Tap the tube in place with a soft-faced hammer. An aluminum or brass drift can be used as shown in **Figure 46**.
6. Lubricate all parts thoroughly with clean engine oil before reassembly.
7. Assembly is the reverse of disassembly. Align the index marks on the side of the rotors, install the cover and tighten the cover retaining screws to the torque listed in **Tables 4-5**. Rotate the pump drive shaft by hand to check for smooth operation.

Inspection

The pump assembly and gears are serviced only as an assembly. If any part is worn or damaged, replace the entire pump.

1. Clean all parts thoroughly in solvent. Brush the inside of the body and the pressure regulator chamber to remove all dirt and metal particles. Dry with compressed air, if available.
2. Check the pump body and cover for cracks or excessive wear.
3. Check the pump gears for damage or excessive wear.
4. Check the drive gear shaft-to-body fit for excessive looseness.
5. Check the inside of the pump cover for wear that could allow oil to leak around the ends of the gears.
6. Check the pressure regulator valve for a smooth fit without any scoring.
7. Measure pump clearances as follows. Refer to **Tables 1-3** for service specifications.
   a. Install the inner rotor/shaft assembly in the pump body, place a straight edge across the rotor and the pump body, then measure the clearance between the rotor and the straight edge.
   b. Install the outer rotor and measure the radial clearance between the rotor and the pump body.
   c. Measure the clearance between the pump shaft and the housing and compare with the specification listed in **Tables 1-3**.
   d. If a spring tester is available, compress the relief spring to the length listed in **Tables 1-3** and compare the pressure measured with the specification listed.

CYLINDER HEAD

Removal

CAUTION

The rocker arm, pivot ball, pushrod and lifter establish a wear pattern to each other and to the valve which it opens. Therefore, always install these parts in their original location. Install the pushrod with the same end up as when originally assembled.

1. Open the engine block drain valves and drain all water from the block.
2. Remove the intake and exhaust manifolds as described in this chapter.

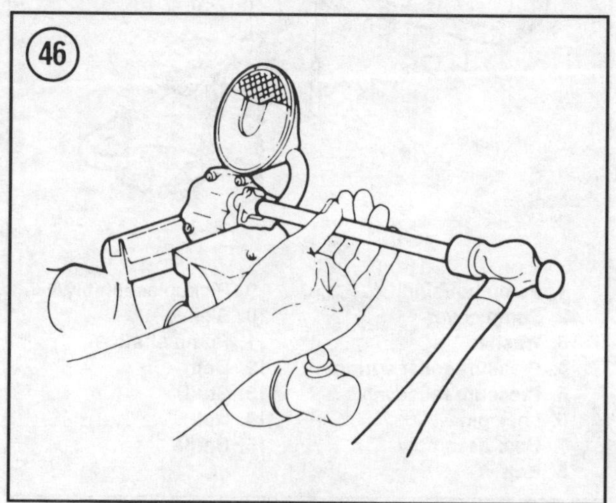

3. Remove the alternator and oil filter mounting brackets.

NOTE

It is not necessary to remove the spark plugs to remove the cylinder head, but the plugs are easier to remove before the head is removed. Also, the plugs are easily broken during cylinder head removal.

4. Disconnect the wires from the spark plugs and detach the wire looms.
5. Remove the valve covers as described in this chapter.
6A. If the rocker arms are retained by nuts, loosen the rocker arm adjusting nuts, swivel the arms away from the pushrods, then remove the pushrods. Identify each pushrod for reinstallation in its original location.
6B. If the rocker arms are retained by shoulder bolts, loosen the bolts, then remove the bolts, rocker arm, pivot ball and pushrods. Identify the removed parts so that each can be reinstalled in its original location.

NOTE

A rack can be made or purchased to hold the bolts, rocker arm, pivot ball and pushrods in the same order and with the same end of the pushrods down as originally installed. Marks on the rack identify the front of the engine.

7. Loosen the cylinder head bolts, beginning in the center of the head and working in each direction toward the ends.
8. Remove the bolts, then carefully lift the head from the engine and move it to a workbench.

NOTE

It may be necessary to bump the head with a soft-faced hammer to break the gasket seal.

CAUTION

Be careful to place the head in a safe location and in a safe position to prevent damage to the valves or gasket surfaces.

9. Remove and discard the head gasket. Clean all gasket residue from the valve (rocker arm) cover, cylinder head and block mating surfaces.

Decarbonizing

Check for any sign of oil or water leaks before cleaning the cylinder head.

1. Before removing the valves, clean all deposits from the combustion chambers, intake ports and exhaust ports. Use a fine wire brush dipped in solvent or make a scraper from hardwood. Be careful not to scratch or gouge the combustion chambers.
2. After all carbon is removed from the combustion chambers and ports, clean the entire head with solvent.
3. Clean carbon from the tops of the pistons.
4. Clean the pushrod guides, valve guide bores and all bolt holes. Use cleaning solvent to remove dirt and grease.
5. Remove the valves as described in this chapter.
6. Clean the valves with a fine wire brush or buffing wheel.

Inspection

1. Check the cylinder head for any signs of oil or water leaks before cleaning.
2. Clean the cylinder head thoroughly in solvent. While cleaning, look for cracks or other visible damage. Look for corrosion or foreign material in the oil and water passages (**Figure 47**). Clean the passages with a stiff spiral brush, then blow them out with compressed air.
3. Check the cylinder head studs for damage and replace if necessary.
4. Check the threaded rocker arm studs or bolt holes for damaged threads and repair if necessary.
5. Check for warpage of the cylinder head-to-block surface with a straightedge and feeler gauge (**Figure 48**). Measure diagonally, as well as end-to-end. If the gap exceeds specification

(**Tables 1-3**), have the head resurfaced at a machine shop. If head resurfacing is necessary, do not remove more than 0.010 in. (0.25 mm). Replace the head if a greater amount must be removed to correct warpage.

Installation

1. Make sure that all gasket surfaces (on the cylinder head and block) and bolt holes are clean. Dirt in bolt holes or on the bolt threads will affect bolt torque.
2. Recheck all visible oil and water passages for cleanliness.

CAUTION
Use only the marine cylinder head gasket available from Volvo Penta. Damage may result from installing an automotive head gasket.

3. Fit a new head gasket over the dowels in the block.
4. Carefully position the head onto the cylinder block, engaging the dowel pins. Do not damage the gasket by sliding the cylinder head into position. Do not crush the gasket by dropping the head on 1 side or 1 corner.
5. Wipe all head bolt threads with Permatex or equivalent sealer. Install and tighten the head bolts finger-tight.

NOTE
*On V6 engines, refer to **Figure 49** and **Table 4**. On small block V8 (5.0 and 5.7 L) engines, refer to **Figure 50** and **Table 4**. On big block (7.4 or 8.2 L) engines, refer to **Figure 51** and **Table 5**.*

6. Tighten the cylinder head retaining screws evenly using a 3-step procedure as follows:
   a. Tighten the head bolts in the sequence shown in **Figure 49**, **Figure 50** or **Figure 51** until the Step 1 torque specified in **Table 4** or **Table 5** is reached. Make sure that all screws are tightened evenly before continuing to the next step.

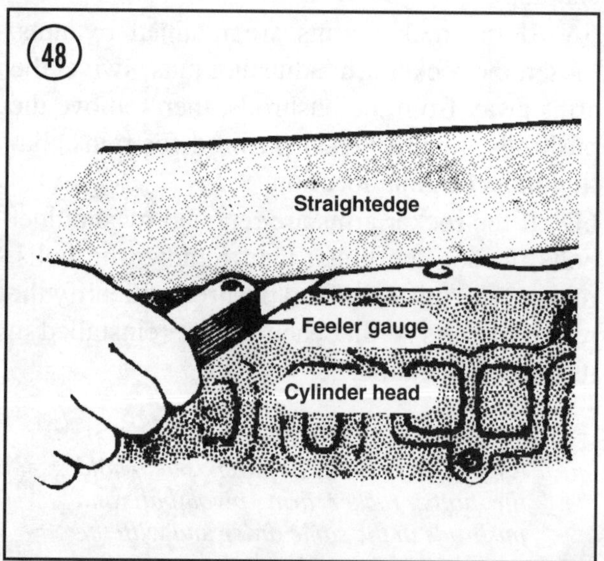

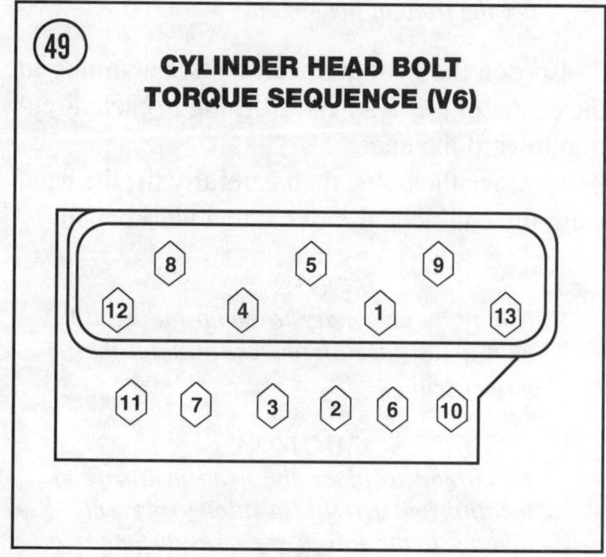

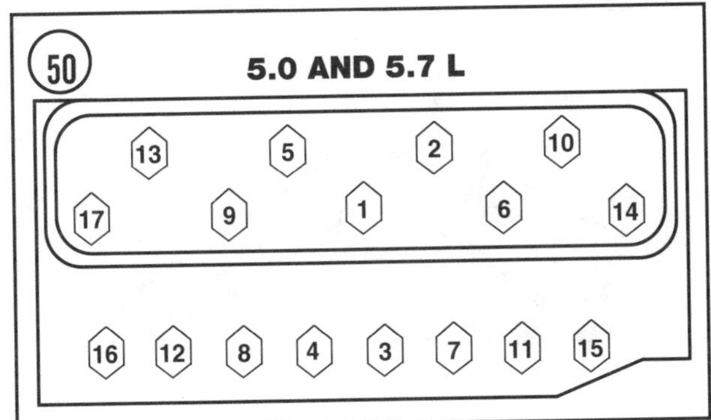

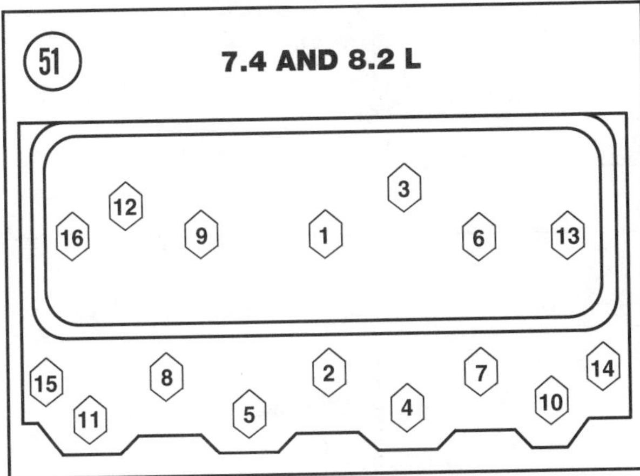

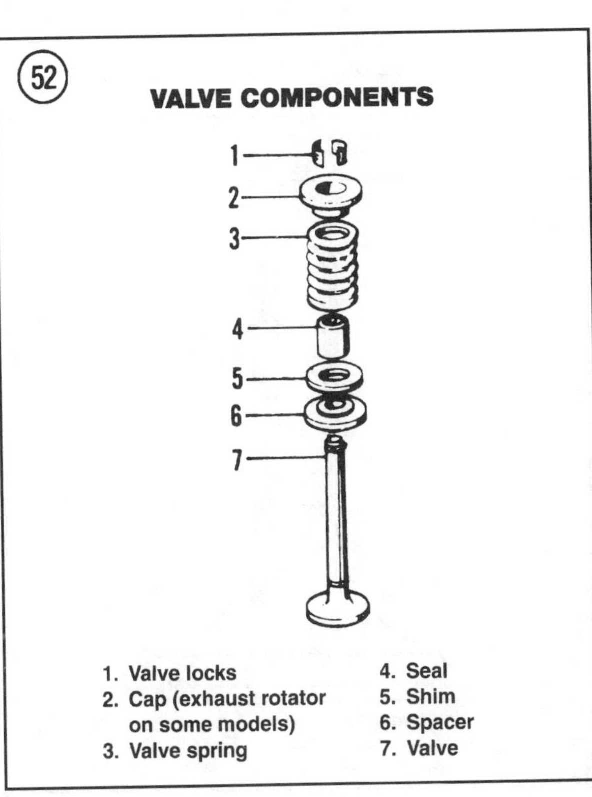

1. Valve locks
2. Cap (exhaust rotator on some models)
3. Valve spring
4. Seal
5. Shim
6. Spacer
7. Valve

b. Tighten the head bolts to the torque specified in **Table 4** or **Table 5**, Step 2 in the sequence shown in **Figure 49**, **Figure 50** or **Figure 51**.

c. Tighten the head bolts to the torque specified in **Table 4** or **Table 5**, Step 3 in the sequence shown in **Figure 49**, **Figure 50** or **Figure 51**.

7. Reverse Steps 1-6 of *Cylinder Head Removal* in this chapter to complete installation. Adjust the valves on models with adjustable valves as described in this chapter. Check and adjust ignition timing as required. See Chapter Four.

VALVES AND VALVE SEATS

Servicing the valves, guides and valve seats must be done at a dealership or machine shop, with trained technicians and the proper machine tools. A general practice for many who do their own service is to remove the cylinder head, perform all disassembly except valve removal and take the head to a dealer or machine shop for inspection and service. Since the cost is low relative to the required effort and equipment, this is usually the best approach, even for experienced mechanics. The following procedures are given to acquaint the home mechanic with what the dealership or machine shop will do.

Valve Removal

Refer to **Figure 52** for this procedure.

1. Remove the cylinder head as described in this chapter.
2. Remove the rocker arm assemblies as described in this chapter.

NOTE
Clean and inspect the cylinder head, combustion chamber as described in this chapter before removing the valves.

3. Compress the valve spring with a compressor like the one shown in **Figure 53**. Remove the valve keys or locks and release the spring tension.
4. Remove the valve spring cap (exhaust valve rotator is used on some models) and spring assembly.

NOTE
*On some models, a small O-ring seal is used on all valves and the larger seals (4, **Figure 52**) are used only on inlet valves. The small O-ring must seat in the groove of the valve as shown in **Figure 54**.*

5. Remove and discard the valve stem seal. See **Figure 52**. Check the cylinder head and remove the shim or spacer located under the spring, if used.

CAUTION
Remove any burrs from the valve stem lock grooves before removing the valve or the valve guide will be damaged. The valve stem will develop a small burr as a result of the locks pounding against the groove.

6. Remove the valve and repeat Steps 3-5 on each remaining valve.
7. Arrange the parts in order so they can be returned to their original positions during reassembly.

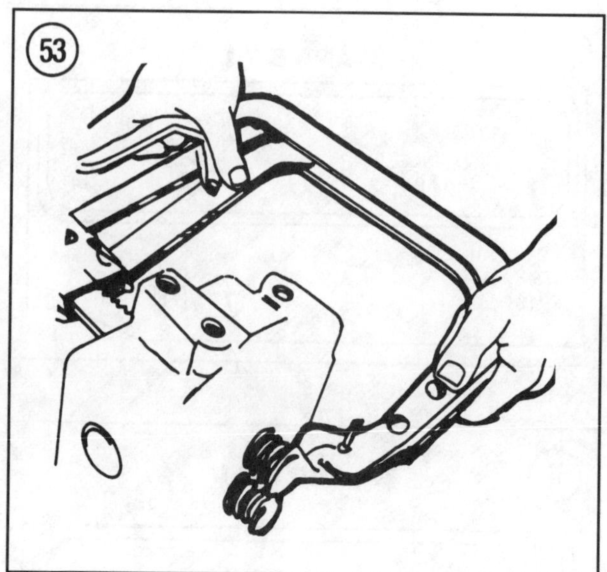

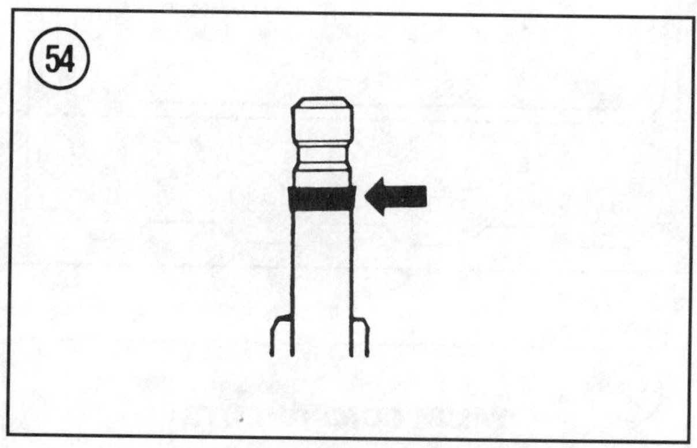

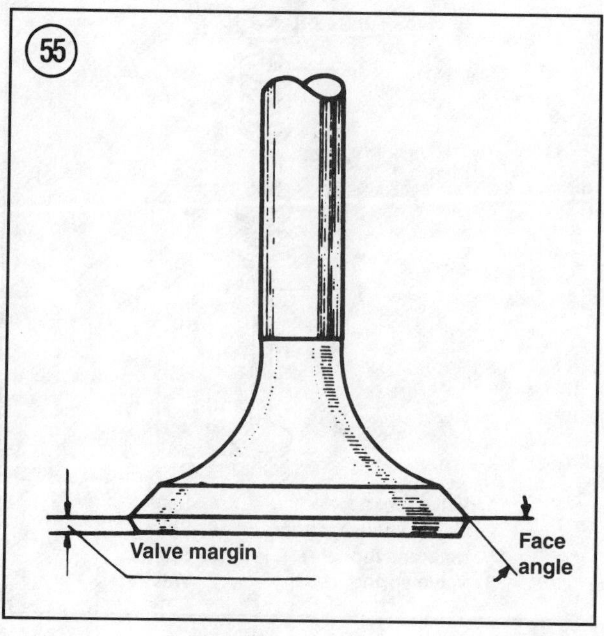

Inspection

1. Clean the valves with a fine wire brush or buffing wheel. Discard any cracked, warped or burned valves.
2. Measure valve stems at the top, center and bottom for wear. A machine shop can do this when the valves are ground. Also measure the length of each valve and the diameter of each valve head.

NOTE

*Check the thickness of the valve edge or margin, after the valves have been ground. See **Figure 55**. Discard any valve with a margin of less than 1/32 in. (0.8 mm).*

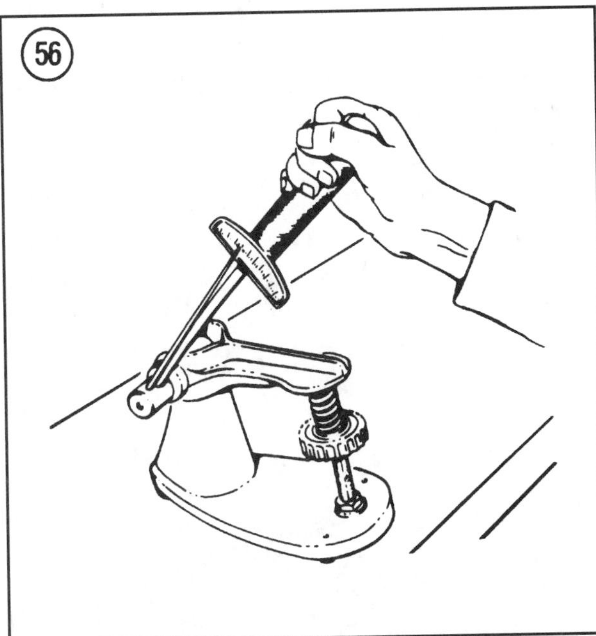

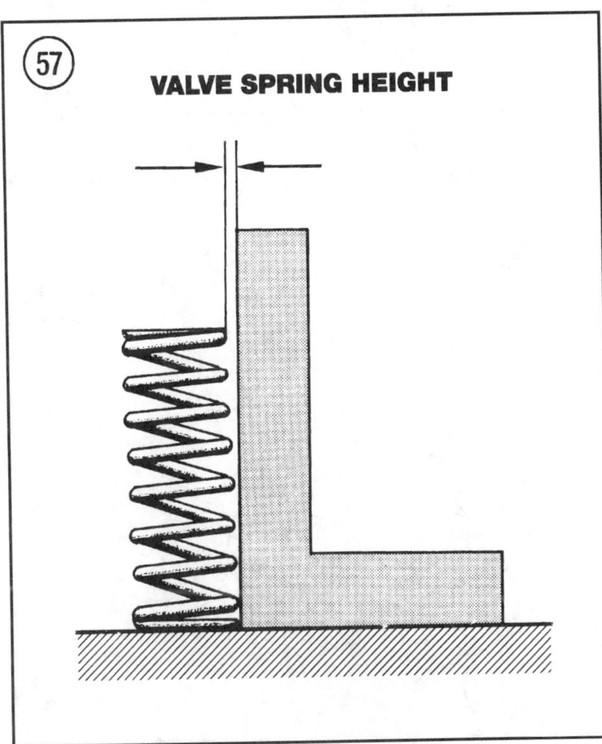

3. Remove all carbon and varnish from the valve guides with a stiff spiral wire brush.

NOTE

The next step assumes that all valve stems have been measured and are within specification. Replace valves with worn stems before performing this step.

4. Insert each valve into the guide from which it was removed. Holding the valve just slightly off its seat, rock it back and forth in a direction parallel to the rocker arms. This is the direction in which the greatest wear normally occurs. If the valve stem rocks more than slightly, the valve guide is probably worn.
5. If there is any doubt about valve guide condition after performing Step 4, have the valve guide measured with a valve stem clearance checking tool. Compare the results with specification in **Tables 1-3**. Worn guides must be reamed for the next oversize valve stem.
6. Test the valve springs under load on a spring tester (**Figure 56**). Replace any weak springs.
7. Inspect the valve seat inserts. If worn or burned, they must be reconditioned. This is a job for a dealership or machine shop, although the procedure is described in this chapter.
8. Check each spring on a flat surface with a steel square. See **Figure 57**. Slowly revolve the spring 360° and note the space between the top of the coil and the square. Replace the spring if it is not straight.
9. Check each valve lifter to make sure it fits freely in the block and that the end that contacts the camshaft lobe is smooth and not worn excessively.

Valve Guide Reaming

Worn valve guides must be reamed to accept a valve with an oversize stem. These are available in 3 sizes for both intake and exhaust valves. Reaming must be done by hand (**Figure 58**) and is a job best left to experienced machine shop personnel. The valve seat must be refaced after the guide has been reamed.

Valve Seat Reconditioning

1. Cut the valve seats to the angle specified in **Tables 1-3**. Use a dressing stone and remove only enough metal to obtain a good finish.
2. Use stones of larger or smaller angles to obtain the specified seat width as necessary.
3. Coat the corresponding valve face with Prussian blue (machinist marking compound).
4. Insert the valve into the valve guide.
5. Apply light pressure to the valve and rotate it a small amount (approximately 1/4 turn).
6. Lift the valve out. If it seats properly, the marking compound should transfer evenly around the valve face.
   a. If the marking compound transfers to only part of the valve, the valve or seat may not be concentric with the stem or guide.
   b. If the marking compound transfers to the valve near the edge of the valve face, the seat can be lowered by machining the seat with a stone which has a smaller angle. A stone with a smaller angle will remove metal from the combustion chamber side of the valve seat.
   c. If the marking compound transfers to the bottom of the valve face, closer to the stem, raise the seat by machining the seat with a stone which has a larger angle. A stone with a larger angle will remove metal from inside the port, closer to the valve stem.

Valve Installation

NOTE

Install all parts that were previously removed in their original location.

1. Coat the valves with engine oil and insert them through the guides in the cylinder head.
2. Install new seals on each valve stem. The small O-ring seals should be flat and not twisted in the valve stem grooves. A light coat of oil will help prevent twisting.
3. Position the valve spring shim/spacer (if used) around the valve guide boss.
4. Install the valve spring(s) over the valve, then install the cap or rotator.
5. Compress the springs and install the locks. Make sure both locks seat properly in the groove of the valve stem.
6. Measure the installed spring height between the top of the valve seat and the underside of the cap or rotator, as shown in **Figure 59**. If height

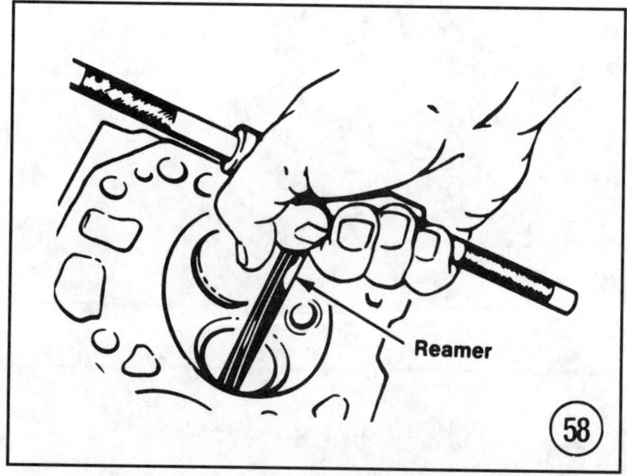

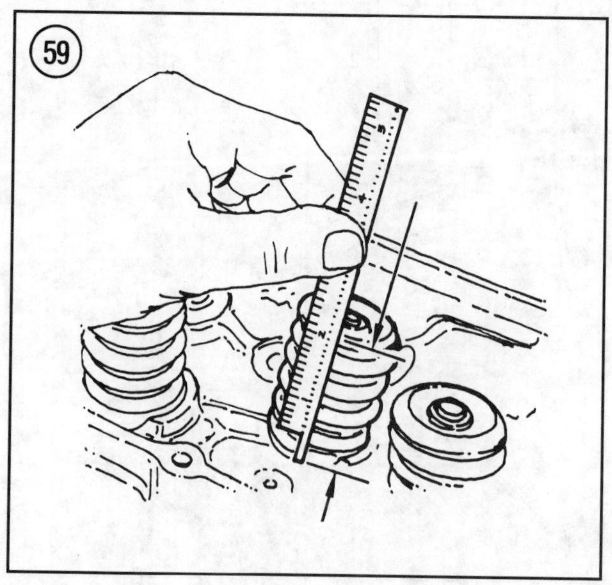

is more than specified in **Tables 1-3**, disassemble the valve, install an appropriately sized spring seat shim under the spring(s). Then, reassemble and remeasure the assembled height.

VALVE LIFTERS

Some models are equipped with roller lifters, while other models are equipped with conventional flat lifters. Service procedures are different for flat and roller lifters. Retaining brackets are used to hold the roller lifters in position, preventing them from turning in their bores, while flat lifters should turn to even the wear and to reduce friction between the lifter and the cam lobe.

Removal/Installation

1. Remove the rocker arm assemblies, pushrods and intake manifold as described in this chapter.

CAUTION
Regardless of the type of lifter installed, each lifter becomes worn to match the cam lobe on which it operates. It is important to reinstall each lifter in its original location. During disassembly, always arrange lifters, rocker arm assemblies and pushrods to identify the original location of each part.

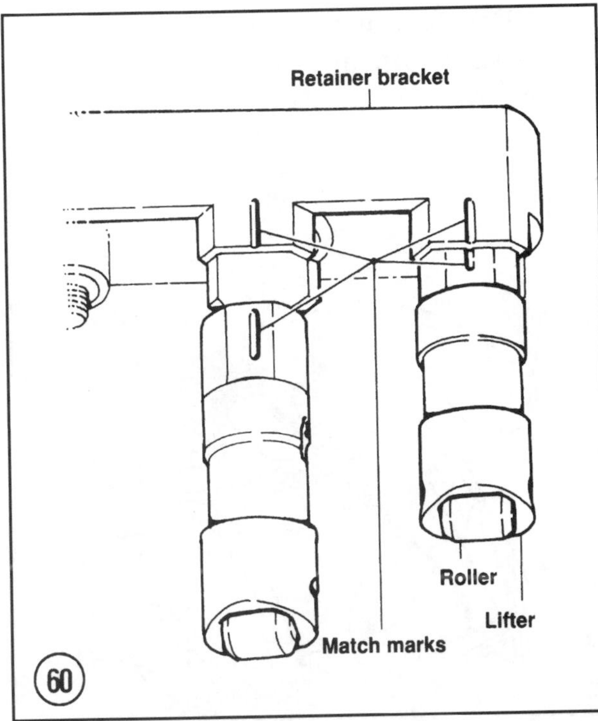

2A. *Flat lifters*—Remove the lifters from their bores. A lifter remover tool is available from most tool sources, which can be used to pull any difficult to remove lifters from their bores.

2B. *Roller lifters*—Use a soft marking pin to apply match marks on each lifter so the lifters can be reinstalled facing the same direction. See **Figure 60**. If reused, the lifter rollers should roll in the same direction. Remove the fasteners securing the lifter retaining brackets. Remove the brackets and lifters.

7

NOTE
Always use new lifters if a new camshaft is installed.

3. Initial lubrication is important to the service life of the camshaft and lifters. Observe the following:

a. Coat the bottom of flat lifters with Molykote or equivalent before installing.

b. Coat the entire lifter assembly and cam lobe with clean engine oil prior to installation.

c. If a new camshaft and lifters are installed, add an additive to the engine oil, such as GM Engine Oil Supplement or a suitable equivalent, containing an extreme pressure (EP) additive.

4A. *Flat lifters*—Install the lifters in their bores. If reusing the original lifters, make certain they are installed in the same location from which they were removed. Initial lubrication such as described in Step 3 is also helpful for used lifters.

4B. *Roller lifters*—Install the lifters in their original bores. Install the lifter retaining brackets and align the match marks made in Step 2B. Install and tighten the retainer fasteners to the torque listed in **Table 4** or **Table 5**.

5. Complete the remaining reassembly by installing the rocker arm assemblies, pushrods and intake manifold as described in this chapter.

Inspection

Keep the lifters in the proper sequence for installation in their original location in the cylinder block. Clean the outside of the lifters in solvent and dry with compressed air. Inspect and test the lifters separately to prevent mixing of their internal components.

Hydraulic lifters are not easily or successfully disassembled, cleaned, reassembled and tested. If any part requires replacement, the entire lifter assembly must be replaced. If lifter failure is suspected, installation of a complete new set is usually the best way of correcting the problem.

Inspect all parts and discard any lifter which is cracked, chipped, pitted, scored or shows excessive wear. If the bottom (flat lifters) or roller (roller lifters) shows excessive wear, the camshaft is probably also damaged. Inspect the camshaft journals and lobes for wear or scoring. If any lifter is galled, chipped, worn, or damaged, the camshaft should also be replaced.

On roller lifters, make sure the roller turns freely without any noticeable roughness.

On flat lifters, the cam contacting surface should be smooth, polished and slightly convex (curved out). The entire surface should be polished indicating the lifter has been rotating freely.

PISTON/CONNECTING ROD ASSEMBLY

Piston/Connecting Rod Removal

1. Remove the engine as described in this chapter.
2. Place a suitable container under the oil pan, remove the drain plug and allow the crankcase oil to drain completely.
3. Remove the intake and exhaust manifolds as described in this chapter.
4. Remove the cylinder heads as described in this chapter.
5. Remove the oil pan and oil pump as described in this chapter.
6. Remove the ridge from the top of the cylinder. Even a small ridge caused by the pistons wearing the cylinder or a buildup of carbon can make removal of the pistons difficult and may damage the piston. Refer to the following:
   a. Turn the crankshaft until the piston is at bottom dead center.

   NOTE
   Special tools (ridge reamer) for removing the ridge from the top of the cylinder are available from most automotive tool suppliers and tool rental agencies. Make sure the tool has the range of operation necessary to work properly on your engine.

   b. Install a ridge reamer in the cylinder following its manufacturer's instructions.
   c. Operate the tool to remove the ridge from the top of the cylinder bore.
   d. Clean the shavings from the cylinder bore. A shop vacuum will remove the shavings easily.

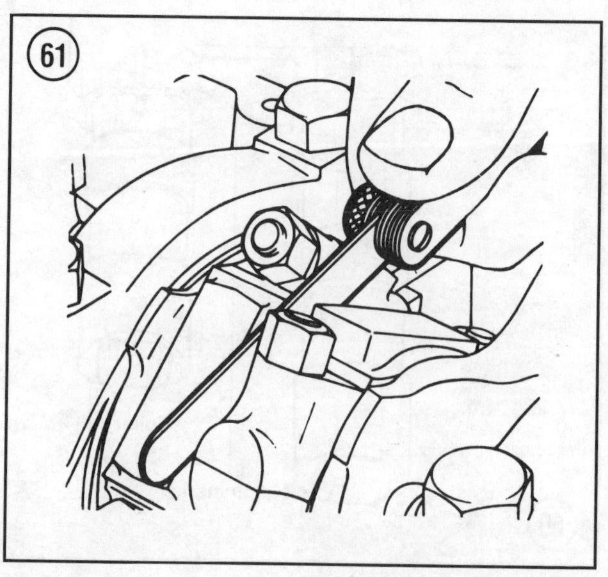

e. Repeat substeps a-d for the remaining cylinders.

7. Measure the side clearance between the side of the connecting rod and the journal flanges of the crankshaft as follows:

a. Rotate the crankshaft until the connecting rods on 1 journal are easily accessible.

b. Measure the clearance between the connecting rod and the crankshaft journal flange with a flat feeler gauge. See **Figure 61**. Measure the clearance for all of the connecting rod journals.

c. Compare the measured side clearance with the clearance listed in **Tables 1-3**. If the clearance is excessive, replace the connecting rods during reassembly.

NOTE

Clean the tops of the pistons before removing them from the cylinders and check for cylinder numbers or identifying marks. Also check for cylinder identifying marks on the connecting rod and cap. If marks are not already located on each part, use a suitable scribe or marker and mark the cylinder number on the piston, connecting rod and rod cap.

8. Mark each connecting rod and its cap with the cylinder number to aid reassembly.

9. Remove the nuts holding the connecting rod cap. Lift off the cap, together with the lower bearing insert. See **Figure 62**.

NOTE

If the connecting rod caps are difficult to remove, tap the studs with a handle of a hammer or similar tool.

10. Use the handle of a hammer to push the piston and connecting rod from the cylinder bore. Be sure to remove the bearing insert.

11. Remove the piston rings with a ring remover (**Figure 63**).

12. Repeat Steps 9-11 for all remaining piston/connecting rods.

62

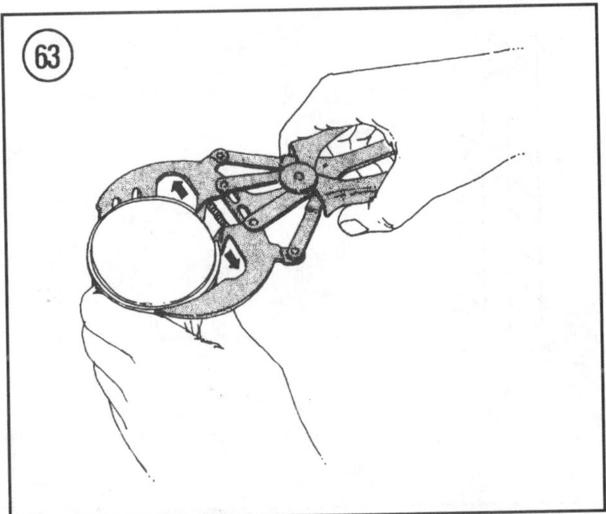

63

7

Piston Pin Removal/Installation

The piston pins are a press fit in the bores of the connecting rods and a light hand fit in the pistons. Do not press the piston pin from the connecting rod unless removal is required. Removal requires the use of a support stand, special removal/installation tool and an arbor press. This is a job for a trained and equipped dealership or machine shop. The piston pin is matched to the piston and the piston and pin are only available as an assembly. The pin should support its own weight in either pin boss when coated with light engine oil with all parts at 60° F (16° C). Differences in temperature will give false indications of clearance.

It is important to assemble the piston and connecting rod correctly as described in this chapter. Incorrect assembly will cause serious damage to the engine.

Piston Clearance Check

Precision measuring equipment and training in its use are required to check this clearance. If you are not properly equipped and trained, have this procedure done at a machine shop.

1. Measure the piston diameter with a micrometer (**Figure 64**) just below the rings at a right angle to the piston pin bore.
2. Measure the cylinder bore diameter with a bore gauge (**Figure 65**). **Figure 66** shows the points of normal cylinder wear. If the diameter at the top of the ring travel (A, **Figure 66**) exceeds the diameter at the bottom, unused part of the cylinder (B, **Figure 66**) by more than 0.003 in., the cylinder must be rebored and a new piston/ring assembly installed.
3. Subtract the piston diameter from the largest cylinder bore reading. If it exceeds the specification in **Tables 1-3**, bore the cylinder and install an oversized piston.

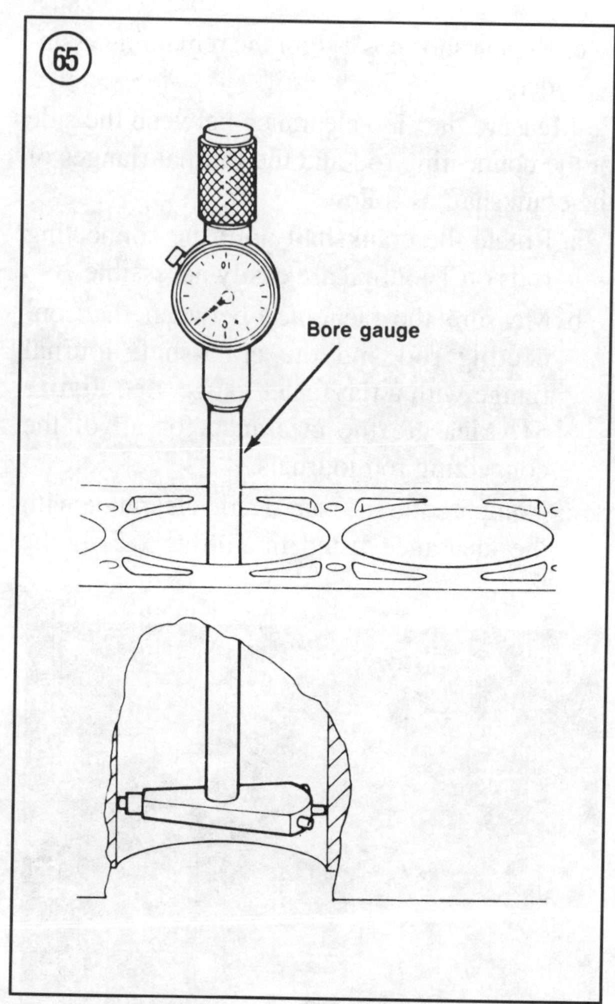

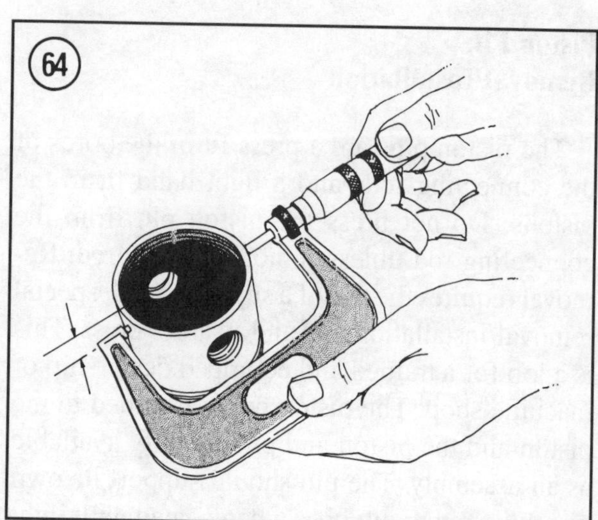

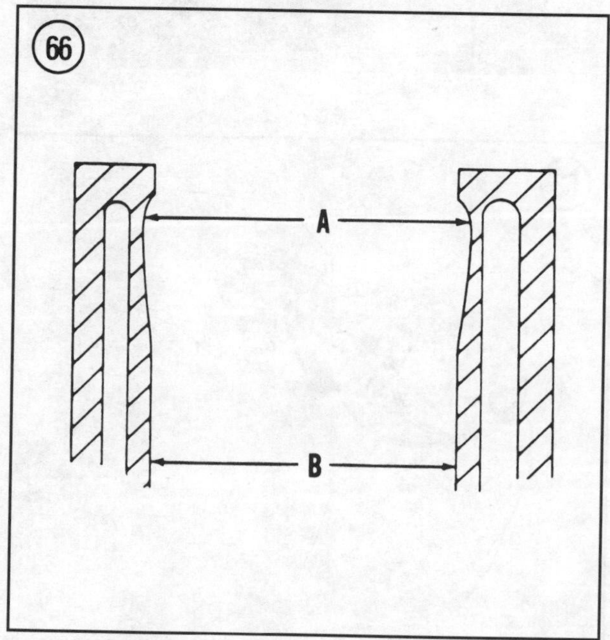

NOTE
Obtain the new piston and measure it to determine the correct cylinder bore oversize diameter.

Piston Ring Fit/Installation

Check the ring gap of each piston ring. Check the gap of new rings, because if the gap is too small the rings will break.

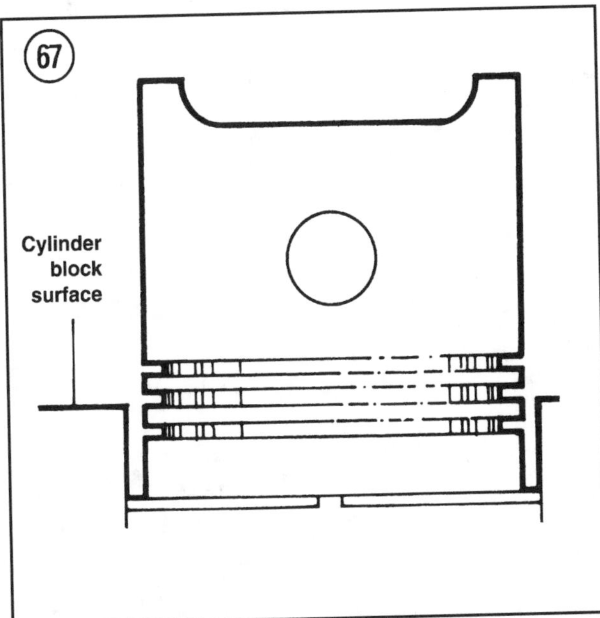

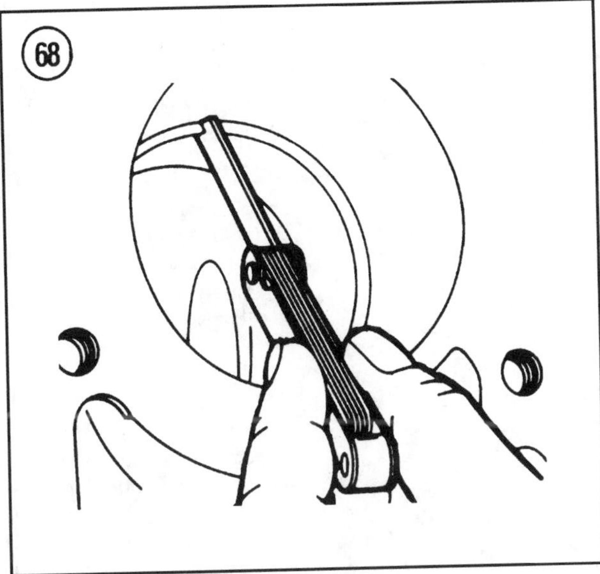

1. Position the ring at the bottom of the ring travel area and square it by moving it gently with an inverted piston. See **Figure 67**.

NOTE
If the cylinders have not been rebored, check the gap at the bottom of the ring travel, where the cylinder is least worn.

2. Measure the end gap of each ring in the cylinder with a feeler gauge as shown in **Figure 68**. Compare the measured gap with the specifications listed in **Tables 1-3**. Gaps should never be more than 1/32 in. (0.8 mm).
3. If the gap is less than the minimum specification, first check to be sure the rings are correct for the size of the cylinder bore. The ends of new rings can be filed to increase the gap slightly. See **Figure 69**.
4. If the end gap measured in Step 2 is too wide, the wrong rings may be installed or the ends of the rings may have been filed too much. If the gap is within specification at the bottom but is too wide at the top of the ring travel, the cylinder is worn (tapered) to the point that it should be

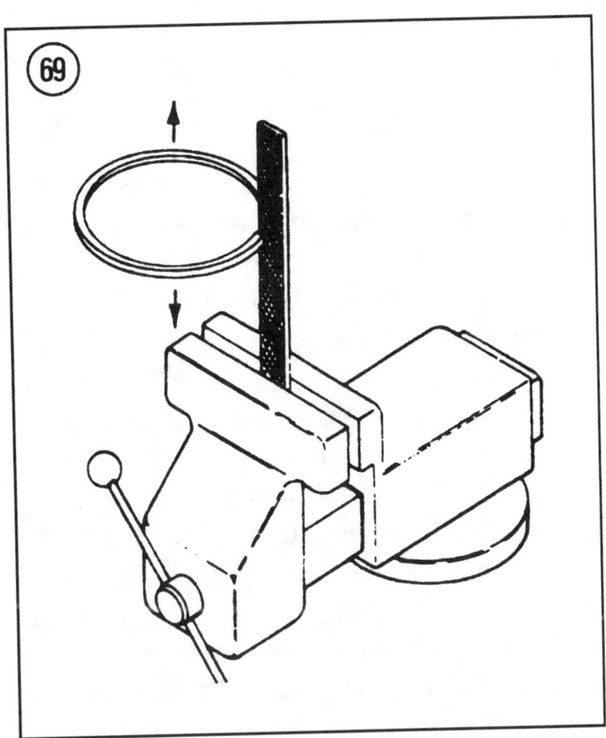

rebored and fitted with the next oversize piston and rings.

5. Check the side clearance of the rings in the grooves as shown in **Figure 70**. Place the feeler gauge alongside the ring all the way into the groove. If the measurement is not within specifications (**Tables 1-3**), either the rings or the ring grooves are worn.

6. Install the oil ring in the lower groove of the piston before installing compression rings. Each oil ring consist of 3 segments. The wavy segment is a spacer for the 2 rails.

NOTE
The correct location of the ring end gaps depends upon whether the piston is installed on the left or right side of the engine. Refer to the appropriate illustration.

a. Install the oil ring expander (**Figure 71**) in the lower groove and engage the tang (that keeps the spacer from turning) with the oil hole. The ends will be approximately in the position indicated by A, **Figure 72**.
b. Hold the spacer with the ends butted (*not overlapped*) and install 1 of the rails at the top of the spacer. The end gap of the rail must be at least 1 in. (25.4 cm) from the gap in the spacer.
c. Install the second rail at the bottom of the spacer. The end gap of the rail (B, **Figure 72**) should be at least 1 in. (25.4 cm) from the gap in the first (top) rail.
d. Check to make sure the lower ring is assembled correctly and moves freely. The antirotation tang should keep the assembly from turning, but it should compress into the groove without binding.

7. Use a ring expander (**Figure 63**) and carefully install the second compression ring. The top of each compression ring is marked and the mark must face toward the top of the piston.

8. Use a ring expander (**Figure 63**) and carefully install the top compression ring. The top of each

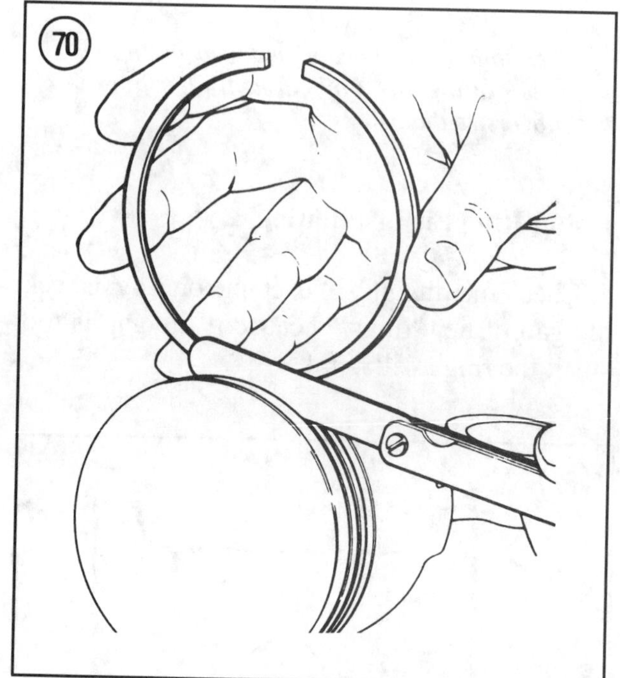

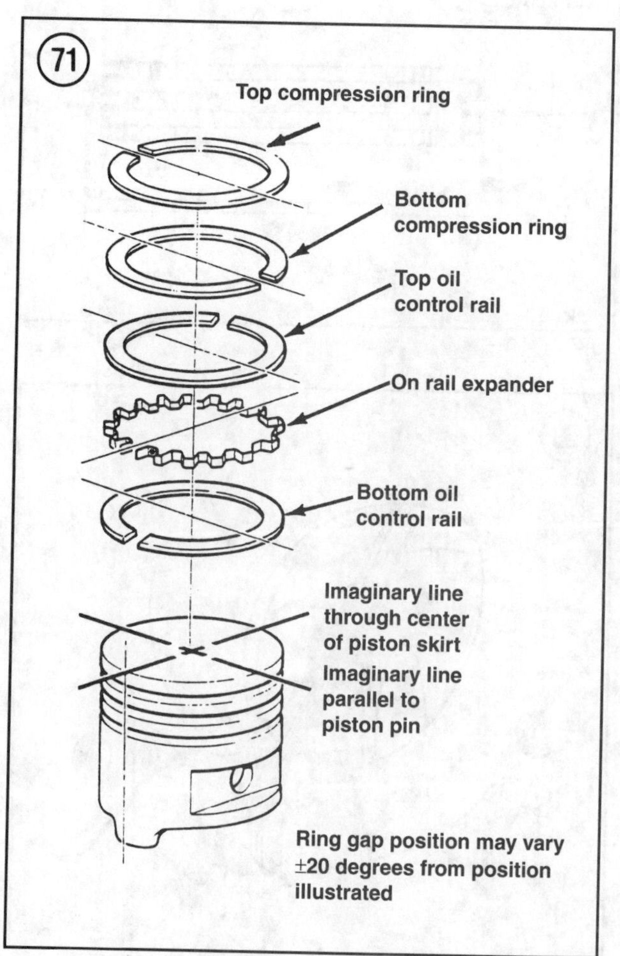

compression ring is marked and the mark must face toward the top of the piston.

9. Move the end gaps of the second and top compression rings if necessary to correctly position the ring gaps. Position the gap in the top ring at the point indicated by C, **Figure 72** and the second compression ring at the point indicated by D, **Figure 72**.

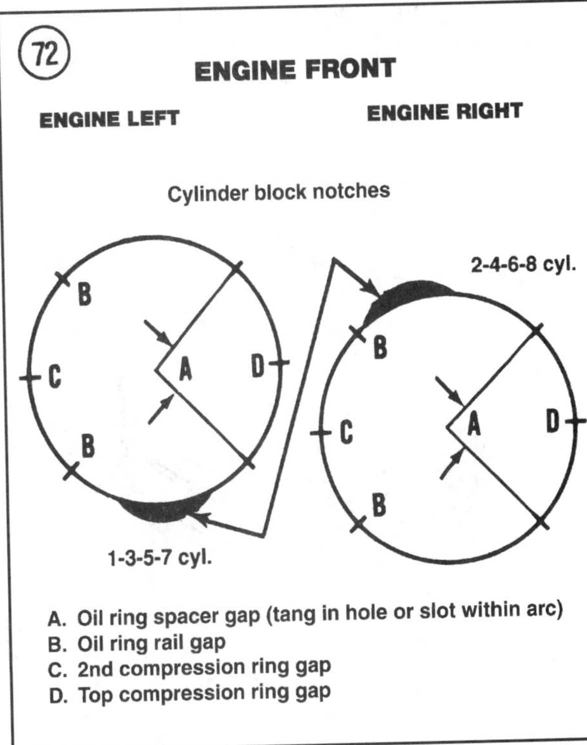

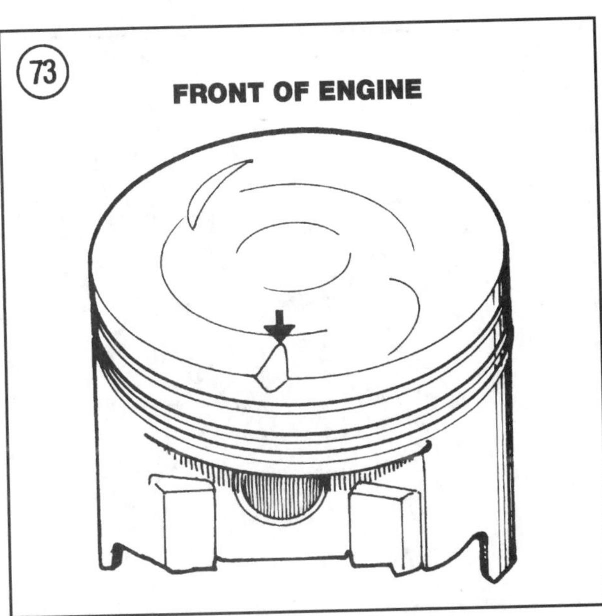

Connecting Rod Inspection

Have the connecting rods checked for straightness at a dealership or machine shop. When installing new connecting rods, have them checked for misalignment before installing the piston and piston pin. Connecting rods can spring out of alignment during shipping or handling.

Piston/Connecting Rod Assembly

The pistons *must* be assembled correctly to the connecting rods or the engine will be damaged. The piston pin hole may be offset and the top of the piston may have clearance slots, notches or relief pockets to allow clearance for the valves to operate. Additionally, the small relief hole between the connecting rod and cap provides lubrication for the camshaft. This hole must be facing toward the camshaft. Assembling the piston and connecting rod incorrectly will probably result in serious engine damage.

On all models, a notch cast in the edge of the piston, such as that shown in **Figure 73**, should be facing the front of the engine. If the valve relief notches are only on 1 side of the piston (**Figure 74**) or if 1 valve notch is of a much larger radius than the other, the large or single valve notch must face toward the center (intake side) of the engine.

On all models, the small hole in the side of the connecting rod and cap (**Figure 75**) must face toward the camshaft.

Connecting Rod Bearing Clearance Measurement

CAUTION

Make sure the bearing bore and bearing insert are both clean. If even the smallest piece of dirt is between the bearing insert and the bearing bore, the clearance will be affected.

1. Install the upper half of the bearing insert in the connecting rod.
2. Install the lower half of the bearing insert in the connecting rod cap.
3. Cut a piece of Plastigage the width of the bearing (**Figure 76**) and place the piece *across* the crankpin journal.

NOTE

In Steps 4-6, be careful not to turn the crankshaft until the rod cap has been removed. Turning the crankshaft will smear the Plastigage and make accurate measurement impossible. Also, be sure to place the Plastigage on a flat surface of the crankpin, not across the oil hole.

4. Position the connecting rod and bearing against the connecting rod journal and install the cap assembly. Make sure the rod is assembled correctly and installed on the correct journal. The numbers stamped on the side of the cap and connecting rod must face the starboard side of the crankshaft.
5. Tighten the connecting rod retaining screws to the torque specified in **Table 4** or **Table 5**. Do not rotate the crankshaft while the Plastigage is in place.
6. Remove the nuts retaining the connecting rod cap, then lift the cap off. The flattened Plastigage may either stick to the crankpin journal or the bearing insert.
7. Determine the bearing clearance by comparing the width of the flattened Plastigage with the markings on the Plastigage envelope. See **Figure 77**.
8. Compare the measured bearing clearance with the specification listed in **Tables 1-3**.
9. If the clearance is excessive, the crankshaft must be machined to a smaller size and undersize bearings fitted. Consult with your dealer or machinist.
10. Refer to the preceding steps. Measure the clearance for the remaining connecting rod bearings.

Piston/Connecting Rod Installation

1. Make sure the pistons are assembled to the connecting rods correctly for the cylinder in which they are being installed. Refer to *Pis-*

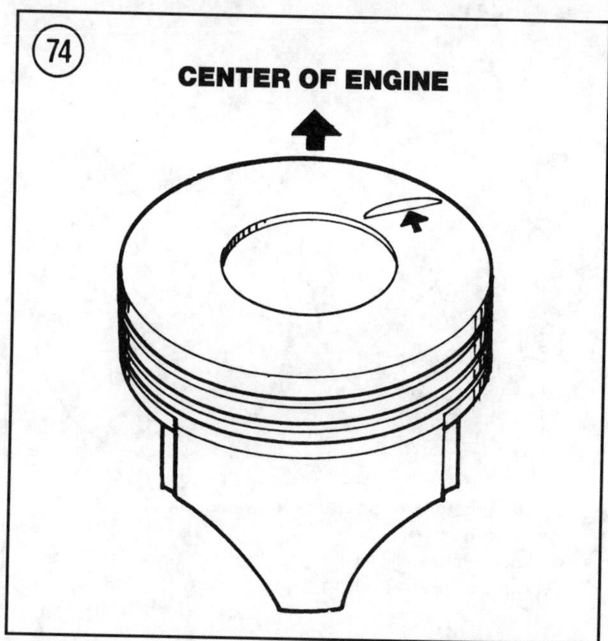

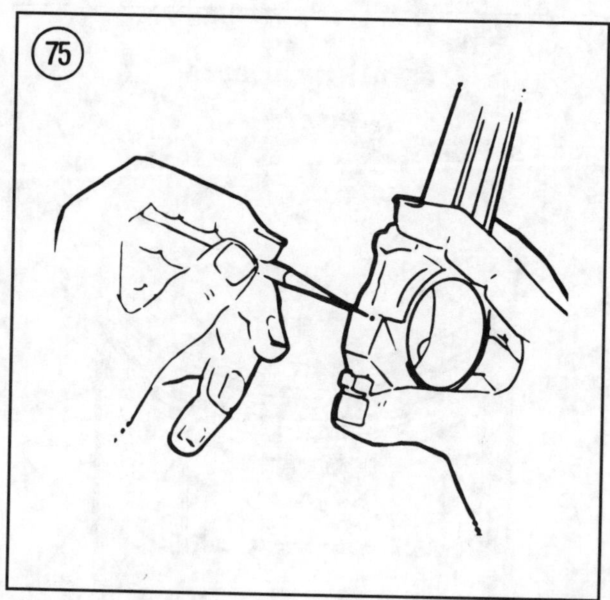

ton/Connecting Rod Assembly in this chapter. On all engines, the connecting rod bearing tangs must face toward the outside of the engine. The small oil hole in the connecting rod and cap (**Figure 75**) will be toward the camshaft.

NOTE
The pistons must be assembled to the connecting rods differently depending upon the position in which it will be installed. If 2 assemblies appear to be incorrect, it may be they are switched (assembled for the other location).

2. Make sure the ring gaps are positioned as described in *Piston Ring Fit/Installation* in this chapter.

NOTE
If the special protector tubes are not available, fit short sections of hose to the rod bolts.

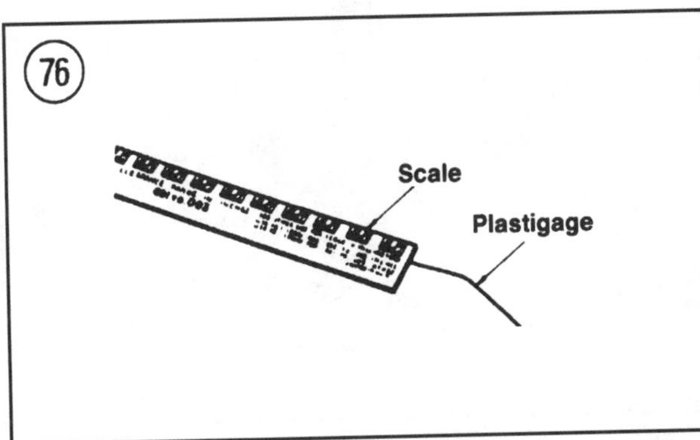

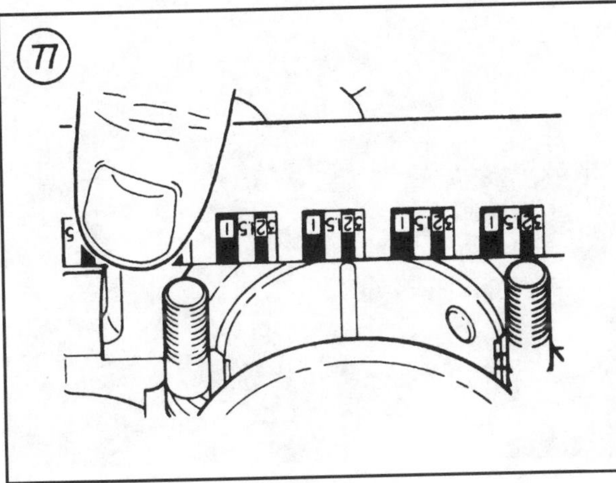

3. Slip special rod protector tubes (available from parts and tool suppliers) over the connecting rod bolts to help guide them into position and keep them from damaging the crankpin journals.
4. Coat the cylinder bore, rings and piston liberally with clean engine oil. The entire piston can be immersed in oil to ensure adequate lubrication.
5. Compress the piston rings using a suitable ring compressor. Be sure to space the ring end gaps as described in this chapter.

CAUTION
Be careful not to damage the piston rings while installing the connecting rod and piston assembly. It is sometimes difficult to buy a single ring. The crankpin can also be damaged easily by hitting 1 of the bolts against a polished bearing journal.

6. Insert the piston and connecting rod assembly into the correct cylinder bore. Align the lower end of the connecting rod with the crankshaft crankpin.

NOTE
Some mechanics protect the crankshaft journal by wrapping it with a protective material before installing the connecting rod and piston assembly. Special protector wraps made of plastic that curl around the journal are available from some tool and parts suppliers. Similar protection is possible by wrapping a piece of thin plastic or card stock (paper) around the journal, then holding this in place with a short piece of tape while assembling. Be careful not to allow adhesive to stick to the journal.

CAUTION
Do not let any part of the connecting rod or the bolts hit the crankpin when installing the piston and rod assemblies. The polished surface of the crankpin can be easily damaged by the connecting rod.

7. Push the piston and rings into the cylinder. Most mechanics use the handle of a hammer to push the piston into the cylinder. See **Figure 78**.

8. Remove the hoses or protector tubes from the connecting rod bolts and make sure the threads are clean.

9. Clean the connecting rod bearing inserts and bore in the connecting rod and cap, then install the bearing insert halves. Make sure the inserts are properly seated.

10. Lubricate the crankpin and connecting rod bearings liberally with clean engine oil.

11. Seat the crankpin firmly against the connecting rod bearing and insert. Make sure the insert is still correctly positioned in the connecting rod.

12. Install the connecting rod cap and install the retaining nuts. See **Figure 79**.

NOTE
Make sure that the bearing tangs on the rod and cap are both on the same side. Also, make sure the pistons are installed correctly.

13. Tighten the cap retaining nuts to the torque specified in **Table 4** or **Table 5**.

14. Check the connecting rod big-end play as described under *Piston/Connecting Rod Removal* in this chapter.

15. Repeat the preceding steps for each of the remaining rod and piston assemblies.

REAR MAIN OIL SEAL

Replacement

A 1-piece rear main seal is used and the seal is contained in a retainer attached to the rear of the engine block. The retainer and seal can be removed and replaced without removing the oil pan or the rear main bearing cap. Replace the seal as follows.

1. Remove the engine from the boat as described in this chapter.

2. Remove the engine coupler and flywheel from the engine.

CAUTION
Be extremely careful not to damage the seal surface of the crankshaft when removing the seal in Step 3.

3. Use a screwdriver inserted into the 3 slots around the seal retainer to carefully pry the rear main seal from the retainer. See **Figure 80**.

4. Thoroughly clean the seal bore in the retainer and the sealing surface of the crankshaft.

5. Lubricate the seal lip with engine oil or grease.

6. Position the seal with its lip facing toward the engine (inward). Use the proper seal installer and

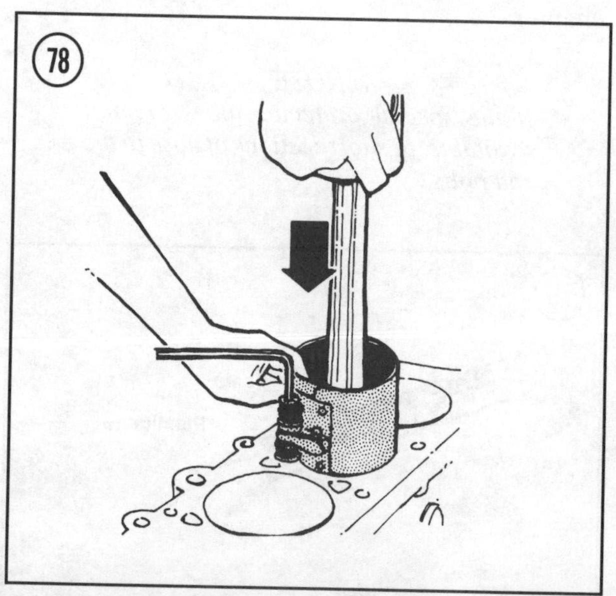
78

79

carefully push the new seal into the cylinder block/bearing cap/seal retainer counterbore. Make certain the seal is not cocked in the counterbore.

NOTE
Use seal installer part No. J-35621 for V6 and small block V8 engines. Use seal installer part No. J-38841 for big block V8 engine.

7. Install the flywheel, engine coupler and the engine into the boat as described in this chapter.

CRANKSHAFT

End Play Measurement

1. Pry the crankshaft to the front of the engine using a pry bar or large screwdriver.

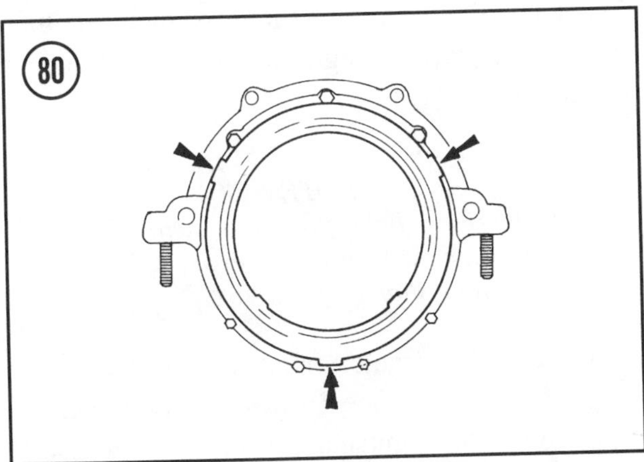

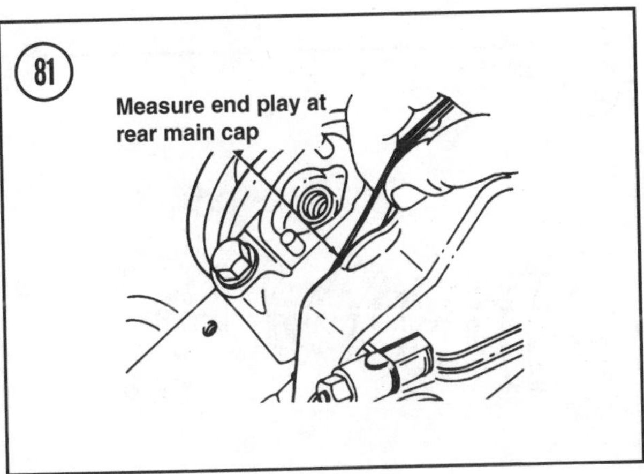

2. Measure the crankshaft end play at the front of the rear main bearing with a flat feeler gauge. See **Figure 81**. Compare end play to that listed in **Tables 1-3**.
3. If the end play is excessive, replace the rear main bearing. If less than specified, check the bearing faces for imperfections.

Removal

Refer to **Figure 82**, typical for this procedure. It is not necessary to remove the cylinder heads and pistons, but often these parts are removed as part of an overhaul before removing the crankshaft. If these parts are already removed, some of the following procedures will have already been accomplished.

1. Remove the engine from the boat as described in this chapter.

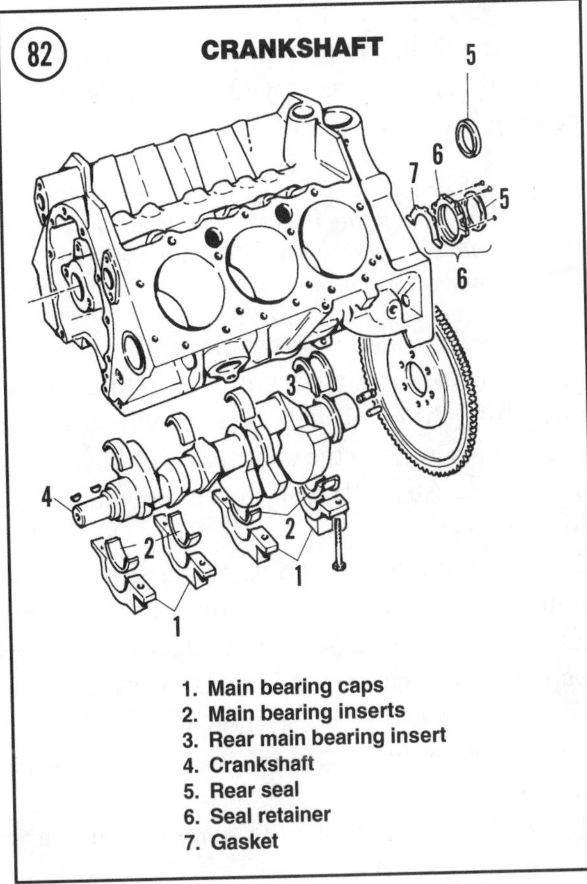

7

2. Remove the flywheel as described in this chapter.
3. Mount the engine on an engine stand, if available.
4. Remove the starter motor. See Chapter Eleven.
5. Invert the engine so the oil pan is at the top.
6. Remove the oil pan and oil pump as described in this chapter.
7. Remove the harmonic balancer, front cover and timing chain as described in this chapter.
8. Remove the spark plugs to allow the crankshaft to turn more easily.
9. Measure crankshaft end play as described in this chapter.
10. Rotate the crankshaft until the connecting rods of 1 journal are easily accessible.

NOTE
Mark each connecting rod and its cap with the cylinder number to aid reassembly.

11. Remove the nuts holding the connecting rod cap. Lift off the cap, together with the lower bearing insert.

NOTE
If the connecting rod caps are difficult to remove, tap the studs with a handle of a hammer or similar tool.

12. Use the handle of a hammer to push the piston and connecting rod into the cylinder bore away from the crankshaft. Be sure to remove the bearing insert from the connecting rod.
13. Repeat Steps 10-12 for each remaining piston/rod assembly.
14. Clean the main bearing caps and check for numbers identifying the location of each cap and an arrow on each indicating the front of the engine. If you cannot find marks, mark the caps so that each can be reassembled in the correct location with the proper side of the cap toward the front.
15. Unbolt and remove the main bearing caps and bearing inserts.

NOTE
If the caps are difficult to remove, lift the bolts partway out, then lever the bolts from side to side.

16. Carefully lift the crankshaft from the engine block and place it on a clean workbench.
17. Remove the bearing inserts from the block. Place the bearing caps and inserts in order on a clean workbench.
18. Remove the main bearing oil seal from the cylinder block and rear bearing cap.

Inspection

1. Clean the crankshaft thoroughly with solvent. Blow out the oil passages with compressed air.
2. Check the main and connecting rod journals for wear, scratches, grooves, scoring or cracks. Check the oil seal surface for burrs, nicks or other sharp edges which might damage a seal during installation.

NOTE
Unless you have precision measuring equipment and know how to use it, have a machine shop perform Step 3.

3. Check all journals for out-of-roundness and taper (**Figure 83**). See **Tables 1-3** for specifications. Have the crankshaft reground, if necessary, and install new undersize bearing inserts.

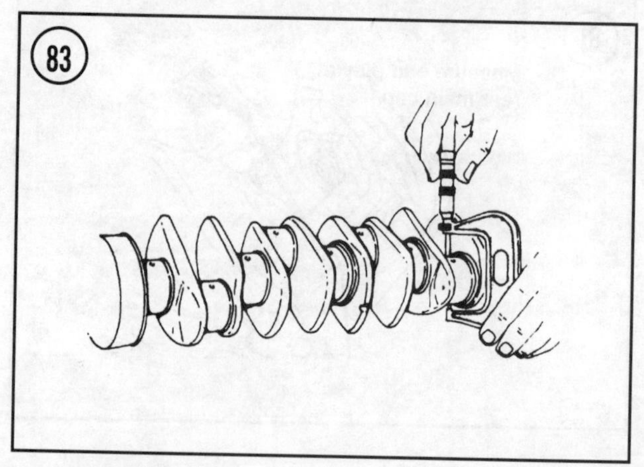

Main Bearing Clearance Measurement

Check main bearing clearance using Plastigage following the same procedure used to measure connecting rod bearing clearance described in this chapter. If clearance is excessive, the bearings should be replaced, and the crankshaft should be reground or both. Bearing inserts 0.001 and 0.002 in. undersize may be available to accommodate small amounts of wear. Check with a bearing supplier for application and availability.

Sprocket Removal/Installation

The crankshaft sprocket that drives the camshaft is keyed to the front of the crankshaft. On some models, the sprocket is a tight fit and a puller is required to remove it and the new sprocket must be driven into place. Refer to *Timing Chain and Sprockets* in this chapter for removal and installation.

Installation

1. Install the main bearing inserts in the cylinder block. Oil holes in the bearing inserts must align with oil passages in the block and the tabs on the inserts must seat in the slots machined in the block.

NOTE
Check cap bolts for thread damage before reuse. If damaged, replace the bolts.

2. Lubricate the bolt threads with clean engine oil.
3. Install the bearing inserts in each cap and lubricate the bearings liberally.
4. Carefully lower the crankshaft into position in the block.
5. Install the bearing caps in their marked positions with the arrows pointing toward the front of the engine.
6. Use the following procedure to align the crankshaft thrust surfaces of the rear main bearing.
   a. Install all screws attaching the main bearing caps and tighten finger-tight.
   b. Tighten screws retaining the front main bearing caps (all except the rear cap) to the torque specified in **Table 4** or **Table 5**.
   c. Tighten the screws retaining the rear main bearing cap to 10-12 ft.-lb. (13.6-16.3 N•m).
   d. Use a heavy soft-faced (lead) hammer to bump the front of the crankshaft and move the crankshaft to the rear.
   e. Bump the rear of the crankshaft to drive it forward.
   f. Tighten the screws attaching the rear main bearing caps to the torque listed in **Table 4** or **Table 5**.
7. Retighten all main bearing caps to the torque listed in **Table 4** or **Table 5**.
8. Rotate the crankshaft to make sure it turns smoothly. If not, remove the bearing caps and crankshaft and check that the bearings are clean and properly installed.
9. Reverse Steps 1-12 of *Removal* in this chapter. Refer to **Table 4** or **Table 5** for tightening torques.
10. Install a new rear main bearing oil seal as described in this chapter.

7

DRIVE COUPLER AND FLYWHEEL

Removal/Installation

1. Remove the engine from the boat as described in this chapter.
2. Unbolt the flywheel and coupler from the crankshaft. Remove the bolts gradually in a diagonal pattern.
3. To install, align the dowel hole in the flywheel with the dowel in crankshaft flange and position the flywheel on studs.

4. Fit the coupler on the studs. Install the washers and locknuts. Tighten nuts to the torque specified in **Table 4** or **Table 5**.
5. Install a dial indicator on the machined surface of the flywheel and check runout. If runout exceeds 0.008 in. (0.20 mm), remove the flywheel and check for burrs on the crankshaft and flywheel mating surfaces. If none are found, replace the flywheel.
6. Reinstall the engine in the boat as described in this chapter.

Inspection

1. Visually check the flywheel for cracks or other damage.
2. Check the condition of the splines and cushion hub of the coupling.
3. Inspect the ring gear for cracks, broken teeth or excessive wear. If the ring gear teeth are damaged, check the starter motor drive teeth for similar wear or damage. If the flywheel ring gear is damaged, it can be removed and replaced at a machine shop.

CYLINDER BLOCK

Cleaning and Inspection

1. Check the block for evidence of fluid leakage. Identify possible problem areas such as leaking plugs, gaskets or cracks. Examine these areas further while cleaning and after cleaning.
2. Clean the block thoroughly. Some cleaning procedures are facilitated by removing plugs from passages.
   a. Clean all gasket or RTV sealant residue from the machined surfaces.
   b. Check all core plugs for leaks and replace any that are suspect. See *Core Plug Replacement* in this chapter.
   c. Check coolant passages for sludge, dirt and corrosion while cleaning. If the passages are very dirty, have the block boiled out at a machine shop. Blow out all passages with compressed air.
   d. Remove plugs from oil passages to permit a more thorough cleaning. Check oil passages for sludge, dirt and corrosion while cleaning. If the passages are very dirty, have the block boiled out at a machine shop. Blow out all passages with compressed air.
   e. Check the threads in the head bolt holes to be sure they are clean. If dirty, use a tap to clean the threads and remove any deposits.
3. Examine the block for cracks. If cracked, the block must be repaired or replaced. A machine shop will be able to confirm suspicions about possible cracks. Another method is as follows:
   a. Mix 1 part of kerosene with 2 parts engine oil.
   b. Dissolve zinc oxide in wood alcohol.
   c. Coat the suspected area with the mixture of kerosene and oil, then wipe the area dry.

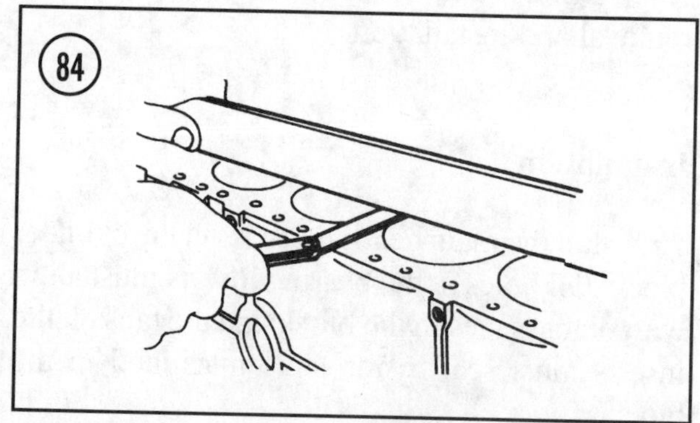

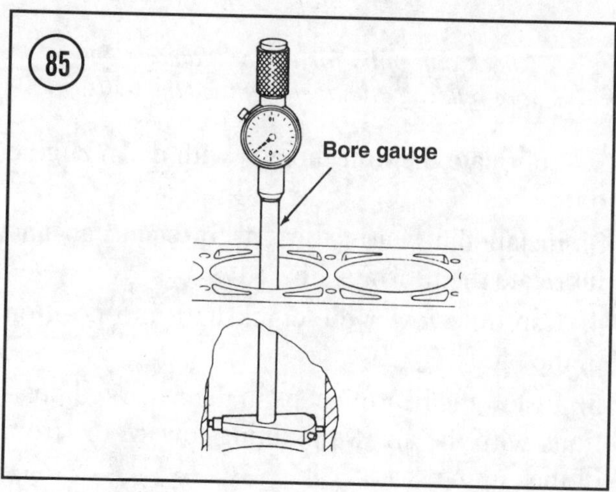

d. Immediately apply the solution of zinc oxide and wood alcohol.

e. A crack will appear as discoloration in the zinc oxide treated area.

4. Check the cylinder block deck (top surface) for flatness. Place an accurate straightedge on the block. If there is any gap between the block and straightedge, measure it with a flat feeler gauge (**Figure 84**). Measure from end to end and from corner to corner. Have the block resurfaced if it is warped more than 0.004 in. (0.102 mm).

5. Measure cylinder bores using a bore gauge (**Figure 85**) for out-of-roundness or excessive wear as described in *Piston Clearance Check* in this chapter. If the cylinders exceed maximum tolerance, they must be rebored. Reboring is also necessary if the cylinder walls are badly scuffed or scored.

79

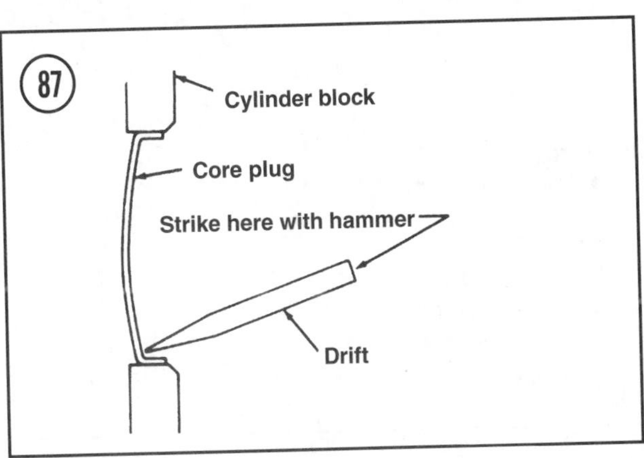

NOTE

*Before boring, install all main bearing caps and tighten the cap bolts to the specification in **Table 2**.*

CORE PLUG REPLACEMENT

Check the condition of all core plugs in the block (**Figure 86**) and cylinder head whenever the engine is out of the boat for service. If any signs of leakage or corrosion are found around 1 core plug, replace them all.

NOTE

Core plugs can be replaced inexpensively at a machine shop. If you are having machine work done on the engine, have the core plugs replaced at the same time.

7

Removal/Installation

CAUTION

Do not drive core plugs into the engine casting. It will be impossible to retrieve them, and they can restrict coolant circulation, resulting in serious engine damage.

1. Tap the bottom edge of the core plug with a hammer and drift. Use several sharp blows to push the bottom of the plug inward, tilting the top out (**Figure 87**).
2. Grip the top of the plug firmly with pliers. Pull the plug from its bore (**Figure 88**) and discard.

NOTE

Core plugs can also be removed by drilling a hole in the center of the plug and prying them out with an appropriate size drift or pin punch. On large core plugs, the use of a universal impact slide hammer is recommended.

3. Clean the plug bore thoroughly to remove all traces of the old sealer. Inspect the bore for any damage that might interfere with proper sealing

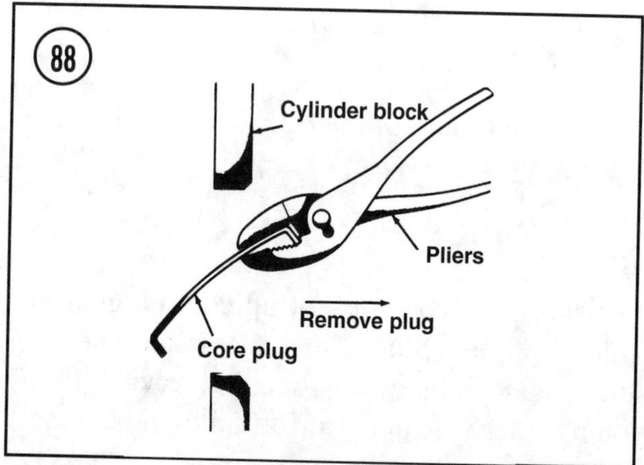

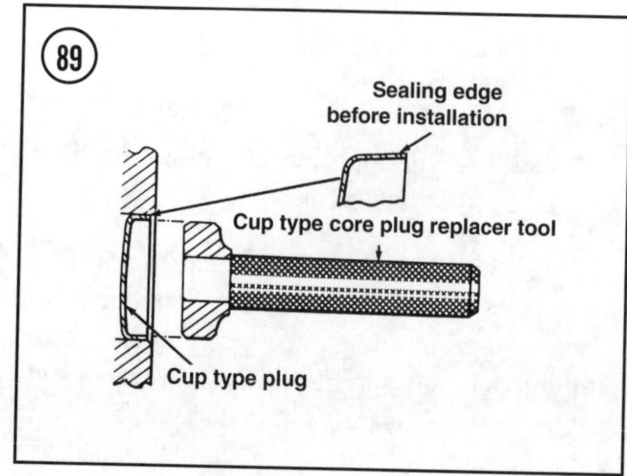

of the new plug. If damage is evident, true the surface by boring for the next oversize plug.

NOTE
Oversize plugs can be identified by an OS stamped in the flat on the cup side of the plug.

4. Coat the inside diameter of the plug bore and the outer diameter of the new plug with sealer. Use an oil-resistant sealer if the plug is to be installed in an oil gallery or a water-resistant sealer for plugs installed in the water jacket.

5. Install the new core plug with an appropriate size core plug installation tool (**Figure 89**), driver or socket. The sharp edge of the plug should be at least 0.02 in. (0.5 mm) inside the lead-in chamfer.

6. Repeat Steps 1-5 to replace each remaining core plug.

Table 1 ENGINE SPECIFICATIONS 4.3 L (262 cid) V6

Type	4.3 L (262 cid) V6
Displacement	262 cid (4.3 L)
Bore	4.0 in. (101.6 mm)
Stroke	3.480 in. (88.4 mm)
Cylinder numbering (front to rear)	
Port	1-3-5
Starboard	2-4-6
Firing order	1-6-5-4-3-2
Piston clearance in cylinder bore	
Production	0.0007-0.0017 in. (0.018-0.043 mm)
Service limit	0.0027 in. maximum (0.069 mm)
Piston rings	
End gap	
Top compression	0.010-0.020 in. (0.25-0.51 mm)
Second compression	0.010-0.025 in. (0.25-0.63 mm)
Oil control (bottom ring)	0.015-0.055 in. (0.38-1.40 mm)

(continued)

Table 1 ENGINE SPECIFICATIONS 4.3 L (262 cid) V6 (continued)

Type	4.3 L (262 cid) V6
Side clearance	
Compression rings	0.0012-0.0032 in. (0.030-0.081 mm)
Oil control (bottom ring)	0.002-0.007 in. (0.05-0.18 mm)
Piston pin	
Diameter	0.9270-0.9273 in. (23.546-23.553 mm)
Fit in connecting rod	0.0016-0.008 in. (0.041-0.20 mm) interference
Fit in piston	
Desired	0.00025-0.00035 in. (0.0063-0.0089 mm)
Service limit	0.001 in. (0.025 mm)
Crankshaft	
Main bearing clearance	
No. 1 (front), production	0.0008-0.0020 in. (0.020-0.051 mm)
Service limit	0.001-0.0015 in. (0.025-0.038 mm)
No. 2 & 3, production	0.0011-0.0023 in. (0.028-0.058 mm)
Service limit	0.001-0.0025 in. (0.025-0.063 mm)
No. 4 (rear), production	0.0017-0.0032 in. (0.043-0.081 mm)
Service limit	0.0025-0.0035 in. (0.063-0.089 mm)
End play (axial)	0.002-0.006 in. (0.051-0.152 mm)
Crankpin diameter	
Production	2.0988-2.0998 in. (53.309-53.334 mm)
Maximum taper	0.001 in. (0.025 mm)
Maximum out-of-round	0.0005 in. (0.013 mm)
Main journals	
Diameter, production	
No. 1 (front)	2.4484-2.4493 in. (62.189-62.212 mm)
No. 2 & 3	2.4481-2.4490 in. (62.182-62.205 mm)
No. 4 (rear)	2.4479-2.4488 in. (62.177-62.199 mm)
Connecting rod	
Side play on crankpin	0.008-0.014 in. (0.20-0.36 mm)
Bearing clearance	
Production	0.0013-0.0035 in. (0.033-0.089 mm)
Service limit	0.0030 in. (0.076 mm)
Camshaft	
End play (axial)	0.004-0.012 in. (0.10-0.30 mm)
Journal diameter	1.8682-1.8692 in. (47.452-47.478 mm)
Maximum out-of-round	0.001 in. (0.025 mm)
Lobe lift	
1994-1996	
Intake	0.234 in. (5.94 mm)
Exhaust	0.2576 in. (6.54 mm)
1997-on	
Intake	0.2763 in. (0.7180 mm)
Exhaust	0.2855 in. (0.7252 mm)
Maximum warpage, between V-blocks	0.0015 in. (0.038 mm)
Valves	
Face angle	45°
Seat angle	46°
Seat width	
1994-1996	
Intake	1/16 to 7/32 in. (1.59-5.56 mm)
Exhaust	1/16 to 3/32 in. (1.59-2.38 mm)
1997-on	
Intake	0.040-0.065 in. (1.016-1.651 mm)
Exhaust	0.065-0.098 in. (1.651-2.489 mm)
Valve stem clearance	0.0010-0.0027 in. (0.025-0.069 mm)

(continued)

7

Table 1 ENGINE SPECIFICATIONS 4.3 L (262 cid) V6 (continued)

Type	4.3 L (262 cid) V6
Valve springs	
Free length	2.03 in. (51.6 mm)
Installed height	1.70 in. (43.2 mm)
Pressure	
Valve closed	76-84 lb. @ 1.70 in. (338-374 N @ 43.2 mm)
Valve open	194-206 lb. @ 1.25 in. (863-916 N @ 31.7 mm)
Oil pump pressure	
1994-1996	15-30 psi (103-207 kPa) @ 800 rpm
	40-60 psi (276-414 kPa) @ 2,000 rpm
1997-on	6 psi (41.4 kPa) @ 1,000 rpm
	18 psi (24.1 kPa) @ 2,000 rpm
	24 psi (165.5 kPa) @ 4,000 rpm

Table 2 ENGINE SPECIFICATIONS 5.0 AND 5.7L (305 AND 350 cid) V8

Type	5.0 and 5.7 L (305 and 350 cid) V8
Displacement	
	5.0 L (305 cid)
	5.7 L (350 cid)
Bore	
5.0 L	94.89 mm (3.736 in.)
5.7 L	101.6 mm (4.00 in.)
Stroke	88.39 mm (3.480 in.)
Cylinder numbering (front to rear)	
Port	1-3-5-7
Starboard	2-4-6-8
Firing order	1-8-4-3-6-5-7-2
Piston clearance	
Production	
1994-1997 5.7 L	0.018-0.043 mm (0.0007-0.0017 in.)
1998-on 5.0 and 5.7 L	0.018-0.053 mm (0.0007-0.0021 in.)
Service limit	
1994-1997 5.7 L	0.069 mm (0.0027 in.) Maximum
1998-on 5.0 and 5.7 L	0.018-0.068 mm (0.0007-0.0026 in.)
Piston ring end gap	
Top compression	
1994-1997 5.7 L	0.25-0.51 mm (0.010-0.020 in.)
1998-on 5.0 and 5.7 L	0.30-0.51 mm (0.012-0.020 in.)
Second compression	
1994-1997 5.7 L	0.25-0.63 mm (0.010-0.025 in.)
1998-on 5.0 and 5.7 L	0.51-0.66 mm (0.020-0.026 in.)
Oil control (bottom ring)	
1994-1997 5.7 L	0.38-1.40 mm (0.015-0.055 in.)
1998-on 5.0 and 5.7 L	0.25-0.76 mm (0.010-0.030 in.)
Side clearance	
Compression rings	
1994-1997 5.7 L	0.030-0.081 mm (0.0012-0.0032 in.)
1998-on 5.0 and 5.7 L	0.030-0.070 mm (0.0012-0.0027 in.)
Oil control (bottom ring)	
1994-1997 5.7 L	0.030-0.081 mm (0.0012-0.0032 in.)
1998-on 5.0 and 5.7 L	0.051-0.170 mm (0.002-0.006 in.)
Piston pin	
Diameter	
1994-1997 5.7 L	23.546-23.553 mm (0.9270-0.9271 in.)
1998-on 5.0 and 5.7 L	23.545-23.548 mm (0.9270-0.9271 in.)

(continued)

Table 2 ENGINE SPECIFICATIONS 5.0 AND 5.7L (305 AND 350 cid) V8

Fit in connecting rod (interference)	0.041-0.20 mm (0.0016-0.008 in.)
Fit in piston	
Production	
1994-1997 5.7 L	0.0063-0.0089 mm (0.00025-0.00035 in.)
1998-on 5.0 and 5.7 L	0.013-0.023 mm (0.0005-0.0009 in.)
Service limit	
1994-1997 5.7 L	0.025 mm (0.001 in.)
1998-on 5.0 and 5.7 L	0.013-0.0254 mm (0.0005-0.0010 in.)
Crankshaft	
Main bearing clearance	
No.1 (front), production	0.018-0.53 mm (0.0007-0.0021 in.)
Service limit	0.025-0.063 mm (0.001-0.0025 in.)
No. 2, 3, and 4 production	0.022-0.061 mm (0.0009-0.0024 in.)
Service limit	0.025-0.063 mm (0.001-0.0025 in.)
No.5 (rear), production	0.0254-0.069 mm (0.0010-0.0027 in.)
Service limit	0.038-0.076 mm (0.0015-0.003 in.)
End play (axial)	0.05-0.20 mm (0.002-0.008 in.)
Crank pin diameter	
Production	53.2840-53.3340 mm (2.0978-2.0998 in.)
Maximum taper	0.025 mm (0.001 in.)
Maximum out-out-round	0.025 mm (0.001 in.)
Main journal diameter	
Production	
No.1, (front)	62.189-62.212 mm (2.4484-2.4493 in.)
No. 2, 3, and 4	62.182-62.205 mm (2.4481-2.4490 in.)
No. 5	62.177-62.199 mm (2.4479-2.4488 in.)
Connecting rod	
Side play on crank pin	
1994-1997 5.7 L	0.20-0.36 mm (0.008-0.014 in.)
1998-on 5.0 and 5.7 L	0.16-0.61 mm (0.006-0.024 in.)
Bearing clearance	
Production	0.033-0.089 mm (0.0013-0.0035 in.)
Service limit	0.076 mm (0.0030 in.)
Camshaft	
End play (axial)	0.10-0.30 mm (0.004-0.012 in.)
Journal diameter	47.44-47.49 mm (1.8677-1.8697 in.)
Maximum out-of-round	0.025 mm (0.001 in.)
Lobe lift	0.05 mm (0.002 in.)
Intake	
1994-1997 5.7 L	6.83 mm (0.269 in.)
1998-on 5.0 and 5.7 L	6.97-7.07 mm (0.274-0.278 in.)
Exhaust	
1994-1997 5.7 L	7.01 mm (0.276 in.)
1998-on 5.0 and 5.7 L	7.07-7.20 mm (0.278-0.283 in.)
Valves	
Face angle	45°
Seat angle	46°
Seat width	
Intake	1.14-1.65 mm (0.045-0.065 in.)
Exhaust	1.65-2.49 mm (0.065-0.098 in.)
Valve stem clearance	0.025-0.069 mm (0.0010-0.0027 in.)
Valve spring 1994-1998	
Free length	51.6 mm (2.03 in.)
Installed height	43.2 mm (1.70 in.)
Pressure	
Valve closed	338-374 N @ 43.2 mm (76-84 lb. @ 1.70 in.)

(continued)

7

Table 2 ENGINE SPECIFICATIONS 5.0 AND 5.7L (305 AND 350 cid) V8 (continued)

Pressure (continued)	
Valve open	
1994-1997 5.7 L	863-916 N @ 3.17 mm (194-206 lb. @ 1.25 in.)
1998-on 5.0 and 5.7 L	832-903 N @ 32.3 mm (187-203 lb. @ 1.27 in.)
Oil pump pressure	103-207 kPa (15-30 psi) @ 800 rpm 276-414 kPa (40-60 psi) @ 2000 rpm

Table 3 ENGINE SPECIFICATIONS 7.4 AND 8.2 L (454 AND 502 cid) V8

Type	7.4 L (454 cid) V8	8.2 L (502 cid) V8
Displacement	454 cid (7.4 L)	502 cid (8.2 L)
Bore	4.250 in. (107.95 mm)	4.468 in. (113.5 mm)
Stroke	4.000 in. (101.6 mm)	4.000 in. (101.6 mm)
Cylinder numbering (front to rear)		
Port	1-3-5-7	1-3-5-7
Starboard	2-4-6-8	2-4-6-8
Firing order	1-8-4-3-6-5-7-2	1-8-4-3-6-5-7-2
Piston clearance		
Production	0.003-0.004 in. (0.08-0.10 mm)	0.004-0.005 in. (0.10-0.13 mm)
Service limit	0.005 in.) (0.13) mm	0.005 in. (0.13 mm)
Piston rings		
End gap		
Top compression	0.010-0.018 in. (0.25-0.46 mm)	0.010-0.018 in. (0.25-0.46 mm)
Second compression	0.016-0.024 in. (0.41-0.61 mm)	0.016-0.024 in. (0.41-0.61 mm)
Oil control (bottom ring)	0.010-0.030 in. (0.25-0.76 mm)	0.010-0.030 in. (0.25-0.76 mm)
Side clearance		
Compression rings	0.0012-0.0029 in. (0.030-0.074 mm)	0.0012-0.0029 in. (0.030-0.074 mm)
Oil control (bottom ring)	0.005-0.0065 in. (0.13-0.165 mm)	0.005-0.0065 in. (0.13-0.165 mm)
Piston pin		
Diameter	0.9895-0.9897 in. (25.133-25.138 mm)	0.9895-0.9897 in. (25.133-25.138 mm)
Fit in connecting rod (interference)	0.0021-0.0031 in. (0.053-0.079 mm)	0.0021-0.0031 in. (0.053-0.079 mm)
Fit in piston		
Desired	0.0002-0.0007 in. (0.005-0.018 mm)	0.0002-0.0007 in. (0.005-0.018 mm)
Service limit	0.001 in. (0.025 mm)	0.001 in. (0.025 mm)
Crankshaft		
Main bearing clearance		
No. 1, 2, 3 & 4	0.0010-0.0030 in. (0.025-0.076 mm)	0.0010-0.0030 in. (0.025-0.076 mm)
No. 5 (rear)	0.0025-0.0040 in. (0.063-0.102 mm)	0.0025-0.0040 in. (0.063-0.102 mm)

(continued)

Table 3 ENGINE SPECIFICATIONS 7.4 AND 8.2 L (454 AND 502 cid) V8 (continued)

Type	7.4 L (454 cid) V8	8.2 L (502 cid) V8
Crankshaft (continued)		
End play (axial)	0.006-0.010 in. (0.15-0.25 mm)	0.006-0.010 in. (0.15-0.25 mm)
Crankpin diameter	2.199-2.1996 in. (55.85-55.870 mm)	2.2000 in. (55.880 mm)
Maximum taper	0.001 in. (0.025 mm)	0.001 in. (0.025 mm)
Maximum out-of-round	0.001 in. (0.025 mm)	0.001 in. (0.025 mm)
Main journal diameter		
Production	2.7482-2.7489 in. (69.804-69.822 mm)	2.7500 in. (69.85 mm)
Maximum taper	0.001 in. (0.025 mm)	0.001 in. (0.025 mm)
Maximum out-of-round	0.001 in. (0.025 mm)	0.001 in. (0.025 mm)
Connecting rod		
Side play on crankpin	0.0013-0.023 in. (0.033-0.58 mm)	0.0013-0.023 in. (0.033-0.58 mm)
Bearing clearance		
Production	0.0011-0.0029 in. (0.028-0.074 mm)	0.0011-0.0029 in. (0.028-0.074 mm)
Service limit	0.0030 in. (0.076 mm)	0.0030 in. (0.076 mm)
Camshaft		
Journal diameter	1.9482-1.9492 in. (49.484-49.510 mm)	1.9482-1.9492 in. (49.484-49.510 mm)
Lobe lift		
Intake		
1994-1996	0.2323-0.2363 in. (5.900-6.002 mm)	0.249-0.253 in. (6.32-6.43 mm)
1997-on	0.2343 in. (5.9512 mm)	0.510 in. (12.954 mm)
Exhaust		
1994-1996	0.2510-0.2550 in. (6.375-6.477 mm)	0.249-0.253 in. (6.32-6.43 mm)
1997-on	0.2530 in. (6.426 mm)	0.510 in. (12.954 mm)
Valves		
Face angle	45°	45°
Seat angle	46°	46°
Seat width		
Intake	1/32 to 1/16 in. (1.59-5.56 mm)	1/32 to 1/16 in. (1.59-5.56 mm)
Exhaust	1/16 to 3/32 in. (1.59-2.38 mm)	1/16 to 3/32 in. (1.59-2.38 mm)
Valve stem clearance		
Intake	0.0010-0.0027 in. (0.025-0.069 mm)	0.0010-0.0027 in. (0.025-0.069 mm)
Exhaust	0.0012-0.0029 in. (0.030-0.074 mm)	0.0010-0.0029 in. (0.030-0.074 mm)

(continued)

Table 3 ENGINE SPECIFICATIONS 7.4 AND 8.2 L (454 AND 502 cid) V8 (continued)

Type	7.4 L (454 cid) V8	8.2 L (502 cid) V8
Valve stem clearance (continued)		
Service limit		
Intake	0.0037 in. (0.094 mm)	0.0037 in. (0.094 mm)
Exhaust	0.0039 in. (0.099 mm)	0.0039 in. (0.099 mm)
Valve springs		
Free length	2.15 in. (54.6 mm)	2.15 in. (54.6 mm)
Installed height	1 51/64 in. (45.6 mm)	1 51/64 in. (45.6 mm)
Pressure		
Valve closed	74-86 lb. @ 1.80 in. (329-382 N @ 45.7 mm)	76-86 lb. @ 1.80 in. (338-382 N @ 45.7 mm)
Valve open	195-215 lb. @ 1.40 in. (867-956 N @ 35.6 mm)	195-215 lb. @ 1.40 in. (867-956 N @ 35.6 mm)
Oil pump pressure		
@ 500 rpm	10 psi (69 kPa)	10 psi (69 kPa)
@ 2,000 rpm	40-60 psi (276-414 kPa)	40-60 psi (276-414 kPa)

Table 4 TIGHTENING TORQUES 4.3 L (262 cid) V6; 5.0 L (305 cid) & 5.7 L (350 cid) V8

	N·m	in.-lb.	ft.-lb.
Balance shaft (V6 only)			
Drive gear stud	16	–	12
Driven gear*			
First step	20	–	15
Second step	35°		
Shaft retainer	14	120	–
Camshaft			
Sprocket	28	–	21
Thrust plate (V6 only)	12	106	–
Connecting rod	60	–	45
Connecting rod nut			
1994-1996	60	–	45
1997 (4.3L)	27 plus additional 70°	20	–
1998-on (5.0 & 5.7 L)			
First step	27	–	20
Second step	Additional 55°		
Coolant circulating pump	41	–	30
Cylinder head*			
1994-1996			
First step	34	–	25
Second step	61	–	45
Third step	88	–	65
1997-on			
First step	30	–	22
Second step			
Short length bolt	55°		
Medium length bolt	65°		
Large length bolt	75°		

(continued)

Table 4 TIGHTENING TORQUES
4.3 L (262 cid) V6; 5.0 L (305 cib) & 5.7 L (350 cid) V8 (cont)

	N·m	in.-lb.	ft.-lb.
Dipstick tube flare	20-24	–	15
Distributor clamp (1994-1996)	27	–	20
Distributor clamp (1997-on)	25	–	18
Engine mounts			
Front			
Adjustment nuts	136-163	–	100-120
Mount to engine	43-54	–	32-40
Rear			
Center screw to square nut	60-71	–	44-52
Lock nuts	38-40	–	28-30
Mount plate to transom	27-34	–	20-25
Exhaust elbow to manifold	16-24	–	12-18
Exhaust pipe to transom shield	27-34	–	20-25
Flame arrestor			
Nut	3.4-4.5	30-40	–
Stud	7-9	65-80	–
Flywheel and coupler	54-61	–	40-45
Flywheel housing	43-54	–	32-40
Harmonic balancer (7/16 × 20)	75-84	–	55-62
Lift bracket	20-39	–	15-29
Lifter retainer (V6 only)	16.4	145	12
Main bearing caps			
Outer bolts of center caps	95	–	70
Other bolts	110	–	80
Manifold			
Exhaust to cylinder head			
1994-1997	27-35	–	20-26
1998-on			
First step	15	–	11
Final step	30	–	22
Intake to cylinder head			
1994-1997	41	–	30
1998-on			
First step	3	27	–
Second step	12	106	–
Third step	15	–	11
Oil drain retainer	20-24	–	15-18
Oil filter bypass valve	27	–	20
Oil pan			
1/4 × 20	9	80	–
5/16 × 18	18.6	165	–
Oil pressure sender	14-19	–	10-14
Oil pump			
Attachment	90	–	65
Cover	8-12	–	6-9
Oil seal retainer (rear)	15.3	135	11
Oil withdrawl tube to elbow	20-24	–	15-18

(continued)

7

Table 4 TIGHTENING TORQUES
4.3 L (262 cid) V6; 5.0 L (305 cib) & 5.7 L (350 cid) V8 (continued)

	N•m	in.-lb.	ft.-lb.
Power steering pump bracket			
Nut	18-20	–	13-15
Screw	35-41	–	26-30
Raw water pump bracket			
1994-1996	41		30
1997-on	45		33
Rear oil seal retainer	15.3	135	11
Remote oil filter adapter	27-34	–	20-25
Rocker arm pivots			
V6 models	54	–	40
Small block V8	See text to adjust lash		
Spark plugs (not oiled)	30	–	22
Starter motor	41-49	–	30-36
Temperature sender	24-30	–	18-22
Thermostat housing	16-22	–	12-16
Timing gear cover	9	80	–
Valve cover screws			
V6 models	7-13	62-115	–
Small block V8	5	45	–
Valve lifter restrainer (V6 only)	16.4	145	12
Valve lifter restrainer (small V8)	25	–	18

* Refer to the text for tightening instructions.

Table 5 TIGHTENING TORQUES 7.4 AND 8.2 L (454 AND 502 cid) V8

	N.m	in.-lb.	ft.-lb.
Camshaft sprocket			
7.4 L	27	–	20
8.2 L	34	–	25
Connecting rod			
7.4 L	65	–	48
8.2 L	99	–	73
Coolant circulating pump	40	–	30
Cylinder head[1]			
First step	47	–	35
Second step	88	–	65
Third step	115	–	85
Dipstick tube flare	20-24	–	15-18
Distributor clamp	34	–	25
Engine mounts			
Front			
Adjustment nuts	136-163	–	100-120
Mount to engine	43-54	–	32-40
Rear			
Center screw to square nut	60-71	–	44-52
Lock nuts	38-40	–	28-30
Mount plate to transom	27-34	–	20-25
Exhaust elbow to manifold	16-24	–	12-18
Exhaust pipe to transom shield	27-34	–	20-25
Flame arrestor	2.8-4.0	25-35	–
Flame arrestor cover	3.4-4.0	30-35	–

(continued)

Table 5 TIGHTENING TORQUES 7.4 AND 8.2 L (454 AND 502 cid) V8 (continued)

	N•m	in.-lb.	ft.-lb.
Flywheel and coupler	54-61	–	40-45
Flywheel housing	43-54	–	32-40
Flywheel housing cover	7-9	60-84	–
Harmonic balancer			
7.4 L (1994-1996)	65		48
7.4 L (1997-on)	115		85
8.2 L (1994-1996)	99		73
8.2 L (1997-on)	122		90
Main bearing caps			
7.4 L	135	–	100
8.2 L	149	–	110
Manifolds			
Exhaust to cylinder head			
Nuts	27-35	–	20-26
Screws	33.38	–	24-28
Intake to cylinder head			
7.4L[2]	40	–	30
8.2L	47	–	35
Oil pan			
To front cover	7.9	70	–
Other screws	22	200	–
Oil pump			
Attachment			
7.4L	90	–	65
8.2L	95	–	70
Cover	9	80	
Oil withdrawl tube to elbow	20-24	–	15-18
Power steering pump bracket			
Nut	18-20	–	13-15
Screw	35-41	–	26-30
Raw water pump bracket			
7.4 L	40	–	30
8.2 L	47	–	35
Remote oil filter adapter	27-34	–	20-25
Rocker arm bolts	54	–	40
Spark plugs (not oiled)	30	–	22
Starter motor	41-49	–	30-36
Thermostat housing	16-22	–	12-16
Timing chain cover			
7.4 L	12	106	–
8.2 L	13.6	120	–
Valve cover screws	13	115	–

1. Refer to the text for tightening instructions.
2. Lower manifold only on models with fuel injection.

7

Chapter Eight

5.0 Liter and 5.8 Liter V8 Engines

Volvo Penta stern drive installations may use a 302 cid (5.0 L) or 351 cid (5.8 L) V8 engines. Most of the repair and service procedures described in this chapter are typical and apply to both of these engines. Exceptions are specifically noted.

The cylinders are numbered from front to rear (1-2-3-4 on the starboard side and 5-6-7-8 on the port side). These engines have been manufactured with 2 different firing orders. Parts must be correctly matched for the engine to run or perform properly. Be sure to install the correct parts when servicing these engines.

The arrangement of the valves alternate from front to rear beginning with the intake valve at the front of the head on the starboard side and with the exhaust valve at the front of the head on the port side.

The cast iron cylinder head contains intake valves, exhaust valves and valve guides. Rocker arms operate on individual rocker arm seats which are retained by special bolts. Camshaft motion opens the valves via hydraulic lifters, pushrods and the rocker arms.

The chain-driven camshaft is located above the crankshaft between the 2 cylinder banks and is supported by 5 bearings. The oil pump, mounted at the bottom of the engine block, is driven by the camshaft via the distributor.

The crankshaft is supported by 5 main bearings, with the center bearing thrust surfaces limiting the crankshaft end play. Crankshaft rotation is counterclockwise when seen from the drive unit (rear) end of the engine.

Engine specifications (**Table 1**) and tightening torques (**Table 2**) are at the end of the chapter.

ENGINE MODEL AND SERIAL NUMBERS

The engine serial number and model designation is on a plate or decal (**Figure 1**) attached to the port (left) side valve (rocker arm) cover of the engine.

This information identifies the engine and indicates if there are any unique parts or if internal changes have been made during its manufacture. The specific model number and serial number are important when ordering replacement parts for the engine. Provide these numbers to the parts department when obtaining or ordering parts.

SPECIAL TOOLS

If special tools are required or recommended for engine overhaul, the tool numbers are provided. Special tools can often be rented. They can also be purchased from OTC Division of SPX Corporation, 655 Eisenhower Dr., Owatonna, Minnesota 55060. If a special tool is required, the procedure may be more efficiently accomplished at a Volvo Penta dealer who is trained to use the special tools.

GASKET SEALANT

Gasket sealant is used instead of preformed gaskets between some mating surfaces on the engines covered in this chapter. Two types of gasket sealant are commonly used room temperature vulcanizing (RTV) and anaerobic. Since these 2 materials have different sealing properties, they cannot be interchanged.

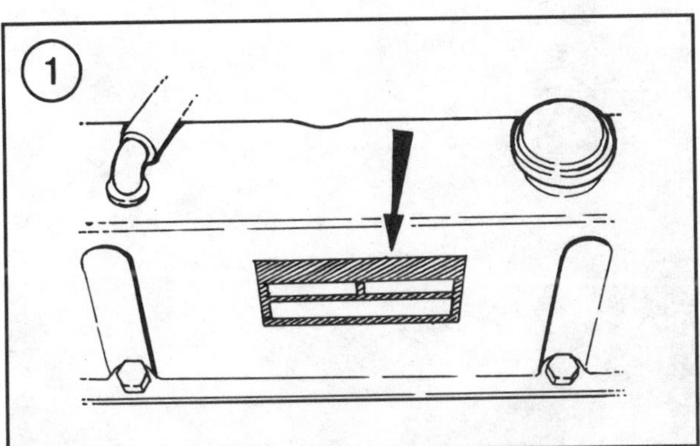

Room Temperature Vulcanizing (RTV) Sealant

This silicone gel is available in tubes that are available from most parts suppliers and Volvo Penta dealers. Moisture in the air causes RTV to cure. Always place the cap on the tube as soon as possible when using RTV. RTV has a shelf life of approximately 1 year and will not cure properly if the shelf life has expired. Check the expiration date on RTV tubes before using and keep partially used tubes tightly sealed.

8

Applying RTV Sealant

Clean all gasket residue from mating surfaces. They should be clean and free of oil and grease. Remove all RTV gasket material from blind attaching holes, as it can cause a hydraulic lock and affect bolt torque.

Unless otherwise specified, apply RTV sealant in a continuous bead 3-5 mm (1/8-3/16 in.) thick. Apply the sealant to the inner side of all mounting bolts. Torque mating parts within 10-15 minutes after application, or the sealant will have started to cure. If this happens, the old sealant must be removed and new sealant applied.

Anaerobic Sealant

This is also a gel that is supplied in tubes. It cures only in the absence of air, as when squeezed tightly between 2 machined mating surfaces. For this reason, it will not spoil if the cap is left off the tube. Do not use anaerobic sealant if 1 mating surface is flexible.

Applying Anaerobic Sealant

Clean all gasket residue from the mating surfaces. They must be clean and free of oil and grease. Remove all gasket material from blind attaching holes, as it can cause a hydraulic lock and affect bolt torque.

Unless otherwise specified, apply anaerobic sealant in a 1 mm (0.04 in.) or less continuous bead to 1 sealing surface. Apply the sealant to the inner side of all mounting holes.

REPLACEMENT PARTS

Various changes are made to automotive engines before they are used for marine applications. Numerous part changes are required due to operation in the marine environment. For example, the cylinder head gasket must be corrosion resistant. Marine engines may use head gaskets of copper or stainless steel instead of the standard steel used in automotive applications. Expansion or core plugs are also made of different material than used in automotive applications.

Since marine engines are run at or near maximum speed most of the time, the use of special valve lifters, springs, pistons, bearings, camshafts and other heavy-duty components is necessary for maximum life and performance.

For these reasons, never substitute automotive-type parts for marine components. In addition, Volvo Penta recommends that only parts available through authorized Volvo Penta dealers be used. Parts offered by other manufacturers may look similar, but may not be manufactured to Volvo Penta's specifications. Any damage resulting from the use of incorrect parts will be the sole responsibility of the installer.

PRECAUTIONS

The engine is heavy, awkward to handle and has sharp edges. It may shift or drop suddenly

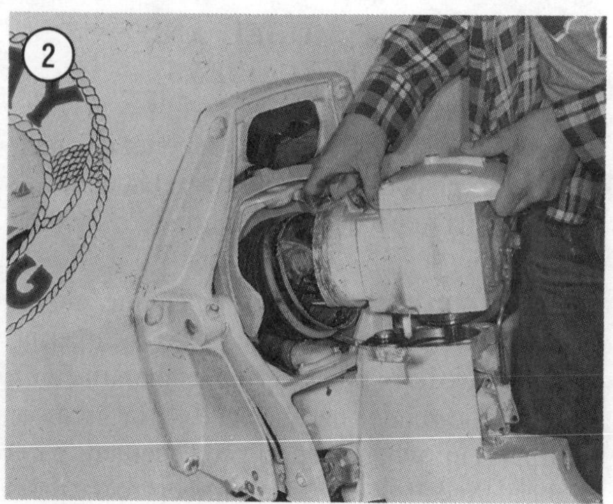

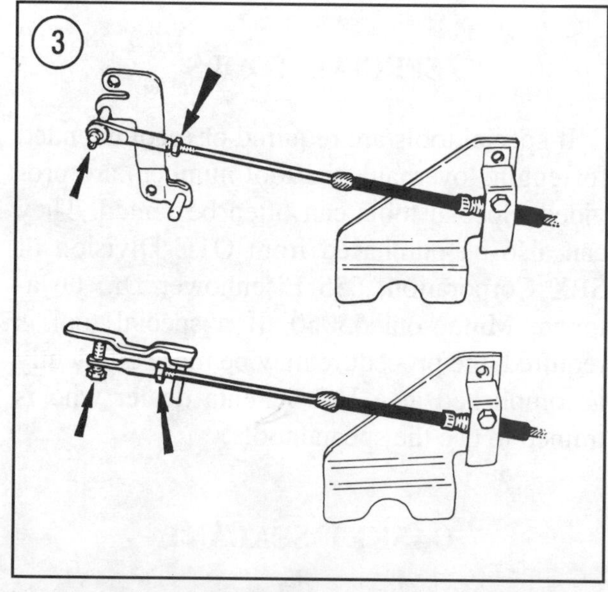

during removal. To prevent serious injury, always observe the following precautions.

1. Never place any part of your body where a moving or falling engine may trap, cut or crush you.
2. If you must push the engine during removal, use a board or similar tool to keep your hands out of danger.
3. Be sure the hoist is designed to lift engines and has enough load capacity for your engine.
4. Be sure the hoist is securely attached to safe lifting points on the engine.
5. The engine should not be difficult to lift with a proper hoist. If it is, stop lifting, lower the engine back onto its mounts and make sure the engine has been completely separated from the vessel.

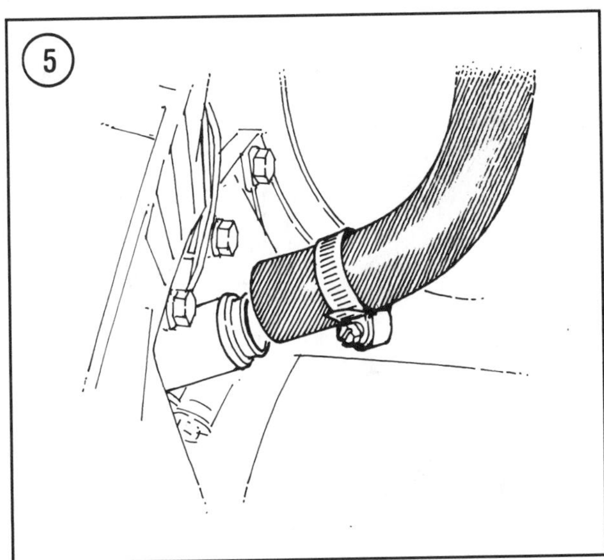

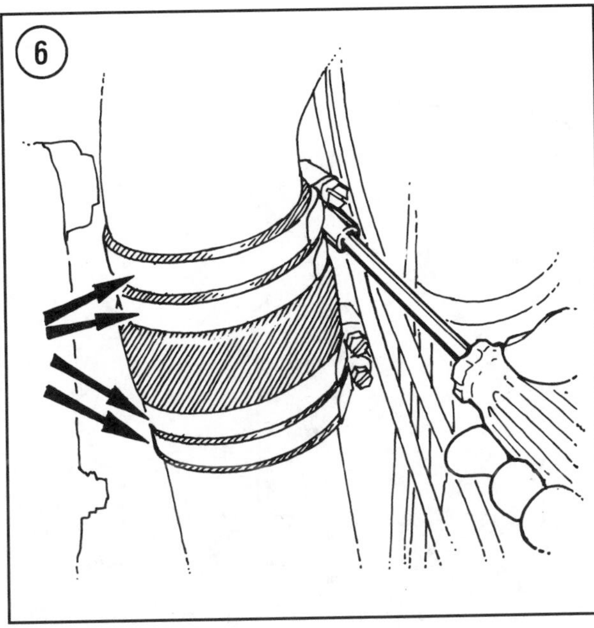

ENGINE REMOVAL

Some service procedures can be performed with the engine in the boat, but others require removal. The boat design and service procedure to be performed will determine whether the engine must be removed.

1. Remove the engine cover and all panels that interfere with engine removal. Move the cover and other parts out of the way.
2. Disconnect the cable from the negative battery terminal, then disconnect the positive battery cable. As a precaution, remove the battery from the boat.
3. Remove the stern drive upper gear housing (**Figure 2**). Refer to Chapter Twelve.
4. Disconnect the throttle cable from the carburetor or fuel control linkage (**Figure 3**, typical). Detach and remove the cable from the anchor plates attached to the engine.
5. Detach electrical cables from the engine. Separate the cables at the connectors.
6. Disconnect the fuel delivery line from the fuel pump. Plug the line and fitting to prevent leakage and the entry of contamination. See **Figure 4**, typical.
7. Loosen the hose clamp and detach the raw water line from the transom shield water tube. See **Figure 5**, typical.
8. Open the engine drain cocks or remove the drain plugs and drain all coolant and water from the engine.
9. Loosen the clamps on the exhaust manifold bellows, then pull the bellows free from the manifolds. See **Figure 6**.

8

10. Remove the shift mechanism cover from the stern drive and disconnect the shift cable from the lever. Remove the cable lock plate from the front of the stern drive intermediate housing.

11. If equipped with power steering, disconnect both power steering hydraulic lines from the control valve. See **Figure 7**. Cap the lines and plug the control valve fittings to prevent leakage and the entry of contamination. Secure the lines at a point higher than the engine power steering pump during the remainder of this procedure to prevent damage or loss of fluid.

12. Detach any wires, hoses or accessories connected to the engine that will interfere with removal.

NOTE
At this point, there should be no hoses, wires or linkage connecting the engine to the boat or stern drive unit. Make sure that nothing remains to hamper removal or to be broken during removal of the engine.

13. Attach a suitable hoist to the engine lifting brackets. The hoist must have a minimum lift capacity of 1,500 lb. (680 kg). Raise the hoist enough to remove all slack. See **Figure 8**.

NOTE
Do not loosen or move the mounts at the engine attaching points or a complete realignment will be required when the engine is reinstalled. Engine alignment should not be disturbed if mounts are detached as described in Step 14.

14. Remove the lag screws (**Figure 9**) from the front engine mount, then remove the locknuts (A, **Figure 10**) and washers (B) from the rear engine mounts.

15. Remove mounting bolts (**Figure 11**) from the clamp ring at the rear.

16. Slide the engine forward until the flywheel cover is clear, then lift the engine from the boat.

ENGINE INSTALLATION

Engine installation is the reverse of removal, plus the following:

1. Clean the engine coupling splines and lubricate lightly.

2. Reinstall any shims or adapters used with the engine mounts.

7

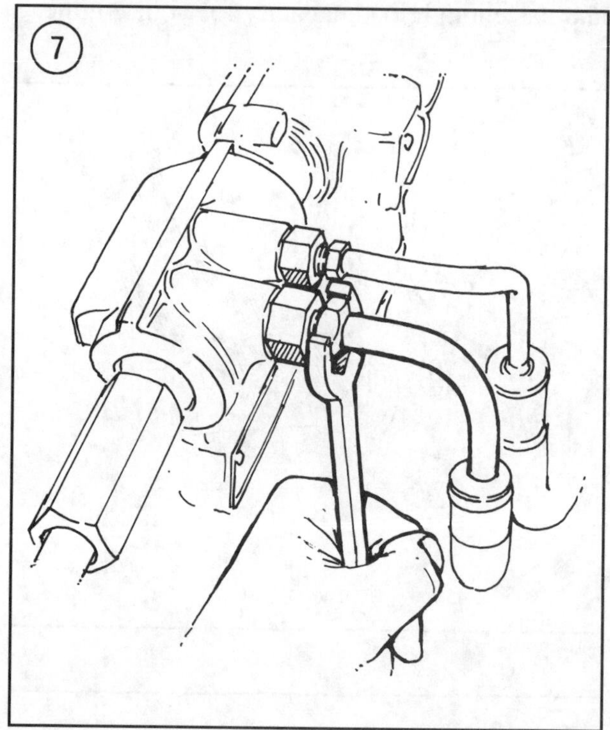

8

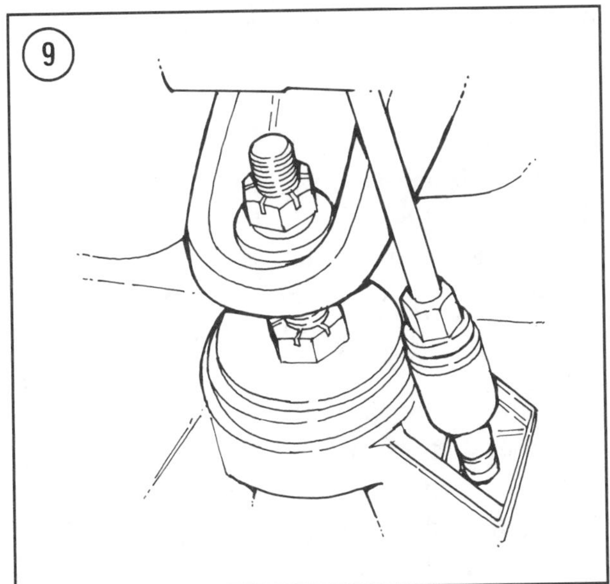

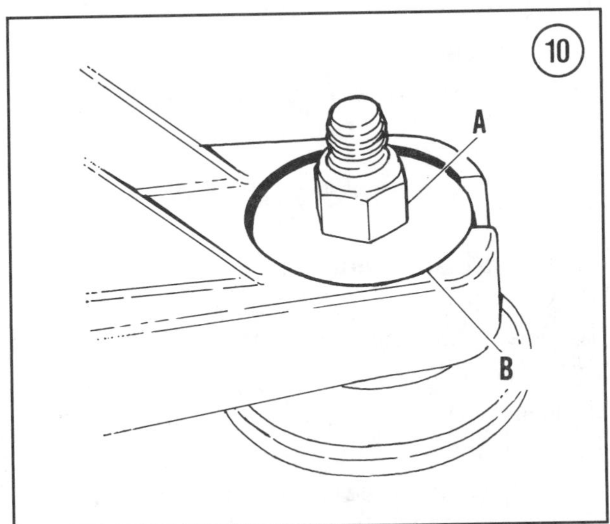

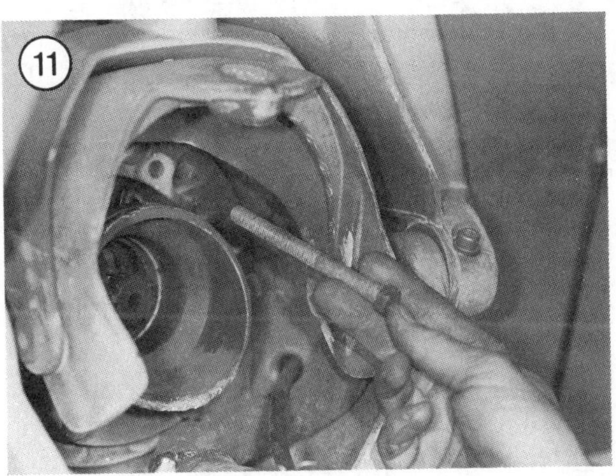

3. Inspect all self-locking nuts, hoses, bellows and other parts for wear or deterioration. The manufacturer recommends replacing the exhaust bellows every 2 years. Also, elastic stop nuts should never be installed more than twice. It is a good idea to replace these parts each time the engine is removed.
4. Guide bolts may be used to align the engine at the rear.
5. Tighten all fasteners to the specifications listed in **Table 2**.
6. If equipped with power steering, tighten the hose fittings and bleed the power steering system as described in Chapter Sixteen.
7. Fill the engine with the quantity, type and viscosity of oil recommended in Chapter Four.
8. If equipped with a closed cooling system, fill the system with a 50:50 mixture of antifreeze and pure water. See Chapter Four.
9. Adjust the accessory drive belts. See Chapter Four.
10. Make sure all hoses, wires and linkage are reattached before starting the engine.

DISASSEMBLY CHECKLIST

To use the checklists, remove and inspect each part in the order mentioned. To reassemble, go through the checklists in reverse order, installing the parts in order. Each major part is covered in its own section in this chapter, unless otherwise noted.

Decarbonizing or Valve Service

1. Remove the valve covers.
2. Remove the intake and exhaust manifolds.
3. Remove the rocker arms.
4. Remove the cylinder heads.
5. Remove and inspect the valves. Inspect the valve guides and seats, repairing or replacing as required.
6. Assemble by reversing Steps 1-5.

Valve and Ring Service

1. Perform Steps 1-5 of *Decarbonizing or Valve Service*.
2. Remove the oil pan and oil pump.
3. Remove the pistons and connecting rods.
4. Remove the piston rings.

NOTE
It is not necessary to separate the pistons from the connecting rods unless a piston, connecting rod or piston pin requires replacement.

5. Assemble by reversing Steps 1-4.

General Overhaul

1. Remove the engine from the boat.
2. Remove the flywheel.
3. Remove the mount brackets and oil pressure sending unit from the engine.
4. If available, mount the engine on an engine stand. These can be rented. The stand is not absolutely necessary, but it will make the job much easier.
5. Remove the following accessories or components from the engine, if present:
   a. Alternator and mounting bracket.
   b. Power steering pump and mounting bracket.
   c. Spark plug wires and distributor cap.
   d. Carburetor and fuel lines.
   e. Oil dipstick and tube.
   f. Raw water pump, if so equipped.

NOTE
Coolant or oil leaks indicate the possibility of a crack, leaking gasket, warped sealing surface or damaged part and should be inspected further when the engine is disassembled.

6. Check the engine for signs of leakage. Record the location of any possible leaks for further inspection or repair.
7. Clean the outside of the engine.
8. Remove the distributor. See Chapter Eleven.
9. Detach or remove all hoses and tubes that will interfere with disassembly.
10. Remove the fuel pump. See Chapter Nine.
11. Remove the intake and exhaust manifolds. On fuel-injected models refer to Chapter Nine. Remove the upper intake manifold first, then remove the lower manifold.
12. Remove the valve cover and rocker arms.
13. Remove the crankshaft pulley, vibration damper, timing case cover and water pump. Remove the timing chain and sprockets.
14. Remove the camshaft.
15. Remove the cylinder heads.
16. Remove the oil pan and oil pump.
17. Remove the pistons and connecting rods.
18. Remove the flywheel and coupler.
19. Remove the crankshaft.
20. Inspect the cylinder block.
21. Assemble by reversing Steps 1-19.

VALVE COVERS

Removal/Installation

1. Detach the crankcase ventilation hose from the valve cover.
2. Remove the exhaust manifold(s) as described in this chapter.
3. Remove any other accessory unit that might interfere with valve cover removal.
4. Remove the cover attaching fasteners.
5. Tap 1 end of the valve cover with a soft-faced hammer to break the gasket or RTV seal. Remove the valve cover.
6. Remove all of the gasket or RTV sealant from the cylinder head and valve cover. Use a cleaning solvent and a gasket scraper to remove any residue remaining on the sealing surfaces.
7. Attach a new gasket to the valve cover, then position the cover and gasket on the cylinder head.
8. Install the valve cover attaching fasteners and tighten to the torque listed in **Table 2**.

9. Install the exhaust manifold(s) as described in this chapter.
10. Install the PCV valve in the cover and attach the crankcase ventilation hose to the valve cover.
11. Install or attach any brackets or accessories that were removed or detached.

INTAKE MANIFOLD

The intake manifold used on fuel-injected models is different from that used for carbureted models and some of the following procedures may be different. The fuel rail and fuel injectors are attached to the lower intake manifold and can be removed with the manifold. Refer to Chapter Nine for removal of the manifolds (upper and lower) used on fuel-injected models.

Removal/Installation (Carbureted Models)

Figure 12 is typical of all models equipped with a carburetor.

1. Disconnect the cable from the negative terminal of the battery.
2. Remove any covers, then detach hoses from both valve covers.
3. Remove the flame arrestor.

NOTE
It may be necessary to remove sediment from the drain by inserting a wire into the opening.

4. Open or remove the cylinder block water drains and allow all of the water to drain. A drain is located on each side of the cylinder block.
5. Remove the exhaust manifolds as described in this chapter.
6. Disconnect the water hoses from the intake manifold, thermostat housing and water pump. See **Figure 12**.
7. Disconnect the throttle cable linkage from the carburetor.
8. Disconnect the wire from the coolant temperature sending unit.
9. Remove the fuel line between the carburetor and fuel pump.
10. Detach the plug wires from the spark plugs and the coil wire from the distributor cap.
11. Remove the distributor cap and place it (with plug wires attached) out of the way.

NOTE
If you mark the position of the distributor rotor in relation to the intake manifold before removing the distributor, it will be easier to install, but only if the crankshaft is not moved. If, however, the engine crankshaft is turned while the distributor is removed, refer to Chapter Eleven for initial installation of the distributor.

12. Mark the position of the distributor rotor on the intake manifold, remove the screw attaching the distributor hold-down clamp and the clamp, then withdraw the distributor.

NOTE
When withdrawing the distributor, the rotor will turn as the drive gears separate. Observe the direction that the rotor turns and its final location when the distributor is free. Knowing this angle will help you install the distributor in its original position.

13. Unbolt and remove the coil and bracket from the manifold.
14. Disconnect the wire from the electric choke and any other electrical wires that will interfere with manifold removal.
15. Loosen all 12 screws attaching the intake manifold, then remove the fasteners. Pry the manifold loose, then lift it from the engine block.
16. Remove and discard the intake manifold gaskets and end seals.
17. Clean all gasket and sealer residue from the block, cylinder heads and intake manifold with degreaser and a gasket scraper.

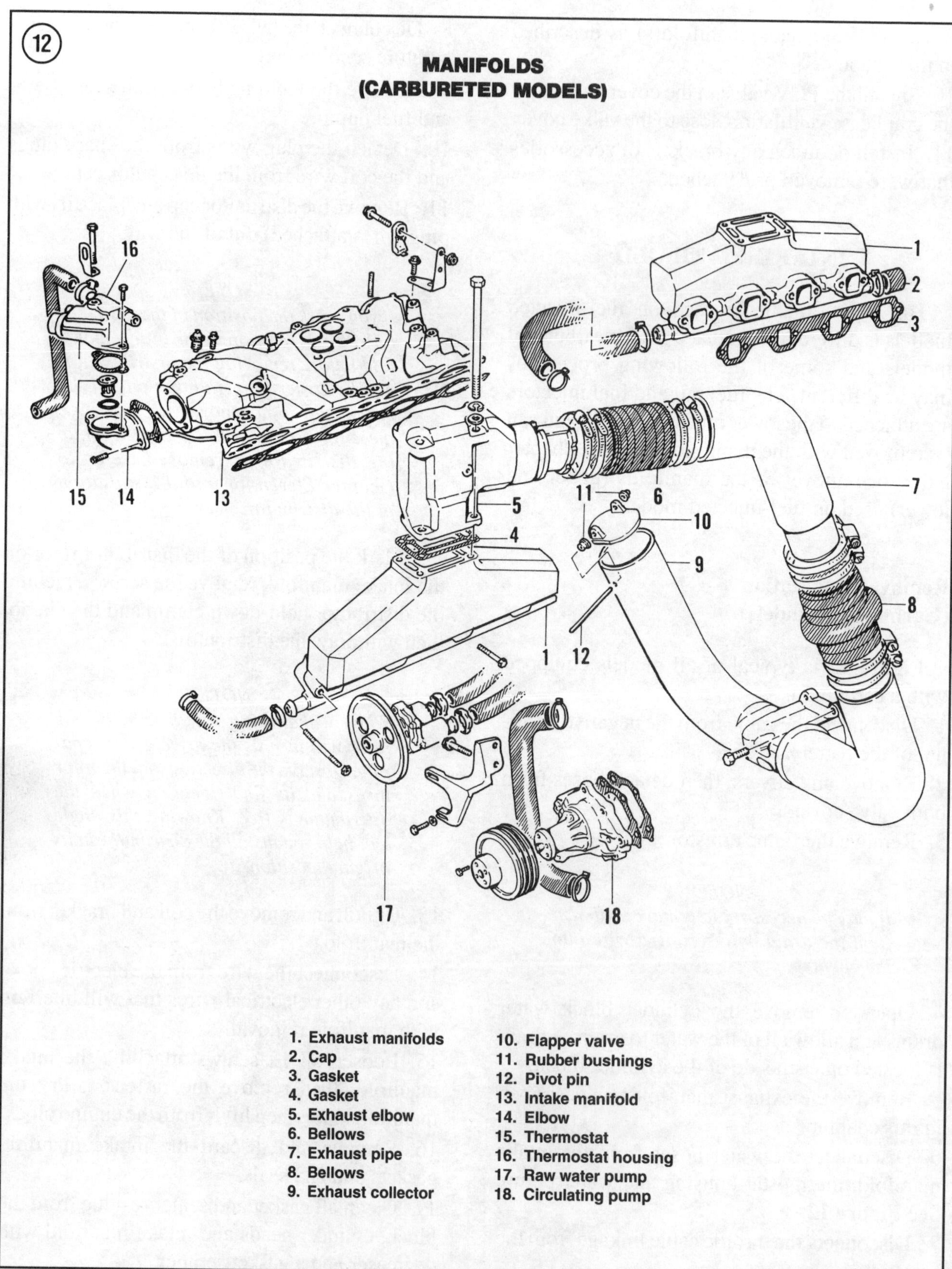
12
MANIFOLDS
(CARBURETED MODELS)
1
2
3
16
7
15
14
13
11
6
5
10
4
9
8
1
12
17
18
1. Exhaust manifolds
2. Cap
3. Gasket
4. Gasket
5. Exhaust elbow
6. Bellows
7. Exhaust pipe
8. Bellows
9. Exhaust collector
10. Flapper valve
11. Rubber bushings
12. Pivot pin
13. Intake manifold
14. Elbow
15. Thermostat
16. Thermostat housing
17. Raw water pump
18. Circulating pump

18. If the intake manifold is being replaced, transfer the carburetor, thermostat and housing, throttle cable anchor block, temperature sending unit and any other hardware from the old to the new manifold.

19. Apply a 1/8 in. (3.2 mm) bead of RTV sealer along the seam at the 4 corners between the cylinder head and the block. See **Figure 13**. Apply the bead of sealer the full width of the seam.

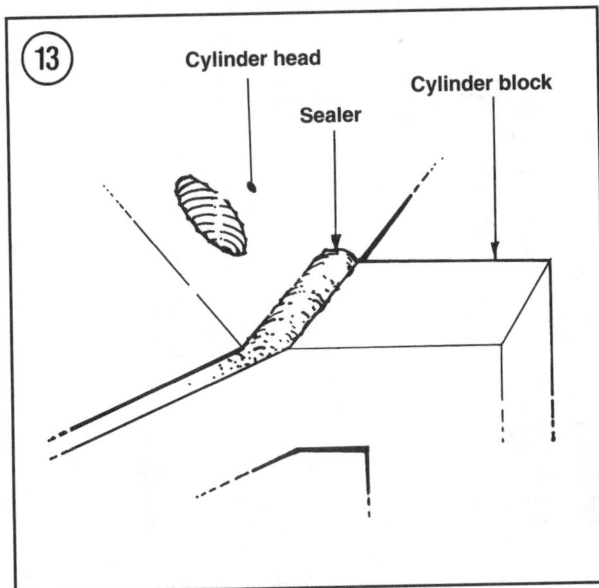

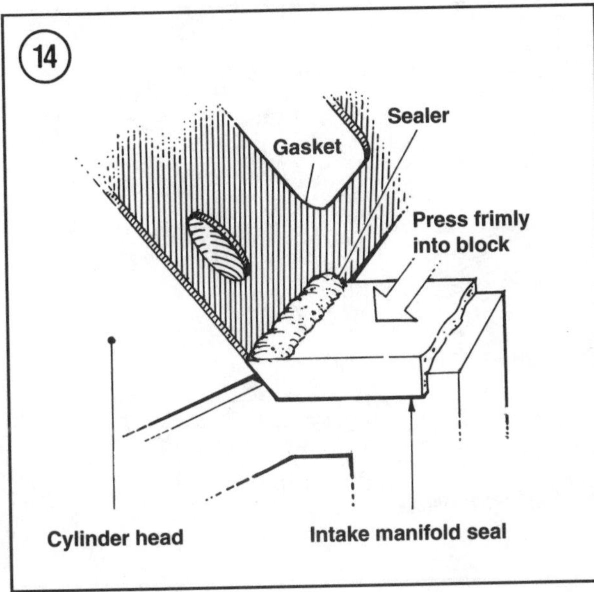

20. Install the new gaskets against the cylinder heads and new front and rear end seals.

21. Apply a 1/16 in. (1.6 mm) diameter bead of RTV sealer at the joint of the gaskets and the end seals. See **Figure 14**. Apply the bead of sealer the full width of the joint.

22. Lower the intake manifold straight down into position against the cylinder heads and block. Check the seal area to make sure the seals are in their proper positions. If not, remove the manifold, correct the seal position and reinstall the manifold.

23. Install the manifold attaching screws. Tighten the screws to the torque specified in **Table 2**, in the sequence shown in **Figure 15**.

24. Reverse Steps 1-14 to complete installation. Coat all electrical connections with a neoprene dip.

8

Removal/Installation (Fuel Injected Models)

1. Make sure the ignition is turned OFF, then disconnect the cable from the negative terminal of the battery.

2. Remove any cover attached to the top of the engine.

3. Separate wiring connectors from the idle speed control (ISC) and the throttle position sensor (TPS). See **Figure 16**.

4. Remove the locknut and washer attaching the throttle cable to the throttle lever. Remove the 2 screws attaching the throttle linkage bracket to the upper intake manifold and move the bracket and cable out of the way.

5. Detach the hose from the PCV valve in the valve cover.

NOTE
It may be necessary to remove sediment from the drain by inserting a wire into the opening.

6. Open or remove the cylinder block water drains and allow all water to drain. A drain is located on each side of the cylinder block.

7. Remove the exhaust manifolds as described in this chapter.

8. Disconnect the water hoses from the intake manifold, thermostat housing and water pump.

9. Remove the clamp from the vacuum hose attached to the fuel pressure regulator valve (**Figure 17**), then detach the hose from the valve.

10. Remove the clamp from the fuel reservoir hose (**Figure 17**), then detach the hose from the reservoir.

11. Detach the shift interrupter switch from the 4-pin connector. Remove the locknuts and washers attaching the shift bracket to the engine, then move the shift bracket out of the way, leaving the shift cables attached.

12. Remove the clamp from the vacuum hose to the manifold absolute pressure (MAP) sensor

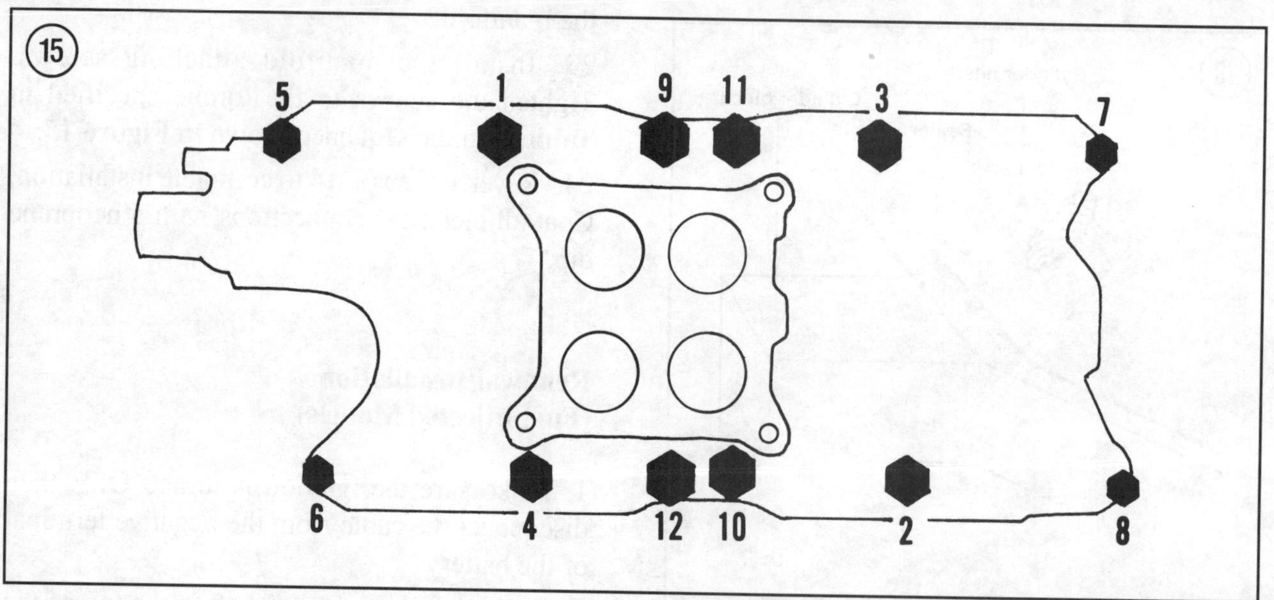

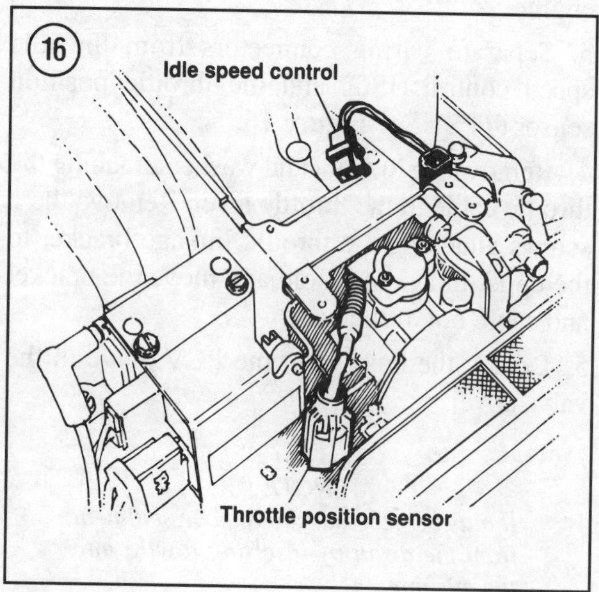

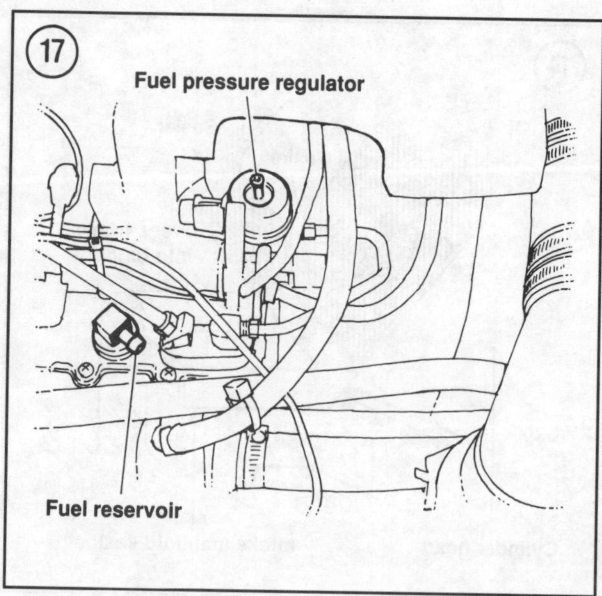

(**Figure 18**), then detach the hose from the MAP sensor.

13. Disconnect the high tension lead (A, **Figure 19**) and the primary connector (C, **Figure 19**) from the ignition coil. Remove the connector (B, **Figure 19**) from the thick film ignition (TFI) module.

14. Remove the screws (**Figure 20** and **Figure 21**) attaching the upper manifold, then lift the manifold and throttle body as an assembly from the engine.

15. Disconnect the wire from the coolant temperature sending unit.

16. Detach the plug wires from the spark plugs and the distributor cap, then remove the distributor cap and place it (with plug wires attached) out of the way.

NOTE
If you mark the position of the distributor rotor in relation to the intake manifold before removing the distributor it will be easier to install, but only if the crankshaft is not moved. If, however, the en-

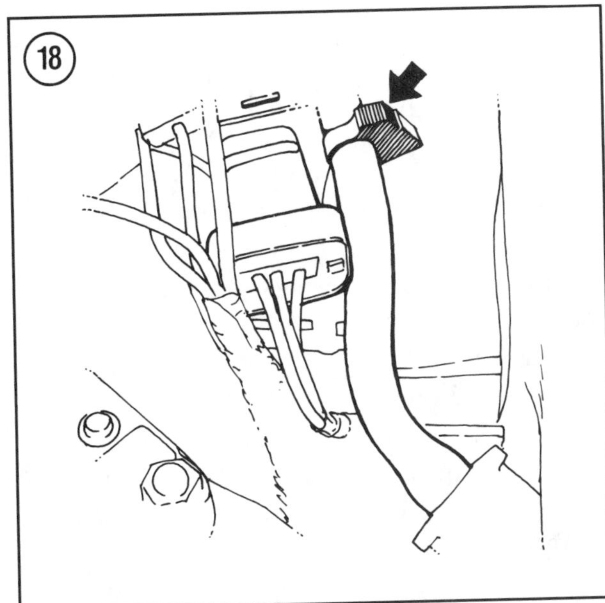

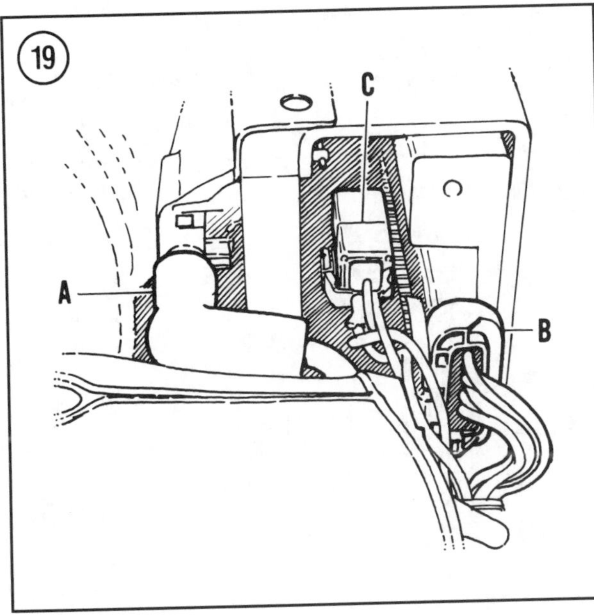

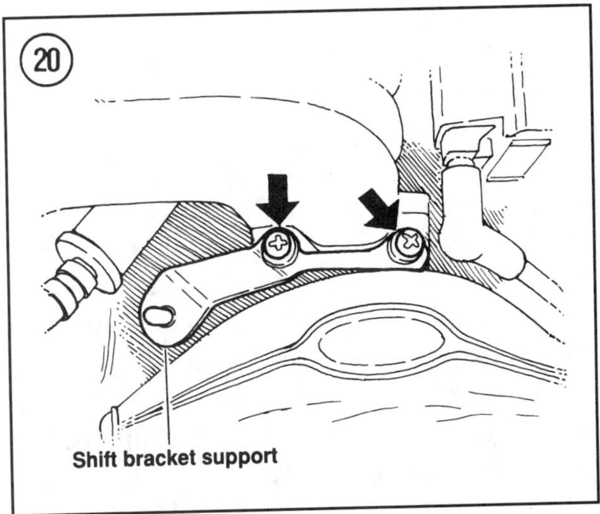

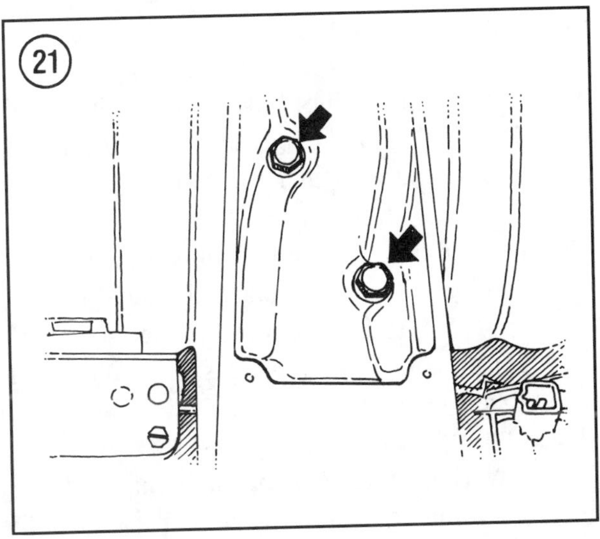

gine crankshaft is turned while the distributor is removed, refer to Chapter Eleven for initial installation of the distributor.

17. Mark the position of the distributor rotor on the intake manifold, remove the screw attaching the distributor hold-down clamp and the clamp, then withdraw the distributor.

NOTE
When withdrawing the distributor, the rotor will turn as the drive gears separate. Observe the direction that the rotor turns and its final location when the distributor is free. Knowing this angle will help you install the distributor in its original position.

18. Make sure all hoses and wires that will interfere with manifold removal have been removed or detached.
19. Loosen all 12 screws attaching the lower intake manifold, then remove the fasteners. Pry the manifold loose, then lift it from the engine block.
20. Remove and discard the intake manifold gaskets and end seals.
21. Clean all gasket and sealer residue from the block, cylinder heads and intake manifold with degreaser and a gasket scraper.
22. If the intake manifold is being replaced, transfer parts and any other hardware from the old to the new manifold.
23. Apply a 1/8 in. (3.2 mm) bead of RTV sealer along the seam at the 4 corners between the cylinder head and the block. See **Figure 13**. Apply the bead of sealer the full width of the seam.
24. Install the new gaskets against the cylinder heads and new front and rear end seals.
25. Apply a 1/16 in. (1.6 mm) diameter bead of RTV sealer at the joint of the gaskets and the end seals. See **Figure 14**. Apply a bead of the sealer that is the full width of the joint.
26. Lower the intake manifold straight down into position against the cylinder heads and block. Check the seal area to make sure the seals are in their proper positions. If not, remove the manifold, correct the seal position and reinstall the manifold.
27. Install the screws attaching the lower manifold to the cylinder heads. Tighten the screws to the torque specified in **Table 2**, in the sequence shown in **Figure 22**.
28. Make sure the gasket surfaces between the upper and lower manifolds is clean and dry, then position a new gasket on the lower manifold.

NOTE
Guide studs can be used to hold the gasket while installing the upper manifold in Step 25.

29. Position the upper manifold and throttle body as an assembly onto the lower manifold. Install the 2 long screws (**Figure 21**) retaining the upper manifold.
30. Install the shift bracket. Install and tighten the screws (**Figure 20**) finger-tight.
31. Check to make sure the gasket between the upper and lower manifold is still aligned, then tighten the 6 attaching screws to the torque listed in **Table 2**.

NOTE
Check the tightness of the upper and lower manifold fasteners after running the engine at normal operating temperature and allowing it to cool. Afterward,

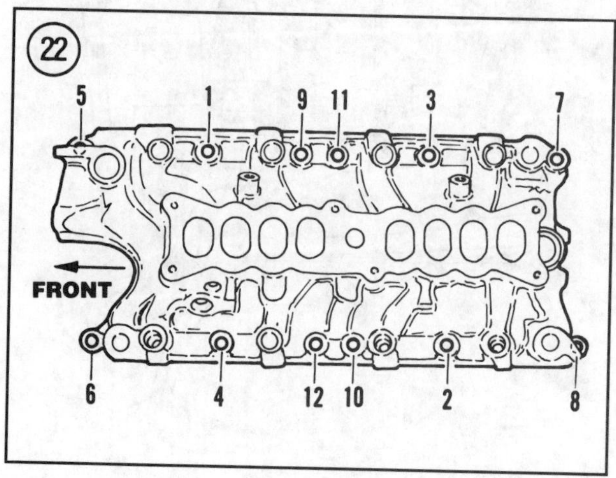

check the tightness of the manifold fasteners once each year.

32. Refer to Chapter Eleven to install and time the ignition distributor.
33. Reverse Steps 1-15 to complete installation.

Inspection

1. Check the intake manifold for cracks or distortion. Replace the manifold if it is distorted or cracked.
2. Check the mating surfaces for nicks or burrs. Small burrs may be removed with a file.
3. Place a straightedge across the manifold sealing surfaces. If there is any gap between the straightedge and the surface, measure it with a flat feeler gauge. Measure each surface from end to end and from corner to corner. If the mating surface is not flat to within 0.003 in. (0.15 mm) per 6 in. (15.2 cm) of length or 0.006 in. (0.30 mm) overall, replace the manifold.

EXHAUST MANIFOLDS

Removal/Installation

Refer to **Figure 23** (typical for this procedure).

1. Disconnect the cable from the negative terminal of the battery.
2. Open the cylinder block and exhaust manifold water drains.
3. Loosen the clamps, then detach the hoses and remove the rubber caps (**Figure 24**) from the exhaust manifold.
4. Loosen the exhaust clamps attaching the exhaust elbow, lubricate the hoses with soapy water and remove the hoses and the exhaust elbow. See **Figure 25**.
5. Detach the spark plug wires from all of the spark plugs.
6. Remove any screws or clamps attaching anything to the manifold. The ECA is attached to the starboard high rise elbow on some models. Also, make sure all hoses are detached.
7. If a high rise elbow can be unbolted and removed if separation from the manifold is required.
8. Remove the 8 nuts and washers, then lift the manifold from the engine.
9. Remove and discard the exhaust manifold gasket.
10. Clean the gasket surfaces of all the old gasket and scale. Make sure the surface is flat.
11. Install a new gasket on the manifold studs and make sure all of the openings are aligned.
12. Slide the manifold onto the studs and install the retaining nuts.
13. Tighten the manifold retaining nuts evenly, beginning in the center and progressing to the ends. Tighten the nuts to the final torque listed in **Table 2**.
14. Attach the hoses and install the plugs on the exhaust manifold.
15. If the exhaust elbow was separated from the manifold, proceed as follows:
    a. Clean the gasket surfaces and make sure they are flat.
    b. Coat the new gasket with high temperature sealer and position it on the manifold.
    c. Install the exhaust elbow and tighten the fasteners to the torque listed in **Table 2**.
16. Attach any components that were removed from the exhaust elbow.

NOTE
Replace any hoses that are hard or damaged.

17. Lubricate the hoses for the exhaust elbow with soapy water and install the clamps and hoses.

Inspection/Cleaning

1. Inspect the exhaust ports for corrosion or damage. Replace the manifold if damage cannot be repaired.

(23)

EXHAUST SYSTEM (Fi AND FSi MODELS)

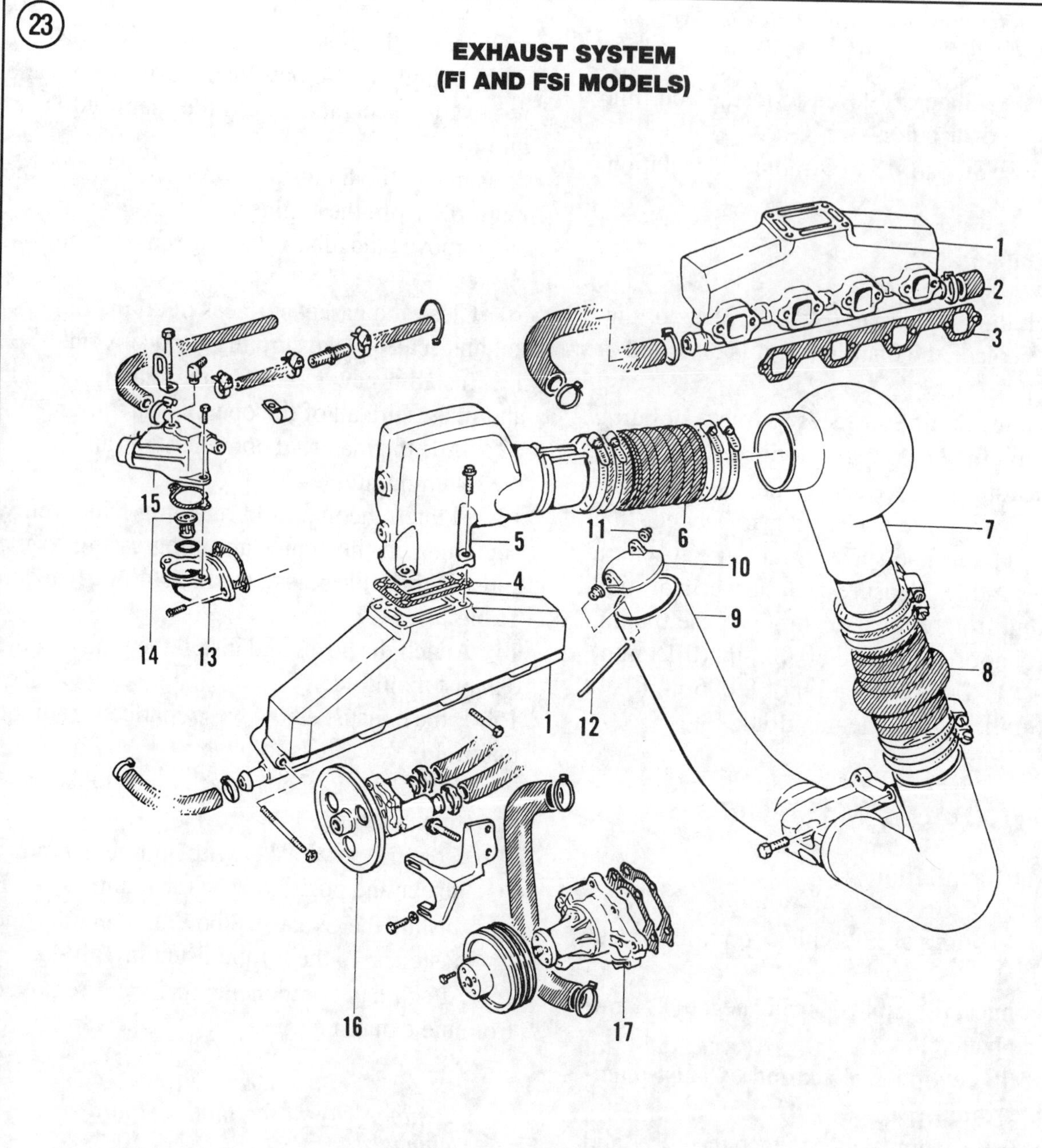

1. Exhaust manifolds
2. Cap
3. Gasket
4. Gasket
5. Exhaust elbow
6. Bellows
7. Exhaust pipe
8. Bellows
9. Exhaust collector
10. Flapper valve
11. Rubber bushings
12. Pivot pin
13. Elbow
14. Thermostat
15. Thermostat housing
16. Raw water pump
17. Circulating pump

2. Check the water passage for clogging. Clean the passage completely.
3. Remove the pipe plugs from the manifold and check for sand, silt or other sediment. Clean the passages thoroughly.
4. Have the manifolds pressure tested at a dealership or radiator repair shop. Repair or replace the manifold if it will not hold 10-15 psi (69-103 kPa).

EXHAUST BELLOWS AND FLAPPER VALVE

Replace the exhaust bellows (6 and 8, **Figure 23**) every other year. Inspect the bellows and replace if it is hard, torn or damaged. Running the engine without proper cooling will quickly damage the bellows as well as other parts.

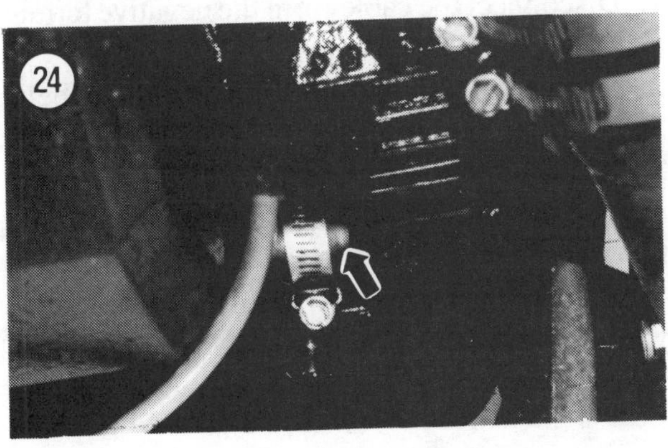

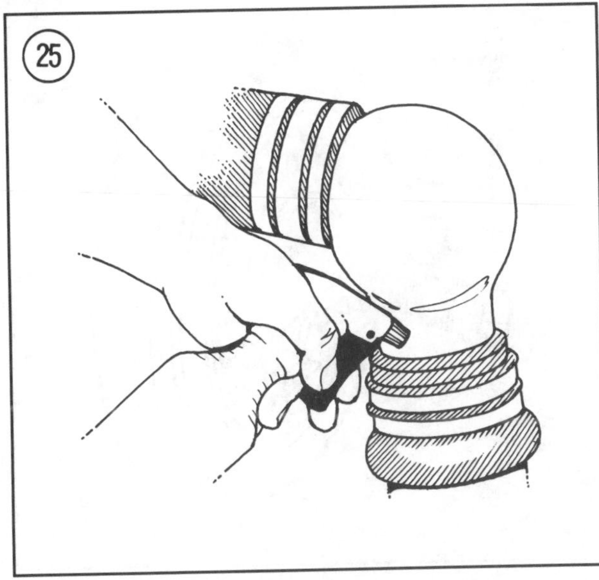

An exhaust flapper valve (10, **Figure 23**) is located in the upper end of the exhaust pipe. Flapper valves are installed to keep the water from backing up into the engine. The valves must move freely. If the valve(s) are stuck, damaged or installed improperly, the exhaust can be restricted and water can back up into the engine. New rubber bushings (11, **Figure 23**) must be installed whenever the valve is removed.

Removal/Installation

1. Loosen the clamps that attach the bellows (8, **Figure 23**) to the exhaust collector and exhaust elbow. Loosen the bellows after the clamps are loose, then slide the bellows up, onto the exhaust elbow.
2. Loosen the clamps that attach the bellows (6, **Figure 23**) to the exhaust riser and exhaust elbow.
3. Loosen the bellows after the clamps are loose, then remove the exhaust elbow and both bellows.
4. Loosen the lower clamps and remove the bellows from the exhaust collector.

NOTE
If the exhaust flapper valve is stuck, damaged or installed improperly, exhaust can be restricted and water can back up into the exhaust, causing engine damage.

5. Check the exhaust flapper valve (10, **Figure 23**) for freedom of movement.
6. If necessary to remove the flapper valve, proceed as follows:
   a. Drive the pivot shaft (12, **Figure 23**) from the valve and bushings using a small diameter punch.
   b. Lift the flapper valve from the exhaust collector pipe.

NOTE
Use care to keep the bushings from falling into the exhaust collector when removing them. The bushing flanges face toward the inside of the pipe.

c. Push (or drive) the rubber bushings from the exhaust collector.

d. Apply Scotch Grip Rubber Adhesive to new bushings and insert them into the bores of the exhaust collector. The flanged side of the bushings must face toward the inside.

e. Position the exhaust flapper valve in the collector, between the bushings with the holes in flanges aligned with the rubber bushings. The long side of the valve must face down.

f. Insert the pin through 1 rubber bushing and the valve flanges, then align the pin with the second bushing and push the pin through the second rubber bushing.

g. Check the valve for freedom of movement. The ends of the pin should be flush with the exhaust collector on both sides. It is important to have the valve correctly installed before completing the reassembling of the exhaust.

NOTE
Lubricate the inside of the bellows with soapy water to ease its installation onto the exhaust pipe and elbow.

7. Position the upper and lower bellows and all of the clamps on the exhaust elbow, then install the exhaust elbow. Leave all of the clamps loose until both bellows are correctly attached to the exhaust riser, exhaust elbow and exhaust collector.

8. Make sure the bellows are on completely and not twisted, then tighten the clamp screws securely.

CRANKSHAFT PULLEY AND VIBRATION DAMPER

The crankshaft pulley and the vibration damper are located on the front of the crankshaft. The crankshaft pulley drives the raw water pump, coolant circulating pump, power steering pump and alternator. The pulley is attached to the vibration damper with screws. The vibration damper is keyed to the front of the crankshaft and is fitted with a large center retaining screw. The vibration damper is sometimes called a torsional damper or harmonic balancer and serves several critical functions.

Removal/Installation

1. Disconnect the cable from the negative terminal of the battery.
2. Loosen, then remove the alternator drive belt. See Chapter Eleven.
3. Remove the screws attaching the pulley, then remove the pulley from the crankshaft and vibration damper.
4. Remove the large screw from the center of the vibration damper.

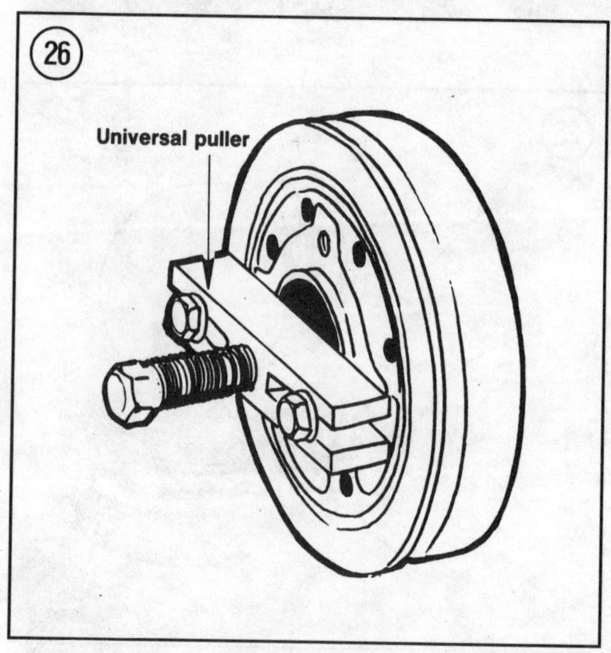

5. Attach a suitable puller (part No. T58P-6316-D or equivalent) to the threaded holes in the vibration damper and pull the damper from the crankshaft. See **Figure 26**, typical.
6. Use clean engine oil to lubricate the lip of the seal located in the front cover, the seal contact surface of the damper and the end of the crankshaft.

NOTE
Use the special installing tool (part No. T58P-6316-A or equivalent) to pull the damper onto the crankshaft.

7. Position the vibration damper over the crankshaft key and install the threaded tool in the end of the crankshaft so that at least 1/2 in. (12.7 mm) of the tool threads are engaged. Install the plate, thrust bearing and nut to complete tool installation.
8. Pull balancer into position as shown in **Figure 27**, typical.
9. Remove the tool and, install the large retaining bolt and washer. Tighten to the specifications listed in **Table 2**.
10. Install the pulley and tighten the attaching bolts.

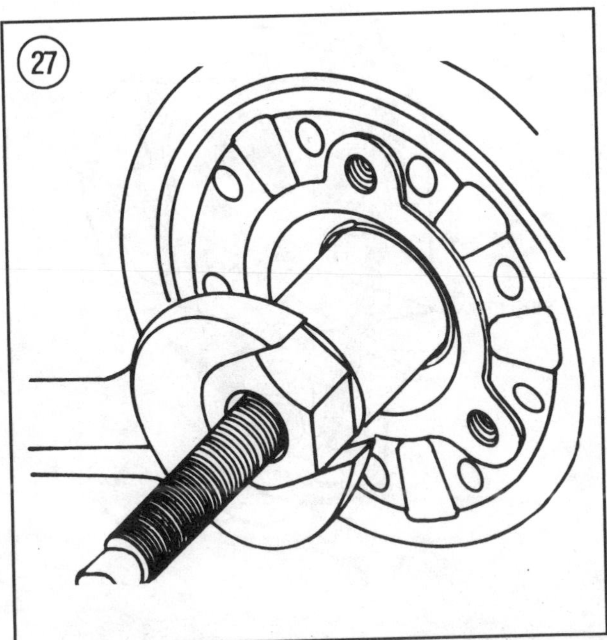

11. Install and adjust the alternator drive belt. See Chapter Eleven.

FRONT COVER AND SEAL

Front Cover Removal/Installation

The oil pan is sealed against the lower surface of the front cover and the lower oil pan gasket is usually damaged during front cover removal. The preferred method of front cover removal is to first remove the oil pan. However, the front cover can be removed without oil pan removal as follows.

1. Open the engine drain valve(s) and drain all the water (or coolant) from the block.
2. Drain the crankcase oil. See Chapter Four.
3. If the oil pan is to be removed, follow the procedure in this chapter.
4. Loosen, then remove belts from the alternator, raw water pump, power steering pump and crankshaft pulleys.
5. Unbolt and remove the pulley from the engine coolant circulating pump.
6. Remove the raw water pump and the mechanical fuel pump (if so equipped) from the front cover.
7. Remove or detach any accessory brackets or hoses attached to the engine coolant circulating pump and front cover.

NOTE
The coolant pump does not need to be removed and can remain attached to the front cover.

8. Unbolt and remove the crankshaft pulley, then pull the vibration damper from the crankshaft as described in this chapter.
9A. If the oil pan is not removed, proceed as follows:
   a. Remove the screws holding the front of the oil pan to the front cover.

b. Unbolt the front cover from the engine, pull the cover away from the block slightly, then use a sharp knife to cut the oil pan gasket flush with the front face of the cylinder block.

9B. If the oil pan has been removed, remove the screws attaching the front cover to the engine.

10. Lift the front cover away from the block and discard the gasket.

11. Clean the oil, grease and gasket residue from the block and front cover sealing surfaces.

12A. If the oil pan has not been removed, proceed as follows:

a. Cut a portion of the front of a new oil pan gasket to match the section that was removed with the front cover.

b. Coat the exposed surface of the oil pan flange with sealer and install the portion of the gasket cut in substep a. Make sure it fits properly.

c. Apply a 1/8 in. (3.2 mm) bead of RTV sealant along the joint on each side where the oil pan, front cover and block meet.

d. Coat the gasket surfaces of the block and front cover with sealer and install a new gasket over the dowel pins on the engine block.

e. Position the front cover on the engine block. Work carefully to prevent damage to the oil seal, front cover gasket or oil pan gasket.

f. Apply downward pressure on the front cover and install the oil pan attaching screws finger-tight. Make sure the cover is correctly installed over the dowel pins.

12B. If the oil pan is removed, proceed as follows:

a. Coat the gasket surfaces of the block and front cover with sealer and install a new gasket over the dowel pins on the engine block.

b. Position the front cover on the engine block.

13. Install the front cover alignment tool (part No. T61P-6019-B or equivalent) over the crankshaft. Install the oil pump as described in this chapter.

14. Install and tighten the screws attaching the front cover and the oil pan (if removed).

15. Reverse Steps 1-8 to complete installation. Be sure to lubricate the lip of the seal, vibration damper bore and the end of the crankshaft with multipurpose grease before installing the damper.

Front Cover Seal Replacement

The crankshaft front seal can be removed and replaced without removing the front cover. Removal and installation of the seal can be easily and safely done using special removal/installation tools (part No. T70P-6B070-B and part No. T70P-6B070-A or equivalent). If special tools are not available, remove the timing cover as described in this chapter, then remove and install the seal with the cover removed.

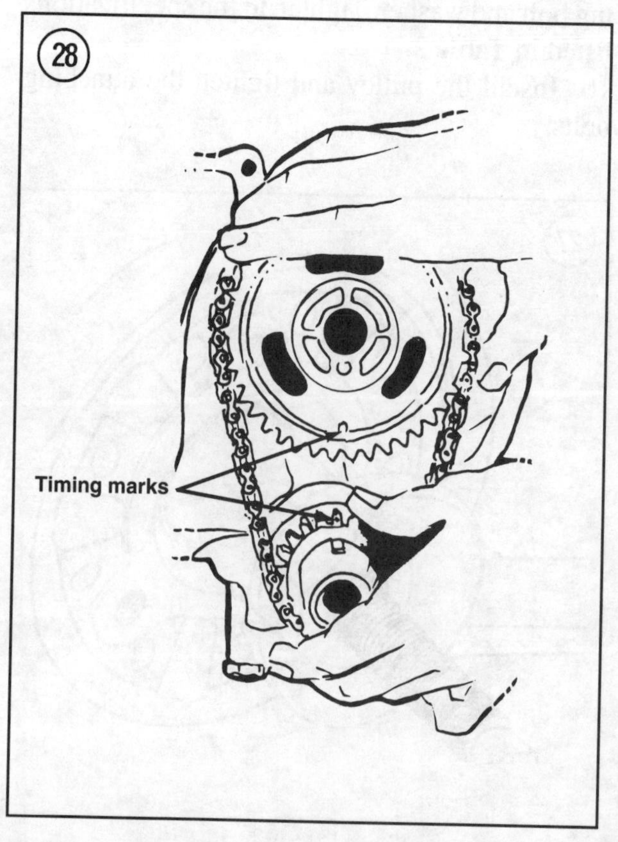

1. Remove the crankshaft pulley and vibration damper as described in this chapter.
2. Attach the special removal tool and pull the seal from the cover.
3. Coat the new seal with multipurpose grease and align the seal with the bore in the front cover.
4. Use the installation tool to push the seal into the cover bore.

TIMING CHAIN AND SPROCKETS

Removal

1. Remove the spark plugs. See Chapter Four.
2. Remove the vibration damper as described in this chapter.
3. Remove the front cover as described in this chapter.
4. Turn the crankshaft clockwise to take up slack on 1 side of the timing chain, then measure chain deflection on the other side. Total deflection should be less than 1/2 in. (12.7 mm).
5. Turn the crankshaft to position the camshaft and crankshaft sprocket marks as shown in **Figure 28**.
6. Remove the screw from the end of the camshaft and remove the washer and fuel pump eccentrics.
7. Remove the camshaft sprocket, crankshaft sprocket and timing chain as an assembly. Both sprockets should slide easily from the shafts.

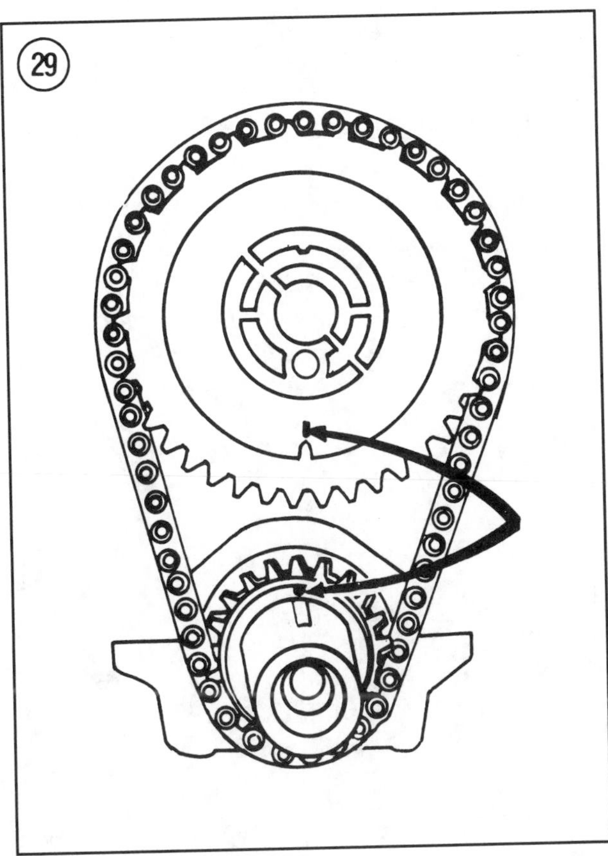

Installation

1. Assemble the timing chain to the camshaft and crankshaft sprockets with the timing marks aligned as shown in **Figure 28**.

NOTE
Lubricate the timing chain with clean engine oil before installing.

2. Install the timing chain/sprocket assembly on the camshaft (**Figure 29**).

NOTE
Before continuing, make sure the timing marks are aligned and that the sprockets correctly engage the drive key in the crankshaft and the drive pin in the camshaft.

3. Install the fuel pump eccentric, washer and retaining screw. Tighten the retaining screw to the torque listed in **Table 2**.
4. Install the front cover as described in this chapter.

ROCKER ARM ASSEMBLIES

Removal/Installation

Each rocker arm moves on its own fulcrum seat, which is retained by a bolt. It is not necessary to remove the rocker arm to remove the pushrod. Loosen the rocker arm retaining bolt, then move the arm away from the pushrod. To remove the entire assembly, proceed as follows:

1. Remove the valve cover(s) as described in this chapter.
2. Turn the crankshaft until the lifter is on the camshaft's base circle (valve closed).
3. Remove the rocker arm retaining bolt, then lift the rocker arm and its seat from the cylinder head.
4. Lift the pushrod from the cylinder block if necessary.

CAUTION

The rocker arm, fulcrum seat, pushrod and lifter establish a wear pattern to each other and to the valve which it opens. Therefore, always reinstall these parts in their original location. Install the pushrod with the same end up as when originally assembled.

5. Repeat Steps 2-4 for each remaining rocker arm, while observing the following:
   a. As they are removed, place each rocker arm and pushrod assembly in a separate container or use a rack that identifies their original location. It is important to keep them separated for reinstallation in the same position from which they were removed.
   b. More than 1 lifter will be on its base circle of the cam at the same time, so more than 1 rocker arm and pushrod can be removed after positioning the camshaft in Step 2.
6. Lubricate the rocker arms and fulcrum seats with engine oil.
7. Install the pushrods, making sure that each fits into its lifter socket.
8. Install the rocker arms, fulcrum seats and retaining bolts. If new rocker arms or fulcrum seats are being installed, coat the contact surfaces with Ford Multipurpose Grease DOAZ-19584-AA or equivalent.
9. Tighten the rocker arm retaining bolts to the torque listed in **Table 2**.
10. Install the valve cover(s) as described in this chapter.

CAMSHAFT

CAUTION

The 5.0 L and 5.8 L engines are manufactured with 2 different firing orders. Parts must be correctly matched for the engine to run or perform properly. Be extremely careful to install the correct parts when servicing these engines.

Removal/Installation

CAUTION

The rocker arm, fulcrum seat, pushrod and lifter establish a wear pattern to each other and to the valve which it opens. Therefore, always reinstall these parts in their original location. Be sure to install the pushrods with the same end up as when originally assembled. When removing, identify the parts for correct assembly.

1. Remove the valve covers as described in this chapter.
2. Remove the intake manifold as described in this chapter.
3. Remove the pushrods and identify each so it can be reinstalled in its original location. The rocker arms can be removed as described in this

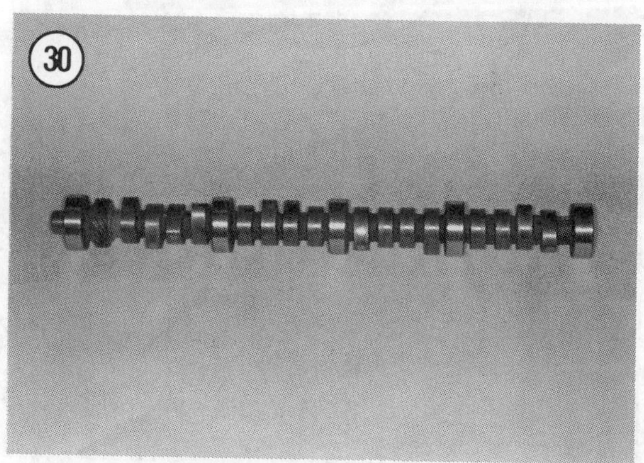

chapter or the rocker arms can remain in place as follows:

a. Loosen the rocker arm retaining shoulder bolts.

b. Swivel the arms away from the pushrods.

c. Lift the pushrods from the lifters.

4. Pull the valve lifters from their bores as described in this chapter. Place each lifter in a rack in the order of removal so they can be reinstalled in their original locations.

NOTE

A rack can be made or purchased to hold the lifters in the same order as originally installed. Marks on the rack identify the front of the engine.

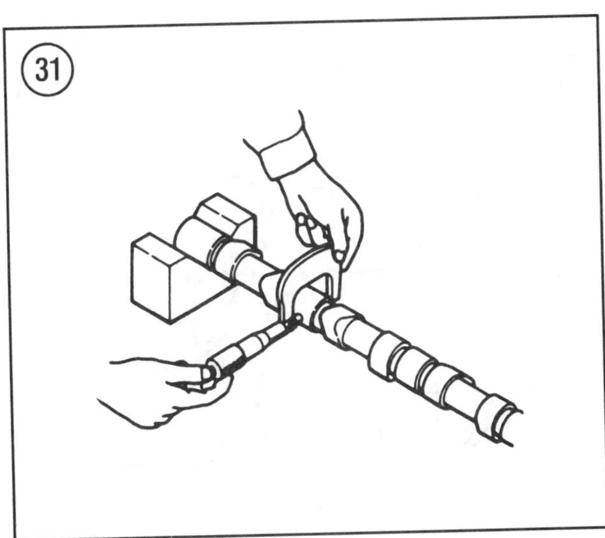

5. If the engine is equipped with a mechanical fuel pump, remove the pump.

6. Remove the front cover, timing chain and camshaft sprocket as described in this chapter.

CAUTION

Do not cock the camshaft during removal. This can damage the camshaft or its bearing surfaces.

7. Carefully withdraw the camshaft (**Figure 30**) from the front of the engine with a rotating motion to avoid damage to the bearings.

8. Installation is the reverse of removal. Coat the bottom of any new lifters with Ford Multipurpose Grease part No. DOAZ-19584-AA or equivalent.

9. Check and adjust ignition timing (Chapter Four).

8

Inspection

1. Inspect the bottom (cam contact surface) of each lifter.

a. The cam contacting surface should be smooth, polished and slightly convex (curved out). The entire surface should be polished indicating the lifter has been rotating freely.

b. If any lifter is galled, chipped, worn, or damaged replace the camshaft and lifters.

2. Inspect the camshaft journals and lobes for wear or scoring.

NOTE

If you do not have precision measuring equipment, a properly equipped machine shop should perform Steps 3 and 4.

3. Measure the camshaft journal diameters with a micrometer (**Figure 31**). Compare measurements with the specifications listed in **Table 1**.

4. Check the distributor drive gear (**Figure 32**) for excessive wear or damage.

5. Replace the camshaft if:

a. Any wear is evident while inspecting the camshaft in Step 2.
b. One or more journals do not meet specifications measured in Step 3.
c. The distributor drive gear is damaged.

Lobe Lift Measurement

The cam lobe lift can be measured by measuring the camshaft lobes directly after the camshaft is removed. In addition, camshaft lobe lift can be measured as follows with the camshaft in the block and the cylinder heads in place.

1. Remove the rocker arm cover as described in this chapter.
2. Remove the rocker arm assemblies as described in this chapter.
3. Remove the spark plugs. See Chapter Four.
4. Attach a dial indicator to the cylinder head with the plunger contacting the end of 1 pushrod. Use a piece of rubber tubing to hold the dial indicator plunger in place against the center of the pushrod. See **Figure 33**, typical.
5. Rotate the crankshaft in the normal direction of rotation until the valve lifter seats against the heel or base circle of the cam (**Figure 34**). This positions the pushrod at its lowest point.
6. Set the dial indicator at zero, slowly rotate the crankshaft until the pushrod reaches its maximum travel and note the dial indicator.
7. Compare the movement of the pushrod with the specification listed in **Table 1**. Movement less than specified indicates the lobe is worn.
8. Repeat Steps 4-7 for each pushrod. If all lobes are within specification, reinstall the rocker arm assemblies.
9. If 1 or more lobes are worn beyond specification, replace the camshaft and lifters as described in this chapter.
10. Remove the dial indicator and reverse Steps 1-3.

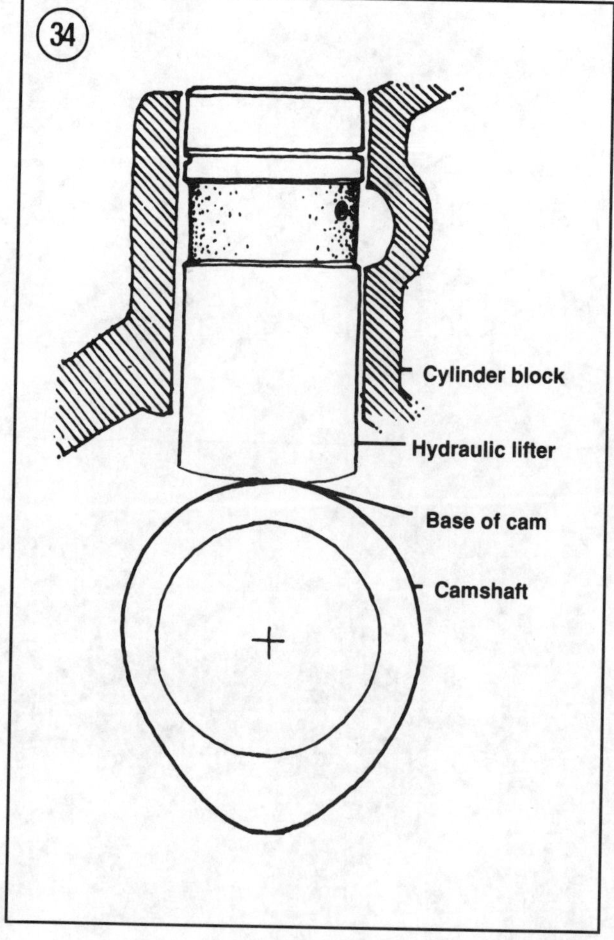

Bearing Replacement

Camshaft bearings can be replaced without complete engine disassembly; however, replacement is often part of a complete overhaul. Replace the bearings only in a complete set. Special camshaft bearing removal and installation tools are required for bearing replacement. Improper use of the special tools or use of the wrong tools can result in severe damage. Bearing replacement should be performed by a properly equipped and qualified service technician.

1. Remove the camshaft as described in this chapter.
2. Remove the crankshaft as described in this chapter. The pistons can remain in cylinder bores.
3. Drive the camshaft core plug from the rear of the cylinder block.
4. Use the special camshaft bearing removal tool to remove the old bearings.

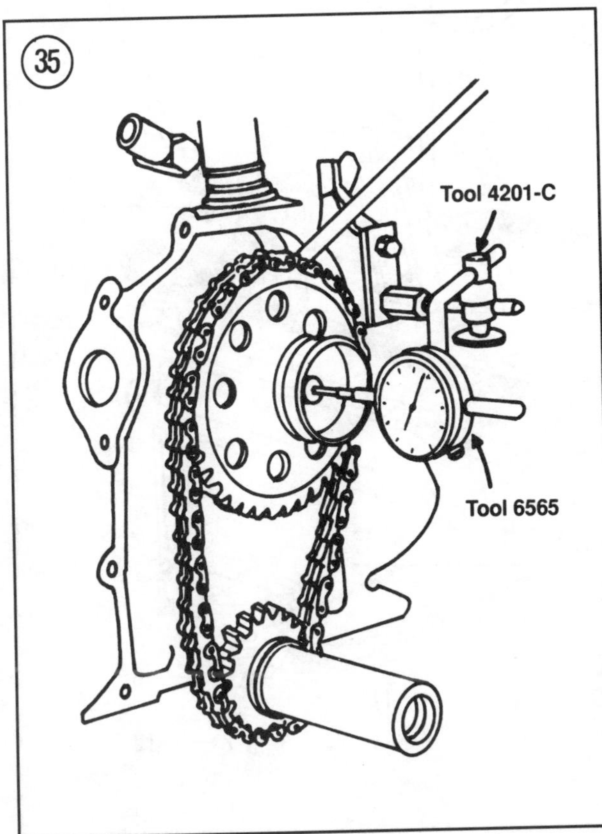

5. Install the new bearings by reversing the removal procedure. Use the same tool to pull the new bearings into their bores, observing the following.
   a. Align the oil holes in the bearings with passages in the block. Since the oil hole is on the top of the bearings, and cannot be seen during installation, align the bearing oil hole with the hole in bore and mark the opposite side of bearing and block at the bore to assist in positioning the oil hole during installation.
   b. Make sure the camshaft front bearing is countersunk the correct amount. Press the front bearing into the block until the front of the bearing is 0.005-0.020 in. (0.13-0.51 mm) from the face of the block.

7. Wipe a new camshaft core plug with sealer and install it flush to 1/32 in. (0.8 mm) deep to maintain a level surface on the rear of the block.

End Play

1. Loosen the rocker arm bolts or remove the rocker arms to reduce the load on the camshaft.
2. Push the camshaft toward the rear as far as possible.
3. Attach a dial indicator to the front of the engine with the tip against the camshaft sprocket. See **Figure 35**.

CAUTION
Be careful not to damage the camshaft sprocket when prying the camshaft forward. Do not pry against any part that will be damaged and do not pry hard enough to damage the sprocket.

4. Set the dial indicator to zero, then gently pry the camshaft toward the front as shown in **Figure 35**.
5. Compare the measured end play with the specification listed in **Table 1**.

6. If end play is excessive, remove the sprocket as outlined in this chapter and replace the thrust plate.

OIL PAN

Ease of oil pan removal depends upon the installation within a given boat. In some cases, the oil pan can be removed without removing the engine. In others, engine removal is required to provide sufficient working space and clearance for oil pan removal.

A kit is attached to the pan on most engines to assist in draining the oil when the engine is in the boat. If not already installed, this kit can be installed on any engine while the engine is removed for service.

Removal

Refer to **Figure 36** for this procedure.

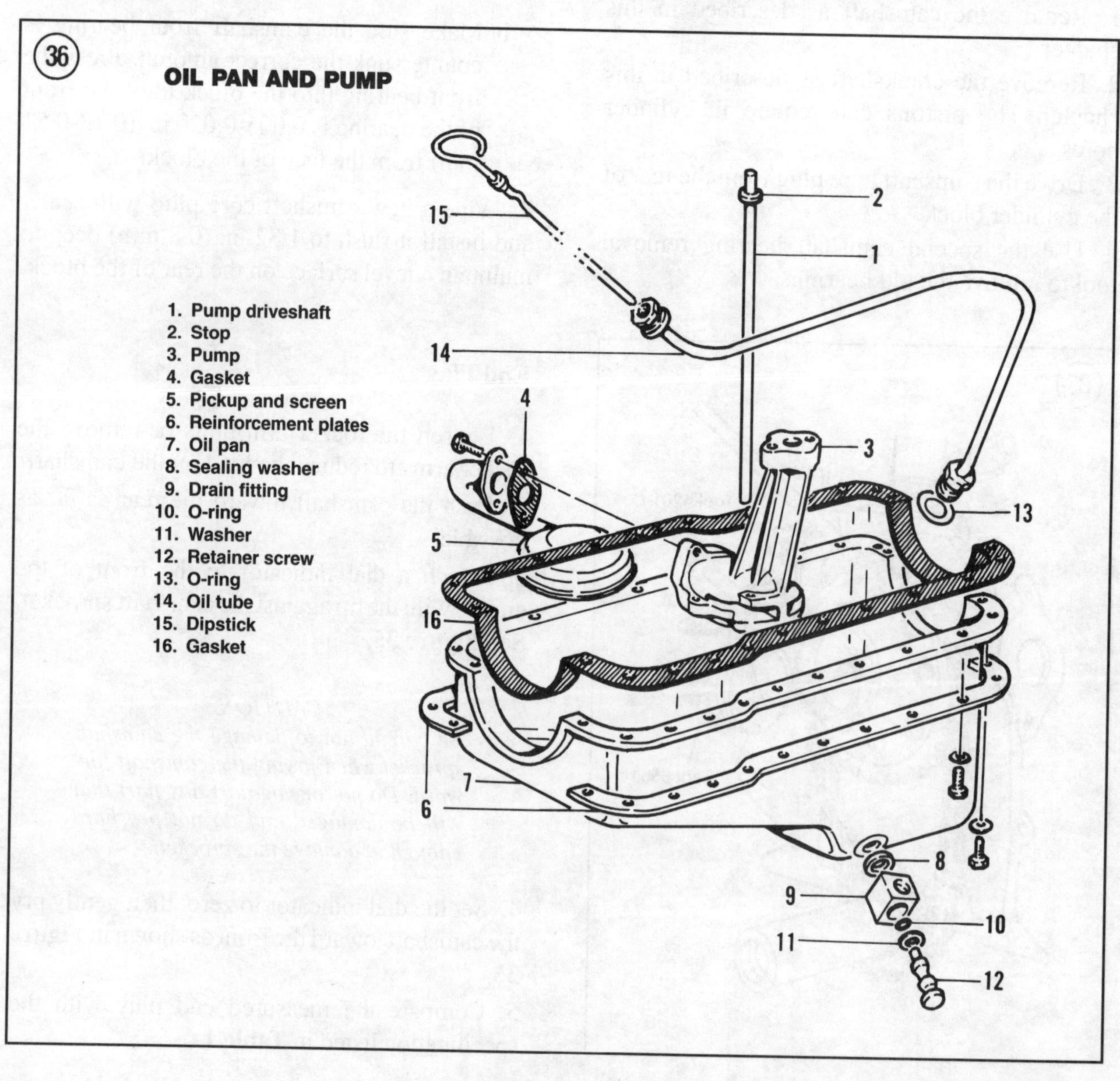

1A. If the pan can be removed with the engine in the boat:
   a. Remove the oil dipstick and siphon the oil from the crankcase. See Chapter Four.
   b. Remove the oil dipstick tube.

1B. If the engine is out of the boat:
   a. Place a suitable container under the oil pan drain plug. Remove the plug and let the crankcase drain. Reinstall the drain plug.
   b. If mounted on an engine stand, rotate the engine 180° to place the oil pan in an upright position.
   c. Remove the oil dipstick and dipstick tube.

2. Remove all of the screws attaching the oil pan. Remove the oil pan.
3. Remove and discard the gasket.

Inspection and Cleaning

1. Clean any gasket residue from the oil pan rail on the engine block, rear main bearing cap, front cover and the oil pan sealing flange with degreaser and a gasket scraper.
2. Clean the pan thoroughly in solvent and check for dents or warped gasket surfaces. Straighten or replace the pan as required.

Installation

1. Position the gasket on the rails of the oil pan and insert a screw at each corner of the pan to hold the gasket in place.
2. Carefully position the oil pan and gasket against the block, make sure the gasket is properly aligned, then install the attaching screws with lockwashers. Tighten the screws to the specifications listed in **Table 2**, working from the center outward in each direction.
3. Reinstall the dipstick.
4. If removed, install the engine in the boat as described in this chapter.
5. Fill the crankcase with the quantity and type of oil recommended in Chapter Four.

OIL PUMP

Removal/Installation

1. Remove the oil pan as described in this chapter.
2. Remove the screw(s) attaching the pump, then remove the pump, intake screen and pump drive shaft. See **Figure 36**.
3. Before installing, prime the pump by pouring clean engine oil into the pump inlet. Turn the pump shaft to fill the pump cavity.

4A. If the engine is attached to a stand that will allow the engine to be inverted, insert the pump drive shaft (1, **Figure 36**) into the distributor socket. Check to make certain the stop (2, **Figure 36**) on the shaft contacts the engine block at the same time the shaft seats in the distributor. Move the stop if necessary.

4B. If the engine can not be inverted, insert the pump drive shaft (1, **Figure 36**) into the distributor socket. Make certain the stop (2, **Figure 36**) on the shaft contacts the engine block at the same time the shaft seats in the distributor. Move the stop if necessary.

5A. If the engine is inverted, install the pump with the tangs on the drive shaft and the pump aligned. If the pump does not seat easily, rotate the pump shaft slightly so it aligns, then reinstall the pump.

5B. If the engine is not inverted, install the drive shaft and pump together. Make sure the pump seats easily against the block before installing the attaching screws.

6. Tighten the pump retaining screw(s) to the torque specified in **Table 2**.
7. Attach the oil inlet tube to the pump and the bracket to the block. Tighten the screws to the torque listed in **Table 2**.
8. Reinstall the oil pan as described in this chapter.

Disassembly/Assembly

Refer to **Figure 37** for this procedure.

1. Remove the screws attaching the pump cover and carefully remove the cover.
2. Remove the inner rotor and shaft assembly.
3. Remove the outer rotor.
4. Remove the pressure relief valve retaining pin, relief spring and valve.
5. Lubricate all parts thoroughly with clean engine oil before assembling.
6. Assemble in the reverse order of disassembly. Align the index marks on the side of the rotors, install the cover and tighten the cover retaining screws to the torque listed in **Table 2**. Rotate the pump drive shaft by hand to check for smooth operation.

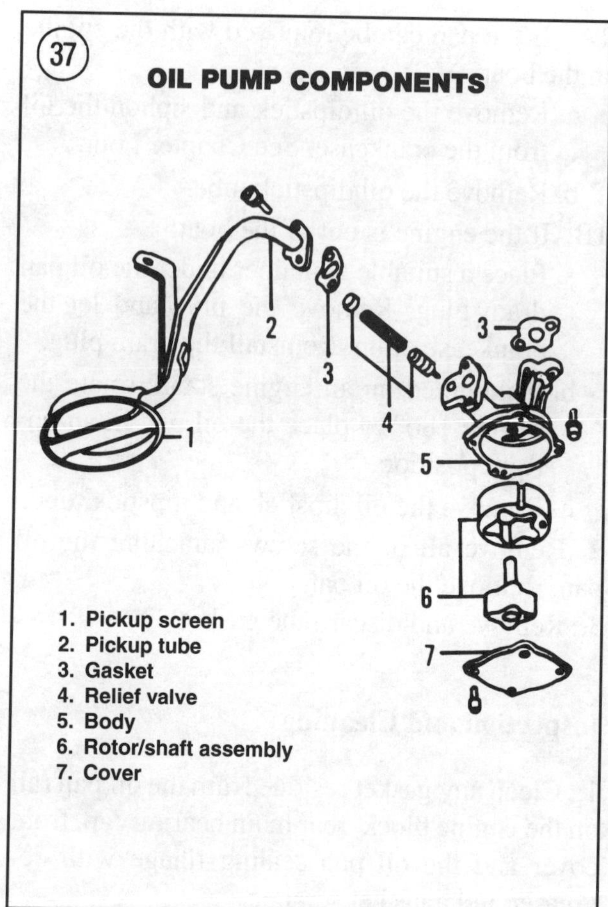

Inspection

The pump assembly and gears are serviced only as an assembly. If any part is worn or damaged, replace the entire pump.

1. Clean all parts thoroughly in solvent. Brush the inside of the body and the pressure regulator chamber to remove all dirt and metal particles. Dry with compressed air, if available.
2. Check the pump body and cover for cracks or excessive wear.
3. Check the pump gears for damage or excessive wear.
4. Check the drive gear shaft-to-body fit for excessive looseness.
5. Check the inside of the pump cover for wear that will allow oil to leak around the ends of the gears.
6. Check the pressure regulator valve for a smooth fit without any scoring.
7. Measure pump clearances as follows and compare to the specification listed in **Table 1**.
   a. Install the inner rotor/shaft assembly in the pump body, place a straightedge across the rotor and the pump body, then measure the clearance between the rotor and the straightedge. See **Figure 38**.

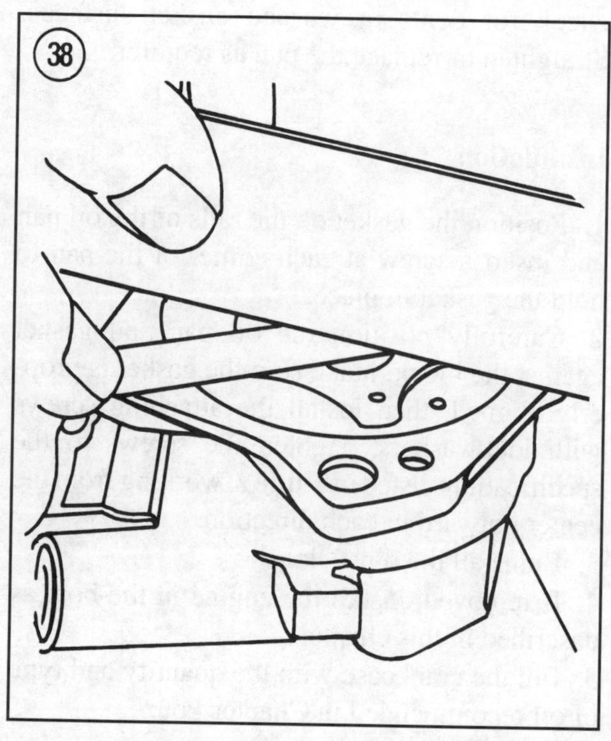

b. Install the outer rotor and measure the radial clearance between the rotor and the pump body. See **Figure 39**.
c. Measure the clearance between the pump shaft and the housing and compare with the specification listed in **Table 1**.
d. If a spring tester is available, compress the relief spring to the length listed in **Table 1** and compare the pressure measured with the specification listed.

CYLINDER HEAD

Removal

1. Open the engine block drain valves and drain all water from the block.
2. Remove the intake and exhaust manifolds as described in this chapter.
3. Remove the alternator and oil filter mounting brackets.

NOTE
It is not necessary to remove the spark plugs to remove the cylinder head, but the plugs are easier to remove before the head is removed. The plugs can also be easily broken during cylinder headremoval.

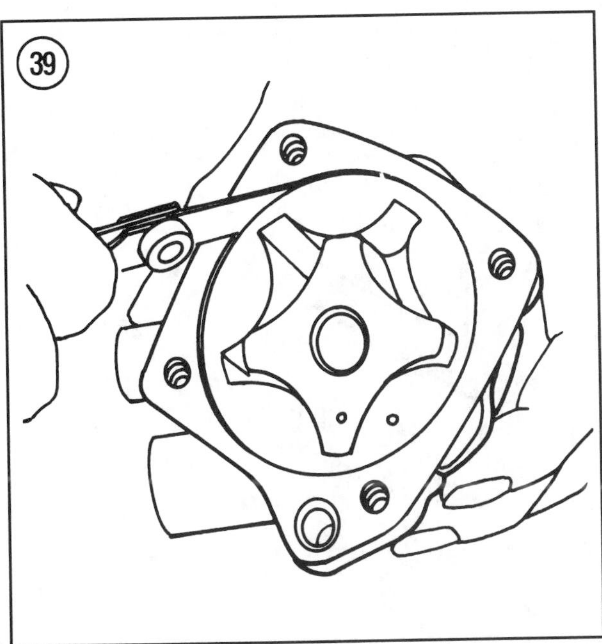

4. Disconnect the wires from the spark plugs and detach the wire looms.
5. Remove the valve covers as described in this chapter.

CAUTION
The rocker arm, fulcrum seat, pushrod and lifter establish a wear pattern to each other and to the valve which it opens. Therefore, always reinstall these parts in their original location. Install the pushrods with the same end up as when originally assembled. When removing, identify the parts for correct assembly.

6. Loosen the rocker arm retaining bolts, then remove the bolts, rocker arm, fulcrum seat and pushrods.

NOTE
A rack can be made or purchased to hold the bolts, rocker arm, fulcrum seat ball and pushrods in the same order and with the same end of the pushrods down as originally installed. Mark the rack to identify the front of the engine.

7. Loosen the cylinder head bolts, beginning in the center of the head and working in each direction toward the ends.
8. Remove and examine the bolts attaching the cylinder head. Two types of bolts are used on 5.0 L (302 cid) engines. Refer to the following:

a. If the engine is equipped with standard type retaining bolts (A, **Figure 40**), they can be reinstalled unless damaged.

b. If the engine is fitted with torque-to-yield bolts (B, **Figure 40**), they should be discarded and new torque-to-yield bolts installed.

9. Carefully lift the head from the engine and move it to a workbench.

NOTE
It may be necessary to bump the head with a soft-faced hammer to break the gasket seal.

CAUTION
Be careful to place the head in a safe location and in a safe position to prevent damage to the valves or gasket surfaces.

10. Remove and discard the head gasket. Clean all gasket residue from the valve (rocker arm) cover, cylinder head and block mating surfaces.

Decarbonizing

Check for any sign of oil or water leaks before cleaning the cylinder head.

1. Before removing the valves, clean all deposits from the combustion chambers, intake ports and exhaust ports. Use a fine wire brush dipped in solvent or make a scraper from hardwood. Be careful not to scratch or gouge the combustion chambers.
2. After all carbon is removed from the combustion chambers and ports, clean the entire head with solvent.
3. Clean carbon from the tops of the pistons.
4. Clean the pushrod guides, valve guide bores and all bolt holes. Use a cleaning solvent to remove dirt and grease.
5. Remove the valves as described in this chapter.
6. Clean the valves with a fine wire brush or buffing wheel.

Inspection

1. Check the cylinder head for any signs of oil or water leaks before cleaning.
2. Clean the cylinder head thoroughly in solvent. While cleaning, look for cracks or other visible damage. Look for corrosion or foreign material in the oil and water passages. Clean the passages with a stiff spiral brush, then blow them out with compressed air.
3. Check the studs in the cylinder head for damage and replace if necessary.
4. Check all of the threaded holes in the cylinder head for damaged threads and repair if necessary.
5. Check for warpage of the cylinder head-to-block surface with a straightedge and feeler gauge. Measure diagonally, as well as end-to-end. If the gap exceeds the specification listed in **Table 1**, have the head resurfaced at a machine shop. If head resurfacing is necessary, do not remove more than the minimum amount necessary to correct the warpage. Replace the cylinder head if more than 0.010 in (0.25 mm) of material must be removed to true the cylinder head.

Installation

1. Make sure that all gasket surfaces (on the cylinder head and block) and bolts holes are clean. Dirt in bolt holes or on the bolt threads will affect bolt torque.
2. Recheck all visible oil and water passages for cleanliness.

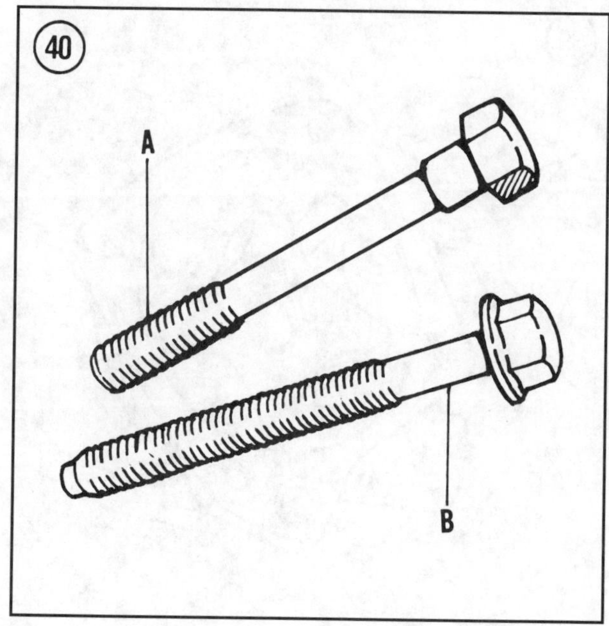

CAUTION
Use only the marine cylinder head gasket available from Volvo Penta. Damage may result from installing an automotive head gasket.

3. Fit a new head gasket over the dowels in the block.
4. Carefully position the head onto the cylinder block, engaging the dowel pins. Do not damage the gasket by sliding the cylinder head into position. Do not crush the gasket by dropping the head on 1 side or 1 corner.

NOTE
*Two types of bolts have been used to attach the cylinder head. Compare the head bolts with those shown in **Figure 40** and continue with Step 5A or 5B as determined by the type of bolt installed. Engines of 5.0 L (302 cid) may be fitted with either torque-to-yield or standard (regular) head bolts; 5.8 L (351 cid) engines use only standard cylinder head bolts.*

5A. If the (5.0 L) engine is fitted with torque-to-yield bolts (B, **Figure 40**), the old bolts should be discarded and new torque-to-yield bolts installed as follows:

a. Tighten the head bolts in the sequence shown in **Figure 41** until the Step 1 torque specified in **Table 2** is reached. Make sure that all screws are tightened evenly before continuing to the next step.

b. Tighten the head bolts in the sequence shown in **Figure 41** to the Step 2 torque specified in **Table 2**.

c. Tighten the head bolts in the sequence shown in **Figure 41** to the final (Step 3) torque specified in **Table 2**.

(41) **CYLINDER HEAD BOLT TORQUE SEQUENCE**

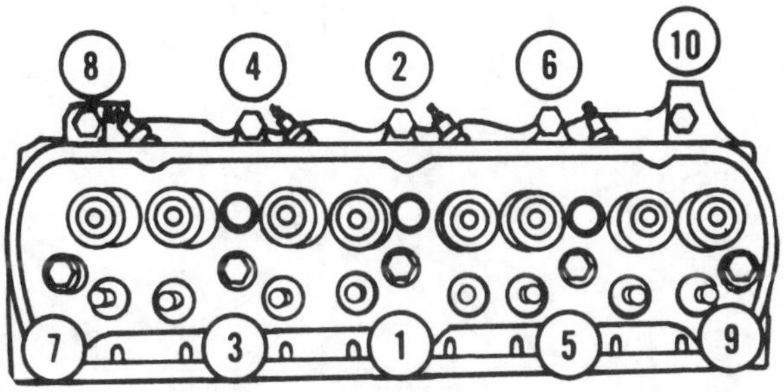

5B. If the engine (either 5.0 L or 5.8 L) is fitted with standard bolts shown at A, **Figure 40**, install and tighten the screws using a 2 step procedure as follows:

a. Tighten the head bolts in the sequence shown in **Figure 41** until the Step 1 torque specified **Table 2** is reached. Make sure that all screws are tightened evenly before continuing to the next step.

b. Tighten the head bolts to the torque specified under Step 2, in **Table 2** in the sequence shown in **Figure 41**.

6. Reverse the *Cylinder Head Removal* in this chapter to complete installation. Check and adjust ignition timing as required. See Chapter Four.

VALVES AND VALVE SEATS

Servicing the valves, guides and valve seats must be done at a dealership or machine shop, with trained technicians and the proper machine tools. A general practice for many who do their own service is to remove the cylinder head, perform all disassembly except valve removal and take the head to a dealership or machine shop for inspection and service. Since the cost is low relative to the required effort and equipment, this is usually the best approach, even for experienced mechanics. The following procedures are given to acquaint the home mechanic with what the dealership or machine shop will do.

Valve Removal

Refer to **Figure 42** for this procedure.

1. Remove the rocker arm assemblies as described in this chapter.
2. Remove the cylinder head as described in this chapter.

NOTE
Clean and inspect the cylinder head, combustion chamber and ports as described in this chapter before removing the valves.

3. Compress the valve spring with a compressor, (**Figure 43**). Remove the valve keys or locks and release the spring tension.
4. Remove the retainer and valve spring. On some valves, there may be a sleeve on top of the retainer, an exhaust valve rotator in place of the retainer or a damper spring inside the valve spring.
5. Remove and discard the valve stem seal. Check the cylinder head and remove the shim or spacer located under the spring, if used.

CAUTION
Remove any burrs from the valve stem lock grooves before removing the valve or the valve guide will be damaged. The valve stem will develop a small burr as a result of the locks pounding against the groove.

6. Remove the valve and repeat Steps 3-5 on each remaining valve.
7. Arrange the parts in order so they can be returned to their original positions when reassembled.

Inspection

1. Clean the valves with a fine wire brush or buffing wheel. Discard any cracked, warped or burned valves.
2. Measure valve stems at the top, center and bottom for wear. A machine shop can do this

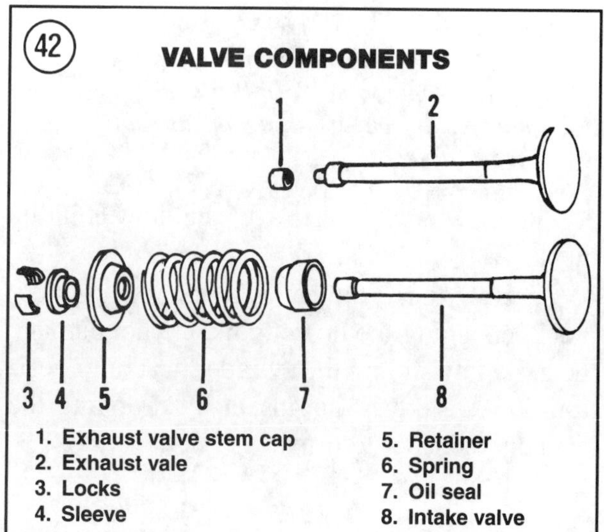

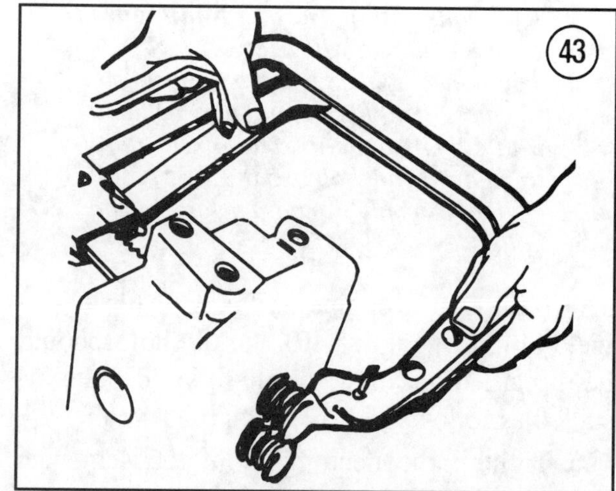

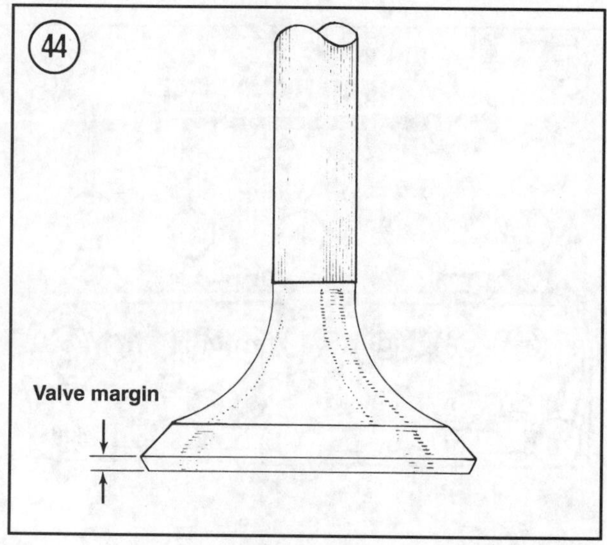

when the valves are serviced. Also measure the length of each valve and the diameter of each valve head.

NOTE
*Check the thickness of the valve edge or margin, after the valves have been ground. See **Figure 44**. Replace any valve with a margin of less than 1/32 in. (0.8 mm).*

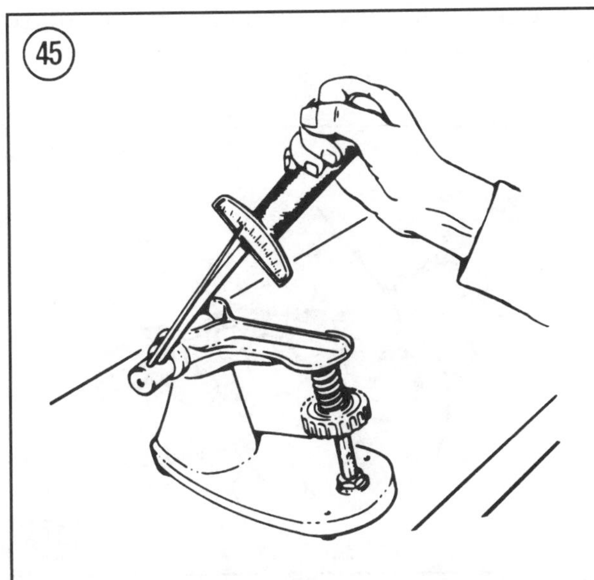

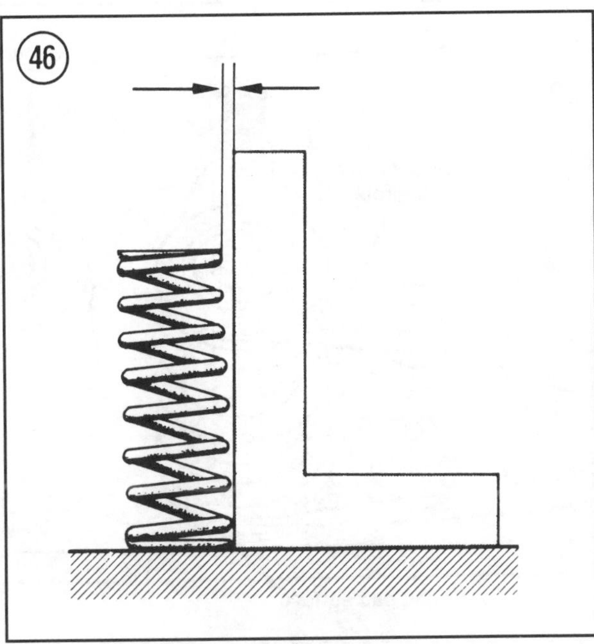

3. Remove all carbon and varnish from the valve guides with a stiff spiral wire brush.

NOTE
The next step assumes that all valve stems have been measured and are within specification. Replace valves with worn stems before performing this step.

4. Insert each valve into the guide from which it was removed. Holding the valve just slightly off its seat, rock it back and forth in a direction parallel with the rocker arms. This is the direction in which the greatest wear normally occurs. If the valve stem rocks more than slightly, the valve guide is probably worn.
5. If there is any doubt about valve guide condition after performing Step 4, have the valve guide measured with a valve stem clearance checking tool. Compare the results with specifications in **Table 1**. Worn guides must be reamed for the next oversize valve stem.
6. Test the valve springs under load on a spring tester (**Figure 45**. Replace any weak springs.
7. Inspect the valve seat inserts. If worn or burned, they must be reconditioned. This is a job for a dealer or machine shop, although the procedure is described in this chapter.
8. Check each spring on a flat surface with a steel square. See **Figure 46**. Slowly revolve the spring 360° and note the space between the top of the coil and the square. Replace the spring if it is not straight.
9. Check each valve lifter to make sure it fits freely in the block and that the end that contacts the camshaft lobe is smooth and not worn excessively.

Valve Guide Reaming

Intake and exhaust valves with oversize stems may be available to compensate for wear in the guides. Worn valve guides must be reamed to accept a valve with an oversize stem. However,

8

valves with oversize stems are not always available. Reaming must be done by hand (**Figure 47**) and should only be accomplished by experienced machine shop personnel. The valve seat must be refaced after the guide has been reamed.

Valve Seat Reconditioning

1. Cut the valve seats to the angle specified in **Table 1**. Use a dressing stone and remove only enough metal to obtain a good finish.
2. Use stones of larger or smaller angles to obtain the specified seat width as necessary.
3. Coat the corresponding valve face with Prussian blue (marking compound).
4. Insert the valve into the valve guide.
5. Apply light pressure to the valve and rotate it a small amount (approximately 1/4 turn).
6. Lift the valve out. If it seats properly, the marking compound will transfer evenly around the valve face.
   a. If the marking compound transfers to only part of the valve, the valve or seat may not be concentric with the stem or guide.
   b. If the marking compound transfers to the valve near the edge of the valve face, the seat can be lowered by machining the seat with a stone which has a smaller angle. A stone with a smaller angle will remove metal from the combustion chamber side of the valve seat.
   c. If the marking compound transfers to the bottom of the valve face, closer to the stem, the seat should be raised by machining the seat with a stone which has a larger angle. A stone with a larger angle will remove metal from inside the port, closer to the valve stem.

Valve Installation

NOTE
Install all parts in their original location.

1. Install new valve stem seals on the guides. Make sure the seal is bottomed on the guide.
2. Coat the valves with engine oil and insert them through the guides and seals in the cylinder head.
3. Position the valve spring shim/spacer (if used) around the valve guide boss.
4. Install the valve spring(s) over the valve, then install the cap or rotator.
5. Compress the springs and install the locks. Make sure that locks seat properly in the groove of the valve stem.

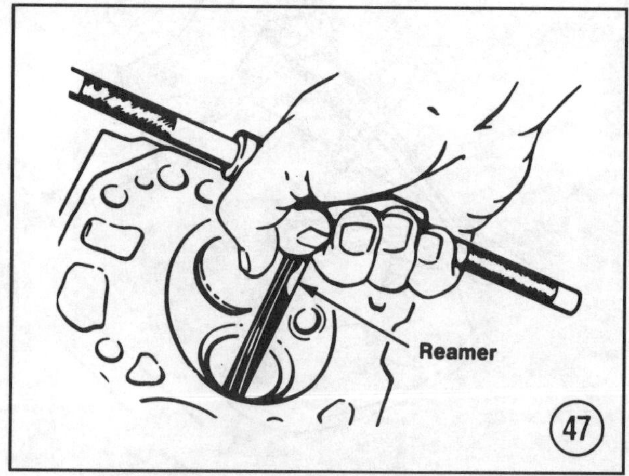

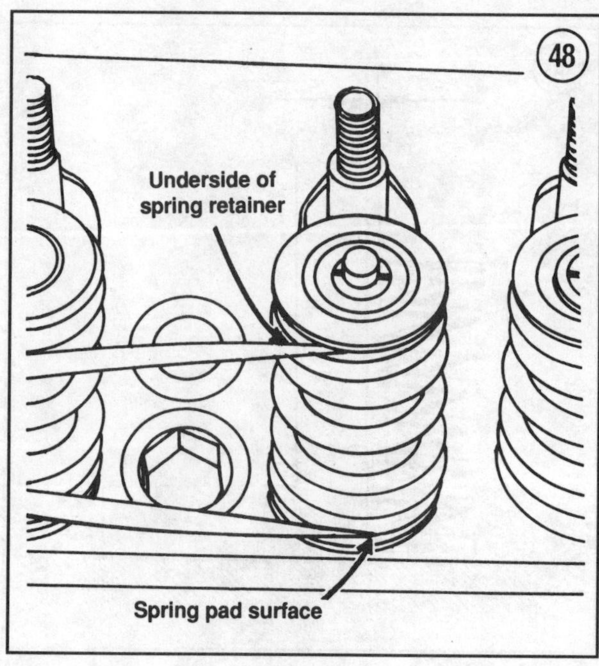

6. Measure the installed spring height between the top of the valve seat and the underside of the cap or rotator, as shown in **Figure 48**. If height is more than specified in **Table 1**, disassemble the valve, install a spring seat shim of the appropriate thickness under the spring(s). Then reassemble the valve and remeasure the assembled height.

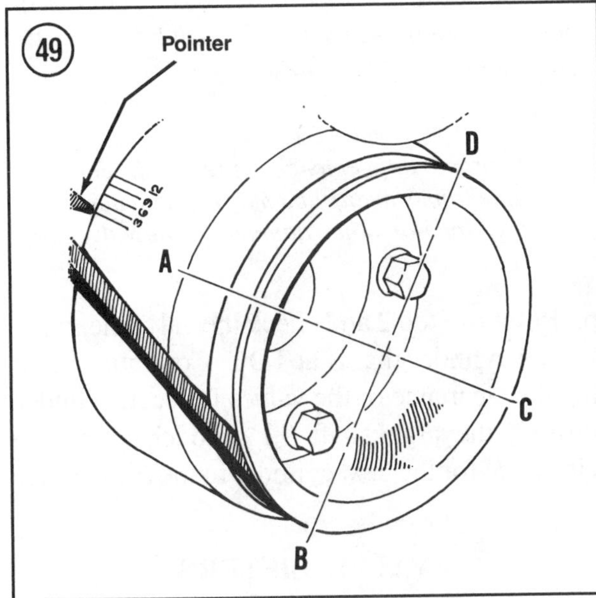

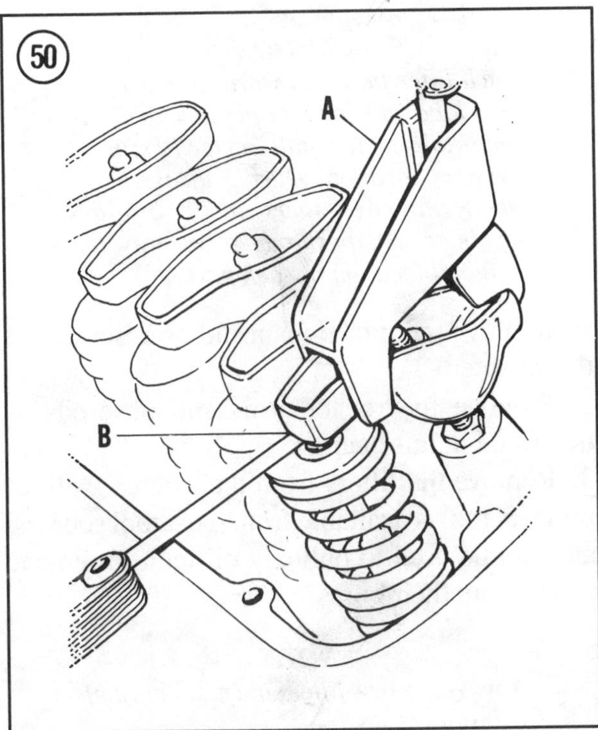

Valve Clearance Measurement

The hydraulic lifters provide adjustment of the valve clearance automatically during operation to compensate for normal wear. Valve clearance should remain within the normal adjustment range unless components of the valve train are worn or damaged. Adjustment is possible only by installing new undamaged and unworn standard parts. Check service clearance as follows with the lifter completely collapsed.

NOTE

If the clearance of one valve is wrong after a period of normal operation, the condition of the lifter and the cam lobe that operates that valve should be checked as described in this chapter.

1. Rotate the crankshaft until the TDC mark on the crankshaft pulley aligns with the timing pointer. See **Figure 49**, typical. This positions the No. 1 cylinder at TDC. Check to make sure the No. 1 cylinder is at the top of its compression stroke by placing your fingers on the No. 1 cylinder rocker arms as the pulley TDC mark nears the pointer. If the valves are moving, the engine is in the firing position for the No. 6 cylinder. Rotate the crankshaft pulley 1 full turn to locate the No. 1 cylinder in firing position.
2. With the engine in the No. 1 firing position, refer to the following procedure and measure clearance of both valves for the No. 1 cylinder (front cylinder on the starboard side).

   a. Attach the hydraulic lifter compressor tool (part No. T71P-6513-B or equivalent) to 1 of the 2 rocker arms. See A, **Figure 50**.

   b. Slowly apply pressure on the special tool to force the lifter to bleed down completely, then hold the hydraulic lifter compressor tool to keep the lifter bottomed.

c. Use a flat feeler gauge to measure the clearance between the rocker arm and the valve stem. See B, **Figure 50**.

d. Compare the clearance with the specification in **Table 1**.

NOTE
If the clearance of 1 valve is wrong after a period of normal operation, the condition of the lifter and the cam lobe that operates that valve should be checked as described in this chapter.

e. Release the hydraulic lifter compressor tool, then remove the tool from the rocker arm.

f. Attach the hydraulic lifter compressor tool to the other valve for the cylinder being tested, then repeat the procedure in substeps b-e for the remaining valves.

NOTE
Temporary marks can be applied to the crankshaft pulley in Step 3. Make sure the marks are accurately positioned in relation to the TDC mark affixed by the manufacturer.

3. Mark the circumference of the crankshaft pulley at 90° increments beginning with the manufacturer's TDC mark. Place each of the 4 marks 90° from the 2 adjacent marks. See **Figure 49**.
4. Place your fingers on the rocker arms for the No. 3 cylinder and turn the crankshaft clockwise 90° aligning the temporary mark (B, **Figure 49**) with the timing pointer.

CAUTION
The 5.0 L and 5.8 L engines are manufactured with 2 different firing orders. Parts must be correctly matched for the engine to run or perform properly. Be extremely careful to install the correct parts when servicing these engines.

5A. If the valves (rocker arms) for the No. 3 cylinder do not move as the temporary mark aligns with the pointer, the firing order is 1-3-7-2-6-5-4-8.
5B. If either of the valves (rocker arms) for the No. 3 cylinder move as the temporary mark aligns with the pointer, turn the crankshaft back (counterclockwise) 90°. Perform Step 4 again with your fingers on the valves for the No. 5 cylinder. If the valves for the No. 5 cylinder do not move, but those for the No. 3 cylinder do, the firing order is 1-5-4-2-6-3-7-8.

CAUTION
Improper adjustment can prevent the engine from starting and may result in bent pushrods or other damage to the valve train.

6. Refer to Step 2 and check the valve clearance for the cylinder that is at TDC. Continue checking the clearance of the valves for each cylinder, turning the crankshaft 90° and checking the clearance for the next cylinder in the firing order.

VALVE LIFTERS

Removal/Installation

CAUTION
Each lifter becomes worn to match the cam lobe on which it operates, and it is important to reinstall each lifter in its original location. During disassembly, always arrange lifters, rocker arm assemblies and pushrods to identify the original location of each part.

1. Remove the intake manifold as described in this chapter.
2. Remove the rocker arms and pushrods as described in this chapter.
3. Remove the lifters from their bores. A lifter removal tool is available from most tool sources, and can be used to pull any difficult to remove lifters from their bores.

NOTE
Always use new lifters if a new camshaft is installed.

4. Initial lubrication is important to the service life of the camshaft and lifters. Observe the following:
   a. Coat the bottom of lifters with Ford Multipurpose Grease part No. DOAZ-19584-AA (or equivalent) before installing.
   b. Coat the entire lifter assembly and cam lobe with clean engine oil prior to installation.
5. Install the lifters in their bores. If reusing the original lifters, make certain they are installed in the same location from which they were removed. Initial lubrication such as described in Step 4 is also helpful for used lifters.

PISTON/CONNECTING ROD ASSEMBLY

Piston Removal

1. Remove the engine as described in this chapter.
2. Place a suitable container under the oil pan, remove the drain plug and allow the crankcase oil to drain completely.
3. Remove the intake and exhaust manifolds as described in this chapter.
4. Remove the cylinder heads as described in this chapter.

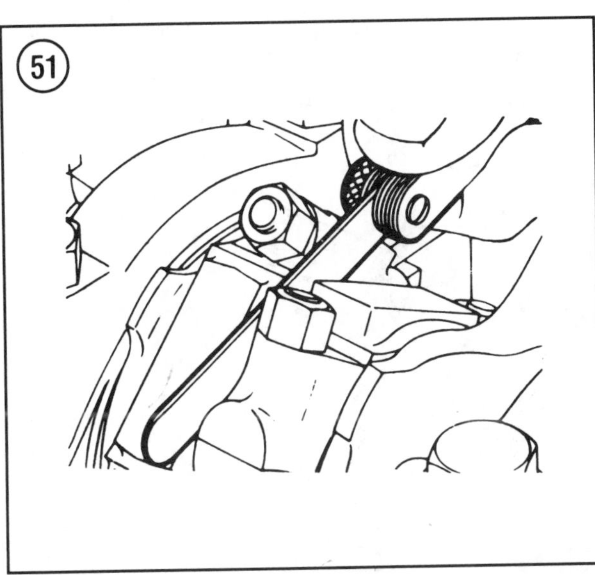

5. Remove the oil pan and oil pump as described in this chapter.
6. Remove the ridge from the top of the cylinder. Even a small ridge caused by the piston wearing the cylinder or a buildup of carbon can make removal of the piston difficult and may damage the piston. Refer to the following.
   a. Turn the crankshaft until the piston is at bottom dead center.
   b. Install a ridge reamer in the cylinder following its manufacturer's instructions.
   c. Operate the tool to remove the ridge from the top of the cylinder bore.
   d. Clean the shavings from the cylinder bore. A shop vacuum will remove the shavings easily.
   e. Repeat substeps a-d for the remaining cylinders.
7. Measure the side clearance between the side of the connecting rod and the journal flanges of the crankshaft as follows:
   a. Rotate the crankshaft until the connecting rods of 1 journal are easily accessible.
   b. Measure the clearance between the connecting rod and the crankshaft journal flange with a flat feeler gauge. See **Figure 51**. Measure the clearance for all of the connecting rod journals.
   c. Compare the measured side clearance with the specification listed in **Table 1**. If the clearance is excessive, replace the connecting rod during reassembly.

NOTE

Clean the tops of the pistons before removing them from the cylinders and check for cylinder numbers or identifying marks. Also check for cylinder identifying marks on the connecting rod and cap. If marks are not already located on each part, use a suitable scribe or marker and mark the cylinder number on the piston, connecting rod and rod cap.

8. Mark each connecting rod and its cap with the cylinder number to aid reassembly. Marks

should be located on the same side of the rod and cap as the cylinder location. Cylinders are numbered 1-2-3-4 on the starboard (left) side, 5-6-7-8 on the port (right) side.

9. Remove the nuts holding the connecting rod cap. Lift off the cap, together with the lower bearing insert. See **Figure 52**.

NOTE
*If the connecting rod caps are difficult to remove, tap the studs with a handle of a hammer or similar tool. See **Figure 53**.*

10. Use the handle of a hammer to push the piston and connecting rod from the cylinder bore. Be sure to remove the bearing insert. See **Figure 54**.

11. Remove the piston rings with a ring remover (**Figure 55**).

12. Repeat Steps 9-11 for all remaining piston/connecting rods.

Piston Pin Removal/Installation

The piston pins are a press fit in the bores of the connecting rods and a light hand fit in the pistons (**Figure 56**). Do not press the piston pin from the connecting rod unless removal is required. Removal requires the use of a support stand, special removal/installation tool and an arbor press. This is a job for a trained and equipped dealership or machine shop. The piston pin is matched to the piston and the piston and pin are only available as an assembly.

It is important to assemble the piston and connecting rod correctly as described in this chapter. Incorrect assembly will cause serious damage to the engine.

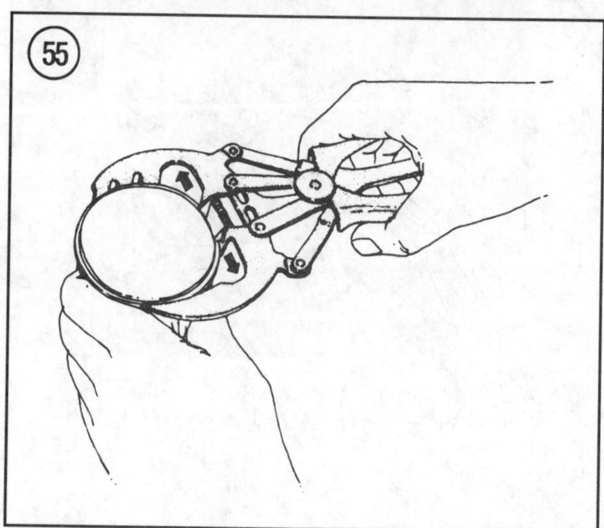

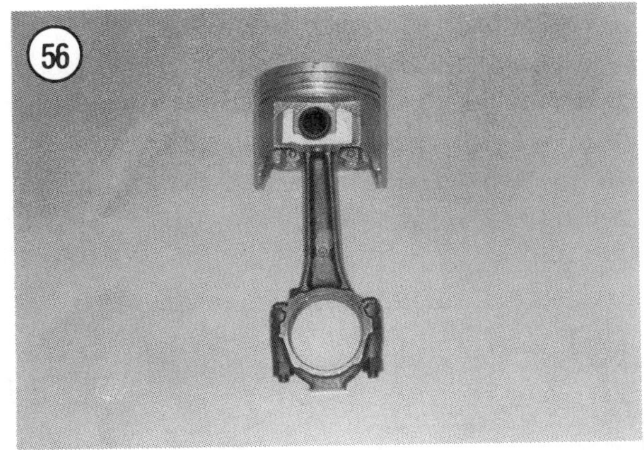

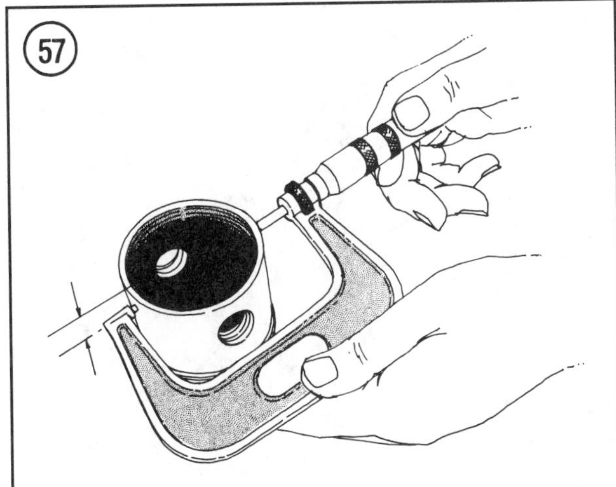

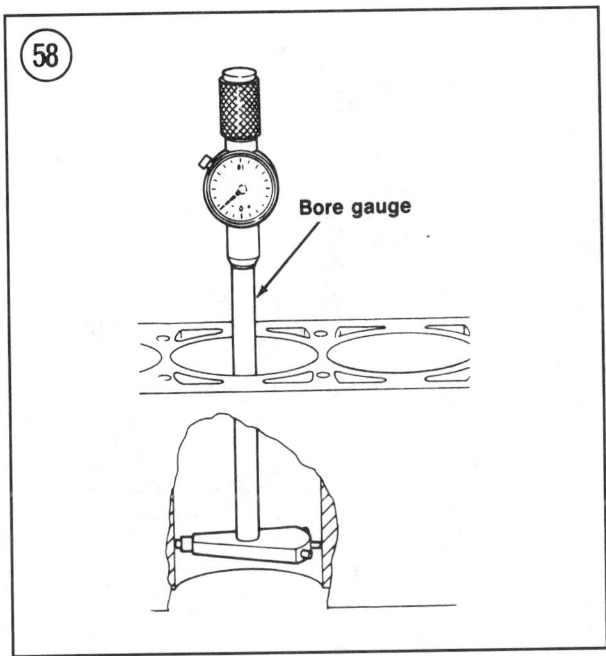

Piston Clearance Check

Precision measuring equipment and training in its use is required to check this clearance. If you are not properly equipped and trained, have this procedure done at a machine shop.

1. Measure the piston diameter with a micrometer (**Figure 57**) just below the rings at a right angle to the piston pin bore.
2. Measure the cylinder bore diameter with a bore gauge (**Figure 58**). **Figure 59** shows the points of normal cylinder wear. If the diameter at the top of the ring travel (A, **Figure 59**) exceeds the diameter at the bottom part of the cylinder (B, **Figure 59**) by more than 0.003 in.(0.076 mm), the cylinder must be rebored and an oversize piston/ring assembly installed.
3. Subtract the piston diameter from the largest cylinder bore reading. If it exceeds the specification in **Table 1**, the cylinder must be rebored and an oversized piston installed.

8

NOTE

Obtain the new piston and measure it to determine the correct cylinder bore oversize diameter.

Piston Ring Fit/Installation

Check the ring the gap of each piston ring. Check gap of new rings, because if the gap is too small the rings will break.

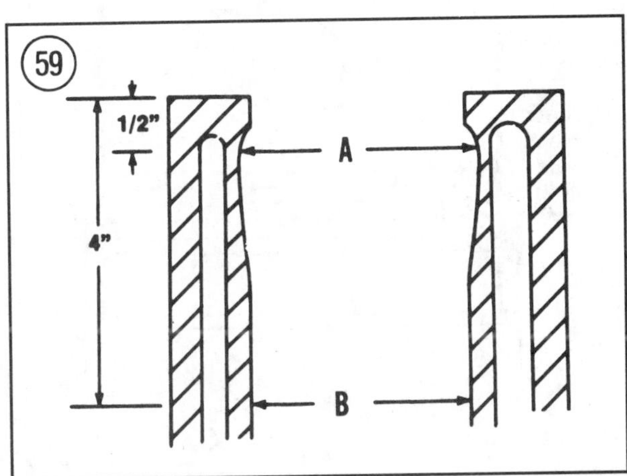

1. Position the ring at the bottom of the ring travel area and square it by moving it gently with an inverted piston. See **Figure 60**.

NOTE
If the cylinders have not been rebored, check the gap at the bottom of the ring travel, where the cylinder is least worn.

2. Measure the end gap of each ring in the cylinder with a feeler gauge as shown in **Figure 61**. Compare the gap with the specifications listed in **Table 1**. Gaps should never be more than 1/32 in. (0.8 mm).
3. If the gap is less than the minimum specification, make sure the rings are correct for the size of the cylinder bore. The ends of new rings can be filed to increase the gap slightly. See **Figure 62**.
4. If the end gap measured in Step 2 is too wide the wrong rings may be installed or the ends of the rings may have been filed too much. If the gap is within specification at the bottom but is too wide at the top of the ring travel, the cylinder is excessively worn (tapered).
5. Check the side clearance of the rings in the grooves as shown in **Figure 63**. Place the feeler gauge alongside the ring all the way into the groove (**Figure 63**). If the measurement is not within specification (**Table 1**), either the rings or the ring grooves are worn.

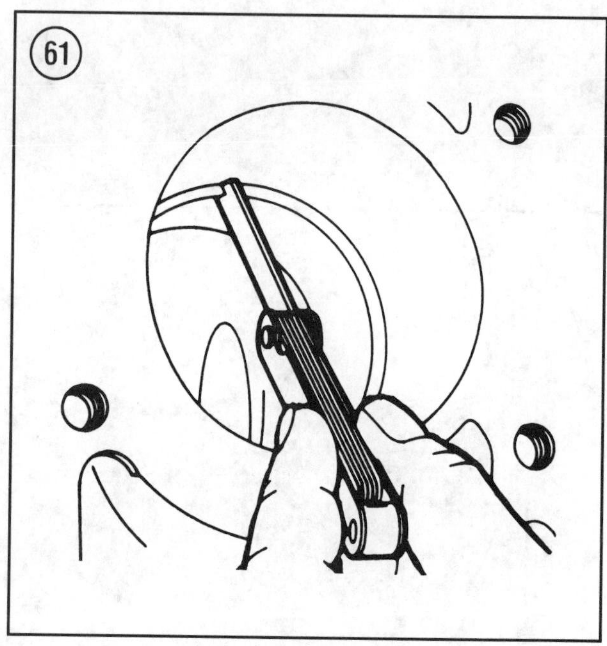

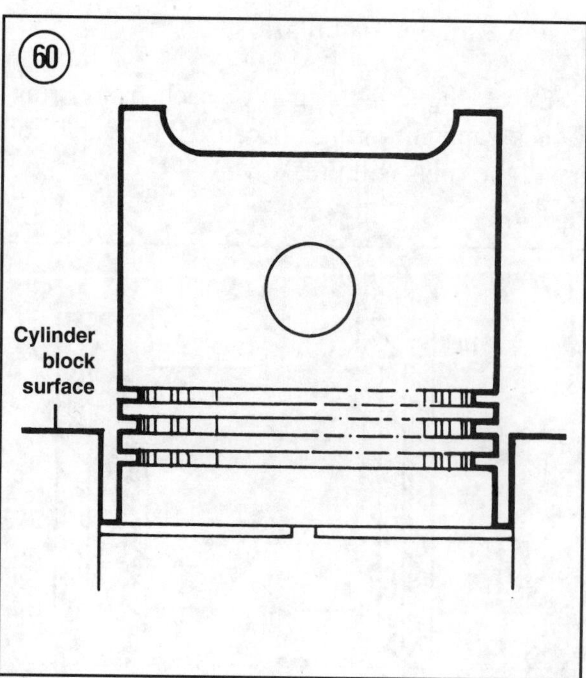

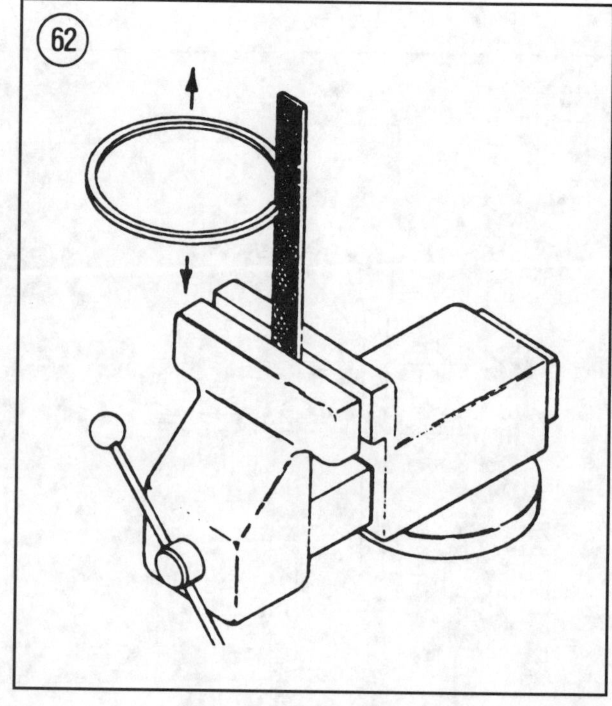

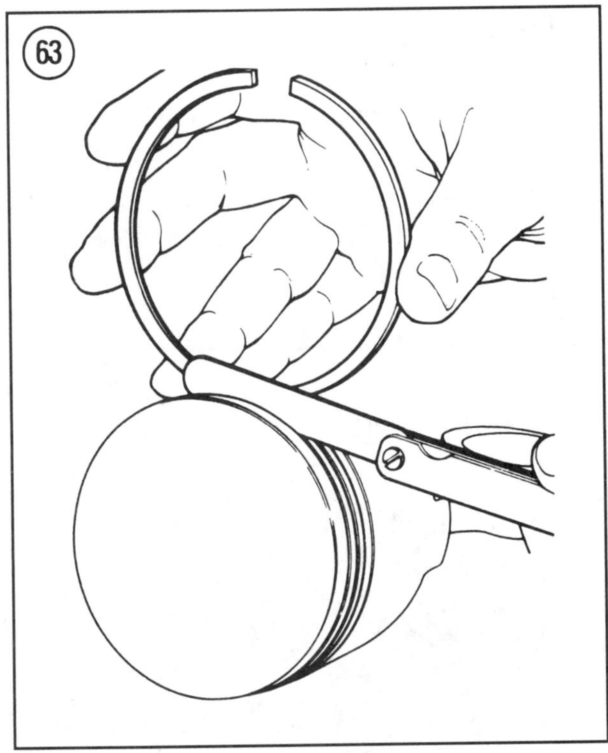

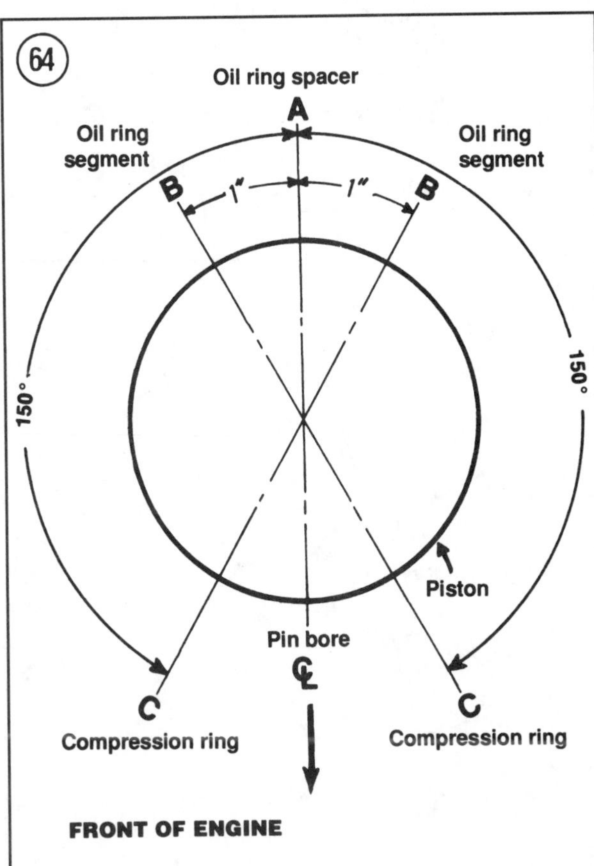

6. Install the oil ring in the lower groove of the piston before installing compression rings. Each oil ring consists of 3 segments.
   a. Install the oil ring expander in the lower groove.
   b. Hold the expander with the ends butted (*not overlapped*) and install 1 of the rails at the top of the expander. The end of the rail must be at least 1 in. (25.4 cm) from the gap in the spacer.
   c. Install the second rail at the bottom of the spacer. The end of the rail should be at least 1 in. (25.4 cm) from the gap in the spacer on the first (top) rail. See B, **Figure 64**.
   d. Make sure the lower ring is assembled correctly and moves freely. It should compress into the groove without binding.
7. Use a ring expander (**Figure 65**) and carefully install the second compression ring. The top of each compression ring is marked and the mark must face toward the top of the piston.
8. Use a ring expander (**Figure 65**) and carefully install the top compression ring. The top of each compression ring is marked and the mark must face toward the top of the piston.
9. Move the end gaps of the second and top compression rings if necessary to correctly position the ring gaps as shown (C, **Figure 64**).

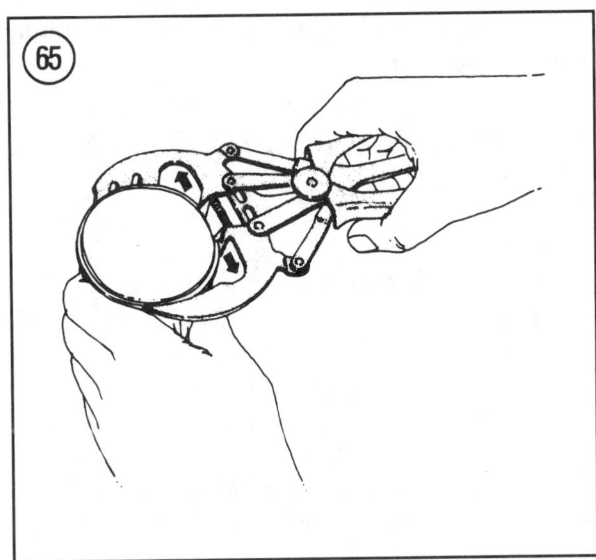

Connecting Rod Inspection

Have the connecting rods checked for straightness at a dealership or machine shop. When installing new connecting rods, have them checked for misalignment before installing the piston and piston pin. Connecting rods can spring out of alignment during shipping or handling.

Piston/Connecting Rod Assembly

The pistons *must* be assembled correctly to the connecting rods or the engine will be damaged. The piston pin hole may be offset and the top of the piston may have clearance slots, notches or relief pockets to allow clearance for the valves to operate. Additionally, the small relief hole between the connecting rod and cap provides lubrication for the camshaft and this hole must face toward the camshaft. Assembling the piston and connecting rod incorrectly will result in serious engine damage.

On all models, the notch cast in the edge of the piston (**Figure 66**) should either be toward the front of the engine or toward the engine valley. If valve relief notches are only on 1 side of the piston (**Figure 66**) or if 1 valve notch is of much larger radius than the other, the large or single valve notch must face toward the center (intake side) of the engine.

The side of the connecting rod and cap marked with the cylinder numbers face outward. See **Figure 66**.

Connecting Rod Bearing Clearance Measurement

CAUTION
Make sure the bearing bore and bearing insert are both clean. If even the smallest piece of dirt is between the bearing insert and the bearing bore, the clearance will be affected.

1. Install the upper half of the bearing insert in the connecting rod.
2. Install the lower half of the bearing insert in the connecting rod cap.
3. Cut a piece of Plastigage the width of the bearing (**Figure 67**) and place the piece *across* the crankpin journal.

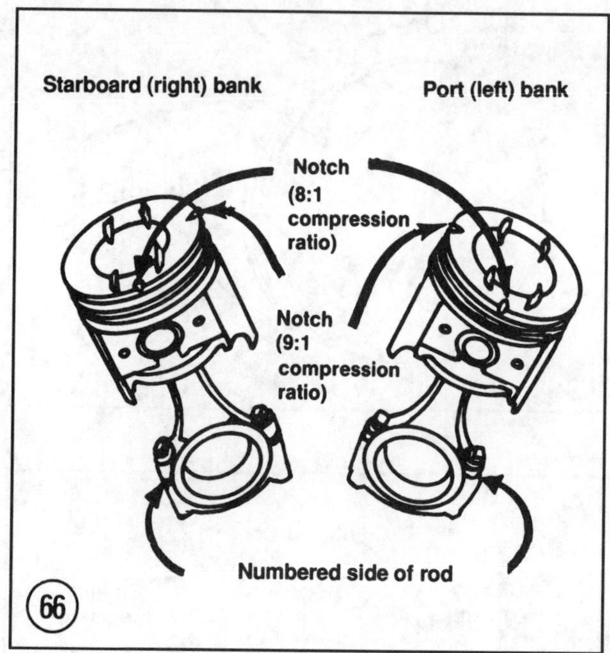

66

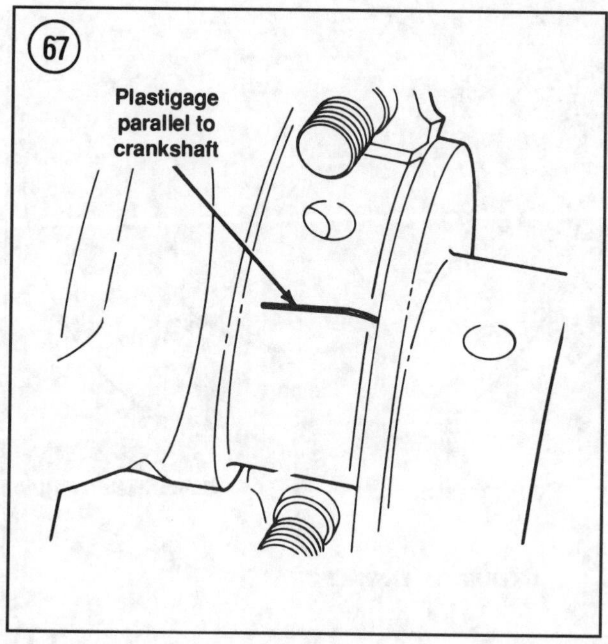

67

NOTE
In Steps 4-6, be careful not to turn (move) the crankshaft until the rod cap has been removed. Turning will smear the Plastigage and make accurate measurement impossible. Also, place the Plastigage on a flat surface of the crankpin, not across the oil hole.

4. Position the connecting rod and bearing against the connecting rod journal and install the cap assembly. Make sure the rod is assembled correctly and installed on the correct journal.
5. Tighten the connecting rod retaining screws to the torque specified in **Table 2**. Do not rotate the crankshaft while the Plastigage is in place.
6. Remove the nuts retaining the connecting rod cap, then lift the cap off. The flattened Plastigage may either stick to the crankpin journal or the bearing insert.
7. Determine the bearing clearance by comparing the width of the flattened Plastigage with the markings on the Plastigage envelope. See **Figure 68**.
8. Compare the bearing clearance with the specification listed in **Table 1**.
9. If the clearance is excessive, the crankshaft must be machined to a smaller size and undersize bearings fitted. Consult with your dealership or machinist.
10. Refer to the preceding steps and measure the clearance for the remaining connecting rod bearings.

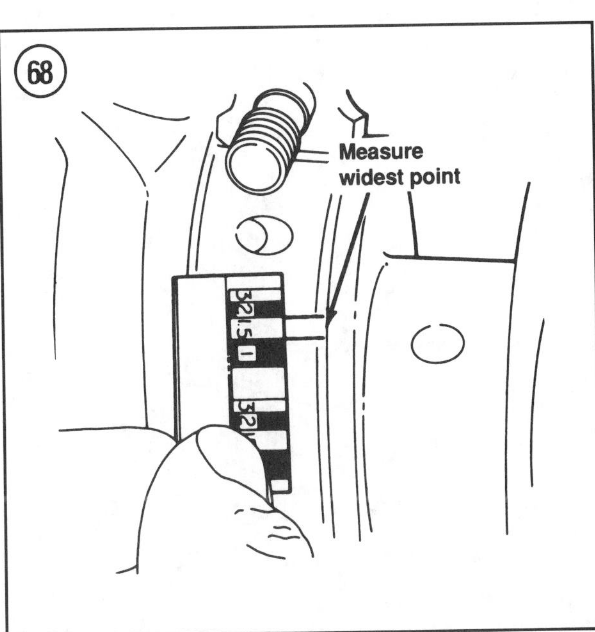

Piston/Connecting Rod Installation

1. Make sure the pistons are attached to the connecting rods correctly for the cylinder in which they are being installed. Refer to *Piston/Connecting Rod Assembly* in this chapter. On all engines, the connecting rod bearing tangs must face toward the outside of the engine.

NOTE
The pistons must be assembled to the connecting rods differently, depending upon the position in which it will be installed. If 2 assemblies appear to be incorrect, they may be switched and belong in the other location.

2. Make sure the ring gaps are positioned as described in *Piston Ring Fit/Installation* in this chapter.

NOTE
If the special protector tubes are not available, short sections of hose can be fitted to the rod bolts in a similar way.

3. Slip special rod protector tubes (available from parts and tool suppliers) over the connecting rod screws to help guide them into position and keep them from damaging the crankpin journals.
4. Coat the cylinder bore, rings and piston liberally with clean engine oil. The entire piston can be immersed in oil to ensure adequate lubrication.
5. Compress the piston rings using a suitable ring compressor. Be sure to space the ring end gaps evenly around the piston.

CAUTION
Be careful not to damage the piston rings while installing the connecting rod and piston assembly. It is sometimes difficult to buy a single ring. The crankpin can also be easily damaged by hitting 1 of the bolts against a polished bearing journal.

6. Insert the piston and connecting rod assembly into the correct cylinder bore. Align the lower end of the connecting rod with the crankshaft crankpin.

NOTE
Some mechanics protect the crankshaft journal by wrapping it before installing the connecting rod and piston assembly. Special protector wraps made of plastic that curl around the journal are available from some tool and parts suppliers. A similar type of protection is possible by wrapping a piece of thin plastic or card stock (paper) around the journal. Hold this in place with a short piece of tape while assembling. Be careful not to allow any adhesive to stick to the journal.

CAUTION
Do not let any part of the connecting rod or the bolts hit the crankpin when installing the piston and rod assemblies. The polished surface of the crankpin can be easily damaged by the connecting rod.

7. Push the piston and rings into the cylinder. Most mechanics use the handle of a hammer to push the piston into the cylinder. See **Figure 69**.
8. Remove the hoses or protector tubes from the connecting rod bolts and make sure the threads are clean.
9. Clean the connecting rod bearing inserts and bore in the connecting rod and cap, then install the bearing insert halves. Make sure the inserts are properly seated.
10. Lubricate the crankpin and connecting rod bearings liberally with clean engine oil.
11. Seat the crankpin firmly against the connecting rod bearing and insert. Make sure the insert is still correctly positioned in the connecting rod.
12. Install the connecting rod cap and install the retaining nuts.

NOTE
Make sure the bearing tangs on the rod and cap are both on the same side. Also, make sure the pistons are installed correctly.

13. Tighten the cap retaining nuts to the torque specified in **Table 2**.
14. Check the connecting rod big-end side play as described under *Piston/Connecting Rod Removal* in this chapter.
15. Repeat the preceding steps for each of the remaining rod and piston assemblies.

REAR MAIN OIL SEAL

Replacement

The 1-piece rear main seal is pressed into the rear of the engine block. The seal can be removed

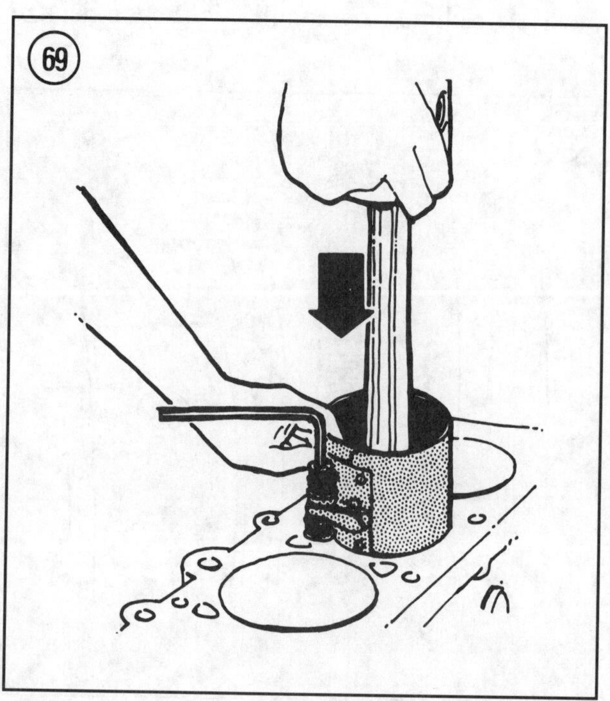

and replaced without removing the oil pan or the rear main bearing cap. Replace the seal as follows.

1. Remove the engine from the boat as described in this chapter.
2. Remove the engine coupler and flywheel from the engine.
3. Remove the starter motor as described in Chapter Eleven.
4. Unbolt and remove the flywheel cover from the rear of the engine.

CAUTION
Be extremely careful not to damage the seal surface of the crankshaft when removing the seal in Step 5.

5. Carefully punch a hole in the metal of the seal with an awl or punch, then use a slide hammer and screw to pull the seal from its bore.
6. Thoroughly clean the seal bore and the sealing surface of the crankshaft.
7. Lubricate the seal lip with engine oil or grease.

NOTE
Use seal installer part No. T-82L-6701-A for 5.0 L (302 cid) engines. Use seal installer part No. T-65P-6701-A for 5.8 L (351 cid) engines.

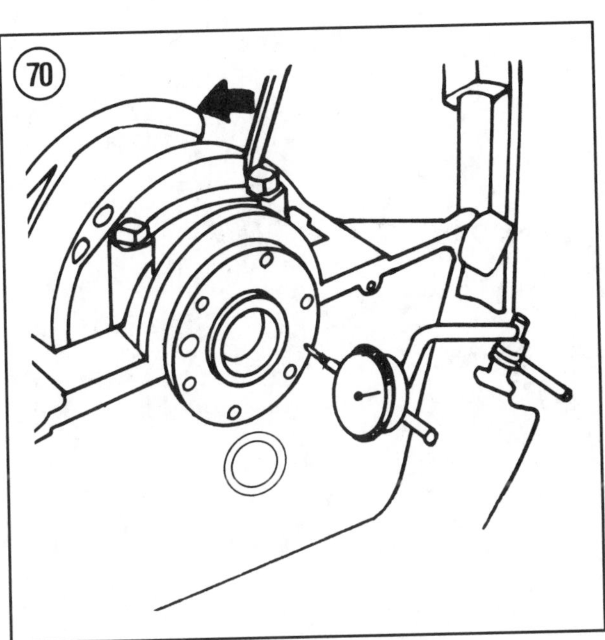

8. Position the seal with its lip facing toward the engine (inward). Use the proper seal installer and carefully push the new seal into the cylinder block/bearing cap bore. Make certain the seal is not cocked. The rear face of the seal should be within 0.005 in. (0.127 mm) of the rear face of the block surface on 5.0 L (302 cid) engines. On 5.8 L (351 cid) engines, the seal installing tool should bottom against the block.
9. Install the flywheel cover and tighten the retaining screws to the torque listed in **Table 2**.
10. Install the starting motor as described in Chapter Eleven and tighten the attaching screws to the torque listed in **Table 2**.
11. Install the flywheel, engine coupler and bellhousing as described in this chapter. Refer to **Table 2** for tightening torques.
12. Install the engine into the boat as described in this chapter.

CRANKSHAFT

End Play Measurement

1. Pry the crankshaft to the front of the engine with a pry bar or large screwdriver.
2. Attach a dial indicator to the rear of the engine block, as shown in **Figure 70**, with its contact point resting against the crankshaft flange. The indicator axis should be parallel with the crankshaft axis.
3. Set the dial indicator to zero. Force the crankshaft forward as far as possible and observe end play measured by the dial indicator.
4. Compare the end play with the specification listed in **Table 1**.
5. If the end play is excessive, replace the center main bearing. If less than specified, check the bearing faces for dirt or imperfections.

Removal

Refer to **Figure 71**, typical for this procedure. It is not necessary to remove the cylinder heads and pistons, but often these parts are removed as part of an overhaul before removing the crankshaft. If these parts are already removed some of the following procedures will have already been accomplished.

1. Remove the engine from the boat as described in this chapter.

2. Remove the flywheel as described in this chapter.

3. Mount the engine on an engine stand, if available.

4. Remove the starter motor. See Chapter Eleven.

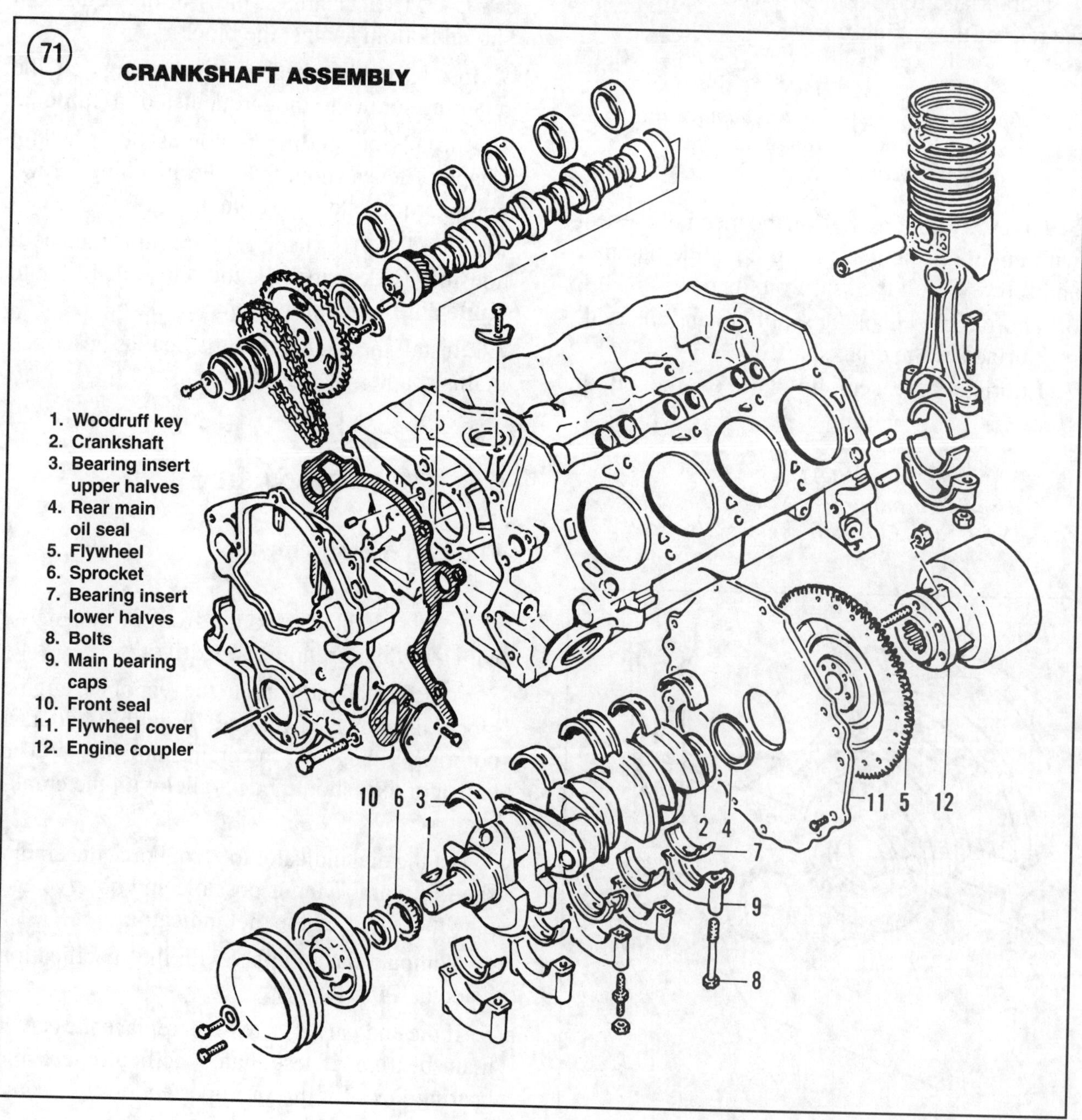

5. Unbolt and remove the flywheel cover (11, **Figure 71**) from the rear of the engine block.
6. Invert the engine so the oil pan is at the top.
7. Remove the oil pan and oil pump as described in this chapter.
8. Remove the harmonic balancer, front cover and timing chain as described in this chapter.
9. Remove the spark plugs to allow the crankshaft to turn easily.
10. Measure crankshaft end play as described in this chapter.
11. Rotate the crankshaft until the connecting rods of 1 journal are easily accessible.

NOTE
Mark each connecting rod and its cap with the cylinder number to aid reassembly. Place the marks on the same side of the rod and cap as the cylinder location. Cylinders are numbered 1-2-3-4 on the starboard (left) side, 5-6-7-8 on the port (right) side.

12. Remove the nuts holding the connecting rod cap. Lift off the cap, together with the lower bearing insert.

NOTE
If the connecting rod caps are difficult to remove, tap the studs with a handle of a hammer or similar tool.

13. Use the handle of a hammer to push the piston and connecting rod into the cylinder bore away from the crankshaft. Be sure to remove the bearing insert from the connecting rod.
14. Repeat Steps 11-13 for each remaining piston/rod assembly.
15. Clean the main bearing caps and check for numbers identifying the location of each cap and an arrow on each indicating the front of the engine. If you cannot find the marks, mark the caps so that each can be reassembled in the correct location with the proper side of the cap toward the front. See **Figure 72**, typical.
16. Unbolt and remove the main bearing caps and bearing inserts. See **Figure 73**.

NOTE
If the caps are difficult to remove, lift the bolts partway out, then lever the bolts from side to side.

17. Carefully lift the crankshaft from the engine block and place it on a clean workbench.
18. Remove the bearing inserts from the block. Place the bearing caps and inserts in order on a clean workbench.

8

Inspection

1. Clean the crankshaft thoroughly with solvent. Blow out the oil passages with compressed air.
2. Check the main and connecting rod journals for wear, scratches, grooves, scoring or cracks. Check the oil seal surface for burrs, nicks or other sharp edges which might damage the seal during installation.

NOTE
Unless you have precision measuring equipment and know how to use it, have a machine shop perform Step 3.

3. Check all journals (**Table 1**) for out-of-roundness and taper. See **Figure 74**. Have the crankshaft reground, if necessary, and install new underside bearing inserts.

Main Bearing Clearance Measurement

Measure main bearing clearance using Plastigage. Follow the same procedure as used to measure connecting rod bearing clearance. See *Connecting Rod Bearing Clearance Measurement* in this chapter.

Main bearings 0.001 and 0.002 in. undersize may be available to accommodate small amounts of crankshaft journal wear.

Installation

Refer to **Figure 71**, typical for this procedure.

1. Install the upper halves of the main bearing inserts in the cylinder block. Oil holes in the bearing inserts must align with oil passages in the block, and the tabs on the inserts must seat in the slots machined in the block.

NOTE
Check all bolts for thread damage before reuse. If damaged, replace the bolts.

2. Lubricate the bolt threads with clean engine oil.
3. Install the main bearing inserts in each cap and lubricate the bearings liberally.

CAUTION
Be careful not to bump the connecting rod or main bearing surfaces of the crankshaft while installing the crankshaft. If the connecting rods are not removed, it may be difficult to keep the protruding studs from hitting the journals while installing the crankshaft. Special rod protector tubes (available from parts and tool suppliers) should be slipped over the connecting rod screws to help guide them into position and keep them from damaging the crankpin journals. If the special protector tubes are not available, short sections of hose can be fitted to the rod bolts in a similar way.

4. Carefully lower the crankshaft into position in the block.
5. Install the bearing caps in their marked positions with the arrows pointing toward the front of the engine. See **Figure 72**.
6. Use the following procedure to align the crankshaft thrust surfaces of the rear main bearing.

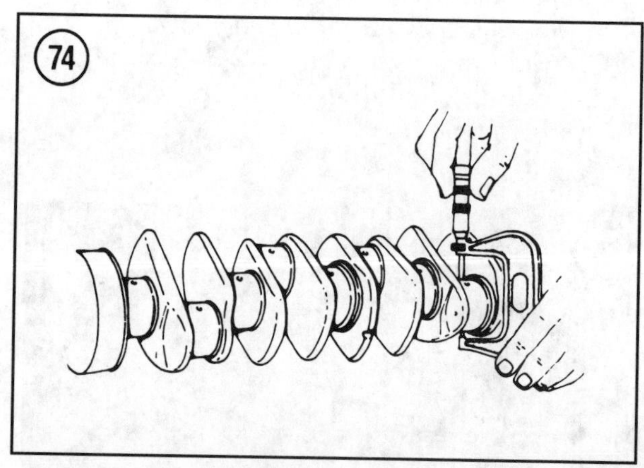

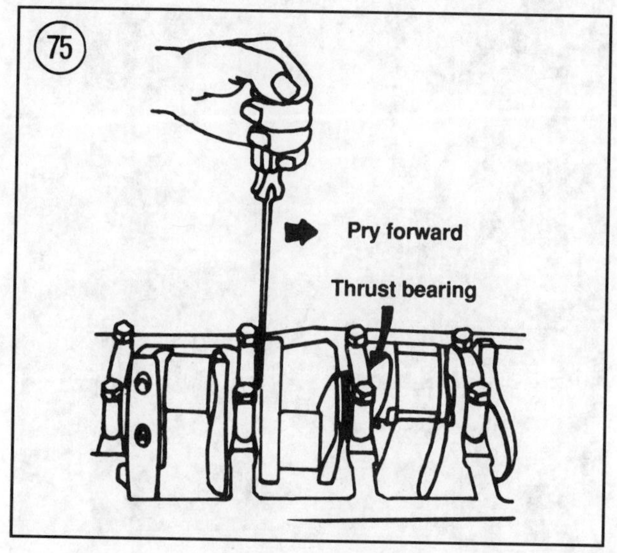

a. Install all the main bearing cap bolts, then tighten the bolts finger-tight.

b. Next tighten the main bearing bolts, except the center cap, to the specification in **Table 2**.

c. Pry the crankshaft forward against the thrust surface of the upper half of the center main bearing. See **Figure 75**.

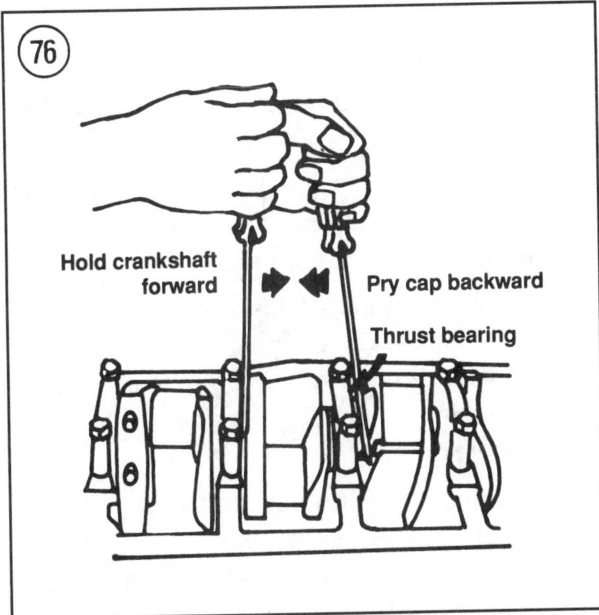

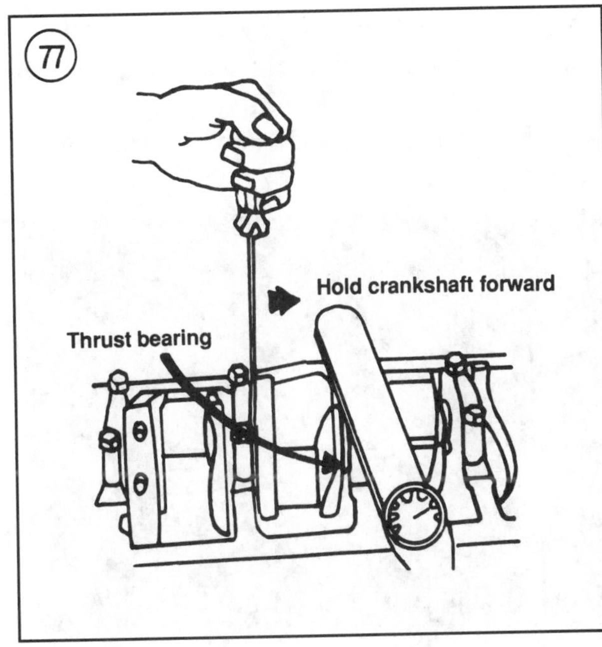

d. Hold the crankshaft in this position (forward) and pry the center main bearing cap toward the rear to align the thrust surfaces of both halves of the bearing insert. See **Figure 76**.

e. Continue to hold the crankshaft forward and tighten the screws attaching the center main bearing cap to the torque listed in **Table 2**. See **Figure 77**.

7. Retighten all main bearing caps to the torque listed in **Table 2**.

8A. If the connecting rods are removed, proceed as follows:

a. Rotate the crankshaft to make sure it turns smoothly.

b. If any binding is noticed, remove the main bearing caps and make sure the bearings are clean, properly installed and the correct size.

c. Refer to *Piston/Connecting Rod Installation* in this chapter to install the connecting rod bearing inserts and attach the connecting rods to the crankshaft.

d. Rotate the crankshaft to make sure it turns smoothly.

e. If any binding is noticed, remove the connecting rod bearing caps and make sure the bearings are clean, properly installed and the correct size. Correct any problems before continuing assembly.

8B. If the connecting rods and pistons were not removed, proceed as follows:

a. Refer to *Piston/Connecting Rod Installation* in this chapter to install the connecting rod bearing inserts and attach the connecting rods to the crankshaft.

b. Rotate the crankshaft to make sure it turns smoothly.

c. If any binding is noticed, remove the bearing caps and make sure that all of the main and rod bearings are clean, properly installed and the correct size. Correct any problems before continuing assembly.

9. Reverse Steps 1-9 of *Removal* in this chapter. Refer to **Table 2** for tightening torques.
10. Install a new rear main bearing oil seal as described in this chapter.

DRIVE COUPLER AND FLYWHEEL

Removal/Installation

1. Remove the engine from the boat as described in this chapter.
2. Unbolt the flywheel and coupler from the crankshaft. Remove the bolts gradually in a diagonal pattern.
3. To install, align the dowel hole in the flywheel with dowel in the crankshaft flange and position the flywheel on the studs.
4. Fit the coupler on the studs. Install the washers and locknuts. Tighten the nuts to the torque specified in **Table 2**.
5. Install a dial indicator on the machined surface of the flywheel and check runout. If runout exceeds 0.008 in. (0.20 mm), remove the flywheel and check for burrs on the crankshaft and flywheel mating surfaces. If none are found, replace the flywheel.
6. Reinstall the engine in the boat as described in this chapter.

Inspection

1. Visually check the flywheel for cracks or other damage.
2. Check the condition of the splines and cushion hub of the coupling.
3. Inspect the ring gear for cracks, broken teeth or excessive wear. If the ring gear teeth are damaged, check the starter motor drive teeth for similar wear or damage. If the flywheel ring gear is damaged, it can be removed and replaced at a machine shop.

CYLINDER BLOCK

Cleaning and Inspection

1. Before cleaning the cylinder block, check it for evidence of fluid leakage. Identify possible problem areas such as leaking plugs, gaskets or cracks. Examine these areas further while cleaning and after cleaning.
2. Clean the block thoroughly. Some cleaning procedures are facilitated by removing plugs from passages.
   a. Clean all gasket or RTV sealant residue from the machined surfaces.
   b. Check all core plugs (**Figure 78**, typical) for leaks and replace any that are suspect. See *Core Plug Replacement* in this chapter.
   c. Check coolant passages for sludge, dirt and corrosion while cleaning. If the passages are very dirty, have the block boiled out at a machine shop. Blow out all passages with compressed air.
   d. Remove plugs from oil passages to permit a more thorough cleaning. Check oil passages for sludge, dirt and corrosion while cleaning. If the passages are very dirty, have the block boiled out at a machine shop. Blow out all passages with compressed air.
   e. Check the threads in the head bolt holes to be sure they are clean. If dirty, use a tap to clean the threads and remove any deposits.

3. Examine the block for cracks. If cracked, the block must be repaired or replaced. A machine shop will be able to confirm suspicions about possible cracks. Another method is as follows:

a. Mix 1 part of kerosene with 2 parts engine oil.

b. Dissolve zinc oxide in wood alcohol.

c. Coat the suspected area with the mixture of kerosene and oil, then wipe the area dry.

d. Immediately apply the solution of zinc oxide and wood alcohol.

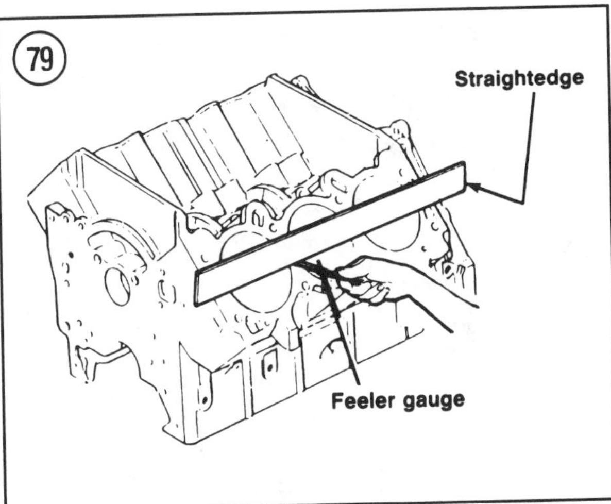

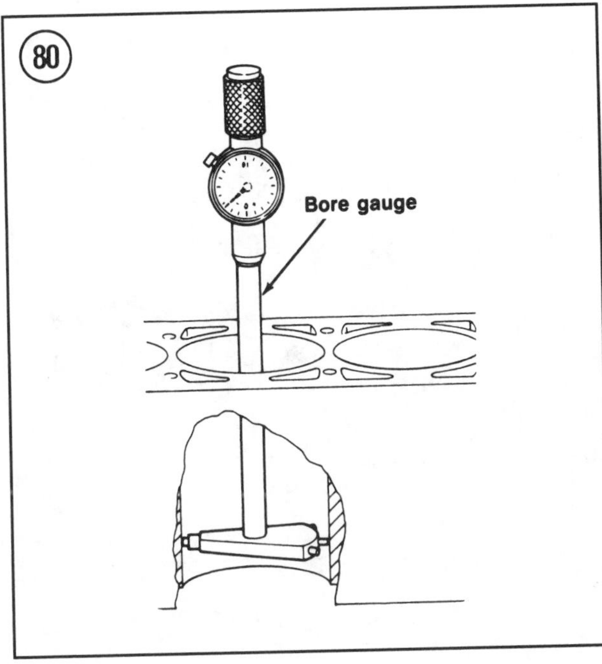

e. A crack will appear as discoloration in the zinc oxide treated area.

4. Check the cylinder block deck (top surface) for flatness. Place an accurate straightedge on the block. If there is any gap between the block and straightedge, measure it with a flat feeler gauge (**Figure 79**, typical). Measure from end to end and from corner to corner. Have the block resurfaced if it is warped more than 0.004 in. (0.102 mm).

5. Measure cylinder bores with a bore gauge (**Figure 80**) for out-of-roundness or excessive wear as described in *Piston Clearance Check* in this chapter. If the cylinders exceed maximum tolerances, they must be rebored. Reboring is also necessary if the cylinder walls are badly scuffed or scored.

NOTE

*Before boring, install all main bearing caps and tighten the cap bolts to the specification in **Table 2**.*

CORE PLUG REPLACEMENT

Check the condition of all core plugs in the block (**Figure 78**) and cylinder head whenever the engine is out of the boat for service. If any signs of leakage or corrosion are found around 1 core plug, replace them all.

NOTE

Core plugs can be replaced inexpensively at a machine shop. If you are having machine work done on the engine, have the core plugs replaced at the same time.

Removal/Installation

CAUTION

Do not drive core plugs into the engine casting. It will be impossible to retrieve them and they can restrict coolant circulation, resulting in serious engine damage.

1. Tap the bottom edge of the core plug with a hammer and drift. Use several sharp blows to push the bottom of the plug inward, tilting the top out (**Figure 81**).
2. Grip the top of the plug firmly with pliers. Pull the plug from its bore (**Figure 82**) and discard.

NOTE

Core plugs can also be removed by drilling a hole in the center of the plug and prying them out with an appropriate size drift or pin punch. On large core plugs, the use of a universal impact slide hammer is recommended.

3. Clean the plug bore thoroughly to remove all traces of the old sealer. Inspect the bore for any damage that might interfere with proper sealing of the new plug. If damage is evident, true the surface by boring for the next oversize plug.

NOTE

Oversize plugs can be identified by an OS stamped in the flat on the cup side of the plug.

4. Coat the inside diameter of the plug bore and the outer diameter of the new plug with sealer. Use an oil-resistant sealer if the plug is to be installed in an oil gallery or a water-resistant sealer for plugs installed in the water jacket.
5. Install the new core plug with an appropriate size core plug replacer tool (**Figure 83**), driver or socket.

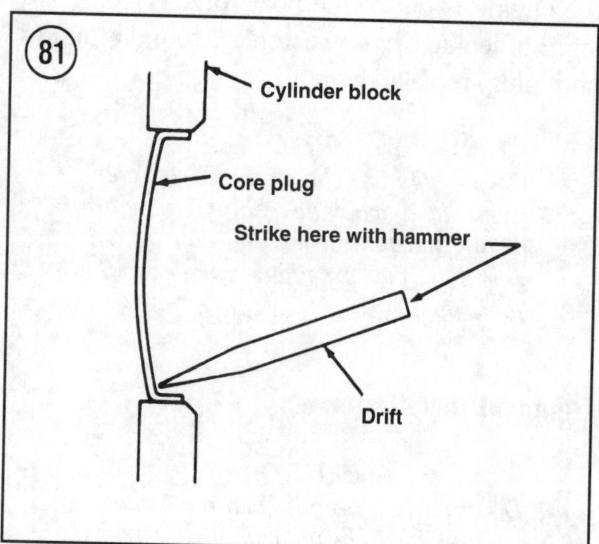

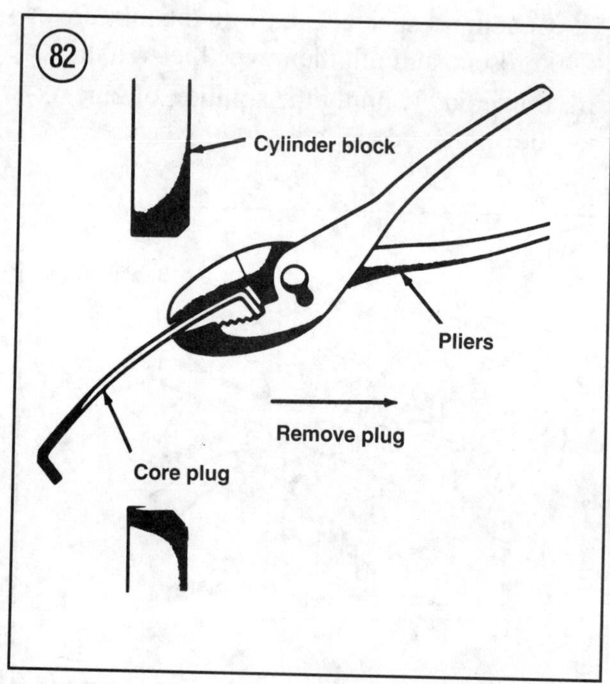

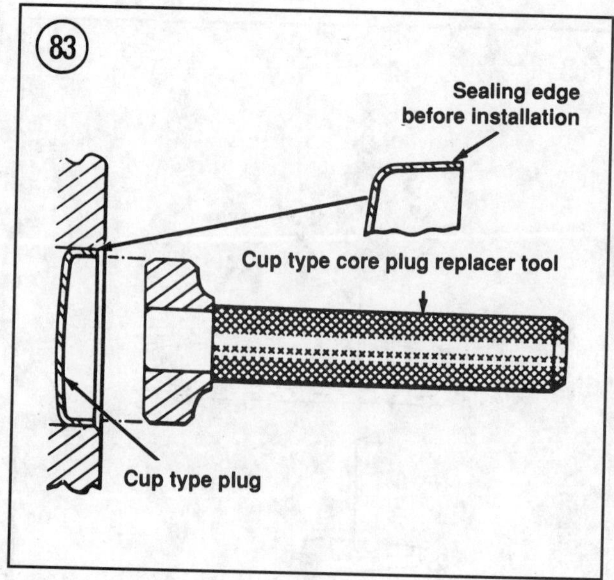

Table 1 ENGINE SPECIFICATIONS
5.0 AND 5.8 L (302 AND 351 cid) V8 MODELS

Type	5.0 L (302 cid) V8 cylinder	5.8 L (351 cid) V8 cylinder
Displacement	302 cid (5.0 L)	351 cid (5.8 L)
Bore	4.000 in. (101.6 mm)	4.000 in. (101.6 mm)
Stroke	3.000 in. (76.20 mm)	3.500 in. (88.90 mm)
Cylinder numbering (front to rear)		
Port	5-6-7-8	5-6-7-8
Starboard	1-2-3-4	1-2-3-4
Firing order[1]	1-3-7-2-6-5-4-8	1-3-7-2-6-5-4-8
Camshaft		
End play (axial)		
Production	0.001-0.007 in. (0.025-0.18 mm)	0.001-0.007 in. (0.025-0.18 mm)
Service limit	0.009 in. (0.23 mm)	0.009 in. (0.23 mm)
Bearing clearance		
Production	0.001-0.003 in. (0.025-0.076 mm)	0.001-0.003 in. (0.025-0.076 mm)
Service limit	0.006 in. (0.15 mm)	0.006 in. (0.15 mm)
Journal diameter		
No. 1 (front)	2.0805-2.0815 in. (52.845-52.870 mm)	2.0805-2.0815 in. (52.845-52.870 mm)
No. 2	2.0655-2.0665 in. (52.464-52.489 mm)	2.0655-2.0665 in. (52.464-52.489 mm)
No. 3	2.0505-2.0515 in. (52.083-52.108 mm)	2.0505-2.0515 in. (52.083-52.108 mm)
No. 4	2.0355-2.0365 in. (51.702-51.727 mm)	2.0355-2.0365 in. (51.702-51.727 mm)
No. 5 (rear)	2.0205-2.0215 in. (51.321-51.346 mm)	2.0205-2.0215 in. (51.321-51.346 mm)
Maximum out-of-round	0.005 in. (0.13 mm)	0.005 in. (0.13 mm)
Lobe lift		
Intake		
Production	0.2600 in. (6.604 mm)	0.2780 in. (7.061 mm)
Service limit	0.2550 in. (6.477 mm)	0.2730 in. (6.934 mm)
Exhaust		
Production	0.2780 in. (7.061 mm)	0.2830 in. (7.188 mm)
Service limit	0.2730 in. (6.934 mm)	0.2780 in. (7.061 mm)
Maximum timing chain deflection	0.5 in. (12.7 mm)	0.5 in. (12.7 mm)
Connecting rod		
Bearing clearance		
Production	0.0008-0.0015 in. (0.020-0.038 mm)	0.0008-0.0015 in. (0.020-0.038 mm)
Service limit	0.0008-0.0025 in. (0.020-0.063 mm)	0.0008-0.0025 in. (0.020-0.063 mm)
Side play		
Desired	0.010-0.020 in. (0.25-0.51 mm	0.010-0.020 in. (0.25-0.51 mm)
Service limit	0.023 in. (0.58 mm)	0.023 in. (0.58 mm)
Crankshaft		
Crankpin diameter		
Production	2.1228-2.1236 in. (53.919-53.939 mm)	2.3103-2.3111 in. (58.682-58.702 mm)
Maximum taper	0.0006 in. (0.015 mm)	0.0006 in. (0.015 mm)
Maximum out-of-round	0.0006 in. (0.015 mm)	0.0006 in. (0.015 mm)

(continued)

8

Table 1 ENGINE SPECIFICATIONS
5.0 AND 5.8 L (302 AND 351 cid) V8 MODELS (continued)

Type	5.0 L (302 cid) V8 cylinder	5.8 L (351 cid) V8 cylinder
Crankpin diameter (continued)		
End play (axial).	0.002-0.008 in. (0.05-0.20 mm)	0.002-0.008 in. (0.05-0.20 mm)
Main bearing clearance		
No. 1 (front), production	0.0001-0.0015 in. (0.002-0.038 mm)	0.0008-0.0015 in. (0.002-0.038 mm)
Service limit	0.0001-0.0020 in. (0.002-0.051 mm)	0.0008-0.0026 in. (0.020-0.066 mm)
Other main bearings, production	0.0005-0.0015 in. (0.013-0.038 mm)	0.0008-0.0015 in. (0.020-0.038 mm)
Service limit	0.0005-0.0024 in. (0.013-0.061 mm)	0.0008-0.0026 in. (0.020-0.066 mm)
Main journal diameter	2.2482-2.4490 in. (57.104-62.205 mm)	2.9994-3.0002 in. (76.185-76.205 mm)
Oil pump		
Relief spring pressure	10.6-12.2 lb. @ 1.7 in. (47-54 N @ 43.2 mm)	18.2-20.2 lb. @ 2.49 in. (81-90 N @ 63.2 mm)
Relief valve clearance	0.0015-0.0030 in. (0.038-0.076 mm)	0.0015-0.0030 in. (0.038-0.076 mm)
Drive shaft clearance	0.0015-0.0030 in. (0.038-0.076 mm)	0.0015-0.0030 in. (0.038-0.076 mm)
Rotor end clearance	0.001-0.004 in. (0.025-0.10 mm)	0.001-0.004 in. (0.025-0.10 mm)
Outer race/housing clearance	0.001-0.004 in. (0.025-0.10 mm)	
Piston clearance		
Production	0.0018-0.0026 in. (0.046-0.066 mm)	0.0018-0.0026 in. (0.046-0.066 mm)
Piston pin diameter	0.9120-0.9123 in. (23.165-23.172 mm)	0.9120-0.9123 in. (23.165-23.172 mm)
Fit in connecting rod	interference fit	
Fit in piston	0.0002-0.0004 in. (0.005-0.010 mm)	0.0002-0.0004 in. (0.005-0.010 mm)
Piston rings		
End gap		
Top compression	0.010-0.020 in. (0.25-0.51 mm)	0.010-0.020 in. (0.25-0.51 mm)
Second compression	0.010-0.020 in. (0.25-0.51 mm)	0.010-0.020 in. (0.25-0.51 mm)
Oil control (bottom ring)	0.015-0.055 in. (0.38-1.40 mm)	0.015-0.055 in. (0.38-1.40 mm)
Side clearance		
Compression rings	0.002-0.004 in. (0.05-0.10 mm)	0.002-0.004 in. (0.05-0.10 mm)
Valves		
Face angle	44°	44°
Seat angle	45°	45°
Seat width	0.060-0.080 in. (1.52-2.03 mm)	0.060-0.080 in. (1.52-2.03 mm)

(continued)

Table 1 ENGINE SPECIFICATIONS 5.0 AND 5.8 L (302 AND 351 cid) V8 MODELS (continued)

Type	5.0 L (302 cid) V8 cylinder	5.8 L (351 cid) V8 cylinder
Valves (continued)		
Clearance, with lifter colapsed[2]		
Desired	0.096-0.165 in. (2.43-4.19 mm)	0.123-0.173 in. (3.12-4.39 mm)
Service limit	0.071-0.193 in. (1.80-4.90 mm)	0.098-0.198 in. (2.49-5.03 mm)
Valve guides		
Bore diameter	0.3433-0.3443 in. (8.720-8.745 mm)	0.3433-0.3443 in. (8.720-8.745 mm)
Valve stem clearance		
Intake	0.0010-0.0027 in. (0.025-0.069 mm)	0.0010-0.0027 in. (0.025-0.069 mm)
Exhaust	0.0015-0.0032 in. (0.038-0.081 mm)	0.0015-0.0032 in. (0.038-0.081 mm)
Valve springs		
Free length		
Intake	2.056 in. (52.22 mm)	2.056 in. (52.22 mm)
Exhaust	1.877 in. (47.68 mm)	1.877 in. (47.68 mm)
Installed height		
Intake	1.78 in. (45.21 mm)	1.78 in. (45.21 mm)
Exhaust	1.60 in.[3] (40.6 mm)	1.60 in.[3] (40.6 mm)
Pressure		
Intake valve closed	74-82 lb. @ 1.78 in. (329-365 N @ 45.2 mm)	74-82 lb. @ 1.78 in. (329-365 N @ 45.2 mm)
Intake valve open	194-214 lb. @ 1.15 in. (863-952 N @ 29.2 mm)	194-214 lb. @ 1.15 in. (863-952 N @ 29.2 mm)
Exhaust valve closed	71-79 @ 1.33	71-79 @ 1.33
Exhaust valve open	195-215 @ 1.15	195-215 @ 1.15

1. Other 5.0L and 5.8L engines have also been manufactured with firing order of 1-3-7-2-6-5-4-8.
2. Refer to text for procedure.
3. Distance from pad to retainer.

8

Table 2 TIGHTENING TORQUES 5.0 L AND 5.8 L (302 AND 351 cid) V8 MODELS

	N·m	ft.-lb.
Camshaft sprocket	55-61	40-45
Circulating (coolant) pump		
Mounting	17-24	12-18
Pulley	19-27	14-20
Connecting rod		
5.0 L (302 cid)	26-33	19-24
5.8 L (351 cid)	54-61	40-45
Crankshaft pulley	30-43	22-32
Cylinder head[1]		
5.0L (302 cid)		
First step	33.8-47.4	25-35
Second step	61.0-74.5	45-55
Third step	an additional 1/4 turn	an additional 1/4 turn

(continued)

Table 2 TIGHTENING TORQUES 5.0 L AND 5.8 L (302 AND 351 cid) V8 MODELS (continued)

	N·m	ft.-lb.
Cylinder head[1] (continued)		
5.8 L (351 cid)		
First step	129.143	95-105
Second step	143-151	105-112
Distributor clamp	23-34	17-25
Engine mounts		
Front		
Top nut	68-95	50-70
Mount to block	43-54	32-40
Bolt	81-102	60-75
Rear		
Center screw to square nut	60-71	44-52
Lock nuts	38-40	28-30
Mount plate to transom	27-34	20-25
Exhaust elbow to manifold	16-24	12-18
Flywheel and coupler		
Nut	54-61	40-45
Stud	14-20	10-15
Flywheel cover	6.7-9.5	5-7
Flywheel housing	38-49	28-36
Fuel pump	24-27	18-20
Main bearing caps		
5.0 L (302 cid)	81-95	60-70
5.8 L (351 cid)	129-142	95-105
Manifold		
Exhaust to cylinder head	27-35	20-26
Intake to cylinder head	31-34	23-25
Upper manifold (Fi & FSi)	16-24	12-18
Oil pressure sender	14-19	10-14
Oil pump cover	8-16	6-10
Oil pump to block	30-43	22-32
Oil tube bracket	30-43	22-32
Oil tube to pump	14-20	10-15
Oil pan		
1/4 × 20	12-15	9-11
5/16 × 18	12-15	9-11
Oil withdrawl tube nut	20-24	15-18
Power steering pump bracket		
Nut	18-20	13-15
Screw	35-41	26-30
Raw water pump bracket	17-24	12-18
Rocker arm	24-34	18-25
Rocker arm (valve) cover	4-6	35-53 in.-lb.
Spark plugs	14-20	10-15
Starter motor	33-41	24-30
Bracket	22-26	16-19
Thermostat housing	16-22	12-16
Throttle body (Fi & FSi)	16-24	12-18
Vibration damper	95-122	70-90
Water outlet housing	14-20	10-15
Water temperature sender	24-30	18-22

1. Refer to the text for tightening instructions.

Chapter Nine

Fuel Delivery Systems

On models equipped with a conventional carburetor, the fuel delivery system consists of the fuel tank(s), a water-separating fuel filter (some models), a fuel pump, connecting lines or hoses and the carburetor. Fuel stored in the tank(s) is moved through the lines and various components to the carburetor by a fuel pump. The carburetor mixes air with the fuel and delivers that mixture to the engine intake. The amount of fuel mixed with air in the carburetor is controlled by various mechanical and vacuum devices. Some adjustment of the fuel/air ratio is possible, but the manufacturer designs and selects components and settings that will deliver the optimum fuel/air ratio.

On models with electronic fuel injection, the fuel delivery system includes the fuel tank(s), filters, fuel lines and a pump(s) that moves the fuel to the electronic fuel injectors.

Several different systems are used on these models, but all use electrical components to determine the needs of the engine, then control the amount of fuel that is delivered to the engine. The ignition system may also be incorporated with the fuel system for a complete, balanced engine control system. In normal operation, the electronic fuel injection systems used on these engines are reasonably trouble free, but many of the sensitive electrical components are easily and quickly damaged by improper testing and service procedures. If problems occur, special equipment and training is necessary to determine the proper corrective action. If problems are encountered and the electronic fuel system is suspected, it should be tested and serviced by properly trained and equipped technicians.

Many fuel system malfunctions (both carburetor and injection) are caused by the fuel used. Using the proper type of fresh, good quality fuel and storing it properly, together with regular maintenance of all fuel filters will reduce fuel system problems. Refer to Chapter Four.

FLAME ARRESTOR

All Volvo Penta engines are equipped with a flame arrestor (**Figure 1**, typical). A flame arrestor cover may also be designed to protect the distributor from water and provide some trim for the engine.

Removal/Installation

1. Remove the engine compartment cover or hatch and move it out of the way.
2. Remove any interfering covers from the engine.
3. Disconnect the crankcase vent hose(s) (A, **Figure 2**) from the flame arrestor.

NOTE
On some models, the flame arrestor may be clamped to the air intake horn. On these models, loosen the clamp to remove the flame arrestor.

4. Remove the nut (B, **Figure 2**) holding the flame arrestor and cover, if so equipped, to the air intake horn or carburetor.
5. Remove the cover, flame arrestor screen and gasket (if used) from the air intake horn or carburetor.
6. Installation is the reverse of removal.

Cleaning

CAUTION
Gasoline presents an extreme fire hazard and should never be used as a cleaning solvent. Many good cleaning solvents are available from local suppliers that will remove residue from the flame arrestor screen. Select a cleaner that will not damage the parts. Always follow the solvent manufacturer's directions.

1. Remove the flame arrestor as described in this chapter.
2. Submerge the flame arrestor in a container of clean solvent for several minutes to let the solution penetrate residue. 3. Slosh the flame arrestor in the solvent container and resubmerge for a few minutes.
4. Remove the flame arrestor from the solvent and allow it to drain, then blow dry with compressed air.
5. If the air inlet screen is deformed in any way, replace the flame arrestor.
6. Reinstall the flame arrestor.

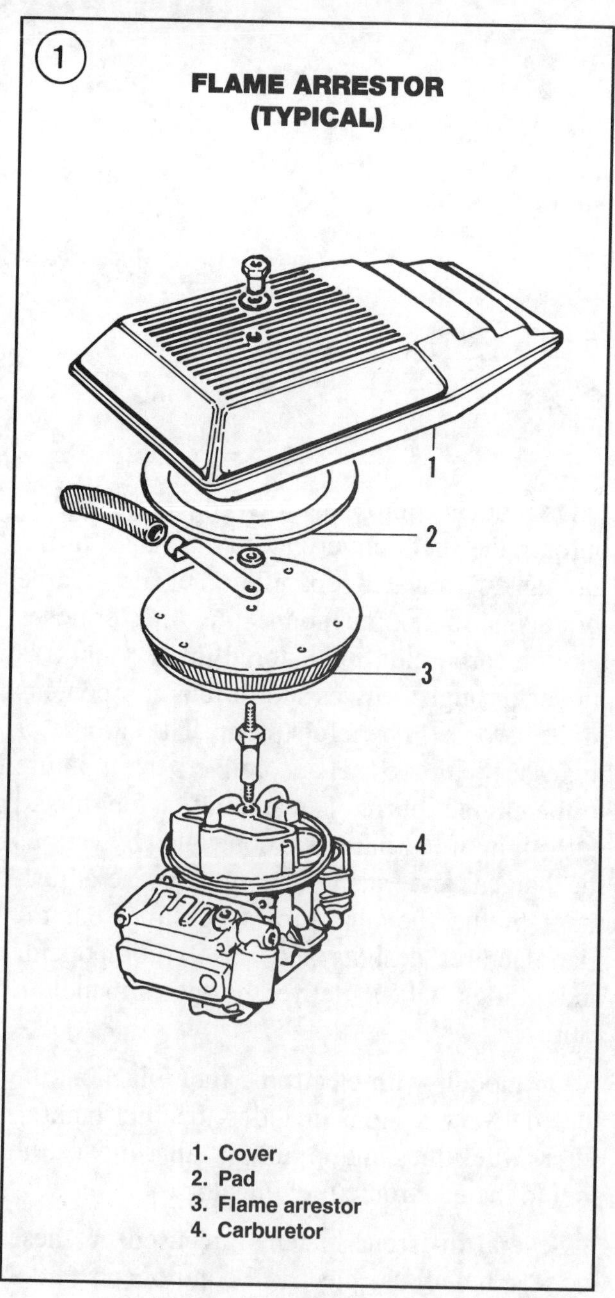

FUEL QUALITY

Sour Fuel

Fuel plays a large role in satisfactory engine performance. In temperate climates, fuel will start to break down after it has been in the fuel tank a few months. When this happens, it forms a gum-like substance that settles to the bottom of the tank where it can clog the in-tank filter. If drawn out of the tank by the fuel pump, this substance will affect the other fuel filters. It will also start to clog the jets and other small passages inside the carburetor or fuel injection system.

You should drain the fuel tank whenever the boat will not be in service for a period of time. The gasoline can be used in an automobile without harm, since it will be burned within a few days. If it is not possible or desirable to drain the tank, the use of gasoline stabilizer is recommended to prevent the fuel from spoiling. Regular use of this additive is also recommended to prevent corrosion and gum formation in the fuel system.

Gasohol

As mentioned in Chapter Four, some gasoline sold for marine use may contain alcohol, although this fact may not be advertised. Using such fuel is not recommended, unless you can determine the nature of the blend. Marine manufacturers suggest that the following precautions be observed if gasohol must be used.

1. Buy fuel only as needed and use it as soon as possible.
2. Do not spill gasohol on painted surfaces.
3. Expect a slight decrease in power, stalling at lower speeds and somewhat greater fuel consumption.
4. Alternate the use of gasohol with regular unleaded gasoline. If it is necessary to operate an engine on gasohol, do not store such fuel in the tank(s) for more than a few days, especially in climates with high humidity.
5. Numerous problems have been identified with the use of improperly blended or stored alcohol/gasoline fuels. Some of the most important problems are:
   a. Corrosion formation on the inside of fuel tanks and steel fuel lines.
   b. Corrosion formation inside carburetor (zinc and aluminum alloys are especially susceptible).
   c. Deterioration and failure of synthetic rubber or plastic materials such as O-ring seals, diaphragms, accelerator pump cups and gaskets.
   d. Premature failure of fuel hoses.

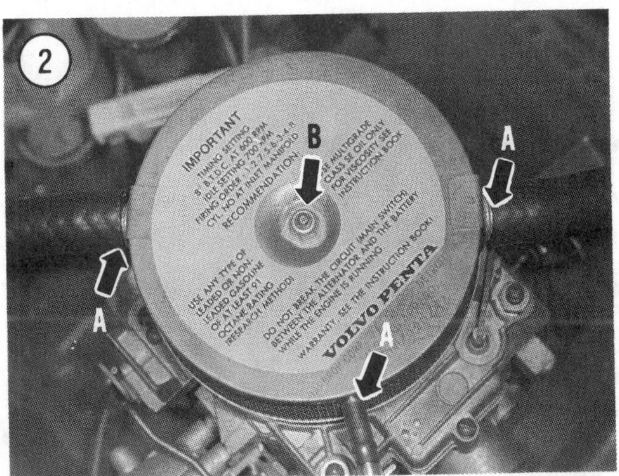

CARBURETOR FUNDAMENTALS

A gasoline engine must receive fuel and air mixed in precise proportions to operate efficiently at various loads and speeds. Carburetors are designed to maintain these fuel/air proportions while providing for sudden acceleration and increased loads.

A mixture with too much fuel is said to be too *rich*. One with too little fuel is said to be too *lean*. Incorrect mixture proportions can result from a variety of factors such as a dirty flame arrestor, defective choke, improperly adjusted idle mixture or speed screws, a leaking needle valve or a float that has absorbed fuel.

The choke valve in a carburetor provides a richer than normal mixture of fuel and air until the engine warms up. If the choke valve sticks in an open position, the engine will not start properly. A choke that sticks in a closed position will cause a flooding condition.

The throat of a carburetor is sometimes called a *barrel*. A single-barrel (1-bbl.) carburetor has only one throat. Two-barrel carburetors have 2 throats and 2 complete sets of metering devices. A 4-barrel carburetor has 4 throats and 4 complete sets of metering devices.

CARBURETORS

During the years covered by this manual, the following carburetors have been used:

a. Holley 2-bbl.

b. Holley 4-bbl.

Removal, overhaul and installation procedures are provided for these carburetor models.

WARNING
Carburetors used on these engines are designed for marine use. Although they may appear to be identical to carburetors installed on automobiles, their internal components are not the same. Automotive carburetors are externally vented and will allow fuel vapor to enter the bilge. Marine carburetors are internally vented to prevent this dangerous situation from occurring. Even the gaskets used in marine carburetors differ from those used in automotive applications. Any fuel vapor that is allowed to escape will create a fire or explosion hazard. Use only NMMA marine-approved parts.

Carburetor specifications may vary with type and model year. Calibration may be changed during production and subsequent modifications may be made to suit an individual boating application. The necessary specifications are provided on instruction sheets accompanying overhaul kits, along with any specific procedures required for adjustment. The specifications provided in **Table 1** should be used only if the overhaul kit instruction sheet is not available.

The carburetor model identification may be stamped on the carburetor air horn casting or on a tag attached to the carburetor (**Figure 3**). This information and the year and model of the engine is necessary to obtain the proper overhaul kit from your dealer.

Carburetor Removal/Installation

1. Remove the flame arrestor as described in this chapter. If the carburetor uses a spacer on the

3

4

flame arrestor mounting stud, remove and store it where it will not be lost.

2. Close the fuel tank supply valve, if so equipped.

3. Place a container under the fuel line connection to catch any spillage. Disconnect the fuel line from the carburetor. See **Figure 4**, typical. Use one wrench to hold the fuel inlet nut while you loosen the fuel line fitting nut with a second wrench. Cap the line and fitting to prevent leakage and the entry of contamination.

4. Remove and discard any tie straps holding hoses, vacuum lines or electrical wiring to the carburetor.

5. Disconnect the wires (**Figure 5**) for the electric choke heater from the carburetor.

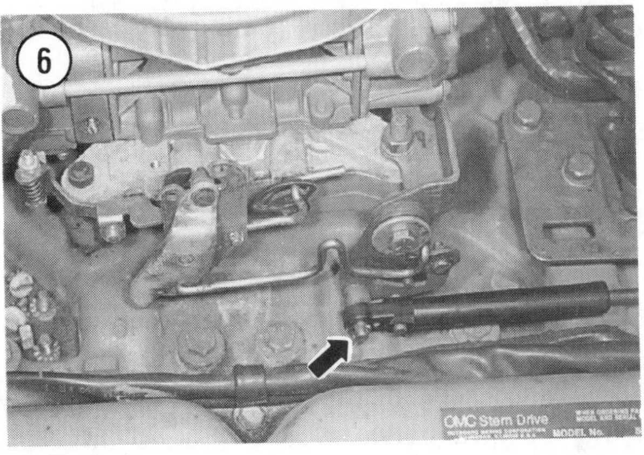

6. Detach the crankcase ventilation hose, if so equipped, from the carburetor.

7. Disconnect the throttle linkage from the carburetor (**Figure 6**).

8. Check for any other hoses or wires connected to the carburetor and disconnect any that will prevent removal.

9. Remove the fasteners attaching the carburetor to the intake manifold. Remove the lockwashers, then lift the carburetor from the manifold.

10. Cover the opening in the intake manifold to prevent small parts or anything else from falling into the opening. A clean cloth can be stuffed into the opening or the opening can be covered with tape.

11. Before installing the carburetor, clean all gasket residue from the intake manifold and carburetor mating surfaces.

12. Position a new gasket between the carburetor and the manifold, then install the carburetor.

13. To prevent warpage of the carburetor base, tighten the fasteners in a crisscross pattern until snug, then tighten to the torque listed in **Table 2**.

Preparations for Overhaul

Before removing and disassembling any carburetor, be sure you have the proper marine carburetor overhaul kit, a sufficient quantity of fresh carburetor cleaner and the proper tools. Work slowly and carefully. *Don't try to hurry or take short-cuts.* Follow the disassembly and assembly procedures. Refer to the exploded drawing of your carburetor when necessary. Do not apply excessive force at any time.

It is not necessary to disassemble the carburetor linkage or remove linkage adjusting screws when overhauling a carburetor. Solenoids, dashpots and other diaphragm-operated assist devices attached to the carburetor body should be removed, because carburetor cleaner will damage them. Clean such parts using a suitable aerosol carburetor cleaner and dry with compressed air or wipe dry with a cloth.

Use a carburetor holding fixture or similar device to prevent damage to the throttle plate(s) while working on the carburetor. If a holding fixture is not available, thread a nut onto each of four 2-1/4 in. bolts. Install a bolt into each mounting hole, then thread a second nut onto the bolt to clamp it to the carburetor mounting flange. These bolts will hold the carburetor up, allowing clearance for the throttle plates, and serve the same purpose as a holding fixture.

CAUTION

Do not use the carburetor-to-manifold gasket supplied in any overhaul, gasket or repair kit unless it is specifically designed for marine application. Current carburetor kits available from Volvo Penta contain the correct gasket. If using a kit provided by a different manufacturer, order the correct mounting gasket from your Volvo Penta dealer.

Inspection and Overhaul

Dirt, varnish, gum, water, carbon or other contamination in or on the carburetor are often the cause of unsatisfactory performance. Gaskets and accelerating pump cups or diaphragms may swell or leak, resulting in carburetion problems. Efficient carburetion depends upon careful cleaning, inspection and proper installation of new parts.

The new gaskets and parts provided in a marine carburetor overhaul kit should be installed when overhauling the carburetor and the old parts discarded. Automotive carburetor kits should not be used. The gaskets included in automotive overhaul kits may allow the carburetor to vent fuel vapors directly into the engine compartment. Any external venting of vapors presents a fire and explosion hazard.

WARNING

Be extremely careful about getting any of the cleaning solvent in your eyes or on your body. Study the manufacturer's cautions carefully and be prepared to perform countermeasures immediately as directed by the manufacturer.

The outside of some carburetors is painted and the inside of some carburetors is coated with a substance designed to reduce porosity of the carburetor castings and prevent corrosion. If this internal coating is removed, the carburetor will be prone to corrosion which will clog the passages. Do not use any cleaner strong enough to remove either the external paint or the internal coating. If it does, carburetor performance will probably be unsatisfactory when reinstalled on the engine.

CAUTION

Many good carburetor cleaning solutions are available from parts and tool suppliers, but you must exercise caution when selecting and using any cleaning solvent. Some solvents are too harsh and can erode, dissolve, etch or otherwise damage even the metal parts of these carburetors. Select the solvent carefully and follow its manufacturer's instructions. If you suspect that it is too harsh and might cause damage, it probably will.

If you are unsure, an aerosol type carburetor cleaner and a clean brush is probably the safest cleaning method. If a commercial carburetor cleaning solvent is used and the parts are to be submerged in the solution, it should be weak enough so that it will not remove the external paint or internal coating. If parts are submerged, do not leave them in the carburetor cleaner longer than necessary to loosen the gum and dirt.

Do not immerse the throttle body on Holley carburetors in carburetor cleaning solution. The Delrin cam for the accelerator pump cam and the Teflon bushings for the throttle shafts will be damaged by most commercial solvents.

Rinse cleaned parts with hot water as directed by the manufacturer of the cleaning solvent. Blow all parts dry with compressed air. Wipe all parts which cannot be immersed in solvent (such as diaphragms, solenoids and dashpots) with a soft cloth slightly moistened with solvent. Then use a clean, dry cloth on the parts. Force compressed air through all passages in the carburetor.

Do not use a wire brush to clean any part of a carburetor. Do not use a drill or wire to clean any opening or passage in the carburetor. A drill or wire may enlarge the orifice or passage and change the calibration. If the carburetor passages are so clogged that cleaning as described with solvent will not clear them, replace the carburetor.

Check the choke and throttle plate shafts for grooves, wear or excessive looseness or binding. Inspect the choke and throttle plates for nicked edges or burrs which prevent proper closure. Choke and throttle plates are correctly positioned during production and should not be removed unless damaged.

Clean all gasket residue from the air horn, main body and throttle body sealing surfaces carefully. The soft metal castings of the carburetor are easily nicked or gouged by sharp cleaning instruments.

Inspect all components for cracks or warpage. Check floats for wear on the lip and hinge pin. Check hinge pin holes in the air horn, bowl cover or float bowl for wear and elongation. Check composition floats for fuel absorption by gently squeezing and applying fingernail pressure. If moisture appears, replace the float. Replace the float if the arm needle contact surface is grooved. If the float or floats are serviceable, gently polish the needle contact surface of the arm with crocus cloth or steel wool. Replace the float if the shaft is worn.

NOTE

Some gasolines contain additives that will cause the Viton tip of the fuel inlet needle to swell. This problem is also caused by gasoline and alcohol blends. If carburetor problems are traced to a deformed inlet needle tip, change brands of gasoline used.

Check the Viton tip of the fuel inlet needle for swelling or distortion. Discard the needle if the overhaul kit contains a new needle for assembly.

Replace all screws and nuts that have stripped threads. Replace all distorted or broken springs. Inspect all gasket mating surfaces for nicks or burrs.

Reassemble all parts carefully. It should not be necessary to apply force to any parts. If force seems to be required, you are doing something wrong. Stop and refer to the exploded drawing for your carburetor that is included in the overhaul kit.

Holley 2-bbl. Disassembly

Refer to **Figure 7**, typical for this procedure.

NOTE

Use a carburetor holding fixture or 4 screws and nuts to provide legs for the carburetor mounting flange as described in Preparations for Overhaul in this chapter. The throttle plates and linkage may be easily bent or damaged if precautions are not taken during service.

1. Attach the carburetor mounting flange to a service jig.
2. Remove the screws attaching the fuel bowl and metering block (52 and 71, **Figure 7**) to the main body, then remove the float bowl and metering block. Install new gaskets when reassembling. See **Figure 8**.
3. Turn the idle mixture adjustment needles (66 and 73, **Figure 7**) in (clockwise) and count the number of turns from the original position until the screw is lightly seated. Record this original setting for each screw, then remove the idle air screw, by turning it counterclockwise.
4. Remove the main jets (67 and 70, **Figure 7**) using a wide blade screwdriver. **Figure 9** shows the location of the jets.
5. Loosen the power valve (**Figure 10**) using a properly fitting wrench, then remove the valve and discard the gasket.

7

HOLLEY 2-BBL. CARBURETOR

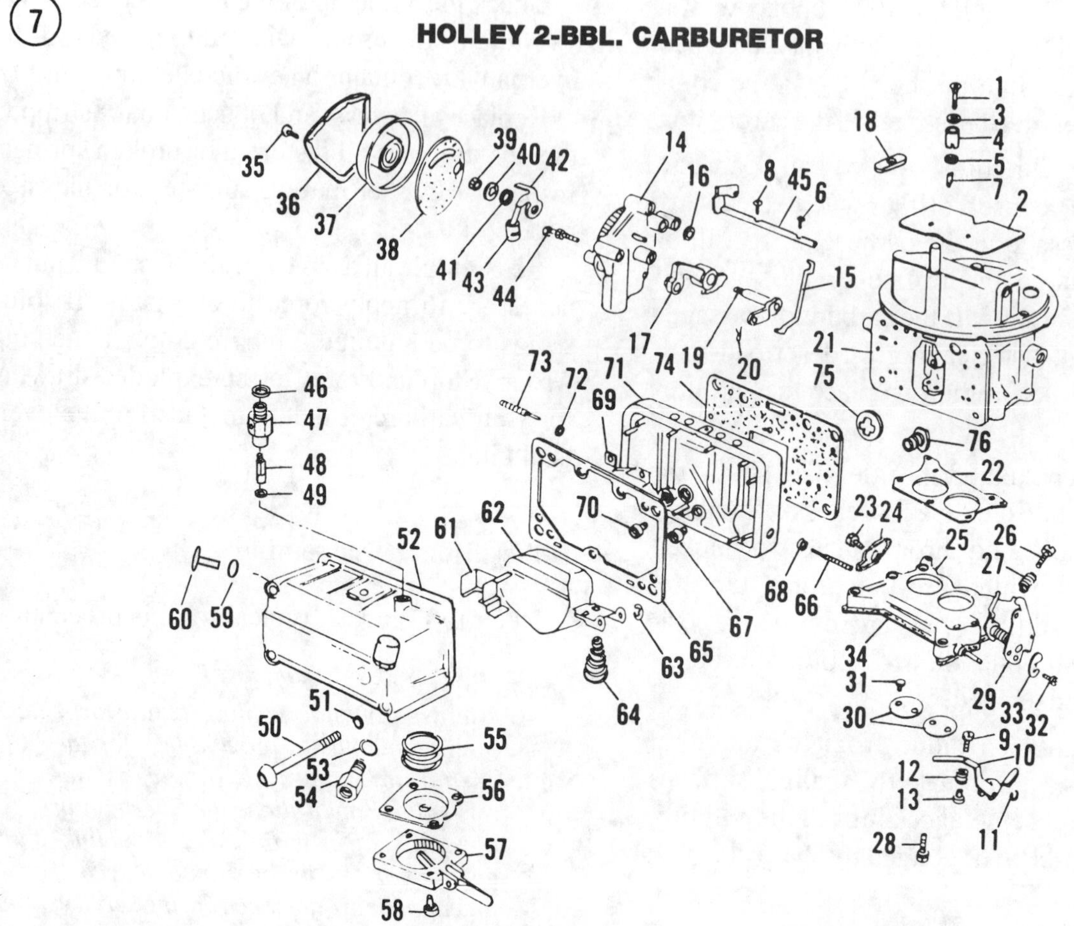

1. Screw
2. Choke plate
3. Gasket
4. Accelerating pump discharge nozzle
5. Gasket
6. Screw
7. Accelerating pump discharge needle
8. Screw
9. Screw
10. Accelerating pump operating lever
11. Retainer
12. Spring
13. Sleeve nut
14. Choke housing
15. Choke rod
16. Gasket
17. Fast idle cam assembly
18. Choke rod seal
19. Choke housing shaft and lever
20. Retainer
21. Main body
22. Throttle body gasket
23. Screw
24. Diaphragm lever assembly
25. Throttle body
26. Idle stop screw
27. Spring
28. Screw
29. Throttle shaft assembly
30. Throttle plate
31. Screw
32. Screw
33. Accelerating pump cam
34. Gasket
35. Screw
36. Choke thermostat clamp
37. Choke thermostat
38. Choke thermostat gasket
39. Nut
40. Lockwasher
41. Spacer
42. Choke lever
43. Choke link and piston
44. Screw and washer
45. Choke shaft
46. Gasket
47. Inlet valve seat
48. Inlet valve needle
49. Pull clip
50. Screw
51. Gasket
52. Fuel bowl
53. Gasket
54. Fuel inlet fitting
55. Diaphragm spring
56. Diaphragm assembly
57. Accelerating pump cover
58. Retaining screw/lockwasher
59. Gasket
60. Fuel level sight plug
61. Baffle plate
62. Float
63. E-ring
64. Float spring
65. Fuel bowl gasket
66. Idle mixture needle
67. Main jet
68. Seal
69. Baffle plate
70. Main jet
71. Metering block
72. Seal
73. Idle mixture needle
74. Metering block gasket
75. Power valve gasket
76. Power valve

8

9

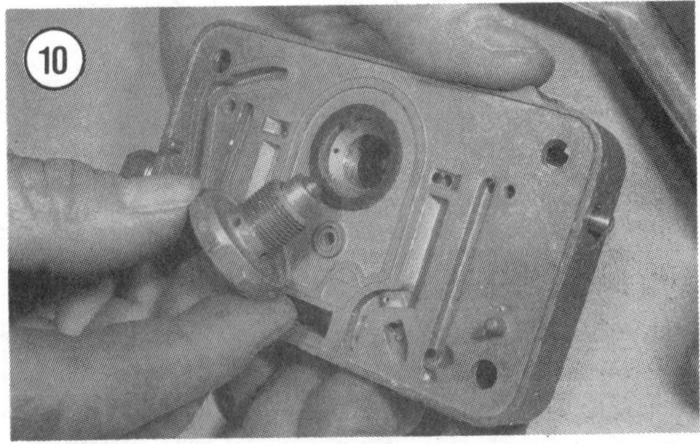

10

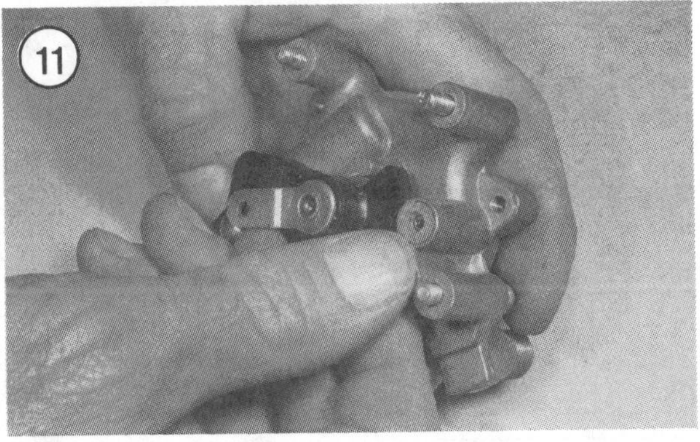

11

6. Remove the float and inlet valve assembly as follows:

a. Use needlenose pliers to remove the E-ring (63, **Figure 7**) retaining the float on the float shaft.

b. Slide the float from the shaft and remove the baffle plate and spring (61 and 64, **Figure 7**) from the fuel bowl.

c. Remove the fuel inlet needle and seat assembly (46-49, **Figure 7**) from the fuel bowl. The needle can be withdrawn from the seat after removing the clip (49, **Figure 7**).

7. Remove the fuel inlet fitting and gasket. Some models are equipped with a screen permanently attached to the inside of the fitting, while others may be equipped with a removable filter. Clean or install a new filter before assembling.

8. Invert the fuel bowl, then remove the accelerator pump cover, diaphragm and spring. The accelerator pump check ball is not serviceable and should not be removed from the fuel bowl. The check ball, however, must be free to move to allow the accelerator pump to function properly.

9. Invert the carburetor and remove the screws and lockwashers attaching the throttle body (25, **Figure 7**) to the main body. Separate the throttle body from the body and discard the gasket. Install a new gasket when reassembling.

10. Remove the retainer pin (20, **Figure 7**) from the choke rod (15, **Figure 7**) and separate the rod from the lever (19, **Figure 7**).

11. Remove the electric choke or thermostatic spring cover (37, **Figure 7**).

12. Remove the housing (14, **Figure 7**) and make sure the small O-ring is removed from the port (**Figure 11**).

13. Remove nut, lockwasher and spacer (**Figure 12**) from the choke housing shaft. Remove the shaft and fast idle cam.

14. Remove the choke piston/lever assembly (42 and 43, **Figure 7**).

15. Remove the choke rod and seal (15 and 18, **Figure 7**).

16. Remove the retaining screw (1, **Figure 7**), then lift the accelerating pump discharge nozzle and gasket (**Figure 13**) from the body.

17. Invert the body and catch the discharge needle (7, **Figure 7**) as it falls out.

18. Remove the accelerating pump operating lever (10, **Figure 7**).

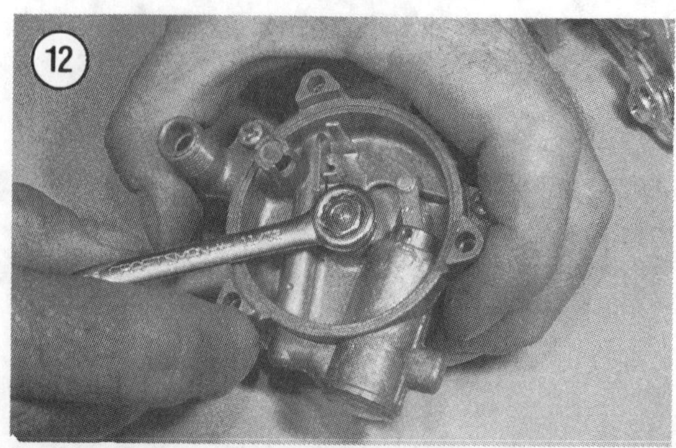

Holley 2-bbl. Assembly

Refer to **Figure 7** for this procedure. Compare the new gaskets with the old gaskets to make sure the replacement gaskets have the proper openings. Always install new gaskets when assembling the carburetor.

1. Attach the accelerating pump operating lever (10, **Figure 7**) to the body.
2. Drop the discharge needle into the pump well and tap the needle gently with a brass punch to seat it lightly, then install a new gaskets and the pump nozzle. Tighten the retaining screw securely. Refer to (**Figure 14**).
3. Install the choke lever link/piston assembly in the choke housing (**Figure 15**), then install the shaft, spacer, lockwasher and nut.
4. Install the choke housing using new gaskets. Insert the choke rod in the shaft lever while installing the choke housing. The projection on the rod must be located under the fast idle cam to lift the cam when the choke is closed. Install a new pin (20, **Figure 7**) when attaching the rod to the lever (19, **Figure 7**).
5. Install a new gasket on the thermostatic coil housing (37, **Figure 7**). Engage the spring loop on the spring lever, then install the retainer(s) and screws. Turn the index marks on the housing/coil assembly as described in the overhaul kit and tighten the screws.
6. Invert the main body and attach the throttle body using a new gasket. The fuel inlet fitting must be on the same side as the accelerating pump operating lever. Tighten the retaining screws securely.

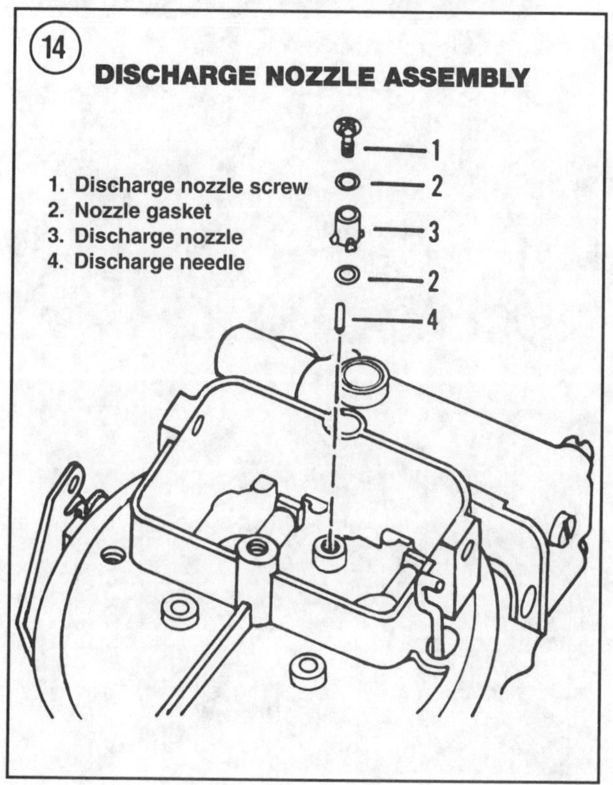

7. Position the accelerating pump diaphragm spring and diaphragm in the pump chamber with the large end of the lever disc against the operating lever. Install the cover and tighten the retaining screws with your fingers.

8. Make sure the diaphragm is centered, then operate the lever to compress the spring completely and tighten the cover retaining screws.

9A. If the fuel inlet fitting is equipped with a renewable filter, install the spring, fuel filter and inlet fitting. Tighten the fitting to the torque listed in **Table 2**.

9B. If the fuel inlet fitting does not have a removable filter, install the fitting using a new gasket. Tighten the fitting to the torque listed in **Table 2**.

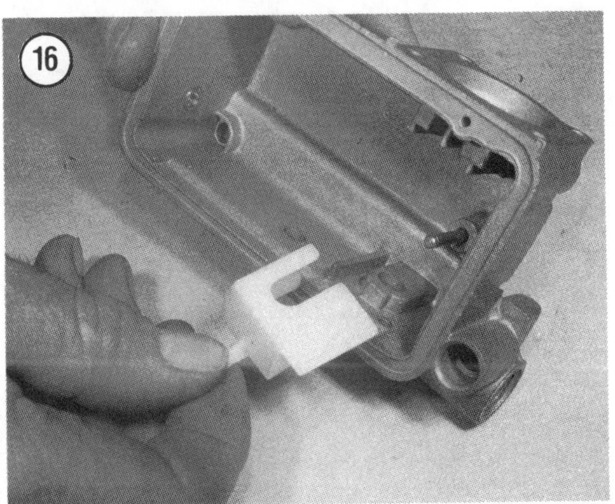

10. Install the float in the fuel bowl as follows:
   a. Install a new fuel inlet valve and seat. Use a new gasket and tighten to the torque listed in **Table 2**. Do not distort the seat by overtightening.
   b. Install a new pull clip on the new inlet valve needle, invert the fuel bowl and insert the inlet needle and clip into the seat.
   c. Slide the baffle plate into the fuel bowl. See **Figure 16**.
   d. Install the spring onto the float and slide the float over the float shaft. Make sure the float spring is seated between the ridges on the boss in the fuel bowl floor.
   e. Install the float retainer E-ring using needlenose pliers after the float, spring and baffle plate are properly located.
   f. Refer to the *Float level adjustment* in this chapter to check and adjust the float level.

NOTE
Several different power valves have been used, so make sure the correct valve is installed. The valves are identified by numbers stamped on the face of the valve. Also, the valve must be installed using the correct gasket. If the power valve has several round fuel opening holes, use a gasket which has 3 internal projections. If the power valve has 2 rectangular fuel openings, the gasket should not have any internal projections.

11. Install a new gasket on the power valve and install the valve on the metering block. Tighten the power valve to the torque listed in **Table 2**.

12. Install the main jets in the metering block using a screwdriver and tightening to the torque listed in **Table 2**.

NOTE
The mixture adjusting screws will probably require additional adjustment to provide optimal idle mixture adjustment. Also the setting may be different between the adjuster on the port side and starboard side.

13. Install the idle mixture adjusting screws in the metering block using new gaskets. Turn the screws in until lightly seated, then back the screws out the number of turns recorded during disassembly. If the original setting is not known, turn the screws in until seated, then turn the screws out (counterclockwise) 1/2 to 1 turn.
14. Install a new inner gasket on the metering block using the dowels on the back of the block for alignment. Fit the metering block and gasket to the main body.
15. Position the outer gasket on the outer dowels of the metering block and hold the parts in place.
16. Install new compression gaskets on the 4 screws that retain the fuel bowl and metering block.
17. Position the fuel bowl and float assembly against the metering block and gasket, then install the retaining screws. See **Figure 17**. Tighten the screws securely.
18. Adjust the accelerating pump as described in this chapter.

Holley 2-bbl. Adjustments

If the carburetor has been completely disassembled and overhauled, perform the adjustment and setup procedures in the following sequence. If only partial disassembly has been performed, complete the necessary adjustments only.

Float level adjustment

1. Invert the removed float bowl (**Figure 18**, typical). The top of the float should be parallel to the float bowl.
2. To adjust the float, carefully bend the curved part of the float arm that contacts the fuel inlet needle. See **Figure 18**.

NOTE

*Install new gaskets (65 and 74, **Figure 7**) on both sides of the metering block each time the fuel bowl is removed. Also, install new gaskets (51, **Figure 7**) on the retaining screws.*

3. Install the fuel bowl and float assembly as described in this chapter and tighten the screws securely.

Accelerating pump stroke adjustment

The correct amount of fuel delivered by the accelerating pump is controlled by the position of the Delrin (plastic) pump cam (33, **Figure 7**)

17

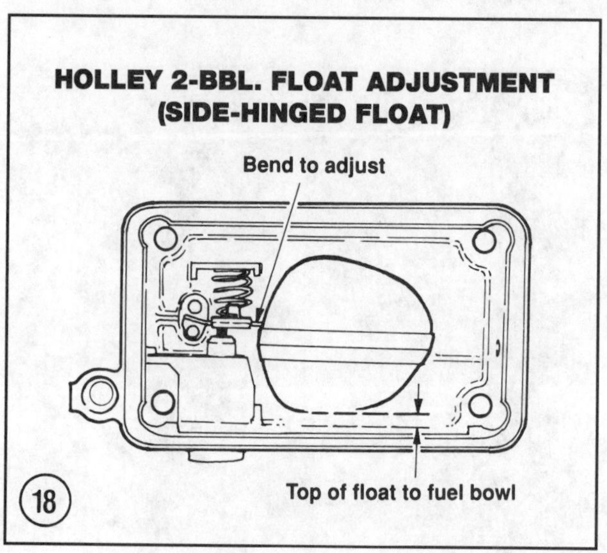

18

attached to the throttle arm. For correct pump stroke, the cam must be installed in the specified hole in the cam and throttle arm. The correct cam location is included in the instructions in the overhaul kit and (for some models) is listed in **Table 1**.

Accelerator pump clearance adjustment

The correct accelerator pump clearance is necessary to prevent hesitation during acceleration and to ensure the maximum pump output. If clearance is insufficient, the throttle valves may not open fully and the accelerating pump diaphragm may be damaged by over-extension.

1. Hold the throttle in the wide-open position, while manually depressing the pump lever.
2. Measure the clearance between the pump lever and the head of the screw on the pump arm as shown in **Figure 19**.
3. Compare the clearance to the specification listed in the instructions included in the overhaul kit or in **Table 1**.
4. If the clearance is incorrect, turn the adjusting nut as required to correct the clearance.

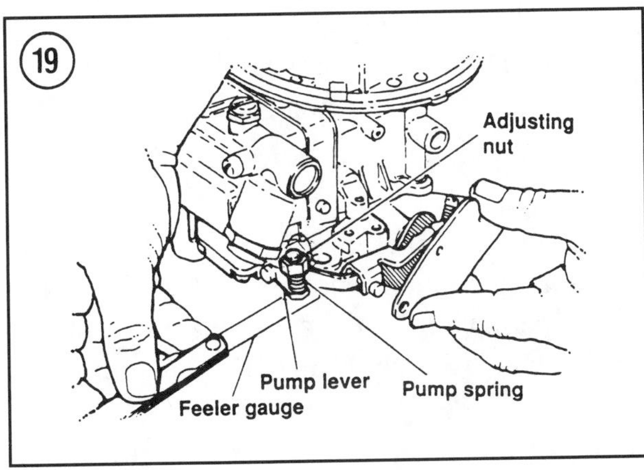

NOTE
The accelerator pump should begin to move at the same time as the throttle. If the pump hesitates, check for worn or bent components, an improperly positioned pump cam or incorrect pump clearance.

Choke vacuum qualification

1. Remove the choke housing cover (37, **Figure 7**).
2. Push the choke linkage so the piston contacts the adjusting screw. See **Figure 20**.

NOTE
Measure the clearance in Step 3 using a drill bit or a carburetor plug gauge of the correct size.

3. Hold the piston against the adjusting screw, and measure the clearance between the lower edge of the choke plate and the inner wall of the air horn.
4. Compare the clearance with the specification listed in **Table 1** or the instructions included with the overhaul kit.
5. If the opening is not as specified, turn the adjustment screw (**Figure 20**) as required.

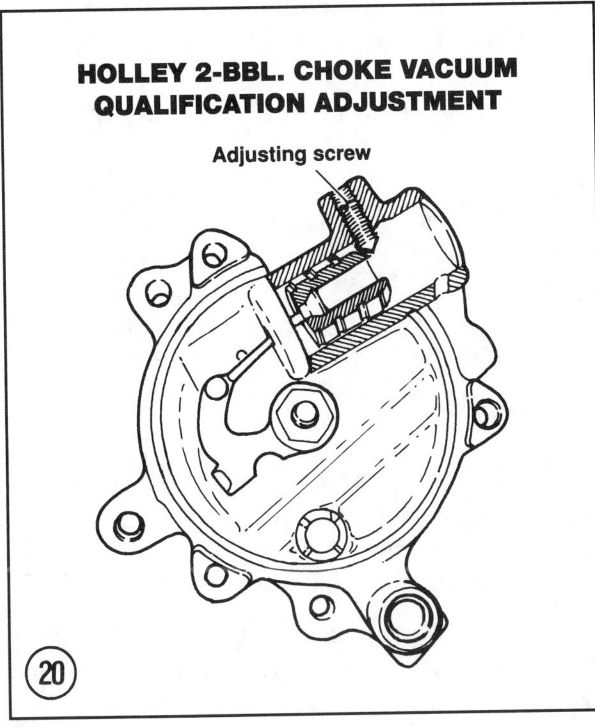

9

Automatic choke adjustment

1. Loosen the 3 screws (35, **Figure 7**), until the cover can be turned.
2. Align the mark on the cover with the index mark specified in **Table 1** or in the instructions included with the overhaul kit. Tighten the 3 screws after the marks are aligned.

NOTE
It should not be necessary to change the setting more than 2 index marks from the standard setting.

3. The choke may require changes from the standard setting, depending upon operating conditions. To set the choke to open more quickly, turn the cover clockwise. To set the choke to remain closed longer, turn the cover counterclockwise.

Holley 4-bbl. Disassembly

The primary stage of this 4-bbl. carburetor includes 2 of the throats (barrels), a fuel bowl, metering block and accelerating pump. The secondary stage includes the other 2 throats, a fuel bowl, metering block and a secondary throttle operating diaphragm. Other features may be included with some carburetor models. Refer to **Figure 21**, typical for this procedure.

1. Attach the carburetor mounting flange to a mounting fixture.
2. Remove the screws attaching the primary fuel bowl and metering block (12 and 18, **Figure 21**) to the main body, then remove the float bowl and metering block. See **Figure 22** and **Figure 23**.
3. Pull the balance tube from between the primary and secondary fuel bowls and remove the O-rings.
4. Turn the idle mixture adjustment needles (20, **Figure 21**) in (clockwise) and count the number of turns from the original position until the screw is lightly seated. Record this original setting for each screw, then remove the idle adjustment screws, by turning counterclockwise.
5. Remove the main jets (26, **Figure 21**) with a wide-blade screwdriver. **Figure 24**, typical shows the location of the jets.
6. Loosen the power valve (**Figure 25**) with a properly fitting wrench, then remove the valve and discard the gasket.
7. Remove the float and inlet valve assembly as follows:
   a. Use needlenose pliers to remove the retainer (25, **Figure 21**) retaining the float on the float shaft.
   b. Slide the float from the shaft and remove the baffle plate and spring (14 and 24, **Figure 21**) from the fuel bowl.
   c. Remove the fuel inlet needle and seat assembly (3 and 4, **Figure 21**) from the fuel bowl.
8. Remove the fuel inlet fitting (7, **Figure 21**) and gasket. Some models are equipped with a screen permanently attached to the inside fitting, while others may be equipped with a removable filter.
9. Invert the fuel bowl, then remove the accelerator pump cover, diaphragm and spring. See **Figure 26**. The accelerator pump check ball is not serviceable and should not be removed from the fuel bowl. The check ball, however, must be free to move for the accelerator pump to function properly.

NOTE
With the fuel bowl inverted, there should be 0.011-0.013 in. (0.28-0.33 mm) clearance between the check ball and the retainer. If clearance is wrong, bend the retainer as necessary. Be careful not to break the retainer.

10. Remove the screws attaching the secondary fuel bowl, then remove the fuel bowl (69, **Figure 21**) and gasket.
11. Use a No. 2 clutch type screwdriver to remove the screws attaching the metering body, plate and gaskets. See **Figure 27**. Remove and discard the gaskets.

(21)

HOLLEY 4-BBL. CARBURETOR

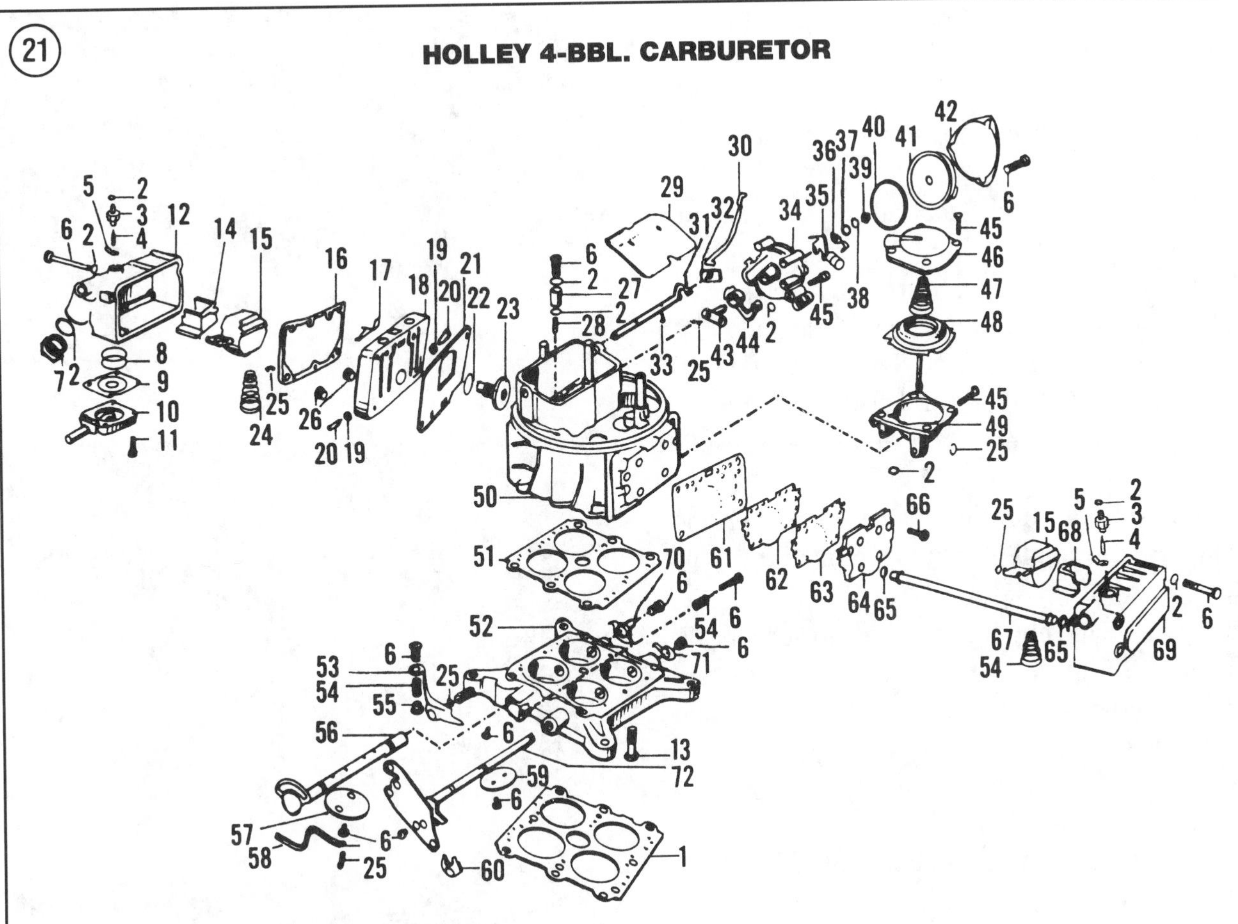

1. Throttle body gasket
2. Gasket
3. Seat
4. Needle
5. Clip
6. Screw
7. Fuel inlet fitting
8. Diaphragm spring
9. Diaphragm assembly
10. Accelerating pump cover
11. Retaining screw/lockwasher
12. Primary fuel bowl
13. Screw
14. Baffle plate
15. Float
16. Primary fuel bowl gasket
17. Baffle plate
18. Primary metering block
19. Seal
20. Idle mixture needle
21. Primary metering block gasket
22. Power valve gasket
23. Power valve
24. Float spring
25. Retainer
26. Main jet
27. Accelerating pump discharge nozzle
28. Accelerating pump discharge needle
29. Choke plate
30. Choke rod
31. Choke shaft
32. Choke rod seal
33. Screw
34. Choke housing
35. Choke link and piston
36. Choke lever
37. Spacer
38. Lockwasher
39. Nut
40. Choke housing gasket
41. Choke thermostat
42. Choke housing clamp
43. Choke housing shaft/lever
44. Fast idle cam
45. Screw/washer
46. Cover
47. Diaphragm spring
48. Diaphragm assembly
49. Secondary housing
50. Main body
51. Throttle body gasket
52. Throttle body
53. Accelerating pump operating lever
54. Spring
55. Sleeve nut
56. Secondary throttle shaft
57. Secondary throttle plate
58. Throttle connecting rod
59. Primary throttle plate
60. Accelerating pump cam
61. Gasket
62. Secondary plate
63. Metering body gasket
64. Secondary metering body
65. O-ring seal
66. Clutch screw
67. Fuel balance tube
68. Baffle plate
69. Secondary fuel bowl
70. Fast idle cam lever
71. Diaphragm lever assembly
72. Primary throttle shaft

12. Refer to Step 6 and remove the float, baffle and fuel inlet valve from the secondary fuel bowl.
13. Remove the flame arrestor anchor stud from the center of the air horn.
14. Remove the C-clip that attaches the secondary diaphragm link.
15. Invert the carburetor and remove the screws and lockwashers attaching the throttle body (52, **Figure 21**) to the main body. Separate the throttle body from the main body and discard the gasket.
16. Remove the electric choke or thermostatic spring cover (41, **Figure 21**).
17. Remove the housing (34, **Figure 21**) and make sure the small O-ring is removed from the port. See **Figure 28**.
18. Remove the nut, lockwasher and spacer (37, 38 and 39, **Figure 21**) from the choke housing shaft. Remove the shaft and fast idle cam (43 and 44, **Figure 21**).
19. Remove the choke piston/lever assembly (35 and 36, **Figure 21**).
20. Remove the choke rod and seal (30 and 32, **Figure 21**).
21. Remove the retaining screw (6, **Figure 21**), then lift the accelerating pump discharge nozzle and gasket (**Figure 29**) from the body.
22. Invert the body and catch the discharge needle (4, **Figure 30**) as it falls out.
23. Remove the accelerating pump operating lever (53, **Figure 21**).
24. Clean and inspect the carburetor thoroughly as described in this chapter.

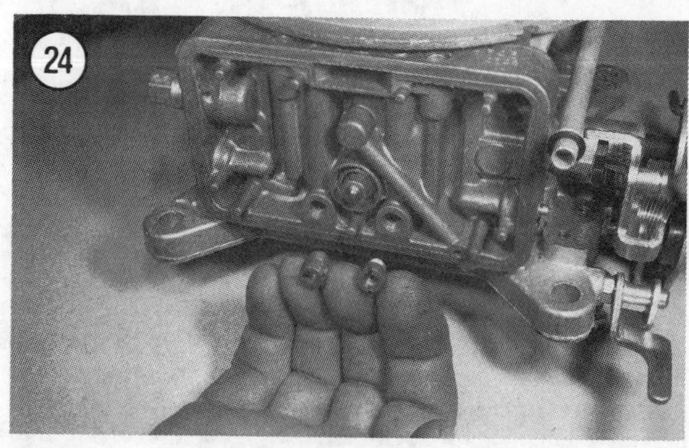

Holley 4-bbl. Assembly

Refer to **Figure 21** for this procedure. Compare the new gaskets to the old gaskets to be sure the replacement gaskets have the proper openings. Always install new gaskets when assembling the carburetor.

1. Attach the accelerating pump operating lever (53, **Figure 21**) to the body.

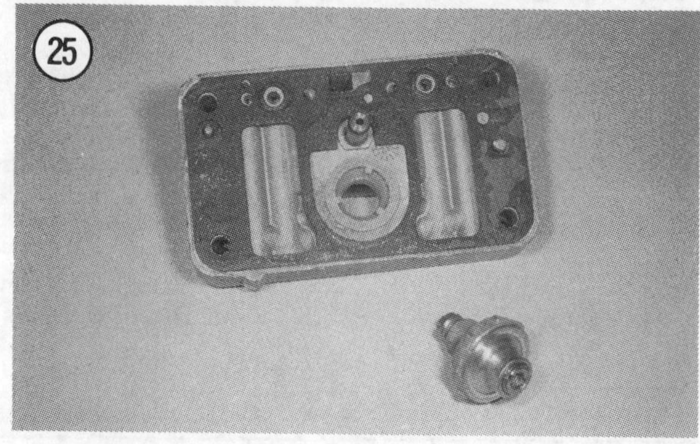

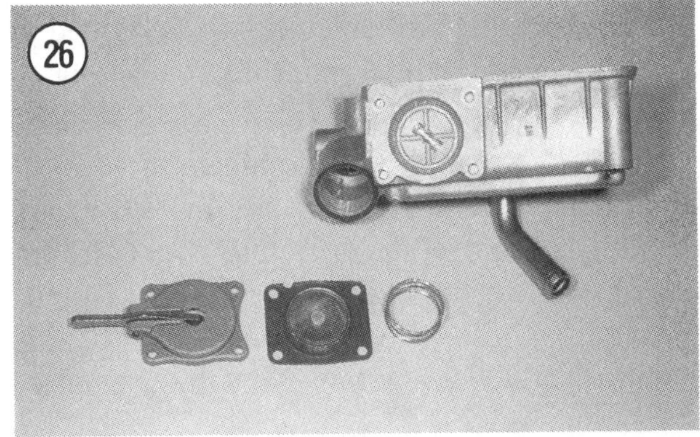

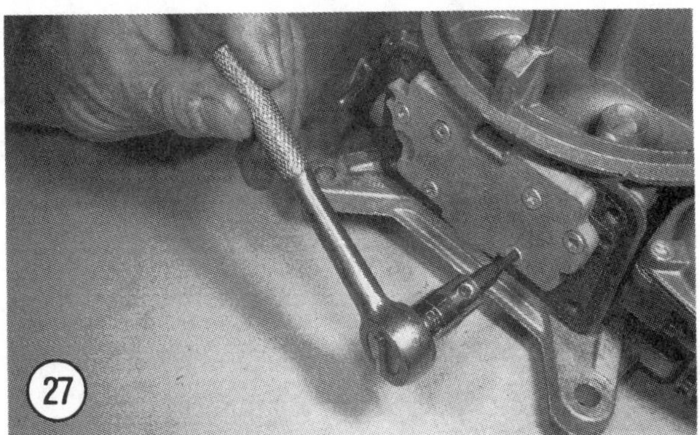

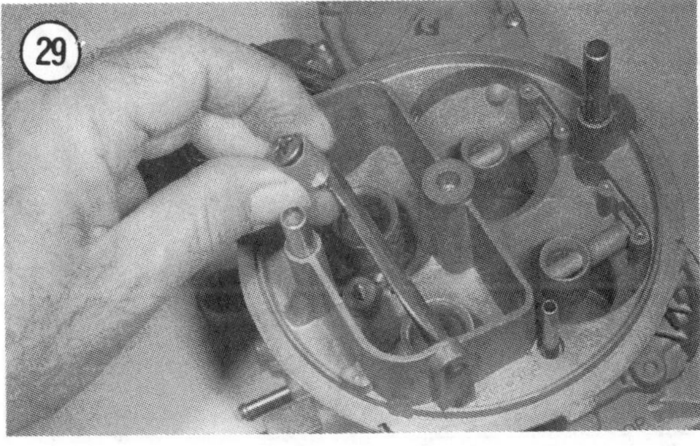

2. Drop the discharge needle (4, **Figure 30**) into the pump well, tap the needle gently with a brass punch to seat it lightly, then install new gaskets and the pump nozzle. Tighten the retaining screw securely, then stake the screw lightly in place with a punch.

3. Position the secondary diaphragm in the housing and the spring in the cover. Push the cover against the housing and install the screws that attach the cover to the housing, but tighten the screws only finger-tight. See **Figure 31**.

4. Pull the diaphragm rod downward as far as possible, then hold the rod in this position while tightening the screws snugly.

5. Fit a new gasket to the secondary vacuum passage opening in the main body and attach the diaphragm housing to the body.

DISCHARGE NOZZLE ASSEMBLY

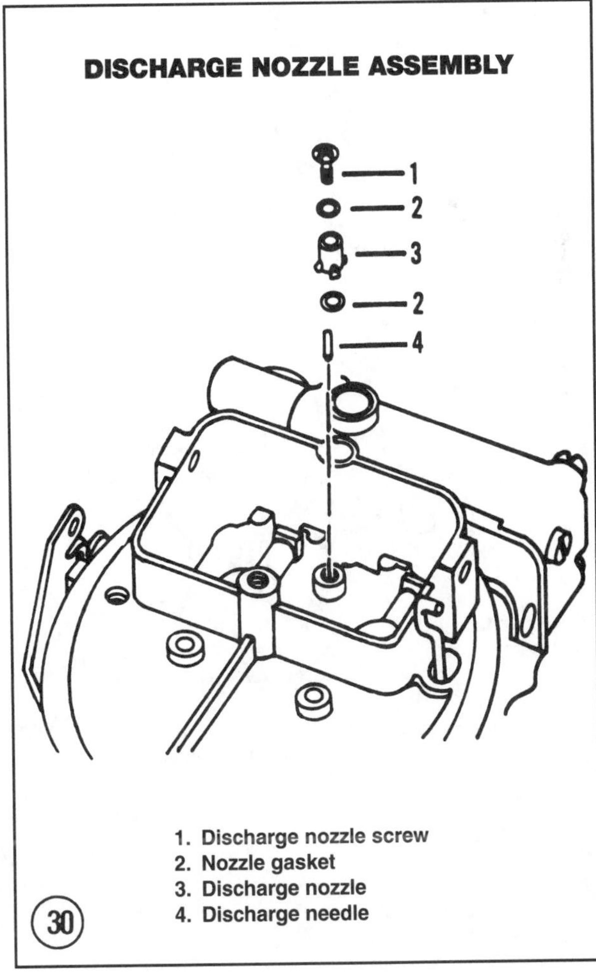

1. Discharge nozzle screw
2. Nozzle gasket
3. Discharge nozzle
4. Discharge needle

6. Fit the seal on the choke rod and install the rod with the seal fitted into the grooves under the flame arrestor mounting flange. See **Figure 32**.
7. Assemble and install the choke assembly (**Figure 32**) as follows:
   a. Install the choke split link lever/piston assembly in the choke housing, then install the choke shaft, fast idle cam, choke housing lever, spacer, lockwasher and nut. See **Figure 32**.
   b. Install the overcenter spring as shown in **Figure 33**.
   c. Install the choke housing assembly using new gaskets. Insert the choke rod in the shaft lever while installing the choke housing. The projection on the rod must be located under the fast idle cam to lift the cam when the choke is closed. Install new retainer pins (25, **Figure 21**) when attaching the rod to the levers.
   d. Install a new gasket and install the choke thermostatic coil, engaging the spring loop with the spring lever.
   e. Install the cover, retainer(s) and screws. Turn the cover to align the index marks on the housing/coil assembly as described in the overhaul kit and tighten the clamp screws.
8. Invert the main body and attach the throttle body using a new gasket. Slide the secondary diaphragm rod over the operating lever (71, **Figure 21**) while installing the throttle body. Tighten the retaining screws to the torque listed in **Table 2** and install a new retainer on the secondary diaphragm rod.
9. Assemble the primary fuel bowl as follows:
   a. If the inlet fitting is equipped with a renewable filter, install the spring, fuel filter and inlet fitting. If the fuel inlet fitting does not

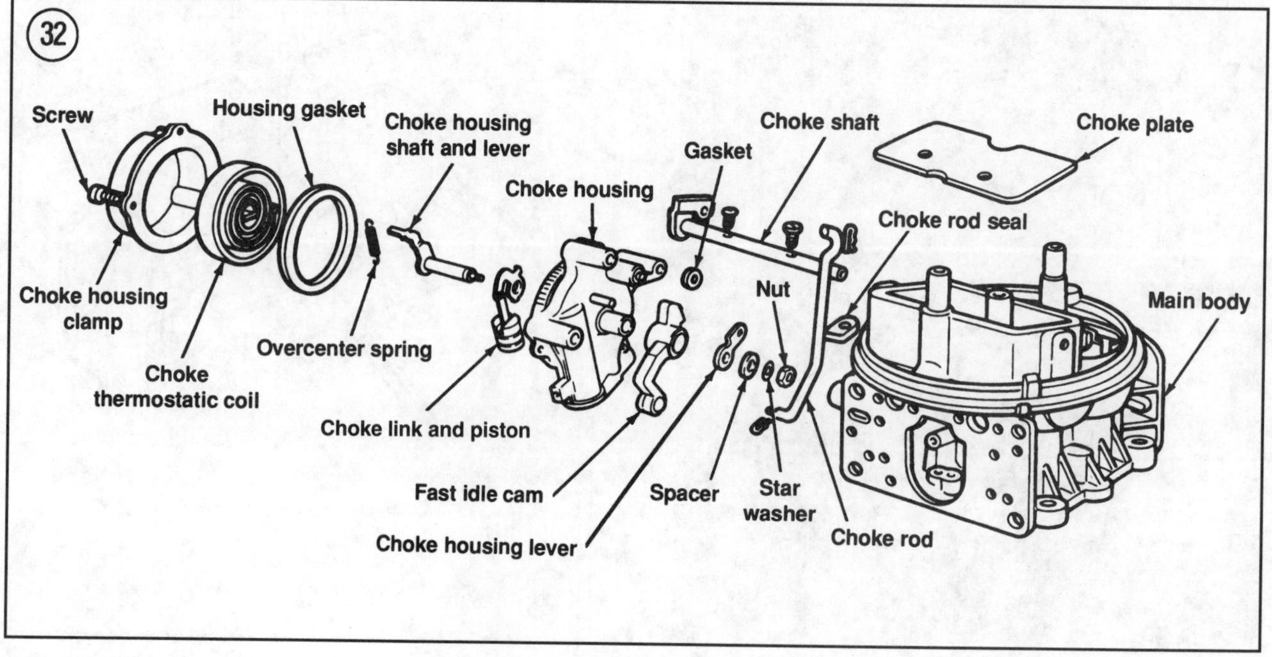

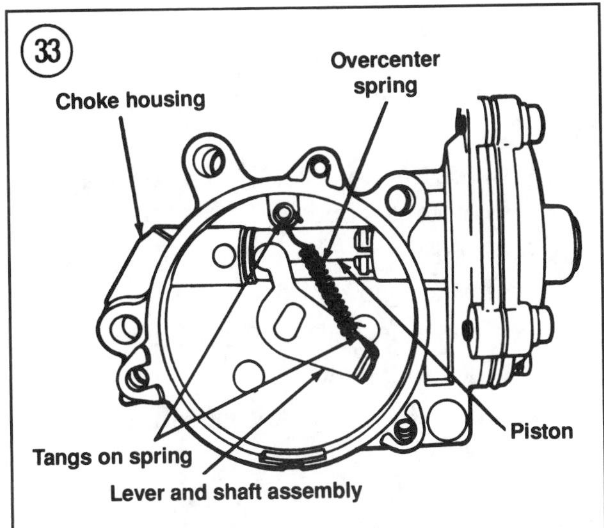

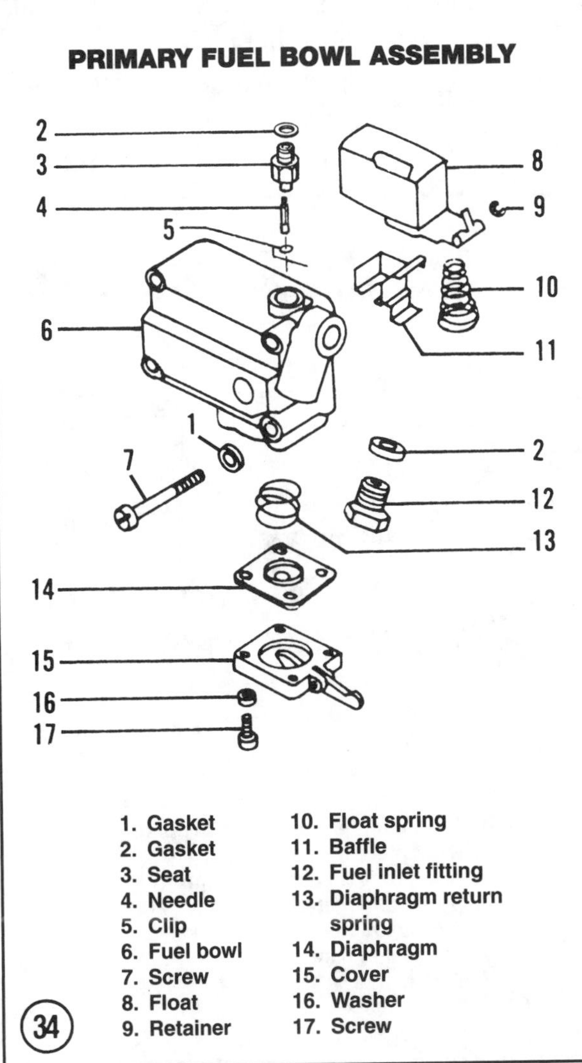

1. Gasket
2. Gasket
3. Seat
4. Needle
5. Clip
6. Fuel bowl
7. Screw
8. Float
9. Retainer
10. Float spring
11. Baffle
12. Fuel inlet fitting
13. Diaphragm return spring
14. Diaphragm
15. Cover
16. Washer
17. Screw

have a removable filter, install the fitting using a new gasket. Tighten the fitting (12, **Figure 34**) to the torque listed in **Table 2**.

b. Position the accelerating pump diaphragm spring and diaphragm (14, **Figure 34**)in the pump chamber with the large end of the lever disc against the operating lever. Install the cover and tighten the retaining screws with your fingers.
c. Make sure the diaphragm is centered, then operate the lever to compress the spring completely and tighten the cover retaining screws (17, **Figure 34**).
d. Install a new fuel inlet valve and seat. Use a new gasket and tighten the seat to the torque listed in **Table 2**. Do not distort the seat by overtightening.
e. Install a new pull clip on the new inlet valve needle, invert the fuel bowl and insert the inlet needle and clip into the seat.
f. Slide the baffle plate into the fuel bowl.
g. Install the spring onto the float and slide the float over the float shaft. Make sure the float spring is seated between the ridges on the boss in the fuel bowl floor.
h. Install the float retainer E-ring using needlenose pliers after the float, spring and baffle plate are properly located.
i. Refer to the *Float level adjustment* in this chapter to check and adjust the float level.

10. Assemble the primary metering block as follows:

a. Install the main jets in the metering block using a screwdriver and tighten to the torque listed in **Table 2**. See **Figure 24**.

NOTE
The mixture adjusting screws will probably require additional adjustment to provide optimal idle mixture adjustment. Also, the setting may be different between the adjuster on the port side and starboard side.

b. Install the idle mixture adjusting screws (20, **Figure 21**) in the metering block using new seals. Turn the screws in until lightly seated, then back the screws out the number of turns recorded during disassembly. If the original setting is not known, turn the screws in until seated, then turn the screws out (counterclockwise) the number of turns listed in the instructions included in the overhaul kit or in **Table 1**.

NOTE

Several different power valves are used, so make sure the correct valve is installed. The valves are identified by numbers stamped on the face of the valve. Also, the valves must be installed using the correct gasket. If the power valve has several round fuel opening holes, use a gasket which has 3 internal projections. If the power valve has 2 rectangular fuel openings, the gasket should not have any internal projections.

c. Install a new gasket on the power valve and install the valve on the metering block. Tighten the power valve to the torque listed in **Table 2**.

d. On models so equipped, install new O-rings on the accelerator passage tube, then push the tube into position in the primary metering block.

11. Install the primary metering block and fuel bowl as follows:

a. Install a new inner gasket on the metering block using the dowels on the back of the block for alignment. Fit the metering block and gasket to the main body.

b. Position the outer gasket on the outer dowels of the metering block and hold the parts in place.

c. Install the baffle plate (17, **Figure 21**).

d. Install new compression gaskets on the 4 screws that retain the fuel bowl and metering block.

e. Position the fuel bowl and float assembly against the metering block and gasket, then install the retaining screws. Tighten the screws securely.

12. Install the secondary metering block as follows:

a. Position a new gasket (7, **Figure 35**) against the carburetor body.

b. Position the metering plate (6, **Figure 35**) against the gasket.

c. Position a new gasket (5, **Figure 35**) against the metering plate.

d. Position the secondary metering body (4, **Figure 35**) against the gasket.

e. Align parts (4, 5, 6 and 7, **Figure 35**), then install the retaining screws.

13. Install the secondary fuel bowl as follows:

a. Assemble the secondary float and fuel inlet valve as described in Step 9.

b. If an external fuel balance tube (67, **Figure 21**) is used, install new O-rings on the bal-

35

SECONDARY FUEL BOWL AND METERING BODY ASSEMBLY

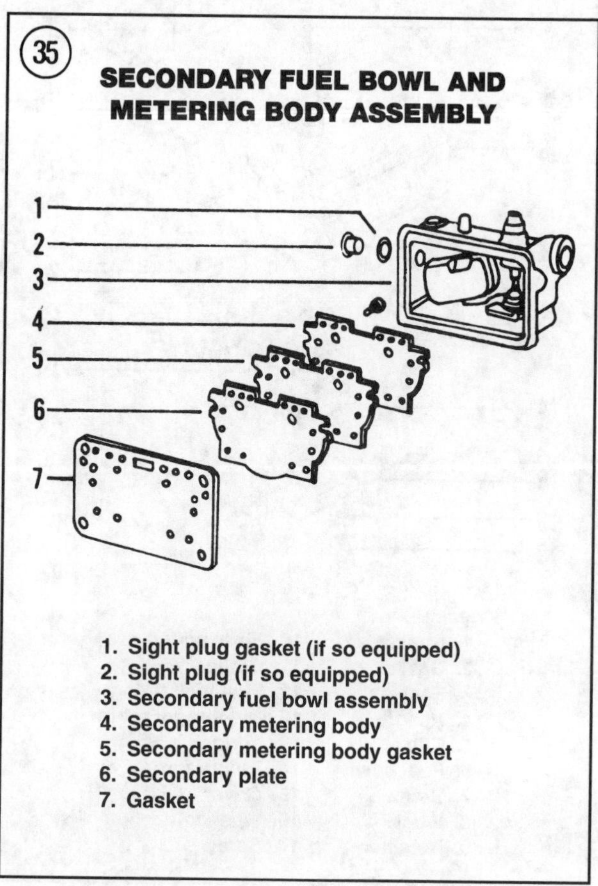

1. Sight plug gasket (if so equipped)
2. Sight plug (if so equipped)
3. Secondary fuel bowl assembly
4. Secondary metering body
5. Secondary metering body gasket
6. Secondary plate
7. Gasket

ance tube and hold the balance tube in position while installing the secondary fuel bowl.

c. Install new compression gaskets on the 4 screws that retain the fuel bowl.

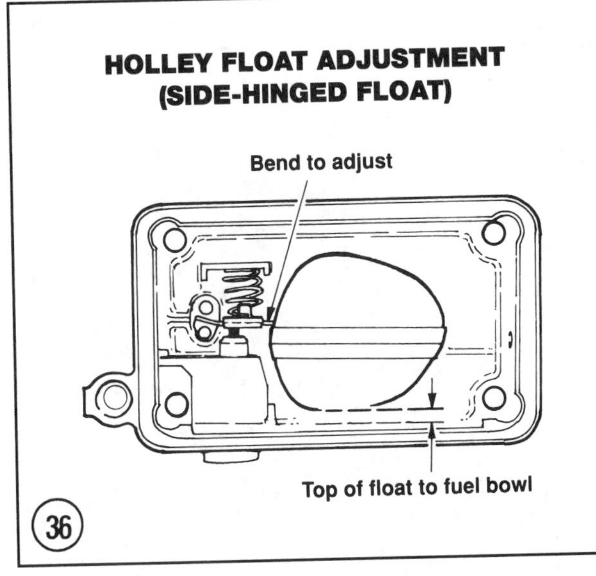

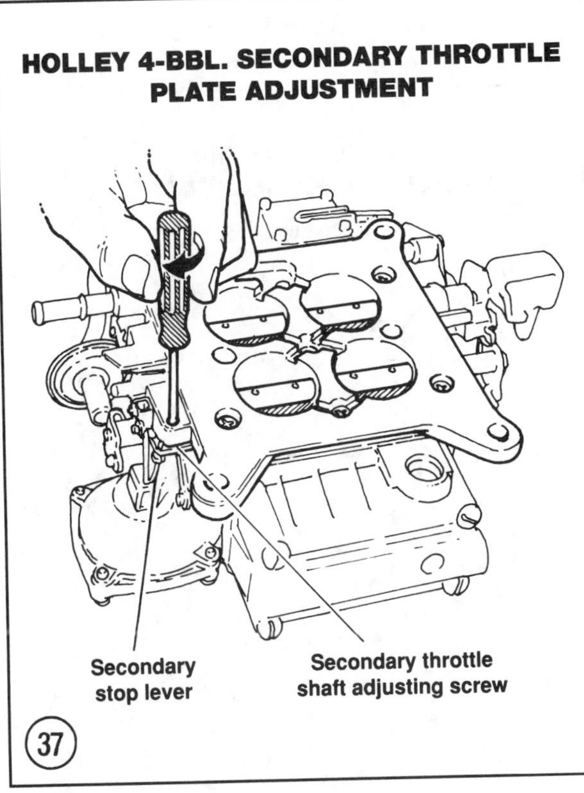

d. Position the fuel bowl and float assembly against the gasket, then install the retaining screws. Tighten the screws securely.

14. Adjust the accelerating pump as described in this chapter.

Holley 4-bbl. Adjustments

If the carburetor has been completely disassembled and overhauled, perform the adjustment and setup procedure in the following sequence. If only partial disassembly has been performed, complete the necessary adjustments only.

Float level adjustment

1. Invert the float bowl (**Figure 36**, typical). The top of the float should be parallel to the float bowl.
2. To adjust the float, carefully bend the curved part of the float arm that contacts the fuel inlet needle.

NOTE
*Install new gaskets (16 and 21 or 61, **Figure 21**) each time the fuel bowl is removed. Also, install new gaskets on the retaining screws.*

3. Install the fuel bowl and float assembly as described in this chapter and tighten the screws securely.

Secondary throttle plate adjustment

1. Turn the adjusting screw (**Figure 37**) out (counterclockwise) until the secondary throttle plates are completely closed.
2. Open the secondary throttle, then release it allowing the throttle valves to snap closed.
3. Turn the adjusting screw in (clockwise) until it *just* contacts the secondary stop lever. See **Figure 37**.

4. Next, turn the screw (**Figure 37**) in (clockwise) an additional 1/4 turn from the setting in Step 3.
5. Check for correct adjustment by opening the throttle, then releasing it to allow the secondary throttle valves to snap closed. The throttles should not stick in the throttle bores. If the throttles stick, readjust the screw beginning at Step 3.

Accelerating pump stroke adjustment

The correct amount of fuel delivered by the accelerating pump is controlled by the position of the Delrin (plastic) pump cam (60, **Figure 21**) attached to the throttle arm. For correct pump stroke, the cam must be installed in the specified hole in the cam and throttle arm. The correct cam location is included in the instructions in the overhaul kit and (for some models) is listed in **Table 1**.

Accelerator pump clearance adjustment

The correct accelerator pump clearance is necessary to prevent hesitation during acceleration and to ensure the maximum pump output. If clearance is insufficient, the throttle valves may not open fully and the accelerating pump diaphragm may be damaged by over-extension.

1. Hold the throttle in the wide-open position, while manually depressing the pump lever.
2. Measure the clearance between the pump lever and the head of the screw on the pump arm as shown in **Figure 38**.
3. Compare the clearance to the specification listed in the instructions included in the overhaul kit or in **Table 1**.
4. If the clearance is incorrect, turn the adjusting nut as required to correct the clearance.

NOTE

The accelerator pump should begin to move at the same time as the throttle. If the pump hesitates, check for worn or bent components, improperly positioned pump cam or incorrect pump clearance.

Choke vacuum qualification

1. Remove the choke thermostat (41, **Figure 21**).
2. Push the choke linkage so the piston contacts the adjusting screw. See **Figure 39**.

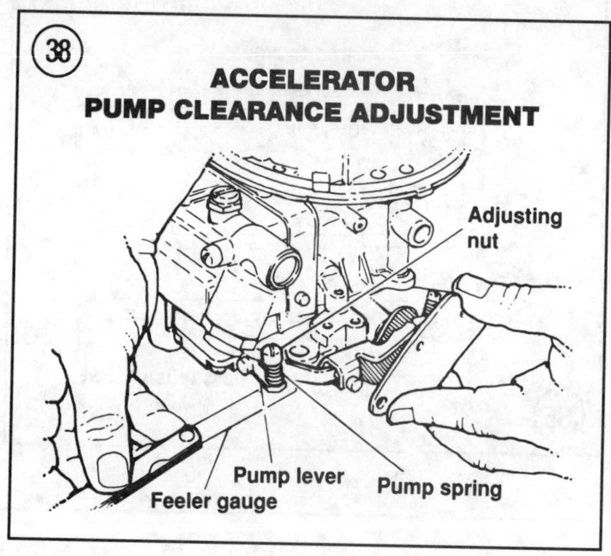

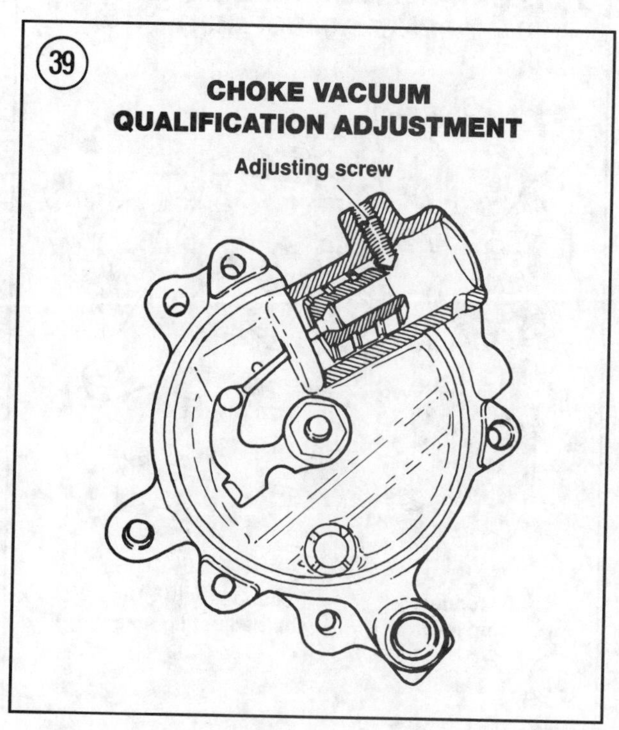

NOTE
Measure the clearance in Step 3 using a drill bit or a carburetor plug gauge of the correct size.

3. Hold the piston against the adjusting screw, and measure the clearance between the lower edge of the choke plate and the inner wall of the air horn.
4. Compare the clearance with the specification listed in **Table 1** or the instructions included with the overhaul kit.
5. If the opening is not the same as specified, turn the adjustment screw (**Figure 39**) as required.

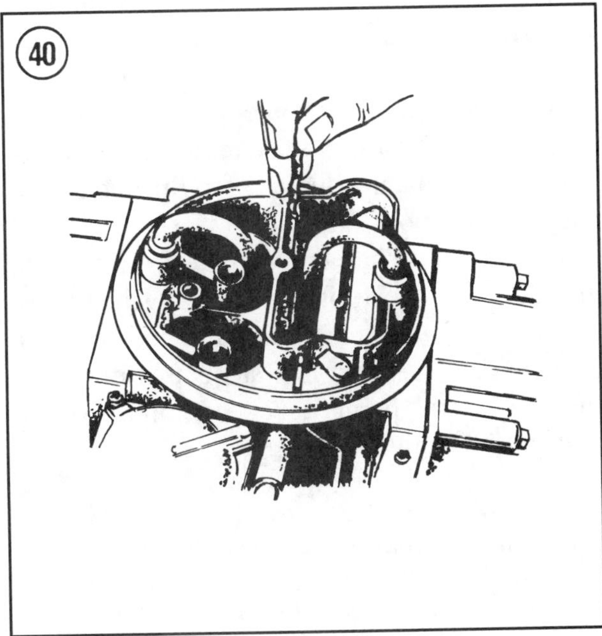

Automatic choke adjustment

1. Loosen the 3 screws holding the retainer (42, **Figure 21**), until the cover can be turned.
2. Align the mark on the cover with the index mark specified in **Table 1** or in the instructions included with the overhaul kit. Tighten the 3 screws after marks are aligned.

NOTE
It should not be necessary to change the setting more than 2 index marks from the standard setting.

3. The choke may require changes from the standard setting, depending upon operating conditions. To set the choke to open more quickly, turn the cover clockwise. To set the choke to remain closed longer, turn the cover counterclockwise.

NOTE
On models with an electric choke, make sure the choke cap is properly grounded with the external ground wire. Also make sure all electrical connections are clean and tight.

Choke unloader adjustment

1. Hold the throttle valves wide open and insert a 19/64 in. drill or plug gauge between the lower edge of the choke valve and the inner wall of the air horn. See **Figure 40**.
2. Use your finger to press the choke lever lightly while pulling the gauge out. A slight drag should be felt.
3. To adjust the choke unloader, bend the tab on the kick-down lever (**Figure 41**).

Idle mixture adjustment

Initial setting for the idle mixture adjusting screws (20, **Figure 21**) is listed in the instructions included in the overhaul kit. Initial setting is also included in **Table 1** for some models. Turn the screws in until lightly seated, then back the screws out (counterclockwise) the number of turns listed in **Table 1**. This is only an approximate setting and the screws will probably require additional adjustment to provide optimal idle mixture adjustment.

NOTE
The setting may be different between the adjuster on the port side and starboard side.

FUEL INJECTION SYSTEMS (GASOLINE ENGINES)

Operating Principals

Constant efforts to improve engine performance, increase fuel efficiency and reduce the impact of gasoline engines on the environment have lead to the development of sophisticated electronically monitored and controlled fuel delivery systems.

The following engine models are equipped with electronic fuel injection (EFI).

a. 4.3 Gi
b. 5.0 Fi
c. 5.0 Gi
d. 5.7 Gi and 5.7 Gsi
e. 5.8 Fi and FSi
f. 7.4 Gi and GSi
g. 8.2 Gsi

Several different EFI systems are used on the engines covered by this book, but all include electronic sensors, an electronic control and fuel delivery system.

The sensors monitor the engine's condition and send electronic data to the electronic control unit. Sensors may include those to check the temperature of the outside (ambient) air, engine cooling system temperature, position of the throttle, amount of air flowing into the engine, oxygen remaining in the exhaust, manifold pressure, barometric pressure, knock control, crankshaft position, crankshaft speed or other conditions. The selection of sensors used on a specific application is determined by the manufacturer. Sensors are carefully selected to provide the information needed by the control assembly.

The decision of how much fuel to inject and when to inject it is made by the control assembly, often called the electronic control unit (ECU) or electronic control module (ECM). The electronic control unit receives information from the various sensors, processes this information, then determines how much fuel should be injected and when it should be injected. After determining the fuel requirements, the control unit sends a control signal to open the fuel injectors. This control signal determines when the injector opens and the how long it opens (duration). On some systems, the electronic control assembly may also control the ignition system as well as the fuel system.

Fuel can be injected into the air entering the engine at a central location or at each cylinder's intake port. The type of system used is determined by the manufacturer. On engines equipped with throttle body injection (TBI), fuel is injected into the air stream as it passes through the throttle body. The throttle body is attached to the intake manifold in much the same location as a conventional carburetor. Systems that inject the fuel at several points is called multipoint or multiport injection (MFI).

WARNING
The electronic fuel injection systems used on these engines are designed for marine use and although they appear similar to systems installed on automobiles, their components are not the same. Any escaping fuel vapor will create a fire or explosion hazard, and it is important to install only parts designed and selected for marine use and available from Volvo Penta.

Acronyms

Acronyms are letters used as an abbreviation used frequently to identify components, systems or subsystems of the ignition/fuel control system. Some acronyms (such EEC-IV) may be pronounced as if they were a word instead of being spelled out. Refer to **Table 9** for a list of common acronyms and their definition.

TROUBLESHOOTING

CAUTION
In normal operation, the electronic fuel injection system used on these engines is reasonably trouble free, but are easily and quickly damaged by improper testing and service procedures. Special equipment and training are necessary to determine the cause of fuel system problems. If problems are encountered and the electronic fuel system is suspected, it should be tested and serviced only by properly trained and equipped technicians.

Many fuel system problems are caused by dirty or contaminated fuel. It is important that owners understand the value of using the proper type of fresh, good quality fuel and storing it properly. This is important for all fuel systems and together with regular maintenance of all fuel filters will reduce fuel system problems. *Do not use old or contaminated fuel in these fuel systems.* Refer to Chapter Four.

Fuel system problems can be divided into 2 categories, either too much fuel or not enough fuel, but the symptoms can take many forms. A fuel/air mixture with too much fuel is said to be *rich* and one with too little fuel is said to be *lean*. All of the electronic fuel injection systems used on these models include on-board diagnostics that can help discover the fault; however, components can be easily and quickly damaged by improper testing procedures. If problems are encountered and the electronic fuel system is suspected, it should be tested and serviced *only* by properly trained and equipped technicians.

Specifications for the fuel injection system may vary with type and model year. Calibration may be changed during production and subsequent modifications may be made to suit an individual boating application. Authorized Volvo Penta service technicians have the special tools, training and specifications necessary to test, adjust and repair the electronic fuel injection systems used on these engines.

Refer to the service procedures included in the appropriate following sections of this chapter for testing and service.

MULTIPOINT FUEL INJECTION (5.0 AND 5.8 L ENGINES)

These engines use the EEC-IV (electronic engine control, fourth generation) engine management system. Complete testing requires the use of the following tools or their equivalent.

a. MFI tester (part No. 3851324-8).
b. A breakout box. A breakout box connects in series between the ECA and the engine wiring harness and is used to isolate each circuit for voltage and resistance tests. An EEC-IV monitor can be used in place of a breakout box for many tests.
c. Digital volt-ohmmeter that is capable of also measuring frequency.
d. Fuel pressure tester (part No. OTC-7211) and adapter (part No. OTC-7272).
e. Variable advance timing light.
f. Kilovolt tester—used to check ignition system spark output voltage. A kilovolt tester is available from Snap-on Tool Company and other tool manufacturers.

Pre-Service Procedures

WARNING
Gasoline is a dangerous fire and explosion hazard, so it is important to release pressure from the system before beginning most service procedures to prevent accidentally spraying fuel as components are loosened, disconnected or removed. The following procedure will help reduce the hazard, but it is always

important to exercise extreme caution whenever servicing any part of the fuel system. Always have an approved fire extinguisher immediately available.

1. Disconnect and insulate the leads to both (low- and high-pressure) electric fuel pumps.
2. Crank the engine for at least 10 seconds. If the engine starts, let it continue to run until it stops, then crank the engine for an additional 5 seconds.
3. Attach the electrical leads to the fuel pumps that were detached in Step 1.
4. Disconnect the ground cable from the battery. Make sure the cable cannot move back to its original location and provide incidental contact. It may be necessary to temporarily tie the cable away from the battery until service is completed.

Post-Service Procedures

WARNING
The danger of fire or explosion continues to exist even after service. Make sure the area is cleaned as completely as possible after servicing, then provide ventilation to the area to remove as much of the vapor as possible.

1. Connect the ground cable to the battery.
2. Turn the ignition switch ON, then OFF several times and check for leaking fuel. Correct any leaks before continuing. Move (wiggle) fuel lines if possible to make sure that all lines (especially those that were loosened during service) are tight.
3. Start the engine and run until warm.
4. Perform any available self-tests and make sure the system has not set any fault codes.

Flame Arrestor Removal/Installation

1. Remove the 4 screws attaching the plastic cover to the top of the engine, then remove the cover.
2. Hold the lower bracket and remove the 2 retaining screws (**Figure 42**) attaching the flame arrestor to the throttle body.
3. Cut the strap securing the flame arresting hose to the oil fitting, then slide the hose from the fitting.
4. Remove the flame arrestor.
5. Inspect the rubber gasket for condition and position. Install a new gasket if cracked, torn or otherwise damaged. The small nipple should be facing down.
6. Clean the flame arrestor and blow dry with air.
7. Position the flame arrestor and the lower bracket. The nipple on the gasket should fit in the hole in the bracket.

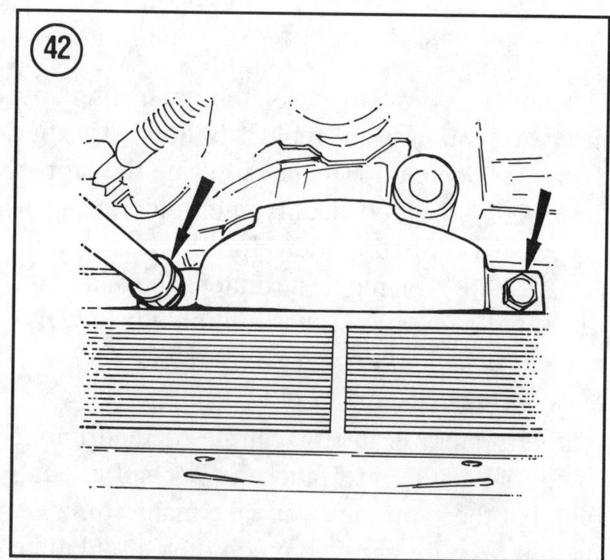

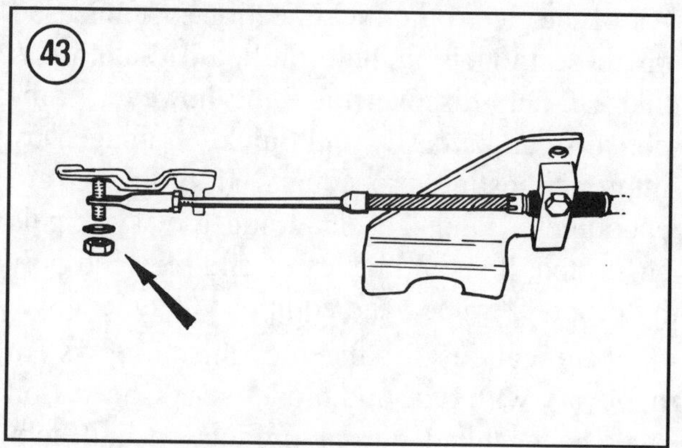

8. Install the 2 retaining screws (**Figure 42**), but tighten only finger-tight.

9. Push the flame arrestor in (toward the throttle body), while tightening the 2 retaining screws to the torque listed in **Table 3**.

10. Attach the flame arrestor to the oil fill fitting and secure with a strap.

11. Install the plastic cover on the top of the engine and tighten the retaining screws to the torque listed in **Table 3**.

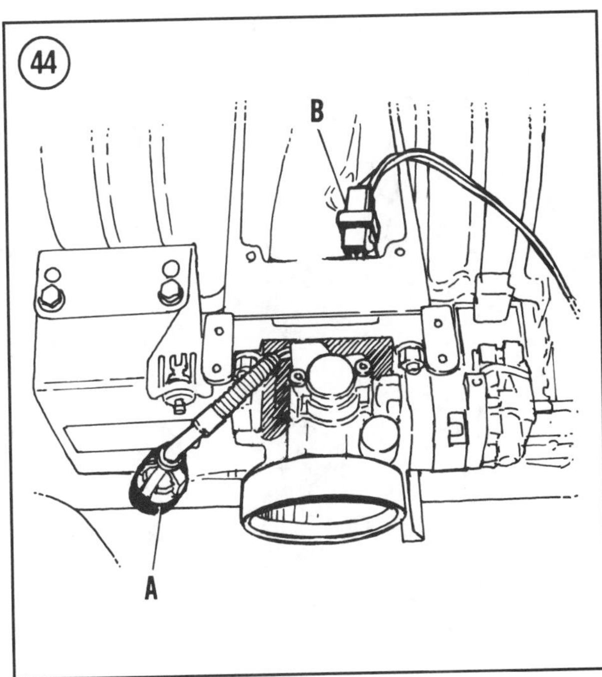

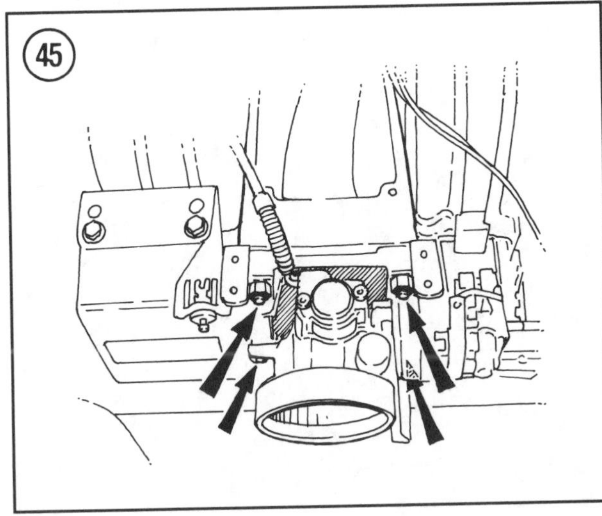

Throttle Body Removal/Installation

1. Remove the flame arrestor as described in this chapter.

2. Remove the locknut and flat washer (**Figure 43**), then disconnect the throttle cable from the throttle body arm.

3. Move the locking tabs outward and disconnect the throttle position sensor connector (A, **Figure 44**) and ISC solenoid connector (B, **Figure 44**).

4. Remove the 4 screws (**Figure 45**) and separate the throttle body from the upper manifold.

5. Remove and discard all gaskets, then clean all sealing surfaces.

CAUTION

Be careful when cleaning. Do not nick or gouge the surfaces between the throttle body and the upper manifold. There is a special coating inside the throttle bore that is easily damaged by strong solvents, including some spray carburetor cleaners.

9

6. Clean and inspect the gasket surfaces of the throttle body and the upper manifold.

7. Install the gasket between the upper manifold and the E-coil bracket. The tab on the gasket should be down and toward the rear.

8. Install the E-coil bracket, then the second gasket with its tab facing down and toward the rear.

9. Attach the throttle body to the upper manifold and tighten the 4 nuts to the torque listed in **Table 3**.

10. Attach the throttle cable, installing the flat washer and tighten the locknut.

11. Apply electric terminal grease (Ford part No. F2AZ-19584-A or equivalent) to all electrical terminals and connectors.

12. Attach the ISC solenoid and the TP sensor connectors (A and B, **Figure 44**).

13. Install the flame arrestor as described in this chapter.

14. Adjust the throttle cable if necessary.

Air Intake Upper Manifold Removal

The throttle body can be removed with the upper manifold. Refer to *Throttle Body Removal/Installation* in this chapter if the throttle body must be separated from the upper manifold.

1. Unbolt and remove the plastic cover from the top of the engine and intake manifold.
2. Detach the connectors (A and B, **Figure 46**) from the ISC solenoid and the TP sensor.
3. Remove the locknut (**Figure 47**), then disconnect the throttle cable from the throttle body assembly.

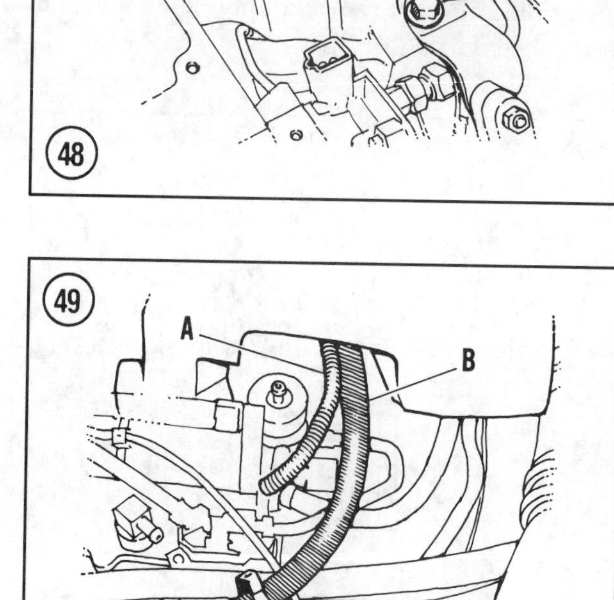

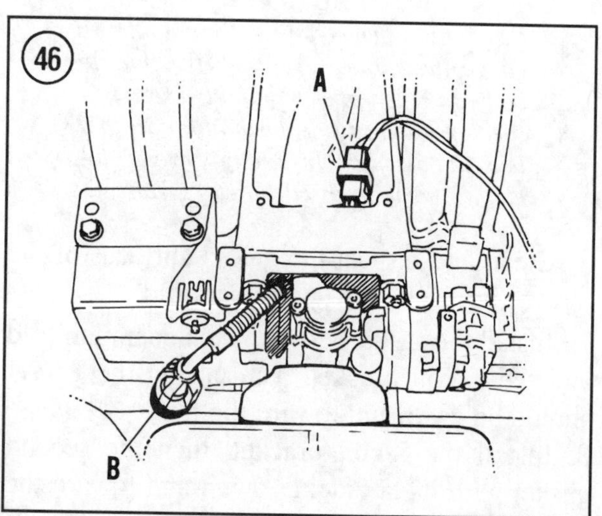

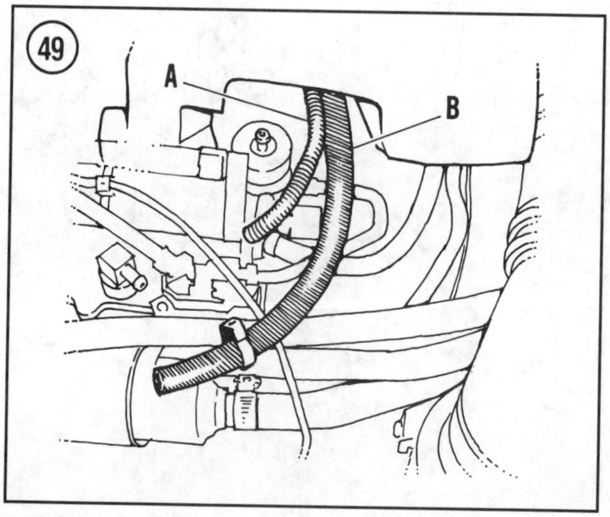

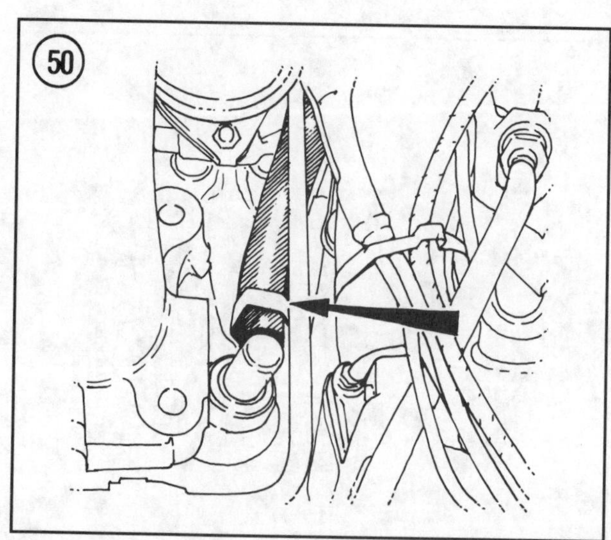

4. Remove the 2 screws (**Figure 48**) attaching the throttle linkage bracket, then move the cable out of the way.

5. Loosen or remove the hose clamps, then disconnect fuel pressure regulator vacuum hose (A, **Figure 49**) and fuel reservoir hose (B, **Figure 49**).

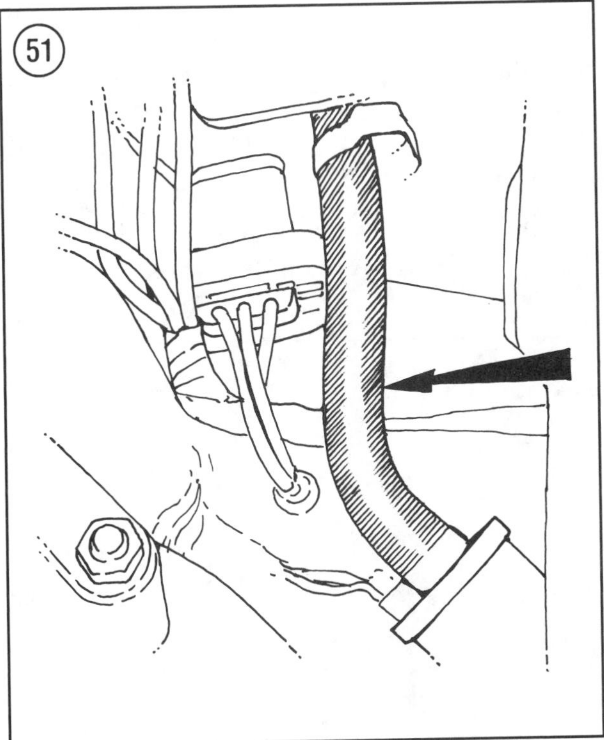

6. Loosen or remove the hose clamps, then disconnect the vacuum hose (**Figure 50**) from the PCV valve.

7. Loosen or remove the hose clamps, then disconnect the MAP sensor vacuum hose (**Figure 51**).

8. Remove the 2 screws (**Figure 52**), then set the shift bracket support aside.

9. Disconnect the high tension lead, E-core primary connector and the TFI-IV connector. See **Figure 53**.

10. Remove the 2 remaining screws (**Figure 54**) attaching the upper manifold to the lower mani-

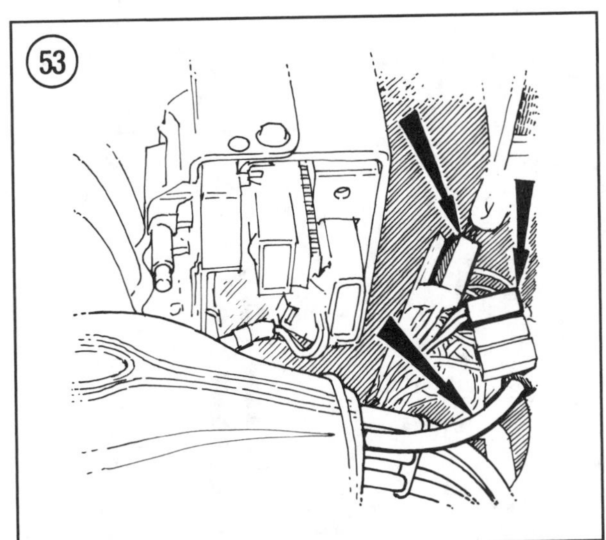

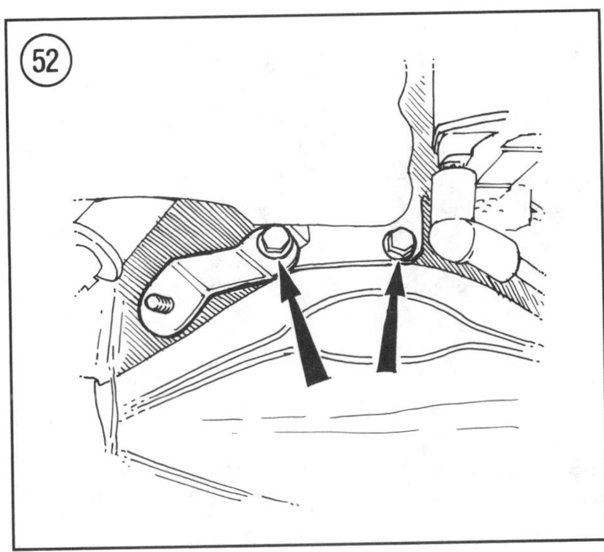

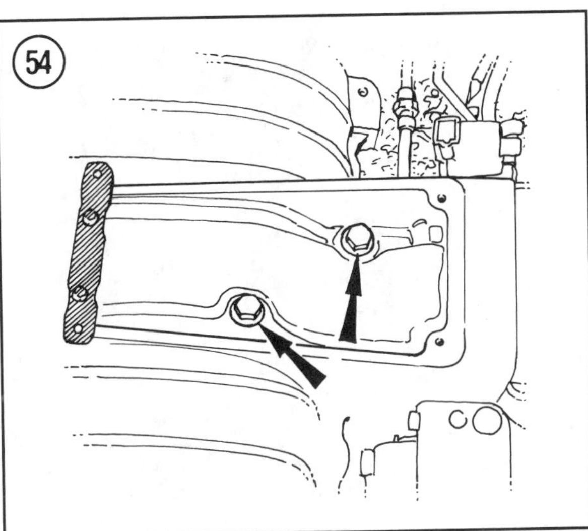

fold, then lift the upper manifold and the throttle body assembly from the engine.

CAUTION

Be careful not to drop anything into the exposed ports of the lower manifold. If the lower manifold is to remain in place, cover the openings while cleaning the gasket and sealer from the lower manifold. Cover the openings in the lower manifold with tape or similar protection while the upper manifold is off.

Air Intake Upper Manifold Installation

1. Clean and inspect the sealing surfaces between the lower and upper manifolds. Use caution to make sure that nothing falls into the open ports in the lower manifold. Vacuum hoses should be tie-strapped in their correct position under the plenum of the upper manifold as shown in **Figure 55** to avoid collapsing or pinching.

2. Position a new gasket on the lower manifold. It is not necessary to use guide studs, but alignment of the gasket and manifolds is easier if guide studs are used. Make sure that guide studs are long enough to remove easily.

3. Install the upper manifold and install the 2 center screws (**Figure 54**). Tighten the screws only finger-tight until all of the retaining screws are installed.

4. Apply electrical terminal grease (Ford part No. F3AZ-19584-A or equivalent) to the termi-

55

VACUUM HOSES

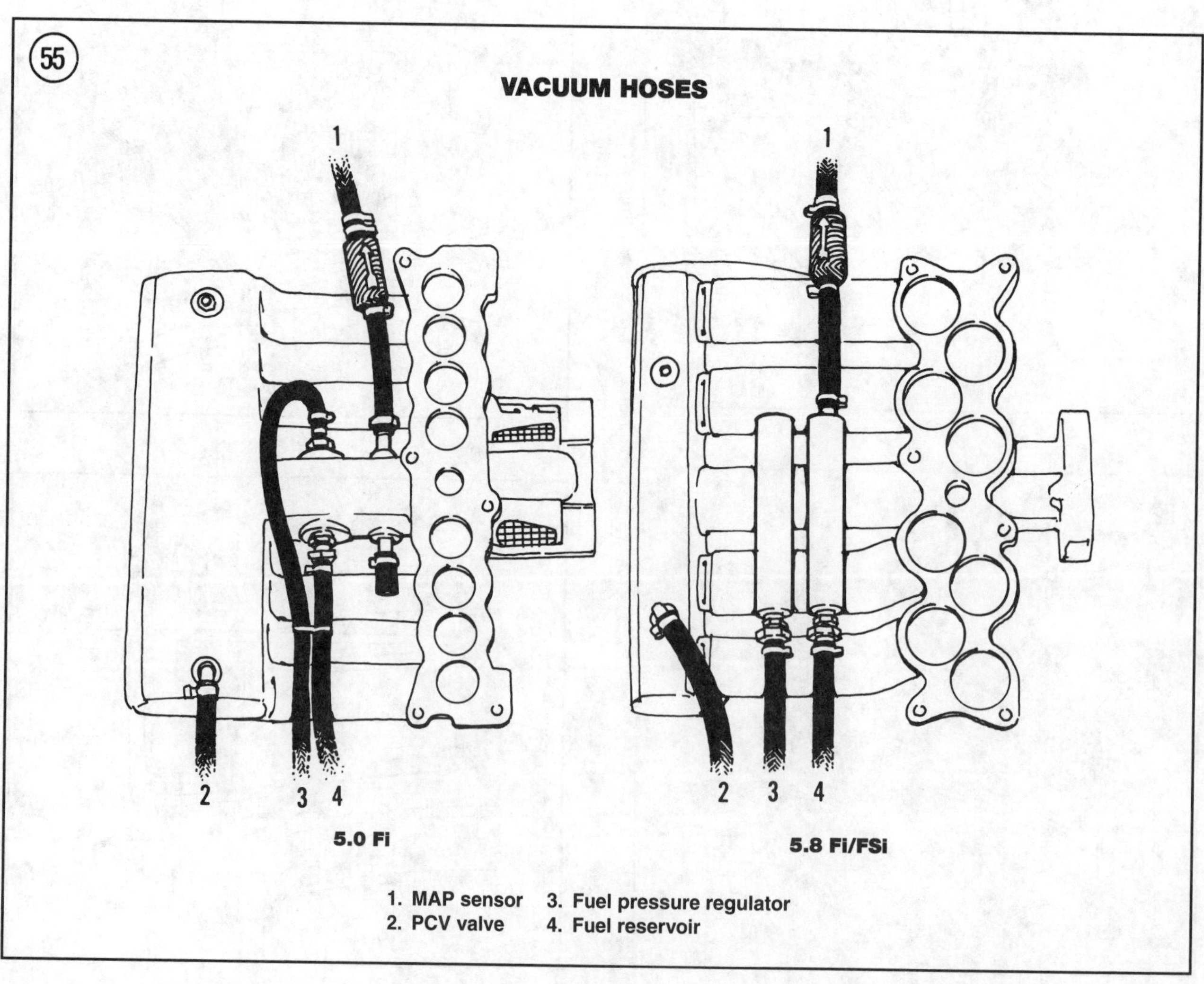

1. MAP sensor
2. PCV valve
3. Fuel pressure regulator
4. Fuel reservoir

nals, then attach the high tension lead, E-core primary connector and the TFI-IV connector (**Figure 53**).

5. Install the shift support bracket and tighten the retaining screws (**Figure 52**) finger-tight.
6. Install the throttle cable bracket with the 2 remaining screws attaching the upper manifold. See **Figure 48**.
7. Tighten the 6 screws attaching the upper manifold in a crossing pattern evenly to the torque listed in **Table 3**.
8. Attach the vacuum hose (**Figure 51**) to the MAP sensor and tighten the clamp.
9. Attach the hose (**Figure 50**) to the PCV valve and tighten clamp.
10. Attach hoses to the fuel pressure regulator (A, **Figure 49**) and fuel reservoir (B, **Figure 49**). Install and tighten the hose clamps.
11. Attach the throttle cable to the throttle body lever and secure with the flat washer and locknut (**Figure 47**).
12. Attach the 2 pin connector to the ISC solenoid (A, **Figure 46**) and the 3 pin connector (B, **Figure 46**) to the TP sensor.
13. Adjust the throttle cable if necessary.
14. Attach the plastic cover to the top of the engine and tighten the retaining screws to the torque listed in **Table 3**.

Air Intake Lower Manifold Removal/Installation

1. Refer to *Pre-Service Procedures* in this chapter and relieve the fuel pressure.
2. Refer to the *Air Intake Upper Manifold Removal* procedure and remove the upper manifold assembly.
3. Remove the fuel rail as described in this chapter.
4. Remove the fuel injectors as described in this chapter.
5. Disconnect the wire from the coolant temperature sending unit.
6. Detach the spark plug wires from the distributor cap, then remove the distributor cap and place it (with plug wires attached) out of the way.

NOTE

If you mark the position of the distributor rotor in relation to the intake manifold before removing the distributor it will be easier to install, but only if the crankshaft is not moved. If, however, the engine crankshaft is turned while the distributor is removed, refer to Chapter Eleven for initial installation of the distributor.

7. Mark the position of the distributor rotor on the intake manifold, remove the screw attaching the distributor hold-down clamp and the clamp, then withdraw the distributor.

NOTE

When withdrawing the distributor, the rotor will turn as the drive gears separate. Observe the direction that the rotor turns and its final location when the distributor is free. This information will help you install the distributor in its original position.

8. Make sure all hoses and wires that will interfere with manifold removal are removed or detached.
9. Loosen all 12 screws attaching the lower intake manifold, then remove the fasteners. Pry the manifold loose, then lift it from the engine block.
10. Remove and discard the intake manifold gaskets and end seals.
11. Clean all gasket and sealer residue from the block, cylinder heads and intake manifold with degreaser and a gasket scraper.
12. If the intake manifold is being replaced, transfer all parts and any other hardware from the old to the new manifold.
13. Apply a 1/8 in. (3.2 mm) bead of RTV sealer along the seam at the four corners between the cylinder head and the block. See **Figure 56**. Apply the bead of sealer the full width of the seam.

14. Install the new gaskets against the cylinder heads. Install the new front and rear end seals.
15. Apply a 1/16 in. (1.6 mm) diameter bead of RTV sealer at the joint of the gaskets and the end seals. See **Figure 57**. Apply a bead of sealer that is the full width of the joint.
16. Lower the intake manifold straight down into position against the cylinder heads and block. Check the seal area to make sure the seals are in their proper positions. If not, remove the manifold, correct the seal position and reinstall the manifold.
17. Install the screws attaching the lower manifold to the cylinder heads. Tighten the screws to the torque specified in **Table 3**, in the sequence shown in **Figure 58**.
18. Install the fuel injectors, fuel rail and air intake upper manifold as described in this chapter.

NOTE
Check the tightness of all upper and lower manifold fasteners after the engine is operated at normal operating temperature and allowed to cool, then once per year thereafter.

19. Refer to Chapter Eleven to install and time the ignition distributor.
20. Refer to *Post-Service Procedures* in this chapter.

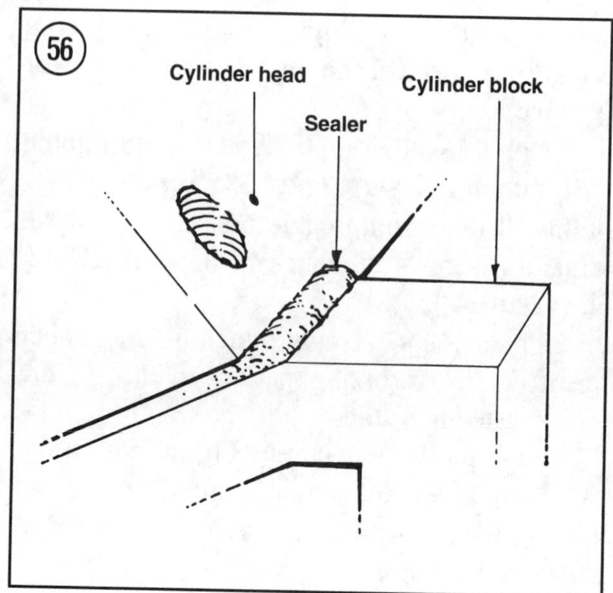

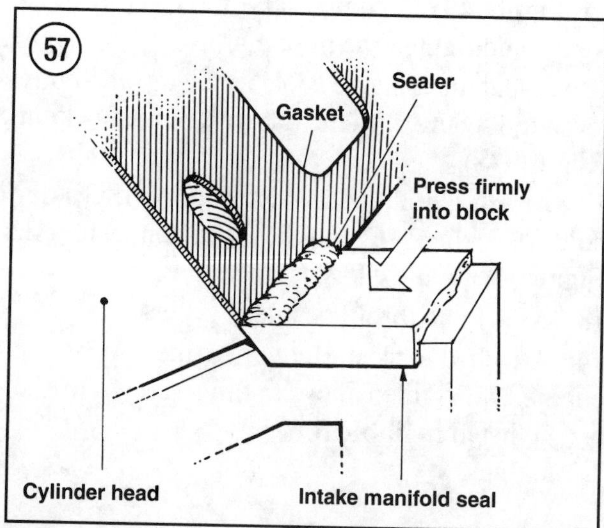

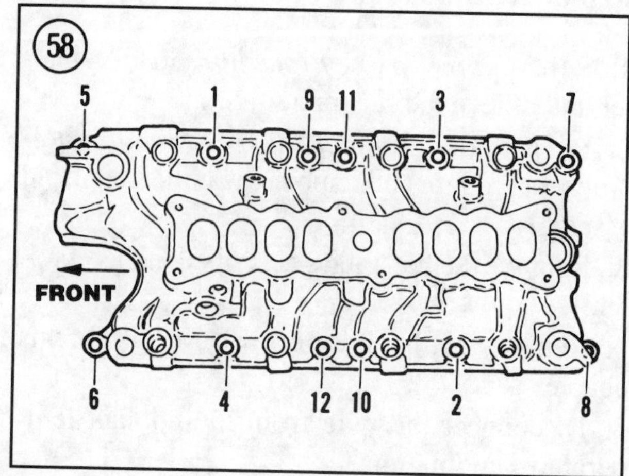

Intake Manifold Inspection

1. Check the intake manifold for cracks or distortion. Replace the manifold if it is distorted or any cracks are found.
2. Check the mating surfaces for nicks or burrs. Small burrs may be removed with a file.
3. Place a straightedge across the manifold sealing surfaces. If there is any gap between the straightedge and the manifold surface, measure it with a flat feeler gauge. Measure each surface from end to end and from corner to corner. If the

mating surface is not flat to within 0.003 in. (0.08 mm) per 6 in. (15.2 cm) of length or 0.006 in. (0.15 mm) overall, replace the manifold.

Fuel Rail

Removal/Installation

1. Refer to *Pre-Service Procedures* in this chapter and relieve the fuel pressure.
2. Refer to the *Air Intake Upper Manifold Removal* procedure and remove the upper manifold assembly.

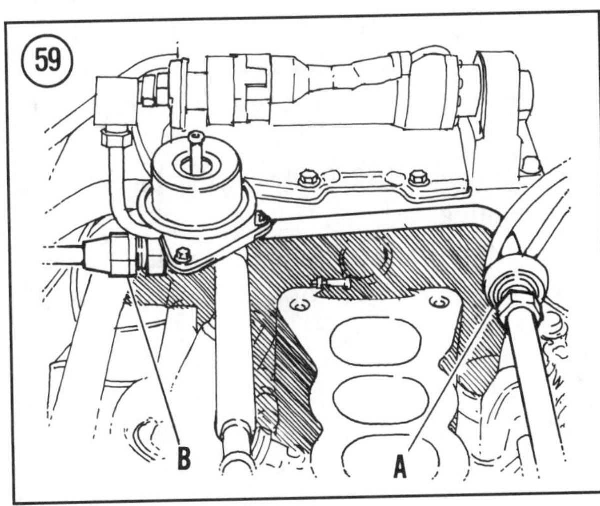

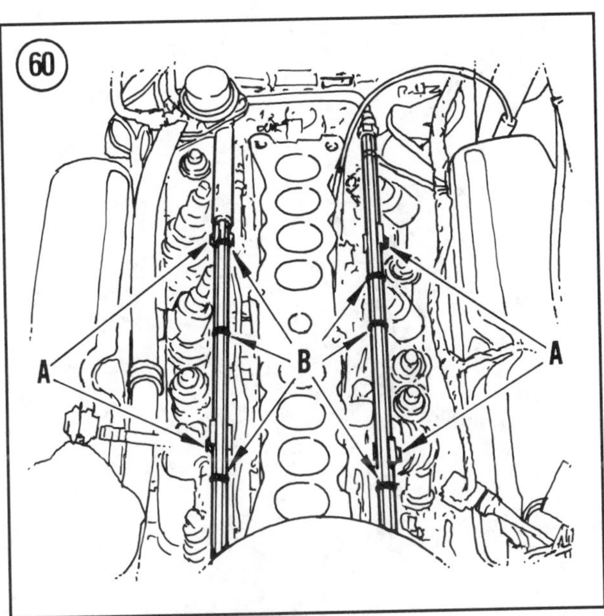

3. Clean any debris from around the injectors to keep it from falling into the intake ports.
4. Detach the fuel supply and return lines (A and B, **Figure 59**) from the fuel rail.
5. Observe where and how the wiring harness is attached to the fuel rail, then cut the tie wraps.
6. Remove the 4 screws (A, **Figure 60**) attaching the fuel rails.

NOTE
Some of the injectors may be withdrawn from the lower manifold while detaching the rails from the injectors in Step 7.

7. Carefully disengage the fuel rails from each injector, then lift the rails from the engine.
8. Check all electrical terminals to make sure they are straight and not corroded or dirty. Clean the terminals and connectors with electronic contact cleaner.

CAUTION
*Do not twist, nick or cut the O-rings (**Figure 61**) when installing the injectors. The O-rings are made of special material that is resistant to fuel. Do not substitute another type of O-ring.*

9. Check the ends of the injectors to be sure they are clean and install new O-rings (**Figure 61**).

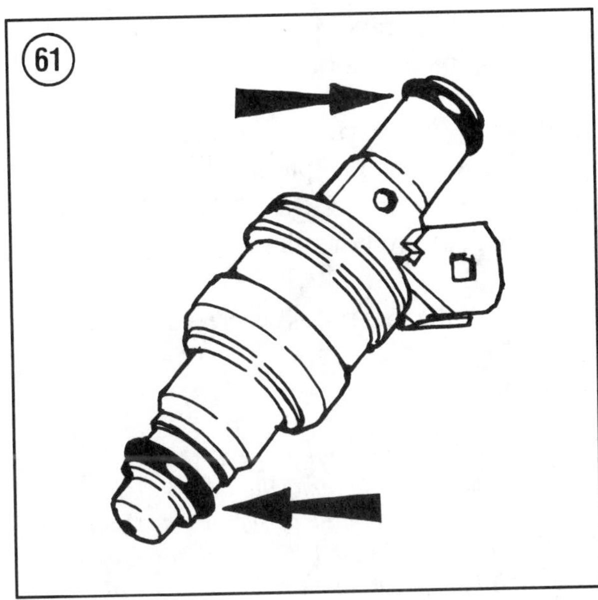

10. Lubricate the O-rings (**Figure 61**) lightly with clean engine oil.
11. Check the cups in the fuel rail and make sure they are clean and smooth.
12. Place the rail over the injectors and press down onto the injector. It may help seat the rail if the injector is turned while pressing down. When properly seated, the O-ring will snap into position in the cup.
13. Attach the rail to the intake manifold and tighten each of the 4 screws (A, **Figure 60**) to the torque listed in **Table 3**.
14. Secure the wiring harness to the fuel rail at the original locations. The 6 positions (B, **Figure 60**) are the usual locations of the tie wraps.
15. Attach the fuel supply and return lines (A and B, **Figure 59**). Tighten the fittings to the torque specified in **Table 3**.
16. Apply electric terminal grease (Ford part No. F2AZ-19584-A or equivalent) to the terminals and attach the connectors.
17. Energize the fuel pumps and check for leaks before proceeding.
18. Install the air intake upper manifold as described in this chapter.
19. Refer to *Post-Service Procedures* in this chapter.

Fuel Pressure Regulator Removal/Installation

1. Refer to *Pre-Service Procedures* in this chapter and relieve the fuel pressure.
2. Refer to *Air Intake Upper Manifold Removal* procedure and remove the upper manifold assembly.
3. Remove the fuel rail as described in this chapter.

NOTE

A new gasket and O-ring should be available before removing the regulator. The O-ring is made of special material that is resistant to fuel. Do not substitute another type of O-ring.

4. Remove the 3 Allen screws (**Figure 62**), then remove the regulator housing.
5. Remove and discard the gasket and O-ring from the regulator. If it is necessary to scrape the gasket from the sealing surfaces, be careful that surfaces are not scratched and damaged.

CAUTION

Do not twist, nick or cut the O-ring when installing the regulator. The O-ring is made of special material that is resistant to fuel. Do not substitute another type of O-ring.

6. Install a new O-ring on the regulator and lubricate it with light oil (part No. ESE-M2C39-F or equivalent). Do not use silicone grease to lubricate the O-ring, because it will clog the injectors.
7. Install a new gasket between the regulator and the mounting surface.
8. Install the regulator and tighten the 3 screws to the torque listed in **Table 3**.

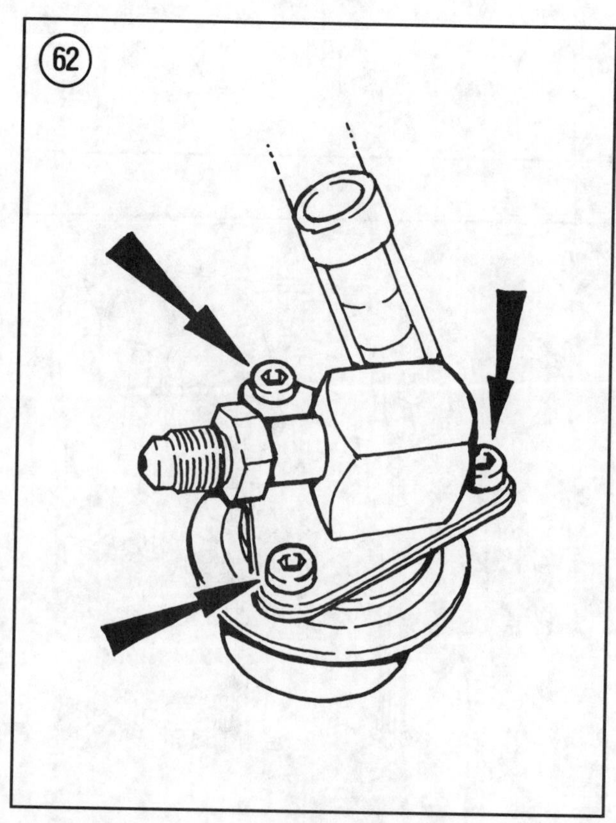

9. Follow the instructions in this chapter to install the fuel rail and air intake upper manifold.
10. Refer to *Post-Service Procedures* in this chapter.

Fuel Injector Removal/Installation

1. Refer to the *Pre-Service Procedures* in this chapter and relieve the fuel pressure.
2. Remove the air intake upper manifold and fuel rail assemblies as described in this chapter.
3. Detach the electrical connector from each injector that is to be removed.
4. Pull the injector body out of its bore while gently rocking the injector from side to side.
5. Check the ends of the injectors to make sure they are clean. Clean the injectors using Rotunda Injector Cleaner/Tester (part No. 113-00001 or equivalent).

CAUTION
Do not attempt to clean the injector orifice with tools or brushes.

6. Check all electrical terminals to make sure they are straight and not corroded or dirty. Clean the terminals and connectors with electronic contact cleaner.

CAUTION
*Do not twist, nick or cut the O-rings (**Figure 61**) when installing the injectors. The O-rings are made of special material that is resistant to fuel. Do not substitute another type of O-ring.*

7. Install new O-rings (**Figure 61**). Lubricate the O-rings lightly with clean engine oil. Do not use silicone grease, because it will clog the injectors.
8. Push the injectors into the manifold using a slight twisting motion. When properly seated, the O-ring will snap into position.
9. Install the fuel rails as described in this chapter.
10. Apply electric terminal grease (Ford part No. F2AZ-19584-A or equivalent) to the terminals and attach connectors.
11. Energize the fuel pumps and check for leaks before proceeding.
12. Install the air intake upper manifold as described in this chapter.
13. Refer to *Post-Service Procedures* in this chapter.

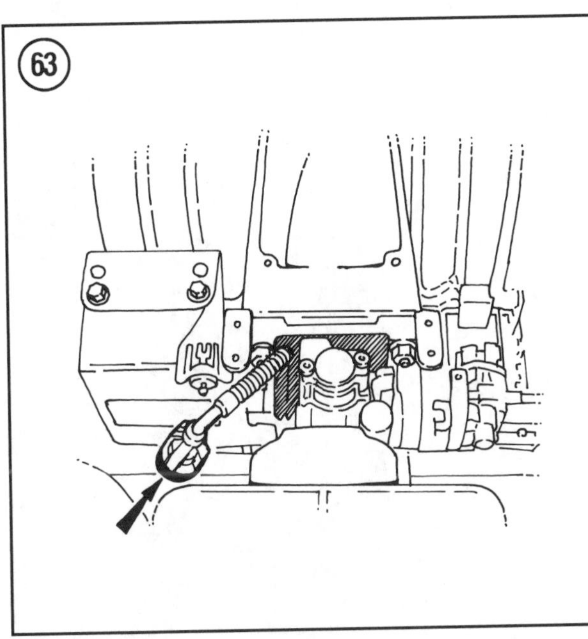

Throttle Position Sensor Removal/Installation

1. Remove the 4 screws attaching the plastic cover to the top of the engine, then remove the cover.
2. Detach the wiring connector (**Figure 63**) from the throttle position sensor.
3. Use a felt-tipped pin to mark across the edge of the sensor and throttle body to facilitate installation. See A, **Figure 64**.
4. Remove the 2 screws (B, **Figure 64**) retaining the sensor.
5. When installing the throttle position sensor, the wiring harness must be parallel with the

throttle bore. Align the reference marks (A, **Figure 64**).

6. Install the retaining screws (B, **Figure 64**) and tighten to the torque listed in **Table 3**.

7. Install the plastic cover on top of the engine and tighten the retaining screws to the torque listed in **Table 3**.

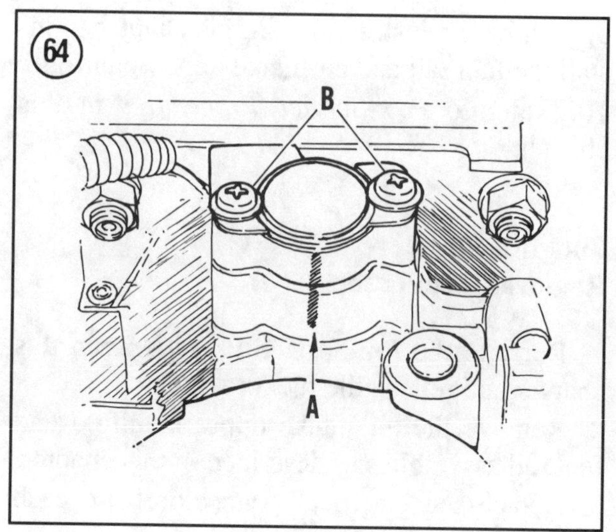

Idle Speed Control (ISC) Solenoid Removal/Installation

1. Remove the 4 screws attaching the plastic cover to the top of the engine, then remove the cover.

2. Detach the 2-pin wiring connector (B, **Figure 65**) from the ISC solenoid.

3. Remove the 2 attaching screws (**Figure 66**), then remove the solenoid.

4. The solenoid adaptor can be removed after removing the 2 attaching screws.

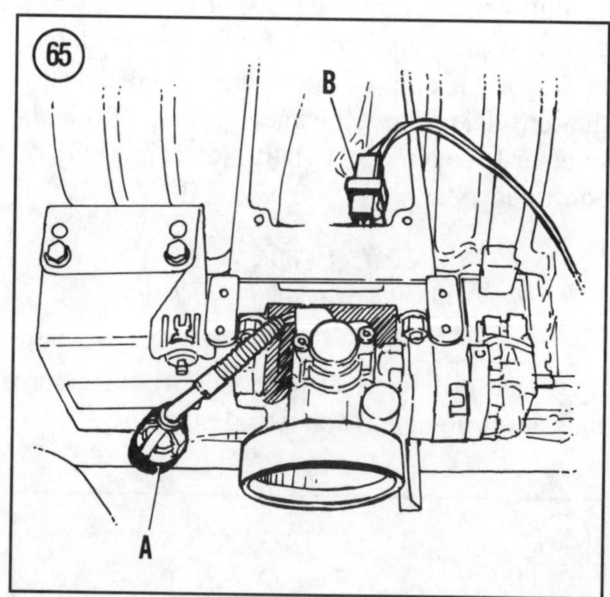

NOTE
Be careful not to damage the adaptor or the muffler foam while cleaning. Install new parts if damaged.

5. Remove the foam muffler from the adaptor and clean the adaptor, gasket surfaces and muffler foam. Discard the old gaskets and dry the muffler foam with air.

6. Push the muffler foam into the adaptor until flush or below flush with the adaptor.

7. Position a new gasket between the throttle body and the adaptor and install the retaining screws. Tighten the screws to the torque listed in **Table 3**.

8. Position a new gasket between the adaptor and the solenoid and install the retaining screws. Tighten the screws to the torque listed in **Table 3**.

9. Apply electric terminal grease (Ford part No. F2AZ-19584-A or equivalent) before attaching the ISC solenoid terminal. See B, **Figure 65**.

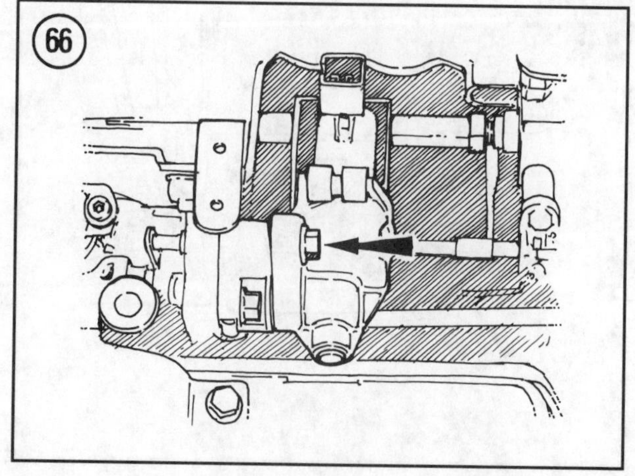

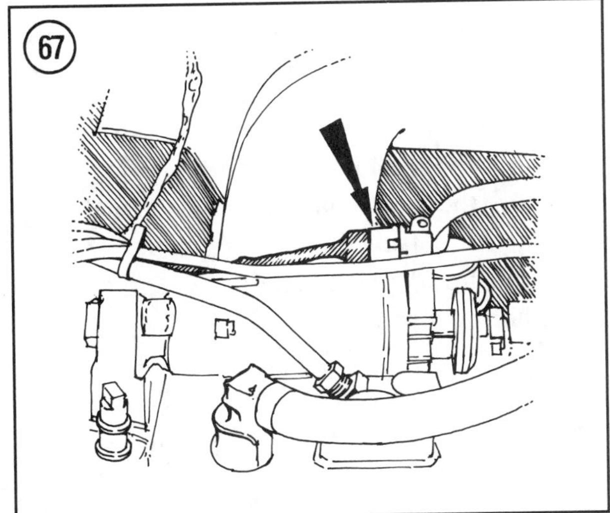

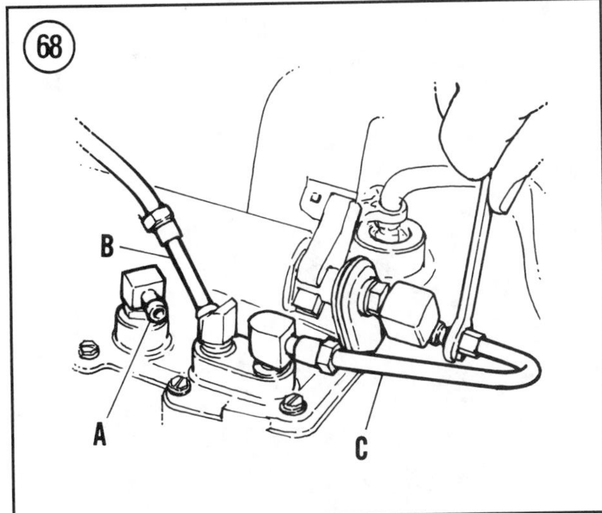

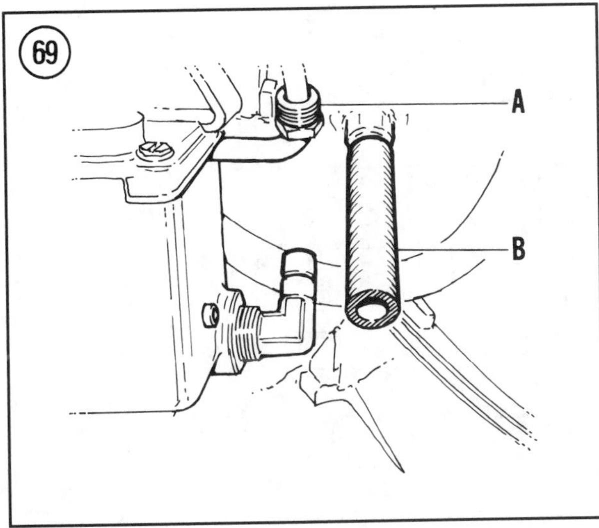

10. Install the plastic cover on the top of the engine and tighten the retaining screws to the torque listed in **Table 3**.

Fuel Reservoir Removal/Installation

1. Loosen or remove the hose clamps and detach the water inlet and outlet hoses from the fuel reservoir.
2. Remove the nut attaching the power steering cooler to the fuel reservoir, then move the cooler out of the way. Remove and save the flat washer located behind the cooler.
3. Cut the tie strap and unplug the electrical connector from the high pressure fuel pump. See **Figure 67**.
4. Loosen the clamp, then detach the vent hose from the reservoir fitting (A, **Figure 68**).
5. Loosen the fitting and detach the low-pressure inlet line (B, **Figure 68**).
6. Loosen the fittings and remove the line (C, **Figure 68**) between the regulator and the reservoir.
7. Loosen the fitting and detach the fuel pump outlet line (A, **Figure 69**).
8. Loosen the clamp, then detach the cooling outlet hose (B, **Figure 69**).
9. Remove the 2 attaching screws and lift the reservoir from the engine.
10. Install and tighten the 2 screws attaching the reservoir to the engine to the torque listed in **Table 3**.
11. Attach the cooling hose to the reservoir and tighten the hose clamp.
12. Attach the high pressure fuel line to the pump.
13. Install the fuel line (C, **Figure 68**) and tighten the fittings to the torque listed in **Table 3**.
14. Attach the low-pressure fuel line (B, **Figure 68**) and tighten the fitting to the torque listed in **Table 3**.

15. Attach the vent hose to the fitting (A, **Figure 68**) and tighten the hose clamp.

16. Apply electric terminal grease (Ford part No. F2AZ-19584-A or equivalent) before attaching the electrical terminal to the high pressure fuel pump. Secure the connection with a strap.

17. Position the thick flat washer onto the reservoir stud and install the power steering cooler.

18. Install the thin flat washer and locknut. Tighten the nut to the torque listed in **Table 3**.

19. Attach the inlet and outlet cooling hoses (A and B, **Figure 70**).

20. Energize the fuel pumps and check for leaks. Refer to *Post-Service Procedures* in this chapter.

Fuel level setting

1. Perform Steps 1-9 of the *Fuel Reservoir Removal* procedure described in this chapter.

2. Remove the screws attaching the cover on the reservoir, then remove the cover. Discard the old gasket.

3. Invert the reservoir cover and allow the float to close the fuel inlet needle. See **Figure 71**.

NOTE
Do not force the needle into the seat. The Viton tipped needle or seat may be damaged.

4. Measure the distance (A, **Figure 71**) between the cover and the float and the cover. Distance should be 3/16 in. (4.76 mm). If the clearance is incorrect, bend tab (B, **Figure 71**) as necessary. Be sure the float moves freely, especially after adjusting.

5. Position a new gasket on the reservoir and install the cover and float assembly.

6. Complete the assembly, referring to Steps 12-20 of the *Fuel Reservoir Installation* procedure described in this chapter.

Low-Pressure Fuel Pump Removal/Installation

1. Refer to *Pre-Service Procedures* in this chapter and relieve the fuel pressure.

2. Detach the fuel supply line from the fuel filter and plug the detached line.

3. Cut the tie strap that holds the electrical wires to the pump, then detach the connector (**Figure 72**).

4. Detach the fuel line (**Figure 73**) from the elbow at the top of the pump. Use 2 wrenches to prevent damage.

NOTE
If the end cap is not held when loosening the locknut and removing the elbow, the O-rings in the pump may leak.

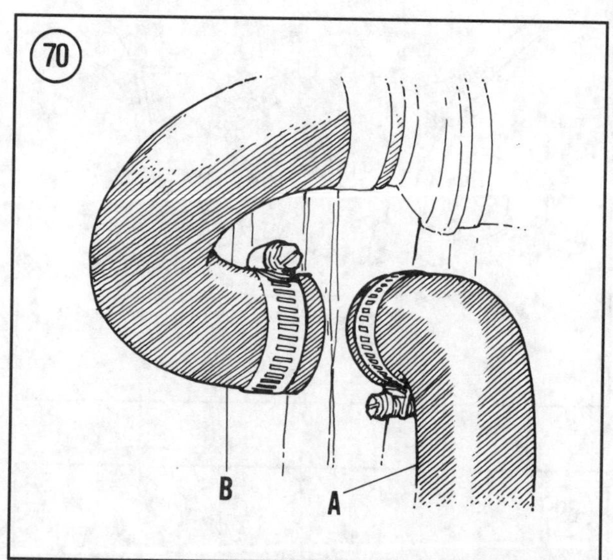

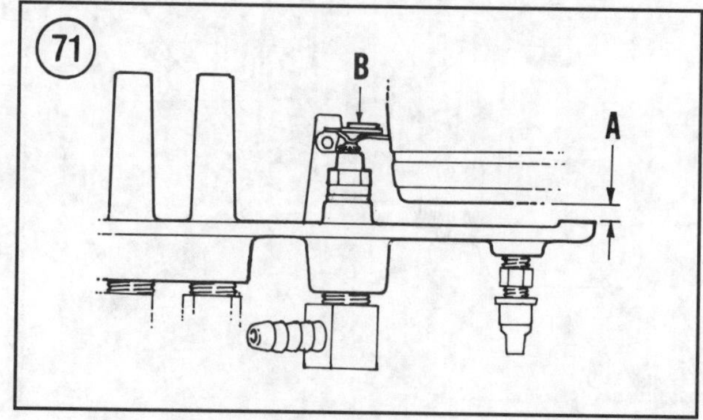

5. Hold the pump end cap with an open-end wrench and loosen the locknut located at the bottom of the elbow.

6. Remove the elbow from the top of the pump.

7. Remove the 2 bolts retaining the filter bracket.

WARNING
Be careful not to spill the fuel that may remain in the pump and filter.

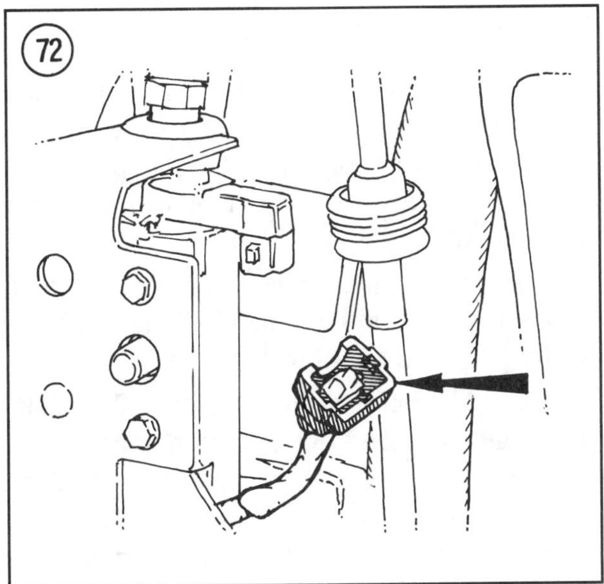

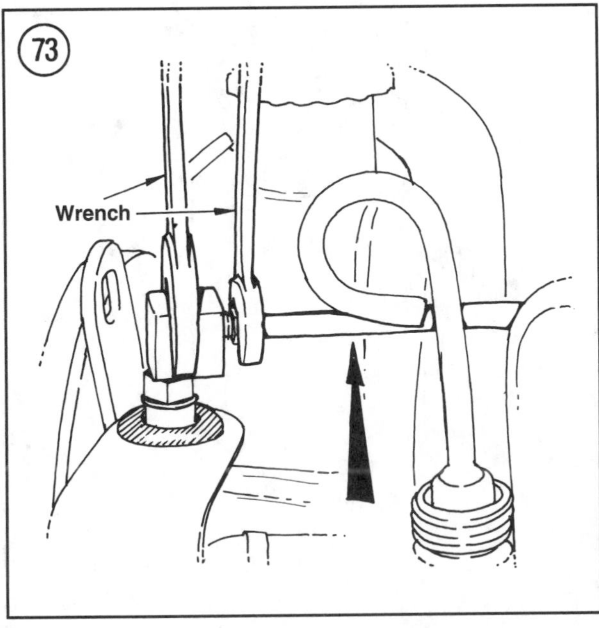

8. Slide the pump from the upper grommet and remove the pump and filter.

9. To separate the fuel pump from the filter, hold the pump end cap with an open-end wrench and remove the adapter from the base of the pump.

CAUTION
Do not nick or cut the O-ring when installing it in Step 10. The O-ring is made of special material that is resistant to fuel. Do not substitute another type of O-ring.

10. Before installing the fuel pump, position a new O-ring on the filter bracket adapter and move it against the hex.

11. Screw the filter bracket into the pump, hold the pump's lower end cap with an open-end wrench and tighten the adapter to the torque listed in **Table 3**.

12. Slide the pump through the grommet at the top and install the 2 screws attaching the filter bracket. Tighten the screws to the torque listed in **Table 3**.

CAUTION
Do not nick or cut the O-ring when installing it. The O-ring is made of special material that is resistant to fuel. Do not substitute another type of O-ring.

13. Turn the locknut against the elbow of the upper adapter and install the washer, then install a new O-ring on the adapter against the washer.

14. Insert the adapter elbow (with the washer and O-ring installed) through the grommet and into the pump. Tighten the adapter elbow all the way into the pump, then back the fitting up enough to align the fitting with the fuel line.

15. Attach the fuel line to the adapter. Hold the elbow with a wrench while tightening the fuel line.

CAUTION
If the pump end cap is not held securely while tightening the banjo bolt in Step 8, the end cap may turn and damage the internal pump seals.

16. Hold the pump end cap with an open-end wrench and tighten the locknut on the adapter to the torque listed in **Table 3**.

17. Apply electric terminal grease (Ford part No. F2AZ-19584-A or equivalent) before attaching the connector to the pump terminal. Connect the terminal and make sure it is secure. The connector should snap into place and be secured with a tie wrap to prevent it from accidentally becoming disconnected.

18. Attach the fuel line from the boat to the fuel filter.

19. Refer to *Post-Service Procedures* in this chapter for attaching the battery and checking for leaks.

High Pressure Fuel Pump Removal/Installation

1. Refer to the Pre-Service Procedures in this chapter and relieve the fuel pressure.

2. Observe and record the position of the elbow (**Figure 74**) so that the elbow can be properly located upon reassembly, then loosen the locknut and unscrew the fitting from the pump.

3. Remove the 2 screws attaching the end bracket to the reservoir and separate the bracket from the pump.

4. Unscrew the banjo fitting attaching the reservoir to the end of the pump, then remove the pump. Discard old O-rings.

WARNING
The O-rings used to seal the fuel fittings are made of special fuel resistant material. Do not attempt to use standard O-rings in this application. Make sure the O-rings are not twisted or damaged when installing.

5. Lubricate one of the small special O-rings with engine oil and install it on the threaded end of the fitting (**Figure 74**).

6. Lubricate one of the large special O-rings with engine oil and install it on the banjo bolt. Make sure the O-ring is correctly positioned in the groove near the head of the banjo bolt.

7. Install the banjo bolt into the hole in the reservoir cover, lubricate the other large special O-ring and install it on the exposed threaded end of the banjo bolt. See **Figure 75**.

CAUTION
If the pump end cap is not held securely while tightening the banjo bolt in Step 8, the end cap may turn and damage internal pump seals.

8. Thread the banjo bolt into the high-pressure fuel pump, position the pump at a 45° angle and tighten the banjo bolt. Hold the pump end cap while tightening the banjo bolt to the torque listed in **Table 3**.

9. Place the pump support bracket over the end of the pump and tighten the retaining screws to the torque listed in **Table 3**.

10. Attach the elbow fitting (**Figure 74**) to the pump and position the fitting at the same angle as it was originally installed.

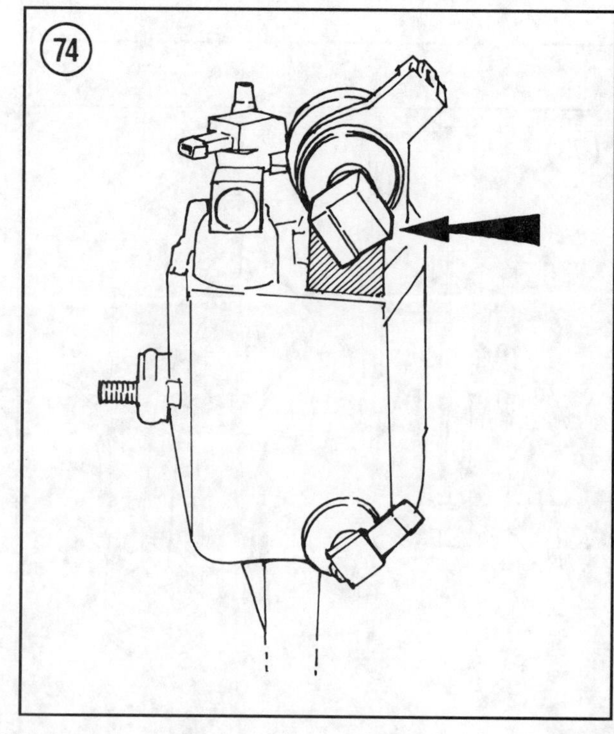

11. Hold the pump end cap and tighten the locknut to the torque listed in **Table 3**.
12. Energize the fuel pumps and check for leaks. Refer to *Post-Service Procedures* in this chapter.

Electronic Control Assembly (ECA) Removal/Installation

CAUTION
The ECA will be damaged if the battery is disconnected or connected with the key switch in the ON position.

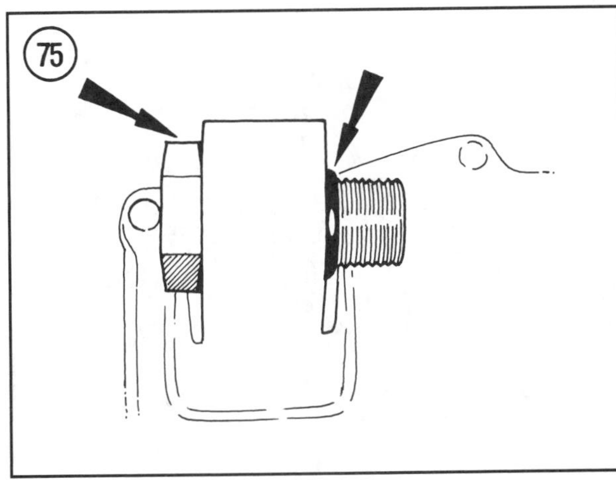

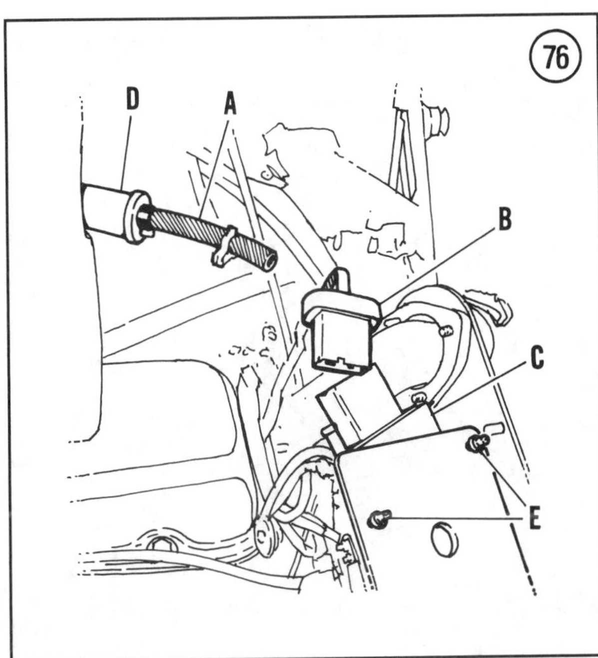

1. Make sure the key switch is OFF, then disconnect the battery.
2. Cut the tie strap from the rubber boot to the ECA cover, then peel the boot back to expose the 60-pin connector.
3. Unscrew the hex screw while separating the connector. When the connector is separated, move the connector out of the way.
4. Remove the 4 screws attaching the ECA cover to the bracket, then remove the ECA from the plastic cover.

NOTE
The ECA can be installed in the plastic cover only one way. Make sure the cover fits properly.

5. Install the ECA in the plastic cover and attach the cover to the bracket with 4 screws. Tighten the screws to the torque listed in **Table 3**.
6. Apply electric terminal grease (Ford part No. F2AZ-19584-A or equivalent) before attaching the 60-pin connector to the terminal to the ECA.
7. Attach the 60-pin connector to the ECA terminal. Tighten the retaining screw to the torque listed in **Table 3**.
8. Cover the connection with the rubber boot, then secure with a new tie strap.
9. Connect the battery cable(s) and check operation.

MAP Sensor Removal/Installation

1. Detach the ground terminal from the battery. Make sure the ground terminal is tied back so that it cannot accidentally contact the battery.
2. Remove the self-test connector and cover from the top of the ECA bracket. Move the cover out of the way.
3. Remove the 3 screws attaching the ECA bracket to the engine.
4. Loosen or remove the hose clamp, then detach the vacuum hose (A, **Figure 76**) from the map sensor (C).

5. Detach the connector (B, **Figure 76**) from the MAP sensor (C).

6. Remove the 2 attaching screws (E, **Figure 76**) and lift the MAP sensor from the bracket.

NOTE
The arrow on the filter must point toward the MAP sensor to allow the filter to drain properly.

7. Remove the MAP sensor filter (D, **Figure 76**). Clean the filter with a mild solvent and dry with air or install a new filter. Secure the filter with a clamp.

NOTE
The MAP sensor is attached to the bracket upside down to prevent the accumulation of condensation and damage to components.

8. Position the MAP sensor on the bracket with the *flat side up* and install the 2 attaching screws. Tighten the screws to the torque listed in **Table 3**.

9. Apply electric terminal grease (Ford part No. F2AZ-19584-A or equivalent) before attaching the electrical connector.

10. Attach the 3-wire connector to the MAP sensor.

11. Attach the vacuum hose (A, **Figure 76**) to the MAP sensor and secure with a clamp.

12. Attach the ECA bracket to the engine and tighten the 3 screws to the torque listed in **Table 3**.

13. Attach the self-test connector and cover to the ECA bracket.

14. Reattach the battery and check for proper operation.

EEC Power Relay Removal/Installation

1. Detach the ground terminal from the battery. Make sure the ground terminal is tied back so that it cannot accidentally contact the battery.

2. Remove the self-test connector and cover from the top of the ECA bracket. Move the cover out of the way.

3. Remove the 3 screws attaching the ECA bracket to the engine.

4. Detach the connector from the EEC Power Relay (**Figure 77**).

5. Cut the tie strap (A, **Figure 78**) and remove the screw (B) attaching the relay (C).

6. Attach the relay to the ECA bracket with a screw (B, **Figure 78**) and a tie strap (A).

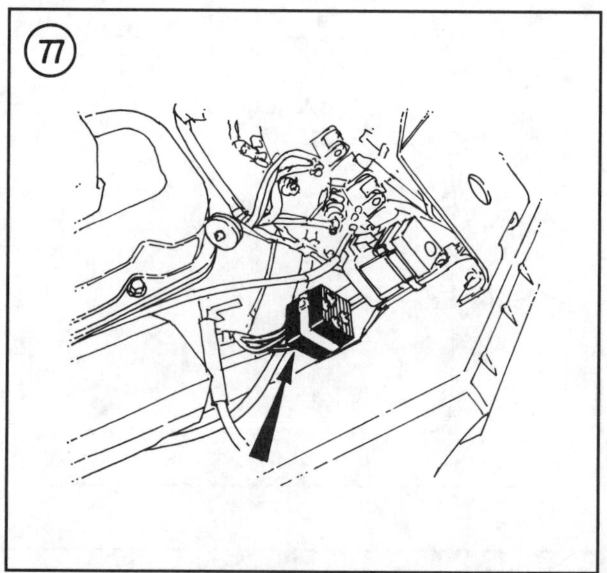

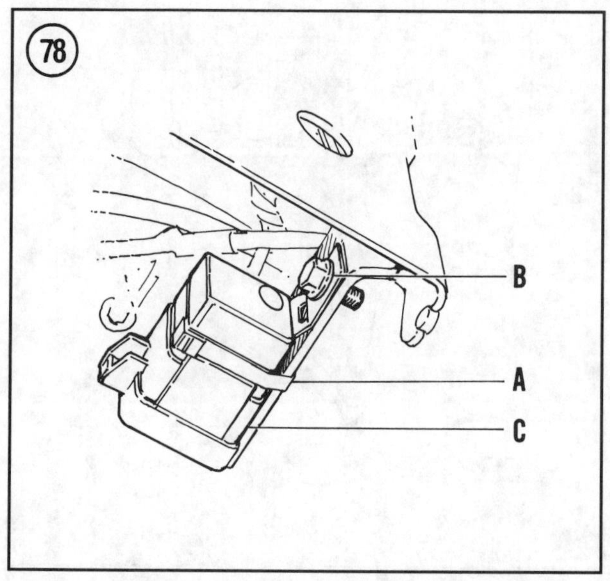

7. Apply electrical terminal grease (Ford part No. F2AZ-19584-A or equivalent) before attaching the electrical connector. Make sure the terminal is attached securely.

8. Attach the vacuum hose (A, **Figure 76**) to the MAP sensor and secure with a clamp.

9. Attach the ECA bracket to the engine and tighten the 3 screws to the torque listed in **Table 3**.

10. Attach the self-test connector and cover to the ECA bracket.

11. Reattach the battery and check for proper operation.

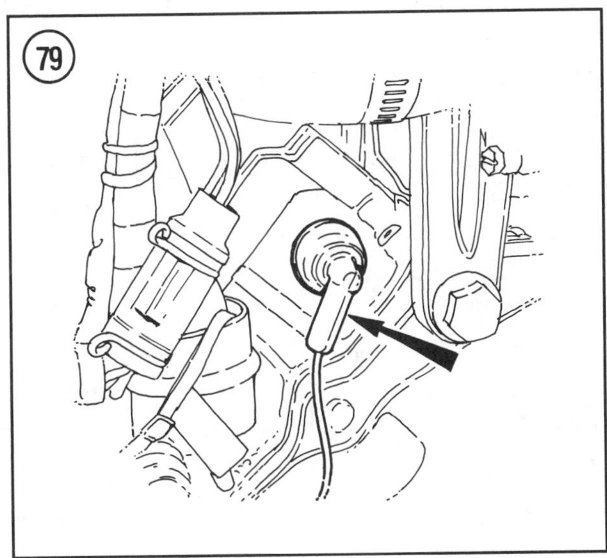

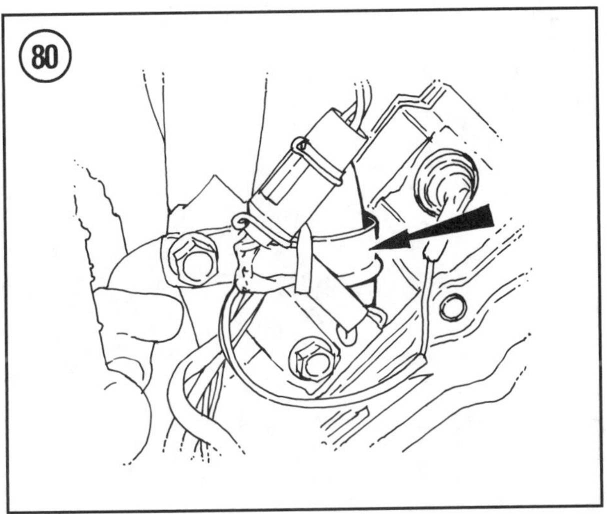

Knock Sensor Removal/Installation

1. Pull the connector from the knock sensor (**Figure 79**), then unscrew the sensor from the cylinder head.

NOTE
The knock sensor is a very sensitive unit that can be easily damaged by improper handling. If it is dropped or struck sharply, it is probably damaged. Install a new knock sensor.

2. Make sure the threads of the sensor and the threads in the cylinder head are clean and free of paint, corrosion or anything that will prevent a good electrical connection. The knock sensor must ground electrically through these threads.

3. Install the knock sensor and tighten to the torque listed in **Table 3**.

4. Attach the electrical connector to the sensor.

Knock Sensor Amplifier Removal/Installation

1. Cut the tie strap from the amplifier (**Figure 80**) and lift the amplifier from its bracket.

2. Remove the retainer from the connector and detach the amplifier from the terminal.

3. Apply electrical terminal grease (Ford part No. F2AZ-19584-A or equivalent) to the connector terminal pins before attaching the electrical connector. Make sure the connector is attached securely.

4. Position the amplifier in the bracket and secure with a tie wrap.

ACT and ECT Sensor Removal/Installation

1. Remove the 4 screws attaching the plastic cover to the top of the engine, then remove the cover.

2. Disconnect the high tension lead, the E-coil connector and the TFI-IV connector and move them out of the way.

3. Detach the lead from the sensor. The ACT sensor is shown in **Figure 81**. The ECT sensor is shown in **Figure 82**.

4. Unscrew the sensor from the block.

5. Install and tighten the sensor to the torque listed in **Table 3**. The ACT sensor and the ECT sensor are tightened to different torque values.

6. Apply electrical terminal grease (Ford part No. F2AZ-19584-A or equivalent) to the terminal pins before attaching the electrical connector. Make sure the terminal is attached securely.

7. Complete the assembly by reversing the removal procedure. Tighten the 4 screws attaching the plastic cover to the torque listed in **Table 3**.

Circuit Breaker Removal/Installation

1. Disconnect the ground cable from the negative terminal of the battery, then secure the cable so that it cannot accidentally touch the battery terminal.

CAUTION
The ECA will be damaged if the battery is disconnected or connected with the key switch in the ON position.

2. Detach wires from both terminals of the circuit breaker.

3. Remove the screws attaching the circuit breaker then lift the circuit breaker from its bracket.

4. Install the circuit breaker and tighten the attaching screws to the torque listed in **Table 3**.

5. Attach the red lead to one terminal and the red/purple lead to the other terminal. Tighten retaining nuts to the torque listed in **Table 3**, then coat with liquid neoprene.

THROTTLE BODY FUEL INJECTION (4.3, 5.0 AND 5.7 L Gi AND GSi MODELS)

Some Volvo Penta models are equipped with a Marine Electronic Fuel Injection (MEFI) system that injects fuel into the incoming air stream at the throttle body unit. Complete testing requires the use of the following tools or their equivalent.

1. Digital volt-ohmmeter (DVOM) part No. J34029-A, or equivalent. Use a DVOM only to perform voltage and resistance tests on any engine management circuit or component. Using an analog meter will result in damaged components.

2. Vacuum pump part No. J23738-A, or equivalent.

3. Twelve-volt test lamp (unpowered) part No. J341142-B, or equivalent. Use the test lamp to check circuit integrity.

4. Inductive tachometer.

5. Metri-Pack terminal remover tool part No. J35689, or equivalent.

6. Weather pack terminal remover tool part No. J28742-A or BT-8234-A, or equivalent.

7. Marine Diagnostic Trouble Code (MDTC) tool part No. TA06075, or equivalent. Use the

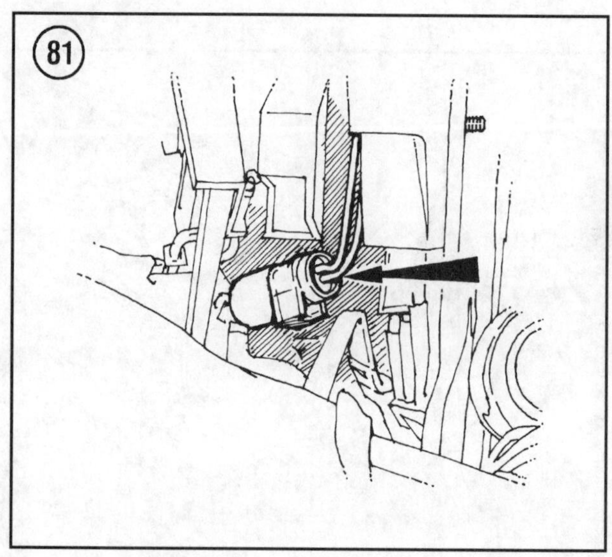

MDTC to retrieve stored trouble codes from ECM. A trouble code is indicated anytime the malfunction indicator light (MIL) is ON.

8. Fuel pressure gauge part No. J29658-D, or equivalent.
9. Injector harness test light part No. J34703-2C or J34730-350 or BT 8329, or equivalent. Provides a visual check for voltage delivered to the injector from the ECM.
10. Idle air control (IAC) wrench part No. J33031, or equivalent.
11. Harness adapter kit part No. J35616. The harness adapter provides test connections for voltage and resistance tests.
12. Diagnostic connector cable part No. TA06076, or equivalent. Use the connector cable to connect the Tech 1 scan tool to the diagnostic link connector (DLC).
13. Fuel line quick disconnector separator tool part No. J37088-A or BT9171, or equivalent.
14. Injector tester part No. J39021, or equivalent.Use the injector tester to test individual injectors.
15. Tech 1 Scan Tool part No. TK00450, or equivalent. Provides trouble code output in addition to serial data stream information.

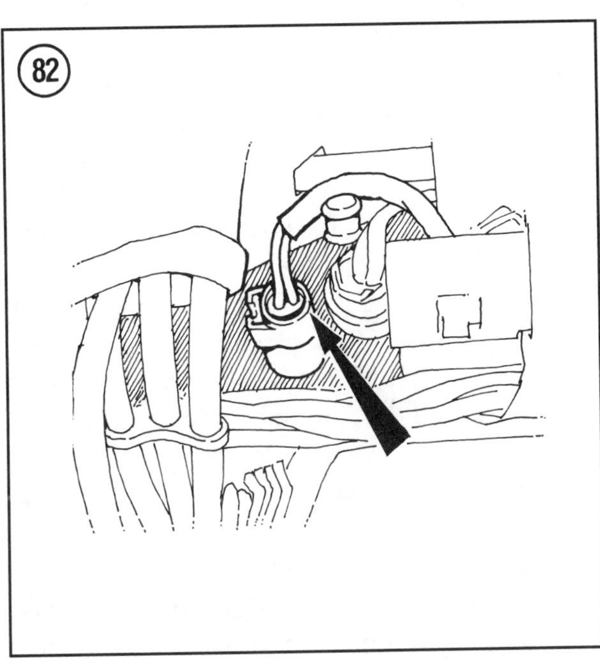

Scan Tool

A scan tool can communicate with the ECM when connected to the diagnostic link connector (DLC) and relay a wide variety of information. With an understanding of the circuits involved, the information provided by the scan tool can be used to troubleshoot the entire engine management system. A scan tool is especially useful when troubleshooting an intermittent malfunction because it can be connected to the DLC and observed while running the boat under the conditions that the malfunction occurs.

The following is a list of system parameters that could be expected from a normally running engine. Compare the operating parameters from a malfunctioning engine with the normal operating parameters to isolate a problem area.

1. *Idle speed*—The ECM receives engine speed information from the ignition reference input and compensates for engine load and maintains the preferred idle speed of 550-650 rpm. 9
2. *Engine coolant temperature*—The engine coolant temperature (ECT) sensor is a thermistor that is installed in the cooling system. The ECT sensor's internal resistance changes as its temperature changes. When the sensor is cold, its internal resistance is high and when the sensor is hot, its internal resistance is low. Because the ECM provides the sensor with a 5-volt reference signal, it can calculate engine temperature by the voltage returned from the ECT. Among other functions, the ECM uses engine temperature information to determine if fuel enrichment (cold engine) is necessary. The normal range of engine coolant temperature is –40 to 151° C (–40 to 304° F).
3. *Manifold absolute pressure (MAP)*—The map sensor provides the ECM with intake manifold pressure information, which relates to changes in engine speed and load. Intake manifold pressure is directly related to air density. The ECM uses this information (in addition to other inputs) to determine if an increase or decrease in

fuel is required. The normal range of the MAP signal is 0.0 volts at 11 kPa barometric pressure to 5.10 volts at 105 kPa barometric pressure.

4. *Knock retard*—The normal range of spark retard is 0-45° and indicates how much the ECM is retarding the ignition spark in response to input from the knock sensor.

5. *Knock sensor*—During normal operating (no knock occurring), the scan tool should display NO, at idle speed. This indicates that a knock signal is not being detected by the ECM. If YES is displayed, the knock sensor is detecting engine knocking or detonation and timing retard is activated.

6. *Barometric (BARO) sensor*—Provides barometric information to the ECM. The ECM uses the baro sensor input to compensate for changes in altitude. The normal range of the baro signal is 0.0 volts at 11 kPa barometric pressure to 5.10 volts at 105 kPa barometric pressure.

7. *Throttle position (TP) sensor*—Provides throttle position information to the ECM. Throttle position voltage should be 0.36-0.96 volts at idle to above 4 volts at wide-open throttle.

8. *Throttle angle*—The throttle angle is determined by the ECM from input from the TP sensor. The scan tool should display 0% at idle to 100% at wide-open throttle.

9. *Spark advance*—The scan tool can display the amount of spark advance from 90° retarded to 90° advanced. The ECM determines the optimum spark advance by processing information such as the current engine temperature, engine speed, engine load, throttle position, vehicle speed and operating mode.

10. *Idle air control*—The scan tool displays the idle air control position in counts. The normal range of operation is 0-255 counts. Higher count numbers indicate more idle air opening. The idle air control opens and closes idle air to increase or decrease engine idle speed.

11. *Injector pulse width*—Injector pulse width is the time in milliseconds that the injectors are activated. Higher pulse width results in more fuel delivery. The normal range of operation is 0.0-999.9. Higher display numbers mean increased pulse width.

12. *PROM ID*—The scan tool can identify the particular PROM (programmable read only memory) installed in the ECM. PROM ID ranges from 0-99999.

13. *System voltage*—The scan tool displays the system voltage as determined by the ECM. The normal range of system voltage is 0.0-25.5 volts.

14. *Intake air temperature (IAT)*—The intake air temperature sensor provides the ECM with intake air temperature. The ECM calculates air density from temperature information and uses this input to adjust fuel delivery and spark advance as required.

Diagnostic Trouble Codes

Diagnostic Trouble Codes (DTC) are stored and can be retrieved using a Marine Diagnostic Trouble Code (MDTC) tool. If multiple codes are stores, always troubleshoot and repair lower numbered codes first. The following DTC are listed with their possible causes:

a. Code 12 is a normal code when the engine is not running.

b. Code 14 indicates the engine coolant temperature sensor voltage is too high or too low. It could also be caused by grounded or an open wire from the signal sensor. If DTC 33 is also set, check for an open in the ground connection (between the sensor and the ECM).

c. Code 21 indicates the signal from the throttle position (TP) sensor is not consistent with the RPM and MAP sensors. It could be caused by a grounded or open wire from the signal sensor. The sensor is provided with a 5 volt reference and should return a sensor voltage of 0.36-0.96 volts at idle, and over 4 volts at wide-open throttle.

d. Code 23 indicates the signal from the intake air temperature (IAT) sensor is too high or too low. It could be caused by a grounded or open wire from the signal sensor.

e. Code 33 indicates the signal from the manifold absolute pressure (MAP) is not consistent with the RPM and throttle position. The sensor output may be either too high or too low with the engine running. If DTC 14 is also set, check for an open in the ground connection (between the sensor and the ECM).

f. Code 42 indicates the ignition control (IC) system is not receiving the correct voltage. DTC 42 may indicate a faulty ignition control (IC) module, but the condition could be caused by a grounded or open IC or a bypass circuit.

g. Code 43 indicates the knock sensor (KS) voltage is too high or too low. It may be caused by the wire from the sensor being open or grounded for more than 58 seconds. Abnormal engine noises or improper fuel may cause DTC 43 to be set.

h. Code 51 indicates a faulty PROM or electronic control module (ECM). The failure may be intermittent and may sometimes be sensitive to temperature changes.

Clearing trouble codes

Clear the trouble codes using the Marine Diagnostic Trouble Code (MDTC) tool or the Tech 1 Scan tool. The battery must be fully charged when clearing the trouble codes and the cranking speed must be at least 200 rpm. If the battery is not fully charged, it may be impossible to clear the trouble codes. Refer to the appropriate following procedure depending upon the tool used.

Marine diagnostic trouble code (MDTC) tool

1. Attach the MDTC tool following its manufacturer's instructions.
2. Turn the ignition ON, but do not start the engine.
3. Select the SERVICE mode on the tool.
4. Move the throttle from idle to wide open then back to idle.
5. Select the NORMAL mode on the tool. If this procedure is not followed, the engine may not start.
6. Start the engine and allow it to run for at least 20 seconds.
7. Turn the ignition OFF for at least 20 seconds.
8. Turn the ignition ON, but do not start the engine.
9. Select the SERVICE mode on the tool and verify the only service code is 12. If no other codes are stored, remove the tool. If other codes are stored, problems are indicated and system checks should be continued.

Tech 1 scan tool

1. Attach the scan tool.
2. Start the engine.
3. Select CLEAR DTC function.
4. Clear the trouble codes.
5. Turn the ignition OFF for at least 20 seconds.
6. Turn the ignition ON and check for trouble codes. If codes are stored, problems are indicated and system checks should be continued. Make sure the battery is fully charged.

9

Pre-Service Procedure

WARNING

Fuel is a dangerous fire and explosion hazard, so it is important to release pressure from the system before beginning most service procedures. This will prevent accidental spraying fuel as components are loosened, disconnected or removed. The following procedure will help reduce the hazard, but it is always important to exercise extreme caution whenever servicing any part of the fuel system. Always have an approved fire extinguisher immediately available.

1. Disconnect the ground cable from the battery. Make sure the cable cannot move back to its original location and provide incidental contact. It may be necessary to temporarily tie the cable away from the battery until service is completed.

2. Loosen the fuel filler cap to relieve any pressure from the fuel tank.

WARNING
Even when following the safest procedures, some fuel will be spilled during many operations and even a very small amount of fuel is dangerous. Always have an approved fire extinguisher ready and do not allow anyone to be in a position where they cannot escape the area quickly and easily.

3. The TBI fuel system is provided with internal bleeding that relieves pressure from the system when the engine is OFF. No additional procedure is necessary to release fuel pressure.

Post-Service Procedure

WARNING
The danger of fire or explosion due to fuel or fuel vapor continues to exist even after service. Make sure the area is cleaned as completely as possible after servicing, then provide ventilation to the area to remove as much of the vapor as possible.

1. Connect the ground cable to the battery.

2. Turn the ignition switch ON, then OFF several times and check for leaking fuel. Correct any leaks before continuing. Move the (wiggle) fuel lines if possible to make sure that all lines (especially those that were loosened during service) are tight.

3. Start the engine and run until warm.

4. Perform any available self-tests and make sure the system has not set any trouble codes.

Engine Control Module (ECM) Removal/Installation

CAUTION
The ECM can be easily damaged by improper or careless service procedures. Make sure the ignition system is OFF and the battery is disconnected before detaching or attaching the J1 and J2 terminals of the ECM. The ECM can also be easily damaged by electrostatic discharge, so make sure that you are grounded before touching the ECM, especially the connector pins. The ECM is carefully packaged, but be careful not to damage the unit by soaking it in cleaning

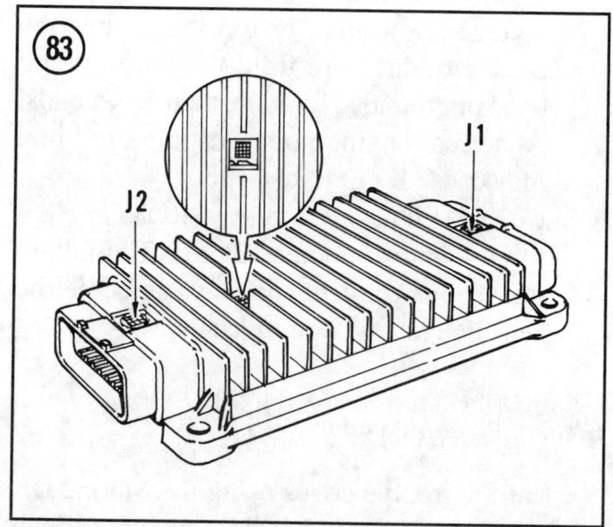

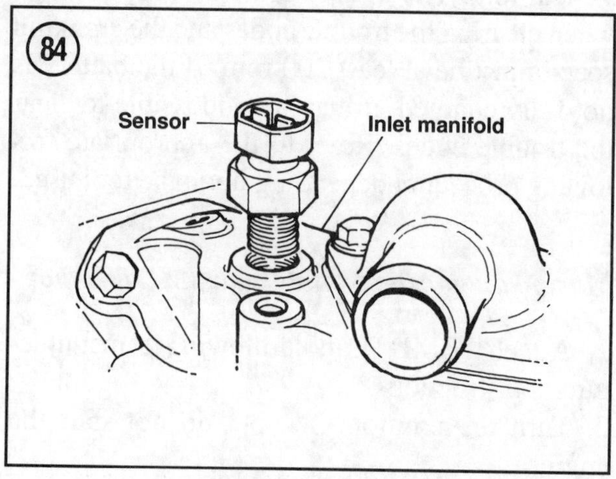

solvent or, bending or breaking the housing or seals.

1. Disconnect the ground cable from the battery negative terminal.
2. Detach the cable connectors from the J1 and J2 terminals of the ECM. See **Figure 83**.
3. Remove the 4 screws attaching the ECM and remove the ECM from its mounting bracket.

NOTE
If the ECM is being replaced with another unit, make sure the new unit has the same number. If the numbers are different, check with the parts supplier or dealership to make sure the unit is correct for your engine.

4. Attach the ECM to its mounting bracket and tighten the 4 screws to the torque listed in **Table 4**.
5. Attach the wiring harness to the J1 and J2 terminals.
6. Connect the ground cable to the battery.
7. Perform any available self-tests and make sure the system has not set any trouble codes.

Engine Coolant Temperature (ECT) Sensor Removal/Installation

1. Disconnect the ground cable from the battery negative terminal.

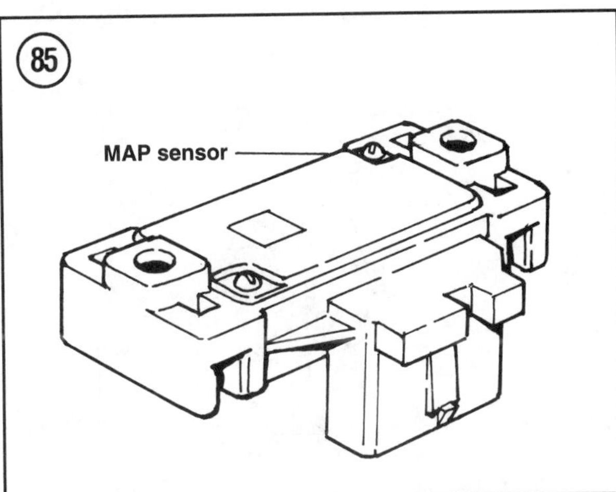

2. Detach the electrical connector from the sensor.
3. Remove the sensor from the intake manifold. See **Figure 84**.
4. Coat the threads of the sensor with teflon tape, then install and tighten the sensor.
5. Attach the electrical connector to the sensor.
6. Connect the ground cable to the battery.
7. Perform any available self-tests and make sure the system has not set any trouble codes.

Manifold Absolute Pressure (MAP) Sensor Removal/Installation

1. Disconnect the ground cable from the battery negative terminal.
2. Detach the electrical connector from the MAP sensor.
3. Remove the screws attaching the sensor. See **Figure 85**.
4. Detach the vacuum line from the MAP sensor, then remove the sensor.

NOTE
Do not soak the MAP sensor in any cleaning solvent.

5. Attach the vacuum hose to the MAP sensor.
6. Attach the MAP sensor and tighten its retaining screws to the torque listed in **Table 4**.
7. Attach the electrical connector to the sensor.
8. Connect the ground cable to the battery.
9. Perform any available self-tests and make sure the system has not set any trouble codes.

Throttle Position (TP) Sensor Removal/Installation

1. Disconnect the ground cable from the battery negative terminal.
2. Remove the flame arrestor as described in this chapter.
3. Detach the electrical connector from the TP sensor.

4. Unbolt and remove the sensor. See **Figure 86**.

NOTE
The TP sensor is an electrical component and can be damaged by improper cleaning. Do not soak in any cleaning solvent.

5. Check to make sure the throttle valve is closed, then install the TP sensor. Tighten the attaching screws to the torque listed in **Table 4**.
6. Attach the electrical connector to the sensor.
7. Connect the ground cable to the battery.
8. Check the TP sensor output voltage after installation. Connect a digital voltmeter to the TP sensor connector terminals B and C by backprobing the sensor connector. With the ignition (key) switch ON (engine not running) TP sensor output voltage must be approximately 0.7 volt at idle and 5 volts at wide-open throttle.
9. Reinstall the flame arrestor as described in this chapter.

Idle Air Control (IAC) Valve Removal/Installation

1. Disconnect the ground cable from the battery negative terminal.
2. Remove the flame arrestor as described in this chapter.
3. Detach the electrical connector from the IAC valve.
4. Remove the attaching screws (**Figure 87**).
5. Withdraw the IAC from the throttle body.

CAUTION
A used, but serviceable IAC valve may be damaged by pushing or pulling the pintle. The threads on the worm drive that move the pintle can be easily damaged.

6. Clean the IAC sealing surfaces, pintle valve seat and air passages. Certain carburetor cleaning solvents can be used, but should not contain methyl ethyl ketone or other extremely strong cleaning agents.
7. Inspect the pintle and seat. Shiny spots are normal and do not indicate misalignment.

NOTE
If the IAC valve is being replaced make sure the new unit has the same number. If the numbers are different, check with the parts supplier or dealership to make sure the unit is correct for your engine.

8. If a new IAC valve is being installed, measure the distance between the end of the pintle and the mounting surface. If the distance is greater than 28 mm (1.10 in.), gently push the valve to retract the pintle.

NOTE
Gentle finger pressure should not damage a new valve, but may damage a used part. New valves are adjusted at the fac-

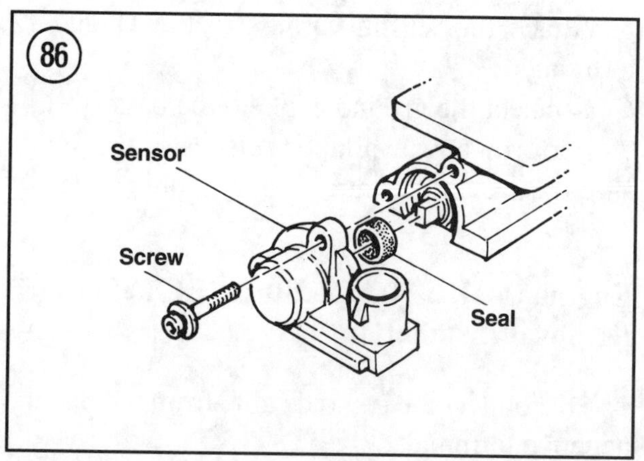

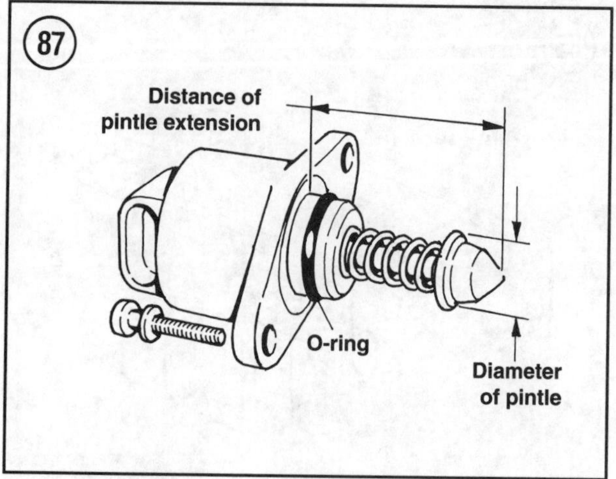

tory and adjustment should not be necessary.

9. Install a new O-ring and lubricate it lightly.
10. Install the IAC valve and tighten the mounting screws to the torque listed in **Table 4**.

NOTE
Attaching screws are coated with threadlocking compound by the manufacturer, which should not be cleaned from the threads. New valves are provided with new attaching screws.

11. Attach the electrical connector to the sensor.
12. Connect the ground cable to the battery.
13. Reset the IAC valve pintle position as follows:
 a. Turn the ignition OFF for 10 seconds.
 b. Start and run the engine for 5 seconds.
 c. Turn the ignition OFF for 10 seconds.
14. Perform any available self-tests and make sure the system has not set any trouble codes.

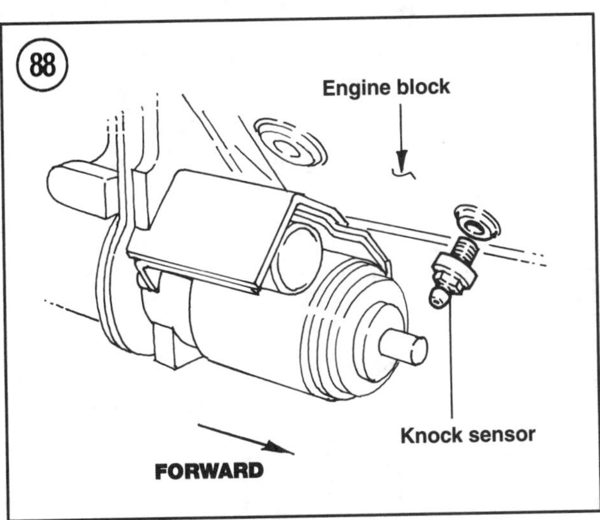

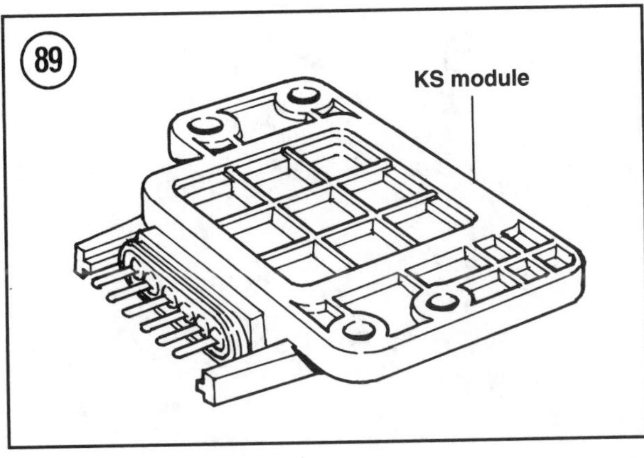

Knock Sensor (KS) Removal/Installation

1. Disconnect the ground cable from the negative battery terminal.
2. Detach the electrical connector from the knock sensor.
3. Unscrew the knock sensor from the engine block. See **Figure 88**.
4. Be sure the threads in the block and on the knock sensor are clean.
5. Install the knock sensor and tighten to the torque listed in **Table 4**.
6. Attach the electrical connector to the sensor.
7. Connect the ground cable to the battery.
8. Perform any available self-tests and make sure the system has not set any trouble codes.

9

Knock Sensor (KS) Module Removal/Installation

1. Disconnect the ground cable from the negative battery terminal.
2. Detach the electrical connector from the knock sensor module.
3. Unbolt and remove the knock sensor module. See **Figure 89**.

NOTE
The knock sensor module is an electrical component and can be damaged by improper cleaning. Do not soak in any cleaning solvent.

4. Attach the knock sensor module and tighten the screws securely.
5. Attach the electrical connector to the module.
6. Connect the ground cable to the battery.
7. Perform any available self-tests and make sure the system has not set any trouble codes.

Flame Arrestor Removal/Installation

1. Detach the hose from the flame arrestor.
2. Loosen the retaining clamp, then lift the flame arrestor from the engine.
3. Check the element for damage and clean or replace as necessary.
4. Reinstall by reversing the removal procedure.

Throttle Body Injector (TBI) Unit Removal/Installation

Use a carburetor holding fixture or similar device to prevent damage to the throttle plate(s) while working on the throttle body assembly. If a holding fixture is not available, long threaded bolts (of appropriate length) can be threaded into each of 3 bolt holes in the throttle body. These bolts will hold the throttle body up allowing clearance for the throttle plates.

1. Follow *Pre-Service Procedures* in this chapter. Be sure that electrical power is disconnected and fuel pressure is relieved.
2. Remove the flame arrestor as described in this chapter.
3. Detach electrical connectors from the idle air control (IAC) valve, throttle position (TP) sensor and fuel injectors. To detach the connectors from the injectors, squeeze the tabs before pulling the connectors from the injectors.
4. Detach the wires from the grommets on the throttle body.
5. Detach the throttle linkage and throttle return springs.
6. Detach the fuel lines. Remove and discard the O-rings from the fittings.
7. Check for any other attaching hardware. Detach anything that would prevent removal.
8. Remove the 3 screws attaching the throttle body to the adapter plate and lift the throttle body from the engine. See **Figure 90**.
9. Attach the throttle body to an appropriate holding fixture to prevent damage to the throttle plates.

CAUTION
Cover the openings in the intake manifold to prevent the entrance of any foreign object into the engine.

10. The adapter plate located under the throttle body can be unbolted and removed if necessary.
11. Clean all gasket material from the throttle body, adapter plate and manifold. Do not drop parts of the gasket or anything else into the intake manifold.
12. If removed, install the adapter plate using a new gasket.
13. Install the throttle body using a new gasket. Tighten the retaining screws to the torque listed in **Table 4**.
14. Attach the fuel line using a new O-ring. Tighten the fitting to the torque listed in **Table 4**.
15. Attach the throttle linkage and install the return springs.

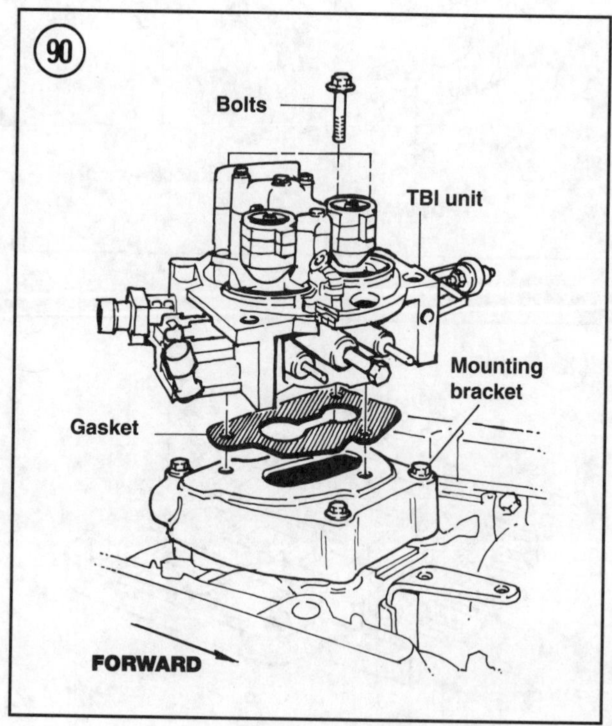

16. Attach the wiring harness to the throttle body through the grommets.
17. Attach the electrical connectors, making sure that each is seated completely.
18. Move the throttle from idle to wide open and check for complete movement with no restrictions.
19. Connect the ground cable to the battery.
20. Turn the ignition ON, but do not start the engine and check for fuel leaks.
21. Install the flame arrestor as described in this chapter.
22. Start the engine and check for proper operation and leaks.
23. Perform any available self-tests and make sure the system has not set any trouble codes.

Fuel Meter Cover Removal/Installation

The fuel meter cover contains the fuel pressure regulator assembly, which has been preset at the factory. Service the regulator and the fuel meter cover as an assembly. See **Figure 91**.

1. Disconnect the ground cable from the negative battery terminal.
2. Remove the flame arrestor as described in this chapter.
3. Detach the electrical connectors from the fuel injectors. Squeeze the tabs of the connectors before pulling the connectors from the injectors.
4. Remove the screws attaching the fuel metering cover to the throttle body. Some of the screws are long and others are short.
5. Lift the fuel metering cover from the throttle body.

NOTE
Do not attempt to remove the pressure regulator from the cover. A large spring is compressed in the regulator and may cause injury if accidentally released. The diaphragm located in the regulator may also be damaged by disassembling.

6. Remove the gaskets and seals from between the cover and body.
7. Clean the assembly and check for warpage or other damage.
8. Install new gaskets and seals between the cover and the throttle body.

NOTE
Coat the threads of the screws with locking compound included in the service repair kit. If not available, use Loctite 262 or equivalent locking compound. Do not use locking compound of higher strength, because it could make subsequent disassembly difficult and cause damage.

9. Install the fuel meter cover assembly. Make sure the screws are installed in the proper locations. The short screws are nearest the injectors. Tighten the screws to the torque listed in **Table 4**.
10. Attach the electrical connectors to the fuel injectors.
11. Connect the ground cable to the battery.
12. Turn the ignition ON, but do not start the engine, and check for fuel leaks.
13. Install the flame arrestor as described in this chapter.
14. Start the engine and check for proper operation and leaks.
15. Perform any available self-tests and make sure the system has not set any trouble codes.

Fuel Injector Removal/Installation

The injectors are serviced only as an assembly and no attempt should be made to disassemble them. The injector is an electrical component and can be damaged by improper cleaning. Do not soak in any cleaning solvent.

1. Remove the fuel meter cover as described in this chapter.

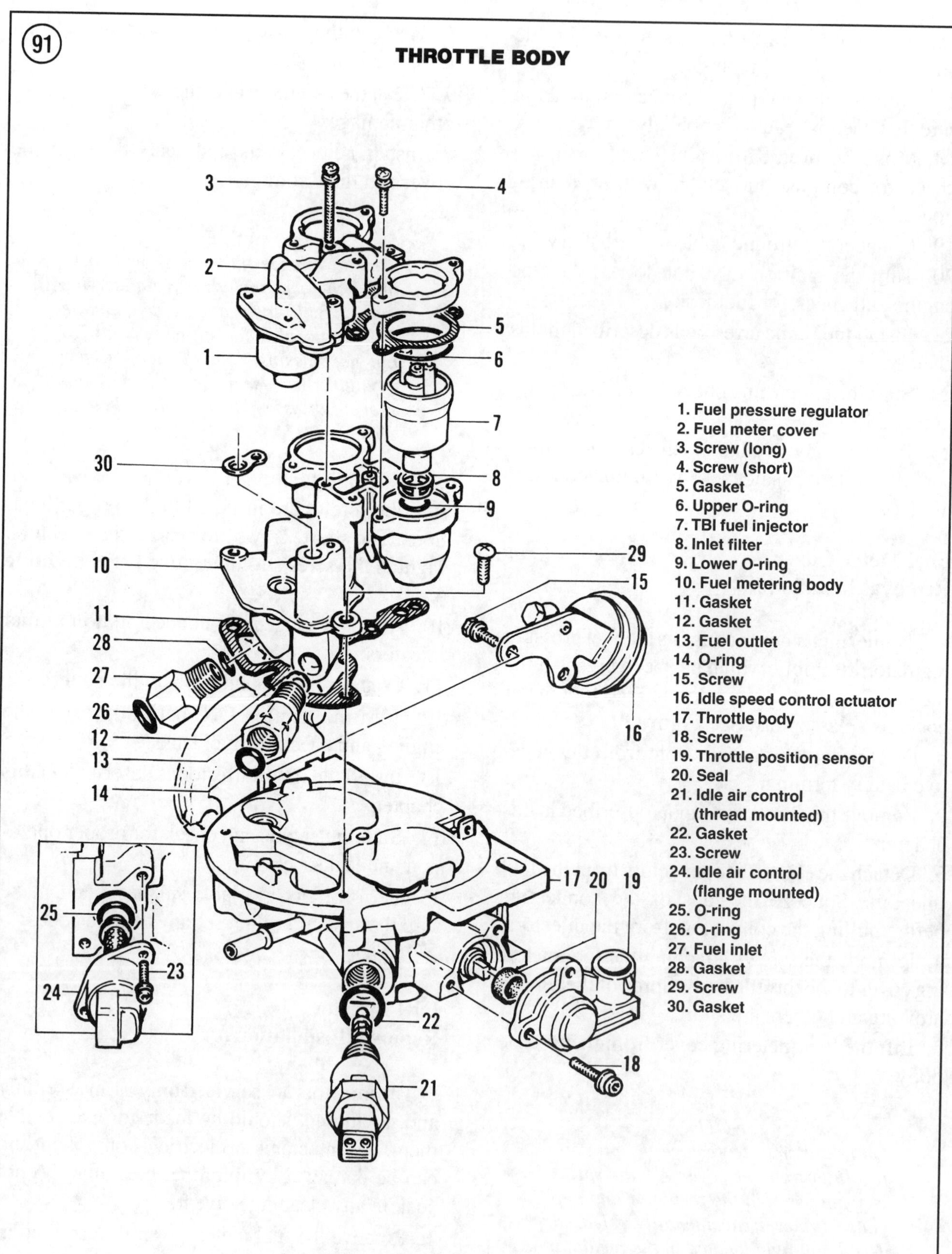
91
THROTTLE BODY
1
2
3
4
5
6
7
8
9
10
11
12
13
14
15
16
17
18
19
20
21
22
23
24
25
26
27
28
29
30
1. Fuel pressure regulator
2. Fuel meter cover
3. Screw (long)
4. Screw (short)
5. Gasket
6. Upper O-ring
7. TBI fuel injector
8. Inlet filter
9. Lower O-ring
10. Fuel metering body
11. Gasket
12. Gasket
13. Fuel outlet
14. O-ring
15. Screw
16. Idle speed control actuator
17. Throttle body
18. Screw
19. Throttle position sensor
20. Seal
21. Idle air control (thread mounted)
22. Gasket
23. Screw
24. Idle air control (flange mounted)
25. O-ring
26. O-ring
27. Fuel inlet
28. Gasket
29. Screw
30. Gasket

2. Leave the old fuel meter cover gasket in place to prevent damage to the fuel meter body when prying injectors out in Step 3.

3. Use a screwdriver and fulcrum as shown in **Figure 92** to pry the injector from the body.

4. Remove and discard the small O-rings from around the injector nozzles. Also, remove and discard the gaskets from between the body and fuel meter cover.

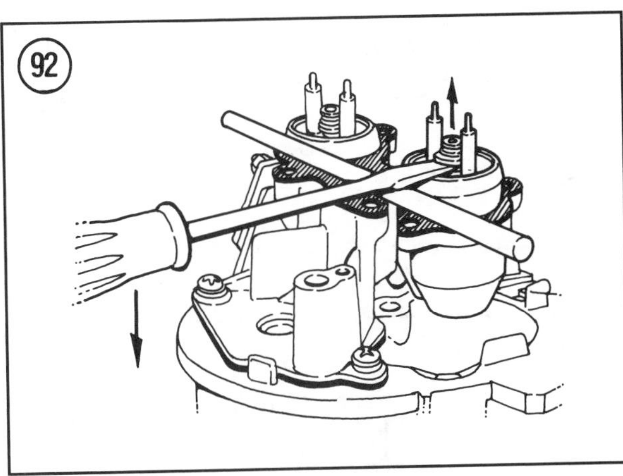

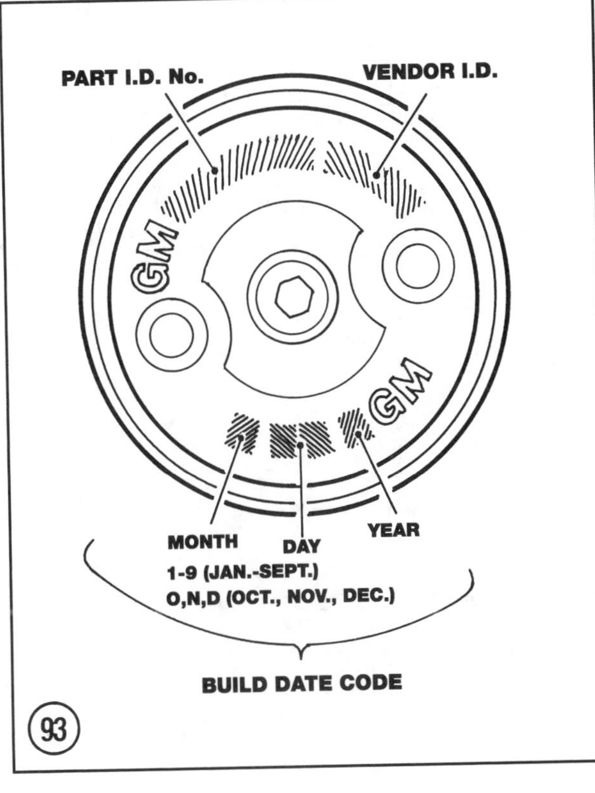

5. Remove and discard the large upper O-rings and steel backup washers from the injector cavities.

6. Inspect the injector filter (8, **Figure 91**). If the filter is dirty, it may indicate that the fuel tank should be cleaned too.

CAUTION

*If an injector is being replaced, make sure the new unit has the same number. Refer to **Figure 93** for identification. Injectors from other units may fit, but have incorrect flow rates that will prevent the engine from running properly. If the numbers are different, check with the parts supplier or dealership to make sure the unit is correct for your engine.*

7. Slide the filter into position on the injector.

8. Lubricate the small lower O-rings with automatic transmission fluid and press the O-ring into position against the filter.

9. Install the steel injector backup washer in the fuel meter body counterbore.

10. Lubricate the large upper O-rings with automatic transmission fluid and position directly over the backup washers installed in Step 9. Make sure the O-rings are properly seated and flush with the top of the fuel metering body surface.

NOTE

Make sure the backup washers (Step 9) and large O-rings (Step 10) are properly seated and lubricated before attempting to install the injectors. Improper installation of the backup rings and O-rings could result in fuel leakage.

11. Align the raised lug on the injector base with the notch in the fuel meter body cavity, then push the injector down until seated in the fuel meter body. See **Figure 94**. The electrical terminals should be parallel with the throttle shaft.

12. Install the fuel metering cover gasket.

13. Install the fuel metering cover as described in this chapter.

Fuel Meter Body Removal/Installation

Refer to **Figure 91** for this procedure.

1. Remove the fuel injectors as described in this chapter.
2. Detach the fuel inlet and return lines. Discard the old O-rings and install new O-rings when assembling.

NOTE

Observe (and mark) the original location of the fuel inlet and return fittings removed in Step 3. The inlet fitting has a larger fuel passage than the return fitting.

3. Remove the fuel inlet and return fittings from the fuel meter body assembly. Remove and discard the gaskets.
4. Remove the screws attaching the fuel meter body to the throttle body, then separate the fuel meter body from the throttle body.
5. Remove the gasket from the mating surfaces of the fuel metering body and throttle body.
6. Position a new gasket on the throttle body, matching the openings of a new gasket to those in the throttle body.

NOTE

Coat the threads of the screws with locking compound included in the service repair kit. If not available, use Loctite 262 or equivalent locking compound. Do not use locking compound of higher strength, because it could make subsequent disassembly difficult and cause damage.

7. Position the fuel meter body against the gasket and throttle body and install the retaining screws. Tighten the screws to the torque listed in **Table 4**.
8. Position new gaskets in the fitting bores, then install and tighten the fuel inlet and outlet fittings to the torque listed in **Table 4**.

NOTE

Install the fitting with the larger opening in the inlet passage. The recommended

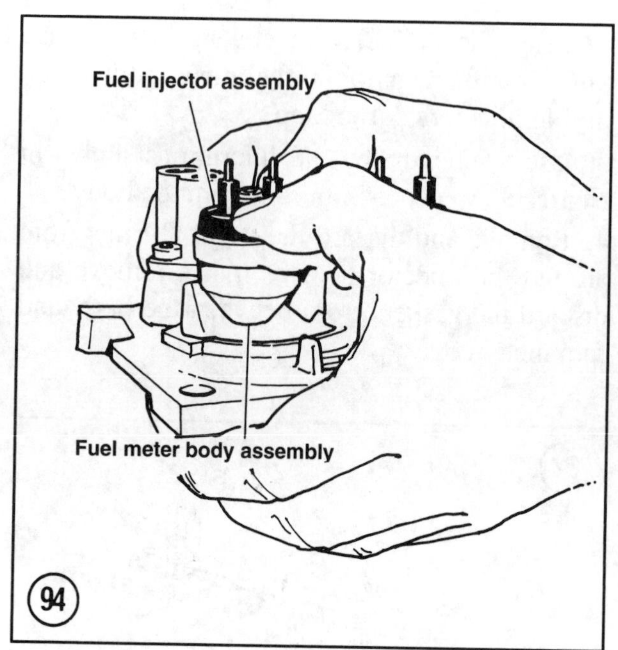

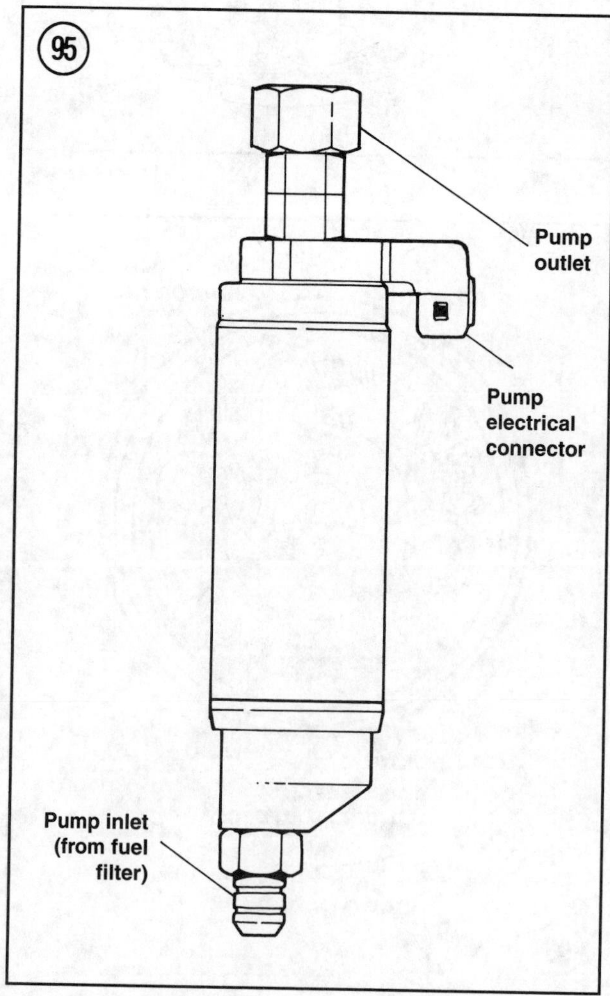

tightening torque is different for the inlet and return fittings.

9. Complete assembly by reversing the disassembly procedure. Install new O-rings and use 2 wrenches when tightening the fuel lines to the fittings.
10. Connect the ground cable to the battery.
11. Turn the ignition ON, but do not start the engine, and check for fuel leaks.
12. Install the flame arrestor as described in this chapter.
13. Start the engine and check for proper operation and leaks.
14. Perform any available self-tests and make sure the system has not set any trouble codes.

Fuel Pump Removal/Installation

1. Disconnect the ground cable from the negative battery terminal.

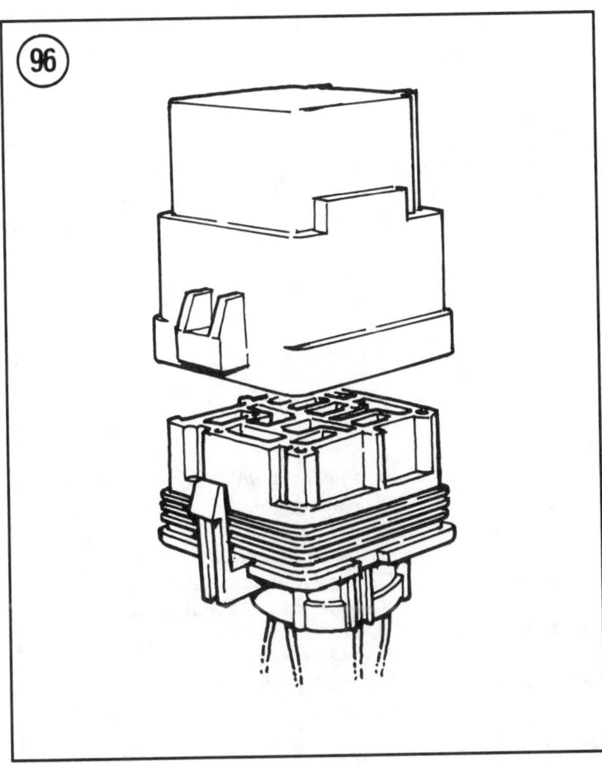

2. Detach the electrical connector from the fuel pump. See **Figure 95**.
3. Detach the fuel inlet and outlet lines from the pump fittings.
4. Detach the vapor return line from its fitting.
5. Unbolt and remove the fuel pump.

CAUTION
If the pump is being replaced, make sure the new unit has the same part number. If the numbers are different, check with the parts supplier or dealership to make sure the unit is correct for your engine.

6. Install the pump by reversing the removal procedure.
7. Attach the electrical connections and connect the battery ground.
8. Before starting the engine, turn the ignition switch ON to prime the fuel lines and check for fuel leaks.

9

Fuel Pump Relay Removal/Installation

1. Remove the retainer (cover), if so equipped. See **Figure 96**.
2. Detach the electrical connector from the fuel pump relay.
3. Remove the relay.
4. Install a new relay by reversing the removal procedure.

MULTIPOINT FUEL INJECTION (7.4 L Gi AND GSi ENGINES)

Some Volvo Penta models with 7.4 L engines are supplied fuel by a Marine Electronic Fuel Injection (MEFI) system that injects fuel into the incoming air stream at each (intake port). See **Figure 97**. Complete testing requires the use of the following tools or their equivalent.

1. Digital volt-ohmmeter (DVOM) part No. J34029-A, or equivalent. Use a DVOM only to perform voltage and resistance tests on any en-

(97)

FUEL INJECTED MODELS 7.4 L

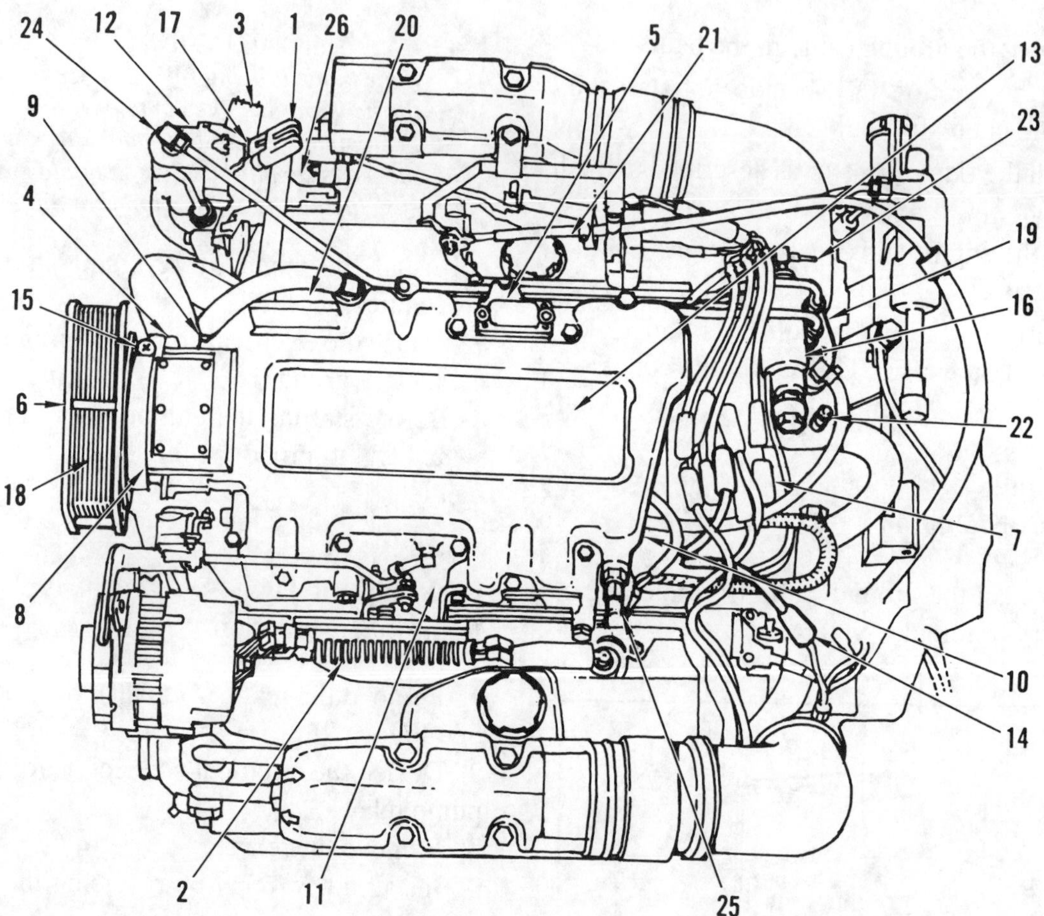

1. Data link connector (DLC)
2. Electronic control module (ECM)
3. Check engine light connector
4. Throttle position sensor (TPS)
5. Manifold absolute pressure (MAP)
6. Flame arrestor
7. Distributor/ignition module
8. Throttle body
9. Idle air control (IAC) motor
10. Pulse limiter
11. Fuel pressure regulator
12. Fuel injectors
13. Fuel rail
14. Ignition coil
15. Engine coolant temperature sensor (CTS or ECT)
16. High pressure fuel pump
17. Alternator
18. Coolant temperature gauge sensor
19. Fuel reservoir/vapor separator
20. Knock module
21. Knock sensor
22. Low pressure test point
23. High pressure test point
24. Low pressure fuel pump
25. Intake air temperature (IAT) sensor
26. Starter relay

gine management circuit or component. Using an analog meter will result in damaged components.

2. Vacuum pump part No. J23738-A, or equivalent.

3. Twelve-volt test lamp (unpowered) part No. J341142-B, or equivalent. Use the test lamp to check circuit integrity.

4. Inductive tachometer.

5. Metri-Pack terminal remover tool part No. J35689, or equivalent.

6. Weather pack terminal remover tool part No. J28742-A or BT-8234-A, or equivalent.

7. Marine Diagnostic Trouble Code (MDTC) tool part No. TA06075, or equivalent. Use the MDTC to retrieve stored trouble codes from ECM. A trouble code is indicated anytime the malfunction indicator light (MIL) is ON.

8. Fuel pressure gauge part No. J34730-1A, or equivalent.

9. Injector harness test light part No. J34703-2C or J34730-350 or BT 8329, or equivalent. Provides a visual check for voltage delivered to the injector from the ECM.

10. Idle air control (IAC) wrench part No. J35632 or BT-8514A, or equivalent.

11. Harness adapter kit part No. J35616. The harness adapter provides test connections for voltage and resistance tests.

12. Diagnostic connector cable part No. TA06076, or equivalent. Use the connector cable to connect the Tech 1 scan tool to the diagnostic link connector (DLC).

13. Fuel line quick disconnect separator tool part No. J37088-A or BT9171, or equivalent.

14. Injector tester part No. J39021, or equivalent. Use the injector tester to test individual injectors.

15. Tech 1 Scan Tool part No. TK00450, or equivalent. Provides trouble code output in addition to serial data stream information.

Scan Tool

A scan tool can communicate with the ECM when connected to the diagnostic link connector (DLC) and access a wide variety of information. With an understanding of the circuits involved, the information provided by the scan tool can be used to troubleshoot the entire engine management system. A scan tool is especially useful when troubleshooting an intermittent malfunction because it can be connected to the DLC and observed while running the boat under the conditions that the malfunction occurs.

The following is a list of system parameters that could be expected from a normally running engine. Compare the operating parameters from a malfunctioning engine with the normal operating parameters to isolate a problem area.

1. *Idle speed*—The ECM receives engine speed input (ignition control reference) from the ignition control (IC) module inside the distributor and maintains the preferred idle speed of 550-600 rpm. A failure in the ignition control circuit will store a trouble code 42.

2. *Engine coolant temperature*—The engine coolant temperature (ECT) sensor is a thermistor that is installed in the cooling system. The ECT sensor's internal resistance changes as its temperature changes. When the sensor is cold, its internal resistance is high and when the sensor is hot, its internal resistance is low. Because the ECM provides the sensor with a 5-volt reference signal, it can calculate engine temperature by the voltage returned from the ECT. Among other functions, the ECM uses engine temperature information to determine if fuel enrichment (cold engine) is necessary. Also, if engine temperature exceeds 93.3°C (200°F), the ECT will activate the SLOW safety mode. In the SLOW safety mode, the ECM limits engine speed to 2,500 rpm by disabling 4 fuel injectors and fixing ignition timing at 8° BTDC. The SLOW safety mode stays activated until engine temperature drops to 82°C (180°F) or engine speed drops to 1,200

rpm. A failure in the ECT circuit will store a diagnostic trouble code 14.

3. *Manifold absolute pressure (MAP)*—The map sensor provides the ECM with intake manifold pressure information, which relates to changes in engine speed and load. Intake manifold pressure is directly related to air density. The ECM uses this information (in addition to other inputs) to determine if an increase or decrease in fuel is required. The normal range of the MAP signal is approximately 1.0-1.5 volts at closed throttle (high vacuum) to approximately 4.0-5.0 volts at wide-open throttle (low vacuum). During engine starting (key on/engine off), the MAP sensor also provides the ECM with barometric pressure information. The ECM uses this data to compensate for changes in altitude. If a MAP circuit failure occurs, a trouble code 33 is stored in the ECM.

4. *Knock sensor*—During normal operating (no knock occurring), the scan tool should display NO, at idle speed. This indicates that a knock signal is not being detected by the ECM. If YES is displayed, the knock sensor is detecting engine knocking or detonation and timing retard is activated. The knock sensor module monitors the AC voltage signal from the knock sensor and delivers a constant 8-10 volt signal to the ECM as long as detonation is not occurring. If knock is detected, the module discontinues the 8-10 volt signal and the ECM immediately adds 5-10% more fuel in an attempt to stop detonation. If detonation continues, the ECM retards spark timing up to a maximum of 10° retard from the initial starting point. A failure in the knock sensor circuit will store a trouble code 43.

5. *Throttle position (TP) sensor*—Provides throttle position information to the ECM. The TP sensor is a potentiometer and is directly connected to the throttle body's throttle shaft. Normal throttle position voltage is approximately 0.5 volt at idle to approximately 5.0 volts at wide-open throttle. A failure in the TP sensor circuit will store a trouble code 21. The throttle angle is determined by the ECM from input from the TP sensor. The scan tool should display 0% at idle to 100% at wide-open throttle.

6. *Air intake temperature (IAT) sensor*—The IAT provides the ECM with intake air temperature data. The sensor is a thermistor and is installed in the induction plenum. IAT sensor resistance is high if intake air is cold and low if intake air is hot. The ECM supplies the IAT sensor with a 5-volt reference and determines intake air temperature by the voltage input from the sensor. An IAT sensor circuit failure will store a trouble code 23.

7. *Idle air control (IAC) valve*—The IAC valve controls engine idle speed by increasing or decreasing bypass air around the throttle valves, therefore compensating for changes in engine load. If idle speed is too slow, the IAC valve allows more air to bypass the throttle valves. If idle speed is too fast, the IAC valve decreases air bypass. The ECM controls the IAC and moves its pintle valve in small steps called counts. The scan tool displays the position of the IAC valve in counts from 0-60. The larger the count number the larger the air bypass opening.

8. *Spark advance*—The scan tool can display the amount of spark advance from 90° retarded to 90° advanced. The ECM determines the optimum spark advance by processing information such as the current engine temperature, engine

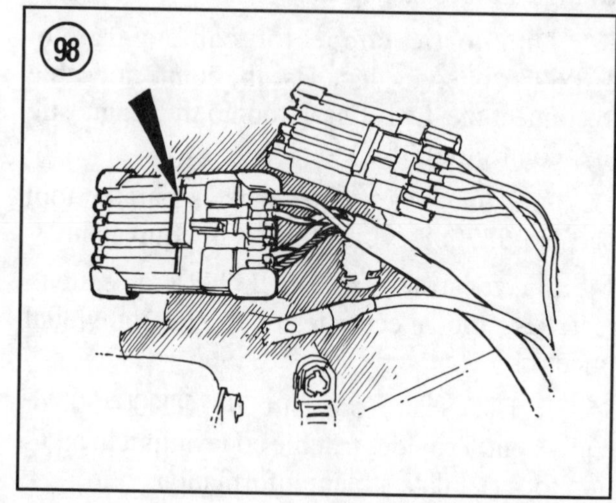

speed, engine load, throttle position, vehicle speed and operating mode.

9. *Injector pulse width*—Injector pulse width is the time in milliseconds that the injectors are activated. Higher pulse width results in more fuel delivery. The normal range of operation is 0.0-999.9. Higher display numbers mean increased pulse width.

10. *PROM ID*—The scan tool can identify the particular PROM (programmable read only memory) installed in the ECM. PROM ID ranges from 0-99999.

11. *System voltage*—The scan tool displays the system voltage as determined by the ECM. The normal range of system voltage is 0.0-25.5 volts.

Diagnostic Trouble Codes

Diagnostic Trouble Codes (DTC) are stored in the ECM and can be retrieved using a Marine Diagnostic Trouble Code (MDTC) tool. To retrieve the codes, proceed as follows.

1. Make sure the ignition switch is OFF.
2. Locate and remove the cover (**Figure 98**) from the data link connector (DLC).

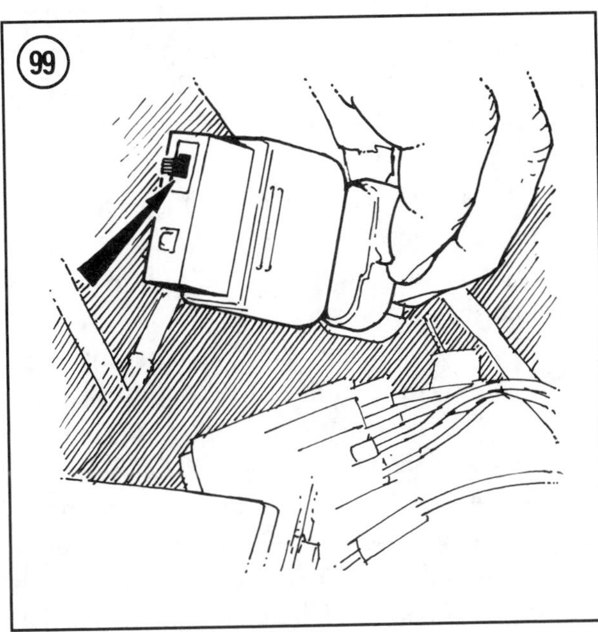

3. Push the switch (**Figure 99**) on the MDTC to the OFF position, then attach the tool to the DLC as shown.
4. Turn the ignition ON and observe the light on the MDTC tool. The light should glow steady. If it does not light, it indicates that the ECM is not receiving current. Check the ECM circuit breaker for faulty electrical connections and bad grounds. Another possible cause is the bulb in the MDTC is burned out.
5. With the engine still not running, push the switch on the MDTC tool (**Figure 99**) to the ON position and observe the light on the tool.

NOTE
DTC 12 is indicated by 1 flash, a long pause, followed by 2 short flashes.

6. The light on the test light should flash DTC 12 three times. If other trouble codes are stored in the ECM memory, they will also be indicated.
7. Trouble codes are stored (and retrieved) in the order in which they occurred. If multiple codes are stored, always troubleshoot and repair lower numbered codes first.
8. The following DTC are listed with their possible causes:
   a. Code 12 is a normal code when the engine is not running.
   b. Code 14 indicates the engine coolant temperature (ECT) sensor voltage is too high or too low. Code 14 could also be caused by grounded or open wire from the ECT signal sensor. If DTC 33 is also set, check for an open in the ground connection (black/orange wire between the sensor and the ECM J1-29 terminal). Resistance across the sensor terminals changes with the temperature, but should be approximately 3,400 ohms at 70° F (20° C) and 450 ohms at 160° F (70° C).
   c. Code 21 indicates the signal from the throttle position (TP) sensor is not consistent with the RPM and MAP sensors. Could be caused by grounded or open wire from the signal sensor. The sensor is provided with a

reference voltage of 5 volts and should return a sensor voltage of approximately 0.5-0.7 volt at idle and 5 volts at wide-open throttle. The gray/orange wire from the ECM delivers the reference voltage to the sensor.

d. Code 23 indicates the signal from the intake air temperature (IAT) sensor is too high or too low. Could be caused by grounded or open wire from the signal sensor. Resistance across the sensor terminals changes with the temperature, but should be approximately 3,400 ohms at 70° F (20° C) and 1,800 ohms at 100° F (38° C). If DTC 21 is also set, check for an open in the ground connection (black/white wire between the sensor and the ECM J1-13 terminal).

e. Code 33 indicates the signal from the manifold absolute pressure (MAP) is not consistent with the RPM and throttle position. The sensor output may be either too high or too low with the engine running. If DTC 14 is also set, check for an open in the ground connection (black/orange wire between the sensor and the ECM J1-29 terminal). The sensor is provided with a reference voltage of 5 volts and should return a signal voltage of approximately 1.0-1.5 volts at idle (closed throttle, high vacuum) to 4.0-4.5 volts at wide open throttle (low vacuum). The gray/orange wire from the ECM delivers the reference voltage to the sensor and the signal voltage is returned to terminal J1-9 of the ECM (light green wire).

f. Code 42 indicates the ignition control (IC) system is not receiving the correct voltage. DTC 42 may indicate a faulty ignition control (IC) module, but the condition (especially if it is intermittent) could be caused by grounded or open IC or bypass circuit wiring. When cranking the engine, there is no voltage in the bypass circuit (ECM J2-24 terminal white/tan wire) and the IC module grounds the IC signal (ECM terminal J2-23 gray/white wire). When the engine is running normally above about 400 rpm, bypass voltage is applied and the IC circuit should no longer ground the signal. If the bypass circuit (ECM J2-24 terminal white/tan wire) is either open or grounded, the IC module will not switch and the DTC 42 will be set. See **Figure 100**.

9. Resistance through the IC module can be checked as follows to determine the condition of the module:

a. Detach the connectors from the JI and J2 terminals of the ECM.
b. Attach one probe of an ohmmeter to the 23 terminal (gray/white wire) of the detached J2 harness connector.
c. Attach the other probe of the ohmmeter to an engine ground.
d. Observe the measured resistance between the D terminal of the IC module (gray/white wire) to engine ground.
e. Resistance should be 3,000-6,000 ohms. Low resistance indicates short to ground or faulty IC module.
f. Leave the ohmmeter attached and proceed with Step g.
g. Attach one lead of a test light to a battery positive connection, then temporarily touch the other lead of the test light to the 24 terminal (white/tan wire) of the detached J2 harness connector.
h. Observe the resistance as voltage is applied to the terminal in Step g. Resistance should drop from more than 3,000 ohms to less than 1,000 ohms.
i. Code 43 indicates the knock sensor (KS) voltage is too high or too low. If the wire from the sensor is either open or grounded for more than 58 seconds DTC 43 may be set. Abnormal engine noises or improper fuel may cause DTC 43 to be set. Resistance through the knock sensor should be 3,300-4,500 ohms. The KS module should receive

8-10 volts from the J1-1 terminal of the ECM.

j. Code 51 indicates a faulty EEPROM or electronic control module (ECM). The failure may be intermittent and may sometimes be sensitive to temperature changes.

Clearing Diagnostic Trouble Codes (DTC)

The diagnostic trouble codes will automatically clear from the ECM memory if they have not reoccurred within 25 powerups. The codes can also be cleared using the Marine Diagnostic Trouble Code (MDTC) tool or the Tech 1 Scan tool. It is important that the battery be fully charged when clearing the trouble codes and the cranking speed should be at least 200 rpm. If the battery is not fully charged, it may be impossible to clear the trouble codes. Refer to the appropriate following procedure depending upon the tool used.

Marine diagnostic trouble code (MDTC) tool

1. Attach the MDTC tool following its manufacturer's instructions.
2. Turn the ignition ON, but do not start the engine.

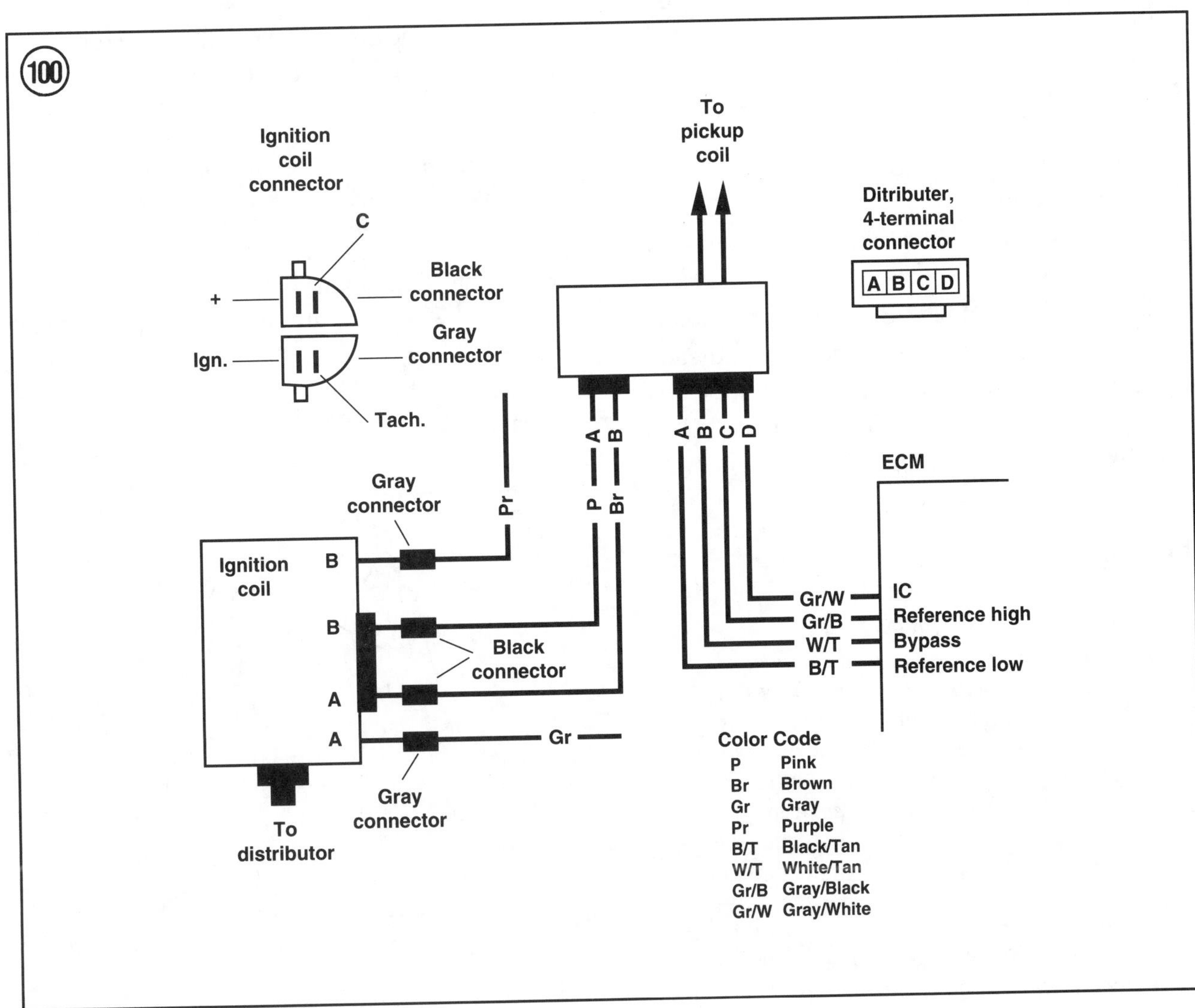

9

3. Select the SERVICE mode on the tool.
4. Move the throttle from idle to wide-open then back to idle.
5. Select the NORMAL mode on the tool. If this procedure is not followed, the engine may not start.
6. Start the engine and allow it to run for at least 20 seconds.
7. Turn the ignition OFF for at least 20 seconds.
8. Turn the ignition ON, but do not start the engine.
9. Select the SERVICE mode on the tool and verify the only service code is 12. If no other codes are stored, remove the tool. If other codes are stored, problems are indicated and system checks should be continued.

Tech 1 scan tool

1. Attach the scan tool.
2. Start the engine.
3. Select clear DTC function.
4. Clear the trouble codes.
5. Turn the ignition OFF for at least 20 seconds.
6. Turn the ignition ON and check for indicated DTC. If codes are stored, problems are indicated and system checks should be continued. Make sure the battery is fully charged.

Pre-Service Procedure

WARNING
Gasoline is a fire and explosion hazard, so it is important to release pressure from the system before beginning most service procedures to prevent accidentally spraying fuel as components are loosened, disconnected or removed. The following procedure will help reduce the hazard, but it is always important to exercise extreme caution whenever servicing any part of the fuel system. Always have an approved fire extinguisher immediately available.

1. Disconnect the ground cable from the battery. Make sure the cable cannot move back to its original location and provide incidental contact. It may be necessary to temporarily tie the cable away from the battery until service is completed.
2. Loosen the fuel filler cap to relieve pressure from the fuel tank.

WARNING
Even when following the safest procedure, some fuel will be spilled during many operations and even a small amount of fuel is dangerous. Always have an approved fire extinguisher ready and do not allow anyone to be in a position where they cannot escape the area quickly and easily.

3. Remove the protective cap from the fuel pressure relief valve (**Figure 101**).

NOTE
Wrap a shop cloth around the relief valve and adapter to catch spilled fuel when attaching it in Step 4.

4. Attach adapter part No. OTC-72723 and part No. OTC-7211 fuel pressure gauge to the relief valve.
5. Place the bleed hose in a container approved to catch fuel.

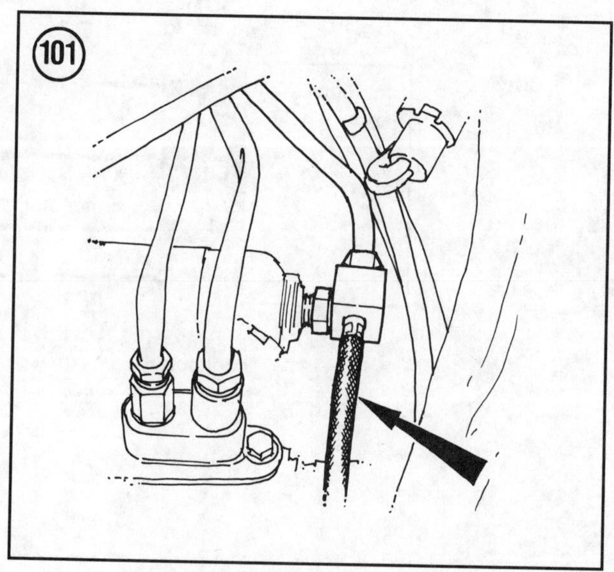

6. Open the bleed valve and allow fuel to drain into the container.
7. Remove the gauge and adapter and drain fuel into the container.
8. Dispose of the drained fuel in an appropriate manner.

Post-Service Procedure

WARNING
The danger of fire or explosion due to fuel or fuel vapor continues to exist even after service. Make sure the area is cleaned as completely as possible after servicing, then provide ventilation to the area to remove as much of the vapor as possible.

1. Connect the ground cable to the battery.
2. Turn the ignition switch ON, then OFF several times and check for leaking fuel. Correct any leaks before continuing. Move (wiggle) fuel lines if possible to make sure that all lines (especially those that were loosened during service) are tight.

NOTE
Steps 3-4 are the procedure to reset the idle air control (IAC) pintle position following service.

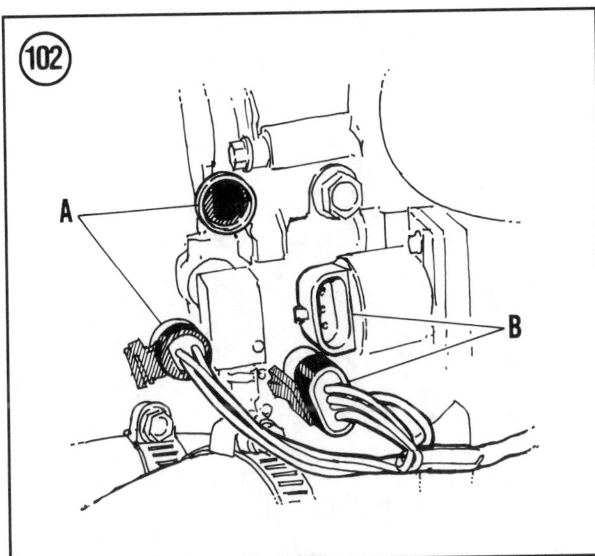

3. Start the engine and allow it to run for 30 seconds.
4. Turn the engine OFF for 10 seconds.
5. Start the engine and check for proper idle operation. Allow the engine to run until it is warm.
6. Perform any available self-tests and make sure the system has not set any trouble codes.

Flame Arrestor Removal/Installation

1. Disconnect the hoses from the flame arrestor.
2. Remove the nut and washer retaining the flame arrestor.
3. Pull the flame arrestor from the throttle body.
4. Remove and inspect the gasket located between the throttle body and the flame arrestor. Install a new gasket if it is cracked, torn or otherwise damaged.
5. Inspect the flame arrestor housing and element. The unit is baffled for correct air distribution and to prevent igniting any bilge vapor. Clean or replace the flame arrestor element and housing as necessary.
6. Install the gasket on the flame arrestor.
7. Push the flame arrestor and gasket onto the throttle body. Make sure the gasket is properly seated.
8. Install the washer and retaining nut. Tighten the nut securely.
9. Attach hoses to the flame arrestor.

Throttle Body Removal

1. Remove the flame arrestor as described in this chapter.
2. Detach the electrical connectors from the throttle positioning (TP) sensor (A, **Figure 102**) and the idle air control (IAC) valve (B).
3. Remove the nut attaching the throttle link to the throttle body arm, then detach the link.

4. Remove the 4 retaining screws (**Figure 103**) and lift the throttle body assembly from the plenum.

Throttle Body Disassembly

1. Remove the IAC valve as described in this chapter.
2. Remove the screws attaching the coolant cover to the throttle body.
3. Clean the assembly and make sure that all of the old gasket is removed. Do not damage the sealing surfaces.

CAUTION
The throttle body is coated at the factory with an approved sealing compound that should not be removed. Do not soak the throttle body in any cleaning solvent.

4. Install the cover using a new gasket. Tighten the screws to the torque listed in **Table 5**.
5. Install the IAC valve as described in this chapter.

Throttle Body Installation

CAUTION
The throttle body is coated at the factory with an approved sealing compound that should not be removed. Do not soak the throttle body in any cleaning solvent.

1. Clean the throttle body with a spray carburetor/choke cleaner and remove all old gasket material from the throttle body and plenum. Do not gouge the sealing surfaces.
2. Position the throttle body against the plenum with a new gasket between the sealing surfaces.
3. Install and tighten the 4 retaining screws to the torque specified in **Table 5**.
4. Make sure the throttle moves from idle to wide open, then to idle freely.
5. Attach the throttle link to the throttle body arm and secure it with the nut. Make sure the washer is installed and use a new cotter pin to lock the nut.
6. Attach the electrical connectors to the throttle positioning (TP) sensor (A, **Figure 102**) and the idle air control (IAC) valve (B).
7. Install the flame arrestor as described in this chapter.
8. Attach the battery ground cable and refer to *Post-Service Procedure* in this chapter. Make sure to reset the IAC pintle position as described.

Air Intake Upper Plenum Removal

1. Detach the ground cable from the negative terminal of the battery.

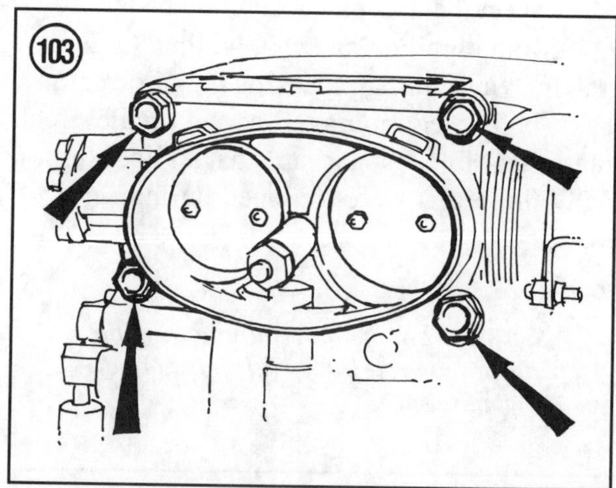

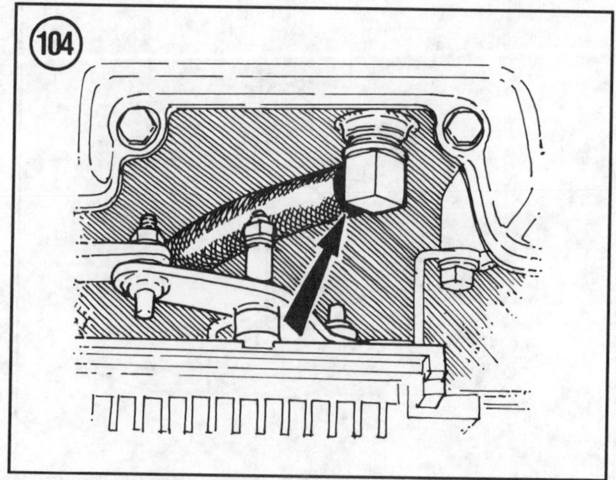

2. Remove the flame arrestor as described in this chapter.
3. Remove the nut attaching the throttle link to the throttle body arm, then detach the link.
4. Detach the wiring harness connectors from the J1 and J2 terminals of the ECM.
5. Detach the electrical connectors from the KS module, TP sensor, IAC valve, MAP sensor and the IAT sensor. See **Figure 97**.
6. Detach the pressure regulator vacuum hose from the fitting on the upper intake plenum. See **Figure 104**.
7. Detach the vapor hose from the pulse limiter. See **Figure 105**.

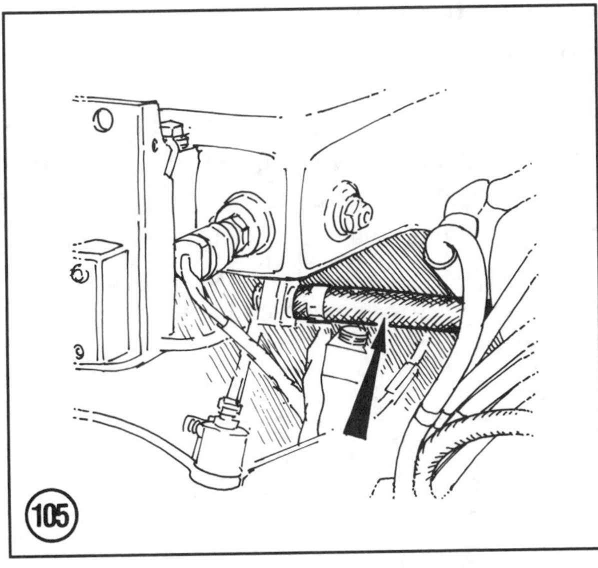

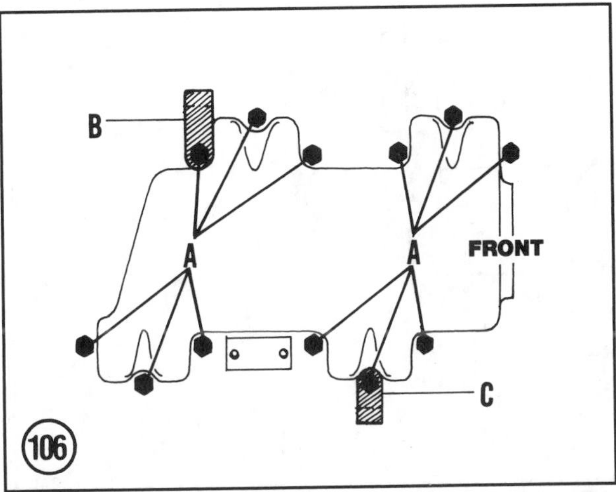

8. Remove the 12 screws (A, **Figure 106**) attaching the upper plenum to the lower intake manifold.
9. Observe the position of the throttle bracket and fuel line bracket (B and C, **Figure 106**), then lift the upper plenum carefully from the engine.
10. Remove the 8 O-ring seals from between the plenum and the lower manifold.

CAUTION
Be careful not to drop anything into the exposed ports of the lower manifold. If the lower manifold is to remain in place, cover the openings while cleaning the gasket and sealer from the lower manifold. Cover the openings in the lower manifold with tape or similar protection while the upper manifold is off.

Air Intake Upper Plenum Installation

9

NOTE
Be careful when cleaning aluminum surfaces. The material is easily gouged by hard scrapers and may be damaged by strong cleaners. If the throttle body is still attached, refer to the CAUTION in the Throttle Body Removal/Installation section of this chapter.

1. Clean and inspect the sealing surfaces between the lower and upper manifolds. Use caution to make sure that nothing falls into the open ports in the lower manifold.
2. Coat the 8 sealing rings with light grease, then install them in the grooves of the lower manifold.

NOTE
It is not necessary to use guide studs when installing the upper plenum, but alignment may be easier if guide studs are used. Make sure that guide studs are long enough to remove easily.

3. Position the upper plenum on the lower manifold carefully. Make sure none of the 8 sealing

rings move out of position when the plenum is installed.

4. Coat the threads and shafts of the 12 retaining screws (A, **Figure 106**) with Lubriplate 777 or equivalent before installing.

5. Install the 12 retaining screws (A, **Figure 106**) and tighten them all finger-tight.

6. Tighten screws (A, **Figure 106**) in several steps (gradually and evenly) in the sequence shown in **Figure 107** to the final torque listed in **Table 5**.

7. Attach the vapor hose to the pulse limiter and secure with a clamp. See **Figure 105**.

8. Attach the pressure regulator vacuum hose to the fitting on the upper intake plenum. See **Figure 104**.

9. Attach the electrical connectors to the KS module, TP sensor, IAC valve, MAP sensor and the IAT sensor. See **Figure 97**.

10. Attach the wiring harness connectors to the J1 and J2 terminals of the ECM.

11. Attach the throttle link to the throttle body arm and secure with the nut. Make sure the washer is installed and use a new cotter pin to lock the nut.

12. Install the flame arrestor as described in this chapter.

13. Attach the battery ground cable and refer to *Post-Service Procedure* in this chapter. Make sure to reset the IAC pintle position as described.

Air Intake Lower Manifold Removal/Installation

Remove the air intake upper manifold, and the fuel rail assembly as described in this chapter, then refer to the intake removal procedure in Chapter Seven to remove the lower manifold.

Fuel Rail Assembly Removal

Remove the fuel rails as an assembly with the injectors attached. Use care to prevent damage to the nozzle tips and the electrical terminals when removing, while the assembly is removed and when installing. Plug all openings and cover all components to prevent contamination of the fuel system.

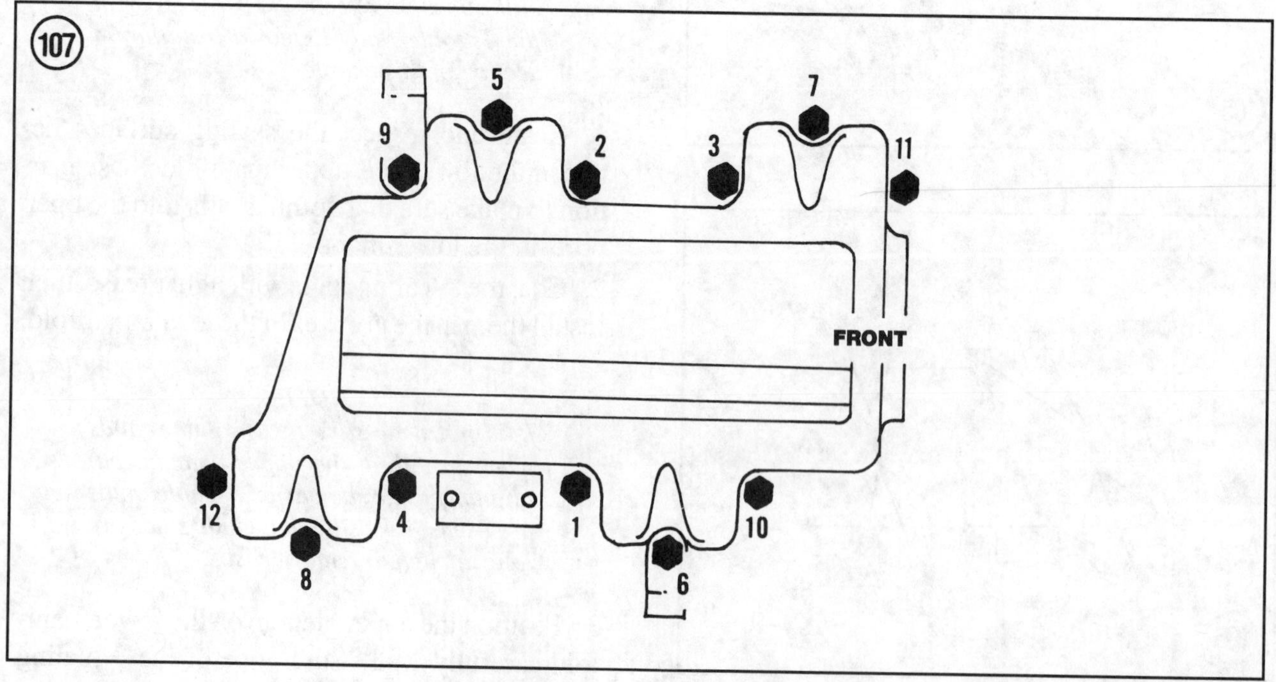

1. Detach the ground cable from the negative terminal of the battery.

2. Refer to *Pre-Service Procedure* in this chapter and relieve the fuel system pressure.

3. Remove the flame arrestor and the air intake upper plenum as described in this chapter.

4. Cover all openings and clean the area, especially around the injectors. Blow all dirt and cleaner from around the injectors to prevent contamination and damage.

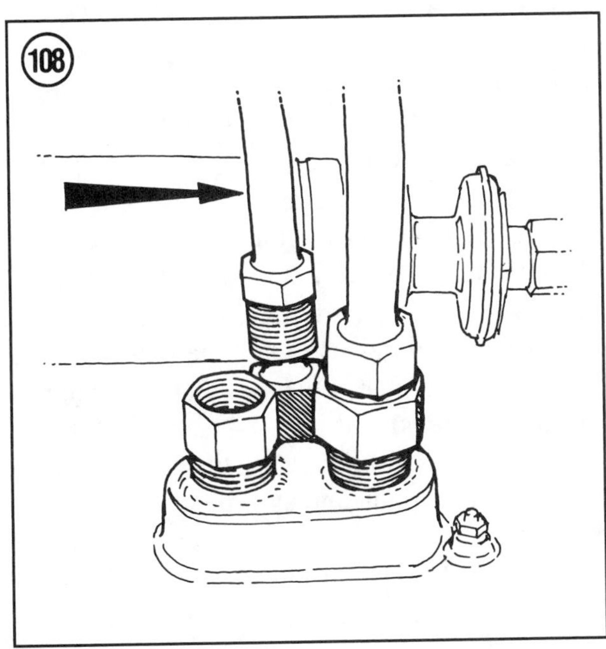

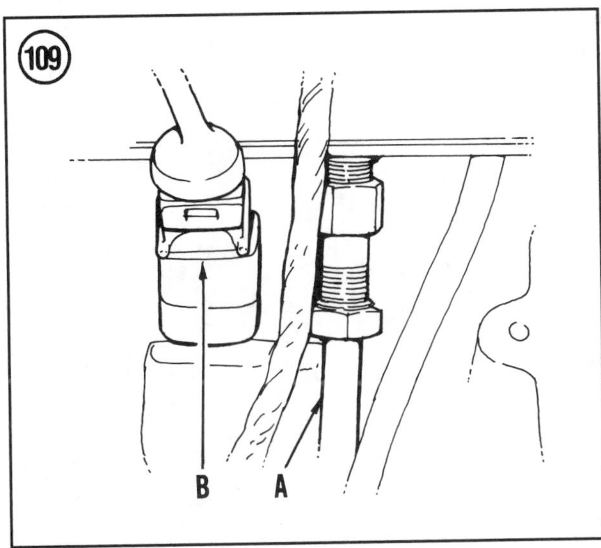

WARNING
Be prepared to catch any fuel that drains from the lines disconnected in Steps 5 and 6. Also have an approved fire extinguisher immediately ready in case of a fire. Any fuel or fuel vapor is potentially hazardous and anyone servicing components that contain fuel should exercise every precaution.

5. Disconnect the fuel return line (**Figure 108**).

6. Disconnect the fuel pressure line (A, **Figure 109**).

7. Observe the location of the tie wraps securing the wiring harness to the fuel rail and securing the injector connectors, then cut and remove the tie wraps.

8. Press the retaining clips on the connectors, then detach the connectors (B, **Figure 109**) from the injectors.

9. Remove the 4 screws attaching the fuel rail to the intake manifold.

10. Lift the fuel rails and injectors from the engine as an assembly.

11. If the injectors must be removed, refer to the appropriate section in this chapter.

12. Clean the fuel rail assembly using a spray type engine degreaser. Do not soak the assembly in solvent or use a harsh solvent.

Fuel Rail Assembly Installation

1. Make sure the fuel rail and the engine are both clean before beginning installation.

2. Check all electrical terminals to make sure they are straight and not corroded or dirty. Clean the terminals and connectors with electronic contact cleaner.

3. Check the bores for the fuel injectors for dirt, nicks or scratches.

CAUTION
Do not twist, nick or cut O-rings when installing. The O-rings are made of spe-

cial material that is resistant to fuel. Do not substitute another type of O-ring.

4. Check the ends of the injectors to make sure they are clean and install new O-rings.
5. Lubricate the O-rings lightly with clean engine oil.
6. Check the cups in the fuel rail and make sure they are clean and smooth.
7. Install the fuel rails and injectors as an assembly. If the injectors are aligned, they should slide in easily with gentle pressure.
8. Make sure the injectors are seated fully, then install the 4 attaching screws and tighten to the torque listed in **Table 5**.
9. Attach the electrical connectors to the injectors. Make sure each connector is fully seated, then secure the connection with a tie wrap.
10. Attach the high pressure fuel line and the return fuel line. Tighten the fittings to the torque listed in **Table 5**.
11. Follow the instructions in *Intake Upper Plenum Installation* in this chapter.
12. Connect the ground cable to the battery.
13. Turn the ignition ON, but do not start the engine and check for fuel leaks.
14. Start the engine and check for proper operation and leaks.
15. Refer to *Post-Service Procedure* described in this chapter. Make sure to reset the IAC pintle position as described. Perform any available self-tests and make sure the system has not set any trouble codes.

Fuel Pressure Regulator Assembly Removal/Installation

The fuel pressure regulator assembly is serviced as a complete unit only. Do not attempt to disassemble the unit.

1. Detach the ground cable from the negative terminal of the battery.
2. Refer to *Pre-Service Procedure* in this chapter and relieve the fuel system pressure.
3. Remove the flame arrestor, the air intake upper plenum and the fuel rail assembly as described in this chapter.
4. Remove the vacuum hose from the fuel pressure regulator (A, **Figure 110**).
5. Remove the fuel return line and fitting (B, **Figure 110**) from the regulator. Use a wrench on the regulator when loosening the return line fitting to prevent damage to the regulator.
6. Remove the retaining screw, then pull the regulator from the fuel rail.
7. Remove and discard the O-ring from the regulator.
8. Use a small pick to remove the filter screen from the fuel inlet port. If the screen is removed, install a new screen.
9. Lubricate a new O-ring with clean engine oil and install it on the regulator. Make sure the O-ring is not twisted or cut when installing.
10. Push the regulator into the fuel rail and install the retaining screw. Tighten the screw to the torque listed in **Table 5**. Install the fuel return line and tighten the fitting (B, **Figure 110**) to the torque listed in **Table 5**. Hold the regulator with a wrench to prevent damage when tightening the return line fitting.
11. Attach the vacuum line to the regulator fitting (A, **Figure 110**).

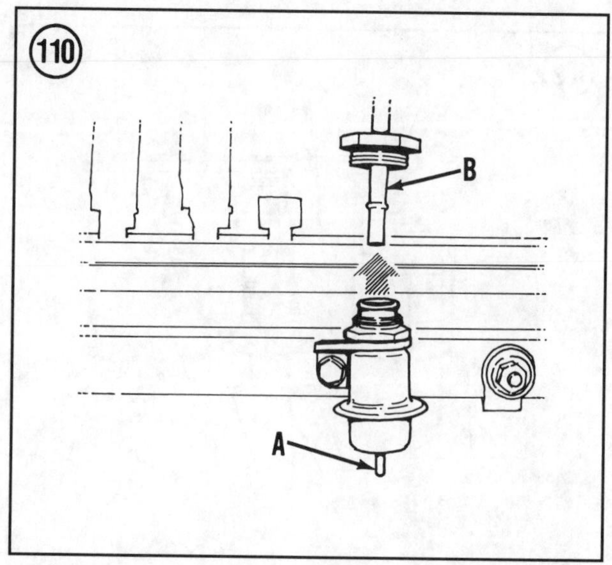

12. Install the fuel rail assembly as described in this chapter. Tighten the fittings to the torque listed in **Table 5**.

13. Follow the procedure in this chapter to install the air intake upper plenum.

14. Connect the ground cable to the battery.

15. Turn the ignition ON, but do not start the engine. Check for fuel leaks.

16. Start the engine and check for proper operation and leaks.

17. Refer to *Post-Service Procedure* in this chapter. Reset the IAC pintle position as described. Perform any available self-tests and make sure the system has not set any trouble codes.

Fuel Injectors Removal/Installation

1. Detach the ground cable from the negative terminal of the battery.

2. Refer to *Pre-Service Procedure* in this chapter and relieve the fuel system pressure.

3. Remove the flame arrestor, the air intake upper plenum and the fuel rail assembly as described in this chapter.

4. Slide the retaining clip to the side, then pull the injector from the fuel rail.

5. Check all electrical terminals to make sure they are straight and not corroded or dirty. Clean the terminals and connectors with electronic contact cleaner.

6. Check the fuel injector bores for dirt, nicks or scratches.

CAUTION
Do not twist, nick or cut the O-rings when installing them. The O-rings are made of special material that is resistant to fuel. Do not substitute another type of O-ring.

7. Check the ends of the injectors to make sure they are clean and install new O-rings.

8. Lubricate the O-rings lightly with clean engine oil.

9. Check the bores in the intake manifold and in the fuel rail to make sure they are clean and smooth.

10. Attach a new retaining clip to each injector.

11. Push the injector into the bore of the fuel rail with the electrical connector toward the front of the engine. Make sure the injector is fully seated and snap the retaining clip into the groove in the fuel rail.

12. Repeat Steps 10 and 11 for all injectors.

13. Install the fuel rails and injectors as described in this chapter. If the injectors are aligned, they should slide into place easily with gentle pressure.

14. Make sure the injectors are seated fully, then install the 4 attaching screws and tighten to the torque listed in **Table 5**.

15. Attach the electrical connectors to the injectors. Make sure each connector is fully seated, then secure the connection with a tie wrap.

16. Follow the instructions in this chapter and install the air intake upper plenum.

17. Connect the ground cable to the battery.

18. Turn the ignition ON (but do not start the engine), and check for fuel leaks.

19. Start the engine and check for proper operation and leaks.

20. Refer to *Post-Service Procedure* in this chapter. Reset the IAC pintle position as described. Perform any available self-tests and make sure the system has not set any trouble codes.

Low-Pressure Fuel Pump Removal/Installation

1. Refer to *Pre-Service Procedure* in this chapter and relieve the fuel pressure.

2. Detach the fuel supply line from the fuel filter and plug the detached line.

3. Cut the tie wrap that holds the electrical wires to the pump, then detach the electrical connector from the pump suppressor.
4. Use 2 wrenches and detach the fuel line from the elbow at the top of the pump.

NOTE
If the end cap is not held when loosening the locknut and removing the elbow, the O-rings in the pump may be damaged.

5. Hold the pump end cap with an open-end wrench and loosen the locknut located at the bottom of the elbow.
6. Remove the elbow from the top of the pump.
7. Remove the 2 bolts retaining the filter bracket.

WARNING
Be careful not to spill the fuel that may remain in the pump and filter.

8. Slide the filter and bracket from the pump.
9. Hold the pump end cap with an open end wrench and remove the adapter from the base of the pump.

CAUTION
Do not nick or cut the O-ring when installing it. The O-ring is made of special material that is resistant to fuel. Do not substitute another type of O-ring.

10. Before installing, position a new O-ring onto the filter bracket adapter and move it against the hex.
11. Screw the filter bracket into the pump, hold the pump's lower end cap with an open-end wrench and tighten the adapter to the torque listed in **Table 5**.
12. Slide the pump through the grommet at the top and install the 2 screws attaching the filter bracket. Tighten the screws to the torque listed in **Table 5**.

CAUTION
Do not nick or cut the O-ring when installing it. The O-ring is made of special material that is resistant to fuel. Do not substitute another type of O-ring.

13. Turn the locknut against the elbow of the upper adapter and install the washer, then install a new O-ring on the adapter against the washer.
14. Insert the adapter elbow (with the washer and O-ring installed) through the grommet and into the pump. Tighten the adapter elbow all the way into the pump, then back the fitting up enough to align the fitting with the fuel line.
15. Attach the fuel line to the adapter. Hold the elbow with a wrench while tightening the fuel line.

CAUTION
If the pump end cap is not held securely while tightening the banjo bolt in Step 8, the end cap may turn and damage internal pump seals.

16. Hold the pump end cap with an open-end wrench and tighten the locknut on the adapter to the torque listed in **Table 5**.
17. Connect the electrical connector to the terminal and make sure it is secure. The connector

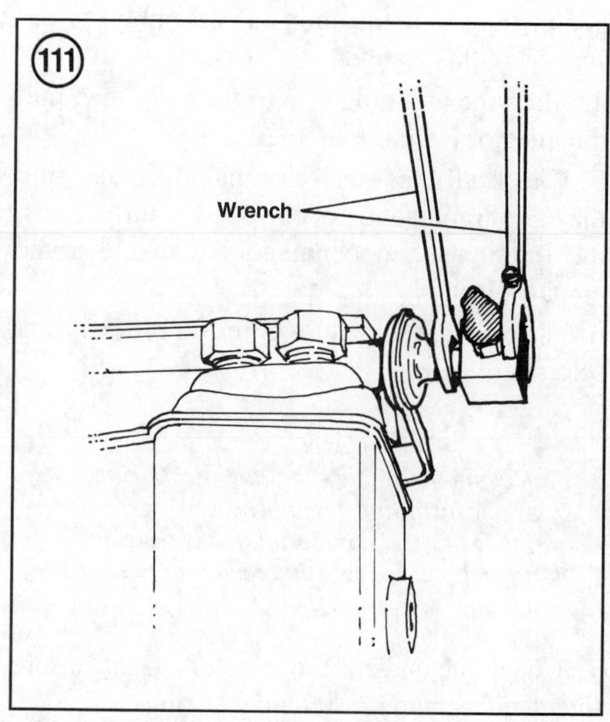

should snap into place, then be secured with a tie wrap to prevent it from accidentally becoming disconnected.

18. Attach the fuel delivery line to the fuel filter.

19. Refer to *Post-Service Procedure* in this chapter for attaching the battery and checking for leaks.

High-Pressure Fuel Pump Removal/Installation

The pump can be removed with the reservoir either off or on the engine.

1. Refer to *Pre-Service Procedure* in this chapter and relieve the fuel pressure.

2. Observe and record the position of the elbow so that the elbow can be properly located upon reassembly, then loosen the locknut and unscrew the fitting from the pump. Use 2 wrenches as shown in **Figure 111**.

3. Remove the 2 screws attaching the end bracket to the reservoir and separate the bracket from the pump.

4. Unscrew the banjo fitting attaching the reservoir to the end of the pump, then remove the pump. Discard old O-rings.

WARNING
The O-rings used to seal the fuel fittings are made of special fuel resistant material. Do not install standard O-rings in this application. Make sure the O-rings are not twisted or damaged during installation.

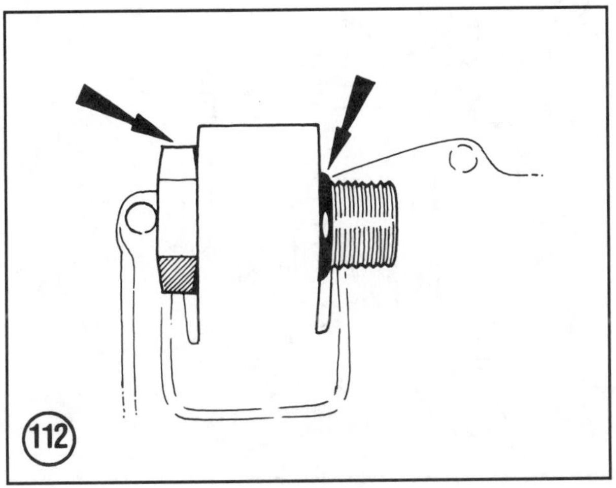

5. Lubricate one of the small special O-rings with engine oil and install it on the threaded end of the fitting.

6. Lubricate one of the large special O-rings with engine oil and install it on the banjo bolt. Make sure the O-ring is correctly positioned in the groove near the head of the banjo bolt.

7. Install the banjo bolt into the hole in the reservoir cover, lubricate the other large special O-ring and install it on the exposed threaded end of the banjo bolt. See **Figure 112**.

CAUTION
If the pump end cap is not held securely while tightening the banjo bolt in Step 8, the end cap may turn and damage internal pump seals.

8. Thread the banjo bolt into the high-pressure fuel pump, position the pump at 45° angle and tighten the banjo bolt. Hold the pump end cap while tightening the banjo bolt to the torque listed in **Table 5**.

9. Place the pump support bracket over the end of the pump and tighten the retaining screws to the torque listed in **Table 5**.

10. Attach the elbow fitting to the pump and position the fitting at the same angle as it was originally installed.

11. Hold the pump end cap and tighten the locknut to the torque listed in **Table 5**.

12. Energize the fuel pumps and check for leaks. Refer to *Post-Service Procedure* in this chapter.

Fuel Reservoir Removal/Installation

1. Loosen or remove the hose clamps and detach the water inlet and outlet hoses from the fuel reservoir.

2. Remove the nut attaching the power steering cooler to the fuel reservoir, then move the cooler

out of the way. Remove and save the flat washer located behind the cooler.

3. Cut the tie strap and unplug the electrical connector from the high-pressure fuel pump. See **Figure 113**.

4. Loosen the clamp, then detach the vent hose from the reservoir fitting (A, **Figure 114**).

5. Loosen the fitting and detach the low pressure inlet line (B, **Figure 114**).

6. Loosen the fittings and remove the line (C, **Figure 114**) between the regulator and the reservoir.

7. Loosen the fitting and detach the fuel pump outlet line (A, **Figure 115**).

8. Loosen the clamp, then detach the cooling outlet hose (B, **Figure 115**).

9. Remove the 2 attaching screws and lift the reservoir from the engine.

10. Install and tighten the 2 screws attaching the reservoir to the engine to the torque listed in **Table 5**.

11. Attach the cooling hose to the reservoir and tighten the hose clamp.

12. Attach the high-pressure fuel line to the pump.

13. Install the fuel line (C, **Figure 114**) and tighten the fittings to the torque listed in **Table 5**.

14. Attach the low-pressure fuel line (B, **Figure 114**) and tighten the fitting to the torque listed in **Table 5**.

15. Attach the vent hose to fitting (A, **Figure 114**) and tighten the hose clamp.

16. Attach the electrical terminal to the high pressure fuel pump and secure it with a strap.

17. Position the thick flat washer on the reservoir stud and install the power steering cooler.

18. Install the thin flat washer and locknut. Tighten the nut to the torque listed in **Table 5**.

19. Attach the inlet and outlet cooling hoses (A and B, **Figure 116**).

20. Energize the fuel pumps and check for leaks. Refer to *Post-Service Procedure* in this chapter.

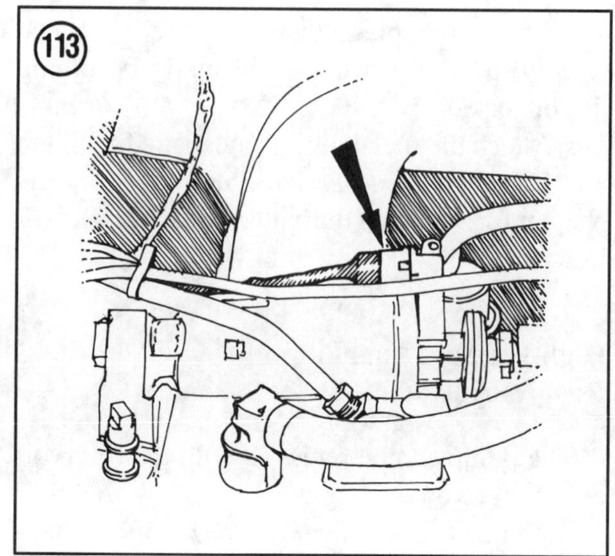

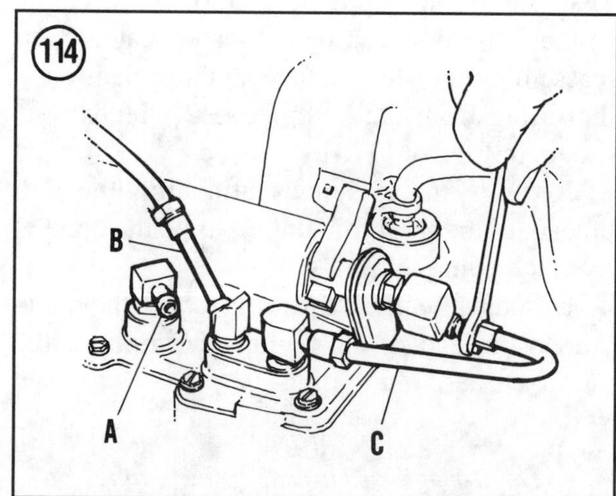

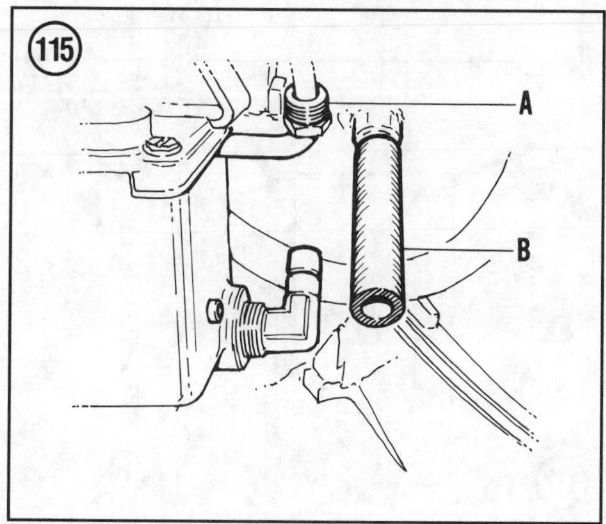

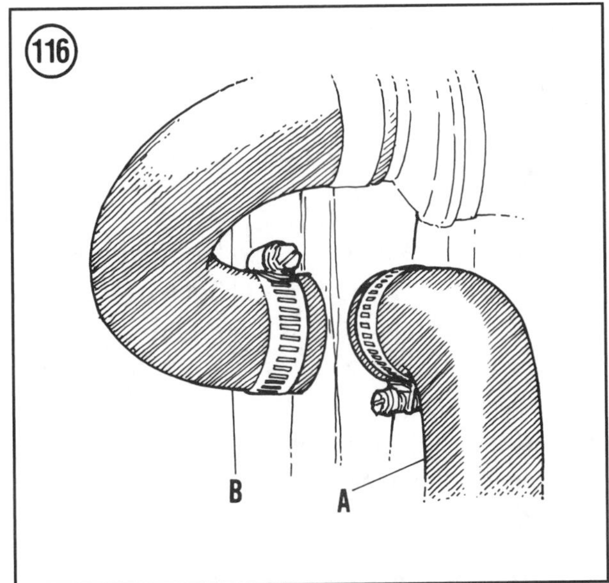

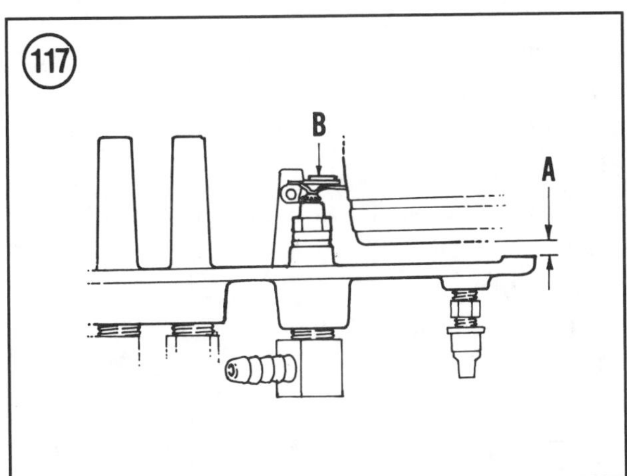

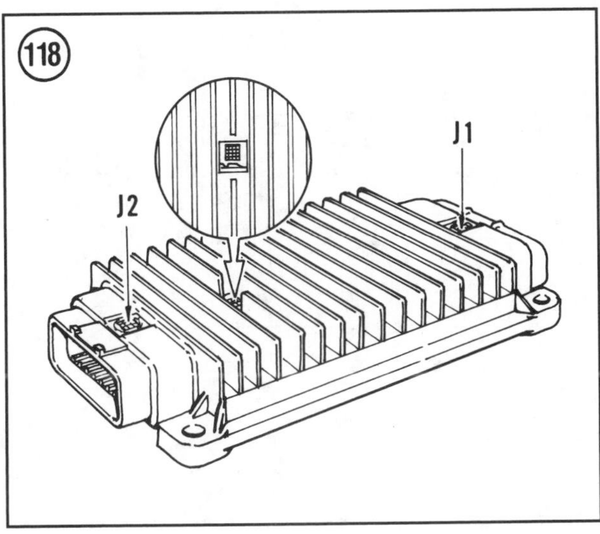

Fuel level setting

1. Perform Steps 1-9 of the *Fuel Reservoir Removal* procedure described in this chapter.
2. Remove the screws attaching the cover to the reservoir, then remove the cover. Discard the old gasket.
3. Turn the reservoir cover over and allow the float to close the fuel inlet needle. See **Figure 117**.

NOTE
Do not force the needle into the seat. The Viton tipped needle or seat may be damaged.

4. Measure the distance (A, **Figure 117**) between the cover and the float and the cover. The distance should be 3/16 in. (4.76 mm). If the clearance is incorrect, bend the tab (B, **Figure 117**) as necessary. Make sure the float moves freely, especially after adjusting it.
5. Position a new gasket on the reservoir and install the cover and float assembly.
6. Complete the assembly, referring to Steps 12-20 of the *Fuel Reservoir Installation* procedure described in this chapter.

9

Engine Control Module (ECM) Removal/Installation

CAUTION
The ECM can be easily damaged by an improper or careless service procedure. Make sure the ignition system is OFF and the battery is disconnected before detaching or attaching the J1 and J2 terminals of the ECM. The ECM can also be easily damaged by electrostatic discharge, so make sure that you are grounded to the engine before touching the ECM, especially the connector pins.

1. Disconnect the ground cable from the negative battery terminal.
2. Detach the cable connectors from the J1 and J2 terminals of the ECM. See **Figure 118**.

3. Remove the 4 screws attaching the ECM and remove the unit from its mounting bracket.

NOTE
*If the ECM (2, **Figure 97**) is being replaced, make sure the new unit has the same number. If the numbers are different, check with the parts supplier or dealership to make sure the unit is correct for your engine.*

4. Attach the ECM to its mounting bracket. Tighten the 4 screws to the torque listed in **Table 5**.
5. Attach the wiring harness to the J1 and J2 terminals.
6. Connect the ground cable to the battery.
7. Perform any available self-tests and make sure the system has not set any trouble codes.

Engine Coolant Temperature (ECT) Sensor Removal/Installation

1. Disconnect the ground cable from the negative battery terminal.
2. Detach the electrical connector from the sensor.
3. Remove the sensor (15, **Figure 97**) from the intake manifold.
4. Coat the threads of the sensor with teflon tape, then install and tighten the sensor.
5. Attach the electrical connector to the sensor.
6. Connect the ground cable to the battery.
7. Perform any available self-tests and make sure the system has not set any trouble codes.

Manifold Absolute Pressure (MAP) Sensor Removal/Installation

1. Disconnect the ground cable from the negative battery terminal.
2. Detach the electrical connector from the MAP sensor.
3. Remove the screws attaching the sensor (5, **Figure 97**).
4. Detach the vacuum line from the MAP sensor, then remove the sensor.

NOTE
Do not soak the MAP sensor in any cleaning solvent.

5. Attach the vacuum hose to the MAP sensor.
6. Attach the MAP sensor and tighten the retaining screws to the torque listed in **Table 5**.
7. Attach the electrical connector to the sensor.
8. Connect the ground cable to the battery.
9. Perform any available self-tests and make sure the system has not set any trouble codes.

Throttle Position (TP) Sensor Removal/Installation

1. Disconnect the ground cable from the negative battery terminal.
2. Remove the flame arrestor as described in this chapter.
3. Detach the electrical connector from the TP sensor.
4. Unbolt and remove the sensor (4, **Figure 97**). Do not lose or damage the seal located under the TP sensor.

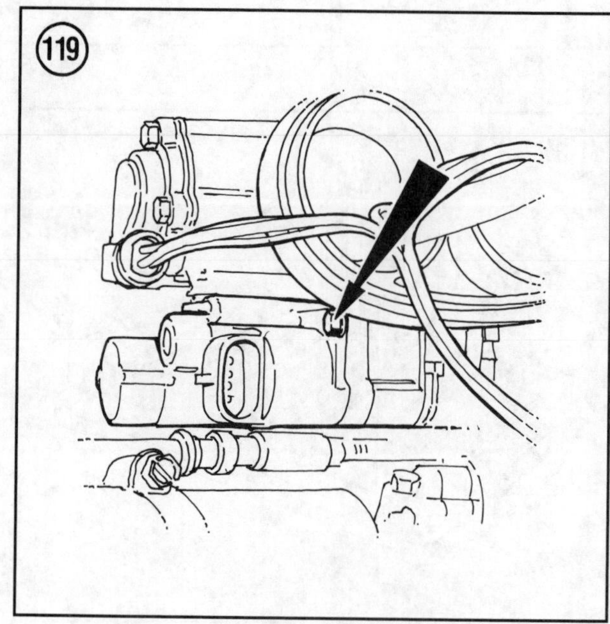

NOTE
The TP sensor is an electrical component and can be damaged by improper cleaning. Do not soak in any cleaning solvent.

5. Make sure the throttle valve is closed, then install the TP sensor. Tighten the attaching screws to the torque listed in **Table 5**.
6. Attach the electrical connector to the sensor.
7. Connect the ground cable to the battery.
8. Reinstall the flame arrestor as described in this chapter.

Intake Air Temperature (IAT) Sensor Removal/Installation

1. Disconnect the ground cable from the negative battery terminal.
2. Detach the electrical connector from the sensor.
3. Remove the sensor (25, **Figure 97**).
4. Install the IAT sensor by reversing the removal procedure.

Idle Air Control (IAC) Valve Removal/Installation

1. Disconnect the ground cable from the negative battery terminal.
2. Remove the flame arrestor as described in this chapter.
3. Detach the electrical connector from the IAC valve.
4. Remove the 2 screws attaching the valve to the throttle body. See **Figure 119**.
5. Withdraw the IAC from the throttle body.

CAUTION
A used, but serviceable IAC valve may be damaged by pushing or pulling the pintle. The threads on the worm drive that move the pintle can be easily damaged.

6. Clean the IAC sealing surfaces, pintle valve seat and air passages. Certain carburetor cleaning solvents can be used, but should not contain methyl ethyl ketone or other extremely strong cleaning agents.
7. Inspect the pintle and seat. Shiny spots are normal and do not indicate misalignment.

NOTE
If the IAC valve is being replaced, make sure the new unit has the same number. If the numbers are different, check with the parts supplier or dealership to make sure the unit is correct for your engine.

8. If a new IAC valve is being installed, measure the distance between the end of the pintle and the mounting surface. If the distance is greater than 1.102 in. (28 mm), gently push the valve to retract the pintle.

NOTE
Gentle finger pressure should not damage a new valve, but may damage a used part. New valves are adjusted at the factory, and adjustment should not be necessary.

9. Install a new O-ring and lubricate it lightly.
10. Install the IAC valve and tighten the mounting screws to the torque listed in **Table 5**.

NOTE
Attaching screws are coated with threadlocking compound by the manufacturer, which should not be cleaned from the threads. New valves are provided with new attaching screws.

11. Attach the electrical connector to the sensor.
12. Reset the IAC valve pintle position as follows:
    a. Start and run the engine for 30 seconds.
    b. Turn the ignition OFF for 10 seconds.
    c. Start the engine and check that it idles properly.
13. Connect the ground cable to the battery.
14. Perform any available self-tests and make sure the system has not set any trouble codes.

Knock Sensor (KS) Removal/Installation

1. Disconnect the ground cable from the negative battery terminal.
2. Detach the electrical connector from the knock sensor.
3. Unscrew the knock sensor from the engine block. See **Figure 120**.
4. Make sure the threads in the block and on the knock sensor are clean.
5. Install the knock sensor and tighten to the torque listed in **Table 5**.
6. Attach the electrical connector to the sensor.
7. Connect the ground cable to the battery.
8. Perform any available self-tests and make sure the system has not set any trouble codes.

Knock Sensor (KS) Module Removal/Installation

1. Disconnect the ground cable from the negative battery terminal.
2. Detach the electrical connector from the knock sensor module.
3. Unbolt and remove the knock sensor module (20, **Figure 97**).

NOTE
The knock sensor module is an electrical component and can be damaged by improper cleaning. Do not soak in any cleaning solvent.

4. Attach the knock sensor module and tighten the screws securely.
5. Attach the electrical connector to the module.
6. Connect the ground cable to the battery.
7. Perform any available self-tests and make sure the system has not set any trouble codes.

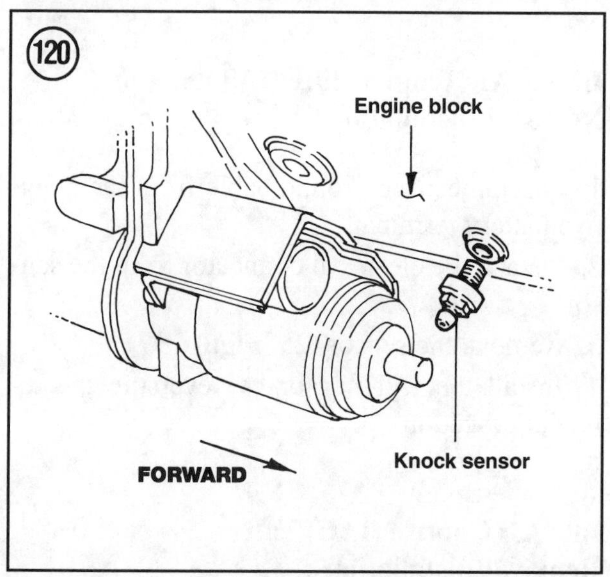

Table 1 HOLLEY CARBURETOR SPECIFICATIONS

Holley list No.	80312
1994-1997	80312
1998-1999	R75006A
Model	500 cfm 2300-2V
Used on engine model	4.3L GL
Initial idle mixture needle setting	5/8 turn out
Pump lever clearance	0.25-0.38 mm (1/8-9/64 in.)
Choke unloader	9.5 mm (3/8 in.)
Choke setting	5 notches lean
Main jets	No. 70
Power valve	2.5
Float setting	Level
Choke vacuum qualification	6.3 mm (1/4 in.)
Pump cam	
Identification	Red
Position	No. 1 hole
Holley list No.	80316
Model	500 cfm 2300-2V
Used on engine model	3.0L GS
Initial idle mixture needle setting	
Starboard	1 turn out
Port	1/2 turn out
Pump lever clearance	0.25-0.38 mm (1/8-9/64 in.)
Choke unloader	7.6 mm (7/16 in.)
Choke setting	5 notches lean
Main jets	No. 75
1994-1996	No. 75
1997-1999	No. 71
Power valve	2.5
Float setting	Level
Choke vacuum qualification	9.3 mm (1/2 in.)
Pump cam	
Identification	Orange
Position	No. 2 hole
Holley list No.	80321
Model	350 cfm 2300-2V
Used on engine model	3.0L GL (1994-1996)
Initial idle mixture needle setting	3/4 turn out
Pump lever clearance	0.25-0.38 mm (1/8-9/64 in.)
Choke unloader	9.6 mm (33/64 in.)
Choke setting	3 notches lean
Holley list No.	
Model	
Main jets	No. 63
Power valve	2.5
Float setting	Level
Choke vacuum qualification	6.3 mm (1/4 in.)
Pump cam	
Identification	Orange
Position	No. 2 hole
Holley list No.	80330-1
Model	850 cfm 4150-4V (Dual feed)
Used on engine model	8.2L GL (1994-1996)
Initial idle mixture needle setting	1 1/2 turns out
Pump lever clearance	0.25-0.38 mm (1/8-9/64 in.)

(continued)

Table 1 HOLLEY CARBURETOR SPECIFICATIONS (continued)

Holley List No. (continued)	
Model (continued)	
Choke unloader	8.1 mm (29/64 in.)
Choke setting	5 notches lean
Main jet	
Primary	No. 88
Secondary	No. 94
Power valve	
Primary	65
Secondary	35
Float setting	Level
Secondary throttle setting	1/8-1/4 turn in
Choke vacuum qualification	11.7-12.7 mm (39/64-1/2 in.)
Pump cam	
Identification	Brown
Position	No. 1 hole
Holley list No.	80378-1
Model	750 cfm 4150-4V (Single feed)
Used on engine model	7.4L GL (1994-1997)
Initial idle mixture needle setting	1 1/2 turns out (1994-1996) 1/4 turn out (1997)
Pump lever clearance	0.25-0.38 mm (1/8-9/64 in.)
Choke unloader	8.9 mm (31/64 in.)
Choke setting	5 notches lean (1994-1996) 6 notches lean (1997)
Main jet	
Primary	No. 73
Secondary	No. 56
Power valve	
Primary	25
Secondary	25
Float setting	Level
Secondary throttle setting	1/8-1/4 turn in (1994-1996) 1/8 beyond contact (1997)
Choke vacuum qualification	7.4-8.4 mm (27/64-15/32 in.)
Pump cam	
Identification	Orange
Position	No. 1 hole
Holley list No.	R-75004A
Model	500 cfm 2300-2V
Used on engine model	5.0 GL and 5.7 GS
Initial idle mixture needle setting	3/4 to 1 turn off seat
Pump lever clearance	0.254-0.381 mm (0.010-0.015 in.)
Choke setting	5 notches lean
Main jets	69
Power valve	4.5
Float setting	level
Choke vacuum qualification	8.00 mm (0.315 in.)
Pump cam	
Identification	Yellow
Position	No. 1 hole
Holley list No.	80382
Model	490 cfm 2300-2V
Used on engine model	5.0L FL
Initial idle mixture needle setting	1 turn out

(continued)

Table 1 HOLLEY CARBURETOR SPECIFICATIONS (continued)

Holley list No. (continued)	
Pump lever clearance	0.25-0.38 mm (1/8-9/64 in.)
Choke unloader	7.9 mm (29/64 in.)
Choke setting	3 notches lean
Holley list No.	
Model	
Main jets	No. 72
Power valve	3.5
Float setting	Level
Choke vacuum qualification	5.6 mm (0.221 in.)
Pump cam	
Identification	Orange
Position	No. 1 hole
Holley list No.	80383
Model	600 cfm 4160-4V
Used on engine model	5.8L FL
Initial idle mixture needles setting	7/8 turn out
Pump lever clearance	0.25-0.38 mm (1/8-9/64 in.)
Choke unloader	7.6 mm (7/16 in.)
Choke setting	3 notches lean
Main jets	No. 67
Power valve	2.5
Float setting	Level
Secondary throttle setting	1/8 turn in
Choke vacuum qualification	5.8 mm (3/8 in.)
Pump cam	
Identification	Orange
Position	No. 1 hole
Holley list No.	80402-1
Model	500 cfm 2300-2V
Used on engine model	5.7L GL
Initial idle mixture needle setting	3/4-1 turn out
Pump lever clearance	0.25-0.38 mm (1/8-9/64 in.)
Choke unloader	7.6 mm (7/16 in.)
Choke setting	5 notches lean
Main jets	No. 75
Power valve	4.5
Float setting	Level
Choke vacuum qualification	8.0 mm (29/64 in.)
Pump cam	
Identification	Red
Position	No. 1 hole
Holley list No.	80390
Model	650 cfm 4175 spread bore
Used on engine model	5.7 Gs
Initial idle mixture needle setting	1/2 turn out
Pump lever clearance	0.25-0.38 mm (1/8-9/64 in.)
Choke setting	index
Main jets	60
Power valve	2.5
Float setting	level
Choke vacuum qualification	5.8 mm (0.228 in.)
Pump cam	
Identification	Orange
Position	No. 2 hole

Table 2 TORQUE SPECIFICATIONS (HOLLEY CARBURETORS) (continued)

	in.-lb.	ft.lb.	N·m
Fuel bowl	45	–	5.5
Fuel inlet fitting	80	–	9.0
Fuel inlet needle seat	10	–	1.1
Main jets	10	–	1.1
Power valve	100	–	11.3
Pump discharge nozzle	15	–	1.7
Throttle body	50	–	5.6
Throttle plate	10	–	1.1

Table 3 TORQUE SPECIFICATIONS (5.0 AND 5.8 L Fi AND FSi MODELS)

	in.-lb.	ft.-lb.	N·m
ACT sensor	–	12-18	16.3-24.4
ECT sensor	–	10-15	13.6-20.3
Adaptor to throttle body	71-102	–	8-11
ECA bracket to engine	60-84	–	6.8-9.5
ECA cover	24-36	–	2.7-4.1
ECA module to bracket	24-36	–	2.7-4.1
ECA 60-pin connector	46-64	–	5-7
EEC relay to bracket	24-36	–	2.7-4.1
Elbow locknut	60-84	–	6.8-9.5
Flame arrestor	24-48	–	2.7-5.4
Fuel line fittings	–	10-12	13.6-16.3
Fuel pressure regulator to fuel rail	27-40	–	3.0-4.5
Fuel pump banjo fitting	–	18-22	24.4-29.8
Fuel rail to lower intake manifold	70-105	–	7.9-11.7
Fuel reservoir cover screws	25-35	–	2.8-4.0
Fuel reservoir to engine	–	24-36	38-49
Knock sensor	–	7-10	
MAP sensor to bracket	24-36	–	2.7-4.1
Power steering cooler to engine	–	20-25	27-34
Shift bracket			
Large locknut	–	20-25	27-34
Small locknut	60-84	–	6.8-9.5
Solenoid to adaptor	71-102	–	8-11
Throttle body to upper manifold	–	12-18	16-24
Throttle position sensor to throttle body	18-26.5	–	2.0-3.0
TP sensor	18-26	–	2.0-3.0
Upper manifold to lower manifold	–	12-18	16-24

Table 4 TORQUE SPECIFICATIONS (4.3 AND 5.7 L Gi AND GSi MODELS)

	in.-lb.	ft.-lb.	N·m
ECT sensor	108	–	12
ECM attachment	88-124	–	10-14
IAC valve	28	–	3.2
KS	–	11-16	15-22
MAP sensor attachment	44-62	–	5-7
TBI fuel metering cover	28	–	3
TBI fuel meter body	30	–	4
TBI fuel return fitting	–	21	29
TBI fuel inlet fitting	–	30	40
TBI fuel inlet and return lines to fittings	–	17	23
TBI unit mounting screws	–	12	16
Throttle positioning sensor attachment	18	–	2

9

Table 5 TORQUE SPECIFICATIONS (7.4 L Gi AND GSi MODELS)

	in.-lb.	ft.-lb.	N·m
ECM attachment	88-124	–	10-14
ECT sensor	108	–	12
Fuel lines			
High-pressure inlet and return	–	13	17.5
Other fuel lines	–	10-12	13.6-16.3
Fuel pressure regulator retaining screw	84	–	9.5
Fuel pump			
Banjo fitting	–	18-22	24.7-29.8
Bracket screws			
High-presure pump	27-35	–	2.8-4.0
Bracket screws			
Low-pressure pump	–	20-25	27-34
Elbow lock nut	60-84	–	6.8-9.5
Fuel rails to intake manifold	88	–	10
Fuel regulator mounting screw	84	–	9.5
Fuel reservoir top cover	–	27-36	38-49
IAC valve	28	–	3.2
TB upper cover	28	–	3
Throttle body to plenum	–	11	15
Throttle positioning sensor attachment	18	–	2
Upper plenum	124	–	14

Table 6 DIAGNOSTIC TROUBLE CODES (4.3, 5.0, 5.7, & 7.4 Gi; 7.4, 8.2 Gsi)

Code	Problem
12	No ignition reference signal from distributor. This code is normal if the engine is not running.
14	Engine Coolant Temperature (ECT) sensor indicates that temperature is too low. This code will also be set if the signal for the circuit is grounded or if the wires are open for 3 seconds.
15	Engine Coolant Temperature (ECT) sensor indicates that temperature is too high. This code will also be set if the signal for the circuit is grounded or if the wires are open for 3 or more seconds.
21	Throttle position (TP) sensor signal too high. This code will be stored if the TP is inconsistent with the rpm and MAP signal or if the signal circuit is grounded or open.
22	Throttle position (TP) sensor signal too low. This code will be stored if the TP is inconsistent with the rpm and MAP signal or if the signal circuit is grounded or open.
23	Intake Air Temperature (IAT) sensor indicates that temperature is too low. This code will also be set if the signal for the circuit is open or if the wires are grounded for 3 or more seconds.
25	Intake Air Temperature (IAT) sensor indicates that temperature is too high. This code will also be set if the signal for the circuit is open or if the wires are grounded for 3 or more seconds.
33	Manifold Absolute Pressure (MAP) sensor. This code will be set if the signal voltage for the circuit is too high for 3 or more seconds or if the circuit is open. Code will be stored if MAP output is inconsistent with rpm and throttle position (TP) signal.
34	Manifold Absolute Pressure (MAP) sensor. This code will be set if the signal voltage for the circuit is too low (or no output) with the engine running. Code will be stored if MAP output is inconsistent with rpm and throttle position (TP) signal.
41	Ignition Control (IC) system is not receiving the correct voltage. The ECM has responded to an open IC or bypass circuit.
42	Ignition Control (IC) system is not receiving the correct voltage. The ECM has responded to a grounded IC or bypass circuit.
43	Knock Sensor (KS) voltage signal is either too high or too low. This code can also be stored as a result of an open or grounded circuit longer than 58 seconds.
44	Knock sensor (KS) circuit inactive.
51	Electronic Erasable Programmable Read Only Memory (EEPROM) or Electronic Control Module (ECM) faulty.

Table 7 FUEL SYSTEM VOLTAGE REFERENCE VALUES (5.0 Fi, 5.8 Fi & 5.8 FSi)

Sensor	Breakout box Black lead	Red lead	Test value
VREF	Pin 46	Pin 26	4.74-5.25 VDC
TP	Pin 46	Pin 47	Closed throttle – 0.9-1.15 VDC Wide-open throttle – 4.65 VDC
ECT	Pin 46	Pin 7	0.87-1.17 VDC
ACT	Pin 46	Pin 25	1.13-1.53 VDC
MAP	Pin 46	Pin 45	147 Hz @ 30.0 in. Hg.[1]
PIP	Pin 46	Pin 56	0-0.3 VDC – opening aligned[2] Battery VDC – vane aligned[3]
KS	Pin 46	Pin 2	0.3 VDC

(continued)

Table 7 FUEL SYSTEM VOLTAGE REFERENCE VALUES (5.0 Fi, 5.8 Fi & 5.8 FSi) (continued)

Sensor	Breakout box Black lead	Red lead	Test value
INJ			
Bank No. 1	Pin 40	Pin 58	Battery VDC
Bank No. 2	Pin 40	Pin 59	Battery VDC
ISC-BPA	Pin 40	Pin 21	Battery VDC
FP	Pin 40	Pin 52	Battery VDC
KAPWR	Pin 40/60	Pin 1	Battery VDC – Key ON and OFF
VPWR	Pin 40/60	Pin 37/57	Battery VDC – Key ON only
IGN GND	Pin 40/60	Pin 16	0
CSE GND	Pin 40/60	Pin 20	0
PWR GND	Pin 40/60	Pin 20	0

1. Hertz signal will increase as barometric pressure increases.
2. Opening in the distributor cup is aligned with the Hall effect device.
3. Vane of the distributor cup is aligned with the Hall effect device.

Table 8 FUEL SYSTEM SPECIFICATIONS (7.4 Gi AND 7.4 GSi)

7.4 L Gi & GSi models	
Fuel system pressure	
Low-pressure pump	
Static (not running)	4.5-7 psi (31-48 kPa)
Cranking/idle speed	5.9-8.4 psi (40.68-57.93 kPa)
Wide-open throttle	4.0 psi (27.5 kPa)
High-pressure pump	
Static (not running)	36-42 psi (248-290 kPa)

Table 9 ACRONYMS AND TERMS

ACT	Air Charge Temperature, such as ACT sensor.
BASE	Initial or not changed, such as the BASE ignition timing that occurs when the SPOUT signal is interupted.
BPA	Bypass Air valve. A valve attached to the ISC solenoid.
CEL	Check Engine Light.
CKP	Crankshaft Postiton sensor.
DTC	Diagnostic Trouble Code.
DLC	Diagnostic Link Connector. The electrical connector provided for attaching test equipment to the system.
E-Core or E-Coil	The high-tension coil used to generate current sufficient to provide the spark at the spark plugs.
ECA	Electronic Control Assembly.
ECT	Engine Coolant Temperature sensor or circuit.
EEC-IV	Electronic Engine Control, fourth generation that combines air, fuel and ignition control systems.
FPM	Fuel Pump Monitor.
IAC	Idle Air Control.
IAT	Intake Air Temperature sensor or circuit.
IDM	Ignition Diagnositics Monitor. A system that continuously monitors the ignition.
ISC	Idle Speed Control, such as ISC solenoid or ISC circuit. The ISC solenoid may attach to the throttle body assembly.

(continued)

Table 9 ACRONYMS AND TERMS (continued)

KAM	Keep Alive Memory is a series of battery powered memory locations that allow the microprocessor to store input about failures that are identified during operation.
KAPWR	Keep Alive Power is the battery current supplied to KAM.
KS	Knock Sensor. The KS is a device that generates a signal current when it senses a specific frequency of vibration to identify knocking.
KOEO	Key On Engine Off, such as the KOEO self test.
LCD	Liquid Crystal Display.
MAP	Manifold Absolute Pressure. May be used when referring to the MAP sensor or circuit.
MDTC	Marine Diagnostic Trouble Code.
MEFI	Marine Electronic Fuel Injection.
MFI	Multipoint Fuel Injection.
OBD	On Board Diagnostics.
PIP	Profile Ignition Pickup. A switch such as that housed in the distributor provides crankshaft position information to the ECA.
Plenum	The upper part of the engine's intake manifold.
Relay	A switching device operated by low current to control the opening and closing of another (higher capacity) circuit.
Sensor	A monitoring device that transmits information, such as the coolant temperature sensor that provides temperature information to the ECA.
S.L.O.W. (or SLOW)	Speed Limiting Operational Warning system. The system incorporates sensors to monitor coolant temperature and oil pressure as well as other operating conditions.
SPOUT	SPark OUTput, such as the SPOUT connector. The SPOUT signal from the EEC-IV controls operation of the ignition module and loss of the signal puts the engine in BASE timing mode.
STI	Self Test Input. May be used to refer to the STI connector.
STO	Self Test Output, such as the circuit transmits service codes. May be used to identify the STO connector.
TBI	Throttle Body Injection.
TFI	Thick Film Integrated Ignition System. TFI-IV is the fourth generation of the TFI system.
TP	Throttle Position. May be used in reference to the TP sensor.
VREF	Voltage REFerence, such as the regulated VREF signal supplied to some sensors.

Chapter Ten

Cooling System

This chapter covers service procedures for the thermostat, engine circulating pump, seawater pump, oil cooler and connecting hoses. Procedures for flushing the system are included in Chapter Four. Draining and filling procedures are described in Chapter Five.

Some engines are equipped with a closed cooling system that is divided into 2 separate subsystems. One system is a closed system of coolant (antifreeze mixture) circulating in the engine's cooling passages and absorbing the engine's heat. Heat absorbed by coolant in the closed system is then transferred (exchanged) to seawater in a heat exchanger. The seawater system delivers water from around the boat to a heat exchanger where it absorbs heat from the closed system. The seawater is then directed to the exhaust manifold where it is expelled with the exhaust gases.

Other models are equipped with an open cooling system; water in which the boat is being operated is used as the coolant to absorb engine heat. Cooling water is picked up at the stern drive lower unit and circulated throughout the engine to cool the engine directly. Water that has absorbed heat while cooling the engine is routed to the exhaust manifold where it is mixed with the exhaust gases and expelled with the exhaust.

Refer to **Figure 1** for a typical closed system or to **Figure 2** for a typical open system. The location of the pumps and path of the flow may differ slightly from those shown in the illustrations.

THERMOSTAT

The thermostat controls water circulation to provide quick engine warmup and maintain a constant operating temperature. When the engine is cold, the thermostat is closed and cooling water is sent directly to the exhaust manifold where it is expelled. When the engine warms up, the thermostat opens and water is used to cool the engine (open system) or the coolant in the heat exchanger before being sent to the exhaust manifold to be expelled.

CAUTION
The engine may be seriously damaged by running without a thermostat. Do not operate the engine with a faulty or missing thermostat. Either condition can cause the engine to overheat or not warm up.

Thermostats are rated according to their opening temperature. The opening temperature value is stamped in the thermostat flange or other area. The thermostat should start to open at the temperature stamped on the thermostat and should be fully open at 25° above that temperature. Check the thermostat rating after removing the thermostat. It should generally be as specified in **Table 2**.

If the boat is used extensively in cold-water operation at low engine speed, it may be necessary to install a thermostat that is rated about 20° F warmer than originally specified for normal

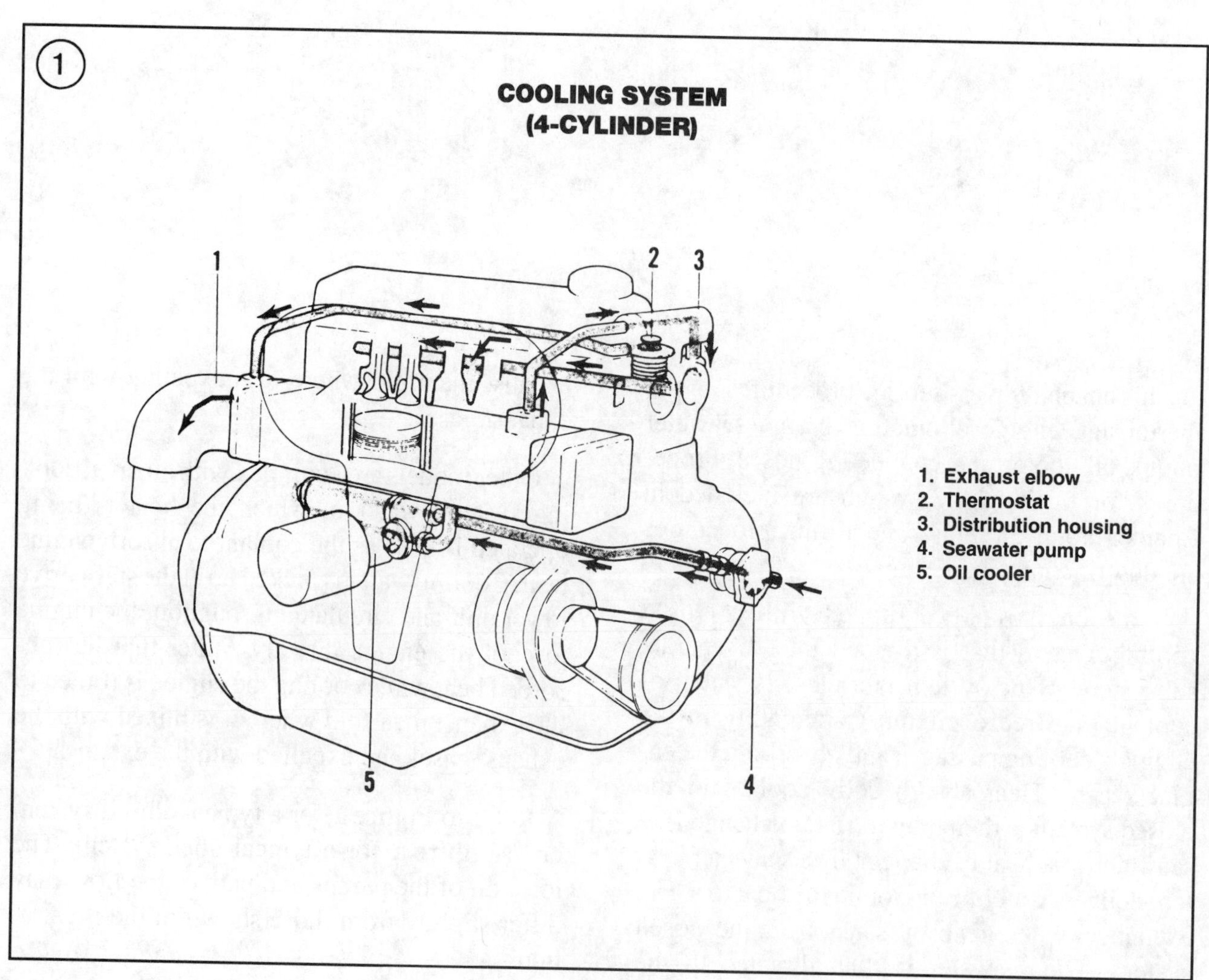

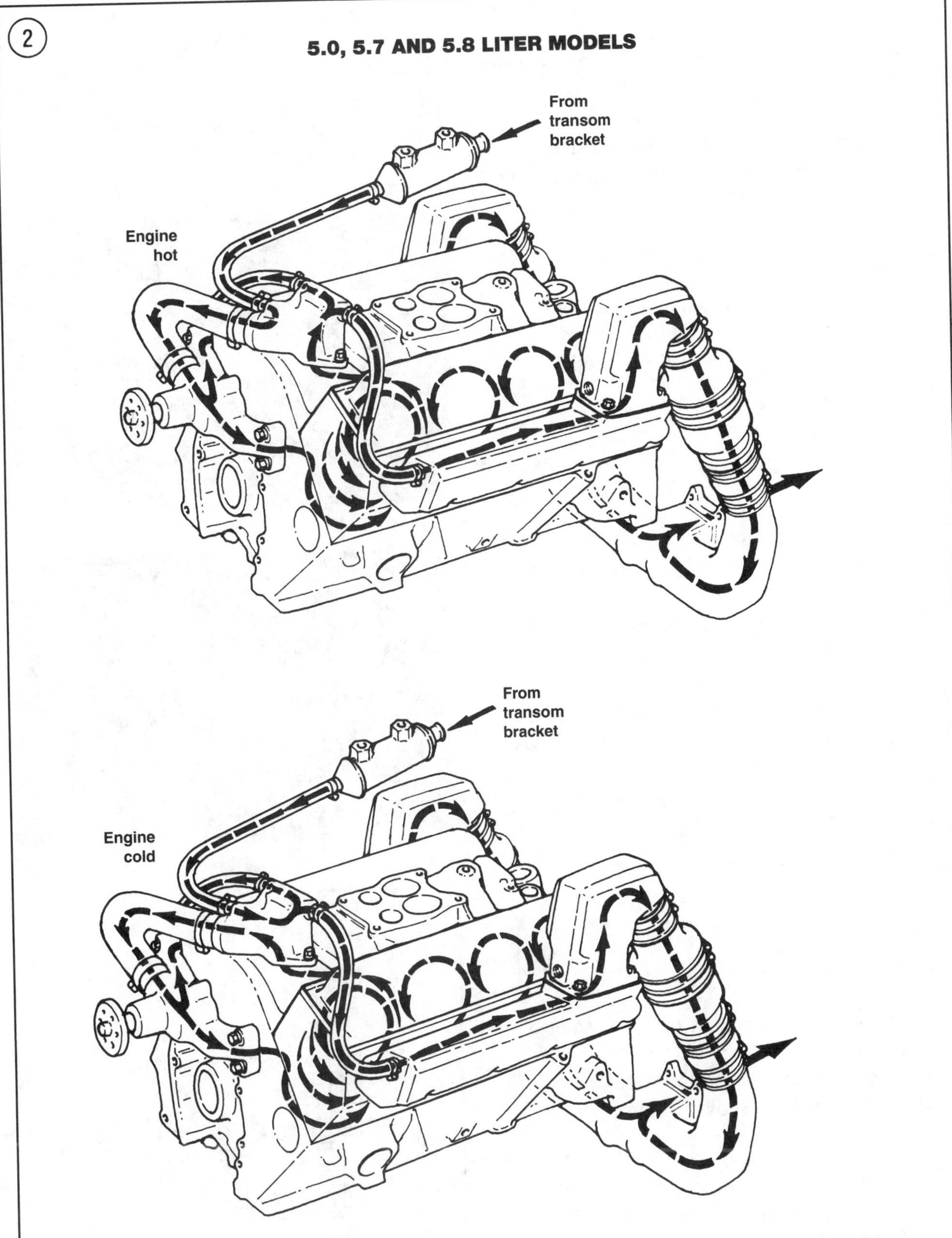
2
5.0, 5.7 AND 5.8 LITER MODELS
From
transom
bracket
Engine
hot
From
transom
bracket
Engine
cold

operation. This may be necessary to maintain normal engine operating temperature, improve low-speed operation and prevent excessive crankcase condensation. You should, however, avoid wide-open throttle operation when using a hotter thermostat, and always reinstall the recommended thermostat when resuming operation in warmer waters.

CAUTION
*Do **not** substitute an automotive-type thermostat. Its higher rating will cause the engine to run hotter than normal and could cause engine damage. Make sure any thermostat that is installed has been approved for use by Volvo Penta.*

Removal

1. Drain the engine coolant or water from the block and exhaust manifold(s). See Chapter Five.
2. Loosen the hose clamps and disconnect the hoses from the thermostat cover or coolant reservoir.
3. Refer to the appropriate illustration (**Figure 3** or **Figure 4**, typical) and remove the screws attaching the thermostat housing or cover.
4. Remove the housing or cover with the gasket(s) and discard the gasket(s).
5. Remove the thermostat.

Testing (Out of Engine)

1. Pour some tap water (not distilled water or coolant) into a container that can be heated. Submerge the thermostat in the water and suspend a thermometer as shown in **Figure 5**.

NOTE
Suspend the thermostat with wire so it does not touch the sides or bottom of the pan.

2. Heat the water until the thermostat starts to open. Check the water temperature on the thermometer. It should be approximately the same as the temperature value stamped on the thermostat. If the thermostat has not started to open at this temperature, replace it.

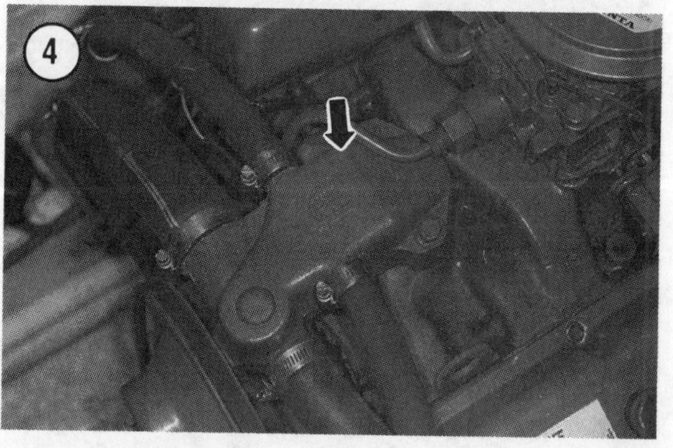

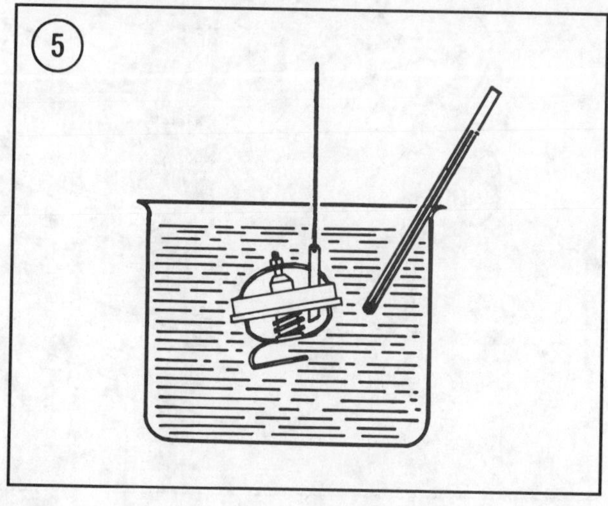

3. Heat the water another 25° F above the temperature value stamped on thermostat. The thermostat should now be fully open. If it is not, replace it.
4. Allow the water to cool to 10° F *under* the thermostat's rated opening temperature. If the thermostat valve is not fully closed at this temperature, replace it.
5. Remove the thermostat from the water and let it cool to room temperature. Hold it close to a light bulb and check for leakage. If light can be seen at more than 1 or 2 tiny points around the edge of the valve, replace the thermostat.

Testing (In Engine)

Thermostat operation can be tested without removing it from the engine or reservoir. This procedure requires the use of 2 thermomelt sticks (**Figure 6**) available from marine supply or automotive parts stores. A thermomelt stick looks like a carpenter's pencil and is made of a chemically impregnated wax material which melts at a specific temperature. The following technique can be used to check the thermostat opening without removing the thermostat.

1. Mark the thermostat housing with 1 thermomelt stick which melts about 10° lower (cooler) than the temperature at which the thermostat opens.
2. Mark the thermostat housing with a second thermomelt stick which melts about 10° higher (hotter) than the thermostat opening temperature.
3. Start the engine and observe the 2 marks made by the thermomelt sticks.
4. As the coolant or water reaches the first temperature, the mark made by the lower temperature stick should melt.
5. If the mark made by the second stick melts, it indicates the coolant or water has increased to that temperature.

WARNING
Do not remove the pressure fill cap from closed cooling systems when the engine is warm. Coolant may blow out of the heat exchanger and cause serious personal injury.

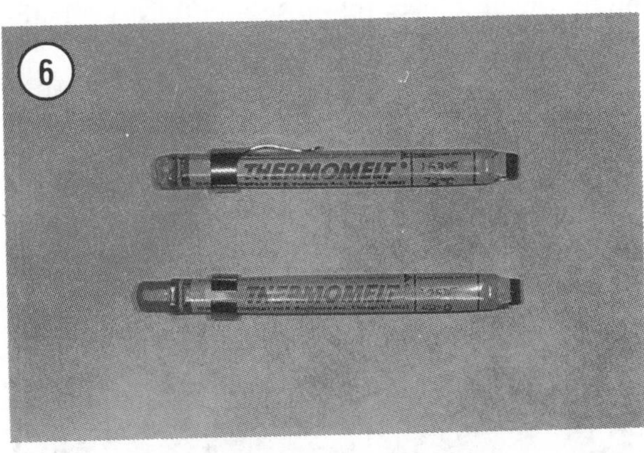

Overheated engine

1. Relieve the freshwater cooling system pressure on a closed cooling system by carefully removing the pressure fill cap from the heat exchanger. See **Figure 7**, typical.
2. Mark the thermostat cover with a thermomelt stick that melts at approximately 180° F.
3. Start the engine and run at a fast idle.
4. If no coolant or water flows through the housing-to-manifold or housing-to-exhaust elbow hoses by the time the mark starts to melt, either the thermostat is stuck closed or the water pump is failing. Remove the thermostat and test it as

described in this chapter. If the thermostat is satisfactory, check the condition of the water pumps.

Slow engine warmup

1. On models with a closed cooling system, allow the engine to cool and slowly remove the pressure fill cap from the heat exchanger to relieve pressure from the system. See **Figure 7**, typical.
2. Rub the 140° F thermomelt stick on the thermostat cover.
3. Start the engine and run at a fast idle.
4. If coolant or water flows through the housing-to-manifold or housing-to-exhaust elbow hoses before the mark starts to melt, the thermostat is stuck open and must be replaced.

Installation

1. If a new thermostat is being installed, test it as described in this chapter.
2. Clean all gasket residue from the thermostat cover and housing mating surfaces.
3. Install the thermostat in the housing with its thermostatic element toward the engine. The thermostat flange must fit into the housing recess.
4. Coat both sides of a new gasket with a water-resistant sealer and stick the gasket to the thermostat cover.
5. Install the cover and tighten the bolts to specification (**Table 1**).
6. Complete the installation by reversing the removal procedure.
7. On models with a closed cooling system, service the coolant as described in Chapter Five.

HOSE REPLACEMENT

Replace any hoses that are cracked, brittle, mildewed or very soft and spongy. If a hose is in questionable condition, replace it to be safe. Attention to hose condition can prevent a failure while you are offshore. Hoses in some installations may be extremely difficult to change.

Hose manufacturers generally suggest that new hoses be installed every 2 years. How long the hoses will last depends a great deal on how much you use your boat and how well you maintain the system; however, it is a good practice to change all hoses every 2 years. Replace cooling system hoses with the same type as removed. Pleated rubber hoses do not allow the same amount of coolant to flow and do not have the same strength as reinforced molded hoses. Check the condition of hose clamps and install new worm screw-type clamps, if necessary.

The seawater section of closed marine grade, cooling systems can be partially drained when replacing upper hoses, but must be completely drained when replacing lower hoses.
1. Loosen the clamp at each end of the hose to be removed. Grasp the hose and twist it off the fitting with a pulling motion.
2. If the hose is corroded to the fitting and will not twist free, cut it off with a sharp knife about 1 in. (25.4 mm) beyond the fitting. Remove the clamp and slit the remaining piece of hose lengthwise, then peel it off the fitting.
3. Clean any rust or corrosion from the fitting by wrapping a piece of medium grit sandpaper

around it and rotating until the fitting surface is relatively clean and smooth.

4. Wipe the inside diameter of the hose with liquid detergent and install the hose ends on the fittings with a twisting motion.

5. Position the new clamps at least 1/4 in. (6.3 mm) from the end of the hose. Make sure the clamp screw is positioned for easy access with a screwdriver or nut driver. Tighten each clamp snugly.

6. Refill the cooling system. Start the engine and check for leaks. Recheck clamps for tightness after operating the engine for a few hours.

ENGINE CIRCULATING PUMP

If the circulating pump is making noise, it may be an indication of impending failure. If the seal is defective, coolant or water may leak from behind the pump pulley. The pump is serviced as an assembly and can be replaced on all models with the engine in the boat. Marine engine water pumps contain stainless steel components and use a special marine shaft seal assembly. Do *not* replace it with an automotive-type water pump.

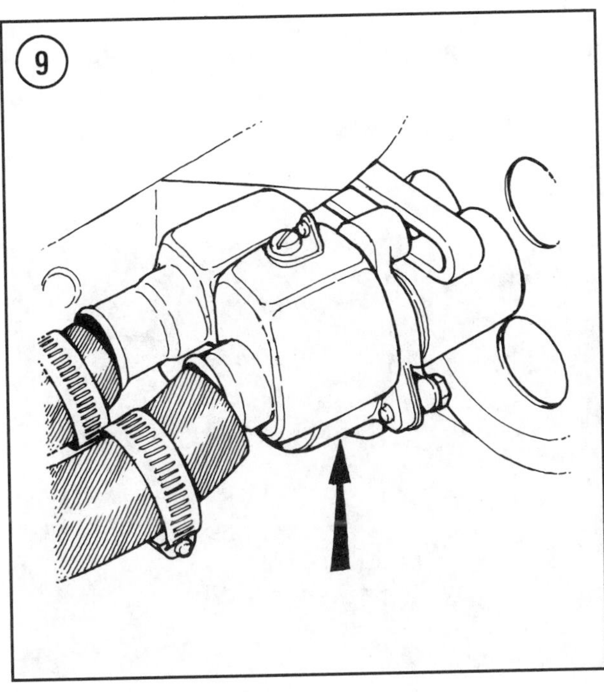

Removal/Installation

1. Disconnect the ground cable from the negative battery terminal.
2. Drain the cylinder block. See Chapter Five.
3. Loosen, but do not remove, the pump pulley fasteners.
4. Loosen the drive belts that contact the circulating pump pulley.
   a. Loosen the alternator adjusting and pivot bolts (**Figure 8**, typical), then move the alternator toward the engine and remove the drive belt.
   b. If equipped with power steering, repeat the procedure in substep 4a to remove the power steering drive belt.
   c. On 5.0 and 5.8 L engines, loosen the seawater pump following a procedure similar to substep 4a.
5. Remove any accessory brackets attached to the water pump which will interfere with its removal.
6. Remove the pump pulley fasteners and remove the pulley.
7. Loosen the clamps and detach the hoses from the circulating pump.
8. Remove the pump-to-cylinder block bolts. Remove the pump and discard the gasket.
9. Clean all gasket residue from the pump and engine block mounting surfaces.
10. Install the pump by reversing the removal procedure. Tighten the water pump fasteners to specification (**Table 1**). Adjust drive belts as described in this chapter. Fill the closed section of the cooling system (if so equipped) with coolant as described in Chapter Five. Start the engine and check for leaks.

SEAWATER PUMP

A sea (raw) water pump with a rubber impeller is used on all models. On other models, the seawater pump is typically located on the starboard side of the engine as shown in **Figure 9**.

Removal/Installation

Refer to **Figures 9** and **10**.

1. Loosen the hose clamps and detach the hoses from the pump.
2. Remove the nut and washer attaching the support bracket to the base of the pump, if so equipped.
3. Remove the screws attaching the pump and lift the pump away from the engine.
4. Install the pump by reversing the removal procedure.
5. Hand-tighten all fasteners until the pump is properly positioned, then tighten fasteners to the torque listed in **Table 1**.

Overhaul

The starboard mounted pump used on most models can be disassembled and a new impeller installed. The water pump repair kit includes the impeller, end plate, screws, washers, gasket and O-ring. The impeller is also available for some models. See **Figure 11**.

1. Remove the 3 screws attaching the impeller housing to the bearing housing.
2. Remove the impeller housing by turning it counterclockwise, while lifting it off.
3. If the impeller remains in the housing, remove it by turning counterclockwise.
4. Remove and discard the O-ring

NOTE
Do not remove the screw and sealing washer from the side of the housing. Do not remove the impeller cam unless replacement is necessary.

5. If the impeller is still on the shaft, remove the impeller.
6. Remove the drive key from the shaft.
7. Remove the end plate and gasket.

NOTE
The snap ring and ceramic seal can be removed from the shaft for inspection, but are not available separately.

8. Remove the snap ring from the shaft and inspect the ceramic seal for cracks.
9. Turn the shaft and check the bearings for smooth rotation.
10. Check the housing for cracks, wear, scoring or distortion.

NOTE
Do not lubricate the ceramic seal with grease.

11. If the snap ring and ceramic seal have been removed, push them onto the shaft until the snap ring seats in the shaft groove.
12. Install the impeller drive key into the shaft.
13. Coat a new gasket lightly with sealer and position it on the bearing housing with the holes aligned.
14. Position the end plate over the gasket with the holes aligned.
15. Slide the impeller onto the shaft and drive key.
16. If the impeller cam has been removed, install the cam using a new seal washer. Coat threads of the retaining screw with sealer and tighten securely.

17. Coat the impeller blades and the O-ring groove lightly with grease and position the sealing O-ring in the groove.
18. Install the impeller housing while rotating it counterclockwise over the impeller.
19. Align the cam attaching screw on the impeller housing with the bearing housing screw next to the boss on the bearing housing.
20. Install and tighten the housing screws securely.

DRIVE BELTS

Inspect all drive belts at regular intervals to make sure they are in good condition and are properly tensioned. Replace worn, frayed, cracked or glazed belts immediately. The components to which they direct power are essential to the safe and reliable operation of the boat. If correct adjustment is maintained on each belt, all will usually give the same service life. For this reason and because of the cost involved in replacing an inner belt (requiring the removal of the outer belt), it is a good idea to replace all belts as a set. The added expense is small compared to the cost of replacing the belts individually and eliminates the possibility of a breakdown on the water which could cost far more in time and money.

Drive belts should be properly tensioned at all times. If loose, the belt(s) will not permit the driven components to operate at maximum efficiency. The belt(s) will also wear rapidly because the increased friction caused by slippage. Belts

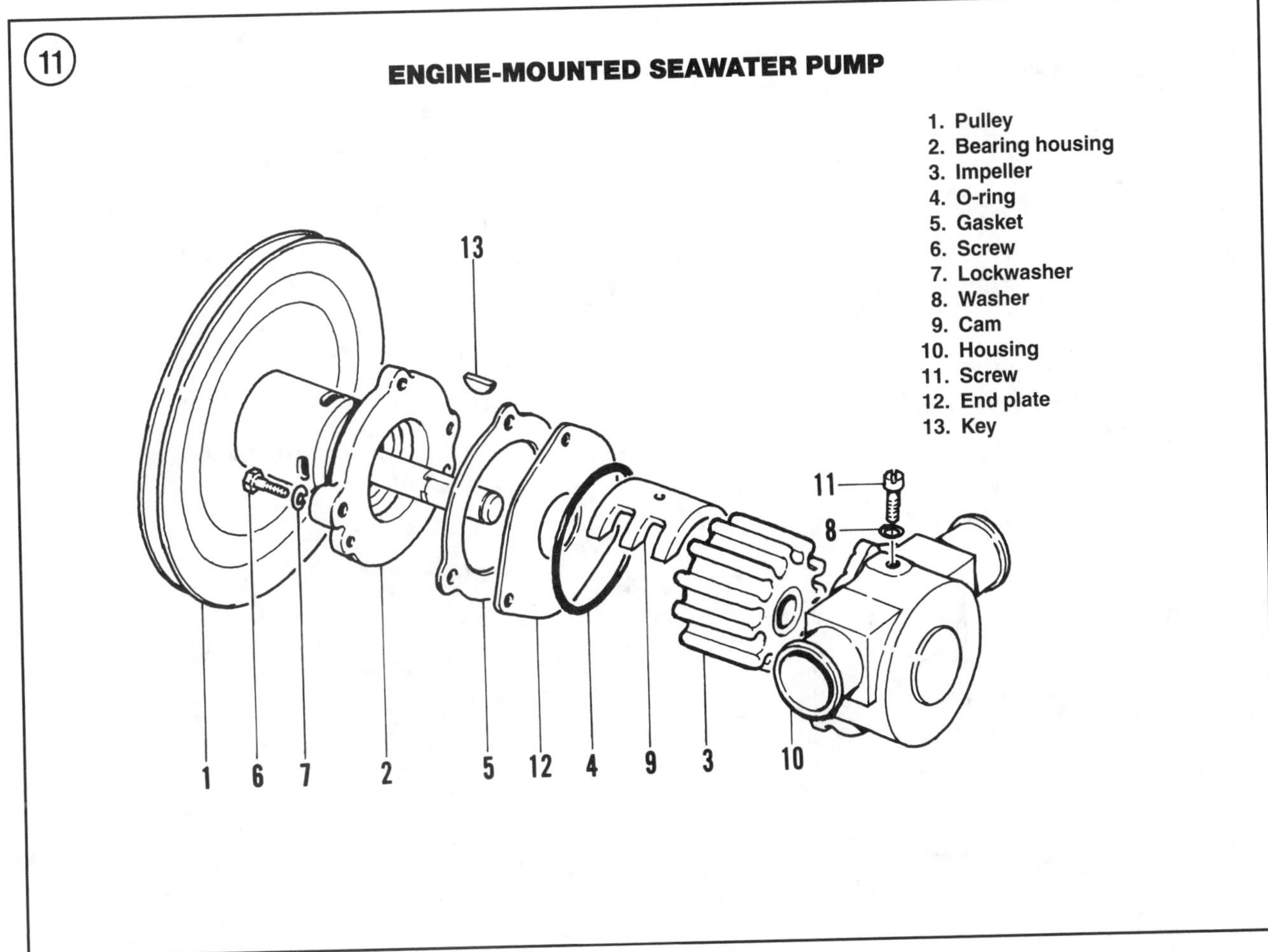

10

that are too tight will be overstressed and prone to premature failure. An excessively tight belt will also overstress the accessory unit's (pump or alternator) bearings, resulting in the unit's premature failure.

Drive belts used on marine engines are heavy-duty belts and should not be replaced with drive belts designed for use with automobiles. **Figure 12** shows typical drive belt routing.

When properly tensioned, the drive belt should deflect approximately 1/4-1/2 in. (6-13 mm) when depressed firmly at a point midway between the pulleys. Drive belt tension should be 44-55 lb. (20-25 kg.) when checked using a

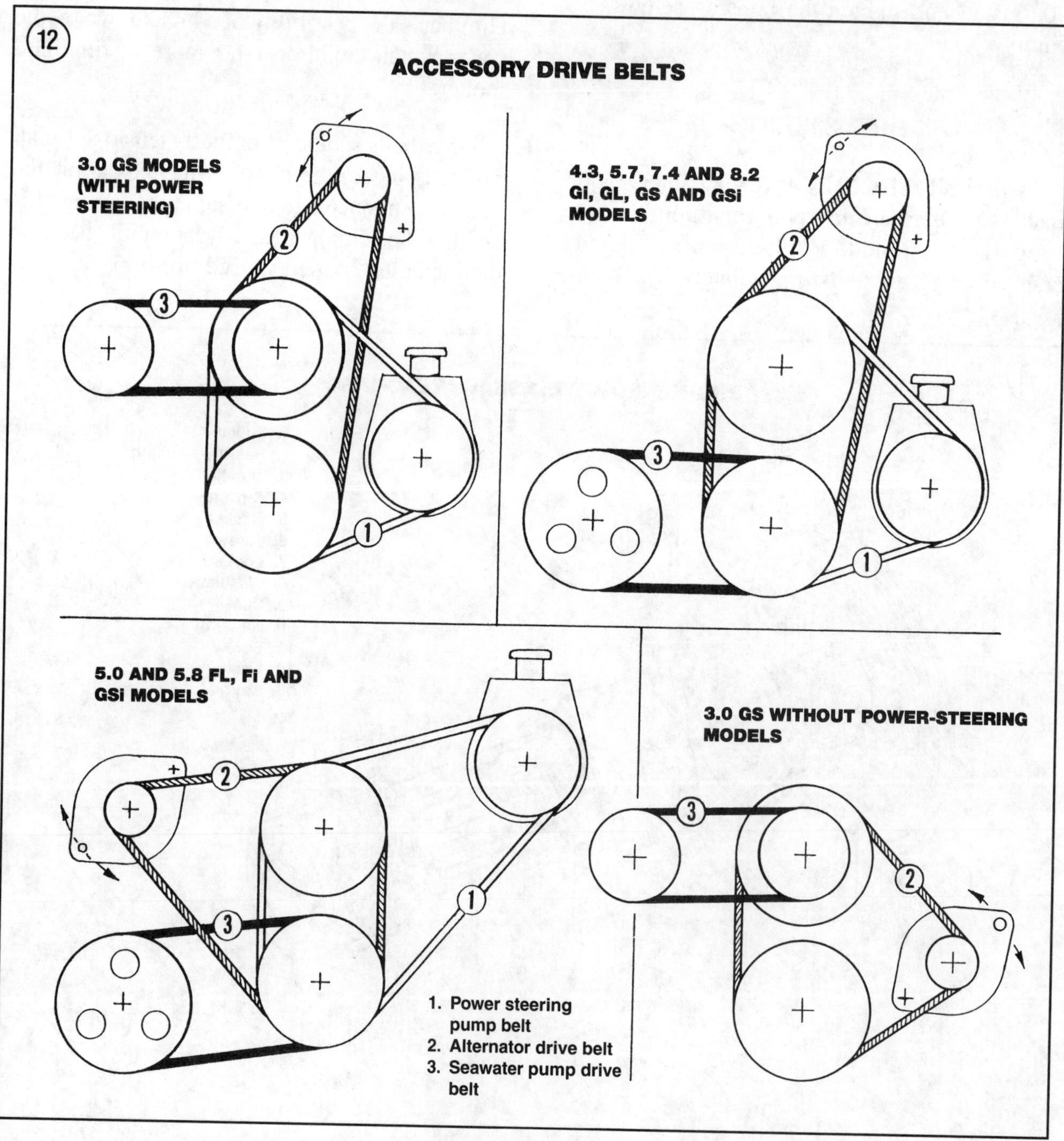

special Volvo Penta drive belt tension gauge (part No. 1159660-8). If the tension is incorrect, perform the procedure below.

Adjustment

On many models, the belt that drives the circulation pump also drives the alternator, and adjustment is accomplished by moving the alternator. On some engines, the power steering pump also drives the circulating pump and adjustment of this belt is accomplished in a similar way—by moving the power steering pump. The belt that drives the seawater pump (that are belt driven) is similarly adjusted—by moving the seawater pump to tighten the belt. The following describes adjusting a typical pump by moving the alternator.

1. Loosen the alternator bracket and pivot bolts. See **Figure 8**, typical.
2. Move the alternator toward the engine to loosen the belt or move it away from the engine to tighten the belt, as required.
3. Tighten the bracket bolt, then tighten the pivot bolt.
4. Recheck belt tension. If necessary, repeat the procedure to obtain the correct tension.

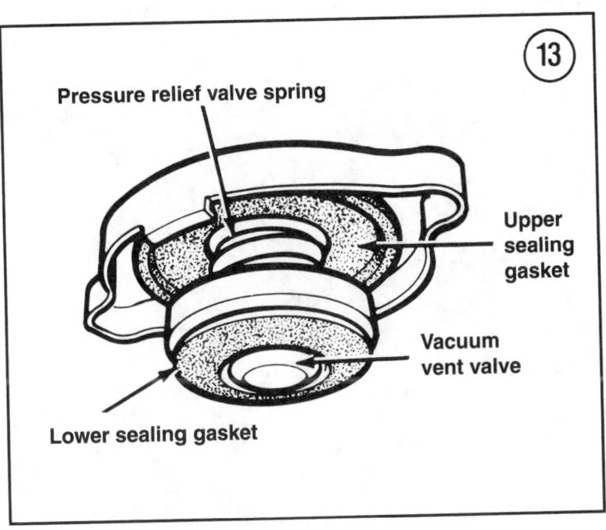

Replacement

If the belt is located behind other belts, it is necessary to remove other drive belts before replacing the drive belt. Refer to **Figure 12**.

1. Loosen the alternator bracket and pivot bolts. See **Figure 8**, typical.
2. Move the alternator toward the engine and slip the belt off the crankshaft and alternator pulleys.
3. Install a new belt over the pulleys and move the alternator away from the engine until the correct deflection or tension is obtained.
4. Tighten the bracket and pivot bolts securely.

CLOSED COOLING SYSTEM MAINTENANCE

Pressure Testing the Freshwater Section

If the freshwater section of a closed cooling system requires frequent topping up, it probably has a leak. Small leaks in a cooling system may not be easy to locate, because the hot coolant evaporates as fast as it leaks out, preventing the formation of tell-tale rusty or grayish-white stains.

A pressure test of the closed section (containing antifreeze) will usually help pinpoint the source of the leak. The procedure is very similar to that used in pressure testing an automotive cooling system and requires the same type of pressure tester.

1. Remove the pressure fill cap from the heat exchanger or reservoir. See **Figure 7**, typical.
2. Wash the cap with clean water to remove any debris or deposits from its sealing surfaces.
3. Check the gasket, if so equipped, and rubber seal on the cap for cuts, cracks, tears or deterioration. See **Figure 13**. Replace the cap if the seal is damaged. Make sure the locking tabs on the cap are not damaged or bent.

4. Dip the cap in water and attach it to a cooling system pressure tester, using the adapters supplied with the tester. See **Figure 14**.
5. Pump the pressure to 14 psi (96 kPa). If the cap fails to hold pressure for 30 seconds without dropping under 11 psi (76 kPa), replace it.
6. Inspect the filler neck seat and sealing surface (**Figure 15**) for nicks, dents, distortion or contamination. Wipe the sealing surface with a clean cloth to remove any rust or dirt. Make sure the locking cams are not bent or damaged.
7. Check coolant level. It should be within 1 in. (25.4 mm) of the filler neck. Top up if necessary.
8. Connect the cooling system pressure tester to the filler neck and pressurize the freshwater section to 17 psi (116 kPa). If pressure does not hold constant for at least 2 minutes, check all hoses, gaskets, drain plugs, drain valves, core plugs and other potential leak points for leakage. Listen for a hissing or bubbling sound while the system is under pressure.
9. If no leaks are found, refer to the appropriate cooling system flow diagram (**Figures 4** and **5**) and disconnect the sea (raw) water outlet hose from the heat exchanger. Repressurize the system to 17 psi (16 kPa) and note the outlet connection on the heat exchanger. If water flows from the connection, air bubbles are seen in the water or a bubbling or hissing noise is heard, there is probably a leak between the fresh and seawater sections inside the heat exchanger.
10. If no signs of leakage can be found in Step 8 or Step 9, yet the coolant level continues to require frequent topping up, there is probably an internal leak. This could be caused by a blown head gasket, loose cylinder head, intake manifold, exhaust elbow or distributor block bolts. A cracked or porous head, block or manifold may also be leaking.

Alkalinity Test

Replace the coolant used in the closed section of a closed cooling system every 2 years. Refer to Chapter Five for the correct coolant. After a year of service, test the coolant for alkalinity with pink litmus paper obtained from a local drug store.

1. With the engine cold, remove the pressure fill cap from the heat exchanger.
2. Insert one end of the litmus paper into the coolant, wait a few seconds and then withdraw it.
   a. If the pink litmus paper turns blue, the coolant alkalinity is satisfactory.
   b. If the litmus paper does not change color, the coolant has lost its alkalinity and should be replaced. Drain and refill the freshwater section of the cooling system. See Chapter Five.

Cleaning the Freshwater Section

Clean and flush the freshwater section every other season or after every 200 hours of operation. Any high-quality, automotive cooling system cleaning solution can be used to remove scale, rust, mineral deposits or other contamination. Use the cleaning solution according to its manufacturer's directions.

If it is extremely dirty or corroded, remaining deposits may be flushed out with a pressure flushing device. Refer to the appropriate cooling system flow diagram and follow the manufacturer's instructions regarding the connection of

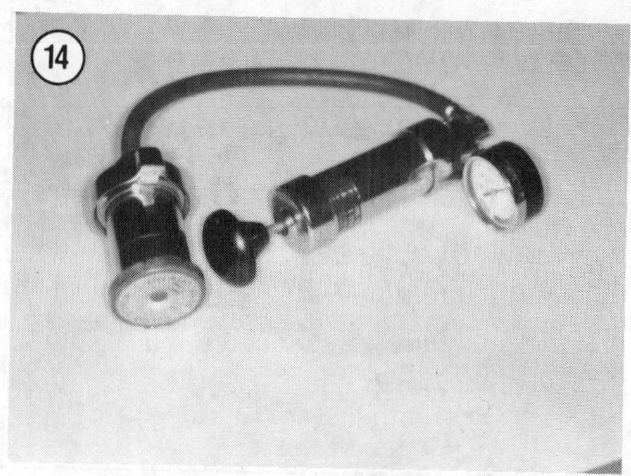

the pressure flushing device and procedure to be followed.

Cleaning the Seawater Section of the Heat Exchanger

Contaminants and minerals will collect inside the copper tubes in the seawater section of the heat exchanger during engine operation. Such foreign material reduces the ability of the heat exchanger to operate efficiently and, if not removed periodically, will eventually lead to engine overheating. It is a good idea to remove and clean the heat exchanger whenever the coolant is changed.

1. Drain both sections of the closed cooling system as described in Chapter Five. Loosen the hose clamps and disconnect all hoses from the heat exchanger. Remove the bolts attaching the heat exchanger, then lift off the unit.
2. Unbolt and remove the heat exchanger end plate(s). Remove and discard the seal washer(s) and gasket(s).

NOTE
If the heat exchanger is plugged or contains heavy scale deposits or if disassembly is difficult, take it to an automotive radiator repair shop for proper cleaning to avoid potential damage to the unit.

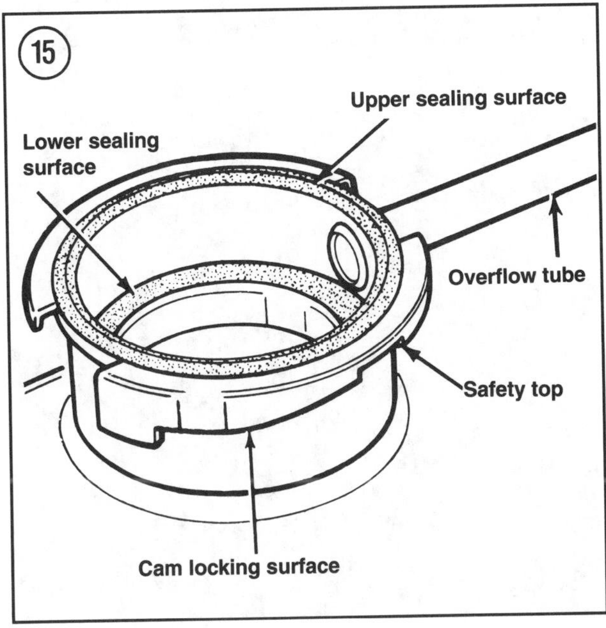

3. Clean all gasket residue from the end plate(s) and heat exchanger sealing surfaces.
4. Insert an appropriate size wire brush into each passage in the heat exchanger. Work the brush back and forth with a vigorous motion, but work carefully to avoid damage to the soldered joints.
5. Remove the brush, hold the heat exchanger vertically and blow loosened particles out with compressed air.
6. Repeat Step 4 and Step 5 as necessary to remove as much of the accumulated deposits as possible.
7. Remove the sacrificial anode, if so equipped, and check for erosion. If more than 25% is gone, install a new anode. Coat anode threads with waterproof sealant.
8. Coat both sides of new end plate gasket(s) with waterproof sealant and reinstall the end plate(s) with a new seal washer.
9. Install the heat exchanger. Check all hoses and clamps. Replace any that have deteriorated. Connect the hoses and tighten hose clamps securely.
10. Fill the freshwater section with coolant. See Chapter Five. Start the engine and check for leaks.

STANDARD COOLING SYSTEM MAINTENANCE

The only maintenance required for an open cooling system is a periodic cleaning of the exhaust manifold. See the appropriate chapter for your engine. However, if the water pump is the cause of an overheating condition, be sure to disassemble the exhaust system and check the condition of the exhaust flapper valves. If burned or otherwise damaged, replace the flapper valves.

OIL COOLER

Some engines are equipped with an engine oil cooler installed on either side of the cylinder block. The cooler may be installed in either vertical or horizontal position. **Figure 16** shows the horizontal installation. Similar coolers may be installed to cool the power steering fluid on some models. Some coolers have a welded construction and cannot be disassembled.

16

Removal/Installation

1. Drain the crankcase and remove the oil filter as described in Chapter Four.

CAUTION
The coolant inlet and outlet lines are sealed to the oil cooler with O-rings. Do not try to separate the lines from the oil cooler without disconnecting them as described in Steps 2 and 3.

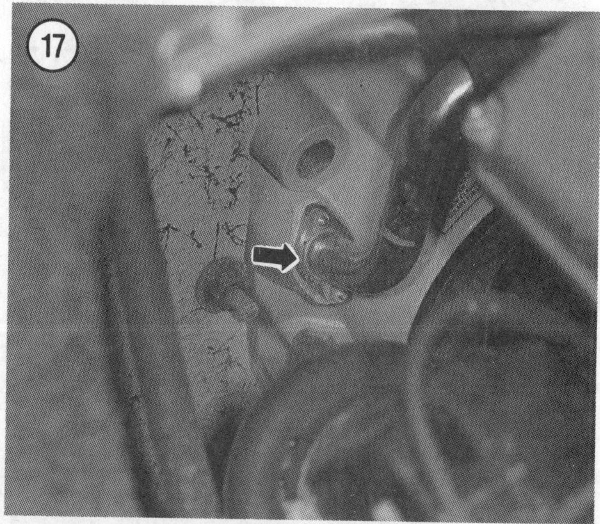

17

2. Remove the screws attaching the water inlet line (**Figure 17**, typical).

3. Detach the water outlet line from the seawater pump. On some installations, the fixture (**Figure 18**) is attached by screws. Other installations may have the outlet attached to a hose which can be disconnected by loosening the clamp and detaching the hose.

4A. On models so equipped, remove the oil filter adapter nut and washer.

4B. On models attached by a bracket, detach the cooler from the engine.

5. Make sure that all attachments are detached, then remove the cooler assembly.

18

WARNING
Be careful to limit spillage and clean any spilled oil immediately after removing the unit.

6. Refer to **Figure 19** for a typical unit that can be taken apart for cleaning. Some coolers have a welded construction and cannot be disassembled.

7. Installation is the reverse of the disassembly procedure. Always use new gaskets, seals and O-rings of the proper type when assembling and installing.

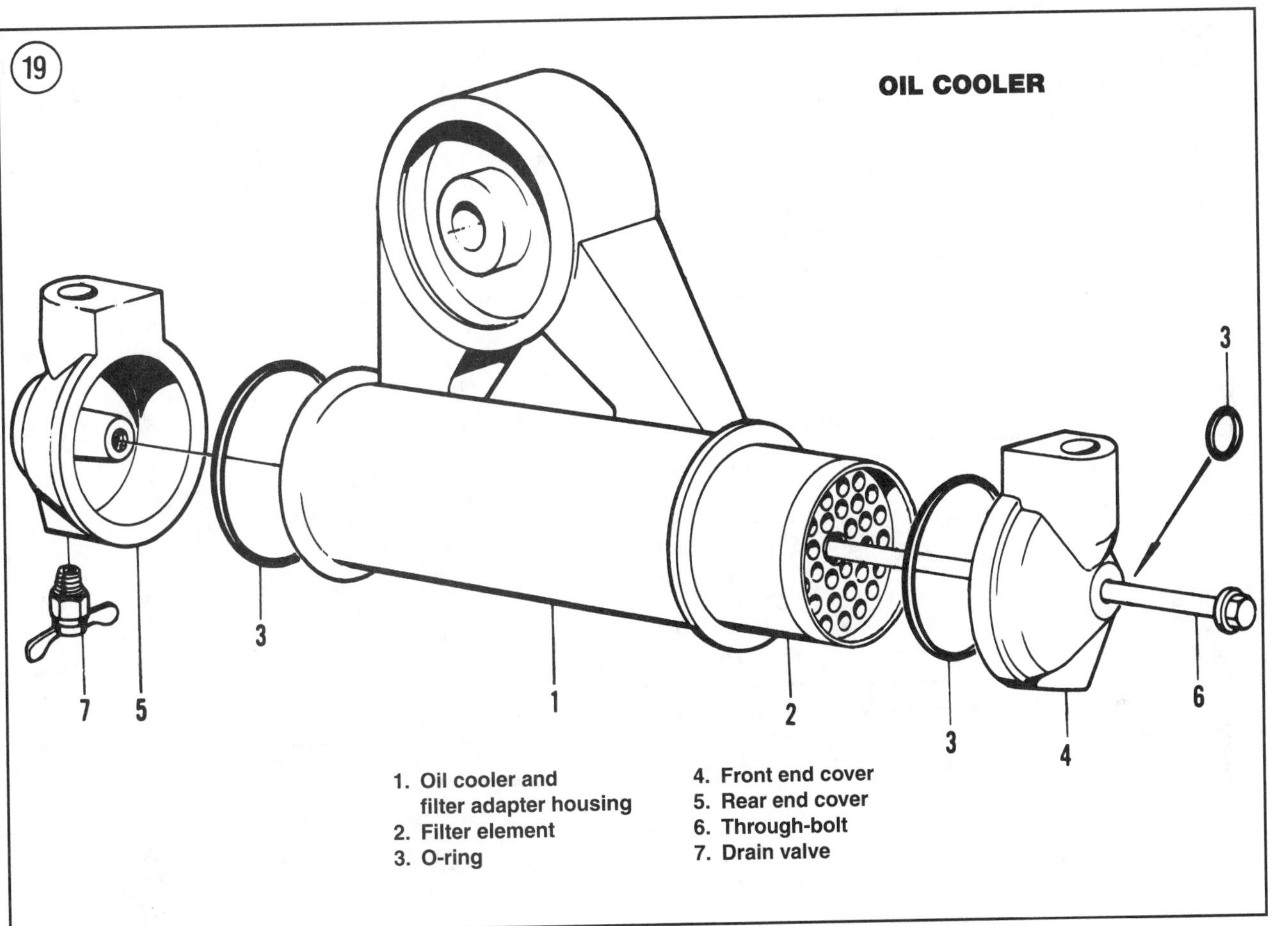

Table 1 TIGHTENING TORQUES

	ft.-lb.	in.-lb.	N.m
Oil cooler center bolt22-25	–	30-34	
Thermostat housing			
3.0 L (GM)	–	60-84	7-9
4.3, 5.0, 5.7, 7.4 and 8.2 L (GM)	20-25	–	27-34
Water pump			
4.3, 5.1, 5.7, 7.4 and 8.2 L (GM)	30	–	41
5.0 and 5.8L (Ford)	10-15	–	15-20
Standard fasteners			
1/4-20	5-7	–	6.8-9.5
5/16-1	14	–	19
3/8-16	20-25	–	27-34
7/16-14	32-40	–	43-54
1/2-13	55-80	–	76-108

Table 2 RECOMMENDED THERMOSTAT

	Starts opening ° F (C)	Fully open ° F (C)
3.0 L	157-163 (69.5-72.8)	182 (83.4)
4.3 L	157-163 (69.5-72.8)	182 (83.4)
5.0/5.8 L	157-163 (69.5-72.8)	182 (83.4)
5.0/5.7 L	157-163 (69.5-72.8)	182 (83.4)
7.4/8.2 L	138-142 (58.9-61.1)	162 (72.3)
All models with closed cooling systems: A 158° F (70°C) is standard.		

Chapter Eleven

Electrical Systems

All engines covered in this manual are equipped with a 12-volt, negative-ground electrical system. Many electrical problems can be traced to a simple cause such as a blown fuse, a loose or corroded connection, a loose alternator drive belt or a frayed wire. While these are easily corrected problems which may not appear to be important, they can quickly lead to serious difficulty if allowed to go uncorrected.

Complete overhaul of electrical components such as the alternator, distributor or starter motor is neither practical nor economical. In some cases, the necessary bushings, bearings or other worn parts are not available for individual replacement.

If tests indicate a unit has problems other than those discussed in this chapter, replace it with a new or rebuilt marine unit. Make certain, however, that the new or rebuilt part to be installed is an exact replacement for the defective one removed. Also, isolate and correct the cause of the failure before installing a replacement. For example, an uncorrected short in an alternator circuit will most likely damage a new alternator as quickly as it damaged the old one. If in doubt, always consult an expert.

This chapter provides service procedures for the battery, charging system, starting system, ignition system and switches. Wiring diagrams are included at the end of the book. **Tables 1-3** are at the end of the chapter.

BATTERY

Since batteries used in marine applications endure far more rigorous treatment than those used in automotive charging systems, they are constructed differently. Marine batteries have a thicker exterior case to cushion the plates. Thicker plates are also used, with each one individually fastened within the case to prevent failure. Spill-proof caps on the battery cells prevent electrolyte from spilling into the bilge. Automotive batteries should be used *only* in an emergency situation when a suitable marine battery is not available. If used, replace the automotive battery with a suitable marine battery as soon as possible.

To ensure sufficient cranking power, install a 12-volt marine battery with a minimum cold cranking amperage rating as specified by the manufacturer. The battery used should have a reserve capacity of at least 100 minutes.

NOTE

Deep cycle batteries are not suitable to start and operate Volvo Penta marine engines. Such batteries are designed to charge and discharge at moderate current levels. If the battery does not have a specified cold cranking amperage rating, it should not be used.

A good state of charge must be maintained in the battery. Any battery that cannot deliver at least 9.6 volts under a starting load should be recharged. If recharging does not bring it up to strength or if it does not hold the charge, replace the battery.

Care and Inspection

1. Disconnect both battery cables (negative first, then positive) and remove the battery hold-down or retainer clamp. See **Figure 1** for a typical open installation and **Figure 2** for a typical enclosed installation.

NOTE

Some batteries have a built-in carry strap for use in Step 2. See ***Figure 3****.*

2. Attach a battery carrier or carrier strap to the battery and lift it from the battery tray. Remove the battery from the engine compartment.
3. Check the entire battery case for cracks or other damage.
4. If the battery has removable vent caps, cover the vent holes in each cap with small pieces of masking tape.

NOTE

Keep cleaning solution out of the battery cells in Step 5 or the electrolyte will be seriously weakened.

5. Scrub the top of the battery with a stiff bristle brush, using a baking soda and water solution

1

2

3

(**Figure 4**). Rinse the battery case with clear water and wipe it dry with a clean cloth or paper towels. Remove the masking tape from the filler cap vent holes, if so equipped.

6. Inspect the battery tray or container in the engine compartment for corrosion. Remove and clean the tray or container, if necessary, with the baking soda and water solution. Rinse with clear water and wipe dry, then reinstall.

7. Clean the battery cable clamps with a stiff wire brush or one of the many tools made for this purpose (**Figure 5**). The same tool is used for cleaning the battery posts (**Figure 6**).

8. Reposition the battery on the battery tray or container and remove the carrier or strap. Install and tighten the hold-down device.

9. Reinstall the positive battery cable, then the negative battery cable.

CAUTION
Be sure the battery cables are connected to their proper terminals. Connecting the battery backward will reverse the polarity and can damage the alternator and ignition system.

10. Tighten the battery cable connections to 9 ft.-lb. (12 N•m). Tightening the connections more than this can cause damage to the battery case. Coat the connections with a petroleum jelly

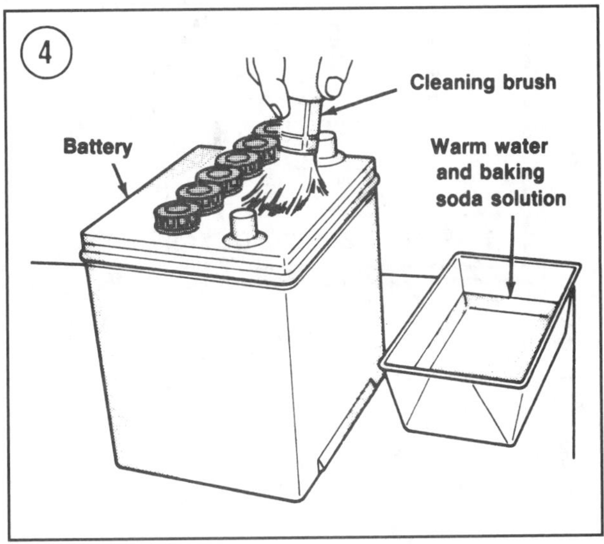

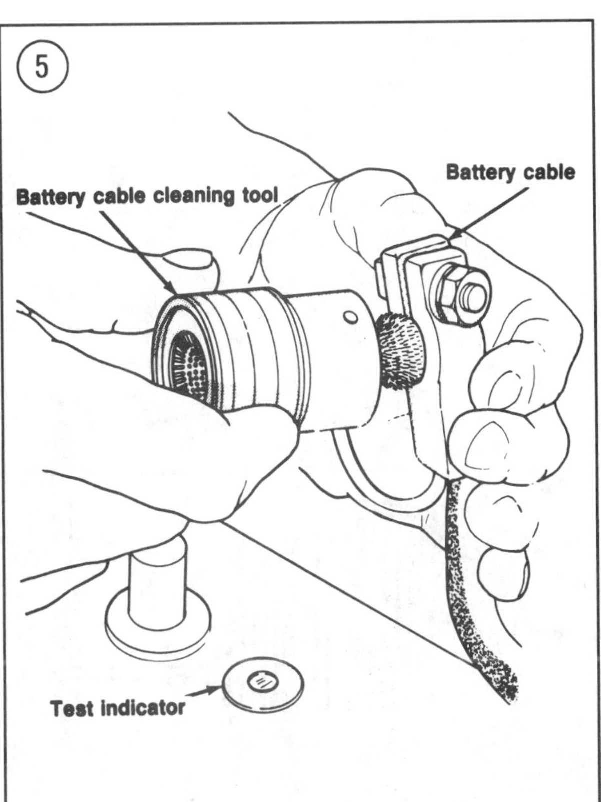

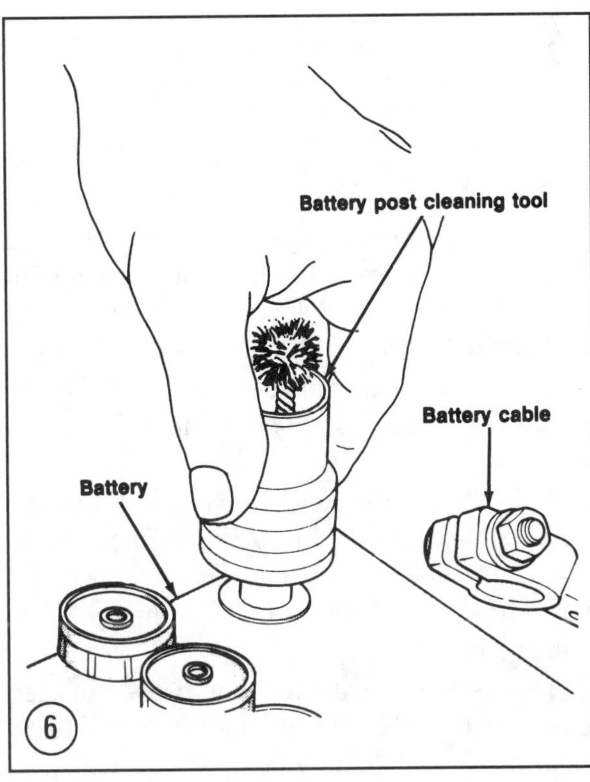

such as Vaseline or a light mineral grease. Aerosol anticorrosion sprays can also be used.

NOTE
Do not overfill the battery cells in Step 11. The electrolyte expands due to heat from charging and may overflow if the level is more than 1/4 in. (6 mm) above the battery plates.

11. Remove the filler caps and check the electrolyte level. The electrolyte should cover the battery plates by at least 3/16 in. (4.8 mm). See **Figure 7**. Top up with distilled water to the bottom of the fill ring in each cell, if necessary.

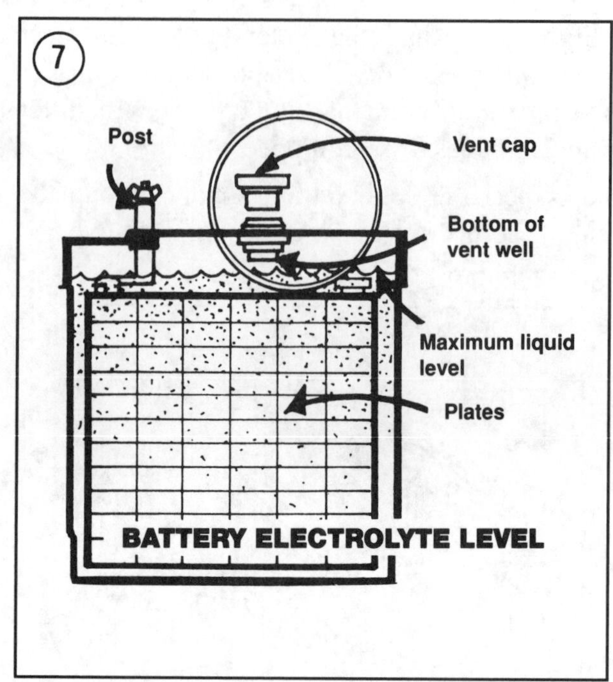

Battery Testing

Hydrometer testing is the best way to check battery condition. Use a hydrometer with numbered graduations from 1.100-1.300 rather than one with just color-coded bands. To use the hydrometer, squeeze the rubber ball, insert the tip in a cell and release the ball (**Figure 8**).

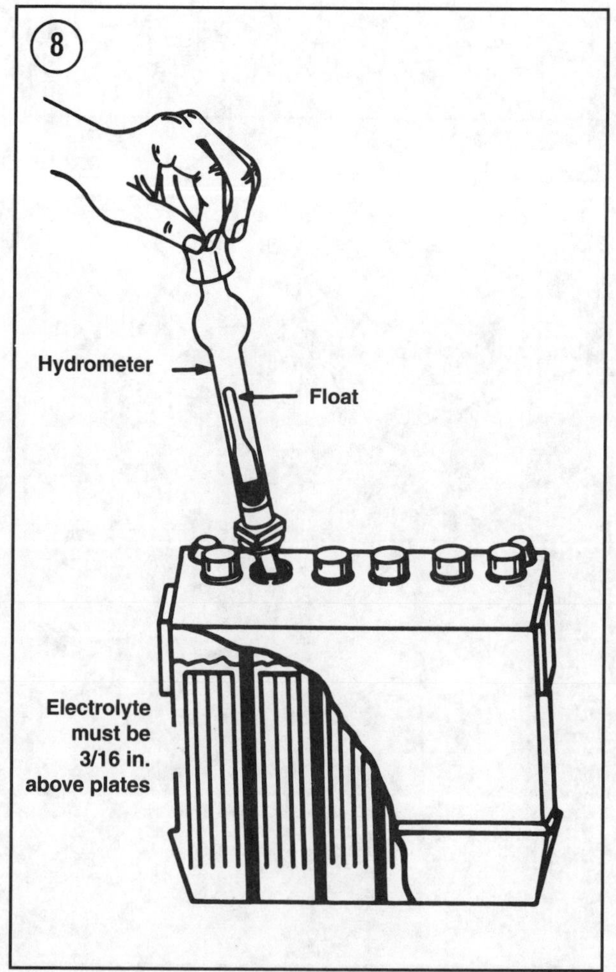

NOTE
Do not attempt to test a battery with a hydrometer immediately after adding water to the cells. Run the engine or charge the battery for 15-20 minutes prior to testing.

Draw enough electrolyte to float the weighted float inside the hydrometer. When using a temperature-compensated hydrometer, release the electrolyte and repeat this process several times to make sure the thermometer has adjusted to the electrolyte temperature before taking the reading.

Hold the hydrometer vertically and note the number aligned with the surface of the electrolyte (**Figure 9**). This is the specific gravity for the cell. Return the electrolyte to the cell from which it came.

The specific gravity of the electrolyte in each battery cell is an excellent indicator of that cell's state of charge. A fully charged cell will read

1.260 or more at 80° F (27° C). If the cells test below 1.220, the battery must be recharged. Charging is also necessary if the specific gravity varies more than 50 points from cell to cell.

NOTE
If a temperature-compensated hydrometer is not used, add 0.004 to the specific gravity reading for every 10° above 80° F (27° C). For every 10° below 80° F (27° C), subtract 0.004.

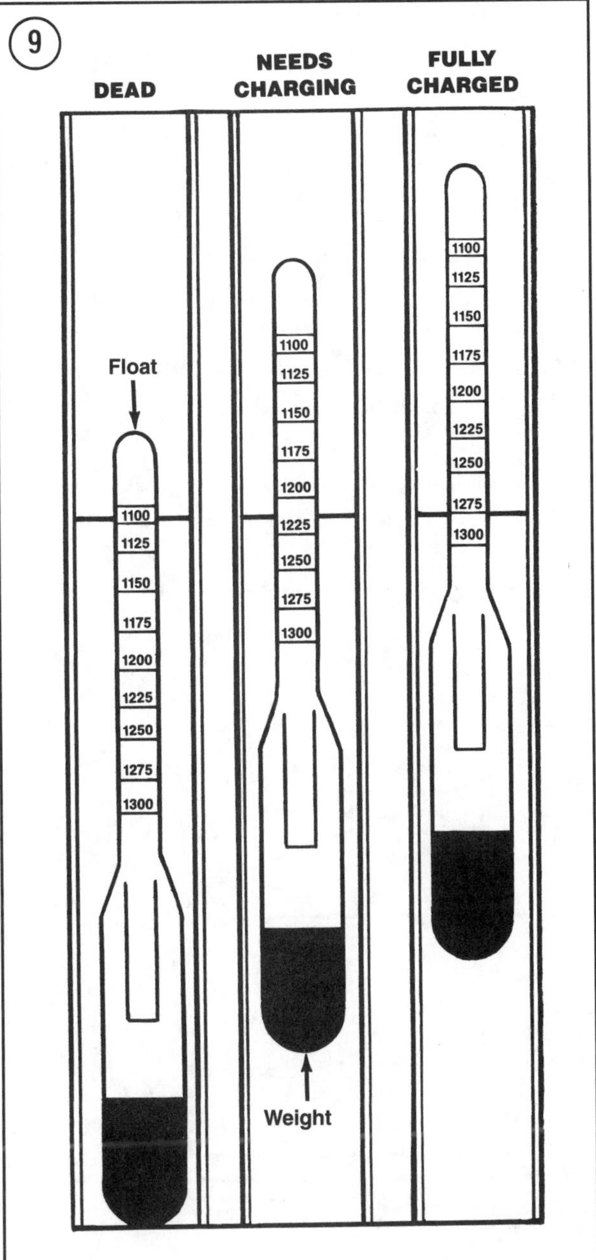

Safety Precautions

When working with batteries, use extreme care to avoid spilling or splashing the electrolyte. This solution contains sulfuric acid, which can ruin clothing and cause serious chemical burns. If any electrolyte is spilled or splashed on clothing or skin, immediately neutralize it with a solution of baking soda and water, then flush with an abundance of clean water.

WARNING
Electrolyte splashed into the eyes is extremely dangerous. Always wear safety glasses while working with batteries. If electrolyte is splashed into the eyes, call a physician immediately, force the eyes open and flood with cool, clean water for approximately 5 minutes.

If electrolyte is spilled or splashed onto any surface, it should be immediately neutralized with baking soda and water solution and then rinsed with clean water.

While batteries are being charged, highly explosive hydrogen gas forms in each cell. Some of this gas escapes through filler cap openings and may form an explosive atmosphere in and around the battery. This condition can persist for several hours. Sparks, an open flame or a lighted cigarette can ignite this gas, causing an internal battery explosion and possible serious personal injury.

Take the following precautions to prevent injury.

1. Do not smoke or permit any open flame near any battery being charged or which has been recently charged.
2. Do not disconnect live circuits from the battery terminals, since a spark usually occurs when a live circuit is broken.
3. Take care when connecting or disconnecting any battery charger. Be sure its power switch is

off before making or breaking any connection. Poor connections are a common cause of electrical arcs which cause explosions.

Charging

A good state of charge must be maintained in batteries used for starting. Check the battery with a voltmeter as shown in **Figure 10**. Any battery that cannot deliver at least 9.6 volts under a starting load should be recharged. If recharging does not bring it up to strength or if it does not hold the charge, replace the battery.

A cold battery will not accept a charge readily. If the temperature is below 40° F (5° C), allow the battery to warm up to room temperature before charging. The battery does not have to be removed from the boat before charging, but it is a recommended procedure since a charging battery produces highly explosive hydrogen gas. In many boats, the area around the battery is not well-ventilated and the gas may remain in the area for several hours after the charging procedure has been completed. Sparks or flames occurring near the battery can cause it to explode, spraying battery acid over a wide area.

Disconnect the negative battery cable first, then the positive battery cable. Make sure the electrolyte is filled to the top. Remove the vent caps and place a folded paper towel over the vent openings to absorb any electrolyte that may spew as the battery charges.

Connect the charger to the battery: negative-to-negative and positive-to-positive. If the charger output is variable, select a 10-12 amp setting. Set the voltage selector to 12 volts and plug the charger in. Once the battery starts to accept a charge, the charge rate should be reduced to a level that will prevent excessive gassing and electrolyte spewing.

The length of time required to recharge a battery depends upon its size, state of charge and temperature. Generally speaking, the current input time should equal the battery amp-hour (AH) rating. For example, a 45 AH battery will require a 9 amp charging rate for 5 hours ($9 \times 5 = 45$) or a 15 amp charging rate for 3 hours ($15 \times 3 = 45$). Check the charging progress with the hydrometer.

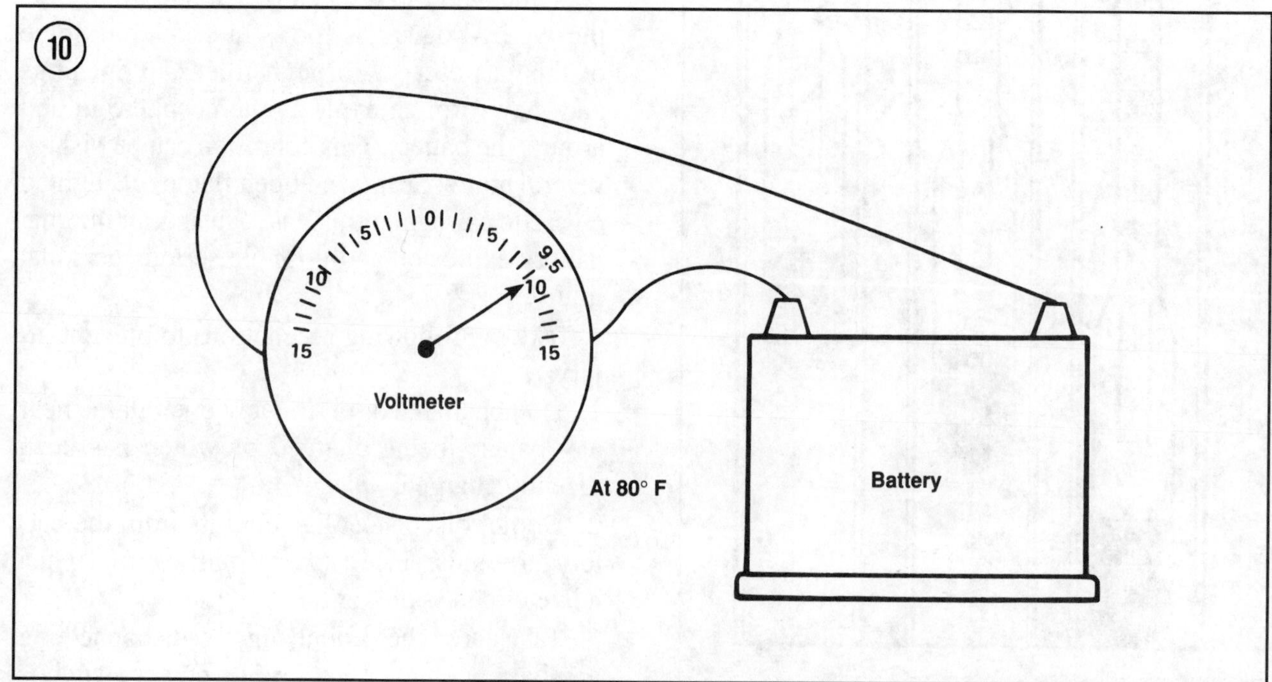

Jump Starting

If the battery becomes severely discharged, it is possible to start and run an engine by jump starting it from another battery. Volvo Penta does not recommend that you jump start a discharged battery due to the possible danger of explosion. Since many owners will disregard this warning, however, the following procedure is provided as the safest method to use.

Before jump starting a battery when temperatures are 32° F (0° C) or lower, check the condition of the electrolyte. If it is not visible or if it appears to be frozen, do *not* attempt to jump start the battery, as the battery may explode or rupture.

WARNING
Use extreme caution when connecting a booster battery to one that is discharged to avoid personal injury or damage to the system.

1. Connect the jumper cables in the order and sequence shown in **Figure 11**.

WARNING
An electrical arc may occur when the final connection is made. This could cause an explosion if it occurs near the battery. For this reason, the final connection should be made to the alternator mounting bracket or another good engine ground and not the battery itself.

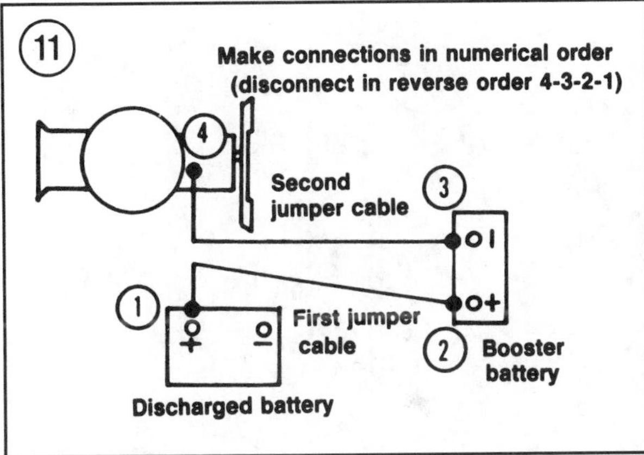

2. Check that all jumper cables are out of the way of moving parts on both engines.
3. Start the engine with the good battery and run at a moderate speed.
4. Start the engine with the discharged battery. Once it starts, run it at a moderate speed.

CAUTION
Excessive engine speed may damage the electrical system.

5. Remove the jumper cables in the exact reverse order shown in **Figure 11**. Begin at point 4, then disconnect at points 3, 2 and 1.

Battery Cables

Poor terminal connections will cause excessive resistance. Defective cable insulation can cause partial short circuits. Both conditions may result in an abnormal voltage drop in the starter motor cable. When this happens, the resulting hard-start condition will place further strain on the battery. Cable condition and terminal connections should be checked periodically.

CHARGING SYSTEM

The charging system consists of the battery, alternator, voltage regulator, ignition switch, ammeter and connecting wiring. The models covered in this manual may be equipped with a Motorola or Prestolite.

Preliminary Testing

The first indication of charging system trouble is usually a slow engine cranking speed during starting or running lights that dim as engine speed decreases. This will often occur long before the ammeter or voltmeter indicates there is a potential problem. When charging system trouble is first suspected, perform the following checks.

1. Check the alternator drive belt for correct tension (Chapter Ten).
2. Check the battery to make sure it is in satisfactory condition and fully charged and that all connections are clean and tight.
3. Check all connections at the alternator to make sure they are clean and tight.

If there are still indications that the charging system is not performing as it should after each of the above points has been carefully checked and any unsatisfactory conditions corrected, refer to Chapter Three and perform the *Charging System Test*.

This section provides alternator replacement procedures. Complete alternator overhaul is not practical for the amateur mechanic. Rebuilt marine-approved alternators can be purchased quite inexpensively compared to the time and effort involved in disassembly, testing, repair and reassembly. In some cases, such overhaul is not even possible since replacement components are not available.

Alternator Removal/Installation

This procedure is generalized to cover all applications. Access to the alternator is quite limited in some engine compartments and care should be taken to avoid personal injury.

1. Disconnect the negative battery cable.
2. Disconnect all wiring harnesses and leads from the rear of the alternator. See **Figure 12**, typical.
3. Loosen the alternator adjusting and pivot bolts (**Figure 13**, typical).
4. Swivel the alternator toward the engine and remove the drive belt from the alternator pulley.
5. Support the alternator with one hand and remove the adjusting and pivot bolts, noting the position of any washers or spacers used. Remove the alternator.
6. Installation is the reverse of removal. Tighten fasteners securely and adjust drive belt tension (Chapter Ten) before attaching the wiring harnesses and leads to the rear of the alternator.

STARTING SYSTEM

The starting system consists of the starter motor, starter solenoid, assist solenoid (relay), ignition switch, neutral switch, battery and one or more fuses or circuit breakers. The neutral switch is located in the remote control assembly and prevents starter operation if the remote control is not in NEUTRAL.

All 1994 models except the Ford based 5.0 L and 5.8 L engines are equipped with a conventional field-wound starter motor. The 1994 5.0 L and 5.8 L models and all 1995-on General Motors based engines are equipped with a permanent magnet, gear reduction type starter motor.

12

13

The permanent magnet starter motor has no field coil or pole shoe. The magnetic field is provided by a series of small permanent magnets. As a result, there is no motor field circuit and thus no potential field wire-to-frame short circuits or other related electrical problems. The permanent magnet motor contains only an armature circuit.

The permanent magnets mounted inside the starter frame (**Figure 14**) are made from an alloy of iron and rare-earth materials that deliver a magnetic field strong enough to operate the motor with the same cranking performance as a comparable starter motor with electromagnetic fields. A planetary gear train transmits power between the armature and the pinion shaft, resulting in a low-speed, high-torque starter motor.

Like any other permanent magnet motor, permanent magnet starters require care in handling. The permanent magnets are quite brittle, and the magnetic field can be destroyed by a sharp impact or by dropping the starter motor.

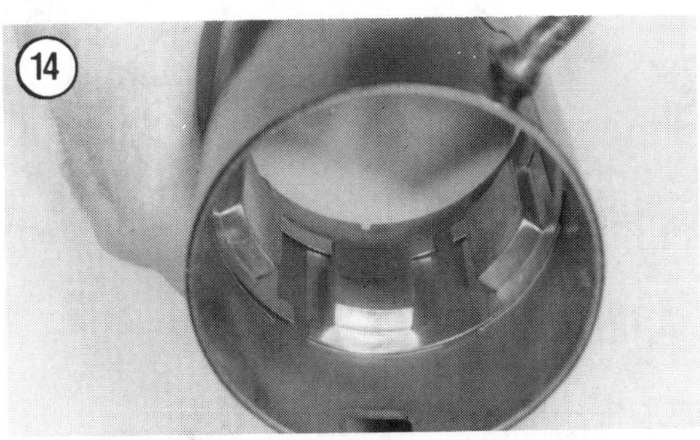
14

15

Starter service requires experience and special tools. Troubleshooting procedures are provided in Chapter Three. The procedures described below consist of removal, installation and brush replacement. Any repairs inside the unit itself (other than brush replacement) should be done at a dealership or certified electrical shop. Installation of a professionally rebuilt marine-type unit is generally less expensive and thus more practical.

Starter Solenoid Replacement

1. Remove the starter motor as described in this chapter.
2. Disconnect the field strap from the starter from the motor terminal.
3. Remove the solenoid-to-drive housing screws and the motor terminal bolt.
4. Rotate the solenoid 90° and remove it from the drive housing with the plunger return or torsion spring.
5. Installation is the reverse of removal.

Assist Solenoid Removal/Installation

1. Detach the ground cable from the negative terminal of the battery.
2. Detach the wires from the solenoid terminals.
3. Remove the nuts holding the starter and battery cables to the solenoid then detach the cables and reinstall the nuts to prevent their loss.
4. Remove the solenoid attaching screws. Remove the solenoid.
5. Installation is the reverse of removal.

Starter Removal/Installation

1. Detach the ground cable from the negative terminal of the battery.
2. *All other starters*—Disconnect the solenoid terminal wires. See **Figure 15**, typical.

3. Remove the starter motor mounting bolts. Pull the starter motor away from the flywheel and remove it from the engine. Retrieve any mounting shims that may fall out.
4. Installation is the reverse of removal. Reinstall any shims to ensure proper pinion-to-flywheel mesh. Tighten mounting bolts securely and apply liquid neoprene to all terminal connections to prevent corrosion.

Starter Brush Replacement (Permanent Magnet Starter)

Brushes cannot be replaced individually or in sets. Brush replacement requires replacement of the entire brush holder assembly (**Figure 16**). New brush holder assemblies come complete with new brushes. To disassemble the starter motor and check brush condition:

1. Remove the nut holding the brush terminal to the solenoid stud. Disconnect the terminal from the stud (**Figure 17**).
2. Remove the 2 through-bolts holding the end cap to the field frame (**Figure 18**). If the cap does not come off easily, tap on its ears with a soft-faced hammer.
3. Remove the end cap (**Figure 19**). Note that there are 6 locating dowels in the cap that must align and engage the brush holder during reassembly.
4. Disengage the brush terminal insulator from the field frame. Then, slide the brush holder from the armature shaft and remove the complete assembly (**Figure 20**). The brushes appear to be removable but they are not. If one or more brushes require replacement, the entire assembly must be replaced.
5. Check the brushes for length and condition. Replace the brush holder if any are oil-soaked or worn to 1/4 in. (6 mm) or less.
6. Make sure the brush holder is clean and that the brushes do not bind in their individual holders.
7. Check the brush springs and replace the entire assembly if distorted or discolored.
8. Installation is the reverse of removal.

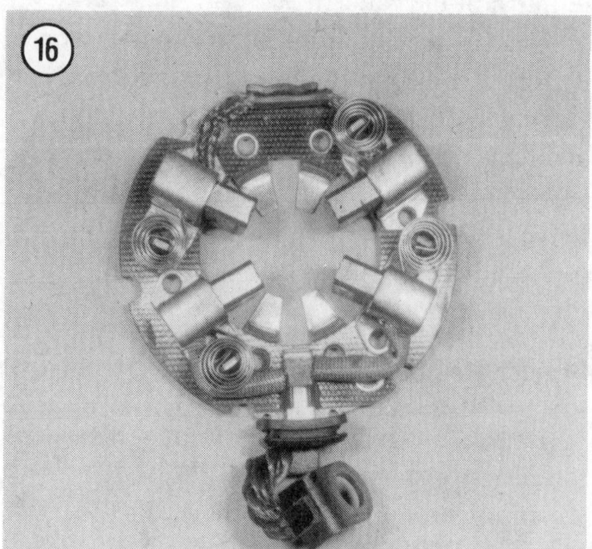
16

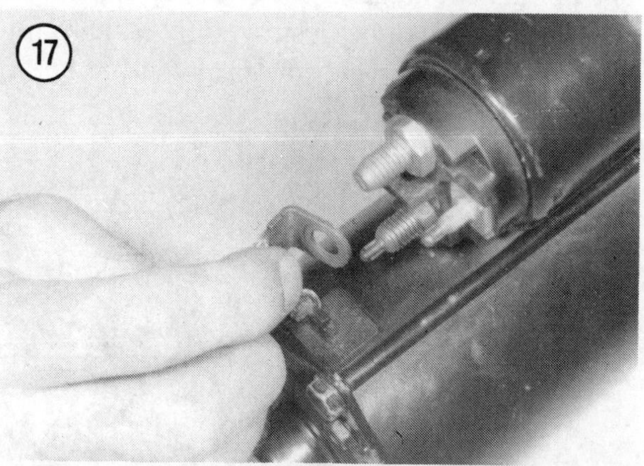
17

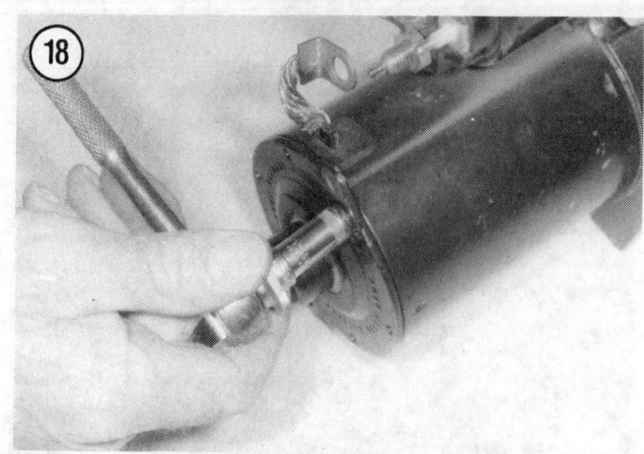
18

Starter Brush Replacement (Field Wound Starter)

Brush replacement requires partial disassembly of the starter. Always replace brushes in complete sets. Refer to **Figure 21** for this procedure.

1. Remove the terminal nut and disconnect the field lead from the solenoid terminal. See **Figure 22**.
2. Remove the 2 through-bolts. Separate the end frame and field frame assembly from the solenoid and drive assembly. See **Figure 23**.
3. Remove the brush and lead attaching screws (**Figure 24**).
4. Remove the brush holder pivot pins.
5. Remove the 2 brush holder and spring assemblies from the field housing. See **Figure 25**.

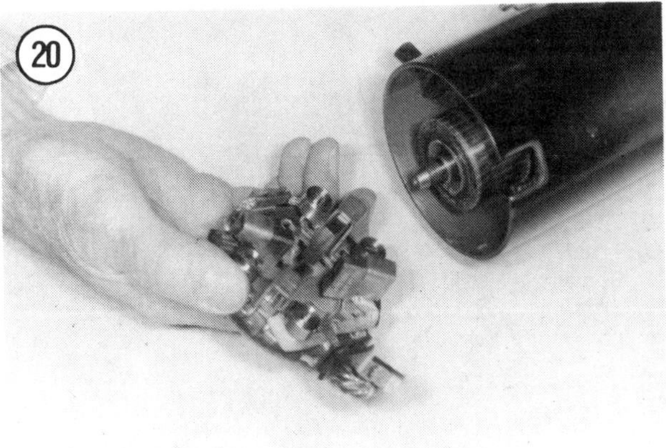

6. Check the brushes for length and condition. Replace all if any are oil-soaked or worn to 1/4 in. (6 mm) or less in length.
7. Make sure the brush holders are clean and that the brushes do not bind in the holder.
8. Check the brush springs and replace if distorted or discolored.
9. Secure new brushes to the leads with the attaching screws.
10. Reverse Steps 1-3 to complete brush installation.

IGNITION SYSTEM

Volvo Penta marine engines are equipped with a Delco EST (Electronic Spark Timing) ignition, Prestolite BID (Breakerless Integral Distributor) ignition, or TFI-IV (Thick Film Integrated) ignition system.

The Delco EST (Electronic Spark Timing) is a breakerless, electronic ignition system consisting of a distributor, magnetic pickup coil, ignition module, ignition coil, battery, ignition switch and related circuitry. A centrifugal spark advance mechanism is not used. Spark advance is controlled electronically by the ignition module. The ignition module and pickup coil are contained inside the distributor. See **Figure 26**. This system may be incorporated with electronic fuel injection and both the ignition and fuel can be controlled by the ECM (Engine Control Module).

The Prestolite BID (Breakerless Integral Distributor) is a breakerless electronic ignition system consisting of a distributor assembly and a high tension ignition coil. The distributor includes a centrifugal advance assembly, magnetic timing system and the ignition electronic control module as well as the rotor and distributor cap. See **Figure 27**.

The TFI-IV (Thick Film Integrated Ignition) ignition system consists of a distributor (with trigger or sensor assembly), ignition coil, ignition amplifier, ignition switch, battery, spark

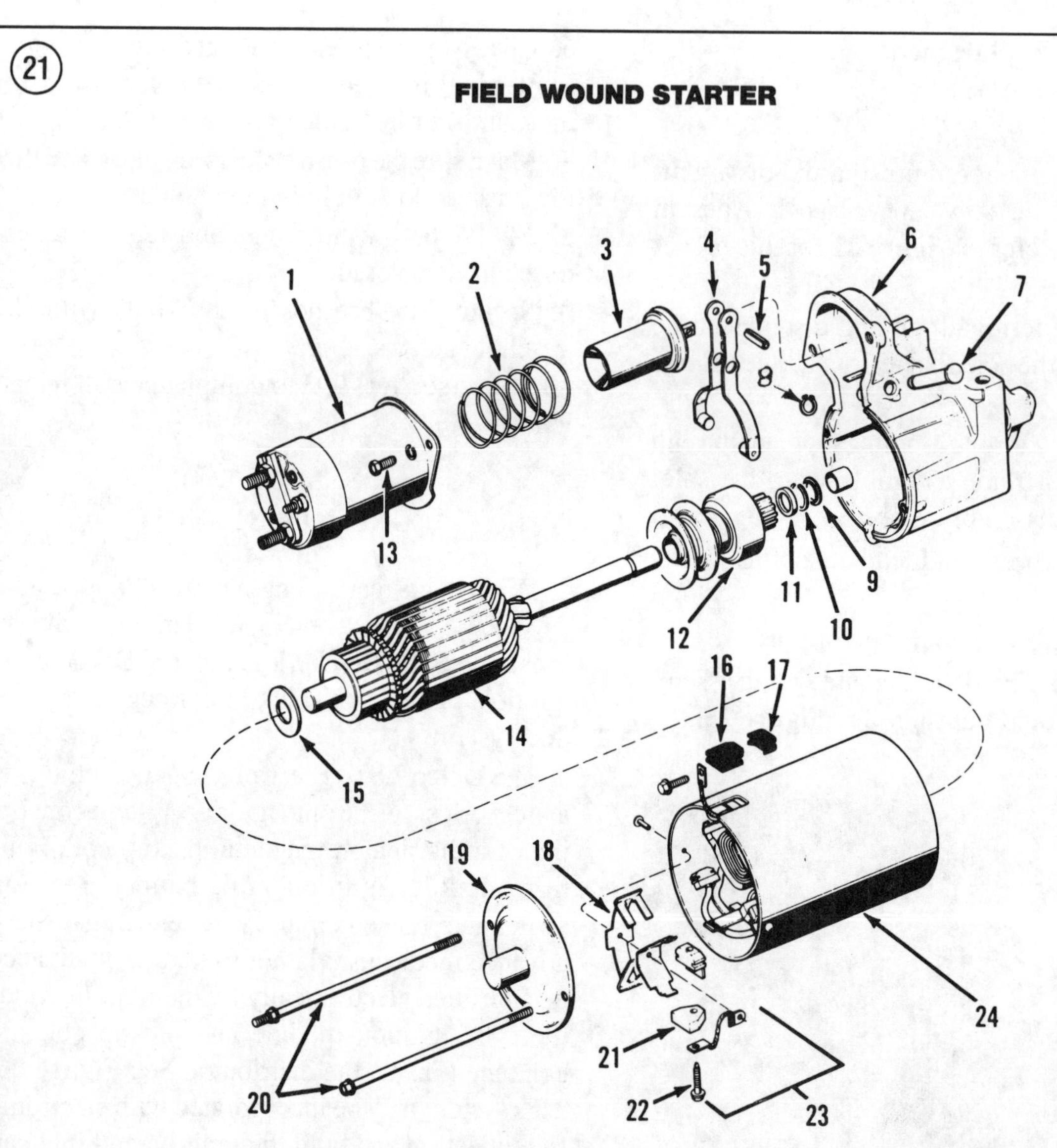

1. Solenoid switch
2. Plunger return spring
3. Plunger
4. Shift lever
5. Plunger pin
6. Drive end housing
7. Shift lever shaft
8. Lever shaft retaining ring
9. Thrust collar
10. Pinion stop retainer ring
11. Pinion stop collar
12. Drive
13. Screw
14. Armature
15. Washer
16. Grommet
17. Grommet
18. Brush holder
19. Commutator end frame
20. Through bolt
21. Brush
22. Screw
23. Brush and holder assembly
24. Frame and field winding

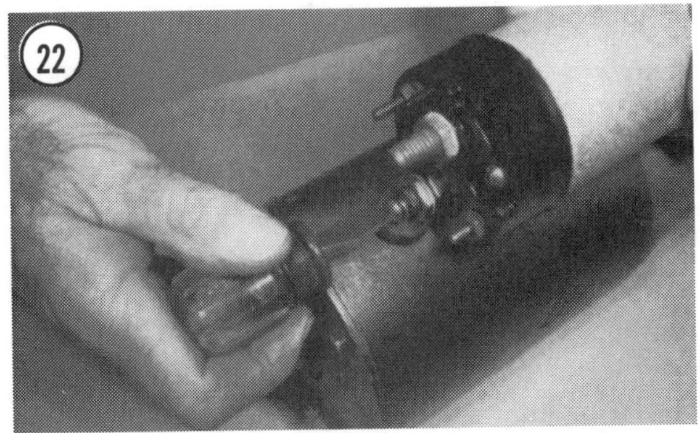

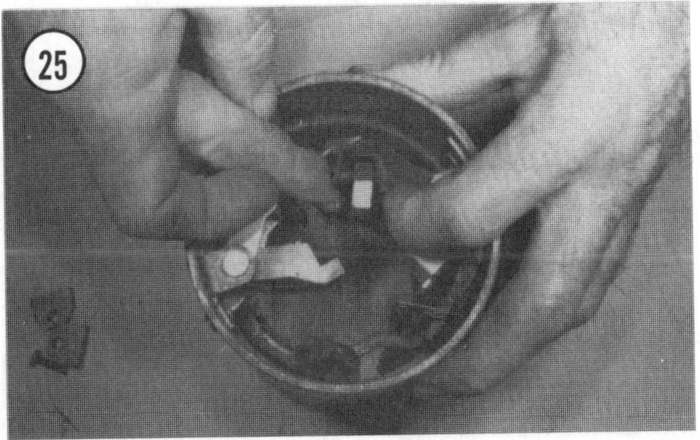

plugs and connecting wiring. See the wiring diagrams at the end of the manual. This system may be incorporated with electronic fuel injection and both the ignition and fuel can be controlled by the ECM (Engine Control Module).

Most troubleshooting procedures and service to electronic ignition and electronic fuel injection systems is beyond the scope of this book. If difficulty is encountered and either the electronic ignition or fuel injection is suspected, the system should be tested and repaired by technicians. Both Volvo Penta and the ignition system manufacturers have trained personnel with the special test equipment necessary to quickly and accurately service these systems.

EST AND DI IGNITION

The Delco EST and Di ignition system used on some engines is manufactured with a special housing, distributor cap, electrical components and other parts designed and selected for marine use. They are designed to withstand climatic and environmental abuse that is much more severe than automotive application. For this reason, automotive parts should not be substituted. Periodic care, cleaning and lubrication is necessary to ensure long service life. Improper or careless testing and servicing procedures can quickly damage the system.

Distributor Assembly
Removal

The distributor can be removed without noting its location, but installation is easier if the following procedure is followed. Steps 2-6 set the crankshaft at the ignition position for the No. 1 piston. At this position the camshaft and crankshaft are correctly positioned to locate the No. 1 piston near top dead center of its compression stroke. If the engine's crankshaft is not moved, installation of the distributor and initial timing

(26)

DISTRIBUTOR ASSEMBLY (EST AND DI IGNITION)

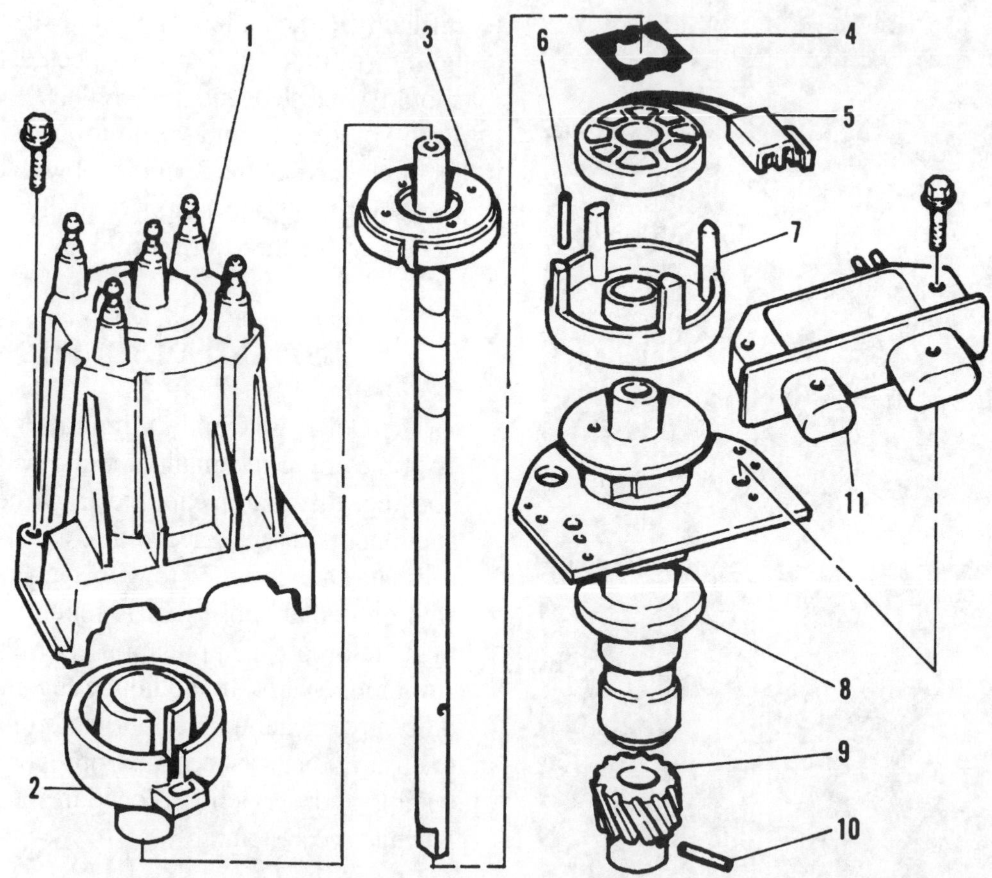

1. Distributor cap
2. Rotor
3. Shaft
4. Retainer
5. Pickup coil
6. Locating pin
7. Pole piece
8. Housing
9. Driven gear
10. Roll pin
11. Ignition module

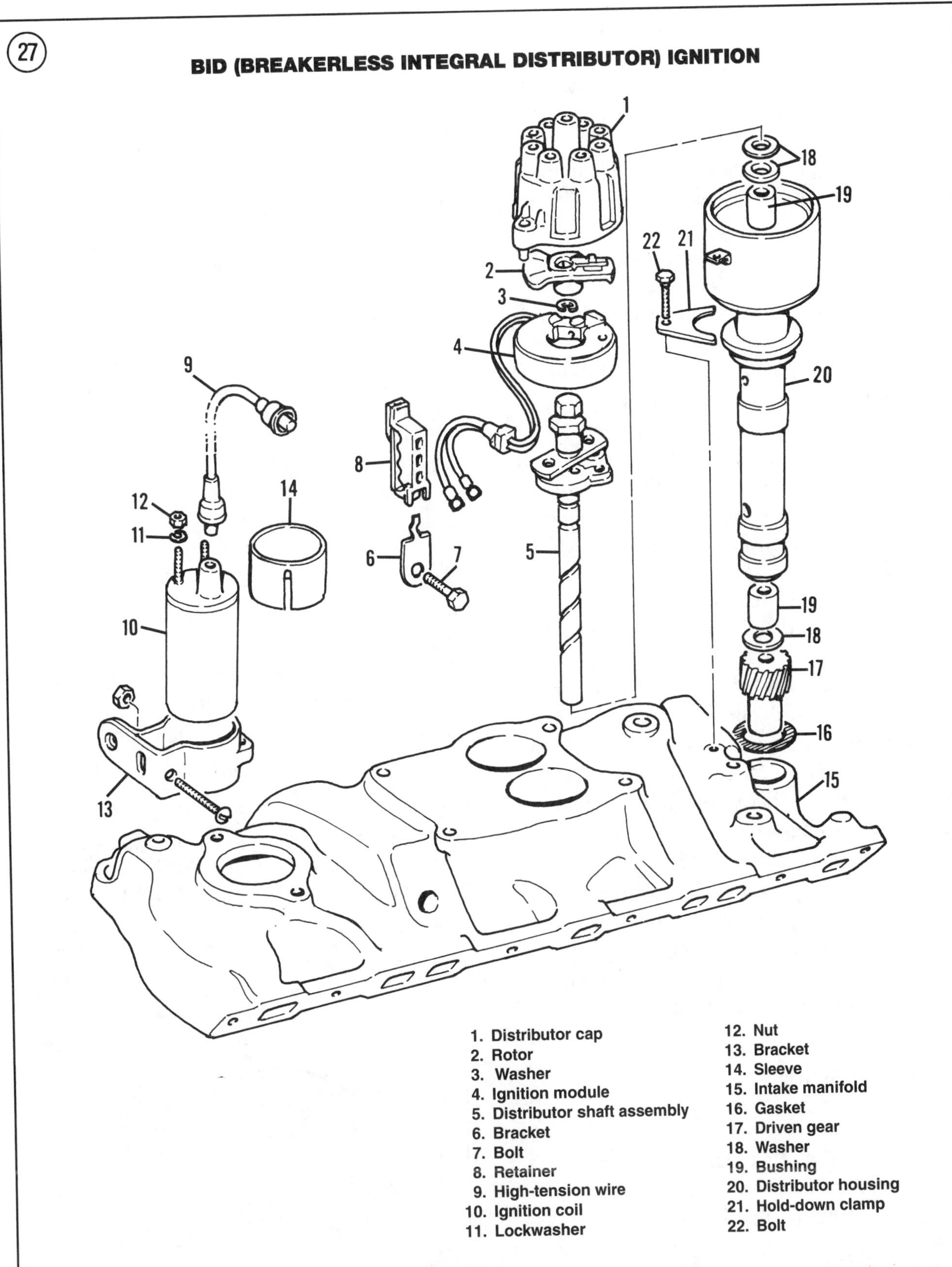

1. Distributor cap
2. Rotor
3. Washer
4. Ignition module
5. Distributor shaft assembly
6. Bracket
7. Bolt
8. Retainer
9. High-tension wire
10. Ignition coil
11. Lockwasher
12. Nut
13. Bracket
14. Sleeve
15. Intake manifold
16. Gasket
17. Driven gear
18. Washer
19. Bushing
20. Distributor housing
21. Hold-down clamp
22. Bolt

will be easier if the rotor, housing and engine are marked as described in these steps:

1. To prevent accidental damage, detach the ground cable from the negative terminal of the battery.
2. Turn the engine crankshaft until the ignition timing mark is aligned as described in Chapter Four.
3. Remove the distributor cap retaining screws.
4. Lift the distributor cap and check to see if the rotor is pointing toward the No. 1 spark plug wire terminal in the distributor cap.
5. If the rotor is pointing to the No. 1 cylinder terminal in the cap, continue to Step 7.
6. If the rotor is pointing opposite the No. 1 spark plug wire terminal, turn the crankshaft 180° (exactly 1 complete revolution) until the timing marks again align, then repeat Step 4. If the rotor does not move, the distributor drive is not working properly.
7. Remove the distributor cap with the spark plug wires attached and place to one side out of the way.
8. Separate the connector containing the small wires from the distributor.
9. Mark the distributor housing in line with the rotor tip. See **Figure 28**, typical. This mark will help locate the distributor shaft in relation to the distributor housing.
10. Mark across the base of the distributor housing and the engine. This mark will help locate the distributor housing in relation to the engine.
11. Remove the distributor hold-down bolt and clamp located at the base of the distributor.
12. Lift the distributor from the engine.

Distributor Assembly Installation

If the crankshaft and camshaft positions are not known, they must be set as described in Steps 1-3 before installing the distributor. If the distributor rotor, housing and engine has been marked as described during the removal procedure *and the crankshaft has not been moved*, then the crankshaft is positioned correctly and the distributor can be installed as described in Steps 4-12.

1. Remove the No. 1 spark plug. See Chapter Four.
2. Press a finger tightly over the spark plug hole, then turn the engine crankshaft pulley in the normal direction of rotation until compression pressure is felt.
3. Continue to turn the crankshaft slowly until the ignition timing mark on the crankshaft pulley and the timing pointer are aligned as described in Chapter Four.

NOTE
Always rotate the engine in the direction of normal rotation. Do not turn the engine backward (back the engine up) to align the timing marks.

4. Position a new distributor gasket (if used) on the distributor housing.
5. Turn the distributor shaft until the rotor tip points in the direction of the No. 1 terminal in the distributor cap. If the distributor housing was marked upon disassembly, align the mark.

NOTE
Step 6 is necessary to compensate for the slight spiral cut of the distributor drive gears. It may be necessary to position the

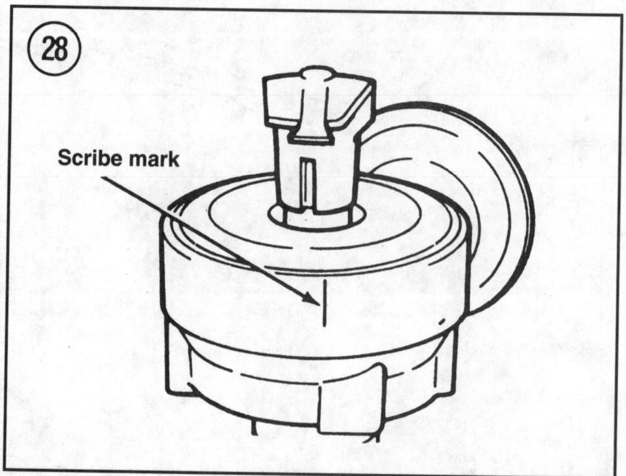

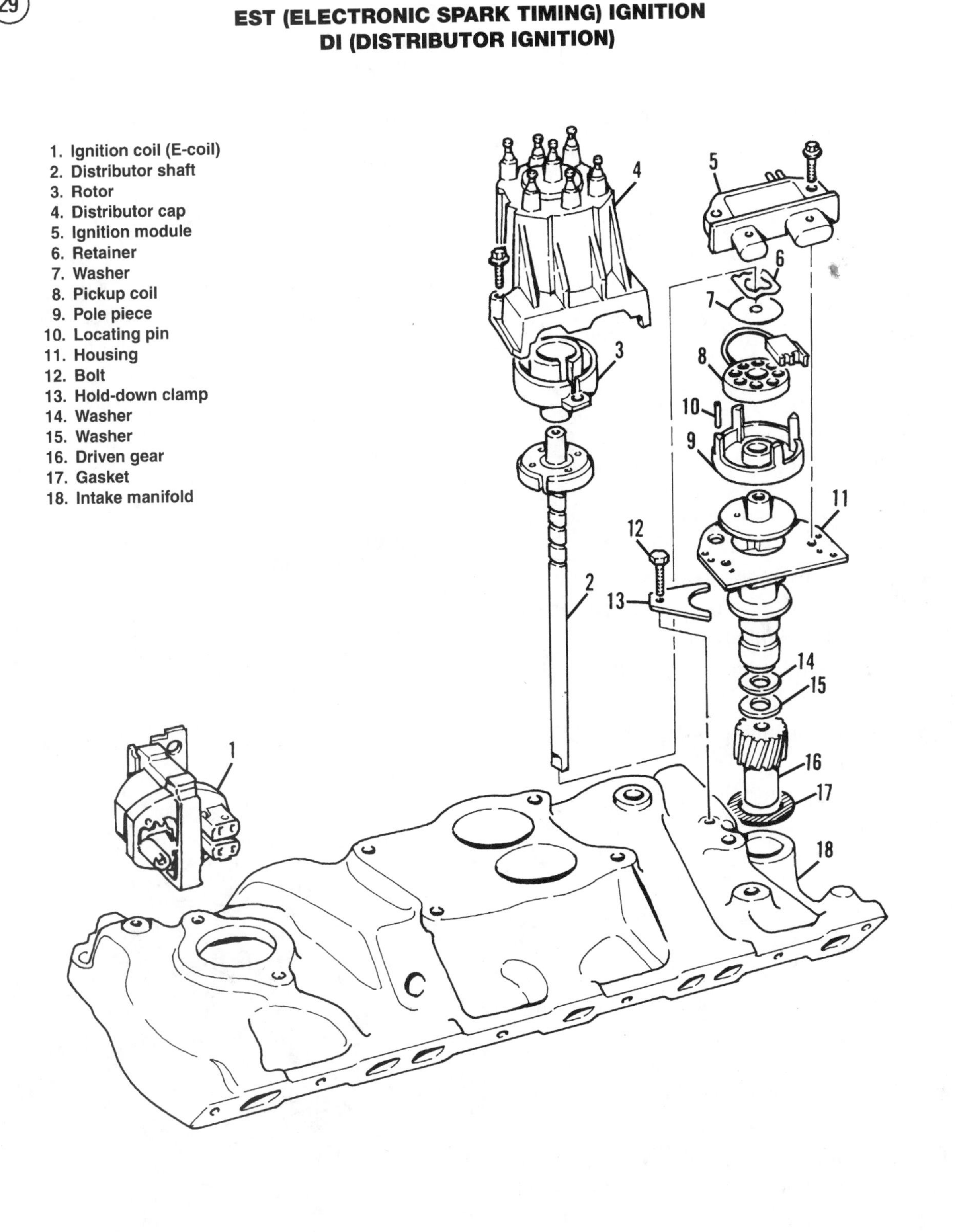
29
EST (ELECTRONIC SPARK TIMING) IGNITION
DI (DISTRIBUTOR IGNITION)
1. Ignition coil (E-coil)
2. Distributor shaft
3. Rotor
4. Distributor cap
5. Ignition module
6. Retainer
7. Washer
8. Pickup coil
9. Pole piece
10. Locating pin
11. Housing
12. Bolt
13. Hold-down clamp
14. Washer
15. Washer
16. Driven gear
17. Gasket
18. Intake manifold

rotor as much as 1/8 turn away from the No. 1 terminal.

6. Turn the rotor counterclockwise slightly past the No. 1 terminal position.
7. Slide the distributor into the engine and check the position of the rotor.

NOTE
If the rotor has moved away from the No. 1 terminal, it may be necessary to remove the distributor, turn the shaft and rotor slightly, then reinstall the distributor. It may also be necessary to remove the distributor and turn the oil pump drive shaft slightly. When correctly assembled, the rotor should align with the No. 1 terminal when the distributor is firmly in place.

8. Install the distributor hold-down clamp and bolt, but do not tighten it more than finger tight.
9. Install the distributor cap on the housing. Be sure the tang on the housing engages the cap slot and that the cap fits snugly on the housing.
10. Attach the wire connector from the distributor to the coil and wiring harness.
11. Set the ignition timing as described in Chapter Four.
12. When timing is correctly adjusted, tighten the distributor hold-down bolt snugly.

Pickup Coil Removal/Installation

1. Remove the distributor as described in this chapter.
2. Place match marks on the distributor drive gear and shaft so the gear can be reinstalled on the shaft in its original position.
3. Carefully drive out the roll pin securing the gear to the shaft. Slide the shaft assembly out of the distributor housing.
4. Disconnect the pickup coil connector (A, **Figure 30**) from the ignition module.
5. Carefully pry off the pickup coil retainer (B, **Figure 30**). Lift the pickup coil off the distributor housing.
6. To reinstall the pickup coil, align the locating tab as shown in **Figure 31** and place the coil onto the pole piece. Make sure the pickup coil is properly seated on the pole piece.
7. Install the pickup coil retainer making sure the locking tabs are securely engaged in the groove.
8. Lubricate the distributor shaft with clean engine oil and insert the shaft into the distributor housing.
9. Install the drive gear onto the distributor shaft, aligning the match marks made in Step 2. Drive a *new roll pin* through the gear and shaft. The pin must be flush on both sides of the gear.

Distributor Shaft/Magnet Assembly Removal/Installation

Remove and reinstall the distributor shaft/magnet assembly as described under *Pickup Coil Removal/Installation* in this chapter.

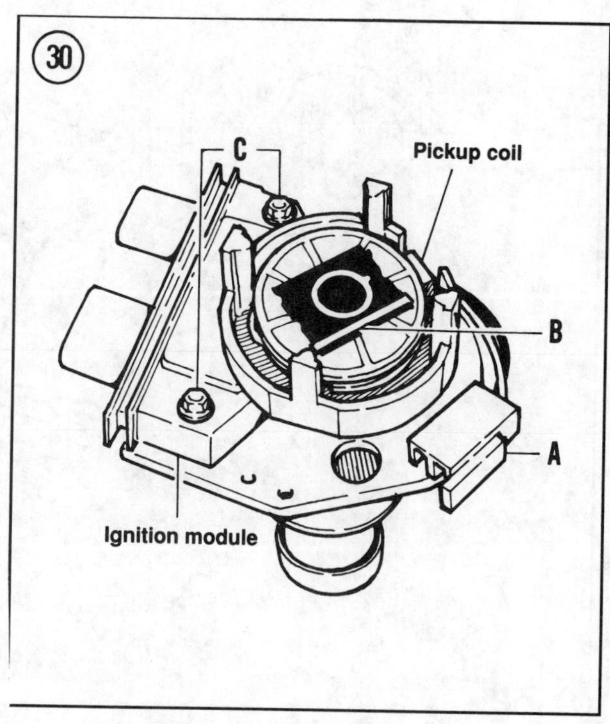

Ignition Module Removal/Installation

The distributor does not normally require removal to replace the ignition module.

1. Remove the 2 screws attaching the distributor cap. Remove the distributor cap and lay it to one side. Remove the distributor rotor.
2. Remove the 4-pin and 2-pin connectors from the ignition module.
3. Remove the 2 module mounting screws (C, **Figure 30**) and lift the module off the distributor.
4. Thoroughly clean all silicone grease from the module and distributor mounting surfaces.
5. To install the module, apply an even coat of silicone grease or a suitable heat sink compound to the mounting surface of the module.
6. Place the module on the distributor, install the mounting screws and tighten securely.
7. Install the rotor and distributor cap.

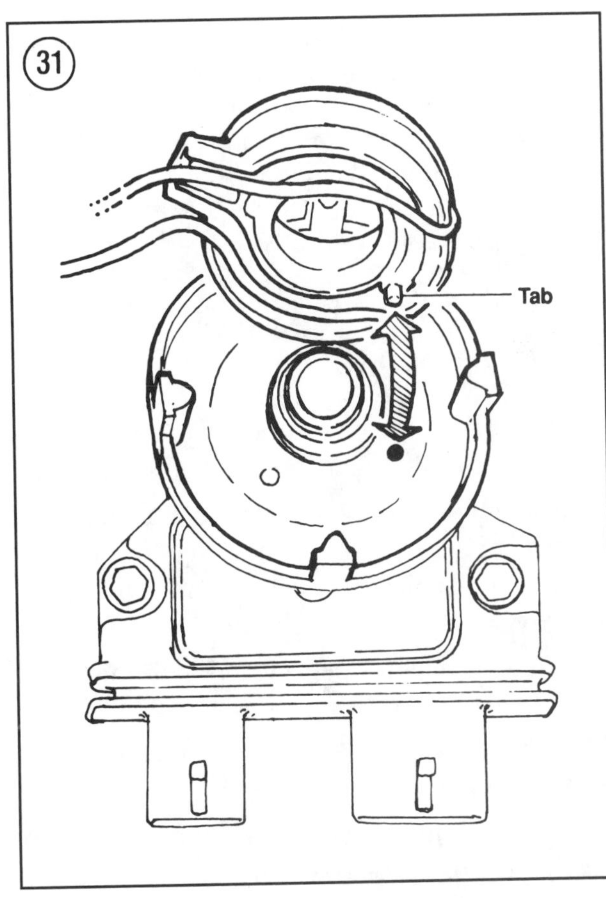

BID IGNITION

The Prestolite BID ignition system used on some engines is manufactured with special electrical and mechanical components designed and selected for marine use. They are designed to withstand climatic and environmental abuse that is much more severe than automotive application. For this reason, automotive parts should not be substituted. Periodic care, cleaning and lubrication is necessary to ensure long service life. Improper or careless testing and servicing procedures can quickly damage the system. See **Figure 27**.

Distributor Assembly Removal

The distributor can be removed without noting its location, but installation is easier if the following procedure is followed. Steps 2-6 set the crankshaft at the ignition position for the No. 1 piston. At this position, the camshaft and crankshaft are correctly positioned to locate the No. 1 piston near top dead center of its compression stroke. If the engine's crankshaft is not moved, installation of the distributor and initial timing will be easier if the rotor, housing and engine are marked as described in these steps.

1. To prevent accidental damage, detach the ground cable from the negative terminal of the battery.
2. Turn the engine crankshaft until the ignition timing mark is aligned as described in Chapter Four.
3. Remove the distributor cap retaining screws.
4. Lift the distributor cap and check to see if the rotor is pointing toward the No. 1 cylinder spark plug wire terminal in the distributor cap.
5. If the rotor is pointing to the No. 1 cylinder terminal in the cap, continue to Step 7.
6. If the rotor is pointing opposite the No. 1 spark plug terminal, turn the crankshaft 180° (exactly 1 complete revolution) until the timing

marks again align, then repeat Step 4. If the rotor does not move, the distributor drive is not working properly.

7. Remove the distributor cap with the spark plug wires attached and place it to one side out of the way.

8. Separate the connector containing the small wires from the distributor.

9. Mark the distributor housing in line with the rotor tip. See **Figure 28**, typical. This mark will help locate the distributor shaft in relation to the distributor housing.

10. Mark across the base of the distributor housing and the engine. This mark will help locate the distributor housing in relation to the engine.

11. Remove the distributor hold-down bolt and clamp located at the base of the distributor.

12. Lift the distributor from the engine.

Distributor Assembly Installation

If the crankshaft and camshaft positions are not known, they must be set as described in Steps 1-3 before installing the distributor. If the distributor rotor, housing and engine has been marked as described in the removal procedure *and the crankshaft has not been moved*, then the crankshaft is positioned correctly and the distributor can be installed as described in Steps 4-12.

1. Remove the No. 1 spark plug. See Chapter Four.

2. Press a finger tightly over the spark plug hole, then turn the engine crankshaft pulley in the normal direction of rotation until compression pressure is felt.

3. Continue to turn the crankshaft slowly until the ignition timing mark on the crankshaft pulley and the timing pointer are aligned as described in Chapter Four.

NOTE

Always rotate the engine in the direction of normal rotation. Do not turn the engine backward (back the engine up) to align the timing marks.

4. Position a new distributor gasket (if used) on the distributor housing.

5. Turn the distributor shaft until the rotor tip points in the direction of the No. 1 terminal in the distributor cap. If the distributor housing was marked upon disassembly, align the mark.

NOTE

Step 6 is necessary to compensate for the slight spiral cut of the distributor drive gears. It may be necessary to position the rotor as much as 1/8 turn away from the No. 1 terminal.

6. Turn the rotor counterclockwise slightly past the No. 1 terminal position.

7. Slide the distributor into the engine and check the position of the rotor.

NOTE

If the rotor has moved away from the No. 1 terminal, it may be necessary to remove the distributor, turn the shaft and rotor slightly, then reinstall the distributor. It may also be necessary to remove the distributor and turn the oil pump drive shaft slightly. When correctly assembled, the rotor should align with the No. 1 terminal when the distributor is firmly in place.

8. Install the distributor hold-down clamp and bolt, but do not tighten it more than finger-tight.

9. Install the distributor cap on the housing. Make sure the tang on the housing engages the cap slot, and make sure the cap fits snugly on the housing.

10. Attach the wire connector from the distributor to the coil and wiring harness.

11. Set the ignition timing as described in Chapter Four.

12. When timing is correctly adjusted, tighten the distributor hold-down bolt snugly.

Module, Sensor and Coil Testing

The ignition sensor (**Figure 32**) creates a magnetic field with current supplied by the ignition module. When the sensor is aligned with a tooth of the impulse sender, the module sends a primary ignition current to the ignition coil. When a tooth passes the sensor, the magnetic field is disturbed, triggering the module to turn off the primary current to the high tension coil.

Dwell (coil charge time) is determined by the air gap between the impulse sender and sensor. The ignition may incorporate a speed limiter designed to interrupt the ignition and prevent the engine speed from exceeding a predetermined value. If the engine will not start, conduct the following tests in the order listed to determine which units are faulty.

1. Remove the coil wire from the distributor cap.
2. Hold the coil wire with a pair of insulated pliers so the exposed end of the wire is approximately 1/4 in. (6.3 mm) from a clean engine ground.
3. Attempt to start the engine while observing the end of the wire for spark.
4. If no spark is noted, remove the distributor cap and rotor.

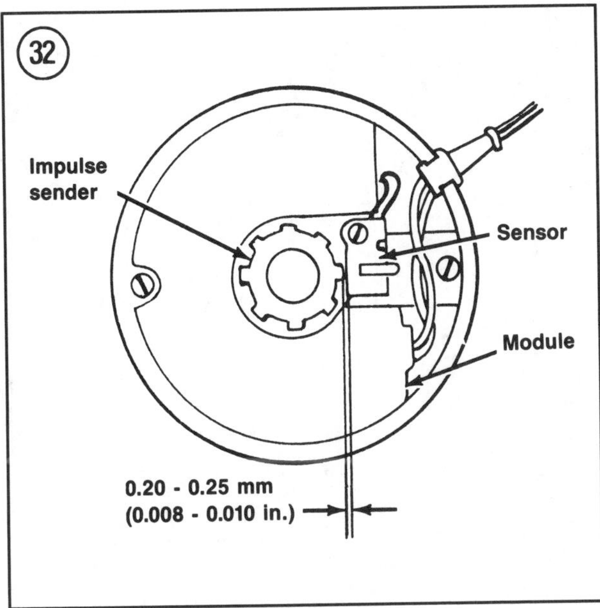

5. Turn the engine so one tooth of the impulse sender is aligned with the sensor as shown in **Figure 32**.
6. Check and adjust the air gap as described in Chapter Four, if necessary. The air gap should be 0.20-0.25 mm (0.008-0.010 in.).
7. Check the battery voltage with a voltmeter. Charge the battery if it is not above 12 volts.
8. Inspect the distributor cap and rotor for contamination, cracks or any other damage. Clean or replace components as needed.
9. Turn the ignition ON and check the voltage between the ignition positive (+) terminal of the high tension coil and the engine ground. The voltage should be within 1 volt of battery voltage. If voltage is less, check for loose or corroded connections or other damage.
10. With the ignition still ON, measure the voltage between the engine ground and the negative (–) terminal of the high tension coil. The voltage should be 4-8 volts.
    a. If voltage is more than 8 volts, the distributor is not properly grounded to the engine or the ignition module is defective.
    b. If voltage is less than 4 volts, detach the black wire from the negative (–) terminal of the ignition high-tension coil and measure the voltage at the terminal of the coil. If the voltage is now near battery voltage, the ignition module is faulty. If the voltage remains less than 4 volts, the coil primary has an open and should be replaced.

11

11. If the voltage measured at the coil negative (–) terminal in Step 10 is 4-8 volts, insert a small screwdriver or other suitable tool between the tooth of the impulse sender and the ignition sensor (**Figure 32**). Note the voltmeter while the tool is inserted.
12. If the voltage measured at the coil negative (–) terminal in Step 11 is near battery voltage, detach the remaining wires from the ignition high-tension coil and check the resistance as described in Step 13.

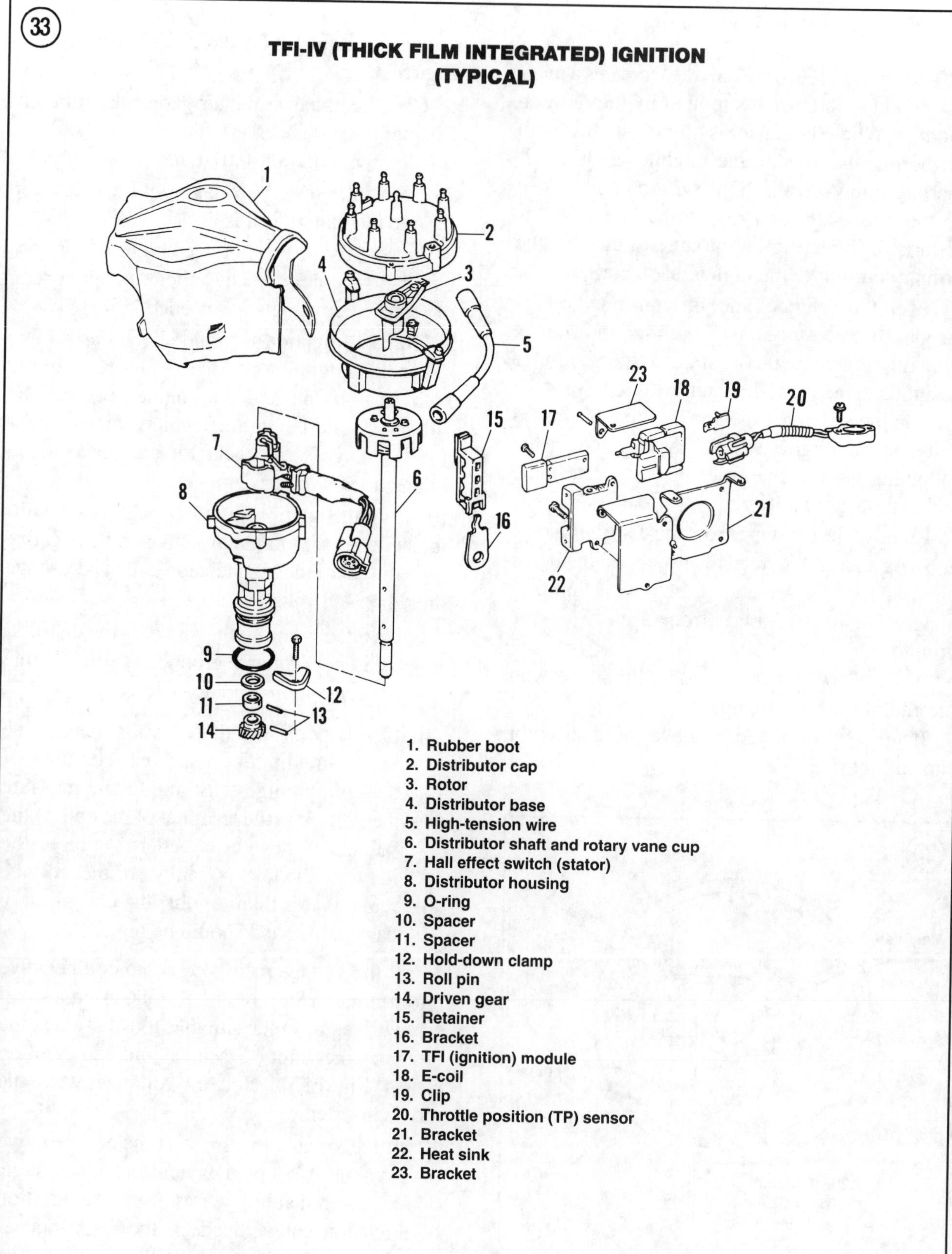

1. Rubber boot
2. Distributor cap
3. Rotor
4. Distributor base
5. High-tension wire
6. Distributor shaft and rotary vane cup
7. Hall effect switch (stator)
8. Distributor housing
9. O-ring
10. Spacer
11. Spacer
12. Hold-down clamp
13. Roll pin
14. Driven gear
15. Retainer
16. Bracket
17. TFI (ignition) module
18. E-coil
19. Clip
20. Throttle position (TP) sensor
21. Bracket
22. Heat sink
23. Bracket

(34) **DISTRIBUTOR (TFI-IV IGNITION)**

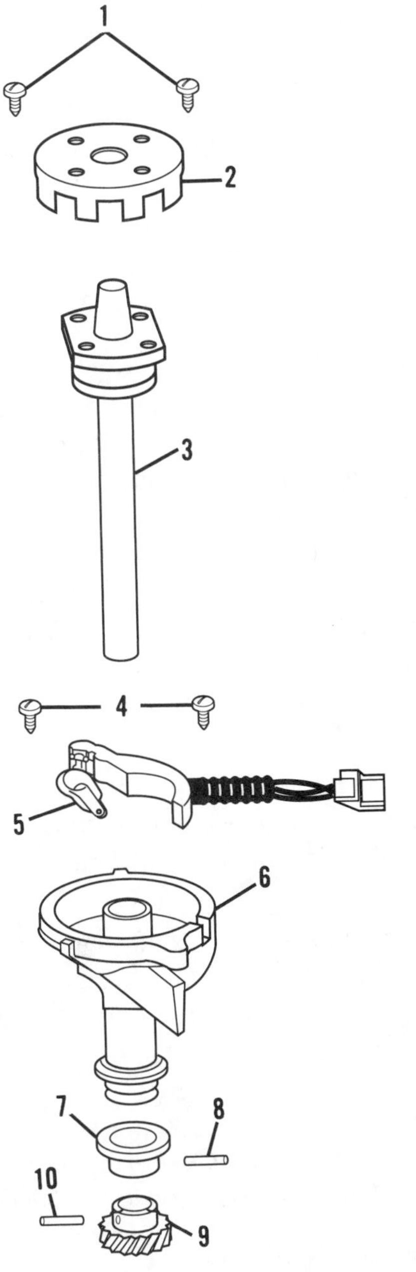

1. Screw
2. Rotary vane cup
3. Shaft
4. Screw
5. Hall effect switch (stator)
6. Housing
7. Washer/spacer
8. Roll pin
9. Driven gear
10. Roll pin

13. Use an accurate ohmmeter and measure the resistance of the primary and secondary windings of the ignition high-tension coil. Resistance of the primary winding should be 1.25-1.4 ohms at 68° F (20° C). Resistance of the secondary winding should be 9,400-11,700 ohms at 68° F (20° C).
14. Install a new high-tension ignition coil if resistance is not as specified.
15. If no other faults are found and the ignition will still not produce a spark (Step 2 and 3), install a new ignition module.

TFI-IV IGNITION

The TFI-IV ignition system used on some engines is manufactured with special housings, caps, electrical components and other parts designed and selected for marine use. These components are designed to withstand climatic and environmental abuse that is much more severe than automotive application. For this reason, automotive parts should not be substituted. Periodic care, cleaning and lubrication is necessary to assure long service life. Improper or careless testing and servicing procedures can quickly damage the system. See **Figure 33**.

The TFI-IV distributor (**Figure 34**) contains a Hall effect trigger device which performs like a switch to make or break current flow when subjected to a magnetic field. This PIP (profile ignition pickup) signal is used to time the ignition spark and fuel injection when starting or if the running spark output (SPOUT) signal is interrupted.

The E-coil on a TFI-IV system serves the same purpose as the high-tension coil used in a conventional ignition system. The name is derived from its appearance.

The TFI-IV ignition module, mounted on a heat sink located near the E-coil, controls the ignition coil's primary current. When starting, the protile ignition pickup (PIP) signal from the module in the distributor determines the timing of the electrical pulses to the E-Coil. When the engine is running, timing is determined by the spark output (SPOUT) signal received from the electronic Control Assembly (ECA).

Distributor Removal/Installation

The distributor can be removed without noting its location, but installation is easier if the following procedure is followed. Steps 2-6 set the crankshaft at the ignition position for the No. 1 piston. At this position the camshaft and crankshaft are correctly positioned to locate the No. 1 piston near top dead center of its compression stroke. If the crankshaft is not moved, installation of the distributor and initial timing will be easier if the rotor, housing and engine are marked as described in these steps.

1. To prevent accidental damage, detach the ground cable from the negative terminal of the battery.
2. Turn the crankshaft until the ignition timing mark is aligned as described in Chapter Four.
3. Remove the distributor cap retaining screws.
4. Lift the distributor cap and check if the rotor is pointing toward the No. 1 spark wire terminal in the distributor cap.
5. If the rotor is pointing to the No. 1 cylinder terminal in the cap, continue to Step 7.
6. If the rotor is pointing opposite the No. 1 spark plug wire terminal, turn the crankshaft 180° (exactly 1 complete revolution) until the timing marks again align, then repeat Step 4. If the rotor does not move, the distributor drive is not working properly.
7. Remove the distributor cap with the spark plug wires attached and place to one side out of the way.
8. Separate the connector containing the small wires from the distributor.
9. Mark the distributor housing in line with the rotor tip. See **Figure 28**, typical. This mark will help locate the distributor shaft in relation to the distributor housing.
10. Mark across the base of the distributor housing and the engine. This mark will help locate the distributor housing in relation to the engine.
11. Remove the distributor hold-down bolt and clamp located at the base of the distributor.
12. Lift the distributor from the engine.

Distributor Assembly Installation

If the crankshaft and camshaft positions are not known, they must be set as described in Steps 1-3 before installing the distributor. If the distributor rotor, housing and engine has been marked as described in the removal procedure *and the crankshaft has not been moved*, then the crankshaft is positioned correctly and the distributor can be installed as described in Step 4 and following.

1. Remove the No. 1 spark plug. See Chapter Four.
2. Press a finger tightly over the spark plug hole, then turn the engine crankshaft pulley in the normal direction of rotation until compression pressure is felt.
3. Continue to turn the crankshaft slowly until the ignition timing mark on the crankshaft pulley and the timing pointer are aligned as described in Chapter Four.

NOTE

Always rotate the engine in the direction of normal rotation. Do not turn the engine backward (back the engine up) to align the timing marks.

4. Position a new distributor gasket (if used) on the distributor housing.
5. Turn the distributor shaft until the rotor tip points in the direction of the No. 1 terminal in the distributor cap. If the distributor housing was marked upon disassembly, align the mark.

NOTE
Step 6 is necessary to compensate for the slight spiral cut of the distributor drive gears. It may be necessary to position the rotor as much as 1/8 turn away from the No. 1 terminal.

6. Turn the rotor counterclockwise slightly past the No. 1 terminal position.
7. Slide the distributor into the engine and check the position of the rotor.

NOTE
If the rotor has moved away from the No. 1 terminal, it may be necessary to remove the distributor, turn the shaft and rotor slightly, then reinstall the distributor. It may also be necessary to remove the distributor and turn the oil pump drive shaft slightly. When correctly assembled, the rotor should align with the No. 1 terminal when the distributor is firmly in place.

8. Install the distributor hold-down clamp and bolt, but do not tighten it more than finger tight.
9. Rotate the distributor as required to align the leading edge of the metal rotary vane cup (2, **Figure 34**) is aligned with the center of the Hall effect switch (5, **Figure 34**).
10. Install the distributor cap on the housing. Be sure the tang on the housing engages the cap slot and that the cap fits snugly on the housing.
11. Attach the wire connector from the distributor to the coil and wiring harness.
12. Set the ignition timing as described in Chapter Four.
13. When timing is correctly adjusted, tighten the distributor hold-down bolt snugly.

Distributor Disassembly/Assembly

The distributor shaft, drive gear and housing are not available separately. If necessary to replace these parts, replace the distributor assembly. Refer to **Figure 34** for this procedure.

1. Remove the distributor as described in this chapter.
2. Remove the 2 screws attaching the rotary vane cup, then lift the cup from the shaft.
3. Drive both pins (8 and 10, **Figure 34**) from the gear, spacer and shaft.
4. Use a bearing splitter and press to remove the gear from the shaft.
5. Polish any burrs from the shaft, then lift the shaft from the housing.
6. Remove the retaining screws and lift the Hall effect switch (5, **Figure 34**) from the housing.
7. Clean all parts before assembling.
8. Install the Hall effect switch (5, **Figure 34**) as in the housing as follows:
   a. Press the Hall effect switch into the housing until it is firmly seated.
   b. Align the connector tab with the notch of the housing and mounting tabs with attaching holes in the housing.
   c. Install the attaching screws. Tighten the screws to 1.7-4.0 N•m (15-35 in.-lb.).
9. Lubricate the shaft and install it into the housing.
10. Install the spacer (7, **Figure 34**) with its flange facing toward the distributor housing and secure with a new roll pin. 11
9. Press the distributor drive gear onto the shaft as follows:
   a. Slip a deep well 5/8 in. socket over the upper end of the distributor shaft.
   b. Invert the distributor and shaft assembly.
   c. Position the drive gear onto the shaft, aligning the holes for the roll pin.

NOTE
It is important to align the holes in the gear and shaft while pressing the gear into position. If the holes are not aligned, the gear must be pressed from the shaft, then reinstalled with the holes aligned. The gear cannot be moved on the shaft with a punch.

   d. Make sure the holes in the gear and shaft are aligned, then use a deep well 5/8 in.

socket to press the gear completely onto the shaft.

e. Install a new roll pin through the gear and shaft.

f. Install the rotary vane cup (2, **Figure 34**) and attach with the 2 screws. Tighten the screws to 2.8-4.0 N.m (25-35 in.-lb.).

g. Turn the distributor shaft and check for freedom of rotation. If the rotary vane cup contacts the Hall effect switch, indicating that the shaft is bent, install a new distributor assembly.

E-Coil Removal/Installation

1. Remove the plastic engine cover.
2. Detach the high tension lead from the coil.
3. Detach the wiring harness connector from the E-coil. Use a small screwdriver or similar tool to release the connector's latch.
4. Remove the 2 screws (**Figure 35**) from the top of the E-coil that secure the coil to the TFI-IV mounting bracket.
5. Remove the 2 small screws (**Figure 36**) from the side of the mounting bracket, then lift the E-coil from the bracket.
6. Refer to the *Ignition Module Removal/Installation* procedure in this chapter to separate the module from the coil.
7. nstall the coil by reversing the removal procedure. Observe the following:
   a. Tighten the 2 smaller screws to 2.7-4.1 N.m (34-36 in.-lb.) and the 2 larger mounting screws to 6.8-9.5 N.m (60-84 in.-lb.). Apply electrical terminal grease to the connector terminals, then attach the connector to the E-coil.

TFI-IV Module Removal/Installation

The module is attached to the E-coil. It is important that the correct unit is installed. Automotive units are similar, but should not be used in marine applications. The correct Volvo unit is black. Automotive units are gray and the connectors are different from the Volvo unit.

1. Remove the E-coil as described in this chapter.
2. Detach the connector from the TFI-IV module by pushing the 2 side clips while pulling the connector.
3. Remove the 2 screws (**Figure 37**) attaching the TFI-IV heat sink to the bracket, then remove the bracket and module as a unit.

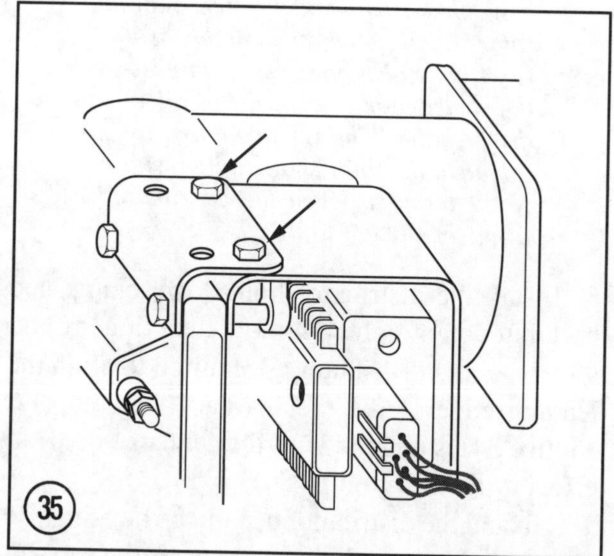

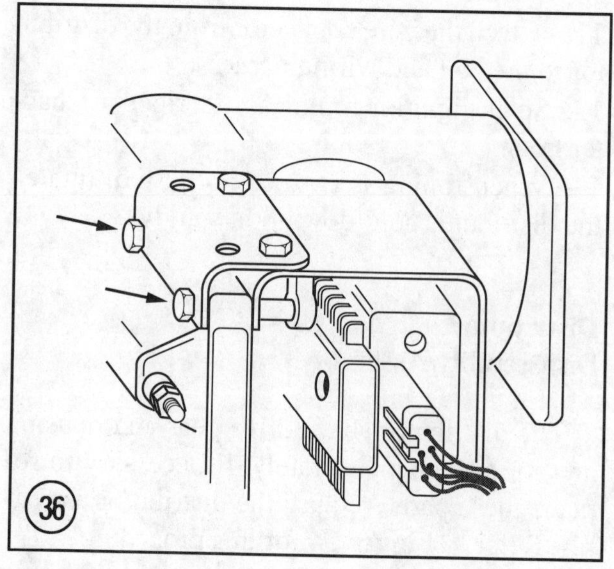

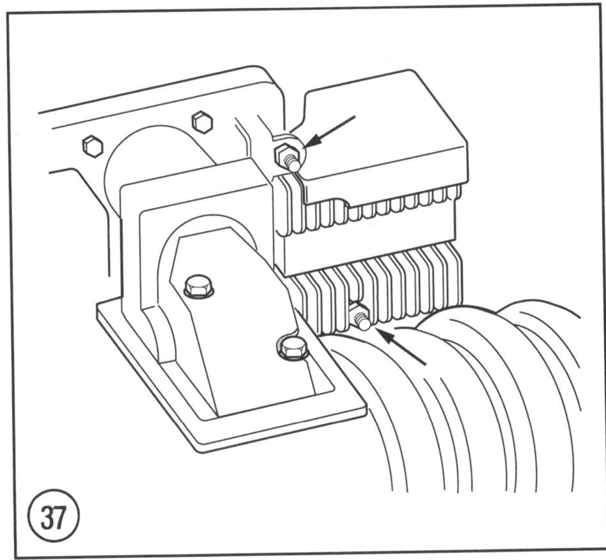

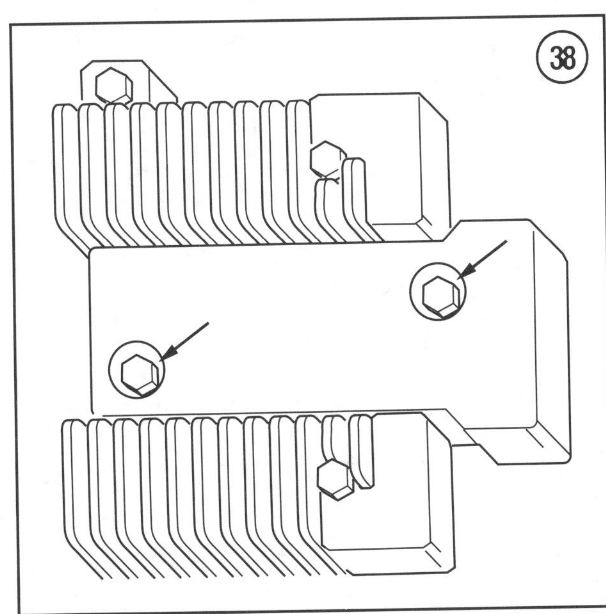

4. Remove the 2 screws attaching the module to the heat sink. See **Figure 38**.

CAUTION
Failure to apply sufficient heat sink compound to the module when assembling, may cause failure of the module.

5. Apply heat sink compound 0.79 mm (1/32 in.)thick to the back of the TFI-IV module before installing the module.

6. Attach the module to the heat sink bracket and tighten the 2 screws to 6.8-9.5 N•m (60-84 in.-lb.).

7. Apply electrical terminal grease to the connector terminal and attach the plug. Make sure the latching tabs lock in place.

8. Install the E-coil as described in this chapter.

IGNITION COIL

The high-tension ignition coil used may be of conventional design in a cylindrical container or of the E-Coil design, but it is important that the correct coil be installed system used. **Figure 39** shows a typical installation.

Each time the secondary (high tension) lead is removed from the ignition coil or distributor cap, pack a small amount of insulating compound into the secondary nipple to waterproof the connection. Wipe off any excess compound after the lead is fully seated.

Ignition coils can be tested using an ohmmeter; however, resistance tests generally only detect open or shorted windings. For this reason, do not fail a coil that is only slightly out of specification. Refer to Chapter Three for testing procedures. A more reliable test for ignition coils can be performed using a suitable ignition analyzer. Follow the instructions included with the analyzer.

Ignition Coil Removal/Installation

Refer to the E-Coil Removal/Installation procedure in this chapter for removal of the ignition coil use with TFI-IV ignition system. Refer to the following for removal of other coils.

1. Disconnect the high tension lead from the coil.

2A. *Except EST ignition*—Disconnect the primary ignition wires from the coil. Reinstall the nuts onto the coil studs to prevent loss.

2B. *EST ignition*—Disconnect the distributor harness connector and engine harness connector from the coil.

3. Remove the coil mounting fasteners and remove the coil.

4. Reverse the removal procedure to install the coil. Tighten the mounting fasteners securely.

SWITCHES AND CONNECTORS

Switches can be tested with an ohmmeter or a self-powered test lamp. If a switch does not perform properly, replace it.

Many electrical problems encountered are due to poor connections in the waterproof connectors. If the pins and sockets are improperly seated in their connectors, the resulting electrical connection will be poor or non-existent.

Ignition Switch

Detach the ground cable from the negative terminal of the battery when testing the ignition switch in the boat. Refer to **Figure 40** and **Figure 41** for this procedure.

1. Test all switch terminals (**Figure 40**) with an ohmmeter or self-powered test lamp and the ignition key in the OFF position. There should be no continuity between the switch terminals.

2. Turn the key (switch) to the RUN position (No. 2, **Figure 41**) and test terminals. There should be no continuity between terminals B and A and between B and 1. There should be no continuity between the C terminal and any of the other terminals.

3. Turn the key (switch) to the START position (No. 3, **Figure 41**) and test terminals. There should be continuity between terminals B and A, B and 1 and B and C.

4. Make sure the terminals make contact when the key is turned to the angles shown in **Figure**

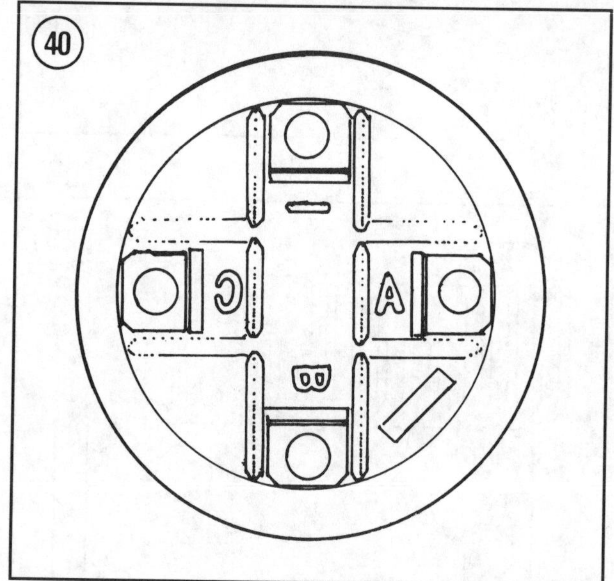

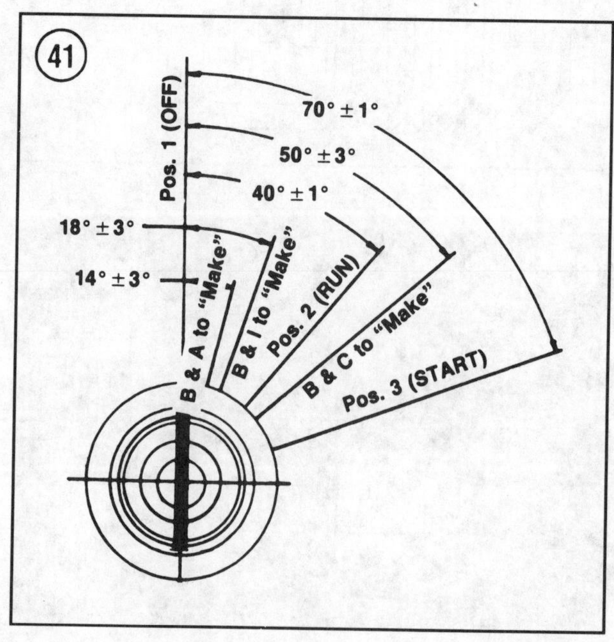

41. They must remain in contact as the switch is rotated to the START position.

5. If any switch position does not check out as described, unsolder the wires and remove the switch. Repeat Steps 1-3 with the switch out of the instrument panel. If the switch now performs as specified, the problem is in the wiring. If the switch still fails the continuity check, replace it.

SOLENOIDS

Solenoids are used with the starter and tilt motors to carry the large amount of electrical current used by the motors. The solenoid is a completely sealed and nonserviceable unit. The 2 large terminals are the battery and motor terminals. The small terminal is the switch control. The ground is internal through the solenoid bracket. If a solenoid is suspected of faulty operation, test it as follows:

1. Connect a volt/ohmmeter between the 2 large solenoid terminals.
2. Connect a carbon pile as shown in **Figure 42** and reduce the voltage to under 6 volts.
3. Adjust the carbon pile until the ohmmeter or test lamp shows a complete circuit. At this point, the voltmeter should show a reading of 6-8 volts. If more than 8 volts are required to complete the circuit, replace the solenoid.

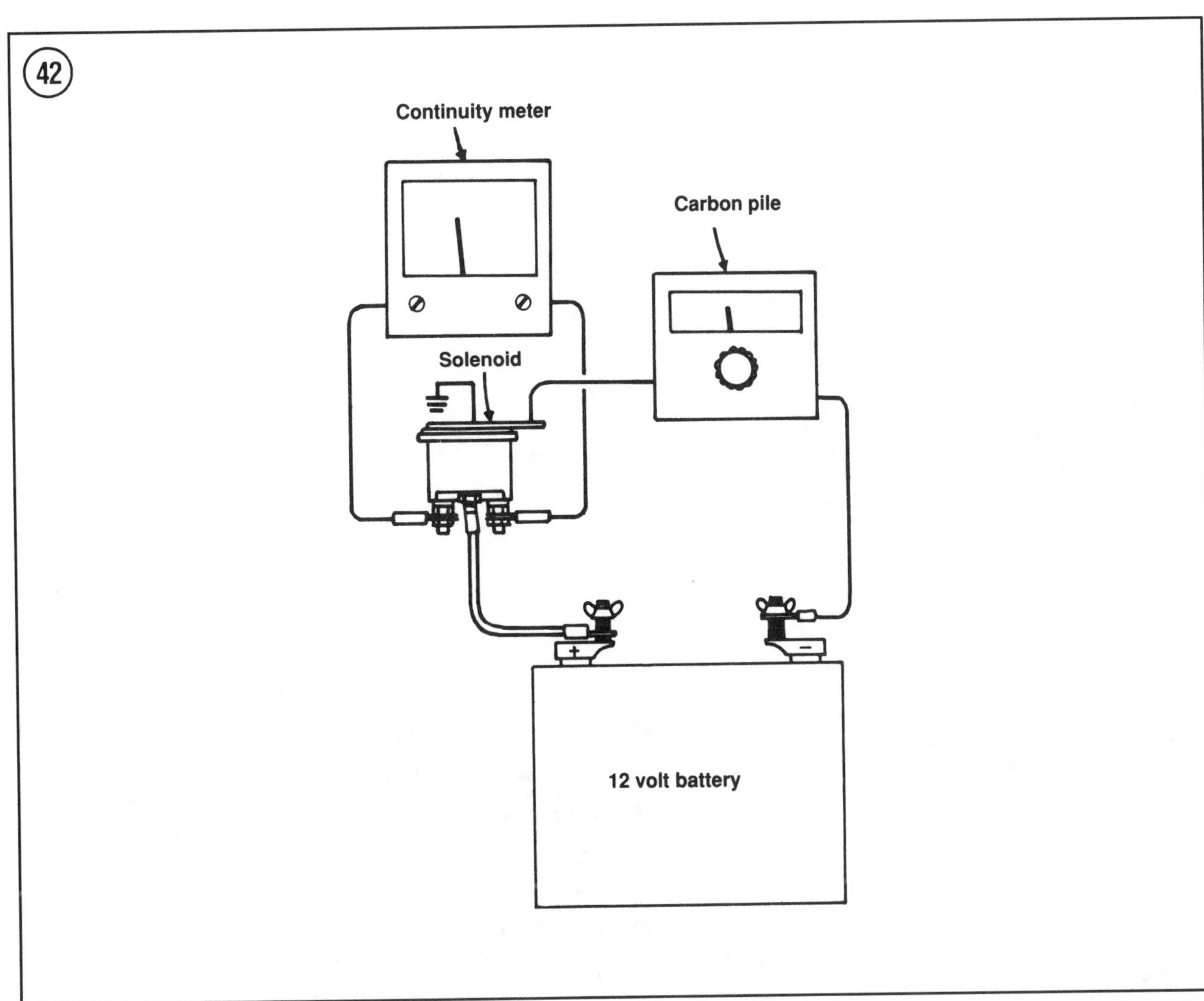

ELECTRICAL PROTECTION

All engines are equipped with a 50- or 60-amp circuit breaker installed in the wiring harness between the ignition switch and starter motor. Individual circuits are fused. If additional electrical accessories are added to any installation, install individual fused circuits for each accessory with power takeoff at the terminal block.

Whenever a failure occurs in any part of the electrical system, always check the fuse first to see if it is blown. Usually, the problem is a short circuit in the wiring. This may be caused by worn-through insulation or by a wire that has worked its way loose and shorted to ground. Occasionally, the electrical overload which causes a fuse to blow may occur in a switch or motor.

A blown fuse should be treated as more than a minor annoyance. It should serve as a warning that something is wrong in the electrical system. Before replacing a fuse, determine what caused it to blow and correct the problem. Always carry several spare fuses of the proper amperage values onboard. Never replace a fuse with one of higher amperage rating than that specified for use. Failure to follow these basic rules could result in heat or fire damage to major parts or even the loss of the entire vessel.

Table 1 ALTERNATOR SPECIFICATIONS

Alternator model	Maximum output @ engine speed
51 amp	20 amps @ 650 rpm
	47 amps @ 1,500 rpm
	51 amps @ 2,000 rpm
65 amp	20 amps @ 650 rpm
	53 amps @ 1,500 rpm
	56 amps @ 2,000 rpm
Regulated voltage range	13.5-14.8 volts (all models)

Table 2 IGNITION SYSTEM APPLICATION

Model	Fuel system	Ignition type	Firing order
3.0	Carburetor	Delco EST[1]	1-3-4-2
4.3	Carburetor	Delco EST[1]	1-6-5-4-3-2
4.3	Fuel injection	Delco EST[1]	1-6-5-4-3-2
5.0	Carburetor	Prestolite BID[2]	1-3-7-2-6-5-4-8
5.0	Fuel injection	TFI-IV[3]	1-3-7-2-6-5-4-8
5.0	Carburetor	Prestolite BID[2]	1-8-4-3-6-5-7-2
5.0	Fuel injection	Delco Di[4]	1-8-4-3-6-5-7-2
5.7	Carburetor	Prestolite BID[2]	1-8-4-3-6-5-7-2
5.7	Fuel injection	Delco EST[1]	1-8-4-3-6-5-7-2
5.8	Carburetor	Prestolite BID[2]	1-3-7-2-6-5-4-8
5.8	Fuel injection	TFI-IV[3]	1-3-7-2-6-5-4-8
7.4	Carburetor	Prestolite BID[2]	1-8-4-3-6-5-7-2
7.4	Fuel injection	Delco EST[1]	1-8-4-3-6-5-7-2
8.2	Carburetor	Prestolite BID[2]	1-8-4-3-6-5-7-2

1. (EST) Delco Electronic Spark Timing System
2. (BID) Prestolite Integral Breakerless Inductive Distributor
3. (TFI-IV) Thick Film Integrated Ignition System
4. (Di) Distributor ignition system.

Table 3 IGNITION SYSTEM SPECIFICATIONS

EST coil	
Primary resistance	1.35-1.45 ohms
Secondary resistance	7,500-9,000 ohms
Pickup coil resistance	700-900 ohms
Operating amperage @ 75° F (24° C)	1.0 amp maximum
(Coil must be able to sustain 25-30 kilovolts for 30 seconds).	
BID coil	
Primary resistance	1.43-1.58 ohms
Secondary resistance	9,400-11,000 ohms
Operating amperage @ 75° F (24° C)	1.0 amp maximum
(Coil must be able to sustain 25-30 kilovolts for 30 seconds).	
BID sensor air gap	0.203 mm (0.008 in.)

Chapter Twelve

Drive Unit and Upper Gearcase

This chapter provides drive unit removal/installation and upper gearcase rebuilding and resealing procedures for Volvo Penta SX Cobra, DuoProp and DPX models. Service procedures for the lower gearcase and transom shield/transom bracket are covered in subsequent chapters. **Table 1** lists the recommended gear ratio for each engine model, **Table 2** and **Table 3** list all drive unit specifications, **Table 4** and **Table 5** list all special torque values and **Table 6** lists all recommended lubricants, sealants and adhesives. **Table 7** and **Table 8** list manufacturer recommended tools, **Table 9** and **Table 10** list standard torque values and **Table 11** lists other recommended special tools, fixtures and their manufacturers. **Table 12** lists gear lash and gear pattern correction procedures for SX and DP-S upper gearcases. **Tables 1-12** are at the end of the chapter.

Exploded illustrations of each drive unit upper gearcase are located in the appropriate *Disassembly* section and are helpful references for many service procedures.

DRIVE UNIT IDENTIFICATION

Volvo Penta and Outboard Marine Corporation formed a joint venture in 1993 to develop a new series of stern drives. The joint venture is called the Volvo Penta Marine Products, Limited Partnership (VPMP, LP). The outcome of the joint venture is product incorporating the best features of both the OMC Cobra and Volvo Penta stern drives. Volvo has continued to produce its original product along with the joint venture product. There are 4 series of drive units produced by Volvo Penta and the VPMP, LP during 1994-1996.

Model identification tags are riveted to the upper gearcase. The model tag lists the product designation (DP-C, DP-D, DPX, SX or DP-S), model number, serial number and the drive unit's original overall gear ratio. Additional numbers or letters printed after the product designation are to identify the production version of the unit. Examples of drive production version codes are DP-C1, SX-S and DPX-S1. Production version codes are most important when ordering replace-

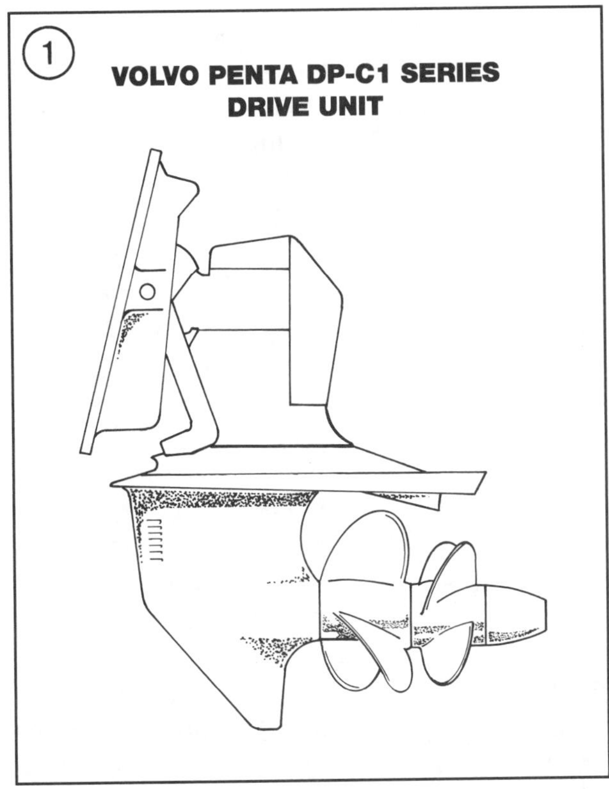

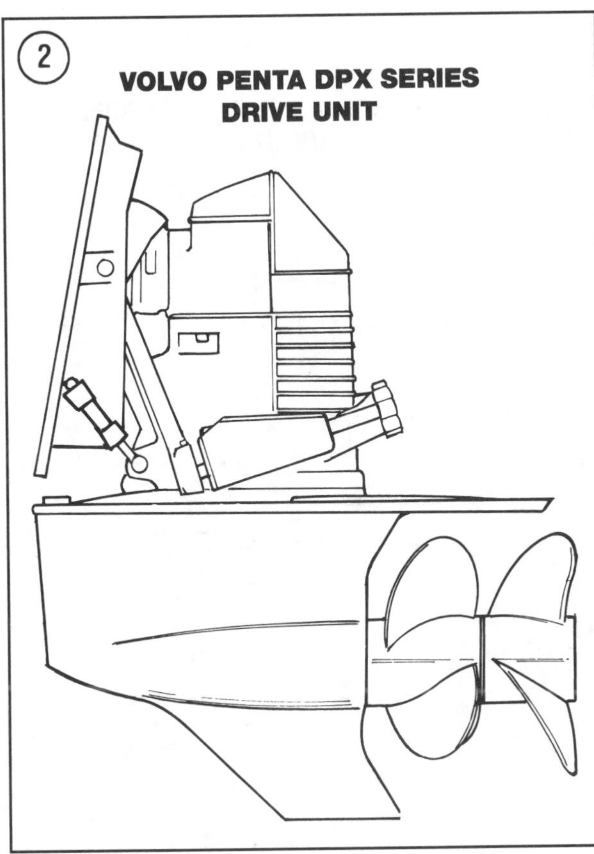

ment parts. Refer to **Table 1** for a list of all drive units by model number and production designation. Any specific service procedure that differs because of production codes is so noted in the text of this chapter.

Volvo Penta DuoProp (C1 and D1 series)

The DuoProp C1 and D1 series drive units (**Figure 1**) are not a product of the joint venture. These drives are fashioned after the original Aquamatic 290 series of drive units. The transom shield is an original Volvo design and does not fit industry standard transom cutouts. The exhaust exits the drive unit through a port in the antiventilation plate. The DP-C1 lower gearcase has an adjustable trim tab, the DP-D1 does not. These drives are referred to as DP-C1/D1 in this chapter. These drives use 2 counter-rotating Volvo Penta B series aluminum or C series stainless steel propellers in matched pitch sets only. DP-C1/D1 drive unit propellers will not fit any of the other drives listed in this chapter.

Volvo Penta DPX

The DPX series drive unit (**Figure 2**) is not a product of the joint venture. DPX-S is the specific production version used on 1994-1996 models. This drive and transom shield are based on the DP-D1 series drive unit. The DPX features heavy-duty components and a special lower gearcase with high-speed hydrodynamics. A mechanical trim position indicating system is standard equipment. The DPX also features Volvo Penta's X-act hydraulic steering as standard equipment. The exhaust exits through the propeller hubs and a port in the anti-ventilation plate. This drive is referred to as DPX in this chapter. This system is used only on selected 7.4 and 8.2 liter models. This drive uses 2 counter-rotating Volvo Penta E series stainless steel propellers in matched pitch sets only. DPX drive unit propellers will not fit any of the other drives listed in this chapter.

Volvo SX and Volvo Penta SX Cobra

The Volvo SX and Volvo Penta SX Cobra (**Figure 3**) are basically the same drive unit. In 1994 it was called the Volvo SX. On later models it was renamed the Volvo Penta SX Cobra. This drive is a product of the joint venture and incorporates the best features of OMC and Volvo Penta. The engine and transom bracket are generally of OMC Cobra design, with the exception of the engine mounted water supply pump (replacing the water pump in the drive unit). The transom cutout is the industry standard that MerCruiser has been using for decades. The upper gearcase housing is an OMC Cobra style casting with Volvo Penta gears, shafts and cone clutch shift mechanism. The lower gearcase housing, propshaft bearing carrier and all bearings are from the OMC King Cobra, while the shafts and gears are from Volvo Penta. The exhaust exits through the propeller hub with additional exhaust relief ports present in the transom bracket and lower gearcase (above the antiventilation plate). These drives use a single propeller with a special spline pattern unique to the joint venture. Normal rotation of the drive unit is clockwise as viewed from the rear. The rotation can be changed for twin engine applications with a simple shift linkage adjustment at the upper gearcase. Model suffixes of SX-S, SX-C and SX-C1 are used. However, these drives are referred to as SX in this chapter.

Volvo Penta DuoProp (S series)

The Volvo Penta DuoProp S-series (**Figure 4**) is a product of the joint venture and was first introduced in 1996. This drive unit uses the same upper gearcase as the SX drive unit. The lower gearcase features internal components similar to the DPX series drive unit and an improved hydrodynamic shape. The exhaust exits through the propeller hubs, with additional exhaust relief ports in the transom bracket and lower gearcase antiventilation plate. These drives use 2 counter-rotating Volvo Penta D series aluminum or F series stainless steel propellers in matched pitch sets only. DP-S drive unit propellers will not fit any of the other drives listed in this chapter. This drive is referred to as DP-S in this chapter.

DRIVE UNIT OPERATION

All of these outdrives use the Volvo Penta cone clutch shift mechanism in the upper gearcase. While there have been many minor variations, the basic operating principle is the same on all models. The upper gearcase contains 3 gears, the driven gear and the upper and lower output gears. All gears are permanently meshed and turn any

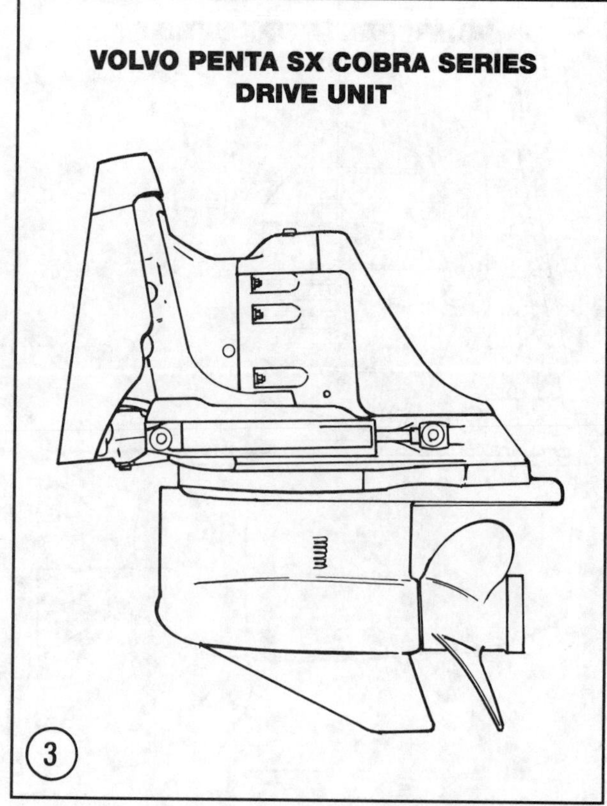

time the engine is running. A sliding cone clutch is positioned between the upper and lower output gears and is connected to the output shaft with helical splines. A spring loaded shift shoe moves the sliding cone clutch up or down to engage the appropriate output gear.

Whenever the cone clutch contacts the spinning sleeve of an output gear, friction begins to turn the cone clutch in the same direction as the output gear. Because of the helical splines on the output shaft, the cone clutch is forced tighter into the output gear sleeve and power is transferred to the lower gearcase through the output shaft to the direct drive lower gearcase. The more power applied, the tighter the wedging action and the more positive the engagement.

To shift out of gear, it is necessary to break the seal between the cone clutch and gear sleeve. An eccentric is machined into the shift shoe groove on the clutch cone which causes the shift shoe to move in and out slightly as the cone clutch rotates, much like a lifter on a camshaft. As the shift shoe attempts to lift the cone clutch out of gear, the shift shoe will begin to compress its internal spring and ride up and away from the engaged side of the cone clutch until it bottoms against the shimmed stop bolt in the shift housing arm. When the shift shoe bottoms and is pinched between the shift shoe stop bolt and the eccentric on the clutch cone, an impact is transferred to the clutch cone eccentric groove, breaking the cone free from the gear sleeve. Once the cone clutch is free, the shift shoe returns to the bottom of the eccentric groove and rides the groove normally.

It is important that the shift shoe be properly shimmed. Too many shims under the stop bolt can make it difficult to shift out of gear. Too few shims will cause mechanical binding resulting in shift shoe or cone clutch failure.

(4) VOLVO PENTA DP-S SERIES DRIVE UNIT

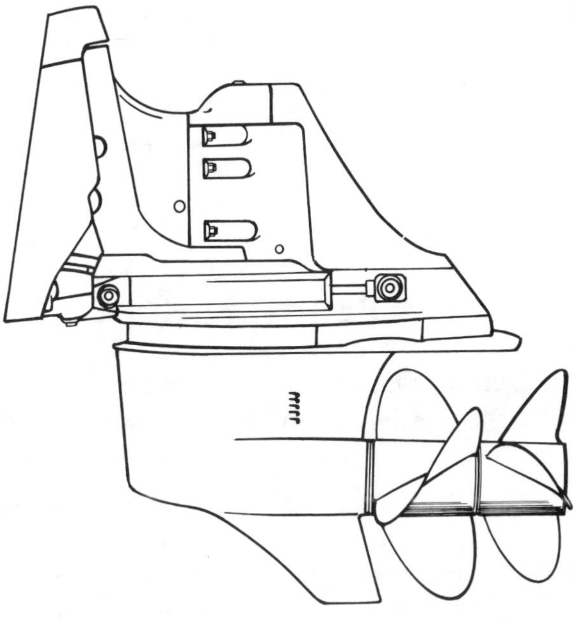

DRIVE UNIT GEAR RATIO

The overall gear ratio refers to the amount of gear reduction between the crankshaft and the propeller and includes the ratios of both the upper and lower gearcases. Overall gear ratios range from as low as 2.30:1 on DuoProp models to as high as 1.43:1 on SX models. The factory installed overall gear ratio is stamped on the model identification plate. An overall gear ratio of 2.30:1 means that the crankshaft turns 2.3 times for every 1 turn of the propeller shaft. Higher number ratios are easier for the engine to turn.

If the model identification plate is missing or the gear ratio is suspected as being incorrect, the gear ratio can be determined by two different methods. The first method requires removing the drive unit. Mark the input shaft and a propeller blade for counting purposes. Manually shift the drive unit into either gear. While counting, turn the input shaft in the normal direction of rotation (counterclockwise as viewed from the rear of the drive unit) until the propshaft has made exactly

10 turns. Divide the number of drive shaft rotations counted by 10 and compare the result with the list of gear ratios in **Table 1**. Round the result to the nearest ratio listed.

The second method of determining gear ratio involves counting the actual number of teeth on the drive unit gears. This method requires at least partial disassembly of the drive unit. Since a drive unit has 2 sets of gears, (upper and lower gear sets) both gear sets must be counted. To determine the overall gear ratio, first divide the upper driven gear tooth count by the upper drive gear tooth count. Divide the lower driven gear tooth count by the lower drive gear tooth count. Multiply the upper and lower ratios together.

For example, an upper gearcase with a 22:23 (drive to driven) tooth count and a lower gearcase with 17:30 (drive to driven) tooth count. Divide 23 (driven) by 22 (drive) = 1.05 ratio upper. Divide 30 (driven) by 17 (drive) = 1.76 ratio lower. Multiply 1.05 (upper ratio) by 1.76 (lower ratio) = 1.85 overall gear ratio drive unit.

It is very important that the engine be operated with the factory recommended gear ratio. Running the engine with an incorrect gear ratio can cause poor performance, poor fuel economy and make it difficult or impossible to obtain the correct wide-open throttle engine speed, which will lead to power head failure.

Some engines have a choice of several factory ratios, depending on boat size and weight. Light, fast boats should run the lower number ratio, while heavy, slow boats should run the higher number ratio. If there is any doubt as to which ratio should be used, contact the boat manufacturer or Volvo Penta Customer Service.

No matter which gear ratio is being used, it is imperative that the engine operate within the recommended speed range at wide-open throttle. Change propeller(s) pitch and diameter as necessary to adjust engine speed. Increasing pitch or diameter increases the load on the engine and reduces the wide-open throttle speed. Decreasing the pitch or diameter reduces the load on the engine and increases the wide-open throttle engine speed. Use an accurate shop tachometer for wide-open throttle engine speed verification.

HIGH ALTITUDE OPERATION

The factory recommended gear ratio is adequate for altitudes up to 3500 ft (1067 m). At higher altitudes, it is recommended to change the gear ratio to a higher number ratio (more gear reduction) to compensate for the loss of horsepower caused by the thinner air. Refer to **Table 1** for gear ratio recommendations. Normally only the lower gears require change.

The propeller(s) will most likely have to be changed to maintain the recommended wide-open throttle engine speed range.

If the boat is returned to lower altitudes, it is recommended that the gear ratio be changed back to the factory recommended ratio and the wide-open throttle speed be checked and adjusted with propeller changes as necessary.

NOTE

If the boat is being operated in a high-altitude environment temporarily (such as a vacation trip), it is recommended that only the propeller(s) be changed to achieve the correct wide-open throttle speed during the stay at high altitude. Change back to the original propeller(s) when the boat is returned to its normal altitude.

SERVICE PRECAUTIONS

When working on a drive unit, there are several good procedures to keep in mind that will make your work easier, faster and more accurate.

1. Never use elastic locknuts more than twice. It is a good practice to replace such nuts each time they are removed. Never use an elastic locknut that can be turned by hand (without the aid of a wrench).

2. Use special tools where noted. **Table 7** and **Table 8** list all manufacturer recommended special tools. The use of makeshift tools can damage components and cause serious personal injury. **Table 11** lists recommended aftermarket tool manufacturers.

3. Use the appropriate fixtures to hold gearcase housings whenever possible. A vise with protective jaws should be used to hold smaller housings or individual components. If protective jaws are not available, insert blocks of wood or similar padding on each side of the housing or component before clamping. Fixture manufacturers are listed in **Table 11**.

4. Remove and install pressed-on parts with an appropriate mandrel, support and press (arbor or hydraulic). Do not attempt to pry or hammer press-fit components on or off.

5. Refer to **Table 4** or **Table 5** for special torque values and **Table 9** or **Table 10** for standard torque values. Proper torque is essential to ensure long life and satisfactory service from drive unit components.

6. To help reduce corrosion, especially in saltwater areas, apply Volvo White Sealing Compound or equivalent (**Table 6**) to all external surfaces of bearing carriers, housing mating surfaces and fasteners unless otherwise specified. Do not apply sealing compound where it can get into gears or bearings.

7. Discard all O-rings, seals and gaskets during disassembly. Apply OMC Triple Guard Grease or equivalent (**Table 6**) to new O-rings and seal lips to provide initial lubrication.

8. All drive units use precision shimmed gears. Tag all shims with the location and measured thickness of each shim as it is removed from the gearcase. Shims are reusable as long as they are not physically damaged or corroded. Follow shimming instructions closely and carefully. Shims control gear location and bearing preload. Incorrectly shimming a gearcase can cause failure of the gears and/or bearings.

9. Work in an area of good lighting and with sufficient space for component storage. Keep an ample number of clean containers available for parts storage. When not being worked on, cover parts and assemblies with clean shop towels or plastic bags.

CAUTION

Metric and U.S. fasteners are used on Volvo drive units. Always match a replacement fastener to the original. Do not run a tap or thread chaser into a hole (or over a bolt) without first verifying the thread size and pitch. SX and DP-S upper gearcases are equipped with Heli-Coil stainless steel locking thread inserts in all holes except the water passage cover and shift housing. Never run a tap or thread chaser into a Heli-Coil equipped hole. Heli-Coil inserts are replaceable, if damaged.

10. Whenever a threadlocking adhesive is specified, first spray the threads of the bore and the screw with Locquic Primer (**Table 6**). Allow the primer to air dry before proceeding. Loquic primer will clean the surfaces and allow better adhesion. Locquic primer will also accelerate the cure rate of threadlocking adhesives from an hour or longer, to 15-20 minutes.

CORROSION CONTROL

Sacrificial zinc or aluminum anodes are standard equipment on all models. The anodes must have good electrical continuity to ground or they will not function. Anodes are inspected visually and tested electrically. Anodes must not be painted or coated with any material. Anodes are mounted as follows:

a. *DP-C1/D1*—Anodes are mounted on the rear of the lower gearcase and bottom of the transom shield. An accessory anode may be mounted to the suspension fork.

b. *DPX*—Anodes are mounted on top of the leading edge of the lower gearcase, on the lower aft portion of the intermediate housing and on the bottom of the transom bracket.

c. *SX and DP-S*—Anodes are mounted on top of the leading edge of the lower gearcase and on the bottom of the transom bracket. The SX also has an additional anode mounted in the propshaft bearing carrier area of the lower gearcase.

If the unit is operated exclusively in freshwater, magnesium anodes are available from Volvo Penta parts and accessories. Magnesium anodes provide better protection in freshwater, but must *not* be used in saltwater. Magnesium anodes will overprotect the unit in saltwater and cause the paint to blister and peel off.

Electronic corrosion control, called the Active Protection System is also available from Volvo Penta Parts and Accessories and operates similar to the Mercury Marine MerCathode system. Two versions are available, one to fit directly to the 1996 SX and DP-S series transom bracket and a transom mount version for all other drive units.

Sacrificial Anode Visual Inspection

Check for loose mounting hardware, verify that the anodes are not painted and check the amount of deterioration present. Replace anodes when they are 2/3rds their original size. Test the electrical continuity of each anode after installation as described in the next section.

Sacrificial Anode Electrical Testing

This test requires an ohmmeter.

1. Calibrate the ohmmeter on the lowest ohms scale available.
2. Connect 1 ohmmeter lead to the anode being tested. Connect the other ohmmeter lead to a good ground point on the gearcase that the anode is mounted to. The meter should indicate a very low reading (zero or very near zero), which indicates electrical continuity.
3. If the reading is not very low, remove the anode and clean the mounting surfaces of the anode, gearcase and mounting hardware. Reinstall the anode and retest continuity.
4. Test the continuity of the gearcase to the engine and negative battery post by connecting 1 ohmmeter lead to the negative battery cable and the other ohmmeter lead to a good ground point on the lower gearcase. The meter should indicate

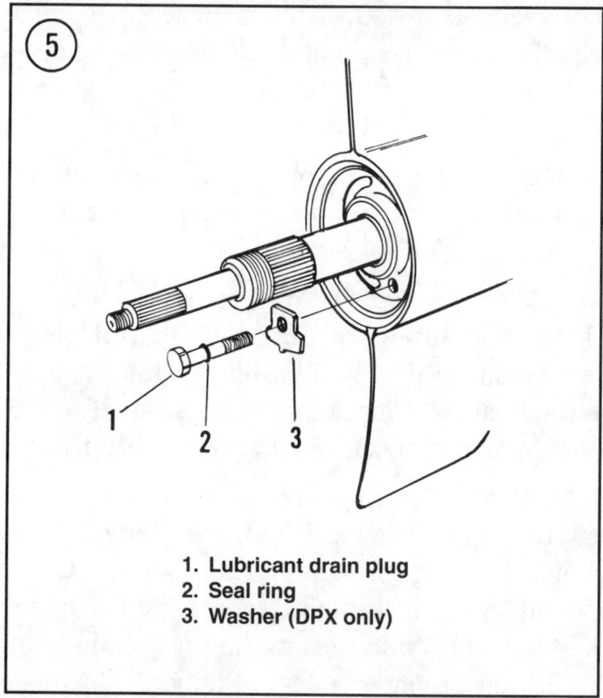

1. Lubricant drain plug
2. Seal ring
3. Washer (DPX only)

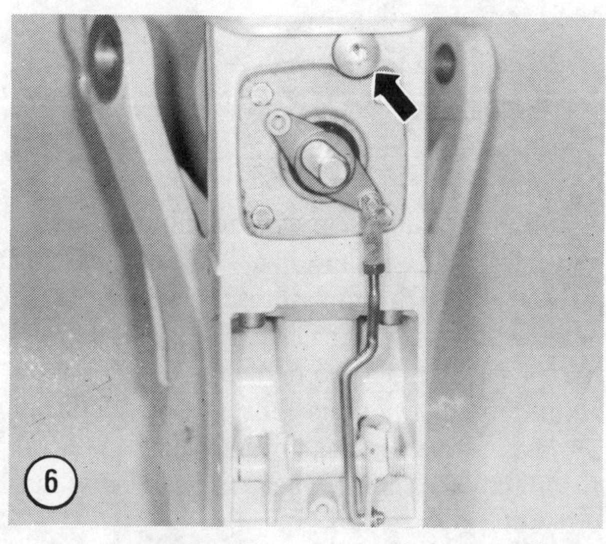

a very low reading (zero or very near zero), which indicates electrical continuity.

5. If the reading is not very low, check the electrical continuity of the lower gearcase to the upper gearcase, the upper gearcase to each component of the transom bracket and transom bracket to the engine. Check for loose mounting hardware, broken or missing ground straps, or excessive corrosion. Repair as necessary to establish a good electrical ground path.

DRIVE UNIT LUBRICATION

To ensure maximum performance and durability, the drive unit requires periodic lubrication. Change the drive lubricant every 100 hours of operation or once each season. The recommended lubricant for all models is Volvo Penta DuraPlus Synthetic GL-5 lubricant or equivalent.

Remove the drive unit from the transom bracket at least once a year to lubricate the drive shaft universal joints and on SX and DP-S models, the transom bracket gimbal bearing. Verify engine alignment on the SX and DP-S series drive and each time the drive unit is removed.

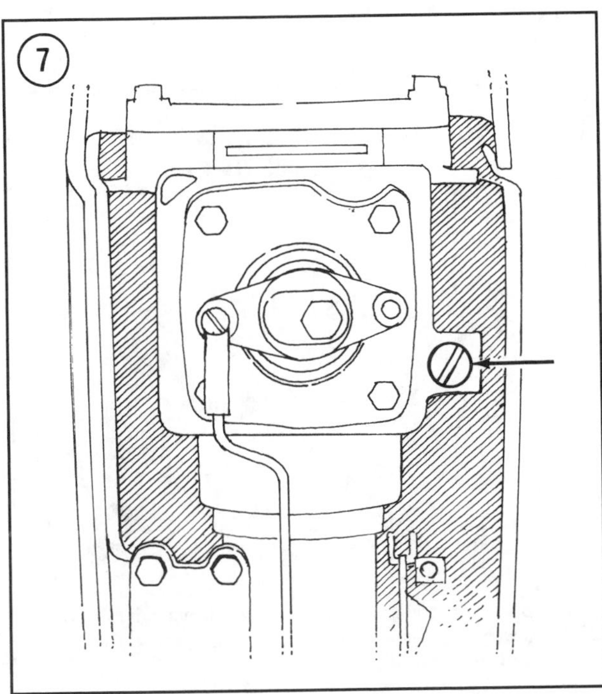

Drive Lubricant Change

The propellers must be removed on DPX and DP-S drive units. Refer to *Propeller Removal* in Chapter Thirteen.

1. *DPX and DP-S units*—Remove both propellers as described in Chapter Thirteen.

2. Tilt the drive unit fully down and place a suitable container under the lower gear case.

3A. *DP-C1/D1 units*—Remove the 2 screws securing the shift cover to the rear of the intermediate housing and upper gearcase. Remove the shift cover.

3B. *DPX units*—Remove the single screw securing the shift cover to the rear of the gearcase. Remove the shift cover.

3C. *SX and DP-S units*—Remove the 3 screws securing the plastic rear cover to the upper gearcase. Remove the rear cover.

4. Remove the lubricant level dipstick located in the center of the drive unit top cover.

5A. *DP-C1/D1 and SX units*—Remove the drain plug near the front of the lower gearcase and allow the unit to drain. Tilt the unit up slightly to position the propshaft just above horizontal and allow any remaining lubricant to drain.

5B. *DPX and DP-S units*—Remove the drain plug in the propshaft bearing carrier. Remove the washer on DPX units. See **Figure 5**.

6A. *DP-C1/D1 and DPX units*—Remove the fill plug near the top starboard corner of the shift housing. See **Figure 6**, typical.

6B. *SX and DP-S units*—Remove the lubricant level plug near the bottom starboard corner of the shift housing. See **Figure 7**.

7. Remove and discard the sealing washers from the drain plug, fill/lubricant level plug and lubricant level dipstick.

8. Install new sealing washers on the drain plug, fill/lubricant level plug and lubricant level dipstick.

9A. *DP-C1/D1 units*—Install the lower drain plug and tighten to specifications (**Table 4**). Tilt the unit to the full up position and fill the gearcase through the upper gearcase fill plug hole (**Figure 6**) until lubricant is present at the dipstick hole. Install the fill plug and tighten to specification (**Table 4**).

9B. *DPX units*—Install the lower drain plug and washer and tighten to specification (**Table 4**). Tilt the unit to the full up position and fill the gearcase through the upper gearcase fill plug (**Figure 6**) until lubricant is present at the dipstick hole. Install the fill plug (and washer) and tighten to specification (**Table 4**).

9C. *SX units*—Fill the drive unit from the lower gearcase drain hole until gear lubricant is present at the lubricant level hole (**Figure 7**). Install the lubricant level plug and dipstick hand-tight, then install the drain plug. Tighten the drain plug and lubricant level plug to specification (**Table 5**).

NOTE
Gearcase fill adaptor part No. 3855932-4 is required to fill the DP-S drive unit with lubricant.

9D. *DP-S units*—Fill the drive unit from the drain hole in the propshaft bearing carrier, using gearcase fill adaptor part No. 3855932-4. Fill until gear lubricant is present at the lubricant level hole (**Figure 7**). Install the level plug and dipstick hand-tight, then install the drain plug. Tighten the drain plug and level plug to specification (**Table 5**).

10. *DP-C1/D1 and DPX units*—Tilt the drive unit down until the propshaft is horizontal.

11. Recheck fluid level after 5-10 minutes. The fluid level must be present on the machined flat area of the dipstick. Add more lubricant as necessary through the dipstick hole. Do not overfill. Tighten the dipstick to specification (**Table 4** or **Table 5**) when the lubricant level has been verified.

12A. *DP-C1/D1 and DPX*—Install the shift cover and tighten the screw(s) securely.

12B. *SX and DP-S*—Install the rear plastic cover and tighten the 3 screws securely.

Universal Joint and Gimbal Bearing Lubrication

All SX and DP-S drive units come from the factory equipped with grease fittings on the universal joints. DP-C1/D1 and DPX may or may not be equipped with grease fittings. If grease fittings are not present, the universal joints must be disassembled and greased. Universal joint disassembly is covered later in this chapter. All SX and DP-S drive units are also equipped with a gimbal bearing in the transom bracket. Refer to **Figure 8** for DP-C1/D1 and DPX models and **Figure 9** for SX and DP-S models.

1. Remove the drive unit as described in the next section.

2. Wipe all old grease from the universal joints and center coupler.

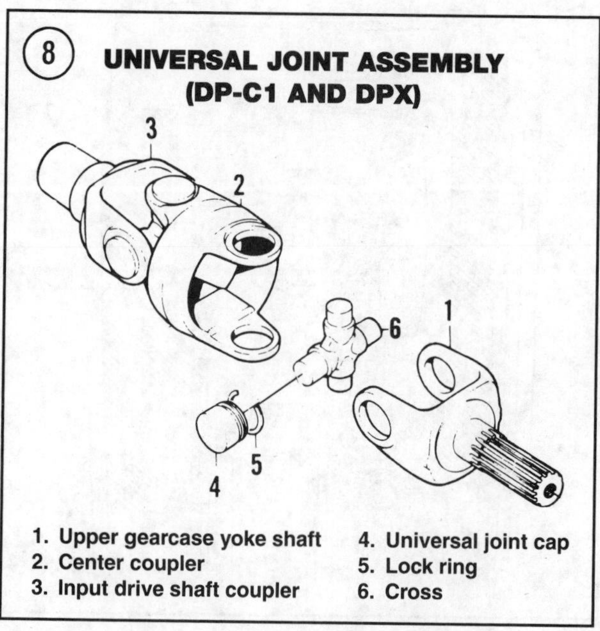

3A. *Models with grease fittings*—Apply an extreme pressure grease, such as OMC EP/Marine wheel bearing grease or equivalent (**Table 6**) to each universal joint grease fitting. Apply grease slowly until fresh grease is present at all caps.

NOTE
In the next step, the universal joint needle bearings and universal joint caps should be kept separate to allow reassembly in their original locations. Do not apply excessive amounts of grease into the universal joint caps or hydraulic lock will occur during reassembly.

3B. *Models without grease fittings*—Disassemble the universal joint as described in this chapter. Wash all of the universal joint components in clean solvent and blow dry. Pack each cross assembly and all needle bearings with an extreme pressure grease, such as OMC EP/Wheel bearing grease or equivalent (**Table 6**). Reassemble each universal joint assembly as described in this chapter.

4. Wipe up any excess grease.

5A. *SX and DP-S models*—Clean the input drive shaft splines thoroughly. Liberally apply a Molybdenum grease, such as OMC Moly Lube or equivalent (**Table 6**), to the input shaft splines.

5B. *DP-C1/D1 and DPX models*—Clean the input drive shaft internal splines thoroughly. Reach into the universal joint bellows and clean the primary drive shaft splines thoroughly. Liberally apply a Molybdenum grease, such as OMC Moly Lube or equivalent (**Table 6**), to the input shaft internal splines and the primary drive shaft external splines.

6. *SX and DP-S models*—Apply an extreme pressure grease, such as OMC Marine wheel bearing grease or equivalent, to the transom bracket gimbal bearing grease fitting, located on the starboard side of the transom plate. Apply grease until fresh grease is visible and all old grease has been displaced.

7. Wipe up any excess grease.

8. Reinstall the drive unit as described in the next section.

DRIVE UNIT REMOVAL/INSTALLATION

DP-C1/D1 and DPX Models

Removal

1. Disconnect the negative battery cable.

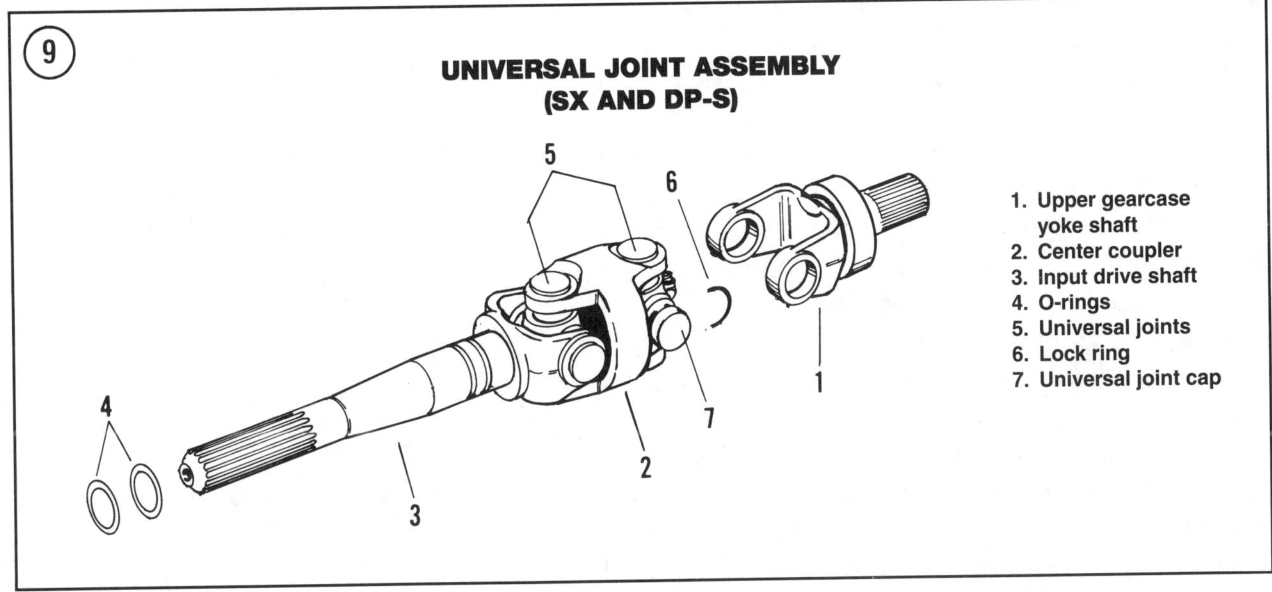

2. If the propeller removal is necessary for the service scheduled to be performed, remove both propellers at this time. See Chapter Thirteen.

NOTE
A steering helmet is used on the DP-C1/D1 drive unit and is considered a structural member of the transom shield. A steering cover is used on the DPX drive unit and is present to protect the bellows and for aesthetic purposes.

3. *DP-C1/D1 models*—Remove the 2 screws from the steering helmet on the front of the upper gearcase (1, **Figure 10**). Remove the steering helmet sleeve by threading 2 part No. 966868-2 screws into the 2 threaded holes of the sleeve (2, **Figure 10**). Tighten each screw 1/2 turn at a time until the sleeve is pushed from the steering helmet. After the sleeve is removed, rotate the steering helmet (6, **Figure 10**) to the full tilt UP position.

NOTE
The steering bushing in the steering helmet is replaceable on DP-C1/D1 models.

4. *DPX models*—Remove the 4 screws securing the trim plate to the top portion of the transom plate. Remove the trim plate. See **Figure 11**.
5. *DPX models*—Remove the 2 screws securing the steering cover to the front of the upper gear housing. Remove the steering cover. See **Figure 11**.
6A. *DP-C1/D1 models*—Remove the 2 screws securing the shift cover to the rear of the intermediate housing. Remove the shift cover. See **Figure 10**.
6B. *DPX models*—Remove the single screw (4, **Figure 10**) securing the shift cover to the rear of the intermediate housing. Remove the shift cover.
7. *DPX models*—Remove the cotter pins from the 2 steering pins securing the 2 hydraulic steering rams to the rear of the intermediate housing. Note the location of any washers present on the steering pins for reassembly purposes. Remove both steering pins and any washers present.
8. Remove the cotter pin and washer holding the remote control shift cable to the shift bellcrank located inside the rear of the intermediate housing. See **Figure 12**. Discard the cotter pin and disconnect the shift cable from the shift bellcrank. Remove the brass cube nut from the shift cable.

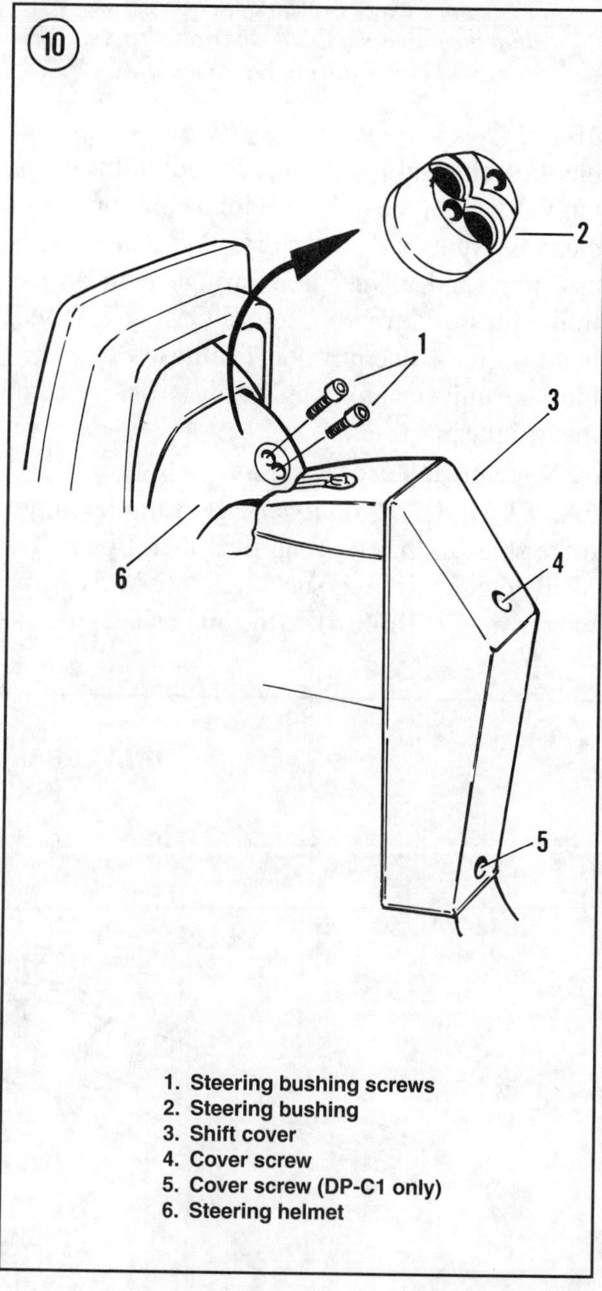

1. Steering bushing screws
2. Steering bushing
3. Shift cover
4. Cover screw
5. Cover screw (DP-C1 only)
6. Steering helmet

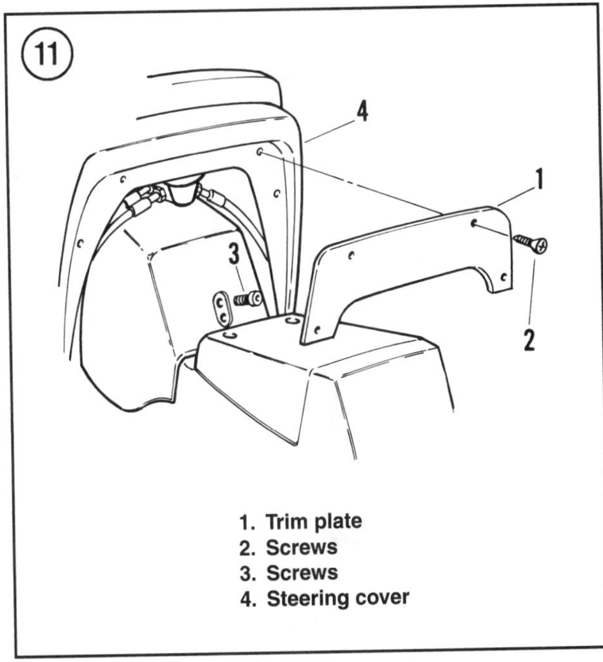

1. Trim plate
2. Screws
3. Screws
4. Steering cover

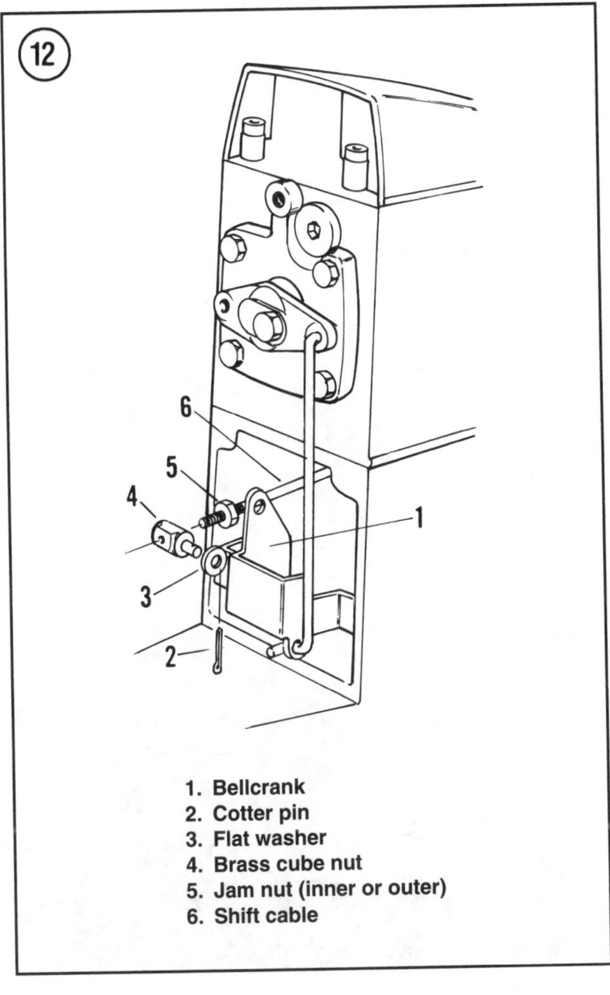

1. Bellcrank
2. Cotter pin
3. Flat washer
4. Brass cube nut
5. Jam nut (inner or outer)
6. Shift cable

9. Loosen the screw securing the shift cable locking plate to the front of the intermediate housing. Rotate the locking plate to free the remote control shift cable. Retighten the screw to prevent the locking plate from falling and, preventing shift cable removal.

10. Remove the cotter pins from the 2 tilt pins securing the trim/tilt rams to the suspension fork. Support the drive unit and carefully remove the 2 tilt pins. See **Figure 13**.

CAUTION

The drive must be supported in the full tilt position to prevent personal injury. Tilt suspension tool part No. 885143-8 is the only recommended tool to serve this function. The tool is inexpensive and should be considered a necessary expenditure to service the drive unit.

11. Manually tilt the drive unit to the fully up position. Install the tilt suspension tool (part No. 885143-8) to the starboard side of the steering fork and engage the rod with the starboard tilt pin hole. Rest the drive unit against the tool and verify that it is securely locked in place. See **Figure 14**.

12. Loosen or remove the clamps attaching the universal joint bellows (**Figure 15**) to the upper gear housing, the exhaust bellows (A, **Figure 16**, typical) to the intermediate housing and the

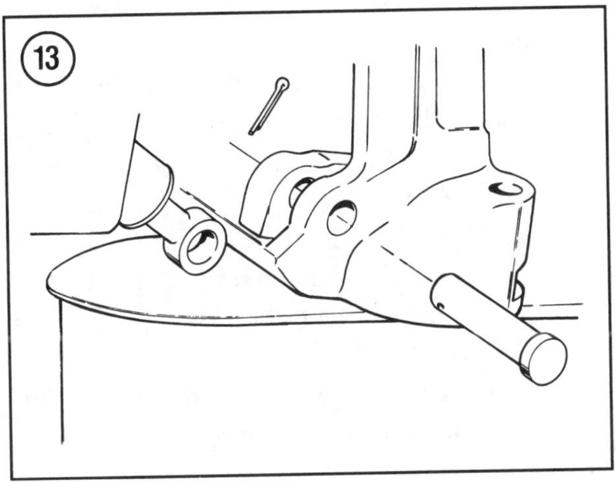

water intake hose (B, **Figure 16**, typical) to the water outlet fitting on the suspension fork.

NOTE

The manufacturer recommends replacement of the universal joint and exhaust bellows and the water hose every 2 years.

13. Remove the bellows and water hose from the drive unit by gently prying them free with a suitable tool. Be careful not to puncture or rip the bellows and water hose if they are to be reused.
14. Support the drive unit and remove the tilt suspension tool, then lower the drive unit and allow it to rest in the fully down position.
15. Remove the pivot pin retaining screw and washer from each side of the transom plate (A, **Figure 17**).

CAUTION

*If the support tool is being used, pull the pivot pins (B, **Figure 17**) out just far enough to support the tool. Then, once the drive is supported by the tool, pull the pivot pins out enough to loosen the drive unit (pins flush with the inside edge of the transom plate) but continue to support the suspension tool. Pivot pin removal tool part No. 885148-7 allows easy control of the pin removal process.*

16A. *Using support tool*:

a. Pull both pivot pins (with pivot pin removal tool [part No. 885148-7 or equivalent]) just enough to support the support 885146-1 tool.
b. Install the suspension tool to the transom plate. Lift the drive unit slightly and connect the drive unit to the suspension tool. See **Figure 18**.
c. Again pull both pivot pins out just far enough to disengage the drive, but no further than flush with the inside edge of the transom plate.
d. Slide the drive unit back on the support tool. Lift and remove the drive unit from the support tool.

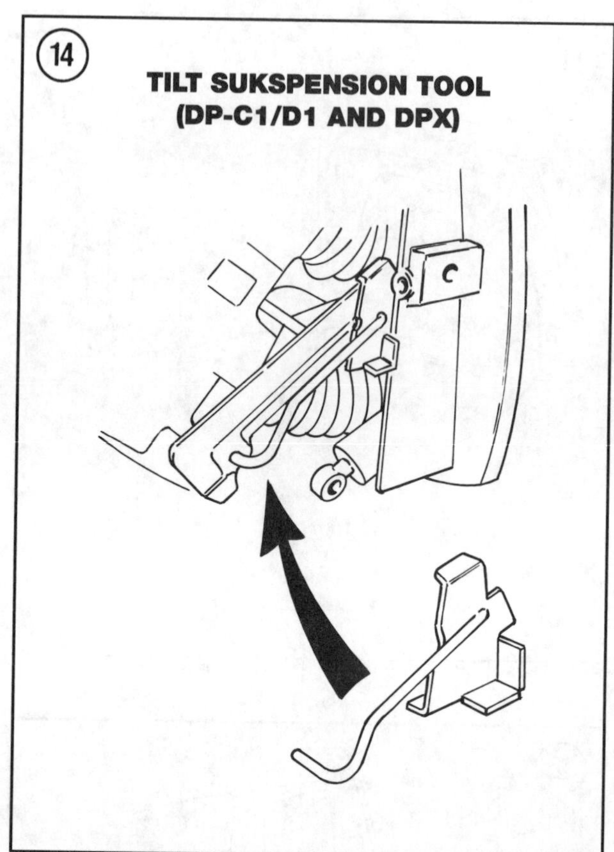

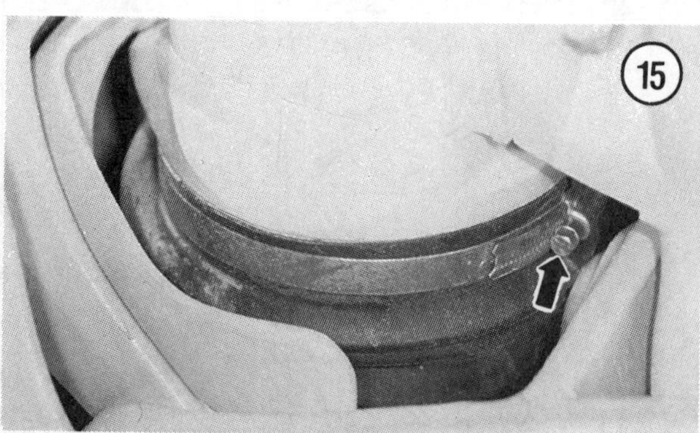

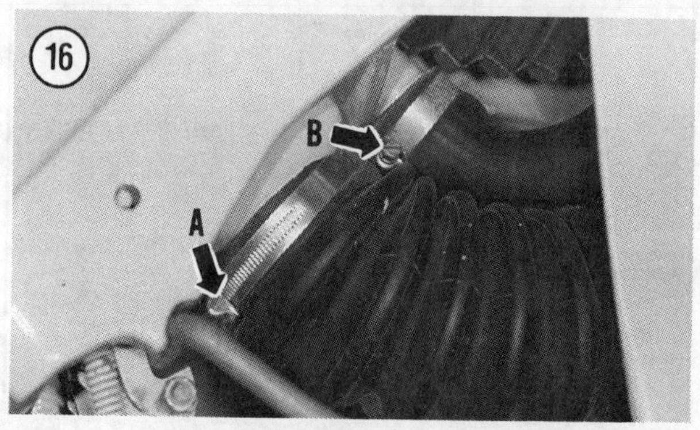

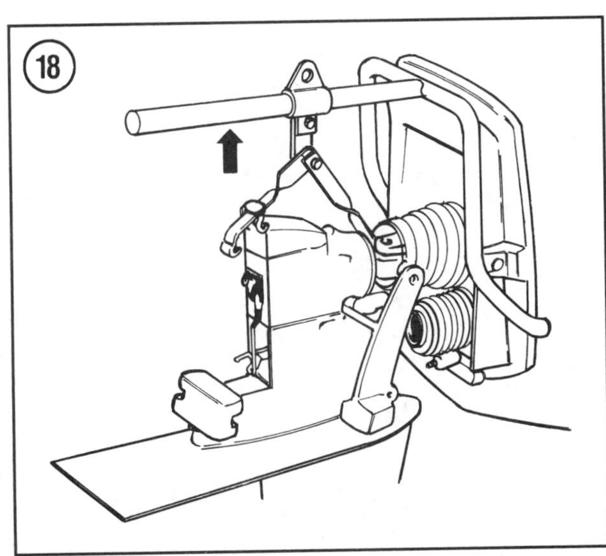

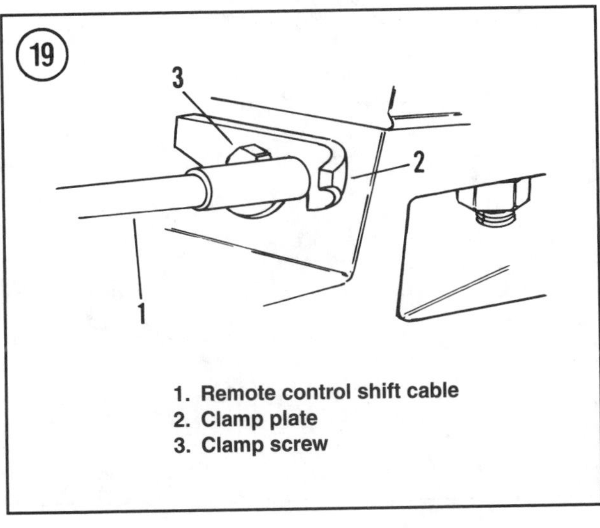

1. Remote control shift cable
2. Clamp plate
3. Clamp screw

16B. *Without support tool*—Support the drive unit with blocks, a suitable hoist or an assistant. Remove both pivot pins with pivot pin removal tool (part No. 885148-7 or equivalent) and remove the drive unit from the transom plate.

17. Secure the drive unit in a suitable holding fixture. Remove and discard both plastic pivot pin bushings from the suspension fork.

Installation

Prior to installing the drive unit, the pivot pins and pivot pin holes should be cleaned with solvent and dried, then cleaned with a fine-grit emery paper to remove all rust or other corrosion. Grease new suspension fork plastic bushings and install them into the suspension fork.

1. Clean the input drive shaft internal splines thoroughly. Reach into the universal joint bellows and clean the primary drive shaft splines thoroughly. Liberally apply a Molybdenum grease, such as OMC Moly Lube or equivalent (**Table 6**), to the input shaft internal splines and the primary drive shaft external splines.
2. Grease the pivot pins (A, **Figure 17**) with Volvo Propeller Shaft Grease (**Table 6**) and install the pins until they are flush with the inside surface of the transom plate.

3A. *Using support tool*—Install the drive support tool (part No. 885146-1) over the transom plate pivot pins. Lift and hang the drive unit from the support tool.

3B. *Without support tool*—Using blocks, a suitable hoist or an assistant, position the drive unit at the correct height to be installed with the drive shaft just ready to enter the universal joint bellows.

4. Insert the shift cable through the intermediate housing. Position the groove in the shift cable at the clamp plate on the front of the intermediate housing. Loosen the clamp plate screw and rotate the clamp plate down to engage the groove on the shift cable and lock it into position. Tighten the clamp screw securely. See **Figure 19**.

5A. *Using support tool*—Slide the drive unit forward on the support tool while guiding the drive shaft and universal joints into the universal joint bellows and onto the primary drive shaft. Rotate the universal joint shaft as necessary to index the splines.

5B. *Without support tool*—Lift the drive unit into position and guide the drive shaft and universal joints into the universal joint bellows and onto the primary drive shaft. Rotate the universal joint shaft as necessary to index the splines. Lift the trim/tilt rams up into position and continue to slide the drive forward, while guiding the suspension fork as necessary.

CAUTION

The pivot pins must be aligned with the suspension fork (and bushing) before they are driven in. Installation tool part No. 3810105-1 is designed to ease alignment and installation of the pivot pins.

6. Carefully align the suspension fork bushing bores with the pivot pins. Using the part No. 3810105-1 installation tool or a *Rubber or Plastic* hammer, drive the pivot pins into the suspension fork. If using the support tool, remove the tool once the pins have securely engaged the suspension fork, then drive the pivot pins the rest of the way into the suspension fork.

7. Position the pivot pins as necessary to align the pivot pin groove with the retaining screw bore. Grease the pivot pin retaining screw threads with Volvo Propeller Shaft Grease (**Table 6**). Install a washer on each retaining screw. Install the screws and washers into each side of the transom plate. Tighten the screws securely. See **Figure 17**.

8. Carefully work the universal joint bellows in place. Do not puncture or tear the bellows. Open the universal joint bellows clamp and install the clamp over the bellows with the clamp screw at the 6 O'clock position with the screw head facing starboard (**Figure 20**). Tighten the clamp securely using clamp tool (part No. 884573-7) or

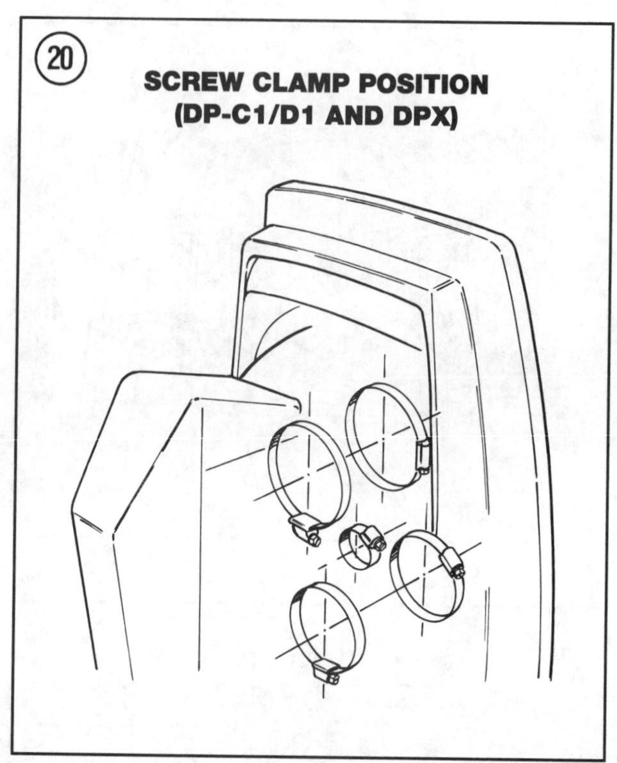

20

SCREW CLAMP POSITION (DP-C1/D1 AND DPX)

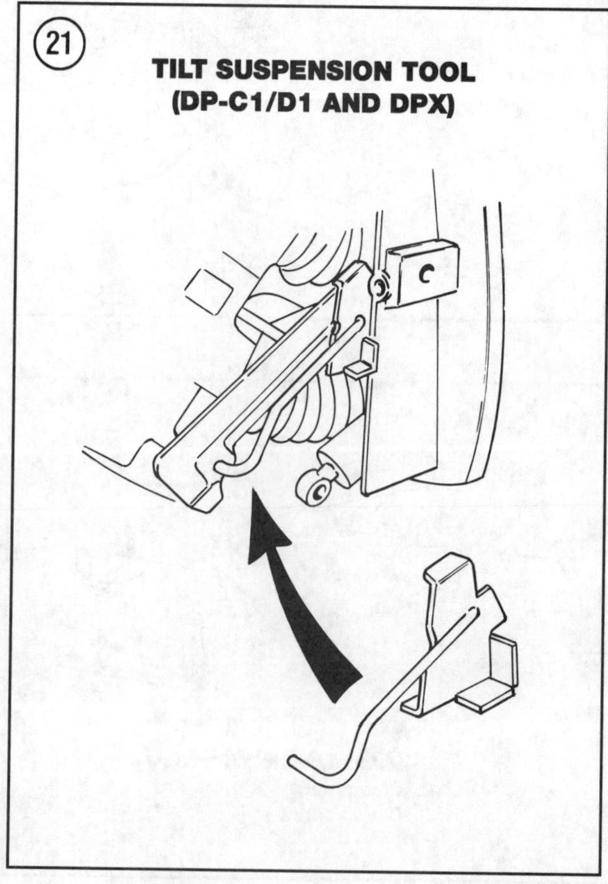

21

TILT SUSPENSION TOOL (DP-C1/D1 AND DPX)

a suitable socket on a 1/4 in. drive swivel and ratchet.

9. Manually tilt the drive unit to the fully up position. Install the tilt suspension tool (part No. 885143-8) to the starboard side of the steering fork and engage the rod into the starboard tilt pin hole. Rest the drive unit against the tool and verify that it is securely locked in place. See **Figure 21**.

CAUTION

*Position the clamp screws as shown in **Figure 20** to avoid the possibility of contact with other bellows during operation. Use great care if the clamp screws are tightened with a screwdriver. If the screwdriver slips, it will probably puncture the bellows.*

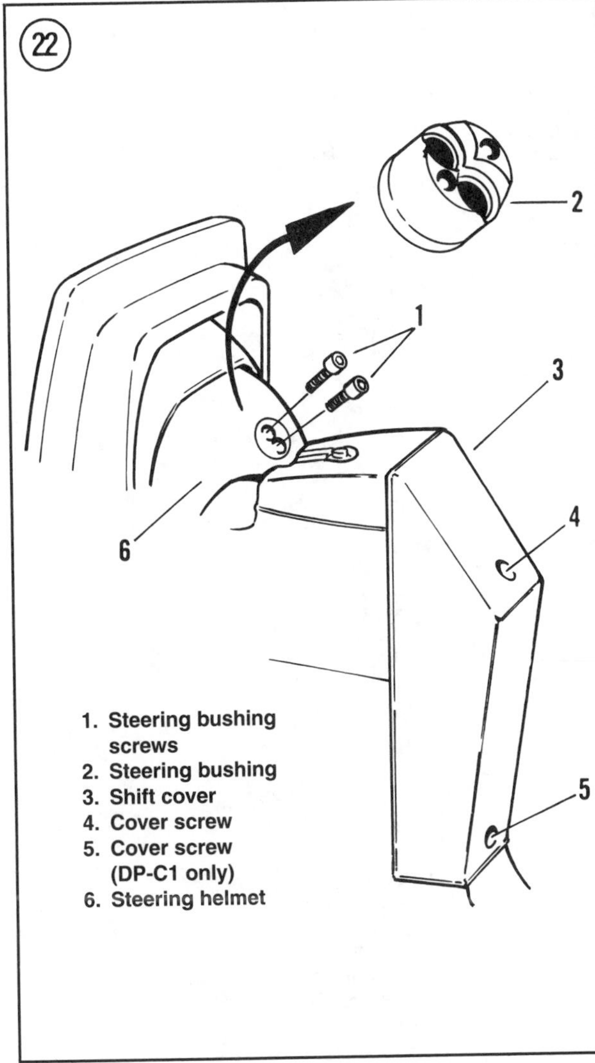

10. Carefully install the water intake hose and exhaust bellows. Position the clamp screws as shown in **Figure 20**. Tighten both clamp screws securely using clamp tool (part No. 884573-7) or a suitable socket on a 1/4 in. drive swivel and ratchet.

11. Support the drive unit and remove the tilt suspension tool, then lower the drive unit and allow it to rest in the fully down position.

12. Move the stern drive from full port to full starboard while visually making sure the clamp screws do not touch another bellows or adjacent hose. Correct any problems noted.

13. Grease the tilt pins with Volvo Propeller Shaft Grease (**Table 6**). Align the trim/tilt rams to the suspension fork and install the 2 tilt pins. Secure each pin with a new stainless steel cotter pin. Bend both prongs of both cotter pins for a secure attachment.

14. *DP-C1/D1 models*—Refer to **Figure 22** for the following procedure:

a. Grease the steering sleeve with Volvo Propeller Shaft Grease (**Table 6**). Lower the steering helmet and install the steering sleeve.

b. Wipe the 2 steering sleeve retaining screw threads with Volvo Propeller Shaft Grease (**Table 6**).

c. Align the steering sleeve screw holes with the upper gearcase holes and install the 2 retaining screws. Tighten the screws to specification (**Table 4**).

15. *DPX models:*

a. Install the steering cover and secure it with 2 screws. Tighten the screws securely. See **Figure 23**.

b. Install the trim plate to the top portion of the transom plate and secure it with 4 screws. Tighten the screws securely. See **Figure 23**.

16. *DPX models*:

a. Reconnect the hydraulic steering rams to rear of the intermediate housing. Grease the washers and pins with Volvo Propeller Shaft Grease (**Table 6**).

b. Place a washer on each lower ear of the intermediate housing so the steering cylinder eye will rest upon it. Align the steering cylinder eyes with the intermediate housing and secure each cylinder with a pin. Make sure the washers were not displaced during the installation process.

c. Secure each pin with new stainless steel cotter pins and bend both prongs of each cotter pin for a secure attachment.

17. Refer to **Figure 24** and connect the remote control cable as follows:

a. Position the remote control box in the neutral detent. Position the drive unit shift linkage in the neutral detent.

b. Thread the brass cube nut onto the shift cable and position it so that when all play in both the remote control cable and the drive unit shift linkage is centered, the brass cube nut will slide freely into the shift bellcrank arm.

c. Secure the brass cube nut to the shift bellcrank with a washer and a new stainless steel cotter pin. Bend both prongs of the cotter pin for a secure attachment.

d. Install the jam nut over the shift cable core wire and tighten it against the brass cube nut.

18A. *DP-C1/D1 models*—Install the shift cover and secure it with 2 screws. Tighten the screws securely. See **Figure 22**.

18B. *DPX models*—Install the shift cover and secure it with a single screw (4, **Figure 22**). Tighten the screw securely.

19. Remove the gearcase lubricant level dipstick and verify that the lubricant level is on the machined flat area of the dipstick. Add gearcase lubricant as necessary through the dipstick hole. When the gearcase lubricant level has been veri-

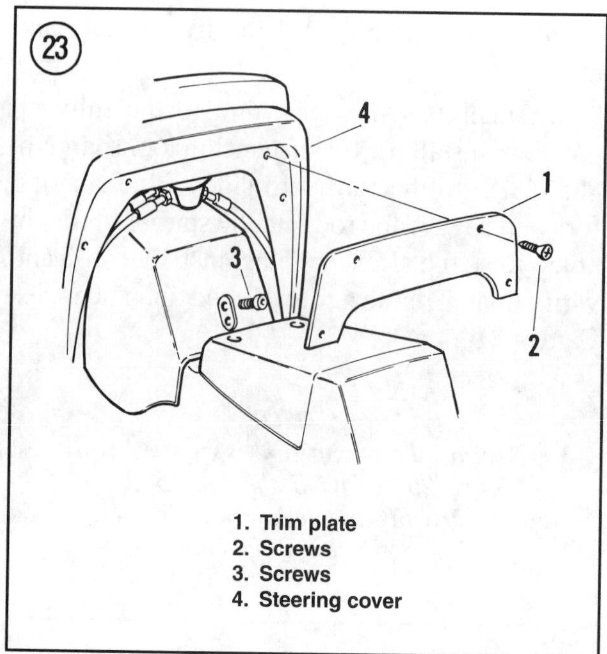

1. Trim plate
2. Screws
3. Screws
4. Steering cover

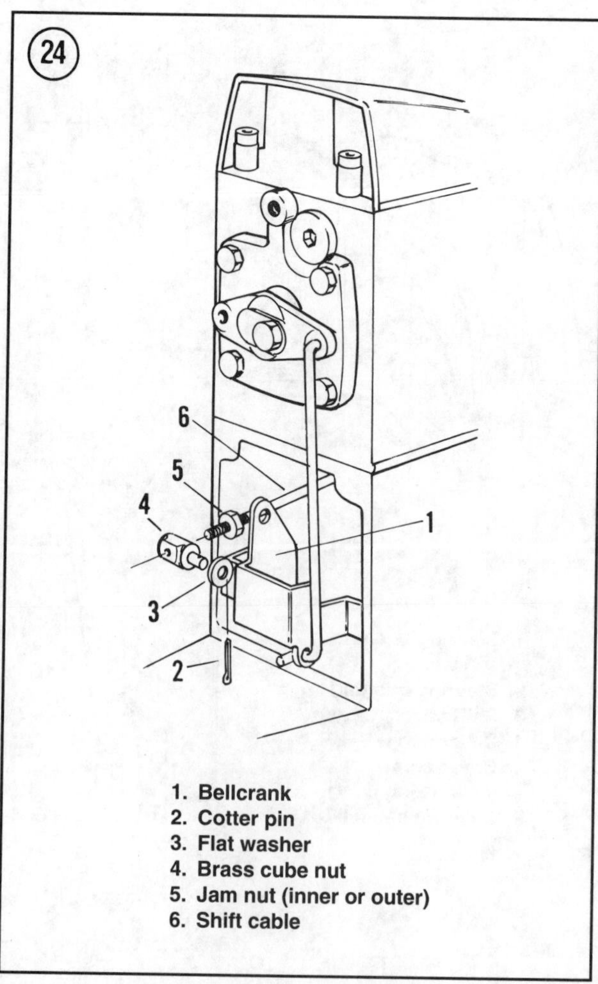

1. Bellcrank
2. Cotter pin
3. Flat washer
4. Brass cube nut
5. Jam nut (inner or outer)
6. Shift cable

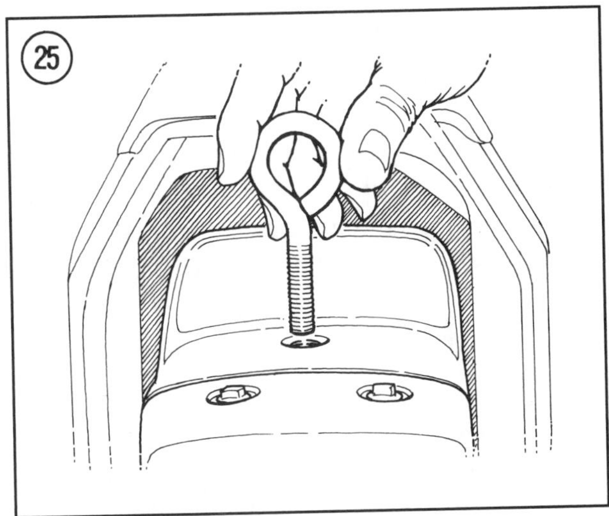

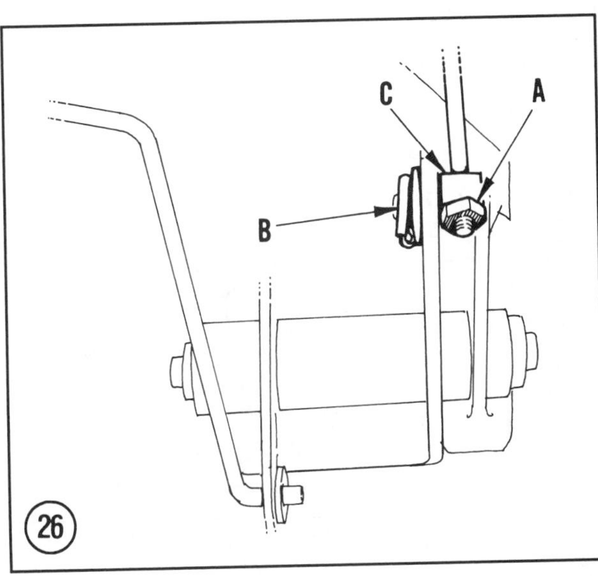

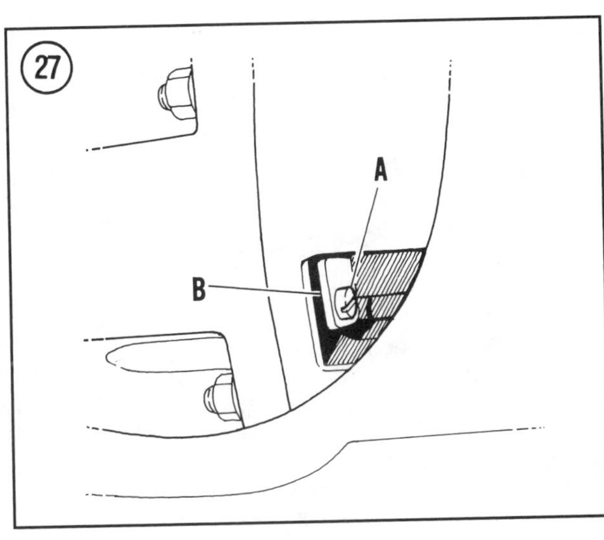

fied, reinstall the dipstick and tighten to specification (**Table 4**).

SX and DP-S Models

Removal

1. Disconnect the negative battery cable.
2. If the propeller removal is necessary for the service scheduled to be performed, remove the propeller(s) at this time. See Chapter Thirteen.

CAUTION
Make sure the lifting eye installed in Step 3 fits the threads properly and is threaded in completely.

3. Unscrew the oil level dipstick from the upper gear housing and thread a 1/2 × 13 lifting eye (available at any hardware store) into this location. See **Figure 25**.
4. Remove the 3 screws securing the plastic rear cover to the upper gearcase. Remove the rear cover.
5. Detach the shift cable as follows:
   a. Remove the locknut (A, **Figure 26**).
   b. Remove the cotter pin and washer (B, **Figure 26**).
   c. Unscrew the brass cube nut (C, **Figure 26**) from the shift cable.
   d. Loosen the screw (A, **Figure 27**) attaching the cable anchor clamp (B, **Figure 27**) to the pivot housing.
   e. Slide the cable anchor clamp to the starboard side to detach the shift cable.
   f. Turn the drive unit to port and remove the shift cable from the drive unit and pivot housing. Make sure that both shift cable rubber grommets are present on the shift cable. Locate the grommets if they are missing.
   g. Allow the shift cable to hang beneath the transom bracket.
6. Detach the trim/tilt hydraulic cylinders as follows:

a. Remove the protective plastic cap, locknut and flat washer from one end of the trim/tilt pivot rod. See **Figure 28**.

b. While supporting the drive, tap one end of the rod from the trim/tilt cylinders and drive unit using a soft-faced hammer and a brass or aluminum punch.

c. Remove the 2 bushings, 2 rubber grommets and 1 ground clip from *each* trim cylinder eyelet.

d. Remove the bushing and rubber grommet from each side of the upper gearcase.

7. Attach a suitable hoist to the lifting eye installed in Step 2. Take up enough pressure with the hoist to support the weight of the drive unit.

8. Remove and discard the 6 washer-faced elastic locknuts (3 on each side [**Figure 29**]) and pull the drive unit away from the transom plate. Support the drive shaft and universal joint assembly as it appears from the pivot housing and prevent it from falling and damaging the pivot housing or drive unit. Support and lower the trim/tilt cylinders carefully as the drive is removed to prevent hydraulic line damage.

9. Once the drive unit is removed, tie the trim cylinders up in the normal running position with a suitable piece of rope.

10. Secure the drive unit in a suitable holding fixture. Remove and discard the 2 input drive shaft O-rings.

Installation

Prior to installing the stern drive, clean both the pivot housing and the drive unit machined mating surfaces thoroughly to remove any corrosion. Remove the water tube seal (molded O-ring) from the pivot housing face (**Figure 30**) and lightly glue a new water tube seal in place with OMC Type M adhesive (**Table 6**). Inspect the universal joint bellows and replace if damaged. Refer to Chapter Fourteen for transom bracket service procedures.

1. Grease the universal joints and gimbal bearing as described in *Drive unit lubrication* previously in this chapter.

2. Check the alignment of the gimbal bearing and engine drive shaft coupler by first assembling the alignment bar (part No. 3851083-0) to the universal drive handle (part No. 3850609-3).

CAUTION

Failure to check and properly adjust alignment will lead to premature engine coupler failure, excessive spline wear and difficult drive unit installation and removal. Misalignment can also cause

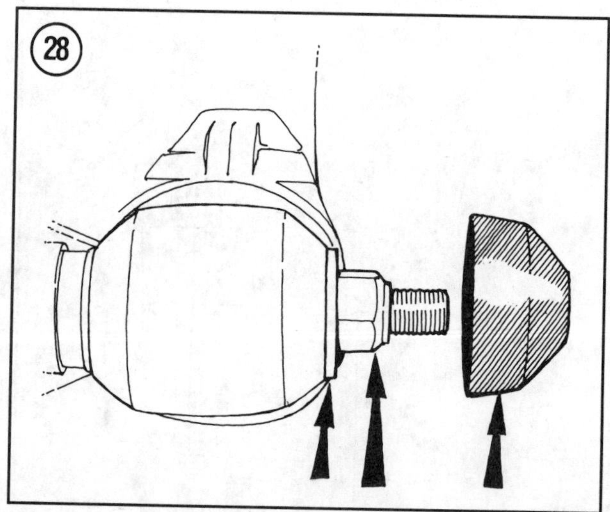

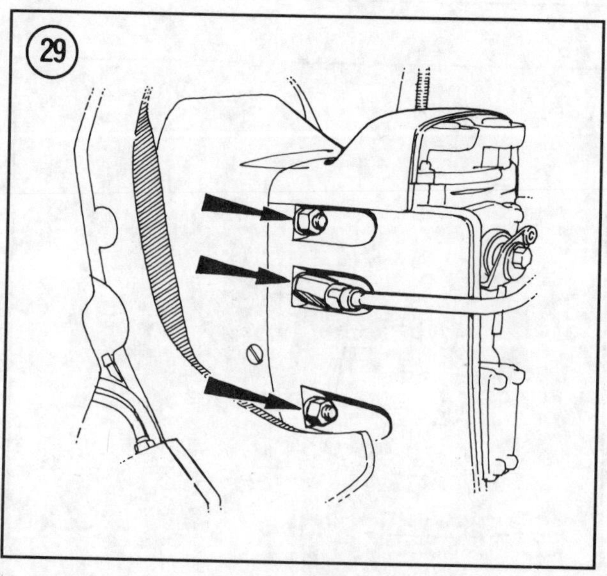

*universal joint **knocking** and vibration when the drive unit is turned under load.*

3. Insert the alignment bar into the pivot housing (**Figure 31**), through the center race of the gimbal bearing and seat it fully into the engine coupler. The alignment bar should slide easily into and out of the engine coupler. If it is difficult to insert and remove the alignment bar, first move the bar from side to side and up and down, to change the position of the gimbal bearing in its carrier. If this does not help, adjust the front engine mount(s) to raise or lower the front of the motor as necessary to correct the alignment and allow easy insertion and removal of the alignment bar.

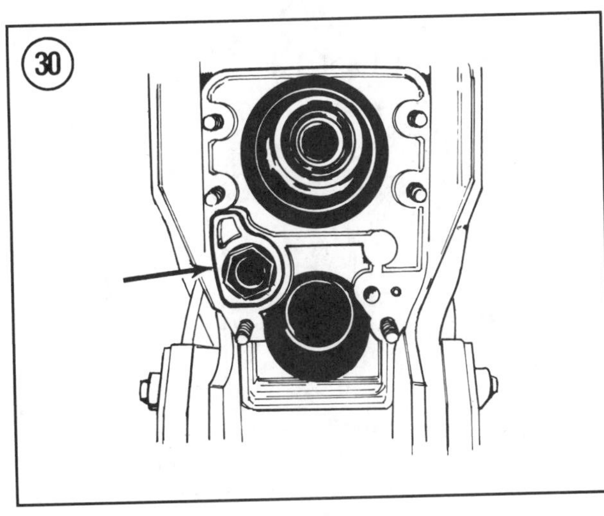

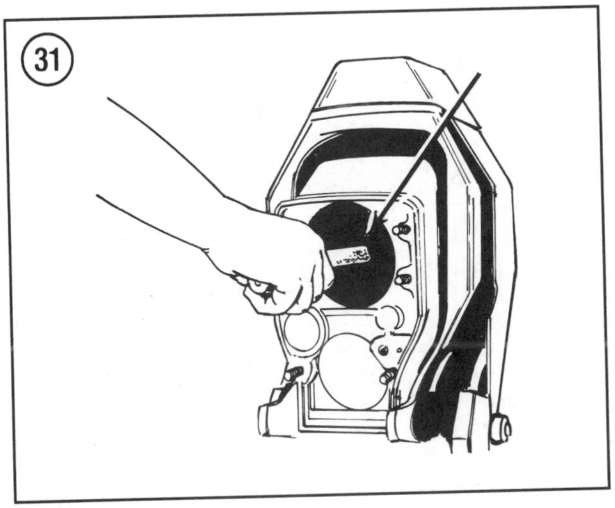

CAUTION
Do not proceed until the alignment bar slides easily into and out of the engine coupler.

4. Apply a light coat of Volvo White Sealing Compound or equivalent (**Table 6**) to the threads of the 6 pivot housing retaining studs and to the pivot housing mating surface.
5. Lubricate the V-shaped lip of the universal joint bellows in the pivot housing bore and the water tube seal on the pivot housing face with OMC Triple Guard Grease or equivalent (**Table 6**).
6. Apply a light coat of OMC Triple Guard Grease or equivalent (**Table 6**) to the extreme leading edge of the drive unit universal joint shaft bearing carrier and the outer diameter of the universal joint center coupler.
7. Clean the input drive shaft splines thoroughly. Liberally apply a Molybdenum grease, such as OMC Moly Lube or equivalent (**Table 6**), to the input shaft splines.

NOTE
Do not grease the O-rings in Step 8. If the drive shaft O-rings are coated with grease, a hydraulic lock situation may occur and prevent the O-rings from seating in the gimbal bearing inner race.

8. Install 2 new O-rings on the input drive shaft. Lubricate the O-rings with any motor or gear oil.
9. Shift the drive unit into either gear by moving the eccentric piston arm (**Figure 32**) either up or down.
10. With a suitable hoist and lift eye, blocks or an assistant, position the drive unit at the correct installation height with the input drive shaft at the entrance to the universal joint bellows.
11. Move the drive unit towards the transom, carefully guiding the input drive shaft and center coupler into the universal joint bellows. Rotate the propeller shaft as necessary to align the input drive shaft splines to the engine coupler splines. Seat the drive unit against the pivot housing.

12. Secure the drive with 6 new washer faced elastic locknuts (**Figure 29**). Tighten the nuts in a crisscross pattern, working from the center out, first to 34 N•m (25 ft.-lb.), then to 68 N•m (50 ft.-lb.).

13. Coat the 6 bushings and 6 rubber grommets with OMC Triple Guard Grease (**Table 6**) and position the rubber grommet (1, **Figure 33**) on each bushing with the beveled edge facing away from the bushing flange. Replace any damaged or missing parts.

14. Install a bushing assembly into each side of the upper gearcase. Install 2 bushing assemblies to each trim/tilt eyelet with a ground clip (3, **Figure 33**) between the 2 bushing assemblies. Align each trim/tilt cylinder eyelet with the upper gearcase bushing.

15. Apply OMC Triple Guard Grease or equivalent (**Table 6**), to the entire length of the trim/tilt rod. Insert the rod through one trim/tilt eyelet, through the upper gearcase bushings and out the other trim/tilt eyelet. Be careful not to displace any ground clips or damage any bushing assemblies. A rubber or plastic mallet may be used to carefully tap the rod into position.

16. Install the flat washer and elastic locknut to the trim/tilt rod. Tighten both elastic locknuts until they are seated, then tighten the nuts to 14-16 N•m (10-12 ft.-lb.). Install the plastic protective covers over the elastic locknuts and tighten them securely.

17. Turn the drive unit to full port. Insert the shift cable through the pivot housing and into the upper gearcase. Verify that the rubber boots are still positioned on the shift cable and position the cable groove at the cable anchor clamp. Slide the cable anchor clamp towards the pivot housing, fully engaging the cable groove. Hold the clamp (B, **Figure 34**) in position and tighten the cable anchor clamp screw (A) securely.

18. Refer to **Figure 35** and connect the remote control cable as follows:

a. Position the remote control box in the neutral detent. Position the drive unit shift linkage in the neutral detent.

b. Thread the brass cube nut (C, **Figure 35**) onto the shift cable and position it so that when all play in both the remote control cable and the drive unit shift linkage is centered, the brass cube nut will slide freely into the shift bellcrank arm.

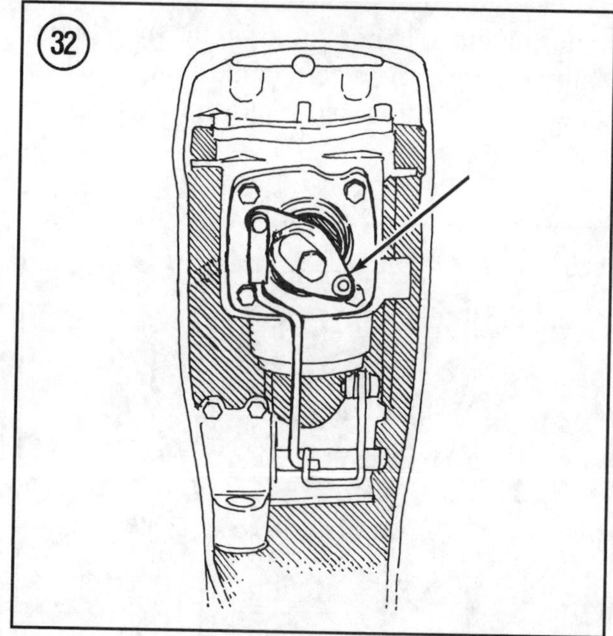

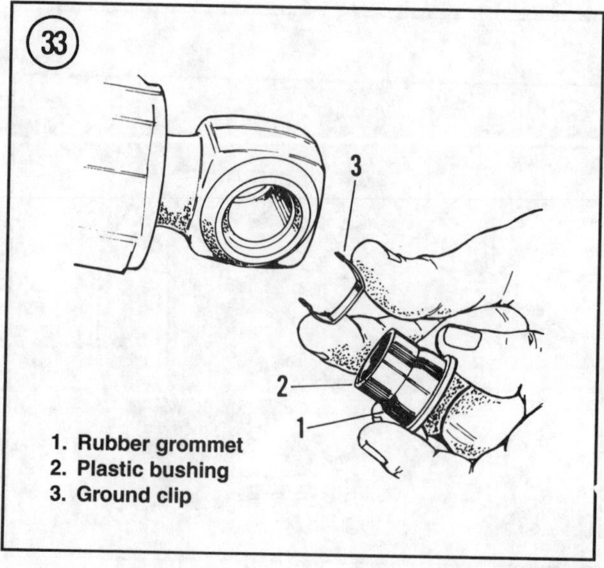

1. Rubber grommet
2. Plastic bushing
3. Ground clip

c. Secure the brass cube nut to the shift bell-crank with a washer and a new stainless steel cotter pin (B, **Figure 35**). Bend both prongs of the cotter pin for a secure attachment.

d. Install the jam nut (A, **Figure 35**) over the shift cable core wire and tighten it against the brass cube nut.

19. Install the upper gearcase rear cover and secure with 3 screws. Tighten the 3 screws securely.

20. Remove the gearcase lubricant level dipstick and verify that the lubricant level is on the machined flat area of the dipstick. Add gearcase lubricant as necessary through the dipstick hole. When the gearcase lubricant level has been verified, reinstall the dipstick and tighten to specification (**Table 5**).

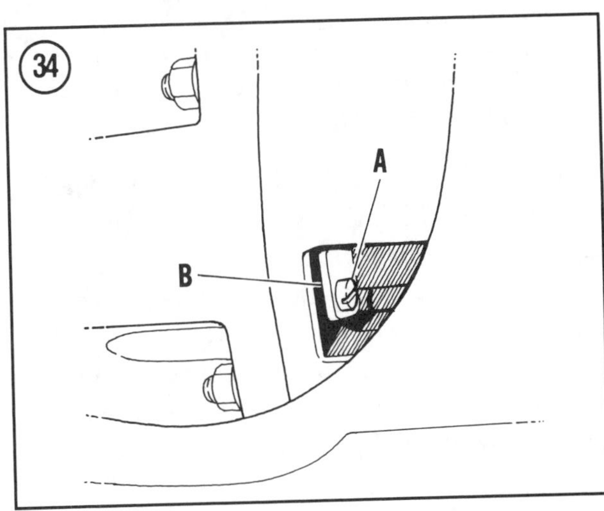

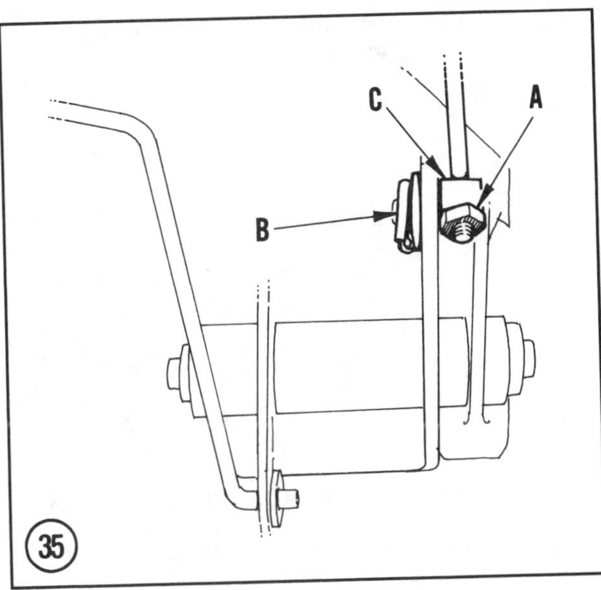

UNIVERSAL JOINT SERVICE

This procedure covers removal and replacement of the universal joints used on DP-C1/D1, DPX, SX and DP-S drive units. If the universal joint is being removed (separated) to service the clamp ring bearing carrier (DP-C1/D1 and DPX) or universal joint bearing carrier (SX and DP-S), only 2 caps need to be removed. These are the 2 caps on the yoke shaft of the clamp ring or universal joint bearing carriers.

On SX and DP-S models, the universal joints can be serviced without removing the yoke shaft from the pinion bearing carrier and without removing the pinion bearing carrier from the upper gearcase.

On DP-C1/D1 and DPX models, the yoke shaft must be removed from the clamp ring bearing carrier to service the universal joint closest the upper gearcase.

NOTE

*Owatonna Tool Company (**Table 11**) part No. T74-46535-C (or OEM-4635) used in conjunction with Volvo adaptor kit part No. 3850628-3 (or equivalent), is recommended for servicing the universal joints. Under no circumstances should the universal joints be beaten apart with a hammer. A pair of suitable sized sockets and a vise or arbor press may be used, if necessary.*

Disassembly

Refer to **Figure 36** or **Figure 37** for this procedure.

1. Remove the lock rings from all of the universal joint bearing caps that are to be removed. Drive the lock rings from the bearing caps with

an appropriate punch and small hammer. Do not strike the bearing caps directly. Discard the lock clips.

CAUTION
Once a lock ring has been removed, it must be discarded. Replacement lock rings are individually available.

2. Clamp the universal joint tool in an appropriate vise. Install the open adaptor from the Volvo adaptor kit into the open end of the universal joint tool.
3. Insert the universal joint and shaft assembly into the tool. Insert the end cap to be removed into the open adaptor from adaptor kit part No. 3850628-3. Tighten the pressing screw to press the universal joint out of its yoke. Do not press the universal joint cap that is against the pressing screw completely through its yoke. When the cap to be removed is sufficiently exposed, remove the shaft from the tool and pull the exposed bearing cap off of the universal joint with a suitable pair of large pliers.

NOTE
If the universal joint is to be reused, keep each bearing cap and loose needle bearings separate from the other caps and bearings. Mark each bearing cap for reassembly in its original location.

4. Rotate the universal joint 180° and reinstall the shaft into the tool with the remaining bearing cap placed into the open adaptor. Tighten the pressing screw against the exposed universal joint cross to press the remaining cap free of its yoke shaft.
5. Repeat Step 3 and Step 4 as necessary to remove all remaining parts to be serviced.
6. Clean and inspect all parts. Replace any parts that are worn, grooved, damaged or corroded.

Reassembly

The SX and DP-S drive unit's universal joints are equipped with grease fittings. The grease fittings should both face away from the upper gearcase and be positioned at a 45° angle to any 2 bearing caps. The DP-C1/D1 and DPX drive unit's universal joints are not normally equipped with grease fittings. If fittings are present, position the fittings as described for the SX and DP-S drive units. If fittings are not present, there is no specific installed position for the universal joint. Refer to **Figure 36** or **Figure 37** for this procedure.

NOTE
Be very careful that none of the needle rollers fall into the bottom bearing cup when pressing the cups into place. If a roller is in the bottom of the bearing cup, it will be difficult or impossible to install the retaining rings and the roller will probably be damaged.

1. Pack all crosses, loose needles and bearing caps with OMC EP/Wheel Bearing Grease or equivalent (**Table 6**).
2. Insert the cross into the appropriate yoke with the grease fittings (if equipped) positioned as described previously. Install 2 bearing caps (on opposing ends of the cross) and press in as far as possible with hand pressure. Slide the cross as-

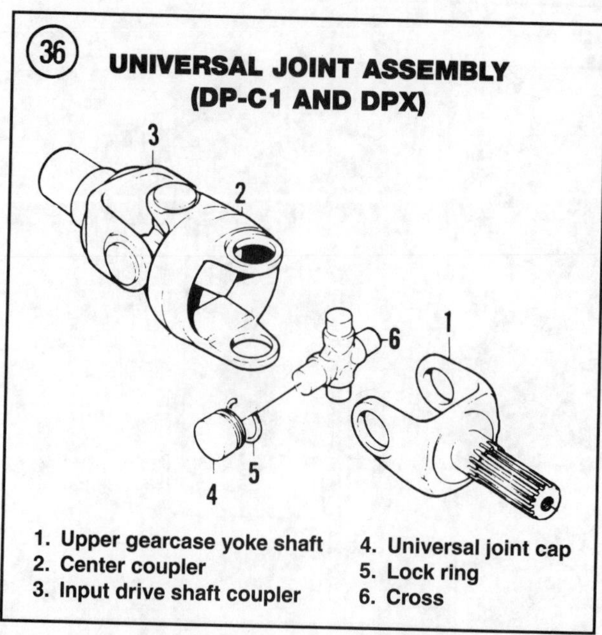

1. Upper gearcase yoke shaft
2. Center coupler
3. Input drive shaft coupler
4. Universal joint cap
5. Lock ring
6. Cross

sembly back and forth between the caps to make sure the caps are correctly aligned.

3. Position the universal joint assembly with one cap piloted in the open adapter and the other cap against the pressing screw. Tighten the pressing screw until lock ring groove is just visible at the yoke inner surface.

4. Install a new lock ring and seat it into the groove.

5. Rotate the universal joint assembly 180° in the tool and repeat Steps 3 and 4 for the remaining bearing cap.

6. Once both lock rings are installed, make sure that the cross assembly pivots freely in the bearing caps. If the cross assembly feels tight, tap the cross assembly sideways with a rubber or plastic mallet to seat the bearing caps out against the lock rings.

7. Repeat Steps 2-6 for all remaining caps and universal joints.

8. On models equipped with grease fittings, slowly apply OMC EP/Wheel bearing grease or equivalent (**Table 6**) to both universal joint grease fittings until fresh grease appears at all 4 bearing cap seals.

UPPER GEARCASE SERVICE (DP-C1/D1 AND DPX MODELS)

The DP-D1 and DPX upper gearcases use a molybdenum coated brass cone clutch, a steel shift shoe and a gear set that can only be used with the molybdenum coated brass cone clutch.

The DP-C1 upper gearcase uses a steel cone clutch and brass plated shift shoe and gear set that can only be used with the steel cone clutch.

Do not attempt to interchange components from one series of drive unit to another. Use only the factory specified replacement parts for service. Always refer to the model identification plate on the top of the upper gearcase when ordering replacement parts.

Upper Gearcase Removal/Installation

The upper gearcase can be removed from the intermediate housing without removing the intermediate housing from the transom plate. However, the drive unit lubricant is pumped from the lower gearcase to the upper gearcase during operation. Therefore, if a failure has occurred in

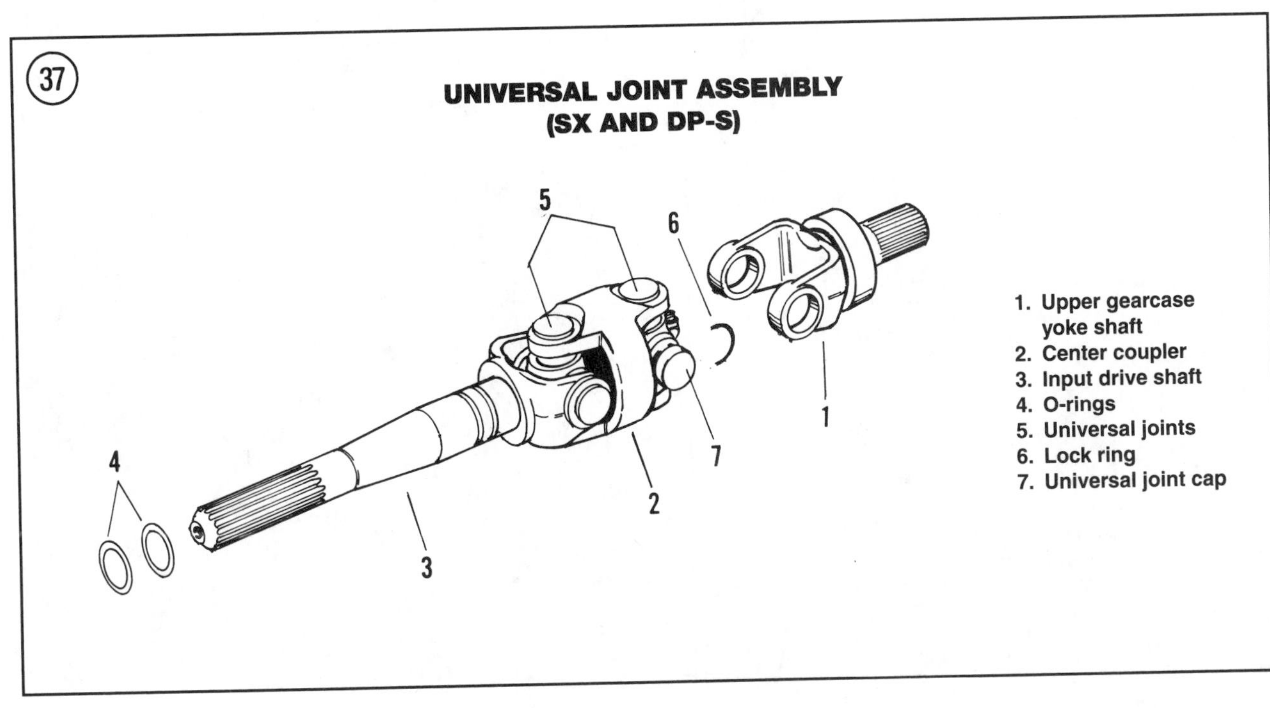

any part of the drive unit, the complete drive unit should be disassembled, cleaned and inspected.

The complete drive unit does not have to be removed for many service operations such as engine removal, universal joint and universal joint bellows service, intermediate shaft/bearing replacement or upper gear housing overhaul. These procedures can be performed by simply removing the upper gear housing from the intermediate housing.

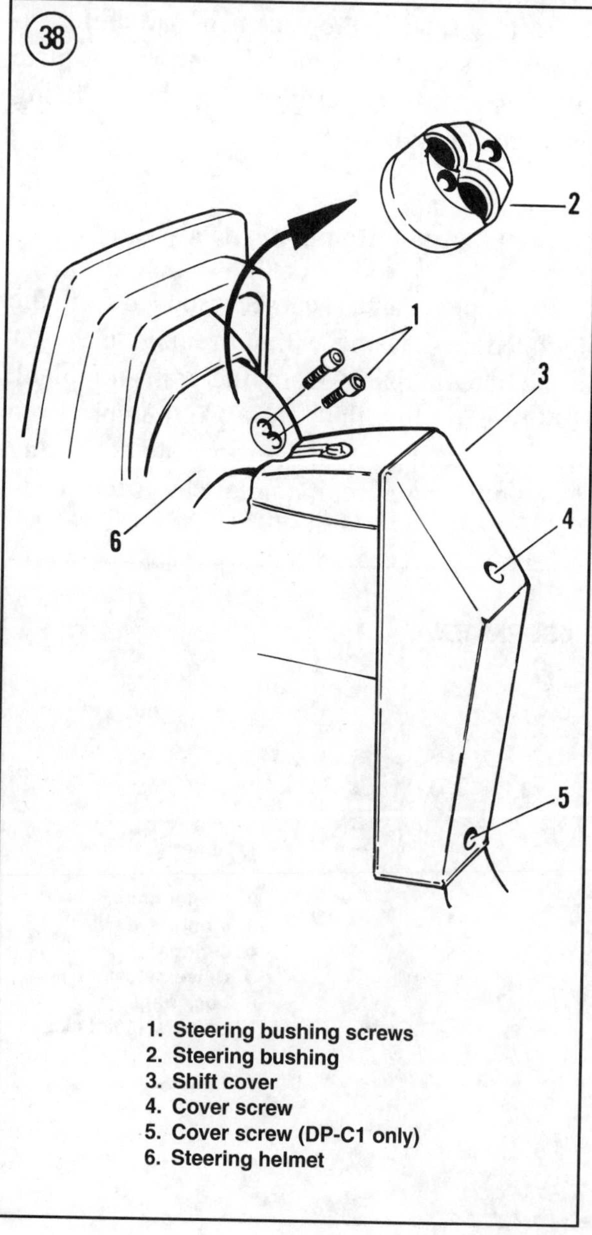

1. Steering bushing screws
2. Steering bushing
3. Shift cover
4. Cover screw
5. Cover screw (DP-C1 only)
6. Steering helmet

Removal with drive unit installed

1. Drain the drive unit lubricant and remove the shift cover as described in *Drive Unit Lubricant Change* previously in this chapter. Leave the dipstick removed.

2. *DP-C1/D1 models*—Remove the 2 screws (1, **Figure 38**) from the steering helmet on the front of the upper gearcase. Remove the steering helmet sleeve (2, **Figure 38**) by threading 2 screws

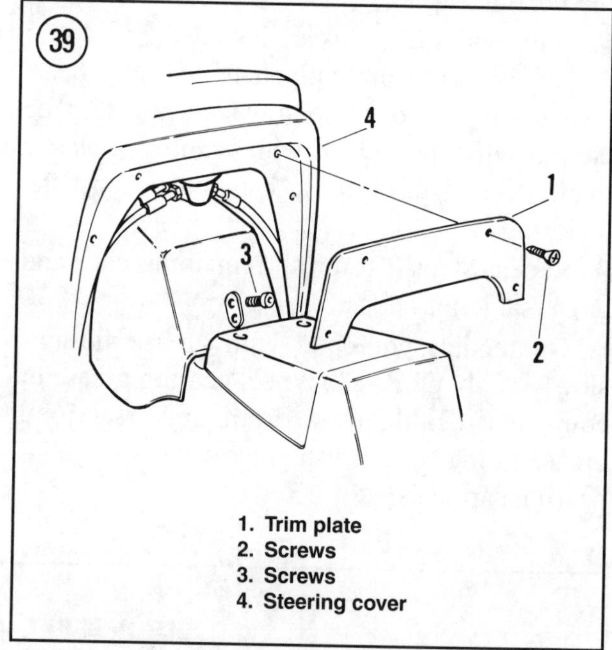

1. Trim plate
2. Screws
3. Screws
4. Steering cover

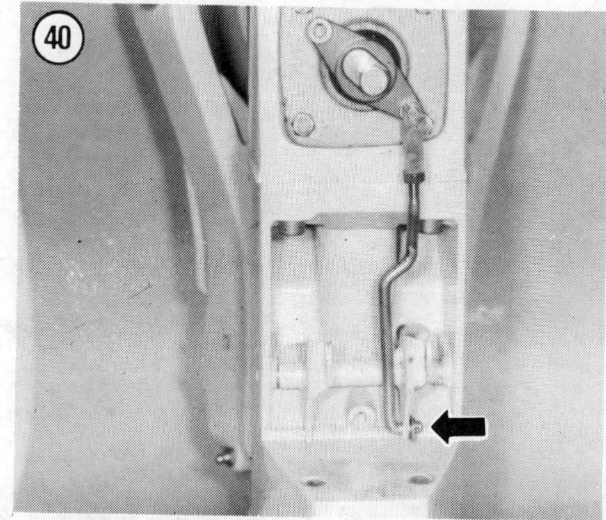

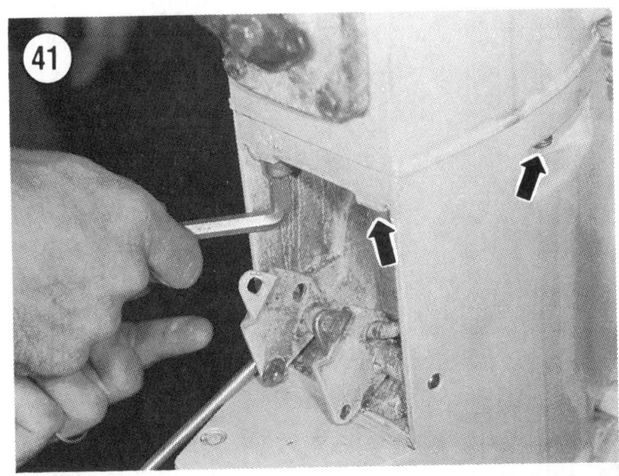

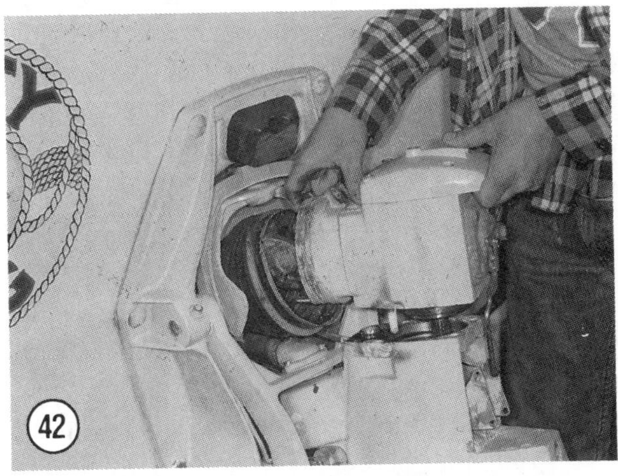

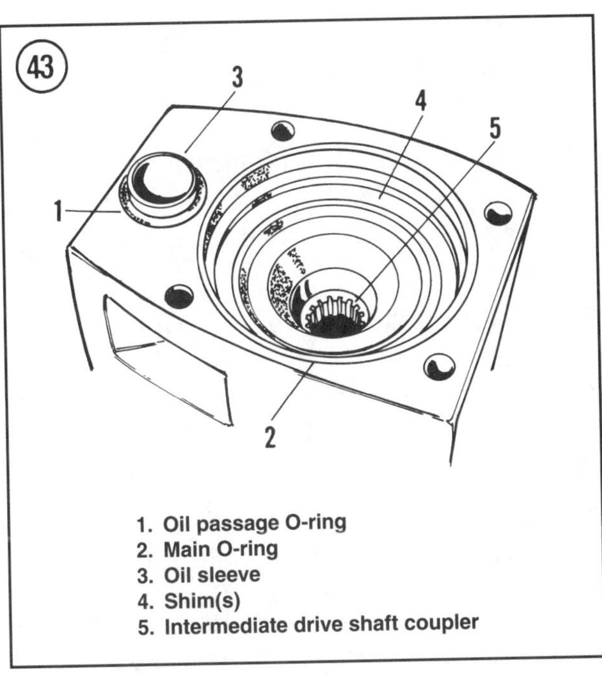

1. Oil passage O-ring
2. Main O-ring
3. Oil sleeve
4. Shim(s)
5. Intermediate drive shaft coupler

part No. 966868-2 (or equivalent) into the 2 threaded holes of the sleeve. Tighten each screw 1/2 turn at a time until the sleeve is pushed from the steering helmet. After the sleeve is removed, rotate the steering helmet (6, **Figure 38**) to the full tilt UP position.

3. *DPX models*—Remove the 4 screws (2, **Figure 39**) securing the trim plate to the top portion of the transom plate. Remove the trim plate (1, **Figure 39**).

4. *DPX models*—Remove the 2 screws (3, **Figure 39**) securing the steering cover to the front of the upper gear housing. Remove the steering cover (4, **Figure 39**).

5. Loosen or remove the clamp attaching the universal joint bellows to the upper gear housing.

6. Remove the universal joint bellows from the upper gearcase by gently prying them free with a suitable tool. Be careful not to puncture or rip the bellows if they are to be reused.

7. Remove the cotter pin and washer securing shift linkage rod to the intermediate housing shift bellcrank. Remove the shift linkage from the bellcrank. See **Figure 40**.

8. Remove the 2 socket head screws and washers from the rear and the 2 nuts from the sides of the intermediate housing securing the upper gearcase to the intermediate housing. See **Figure 41**.

9. Alternately tap the upper gear housing from side to side with a soft hammer to break the upper gearcase seal to the intermediate housing. Lift the upper gear housing from the intermediate housing (**Figure 42**, typical) and place it on a clean workbench or secure it in a suitable holding fixture.

10. Discard the oil passage and main O-rings (1 and 2, **Figure 43**) from the intermediate housing. Locate and remove the oil sleeve (3, **Figure 43**) from either the intermediate housing or the upper gearcase. Locate and remove the intermediate housing shim(s) (4, **Figure 43**) from either the upper gearcase lower bearing or intermediate housing bore.

11. Remove the intermediate drive shaft coupler (5, **Figure 43**) from the intermediate housing.

Installation with drive unit installed

Before installing the upper gearcase to the drive unit, make sure the sealing surfaces are thoroughly clean. Lubricate the universal joints as described in *Universal Joint and Gimbal Bearing Lubrication* located previously in this chapter.

1. Install the oil sleeve into the intermediate housing oil passage bore. Install a new O-ring around the sleeve and seat the O-ring in its groove. Install a new main O-ring in the uppermost groove in the intermediate housing and the predetermined or original shim(s) in the intermediate housing bore. See **Figure 43**.
2. Coat the mating surfaces of the gear housing and intermediate housing with Volvo White Sealing Compound or equivalent (**Table 6**).
3. Clean the input drive shaft internal splines thoroughly. Reach into the universal joint bellows and clean the primary drive shaft splines thoroughly. Liberally apply a molybdenum grease, such as OMC Moly Lube or equivalent (**Table 6**), to the input shaft internal splines and the primary drive shaft external splines.
4. Install the intermediate drive shaft coupler (5, **Figure 43**) into the intermediate housing and engage it to the lower gearcase drive shaft splines with the grooved end facing up.
5. Install the upper gearcase by first guiding the drive shaft and universal joints into the universal joint bellows and onto the primary drive shaft. Keep the rear of the upper gearcase tilted up and away from the intermediate housing. Rotate the universal joint shaft as necessary to index the splines.
6. Once the drive shaft coupler has engaged the primary drive shaft, lower the rear of the upper gearcase into the intermediate housing and engage the output shaft to the intermediate drive shaft coupler. Turn the propshaft as necessary to engage the intermediate shaft coupler splines.
7. Seat the gearcase to the intermediate housing. Coat the threads of the 2 rear screws with Volvo White Sealing Compound or equivalent (**Table 6**). Install the screws and washers hand-tight. Install the 2 locknuts on the sides of the upper gearcase hand-tight. Evenly tighten all 4 fasteners to specification (**Table 4**). See **Figure 41**.
8. Carefully work the universal joint bellows in place. Do not puncture or tear the bellows. Open the universal joint bellows clamp and install the clamp over the bellows with the clamp screw at the 6 O'clock position and the screw head facing starboard. Tighten the clamp securely using clamp tool (part No. 884573-7) or a suitable socket on a 1/4 in. drive swivel and ratchet.
9. *DP-C1/D1 models*—Grease the steering sleeve with Volvo Propeller Shaft Grease (**Table 6**). Lower the steering helmet and install the steering sleeve. Wipe the 2 steering sleeve retaining screw threads with Volvo Propeller Shaft Grease (**Table 6**). Align the steering sleeve screw holes with the upper gearcase holes and install the 2 retaining screws. Tighten the screws to specification (**Table 4**). See **Figure 38**.

10A. *DPX models*—Install the steering cover and secure it with 2 screws. Tighten the screws securely. See **Figure 39**.

10B. *DPX models*—Install the trim plate to the top portion of the transom plate and secure it with 4 screws. Tighten the screws securely. See **Figure 39**.

11. Reconnect the shift linkage to the shift bellcrank (**Figure 40**). Secure the shift linkage with a flat washer and a new stainless steel cotter pin. Bend both prongs of the cotter pin for secure attachment.
12. Pressure test the drive unit with pressure tester part No. 381052-3 as follows:

   a. Make sure the lubricant drain plug and fill plug are installed and tightened securely.

b. Connect the pressure tester to the dipstick hole. Pressurize the drive unit to 48 kPa (7 psi) for 3 minutes, minimum.

c. Rotate the input drive shaft, propshaft(s) and shift the gearcase into and out of gear during the test.

d. If any pressure drop is noted, spray soapy water on all seals and mating surfaces until the leak is found. Correct the leak and retest.

e. Do not proceed until the gearcase holds pressure for at least 3 minutes without any measurable leakage.

NOTE
Make sure the lubricant level is rechecked after the drive has sat for 5-10 minutes after the filling procedure. Running the drive unit with insufficient lubricant will cause drive unit damage.

13. Fill the drive unit with gear lubricant and reinstall the shift cover as described in *Drive Lubricant Change* previously in this chapter.

Removal with drive unit removed

1. Drain the drive unit lubricant and remove the shift cover (if not already removed) as described in *Drive Lubricant Change* previously in this chapter. Leave the dipstick removed.
2. Remove the cotter pin and washer securing shift linkage rod to the intermediate housing shift bellcrank. Remove the shift linkage from the bellcrank. See **Figure 40**.
3. Remove the 2 socket head screws and washers at the rear and the 2 nuts on the sides of the intermediate housing securing the upper gearcase to the intermediate housing. See **Figure 41**.
4. Alternately tap the upper gear housing from side to side with a soft hammer to break the upper gearcase seal to the intermediate housing. Lift the upper gear housing from the intermediate housing and place it on a clean workbench or secure it in a suitable holding fixture.
5. Discard the oil passage and main O-rings from the intermediate housing. Locate and remove the oil sleeve from either the intermediate housing or the upper gearcase. Locate and remove the intermediate housing shim(s) from either the upper gearcase lower bearing or intermediate housing bore. See **Figure 43**.
6. Remove the intermediate drive shaft coupler (5, **Figure 43**) from the intermediate housing.

Installation with drive unit removed

Before installing the upper gearcase to the drive unit, make sure the sealing surfaces are thoroughly clean. If necessary, lubricate the universal joints as described in *Universal Joint and Gimbal Bearing Lubrication* located previously in this chapter.

1. Install the oil sleeve into the intermediate housing oil passage bore. Install a new O-ring around the sleeve and seat the O-ring in its groove. See **Figure 43**.
2. Install a new main O-ring in the uppermost groove in the intermediate housing and the predetermined or original shim(s) in the intermediate housing bore. See **Figure 43**.
3. Coat the mating surfaces of the gear housing and intermediate housing with Volvo White Sealing Compound or equivalent (**Table 6**).
4. Clean the input drive shaft internal splines thoroughly. Reach into the universal joint bellows and clean the primary drive shaft splines thoroughly. Liberally apply a molybdenum grease, such as OMC Moly Lube or equivalent (**Table 6**), to the input shaft internal splines and the primary drive shaft external splines.
5. Install the intermediate drive shaft coupler (5, **Figure 43**) into the intermediate housing and engage it to the lower gearcase drive shaft splines with the grooved end facing up.
6. Install the upper gearcase by guiding the output shaft into the intermediate housing and engaging the output shaft to the intermediate drive

shaft coupler. Turn the propshaft as necessary to engage the intermediate shaft coupler splines.

7. Seat the gearcase to the intermediate housing. Coat the threads of the 2 rear screws with Volvo White Sealing Compound or equivalent (**Table 6**). Install the screws and washers hand-tight. Install the 2 locknuts on the sides of the upper gearcase hand-tight. Evenly tighten all 4 fasteners to specification (**Table 4**). See **Figure 41**.

8. Reconnect the shift linkage to the shift bellcrank (**Figure 40**). Secure the shift linkage with a flat washer and a new stainless steel cotter pin. Bend both prongs of the cotter pin for secure attachment.

9. Pressure test the drive unit with pressure tester part No. 381052-3 as follows:

a. Make sure the lubricant drain plug and fill plug are installed and tightened securely.

b. Connect the pressure tester to the dipstick hole. Pressurize the drive unit to 48 kPa (7 psi) for 3 minutes, minimum.

c. Rotate the input drive shaft, propshaft(s) and shift the gearcase into and out of gear during the test.

d. If any pressure drop is noted, spray soapy water on all seals and mating surfaces until the leak is found. Correct the leak and retest.

e. Do not proceed until the gearcase holds pressure for at least 3 minutes without any measurable leakage.

NOTE

Make sure the lubricant level is rechecked after the drive has sat for 5-10 minutes after the filling procedure. Running the drive unit with insufficient lubricant will cause drive unit damage.

10. Fill the drive unit with gear lubricant and reinstall the shift cover as described in *Drive Lubricant Change* previously in this chapter.

Disassembly

Figure 44 shows an exploded view of a typical DP-C1/D1 and DPX upper gear housing and

UPPER GEARCASE (DO-C1/D1 AND DPX)

1. Lubricant level dipstick and O-ring
2. Top cover
3. Top cover screw
4. Top cover screw and O-ring (hollow)
5. Plastic plug
6. Rear cover (DP-C1/D1 shown)
7. Retaining O-ring
8. Cover screw
9. Cover screw (DP-C1/D1 only)
10. Top cover shim(s)
11. Upper output shaft nut
12. Output gear main bearing
13. Upper output gear shim(s)
14. Double-stacked needle bearing
15. Top cover seal
16. Upper output gear and sleeve
17. Model identification plate
18. Oil fill plug and gasket
19. Output shaft
20. Cone clutch
21. Cone support spring
22. Cone support washer
23. C-clip
24. Lower output gear and sleeve
25. Retaining (thrust) washer
26. Split locking ring
27. Lower output gear shim(s)
28. Shift shoe stop bolt
29. Shim(s)
30. Eccentric piston
31. Ramp follower pin
32. Roll pin
33. Seal
34. Screw
35. Shift housing
36. O-ring
37. Shift shoe spring
38. Shift shoe
39. Gearcase housing
40. Yoke shaft retaining screw
41. Washer
42. Pinion gear
43. Tapered roller bearing (large)
44. Pretension (crush) sleeve
45. O-ring
46. Shim(s)
47. Clamp ring bearing carrier
48. Screw and washer
49. Tapered roller bearing (small)
50. Seal
51. Stud
52. Washer
53. O-ring
54. C-clip
55. Yoke shaft
56. Universal joint
57. Lock clip
58. Center coupler
59. Input drive shaft coupler
60. Bearing cap
61. Clamp
62. Universal joint bellows

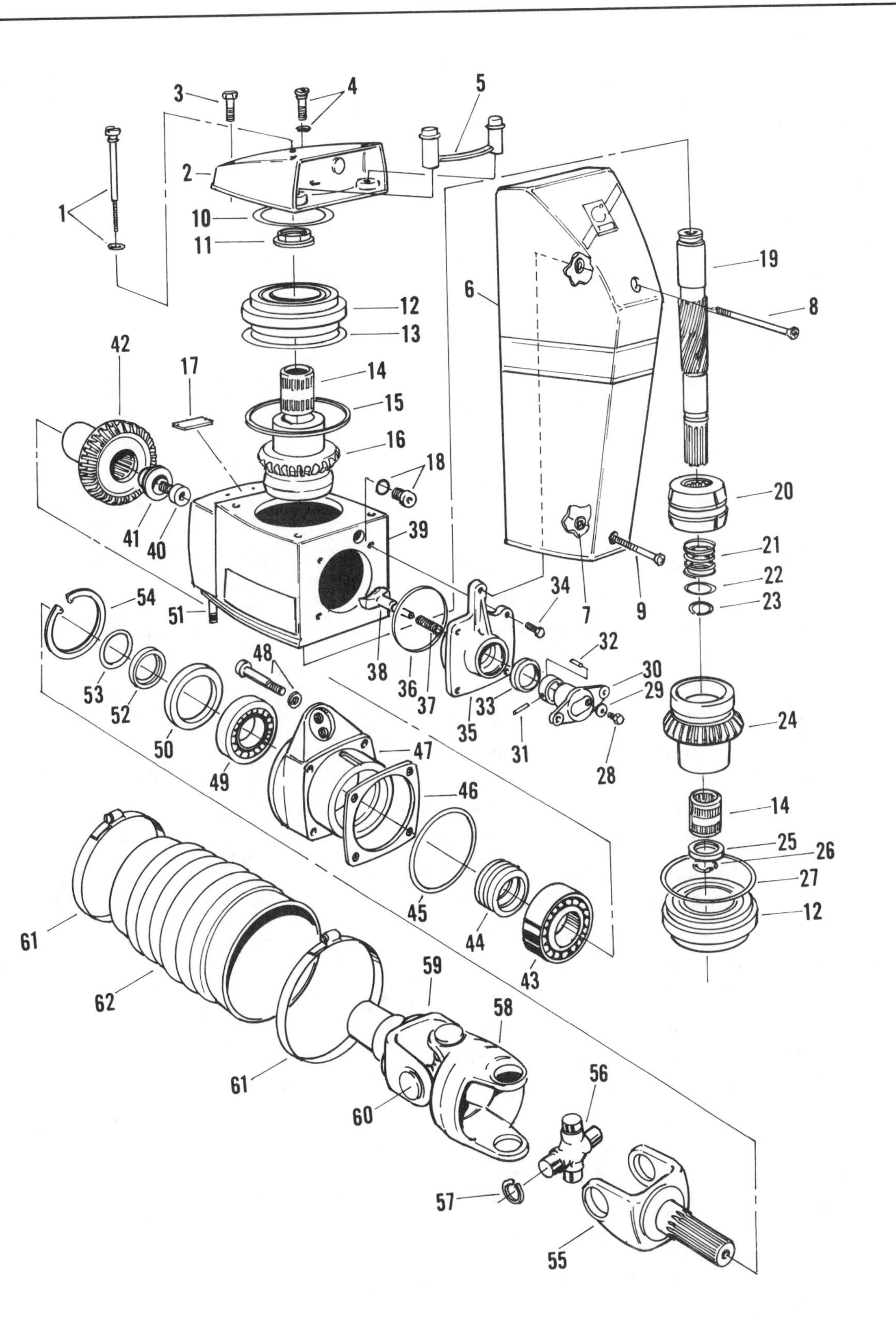
1
2
3
4
5
6
7
8
9
10
11
12
13
14
15
16
17
18
19
20
21
22
23
24
25
26
27
28
29
30
31
32
33
34
35
36
37
38
39
40
41
42
43
44
45
46
47
48
49
50
51
52
53
54
55
56
57
58
59
60
61
62

Figure 45 shows the related intermediate housing. Place the gearcase on a clean workbench or secure the splined support fixture (part No. 884830-1) in a suitable vise and set the upper gearcase output shaft into the fixture.

Record the measurement of all shims as they are removed. Shims can be reused if they are not damaged. Tag the shims by location for reassembly purposes. Do not lose or discard any shims.

All components that are to be reused must be installed in their original location and orientation. Mark components as necessary to ensure correct reinstallation.

NOTE
The shift shoe is spring-loaded and can fall free from the shift housing.

1. Remove the 4 screws (34, **Figure 44**) attaching the shift housing to the rear of the upper gear housing. Remove the shift housing and shift shoe assembly (28-38, **Figure 44**). Discard the housing O-ring.
2. Refer to *Shift Housing Service* in this chapter, if the shift housing seal or any shift housing components are to be serviced.
3. Remove the 4 socket head bolts securing the clamp ring bearing carrier and universal joint shaft assembly to the upper gear housing. See **Figure 46**. Remove the clamp ring bearing carrier and universal joint shaft assembly. A rubber or plastic mallet can be used to help break the bearing carrier free from the upper gearcase.
4. Discard the bearing carrier O-ring. Remove the shim(s). Measure and record the thickness of the shims for later reference. Tag the shim(s) for identification during reassembly.
5. Remove the 4 screws securing the top cover to the upper gearcase. Notice that the starboard, front screw (4, **Figure 44**) has an O-ring seal. Discard the O-ring.
6. Remove the top cover (2, **Figure 44**) from the gearcase. A rubber or plastic mallet can be used to break the top cover free. Discard the top cover seal. Remove the shim(s). Measure and record

INTERMEDIATE HOUSING (DP-C1/D1 AND DPX)

1. O-ring
2. Oil sleeve
3. O-ring
4. Lower output gear preload shim(s)
5. Screw
6. Shift cable clamp plate
7. Screw and washer
8. Elastic locknut
9. Intermediate housing
10. Rear steering pin (DPX only)
11. Steering bushings (DPX only)
12. Steering cotter pin (DPX only)
13. Steering washer (DPX only)
14. Trim/tilt clevis pin
15. Trim/tilt cotter pin
16. Front steering pin (DPX only)
17. Seal
18. Retainer
19. Bushing
20. Steering tube
21. Thrust washer
22. O-ring
23. Water outlet fitting
24. Screw
25. Clamps
26. Exhaust bellows
27. Pivot pin bushings
28. Suspension fork
29. Bellcrank shaft
30. Bellcrank
31. Brass cube nut
32. Shift link
33. Flat washer
34. Cotter pin
35. Flat washer
36. Cotter pin
37. Flat washer

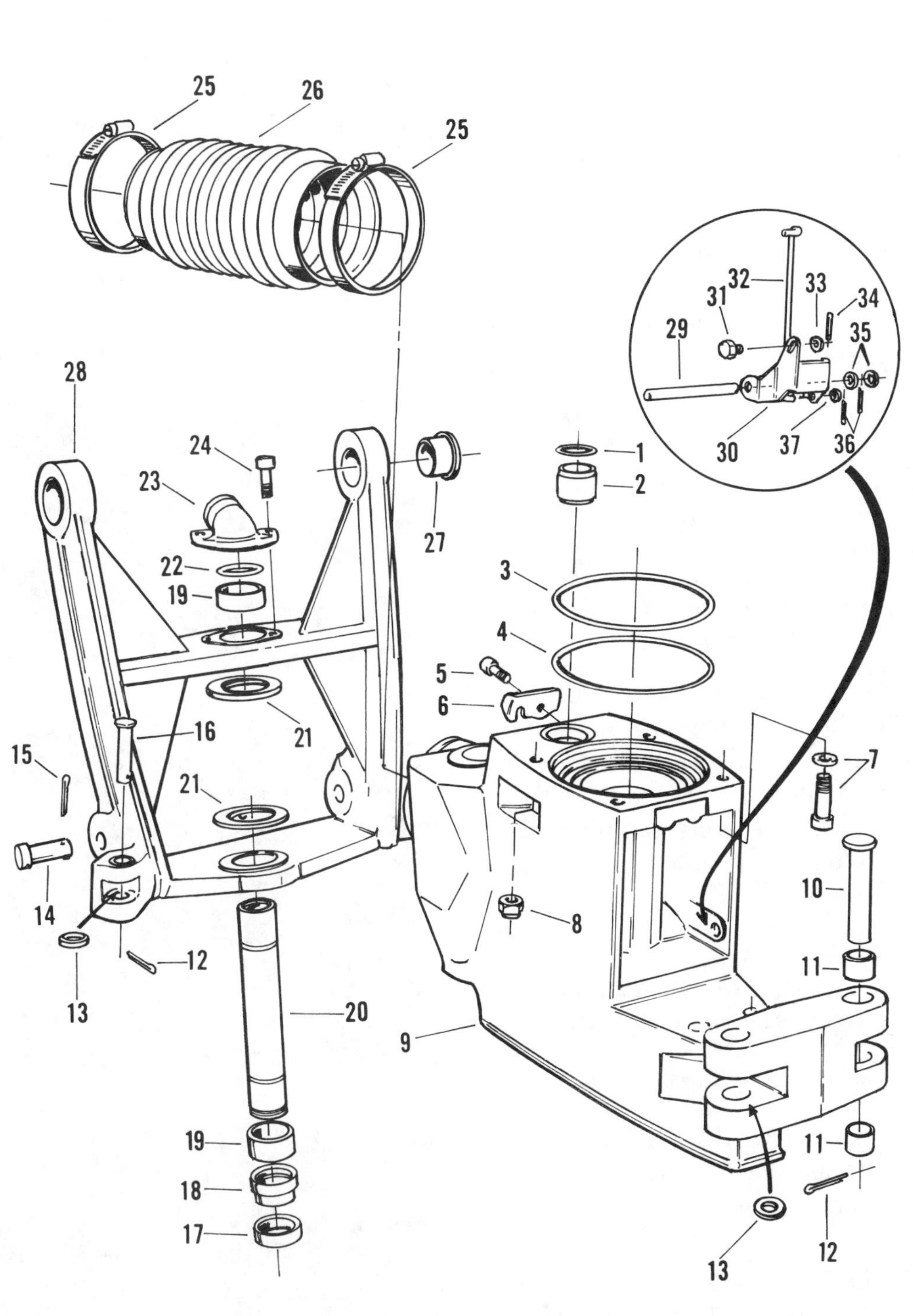
25
26
25
28
24
23
22
19
21
21
15
16
14
13
12
20
19
18
17
27
1
2
3
4
5
6
7
8
9
10
11
11
12
13
29
30
31
32
33
34
35
36
37

the thickness of the shims for later reference. Tag the shim(s) for identification during reassembly.

NOTE
The output shaft nut has left-hand threads and must be turned clockwise to remove. The nut is also a shim. The nut comes in 4 sizes (thickness) to control output shaft end play.

7. Secure the splined support fixture (part No. 884830-1) in a suitable vise and set the upper gearcase output shaft into the fixture. Remove the output shaft nut by turning it *clockwise* with a suitable socket and breaker bar. Record the number stamped into the nut for later reference. See **Figure 47**.

NOTE
If the double stack caged bearing removed in Step 8 is to be reused, mark the bearing as to its location and orientation for reassembly purposes.

8. Remove the upper output gear (**Figure 48**) and the needle bearing assembly (14, **Figure 44**). Remove the shim(s). Measure and record the thickness of the shims for later reference. Tag the shim(s) for identification during reassembly. Remove and mark the needle bearing in the gear hub.

NOTE
*The cone clutch should be stamped with the word **Top** on its upper surface. If the stamping is not visible, be sure to mark the cone for reassembly purposes.*

9. Remove the cone clutch (**Figure 49**) and support spring from the gearcase. Mark the cone clutch as to its orientation for reassembly purposes.

10. Lift the upper gearcase off of the lower output gear and shaft and place it on a clean workbench.

11. Grasp the output shaft and lower output gear assembly and lift it from the splined fixture. Set the shaft and gear assembly on a clean workbench. Remove the shim(s) from the gearcase or lower output gear. Measure and record the thickness of the shims for later reference. Tag the shim(s) for identification during reassembly.

12. Remove the 2 split lock rings and the retaining washer from the lower gear and output shaft assembly (**Figure 50**).

NOTE
If the double stack caged bearing removed in Step 13 is to be reused, mark

46

47

48

the bearing as to its location and orientation for reassembly purposes.

13. Remove the lower output gear and needle bearing assembly (14, **Figure 44**) from the output shaft. Mark the needle bearing as to its location and orientation.

NOTE
Do not remove the output gear main roller bearings unless they are to be replaced. The removal process will damage the bearings.

49

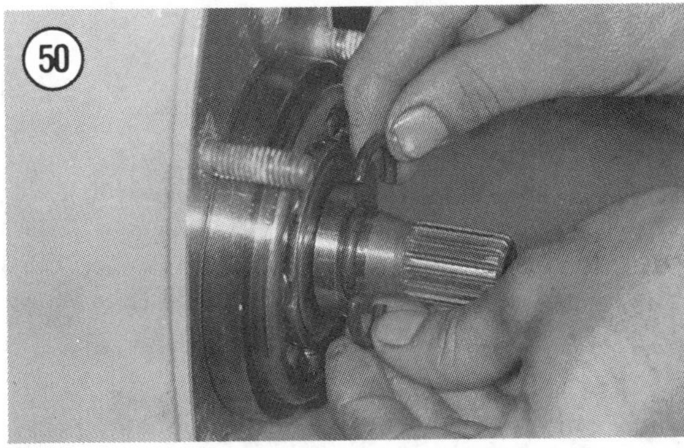

50

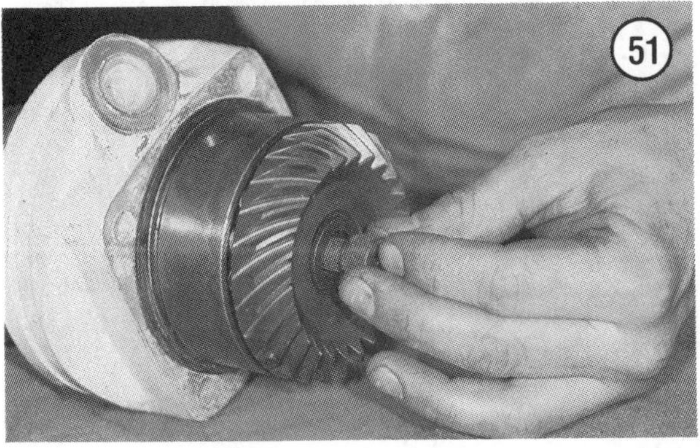

51

14. If the upper or lower output gear main bearings require replacement, proceed as follows:
   a. Place support sleeve part No. 884938-2 into an arbor or hydraulic press with the large end facing up. Place a shop towel into the support sleeve to cushion the gear.
   b. Place the output gear and bearing assembly into the sleeve with the gear facing down.
   c. Place sleeve part No. 884263-5 against the gear hub. Press the gear from the bearing.
   d. Repeat substeps a-c for the remaining output gear. Discard the bearings.

15. Inspect the washer and C-clip (25 and 26, **Figure 44**) on the output shaft. If replacement is necessary, remove the C-clip with a suitable pair of snap ring pliers and slide the washer from the shaft.

NOTE
In Step 16, some early models may be equipped with an internal hex head screw. Later models and all replacement screws are T50 internal Torx head. Socket part No. 885043-0 is available for servicing the T50 Torx head screw.

16. To service the clamp ring bearing carrier, remove the internal hex or Torx head screw and the washer from the center of the drive gear (**Figure 51**). The screw is sealed in place with Loctite and will be difficult to remove. It is necessary to support the assembly in a vise and block the universal joint shaft with a suitable rod. Discard the screw.

17. Remove the universal joints and yoke shaft from the clamp ring bearing carrier. Remove the shoulder washer and O-ring from the clamp ring bearing carrier or yoke shaft. See **Figure 52**.

NOTE
*If the universal joints require service or the yoke shaft requires replacement, refer to **Universal Joint Service** in this chapter.*

18. Remove the snap ring securing the seal with part No. 3850608-5 (or equivalent) snap ring pliers. The seal will be removed in a later operation.

19. To remove the drive gear, proceed as follows:

   a. Place support sleeve part No. 884938-2 in a press with its large end facing up. Place a shop towel in the bottom of the support sleeve.
   b. Set the clamp ring bearing carrier in the support sleeve with the gear facing down.
   c. Place sleeve part No. 884266-8 against the gear hub. Press the gear from the bearing.
   d. Remove and discard the pretension (crush) sleeve (44, **Figure 44**).

20. Turn the clamp ring bearing carrier over and press the roller bearing and seal out with sleeve part No. 884263-5. The bearing and seal can usually be pushed out with hand pressure. Discard the seal.

NOTE

Do not remove the roller bearing from the drive gear, or the bearing races from the clamp ring bearing carrier unless they are going to be replaced.

21. To remove the small bearing cup from the clamp ring bearing carrier, begin by installing bearing remover part No. 884933-3 onto the drive handle part No. 9991801-3. Place the clamp ring bearing carrier in a press with the large diameter facing down. Insert the bearing remover behind the small bearing cup and press the cup from the bearing carrier. Discard the bearing race and the roller assembly removed previously.

22. To remove the large bearing cup, place the support sleeve part No. 884938-2 into a press with its large end facing up. Set the bearing carrier into the support sleeve with its large end facing up. Insert the bearing remover behind the large bearing cup and press the cup from the bearing carrier. Discard the bearing cup.

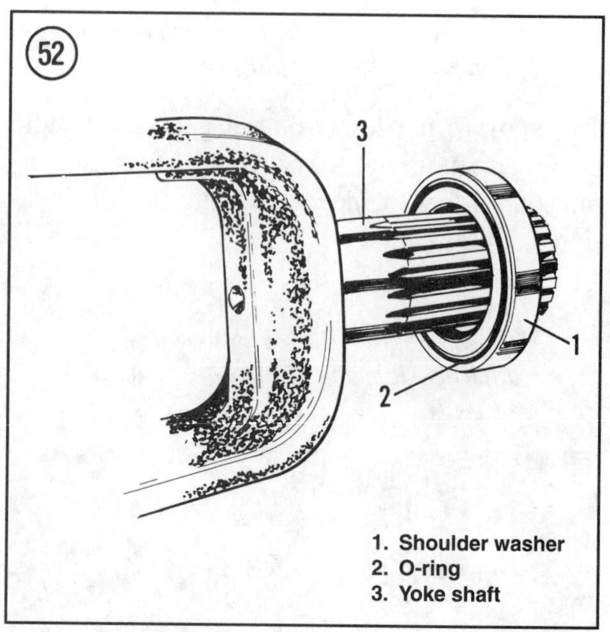

1. Shoulder washer
2. O-ring
3. Yoke shaft

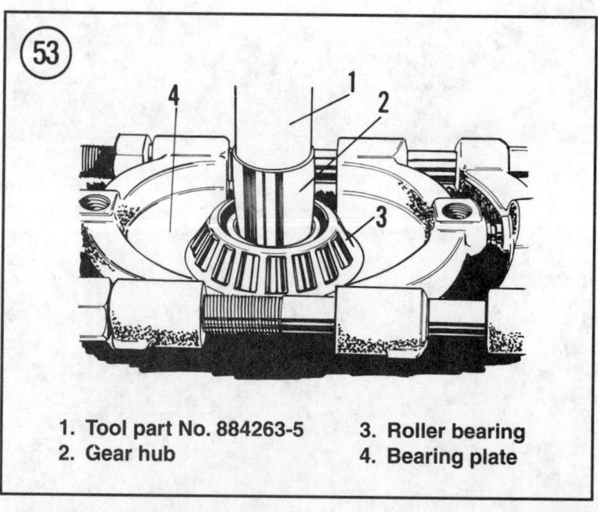

1. Tool part No. 884263-5
2. Gear hub
3. Roller bearing
4. Bearing plate

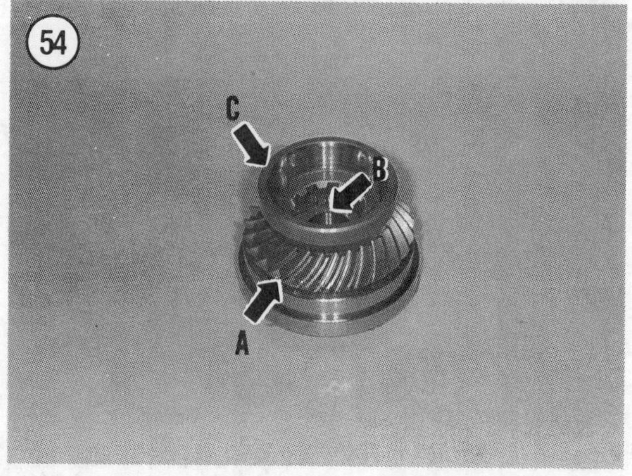

23. To remove the roller bearing from the drive gear, attach a knife-edge bearing plate behind the roller bearing. Press the gear from the bearing with sleeve part No. 884263-5. Discard the roller bearing. See **Figure 53**.

24. Clean and inspect all components as described in the next section.

Cleaning and Inspection

1. Wash all components in clean solvent and blow dry with compressed air.

2. Apply a light coat of oil to all of the cleaned components to prevent rusting.

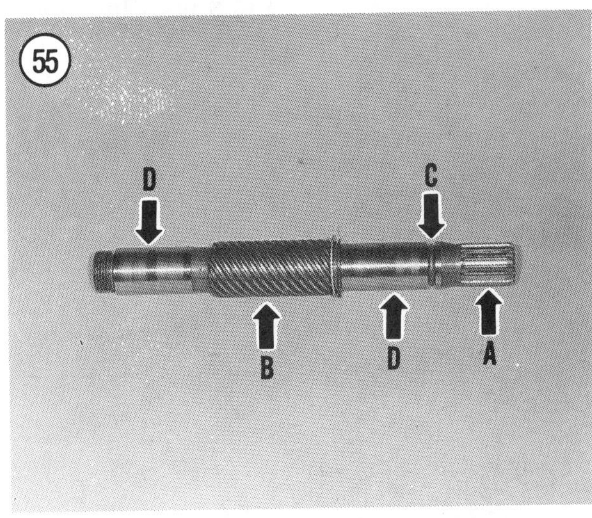

3. Inspect the gears. Check all gear teeth (A, **Figure 54**) and the internal bearing surfaces (B, **Figure 54**) for excessive wear, chips, cracks, nicks or other damage. Inspect the coned sleeve (C, **Figure 54**) of each output gear for scoring, glazing or metal transfer. The sleeve surface may be lightly dressed with emery cloth to remove superficial defects. If one gear is damaged and requires replacement, replace all 3 as an assembly.

CAUTION

One tapered roller bearing consists of the caged tapered roller bearings and cone-shaped inner race, and a cup-shaped outer race. The bearing must be replaced as a set and parts from one bearing must never be mixed with parts from another.

4. Check all of the bearings and bearing races for excessive or uneven wear, scoring, roughness, heat discoloration and binding. Replace any bearings (and corresponding races) as necessary.

5. Check the splines and threads of the input drive shaft coupler and yoke shaft for excessive wear, burring or distortion. Check the seal surfaces for grooving. Replace the shaft(s) if any defects are noticed.

6. Check the output shaft splines (A and B, **Figure 55**) for excessive wear, burring or distortion. Pay particular attention to the spiral splines at the center of the shaft. Inspect the split lock ring groove (C, **Figure 55**) for wear. Inspect the bearing surfaces (D, **Figure 55**) for wear, scoring and indications of overheating. Replace the shaft if any damage is noticed.

7. Inspect the cone clutch (**Figure 56**) for internal spline damage. Check the outer diameter for excessive wear, heat discoloration or damage on the cone-to-output sleeve mating surfaces. Inspect the shift shoe groove. Replace the cone clutch if there is any question as to its condition.

8. Check the cone clutch support spring (21, **Figure 44**) for distortion or loss of tension. Replace as required.
9. Inspect all shims and replace any that are damaged. If shimming adjustment is not required, damaged shims can be replaced with new shims of the same thickness.
10. Check the double stack, caged needle bearing assemblies (14, **Figure 44**) for roughness, heat discoloration, binding or missing needles. Replace each bearing assembly as required.

Assembly

For maximum durability and quiet running, all of the gears must be properly located in the gearcase through shimming procedures. When the gears are properly located, the correct backlash and gear contact pattern will be observed.

Additionally, the tapered bearings in the clamp ring bearing carrier must be properly tensioned or *preloaded*. Preload refers to the tension applied to hold a tapered roller bearing in its cup. Insufficient preload will allow the bearing to move in relation to the bearing cup. Any movement of the bearing from its cup will result in premature bearing and gear failure. Excessive preload will cause the bearings to overheat and fail.

Refer to **Figure 44** for an exploded view of the upper gearcase components and **Figure 45** for an exploded view of the associated intermediate housing components. During assembly procedures, lubricate all components with Volvo DuraPlus GL5 Synthetic Gear Lube (**Table 6**). Do not make any *dry* assemblies.

1. If the clamp ring bearing carrier bearing cups were removed, proceed as follows:
   a. Begin the installation of new bearings and cups by placing the clamp ring bearing carrier in a press with its large end facing down.
   b. Lubricate the large bearing cup and place it into the bearing carrier with its tapered bearing face facing up.
   c. Press the bearing cup into the bearing carrier with the small end of bearing installer part No. 884932-5. Press until the cup is seated in the bearing carrier.
   d. To install the small bearing cup, place the bearing carrier in a press with its small end facing down.
   e. Lubricate the small bearing cup and place it into the bearing carrier with its tapered bearing face facing up.
   f. Press the bearing cup into the bearing carrier with the large end of bearing installer part No. 884932-5. Press until the cup is seated in the bearing carrier.

NOTE
Protect the tips of the drive gear teeth from damage when pressing the tapered roller bearing onto the gear in Step 2.

2. If the bearing was removed from the drive gear, proceed as follows:

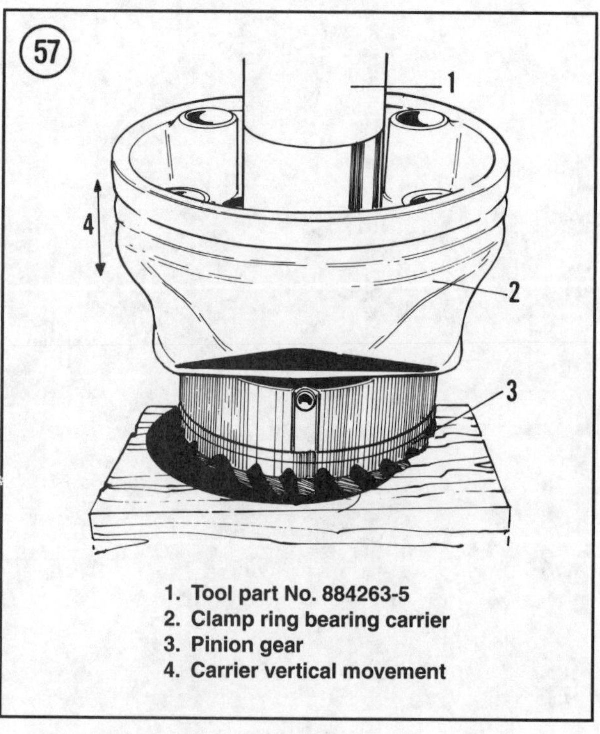

1. Tool part No. 884263-5
2. Clamp ring bearing carrier
3. Pinion gear
4. Carrier vertical movement

a. Begin installation of a new bearing by placing the drive gear in a press with its gear teeth facing down. Protect the gear teeth with a piece of wood, plastic or aluminum. Lubricate the large roller bearing and gear hub.
b. Place the roller bearing onto the gear with its rollers facing up.
c. Press the bearing fully onto the gear with sleeve part No. 884263-5. Make sure the bearing is seated against the gear flange.

CAUTION
A new pretension (crush) sleeve must be installed each time the clamp ring bearing carrier is disassembled. Failure to install a new pretension sleeve will result in premature bearing and gear failure.

3. Place a new pretension (crush) sleeve over the drive gear hub and against the large roller bearing.
4. Install the clamp ring bearing carrier (with the large end up) over the gear and seat it on the large bearing.
5. Lubricate the small bearing and set it into the bearing carrier and on top of the gear hub with its rollers facing down.

CAUTION
Do not press the bearing too far in Step 6. If the pretension sleeve is over-crushed, the bearing carrier must be disassembled and a new pretension sleeve installed.

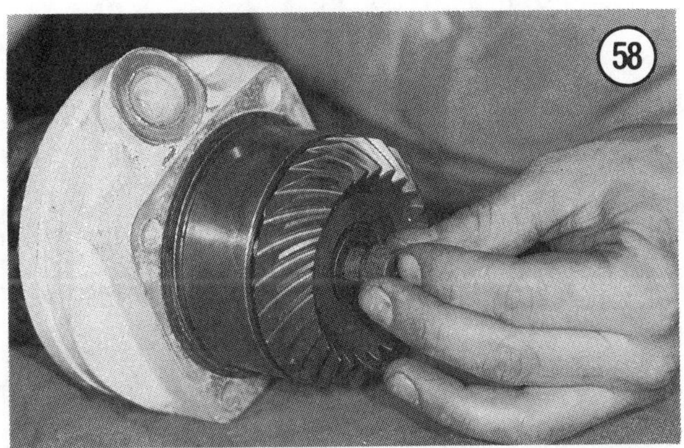

6. Protect the gear teeth with a piece of wood, plastic or aluminum. Press the small bearing onto the gear hub with sleeve part No. 884263-5 until there is almost no play (approximately 1 mm [0.040 in.]) between the bearing carrier and the gear (and bearings). Wiggle the bearing carrier up and down while pressing, to monitor the small bearing's progress. See **Figure 57**.
7. Place support sleeve part No. 884938-2 into a press with the large end facing up. Set the bearing carrier into the support sleeve with its large end facing up. Coat the outer diameter of a new universal joint shaft oil seal with Volvo White Sealing Compound or equivalent (**Table 6**). Press the seal into the bearing carrier with installer 884932-5, until the seal is seated on the bearing carrier shoulder.
8. Secure the seal by installing the snap ring with snap ring pliers part No. 3850608-5 (or equivalent). Make sure the snap ring is fully expanded into its groove. Coat the seal lips with OMC Triple Guard Grease or equivalent (**Table 6**).
9. Coat a new shoulder washer O-ring with OMC Triple Guard Grease or equivalent (**Table 6**) and place it in the shoulder washer groove. Install the shoulder washer onto the yoke shaft with the O-ring facing the yoke. See **Figure 52**.
10. Slide the clamp ring bearing carrier over the yoke shaft (and universal joint assembly). Turn the gear and yoke shaft as necessary to align the splines. Seat the bearing carrier on the yoke shaft.

12

NOTE
In Step 11, all replacement screws are T50 internal Torx head. Socket part No. 885043-0 is available for servicing the T50 Torx head screw.

11. Install the washer into the gear face. Lightly coat the threads of a new Torx head screw with Loctite 271 threadlocking adhesive (**Table 6**). Install the screw into the yoke shaft and hand-tighten. See **Figure 58**.

12. Clamp a 12.7 mm (1/2 in.) diameter or larger metal rod in a vise. Place the yoke shaft and universal joint assembly over the rod so the Torx head screw can be tightened without the yoke shaft rotating, yet the clamp ring bearing carrier can be rotated freely.

NOTE
The next step sets the preload on the tapered roller bearings. Do not over-tighten the Torx head screw or the pretension sleeve will be damaged and will have to be replaced. The preload is checked by wrapping a string around the bearing carrier and pulling on it with a spring scale (part No. 9985494-5). The scale should be pulled slowly and smoothly. The bearings must be well lubricated for this adjustment.

13. Tighten the screw slowly, while rotating the bearing carrier. As the screw is tightened the bearings will be forced closer together as they compress the pretension sleeve. When the bearings begin to preload, a marked increase in the effort required to rotate the carrier will be noticed. Stop tightening the screw when the increase in effort is noted. See **Figure 59**.

CAUTION
*It is typical for a person to tighten the screw and see no immediate results. The person will then tighten the screw too far and damage the pretension sleeve. Do not become frustrated and tighten the screw in large increments. Be patient and tighten the screw a little at a time, checking the preload each time. With experience, the preload can be set very close by **feel** and will only require 1 or 2 spring scale checks to achieve the specified setting.*

14. Check the bearing preload by tying a string to a bearing carrier screw hole. Wrap the string several turns around the bearing carrier O-ring groove. Fasten the loose end of the string to spring scale part No. 9985494-5. Pull the spring scale slowly and smoothly and measure the effort required to rotate the carrier. Compare the spring scale reading to specification (**Table 2**). Carefully and slowly tighten the screw as necessary to obtain the specified preload (**Table 2**). See **Figure 60**.

CAUTION
*If the rolling torque is set too high, the bearing carrier must be disassembled and a new pretension (crush) sleeve installed. Do not continue until the specified bearing preload (**Table 2**) is obtained.*

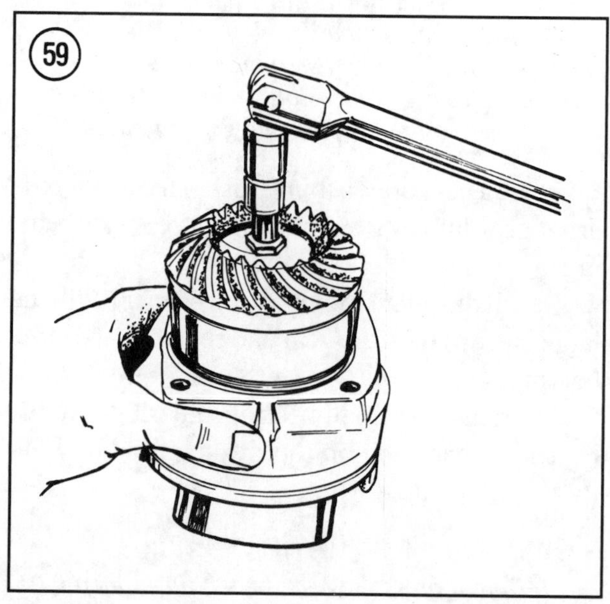

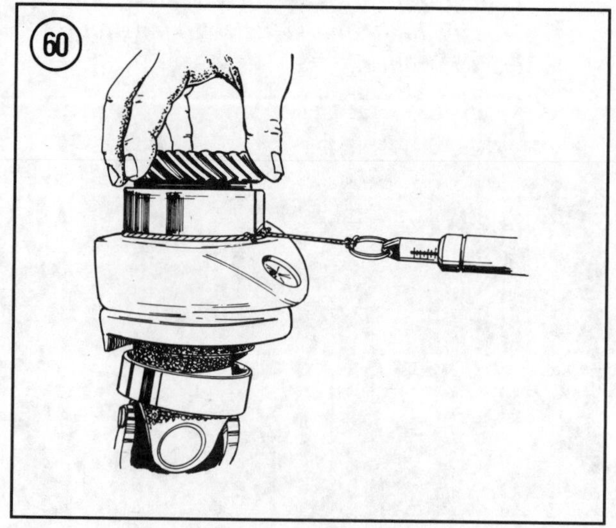

15. If the main bearings were removed from the output gears, proceed as follows:

a. Begin installation of new bearings by placing the output gear in a press with the gear sleeve facing down. Protect the gear sleeve with a piece of wood, plastic or aluminum.

b. Lubricate a new main roller bearing and the gear hub. Place the bearing on the gear hub with its numbered side facing up.

c. Press the bearing fully onto the gear with sleeve part No. 884265-0. Make sure the bearing seats against the gear flange.

d. Repeat substeps a-c for the remaining output gear and bearing.

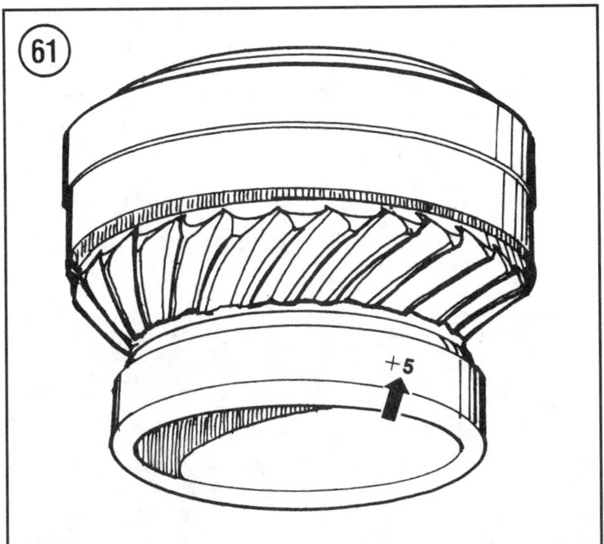

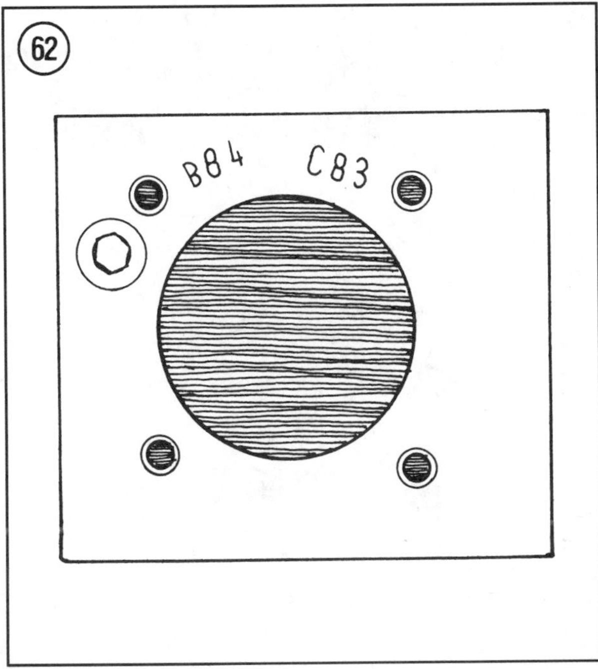

Lower and upper output gear shimming

To determine the correct amount of shims to properly position the lower and upper output gears, keep in mind that the numbers stamped on the gear sleeve and gear housing are correction numbers in hundredths of a millimeter. Both the lower and upper output gears need to be positioned to a fixed dimension of 62.05 mm (2.443 in.) as established by Volvo Penta during design and manufacturing of the product. Housing numbers B and C must have a fixed dimension of 61.00 mm (2.40 in) added to them before the calculations can be made.

Since the gears and housing are stamped using Metric measurements, it is recommended that all calculations be performed in millimeters. Any conversions from Metric to U.S. standard should only be attempted on the final calculated result.

To determine the shims required for output gear location, proceed as follows:

1. Find the correction number etched or stamped on the lower output gear (**Figure 61**, typical). Record this figure as hundredths of a millimeter. For example, if +5 is etched on the gear, write it as +0.05 mm. If -5 is etched on the gear, write it as -0.05 mm.

2. Add or subtract (as indicated by the + or -) the etched number on the gear to the fixed dimension of 62.05 mm. For example, the gear shown in **Figure 61** is 62.05 mm + 0.05 mm or 62.10 mm. Write this number down.

3. Find the dimensions stamped on the housing (**Figure 62**, typical). The number indicated by C is for the lower output gear and the number indicated by B is for the upper output gear. In the example shown in **Figure 62**, the number for the

lower output gear is 83 which is actually 0.83 mm.

4. Add the C number as hundredths of a millimeter to the fixed manufacturing dimension of 61.00 mm (2.40 in.). For example, the housing shown in **Figure 62** is 61.00 mm plus 0.83 mm for a total dimension of 61.83 mm. Record the result.

5. Subtract the dimension of the housing determined in Step 4 from the dimension for the gear determined in Step 2. The result is the thickness of the shims necessary for correct gear position. For example, if the calculation in Step 2 is 62.10 mm and the calculation in Step 4 is 61.83 mm, then we would subtract 61.83 mm from 62.10 mm and the result would be 0.27 mm (62.10 mm —61.83 mm = 0.27 mm). We would install 0.27 mm (0.011 in.) shims between the lower output gear and the gear housing in this example.

6. Repeat this procedure for the upper output gear, using the B dimension on the gear housing and the etched correction number on the upper output gear.

Gear lash verification

Refer to **Figure 44** and assemble the vertical components of the gearcase for the purpose of checking the gear backlash.

1. Install the vertical shaft and double-stacked needle bearing in the lower output gear. Install the split rings and collar on the shaft. Place the calculated amount of shims on top of the bearing (between the bearing and the upper gearcase) as shown in **Figure 63**.

2. Insert the assembled shaft and gear into the upper gear housing.

3. Install the upper output gear with the calculated amount of shims into the bore at the top of the gear housing. Install the double-stacked needle bearing into the upper output gear.

4. Thread the output shaft nut onto the vertical shaft and tighten to the torque listed in **Table 4**. After torquing, make sure the shaft has end play and is not binding the gears toward each other. If so, install a thinner nut and recheck for the presence of end play.

5. Set the top cover onto the gearcase *without* the seal and *with* the original shim(s). While pressing down on the top cover with firm hand pressure, measure the clearance between the top cover and gearcase with a feeler gauge (**Figure 64**). The clearance must be 0.05-0.1 mm (0.002-0.004 in.). Add or subtract shims under the top cover to achieve the specified clearance.

6. Install and evenly tighten the top cover screws to specifications (**Table 4**). Do not install the O-ring under the front, starboard bolt or the top cover seal at this time.

7. Install the clamp ring bearing carrier *without* the O-ring and *with* the original shim(s) *or* an

63

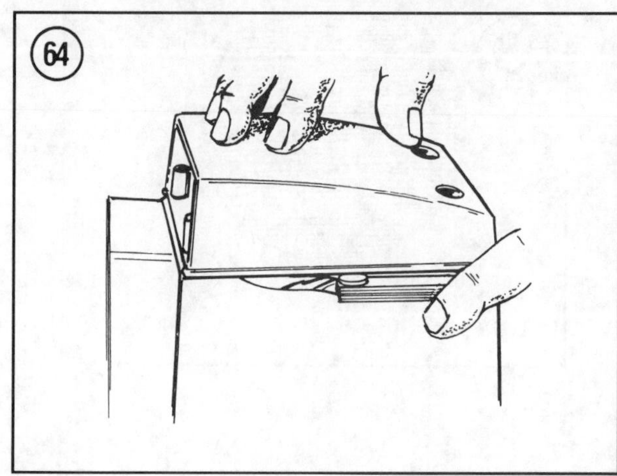
64

initial amount of 0.04 mm (0.016 in.) shims (**Figure 65**). Lubricate the bearing carrier to ease installation and make sure the shim(s) are correctly aligned with the bolt holes. Install and evenly tighten the 4 carrier screws to specifications (**Table 4**).

NOTE
*Gear lash and gear pattern cannot be checked unless the lower output gear is held firmly into the upper gearcase. Plate and shim ring part No. 885152-9 simply take the place of the intermediate housing and shims. If the plate is not available, some sort of fixture must be fabricated to hold the lower output bearing and gear firmly into the upper gearcase. As an alternative, the upper gearcase can be temporarily mounted to the intermediate housing (after performing the **Upper Gearcase to Intermediate Housing Shim Selection**).*

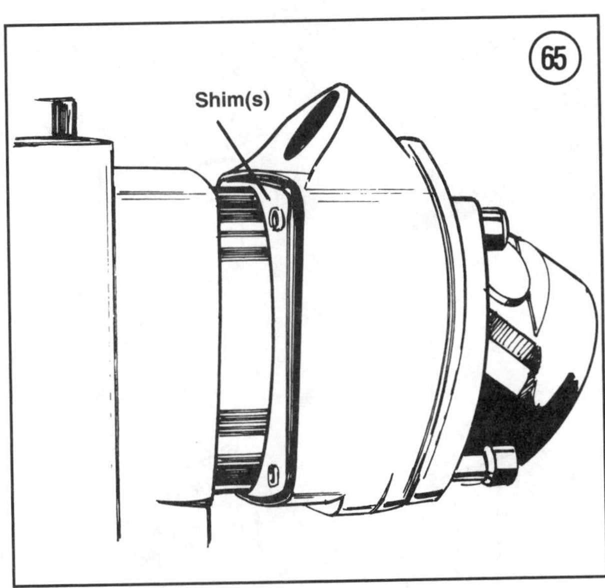

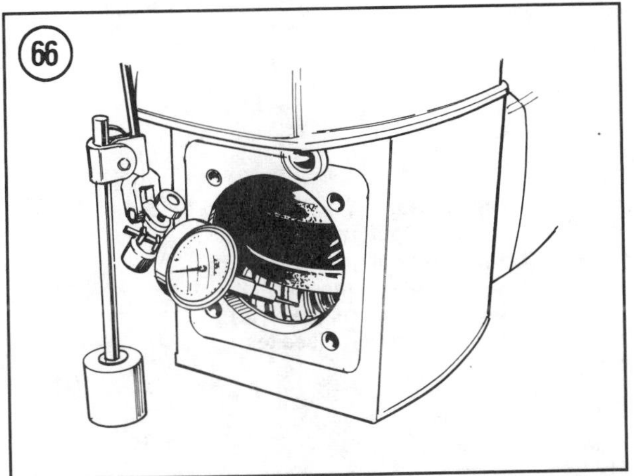

8. Clamp the plate (from kit part No. 885152-9) in a vise and set the shim ring (from kit part No. 885152-9) into the plate's recess. Install the gear housing onto the plate and shim ring. Secure the gearcase to the plate with 2 nuts and 2 screws (and washers). Tighten the fasteners to specifications (**Table 4**).

NOTE
Gear lash is a measurement of the clearance between a drive gear tooth and the output gear tooth. The drive gear must not move during this procedure and the gear teeth must be clean and free of excessive oil, lint, dirt or debris. The gears should make a distinct clicking sound as the output gear is rotated back and forth against the drive gear.

9A. Mount a dial indicator (such as OTC model OEM4635, [**Table 11**]) capable of reading lateral movement to the tool plate. Place the ball tip of the dial indicator arm on the horizontal and vertical midpoint of the lower output gear tooth. Make sure the face of the dial indicator is vertical and that the indicator's arm is pointing directly into the imaginary center of the output shaft. See **Figure 66**. Zero the indicator and rock the output gear lightly back and forth to read the backlash. Record the reading. Lift the dial indicator from the gear tooth, turn the gear 1/2 turn, reposition the indicator and recheck the backlash. Record the reading.

9B. Reposition the indicator and repeat Step 9A for the upper output gear. Record the readings. Remove the dial indicator when finished.

NOTE
If the gear lash requires correction, change approximately 0.03 mm (0.001

in.) of shims for every 0.03 mm (0.001 in.) of correction desired. Move the appropriate gear toward the other gear(s) to decrease gear lash and move the appropriate gear away from the other gear(s) to increase gear lash.

10. Compare the measured gear lash of both gears with the specifications listed in **Table 2**.
    a. If the gear lash of both gears is excessive, reduce the thickness of shims between the clamp ring bearing carrier and the gearcase. Repeat Step 9A and 9B.
    b. If the gear lash of both gears is insufficient, increase the thickness of shims between the clamp ring bearing carrier and the gearcase. Repeat Step 9A and 9B.
    c. If the gear lash on one output gear is correct and the other output gear is incorrect, recheck the calculations used to determine the incorrect output gear's shim(s). If the calculations are correct, add or subtract shims from the calculated shims as necessary to bring the incorrect output gear into the specified backlash range (**Table 2**). Repeat Step 9A and 9B.

Gear pattern verification

Once gear lash has been verified, check the gear contact pattern as follows:

1. Coat 3 teeth of both output gears with a thin coat of GM gear marking compound available from any General Motors automotive dealership.
2. Wedge a wooden hammer handle against the gear sleeves and rotate the drive gear by turning the universal joint yoke counter-clockwise (as viewed from the rear of the drive) several revolutions to produce a tooth pattern on the driven gears. The gears must be loaded to produce a pattern.
3. Withdraw the hammer handle and observe the pattern on the teeth of both output gears through the shift housing bore.

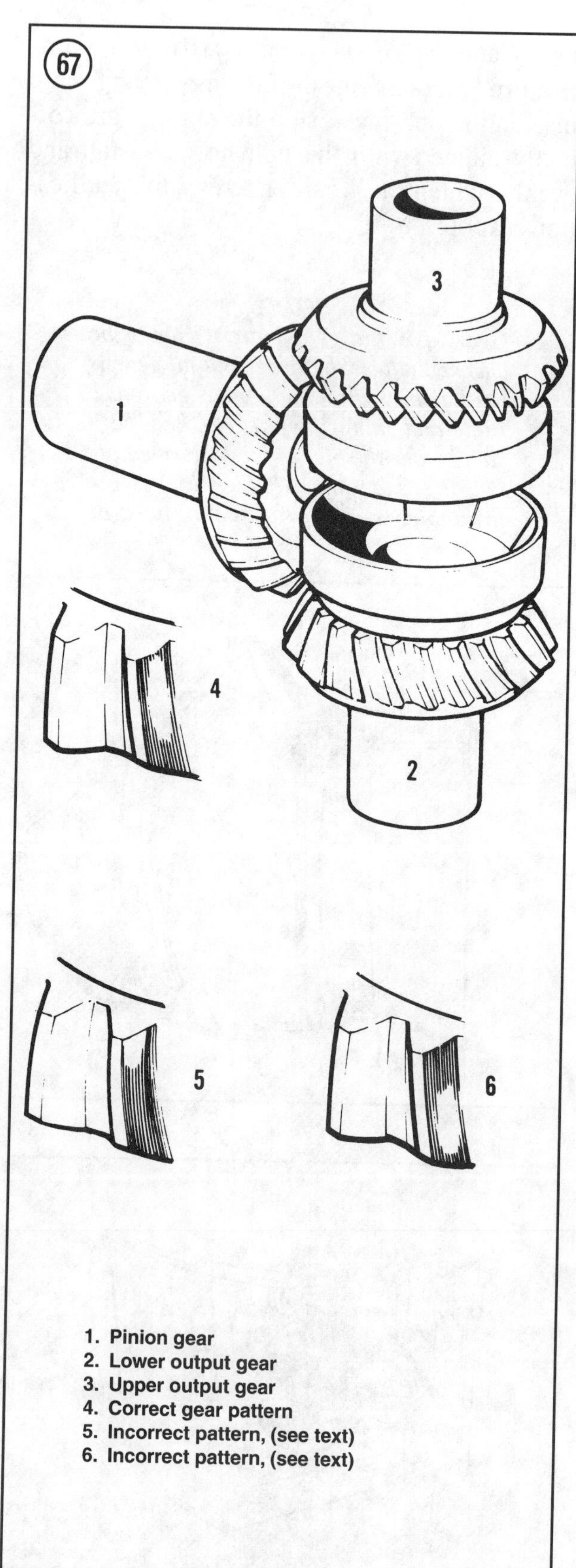

1. Pinion gear
2. Lower output gear
3. Upper output gear
4. Correct gear pattern
5. Incorrect pattern, (see text)
6. Incorrect pattern, (see text)

4. Compare the pattern on the gear teeth with the pattern shown at 4, **Figure 67**.

5. If the pattern is more like that shown at 5, **Figure 67**, add shims to the clamp ring bearing carrier and remove the same amount from both output gears to move the contact pattern toward the center.

6. If the pattern is more like that shown at 6, **Figure 67**, remove shims from the clamp ring bearing carrier and add the same amount to both output gears to move the contact pattern toward the center.

7. Correct the placement of shims as necessary to make the gear tooth pattern match that shown at 4, **Figure 67** before continuing. Remove the gearcase from the plate when finished.

CAUTION

If the contact pattern must be corrected, gear backlash must again be verified after the pattern correction, before continuing with final assembly.

8. Disassemble the gear housing keeping all of the shims in their correct positions. Clean all of the marking compound from the gear teeth and lubricate all internal components with clean gear oil. Proceed with the final assembly after all parts are clean and lubricated.

Final Assembly

Refer to **Figure 68** for this procedure.

1. If removed, install the cone clutch support washer (22, **Figure 68**) and C-clip (23, **Figure 68**) onto the output shaft.

2. Insert the double-stack needle bearing (14, **Figure 68**) into the lower output gear in its original orientation. Insert the output shaft through the gear and needle bearing.

3. Place the thrust washer over the output shaft and secure it with the 2 split locking rings. Pull the output shaft upward to lock the split rings into the thrust washer. See **Figure 69**.

4. Clamp the splined support fixture (part No. 884830-1) into a vise. Set the output shaft and lower output gear assembly into the fixture.

5. Install the predetermined amount of shims on the lower gear bearing flange.

6. Lower the gearcase housing over the output gear and seat it against the lower output gear bearing (and shims). The gearcase may be tapped gently with a rubber or plastic mallet. Make sure the bearing is not cocked in the bore.

7. Install the cone clutch support spring (**Figure 70**) over the output shaft. Install the cone clutch (**Figure 71**) onto the output shaft. Make sure the side stamped TOP or the side marked on disassembly is facing up.

8. Place the predetermined amount of upper output gear shims onto the upper output gear bearing and against the bearing flange. Install the upper output gear and bearing assembly into the gearcase bore. Seat the assembly into the housing. Make sure no shims are displaced or damaged during installation. See **Figure 72**.

9. Install the double-stack needle bearings (14, **Figure 68**) into the upper gear hub in its original orientation.

10. Lubricate the threads of the output shaft and install the output shaft nut (**Figure 73**). Tighten the nut to the torque listed in **Table 2**.

NOTE

Output shaft nuts are available in 4 different sizes (thickness), in 0.2 mm (0.008 in.) increments for output shaft end play adjustment. The nuts are numbered 0, 2, 4 and 6, with 0 being the thinnest. Remember that the nut has left-hand threads.

CAUTION

The output shaft must be held upward and the upper output gear held downward when checking the clearance in the next step.

11. Measure the clearance between the output shaft nut and the gear hub using a feeler gauge (**Figure 74**). If the clearance is not 0.01-0.05 mm

(0.004-0.020 in.), replace the nut with one of the proper thickness, as required. If none of the available nuts will establish the proper clearance, make sure the upper and lower output gear main bearings are seated in the gearcase housing. If the end play still cannot be properly set, the gearcase must be disassembled and all components between the top and bottom of the output shaft inspected for wear or damage.

12. Install the predetermined amount of top cover shims on the upper output gear bearing. Coat a new top cover seal with Volvo White Sealing Compound or equivalent (**Table 6**). Install the seal with the seal ring positioned over the front starboard screw hole (**Figure 75**).

13. Carefully install the top cover without displacing any of the shims or the seal ring. Install a new O-ring coated with Volvo White Sealing Compound or equivalent (**Table 6**) on the front, starboard screw (4, **Figure 68**). Coat all 4 top cover screw threads with sealing compound. Install and evenly tighten the screws to specifications (**Table 2**).

14. Install the predetermined shim(s) onto the clamp ring bearing carrier. Install a new O-ring in the carrier groove. Coat the O-ring and mating surfaces of the bearing carrier and upper gearcase with Volvo White Sealing Compound or equivalent (**Table 6**).

15. Install the clamp ring bearing carrier into the upper gearcase (**Figure 76**). Be careful not to displace the shim(s) and do not cock the carrier in the gearcase bore. A rubber or plastic mallet may be used to lightly tap the carrier into place. Seat the carrier against the gearcase.

16. Apply Loctite 271 (**Table 6**) to the threads of the 4 bearing carrier screws, then install and evenly tighten the screws to specifications (**Table 4**).

17. Install a new O-ring in the shift housing groove. Coat the O-ring, shift housing and gear housing mating surfaces with Volvo White Sealing Compound or equivalent (**Table 6**).

UPPER GEARCASE (DO-C1/D1 AND DPX)

1. Lubricant level dipstick and O-ring
2. Top cover
3. Top cover screw
4. Top cover screw and O-ring (hollow)
5. Plastic plug
6. Rear cover (DP-C1/D1 shown)
7. Retaining O-ring
8. Cover screw
9. Cover screw (DP-C1/D1 only)
10. Top cover shim(s)
11. Upper output shaft nut
12. Output gear main bearing
13. Upper output gear shim(s)
14. Double-stacked needle bearing
15. Top cover seal
16. Upper output gear and sleeve
17. Model identification plate
18. Oil fill plug and gasket
19. Output shaft
20. Cone clutch
21. Cone support spring
22. Cone support washer
23. C-clip
24. Lower output gear and sleeve
25. Retaining (thrust) washer
26. Split locking ring
27. Lower output gear shim(s)
28. Shift shoe stop bolt
29. Shim(s)
30. Eccentric piston
31. Ramp follower pin
32. Roll pin
33. Seal
34. Screw
35. Shift housing
36. O-ring
37. Shift shoe spring
38. Shift shoe
39. Gearcase housing
40. Yoke shaft retaining screw
41. Washer
42. Pinion gear
43. Tapered roller bearing (large)
44. Pretension (crush) sleeve
45. O-ring
46. Shim(s)
47. Clamp ring bearing carrier
48. Screw and washer
49. Tapered roller bearing (small)
50. Seal
51. Stud
52. Washer
53. O-ring
54. C-clip
55. Yoke shaft
56. Universal joint
57. Lock clip
58. Center coupler
59. Input drive shaft coupler
60. Bearing cap
61. Clamp
62. Universal joint bellows

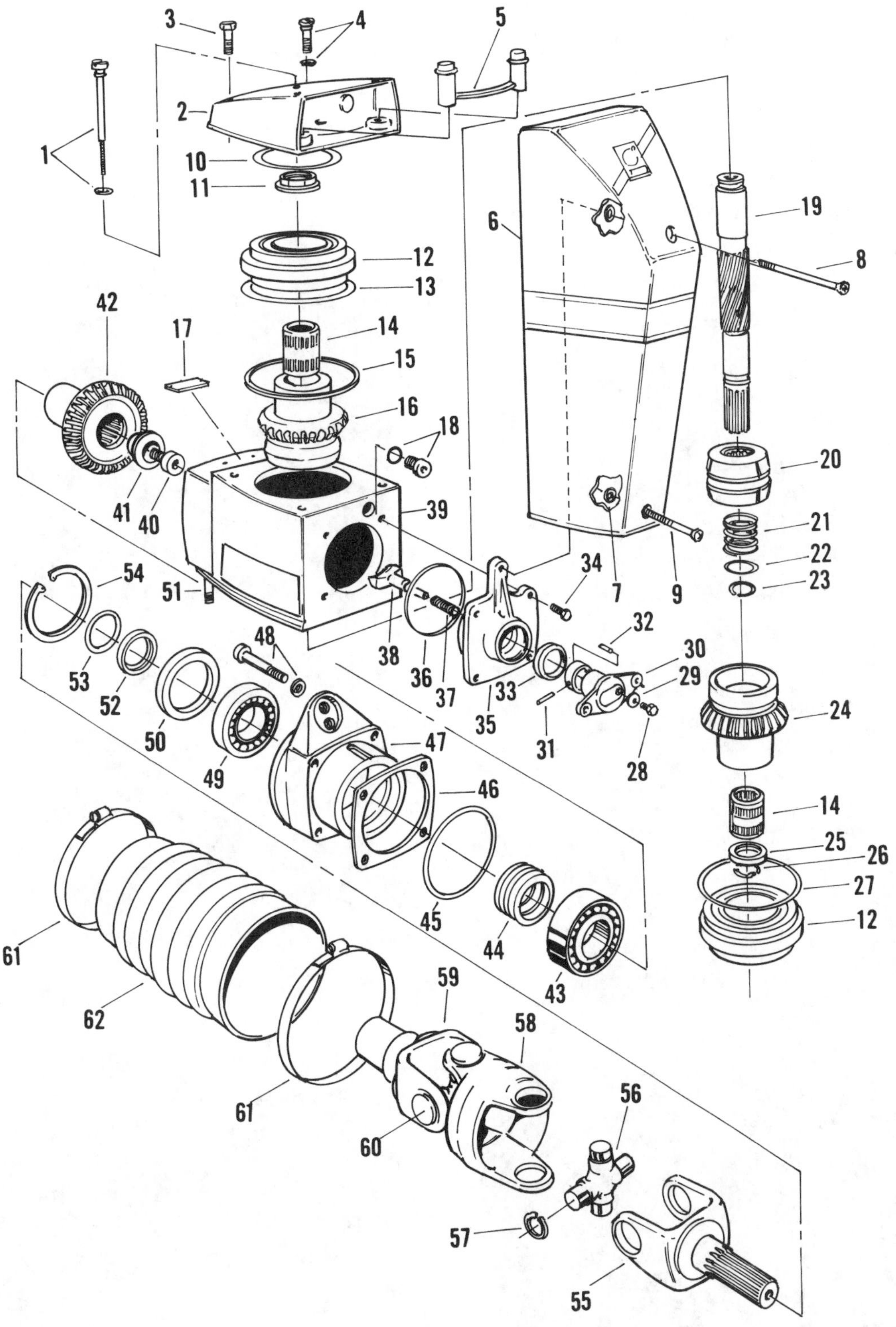

12

18. Install the shift housing assembly (**Figure 77**) into the gearcase bore with the large side (big end) of the shift shoe facing starboard. Coat the threads of the 4 screws with Volvo White Sealing Compound or equivalent (**Table 6**). Install and evenly tighten the screws to specification (**Table 4**).

19. Refer to *Upper Gearcase to Intermediate Housing Shimming* in the next section and determine the shims required to preload the lower output gear bearing against the upper gearcase.

20. Refer to *Shift Shoe Shimming* at the end of this chapter and determine the shims required to properly locate the shift shoe stop bolt. The shift shoe can also be shimmed after the upper gearcase has been installed to the intermediate housing, if so desired.

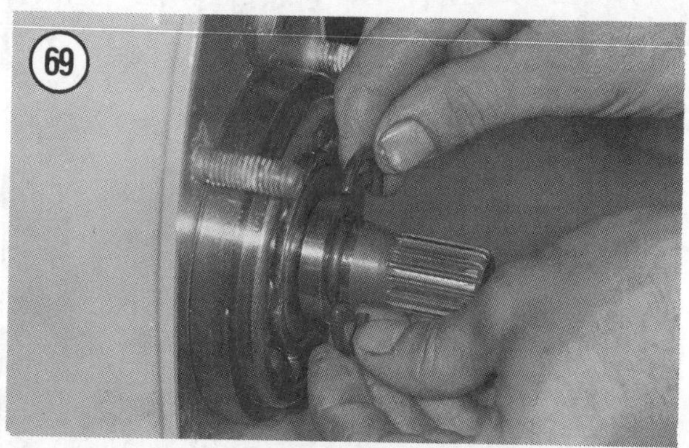

69

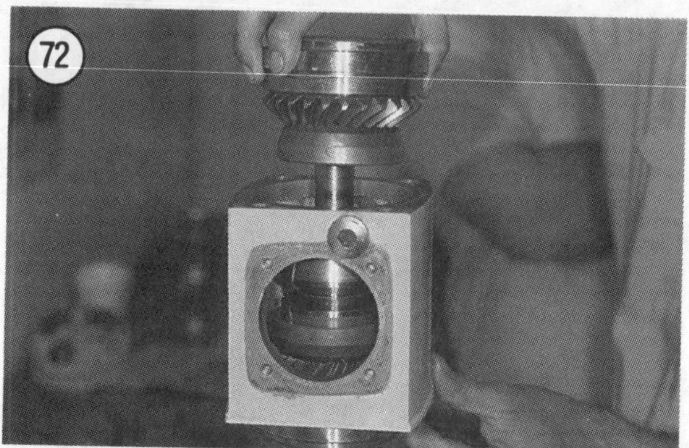

72

70

73

71

74

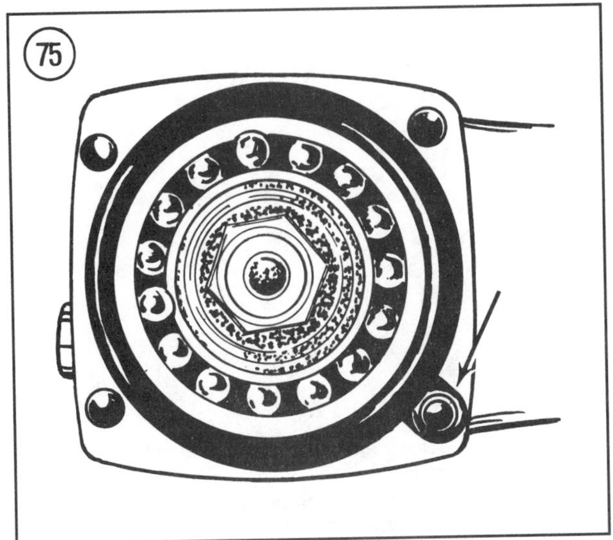

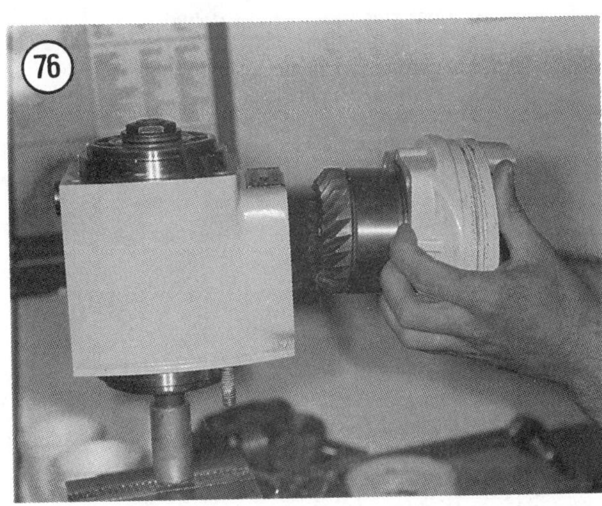

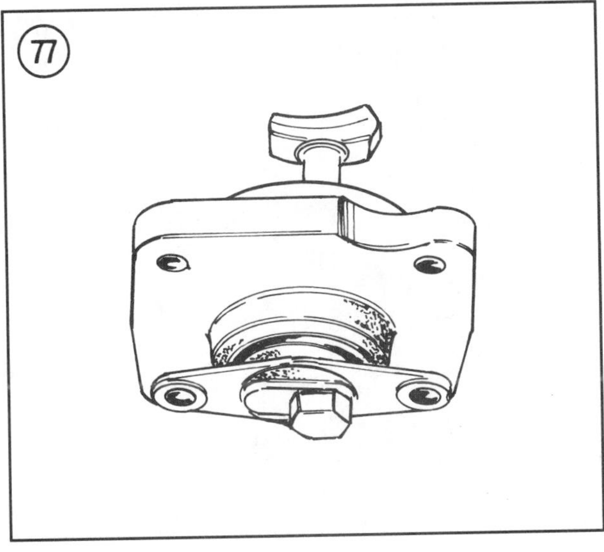

21. Make sure the drive unit is pressure tested as described in *Upper gearcase installation* before the drive unit is filled with lubricant.

Upper Gearcase to Intermediate Housing Shimming Procedure

This procedure determines the amount of shims required to properly preload the lower output bearing against the upper gearcase. If any of the shims or major components in the upper gearcase or the intermediate housing have been changed, the correct amount of shims to preload the lower output bearing should be recalculated. Refer to **Figure 78** for this procedure.

1. Invert the upper gearcase and measure the height from the lower output gear bearing race outside diameter to the mating surface of the upper gearcase (**Figure 79**). Record the measurement.
2. Remove any shims present in the intermediate housing bearing bore, then measure the corresponding depth of the bearing bore (to the shim seating area) from the intermediate housing mating surface (**Figure 80**). Record the measurement.
3. Subtract the depth measured in Step 2 from the height measured in Step 1. Add 0.05 mm to the result to provide the correct amount of bearing preload. The final result is the correct thickness of shims to install in Step 4. For example, if the bearing height is 22.83 mm and the housing depth is 22.73 mm, subtract 22.73 mm from 22.83 mm, resulting in 0.102 mm. Then, add 0.051 mm (preload figure) to the 0.102 mm initial result. The final amount of shims in this example is 0.152 mm (0.006 in.).
4. Install the calculated shim(s) into the bearing bore of the intermediate housing. See **Figure 78**.
5. Refer to *Upper gearcase installation* located previously in this chapter.

12

UPPER GEARCASE SERVICE SX AND DP-S MODELS

SX-S (1994 model year) upper gearcase uses a steel cone clutch with a brass plated shift shoe. The vertical drive shaft O-ring groove is located in the lower gearcase. The tooth count on this gearcase is 22:23 (drive to driven).

SX-C and SX-CT (1995 model year) upper gearcase uses a molybdenum coated brass cone clutch, a steel shift shoe and a new gear set that can only be used with the new cone clutch. This drive is 12.7 mm (1/2 in.) shorter in overall length than the SX-S model. This was done to match the industry standard for transom cutout mounting height. The vertical drive shaft O-ring groove is located in the upper gearcase. A large splash plate was added just below the hydraulic trim/tilt cylinders. The original upper gearcase holding fixture (part No. 3850605-1) had to be modified (4 new holes drilled) to allow it to function with this upper gearcase. Newer releases of this tool are factory modified. The T designates drives shipped with an adjustable trim tab (manual steering models). The tooth count on this gearcase is 22:23 (drive to driven).

SX-C1, SX-CT1 and DP-S (1996 model year) upper gearcase has once again relocated the vertical drive shaft O-ring to the lower gearcase. All other 1995 model year improvements remain unchanged. The DP-S gearcase uses 4 studs to replace the 2 bolts on each side of the drive unit that secure the upper gearcase to the lower gearcase. There are 2 gear ratios available, 22:23 and 21:26 (drive to driven). Shimming dimensions vary between the 2 gear ratios. A ground spring was added to the upper gear housing to ground the trim rod to the upper gearcase to help prevent galvanic corrosion. A kit (part No. 3855829-2) is available to upgrade 1994-1995 gearcases.

Upper Gearcase Removal/Installation

Removal of the upper gearcase requires removal of the drive unit from the transom bracket.

INTERMEDIATE HOUSING (DP-C1/D1 AND DPX)

1. O-ring
2. Oil sleeve
3. O-ring
4. Lower output gear preload shim(s)
5. Screw
6. Shift cable clamp plate
7. Screw and washer
8. Elastic locknut
9. Intermediate housing
10. Rear steering pin (DPX only)
11. Steering bushings (DPX only)
12. Steering cotter pin (DPX only)
13. Steering washer (DPX only)
14. Trim/tilt clevis pin
15. Trim/tilt cotter pin
16. Front steering pin (DPX only)
17. Seal
18. Retainer
19. Bushing
20. Steering tube
21. Thrust washer
22. O-ring
23. Water outlet fitting
24. Screw
25. Clamps
26. Exhaust bellows
27. Pivot pin bushings
28. Suspension fork
29. Bellcrank shaft
30. Bellcrank
31. Brass cube nut
32. Shift link
33. Flat washer
34. Cotter pin
35. Flat washer
36. Cotter pin
37. Flat washer

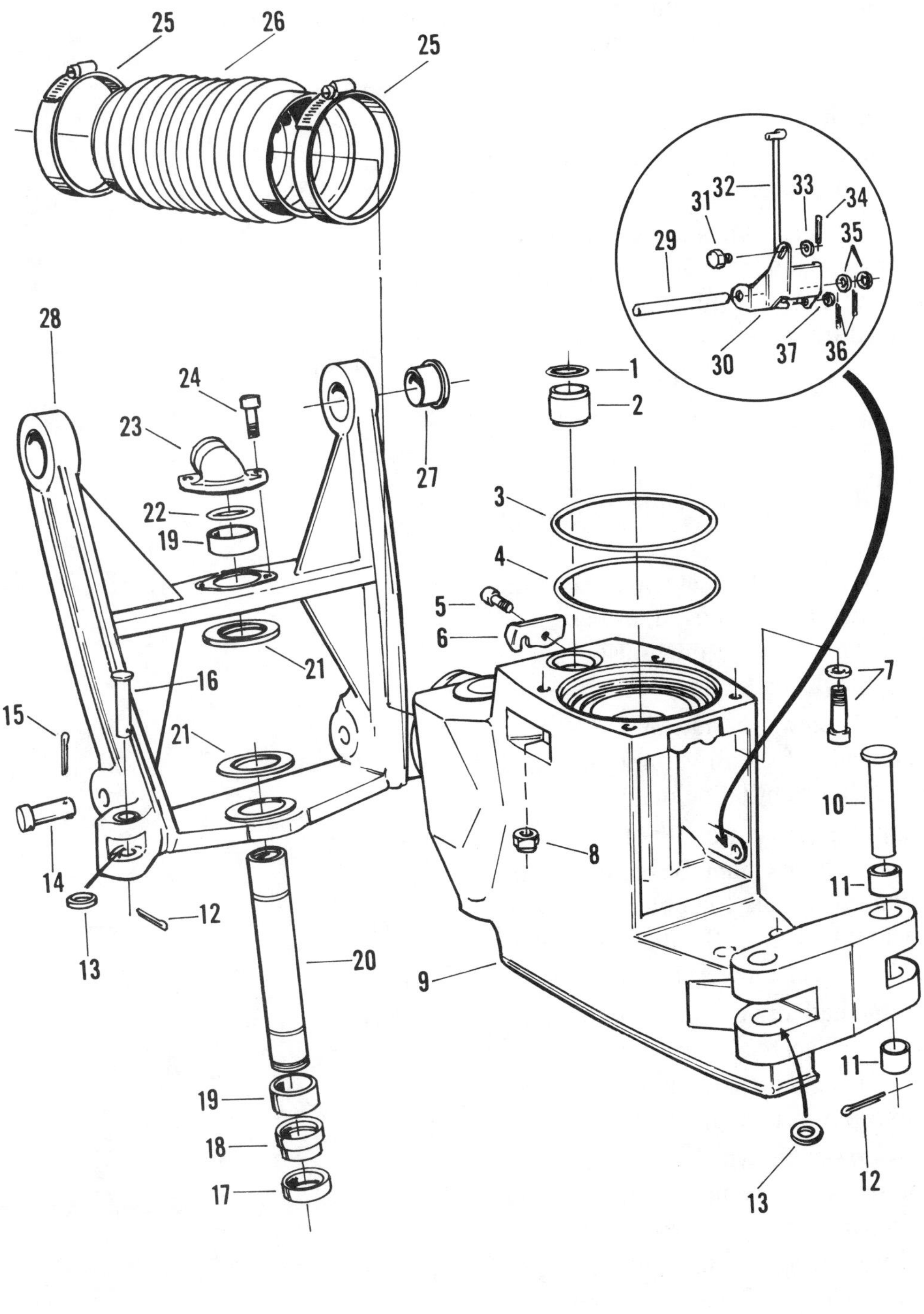

12

Refer to *Drive Unit Removal/Installation* located previously in this chapter. The drive unit pumps lubricant from the lower gearcase to the upper gearcase during operation. If a failure has taken place in any part of the drive unit, the complete drive unit should be disassembled, cleaned and inspected.

The shift shoe housing assembly can be serviced and shimmed without removing the drive unit from the transom bracket.

There is a gear lubricant filter located in the lubricant passage at the front of the upper gearcase. Replace the filter each time the upper gearcase is separated from the lower gearcase.

Removal

1. Secure the drive unit in a suitable holding fixture.
2. Drain the drive unit lubricant and remove the rear cover (if not already removed) as described in *Drive Lubricant Change* previously in this chapter. Leave the dipstick removed.
3. Remove the 4 screws (or nuts on DP-S models), 2 on each side of the drive unit and the 2 screws under the antiventilation plate.
4. Lift the upper gearcase from the lower gearcase with the aid of an assistant. Be ready to catch the intermediate drive shaft coupler and water tube if they should fall free. Set the upper gearcase on its side, on a clean workbench.
5. If the intermediate drive shaft coupler came free with the upper gearcase, reinstall it on the lower gearcase drive shaft with its grooved end facing up (to keep it from being misplaced).
6A. *SX-S models*—Remove the copper water tube and grommet from the upper gearcase. Do not remove the water tube grommet (1, **Figure 81**) from the lower gearcase unless it is going to be replaced. See Chapter Thirteen for replacement procedures.
6B. *All other models*—Remove the copper water tube, upper gearcase grommet, lower gearcase grommet and lower gearcase plastic water guide. See **Figure 81**.
7. Remove and discard the lubricant filter (3, **Figure 82**) located in the lubricant passage at the bottom of the gearcase. Hook the filter with an appropriate tool and pull it from the upper gearcase.

NOTE
The drive shaft bearing O-ring groove is located in the lower gearcase on SX-S and SX-C1 series drive units and located in the upper gearcase on SX-C series drive units.

8. Clean the mating surfaces of the upper and lower gearcases before reassembly. Remove and

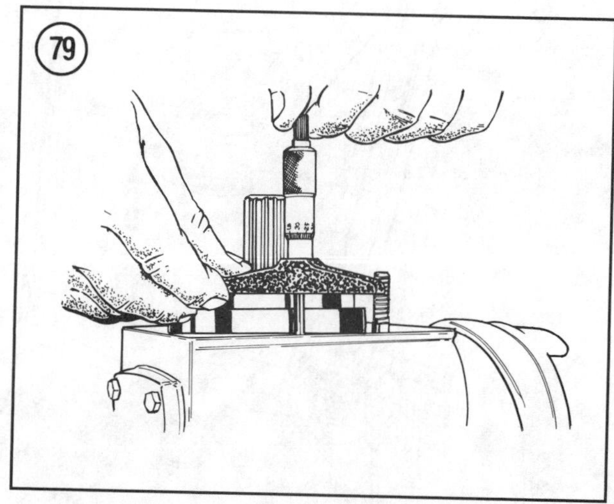

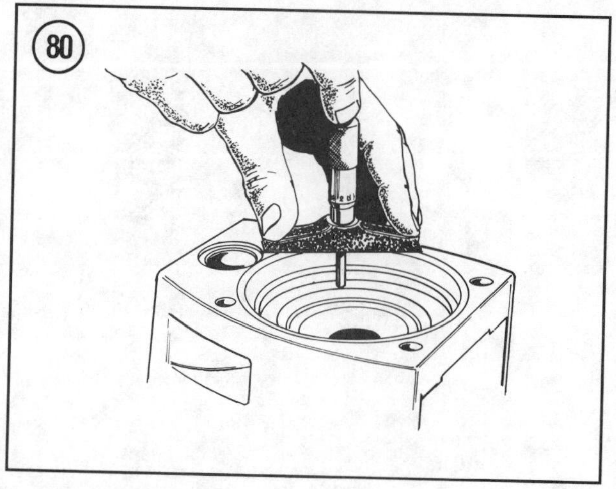

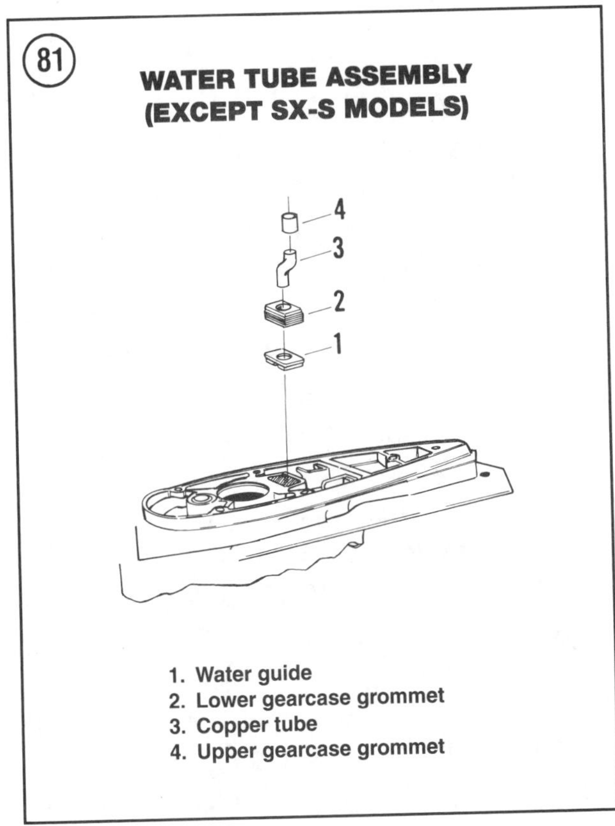

1. Water guide
2. Lower gearcase grommet
3. Copper tube
4. Upper gearcase grommet

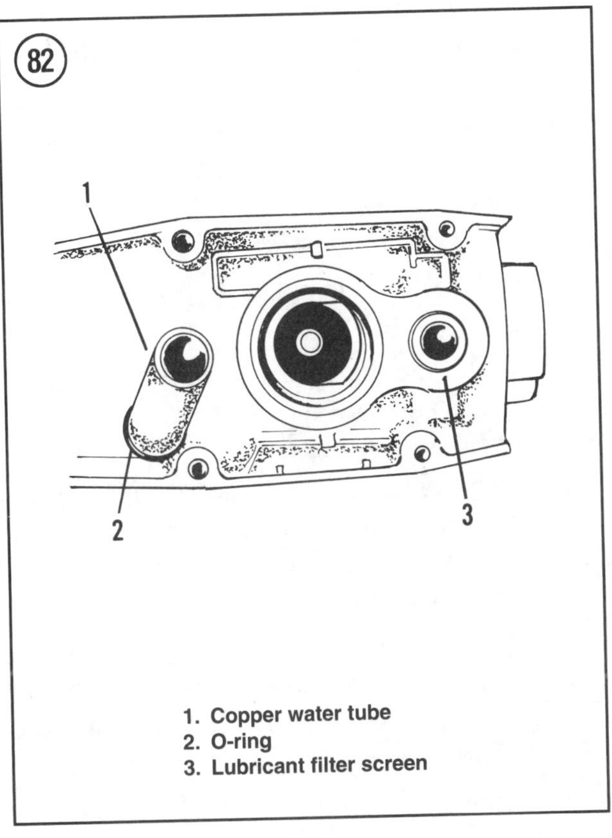

1. Copper water tube
2. O-ring
3. Lubricant filter screen

discard the lubricant filter O-ring (3, **Figure 82**) and drive shaft retainer O-ring (2, **Figure 82**).

Installation

Before installing the upper gearcase to the drive unit, make sure the sealing surfaces are thoroughly clean. If necessary, lubricate the universal joints and gimbal bearing as described in *Universal Joint and Gimbal Bearing Lubrication* located previously in this chapter.

1. Install new lubricated O-rings in the lower gearcase filter passage groove (3, **Figure 82**) and around the drive shaft bearing retainer (2, **Figure 82**).
2. Install a new lubricant filter into the upper gearcase lubricant passage and seat it flush with the gearcase mating surface (3, **Figure 82**).
3. Install the water tube grommet into the upper gearcase. Install the water tube, seating it fully into the upper gearcase grommet. Align the lower end of the water tube to form a straight line through the lubricant filter and drive shaft bores, and the water tube open end. See **Figure 82**.

4A. *SX-S models*—Verify that the water tube guide is secured to the lower gearcase. Wipe the internal water tube seal with OMC Type M adhesive or equivalent (**Table 6**) just before installing the upper gearcase.

4B. *All other models*—Set the water tube plastic guide (1, **Figure 81**) into the lower gearcase with protruding edges facing down. Coat the outside surface of the lower water tube grommet (2, **Figure 81**) with OMC gasket sealing compound or equivalent (**Table 6**). Insert the lower water tube grommet into the lower gearcase on top of the plastic water tube guide.

5. Install the intermediate drive shaft coupler onto the lower gearcase drive shaft with the grooved end facing up (if not already installed).
6. Coat the mating surfaces of the upper and lower gearcases with Volvo White Sealing Com-

pound or equivalent (**Table 6**). This will help prevent corrosion, especially in saltwater.

7. Set the upper gearcase onto the lower gearcase with the aid of an assistant. Be sure to engage the drive shaft coupler splines by rotating the propeller shaft(s) as the gearcase is lowered. Be sure to engage the water tube into the water tube adaptor or lower grommet before seating the upper gearcase to the lower gearcase.

8. Coat the threads of the 6 fasteners with OMC Gasket Sealing Compound or equivalent (**Table 6**). Install the 2 screws under the antiventilation plate and the 2 screws or nuts on each side of the drive unit. Evenly tighten all 6 fasteners to specifications (**Table 5**).

Pressure and vacuum tests

Make sure the lubricant fill/drain plug and lubricant level dipstick are installed and tightened securely before proceeding. Do not fill the drive unit with lubricant until the seal integrity of the drive unit is verified by performing 4 pressure and vacuum tests in the following order.

1. Perform a low pressure test as follows:
   a. Connect a pressure tester (such as Stevens S-34 [**Table 11**]) to the lubricant level hole.
   b. Pressurize the drive unit to 20.7-34.5 kPa (3-5 psi) for a minimum of 3 minutes.
   c. Rotate the input drive shaft, propeller shaft(s) and shift the gearcase into and out of gear during the test.
   d. If any pressure drop is noted, spray soapy water on all seals and mating surfaces until the leak is found. Correct the leak and retest.
   e. Do not proceed until the drive unit holds pressure for at least 3 minutes without measurable leakage.
2. Perform a high pressure test as follows:
   a. Increase the pressure to 110-124 kPa (16-18 psi) for a minimum of 3 minutes.
   b. Rotate the input drive shaft, propeller shaft(s) and shift the gearcase into and out of gear during the test.
   c. If any pressure drop is noted, spray soapy water on all seals and mating surfaces until the leak is found. Correct the leak and retest.
   d. Do not proceed until the drive unit holds pressure, or loses no more than 6.9 kPa (1 psi) after a minimum of 3 minutes.
   e. Remove the pressure tester when finished.
3. If both pressure tests are completed satisfactorily, perform a low vacuum test as follows:
   a. Connect a vacuum tester (such as Stevens V-34 [**Table 11**]) to the lubricant level hole.
   b. Pull a vacuum of 10-16.8 kPa (3-5 in.-Hg) for a minimum of 3 minutes.
   c. Rotate the input drive shaft, propeller shaft(s) and shift the gearcase into and out of gear during the test.
   d. If any vacuum loss is noted, apply gear lubricant to all seals and mating surfaces. The lubricant will be drawn into the drive unit at the point of the leak. Correct the leak and retest.
   e. Do not proceed until the drive unit holds vacuum for at least 3 minutes without measurable leakage.
4. Perform a high vacuum test as follows:
   a. Increase the vacuum to 47-54 kPa (14-16 in.-Hg).
   b. Rotate the input drive shaft, propeller shaft(s) and shift the gearcase into and out of gear during the test.
   c. If any vacuum loss is noted, apply gear lubricant to all seals and mating surfaces. The lubricant will be drawn into the drive unit at the point of the leak. Correct the leak and retest.
   d. Do not proceed until the drive unit holds vacuum, or loses no more than 3.4 kPa (1 in.-Hg) after a minimum of 3 minutes.
   e. Remove the vacuum tester when finished.

5. Fill the drive unit with lubricant and install the rear cover as described in *Drive unit lubrication.*

Disassembly

Figure 83 shows an exploded view of a typical SX/DP-S upper gear housing and components.

Record the measurement of all shims as they are removed. Shims can be reused if they are not damaged. Tag the shims by location for reassembly purposes. Do not lose or discard any shims. All components that are to be reused must be installed in their original location and orientation. Mark components as necessary to ensure correct reinstallation.

Gearcase holding fixture part No. 3850605-1 is designed to hold the upper gearcase securely for all service procedures. The holding fixture fits a standard Bob Kerr Tool Company (**Table 11**) workbench base or floor stand. It is highly recommended that these procedures be performed *with* a holding fixture. Attempting to perform these procedures without a holding fixture will be very difficult, even with the aid of an assistant.

1. Remove the 3 screws (39, **Figure 83**) securing the rear cover (40, **Figure 83**) to the gearcase. Remove the rear cover. Remove and discard the cotter pin securing the clevis pin (1, **Figure 84**) to the eccentric piston arm. Remove the clevis pin and shift linkage (3, **Figure 84**) from the arm.

NOTE
The shift shoe is spring-loaded and can fall free from the shift housing.

2. Remove the 4 screws (2, **Figure 84**) attaching the shift housing to the rear of the upper gear housing. Remove the shift housing and shift shoe assembly. Discard the housing O-ring.
3. Refer to *Shift Housing Service* in this chapter, if the shift housing seal or any shift housing components are to be serviced.
4. Remove the pinion bearing carrier as follows:
   a. Remove the 4 screws (29, **Figure 83**) securing the pinion carrier and universal joint shaft assembly to the gearcase.
   b. Pull the pinion bearing carrier from the gearcase. If the carrier binds, tap on side of the carrier with a rubber or plastic mallet while an assistant pulls on the carrier.
   c. As a last resort, pry the carrier from the gearcase with 2 screwdrivers in the relief slots on each side of the carrier.
   d. Discard the carrier O-ring. Remove the plastic shims. Measure and record the thickness of the shims for later reference. Tag the shim(s) for identification during reassembly.
5. Remove the 4 screws (2, **Figure 83**) securing the top cover (3, **Figure 83**) to the upper gearcase. Remove the top cover from the gearcase. A rubber or plastic mallet can be used to break the top cover free. Discard the top cover seal. Remove the shim(s). Measure and record the thickness of the shims for later reference. Tag the shim(s) for identification during reassembly.

NOTE
*The output shaft nut (**Figure 85**) has left-hand threads and must be turned clockwise to remove. The nut is also a shim. The nut comes in 4 sizes (thickness) to control output shaft end play.*

6A. *With holding fixture*—Remove the output shaft nut by turning it *clockwise* with a 30 mm socket and breaker bar. Record the number stamped into the nut for later reference.

6B. *Without holding fixture*:
   a. With the aid of an assistant, lay the gearcase on its side and secure the lower end of the output shaft with spline socket part No. 3855098-5, 1/2 in. extension and a breaker bar.
   b. Remove the output shaft nut by turning it *clockwise* with a 30 mm socket and breaker

12

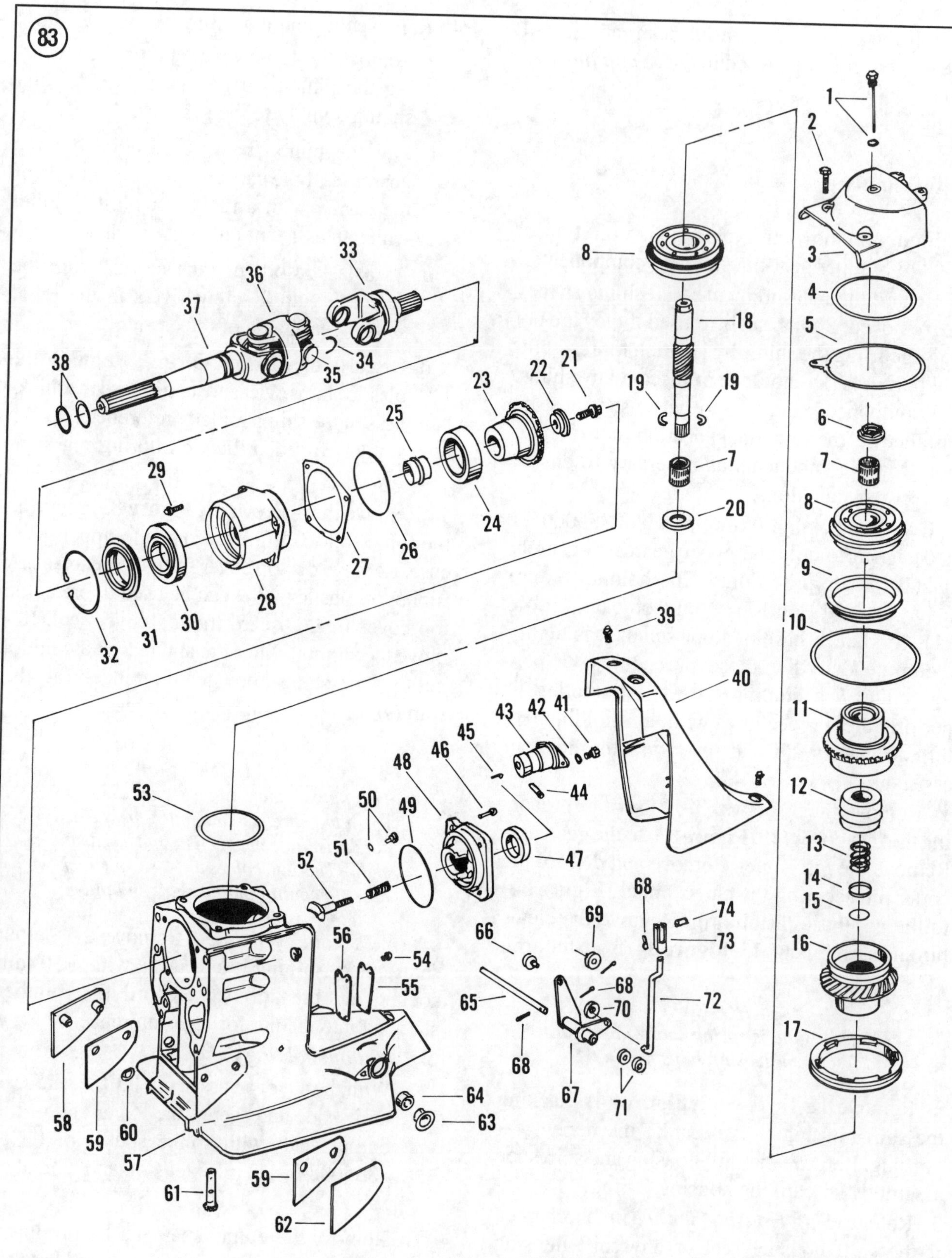
83
1
2
3
4
5
6
7
8
9
10
11
12
13
14
15
16
17
18
19
20
21
22
23
24
25
26
27
28
29
30
31
32
33
34
35
36
37
38
39
40
41
42
43
44
45
46
47
48
49
50
51
52
53
54
55
56
57
58
59
60
61
62
63
64
65
66
67
68
69
70
71
72
73
74

UPPER GEARCASE (SX AND DP-S)

1. Lubricant level dipstick and O-ring
2. Screw
3. Top cover
4. Top cover shim(s)
5. Top cover seal
6. Upper output shaft nut (shim)
7. Double stack caged needle bearing
8. Output gear main bearing
9. Bearing ring (upper gear only)
10. Upper output gear shim(s)
11. Upper output gear
12. Cone clutch
13. Cone support spring
14. Support washer
15. C-clip
16. Lower output gear
17. Lower gear retaining ring
18. Output shaft
19. Split lock ring
20. Thrust washer
21. Torx head screw
22. Washer
23. Pinion gear
24. Large tapered roller bearing
25. Pretension (crush) sleeve
26. O-ring
27. Plastic shim(s)
28. Pinion bearing carrier
29. Screw
30. Small tapered roller bearing
31. Seal
32. Snap ring
33. Yoke shaft
34. Lock ring
35. Bearing cap
36. Center coupler
37. Input drive shaft
38. O-ring
39. Screw
40. Rear cover
41. Shift shoe stop bolt
42. Shim(s)
43. Eccentric piston
44. Ramp follower pin
45. Roll pin
46. Screw
47. Seal
48. Shift housing
49. O-ring
50. Oil level plug and seal
51. Shift shoe spring
52. Shift shoe
53. Lower output gear shim
54. Screw
55. Water cover
56. Gasket
57. Gear housing
58. Starboard thrust plate
59. Thrust plate shim(s)
60. Retaining clip
61. Lubricant filter
62. Port thrust plate
63. Pivot pin bushing
64. Rubber grommet
65. Bellcrank shaft
66. Brass cube nut
67. Bellcrank
68. Cotter pin
69. Flat washer
70. Flat washer
71. Flat washer
72. Shift link
73. Clevis end
74. Clevis pin

bar. Record the number stamped into the nut for later reference.

c. Stuff several shop towels into the drive shaft bore of the gearcase to keep the output shaft from dropping down into the bore, disengaging the split lock rings and thrust washer.

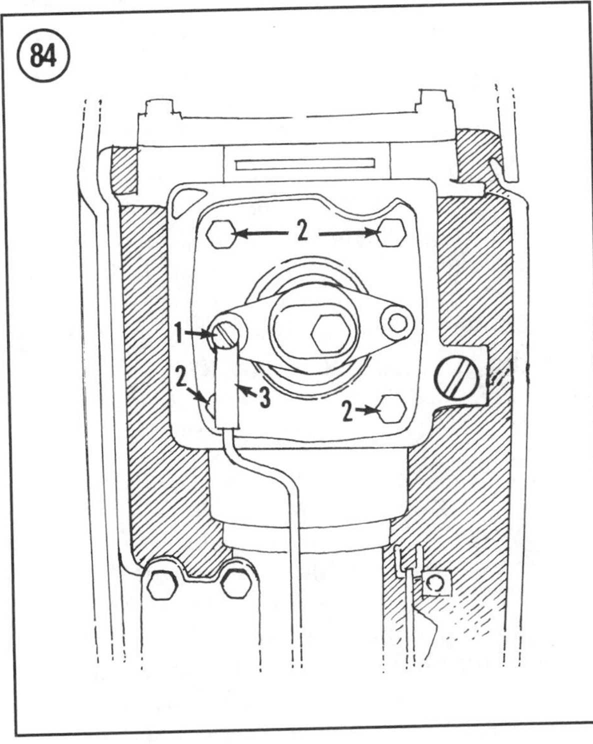

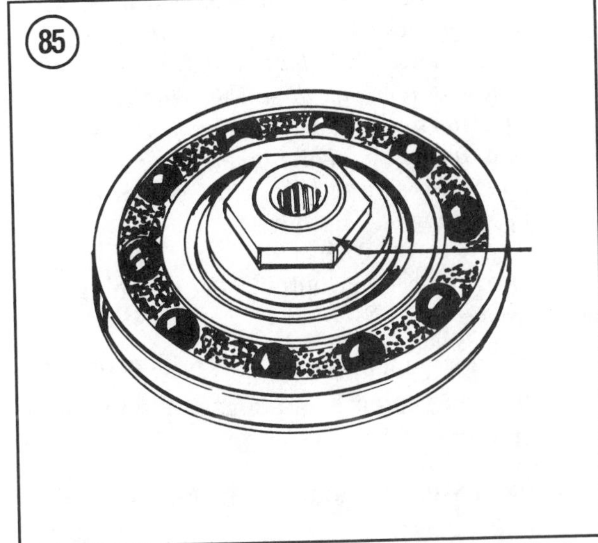

12

NOTE
If the double stack caged bearing removed in Step 7 is to be reused, mark the bearing's location and orientation, for reassembly purposes.

7. Remove the upper output gear and the needle bearing assembly. Remove the shim(s). Measure and record the thickness of the shims for later reference. Tag the shim(s) for identification during reassembly. Remove and mark the needle bearing in the gear hub. See **Figure 86**.

NOTE
The cone clutch should be stamped with the word TOP on its upper surface. If the cone clutch is to be reused, it must be installed in its original orientation.

8. Remove the cone clutch and support spring from the gearcase. See **Figure 87**.

CAUTION
*The lower output gear retaining ring (17, **Figure 83**) is torqued to 197-224 N•m (145-165 ft.-lb.) The gearcase must be secured to holding fixture part No. 3850605-1 or equivalent (**Figure 88**) and spanner wrench part No. 3850604-4 (**Figure 89**) must be used to break the ring free. Make sure that any debris from a gear or bearing failure is cleaned from the ring and housing threads. If necessary, scrape the threads clean with a suitable pick tool and liberally lubricate the area with fresh lubricant. If the ring binds on removal, thread the ring back in, clean and lubricate the threaded area and try again. Forcing the ring will cause the ring to lock in the gearcase, destroying the housing.*

9. Remove the lower output gear retaining ring as follows:
   a. Insert spanner wrench part No. 3850604-4 into the gearcase and engage the retaining ring lugs.
   b. Secure the tool to the gearcase with 2 suitable screws.

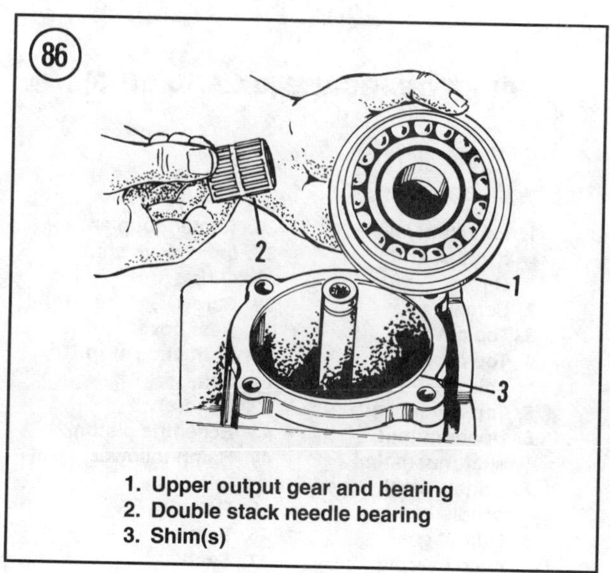

1. Upper output gear and bearing
2. Double stack needle bearing
3. Shim(s)

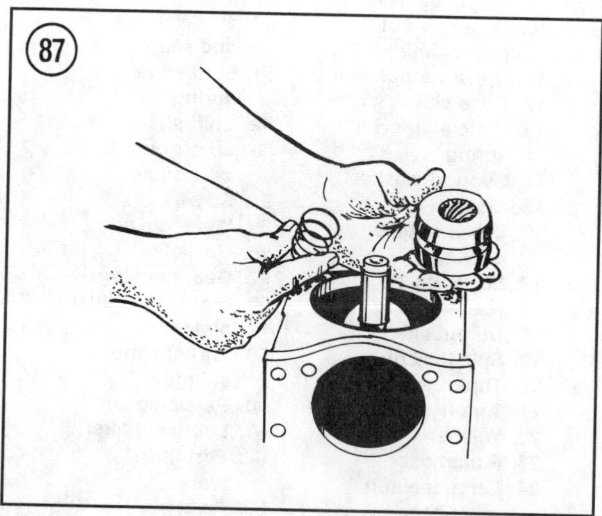

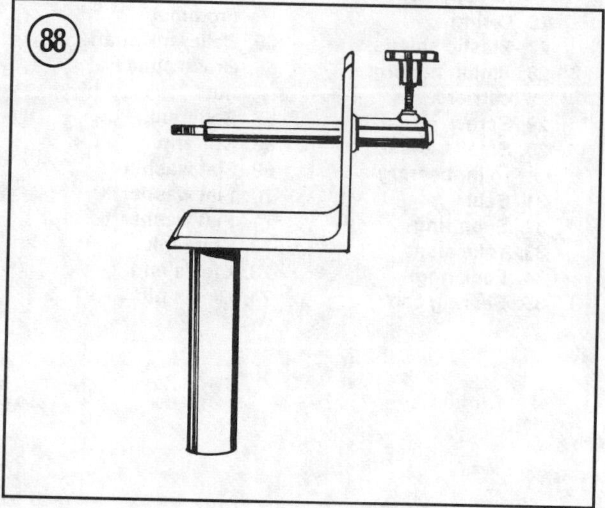

c. Use a 3/4 in. breaker bar and break the ring free with a sudden, quick movement. Do not turn the ring more than 1/4 turn with the breaker bar.

d. Remove the breaker bar and the 2 screws securing the tool to the gearcase.

e. Unscrew the ring the rest of the way by hand.

10. Grasp the output shaft and remove the output shaft and lower output gear assembly from the gearcase. Lay the assembly on a clean workbench. Remove the shim(s) from the gearcase bore or bottom of the output bearing. Measure and record the thickness of the shims for later reference. Tag the shim(s) for identification during reassembly.

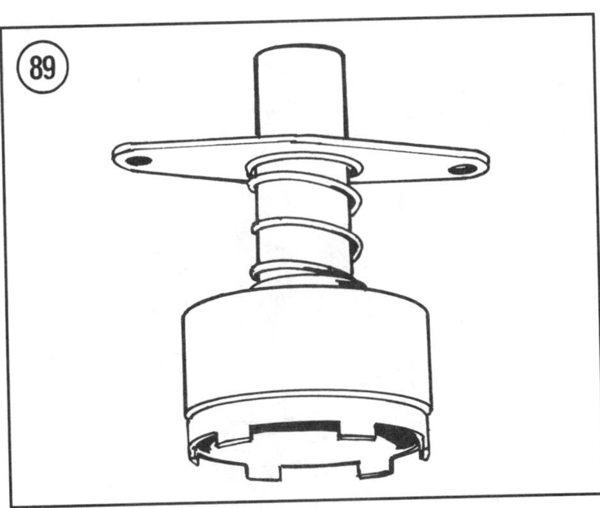

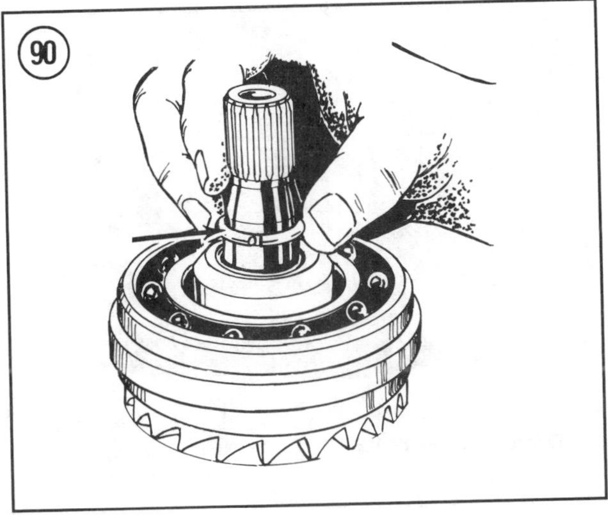

11. Remove the split lock rings (**Figure 90**) and thrust washer from the lower end of the output shaft.

NOTE

If the double stack caged bearing removed in Step 13 is to be reused, mark the bearing's location and orientation, for reassembly purposes.

12. Remove the lower output gear and needle bearing assembly from the output shaft (**Figure 86**, similar). Mark the needle bearing's location and orientation.

NOTE

Do not remove the output gear main roller bearings unless they are to be replaced. The removal process will damage the bearings. The upper output gear assembly is identified by the presence of an additional ring around the bearing. Once the bearings (and ring on the upper gear) are removed, the gears are identical. Mark the gears for reassembly in their original location.

13. If the upper or lower output gear main bearings require replacement, proceed as follows:

a. Begin by removing the bearing ring from the upper output gear. Place the support sleeve part No. 3850606-9 into an arbor or hydraulic press with its large end facing up.

b. Place the upper gear assembly into the support with the gear facing up. Press the gear and bearing from the sleeve with drift part No. 884263-5.

c. Continue the disassembly by removing the main bearing from each gear. Place the support sleeve part No. 884938-2 into a press with its large end facing up.

d. Place a shop towel into the support sleeve to cushion the gear. Place the output gear and bearing assembly into the sleeve with the gear facing down.

e. Place sleeve part No. 884263-5 against the gear hub. Press the gear from the bearing.

f. Repeat substeps d and e for the remaining output gear. Discard the bearings.

14. Inspect the washer and C-clip on the output shaft. If replacement is necessary, remove the C-clip with a suitable pair of snap ring pliers and slide the washer from the shaft.

15. To service the pinion bearing carrier, remove the 2 universal joint bearing caps from the pinion bearing carrier yoke shaft and separate the universal joint from the shaft. Refer to *Universal Joint Service* in this chapter.

16. Fabricate a universal joint yoke shaft support by cutting a 25.4 mm (1 in.) diameter steel or cast iron pipe to a length of 73 mm (2-7/8 in.). Position the pipe in both yokes. Clamp the yoke shaft and pipe securely in a vise. The pipe should absorb all compressive loads and prevent damage to the yoke shaft.

17. Remove the Torx screw (A, **Figure 91**) and washer (B, **Figure 91**) from the center of the drive gear with T50 Torx socket, part No. 885043-0. The screw is sealed with Loctite and is difficult to remove. Discard the screw.

18. Remove the yoke shaft (33, **Figure 83**) from the pinion bearing carrier.

19. Remove the snap ring securing the seal (32, **Figure 83**) with snap ring pliers part No. 3850608-5 (or equivalent). The seal will be removed in a later operation.

20. To remove the drive gear, proceed as follows:

a. Place support sleeve part No. 884938-2 in a press with its large end facing up. Place a shop towel in the bottom of the support sleeve.

b. Set the pinion bearing carrier in the support sleeve with the gear facing down.

c. Place sleeve part No. 884266-8 against the gear hub. Press the gear from the bearing.

d. Remove and discard the pretension (crush) sleeve.

21. Turn the bearing carrier over and press the roller bearing and seal out with sleeve part No. 884263-5. The bearing and seal can usually be pushed out with hand pressure. Discard the seal.

NOTE

Do not remove the roller bearing from the drive gear, or the bearing races from the pinion bearing carrier unless replacement is necessary.

22. To remove the small bearing cup from the pinion bearing carrier, begin by installing bearing remover part No. 884933-3 onto the drive handle part No. 9991801-3. Place the pinion bearing carrier in a press with its large diameter

91

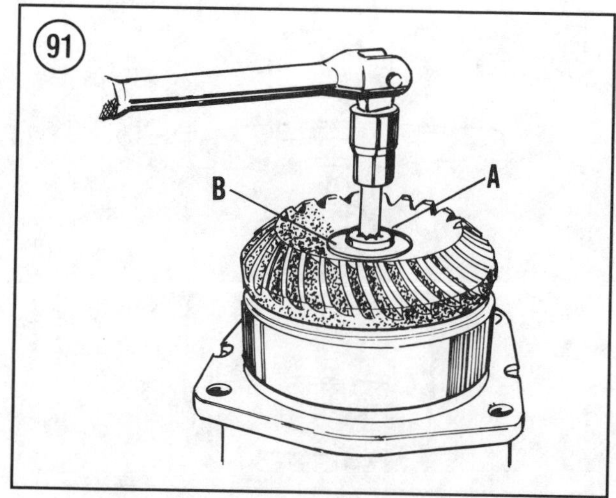

92

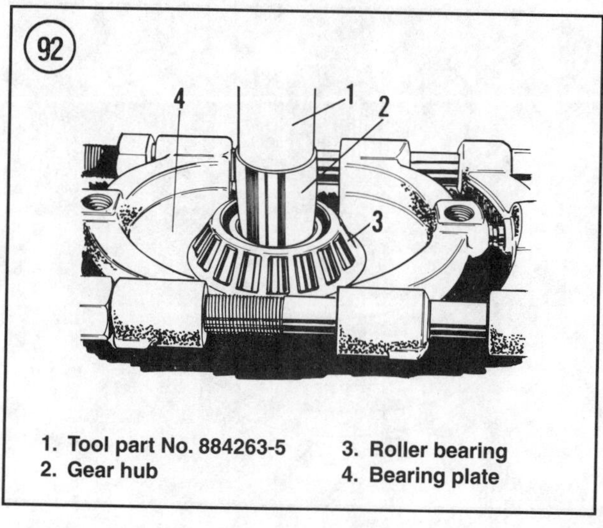

1. Tool part No. 884263-5
2. Gear hub
3. Roller bearing
4. Bearing plate

facing down. Insert the bearing remover behind the small bearing cup and press the cup from the bearing carrier. Discard the bearing race and the roller assembly removed previously.

23. To remove the large bearing cup, place the support sleeve part No. 884938-2 into a press with its large end facing up. Set the bearing carrier into the support sleeve with its large end facing up. Insert the bearing remover behind the large bearing cup and press the cup from the bearing carrier. Discard the bearing cup.

24. To remove the roller bearing from the drive gear, attach a knife-edge bearing plate behind the roller bearing. Press the gear from the bearing with sleeve part No. 884263-5. Discard the roller bearing. See **Figure 92**.

25. Remove the upper gearcase from the fixture. Clean and inspect all components as described in the next section. If service of the shift linkage and bellcrank is desired, refer to *Shift linkage service* in the next section.

Shift linkage service

The shift linkage consists of a bellcrank, pivot shaft, shift link, washers and cotter pins. The shift linkage normally does not need to be disassembled unless corroded or damaged. Verify the shift link overall length anytime major service is performed on the upper gearcase. The shift linkage should measure close to, but no more than 150.8 mm (5-15/16 in.) from center-to-center of each attachment point.

A change to the assembly procedure has been made to reduce the amount of play in the shift linkage. Additional washers are added to the shift link and between the bellcrank and gearcase as shown in **Figure 93**. This will improve shift

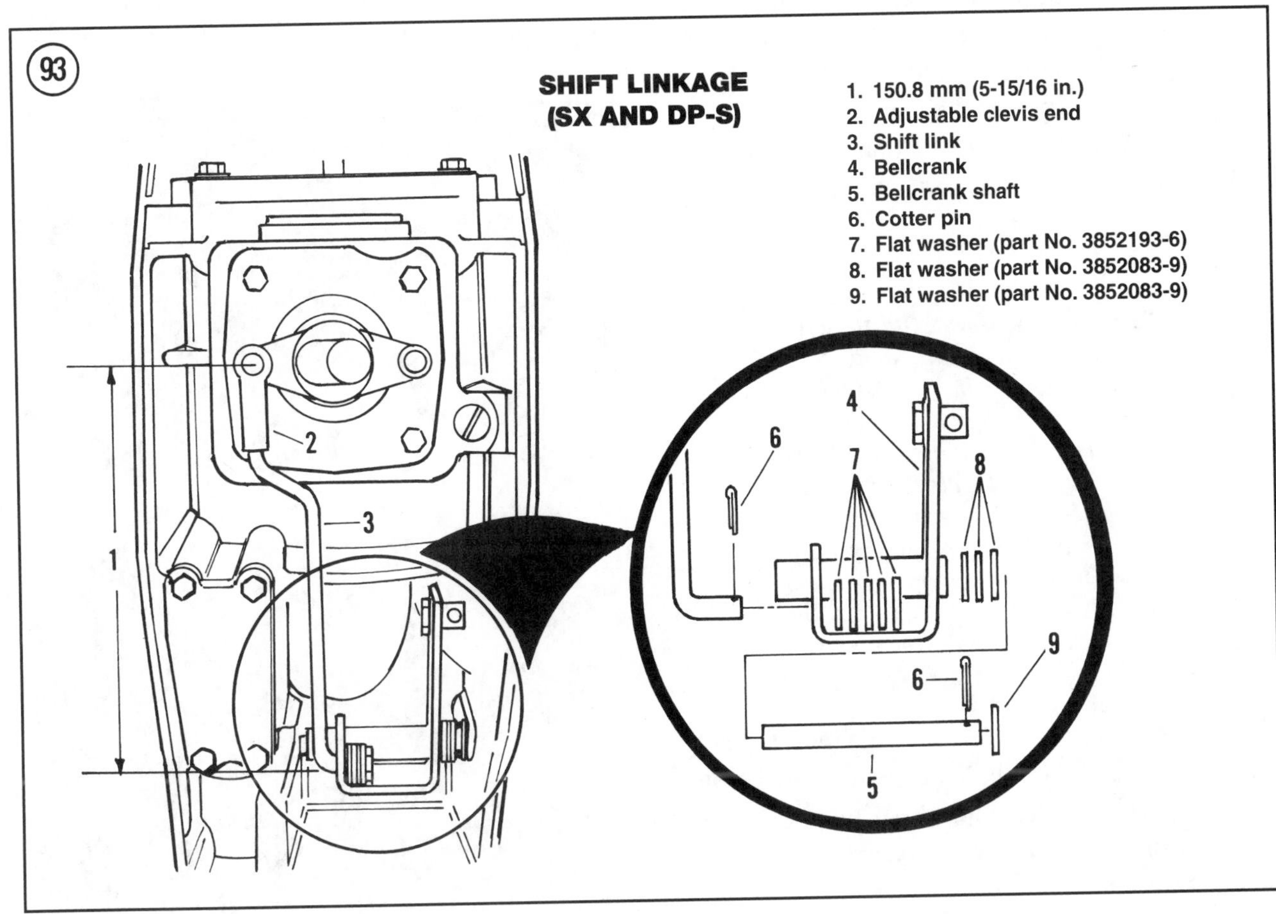

12

quality on all models and is a recommended improvement. An additional 4 washers part No. 3852193-6 and 2 washers part No. 3852083-9 are required for the upgrade. Install a total of 5 washers on the shift link and a total of 3 washers between the bellcrank and the cotter pin. Install the original 1 washer between the cotter pin and the gear housing.

To service the shift linkage, refer to **Figure 83** and **Figure 93** as necessary and proceed as follows.

1. Remove the cotter pin securing the shift link to the bellcrank. Remove the shift link and washer(s). Discard the cotter pin.

NOTE
The starboard end of the bellcrank shaft is slotted. Hold the cotter pin with needlenose pliers and rotate the shaft with a screwdriver to remove the cotter pin.

2. Remove the cotter pin securing the bellcrank shaft to the gearcase. Slide the bellcrank shaft out of the gearcase. Remove the bellcrank and all washers from the gearcase.
3. Clean and inspect all components. Remove any corrosion from the upper gearcase bellcrank shaft bore.

NOTE
If it is impossible to thread the clevis fitting on far enough to achieve the specified dimension in Step 4, it may be necessary to increase the threaded area of the clevis fitting ears. Clamp the full length of the clevis fitting in a vise so the flats of the ears are against the vise jaws. Run a 1/4-20 thread tap into the clevis fitting to increase the threaded area of the clevis ears. This will allow you to thread the clevis end further onto the link.

4. Measure the length of the shift link. Thread the clevis fitting in or out to achieve a dimension close to, but no more than 150.8 mm (5-15/16 in.) measured from center-to-center of each attachment point.
5. Reassemble the bellcrank and pivot rod as follows:
   a. Grease the bellcrank shaft and the bellcrank bore with Volvo Penta Propeller Grease or equivalent (**Table 6**).
   b. Position the bellcrank in the upper gearcase.
   c. Install the bellcrank shaft into the upper gearcase with its slotted end facing starboard. Install 4 washers part No. 3852083-9 over the shaft before piloting the shaft into the bellcrank and into its final position.
   d. Install a new stainless steel cotter pin into the shaft so that 3 washers are to port and 1 washer is to starboard of the cotter pin.
   e. Hold the pin with an appropriate flat blade screwdriver and bend both prongs of the cotter pin for a secure attachment.

NOTE
Install the shift link on the port side of the bellcrank arm (and eccentric piston)

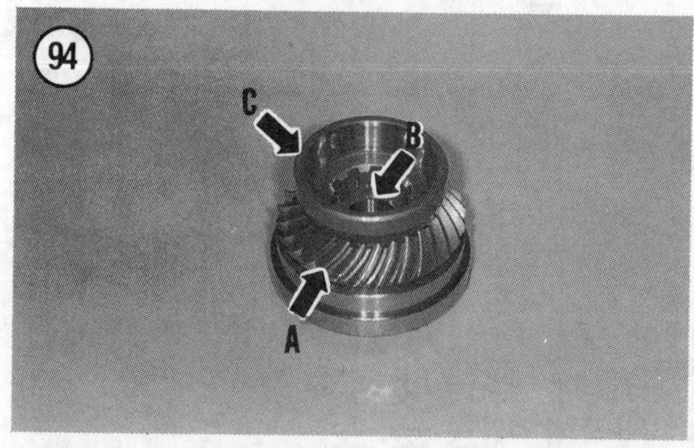

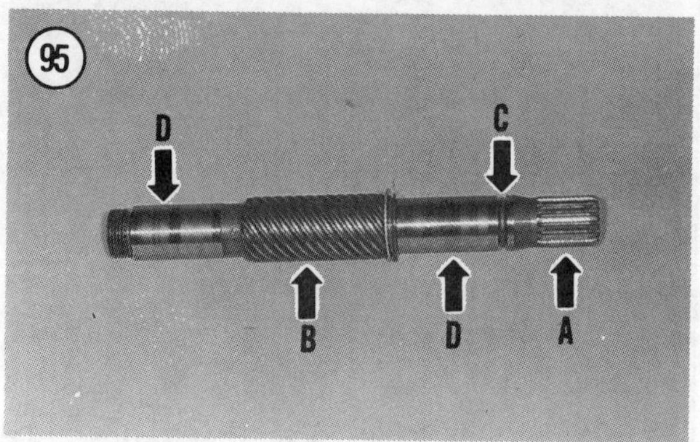

on DP-S and standard rotation SX models. Install the shift link on the starboard side of the bellcrank arm (and eccentric piston) for counter-rotation on SX models only.

6. Install the shift link and place 5 washers part No. 3852193-6 over the rod end. Secure the washers and shift link to the bellcrank with a new stainless steel cotter pin. Bend both prongs of the cotter pin for a secure attachment.

Cleaning and Inspection

CAUTION
Heli-Coil stainless steel locking thread inserts are used in all holes except the water cover and shift housing holes. Do not run a tap or thread chaser into any Heli-Coil equipped hole. Wash the holes with solvent and blow dry with compressed air.

1. Wash all components in clean solvent and blow dry with compressed air.
2. Apply a light coat of oil to all of the cleaned components to prevent rusting.
3. Inspect the gears. Check all gear teeth (A, **Figure 94**) and the internal bearing surfaces (B, **Figure 94**) for excessive wear, chips, cracks, nicks or other damage. Inspect the coned sleeve (C, **Figure 94**) of each output gear for scoring, glazing or metal transfer. The sleeve surface may be lightly dressed with emery cloth to remove superficial defects. If one gear is damaged and requires replacement, replace all 3 as an assembly.

CAUTION
One tapered roller bearing consists of the caged tapered roller bearings and cone-shaped inner race, and a cup-shaped outer race. The bearing must be replaced as a set and parts from one bearing must never be mixed with parts from another.

4. Check all of the bearings and bearing races for excessive or uneven wear, scoring, roughness, heat discoloration and binding. Replace any bearings (and corresponding races) as necessary.
5. Check the splines and threads of the input drive shaft coupler and yoke shaft for excessive wear, burring or distortion. Check the seal surfaces for grooving. Replace the shaft(s) if any defects are noticed.
6. Check the output shaft splines (A and B, **Figure 95**) for excessive wear, burring or distortion. Pay particular attention to the spiral splines at the center of the shaft. Inspect the split lock ring groove (C, **Figure 95**) for wear. Inspect the bearing surfaces (D, **Figure 95**) for wear, scoring and indications of overheating. Replace the shaft if any damage is noticed.
7. Inspect the cone clutch (**Figure 96**) for internal spline damage. Check the outer diameter for excessive wear, heat discoloration or damage on the cone-to-output sleeve mating surfaces. Inspect the shift shoe groove. Replace the cone clutch if its condition is questionable.
8. Check the cone clutch support spring (13, **Figure 83**) for distortion or loss of tension. Replace as required.
9. Inspect all shims and replace any that are damaged. If shimming adjustment is not required, damaged shims can be replaced with new shims of the same thickness.
10. Check the double stack, caged needle bearing assemblies (7, **Figure 83**) for roughness, heat

96

12

discoloration, binding or missing needles. Replace each bearing assembly as required.

11. Water cover service:
    a. Inspect the water passage cover (55, **Figure 83**) for gasket deterioration, loose fasteners and evidence of leakage.
    b. If necessary remove the 4 screws securing the water cover to the gearcase.
    c. Remove the water cover and all gasket material from the gearcase and the cover.
    d. Check the cover for distortion and replace if necessary.
    e. Check the gearcase for corrosion and clean as required.
    f. Install the water cover using a new gasket and *no* sealer. Tighten the screws evenly to specification (**Table 5**).

Thrust plate service

The thrust plates (58 and 62, **Figure 97**) located on each side of the front of the gearcase provide a bearing surface to absorb the side-to-side thrust loads from the propeller(s) and allow the transom bracket gimbal ring to absorb these loads. Inspect and measure the thrust plates each time the upper gearcase receives any major service. If the thrust plate dimension is too small, the drive unit will be able to move laterally during operation, causing excessive stress on the pivot housing pivot pins. If the thrust plate dimension is too large, the thrust plates will bind and break loose from the upper gearcase.

1. Measure the distance across the thrust plates with a 152.4 mm (6 in.) or larger dial caliper. Be sure to compress the plates and remove any air gaps between the plates, shims and the gearcase. Take several measurements up and down the plates and locate the widest dimension. Record this dimension. The thrust plates must measure between 12.72-12.79 cm (5.007-5.036 in.) at the widest point.

UPPER GEARCASE (SX AND DP-S)

1. Lubricant level dipstick and O-ring
2. Screw
3. Top cover
4. Top cover shim(s)
5. Top cover seal
6. Upper output shaft nut (shim)
7. Double stack caged needle bearing
8. Output gear main bearing
9. Bearing ring (upper gear only)
10. Upper output gear shim(s)
11. Upper output gear
12. Cone clutch
13. Cone support spring
14. Support washer
15. C-clip
16. Lower output gear
17. Lower gear retaining ring
18. Output shaft
19. Split lock ring
20. Thrust washer
21. Torx head screw
22. Washer
23. Pinion gear
24. Large tapered roller bearing
25. Pretension (crush) sleeve
26. O-ring
27. Plastic shim(s)
28. Pinion bearing carrier
29. Screw
30. Small tapered roller bearing
31. Seal
32. Snap ring
33. Yoke shaft
34. Lock ring
35. Bearing cap
36. Center coupler
37. Input drive shaft
38. O-ring
39. Screw
40. Rear cover
41. Shift shoe stop bolt
42. Shim(s)
43. Eccentric piston
44. Ramp follower pin
45. Roll pin
46. Screw
47. Seal
48. Shift housing
49. O-ring
50. Oil level plug and seal
51. Shift shoe spring
52. Shift shoe
53. Lower output gear shim
54. Screw
55. Water cover
56. Gasket
57. Gear housing
58. Starboard thrust plate
59. Thrust plate shim(s)
60. Retaining clip
61. Lubricant filter
62. Port thrust plate
63. Pivot pin bushing
64. Rubber grommet
65. Bellcrank shaft
66. Brass cube nut
67. Bellcrank
68. Cotter pin
69. Flat washer
70. Flat washer
71. Flat washer
72. Shift link
73. Clevis end
74. Clevis pin

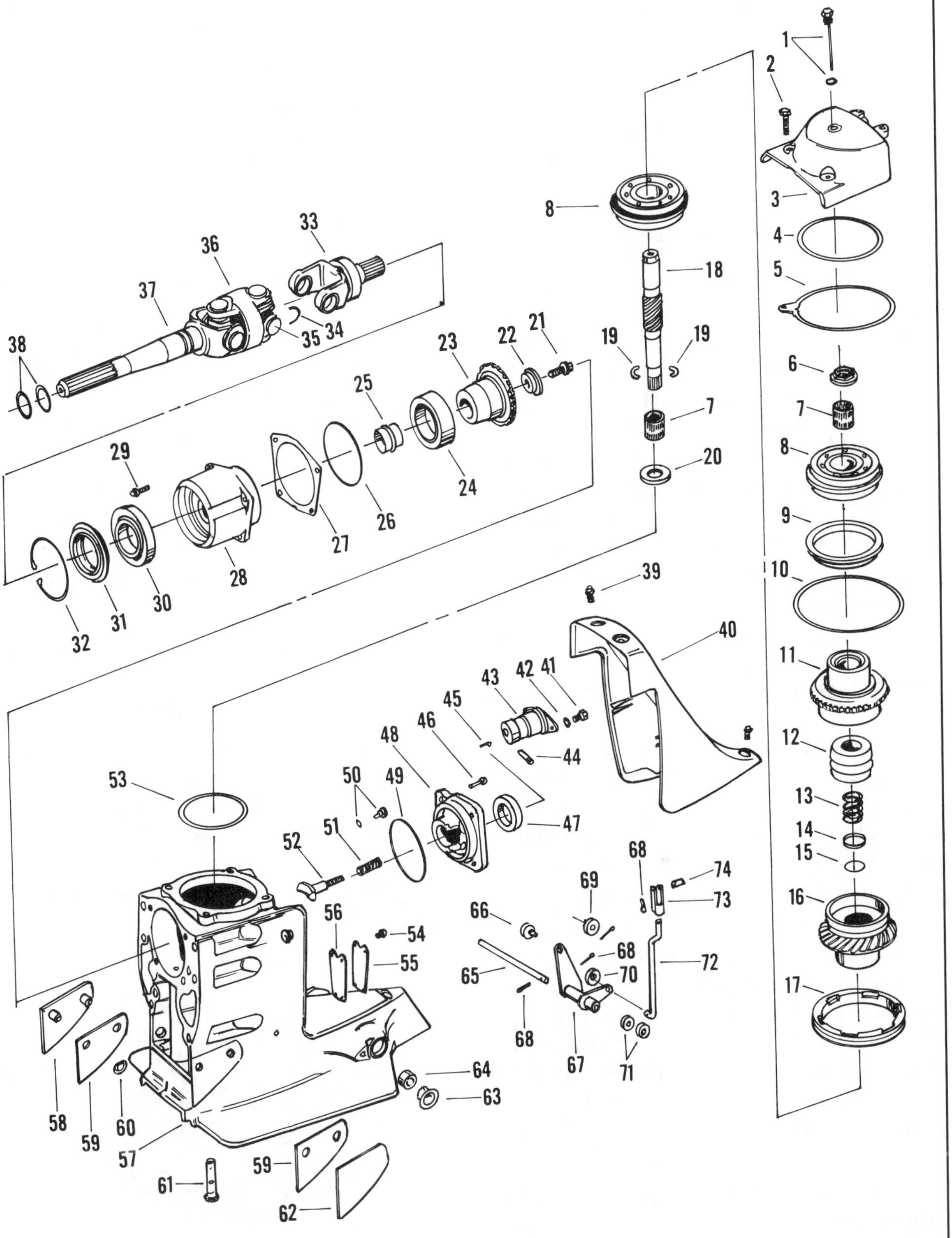

12

NOTE
*Thrust plate shims (59, **Figure 97**) come in one size only, 0.38 mm (0.015 in.). Shims must always be installed or removed equally to each side, with a minimum of 1 shim and a maximum of 4 shims per side. Each side must have the same amount of shims installed to keep the drive centered. If more than 4 shims are required on each side, replace both thrust plates and recheck the dimension.*

2. If the measurement exceeds specification, remove both thrust plates, remove 1 shim from each side, reassemble and recheck the dimension. If the measurement is below specification, remove both thrust plates, add 1 shim to each side, reassemble and recheck the dimension.
3. Install the thrust plates with new retaining rings (60, **Figure 97**). Seat the retaining rings by holding them in the installed position with a 1/2 in. box wrench and tapping the thrust plate toward the gearcase with a soft mallet. Make sure all 4 retaining rings are tightly seated.

Shim Selection

For maximum durability and quiet running, all of the gears must be properly located in the gearcase through shimming procedures. If the gears are properly located, the correct backlash and gear contact pattern will be observed.

Additionally, the tapered bearings in the clamp ring bearing carrier must be properly tensioned or *preloaded*. Preload refers to the tension applied to hold a tapered roller bearing in its cup. Insufficient preload will allow the bearing to move in relation to the bearing cup. Any movement of the bearing from its cup will result in premature bearing and gear failure. Excessive preload will cause the bearings to overheat and fail.

Refer to **Figure 97** for an exploded view of the upper gearcase components. During assembly procedures, lubricate all components with Volvo DuraPlus GL5 Synthetic Gear Lube (**Table 6**). Do not make any *dry* assemblies.

Pinion bearing carrier reassembly

1. If the pinion bearing carrier bearing cups were removed, proceed as follows:
   a. Begin the installation of new bearings and cups by placing the pinion bearing carrier in a press with its large end facing down.
   b. Lubricate the large bearing cup and place it into the bearing carrier with the tapered bearing face facing up.
   c. Press the bearing cup into the bearing carrier with the small end of bearing installer part No. 884932-5. Press until the cup is seated in the bearing carrier.
   d. To install the small bearing cup, place the bearing carrier in a press with its small end facing down.
   e. Lubricate the small bearing cup and place it into the bearing carrier with the tapered bearing face facing up.
   f. Press the bearing cup into the bearing carrier with the large end of bearing installer part No. 884932-5. Press until the cup is seated in the bearing carrier.

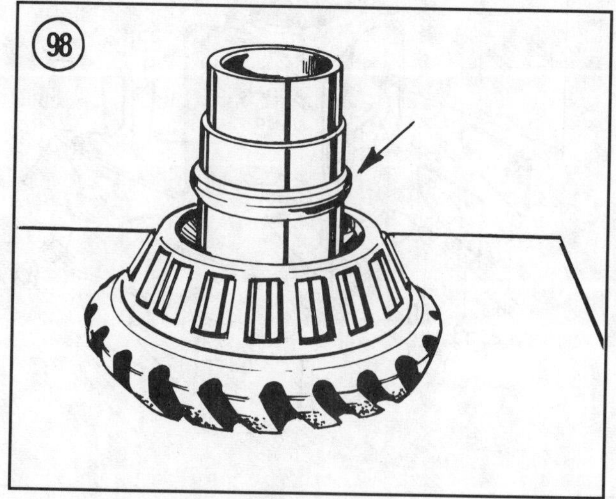

NOTE
Protect the tips of the drive gear teeth from damage when pressing the tapered roller bearing onto the gear in Step 2.

2. If the bearing was removed from the drive gear, proceed as follows:

   a. Begin installation of a new bearing by placing the drive gear in a press with the gear teeth facing down. Protect the gear teeth with a piece of wood, plastic or aluminum. Lubricate the large roller bearing and gear hub.

   b. Place the roller bearing onto the gear with the rollers facing up.

   c. Press the bearing fully onto the gear with sleeve part No. 884263-5. Make sure the bearing is seated against the gear flange.

CAUTION
A new pretension (crush) sleeve (25, ***Figure 97****) must be installed each time the clamp ring bearing carrier is disassembled. Failure to install a new pretension sleeve will result in premature bearing and gear failure.*

3. Place a new pretension (crush) sleeve (**Figure 98**) over the drive gear hub and against the large roller bearing.

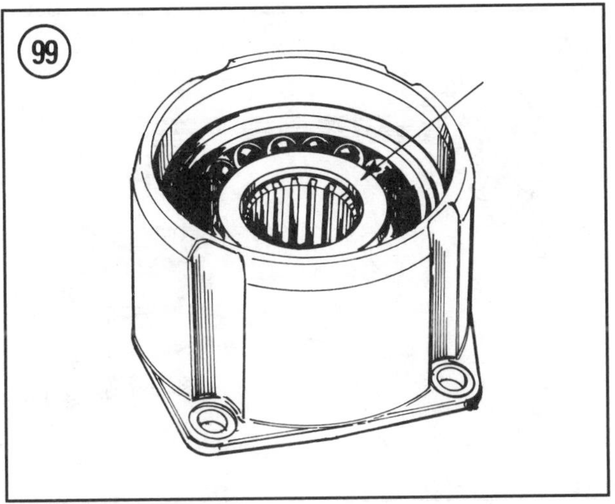

99

4. Install the pinion bearing carrier (with the large end up) over the gear and seat it on the large bearing.

5. Lubricate the small bearing and set it into the bearing carrier and on top of the gear hub with the rollers facing down. See **Figure 99**.

CAUTION
Do not press the bearing too far in Step 6. If the pretension sleeve is overcrushed, the bearing carrier must be disassembled and a new pretension sleeve installed.

6. Protect the gear teeth with a piece of wood, plastic or aluminum. Press the small bearing onto the gear hub with sleeve part No. 884263-5 until there is almost no play (approximately 1 mm [0.040 in.]) between the bearing carrier and the gear (and bearings). Wiggle the bearing carrier up and down while pressing, to monitor the small bearing's progress.

7. Place support sleeve part No. 884938-2 into a press with its large end facing up. Set the bearing carrier into the support sleeve with its large end facing up. Coat the outer diameter of a new universal joint shaft oil seal with Volvo White Sealing Compound or equivalent (**Table 6**). Press the seal into the bearing carrier with its seal lip facing up, using installer part No. 3850607-7. Press the seal until it is seated on the bearing carrier shoulder.

8. Secure the seal by installing the snap ring with snap ring pliers part No. 3850608-5 (or equivalent) (**Figure 100**). Make sure the snap ring is fully expanded into its groove. Coat the seal lips with OMC Triple Guard Grease or equivalent (**Table 6**).

9. Position the universal joint yoke shaft support fabricated during disassembly into both yokes of the yoke shaft. Clamp the yoke shaft and pipe securely in a vise with spline the shaft point up. The pipe should absorb all compressive loads and prevent damage to the yoke shaft.

10. Slide the pinion bearing carrier over the yoke shaft. Turn the gear and yoke shaft as

necessary to align the splines. Seat the bearing carrier on the yoke shaft.

11. Install the washer into the gear face. Lightly coat the threads of a new Torx head screw with Loctite 271 threadlocking adhesive (**Table 6**). Install the screw into the yoke shaft and hand-tighten.

NOTE
The next step sets the preload on the tapered roller bearings. Do not over-tighten the Torx head screw or the pre-tension sleeve will be damaged and will have to be replaced. The preload is checked by measuring the torque required to turn the yoke shaft as the bearing carrier is held stationary. The yoke should be turned slowly and smoothly. The bearings must be well lubricated for this adjustment. A 0-3.4 N•m (0-30 in.-lb.) dial indicator torque wrench is recommended for this procedure

12. Slowly tighten the Torx head screw with T50 Torx socket part No. 885043-0 while rotating the bearing carrier. As the screw is tightened the bearings will be forced closer together as they compress the pretension sleeve. When the bearings begin to preload, a marked increase in the effort required to rotate the carrier will be noticed. Stop tightening the screw when the increase in effort is noted.

CAUTION
*It is typical for a person to tighten the screw and see no immediate results. The person will then tighten the screw too far and damage the pretension sleeve. Do not become frustrated and tighten the screw in large increments. Be patient and tighten the screw a little at a time, checking the preload each time. With experience, the preload can be set very close by **feel** and will only require 1 or 2 torque wrench checks to achieve the specified setting.*

13. Check the bearing preload by gently clamping the carrier into the vise. Attach the T50 Torx socket to a suitable torque wrench. Rotate the pinion gear several turns to align and seat the bearings. Rotate the pinion gear slowly and smoothly while noting the torque wrench reading (**Figure 101**). Compare the reading to specifications (**Table 2**). Clamp the yoke shaft and pipe support into the vise and repeat Step 12 as necessary to obtain the specified preload (**Table 2**).

CAUTION
*If the rolling torque is set too high, the bearing carrier must be disassembled and a new pretension (crush) sleeve installed. Do not continue until the specified bearing preload (**Table 2**) is obtained.*

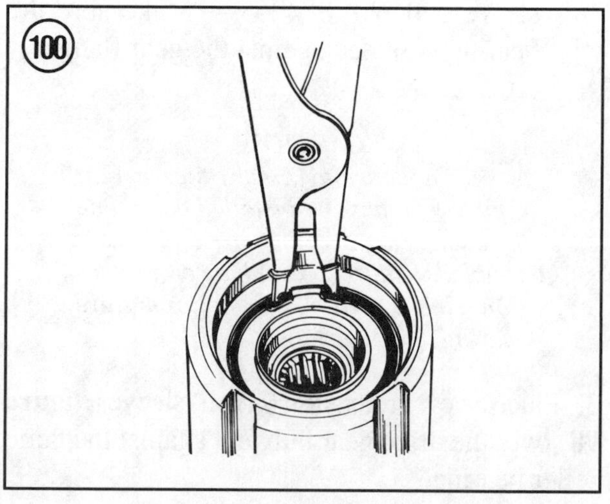

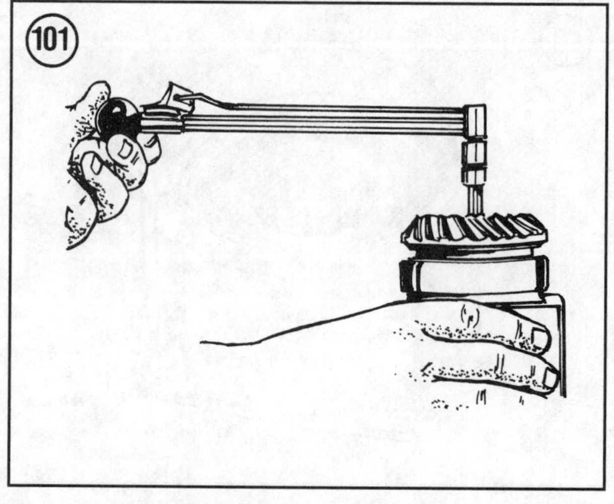

14. Reinstall the input drive shaft and universal joint assembly to the yoke shaft and pinion bearing carrier. Refer to *Universal Joint Service* in this chapter.

15. If the main bearings were removed from the output gears, proceed as follows:

   a. Begin installation of new bearings by placing the output gear in a press with the gear sleeve facing down. Protect the gear sleeve with a piece of wood, plastic or aluminum.
   b. Lubricate a new main roller bearing and the gear hub. Place the bearing on the gear hub with its numbered side facing up.
   c. Press the bearing fully onto the gear with drift part No. 884168-6. Make sure the bearing seats against the gear flange.
   d. Repeat substeps a-c for the remaining output gear and bearing.

16. If removed, install the adaptor ring on the upper output gear and bearing assembly as follows:

   a. Place the support sleeve (1, **Figure 102**) part No. 884938-2 in a press with the large opening facing up.

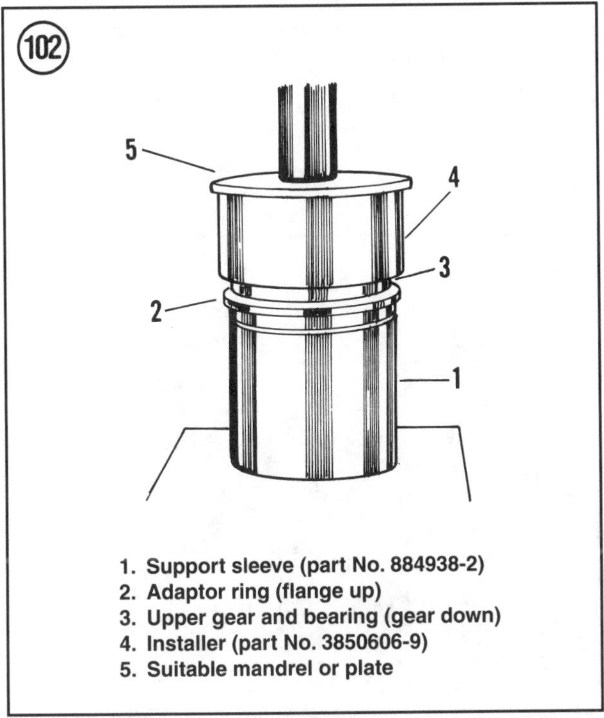

1. Support sleeve (part No. 884938-2)
2. Adaptor ring (flange up)
3. Upper gear and bearing (gear down)
4. Installer (part No. 3850606-9)
5. Suitable mandrel or plate

   b. Lubricate the adaptor ring (2, **Figure 102**) and set it on top of the support sleeve with the largest diameter (flanged lip) facing up.
   c. Set the upper output gear and bearing (3, **Figure 102**) on top of the adaptor ring with the gear facing down.
   d. Place installer part No. 3850606-9 (4, **Figure 102**) on top of the bearing. Place a suitable mandrel (or metal plate) (5, **Figure 102**) over the installer.
   e. Press the bearing and gear assembly into the adaptor ring, until the bearing lip is seated against the adaptor ring.

Lower output gear shimming

To determine the correct amount of shims to properly position the lower output gear, keep in mind that the numbers stamped on the gear sleeves are correction numbers in thousandths of an inch. Both the lower and upper output gears need to be properly positioned through the use of a shim gauge or shim fixture.

Since the gears are stamped using U.S. standard units of measure, it is recommended that all calculations be performed in inches. Any conversions from U.S. to Metric should only be attempted on the final calculated result.

The correct selection of shims and proper gearcase assembly will be confirmed by the gear lash and gear pattern verifications. To determine the shims required to located the lower output gear, proceed as follows.

NOTE

All 3 gears are stamped with a correction number and a match number. The match number always starts with a T. All 3 gears have the same T number. It would be extremely rare for all 3 gears to have the same correction number. Do not confuse the T number with a + (positive) correction number.

1. Find the correction number etched or stamped on the lower output gear sleeve (**Figure**

103). Record this figure as thousandths of an inch. For example, if +5 is etched on the gear, write it as +0.005 in. If -5 is etched on the gear, write it as -0.005 in.

2. Set the lower output gear on a clean workbench with the gear sleeve facing down.

3. Position the machined flat of shim gauge part No. 3850701-8 on the gear hub with the upper measuring tip positioned directly over the outer race of the main bearing.

NOTE

When the correct feeler gauge has been selected, a slight drag will be felt as the feeler gauge blade is moved between the measuring points. To verify, insert the next size larger blade and check for a noticeable increase in the drag. Then insert the next size smaller blade and check for the absence of any drag.

4. While holding the shim gauge firmly in place, take a feeler gauge reading between the shim gauge upper tip and the main bearing outer race (**Figure 104**). Record the feeler gauge reading.

CAUTION

Due to the location of the lower output gear shims, a minus (–) correction number must be ***added*** *to the feeler gauge reading and a positive (+) correction number must be* ***subtracted*** *to the feeler gauge reading.*

5. Add or subtract the correction number to the feeler gauge reading. For example, if the feeler gauge reading is 0.011 in. and the correction number is +5 (positive 5), *subtract* 0.005 in. from 0.011 in., with the result being 0.006 in. If the feeler gauge reading is 0.011 in. and the correction number is -5 (minus 5), *add* 0.005 in. to 0.011 in., with the result being 0.016 in. (0.41 mm). Install 0.016 in. (0.41 mm) shims in this example.

6. Select the correct amount of shims based on the results of Step 5. Install this amount of shims into the upper gearcase, lower output bearing bore.

Upper output gear shimming

To determine the correct amount of shims to properly position the upper output gear, proceed as follows.

1. Find the correction number etched or stamped on the upper output gear sleeve. Record this figure as thousandths of an inch. For example, if +5 is etched on the gear, write it as +0.005 in. If -5 is etched on the gear, write it as -0.005 in.

2. Set the upper output gear on a clean workbench with the gear sleeve facing down.

3. Position the machined flat of shim gauge part No. 3850701-8 on the gear hub with the lower

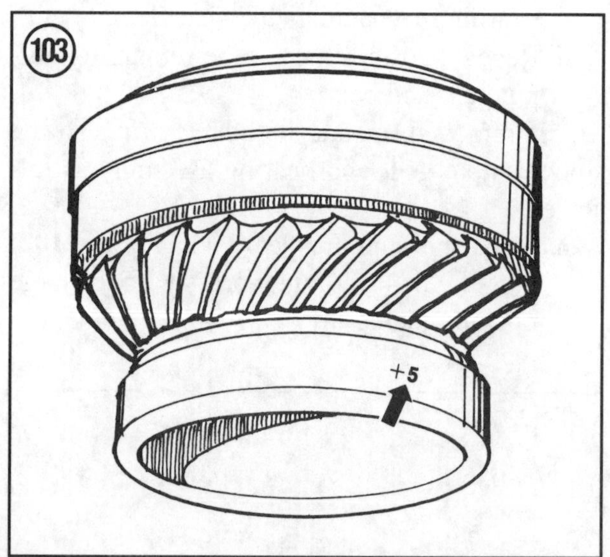

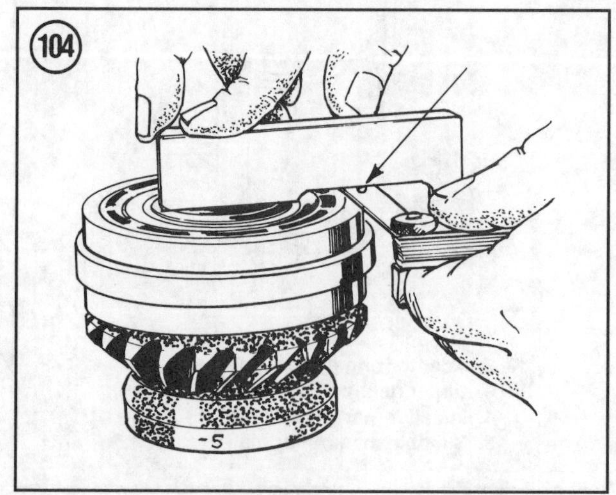

measuring tip positioned directly under the adaptor ring flanged lip.

NOTE
When the correct feeler gauge has been selected, a slight drag will be felt as the feeler gauge blade is moved between the measuring points. To verify, insert the next size larger blade and check for a noticeable increase in the drag. Then insert the next size smaller blade and check for the absence of any drag.

4. While holding the shim gauge firmly in place, take a feeler gauge reading between the shim gauge lower tip and the adaptor ring flanged lip (**Figure 105**). Keep the feeler gauge flat (horizontal) during the reading. Record the feeler gauge reading.

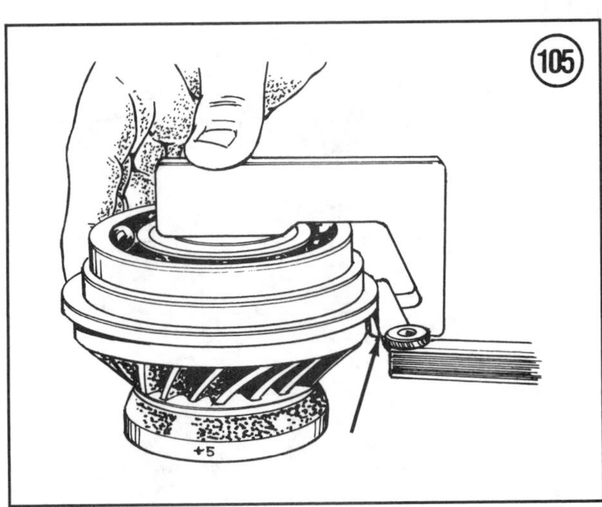

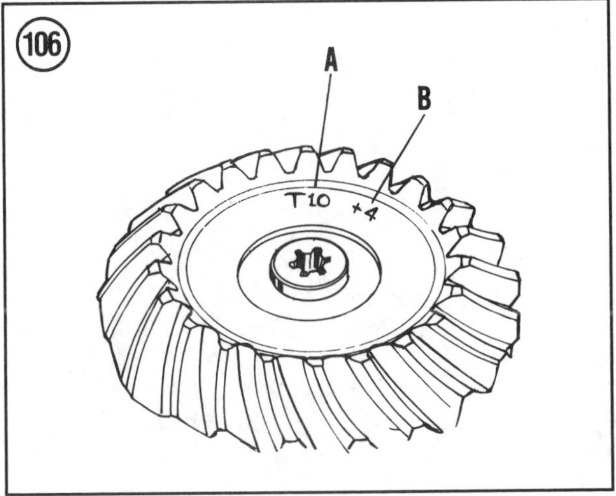

CAUTION
Due to the location of the upper output gear shims, a minus (–) correction number must be ***subtracted*** *from the feeler gauge reading and a positive (+) correction number must be* ***added*** *to the feeler gauge reading.*

5. Add or subtract the correction number to the feeler gauge reading. For example, if the feeler gauge reading is 0.011 in. and the correction number is +5 (positive 5), *add* 0.005 in. to 0.011 in., with the result being 0.016 in. If the feeler gauge reading is 0.011 in. and the correction number is -5 (minus 5), *subtract* 0.005 in. from 0.011 in., with the result being 0.006 in. (0.15 mm). Install 0.006 in. (0.15 mm) shims in this example.
6. Select the correct amount of shims based on the results of Step 5. Place these shims with the upper output gear assembly.

Pinion bearing carrier shimming

To determine the correct amount of shims to properly position the pinion gear, keep in mind that the number etched into the pinion gear face is a correction number in thousandths of an inch. The pinion gear nominal figures listed in **Table 3** are the factory specified dimension required to properly position the pinion gear in the upper gearcase. When the correct amount of shims are installed on the pinion bearing carrier flange, the dimension from the shim surface to the gear teeth should equal the specified nominal dimension. Proceed as follows.

NOTE
All 3 gears are stamped with a correction number and a match number. The match number always starts with a T (A, ***Figure 106****). All 3 gears have the same T number. It would be extremely rare for all 3 gears to have the same correction num-*

ber. Do not confuse the T number with a + (positive) correction number.

1. Find the correction number etched or stamped on the pinion gear face (B, **Figure 106**). Record this figure as thousandths of an inch. For example, if +5 is etched on the gear, write it as +0.005 in. If -5 is etched on the gear, write it as -0.005 in.
2. Lightly clamp the pinion bearing carrier assembly into a vise with the gear facing up.

NOTE
The distance from the pinion gear teeth to the pinion bearing carrier flange must be accurately measured in this procedure. Shim plate part No. 3850600-2 is designed to sit on the gear teeth and provide a stable platform to measure from. The thickness of the shim plate must be compensated for in the calculations. If the shim plate is not used, a wide based depth micrometer, which rests on several gear teeth must be used for accurate results.

3A. *With shim plate*:
  a. Set shim plate part No. 3850600-2 (A, **Figure 107**) on top of the gear teeth with the recessed side facing up.
  b. Measure the distance from the top of the shim plate to the pinion bearing carrier flange (B, **Figure 107**). Do not measure near the bolt holes. Take several readings to ensure accuracy. Record the measurement.
  c. Subtract the thickness of the shim plate (12.70 mm [0.500 in.]) from the recorded measurement. The resulting number is the actual distance from the gear teeth to the pinion carrier flange. Record the actual distance.

3B. *Without shim plate*—Measure the distance from the top of the gear teeth to the pinion bearing carrier flange (**Figure 108**). Do not measure near the bolt holes. Take several readings to ensure accuracy. Record the measurement.

CAUTION
Due to the location of the pinion gear shims, a minus (–) correction number must be ***subtracted*** *from the feeler gauge reading and a positive (+) correction number must be* ***added*** *to the feeler gauge reading.*

4. Add or subtract the etched correction number from the actual distance (gear teeth to the carrier flange). For example, if the actual distance is 1.999 in. and the correction number is +4 (positive 4), *add* 0.004 in. to 1.999 in., with the result being 2.003 in. If the actual distance is 1.999 in. and the correction number is -4 (minus 4), *sub-*

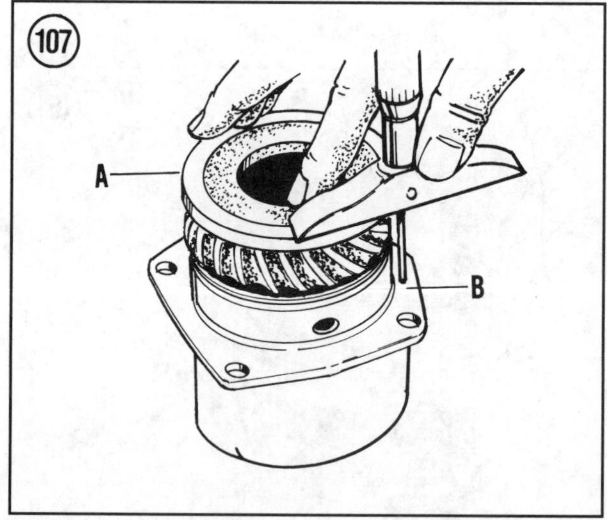

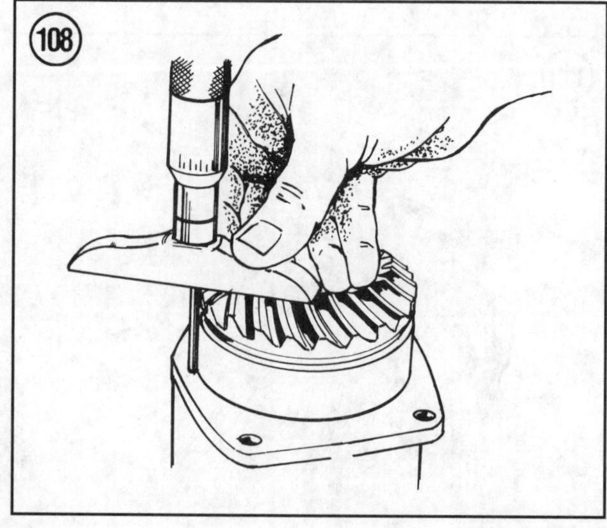

tract 0.004 in. from 1.999 in., with the result being 1.995 in. Record your calculations.

5. Subtract the appropriate pinion gear nominal figure listed in **Table 3** from the result of the calculations in Step 4. For example, if we had a result from Step 4 of 1.995 in. and our gearcase uses a 22:23 upper gear ratio, we would subtract the specified nominal figure of 1.971 in. from 1.995 in. and the result would be .024 in. (0.61 mm). We would install 0.024 in. (0.61 mm) shims in this example.

6. Select the correct amount of plastic shims based on the results of Step 5. Place these plastic shims on the pinion bearing carrier.

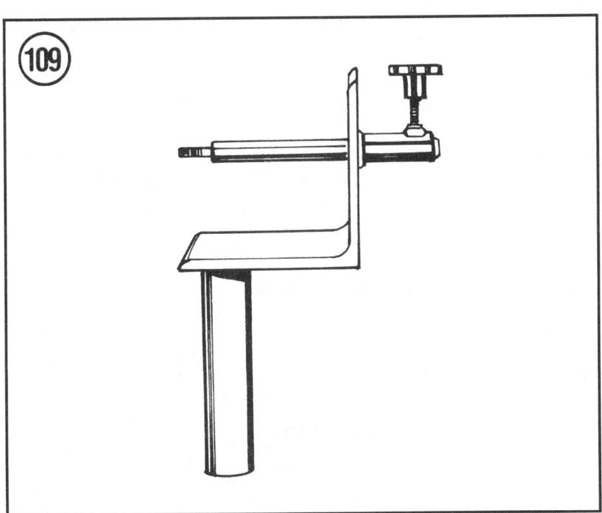

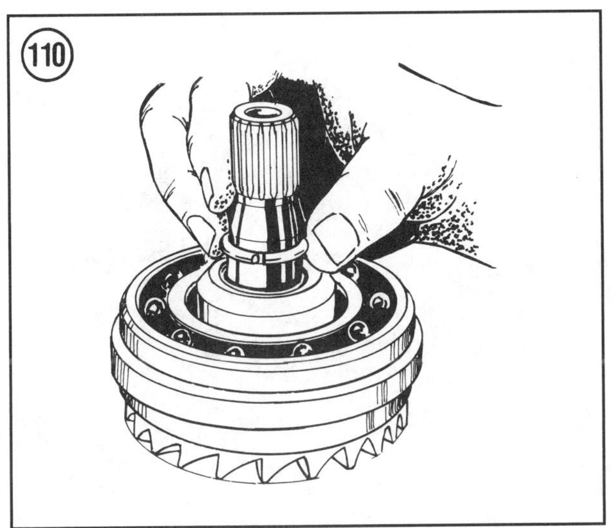

Assembly

Gearcase holding fixture part No. 3850605-1 (**Figure 109**) is designed to hold the upper gearcase securely for all service procedures. The holding fixture fits a standard Bob Kerr Tool Company workbench base or floor stand. It is highly recommended that these procedures be performed *with* a holding fixture. Attempting to perform these procedures without a holding fixture will be very difficult, even with the aid of an assistant.

1. Mount the holding fixture part No. 3850605-1 in a Bob Kerr workbench base or floor stand.
2. Attach the spline socket part No. 38950598-5 to the fixture shaft and tighten the set screw securely.
3. Loosen the shaft lock screw and lower the shaft fully.
4. Set the upper gearcase onto the fixture and align the appropriate bolt holes.

5A. *SX models*—Secure the upper gearcase to the fixture with the 4 screws provided with the fixture. Tighten the 4 screws *hand-tight*.

5B. *DP-S models*—Secure the upper gearcase to the fixture with 4 appropriate nuts and washers on the upper gearcase studs. Tighten the 4 nuts *hand-tight*.

12

Vertical shaft assembly

1. If removed, install the cone clutch support washer and C-clip (14 and 15, **Figure 97**) onto the output shaft.
2. Insert the double-stack needle bearing into the lower output gear in its original orientation. Insert the grooved end of the output shaft through the lower gear and needle bearing assembly.
3. Place the thrust washer over the output shaft with the recess facing out. Coat the 2 split locking rings with OMC Needle Bearing Assembly Grease or equivalent (**Table 6**). Place the 2 split rings into the output shaft groove. Pull the output shaft to lock the split rings into the thrust washer's recess. See **Figure 110**.

CAUTION
When the output shaft and lower bearing are installed into the gearcase, the output shaft must be supported to prevent it from falling, causing the 2 split locking rings to fall out.

4A. *Without holding fixture*:
 a. Verify that the predetermined shims are installed in the bottom of the gearcase bore.
 b. Stuff several shop towels into the drive shaft bore from the bottom of the gearcase to support the output shaft during assembly.
 c. Lower the output shaft and lower output gear assembly into the gearcase bore and seat the gear and bearing on top of the shims.
 d. While still holding the output shaft upward, make sure the shop towels are pressed up against the lower end of the output shaft and will keep it from falling into the drive shaft bore.

4B. *With holding fixture*:
 a. Verify that the predetermined shims are installed in the bottom of the gearcase bore.
 b. Lower the output shaft and lower output gear assembly into the gearcase bore and seat the gear and bearing on top of the shims.
 c. While still holding the output shaft upward, loosen the locking screw on the fixture and raise the shaft and socket up to support the output shaft. Move the gearcase as necessary to align the splines.
 d. Tighten the locking screw on the fixture *snugly*. Verify that the bearing and gear assembly are seated in the gearcase bore and that the output shaft splines are engaged to the shaft and socket. Tighten the 4 screws or nuts securing the gearcase to the fixture securely.

CAUTION
If the lower output gear assembly is not seated in the gearcase bore, the threads of the lock ring will be visible through the pinion bearing carrier bore. If using the fixture, the shaft assembly may be positioned too high, preventing the gear assembly from seating. ***Do not*** *use the spanner wrench to force the gear and retaining ring into position.*

5. Lubricate the lower output gear retaining ring (17, **Figure 97**) and the corresponding threads in the gearcase. Install and thread the ring in as far as possible by hand. The threads of the ring should not be visible when viewed through the pinion bearing carrier bore.

6. Install the spanner wrench part No. 3850604-4 (**Figure 111**) into the gearcase and engage the

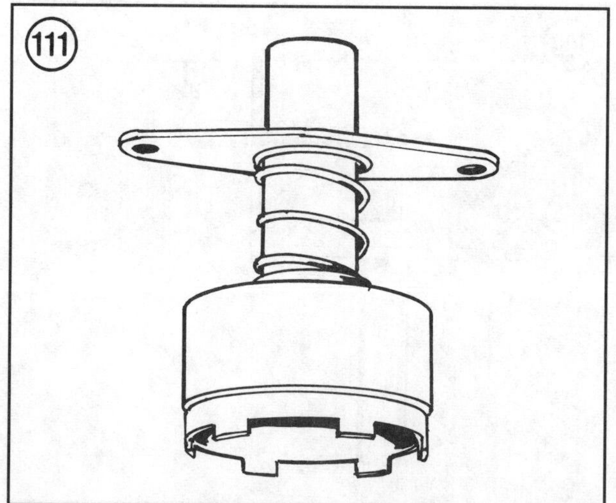

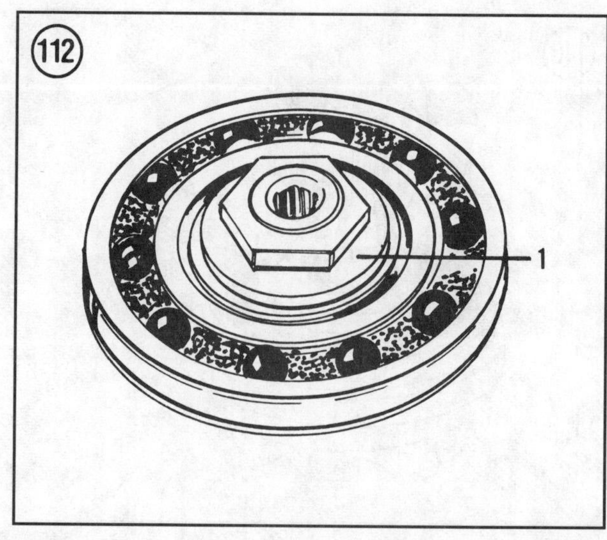

retaining ring lugs. Secure the tool to the gearcase with 2 suitable screws.

7A. *Without holding fixture*—With the aid of an assistant, a 1/2 in. to 3/4 in. adapter and a suitable torque wrench, tighten the retaining ring to specification (**Table 5**).

7B. *With holding fixture*—Using a 1/2 in. to 3/4 in. adapter and a suitable torque wrench, tighten the retaining ring to specification (**Table 5**).

8. Remove the spanner wrench from the gearcase.

9. Install the cone clutch support spring (13, **Figure 97**) over the output shaft.

10. Install the cone clutch onto the output shaft with the TOP mark facing up.

11. Install the predetermined shims to the upper output gear adaptor ring flange. Secure the shims in place with OMC Needle Bearing Assembly Grease or equivalent (**Table 6**).

12. Install the upper output gear and shims into the upper gearcase. Make sure none of the shims are displaced or damaged during the installation process.

NOTE

If using the gearcase fixture, it may be necessary to loosen the 4 fasteners securing the upper gearcase to the fixture and move the upper gearcase slightly to align the output shaft perfectly to install the needle bearing in Step 13.

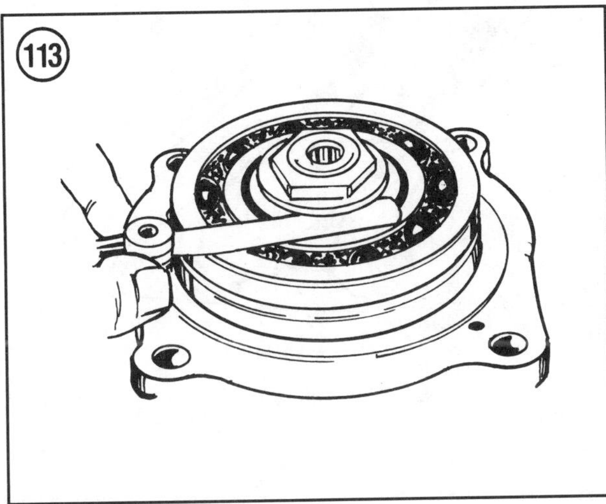

13. Install the double-stack needle bearing (7, **Figure 97**) into the upper output gear in its original orientation.

NOTE

*If the original upper nut has been misplaced, install the thinnest nut first (**Table 3**). If too thick of a nut is installed, the upper and lower output gears will be pinched together when the nut is tightened. This can force the gears to shift in the bearing assemblies, leading to premature gear and bearing failure. Remember that the upper output shaft nut has left hand threads.*

14A. *Without holding fixture*:

a. Lubricate the threads of the output shaft and install the upper drive shaft nut (**Table 3**). See **Figure 112**.

b. Tighten the nut hand-tight. Remove the shop towels from the lower drive shaft bore. Using a flashlight, verify that the 2 split ring retainers are still correctly installed.

c. With the aid of an assistant, secure the output shaft with spline socket part No. 3850598-8, an extension and a breaker bar. Tighten the nut with a 30 mm socket to specification (**Table 5**).

d. With the aid of an assistant, hold the output shaft firmly in the UP position with the spline socket and extension or a suitable tool.

e. While the shaft is being held up, make sure the upper output gear is held firmly against its shims and the upper gearcase.

f. Using a feeler gauge, measure the clearance between the upper output gear hub and the upper nut (**Figure 113**). Compare the feeler gauge reading to the specification (**Table 3**).

14B. *With holding fixture*:

a. Lubricate the threads of the output shaft and install the upper drive shaft nut (**Table 3**). See **Figure 112**.

b. Tighten the nut with a 30 mm socket to specification (**Table 5**).
c. Loosen the fixture lock screw and push the shaft firmly up against the output shaft. Tighten the lock screw securely.
d. Using a feeler gauge, measure the clearance between the upper output gear hub and the upper nut (**Figure 113**). Compare the feeler gauge reading to the specification (**Table 3**).

15. If the clearance is below specification (**Table 3**), install the next size thinner nut and repeat Step 14A or 14B. If the clearance is above specification, install the next size larger nut and repeat Step 14A or 14B.

NOTE
If the specified clearance cannot be obtained with available nut sizes, recheck the assembly of the vertical shaft components. Make sure that both gears are pressed fully into their bearings and that the bearings are not worn. Recheck all shimming calculations and measurements.

16. Lubricate the pinion bearing carrier and gearcase bore. Install the pinion bearing carrier *without* the O-ring and *with* the predetermined shims. Seat the bearing carrier fully into the gearcase and make sure the shims are correctly aligned with the bolt holes. The shims will only fit correctly in one position.
17. Install the 4 bearing carrier screws and tighten to specifications (**Table 5**).

Top cover shimming

The top cover must be shimmed correctly to provide the proper preload required to hold the upper output gear bearing firmly into the upper gearcase bore and prevent the outer race from rotating. If too many shims are installed, the top cover will be warped and will not seal properly. If too few shims are installed, the top bearing will spin in the gearcase and destroy the gearcase housing. To shim the top cover, proceed as follows.

1. Install the original top cover shims or approximately 0.51 mm (0.020 in.) shims into the top cover. Secure the shims in place with OMC Needle Bearing Assembly Grease or equivalent (**Table 6**).
2. Install the top cover to the gearcase *without* the top cover seal. Make sure the shims are not displaced or damaged during installation.
3. Hold the top cover firmly against the upper gearcase. Measure the clearance between the top cover and the upper gearcase along the mating surfaces. Take several readings and average the readings if necessary.
4. Compare the average feeler gauge reading to the specification (**Table 3**). If the reading is less than specified, install additional top cover shims and recheck the measurement as described in Step 3. If the reading is more than specified, remove top cover shims as necessary and recheck the measurement.
5. Once the specified measurement has been obtained, install the 4 cover screws and tighten to specification (**Table 5**).

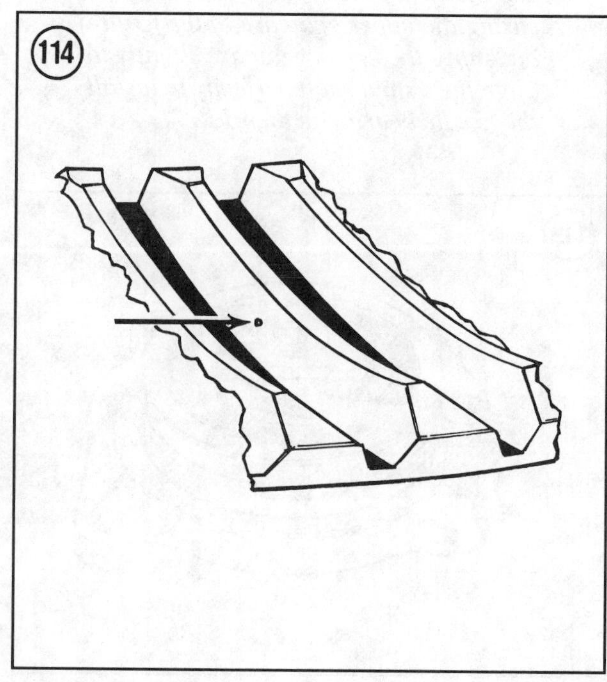

Gear lash verification

Gear lash is a measurement of the clearance between a drive gear tooth and the output gear tooth. The drive gear must not move during this procedure and the gear teeth must be clean and free of excessive oil, lint, dirt or debris. The gears should make a distinct clicking sound as the output gear is rotated back and forth against the drive gear. The output gears are accessed through the shift housing bore.

The simplest way to mount a dial indicator to the upper gearcase is to mount a flat metal plate to one of the rear cover mounting bosses located at the rear of the top cover (3, **Figure 97**). A 76 mm (3 in.) long piece of 12.7 mm (1/2 in.) wide, 3.2 mm (1/8 in.) flat stock with a 7.94 mm (5/16 in.) hole drilled in it will work perfectly. Install the plate to one of the rear cover mounting bosses (on the top cover) with a suitable screw. Use the dial indicator C-clamp to secure the dial indicator to the plate. This setup allows the dial indicator to be centered on the shift housing bore.

1. Mount a dial indicator (such as OTC model OEM4635, [**Table 11**]) capable of reading lateral movement to the upper gearcase. Place the ball tip of the dial indicator arm on the horizontal and vertical midpoint (**Figure 114**) of the lower output gear tooth. Make sure the face of the dial indicator is vertical and that the indicator's arm is pointing directly into the imaginary center of the output shaft. Zero the indicator and rock the output gear lightly back and forth to read the backlash. Record the reading. Lift the dial indicator from the gear tooth, turn the gear 1/2 turn, reposition the indicator and recheck the backlash. Record the reading.
2. Reposition the indicator and repeat Step 1 for the upper output gear. Record the readings. Remove the dial indicator when finished.

NOTE

If the gear lash requires correction, change approximately 0.03 mm (0.001 in.) of shims for every 0.03 mm (0.001 in.) of correction desired. Move the appropriate gear toward the other gear(s) to decrease gear lash and move the appropriate gear away from the other gear(s) to increase gear lash.

3. Compare the measured gear lash of both gears with the specification listed in **Table 3**.
   a. If the gear lash of both gears is excessive, reduce the thickness of shims between the pinion bearing carrier and the gearcase. Repeat Steps 1 and 2.
   b. If the gear lash of both gears is insufficient, increase the thickness of shims between the pinion bearing carrier and the gearcase. Repeat Steps 1 and 2.
   c. If the gear lash on one output gear is correct and the other output gear is incorrect, recheck the calculations used to determine the incorrect output gear's shim(s). If the calculations are correct, add or subtract shims from the calculated shims as specified in **Table 12** to bring the incorrect output gear into the specified gear lash range (**Table 3**). Repeat Steps 1 and 2.

CAUTION

*If either output gear shims are changed, the output shaft end play and top cover shims must be again verified **during** reassembly.*

Any changes to the upper output gear shims must be compensated by changing the exact opposite amount of shims at the top cover. The sum of the changes to the upper output shims and the top cover shims must equal 0 (zero).

Changing Shims at the lower and upper output gears affects output shaft end play. Subtracting lower output shims or adding upper output shims decreases end play and may require that a thinner output shaft nut be installed.

Adding lower output shims or subtracting upper output shims increases end play and may require that a thicker output shaft nut be installed. It is possible for the changes at the lower

12

and upper output gears to cancel out each other as far as output shaft end play is concerned.

Gear pattern verification

Once gear backlash has been verified, check the gear contact pattern as follows.

1. Coat 3 teeth of both output gears with a thin coat of GM gear marking compound available from all General Motors automotive dealerships.
2. Wedge a wooden hammer handle against the gear sleeves and rotate the drive gear by turning the universal joint yoke counterclockwise (as viewed from the rear of the drive) several revolutions to produce a tooth pattern on the driven gears. The gears must be loaded to produce a pattern.
3. Withdraw the hammer handle and observe the pattern on the teeth of the driven gears through the shift housing bore.
4. Compare the pattern on the gear teeth with the pattern shown at 4, **Figure 115**.
5. If the pattern is not as specified (**Figure 115**), refer to **Table 12** and change shims as specified to move the contact pattern toward the center of the tooth.
6. Correct the placement of shims as necessary to make the gear tooth pattern match that shown at 4, **Figure 115** before continuing.

CAUTION
*If the contact pattern must be corrected, the output shaft end play and top cover shims must be verified **during** reassembly. The gear lash must be checked **before** continuing with final assembly.*

7. Remove the top cover and pinion bearing carrier keeping all of the shims in their correct positions. Lubricate all internal components with clean gear oil. Proceed with the final assembly after all parts are lubricated.

Final Assembly

1. Install a new top cover seal on the upper gearcase with the seal protrusion over the starboard front screw hole (A, **Figure 116**). *Lightly* glue the seal to the upper gearcase with OMC Type M adhesive or equivalent (**Table 6**). Make sure the lubricant passage (B, **Figure 116**) in the seal is aligned with lubricant passage in the gearcase and is not blocked with sealant.
2. Install the predetermined top cover shims into the top cover. Secure the shims in place with

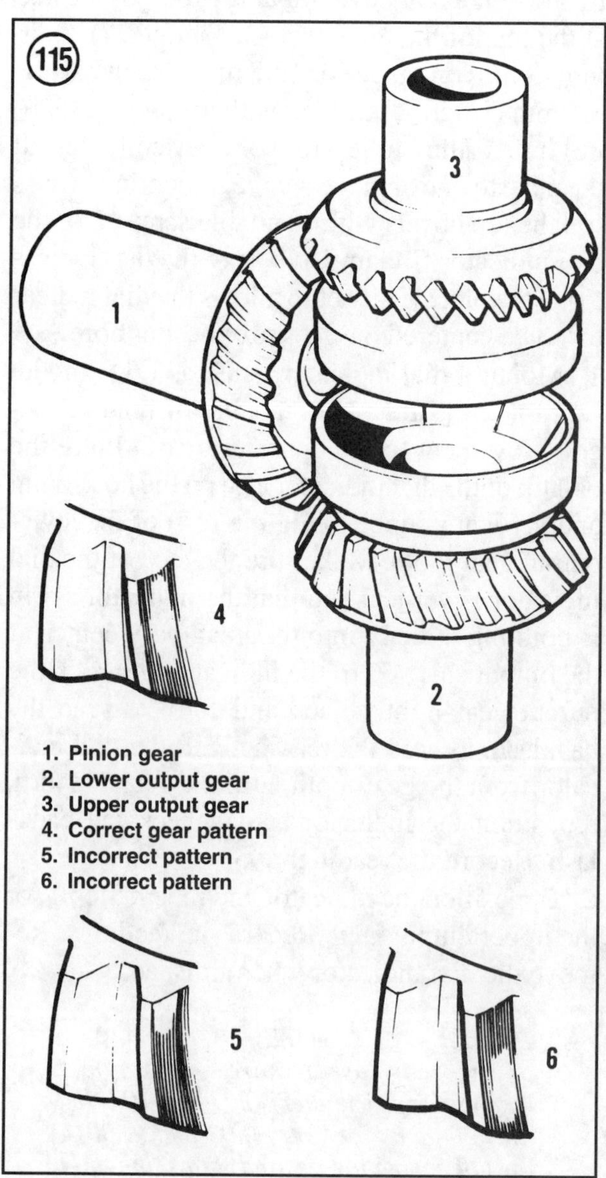

1. Pinion gear
2. Lower output gear
3. Upper output gear
4. Correct gear pattern
5. Incorrect pattern
6. Incorrect pattern

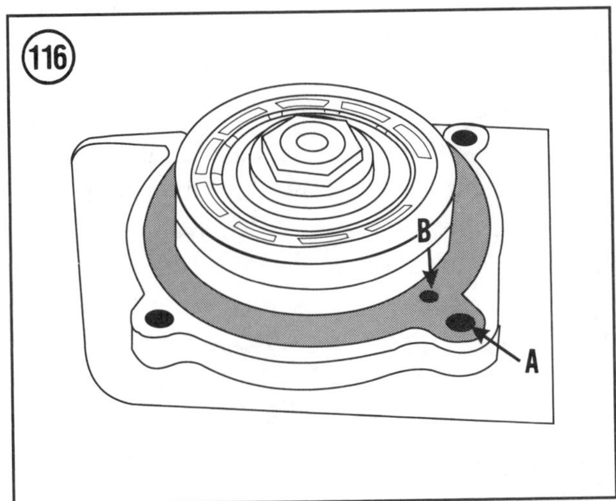

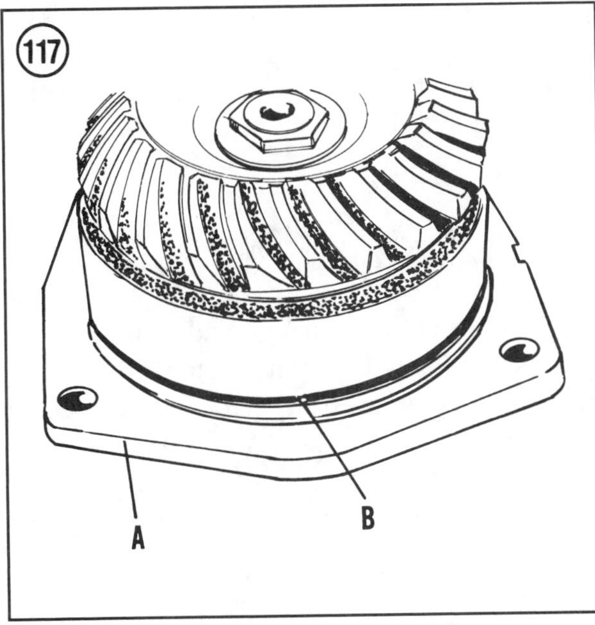

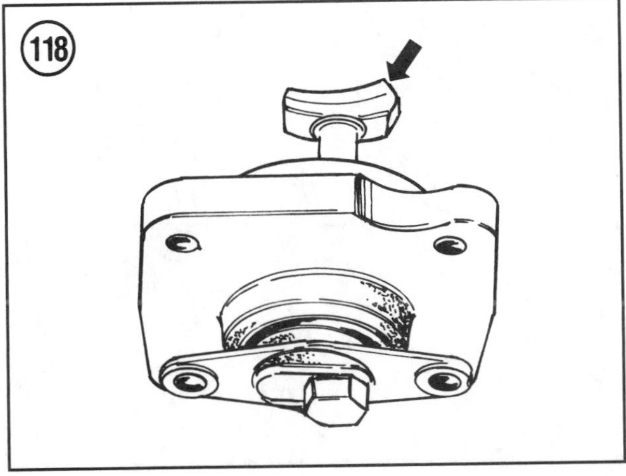

OMC Needle Bearing Assembly Grease or equivalent (**Table 6**).

3. Carefully install the top cover without displacing any of the shims or the seal ring. Coat all 4 top cover screw threads with Volvo White Sealing Compound or equivalent (**Table 6**). Install and evenly tighten the screws to specification (**Table 5**).

4. Install the predetermined shim(s) onto the pinion bearing carrier (A, **Figure 117**). Install a new O-ring (B, **Figure 117**) in the carrier groove. Coat the O-ring and mating surfaces of the bearing carrier and upper gearcase with Volvo White Sealing Compound or equivalent (**Table 6**).

5. Install the pinion bearing carrier into the upper gearcase. Be careful not to displace the shim(s) and do not cock the carrier in the gearcase bore. A rubber or plastic mallet may be used to lightly tap the carrier into place. Seat the carrier against the gearcase.

6. Apply Volvo White Sealing Compound or equivalent (**Table 6**) to the threads of the 4 bearing carrier screws, then install and evenly tighten the screws to specification (**Table 5**).

7. Install a new O-ring in the shift housing groove. Coat the O-ring, shift housing and gear housing mating surfaces with Volvo White Sealing Compound or equivalent (**Table 6**).

8. Install the shift housing assembly into the gearcase bore with the large side (big end) of the shift shoe facing starboard (**Figure 118**). Coat the threads of the 4 screws with Volvo White Sealing Compound or equivalent (**Table 6**). Install and evenly tighten the screws to specifications (**Table 5**).

9. Refer to *Shift Shoe Shimming* in this chapter and determine the shims required to properly locate the shift shoe stop bolt. The shift shoe can also be shimmed after the upper gearcase is installed to the intermediate housing, if so desired.

10. Refer to *Upper gearcase installation* in this section and install the upper gearcase.

11. Make sure that the drive unit is pressure and vacuum tested as described in *Upper gearcase installation* before the drive unit is filled with lubricant.

SHIFT HOUSING SERVICE (ALL MODELS)

All of the upper gearcases covered in this chapter use the same basic shift housing and shift shoe assembly. The only important thing to note is that if the cone clutch is steel, then the shift shoe must be brass. If the cone clutch is brass, then the shift shoe must be steel. Do not attempt to run steel on steel or brass on brass.

The shift mechanism can be serviced without removing the upper gear housing assembly from the drive unit and without removing the drive unit from the transom bracket or transom shield. However, if the shift shoe is damaged or broken, the drive unit (or at least the upper gearcase) should be disassembled and inspected for damage.

The shift shoe stop bolt requires shimming to ensure smooth, positive gear disengagement. Any time the drive unit is difficult to get out of gear, shim the shift shoe as described in *Shift Shoe Shimming* located in this section.

The SX and DP-S upper gearcases use an adjustable shift linkage to connect the bellcrank to the eccentric piston arm. The dimension of the shift link must not exceed 150.8 mm (5-15/16 in.), when measured from center of the clevis pin bore to the center of link rod. Refer to *SX and DP-S Upper Gearcase Service* for adjustment procedures.

Refer to **Figure 119** for a typical shift housing assembly exploded view.

Disassembly

1. Remove the shift cover/rear cover as described in this chapter.

NOTE
The shift shoe is spring-loaded and can fall free from the shift housing.

2. Detach the shift linkage and remove the 4 screws (5, **Figure 119**) securing the shift housing to the upper gearcase, then remove the shift cover and shift shoe assembly. Discard the O-ring.

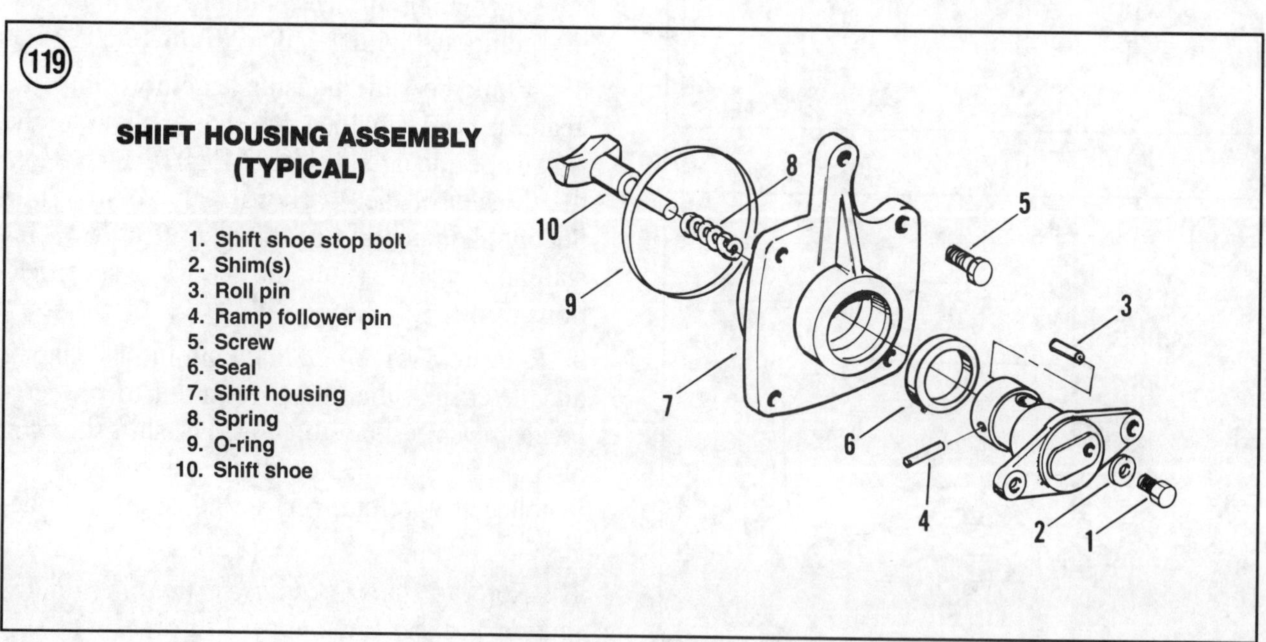

3. Clamp the shift housing in a vise with protective jaws.
4. Remove the shift shoe and spring (8 and 10, **Figure 119**).
5. Using a 1.98 mm (5/64 in.) pin punch (such as Snap-on part No. PPR2-1/2), drive the roll pin (**Figure 120**) into the eccentric piston cavity.
6. Remove the ramp follower pin (4, **Figure 119**) from the eccentric piston with a pair of pliers. Shake the eccentric piston until the roll pin falls out. Discard the roll pin.

CAUTION
The roll pin must be removed from the eccentric piston in Step 5. Failure to remove the roll pin at this time will prevent future disassembly.

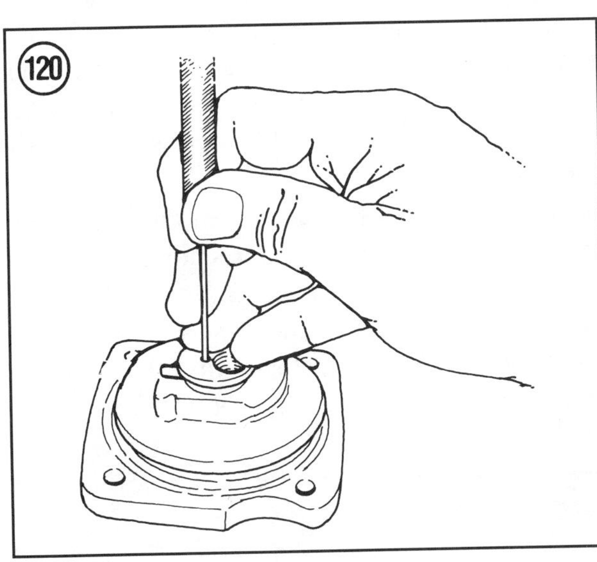

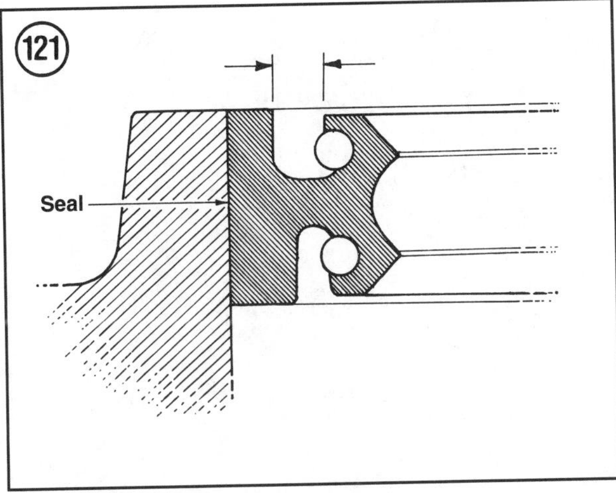

7. Remove the eccentric piston from the shift housing. Pry the seal from the cover bore with an appropriate screwdriver. Do not damage the housing bore. Discard the seal.
8. Clean all parts in solvent and blow dry with compressed air. Check all parts for wear or damage and replace as necessary.
9. Clean the inside of the eccentric piston bore as necessary to remove all corrosion and deposits that could cause binding.

Assembly and Installation

1. Coat the outside diameter of a new shift housing seal with Loctite 271 (**Table 6**). The inner side of the seal is fitted with a steel ring and can be identified by the narrower gap (**Figure 121**). Press the seal into the housing with the steel ring side facing down, using the large end of seal installer part No. 884259-3 or equivalent, until the tool seats against the shift housing (or the seal is flush with the housing).
2. Lubricate the seal lips with OMC Triple Guard Grease or equivalent (**Table 6**).
3. Lubricate the eccentric piston and install it through the seal and into the housing with a rotating motion.
4. Install the ramp follower pin and align the hole in the pin with hole in the eccentric piston.
5. Drive a new roll pin into the eccentric piston and ramp follower pin until the roll pin is flush with the surface of the eccentric piston. Verify that the eccentric piston still turns freely in the shift housing.
6. Lubricate the shift shoe and spring. Install the spring, then the shift shoe into the eccentric piston.
7. Install a new O-ring in the shift housing groove. Coat the O-ring, shift housing and upper gearcase mating surfaces with Volvo White Sealing Compound or equivalent (**Table 6**).

8. Install the shift housing assembly into the gearcase bore with the large side (**Figure 118**) of the shift shoe facing starboard. Coat the threads of the 4 screws with Volvo White Sealing Compound or equivalent (**Table 6**). Install and evenly tighten the screws to specification (**Table 4**).
9. Reconnect the shift linkage. Install a new stainless steel cotter pin. Bend both prongs of the cotter pin for a secure attachment.
10. Shim the shift shoe as described in the next section.

Shift Shoe Shimming

The shift shoe must be shimmed anytime the cone clutch, shift shoe, or any of the shift housing components are changed. The shift shoe should also be shimmed anytime the drive unit is hard to get out of gear. The drive unit does not have to be removed for this procedure.

1. Remove the shift cover/rear cover from the upper gearcase as described in this chapter.
2. Disconnect the remote control shift cable from the shift bellcrank. Discard the cotter pin.
3. Support the eccentric piston arm with an adjustable wrench and remove the shift shoe stop bolt (1, **Figure 119**).
4. Carefully remove the shim(s) (2, **Figure 119**) from the stop bolt or eccentric piston face.
5. Clean all sealer from the stop bolt, shims and eccentric piston face and threads.
6. Install the stop bolt *without* the shims and *without* any sealer.
7. Turn the eccentric piston to position the internal ramp follower pin (A, **Figure 122**) on a *flat* (B, **Figure 122**) of the shift housing ramp, located just past either side of the neutral detent (C, **Figure 122**). The eccentric piston arms will be positioned just above or just below the horizontal position. This positions the eccentric piston (and stop bolt) as close to the clutch cone as possible.

WARNING

The shift shoe is shimmed by rotating the propeller shaft or the upper gearcase output shaft, depending on whether or not the upper gearcase is installed. If the drive unit is installed to the transom shield/bracket, disconnect the negative battery cable to prevent accidental starting.

NOTE

The shift shoe rides an eccentric, machined into the cone clutch groove. During operation the shift shoe moves in and out, much like a lifter on a camshaft. There is only 1 eccentric high point per each revolution of the cone clutch.

8. While rotating the propeller shaft or the upper gearcase output shaft, slowly turn the stop bolt inward in small increments, until the propeller or output shaft binds from the shift shoe being pinched between the cone clutch eccentric and the shift shoe stop bolt. Wait at least 1 revolution of the cone clutch for each incremental turn of the stop bolt.
9. When you feel the binding of the shift shoe, verify that the eccentric arm has not moved from its correct position (internal ramp on a flat, either side of neutral detent). If the eccentric arm is still in the correct position, slowly turn the stop bolt out, while rotating the shaft, until the eccentric

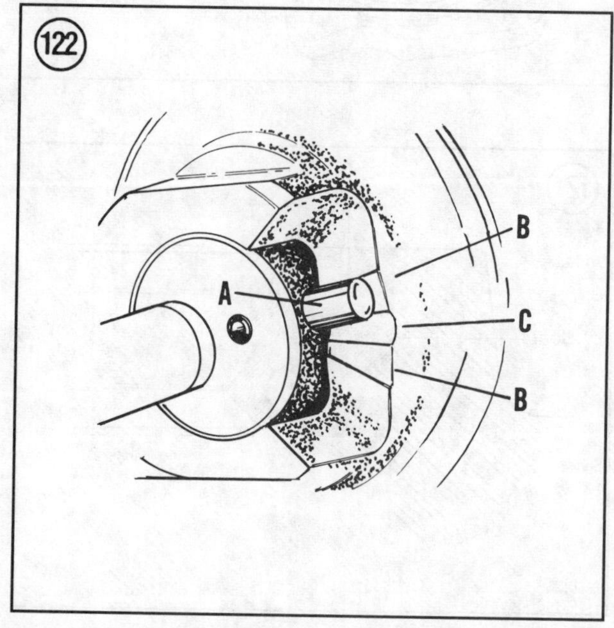

just *cannot* be felt. Do not confuse the resulting friction from the shift shoe spring compressing and relaxing with the mechanical binding of the shift shoe to the cone clutch and stop bolt.

10. Measure the gap between the eccentric piston face and the stop bolt head (**Figure 123**). If the bolt is slightly cocked, measure the smallest and largest gaps and average the measurements. Shift shoe shims come in 0.02 mm (0.008 in.) sizes only. You must install shims at least equal to the size of the feeler gauge reading or larger. You must never install shims of lesser size than the feeler gauge reading.

11. Compare the feeler gauge reading to the 0.02 mm (0.008 in.) shim size. Select a quantity of shims that equals or exceeds the feeler gauge reading. For example, if the feeler gauge reading is 0.48 mm (0.019 in.), install 3 shims for a total thickness of 0.06 mm (0.024 in.). Select the appropriate amount of shims based on your feeler gauge reading and install them on the shift shoe stop bolt.

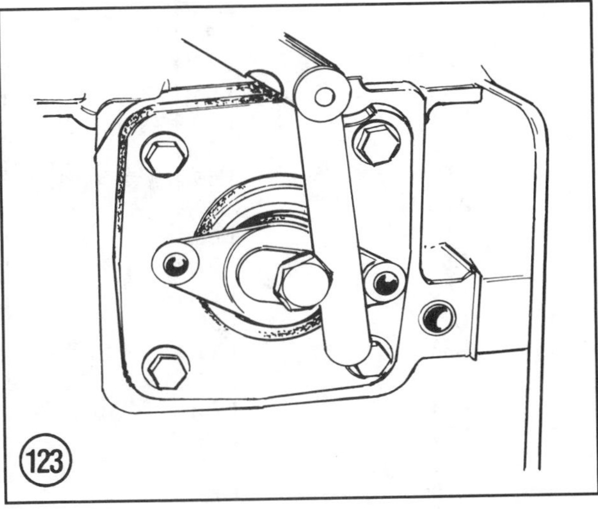

12. Support the eccentric piston arms and tighten the stop bolt to 14-16 N•m (10-12 ft-lb.).

13. Reposition the eccentric piston arm as described in Step 7. Rotate the propeller shaft or output shaft and feel for any binding of the shift shoe against the cone clutch and stop screw. The shift shoe is correctly shimmed if *no* binding is noted. If binding is noted, remove the stop bolt and install 1 more shim. Rotate the propeller shaft or output shaft and recheck for binding.

CAUTION

Do not continue assembly if binding is noted. The shift shoe and cone clutch will be damaged if the unit is operated with an incorrectly shimmed shift shoe. Generally, no less than 1 shim and no more than 5 shims should be required to correctly shim the shift shoe.

14. When the shift shoe is correctly shimmed, remove the stop bolt (while supporting the arm) and shims. Coat the threads of the stop bolt liberally with Loctite PST pipe sealant (**Table 6**). Reinstall the stop bolt and all shims. Support the eccentric arm and torque the stop bolt to 14-16 N•m (10-12 ft.-lb.).

CAUTION

If the stop bolt is not correctly sealed in Step 13, the gearcase will not hold lubricant in and keep water out.

12

15. Reconnect the remote control shift cable to the bellcrank arm. Secure the brass cube nut to the bellcrank with a flat washer and new stainless steel cotter pin. Bend both prongs of the cotter pin for a secure attachment.

16. Reinstall the shift cover/rear cover as described in this chapter.

Tables 1-12 are on the following pages.

Table 1 DRIVE UNIT RECOMMENDED GEAR RATIO SPECIFICATIONS

Engine model	Original drive unit	Original drive No.	Standard gear ratio	3500-5000 ft. (1067-1524 m) gear ratio	5000 ft.-up (1524 m-up) gear ratio
1994–MD models					
3.0 GL/GS	SX-S	3868035	1.85:1	1.85:1	1.85:1
4.3 GL/GS	SX-S	3868077	1.66:1	1.85:1	1.85:1
4.3 GS	DP-C1	3868008	2.30:1	2.30:1	2.30:1
5.0 FL	SX-S	3868077	1.66:1	1.85:1	1.85:1
	DP-C1[1]	3868002	1.95:1	2.30:1	2.30:1
	DP-C1[1]	3868008	2.30:1	2.30:1	2.30:1
5.0 Fi	SX-S[1]	3868068	1.60:1	1.66:1	1.66:1
	SX-S[1]	3868077	1.66:1	1.66:1	1.66:1
	DP-C1[1]	3868002	1.95:1	2.30:1	2.30:1
	DP-C1[1]	3868008	2.30:1	2.30:1	2.30:1
5.7 GL	SX-S	3868068	1.60:1	1.66:1	1.66:1
	DP-C1[1]	3868002	1.95:1	2.30:1	2.30:1
	DP-C1[1]	3868008	2.30:1	2.30:1	2.30:1
5.7 Gi	DP-D1[1]	3868022	1.78:1	1.95:1	2.30:1
	DP-C1[1]	3868002	1.95:1	2.30:1	2.30:1
5.8 FL	SX-S	3868058	1.51:1	1.66:1	1.66:1
5.8 Fi	SX-S	3868058	1.51:1	1.60:1	1.60:1
7.4 GL	DP-D1	3868022	1.78:1	1.78:1	1.95:1
8.2 GL	DPX-S[1]	3868020	1.59:1	1.78:1	1.78:1
	DPX-S[1]	3868021	1.68:1	1.78:1	1.78:1
	DPX-S[1]	3868023	1.78:1	1.78:1	1.78:1
1995–HU models					
3.0 GS	SX-CT	3868159	1.85:1	1.85:1	1.85:1
4.3 GL/GS	SX-C	3868160	1.66:1	1.85:1	1.85:1
4.3 GS/Gi	DP-C1	3868008	2.30:1	2.30:1	2.30:1
5.0 FL	SX-C	3868160	1.66:1	1.85:1	1.85:1
	DP-C1	3868002	1.95:1	2.30:1	2.30:1
5.0 Fi	SX-C	3868161	1.60:1	1.66:1	1.66:1
	DP-C1	3868002	1.95:1	2.30:1	2.30:1
5.7 Gi	DP-C1	3868002	1.95:1	2.30:1	2.30:1
5.8 FL	SX-C	3868162	1.51:1	1.66:1	1.66:1
	DP-C1	3868002	1.95:1	2.30:1	2.30:1
5.8 Fi	SX-C	3868162	1.51:1	1.66:1	1.66:1
5.8 FSi	SX-C	3868208	1.43:1	1.51:1	1.51:1
	DP-D1	3868022	1.78:1	1.95:1	1.95:1
	DP-C1[1]	3868002	1.95:1	1.95:1	1.95:1
7.4 GL/Gi	DP-D1	3868022	1.78:1	1.95:1	1.95:1
7.4 GSi	DPX-S[1]	3868020	1.59:1	1.78:1	1.78:1
	DPX-S[1]	3868021	1.68:1	1.78:1	1.78:1
	DPX-S[1]	3868023	1.78:1	1.78:1	1.78:1
8.2 GL	DPX-S[1]	3868020	1.59:1	1.78:1	1.78:1
	DPX-S[1]	3868021	1.68:1	1.78:1	1.78:1
	DPX-S[1]	3868023	1.78:1	1.78:1	1.78:1
1996–NC models					
3.0 GS	SX-CT1[1,2]	3868396	1.85:1	2.18:1	2.18:1
	SX-CT1[1]	3863937	1.97:1	2.18:1	2.18:1
4.3 GS/GL/Gi	SX-C1[1]	3868395	1.66:1	1.85:1	1.85:1
	SX-C1[1]	3868465	1.85:1	1.85:1	1.85:1
4.3 GS	DP-S	3868163	2.30:1	2.30:1	2.30:1
	DP-C1	3868008	2.30:1	2.30:1	2.30:1

(continued)

Table 1 DRIVE UNIT RECOMMENDED GEAR RATIO SPECIFICATIONS (continued)

Engine model	Original drive unit	Original drive No.	Standard gear ratio	3500-5000 ft. (1067-1524 m) gear ratio	5000 ft.-up (1524 m-up) gear ratio
1996–NC models (continued)					
4.3 Gi	DP-S	3868163	2.30:1	2.30:1	2.30:1
5.0 FL	SX-C1	3868394	1.60:1	1.66:1	1.85:1
	DP-S	3868164	1.95:1	2.30:1	2.30:1
	DP-C1	3868002	1.95:1	2.30:1	2.30:1
5.0 Fi	SX-C1[1]	3868394	1.60:1	1.66:1	1.66:1
	SX-C1[1]	3868395	1.66:1	1.66:1	1.66:1
	DP-S	3868164	1.95:1	2.30:1	2.30:1
	DP-C1	3868002	1.95:1	2.30:1	2.30:1
5.7 GL	SX-C1	3868394	1.60:1	1.66:1	1.66:1
	DP-S	3868164	1.95:1	1.95:1	2.30:1
5.7 Gi	SX-C1	3868393	1.51:1	1.60:1	1.66:1
	DP-S	3868164	1.95:1	1.95:1	2.30:1
	DP-C1	3868002	1.95:1	1.95:1	2.30:1
5.7 GSi	SX-C1	3868392	1.43:1	1.51:1	1.51:1
	DP-S	3868165	1.78:1	1.95:1	1.95:1
5.8 FL	SX-C1	3868393	1.51:1	1.60:1	1.66:1
	DP-S	3868164	1.95:1	2.30:1	2.30:1
	DP-C1	3868002	1.95:1	2.30:1	2.30:1
5.8 Fi/FSi	SX-C1	3868393	1.51:1	1.60:1	1.66:1
	DP-S	3868165	1.78:1	1.95:1	1.95:1
	DP-S	3868164	1.95:1	1.95:1	1.95:1
7.4 GL/Gi	SX-C1	3868392	1.43:1	1.51:1	1.51:1
7.4 GL	DP-S	3868185	1.78:1	1.78:1	1.95:1
	DP-D1	3868022	1.78:1	1.78:1	1.95:1
7.4 Gi	DP-S	3868166	1.68:1	1.78:1	1.95:1
	DP-D1	3868455	1.68:1	1.78:1	1.95:1
7.4 GSi	DPX-S[1]	3868020	1.59:1	1.78:1	1.78:1
	DPX-S[1]	3868021	1.68:1	1.78:1	1.78:1
	DPX-S[1]	3868023	1.78:1	1.78:1	1.78:1
8.2 GL/GSi	DPX-S[1]	3868020	1.59:1	1.78:1	1.78:1
	DPX-S[1]	3868021	1.68:1	1.78:1	1.78:1
	DPX-S[1]	3868023	1.78:1	1.78:1	1.78:1
1997 LK models					
3.0 GS	SX-C	3868392	1.43:1	1.60:1	1.97:1
4.3 GL/GS	SX-C	3868392	1.43:1	1.60:1	1.97:1
4.3 Gi	DP-S	3868166	1.68:1	1.95:1	2.30:1
5.7 GL/GS	SX-C	3868392	1.43:1	1.60:1	1.97:1
5.7 GSi	DP-S	3868166	1.68:1	1.95:1	2.30:1
7.4 GL	DP-S	3868166	1.68:1	1.95:1	2.30:1
7.4 Gi	DPX-S1	3868637	1.59:1	1.68:1	1.78:1
7.4 GSi	DPX-S1	3868637	1.59:1	1.68:1	1.78:1
8.2 GSi	DPX-S1	3868637	1.59:1	1.68:1	1.78:1
1998 BY, 1999 WT and 2000 FS models					
3.0 GS	SX-M	3868895	1.97:1	2.18:1	2.18:1
4.3 GL	SX-M	3868892	1.66:1	1.79:1	1.89:1
	DP-SM	3868913	1.95:1	2.32:1	2.32:1
4.3 GS	SX-M	3868892	1.66:1	1.79:1	1.79:1
	DP-SM	3868913	1.95:1	2.32:1	2.32:1

(continued)

12

Table 1 DRIVE UNIT RECOMMENDED GEAR RATIO SPECIFICATIONS (continued)

Engine model	Original drive unit	Original drive No.	Standard gear ratio	3500-5000 ft. (1067-1524 m) gear ratio	5000 ft.-up (1524 m-up) gear ratio
1998 BY, 1999 WT & 2000 FS (continued)					
4.3 Gi	SX-M	3868892	1.66:1	1.79:1	1.79:1
	DP-SM	3868913	1.95:1	2.32:1	2.32:1
5.0 GL	SX-M	3868890	1.51:1	1.60:1	1.60:1
	DP-SM	3868912	1.78:1	1.95:1	1.95:1
5.0 Gi	SX-M	3868890	1.51:1	1.60:1	1.60:1
	DP-SM	3868912	1.78:1	1.95:1	1.95:1
5.7 GS/GSi	SX-M	3868889	1.43:1	1.51:1	1.51:1
	DP-SM	3868912	1.78:1	1.95:1	1.95:1
7.4 Gi	SX-M	3868889	1.43:1	1.43:1	1.43:1
	DP-SM	3868911	1.68:1	1.78:1	1.95:1
7.4 GSi	DP-SM	3868911	1.68:1	1.78:1	1.78:1
8.2 GSi	DP-SM	3868911	1.68:1	1.78:1	1.78:1

1. Refer to *Drive Unit Gear Ratio* in this chapter.
2. High-altitude gear ratio requires upper and lower gear changes.

Table 2 DRIVE UNIT SPECIFICATIONS (DP-C1/D1 AND DPX MODELS)

Drive unit lubricant capacity	
DP-C1/D1	2.7 L (2.8 qt.)
DPX	2.0 L (2.1 qt.)
Clamp ring bearing carrier preload	
New bearings	500-1000 g (1.1-2.2 lb.)
Used bearings	500-800 g (1.1-1.8 lb.)
Fixed dimensions, output gears and gear housing	
Output gears	62.05 mm (2.443 in.)
Gear housing B and C prefix	61.00 mm (2.402 in.)
Output shaft end play	0.1-0.5 mm (0.004-0.020 in.)
Pressure test	48 kPa (7 psi)
Top cover clearance (preload)	0.05-0.1 mm (0.002-0.004 in.)
Upper gearcase gear lash	
DP-C1/D1 - 1.78:1 and 1.95 ratio	0.15-0.25 mm (0.006-0.010 in.)
DP-C1/D1 - 2.30:1 ratio	0.08-0.18 mm (0.003-0.007 in.)
All DPX	0.15-0.25 mm (0.006-0.010 in.)

Table 3 DRIVE UNIT SPECIFICATIONS (SX AND DP-S MODELS)

Drive unit lubricant capacity	
SX	2.1 L (71 oz.)
DP-S	2.4 L (81 oz.)
Output shaft end play	0.05-0.25 mm (0.002-0.010 in.)
Output shaft nut thickness	
Part No.3852301-5, stamped - 0	0.00 mm (0.000 in.)
Part No. 3852302-3, stamped - 2	0.02 mm (0.008 in.)
Part No. 3852303-1, stamped - 4	0.04 mm (0.016 in.)
Part No. 3852375-9, stamped - 6	0.06 mm (0.024 in.)
Pinion gear nominal dimension	
21:26 upper gear tooth count	48.21 mm (1.898 in.)
22:23 upper gear tooth count	50.06 mm (1.971 in.)

(continued)

Table 3 DRIVE UNIT SPECIFICATIONS (SX AND DP-S MODELS) (continued)

Pressure test specification (3 minute minimum test)	
Low pressure	20.7-34.5 kPa (3-5 psi)
High pressure	110-124 kPa (16-18 psi)
Vacuum test specification (3 minute minimum test)	
Low vacuum	10-16.8 kPa (3-5 in.-Hg)
High vacuum	47-54 kPa (14-16 in.-Hg)
Shift linkage (center to center)	150.8 mm (5-15/16 in.) maximum
Top cover clearance (preload)	0.05-0.1 mm (0.002-0.004 in.)
Thrust plate allowable dimension	12.72-12.79 cm (5.007-5.036 in.)
Universal joint bearing carrier rolling torque	1.0-1.6 N•m (9-14 in.-lb.)
Upper gearcase gear lash	0.15-0.28 mm (0.006-0.011 in.)

Table 4 SPECIAL TORQUE VALUES–DP-C1/D1 AND DPX DRIVE UNITS

Fastener	N•m	in.-lb.	ft.-lb.
Clamp ring bearing carrier	35	–	25.8
Lubricant dipstick	Securely	Securely	Securely
Lubricant drain plug (DP-C1/D1)	10	88	7.4
Lubricant drain plug (DPX)	17	150	12.5
Lubricant fill plug	35	–	25.8
Output shaft top nut (shim nut)	125	–	92.2
Shift housing	6.8-9.5	60-84	–
Shift shoe stop screw	14-16	124-141	10-12
Steering helmet retaining screws (DP-C1/D1)	35	–	25.8
Top cover	15	133	11.1
Upper gearcase mounting screws and nuts	38	–	28.0

Table 5 SPECIAL TORQUE VALUES–SX AND DP-S DRIVE UNITS

Fastener	N•m	in.-lb.	ft.-lb.
Universal joint bearing carrier	16-19	144-168	12-14
Lower output gear retaining ring	197-224	–	145-165
Lubricant dipstick	5.4-8.1	48-72	–
Lubricant drain plug (SX)	6.8-9.5	60-84	–
Lubricant drain plug (DP-S)	14-20	120-180	10-15
Lubricant level plug	5.4-8.1	48-72	–
Output shaft top nut (shim nut)	130-149	–	96-110
Rear cover (plastic)	12-15	108-132	9-11
Shift housing	6.8-9.5	60-84	–
Shift shoe stop screw	14-16	124-141	10-12
Top cover	22-24	192-216	16-18
Upper gearcase mounting hardware			
3/8-16 thread	30-33	–	22-24
7/16-14 thread	43-54	–	32-40
Water cover	6.8-9.5	60-84	–

12

Table 6 RECOMMENDED LUBRICANTS, SEALANTS AND ADHESIVES*

	Part No.
Lubricants	
Volvo DuraPlus GL5 Synthetic Gear Lube	(dealer stock item)
Volvo Penta Propeller Shaft Grease	1141644-3
or Quicksilver Special Lubricant 101	92-13872A-1
Volvo DuraPlus Power Trim/Steering Fluid	3851039-2
OMC EP/Wheel Bearing Grease	(dealer stock item)
OMC Moly Lube	175356
OMC Triple Guard Grease	(dealer stock item)
or Quicksilver 2-4-C Multi-Lube	(dealer stock item)
OMC Needle Bearing Assembly Grease	378642
or Quicksilver Needle Bearing Grease	92-825265A-1
Sealants	
Volvo Master Gasket Sealant	840879-1
Volvo Black silicone sealant	1161277-7
or OMC RTV black silicone sealant	263753
Volvo White Sealing Compound	1141570-0
or OMC Gasket Sealing Compound	508235
or Quicksilver Perfect Seal	92-34227-11
OMC Black Neoprene Dip	909570
or Quicksilver Liquid Neoprene	92-25711-2
OMC Pipe Sealant with Teflon	9100048
or Quicksilver Loctite 567 PST pipe sealant	92-809822
3M Marine sealant 101 (polysulfide [OMC or locally available])	506852
Adhesives	
OMC Type M adhesive	318535
or Scotch grip 1300 adhesive (OMC or locally available)	982551
or Quicksilver Bellows Adhesive (contact cement)	92-86166-1
OMC Locquic Primer	772032
or Quicksilver Locquic Primer	92-809824
OMC Ultra Lock threadlocking adhesive (high strength)	500422
or Quicksilver Loctite 271 threadlocking adhesive	92-809819
OMC Nut Lock threadlocking adhesive (medium strength)	500418
or Quicksilver Loctite 242 threadlocking adhesive	92-809821
Miscellaneous	
Volvo DuraPlus Corrosion Shield	362002-8
Quicksilver Storage Seal Rust inhibitor	92-86145A12
OMC Dielectric grease	503243
or Quicksilver Dielectric silicone grease	92-823506-1

* Obtain Volvo supplies from a Volvo-Penta Dealer, Quicksilver supplies from a Mercury Marine Dealer and OMC supplies from any OMC Stern Drive, Evinrude or Johnson Dealer.

Table 7 VOLVO SPECIAL TOOLS (DP-C1/D1 AND DPX DRIVE UNITS)

Description	Application	Part No.
T50 Torx socket	DP-C1/D1 and DPX	885043-0
Tilt suspension tool	DP-C1/D1 and DPX	885143-8
Drive support tool	DP-C1/D1 and DPX	885146-1
Seal installer	DP-C1/D1 and DPX	884259-3
Sleeve	DP-C1/D1 and DPX	884263-5
Sleeve	DP-C1/D1 and DPX	884265-0
Sleeve	DP-C1/D1 and DPX	884266-8

(continued)

Table 7 VOLVO SPECIAL TOOLS (DP-C1/D1 AND DPX DRIVE UNITS) (continued)

Description	Application	Part No.
Hose clamp installation tool	DP-C1/D1 and DPX	884573-7
Upper gearcase spline fixture	DP-C1/D1 and DPX	884830-1
Bearing installer	DP-C1/D1 and DPX	884932-5
Bearing cup remover	DP-C1/D1 and DPX	884933-3
Support sleeve	DP-C1/D1 and DPX	884938-2
Pivot pin removal tool	DP-C1/D1 and DPX	885148-7
Plate and shim ring kit	DP-C1/D1 and DPX	885152-9
Plate only	884387-2	
Shim ring only	885153-7	
Pivot pin installation tool	DP-C1/D1 and DPX	3810105-1
Pressure tester	DP-C1/D1 and DPX	3810152-3
Drive handle	DP-C1/D1 and DPX	9991801-3
Spring scale for measuring preload	DP-C1/D1 and DPX	9985494-5

Table 8 VOLVO SPECIAL TOOLS (SX AND DP-S DRIVE UNITS)

Description	Application	Part No.
Drift	SX and DP-S	884168-6
Seal installer	SX and DP-S	884259-3
Sleeve	SX and DP-S	884263-5
Sleeve	SX and DP-S	884265-0
Sleeve	SX and DP-S	884266-8
Bearing installer	SX and DP-S	884932-5
Bearing cup remover	SX and DP-S	884933-3
Support sleeve	SX and DP-S	884938-2
T50 Torx socket	SX and DP-S	885043-0
Alignment bar	SX and DP-S	3851082-2
Spline socket	SX and DP-S	3850598-8
Spanner wrench	SX and DP-S	3850604-4
Gearcase holding fixture	SX and DP-S	3850605-1
Remover/installer	SX and DP-S	3850606-9
Seal installer	SX and DP-S	3850607-7
Snap ring pliers	SX and DP-S	3850608-5
Universal drive handle	SX and DP-S	3850609-3
Universal joint adaptor kit	SX and DP-S	3850628-3
Shim gauge	SX and DP-S	3850701-8
Drive handle	SX and DP-S	9991801-3

Table 9 STANDARD TORQUE VALUES (METRIC FASTENERS)

Screw or Nut Size	N.m	in.-lb.	ft.-lb.
M5	4.1	36	–
M6	8.1	70	6
M8	17.6	156	13
M10	35.3	312	26
M12	47.5	–	35
M14	81.3	–	60

Table 10 STANDARD TORQUE VALUES (U.S. FASTENERS)

Screw or Nut Size	N.m	in.-lb.	ft.-lb.
6-32	1.0	9	–
8-32	2.3	20	–
10-24	3.4	30	–
10-32	4.0	35	–
12-24	5.1	45	–
1/4-20	7.9	70	6
1/4-28	9.5	84	7
5/16-18	18.1	160	13
5/16-24	19.0	168	14
3/8-16	30.5	270	23
3/8-24	33.9	300	25
7/16-14	48.8	–	36
7/16-20	54.2	–	40
1/2-13	67.8	–	50
1/2-20	81.3	–	60

Table 11 TOOL AND FIXTURE MANUFACTURERS

Manufacturer of holding fixtures and handling equipment
Bob Kerr Marine Tool Company
P.O. Box 771135
Winter Garden, Florida 34777
Manufacturers of tools and equipment
OTC Division of SPX Corporation
655 Eisenhower Drive
Owatonna, Minnesota 55060
Manufacturers of marine service products
Stevens instruments
111 Greenwood Avenue
Waukegan, illinois 60079-9375

Table 12 GEAR LASH AND PATTERN CORRECTION GUIDE–SX AND DP-S MODELS

Shim location	Pinion	Lower	Upper	Top cover	Upper nut
Gear lash					
Both gears below specifications					
Changes required	add	no change	no change	no change	no change
Both gears above specifications					
Changes required	subtract	no change	no change	no change	no change
Upper gear below specifications					
Changes required[1]:	no change	no change	add	subtract	recheck
Upper gear above specifications					
Changes required[1]:	no change	no change	subtract	add	recheck
Lower gear below specifications					
Changes required[1]:	no change	subtract	no change	no change	recheck
Lower gear above specifications					
Changes required[1]:	no change	add	no change	no change	recheck
Gear pattern					
Pattern too close to outer diameter of gear					
Changes required[1]:	subtract	subtract	add	subtract	recheck[2]
Pattern too close to inner diameter of gear					
Changes required[1]:	add	add	subtract	add	recheck[2]

1. Change equal amounts (thickness) of shims at each location.
2. No change should be necessary, but verification is recommended.

Chapter Thirteen

Lower Gearcase

This chapter provides propeller removal and installation procedures and lower gearcase removal, installation, rebuilding and resealing procedures for Volvo Penta SX Cobra, DuoProp and DPX models. Service procedures for the upper gearcase and drive unit removal/installation are covered in Chapter Twelve. Service procedures for the intermediate housing and transom shield/bracket are covered in Chapter Fourteen.

Table 1 and **Table 2** list gearcase specifications. **Table 3** and **Table 4** list special torque values. **Table 5** lists recommended lubricants, sealants and adhesives. **Table 6** and **Table 7** list manufacturer recommended special tools. **Table 8** and **Table 9** list standard torque values. **Table 10** and **Table 11** list gear lash and gear pattern correction procedures. **Tables 1-11** are at the end of the chapter.

Exploded illustrations of each lower gearcase are located in the appropriate Disassembly and Assembly sections and are helpful references for many service procedures.

LOWER GEARCASE IDENTIFICATION

Complete drive unit identification is covered at the beginning of Chapter Twelve. There are 4 lower gearcases covered in this chapter: Volvo Penta DP-C1/D1 series, Volvo Penta DPX series, Volvo Penta SX Cobra series and the Volvo Penta DP-S series lower gearcases.

LOWER GEARCASE OPERATION

Engine torque is transferred from the upper gearcase to the lower gearcase via a female splined drive shaft coupler. The drive shaft coupler has a deep groove in the middle of the shaft which is designed to provide a breaking point to save the upper gearcase from damage if the lower gearcase should encounter an extreme impact load. A shallow groove on one end is an orientation groove. The shallow groove should always face the upper gearcase (up).

A pinion gear at the lower end of the vertical drive shaft is in constant mesh with a gear (or gears) to drive the horizontal propeller shaft(s) located in the propeller shaft bearing carrier. All of these lower gearcases are considered direct drive, as all shifting is accomplished in the upper gearcase (Chapter Twelve).

DuoProp and DPX models incorporate twin counter rotating propellers. The front propeller is powered by the aft driven gear and turns counterclockwise when viewed from the rear. The rear propeller is powered by the front gear and turns clockwise when viewed from the rear.

All of these gearcases circulate gear lubricant from the lower gearcase to the upper gearcase (whenever the drive unit is in forward or reverse gear). The circulating lubricant helps to cool the upper gearcase and a lubricant filter located at the upper gearcase (or intermediate housing) to lower gearcase parting line traps impurities from reaching the upper gearcase. Clean or replace the filter each time the lower gearcase is removed from the drive unit. SX models incorporate an oil slinger pressed onto the propeller shaft gear to help ensure positive lubricant flow to the upper gearcase.

SERVICE PRECAUTIONS

When working on a drive unit, there are several good procedures to keep in mind that will make your work easier, faster and more accurate.

1. Never use elastic locknuts more than twice. It is a good practice to replace such nuts each time they are removed. Never use an elastic locknut that can be turned by hand (without the aid of a wrench).

2. Use special tools where noted. **Table 6** and **Table 7** list all manufacturer recommended special tools. The use of makeshift tools can damage components and cause serious personal injury.

3. Use the appropriate fixture to hold the gearcase housing whenever possible. A vise with protective jaws should be used to hold smaller housings or individual components. If protective jaws are not available, insert blocks of wood or similar padding on each side of the housing or component before clamping.

4. Remove and install pressed-on parts with an appropriate mandrel, support and press (arbor or hydraulic). Do not attempt to pry or hammer press-fit components on or off.

5. Refer to **Table 3** or **Table 4** for special torque values and **Table 8** or **Table 9** for standard torque values. Proper torque is essential to ensure long life and satisfactory service from drive unit components.

6. To help reduce corrosion, especially in saltwater areas, apply Volvo White Sealing Compound or equivalent (**Table 5**) to all external surfaces of bearing carriers, housing mating surfaces and fasteners (unless specified otherwise). Do not apply sealing compound where it can get into gears or bearings.

7. Discard all O-rings, seals and gaskets during disassembly. Apply OMC Triple Guard Grease

or equivalent (**Table 5**) to new O-rings and seal lips to provide initial lubrication.

8. All drive units use precision shimmed gears. Tag all shims with the location and measured thickness of each shim as it is removed from the gearcase. Shims are reusable as long as they are not physically damaged or corroded. Follow shimming instructions closely and carefully. Shims control gear location and bearing preload. Incorrectly shimming a gearcase can cause failure of the gears and/or bearings.

9. Work in an area of good lighting and with sufficient space for component storage. Keep an ample number of clean containers available for parts storage. When not being worked on, cover parts and assemblies with clean shop towels or plastic bags. See **Figure 1**.

CAUTION

*Metric and U.S. standard fasteners are used on Volvo drive units. Always match a replacement fastener to the original. Do not run a tap or thread chaser into a hole (or over a bolt) without first verifying the thread size and pitch (**Figure 2**). The lower gearcase may be equipped with Heli-Coil stainless steel locking thread inserts in some locations. Never run a tap or thread chaser into a Heli-Coil equipped hole. Heli-Coil inserts are replaceable, if damaged.*

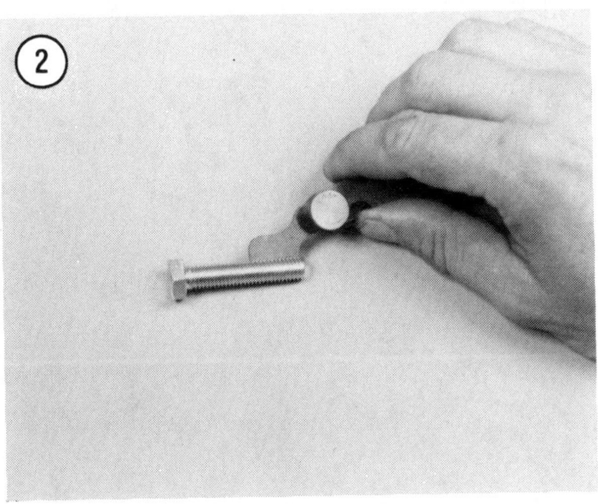

10. Whenever a threadlocking adhesive is specified, first spray the threads of the bore and the screw with Locquic Primer (**Table 5**). Allow the primer to air dry before proceeding. Locquic primer will clean the surfaces and allow better adhesion. Locquic primer will also accelerate the cure rate of threadlocking adhesives from an hour or longer, to 15-20 minutes.

CORROSION CONTROL

Sacrificial zinc or aluminum anodes are standard equipment on all models. The anodes must have good electrical continuity to ground or they will not function. Anodes are inspected visually and tested electrically. Anodes must not be painted or coated with any material. Anodes are mounted as follows:

a. *DP-C1/D1*—Anodes are mounted on the rear of the lower gearcase and bottom of the transom shield. An accessory anode may be mounted to the suspension fork.
b. *DPX*—Anodes are mounted on top of the leading edge of the lower gearcase, on the lower aft portion of the intermediate housing and on the bottom of the transom shield.
c. *SX and DP-S*—Anodes are mounted on top of the leading edge of the lower gearcase and on the bottom of the transom bracket. The SX also has an additional anode mounted in the propshaft bearing carrier area of the lower gearcase.

If the unit is operated exclusively in freshwater, magnesium anodes are available from Volvo Penta parts and accessories. Magnesium anodes provide better protection in freshwater, but must *not* be used in saltwater. Magnesium anodes will overprotect the unit in saltwater and cause the paint to blister and peel off.

Electronic corrosion control, called the Active Protection System is also available from Volvo Penta Parts and Accessories and operates similar to the Mercury Marine MerCathode system. Two versions are available, one to fit directly to the

13

1996 SX and DP-S series transom bracket and a transom mount version for all other drive units.

Sacrificial Anode Visual Inspection

A visual inspection should check for loose mounting hardware, verify that the anodes are not painted and check the amount of deterioration present. Anodes should be replaced when they are 2/3rds their original size. Test the electrical continuity of each anode after installation as described in the next section.

Sacrificial Anode Electrical Testing

This test requires an ohmmeter.

1. Calibrate the ohmmeter on the lowest ohms scale available.
2. Connect 1 ohmmeter lead to the anode being tested. Connect the other ohmmeter lead to a good ground point on the gearcase that the anode is mounted to. The meter should indicate a very low reading (zero or very near zero), which indicates electrical continuity.
3. If the reading is not very low, remove the anode and clean the mounting surfaces of the anode, gearcase and mounting hardware. Reinstall the anode and retest continuity.
4. Test the continuity of the gearcase to the engine and negative battery post by connecting 1 ohmmeter lead to the negative battery cable and the other ohmmeter lead to a good ground point on the lower gearcase. The meter should indicate a very low reading (zero or very near zero), which indicates electrical continuity.
5. If the reading is not near zero, check the electrical continuity of the lower gearcase to the upper gearcase, the upper gearcase to each component of the transom bracket and transom bracket to the engine. Check for loose mounting hardware, broken or missing ground straps, or excessive corrosion. Repair as necessary to establish a good electrical ground path.

PROPELLERS

Propeller Rotation

NOTE

SX and DP-S models require a remote control box setup that retracts the shift cable at the drive unit when the remote control box is shifted into FORWARD gear and extends the shift cable at the drive unit when the remote control box is shifted into REVERSE gear. DP-C1/D1 and DPX models require the opposite remote control box setup.

All DuoProp and DPX model propellers require that the front propeller rotates counterclockwise and the rear propeller rotates clockwise, when in FORWARD gear. To accomplish this, the shift arm (eccentric piston) must rotate clockwise when the remote control is shifted into FORWARD gear. FORWARD gear on all DuoProp and DPX drive units will be the lower output gear.

DP-C1/D1 and DPX models—If the input from the remote control box is correct, the shift link should be in the factory installed position on the starboard side of the shift arm (eccentric piston). See **Figure 3**.

DP-S models—If the input from the remote control box is correct, the shift link should be in

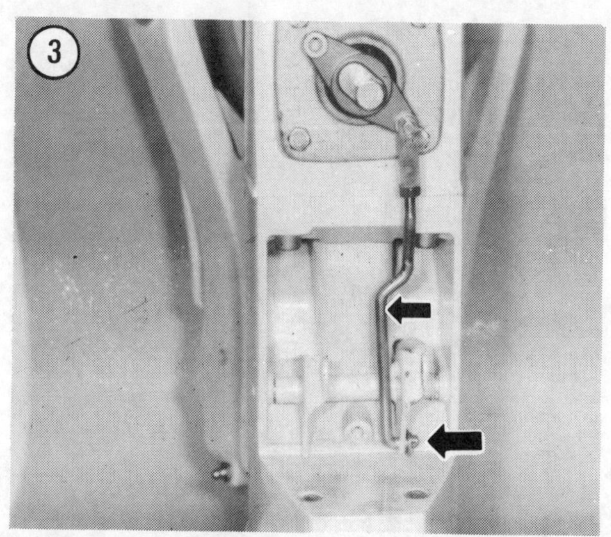

the factory installed position on the port side of the shift arm (eccentric piston). See **Figure 4**.

SX models—The SX drive unit is factory set to provide right hand (clockwise) rotation in FORWARD gear, if the input from the remote control box is correct. The shift link is factory installed on the port side of the shift arm (eccentric piston). See **Figure 4**. The lower output gear is FORWARD gear in this setup.

If twin SX drive units are being used, the starboard drive unit should remain standard (clockwise) rotation, while the port drive unit should be changed to left hand (counter-clockwise) rotation and a matching left hand (counter rotation) propeller installed. Moving the shift link to the starboard side of the shift arm is the only adjustment required to change drive unit rotation. The port (counter rotating) drive unit will use the upper output gear for FORWARD gear in this setup.

Running 2 drive units with counter-rotating propellers reduces steering torque, is generally more efficient and reduces torque roll (the tendency of a boat to lean to one side under way).

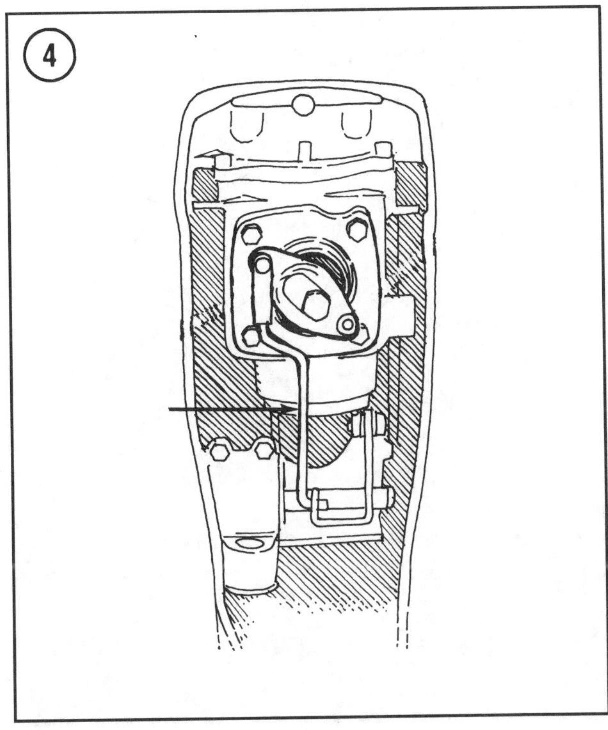

NOTE
Install the shift link on the port side of the bellcrank arm (and eccentric piston) on standard rotation SX models and all DP-S models. Install the shift link on the starboard side of the bellcrank arm (and eccentric piston) for counter-rotation on SX models only.

Refer to Chapter Twelve, *Shift linkage service* to change the rotation of a SX drive unit.

Removal/Installation (DP-C1/D1 Models)

The DP-C1/D1 series drive unit uses 2 counter-rotating Volvo Penta B series aluminum or C series stainless steel propellers in matched pitch sets only. DP-C1/D1 drive unit propellers will not fit any of the other gearcases listed in this chapter. Propeller tool kit part No. 873058-2 is a consumer kit for removing both propellers. This tool kit is recommended for carrying in the boat.

The front propeller nut is an elastic locknut. Replace the front propeller nut if it can be turned by hand (without the aid of a wrench). Refer to **Figure 5** for this procedure.

CAUTION
Use a suitable block of wood between a propeller blade and the antiventilation plate to prevent the propeller from rotating during removal and installation. Do not attempt to hold the propeller(s) with your hands. The propeller blades can damage your hands due to the high torque of the propeller nut(s) and the resultant effort required to hold the blades stationary.

1. Disconnect the negative battery cable to prevent accidental starting.
2. Remove the center bolt (1, **Figure 5**) and washer (if so equipped) from the center of the rear propeller cone nut.
3. Remove the cone nut and plastic washer (3 and 4, **Figure 5**).

CAUTION
The fish line cutters may be very sharp. Careless handling during removal can result in serious personal injury.

4. Pull the rear propeller from the inner shaft splines, then remove the small fish line cutter/thrust washer (6, **Figure 5**).
5. Remove the front propeller retaining nut (7, **Figure 5**) with propeller wrench part No. 3855876-3 (shop tool) or part No. 873058-2 (consumer tool), then remove the propeller from the tube shaft splines.
6. Remove the large fish line cutter/thrust washer (9, **Figure 5**).
7. Lubricate both propeller shaft's splines and both propeller's hub splines with Volvo Penta Propeller Shaft Grease or equivalent (**Table 5**) before installing the propellers.
8. Install the large fish line cutter/thrust washer over the tube shaft splines.
9. Install the front propeller and seat it against the thrust washer.
10. Install the front propeller nut and tighten it to specification (**Table 3**) with propeller wrench part No. 3855876-3 (shop tool) or part No. 873058-2 (consumer tool).
11. Install the small fish line cutter/thrust washer over the inner shaft splines.
12. Install the rear propeller and seat it against the thrust washer.
13. Install the cone nut and tighten it to specification (**Table 3**).
14. Install the center bolt and washer (if so equipped) through the rear propeller cone and into the propshaft. Tighten the center bolt to specification (**Table 3**).
15. Reconnect the negative battery cable.

Removal/Installation (DPX and DP-S Models)

The DPX drive unit uses 2 counter-rotating Volvo Penta E series stainless steel propellers in matched pitch sets only. DPX drive unit propellers will not fit any of the other lower gearcases listed in this chapter. Propeller tool kit part No. 885195-8 is a consumer kit for removing both propellers. This tool kit is recommended for carrying in the boat.

The DP-S drive unit uses 2 counter-rotating Volvo Penta D series aluminum or F series stainless steel propellers in matched pitch sets only. DP-S drive unit propellers will not fit any of the other lower gearcases listed in this chapter. Propeller tool kit part No. 3855516-5 is a consumer kit for removing both propellers. This tool kit is recommended for carrying in the boat.

The front propeller nut on both DPX and DP-S models and the rear propeller nut on DP-S models are elastic locknuts. Replace any elastic pro-

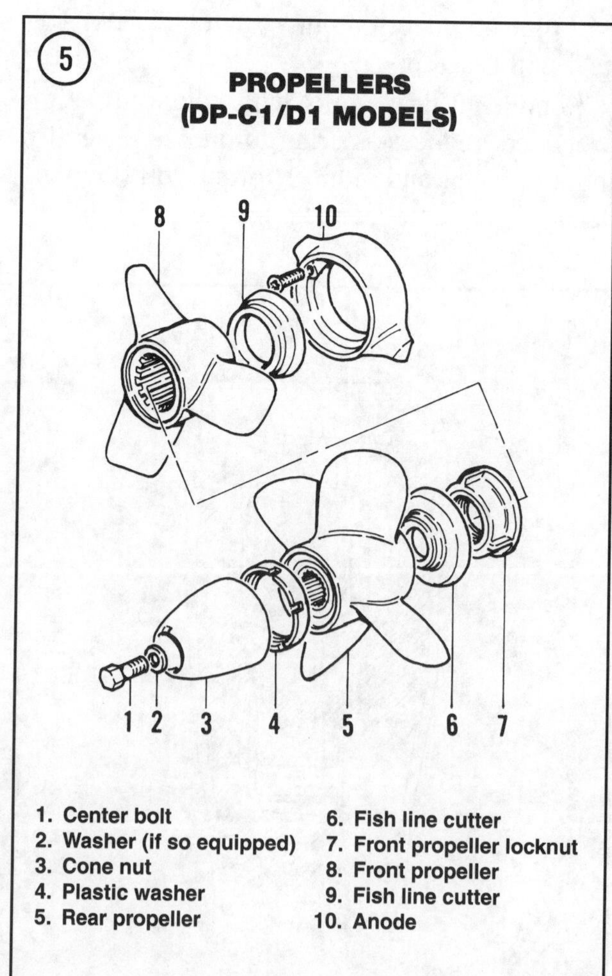

1. Center bolt
2. Washer (if so equipped)
3. Cone nut
4. Plastic washer
5. Rear propeller
6. Fish line cutter
7. Front propeller locknut
8. Front propeller
9. Fish line cutter
10. Anode

peller locknut that can be turned by hand (without the aid of a wrench). The DPX uses a special rear propeller nut that consists of an outer nut and an inner bolt. Tighten the outer nut first, then the inner bolt.

These propellers do not use thrust washers or fish line cutters. The thrust washers are built into the propeller or propeller hub. Refer to **Figure 6** for this procedure.

CAUTION
Use a suitable block of wood between a propeller blade and the antiventilation plate to prevent the propeller from rotating during removal and installation. Do not attempt to hold the propeller(s) with your hands. The propeller blades can damage your hands due to the high torque of the propeller nut(s) and the resultant effort required to hold the blades stationary.

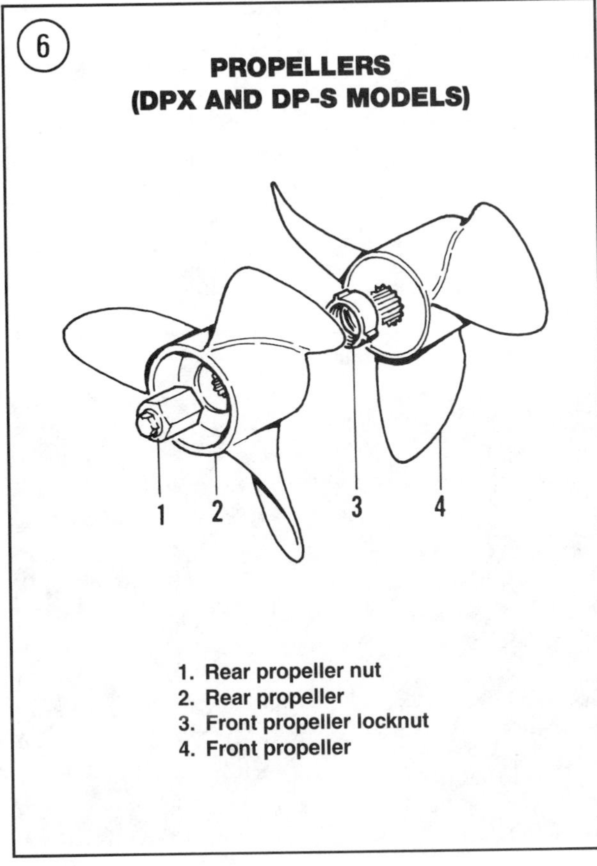

1. Rear propeller nut
2. Rear propeller
3. Front propeller locknut
4. Front propeller

1. Disconnect the negative battery cable to prevent accidental starting.

2A. *DPX models*—Loosen the rear propeller nut inner bolt until it is free of the inner propshaft threads, then remove the rear propeller outer nut assembly (1, **Figure 6**). Pull the rear propeller (2, **Figure 6**) from the inner shaft splines.

2B. *DP-S models*—Remove the rear propeller retaining nut (1, **Figure 6**) and pull the rear propeller (2, **Figure 6**) from the inner shaft splines.

3. Remove the front propeller retaining nut (3, **Figure 6**) with propeller wrench part No. 3855876-3 (shop tool) or the appropriate consumer tool, then pull the front propeller from the tube shaft splines.

4. Lubricate both propeller shaft splines and both propeller hub splines with Volvo Penta Propeller Shaft Grease or equivalent (**Table 5**).

5. Install the front propeller and tighten the retaining nut (3, **Figure 6**) to specification (**Table 3** or **Table 4**).

6A. *DPX models*—Install the rear propeller nut assembly. Tighten the outer nut to specification, then tighten the inner bolt to specification (**Table 3**).

6B. *DP-S models*—Install the rear propeller and tighten the retaining nut (1, **Figure 6**) to specification (**Table 4**).

7. Reconnect the negative battery cable.

Removal/Installation (SX Models)

This series gearcase uses a single propeller with a special spline pattern unique to the Volvo Penta/OMC joint venture. Normal rotation of the drive unit is clockwise as viewed from the rear. The rotation can be changed for twin engine applications with a simple shift linkage adjustment at the upper gearcase. See *Propeller rotation* in this chapter. Propellers are available from Volvo Penta in right and left hand rotation, in a variety of aluminum and stainless steel designs.

The rubber hub and sleeve (6, **Figure 7**) are not consumer serviceable. A propeller shop can replace the hub assembly if it should fail. Refer to **Figure 7** for this procedure.

CAUTION
Use a suitable block of wood between a propeller blade and the antiventilation plate to prevent the propeller from rotating during removal and installation. Do not attempt to hold the propeller with your hands. The propeller blades can damage your hands due to the high torque of the propeller nut and the resultant effort required to hold the blades stationary.

1. Remove the cotter pin and keeper (1 and 2, **Figure 7**). Discard the cotter pin.
2. Remove the retaining nut and splined washer (3 and 4, **Figure 7**).
3. Pull the propeller (5, **Figure 7**) and thrust washer (7, **Figure 7**) from the shaft splines.
4. Lubricate the propeller shaft splines with Volvo Penta Propeller Shaft Grease or equivalent (**Table 5**) before installing the propeller.
5. Install the thrust washer over the propeller shaft, then install the propeller and seat it against the thrust washer.
6. Install the splined washer and index it to the propeller shaft splines.
7. Install and tighten the nut (3, **Figure 7**) to specification (**Table 4**).
8 Install the castellated keeper and a new stainless steel cotter pin (1 and 2, **Figure 7**). Index the keeper as necessary to align the cotter pin hole in the propeller shaft. Bend both prongs to secure the cotter pin.

LOWER GEARCASE SERVICE (DP-C1/D1 AND DPX MODELS)

Removal

The lower gearcase can be removed from the intermediate housing without removing the drive unit from the transom shield.

1. Drain the gear lubricant as described in Chapter Twelve.
2. Remove the propellers as described previously in this chapter.

CAUTION
*If it is necessary to tilt the drive unit to gain the clearance necessary to remove the lower gearcase, the drive unit must be supported with the hydraulic trim system or with suspension tool part No. 885143-8. Refer to **Drive unit removal** in Chapter Twelve.*

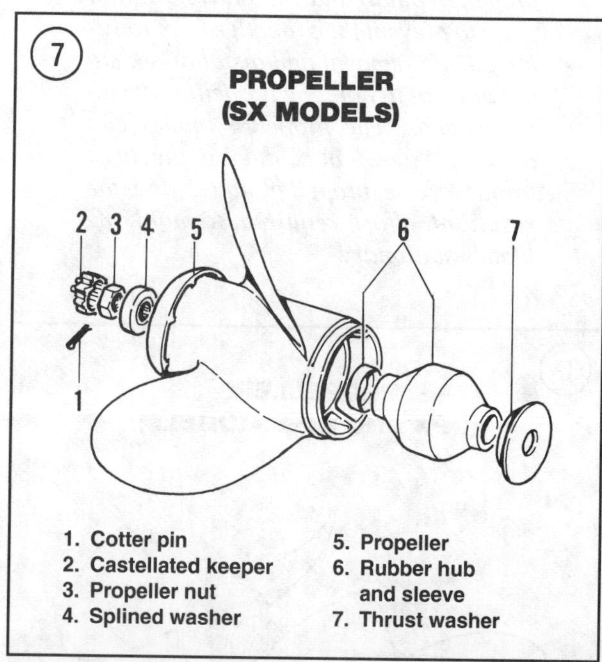

1. Cotter pin
2. Castellated keeper
3. Propeller nut
4. Splined washer
5. Propeller
6. Rubber hub and sleeve
7. Thrust washer

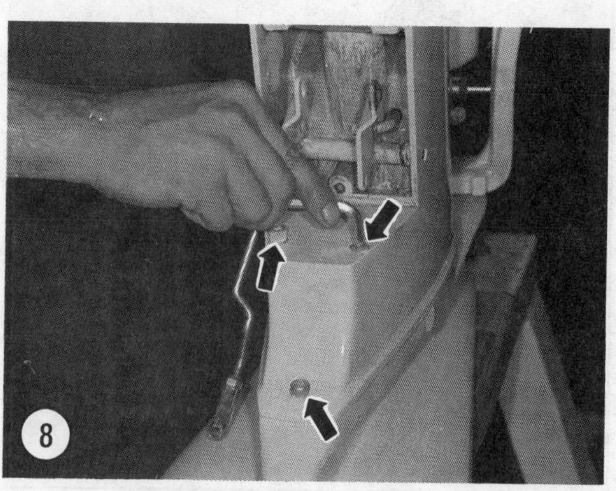

3. Remove the 3 screws from the aft portion of the intermediate housing (**Figure 8**).

4. Remove the 4 screws (2 each side) from the lower gearcase (**Figure 9**). Have an assistant support the lower gearcase as the last screw is removed.

5. Remove the lower gearcase and secure it in a suitable fixture.

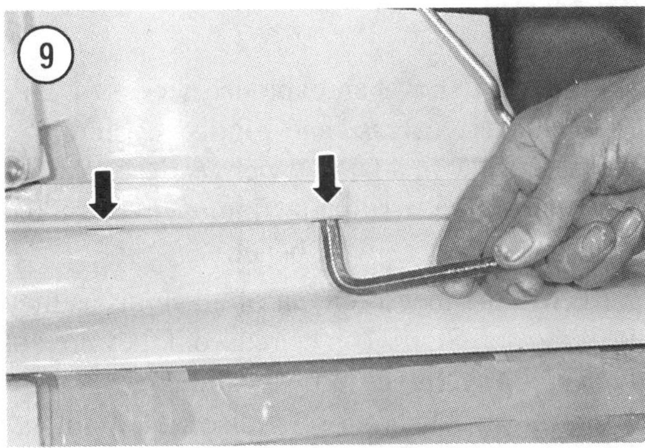

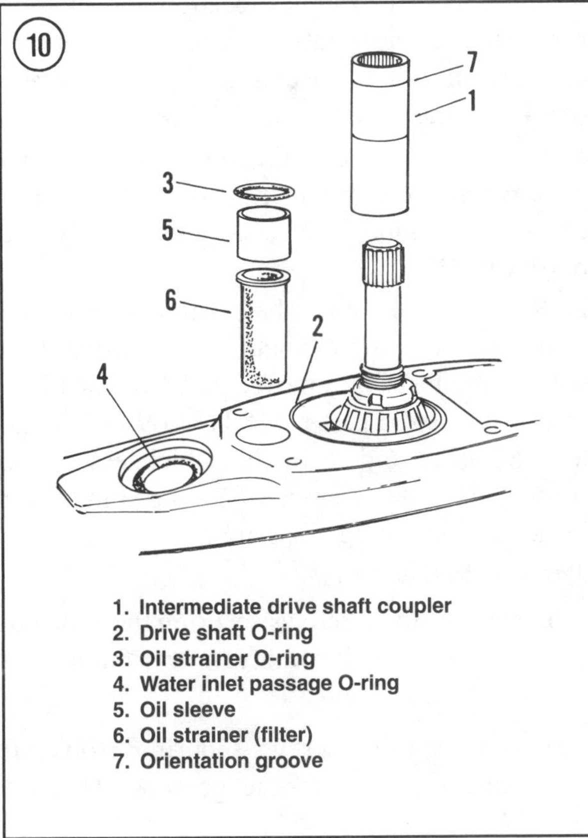

1. Intermediate drive shaft coupler
2. Drive shaft O-ring
3. Oil strainer O-ring
4. Water inlet passage O-ring
5. Oil sleeve
6. Oil strainer (filter)
7. Orientation groove

6. Remove and inspect the intermediate drive shaft coupler (1, **Figure 10**). Replace the coupler if the splines are worn, damaged or distorted.

7. Remove and discard the O-rings or seals around the drive shaft bearing (2, **Figure 10**), oil strainer (3, **Figure 10**) and water inlet (4, **Figure 10**). The oil strainer O-ring will most likely be in the intermediate housing groove around the oil sleeve (5, **Figure 10**).

8. Remove and clean the oil strainer (6, **Figure 10**). Replace the oil strainer if it is damaged or cannot be cleaned satisfactorily. Make sure that the oil sleeve (5, **Figure 10**) is present and accounted for in either the intermediate housing or the lower gearcase.

9. Clean all sealer and any corrosion from the intermediate housing and lower gearcase mating surfaces.

10. If necessary, remove the drive shaft bearing cup and shims from the bottom of the intermediate housing using bearing remover part No. 884140-5 and drive handle part No. 884143-9 or equivalent. Measure and record the thickness of the shim(s) for later reference. Tag the shim(s) for identification during reassembly.

Installation

The *Lower Gearcase to Intermediate Housing Shimming Procedure* must be performed if the lower gearcase, the intermediate housing or any of the drive shaft components were serviced or replaced. Refer to *Lower Gearcase to Intermediate Housing Shimming Procedure* located later in this chapter.

1. Install the oil strainer (6, **Figure 10**) into the lower gearcase.

2. Verify the presence of the oil sleeve (5, **Figure 10**) in the intermediate housing. Install a new sleeve if necessary. Install a new O-ring (3, **Figure 10**) around the sleeve.

3. Install a new O-ring in the groove around the drive shaft (2, **Figure 10**) and a new seal in the water inlet passage (4, **Figure 10**). Apply a lib-

eral coat of Volvo Penta Propeller Shaft Grease or equivalent (**Table 5**) to the water tube seal.
4. Perform the lower gearcase to intermediate housing shimming procedure, if necessary.
5. Coat the mating surfaces of the lower gearcase and intermediate housing with Volvo White Sealing Compound or equivalent (**Table 5**). Do not get any sealer into the roller bearings or lubricant passages.
6. Make sure the intermediate drive shaft coupler is installed on the lower gearcase drive shaft. Position the grooved end of the coupler facing up (7, **Figure 10**).
7. With the aid of an assistant, install the lower gearcase to the intermediate housing. Be careful not to displace any of the O-rings or seals. Turn the propeller shafts as necessary to align the drive shaft splines.
8. Coat the threads of the gearcase mounting hardware with Volvo White Sealing Compound or equivalent (**Table 5**). Install the 3 intermediate housing screws (**Figure 8**) and the 4 lower gearcase screws (**Figure 9**). Tighten the screws evenly to specification (**Table 3**).
9. Pressure test the drive unit with pressure tester part No. 3810152-3 as follows:
   a. Make sure the lubricant drain plug and fill plug are installed and tightened securely.
   b. Connect the pressure tester to the dipstick hole. Pressurize the drive unit to 48 kPa (7 psi) for 3 minutes, minimum.
   c. Rotate the input drive shaft, propshaft(s) and shift the gearcase into and out of gear during the test.
   d. If any pressure drop is noted, spray soapy water on all seals and mating surfaces until the leak is found. Correct the leak and retest.
   e. Do not proceed until the gearcase holds pressure for at least 3 minutes without measurable leakage.

NOTE

Make sure the lubricant level is rechecked after the drive has sat for 5-10 minutes after the filling procedure. Running the drive unit with insufficient lubricant will cause drive unit damage.

10. Fill the drive unit with gear lubricant as described in *Drive Lubricant Change* in Chapter Twelve.
11. Install the propellers as described in this chapter.

Disassembly

Figure 11 shows an exploded view of a DP-C1/D1 lower gearcase and **Figure 12** shows an exploded view of a DPX lower gearcase. Secure the gearcase in a suitable fixture or place the gearcase on a clean workbench.

Record the measurement of all shims as they are removed. Shims can be reused if they are not damaged. Tag the shims by location for reassembly purposes. Do not lose or discard any shims.

All components that are to be reused must be installed in their original location and orientation. Mark components as necessary to ensure correct reinstallation. Refer to **Figure 11** or **Figure 12** for the following procedure.

1. Remove and clean the oil strainer (if not already removed). Replace the oil strainer if it is damaged or cannot be cleaned satisfactorily. See 6, **Figure 10**.
2. Remove the drive shaft bearing race and shims from the intermediate housing drive shaft bore, using bearing remover part No. 884140-5 and drive handle part No. 884143-9 or equivalent. Measure and record the thickness of the shim(s) for later reference. Tag the shim(s) for identification during reassembly.
3. *DP-C1/D1 models:*
   a. Remove the 2 screws securing the anode to the propshaft bearing carrier. Remove the anode. See **Figure 13**.
   b. Remove the 2 screws securing propshaft bearing carrier to the gearcase (**Figure 14**).

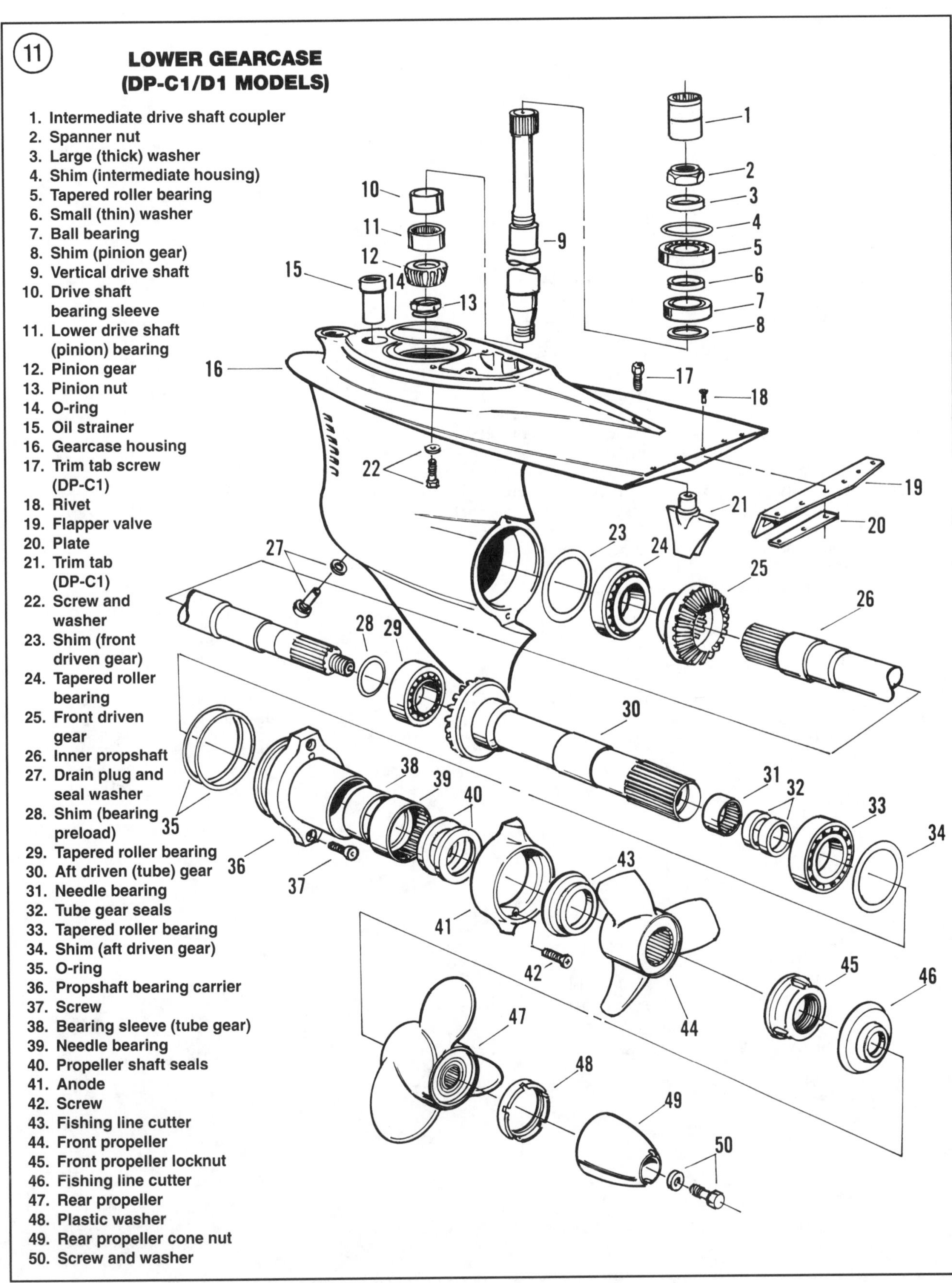
11
LOWER GEARCASE
(DP-C1/D1 MODELS)
1. Intermediate drive shaft coupler
2. Spanner nut
3. Large (thick) washer
4. Shim (intermediate housing)
5. Tapered roller bearing
6. Small (thin) washer
7. Ball bearing
8. Shim (pinion gear)
9. Vertical drive shaft
10. Drive shaft bearing sleeve
11. Lower drive shaft (pinion) bearing
12. Pinion gear
13. Pinion nut
14. O-ring
15. Oil strainer
16. Gearcase housing
17. Trim tab screw (DP-C1)
18. Rivet
19. Flapper valve
20. Plate
21. Trim tab (DP-C1)
22. Screw and washer
23. Shim (front driven gear)
24. Tapered roller bearing
25. Front driven gear
26. Inner propshaft
27. Drain plug and seal washer
28. Shim (bearing preload)
29. Tapered roller bearing
30. Aft driven (tube) gear
31. Needle bearing
32. Tube gear seals
33. Tapered roller bearing
34. Shim (aft driven gear)
35. O-ring
36. Propshaft bearing carrier
37. Screw
38. Bearing sleeve (tube gear)
39. Needle bearing
40. Propeller shaft seals
41. Anode
42. Screw
43. Fishing line cutter
44. Front propeller
45. Front propeller locknut
46. Fishing line cutter
47. Rear propeller
48. Plastic washer
49. Rear propeller cone nut
50. Screw and washer

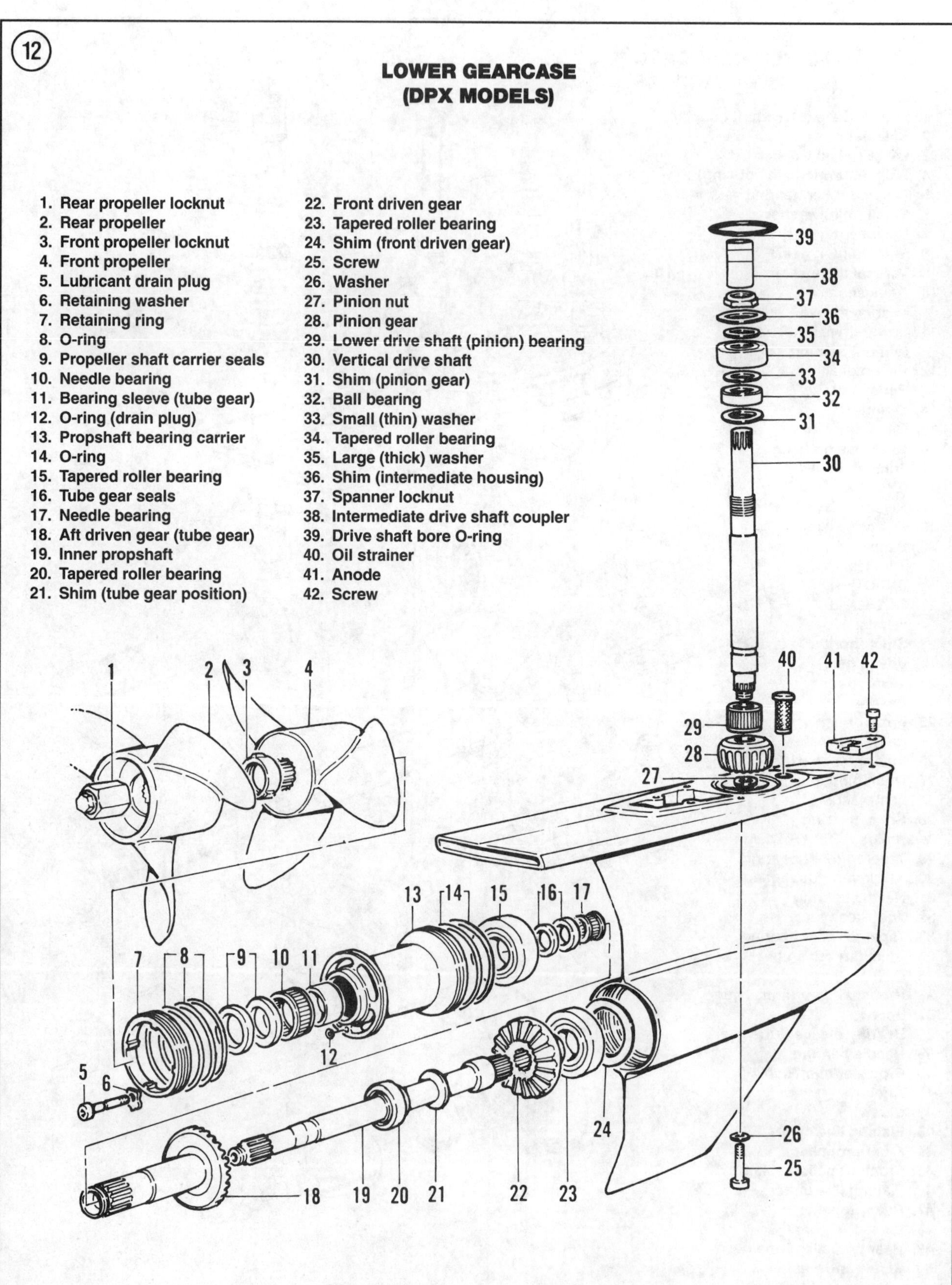

12
LOWER GEARCASE
(DPX MODELS)
1. Rear propeller locknut
2. Rear propeller
3. Front propeller locknut
4. Front propeller
5. Lubricant drain plug
6. Retaining washer
7. Retaining ring
8. O-ring
9. Propeller shaft carrier seals
10. Needle bearing
11. Bearing sleeve (tube gear)
12. O-ring (drain plug)
13. Propshaft bearing carrier
14. O-ring
15. Tapered roller bearing
16. Tube gear seals
17. Needle bearing
18. Aft driven gear (tube gear)
19. Inner propshaft
20. Tapered roller bearing
21. Shim (tube gear position)
22. Front driven gear
23. Tapered roller bearing
24. Shim (front driven gear)
25. Screw
26. Washer
27. Pinion nut
28. Pinion gear
29. Lower drive shaft (pinion) bearing
30. Vertical drive shaft
31. Shim (pinion gear)
32. Ball bearing
33. Small (thin) washer
34. Tapered roller bearing
35. Large (thick) washer
36. Shim (intermediate housing)
37. Spanner locknut
38. Intermediate drive shaft coupler
39. Drive shaft bore O-ring
40. Oil strainer
41. Anode
42. Screw

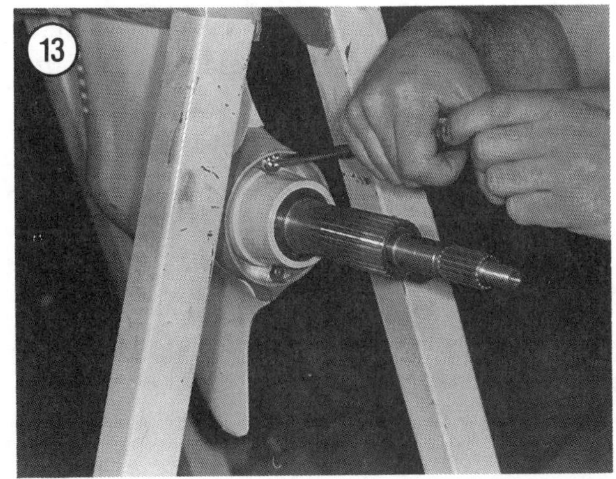

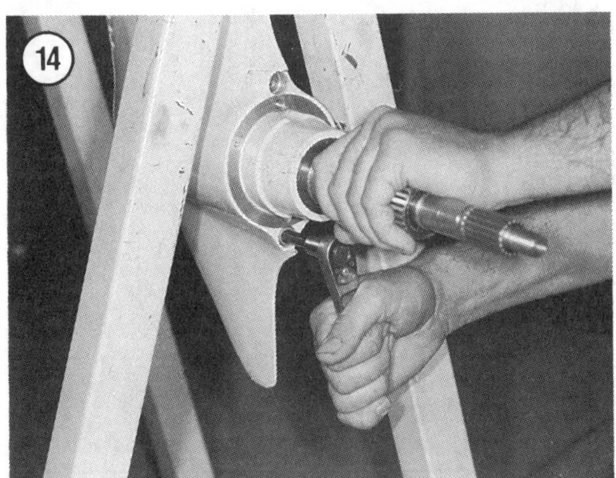

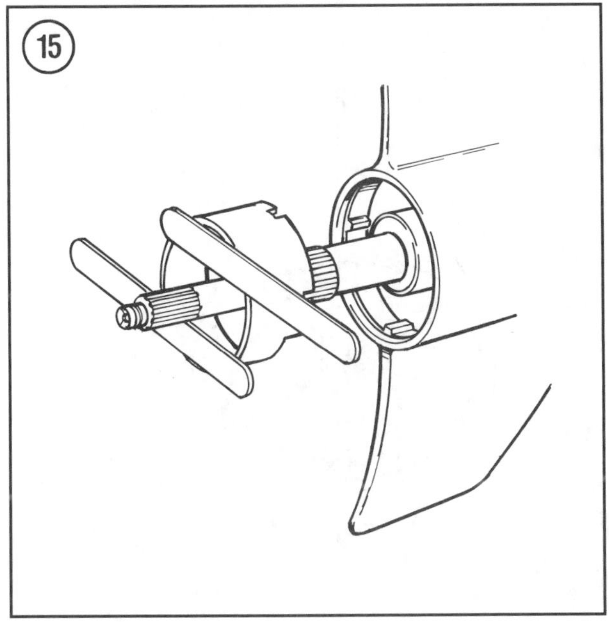

4. *DPX models*—Remove the propshaft bearing carrier retaining ring with spanner wrench part No. 885221-2 (**Figure 15**). Remove and discard the 2 retaining ring O-rings.

5. Thread tube gear remover part No. 884789-9 fully onto the outer propeller shaft (**Figure 16**, DP-C1/D1 shown), then connect a slide hammer (such as part No. 884161-1) to the adapter tool. Use the slide hammer to pull the outer propeller shaft (tube gear) and propshaft bearing carrier from the gearcase (**Figure 17**, [DP-C1/D1 shown]), then remove the slide hammer and tube gear puller.

6. Remove the inner propeller shaft as follows:

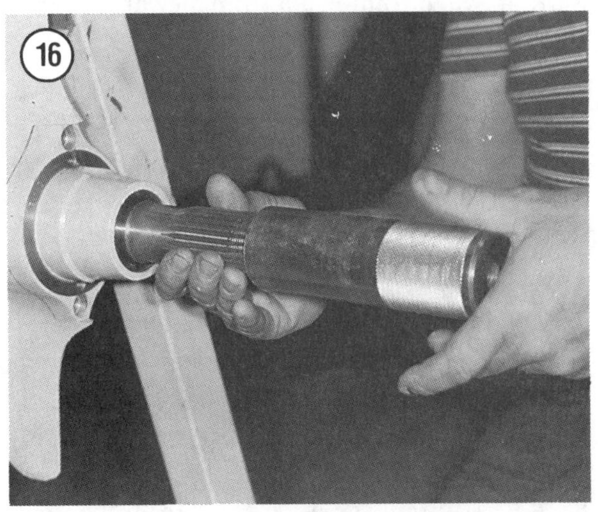

a. Attach adaptor part No. 885197-4 (A, **Figure 18**) to the propeller nut threads.
b. Install sleeve part No. 884802-0 (B, **Figure 18**) over the propeller shaft with its recess over the pinion nut.
c. Lubricate the tool's washer and nut, then install the washer and nut to the tool.
d. Tighten the nut (C, **Figure 18**) while holding the adapter (part No. 885197-4), until the propeller shaft is removed from the front gear.

7. Secure spline socket part No.884830-1 in a suitable vise. Invert the gear housing and engage the drive shaft splines into the spline holding fixture.
8. Remove the pinion nut from the vertical drive shaft with a 23 mm wrench (**Figure 19**).

NOTE
Do not discard the pinion nut at this point. It will be reused for shimming and gear pattern verification, then discarded. A new nut must be used during ***Final assembly***.

9. Reposition the gearcase in the upright position in a suitable fixture or on a clean workbench.
10. Thread drive shaft remover part No. 884267-6 on the end of the drive shaft, then turn the drive shaft with spline socket part No. 884830-1 to pull the drive shaft from the gearcase. Remove the tool when the shaft turns freely. See **Figure 20**.
11. Remove the drive shaft from the housing. Remove the shims from the drive shaft bore. Measure and record the thickness of the shim(s) for later reference. Tag the shim(s) for identification during reassembly.
12. Reach into the propshaft bore and remove the pinion gear and the front driven gear.
13. Remove the front driven gear bearing race (24, **Figure 11** or 23 , **Figure 12**) using bearing remover part No. 884794-9 and slide hammer part No. 884161-1 or a suitable 3 jaw slide hammer, such as OTC part No. OEM-4184. Remove the shim(s) from the bearing race bore. Measure and record the thickness of the shim(s) for later reference. Tag the shim(s) for identification during reassembly.
14. Remove the propeller shaft bearing carrier from the outer propeller shaft (tube gear).
15. Remove the roller bearing and shims from the inner propeller shaft as follows:

a. Place bearing remover part No. 884797-2 (A, **Figure 21**) over the gear end of the propshaft and against the roller bearing (B, **Figure 21**).

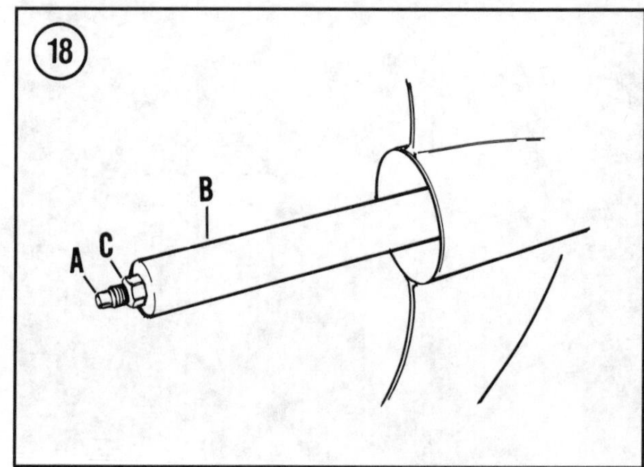

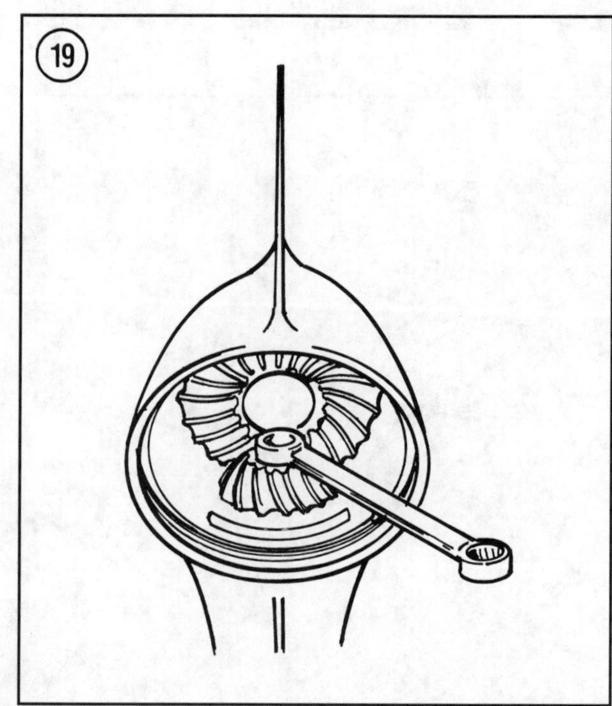

b. Install a suitable nut on the propeller end of the propshaft (C, **Figure 21**) to protect the threads.

c. Place the assembly into a press. Support the propeller nut and press against the tool until the roller bearing is free. *Do not* discard the bearing unless it is damaged.

d. Remove the shim(s) from the propeller shaft shoulder. Measure and record the thickness of the shim(s) for later reference.

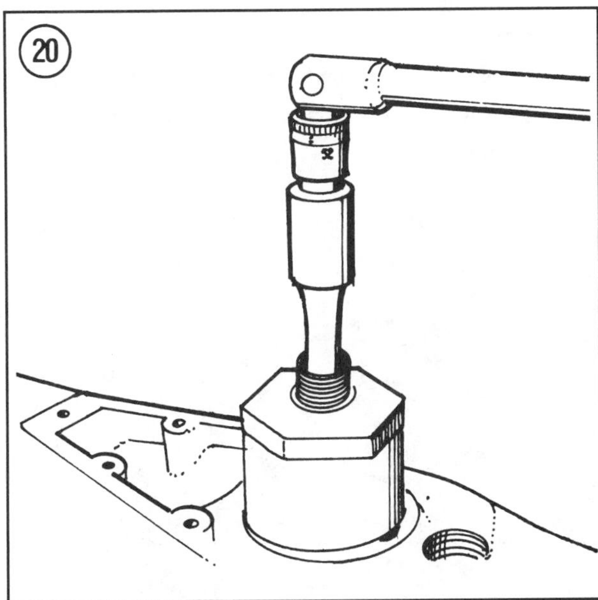

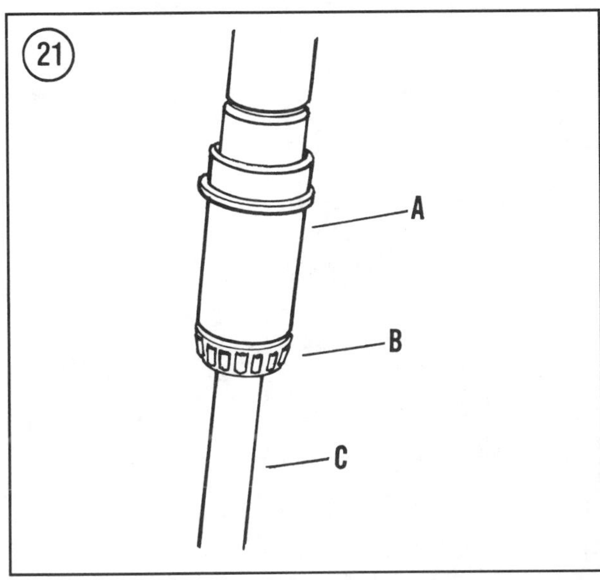

Tag the shim(s) for identification during reassembly.

NOTE
The tube gear inner needle bearing and propshaft seals can be removed at the same time if bearing replacement is required. If bearing replacement is not required, pull the seals with a suitable 2-jaw puller, being careful not to damage the inner surface of the tube gear or the inner needle bearing.

16A. *Seal removal only*—Remove the tube gear propshaft seals with a suitable 2 jaw puller. Do not damage the tube gear inner surfaces or the inner needle bearing. Discard the seals.

16B. *Seal and bearing removal*—If the tube gear inner needle bearing requires replacement, proceed as follows:

a. Install bearing remover part No. 884803-8 onto drive handle part No. 884143-9.

b. Thread an old propeller nut onto the tube gear to protect the threads and splines.

c. Insert the bearing remover and drive handle into the gear end of the tube gear.

d. Place the tool and gear assembly into a press. Support the propeller nut (while allowing room for the seals and bearings to exit) and press against the drive handle until the seals and needle bearing are free.

e. Discard the seals and needle bearing.

CAUTION
Do not remove any additional bearings or bearing races unless new bearings are going to be installed. The removal process is stressful to the bearings and races. However, all seals and O-rings should be removed and replaced each time the gearcase is disassembled.

17. If the lower drive shaft (pinion) bearing requires replacement, proceed as follows:

a. Assemble the appropriate pinion bearing remover (part No. 884791-5 for DP-C1/D1 or part No. 885226-1 for DPX) to the drive handle part No. 884143-9.

b. Place a shop towel in the propshaft bore underneath the pinion bearing.
c. Insert the bearing remover and drive handle into the drive shaft bore.
d. Drive the pinion bearing into the propshaft bore and onto the shop towel. If the bearing proves difficult to remove, apply mild heat to the outside of the gearcase around the pinion bearing with a heat gun or heat lamp. Do not use an open flame or torch.
e. Discard the pinion bearing and remove the tools.

18. If the drive shaft upper bearings require replacement, proceed as follows:
a. Remove the elastic lock spanner nut from the drive shaft with a suitable spanner wrench such as Snap-on part No. AHS301 or equivalent. Hold the drive shaft splines with spline socket part No. 884830-1.
b. Remove the large washer on top of the upper tapered roller bearing (under the spanner nut).
c. Support the tapered roller bearing in a press with a knife edge bearing plate (**Figure 22**). The drive shaft input splines must face up.
d. Press on the top of the drive shaft until the bearing is free from the drive shaft.
e. Remove the spacer washer from the drive shaft (on top of the ball bearing).
f. Support the ball bearing in a press with a knife edge bearing plate. The drive shaft input splines must face up.
g. Press on the top of the drive shaft until the bearing is free from the drive shaft.
h. Discard both bearings and the intermediate housing bearing cup removed previously.

19. *DP-C1/D1 models*—If the drive shaft lower bearing sleeve (race) requires replacement, proceed as follows:
a. Support the drive shaft bearing sleeve (A, **Figure 23**) in a press with a knife edge bearing plate (B, **Figure 23**). The pinion nut must face up.
b. Thread the old pinion nut onto the drive shaft to protect the drive shaft threads.
c. Press against the pinion nut until the sleeve is free from the drive shaft.
d. Discard the drive shaft bearing sleeve.
e. Remove and discard the pinion bearing from the gearcase housing as described previously in this section.

20. If the front driven gear roller bearing requires replacement, proceed as follows:
a. Support the bearing in a press with a knife edge bearing plate. The gear teeth must face down.
b. Press on the gear hub with a suitable mandrel until the bearing is free from the gear.

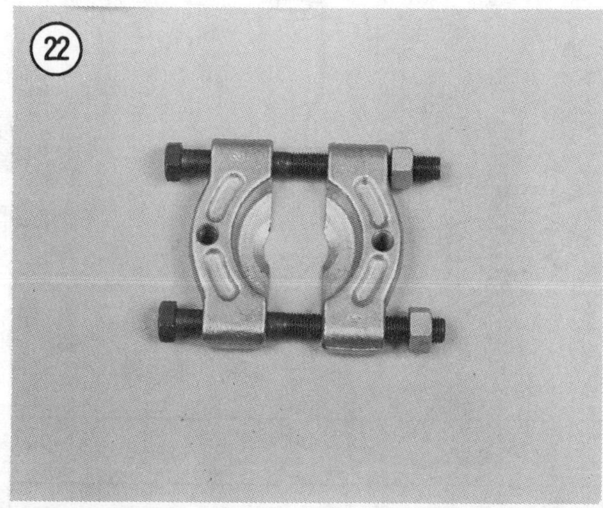

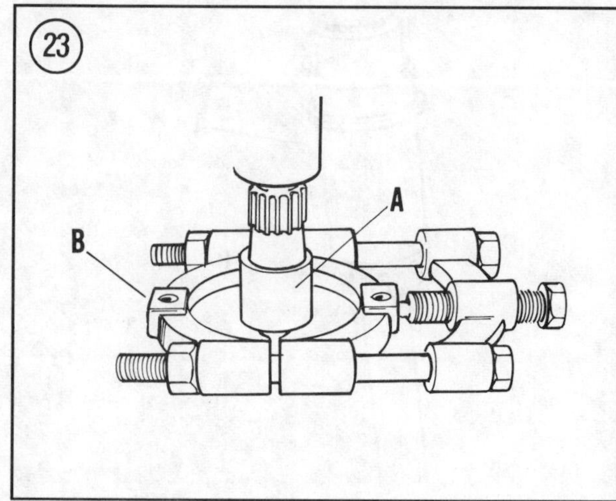

Tube gear roller bearing, race and sleeve removal

If the tube gear large tapered roller bearing requires replacement, the bearing sleeve (inner bearing race) for the propshaft bearing carrier needle bearing must also be removed and replaced. To remove the tube gear roller bearing, bearing sleeve and tube gear tapered roller bearing race, proceed as follows.

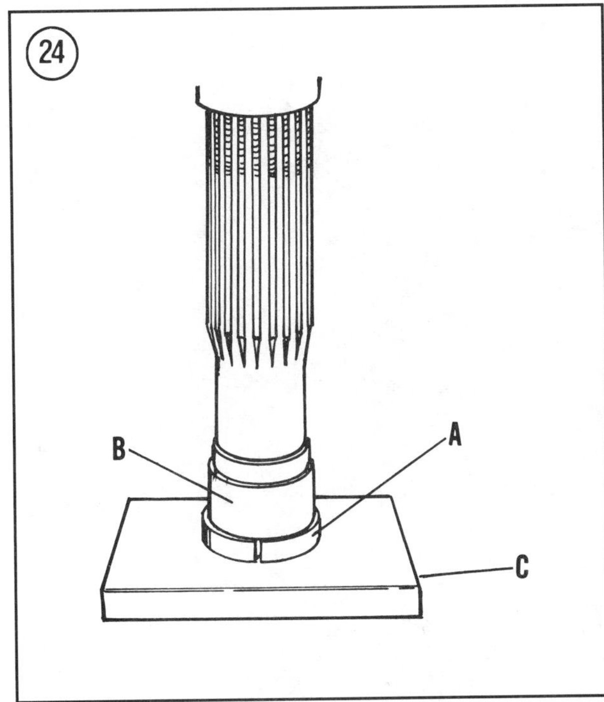

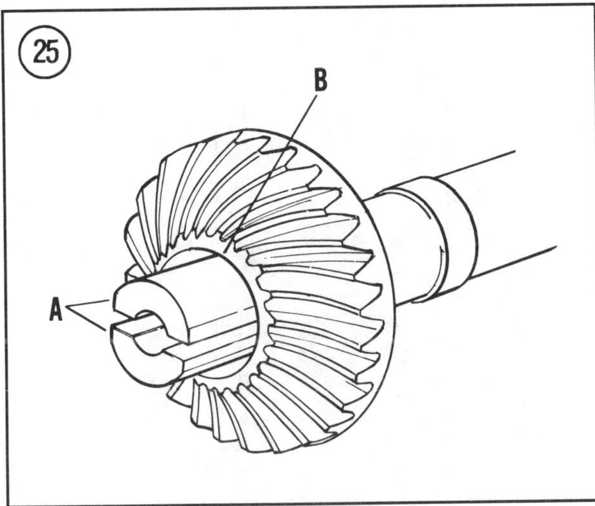

1. Insert the tube gear in sleeve removal tool part No. 884831-9. Position the split sleeves (A, **Figure 24**) on the gear side of the bearing sleeve (B, **Figure 24**) against the remover plate (C, **Figure 24**).
2. Thread an old propeller nut onto the tube gear to protect the threads and splines.

NOTE
If the sleeve proves difficult to remove in Step 3, apply mild heat to the sleeve. A heat lamp, heat gun or propane torch may be used.

3. Support the removal tool plate in a press. Press against the propeller nut until the sleeve is free from the tube gear.
4. Discard the bearing sleeve.
5. Support the tube gear tapered roller bearing in a press with a knife-edge bearing plate. The splined end of the tube gear must face up.
6. Thread an old propeller nut onto the tube gear to protect the threads and splines.
7. Press against the propeller nut until the bearing is free from the tube gear.
8. Discard the bearing.
9. Remove and discard the associated propshaft bearing carrier race as described in *Propshaft bearing carrier service* in this chapter.
10. To remove the small tapered roller bearing race in the tube gear face, proceed as follows:
    a. Insert the split remover halves part No. 884832-7 (A, **Figure 25**) into the gear face (B, **Figure 25**) and position the tool lips behind the bearing race.
    b. Insert the drive handle part No. 884143-9 through the propeller end of the tube gear and pilot it between the split bearing remover.
    c. Support the tube gear in a press. Protect the gear teeth with wood, plastic or aluminum blocks.
    d. Press on the drive handle until the bearing race is free from the tube gear.
    e. Discard the bearing race.

f. Remove and discard the inner propeller shaft tapered roller bearing as described previously.

Propshaft bearing carrier disassembly

The large bearing cup in the DP-C1/D1 propshaft bearing carrier is shimmed. The shim(s) set bearing preload on the propeller shaft assembly. The amount of shims need to be recalculated if any of the propeller shaft components or the housings are disassembled or replaced.

DPX models do not have shims in this location. Do not remove the race unless it is going to be replaced.

1A. *DP-C1/D1 models*—Remove and discard the 2 propshaft bearing carrier O-rings. See **Figure 26**.

1B. *DPX models*—Remove and discard the 3 propshaft bearing carrier O-rings.

NOTE

The propshaft carrier inner needle bearing and propshaft seals can be removed at the same time if bearing replacement is required. If bearing replacement is not required, pull the seals with a suitable 2-jaw puller, being careful not to damage the inner surface of the propshaft bearing carrier or the needle bearing.

2A. *Seal removal only*—Remove the propshaft seals with a suitable 2 jaw puller. Do not damage the carrier inner surfaces or the needle bearing. Discard the seals.

2B. *Seal and bearing removal*—If the propshaft bearing carrier inner needle bearing requires replacement, refer to **Figure 27** (DPX carrier shown) and proceed as follows:

a. Place the appropriate bearing remover (part No. 884797-2 for DP-C1/D1 models or part No. 884265-0 for DPX models) against the needle bearing.
b. Place the tool and carrier assembly into a press. Support the carrier (A, **Figure 27**), while allowing room for the seals and bearings to exit. Press against the tool (B, **Figure 27**) until the seals (C, **Figure 27**) and needle bearing (D, **Figure 27**) are free.
c. Discard the seals and needle bearing.

3. To remove the tapered roller bearing race from the propshaft bearing carrier, refer to **Figure 28** (DPX carrier shown) and proceed as follows:

a. Place bearing remover part No. 884796-4 inside the carrier with the tool's flanges (A, **Figure 28**) behind the bearing race (B, **Figure 28**).

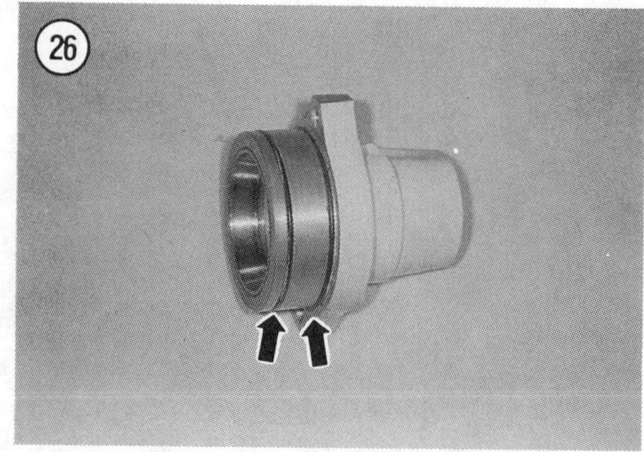

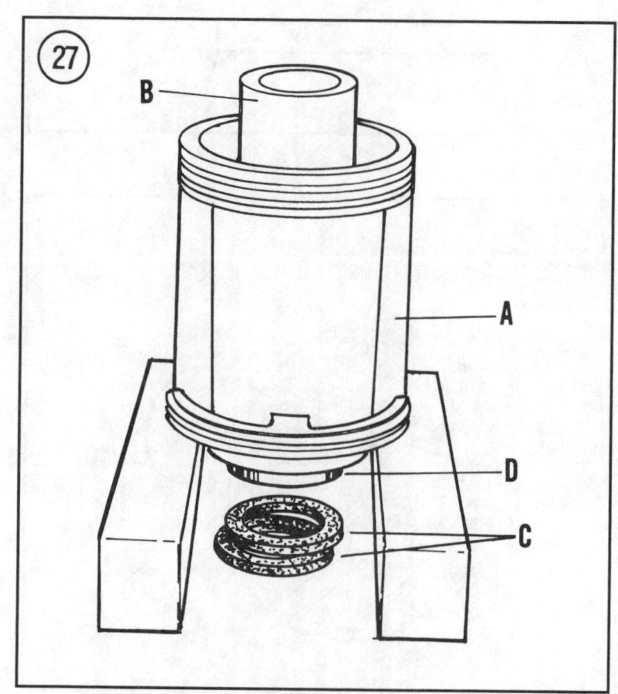

b. Install drive handle part No. 9991801-3 through the prop end of the carrier and pilot the drive handle (C, **Figure 28**) into the bearing remover.

c. Support the carrier in a press. Press on the drive handle until the bearing race is free from the carrier.

d. *DP-C1/D1 models*—Remove the shim(s) from the bearing carrier bore. Measure and record the thickness of the shim(s) for later reference. Tag the shim(s) for identification during reassembly. Discard the bearing race if it is going to be replaced.

e. *DPX models*—Discard the bearing race.

f. If the bearing race is being replaced, remove and replace the tapered roller bearing on the tube gear as described previously.

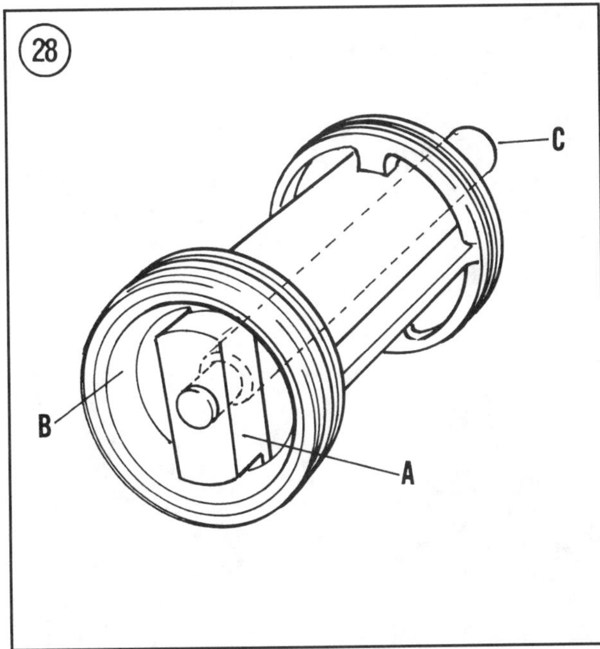

Cleaning and Inspection

1. Clean all parts in a suitable solvent and blow dry with compressed air. Make sure all sealer and gasket residue is removed and blow out all threaded holes, lubricant passages and water intake passages.
2. Apply a light coat of oil to all of the cleaned components to prevent rusting.
3. Inspect the gears. Check all gear teeth and the internal bearing or splined surfaces for excessive wear, chips, cracks, nicks or other damage. If 1 gear is damaged and requires replacement, replace all 3 as an assembly.

CAUTION

One tapered roller bearing consists of the caged tapered roller bearings and cone-shaped inner race, and a cup-shaped outer race. The bearing must be replaced as a set and parts from one bearing must never be mixed with parts from another.

4. Check all of the bearings (**Figure 29**, typical) for scoring, roughness, heat discoloration and binding. Replace any bearing (and corresponding race) as necessary. Follow the procedures in this chapter to remove the bearings. Do not remove pressed-on bearings unless replacement is necessary or the text specifically directs you to do so.
5. Check the splines of the intermediate drive shaft coupler for excessive wear or distortion.
6. Inspect all shims and replace any that are damaged. If shimming adjustment is not required, damaged shims can be replaced with new shims of the same thickness.

7. Check all of the threads, sealing surfaces and splines (internal and external) on the propeller and drive shafts. See **Figure 30** (tube shaft), **Figure 31** (inner propeller shaft) and **Figure 32** (drive shaft). Replace any shaft that displays excessive wear, mechanical damage or distortion. Slight imperfections can be removed with emery cloth.

8. Check the propellers for spline damage, corrosion or wear. Check the propeller blades for cracks, dents, gouged or broken blades. Rebuild or replace the propellers as necessary.

9. Check the gear housing and propeller bearing housing for cracks around the screw holes and bearing bores. Also check for cracks, nicks or burrs on the housing mating surfaces and O-ring surfaces. Slight imperfections can be removed with emery cloth.

10. Inspect the anodes as described in *Corrosion Control* located in this chapter.

Assembly

For maximum durability and quiet running, all of the gears must be properly located in the gearcase by following the correct shim selection procedure. When the gears are properly located, the correct backlash and gear contact pattern will be observed.

Additionally, the tapered bearings in the gearcase must be properly tensioned or *preloaded.* Preload refers to the tension applied to hold a tapered roller bearing in its cup. Insufficient preload will allow the bearing to move in relation to the bearing cup. Any movement of the bearing from its cup will result in premature bearing and gear failure. Excessive preload will cause the bearings to overheat and fail. Correct preload is determined by measuring the torque required to rotate the shafts and gears. This is called *rolling torque*.

During assembly procedures, lubricate all components with Volvo DuraPlus GL5 Synthetic Gear Lube (**Table 6**). Do not make any *dry* assemblies.

Do not install new seals and O-rings until the gear lash, gear pattern and bearing rolling torque have been verified. Seal and O-ring installation will be covered under *Final Assembly*.

Figure 33 is an exploded view of a DP-C1/D1 DuoProp lower gearcase and **Figure 34** is an exploded view of a DPX lower gearcase.

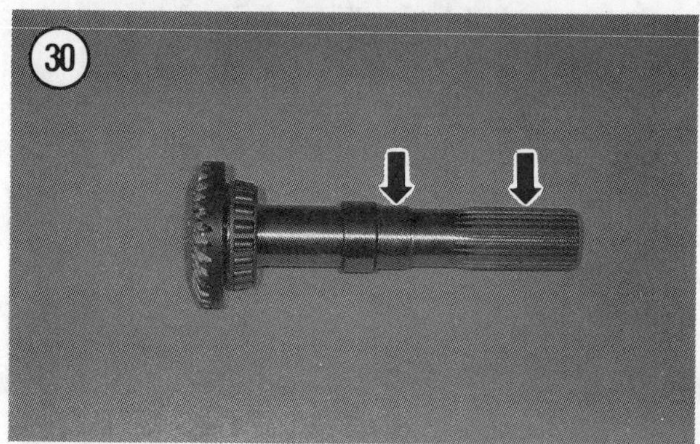

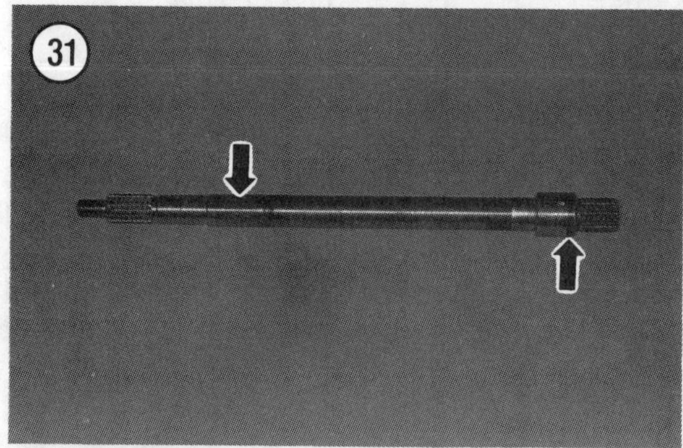

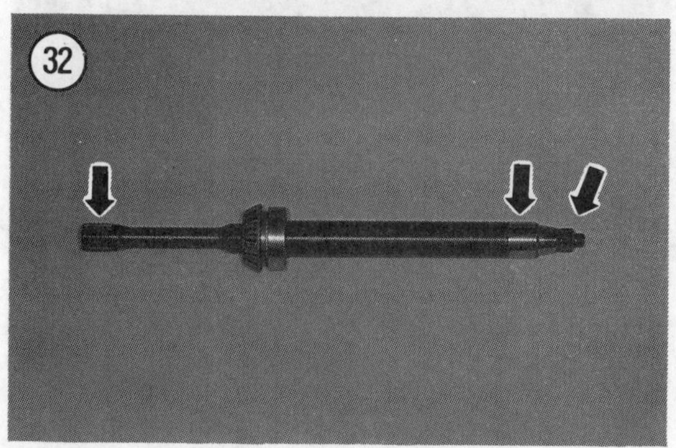

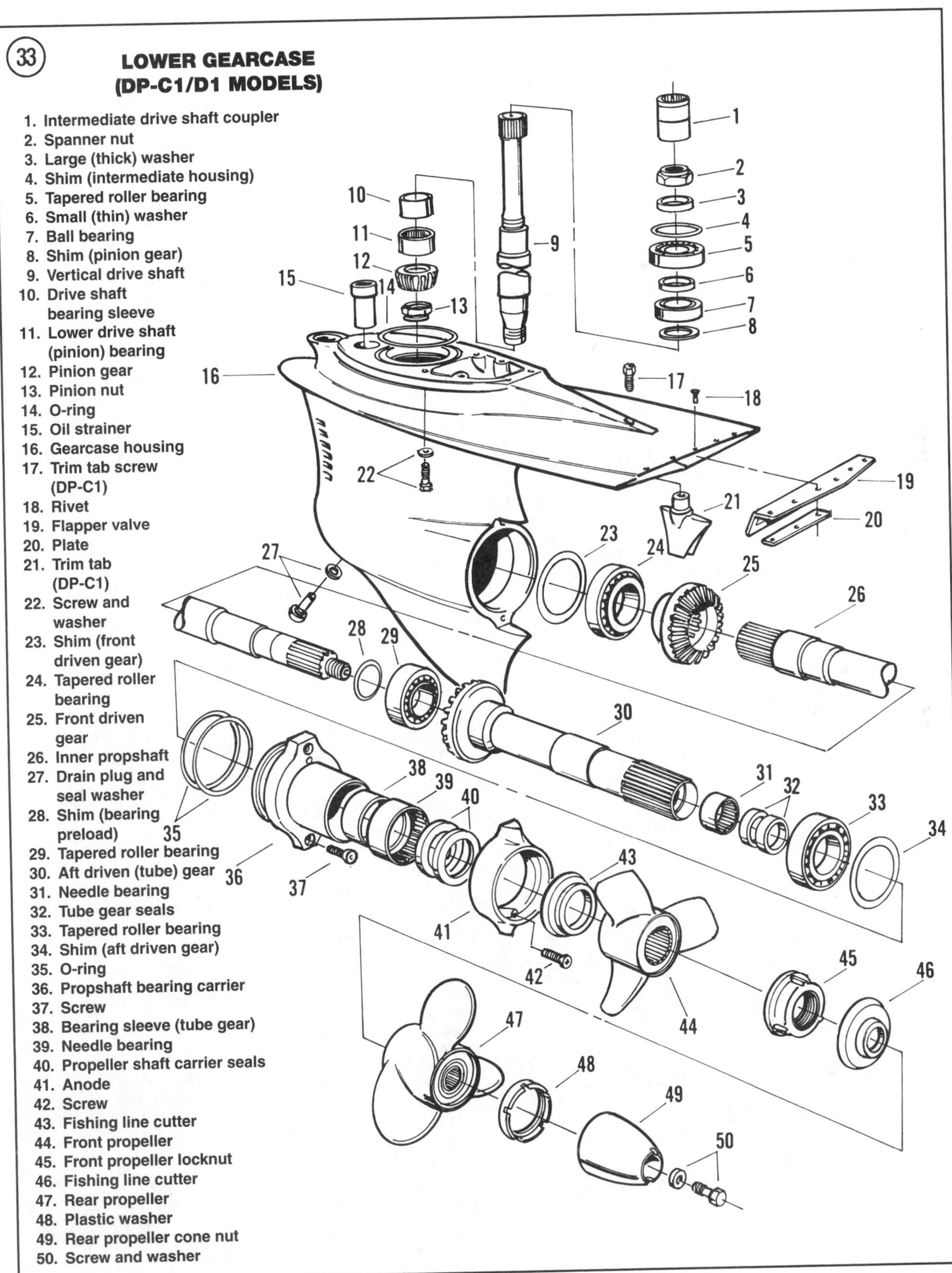
33
LOWER GEARCASE
(DP-C1/D1 MODELS)
1. Intermediate drive shaft coupler
2. Spanner nut
3. Large (thick) washer
4. Shim (intermediate housing)
5. Tapered roller bearing
6. Small (thin) washer
7. Ball bearing
8. Shim (pinion gear)
9. Vertical drive shaft
10. Drive shaft bearing sleeve
11. Lower drive shaft (pinion) bearing
12. Pinion gear
13. Pinion nut
14. O-ring
15. Oil strainer
16. Gearcase housing
17. Trim tab screw (DP-C1)
18. Rivet
19. Flapper valve
20. Plate
21. Trim tab (DP-C1)
22. Screw and washer
23. Shim (front driven gear)
24. Tapered roller bearing
25. Front driven gear
26. Inner propshaft
27. Drain plug and seal washer
28. Shim (bearing preload)
29. Tapered roller bearing
30. Aft driven (tube) gear
31. Needle bearing
32. Tube gear seals
33. Tapered roller bearing
34. Shim (aft driven gear)
35. O-ring
36. Propshaft bearing carrier
37. Screw
38. Bearing sleeve (tube gear)
39. Needle bearing
40. Propeller shaft carrier seals
41. Anode
42. Screw
43. Fishing line cutter
44. Front propeller
45. Front propeller locknut
46. Fishing line cutter
47. Rear propeller
48. Plastic washer
49. Rear propeller cone nut
50. Screw and washer

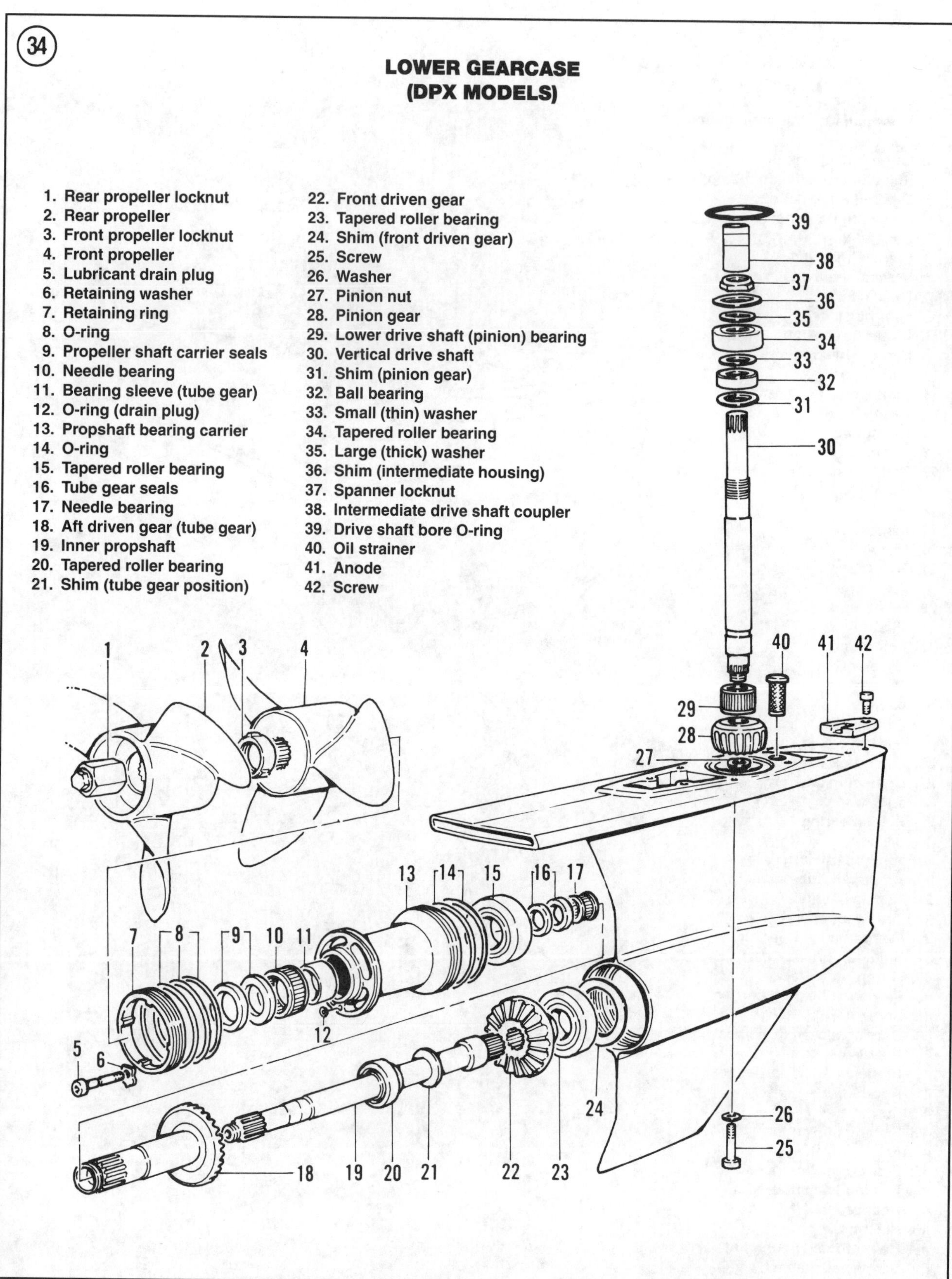
34
LOWER GEARCASE
(DPX MODELS)
1. Rear propeller locknut
2. Rear propeller
3. Front propeller locknut
4. Front propeller
5. Lubricant drain plug
6. Retaining washer
7. Retaining ring
8. O-ring
9. Propeller shaft carrier seals
10. Needle bearing
11. Bearing sleeve (tube gear)
12. O-ring (drain plug)
13. Propshaft bearing carrier
14. O-ring
15. Tapered roller bearing
16. Tube gear seals
17. Needle bearing
18. Aft driven gear (tube gear)
19. Inner propshaft
20. Tapered roller bearing
21. Shim (tube gear position)
22. Front driven gear
23. Tapered roller bearing
24. Shim (front driven gear)
25. Screw
26. Washer
27. Pinion nut
28. Pinion gear
29. Lower drive shaft (pinion) bearing
30. Vertical drive shaft
31. Shim (pinion gear)
32. Ball bearing
33. Small (thin) washer
34. Tapered roller bearing
35. Large (thick) washer
36. Shim (intermediate housing)
37. Spanner locknut
38. Intermediate drive shaft coupler
39. Drive shaft bore O-ring
40. Oil strainer
41. Anode
42. Screw

Begin reassembly by first installing new bearings to replace any that were removed. The small roller bearing on the inner propshaft, the front driven gear race and the propshaft bearing carrier large race (DP-C1/D1 only) cannot be installed until the shims have been determined. Installation of these bearings is covered later in this section.

Pinion bearing installation

If the lower drive shaft (pinion) bearing was removed from the gearcase, install a new pinion bearing as follows.

1. Lubricate a new pinion bearing and place it on bearing installer part No. 884792-3 (A, **Figure 35**) with the lettered side of the bearing facing the installer. Place the tool and bearing into the lower drive shaft bore via the propshaft bore. The lettered side of the pinion bearing must face down when installed.

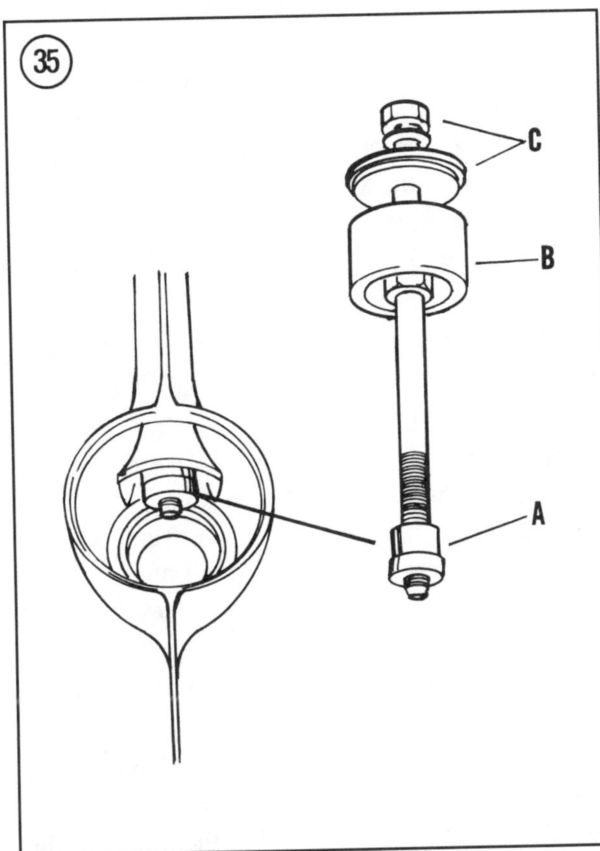

2A. *DP-C1/D1 models*—Insert the threaded rod and plate part No. 884241-1 (C, **Figure 35**) into the drive shaft bore and engage the bearing installer. Thread the bearing installer securely onto the threaded rod.

2B. *DPX models*—Insert the threaded rod and plate part No. 884281-1 (C, **Figure 35**) through remover part No. 884267-6 (B, **Figure 35**) and into the drive shaft bore. Thread the bearing installer securely onto the threaded rod. The remover is needed as an additional spacer due to the DPX gearcase being shorter than the DP-C1/D1 gearcase.

3. Tighten the threaded rod to pull the bearing into position. Stop tightening the rod as soon as the bearing seats in its bore or the bearing will be damaged.

4. Remove the tools and inspect the bearing for damage.

Drive shaft bearing installation

If the bearings or bearing sleeve were removed from the drive shaft, install new components as follows.

1. Lubricate a new lower drive shaft bearing sleeve and place it over the pinion nut end of the drive shaft. Place sleeve installer part No. 884793-1 over the sleeve.

2. Place the drive shaft assembly into a press. Protect the input splines with wood, plastic or an aluminum plate.

3. Press against the sleeve installer until the sleeve is seated on the drive shaft.

4. Lubricate a new ball bearing and place it over the drive shaft input splines with the thickest side of the inner race facing up. Place bearing installer part No. 884266-8 over the drive shaft and bearing.

5. Thread an old pinion nut onto the drive shaft to protect the threads. Place drive shaft assembly into a press.

6. Press against the bearing installer until the bearing is seated against the drive shaft shoulder.

7. Place the thin spacer washer over the input splines and against the ball bearing.
8. Lubricate a new tapered roller bearing and place it over the input splines with the rollers facing up. Place bearing installer part No. 884266-8 over the drive shaft and bearing.
9. Place the drive shaft assembly into a press.
10. Press against the bearing installer until the bearing is seated against the ball bearing and thin spacer washer.
11. Place the thick spacer washer over the drive shaft splines and seat it against the tapered roller bearing.
12. Install a new elastic locking spanner nut. Tighten the nut securely against the bearings with a spanner wrench, such as Snap-on part No. AHS301 or equivalent. Hold the drive shaft splines with spline socket part No. 884830-1.

Tube gear bearing installation

If the tube gear large tapered roller bearing, bearing sleeve, small bearing race or inner needle bearing were removed, install new components as follows.

1. Install a new inner needle bearing by first lubricating the bearing and placing it into the propeller end of the tube gear with the numbered side of the bearing facing out.
2. Set the tube gear into a press with the gear facing down. Protect the gear teeth with wood, plastic or an aluminum plate. Place the large end of bearing installer part No. 884806-1 against the needle bearing.
3. Press against the installer until the tool seats against the tube gear. Remove the installer.
4. Lubricate the large roller bearing and place it over the tube gear splines with the rollers facing up. Place bearing installer part No. 884801-2 over the tube gear splines and against the bearing.
5. Press against the installer until the bearing seats against the gear. Remove the installer.
6. Lubricate a new bearing sleeve and place it over the tube gear splines. Place bearing installer part No. 884801-2 over the tube gear splines and against the sleeve.
7. Press against the installer until the tool seats against the large tapered roller bearing. Leave the installer on the tube gear.
8. Invert the tube gear and bearing installer so the gear is facing up and the bearing installer is against the press support plate.
9. Lubricate a new small roller bearing race and place it into the face of the tube gear with the tapered side facing up. Place the large (longer) end of bearing installer part No. 884797-2 against the bearing race.
10. Press against the installer until the bearing race is seated in the tube gear bearing bore. Remove all tools and the tube gear from the press.

Propshaft bearing carrier assembly

The large bearing race on DP-C1/D1 models is shimmed to control the bearing preload of both propeller shaft assemblies. The large race cannot be installed on these models until the shimming calculations have been performed. Refer to *Propshaft carrier shimming* located later in this chapter.

If the inner needle bearing or large tapered roller bearing race were removed, install new components as follows.

1. Install a new inner needle bearing by first lubricating a new needle bearing and placing it into the propeller end of the propshaft carrier bore with its numbered side facing out.
2A. *DP-C1/D1 models*—Place the small (short) end of the bearing installer part No. 884797-2 against the needle bearing. Place the bearing carrier assembly into a press.
2B. *DPX Models*—Place spacer part No. 885227-9 over the small (short) end of bearing installer part No. 884797-2. Set the tool into the

propshaft bearing carrier so the spacer is against the bearing.

3. Press against the installer until the tool seats against the bearing carrier. Remove the tool(s).

4. Invert the propshaft carrier so its large opening is facing up.

5A. *DP-C1/D1 models*—Set the predetermined shims into the propshaft bearing carrier bearing bore. Lubricate the large roller bearing race and set it into the propshaft bearing carrier with the taper facing up (out). Place the bearing installer part No. 884795-6 against the bearing race.

5B. *DPX models*—Lubricate a new large roller bearing race and set it into the propshaft bearing carrier with the taper facing up (out). Place the bearing installer part No. 884795-6 against the bearing race.

6. Press against the installer until the race is seated in the bearing carrier.

Front driven gear bearing installation

1. To install a new front driven gear roller bearing, begin by lubricating the new roller bearing. Place its bearing over the gear hub with its rollers facing away from the gear.

2. Place the gear assembly into a press. Protect the gear teeth with wood, plastic or an aluminum plate. Place bearing installer part No. 884801-2 against the bearing.

3. Press against the installer until the bearing is seated against the gear.

Lower Gearcase Shimming Procedures (DP-C1/D1 and DPX Models)

To determine the correct amount of shims to position the gear and bearings properly, keep in mind that the numbers stamped on the gear sleeve and gear housing are correction numbers in hundredths of a millimeter. Nominal dimensions are fixed dimensions that are established by Volvo Penta during the design and manufacturing of the product. All fixed (nominal) dimensions are listed in **Table 1**.

Since the gears and housing are stamped using the Metric system, it is recommended that all calculations be performed in millimeters. Any conversions from Metric to U.S. standard units should only be attempted on the final calculated result.

On units that have 2 nominal figures listed, use the larger nominal figure if the stamped correction number on the housing is below 50. Use the smaller nominal figure if the stamped correction number is above 50.

The bearings for each driven gear are dimensionally unique. The front driven gear uses a roller bearing with a nominal dimension of 20.85 mm (0.821 in.). The rear driven gear (tube gear) uses a roller bearing with a nominal dimension of 20.75 mm (0.817 in.). Do not intermix the bearings or races.

The correct selection of shims and proper gearcase assembly will be confirmed by the gear lash and gear pattern verifications and the overall rolling torque check.

CAUTION

It cannot be stated strongly enough that you must clearly record and label all of your shimming calculations. Time spent calculating shim amounts is wasted if the results are not recorded and labeled.

Front driven gear shimming

The following procedure determines the shims required to locate the front driven gear correctly, in the lower gearcase. The shims will be installed behind the roller bearing race at the front of the gearcase housing. To determine the correct thickness of shims (23, **Figure 33** or 24, **Figure 34**), proceed as follows.

NOTE

If the G correction number in Step 1 is above 50, use the nominal dimension of 60.00 mm. If the correction number is less than 50, use the nominal dimension *of 61.00 mm. For example, the G correction number in **Figure 36** is 95. This example would require the use of the 60.00 mm nominal figure.*

1. Locate the stamped G correction number on the top face of the lower gear housing. **Figure 36** shows a G correction number (example) of 95. Record this as 0.95 mm. Record the G dimension from the gearcase as hundredths of a millimeter. Add this number to the nominal figure of 60.00 mm or 61.00 mm. In our example, this would be 60.00 mm plus 0.95 mm equals 60.95 mm, (60.00 + 0.95 = 60.95). Record this result and label it as *total housing dimension*.
2. Locate the correction number etched or stamped on the front driven gear (**Figure 37**, typical). Record this figure as hundredths of a millimeter. For example, if +5 is etched on the gear, write it as +0.05 mm. If -5 is etched on the gear, write it as -0.05 mm.
3. Add or subtract (as indicated by the + or -) the etched number on the gear to the fixed driven gear nominal dimension of 39.50 mm. For example, the gear shown in **Figure 37** is 39.50 mm plus 0.05 mm equals 39.55 mm, (39.50 + 0.05 = 39.55). Record this result and label it as *total gear dimension*.

NOTE

*The front driven gear tapered roller bearing can be identified by the thickness of the bearing and race assembly. Front driven gear bearings should measure 20.85 mm (0.821 in.) total thickness. See **Figure 38**.*

4. Add the result of Step 3 (total gear dimension) to the front bearing thickness of 20.85 mm. Following our example, this would be 39.55 mm (total gear dimension) plus 20.85 mm (front bearing thickness) equals 60.4 mm, (39.55 + 20.85 = 60.4). Record this result and label it as *total gear and bearing dimension*.
5. Subtract the *total gear and bearing dimension* from the *total housing dimension*. Following our example, this would be 60.95 mm (total housing dimension) minus 60.4 mm (total gear and bearing dimension) equals 0.55 mm., (60.95 - 60.4 = 0.55). Record this result and label it *front driven gear shims*. This result is the amount of shims (in hundredths of a millimeter) required to locate the front driven gear.
6. Select and measure the correct amount of shims determined by your calculations. Set these predetermined shims into the lower gearcase, front driven gear bearing race bore.
7. Lubricate the front driven gear bearing race and set it into the propshaft bore with the tapered side facing up (out).

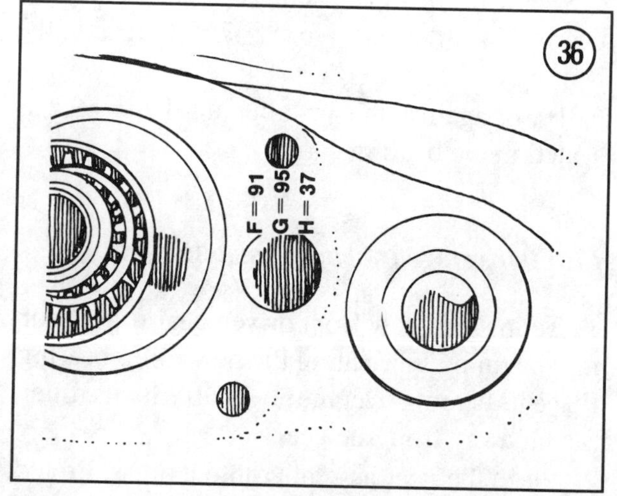

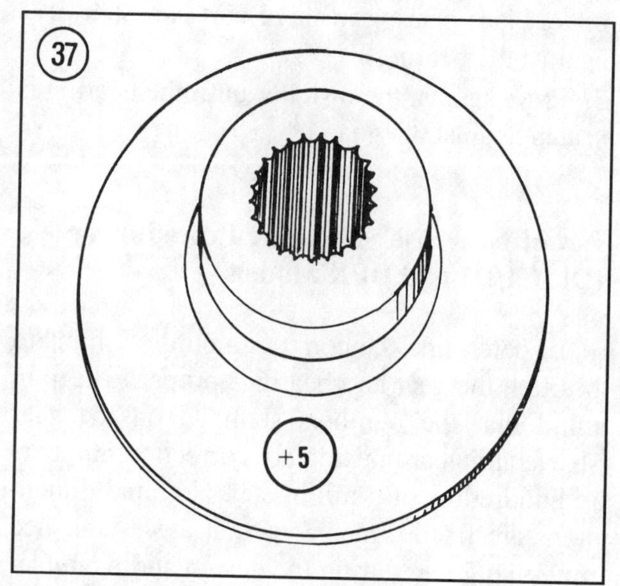

8. Place bearing installer part No. 884795-6 into the propshaft bore and against the bearing race. Press or drive the bearing race into the gearcase until it is seated in its bore. Set the leading edge of the gearcase on a wooden block to prevent damage to the housing.

9. Remove the installer when the bearing race has been properly seated.

10. Press the inner propshaft into the front driven gear as follows:

   a. Lubricate the inner propshaft splines and pilot the splines into the front driven gear splines. Make sure the gear teeth are facing the propeller end of the inner propshaft.

   b. Thread a propeller nut onto the propshaft to protect the threads.

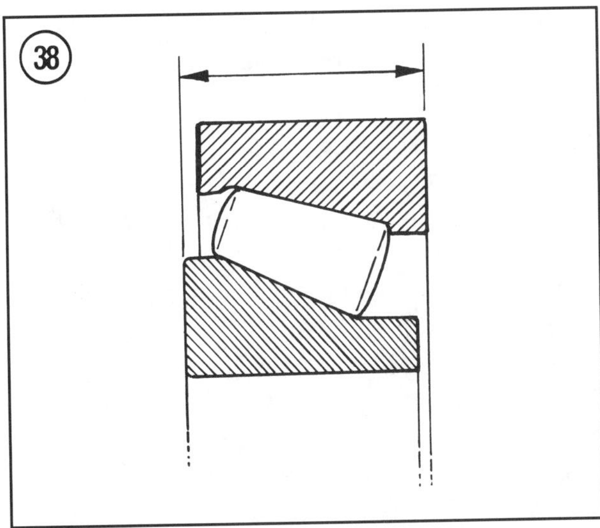

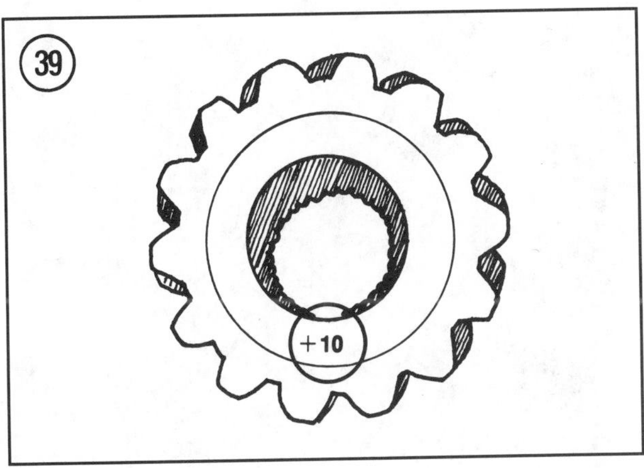

   c. Support the gear on a suitable mandrel to protect the roller bearing.

   d. Press on the propeller nut until the propshaft shoulder is seated against the gear face.

   e. Remove the propeller nut.

Vertical drive shaft shimming (DP-C1/D1 models)

The following procedure determines the shims required to locate the vertical shaft (pinion gear) in a DP-C1/D1 series lower gearcase, correctly. The shims will be installed under the ball bearing at the top of the drive shaft bore of the gearcase housing. To determine the correct thickness of shims (8, **Figure 33**), proceed as follows.

NOTE

*If the H correction number in Step 1 is above 50, use the nominal dimension of 276.00 mm. If the correction number is less than 50, use the nominal dimension of 277.00 mm. For example, the H correction number in **Figure 36** is 37. This example would require the use of the 277.00 mm nominal figure.*

1. Locate the stamped H correction number on the top face of the lower gear housing. **Figure 36** shows an H correction number (example) of 37. Record this as 0.37 mm. Record the H dimension from your gearcase as hundredths of a millimeter. Add this number to the nominal figure of 276.00 mm or 277.00 mm. In our example, this would be 277.00 mm plus 0.37 mm equals 277.37 mm, (277.00 + 0.37 = 277.37). Record this result and label it as *total housing dimension*.

2. Locate the correction number etched or stamped on the pinion gear (**Figure 39**, typical). Record this figure as hundredths of a millimeter. For example, if +10 is etched on the gear, write it as +0.10 mm. If -10 is etched on the gear, write it as -0.10 mm.

3. Add or subtract (as indicated by the + or -) the etched number on the gear to the fixed pinion

gear dimension of 60.00 mm. For example, the gear shown in **Figure 39** is 60.00 mm plus 0.10 mm equals 60.10 mm, (60.00 + 0.10 = 60.10). Record this result and label it as *total gear dimension.*

4. Add the result of Step 3 (total gear dimension) to the fixed vertical shaft nominal dimension of 217.75 mm. Following our example, this would be 60.10 mm (total gear dimension) plus 217.75 mm (vertical shaft nominal dimension) equals 277.85 mm, (60.10 + 217.75 = 277.85). Record this result and label it as *total gear and shaft dimension.*

5. Subtract the *total housing dimension* from the *total gear and shaft dimension.* Following our example, this would be 277.85 mm (total gear and shaft dimension) minus 277.37 mm (total housing dimension) equals 0.48 mm., (277.85 - 277.37 = 0.48). Record this result and label it *vertical shaft shims.* This result is the amount of shims (in hundredths of a millimeter) required to locate the vertical shaft (pinion gear).

6. Select and measure the correct amount of shims determined by your calculations. Set these predetermined shims into the lower gearcase, drive shaft bore.

7. Coat at least 3 teeth of the front driven gear with GM Gear Marking Compound, available from any General Motors automotive dealership.

8. Stand the gearcase on its leading edge. Lubricate the front driven gear, bearing and propshaft assembly. Place the gear assembly into the gearcase and seat it into the front driven gear bearing race.

9. Hold the pinion gear in position and install the drive shaft into the drive shaft bore being careful not to displace any of the predetermined vertical shaft shims (**Figure 40**). Rotate the drive shaft as necessary to engage the pinion gear splines. Seat the drive shaft against the shims.

NOTE
Use the original pinion nut at this time. A new pinion nut will be installed during ***Final Assembly***.

10. Lubricate the original pinion nut and install it to the drive shaft. Tighten the nut hand-tight initially.

11. With the aid of an assistant, torque the pinion nut to specification (**Table 3**). Use a 23 mm wrench to hold the pinion nut. Use spline socket part No. 884830-1, an appropriate adapter and a torque wrench to turn the drive shaft.

Vertical drive shaft shimming (DPX models)

The following procedure determines the shims required to locate the vertical shaft (pinion gear) in a DPX series lower gearcase, correctly. The shims will be installed under the ball bearing at the top of the drive shaft bore of the gearcase housing. To determine the correct thickness of shims (31, **Figure 34**), proceed as follows.

1. Locate the stamped H correction number on the top face of the lower gear housing. **Figure 36** shows an H correction number (example) of 37. Recorded this as 0.37 mm. Record the H dimension from your gearcase as hundredths of a millimeter. Add this number to the nominal figure of 229.10 mm. In our example, this would be 229.10 mm plus 0.37 mm equals 229.47 mm, (229.10 + 0.37 = 229.47). Record this result and label it as *total housing dimension*.

2. Locate the correction number etched or stamped on the pinion gear (**Figure 39**, typical). Record this figure as hundredths of a millimeter. For example, if +10 is etched on the gear, write it as +0.10 mm. If -10 is etched on the gear, write it as -0.10 mm.
3. Add or subtract (as indicated by the + or -) the etched number on the gear to the fixed pinion gear dimension of 60.00 mm. For example, the gear shown in **Figure 39** is 60.00 mm plus 0.10 mm equals 60.10 mm, (60.00 + 0.10 = 60.10). Record this result and label it as *total gear dimension*.
4. Add the result of Step 3 (total gear dimension) to the fixed vertical shaft nominal dimension of 169.85 mm. Following our example, this would be 60.10 mm (total gear dimension) plus 169.85 mm (vertical shaft nominal dimension) equals 229.95 mm, (60.10 + 169.85 = 229.95). Record this result and label it as *total gear and shaft dimension*.
5. Subtract the *total housing dimension* from the *total gear and shaft dimension*. Following our example, this would be 229.95 mm (total gear and shaft dimension) minus 229.47 mm (total housing dimension) equals 0.48 mm., (229.95 - 229.47 = 0.48). Record this result and label it *vertical shaft shims*. This result is the amount of shims (in hundredths of a millimeter) required to locate the vertical shaft (pinion gear).
6. Select and measure the correct amount of shims determined by your calculations. Set these predetermined shims into the lower gearcase, drive shaft bore.
7. Coat at least 3 teeth of the front driven gear with GM Gear Marking Compound, available from any General Motors automotive dealership.
8. Stand the gearcase on its leading edge. Lubricate the front driven gear, bearing and propshaft assembly. Place the gear assembly into the gearcase and seat it into the front driven gear bearing race.
9. Hold the pinion gear in position and install the drive shaft into the drive shaft bore being careful not to displace any of the predetermined vertical shaft shims (**Figure 40**). Rotate the drive shaft as necessary to engage the pinion gear splines. Seat the drive shaft against the shims.

NOTE

Use the original pinion nut at this time. A new pinion nut will be installed during ***Final Assemby.***

10. Lubricate the original pinion nut and install it to the drive shaft. Tighten the nut hand-tight initially.
11. With the aid of an assistant, torque the pinion nut to specification (**Table 3**). Use a 23 mm wrench to hold the pinion nut. Use spline socket part No. 884830-1, an appropriate adapter and a torque wrench to turn the drive shaft.

Propshaft bearing carrier shimming (DP-C1/D1 models)

The following procedure determines the shims required to locate the aft driven gear (tube gear) in a DP-C1/D1 series lower gearcase, correctly. The shims will be installed under the large bearing race in the propshaft bearing carrier. To determine the correct thickness of shims (34, **Figure 33**), proceed as follows.

NOTE

If the F correction number in Step 1 is above 50, use the nominal dimension of 79.00 mm. If the correction number is less than 50, use the nominal dimension of 80.00 mm. For example, the F correction number in ***Figure 36*** *is 91. This example would require the use of the 79.00 mm nominal figure.*

1. Locate the stamped F correction number on the top face of the lower gear housing. **Figure 36** shows an F correction number (example) of 91. Record this as 0.91 mm. Record the F dimension from your gearcase as hundredths of a millimeter. Add this number to the nominal figure of 79.00 mm or 80.00 mm. In our example, this

would be 79.00 mm plus 0.91 mm equals 79.91 mm, (79.00 + 0.91 = 79.91). Record this result and label it as *total gear housing dimension*.

2. Locate the stamped C correction number on the inner face of the propshaft bearing carrier. **Figure 41** shows a C correction number (example) of 25. Recorded this as 0.25 mm. Record the C dimension from your gearcase as hundredths of a millimeter. Add this number to the fixed bearing carrier nominal figure of 19.00 mm. In our example, this would be 19.00 mm plus 0.25 mm equals 19.25 mm, (19.00 + 0.25 = 19.25). Record this result and label it as *total bearing carrier dimension*.

3. Subtract the *total bearing carrier dimension* from the *total gear housing dimension*. Following our example, this would be 79.91 mm (total gear housing dimension) minus 19.25 mm (total bearing carrier dimension) equals 60.66 mm, (79.91 - 19.25 = 60.66). Record this result and label it as *total housing and carrier dimension*.

4. Locate the correction number etched or stamped on the aft driven (tube) gear (**Figure 42**, typical). Record this figure as hundredths of a millimeter. For example, if +10 is etched on the gear, write it as +0.10 mm. If -10 is etched on the gear, write it as -0.10 mm.

5. Add or subtract (as indicated by the + or -) the etched number on the gear to the fixed tube gear dimension of 39.50 mm. For example, the gear shown in **Figure 42** is 39.50 mm plus 0.10 mm equals 39.60 mm, (39.50 + 0.10 = 39.60). Record this result and label it as *total gear dimension*.

NOTE

The aft driven gear (tube gear) tapered roller bearing can be identified by the thickness of the bearing and race assembly. Aft driven gear (tube gear) bearings should measure 20.75 mm (0.817 in.) total thickness. See ***Figure 38****.*

6. Add the result of Step 5 (total gear dimension) to the aft bearing thickness of 20.75 mm. Following our example, this would be 39.60 mm (total gear thickness) plus 20.75 mm (aft bearing thickness) equals 60.35 mm, (39.60 + 20.75 = 60.35). Record this result and label it as *total gear and bearing dimension*.

7. Subtract the *total gear and bearing dimension* from the *total housing and carrier dimension*. Following our example, this would be 60.66 mm (total housing and carrier dimension) minus 60.35 mm (total gear and bearing dimension) equals 0.31 mm., (60.66 - 60.35 = 0.31). Record this result and label it *propshaft bearing carrier shims*. This result is the amount of shims (in hundredths of a millimeter) required to locate the aft driven gear (tube gear).

8. Select and measure the correct amount of shims determined by your calculations. Set these predetermined shims into the propshaft bearing carrier, large bearing race bore.

9. Install the aft driven gear bearing cup into the propshaft bearing carrier as described in *propshaft bearing carrier assembly* located previously in this section.

Inner propshaft bearing shimming (DP-C1/D1 models)

The following procedure determines the amount of shims necessary to properly preload

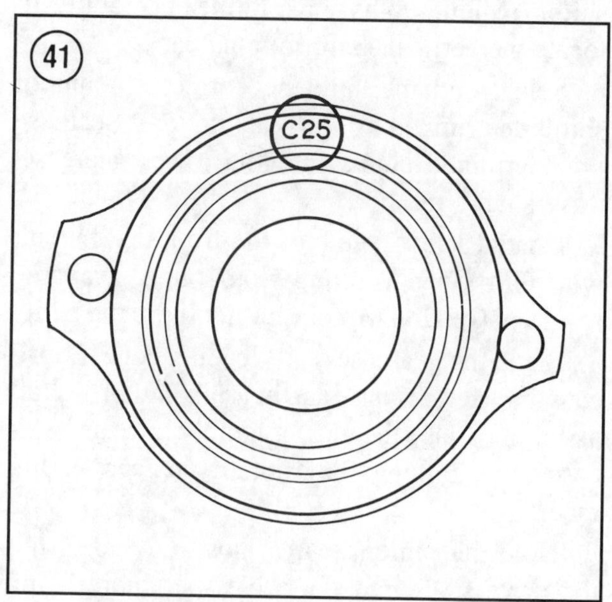

all of the tapered roller bearings in the complete propeller shaft assembly. The result of this procedure is determined strictly from the results of previous shimming calculations. A nominal (fixed) dimension of 120.00 mm (4.724 in.) will be used in this procedure. To determine the correct amount of shims to install under the inner propeller shaft small roller bearing, proceed as follows.

1. Add the total housing dimension from Step 1 of *front driven gear shimming* to the total gear housing dimension in Step 1 of *propshaft bearing carrier shimming (DP-C1/D1 models)*. To continue to follow our example, we would add 60.95 mm (total housing dimension from front driven gear shimming, Step 1) to 79.91 mm (total gear housing dimension from propshaft bearing carrier shimming, Step 1) which equals 140.86 mm, (60.95 + 79.91 = 140.86). Perform the calculation with your gearcase's dimensions, record the result and label it as *total G and F dimension*.

2. Subtract the total bearing carrier dimension from Step 2 of *propshaft bearing carrier shimming (DP-C1/D1 models)* from the *total G and F dimension*. Following our example, we would subtract 19.25 mm (total bearing carrier dimension from propshaft bearing carrier shimming, Step 2) from 140.86 mm (total G and F dimension), which equals 121.61 mm, (140.86 - 19.25 mm = 121.61). Record this result and label it as *complete housing calculated dimension*.

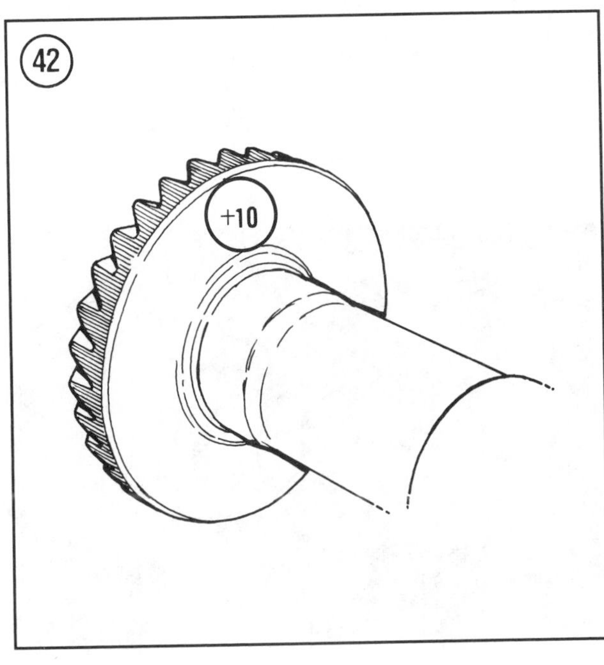

3. Add the predetermined amount of *front driven gear shims* to the total *propshaft bearing carrier shims*. Following our example, this would be 0.55 mm (front driven gear shims) plus 0.31 mm *(propshaft bearing carrier shims)* equals 0.86 mm, (0.55 + 0.31 = 0.86). Record this result and label it *driven gear shim total*.

4. Add the fixed nominal dimension of 120.00 mm to the *drive gear shim total* from Step 3. Continuing our example, we would add 120.00 mm (nominal dimension) to 0.86 (driven gear shim total), which equals 120.86 mm, (120.00 + 0.86 = 120.86). Record this result and label it *total driven gear calculated dimension*.

5. To complete the calculations, subtract the *total drive gear calculated dimension* from the *complete housing calculated dimension*. Completing our example, we would subtract 120.86 mm (total driven gear calculated dimension) from 121.61 mm (complete housing calculated dimension), which equals 0.75 mm, (121.61 - 120.86 = 0.75). Record this result and label it *inner propshaft small roller bearing shims*. This result is the amount of shims (in hundredths of a millimeter) required to correctly preload propeller shafts tapered roller bearings as an assembly.

6. Select and measure the correct amount of shims determined by your calculations. Slide these shims over the propeller end of the inner propeller shaft and up against the inner propeller shaft shoulder.

7. Install the inner propeller shaft and engage the splines to the front driven gear.

8. Lubricate the small roller bearing and slide it over the propshaft with the rollers facing aft (out). Slide the bearing as far down the propshaft as possible with hand pressure.

9. Thread adaptor part No. 885197-4 (A, **Figure 43**) fully onto the inner propeller shaft, then slide bearing installer part No. 884798-0 (B, **Figure 43**) over the propeller shaft. Install the flat washer and nut to the adaptor.
10. Tighten nut (C, **Figure 43**) to press the bearing fully onto the propshaft. Make sure the small roller bearing is fully seated against the shims and propshaft shoulder. Remove the tools.
11. Continue with gearcase assembly by performing the *vertical drive shaft bearing shimming* located later in this section.

Aft driven (tube) gear shimming (DPX models)

The DPX uses a different arrangement to shim the location of aft driven (tube) gear and to set the bearing preload on all of the tapered bearings in the complete propshaft assembly.

The shims behind the small roller bearing on the inner propshaft control the location of the tube gear. Adding shims to this location will move the tube gear away from the pinion gear and will increase gear lash on the tube gear only. Subtracting shims from this location will move the tube gear toward the pinion gear and will decrease gear lash on the tube gear only.

There are no shims behind the large bearing race in the propshaft bearing carrier. Bearing preload is set by simply tightening the large retaining ring securing the propshaft bearing carrier to the gearcase. The tighter the retaining ring, the more preload on the roller bearings and the higher the rolling torque.

Basically, a preset value of inner propshaft small bearing shims is installed, the rolling torque set and then the gear lash and gear patterns are checked. The propshaft bearing carrier will be removed as necessary and shims added or subtracted to the inner propshaft small bearing, until the rear gear backlash is correct and its pattern is the same as the front driven gear. Once this is accomplished, any final adjustments to the gear lash and pattern of both gears are performed.

To facilitate this procedure, it is recommended that an extra inner propshaft small roller bearing be purchased and modified to perform as a special tool. Slightly grind the inner diameter of the roller assembly (with a Dremel tool, small drum sander or equivalent) to allow the bearing to be slipped onto and off of the inner propshaft with hand pressure. This will allow easy shim correction on the inner propeller shaft. Once all adjustments and verifications have been satisfactorily performed, remove the modified bearing and race and install the new bearing and race.

1. Install the inner propeller shaft and engage the splines to the front driven gear.
2. Install an initial amount of 0.6 mm (0.024 in.) shims over the inner propeller shaft and against the shaft shoulder.

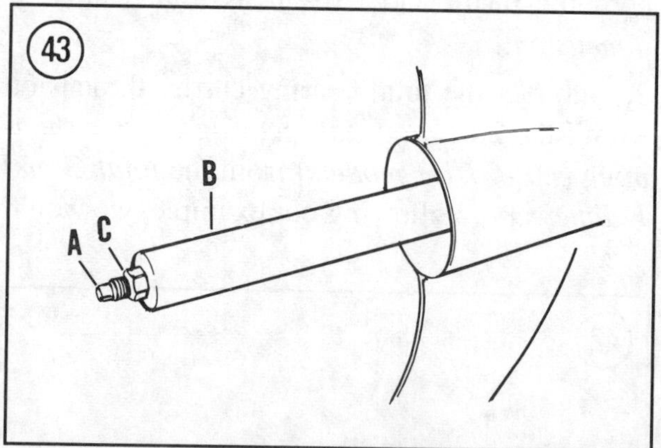

CAUTION

*The gearcase cannot be operated on the modified small roller bearing. The modified bearing is only a tool to simplify tube gear location adjustments. Remove the tool bearing and install the replacement bearing during **Final Assembly**.*

3. Lubricate the modified bearing. Slide the *modified* small roller bearing over the propshaft with its rollers facing aft (out). Seat the bearing against the shaft shoulder and shims.
4. Continue with gearcase assembly by performing the *Vertical drive shaft bearing shimming* in the next section.

Vertical drive shaft bearing shimming

The vertical drive shaft vertical movement is controlled by shims installed behind the tapered roller bearing race in the intermediate housing. A bearing plate part No. 884348-4 (**Figure 44**) is designed to take the place of the intermediate housing and secure the tapered roller bearing race and shims to the lower gearcase.

The vertical drive shaft is allowed to have as much as 0.07 mm (0.003 in.) clearance, which means that the shaft could move vertically up to 0.07 mm (0.003 in.). The drive shaft is also allowed to have as much as 0.02 mm (0.001 in.) preload on the bearings. The recommended assembly specification is to allow 0.02 mm (0.001 in.) clearance on the bearings.

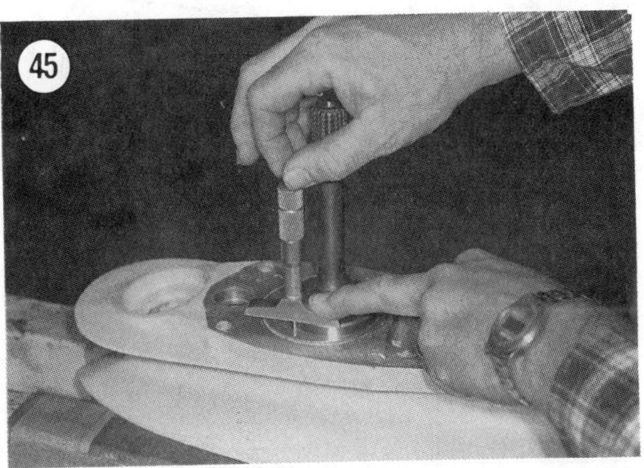

At this point of assembly, we simply want to make sure that the vertical shaft is held securely without any preload on the tapered roller bearing. Install the bearing plate as follows.

1. Install the tapered roller bearing race over the drive shaft and seat it into the gearcase bore against the drive shaft roller bearing. This should be a slip fit and not require excessive force.
2. With the bearing race held against the roller bearing, measure the distance from the top of the bearing race to the gearcase housing deck (**Figure 45**). Record this dimension and label it *bearing dimension*.
3. Lay the bearing plate part No. 884348-4 on a work bench and measure the depth of the bearing recess machined into the plate. Record this dimension and label it *tool dimension*.
4. Subtract the bearing dimension from the tool dimension. Record this result and label it *clearance dimension*.
5. Subtract 0.02 mm (0.001 in.) from the clearance dimension. Record this result and label it *shims-bearing plate*.
6. Select and measure the correct amount of shims determined by your calculations. Set these predetermined shims on top of the drive shaft bearing race.
7. Place the bearing plate part No. 884348-4 over the drive shaft, bearing race and shims. Make sure that no shims are displaced or damaged. Secure the tool to the gearcase with 2 appropriate screws. See **Figure 44**.
8. Rotate the drive shaft and check for preload. The shaft should rotate freely without any noticeable bearing preload. Check the shaft for play, the shaft should have no radial play and no more than 0.02 mm (0.001 in.) vertical play. Recheck your measurements and calculations if the drive shaft is preloaded or has unacceptable play.
9. Continue gearcase assembly by performing the *Overall rolling torque verification* in the next section.

13

Overall rolling torque verification

The overall rolling torque verification confirms or sets the correct preload on all of the tapered roller bearings in the propeller shaft assembly. The tapered roller bearings must be properly preloaded or the gears and bearings will fail prematurely. Since the bearings hold the gears in position, gear lash and gear pattern verifications should not be attempted until the overall rolling torque has been verified.

DP-C1/D1 models control overall rolling torque by adjusting the size of the shim behind the small roller bearing on the inner propshaft.

DPX models control overall rolling torque by simply tightening the propshaft bearing carrier retaining ring until the rolling torque specification is achieved.

To verify, adjust or set the overall rolling torque, proceed as follows.

NOTE
*Do not install any O-rings or seals at this time. The O-rings and seals will be installed during **Final Assembly**.*

1. Coat at least 3 teeth of the aft driven (tube) gear with GM Gear Marking Compound, available from any General Motors automotive dealership.
2. Slide the tube gear over the inner propshaft and seat it against the small roller bearing on the inner propshaft.
3. Lubricate the bearings of the propshaft bearing carrier and install it over the tube gear shaft and seat it in the gearcase housing.

4A. *DP-C1/D1 models*—Secure the propshaft bearing carrier with the 2 screws. Tighten the screws to specification (**Table 3**).

4B. *DPX models*—Lubricate the propshaft bearing carrier retaining ring and install it to the gearcase. Thread the ring as far as possible by hand.

5. Attach a torque wrench capable of reading 1-3 N•m (10-30 in.-lb.) accurately to spline socket part No. 884830-1 with the appropriate adapters. Attach the torque wrench to the drive shaft.

6A. *DP-C1/D1 models*—Rotate the drive shaft at approximately 60 rpm while observing the torque wrench reading. The torque wrench reading should be 1.2-2.3 N•m (10.6-20.4 in.-lb.).

a. If the reading is too low, remove the inner propshaft roller bearing (29, **Figure 33**) as described in this chapter and add shims to the existing small roller bearing shims (28, **Figure 33**). Reassemble and recheck rolling torque.
b. If the reading is too high, remove the inner propshaft roller bearing (29, **Figure 33**) as described in this chapter and remove shims

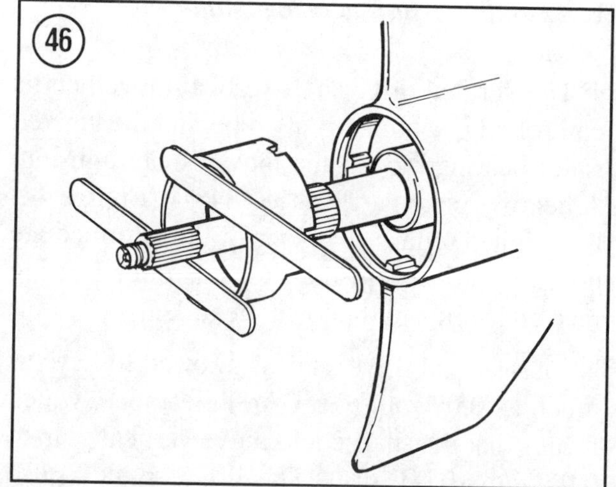

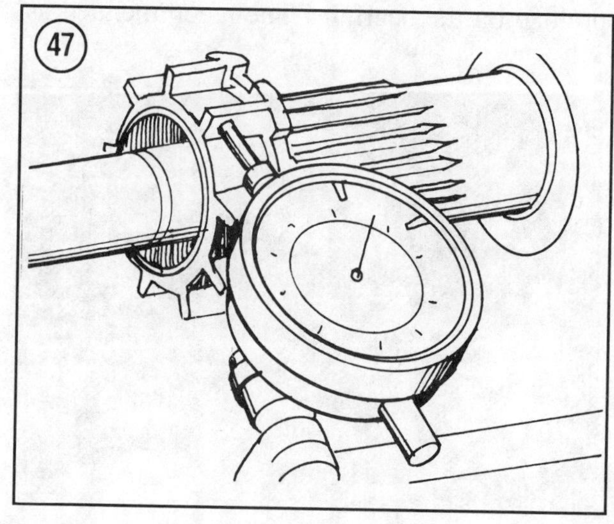

from the existing small roller bearing shims (28, **Figure 33**). Reassemble and recheck rolling torque.

6B. *DPX models*—Tighten the propshaft bearing carrier retaining ring with spanner wrench part No. 885221-2 (**Figure 46**) while observing the torque wrench reading. Tighten the retaining ring until the torque wrench reads 3.0 N•m (26.6 in.-lb.) at approximately 60 rpm.

7. When overall rolling torque has been verified, continue with *Gear lash verification* in the next section.

Gear lash verification

To verify gear lash, 2 older style propeller nuts are required. They are part No. 852196-5 (front nut) and part No. 852201-3 (rear nut). Gear lash is a clearance measurement between 2 gears. If too much clearance is present between the gears, the strength of the gears is reduced and the gears create more gear whine than normal. If too little clearance is present between the gears, there is no room for heat expansion and lubricant film causing the gears to be quickly damaged. The drive shaft must not move during this procedure. The gear lash of each driven gear is checked at each shaft's propeller nut. To verify the gear lash, proceed as follows.

1. Install and tighten the older style propeller nut on each propeller shaft. The nuts must not be loose on the shaft.
2. Securely attach a dial indicator to the gearcase at a convenient location. Position the dial indicator so the indicator contacts the front propeller nut (tube gear) as shown in **Figure 47**. Position the dial indicator tip as far out on the wings of the propeller nut as possible. The indicator tip must be as close to 90° to the wing as possible. Zero the indicator and check the gear lash by rotating the outer propeller shaft (tube gear) lightly back and forth while holding the drive shaft stationary. Record the reading and compare to specification (**Table 1**).
3. Reposition the dial indicator so the indicator contacts the rear propeller nut (inner propshaft) as shown in **Figure 48**. Position the dial indicator tip as far out on the wings of the propeller nut as possible. The indicator tip must be as close to 90° to the wing as possible. Zero the indicator and check the gear lash by rotating the inner propeller shaft back and forth while holding the drive shaft stationary. Record the reading and compare to specification (**Table 1**).

NOTE
If it is necessary to remove or add a large thickness of shims to correct the gear lash, recheck your shimming calculations and measure all shims to check for improper assembly or mathematical mistakes.

4. If the gear lash readings for both gears are within specification, proceed to *Gear pattern verification* in the next section.

NOTE
If the gear lash requires correction, change approximately 0.03 mm (0.001 in.) of shims for every 0.03 mm (0.001 in.) of correction desired. Move the appropriate gear toward the other gear(s) to decrease gear lash and move the ap-

propriate gear away from the other gear(s) to increase gear lash. If two or more gears are being moved, change one-half of the total correction desired at the pinion gear and the other one-half of the correction at the driven gear(s).

5. If the gear lash reading for one or both gears is not within specification, refer to **Table 10** or **Table 11** for gear lash correction procedures. Disassemble the gearcase and change the shims as directed in **Table 10** or **Table 11**. Reassemble the gearcase and recheck rolling torque first, then gear lash. Do not proceed until rolling torque and gear lash are within specifications.
6. Remove the old style propeller nuts and all tools when finished.

Gear pattern verification

Once gear lash has been verified, check the gear contact pattern as follows.
1. Install the spline socket part No. 884830-1 (A, **Figure 49**) over the drive shaft splines. Attach a breaker bar with the appropriate adapters.

NOTE
*The gears must be loaded to produce a contact pattern. A simple clamping brake can be fabricated from two, 2 × 4 pieces of wood approximately 457 mm (18 in.) long. Hinge the boards together so that they can be folded upon each other, pinching the appropriate propeller shaft between them (like a nut cracker). See B, **Figure 49**.*

2. Place an appropriate clamping brake (B, **Figure 49**) over the inner propshaft. Apply clamping pressure to the inner propeller shaft to resist rotation and load the gear. Rotate the drive shaft with a breaker bar 6-8 revolutions in each direction.
3. Place the clamping brake (B, **Figure 49**) over the outer (tube gear) propshaft. Apply clamping pressure to the outer propeller shaft to resist rotation and load the gear. Rotate the drive shaft with a breaker bar 6-8 revolutions in each direction.
4. Remove the outer propeller shaft and propshaft bearing housing assembly as described previously in this chapter.
5. Compare the pattern on the front driven gear and tube gear with the following patterns:

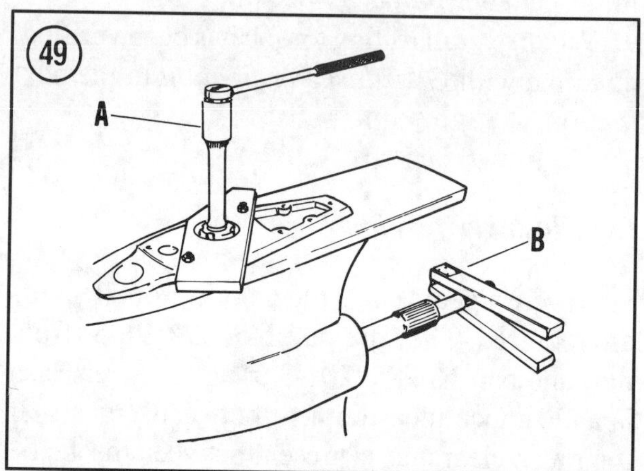

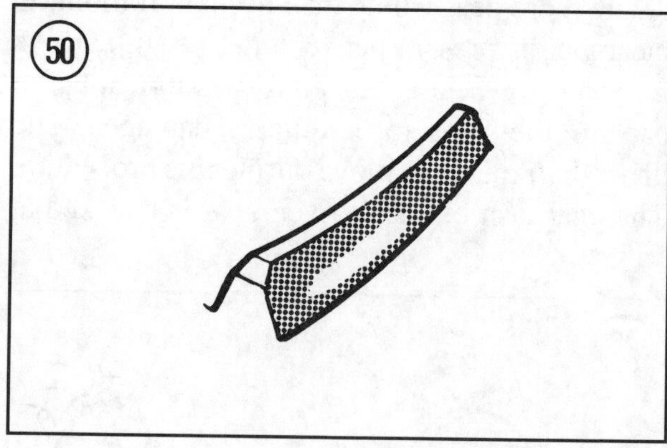

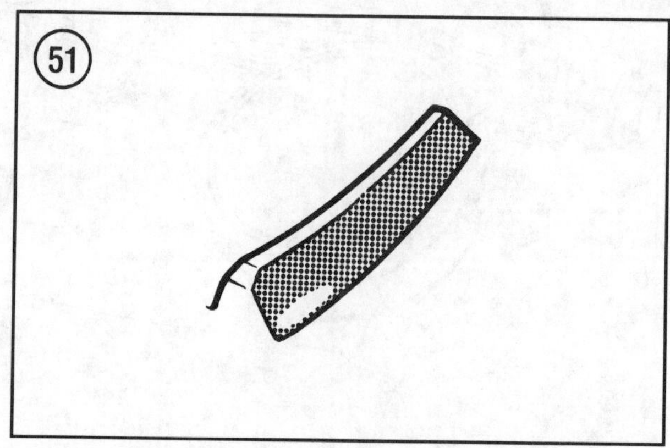

a. **Figure 50** show a satisfactory contact pattern slightly biased toward the root of the tooth and toward the outside diameter of the gear.

b. **Figure 51** shows an unsatisfactory contact pattern too far to the root of the tooth and outside diameter of the gear. It will be necessary to move the pinion gear up and both driven gears toward the pinion gear.

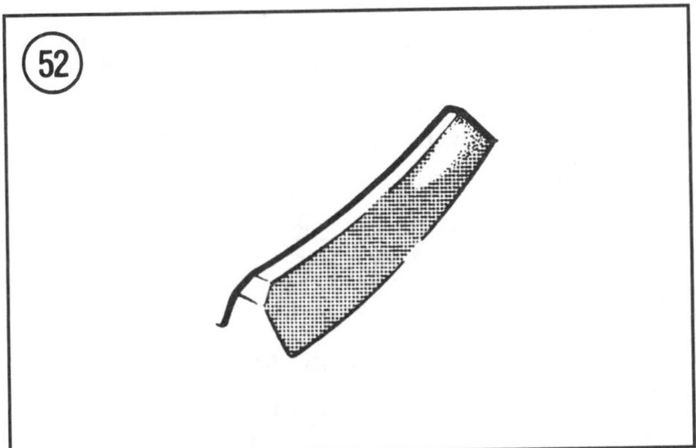

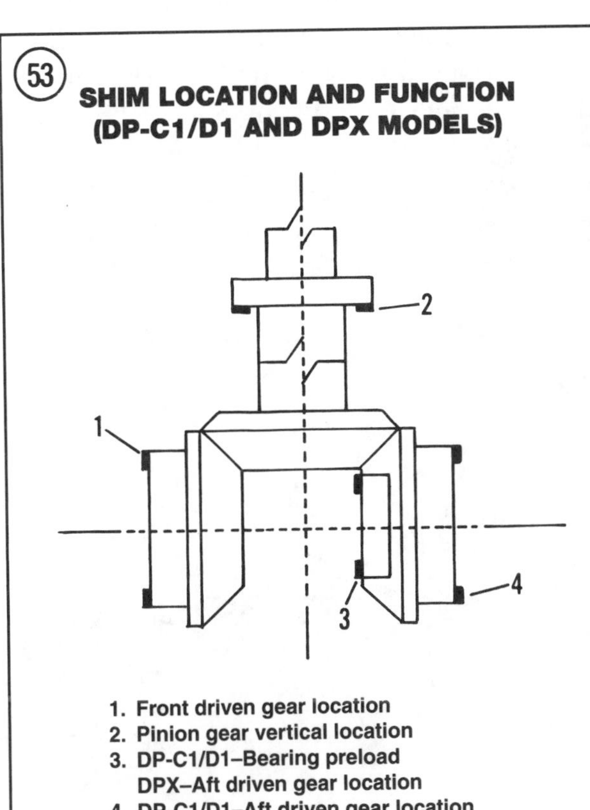

SHIM LOCATION AND FUNCTION (DP-C1/D1 AND DPX MODELS)

1. Front driven gear location
2. Pinion gear vertical location
3. DP-C1/D1–Bearing preload
   DPX–Aft driven gear location
4. DP-C1/D1–Aft driven gear location

c. **Figure 52** shows an unsatisfactory contact pattern too far to the crest of the tooth and inner diameter of the gear. It will be necessary to move the pinion gear down and both driven gears away from the pinion gear.

6. If the pattern is not as specified, refer to **Table 10** or **Table 11** for pattern correction procedures. **Figure 53** shows the location and function of each shim. Disassemble the gearcase and change the shims as directed in **Table 10** or **Table 11**. Make corrections in approximately 0.10 mm (0.004 in.) increments. Reassemble the gearcase and recheck rolling torque first, then gear lash and finally gear pattern. Do not proceed until rolling torque, gear lash and gear pattern are within specifications.

CAUTION

If the contact pattern must be corrected, rolling torque and gear backlash must again be verified after the pattern correction, before continuing with final assembly.

7. Remove the outer propshaft and propshaft bearing carrier, vertical drive shaft and pinion gear and the front driven gear assemblies from the gearcase keeping all of the shims in their correct positions. Discard the pinion nut. Do not remove any pressed bearings from the housings or shafts. Clean all of the marking compound from the gear teeth and lubricate all internal components with clean gear oil. Proceed with the final assembly after all parts are clean and lubricated.

13

Final Assembly (DP-C1/D1 and DPX Models)

1. Reinstall the front driven gear and inner propshaft, pinion gear and drive shaft as described previously. Install and tighten a *new*pinion nut to specification (**Table 3**).

2. *DPX models*—Remove the modified small roller bearing from the inner propshaft. Do not

remove the shims. Install the original or new small roller bearing as follows:

a. Lubricate the unmodified small roller bearing and slide it over the propshaft with the rollers facing aft (out). Slide the bearing as far down the propshaft as possible with hand pressure.

b. Thread adaptor part No. 885197-4 (A, **Figure 54**) fully onto the inner propeller shaft, then slide bearing installer part No. 884798-0 (B, **Figure 54**) over the propeller shaft. Install the flat washer and nut to the adaptor.

c. Tighten nut to (C, **Figure 54**) press the bearing fully onto the propshaft. Make sure the small roller bearing is fully seated against the shims and propshaft shoulder. Remove the tools when finished.

3. Install 2 new propshaft seals into the outer propeller shaft (tube gear) using seal installer part No. 884975-4. Refer to **Figure 55** and proceed as follows:

a. Position the double lip, single case seal onto the deep (wide) shouldered edge of the seal installer with the steel edge facing away from the tool shoulder and into the gearcase.

b. Press the inner (double lip) seal into the propshaft until the tool seats on the propshaft.

c. Position the single lip seal onto the shallow (narrow) shouldered edge of the seal installer with the spring side of the seal facing the tool shoulder and away from the gearcase.

d. Press the outer (single lip) seal into the propshaft until the tool seats on the propshaft. The outer seal should be 1 mm (0.039 in.) from the end of the shaft as shown in **Figure 55**.

e. Lubricate the seals and pack the area between the seals with OMC Triple Guard Grease or equivalent (**Table 5**).

4. Install seal protector part No. 884976-2 into the tube gear seals. Carefully slide the tube gear over the inner propshaft and seat it against the small roller bearing. Remove the seal protector.

5. Install 2 new propshaft seals into the propshaft bearing carrier. Install the seals *back-to-back* with the spring side of each seal facing away from each other. Coat the outer diameter of the seals with OMC Triple Guard Grease or equivalent (**Table 5**). Install the seals as follows:

6A. *DP-C1/D1 models*—Position both seals onto the short end of installer part No. 884801-2. Make sure the seals are oriented *back-to-back* and the outer diameters are greased. Press the seals into the propshaft bearing carrier until the tool seats against the carrier.

6B. *DPX models*—Place spacer ring part No. 885228-7 onto the short end of installer part No. 884801-2. Make sure the seals are oriented *back-to-back* and the outer diameters are greased. Press the seals into the propshaft bearing carrier until the tool seats against the carrier. Remove the installation tool and spacer (DPX models).

7. Lubricate the seals and pack the area between the seals with OMC Triple Guard Grease or equivalent (**Table 5**).

8A. *DP-C1/D1 models*—Coat 2 new O-rings with Volvo White Sealing Compound or equivalent (**Table 5**). Install the O-rings into the prop-

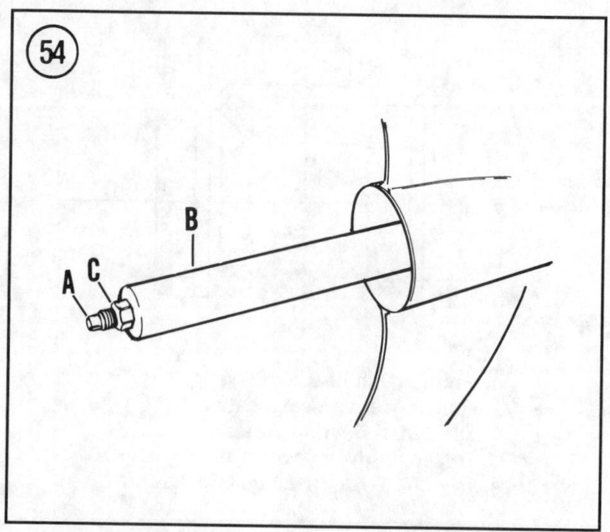

shaft bearing carrier grooves. Coat the propshaft bearing carrier mating surfaces with sealing compound.

NOTE
DPX models use 2 different size O-rings on the propshaft bearing carrier. Be sure to match the O-ring to its groove.

8B. *DPX models*—Coat 3 new O-rings with Volvo White Sealing Compound or equivalent (**Table 5**). Install each O-ring into the correct propshaft bearing carrier groove. Coat the propshaft bearing carrier mating surfaces and the outer diameter of the rear flange with sealing compound.

9. Install seal protector part No. 884807-9 into the propshaft carrier seals. Carefully slide the propshaft bearing carrier over the outer propshaft and seat it against (or into) the gear housing. Remove the seal protector. On DPX models make sure the lubricant drain hole is pointing straight down.

10A. *DP-C1/D1 models*—Coat the 2 propshaft bearing carrier screws with Volvo White Sealing Compound or equivalent (**Table 5**). Install and evenly tighten the 2 screws to specification (**Table 3**).

10B. *DPX models*—Install 2 new O-rings on the propshaft bearing carrier retaining ring. Liberally coat the retaining ring and O-rings with Volvo Penta Propeller Shaft Grease or equivalent

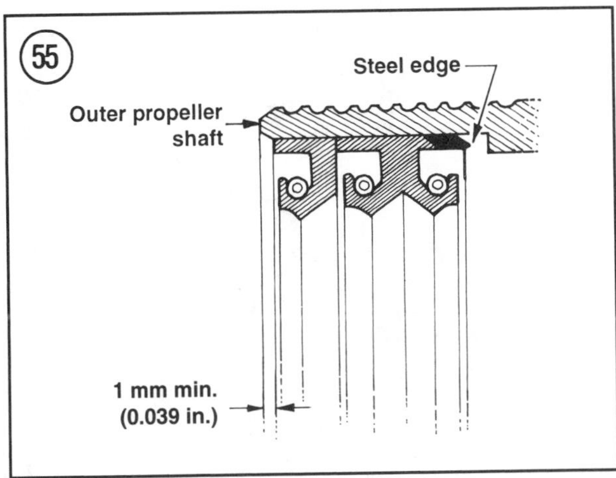

(**Table 5**). Install the retaining ring to the gearcase and thread as far as possible by hand. Refer to *Overall rolling torque verification* in this chapter and set the overall rolling torque.

11A. *DP-C1/D1 models*—Position the anode over the propshaft bearing carrier and secure it with 2 screws. Tighten the screws securely. Refer to *Corrosion Control* at the beginning of this chapter and verify that the anode is grounded to the gearcase.

11B. *DPX models*—Install the lubricant drain plug (with a new O-ring) and the retaining washer. It may be necessary to turn the propshaft bearing carrier retaining ring *slightly* to allow the retaining washer to be installed. Tighten the drain plug to specification (**Table 3**).

12. Perform the *Lower Gear Housing to Intermediate Housing Shimming Procedure (DP-C1/D1 and DPX Models)* as described in the following section.

Lower Gearcase to Intermediate Housing Shimming Procedure (DP-C1/D1 and DPX Models)

The *Lower Gearcase to Intermediate Housing Shimming Procedure (DP-C1/D1 and DPX Models)* must be performed if the lower gearcase, the intermediate housing or any of the drive shaft components were serviced or replaced.

The vertical drive shaft vertical movement is controlled by shims installed behind the tapered roller bearing race in the intermediate housing. The vertical drive shaft is allowed to have as much as 0.07 mm (0.003 in.) clearance, which means that the shaft could move vertically up to 0.07 mm (0.003 in.). The drive shaft is also allowed to have as much as 0.02 mm (0.001 in.) preload on the bearings. The recommended assembly specification is to allow 0.02 mm (0.001 in.) clearance on the bearings.

1. Install the tapered roller bearing race over the drive shaft and seat it into the gearcase bore

against the drive shaft roller bearing. This should be a slip fit and not require excessive force.

2. With the bearing race held against the roller bearing, measure the distance from the top of the bearing race to the gearcase housing deck (**Figure 56**). Record this dimension and label it *bearing dimension*. Remove the bearing race.
3. Remove any shims from the bearing recess in the intermediate housing, then measure the depth of the bearing recess machined into the intermediate housing (**Figure 57**). Record this dimension and label it *housing dimension*.
4. Subtract the bearing dimension from the housing dimension. Record this result and label it *clearance dimension*.
5. Subtract 0.02 mm (0.001 in.) from the clearance dimension. Record this result and label it *shims-intermediate housing*.
6. Select and measure the correct amount of shims determined by your calculations. Place these predetermined shims with the drive shaft bearing race.
7. Position the selected shims in the intermediate housing bore, then position the drive shaft roller bearing race. Use OMC Needle Bearing Assembly Grease or equivalent (**Table 5**) to help hold the shims in position. Drive the bearing race into the intermediate housing with installer part No. 884168-6 and a mallet. Drive the bearing until it is seated in the intermediate housing.
8. Install the lower gearcase as described previously in this chapter.

LOWER GEARCASE (SX AND DP-S MODELS)

The drive unit pumps lubricant from the lower gearcase to the upper gearcase during operation. If a failure has taken place in any part of the drive unit, the complete drive unit should be disassembled, cleaned and inspected.

The lower gearcase can be removed from the upper gearcase without removing the drive unit from the transom bracket.

There is a gear lubricant filter located in the lubricant passage at the front of the upper gearcase. Replace the filter each time the lower gearcase is separated from the upper gearcase.

Removal

1. Drain the gear lubricant as described in Chapter Twelve.
2. Remove the propellers as described previously in this chapter.
3. Raise the drive unit to the full up position.

NOTE
Be prepared to support the unit as the fasteners are removed in Step 3. When the last fastener is removed, the lower gearcase will fall free.

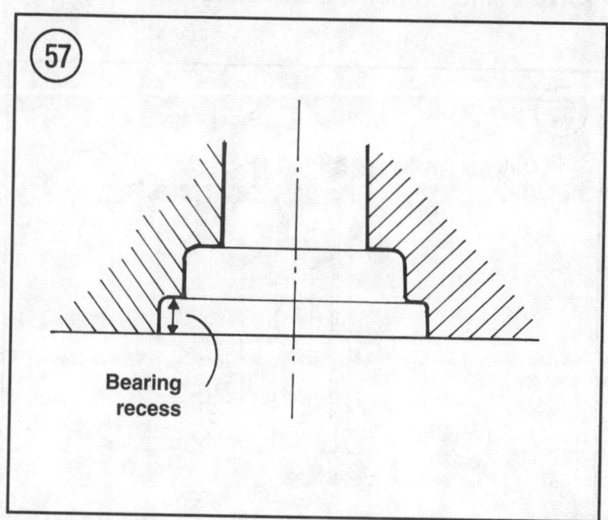

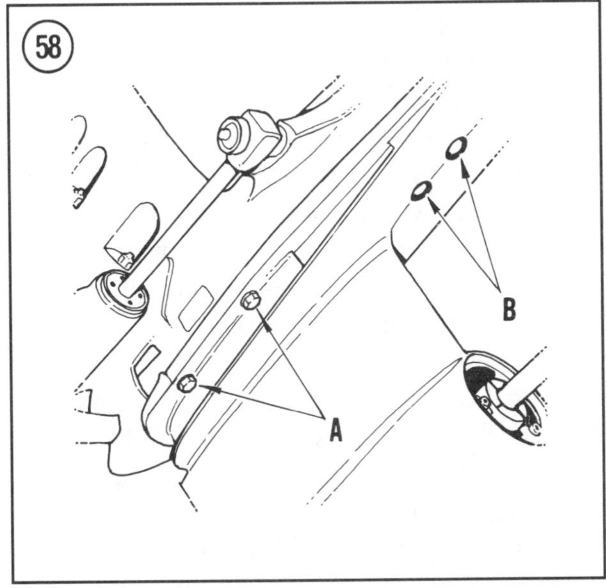

4. Remove the 4 screws (or nuts on DP-S models), (A, **Figure 58**) and the 2 screws under the antiventilation plate (B, **Figure 58**). Support the lower gearcase as the last fastener is removed.

5. Remove the lower gearcase from the upper gearcase with the aid of an assistant. Be ready to catch the intermediate drive shaft coupler and water tube if they should fall free. Set the lower gearcase on its side, on a clean workbench.

6. If the intermediate drive shaft coupler came free with the upper gearcase, temporarily reinstall it on the lower gearcase drive shaft with its grooved end facing up (to keep it from being misplaced).

7A. *SX-S models*—Remove the copper water tube and grommet (1 and 2, **Figure 59**) from the upper gearcase. Do not remove the water tube adaptor (A, **Figure 60**) from the lower gearcase unless it is going to be replaced. Replacement procedures are covered later in this chapter.

7B. *All other models*—Remove the copper water tube, upper gearcase grommet, lower gearcase grommet and lower gearcase plastic water guide. See **Figure 61**.

8. Remove and discard the lubricant filter (3, **Figure 59**) located in the lubricant passage at the bottom of the gearcase. Hook the filter with an appropriate tool and pull it from the upper gearcase.

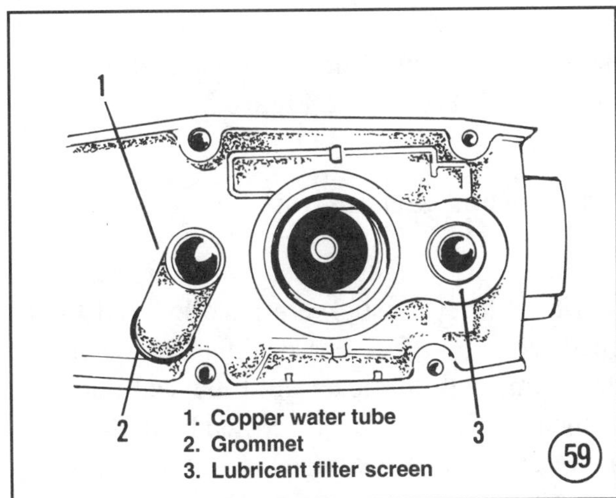

1. Copper water tube
2. Grommet
3. Lubricant filter screen

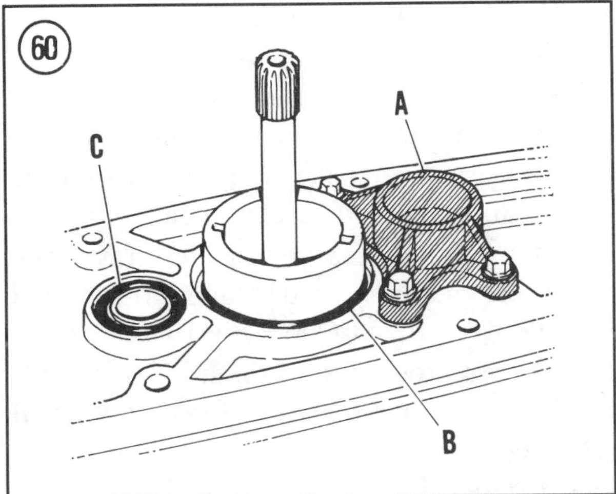

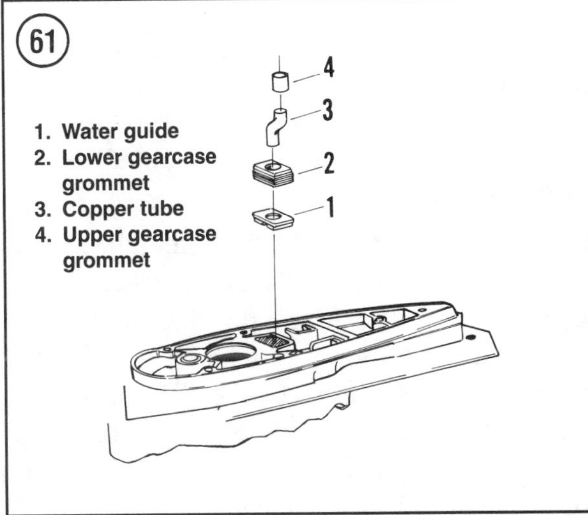

1. Water guide
2. Lower gearcase grommet
3. Copper tube
4. Upper gearcase grommet

NOTE

The drive shaft bearing O-ring groove is located in the lower gearcase on SX-S and SX-C1 series drive units and located in the upper gearcase on SX-C series drive units.

9. Clean the mating surfaces of the upper and lower gearcases before reassembly. Remove and discard the lubricant filter O-ring (C, **Figure 60**) and drive shaft retainer O-ring (B, **Figure 60**).

Installation

Before installing the lower gearcase to the drive unit, make sure the sealing surfaces have been thoroughly cleaned.

1. Install new lubricated O-rings in the lower gearcase filter passage groove (C, **Figure 60**) and around the drive shaft bearing retainer (B, **Figure 60**).

2. Install a new lubricant filter (3, **Figure 59**) into the upper gearcase lubricant passage and seat it flush with the gearcase mating surface.

3. Install the water tube grommet into the upper gearcase. Install the water tube, seating it fully into the upper gearcase grommet. Align the lower end of the water tube to form a straight line through the lubricant filter and drive shaft bores, and the water tube open end. See **Figure 59**.

4A. *SX-S models*—Verify that the water tube guide is secured to the lower gearcase. Wipe the internal water tube seal (A, **Figure 60**) with OMC Type M adhesive or equivalent (**Table 5**) just before installing the upper gearcase.

4B. *All other models*—Set the water tube plastic guide (1, **Figure 61**) into the lower gearcase with its protruding edges facing down. Coat the outside surface of the lower water tube grommet (2, **Figure 61**) with OMC Gasket Sealing Compound or equivalent (**Table 5**). Insert the lower water tube grommet into the lower gearcase on top of the plastic water tube guide.

5. Install the intermediate drive shaft coupler onto the lower gearcase drive shaft with the grooved end facing up (if not already installed).

6. Coat the mating surfaces of the upper and lower gearcases with Volvo White Sealing Compound or equivalent (**Table 5**). This will help prevent corrosion, especially in saltwater.

7. Install the lower gearcase to the upper gearcase with the aid of an assistant. Be sure to engage the drive shaft coupler splines by rotating the propeller shaft(s) as the gearcase is lowered. Be sure to engage the water tube with the water tube adaptor or lower grommet before seating the lower gearcase to the upper gearcase.

8. Coat the threads of the 6 fasteners with OMC Gasket Sealing Compound or equivalent (**Table 5**). Install the 2 screws under the antiventilation plate and the 2 screws or nuts on each side of the drive unit. Evenly tighten all 6 fasteners to specifications (**Table 4**). See **Figure 58**.

Pressure and vacuum tests

Make sure the lubricant fill/drain plug and lubricant level dipstick are installed and tightened securely before proceeding. Do not fill the drive unit with lubricant until the seal integrity of the drive unit has been verified by performing 4 pressure and vacuum tests in the following order.

1. Perform a low pressure test as follows:
   a. Connect a pressure tester (such as Stevens S-34) to the lubricant level hole.
   b. Pressurize the drive unit to 20.7-34.5 kPa (3-5 psi) for a minimum of 3 minutes.
   c. Rotate the propeller shaft(s) and shift the gearcase into and out of gear during the test.
   d. If any pressure drop is noted, spray soapy water on all seals and mating surfaces until the leak is found. Correct the leak and retest.
   e. Do not proceed until the drive unit holds pressure for at least 3 minutes without measurable leakage.
2. Perform a high pressure test as follows:

a. Increase the pressure to 110-124 kPa (16-18 psi) for a minimum of 3 minutes.

b. Rotate the propeller shaft(s) and shift the gearcase into and out of gear during the test.

c. If any pressure drop is noted, spray soapy water on all seals and mating surfaces until the leak is found. Correct the leak and retest.

d. Do not proceed until the drive unit holds pressure, or loses no more than 6.9 kPa (1 psi) after a minimum of 3 minutes.

e. Remove the pressure tester when finished.

3. If both pressure tests have been completed satisfactorily, perform a low vacuum test as follows:

a. Connect a vacuum tester (such as Stevens V-34) to the lubricant level hole.

b. Pull a vacuum of 10-16.8 kPa (3-5 in.-Hg) for a minimum of 3 minutes.

c. Rotate the propeller shaft(s) and shift the gearcase into and out of gear during the test.

d. If any vacuum loss is noted, apply gear lubricant to all seals and mating surfaces, the lubricant will be drawn into the drive unit at the point of the leak. Correct the leak and retest.

e. Do not proceed until the drive unit holds vacuum for at least 3 minutes without measurable leakage.

4. Perform a high vacuum test as follows:

a. Increase the vacuum to 47-54 kPa (14-16 in.-Hg).

b. Rotate the propeller shaft(s) and shift the gearcase into and out of gear during the test.

c. If any vacuum loss is noted, apply gear lubricant to all seals and mating surfaces, the lubricant will be drawn into the drive unit at the point of the leak. Correct the leak and retest.

d. Do not proceed until the drive unit holds vacuum, or loses no more than 3.4 kPa (1 in.-Hg) after a minimum of 3 minutes.

e. Remove the vacuum tester when finished.

5. Fill the drive unit with lubricant and install the rear cover as described in *Drive unit lubrication* in Chapter Twelve.

Disassembly (SX models)

Figure 62 shows an exploded view of a SX-C/C1 series lower gearcase. The only differences between the SX-S gearcase and the subsequent SX-C and SX-C1 gearcases are the water tube guide/grommet style and the location of the drive shaft O-ring. **Figure 60** shows the water tube guide (and integral grommet) used on SX-S models. The drive shaft O-ring groove is located on the lower gearcase on SX-S and SX-C1 models and is located on the upper gearcase on SX-C models.

Secure the gearcase in a suitable fixture or place the gearcase on a clean workbench.

Record the measurement of all shims as they are removed. Shims can be reused if they are not damaged. Tag the shims by location for reassembly purposes. Do not lose or discard any shims.

All components that are to be reused must be installed in their original location and orientation. Mark components as necessary to ensure correct reinstallation. To disassemble the SX lower gearcase, proceed as follows.

1. *Models equipped with a trim tab*—Mark the position of the trim tab to the gearcase with a felt-tipped marker. Remove the screw securing the trim tab to the antiventilation plate, then remove the trim tab. 13

2. *SX-S models*—Remove the 4 screws securing the water tube guide (A, **Figure 60**) to the gearcase deck. Remove and discard the water tube guide.

3. Remove the screw (38, **Figure 62**) securing the propshaft bearing carrier retainer to the lower gearcase. The screw is located inside the exhaust passage and requires 1/4 in. drive tools to access it. Invert the gearcase and let the retainer fall out of the exhaust passage on the gearcase deck.

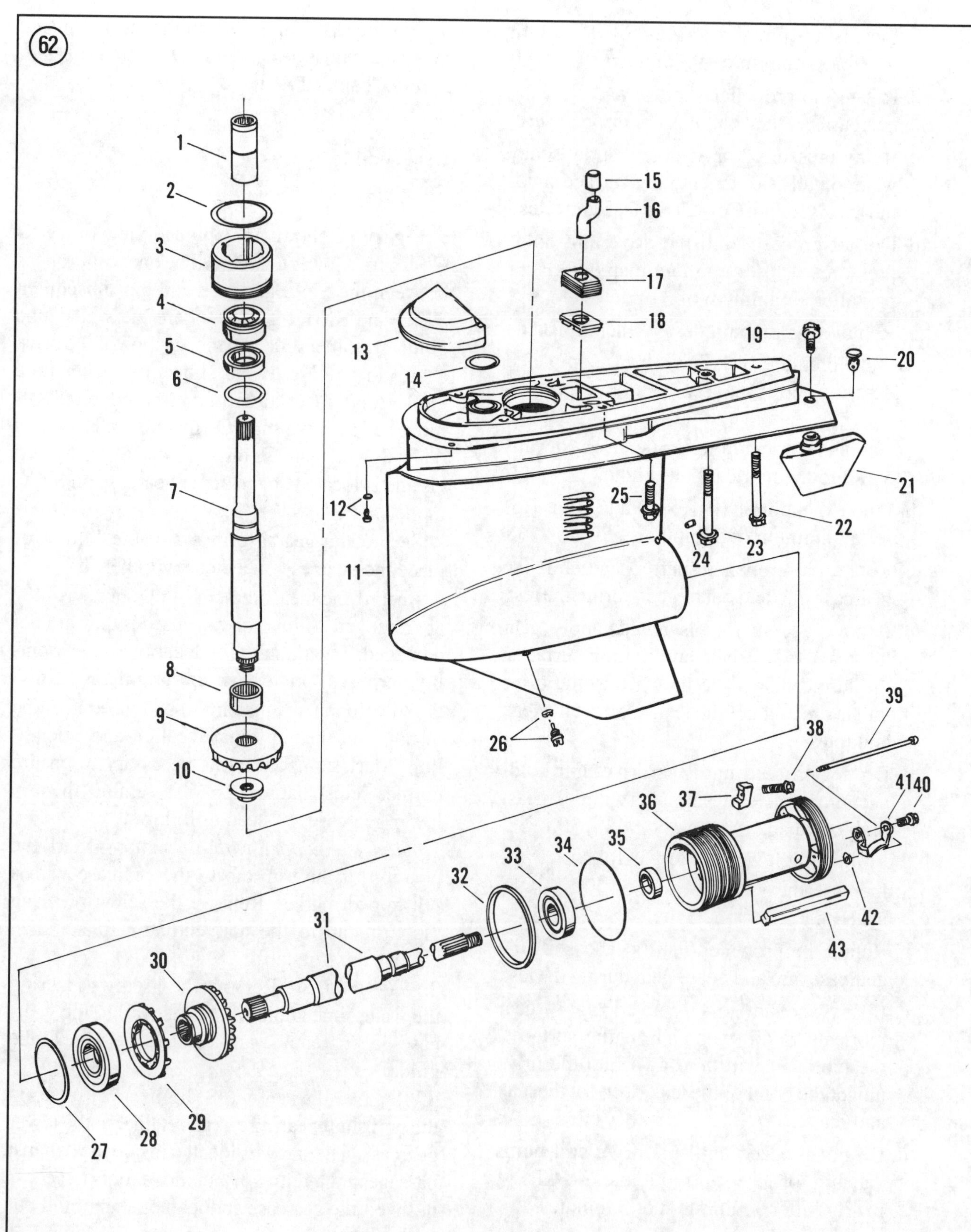
62
1
2
3
4
5
6
7
8
9
10
11
12
13
14
15
16
17
18
19
20
21
22
23
24
25
26
27
28
29
30
31
32
33
34
35
36
37
38
39
40
41
42
43

LOWER GEARCASE (SX MODELS)

1. Intermediate drive shaft coupler
2. Drive shaft O-ring
3. Drive shaft bearing retainer
4. Larger tapered roller bearing
5. Small tapered roller bearing
6. Shim (pinion gear location)
7. Vertical drive shaft
8. Lower drive shaft (pinion) bearing
9. Pinion gear
10. Pinion nut
11. Gearcase housing
12. Anode screw and washer
13. Anode
14. O-ring
15. Water tube grommet (upper gearcase)
16. Water tube
17. Water tube grommet (lower gearcase)
18. Water tube plastic guide
19. Trim tab screw (manual steering models)
20. Plug (power steering models)
21. Trim tab (manual steering models)
22. Screw
23. Screw
24. Set screw
25. Screw
26. Drain/fill plug and seal washer
27. Shim (propshaft gear location)
28. Tapered roller bearing
29. Oil slinger
30. Propshaft gear
31. Propshaft
32. Shim ring (bearing preload)
33. Tapered roller bearing
34. O-ring
35. Seal (double-lip, single case)
36. Propshaft bearing carrier
37. Retainer block
38. Retainer screw
39. Anode screw
40. Bracket screw
41. Anode bracket
42. Wave washer
43. Anode

4. Remove the propshaft bearing carrier setscrew (24, **Figure 62**) located on the port, aft, upper portion of the gearcase torpedo. A T-27 Torx bit is required to remove the screw.

5. Remove the 2 anode bracket screws and washers (40, **Figure 62**) from the propshaft bearing carrier. A T-40 Torx bit is required to remove these screws.

6. Unthread the anode screw (39, **Figure 40**) fully and remove the anode, spring washer and anode bracket as an assembly. A T-30 Torx bit is required to remove the screw.

CAUTION

When removing the propshaft bearing carrier, great care must be taken to prevent damage to the gearcase and carrier threads. Remove any corrosion from the carrier rear flange and the gearcase bore. Liberally lubricate the front and rear flanges of the carrier. If the carrier begins to bind on removal, stop and apply additional lubricant. Let the carrier sit for a few minutes, then turn the carrier back into the gearcase and apply additional lubricant. Forcing the carrier will destroy the carrier and the gearcase housing.

7. With the aid of an assistant, remove the propshaft bearing carrier by turning it counterclockwise with remover part No. 3850707-5. The carrier is tightened to an extremely high torque value and is difficult to break free. See **Figure 63**.

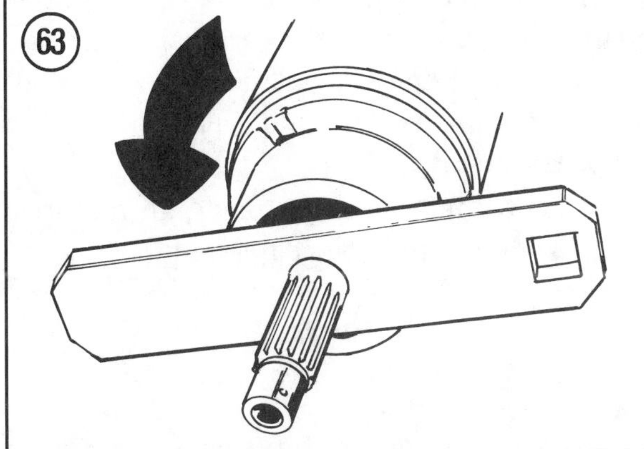

8. Remove and discard the carrier O-ring. Remove the thick shim ring from the carrier shoulder. Measure and record the thickness of the shim ring for later reference. Tag the shim ring for identification during reassembly.

9. Remove the propshaft seal with a small punch and hammer by driving the seal into the carrier. Be careful not to damage the carrier bore with the punch. Discard the seal. See **Figure 64**.

10. Remove the propeller shaft from the gearcase. The shaft should pull freely from the propshaft gear splines. If the shaft sticks, use a suitable slide hammer threaded to the propshaft propeller nut threads.

11. Remove the intermediate drive shaft coupler from the vertical drive shaft if it has not already been removed.

12. Remove the 2 screws securing the anode to the front of the gearcase deck. Remove the anode.

13. Unscrew the drive shaft bearing retainer with spanner wrench part No. 3850601-0 (A, **Figure 65**). Remove the retainer (B, **Figure 65**) from the gearcase.

14. Assemble the following tools to hold the pinion nut. Thread nut holder part No. 3854864-0 (A, **Figure 66**) onto drive handle part No. 3850609-3 (B, **Figure 66**). Insert the tool into the propshaft bore and engage the propeller nut. Slide alignment plate part No. 3850613-5 (C, **Figure 66**) over the drive handle and into the propshaft bore.

15. Loosen the pinion nut by turning the drive shaft counterclockwise with spline socket part No. 3850598-8 and a breaker bar. Once the shaft turns freely, remove the pinion nut tools from the propshaft bore.

16. Remove the pinion nut and pull the drive shaft assembly from the gearcase.

NOTE

Expect the lower drive shaft (pinion) bearing's 19 loose rollers to fall free when the vertical shaft is removed.

17. Collect and remove the 19 loose rollers (from the pinion bearing) and the pinion gear, from the propshaft bore.

18. Remove the propeller shaft gear assembly from the propshaft bore. The drain plug must be removed from the lower gearcase in order to remove the bearing.

CAUTION

The drive shaft bearing race in the top of the drive shaft bore and the propeller gear bearing race at the bottom of the propshaft bore are shimmed bearings. These bearing races must be removed to perform the lower gearcase shimming

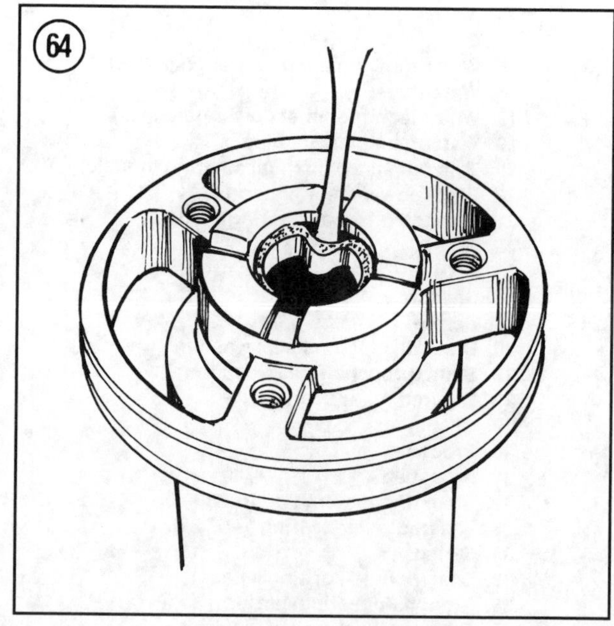

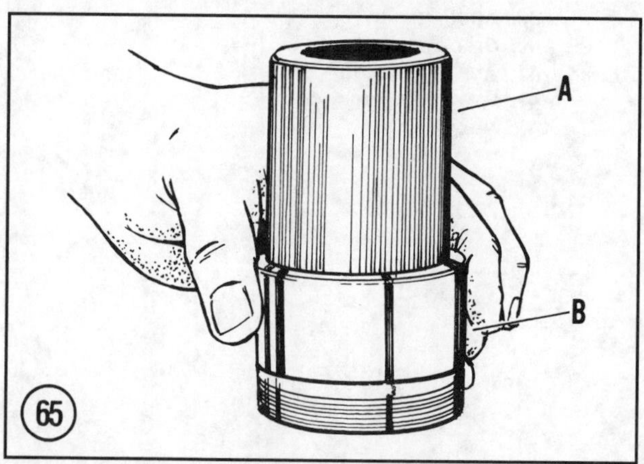

procedures. All other bearings and cups are not shimmed and should not be removed unless they are going to be replaced.

19. Assemble the tools to remove the drive shaft bearing race and shims as follows:

a. Thread bearing remover part No. 3855859-9 (A, **Figure 67**) onto the threaded rod part No. 3855860-7 (B, **Figure 67**). Use guide plate part No. 3850619-2 for SX-S and SX-C1 series gearcases and guide plate part No. 3850218-3 for SX-C series gearcases (C, **Figure 67**).

b. Insert the bearing remover through the bearing race and center it behind the race (D, **Figure 67**). Pilot the guide plate into the drive shaft bore.

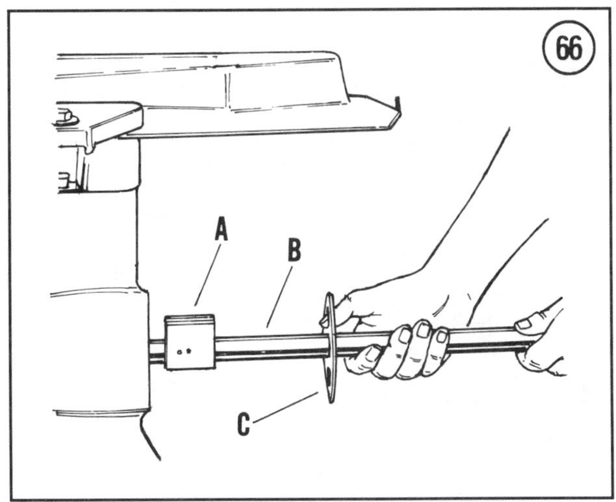

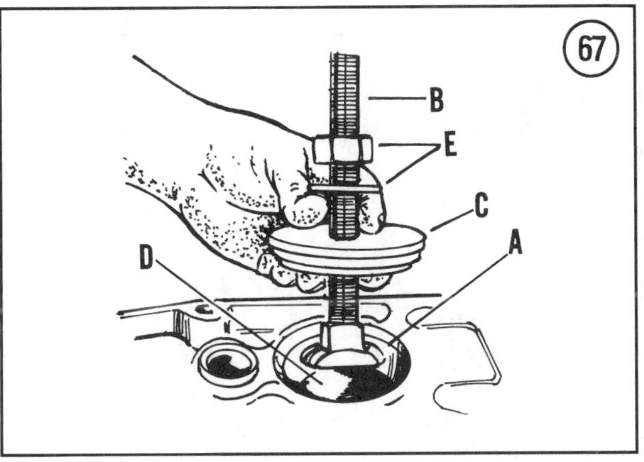

c. Install and tighten the nut and washer (E, **Figure 67**) onto the threaded rod.

d. Tighten the nut to pull the bearing race from the gearcase.

e. Remove the shim(s) from the drive shaft bore or bearing race. Measure and record the thickness of the shim(s) for later reference. If the shims are damaged, they must be discarded. If the shims are not damaged, tag the shim(s) for identification during reassembly.

20. Use an appropriate 3-jaw slide hammer, such OTC part No. OEM-4184 to remove the propeller gear bearing race from the bottom of the propshaft bore. Make sure the bearing is pulled straight from its bore and is not cocked. Remove the shim(s) from the propshaft bore or bearing race. Measure and record the thickness of the shim(s) for later reference. If the shims are damaged, they must be discarded. If the shims are not damaged, tag the shim(s) for identification during reassembly.

21. If no other bearings are to removed, refer to *Cleaning and inspection (SX and DP-S models)* located later in this chapter. If all bearings are to be removed and replaced, continue with *Remaining Bearing Removal (SX Models)* in the next section.

Remaining Bearing Removal (SX Models)

Do not remove any of the following roller bearings and races unless new parts are to be installed.

1. If the propshaft roller bearing and propshaft bearing carrier bearing race are to be replaced, remove the original bearing and race as follows:

a. Place the propshaft bearing carrier on a clean workbench.

b. Assemble the puller jaws part No. 3850612-7 to the threaded rod from bridge puller part No. 3850611-9. Place the puller

b. Slide expanding rod and jaws into the carrier bearing race. Position the jaws behind the carrier bearing race and expand the jaws tightly.

jaws behind the carrier bearing race and expand the jaws tightly.

c. Slide guide plate part No. 3850619-2 over the threaded rod with its largest diameter facing down. Place a flat washer over the threaded rod, then run the nut down against the washer.

d. Tighten the nut to pull the bearing race from the carrier. Remove the tools and discard the bearing race.

e. Support the propshaft roller bearing in a press using a knife edge bearing plate. Position the propshaft with the propeller end facing up. Install the propeller nut onto the propshaft to protect the threads.

f. Press against the propeller nut until the bearing is free of the propshaft. Discard the bearing.

2. If the propeller gear roller bearing or bearing and oil slinger are to be replaced, remove the original roller bearing, or bearing and slinger as follows:

a. Support the propeller gear roller bearing in a press with a knife edge bearing plate.

b. Place bearing remover part No. 3850625-9 onto driver handle part No. 3850610-1.

c. Place the remover and handle assembly against the gear hub.

d. Press on the driver handle until the gear is free from the bearing. Discard the bearing.

e. To remove the slinger, support the oil slinger in a press with a knife edge bearing plate.

f. Press against the gear hub until the slinger is free of the gear hub. Discard the slinger.

3. If the drive shaft bearings are to be replaced, remove the original bearings as follows:

a. Support the drive shaft roller bearings in a press with a knife edge bearing plate. Position the drive shaft input splines facing up. Both bearings are removed at the same time.

b. Press against the drive shaft input splined end until the roller bearings are free from the drive shaft.

c. Discard both roller bearings.

4. If the lower drive shaft (pinion) bearing is to be replaced, remove the bearing as follows:

a. Assemble the bearing remover by sliding the appropriate guide plate (part No. 3850619-2 for SX-S and SX-C1 series gearcases and part No. 3850218-3 for SX-C series gearcases) over the threaded rod part No. 3850623-4 (A, **Figure 68**) with the small diameter end of the guide plate (B, **Figure 68**) facing the threaded end of the bolt. Thread bearing remover part No. 3850622-6 (C, **Figure 68**) onto the threaded rod.

b. Lubricate the 19 loose rollers with OMC Needle Bearing Assembly Grease or equivalent (**Table 5**) and install the loose rollers into the pinion bearing.

c. Insert the bearing remover into the pinion bearing through the drive shaft bore. Place a shop towel into the propshaft bore, underneath the pinion bearing.

d. Drive the bearing from the gearcase with a suitable mallet.

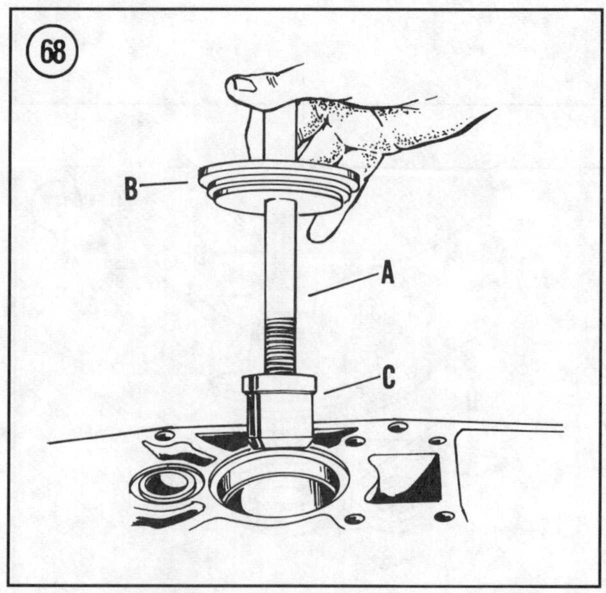

e. Remove the tools and discard the bearing.

5. Refer to *Cleaning and inspection (SX and DP-S models)* in this chapter.

Disassembly (DP-S Models)

Figure 69 shows an exploded view of a DP-S lower gearcase. Secure the gearcase in a suitable fixture such as one from Bob Kerr Marine or place the gearcase on a clean workbench. A special plate (**Figure 70**) must be fabricated to hold the DP-S gearcase into a standard Kerr fixture.

Fabricate the plate out of 1/4 in. mild steel or 3/8 in. aluminum plate. The plate should be approximately 76.5 mm (3 in.) wide and have 2 14.3 mm (9/16 in.) holes located on a centerline of approximately 15.9 mm (5/8 in.) from each end of the plate. The centerline between the holes should match the centerline of the existing retaining bolt holes of your fixture. Glue a piece of cork or rubber to 1 side of the plate to protect the gearcase. Install longer bolts as necessary to allow the plate to be set on top of the gearcase deck and clamp the gearcase down to the fixture.

Record the measurement of all shims as they are removed. Shims can be reused if they are not damaged. Tag the shims by location for reassembly purposes. Do not lose or discard any shims.

All components that are to be reused must be installed in their original location and orientation. Mark components as necessary to ensure correct reinstallation.

1. Verify that the lubricant drain plug (41, **Figure 69**) is removed, then remove the propshaft bearing carrier retaining ring (46, **Figure 69**) with spanner wrench part No. 3855877-1. Turn the ring counterclockwise to remove. Remove and discard the 2 retaining ring O-rings.
2. Remove the bearing housing tabbed retaining washer (45, **Figure 69**). Remove the O-ring underneath the washer.
3. Thread tube gear remover part No. 884789-9 fully onto the outer propeller shaft (A, **Figure 71**). Then tighten the bolt (B, **Figure 71**) to pull the outer propeller shaft (tube gear) and propshaft bearing carrier from the gearcase. Remove the tube gear puller.
4. Remove the inner propeller shaft and loosen the pinion nut as follows:
   a. Attach adaptor part No. 3855919-1 to the propeller nut threads (A, **Figure 72**).
   b. Attach pusher tip part No. 3855921-7 to tube part No. 3855922-5. Tighten the pusher tip setscrew securely.
   c. Install the pusher tip and tube assembly over the inner propshaft. Rotate the drive shaft as necessary to engage the pusher tip to the pinion nut. Seat the tool into the gearcase (B, **Figure 72**).
   d. Install spline socket part No. 3850598-8 onto the drive shaft splines. Attach a breaker bar and loosen the pinion nut several turns (no more than 3), by turning the shaft counterclockwise.
   e. Lubricate the special nut part No. 3855920-9 with grease, then thread the nut onto the adaptor and seat it against the tube assembly.
   f. Tighten the nut (C, **Figure 72**) while holding the tube with a crescent wrench, until the propeller shaft is removed from the front gear.

NOTE

*Do not discard the pinion nut at this point. It will be reused for shimming and gear pattern verification, then discarded. Always install a new nut during **Final Assembly**.*

5. Reach inside the propshaft bore and remove the pinion nut. Retain the pinion nut for shimming purposes.
6. Remove the 2 screws securing the anode to the front of the gearcase deck. Remove the anode.

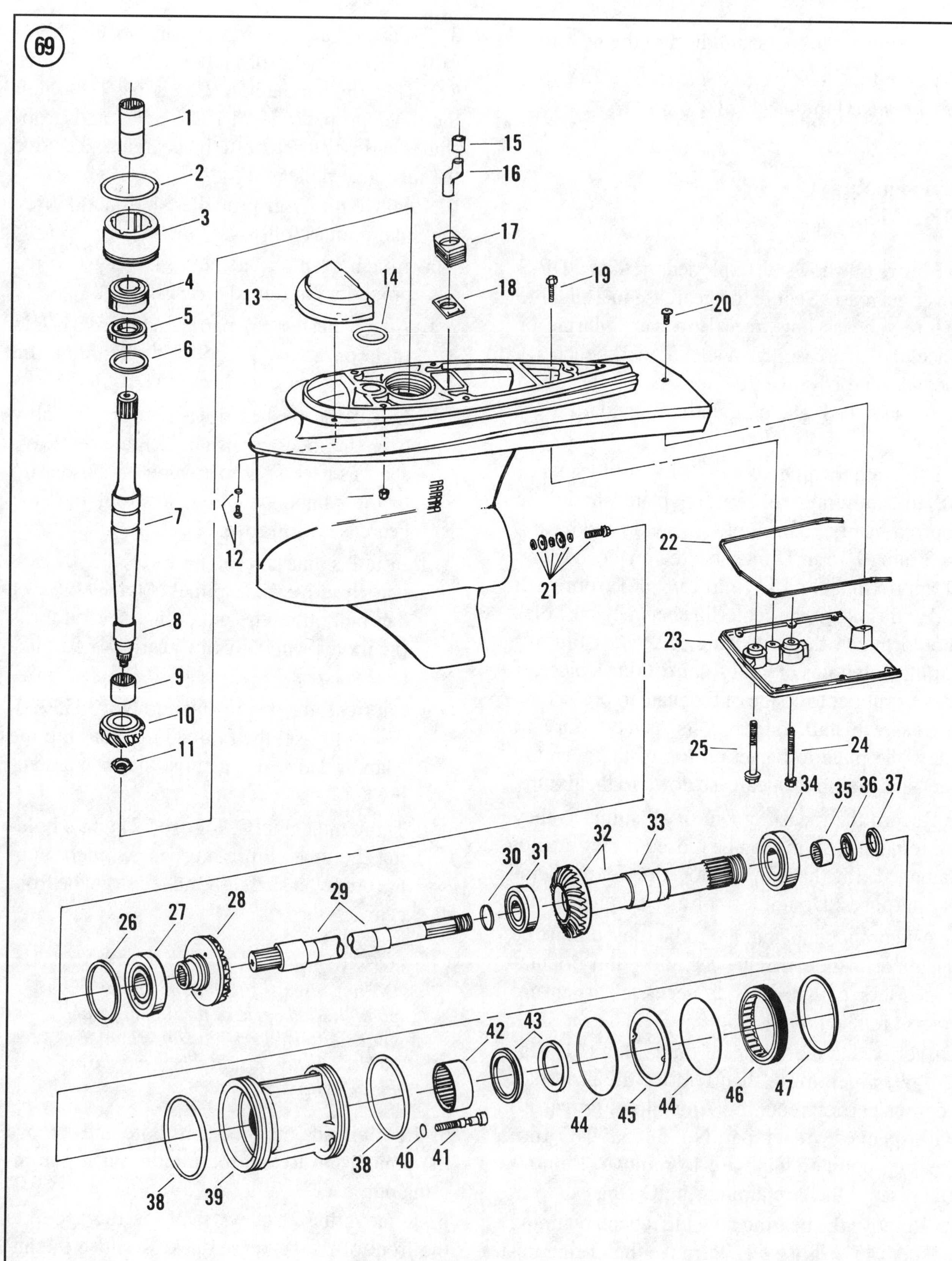
69
1
2
3
4
5
6
7
8
9
10
11
12
13
14
15
16
17
18
19
20
21
22
23
24
25
26
27
28
29
30
31
32
33
34
35
36
37
38
39
40
41
42
43
44
45
46
47

LOWER GEARCASE (DP-S MODELS)

1. Intermediate drive shaft coupler
2. Drive shaft O-ring
3. Drive shaft bearing retainer
4. Larger tapered roller bearing
5. Small tapered roller bearing
6. Shim (pinion gear location)
7. Vertical drive shaft
8. Bearing sleeve
9. Lower drive shaft (pinion) bearing
10. Pinion gear
11. Pinion nut
12. Anode screw and washer
13. Anode
14. O-ring
15. Water tube grommet (upper gearcase)
16. Water tube
17. Water tube grommet (lower gearcase)
18. Plastic water tube guide
19. Exhaust plate screw (hex head)
20. Exhaust plate screw (Torx head)
21. Magnet assembly
22. Exhaust plate seal
23. Exhaust plate
24. Screw (3/8 in. shank)
25. Screw (7/16 in. shank)
26. Shim (propshaft gear location)
27. Tapered roller bearing
28. Propshaft gear
29. Inner propshaft
30. Shim (aft driven gear position)
31. Tapered roller bearing
32. Aft driven (tube) gear
33. Bearing sleeve
34. Tapered roller bearing
35. Needle bearing
36. Seal (double-lip, single case)
37. Seal (single-lip)
38. O-ring
39. Propshaft bearing carrier
40. O-ring (drain/fill plug)
41. Drain/fill plug
42. Needle bearing
43. Seals
44. O-ring
45. Tabbed retaining washer
46. Retaining ring
47. O-ring

7. Unscrew the drive shaft bearing retainer with spanner wrench part No. 3850601-0 (A, **Figure 73**). Remove the retainer (B, **Figure 73**) from the gearcase.

8. To remove the drive shaft, proceed as follows:
   a. Verify that the pinion nut has been removed, then install drive shaft puller part No. 3855923-3 to the drive shaft as shown in **Figure 74**.
   b. Tighten the socket head clamp screws (A, **Figure 74**) securely to hold the tool to the drive shaft.
   c. Tighten the hex head screws (B, **Figure 74**) alternately, 1/2 turn at a time, until the drive shaft is free from the pinion gear.
   d. Remove the tool from the drive shaft and remove the drive shaft from the gearcase.
   e. Reach inside the propshaft bore and remove the pinion gear.
   f. Reach inside the propshaft bore and remove the front driven gear.

9. Remove the screw securing the magnets and spacers at the very bottom of the propshaft bore. Remove the screw, 2 magnets and 3 washers from the propshaft bore. See 21, **Figure 69**.

CAUTION

The drive shaft bearing race in the top of the drive shaft bore, the front driven gear bearing race at the bottom of the propshaft bore and the roller bearing on the inner propshaft are shimmed bearings. These bearing races and roller bearing must be removed to perform the lower gearcase shimming procedures. All other bearings and cups are not shimmed and should not be removed unless they are going to be replaced.

10. Assemble the tools to remove the drive shaft bearing race and shims as follows:
   a. Thread bearing remover part No. 3855859-9 (A, **Figure 75**) onto threaded rod part No. 3855860-7 (B, **Figure 75**).
   b. Insert the bearing remover through the bearing race and center it behind the race

(D, **Figure 75**). Pilot the guide plate part No. 3850619-2 (C, **Figure 75**) into the drive shaft bore.

c. Install and tighten the nut and washer (E, **Figure 75**) onto the threaded rod.
d. Tighten the nut to pull the bearing race from the gearcase.
e. Remove the shim(s) from the drive shaft bore or bearing race. Measure and record the thickness of the shim(s) for later reference. If the shims are damaged, they must be discarded. If the shims are not damaged, tag the shim(s) for identification during reassembly.

11. Assemble the tools and remove the front driven gear bearing race and shims as follows:

a. Insert the threaded rod part No. 3855860-7 (A, **Figure 76**) through the guide plate part No. 3855863-1 (B, **Figure 76**) so the washer and nut (D, **Figure 76**) are on the large diameter side of the guide plate.
b. Thread the bearing remover part No. 3855862-3 (C, **Figure 76**) onto the threaded rod with the snap ring side facing the guide plate.
c. Insert the tool assembly into the propshaft bore. With hand pressure or a rubber or plastic hammer, push the bearing remover through the front driven gear bearing race until it locks behind the race.
d. Tighten the nut to pull the bearing race from the gearcase.
e. Remove the tool and bearing race from the propshaft bore.
f. Remove the shim(s) from the propshaft bore or bearing race. Measure and record the thickness of the shim(s) for later reference. If the shims are damaged, they must

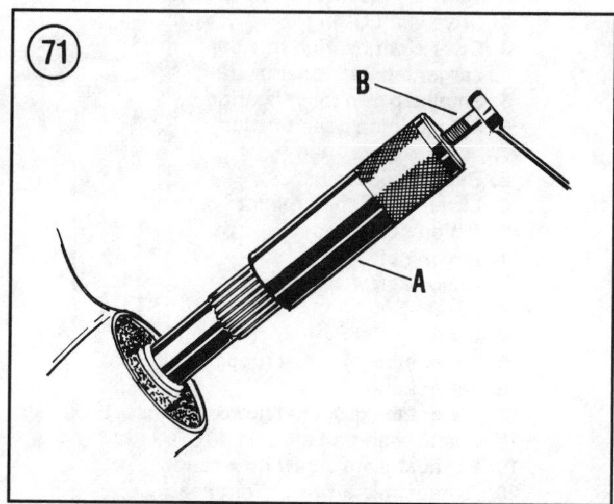

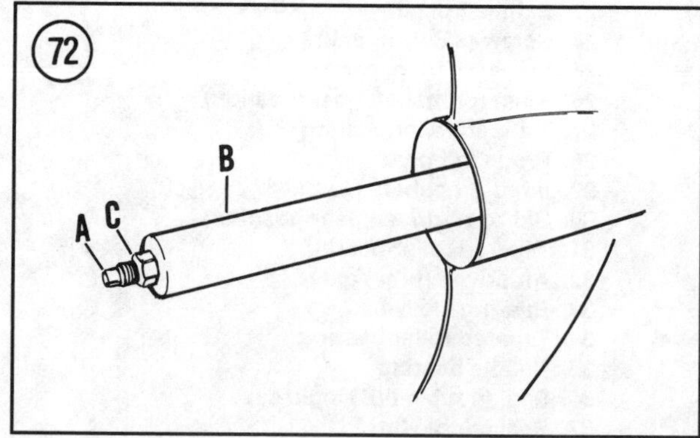

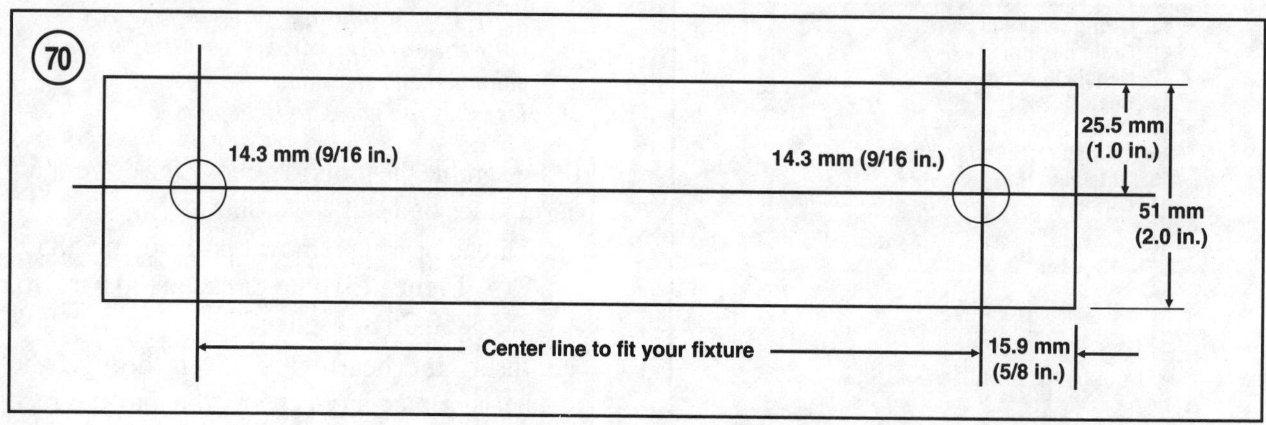

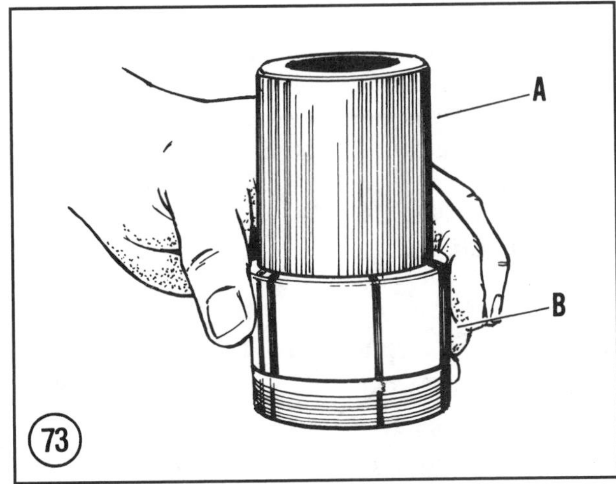

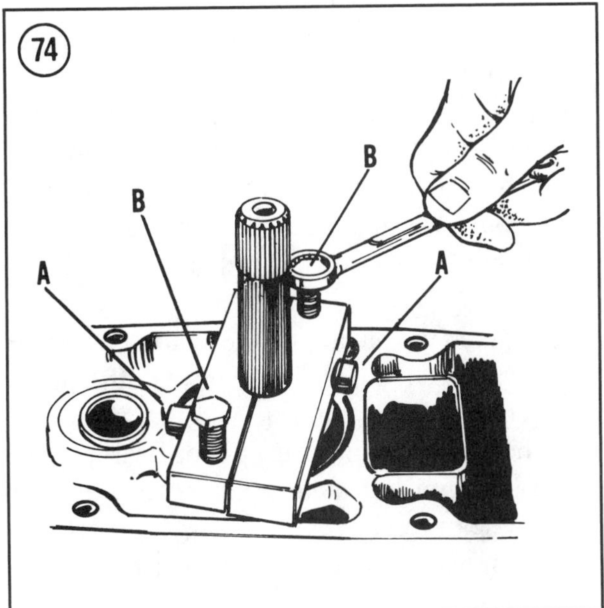

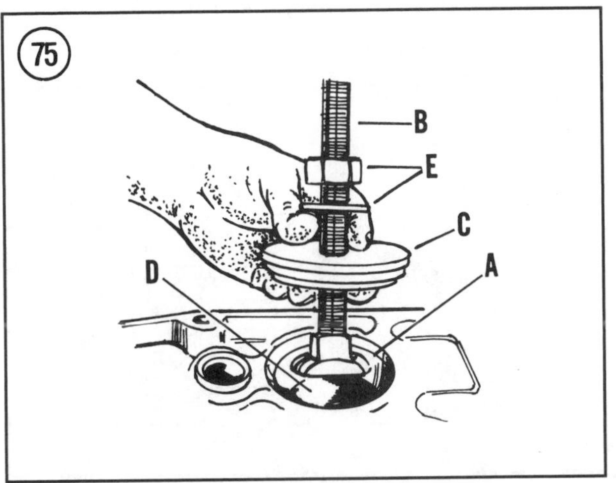

be discarded. If the shims are not damaged, tag the shim(s) for identification during reassembly.

12. Remove the roller bearing and shims from the inner propeller shaft as follows:

a. Place pusher tip part No. 3855921-7 in a press with the setscrew end facing up and the pinion nut relief (A, **Figure 77**) facing down.

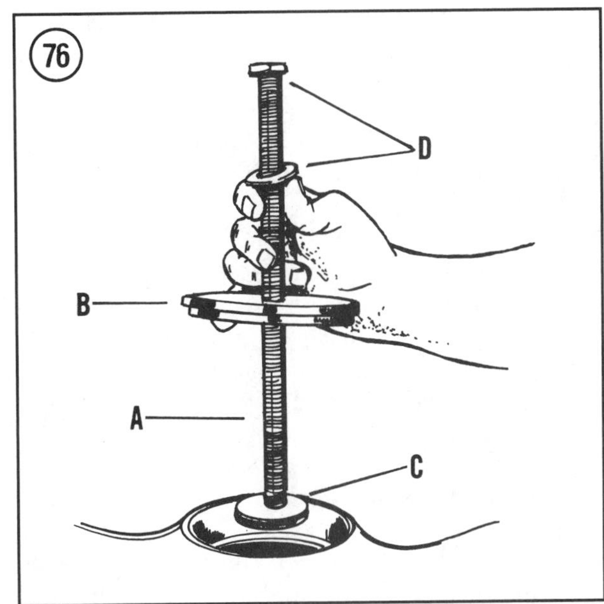

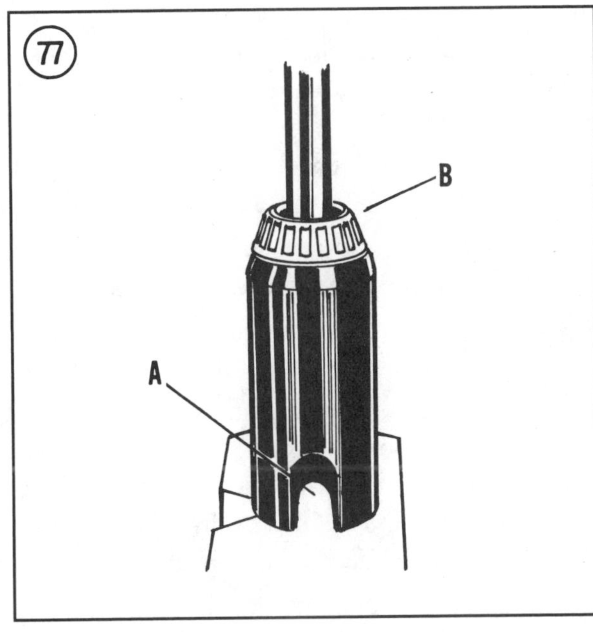

13

b. Install a suitable nut on the propeller end of the propshaft to protect the threads.
c. Place the gear end of the propshaft into the pusher tip with the roller bearing against the pusher tip shoulder (B, **Figure 77**).
d. Press on the propeller nut until the bearing is free. *Do not* discard the bearing unless it is damaged or going to be replaced.
e. Remove the shim(s) from the propeller shaft shoulder. Measure and record the thickness of the shim(s) for later reference. Tag the shim(s) for identification during reassembly.

13. Remove the propeller shaft bearing carrier from the outer propeller shaft (tube gear).

NOTE
The tube gear inner needle bearing and propshaft seals can be removed at the same time if bearing replacement is required. If bearing replacement is not required, pull the seals with a suitable 2-jaw puller, being careful not to damage the inner surface of the tube gear or the inner needle bearing.

14A. *Seal removal only*—Remove the tube gear propshaft seals with a suitable 2 jaw puller. Do not damage the tube gear inner surfaces or the inner needle bearing. Discard the seals.

14B. *Seal and bearing removal*—If the tube gear inner needle bearing requires replacement, proceed as follows:
a. Install bearing remover part No. 884803-8 onto drive handle part No. 884143-9.
b. Thread an old propeller nut onto the tube gear to protect the threads and splines.
c. Insert the bearing remover and drive handle into the gear end of the tube gear.
d. Place the tool and gear assembly into a press. Support the propeller nut (while allowing room for the seals and bearings to exit) and press against the drive handle until the seals and needle bearing are free.
e. Discard the seals and needle bearing.

CAUTION
Do not remove any additional bearings or bearing races unless new bearings are going to be installed. The removal process is stressful to the bearings and races. However, replace all seals and O-rings each time the gearcase is disassembled.

15. If the lower drive shaft (pinion) bearing requires replacement, proceed as follows:
a. Insert the threaded rod part No. 3855860-7 through the guide plate part No. 3850619-2 so that the nut and washer are against the large diameter end of the guide plate.
b. Insert the guide plate and threaded rod into the drive shaft bore and pilot the guide plate into the drive shaft O-ring groove.
c. Position the bearing remover part No. 3855898-0 into the propshaft bore and piloted into the pinion bearing so that the tool shoulder is against the bearing.
d. Thread the threaded rod into the pinion bearing.
e. Tighten the nut to pull the bearing from the gearcase. If the bearing proves difficult to remove, apply mild heat to the outside of the gearcase around the pinion bearing with a heat gun or heat lamp. Do not use an open flame or torch.
f. Remove the tools and discard the pinion bearing.

16. If the drive shaft upper roller bearings require replacement, proceed as follows:

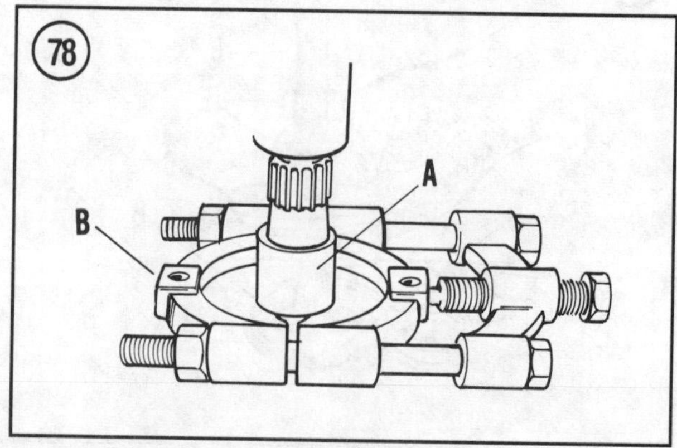

a. Support the drive shaft roller bearings in a press with a knife edge bearing plate. Position the drive shaft input splines facing up. Both bearings will be removed at the same time.

b. Press against the drive shaft input splined end until the roller bearings are free from the drive shaft.

c. Discard both roller bearings.

17. If the drive shaft lower bearing sleeve (race) requires replacement, proceed as follows:

a. Support the drive shaft bearing sleeve (A, **Figure 78**) in a press with a knife edge bearing plate (B, **Figure 78**). The pinion nut must face up.

b. Thread the old pinion nut onto the drive shaft to protect the drive shaft threads.

c. Press against the pinion nut until the sleeve is free from the drive shaft.

d. Discard the drive shaft bearing sleeve.

e. Remove and discard the pinion bearing from the gearcase housing as described previously in this section.

18. If the front driven gear roller bearing requires replacement, proceed as follows:

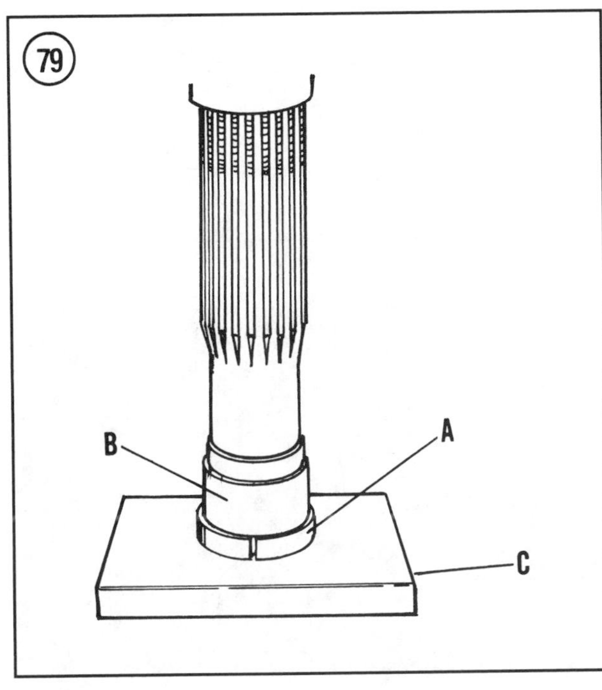

a. Support the bearing in a press with a knife edge bearing plate. The gear teeth must face down.

b. Press on the gear hub with a suitable mandrel until the bearing is free from the gear.

Tube gear roller bearing, race and sleeve removal

If the tube gear large tapered roller bearing requires replacement, the bearing sleeve (inner bearing race) for the propshaft bearing carrier needle bearing must also be replaced. To remove the tube gear roller bearing, bearing sleeve and tube gear tapered roller bearing race, proceed as follows.

1. Insert the tube gear in sleeve removal tool part No. 884831-9. Position the split sleeves (A, **Figure 79**) on the gear side of the bearing sleeve (B, **Figure 79**) against the remover plate (C, **Figure 79**).

2. Thread an old propeller nut onto the tube gear to protect the threads and splines.

NOTE
If the sleeve proves difficult to remove in Step 3, apply mild heat to the sleeve. A heat lamp, heat gun or propane torch may be used.

3. Support the removal tool plate in a press. Press against the propeller nut until the sleeve is free from the tube gear.

4. Discard the bearing sleeve.

5. Support the tube gear tapered roller bearing in a press with a knife-edge bearing plate. The splined end of the tube gear must face up.

6. Thread an old propeller nut onto the tube gear to protect the threads and splines.

7. Press against the propeller nut until the bearing is free from the tube gear.

8. Discard the bearing.

9. Remove and discard the associated propshaft bearing carrier race as described in *Propshaft bearing carrier disassembly* in this chapter.

10. To remove the small tapered roller bearing race in the tube gear face, proceed as follows:
   a. Insert the split remover part No. 884832-7 halves (A, **Figure 80**) into the gear face (B, **Figure 80**) and position the tool lips behind the bearing race.
   b. Insert the drive handle part No. 884143-9 through the propeller end of the tube gear and pilot it between the split bearing remover.
   c. Support the tube gear in a press. Protect the gear teeth with wood, plastic or aluminum blocks.
   d. Press on the drive handle until the bearing race is free from the tube gear.
   e. Discard the bearing race.
   f. Remove and discard the inner propeller shaft tapered roller bearing as described previously.

Propshaft bearing carrier disassembly

NOTE
The propshaft carrier inner needle bearing and propshaft seals can be removed at the same time if bearing replacement is required. If bearing replacement is not required, pull the seals with a suitable 2-jaw puller, being careful not to damage the inner surface of the propshaft bearing carrier or the needle bearing.

1. Remove and discard the O-ring from each carrier flange.
2. *Seal removal only*—Remove the propshaft seals with a suitable 2 jaw puller. Do not damage the carrier inner surfaces or the needle bearing. Discard the seals.
3. *Seal and bearing removal*—If the propshaft bearing carrier inner needle bearing requires replacement, proceed as follows:
   a. Place the support base part No. 3855926-6, notched side up, into a press.
   b. Place the propshaft bearing carrier, seal side down, into the support base.
   c. Place remover part No. 3855924-1 onto driver handle part No. 9991801-3 so that the large diameter of the tool faces the driver handle.
   d. Place the remover assembly into the carrier and press the seals and bearing from the carrier.
   e. Discard the seals and needle bearing.
4. To remove the tapered roller bearing race from the propshaft bearing carrier, proceed as follows:
   a. Place the support base part No. 3855926-6, notched side up, into a press.
   b. Insert remover part No. 3855862-3 into the bearing race until it snaps into place behind the bearing race.
   c. Set the propshaft bearing carrier into the support base with the propeller end facing up.
   d. Insert tool part No. 884789-9 through the carrier bore and against the remover tool.

80

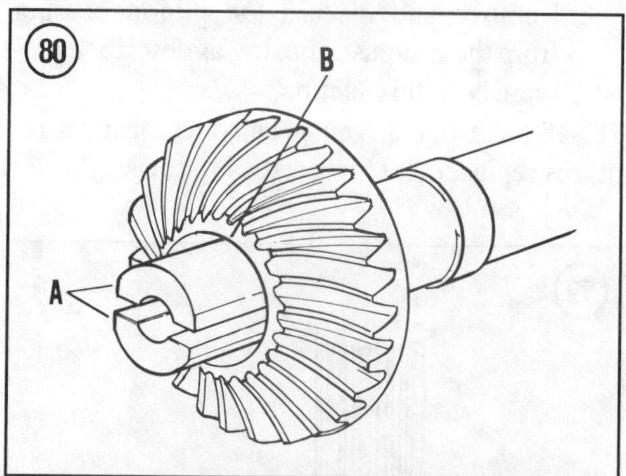

81

e. Press against tool part No. 884789-9 until the bearing race is free from the carrier.

f. Discard the bearing race. Remove and replace the tapered roller bearing on the tube gear as described previously, if you have not already done so.

Cleaning and Inspection (SX and DP-S models)

1. Clean all parts in a suitable solvent and blow dry with compressed air. Make sure all sealer and gasket residue are removed and blow out all threaded holes, lubricant passages and the water intake passages.
2. Apply a light coat of oil to all of the cleaned components to prevent rusting.
3. Inspect the gears. Check all gear teeth and the internal bearing or splined surfaces for excessive wear, chips, cracks, nicks or other damage. If 1 gear is damaged and requires replacement, replace both (SX models) or all 3 (DP-S models) as an assembly.

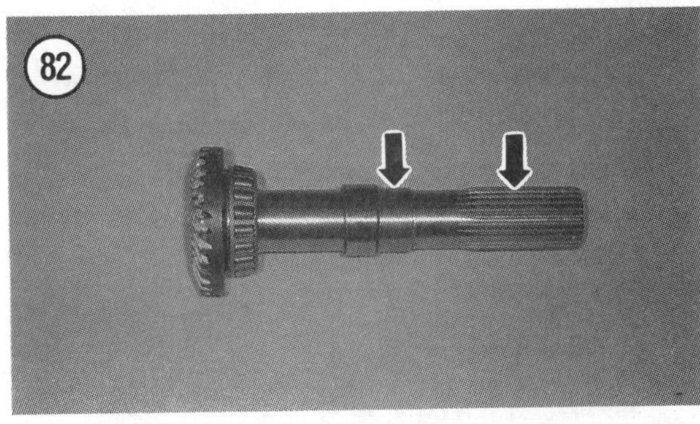

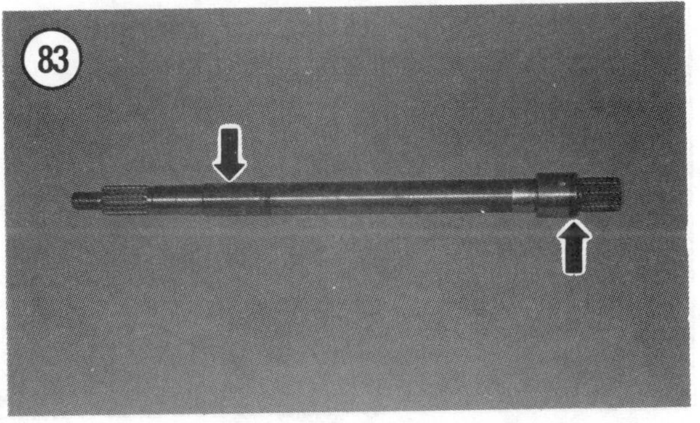

CAUTION

One tapered roller bearing consists of the caged tapered roller bearings and cone-shaped inner race, and a cup-shaped outer race. The bearing must be replaced as a set and parts from one bearing must never be mixed with parts from another.

4. Check all bearings (**Figure 81**, typical) for scoring, roughness, heat discoloration and binding. Replace any bearing (and corresponding race) as necessary. Follow the procedures in this chapter to remove the bearings. Do not remove pressed-on bearings unless replacement is necessary or the text specifically directs you to do so.
5. Check the splines of the intermediate drive shaft coupler for excessive wear or distortion.
6. Inspect all shims and replace any that are damaged. If shimming adjustment is not required, damaged shims can be replaced with new shims of the same thickness.
7. Check all of the threads, sealing surfaces and splines (internal and external) on the propeller and drive shafts. See **Figure 82** (tube shaft, DP-S models) and **Figure 83** (inner propeller shaft, DP-S models). Replace any shaft that displays excessive wear, mechanical damage or distortion. Slight imperfections can be removed with emery cloth.
8. Check the propeller(s) for spline damage, corrosion or wear. Check the propeller blades for cracks, dents, gouged or broken blades. Rebuild or replace the propeller(s) as necessary.
9. Check the gear housing and propeller bearing housing for cracks around the screw holes and bearing bores. Also check for cracks, nicks or burrs on the housing mating surfaces and O-ring surfaces. Remove slight imperfections with emery cloth.
10. Inspect the gear housing threaded area and the propshaft bearing carrier threaded area (SX models) or the retaining ring (DP-S models) for corrosion, damaged threads, nicks, burrs or other damage. Use a thread file to repair minor thread

damage. Remove minor nicks or burrs with emery cloth.

11. Inspect the anodes as described in *Corrosion Control* located previously in this chapter.

12. *DP-S models*—If the upper to lower gearcase mounting studs are damaged, remove the studs with an appropriate stud remover or double-nut the studs. Coat the threads of new studs with Loctite 271 threadlocking adhesive (**Table 5**) and install the studs to a remaining height of 28.95-29.05 mm (1.140-1.144 in.).

13. *DP-S models*—Thoroughly clean the magnet assembly of all metallic particles. Replace any magnet that is cracked or damaged.

Assembly (SX Models)

For maximum durability and quiet running, both gears must be properly located in the gearcase through shimming procedures. When the gears are properly located, the correct backlash and gear contact pattern will be observed.

Additionally, the tapered bearings in the gearcase must be properly tensioned or *preloaded.* Preload refers to the tension applied to hold a tapered roller bearing in its cup. Insufficient preload will allow the bearing to move in relation to the bearing cup. Any movement of the bearing from its cup will result in premature bearing and gear failure. Excessive preload will cause the bearings to overheat and fail. Correct preload is determined by measuring the torque required to rotate the shafts and gears. This is called *rolling torque*.

During assembly procedures, lubricate all components with Volvo DuraPlus GL5 Synthetic Gear Lube (**Table 6**). Do not make any *dry* assemblies.

New O-rings will not be installed until the gear lash, gear pattern and bearing rolling torque have been verified. O-ring installation is covered under *Final Assembly* in this chapter.

Figure 84 is an exploded view of a typical SX series lower gearcase.

LOWER GEARCASE (SX MODELS)

1. Intermediate drive shaft coupler
2. Drive shaft O-ring
3. Drive shaft bearing retainer
4. Larger tapered roller bearing
5. Small tapered roller bearing
6. Shim (pinion gear location)
7. Vertical drive shaft
8. Lower drive shaft (pinion) bearing
9. Pinion gear
10. Pinion nut
11. Gearcase housing
12. Anode screw and washer
13. Anode
14. O-ring
15. Water tube grommet (upper gearcase)
16. Water tube
17. Water tube grommet (lower gearcase)
18. Water tube plastic guide
19. Trim tab screw (manual steering models)
20. Plug (power steering models)
21. Trim tab (manual steering models)
22. Screw
23. Screw
24. Set screw
25. Screw
26. Drain/fill plug and seal washer
27. Shim (propshaft gear location)
28. Tapered roller bearing
29. Oil slinger
30. Propshaft gear
31. Propshaft
32. Shim ring (bearing preload)
33. Tapered roller bearing
34. O-ring
35. Seal (double-lip, single case)
36. Propshaft bearing carrier
37. Retainer block
38. Retainer screw
39. Anode screw
40. Bracket screw
41. Anode bracket
42. Wave washer
43. Anode

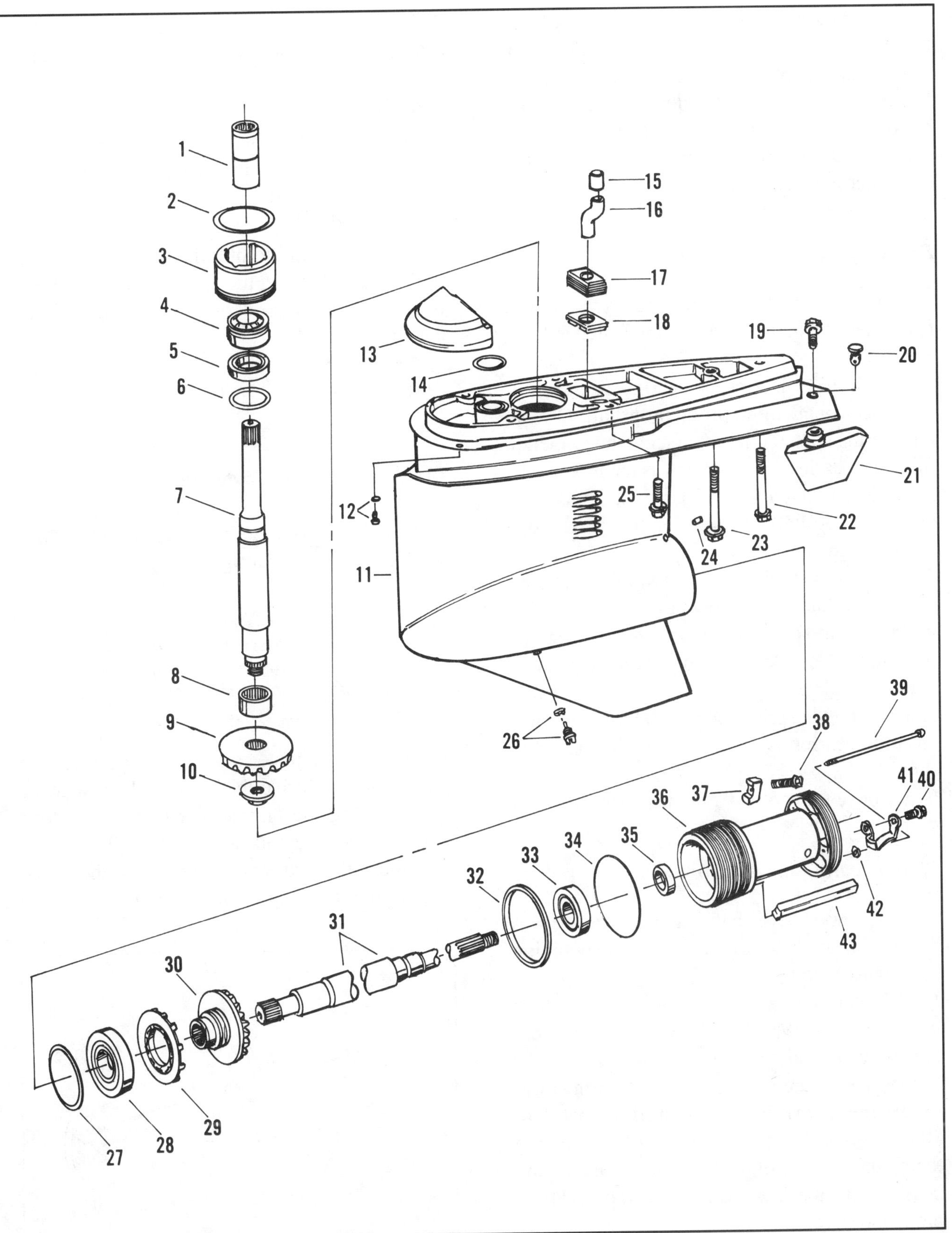
1
2
3
4
5
6
7
8
9
10
11
12
13
14
15
16
17
18
19
20
21
22
23
24
25
26
27
28
29
30
31
32
33
34
35
36
37
38
39
40
41
42
43

Begin reassembly by first installing new bearings to replace any that were removed. The propshaft gear tapered roller bearing race and the lower drive shaft tapered roller bearing race cannot be installed until the correct shims have been determined. Installation of these bearings is covered later in this section.

Propshaft bearing installation

If the propshaft roller bearing was removed from the propshaft, install a new roller bearing as follows.

1. Lubricate a new roller bearing and slide it over the propeller end of the propshaft. Oriente the bearing so the rollers are facing the propeller. Slide the bearing onto the shaft as far as possible.
2. Slide bearing installer part No. 3850617-6 over the propshaft and position the raised edge of the tool against the bearing.
3. Support the tool in a press with the propeller end of the shaft facing down.
4. Protect the splined end of the shaft with spline socket part No. 3850618-4 or a suitable piece of aluminum plate.
5. Press on the spline socket or aluminum plate until the bearing is seated against the propshaft shoulder.
6. Remove the tool(s) from the propshaft.

Pinion bearing installation

If the lower drive shaft (pinion) bearing was removed from the gearcase, install a new pinion bearing as follows.

1. Lubricate a new pinion bearing and rollers liberally with OMC Needle Bearing Assembly Grease or equivalent (**Table 5**). Make sure all 19 bearing rollers are installed into the bearing race. Place the bearing onto installer part No. 3850620-0 with the lettered side of the bearing facing the hex end of the tool. Place the tool and bearing into the lower drive shaft bore via the propshaft bore.
2. Insert the threaded rod part No. 3855860-7 into the guide plate part No. 3850619-2, so the large end of the guide plate is facing the washer and nut.
3. Insert the guide plate and rod into the drive shaft bore and engage the bearing installer. Thread the bearing installer securely onto the threaded rod.
4. Tighten the nut to pull the bearing into position. Stop tightening the nut as soon as the bearing seats in its bore or the bearing will be damaged.
5. Remove the tools and inspect the bearing for damage.

Drive shaft bearing installation

If the bearings were removed from the drive shaft, install new bearings as follows.

NOTE

When installed correctly, the bearing rollers face away from each other. Install the small bearing first and the large bearing second.

1. Lubricate a new small roller bearing and place it over the drive shaft input splines with the rollers facing the pinion gear end of the drive shaft. Place bearing installer part No. 3850617-6 over the drive shaft and bearing with the raised edge of the tool against the bearing.

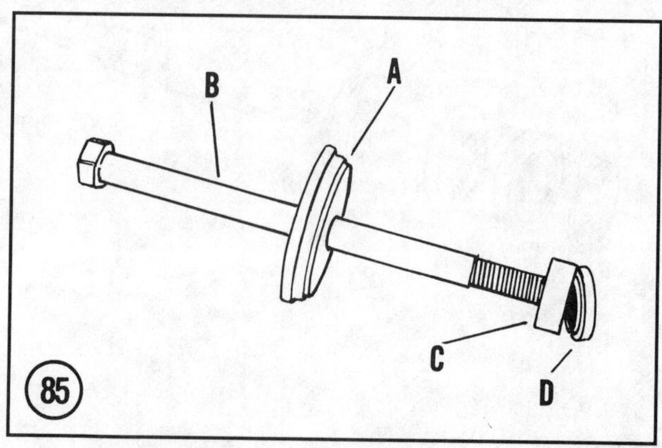

2. Thread an old pinion nut onto the drive shaft to protect the threads. Place the drive shaft assembly into a press. Support the bearing installer with pressing plates.
3. Press against the pinion nut until the bearing is seated against the drive shaft shoulder.
4. Lubricate a new large tapered roller bearing and place it over the input splines with the rollers facing up away from the small bearing. Place bearing installer part No. 3850617-6 over the drive shaft and bearing with the raised edge of the tool against the bearing.
5. Place the drive shaft assembly into a press. Support the bearing installer with pressing plates.
6. Press against the pinion nut until the bearing is seated against the small roller bearing.
7. Remove the pinion nut and tool from the drive shaft.

Propshaft bearing carrier assembly

1. If removed, install a new tapered roller bearing race into the propshaft bearing carrier as follows:
   a. Lubricate the race and set it into the propshaft bearing carrier with the tapered side facing away from the propeller.
   b. Assembly the guide plate part No. 3850619-2 over the large bolt part No. 3850623-4 so the large diameter of the plate is facing the bolt head. Install bearing installer part No. 3850621-8 onto the bolt threads so the beveled edge is facing away from the bolt head.
   c. Insert the tool assembly into the propshaft bearing carrier and engage the installer into the bearing race and the guide plate into the carrier bore.
   d. Support the carrier in a press with the bolt head facing up. Press on the bolt until the bearing race is seated in the propshaft bearing carrier.
2. Install a new propshaft seal into the propshaft bearing carrier as follows:
   a. Assemble the guide plate part No. 3850619-2 (A, **Figure 85**) over the large bolt part No. 3850623-4 (B, **Figure 85**) so the large diameter of the plate is facing the bolt head. Install seal installer part No. 3850627-5 (C, **Figure 85**) onto the bolt threads so the recessed edge is facing away from the bolt head.
   b. Coat the metal case of a new propshaft seal with OMC Gasket Sealing Compound or equivalent (**Table 5**). Set the seal into the installer so the protruding lip of seal is piloted into the recess of the installer (D, **Figure 85**).
   c. Invert the propshaft bearing carrier and set it over the tool and seal. While holding the tool and seal firmly into the carrier, again invert the carrier so the bolt is facing up.
   d. Support the carrier in a press with the bolt head facing up. Press on the bolt until the seal is seated in the propshaft bearing carrier. Do not press with excessive force or the seal will be damaged.
   e. Coat the seal lips with OMC Triple Guard Grease or equivalent (**Table 5**).

Propshaft gear assembly

Begin reassembly of the propeller gear by pressing a new oil slinger onto the gear hub.

1. Set the gear in a press. Protect the gear teeth with wood, plastic or an aluminum plate.
2. Lubricate a new oil slinger and align the pins of the oil slinger with the corresponding holes in the gear hub.
3. Place support tool part No. 3850614-3 over the oil slinger. Place a suitable mandrel (such as installer part No. 3850617-6) over the support tool.
4. Press on the mandrel until the oil slinger is seated against the gear hub.

5. Lubricate a new roller bearing and place it over the oil slinger and gear hub with the rollers facing away from the gear and slinger.
6. Place the gear assembly into a press. Protect the gear teeth with wood, plastic or an aluminum plate. Place bearing installer part No. 3850624-2 against the bearing.
7. Press on the installer until the bearing is seated against the gear.

Lower Gearcase Shimming Procedures (SX Models)

To determine the correct amount of shims to properly position the gears and bearings, keep in mind that the numbers stamped on the gears are correction numbers in thousandths of an inch. Nominal dimensions are fixed dimensions that are established by Volvo Penta during the design and manufacturing of the product. All fixed (nominal) dimensions are listed in **Table 2**.

Since the gears are stamped using U.S. standard units of measure, it is recommended that all calculations be performed in inches. Any conversions from U.S. standard to Metric should only be attempted on the final calculated result.

NOTE
Both gears are stamped with a correction number and a match number. The match number always starts with a T. Both gears will have the same T number. It would be rare for both gears to have the same correction number. Do not confuse the T number with a + (positive) correction number.

The correct selection of shims and proper gearcase assembly will be confirmed by the gear lash and gear pattern verifications and the overall rolling torque check.

CAUTION
It cannot be stated strongly enough that you must clearly record and label all of your shimming calculations. Time spent calculating shim amounts is wasted if the results are not recorded and labeled.

Pinion gear shimming

The drive shaft on SX-S and SX-C/C1 models are different lengths. Make sure the correct tool is used as specified. To determine the proper shims to locate the pinion gear, proceed as follows.

1. Securely clamp spline socket part No. 3850598-8 vertically in a vise. Insert the drive shaft into the spline socket making sure the splines engage fully.
2. Install the small tapered roller bearing race over the drive shaft and against the small roller bearing.
3A. *SX-S models*—Install shim fixture part No. 3850599-6 over the drive shaft and seat it against the small bearing race with the slotted end of the tool facing up.
3B. *SX-C and SX-C1 models*—Install shim fixture part No. 3855098-4 onto the drive shaft and seat it against the small bearing race with the slotted end of the tool facing up.
4. Install the pinion gear to the drive shaft. Install the original (used) nut. Tighten the nut to specification (**Table 4**).
5. Rotate the shim tool several turns to seat the small bearing.

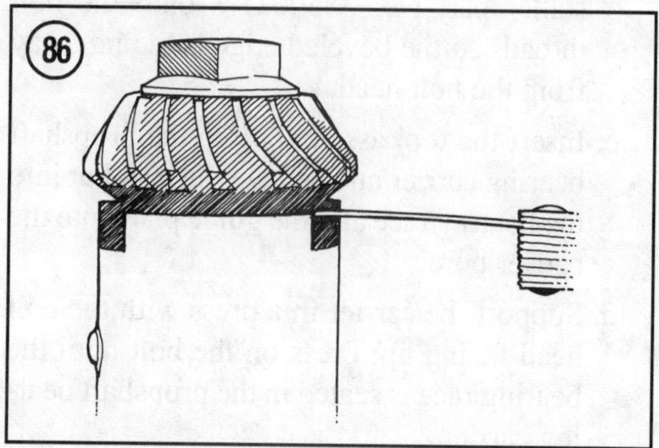

NOTE
When the correct feeler gauge has been selected, a slight drag will be felt as the feeler gauge blade is moved between the measuring points. To verify, insert the next size larger blade and check for a noticeable increase in the drag. Then insert the next size smaller blade and check for the absence of drag.

6. Use a feeler gauge to measure the distance between the shim tool and the pinion gear at each of the 3 slots. See **Figure 86**. It is normal for the measurements to vary slightly. Average the 3 readings by adding the 3 measurements to each other and dividing the result by 3. Round to the nearest thousandth of an inch. Record this result and label it *pinion gear average feeler gauge measurement.*
7. Remove the pinion nut, pinion gear, shim tool and small bearing race.
8. Locate the correction number stamped or etched on the pinion gear (**Figure 87**, typical). Record this figure as thousandths of an inch. For example, if +10 is etched on the gear, write it as +0.010 in. If -10 is etched on the gear, write it as -0.010 in.
9. Add or subtract (as indicated by the + or -) the etched number on the gear to the *pinion gear average feeler gauge measurement.* For example, the gear shown in **Figure 87** is +10. This would be 0.010 in. *plus* the pinion gear average feeler gauge measurement. Record this result and label it as *pinion gear shims.*
10. Select and measure the correct amount of shims determined by your calculations. Set these predetermined shims into the drive shaft small bearing bore in the lower gearcase.
11. Lubricate the small bearing race and set it on top of the shims in the drive shaft bore with the tapered side of the bearing facing up.
12. Assemble the bearing installer as follows:
   a. Assemble the guide plate part No. 3850619-2 for SX-S and SX-C1 series gearcases or guide plate part No. 3850218-3 for SX-C series gearcases over the large bolt part No. 3850623-4 so the large diameter of the plate is facing the bolt head.
   b. Install bearing installer part No. 3850621-8 onto the bolt threads so the beveled edge is facing away from the bolt head.
   c. Insert the tool assembly into the drive shaft bore and engage the installer into the bearing race and the guide plate into the gearcase bore.
   d. Using a mallet, drive the bearing into the gearcase until it is seated in the drive shaft bore.
   e. Remove the tool from the gearcase. Inspect the bearing and make sure that the shim(s) are not displaced or damaged and that the bearing is fully seated.

13

Propshaft gear shimming

A fixed (nominal) dimension of 0.106 in. is used in this process. To determine the proper shims to locate the propshaft gear, proceed as follows:

1. Place the propshaft gear, with the teeth facing down, onto a clean workbench. Install the bearing race over the propshaft gear roller bearing and rotate the race several turns to align the bearing.

2. Position the shim fixture part No. 3850600-2 on top of the bearing race, with its recessed side facing the bearing.

3. Measure the distance from the top surface of the shim fixture to the end of the gear stub shaft (**Figure 88**). Record this reading. Subtract the thickness of the shim fixture (0.500 in.) from this reading. For example, if the reading is 0.599 in., subtract 0.500 in. from 0.599 in. which equals 0.099 in., (0.599 - 0.500 = 0.099). Record this result and label it *actual dimension*.

4. Locate the correction number stamped or etched on the outer diameter of the propshaft gear. Record this figure as thousandths of an inch. For example, if +5 is etched on the gear, write it as +0.005 in. If -5 is etched on the gear, write it as -0.005 in.

5. Add or subtract (as indicated by the + or -) the etched number on the gear to the *actual dimension*. For example, if the gear is stamped +5, then record as 0.005 in. *plus* the actual dimension. Following this example, add 0.005 in. (gear correction figure) to 0.099 in. (actual dimension), which equals 0.104 in., (0.005 + 0.099 = 0.104). Record this result and label it as *corrected dimension*.

6. Subtract the corrected dimension from the fixed (nominal) dimension of 0.106 in. To complete this example, subtract 0.104 in. (corrected dimension) from 0.106 (nominal dimension), which equals 0.002 in., (0.106 - 0.104 = 0.002). This result is the total amount (thickness) of shims to be installed under the propshaft gear bearing race. Record this result and label it *propshaft gear shims*.

7. Select and measure the correct amount of shims determined by your calculations. Set these predetermined shims into the gearcase propshaft gear bearing bore.

8. Lubricate the propshaft gear bearing race and set it on top of the shims in the bearing bore with the tapered side of the bearing facing up.

9. Assemble the bearing installer as follows:

a. Assemble the drive handle part No. 3850609-3 (A, **Figure 89**) to the bearing installer part No. 3850616-8 (B, **Figure 89**) so the large diameter of the installer is facing the drive handle.

b. Install alignment plate part No. 3850613-5 (C, **Figure 89**) over the drive handle.

c. Insert the tool assembly into the drive shaft bore and engage the installer into the bearing race and the alignment plate into the propshaft bore.

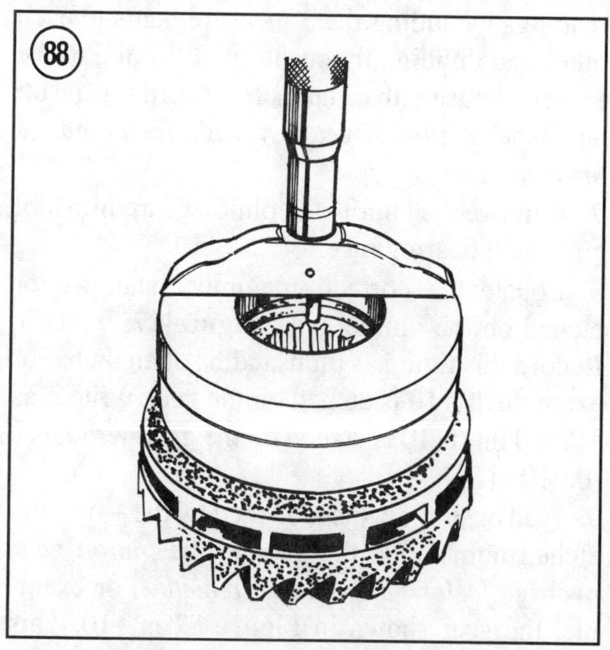

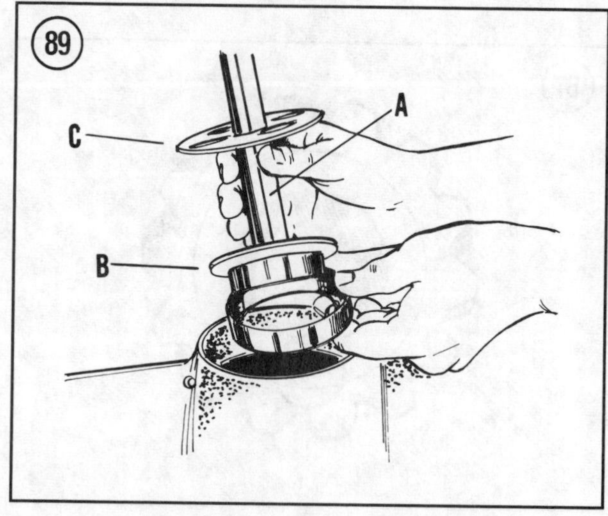

d. Cushion the leading edge of the gearcase with a wooden block. Using a mallet, drive the bearing into the gearcase until it is seated in the drive shaft bore.

e. Remove the tool from the gearcase. Inspect the bearing and make sure that shim(s) are not displaced or damaged and that the bearing is fully seated.

Drive shaft rolling torque verification

This procedure covers propshaft gear and drive shaft component installation and drive shaft rolling torque adjustment. If the gear pattern (optional) is going to be checked, apply marking compound to the gear teeth and use the old pinion nut. If the gear pattern is not going to be verified, do not apply gear marking compound to the gear teeth. Additionally, apply Loctite 271 threadlocking compound to a *new* pinion nut.

1. Verify that all 19 rollers are still present in the lower drive shaft (pinion) bearing. If not, liberally apply OMC Needle Bearing Assembly Grease or equivalent (**Table 5**) to any loose rollers and reinstall them.

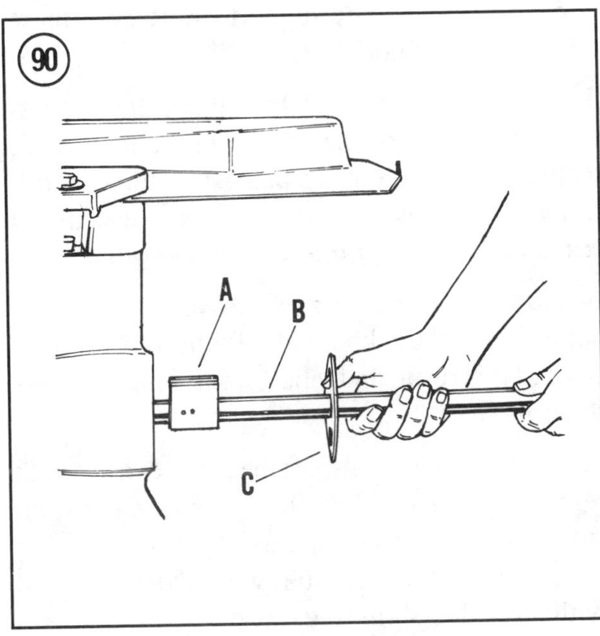

NOTE

If the gear pattern verification (optional) is to be performed, apply GM Gear Marking Compound (available at any GM automotive dealership) to at least 3 teeth of the propshaft gear before performing Step 2.

2. Lubricate the propshaft gear and bearing and set it into the propshaft bore. Seat the roller bearing of the gear to the bearing race.

3. Position the pinion gear in the propshaft bore. Carefully insert the drive shaft through the pinion bearing and engage the splines of the pinion gear.

CAUTION

*If the gear pattern verification (optional) is to be performed, install the original pinion nut without threadlocking adhesive. If the gear pattern verification is not going to be performed, install a new pinion nut and apply Loctite 271 threadlocking adhesive (**Table 5**) to the pinion nut threads in Step 4.*

4. Install the pinion nut and tighten it hand-tight.

5. Install the drive shaft large roller bearing race over the drive shaft and seat it against the large roller bearing. Lubricate the drive shaft bearing retainer and thread it into the drive shaft bore. Tighten the retainer hand-tight.

6. Assemble the following tools to hold the pinion nut. Thread nut holder part No. 3854864-0 (A, **Figure 90**) onto drive handle part No. 3850609-3 (B, **Figure 90**). Insert the tool into the propshaft bore and engage the propeller nut. Slide alignment plate part No. 3850613-5 (C, **Figure 90**) over the drive handle and into the propshaft bore.

7. Torque the pinion nut to 203-217 N•m (150-160 ft.-lb.) by turning the drive shaft clockwise with spline socket part No. 3850598-8 and an appropriate torque wrench. Remove the pinion nut holding tools when finished.

8. Position the gearcase so the propshaft bore is pointing straight up. The propshaft gear must be

held away from the pinion gear (by gravity) to get an accurate rolling torque reading. Set the drive shaft bearing rolling torque as follows:

a. Attach a torque wrench capable of accurately reading 0.23-0.45 N•m (2-4 in.-lb.) to spline socket part No. 3850598-8 with the appropriate adapter(s).
b. Attach the torque wrench to the drive shaft.
c. Turn the drive shaft several turns counterclockwise to seat the bearings. Slow the rotational speed down to approximately 3 rpm. Note the torque wrench reading.
d. If the reading is below specification 0.23-0.45 N•m (2-4 in.-lb.), tighten the drive shaft bearing retainer slightly with spanner wrench part No. 3850601-0. Repeat substep c.
e. If the reading is above specification 0.23-0.45 N•m (2-4 in.-lb.), loosen the drive shaft bearing retainer slightly with spanner wrench part No. 3850601-0. Repeat substep c.
f. Do not proceed until the rolling torque is 0.23-0.45 N•m (2-4 in.-lb.) at approximately 3 rpm. Remove the tools when finished. Do not disturb the bearing retainer position.

Initial propshaft bearing carrier shimming

The purpose of this procedure is to minimize the number of times the propshaft bearing carrier is installed and removed while trying to determine the proper shim ring for the bearing carrier. The shim ring determines the overall rolling torque of the gearcase. If the shim ring is too small, the overall rolling torque will be too high. If the shim ring is too large, the overall rolling torque will be too low.

This procedure will establish a base position of the propshaft bearing carrier. The recorded measurement will be used during the *Final Assembly and overall rolling torque verification* procedure. The shim ring used in this procedure is a special tool and must measure 4.06 mm (.0160 in.) thick. Do not use the original shim ring from your gearcase.

NOTE
*The propeller shaft and carrier O-ring are **not** installed for this procedure.*

1. Locate shim ring tool part No. 3850626-7. Measure the ring and verify that it is 4.06 mm (0.160 in.) thick. Secure the shim ring to the propshaft bearing carrier flange with OMC Needle Bearing Grease or equivalent (**Table 5**). Liberally lubricate the threads and flange of the propshaft bearing carrier with gear lubricant.

2. Install the propshaft bearing carrier into the gearcase bore. Thread the carrier as far as possible by hand. Be careful not to dislodge the shim ring from the propshaft bearing carrier.

3. Tighten the propshaft bearing carrier to 108.5 N•m (80 ft.-lb.) with remover/installer part No. 3850707-5. Attach the torque wrench at a 90° angle to the tool.

4. Measure the distance from the gearcase torpedo trailing edge to the rear of the propshaft bearing carrier flange. Take 3 measurements, one at each carrier flange support rib. Record these readings. See **Figure 91**.

5. Average the readings by adding the 3 measurements together, then dividing the total by 3. Round your result to the nearest hundredth millimeter or thousandth of an inch. Record this result and label it *initial carrier measurement.*

6. Add the *initial carrier measurement* to the shim ring tool thickness of 4.06 mm (0.160 in.). Record this result and label it *total initial carrier measurement.*

7. Remove the propshaft bearing carrier with remover part No. 3850707-5. Remove the shim ring tool part No. 3850626-7 from the bearing carrier and put it away so it will not be confused with any other shim ring.

Gear lash verification

Gear lash is a clearance measurement between 2 gears. If too much clearance is present between the gears, the strength of the gears is reduced and the gears create more gear whine than normal. If too little clearance is present between the gears, there will be no room for heat expansion and lubricant film causing the gears to be quickly damaged. The purpose of this procedure is to verify the correct positioning of the pinion and propshaft gears in the gearcase housing. The position of the gearcase is not important for this procedure. The propshaft bearing carrier will be installed without a shim ring and without the O-ring. The size of the shim ring required will be determined during *Final Assembly*.

1. Lubricate the propeller shaft roller bearing and drive splines. Install the propeller shaft into the propshaft bore and engage it to the propshaft gear splines.
2. Liberally lubricate the threads and flange of the propshaft bearing carrier with gear lubricant.
3. Install the propshaft bearing carrier into the gearcase bore *without* a shim ring and *without* the O-ring. Thread the carrier as far as possible by hand.

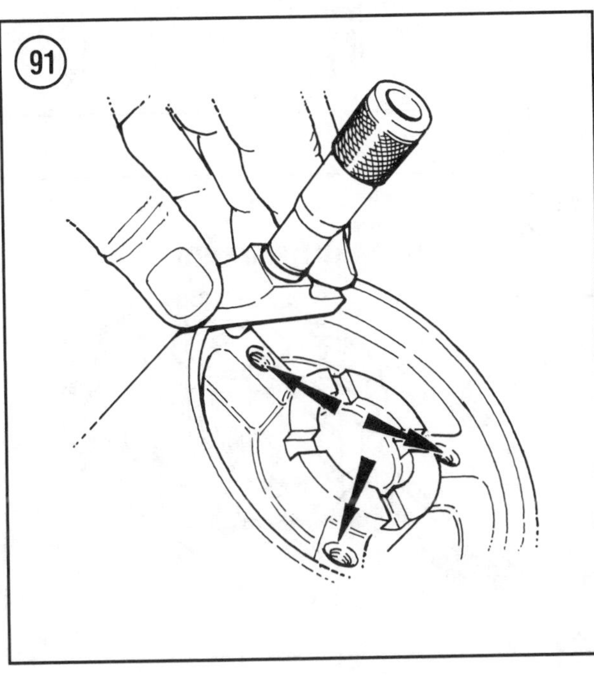

4. Set the overall rolling torque for this procedure as follows:
   a. Attach a torque wrench capable of reading 1.13-3.39 N•m (10-30 in.-lb.) accurately to spline socket part No. 3850598-8 with the appropriate adapter(s).
   b. Attach the torque wrench to the drive shaft.
   c. Turn the drive shaft several turns counterclockwise to seat the bearings. Slow the rotational speed down to approximately 3 rpm. Note the torque wrench reading.

   NOTE

   The specified overall rolling torque varies depending on the drive unit gear ratio. Refer to ***Table 2*** *for the overall rolling torque for your gearcase. Refer to Chapter Twelve if you do not know what gear ratio your unit is.*

   d. If the reading is below specification (**Table 2**), tighten the propshaft bearing carrier slightly with remover/installer part No. 380707-5. Repeat substep c.
   e. If the reading is above specification (**Table 2**), loosen the propshaft bearing carrier slightly with remover/installer part No. 3850707-5. Repeat substep c.
   f. Do not proceed until the rolling torque is within specification for your gear ratio as listed in **Table 2**, when measured at approximately 3 rpm. Remove the tools when finished. Do not disturb the propshaft bearing carrier position.
5. Attach gear lash extension tool part No 3850602-8 (A, **Figure 92**) to the drive shaft splines. The tool is designed to wedge onto the shaft with hand pressure. *Do not* install the tool with a hammer.
6. Securely attach a dial indicator to the gearcase. Position the dial indicator plunger against the machined groove (B, **Figure 92**) on the extension tool arm. The plunger must be at a 90° angle to the extension tool arm. The plunger

must extend perfectly horizontal to the extension arm. See **Figure 92**.

7. Zero the indicator and check the gear lash by lightly rotating the drive shaft back and forth while holding the propshaft stationary. Record the reading.

8. Lift the dial indicator and turn the drive shaft 1/2 turn. Reposition the extension tool and Repeat Steps 6-7 to confirm your first reading.

9. Gear lash should be 0.13-0.30 mm (0.005-0.012 in.). If the reading is within specification, proceed to *Gear pattern verification* or *Final Assembly and overall rolling torque verification* as desired. Both procedures are located later in this chapter.

NOTE

If the gear lash requires correction, change approximately 0.03 mm (0.001 in.) of shims for every 0.03 mm (0.001 in.) of correction desired. Move both gears toward each other to decrease gear lash and move both gears away from each other to increase gear lash. Change 1/2 of the total correction desired at the pinion gear and the other 1/2 of the correction at the propshaft gear. Use 0.20-0.23 mm (0.008-0.009 in.), as the desired target gear lash for your calculations. Always change equal amounts of shims at both locations.

10. If the gear lash is above specification, add shims to the propshaft gear race and subtract shims from the drive shaft race as follows:

a. For example, if the gear lash measures 0.41 mm (0.016 in.) target 0.20 mm (0.008 in.), as the desired gear lash.

b. This would be a total change of 0.20 mm (0.008 in.) shims, (0.41 - 0.20 = 0.21 mm) or (0.016 - 0.008 = 0.008 in.).

c. Divide this total change by 2 to get the actual amount of change at each location. Continuing the example, 0.21 mm (0.008 in.) total change divided by 2 equals 0.105 mm (0.004 in.) change at each location.

d. In this example add 0.105 mm (0.004 in.) shims to the propshaft race and subtract 0.105 mm (0.004 in.) from the drive shaft race.

11. If the gear lash is below specification, subtract shims from the propshaft gear race and add shims to the drive shaft race as follows:

a. For example, if the gear lash measures 0.08 mm (0.003 in.) target 0.23 mm (0.009 in.), as the desired gear lash.

b. This would be a total change of 0.15 mm (0.006 in.) shims, (0.23 - 0.08 = 0.15 mm) or (0.009 - 0.003 = 0.006 in.).

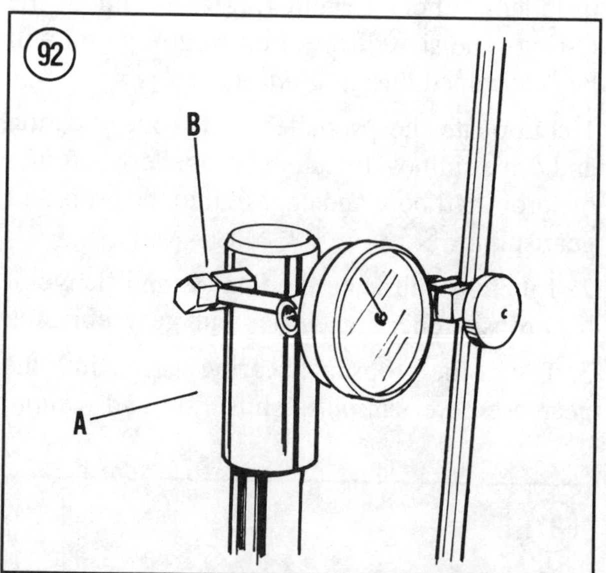

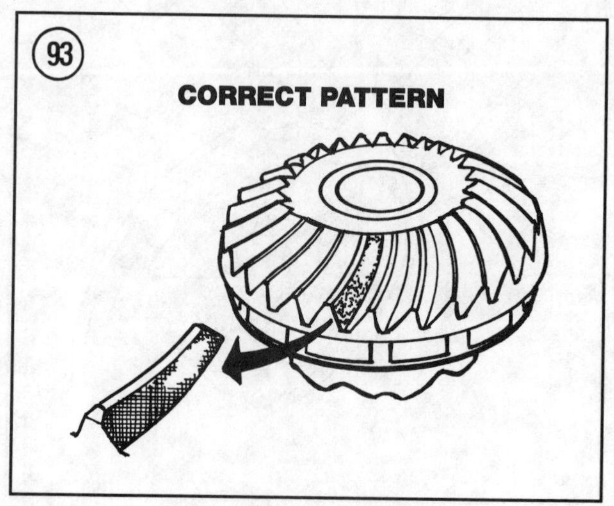

c. Divide this total change by 2 to get the actual amount of change at each location. Continuing the example, 0.15 mm (0.006 in.) total change divided by 2 equals 0.075 mm (0.003 in.) change at each location.

d. In this example subtract 0.075 mm (0.003 in.) shims from the propshaft race and add 0.075 mm (0.003 in.) to the drive shaft race.

12. Disassemble the gearcase as necessary and change the shims as calculated. Reset rolling torque as specified and recheck gear lash as described in this section.

13. Do not proceed until gear lash is confirmed at 0.13-0.30 mm (0.005-0.012 in.). Remove the dial indicator when finished.

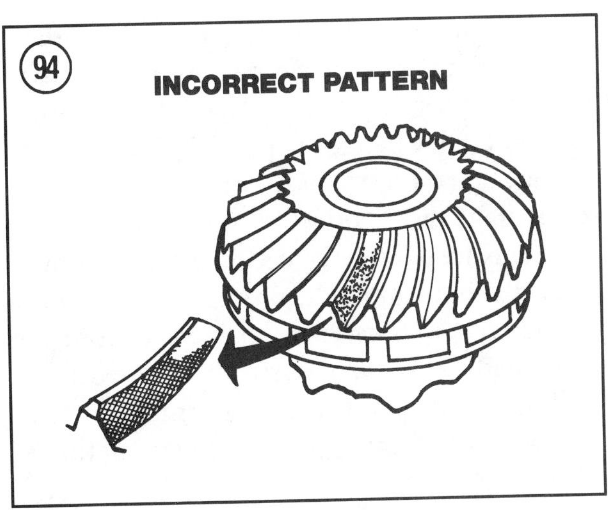
94
INCORRECT PATTERN

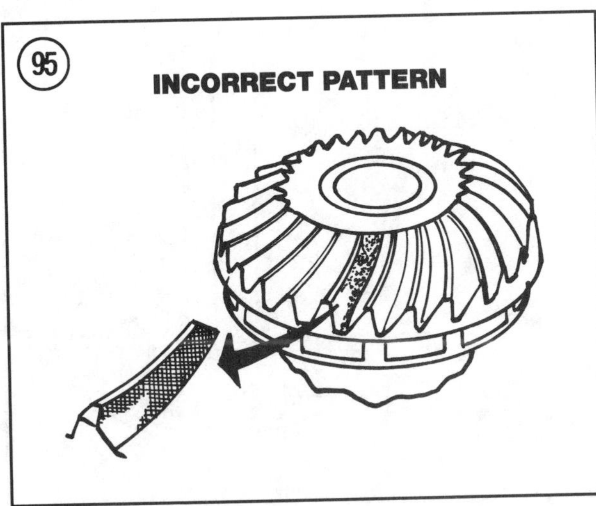
95
INCORRECT PATTERN

CAUTION

*Do NOT disturb the propshaft bearing carrier position if going directly to **Final Assembly and Overall Rolling Torque Verification (SX Models)**.*

Gear pattern verification

Once gear lash has been verified, check the gear contact pattern as follows (if so desired).

1. Install the spline socket part No. 3850598-8 to the drive shaft splines. Attach a breaker bar with the appropriate adapters.

NOTE

*The gears must be loaded to produce a contact pattern. A simple clamping brake can be fabricated from two, 2 × 4 pieces of wood approximately 457 mm (18 in.) long. Hinge the boards together so they can be folded upon each other, pinching the propeller shaft between them (like a nut cracker). See **Figure 49** for reference.*

2. Place an appropriate clamping brake over the propshaft. Apply clamping pressure to the propeller shaft to resist rotation and load the gear. Rotate the drive shaft with a breaker bar 6-8 revolutions in each direction.

3. Disassemble the gearcase sufficiently to examine the propshaft gear and its gear contact pattern.

4. Compare the pattern on the propshaft gear with the pattern shown at **Figure 93**. The pattern should be located completely on the gear tooth with a slight bias toward the inner diameter of the gear tooth.

5. If the pattern is located too close to the gear inner diameter or runs off the inner diameter (**Figure 94**), add equal amounts of shims (approximately 0.10 mm [0.004 in.]) to both the propshaft gear race and the drive shaft race. Reassemble the gearcase, recheck gear lash and repeat the gear pattern verification.

6. If the pattern is located too close to the gear outer diameter or runs off the outer diameter (**Figure 95**), subtract equal amounts of shims

(approximately 0.10 mm [0.004 in.]) from the propshaft gear race and the drive shaft race. Reassemble the gearcase, recheck gear lash and repeat the gear pattern verification.

7. Do not proceed until rolling torque, gear lash and gear pattern are within specification.

CAUTION
If the contact pattern must be corrected, rolling torque and gear backlash must again be verified after the pattern correction, before continuing with ***Final assembly.***

8. Once gear pattern has been verified, perform the following:

a. Disassemble the gearcase as necessary to remove all gear marking compound from the gear teeth and discard the original pinion nut. Do not remove any pressed in bearings or races.

b. Reassemble the gearcase to the point described in *Gear lash verification*. A new pinion nut coated with Loctite 271 threadlocking adhesive must be used.

c. The propshaft bearing carrier must again be installed *without* a shim ring and O-ring. The overall rolling torque must be initially set as described in *Gear lash verification*.

d. Once rolling torque is set, the propshaft bearing carrier must not be disturbed until the carrier position has been measured as described in *Final Assembly and Overall Rolling Torque Verification (SX Models)*.

Final Assembly and Overall Rolling Torque Verification (SX Models)

A part of this procedure determines the correct thickness of the propshaft bearing carrier shim ring. The shim ring controls the gearcase overall rolling torque by controlling the position of the rear propshaft roller bearing race. Remember that drive shaft rolling torque was previously set by tightening the drive shaft bearing retainer.

To determine the correct propshaft bearing carrier shim ring and make the final assembly of the gearcase, proceed as follows.

CAUTION
*At this point there should not be any gear marking compound present on the gear teeth. The pinion gear must be secured with a new pinion nut, sealed with Loctite 271 threadlocking adhesive (**Table 5**) and torqued to specification (**Table 2**).*

NOTE
The propshaft bearing carrier must be installed as described in Steps 1-4 of ***Gear lash verification***.

1. Measure the distance from the gearcase torpedo trailing edge to the rear of the propshaft bearing carrier flange. Take 3 measurements, one at each carrier flange support rib. Record these readings. See **Figure 96**.

2. Average the readings by adding the 3 measurements together, then dividing the total by 3. Round your result to the nearest hundredth millimeter or thousandth of an inch. Record this result and label it *final carrier measurement*.

3. Subtract the *final carrier measurement* from the *total initial carrier measurement* determined

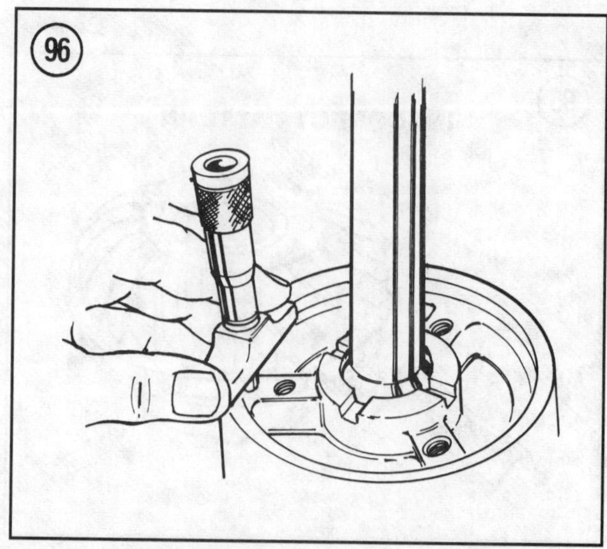

previously. Record this result and label it *propshaft bearing carrier calculated shim ring*.

4. Remove the propshaft bearing carrier with remover part No. 3850707-5.

5. Select and measure the shim ring that comes closest to your calculated dimension. Shim rings come in 15 sizes ranging from 2.44 mm (0.096 in.) to 3.15 mm (0.124 in.).

6. Lubricate a new carrier O-ring and install it into the bearing carrier groove.

7. Grease the predetermined shim ring with OMC Needle Bearing Grease or equivalent (**Table 5**) and install it to the carrier shoulder.

8. Install the propshaft bearing carrier being careful not to dislodge the shim ring or pinch the carrier O-ring. Tighten the carrier as far as possible by hand. The O-ring will offer substantial resistance.

9. With the aid of an assistant, tighten the propshaft bearing carrier to 271-305 N•m (200-225 ft.-lb.) with remover/installer part No. 3850707-5. Attach the torque wrench at a 90° angle to the tool. See **Figure 97**.

10. Verify the overall rolling torque as follows:

  a. Attach a torque wrench capable of reading 1.13-3.39 N•m (10-30 in.-lb.) accurately to spline socket part No. 3850598-8 with the appropriate adapter(s).

  b. Attach the torque wrench to the drive shaft.

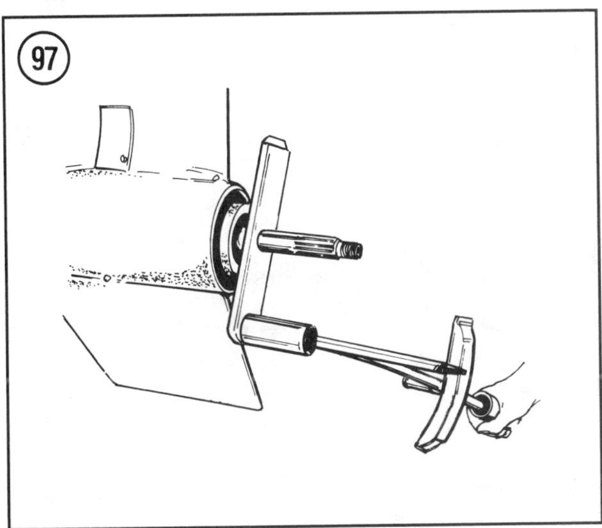

  c. Turn the drive shaft several turns counterclockwise to seat the bearings. Slow the rotational speed down to approximately 3 rpm. Note the torque wrench reading.

NOTE

*The specified overall rolling torque varies depending on the drive unit gear ratio. Refer to **Table 2** for the overall rolling torque for your gearcase. Refer to Chapter Twelve if you do not know what gear ratio your unit is.*

  d. If the reading is below specification (**Table 2**), remove the propshaft bearing carrier and install the next size *smaller* shim ring. Reassemble and repeat substep c.

  e. If the reading is above specification (**Table 2**), remove the propshaft bearing carrier and install the next size *larger* shim ring. Reassemble and repeat substep c.

  f. Do not proceed until the rolling torque is within specification for your gear ratio as listed in **Table 2**, when measured at approximately 3 rpm. Remove the tools when finished and continue final assembly.

NOTE

Be careful not to damage the propshaft bearing carrier by over-tightening the setscrew in the next step.

11. Install the propshaft bearing carrier setscrew located on the port, aft, upper portion of the gearcase torpedo. Coat the screw with Loctite 271 threadlocking adhesive (**Table 5**) and tighten the screw to 4.8-6.4 N•m (42-60 in.-lb.). A T-27 Torx bit is required to torque the screw.

12. Use installer part No. 3850603-6 or a set of mechanical fingers to position the retainer and screw. The retainer screw bore angles up slightly toward the gearcase deck. Make sure the retainer is positioned to allow the screw to angle upwards. Coat threads of the screw with Volvo White Sealing Compound or equivalent (**Table 5**), then install and tighten the screw to 27-34 N•m (20-25 ft.-lb.) torque. This procedure will

usually require 1/4 in. drive tools, depending on the tool manufacturer. See **Figure 98**.

13. Assemble the propshaft anode screw, bracket, wave washer and anode. Coat the threads of the anode screw with Volvo White Sealing Compound or equivalent (**Table 5**). Match the curve of the anode to the curve of the opening in the propshaft bearing carrier. Install the anode in the lowest possible carrier opening. Tighten the anode screw hand-tight (A, **Figure 99**).

14. Coat the threads of the 2 anode bracket screws with sealing compound and install the screws and washers to the propshaft bearing carrier. Tighten both screws to 16-19 N•m (144-168 in.-lb.). A T-40 Torx bit is required to torque these screws (B, **Figure 99**).

15. Torque the anode screw to 6.8-9.5 N•m (60-84 in.-lb.). A T-30 Torx bit is required to torque the screw (A, **Figure 99**).

16. Position the anode at the front of the gearcase deck. Secure the anode to the gearcase with 2 screws and lock washers. Tighten the anode screws to 6.8-9.5 N•m (60-84 in.-lb.).

17. *SX-S models*—Coat the sealing ribs of a new water tube guide with OMC Type M adhesive or equivalent (**Table 5**). See **Figure 100**. Position the guide on the gearcase deck. Coat the guide's 4 screws with Volvo White Sealing Compound or equivalent (**Table 5**). Install and evenly tighten the 4 screws to 14-16 N•m (120-144 in.-lb.).

18. Install the intermediate drive shaft coupler to the vertical drive shaft with the groove end facing up (away from the lower gearcase).

19. *Models equipped with a trim tab*—Coat the trim tab screw threads with Volvo White Sealing Compound or equivalent (**Table 5**). Position the trim tab to the gearcase and align the mark made on disassembly. Install and tighten the screw to 19-22 N•m (14-16 ft.-lb.).

20. Install the lower gearcase to the upper gearcase as described previously in this chapter. Do not fill the drive unit with lubricant until the drive unit has passed the pressure and vacuum tests as described under *Pressure and vacuum tests*, in this chapter.

Assembly (DP-S Models)

For maximum durability and quiet running, all of the gears must be properly located in the gearcase through shimming procedures. When the gears are properly located, the correct backlash and gear contact pattern will be observed.

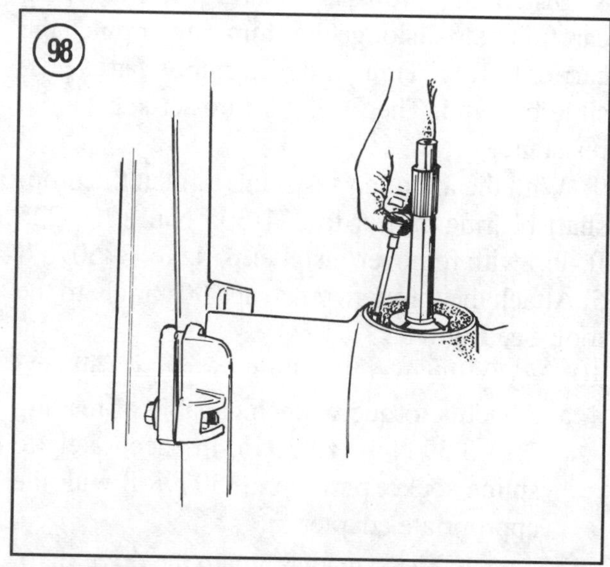

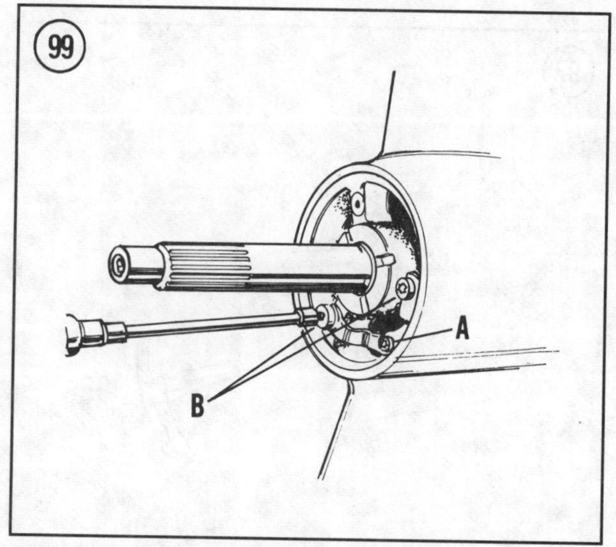

Additionally, the tapered bearings in the gearcase must be properly tensioned or *preloaded*. Preload refers to the tension applied to hold a tapered roller bearing in its cup. Insufficient preload will allow the bearing to move in relation to the bearing cup. Any movement of the bearing from its cup will result in premature bearing and gear failure. Excessive preload will cause the bearings to overheat and fail. Correct preload is determined by measuring the torque required to rotate the shafts and gears. This is called *rolling torque*.

During assembly procedures, lubricate all components with Volvo DuraPlus GL5 Synthetic Gear Lube (**Table 6**). Do not make any *dry* assemblies.

New seals and O-rings must not be installed until the gear lash and tube gear pattern have been verified. Seal and O-ring installation is covered under *Final Assembly (DP-S Models)*.

Figure 101 is an exploded view of a DP-S lower gearcase.

Begin reassembly by first installing new bearings to replace any that were removed. The small roller bearing on the inner propshaft, the lower drive shaft bearing race and the front driven gear race cannot be installed until the shims have been selected. Installation of these bearings will be covered later in this section.

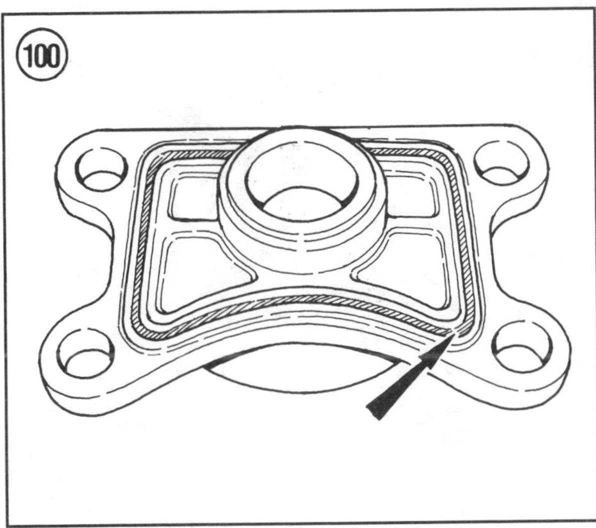

Pinion bearing installation

If the lower drive shaft (pinion) bearing was removed from the gearcase, install a new pinion bearing as follows.

1. Lubricate a new pinion bearing and place it on bearing installer part No. 3855868-0 with the lettered side of the bearing facing the installer. Place the tool and bearing into the lower drive shaft bore via the propshaft bore. The lettered side of the pinion bearing must face down, when installed.
2. Insert the threaded rod part No. 3855860-7 through the drive shaft bore and engage the bearing installer. Thread the bearing installer securely onto the threaded rod.
3. Slide spacer part No. 3855867-2 over the threaded rod and into the drive shaft bore.
4. Install guide plate part No. 3850619-2 over the threaded rod and pilot the guide plate into the drive shaft bore. Install the flat washer and nut over the threaded rod and against the guide plate.
5. Tighten the nut to pull the bearing into position. Stop tightening the nut as soon as the spacer binds between the bearing installer and guide plate.
6. Remove the tools and inspect the bearing.

Drive shaft bearing installation

If the bearings or bearing sleeve were removed from the drive shaft, install new components as follows.

1. Lightly coat the sleeve area of the drive shaft with Loctite 271 threadlocking adhesive. Place the bearing sleeve over the pinion nut end of the drive shaft. Place sleeve installer part No. 3855869-8 over the sleeve.
2. Place the drive shaft assembly into a press. Protect the input splines with wood, plastic or an aluminum plate.
3. Press against the sleeve installer until the sleeve is seated on the drive shaft.

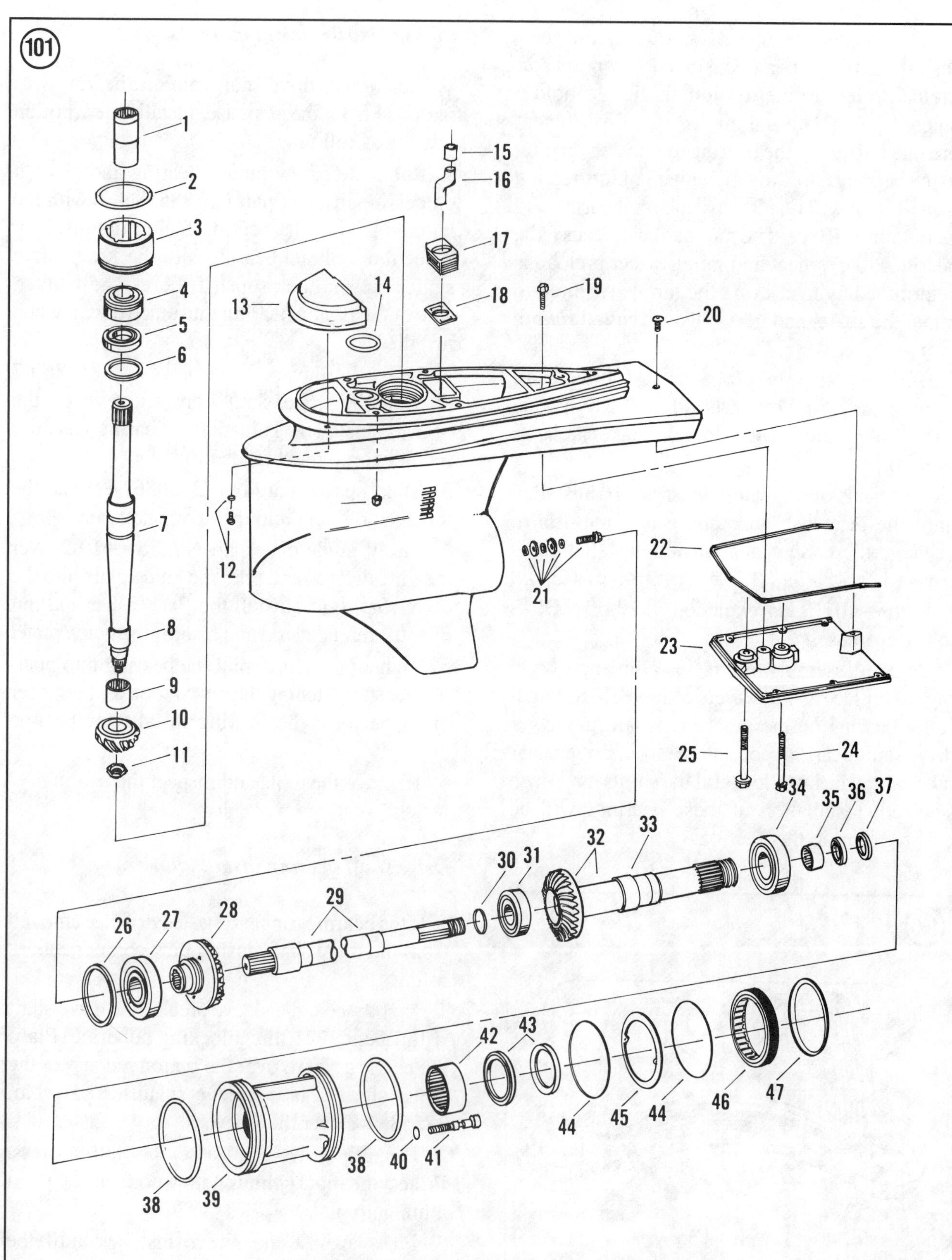
101
1
2
3
4
5
6
7
8
9
10
11
12
13
14
15
16
17
18
19
20
21
22
23
24
25
26
27
28
29
30
31
32
33
34
35
36
37
38
39
40
41
42
43
44
45
44
46
47
38

LOWER GEARCASE
(DP-S MODELS)

1. Intermediate drive shaft coupler
2. Drive shaft O-ring
3. Drive shaft bearing retainer
4. Larger tapered roller bearing
5. Small tapered roller bearing
6. Shim (pinion gear location)
7. Vertical drive shaft
8. Bearing sleeve
9. Lower drive shaft (pinion) bearing
10. Pinion gear
11. Pinion nut
12. Anode screw and washer
13. Anode
14. O-ring
15. Water tube grommet (upper gearcase)
16. Water tube
17. Water tube grommet (lower gearcase)
18. Plastic water tube guide
19. Exhaust plate screw (hex head)
20. Exhaust plate screw (Torx head)
21. Magnet assembly
22. Exhaust plate seal
23. Exhaust plate
24. Screw
25. Screw
26. Shim (propshaft gear location)
27. Tapered roller bearing
28. Propshaft gear
29. Inner propshaft
30. Shim (aft driven gear position)
31. Tapered roller bearing
32. Aft driven (tube) gear
33. Bearing sleeve
34. Tapered roller bearing
35. Needle bearing
36. Seal (double-lip, single case)
37. Seal (single-lip)
38. O-ring
39. Propshaft bearing carrier
40. O-ring (drain/fill plug)
41. Drain/fill plug
42. Needle bearing
43. Seals
44. O-ring
45. Tabbed retaining washer
46. Retaining ring
47. O-ring

4. Lubricate a new small roller bearing and place it over the drive shaft input splines with the rollers facing the pinion gear end of the drive shaft. Place bearing installer part No. 3850617-6 over the drive shaft and bearing with the raised edge of the tool against the bearing.
5. Place sleeve installer part No. 3855869-8 over the drive shaft or thread an old pinion nut onto the drive shaft to protect the threads. Place the drive shaft assembly into a press. Support the bearing installer with pressing plates.
6. Press against the sleeve installer or pinion nut until the bearing is seated against the drive shaft shoulder.
7. Lubricate a new large tapered roller bearing and place it over the input splines with the rollers facing up away from the small bearing. Place bearing installer part No. 3850617-6 over the drive shaft and bearing with the raised edge of the tool against the bearing.
8. Place the drive shaft assembly into a press. Support the bearing installer with pressing plates.
9. Press against the sleeve installer or the pinion nut until the bearing is seated against the small roller bearing.
10. Remove the sleeve installer or pinion nut and the bearing installer from the drive shaft.

Tube gear bearing installation

If the tube gear large tapered roller bearing, bearing sleeve, small bearing race or inner needle bearing were removed, install new components as follows.

1. Install a new inner needle bearing by first lubricating the bearing and placing it into the propeller end of the tube gear with the numbered side of the bearing facing out.
2. Set the tube gear into a press with the gear facing down. Protect the gear teeth with wood, plastic or an aluminum plate. Place the small end of bearing installer part No. 3855928-2 against the needle bearing.

3. Press against the installer until the tool seats against the tube gear. Remove the installer.
4. Lubricate the large roller bearing and place it over the tube gear splines with the rollers facing up. Place bearing installer part No. 3855866-4 over the tube gear splines and against the bearing.
5. Press against the installer until the bearing seats against the gear. Remove the installer.
6. Coat the inner diameter of a new bearing sleeve with Loctite 271 threadlocking adhesive and place the sleeve over the tube gear splines. Place bearing installer part No. 3855866-4 over the tube gear splines and against the sleeve.
7. Press against the installer until the tool seats against the large tapered roller bearing. Leave the installer on the tube gear.
8. Invert the tube gear and bearing installer so that the gear is facing up and the bearing installer is against the press support plate.
9. Lubricate a new small roller bearing race and place it into the face of the tube gear with the tapered side facing up. Place bearing installer part No. 3855865-6 against the bearing race.
10. Press against the installer until the bearing race is seated in the tube gear bearing bore. Remove all tools and the tube gear from the press.

Propshaft bearing carrier assembly

If the inner needle bearing or large tapered roller bearing race were removed, install new components as follows.

1. Place support base part No. 3855926-6 in a press with the recessed end facing up.
2. Set the propshaft bearing carrier into the support with the propeller end facing up.
3 Lubricate a new needle bearing and set it into the propshaft bearing carrier with the lettered side of the bearing facing up.
4. Place the large end of bearing installer part No. 3855925-8 into the needle bearing.
5. Press against the installer until the tool seats against the bearing carrier. Remove the tool when finished.
6. Invert the propshaft carrier so that the large opening is facing up. Set the carrier onto the support base.
7. Lubricate a new large roller bearing race and set it into the propshaft bearing carrier with the taper facing up (out). Place bearing installer part No. 3855864-9 into the bearing race.
8. Press against the installer until the race is seated in the bearing carrier. Remove the tools when finished.

Front driven gear bearing installation

1. To install a new front driven gear roller bearing, begin by lubricating a new roller bearing. Place the bearing over the gear hub with the rollers facing away from the gear.
2. Place the gear assembly into a press. Protect the gear teeth with wood, plastic or an aluminum plate. Place bearing installer 3855861-5 over the bearing.
3. Press against the installer until the bearing is seated against the gear.

Lower Gearcase Shimming Procedures (DP-S Models)

To determine the correct amount of shims to position the gears and bearings properly, keep in mind that the numbers stamped on the gears are correction numbers in thousandths of an inch. Nominal dimensions are fixed dimensions that are established by Volvo Penta during the design and manufacturing of the product. All fixed (nominal) dimensions are listed in **Table 2**.

Since the gears are stamped using U.S. standard units of measure, it is recommended that all calculations be performed in inches. Any conversions from U.S. standard to Metric should only be attempted on the final calculated result.

NOTE
All 3 gears are stamped with a correction number and a match number. The match number always starts with a T. All 3 gears have the same T number. It would be extremely rare for all 3 gears to have the same correction number. Do not confuse the T number with a + (positive) correction number.

The correct selection of shims and proper gearcase assembly will be confirmed by the gear lash and gear pattern verifications and the overall rolling torque check.

CAUTION
It cannot be stated strongly enough that you must clearly record and label all of your shimming calculations. Time spent calculating shim amounts is wasted if the results are not recorded and labeled.

Pinion gear shimming

To determine the proper shims to locate the pinion gear, proceed as follows.

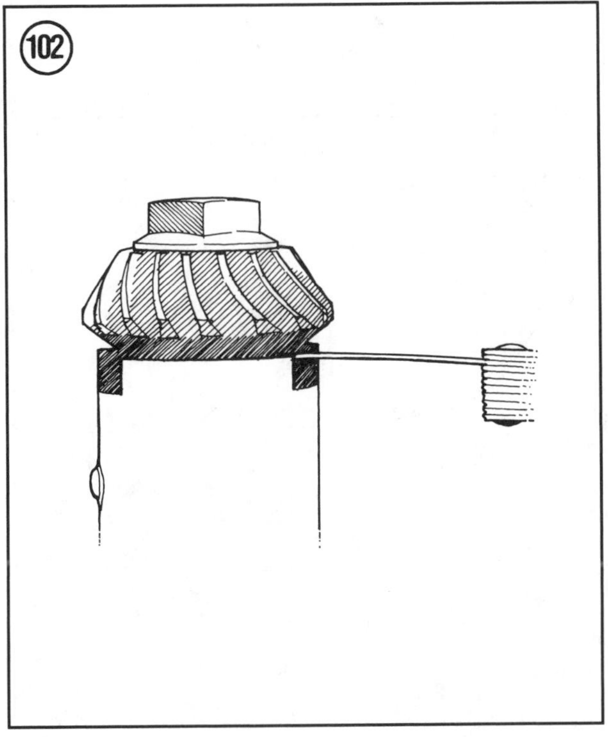

1. Securely clamp spline socket part No. 3850598-8 vertically in a vise. Insert the drive shaft into the spline socket making sure the splines engage fully.
2. Install the small tapered roller bearing race over the drive shaft and against the small roller bearing.
3. Install shim fixture part No. 3855870-6 over the drive shaft and seat it against the small bearing race with the slotted end of the tool facing up.
4. Install the pinion gear to the drive shaft. Install the original (used) nut. Tighten the nut to specification (**Table 4**). Record the exact torque figure used for final assembly.
5. Rotate the shim tool several turns to seat the small bearing.

NOTE
When the correct feeler gauge has been selected, a slight drag will be felt as the feeler gauge blade is moved between the measuring points. To verify, insert the next size larger blade and check for a noticeable increase in the drag. Then insert the next size smaller blade and check for the absence of drag.

6. Use a feeler gauge to measure the distance between the shim tool and the pinion gear at each of the 3 slots. See **Figure 102**. It is normal for the measurements to vary slightly. Average the 3 readings by adding the 3 measurements to each other and dividing the result by 3. Round to the nearest thousandth of an inch. Record this result and label it *pinion gear average feeler gauge measurement*.

NOTE
It may be necessary to loosen the pinion nut 2 or 3 turns, hold the shim tool firmly in one hand, then strike the pinion nut with a plastic or brass hammer to break the pinion gear free of the drive shaft taper.

7. Remove the pinion nut, pinion gear, shim tool and small bearing race.

8. Locate the correction number stamped or etched on the pinion gear (**Figure 103**, typical). Record this figure as thousandths of an inch. For example, if +10 is etched on the gear, write it as +0.010 in. If -10 is etched on the gear, write it as -0.010 in.
9. Add or subtract (as indicated by the + or -) the etched number on the gear to the *pinion gear average feeler gauge measurement*. For example, the gear shown in **Figure 103** is +10. This would be 0.010 in. *plus* the pinion gear average feeler gauge measurement. Record this result and label it as *pinion gear shims*.
10. Select and measure the correct amount of shims determined by your calculations. Set these predetermined shims into the drive shaft small bearing bore in the lower gearcase.
11. Lubricate the small bearing race and set it on top of the shims in the drive shaft bore with the tapered side of the bearing facing up.
12. Assemble the bearing installer as follows:
    a. Assemble the guide plate part No. 3850619-2 over the large bolt part No. 3850623-4 so the large diameter of the plate is facing the bolt head.
    b. Install bearing installer part No. 3850621-8 onto the bolt threads so the beveled edge is facing away from the bolt head.
    c. Insert the tool assembly into the drive shaft bore and engage the installer into the bearing race and the guide plate into the gearcase bore.
    d. Using a mallet, drive the bearing into the gearcase until it is seated in the drive shaft bore.
    e. Remove the tool from the gearcase. Inspect the bearing and make sure that shim(s) are not displaced or damaged and that the bearing is fully seated.

Front driven gear shimming

A fixed (nominal) dimension of 0.055 in. is used in this process. To determine the proper shims to locate the propshaft gear, proceed as follows.

1. Place the propshaft gear, with the teeth facing down, onto a clean workbench. Install the bearing race (A, **Figure 104**) over the propshaft gear roller bearing and rotate the race several turns to align the bearing.
2. Position the shim fixture part No. 3850600-2 (B, **Figure 104**) on top of the bearing race, with its recessed side facing the bearing.
3. Measure the distance from the top surface of the shim fixture to the end of the gear stub shaft (**Figure 104**). Record this reading. Subtract the thickness of the shim fixture (0.500 in.) from

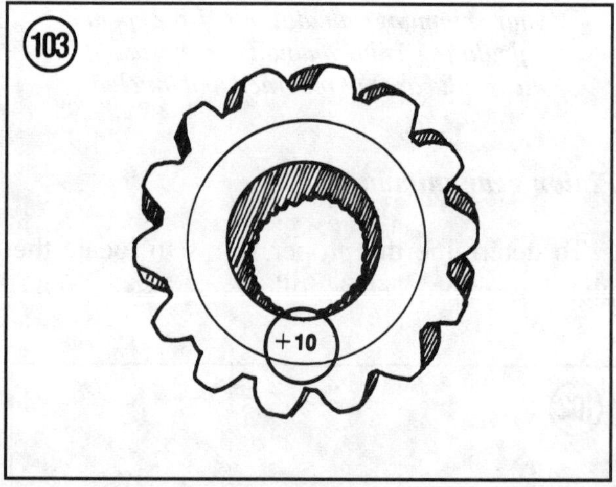

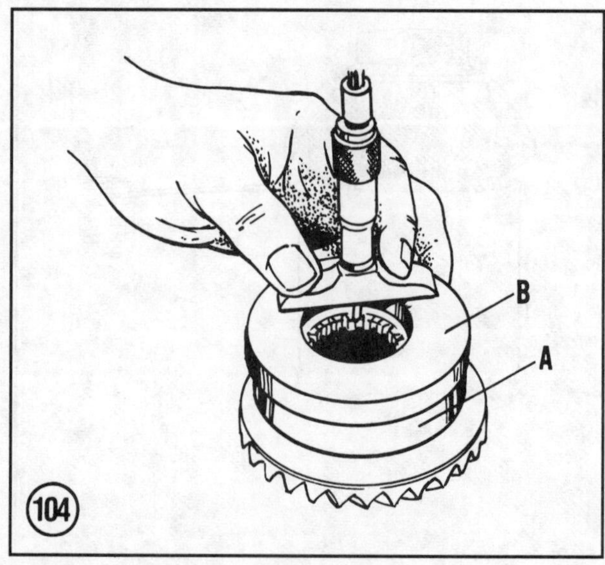

your reading. For example, if the reading is 0.544 in., subtract 0.500 in. from 0.544 in. which equals 0.044 in., (0.544 - 0.500 = 0.044). Record this result and label it *actual dimension*.

4. Locate the correction number stamped or etched on the propshaft gear (**Figure 105**, typical). Record this figure as thousandths of an inch. For example, if +5 is etched on the gear, write it as +0.005 in. If -5 is etched on the gear, write it as -0.005 in.

5. Add or subtract (as indicated by the + or -) the etched number on the gear to the *actual dimension*. For example, the gear shown in **Figure 105** is +5. This would be 0.005 in. *plus* the actual dimension. Following the example, add 0.005 in. (gear correction figure) to 0.044 in. (actual dimension), which equals 0.049 in., (0.005 + 0.044 = 0.049). Record this result and label it as *corrected dimension*.

6. Subtract the corrected dimension from the fixed (nominal) dimension of 0.055 in. To complete the example, subtract 0.049 in. (corrected dimension) from 0.055 in. (nominal dimension), which equals 0.006 in., (0.055 - 0.049 = 0.006). This result is the total amount (thickness) of shims to be installed under the propshaft gear bearing race. Record this result and label it *front driven gear shims*.

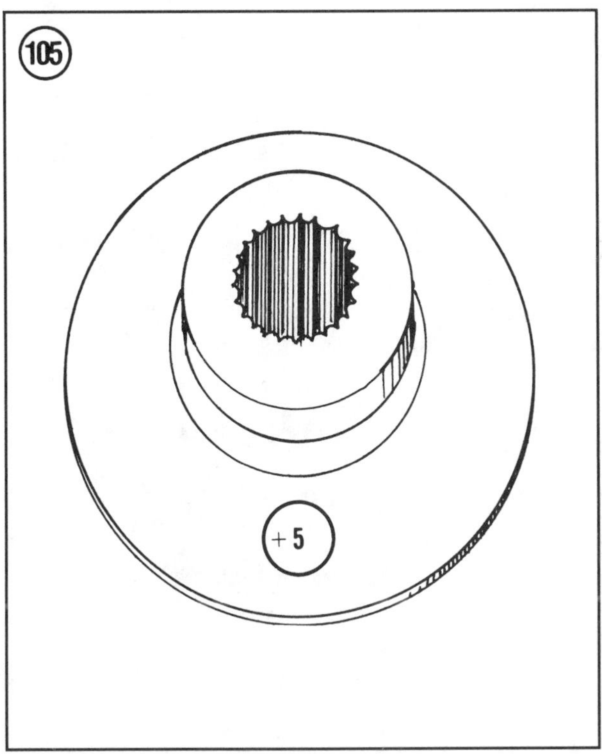

7. Select and measure the correct amount of shims determined by your calculations. Set these predetermined shims into the gearcase propshaft gear bearing bore.

Aft driven (tube) gear shimming

This procedure determines the shims to be installed under the small roller bearing on the inner propshaft. These shims set the location of the aft driven (tube) gear in the gearcase. Shim fixtures part No. 3855871-4 and part No. 3855872-2 are required for this procedure. Do not attempt to shim the tube gear without these shim fixtures.

1. Begin the shimming procedure by pressing the inner propshaft into the front driven gear assembly as follows:
   a. Place bearing installer part No. 3855861-5 in a press with the recessed side facing up.
   b. Set the front drive gear onto the installer with the gear teeth facing up.
   c. Thread an old propeller nut onto the inner propeller shaft. Lubricate the splines of the inner propshaft.
   d. Place the inner propshaft into the front driven gear and engage the splines.
   e. Press against the propeller nut until the propshaft shoulder is seated against the gear face.
   f. Remove the propeller nut and tools.

2. Place shim fixture part No. 3855872-2 onto a clean workbench. Set the front drive gear race into the fixture with the tapered surface facing up. The race should sit on the 3 feet at the bottom of the fixture bore.

3. Place the front driven gear and propshaft assembly into the shim fixture. Make sure the gear

roller bearing is seated in the bearing race. See **Figure 106**.

4. Slide shim fixture part No. 3855871-4 over the propeller shaft and seat it against the propshaft shoulder. See **Figure 107**.

5. Slide the inner propshaft small roller bearing over the propshaft with the rollers facing up and seat it against the shim fixture part No. 3855871-4.

6. Slide the tube gear assembly over the inner propshaft and seat the tube gear small bearing race against the inner propshaft small roller bearing.

7. Rotate the shafts several turns to seat the bearings. Press down on the tube shaft and tighten the 3 fixture setscrews to hold the tube gear centered and stabilized in the fixture.

NOTE

If the measurements in the next step display wide variations, loosen the 3 fixture setscrews, rotate the shafts and retighten the screws. Make sure the tube gear is as centered as possible in the fixture bore.

8. Measure the distance from the top surface of the large shim fixture to the machined ring located on the rear face of the tube gear. See **Figure 108**. Take a reading near each of the 3 setscrews. Average the readings by adding the measurements together and dividing the total by 3. Round the result to the nearest thousandth of an inch. Record this result and label it *initial tube gear dimension*.

9. Disassemble the shim fixtures and both propshafts.

10. Subtract the amount of *front driven gear shims* determined previously from the *initial tube gear dimension*. For example, if the initial tube dimension is 0.040 in., subtract 0.006 in. (front driven gear shim example) from 0.040 in. (initial tube dimension example), which equals 0.034 in., (0.040 - 0.006 = 0.034). Record this result and label it *corrected tube gear dimension*.

11. Locate the correction number stamped or etched on the tube shaft (**Figure 109**, typical). Record this figure as thousandths of an inch. For example, if +5 is etched on the gear, write it as +0.005 in. If -5 is etched on the gear, write it as -0.005 in.

12. Add or subtract (as indicated by the + or -) the etched number on the tube to the *corrected tube gear dimension*. For example, the gear shown in **Figure 109** is +5. This would be 0.005 in. *plus* the corrected dimension. Following the

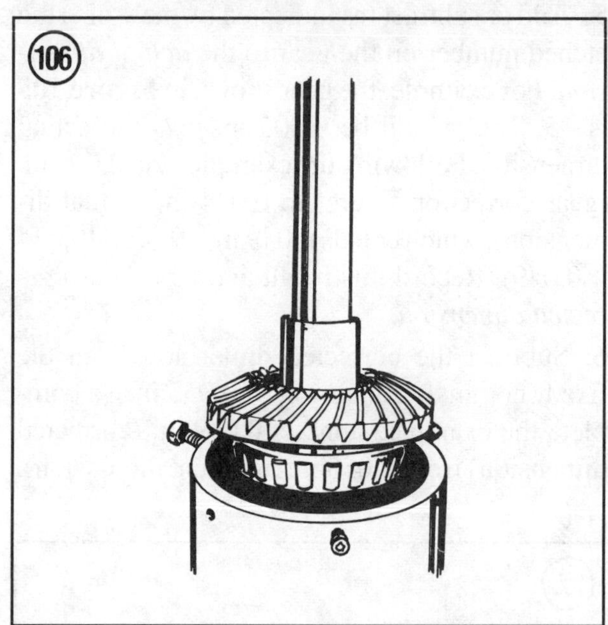

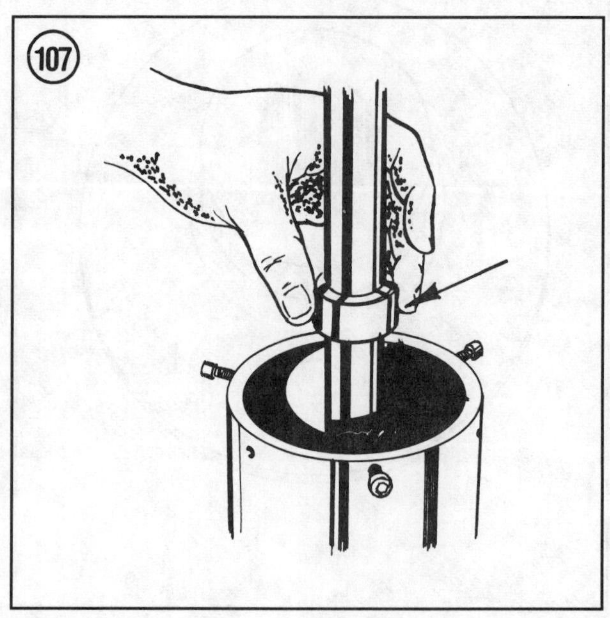

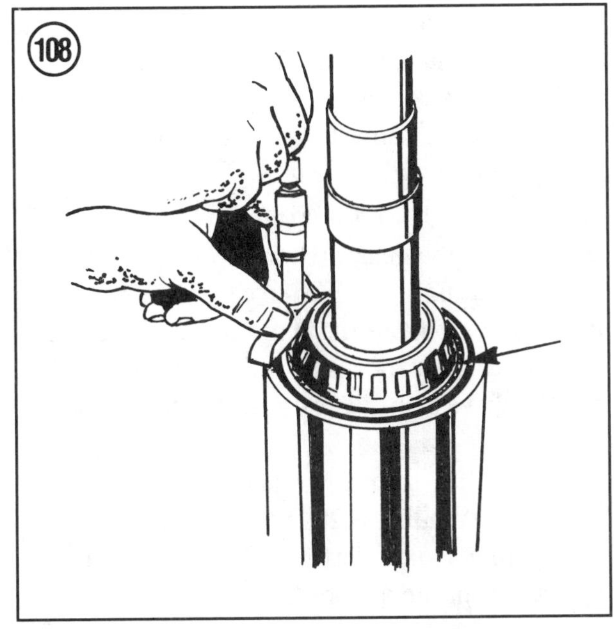

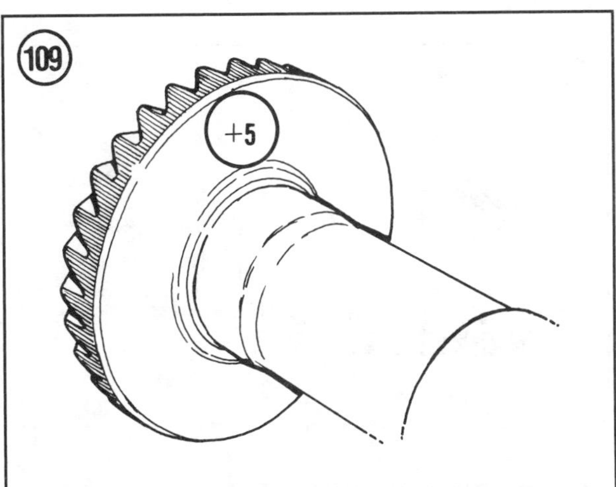

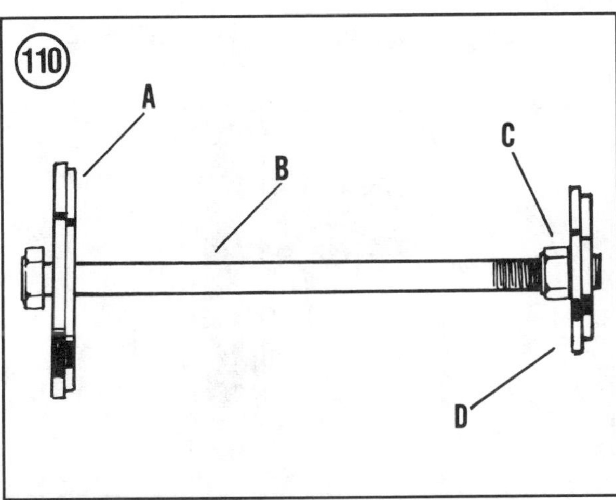

example, add 0.005 in. (gear correction figure) to 0.034 in. (corrected dimension), which equals 0.039 in., (0.005 + 0.034 = 0.039). Record this result and label it as *aft driven (tube gear shims)*.

13. Select and measure the correct amount of shims determined by your calculations. Set these predetermined shims with the inner propshaft roller bearing.

Drive shaft rolling torque verification

This procedure covers the magnet, front driven gear and inner propshaft and drive shaft installation and drive shaft rolling torque adjustment.

1. Assemble the 2 magnets and 3 flat washers over the mounting screw so a flat washer is on each side of each magnet. Coat the threads of the mounting screw with Loctite 242 threadlocking adhesive. Install the assembly to the mounting boss at the very bottom of the propshaft bore. Tighten the mounting screw securely.
2. Lubricate the front driven gear bearing race and set it on top of the shims in the bearing bore with the tapered side of the bearing facing up.
3. Assemble the bearing installer as follows:
   a. Install guide plate part No. 3855863-1 (A, **Figure 110**) over the large bolt part No. 3850623-4 (B, **Figure 110**) so the large diameter of the guide plate is facing the bolt head.
   b. Thread the large nut (C, **Figure 110**) from kit part No. 3855860-7 onto the large bolt, then install the bearing installer part No. 3855864-9 (D, **Figure 110**) onto the large bolt. Tighten the nut securely against the bearing installer.
   c. Insert the tool assembly into the drive shaft bore and engage the installer into the bearing race and the alignment plate into the propshaft bore.
   d. Cushion the leading edge of the gearcase with a wooden block. Using a mallet, drive

13

the bearing into the gearcase until it is seated in the drive shaft bore.

e. Remove the tool from the gearcase. Inspect the bearing and make sure the shim(s) are not displaced or damaged and that the bearing is fully seated.

4. Lubricate the front driven gear and bearing. Set the front gear and inner propshaft assembly into the propshaft bore. Seat the roller bearing of the gear to the bearing race.

NOTE
The pinion gear internal taper and the drive shaft external taper must be clean and dry for assembly.

5. Position the pinion gear in the propshaft bore. Carefully insert the drive shaft through the pinion bearing and engage the splines of the pinion gear.

6. Install a new pinion nut with a pair of mechanical fingers or installer part No. 3855930-8. Tighten the nut hand-tight. Do not attempt to use part No. 3855930-8 to hold the pinion nut during torquing.

7. Install the drive shaft large roller bearing race over the drive shaft and seat it against the large roller bearing. Lubricate the drive shaft bearing retainer and thread it into the drive shaft bore. Tighten the retainer hand-tight.

8. Assemble the following tools to hold the pinion nut:

a. Attach adaptor part No. 3855919-1 to the inner propshaft propeller nut threads.

b. Attach pusher tip part No. 3855921-7 (A, **Figure 111**) to tube part No. 3855922-5 (B, **Figure 111**). Tighten the pusher tip setscrew (C, **Figure 111**) securely.

c. Install the pusher tip and tube assembly over the inner propshaft. Rotate the drive shaft as necessary to engage the pusher tip to the pinion nut. Seat the tool into the gearcase.

d. Thread nut part No. 3855920-9 onto adaptor part No. 3855919-1 *finger-tight.*

e. Install spline socket 3850598-8 onto the drive shaft splines. Attach an appropriate torque wrench and torque the pinion nut to the exact same torque as recorded during *pinion gear shimming*.

f. Remove the tools from the gearcase.

9. Position the gearcase so the propshaft bore is pointing straight up. The front driven gear must be held away from the pinion gear (by gravity) in order to get an accurate rolling torque reading. Set the drive shaft bearing rolling torque as follows:

a. Attach a torque wrench capable of accurately reading 0.23-0.45 N•m (2-4 in.-lb.) to spline socket part No. 3850598-8 with the appropriate adapter(s).

b. Attach the torque wrench to the drive shaft.

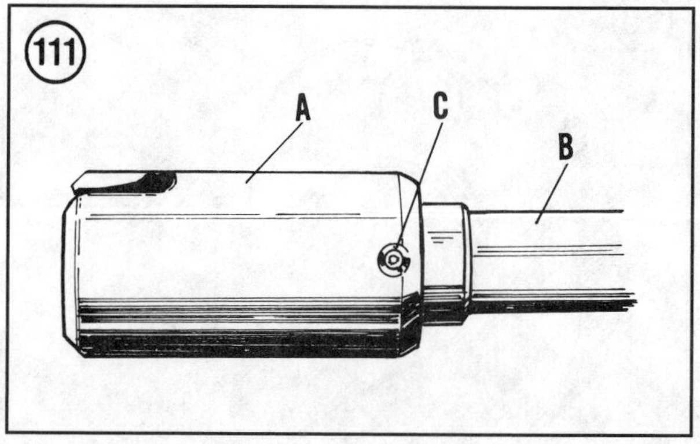

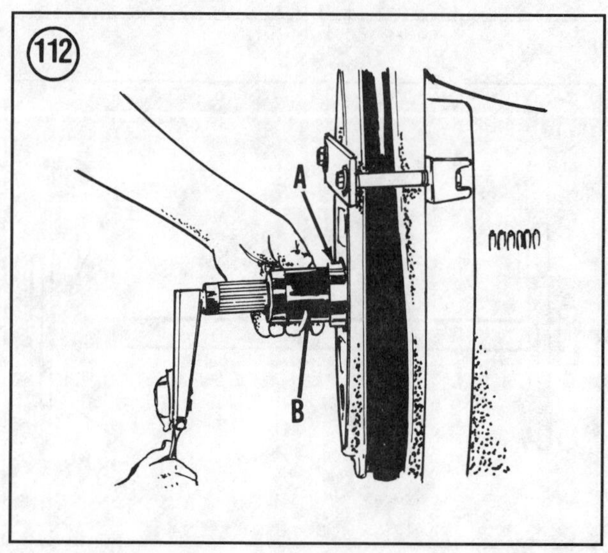

c. Turn the drive shaft several turns clockwise to seat the bearings. Slow the rotational speed down to approximately 3 rpm. Note the torque wrench reading.

d. If the reading is below specification 0.23-0.45 N•m (2-4 in.-lb.), tighten the drive shaft bearing retainer (A, **Figure 112**) slightly with spanner wrench part No. 3850601-0 (B, **Figure 112**). Repeat Step 8c.

e. If the reading is above specification 0.23-0.45 N•m (2-4 in.-lb.), loosen the drive shaft bearing retainer (A, **Figure 112**) slightly with spanner wrench part No. 3850601-0 (B, **Figure 112**). Repeat Step 8c.

f. Do not proceed until the rolling torque is 0.23-0.45 N•m (2-4 in.-lb.) at approximately 3 rpm. Remove the tools when finished. Do not disturb the bearing retainer position.

Overall rolling torque verification

The following procedure covers installation of the aft driven (tube) gear and propshaft bearing carrier and the setting of the gearcase overall rolling torque. No seals or O-rings should be installed at this time. Seal and O-ring installation is covered under *Final Assembly*.

1. Install the predetermined small roller bearing shims over the inner propshaft and against the propshaft shoulder.

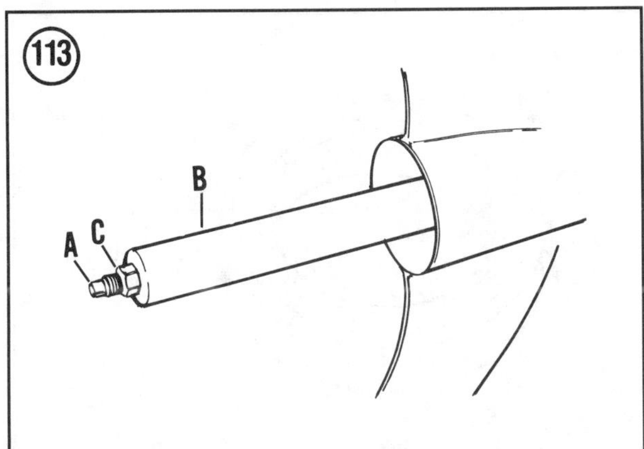

2. Lubricate the small roller bearing and slide it over the inner propshaft with the rollers facing up (out).
3. Press the bearing onto the propshaft as follows:
   a. Attach adaptor part No. 3855919-1 (A, **Figure 113**) to the inner propshaft propeller nut threads.
   b. Slide tube part No. 3855922-5 (B, **Figure 113**) over the propshaft and seat it against the roller bearing.
   c. Lubricate tool nut part No. 3855920-9 (C, **Figure 113**) with grease and thread it onto the adapter as far as possible by hand.
   d. Secure the tube with an adjustable wrench and tighten the nut to press the bearing onto the propshaft.
   e. Remove the tools when the bearing has been fully seated against the propshaft shoulder.
4. Coat at least 3 gear teeth of the aft driven (tube) gear with GM Gear Marking Compound, available from any General Motors automotive dealership.
5. Install the tube gear over the inner propshaft and seat the tube gear bearing against the inner propshaft roller bearing. Lubricate the larger roller bearing on the rear of the aft driven gear.
6. Lubricate both flanges and the bearings of the propshaft bearing carrier. Slide the propshaft bearing carrier over the tube gear shaft and seat it into the propshaft bore. Make sure the lubricant drain/fill hole is facing the skeg (down).
7. Install the tabbed washer. Position the tab into the gearcase hole at the top of the propshaft bore.
8. Liberally lubricate the propshaft retaining ring and thread it into the propshaft bore as far as possible by hand.
9. Set the overall rolling torque as follows:
   a. Attach a torque wrench capable of accurately reading 1.69-4.52 N•m (15-40 in.-lb.) to spline socket part No. 3850598-8 with the appropriate adapter(s).
   b. Attach the torque wrench to the drive shaft.

NOTE
*The specified overall rolling torque varies depending on the drive unit gear ratio. Refer to **Table 2** for the overall rolling torque for your gearcase. Refer to Chapter Twelve if you do not know what gear ratio your unit is.*

c. Turn the drive shaft several turns clockwise to seat the bearings. Slow the rotational speed down to approximately 3 rpm. Note the torque wrench reading.
d. If the reading is below specification (**Table 2**), tighten the propshaft bearing carrier retaining ring slightly with spanner wrench part No. 3855877-1. Repeat substep c.
e. If the reading is above specification (**Table 2**), loosen the propshaft bearing carrier retaining ring slightly with spanner wrench part No. 38558577-1. Repeat substep c.

NOTE
*When rolling torque has been correctly adjusted, record the figure for duplication during **Final assembly**.*

f. Do not proceed until the rolling torque is within specification (**Table 2**) at approximately 3 rpm. Remove the tools when finished. Record the figure for duplication during final assembly. Do not disturb the retaining ring position.

Gear lash verification

Gear lash is a clearance measurement between 2 gears. If too much clearance is present between the gears, the strength of the gears is reduced and the gears create more gear whine than normal. If too little clearance is present between the gears, there is no room for heat expansion and lubricant film causing the gears to be quickly damaged.

The drive shaft must not move during this procedure. The gear lash of each driven gear is checked at each gear's propeller shaft using a special adaptor. To verify the gear lash, proceed as follows.

1. To secure the drive shaft and prevent erroneous gear lash readings, install drive shaft puller part No. 3855923-3 to the drive shaft as shown in **Figure 114**. Tighten the socket head clamp screws (A, **Figure 114**) securely to hold the tool to the drive shaft. Tighten the hex head screws (B, **Figure 114**) *lightly* to lock the drive shaft to the gearcase and prevent drive shaft rotation.
2. Install gear lash tool part No. 3855873-0 (**Figure 115**) to the smooth portion of the inner propshaft. Do not position the tool on the prop-

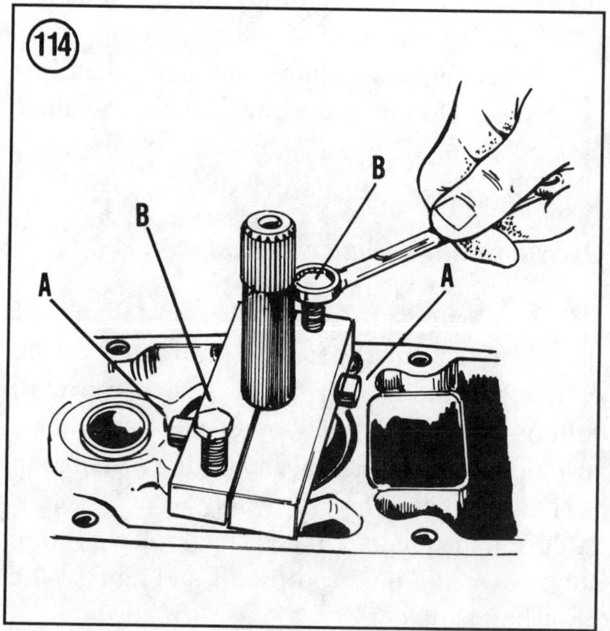

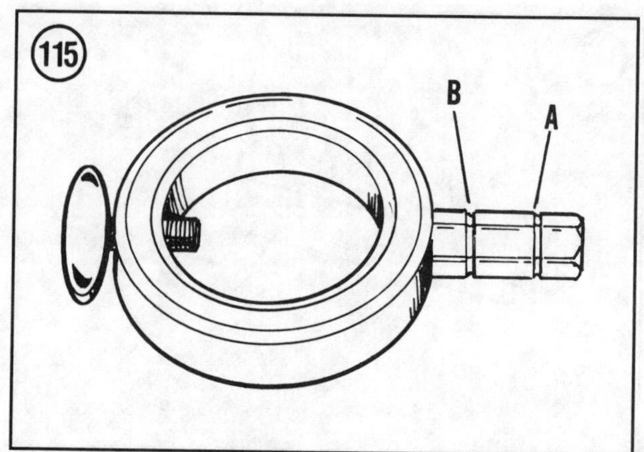

shaft splines. Tighten the tool's thumbscrew securely.

3. Securely attach a dial indicator to the gearcase at a convenient location. Position the dial indicator so that the indicator tip contacts the lash tool's outer index line (A, **Figure 115**). The dial indicator tip must be at a 90° angle to the tool's arm and the dial indicator face (dial) must be parallel to the propshaft centerline. Zero the indicator and check the gear lash by rotating the inner propeller shaft lightly back and forth. Record the reading.

4. Reposition the gear lash tool onto the smooth portion of the outer propeller (tube) shaft. Do not position the tool on the propshaft splines. Tighten the tool's thumbscrew securely.

5. Reposition the dial indicator so the indicator contacts the lash tool's inner index line (B, **Figure 115**). The dial indicator tip must be at a 90° angle to the tool's arm and the dial indicator face (dial) must be parallel to the propshaft centerline. Zero the indicator and check the gear lash by rotating the outer (tube) propeller shaft back and forth. Record the reading and compare to specification (**Table 2**).

NOTE

If it is necessary to remove or add a large thickness of shims to correct the gear lash, recheck your shimming calculations and measure all shims to check for improper assembly or mathematical mistakes.

6. If the gear lash readings for both gears are within specification, proceed to *Tube gear pattern verification* in this chapter.

NOTE

If the gear lash requires correction, change approximately 0.03 mm (0.001 in.) of shims for every 0.03 mm (0.001 in.) of correction desired. Move the appropriate gear toward the other gear(s) to decrease gear lash and move the appropriate gear away from the other gear(s) to increase gear lash. If 2 or more gears are being moved, change 1/2 of the total correction desired at the pinion gear and the other 1/2 of the correction at the driven gear(s).

7. If the gear lash reading for one or both gears is not within specification, refer to **Table 11** for the gear lash correction procedure. Disassemble the gearcase and change the shims as directed in **Table 11**. **Figure 116** shows shim location and function. Reassemble the gearcase and reset rolling torque first, then check gear lash. Do not proceed until rolling torque and gear lash are within specification.

8. Remove the tools when finished.

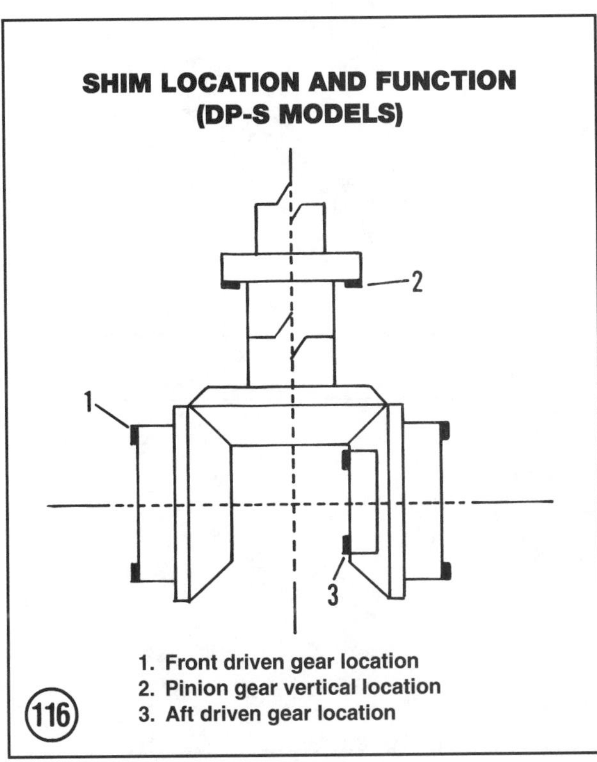

1. Front driven gear location
2. Pinion gear vertical location
3. Aft driven gear location

Tube gear pattern verification

Once gear lash has been verified, check the tube gear contact pattern as follows.

1. Install the spline socket part No. 3850598-8 over the drive shaft splines. Attach a breaker bar with the appropriate adapters.

13

NOTE
*The tube gear must be loaded to produce a contact pattern. A simple clamping brake can be fabricated from two, 2 × 4 pieces of wood approximately 457 mm (18 in.) long. Hinge the boards together so they can be folded upon each other, pinching the tube gear propeller shaft between them (like a nut cracker). See **Figure 117**.*

2. Place the clamping break over the outer (tube gear) propshaft. Apply clamping pressure to the outer propeller shaft to resist rotation and load the gear. Rotate the drive shaft with a breaker bar 6-8 revolutions in each direction.
3. Remove the outer propeller shaft and propshaft bearing housing assembly as described previously in this chapter.
4. Compare the pattern on the tube gear with the pattern shown at **Figure 118**.
5. If the pattern is not as specified, refer to **Table 11** for pattern correction procedures. **Figure 119** shows a pattern located too close to the gear's outer diameter. **Figure 120** shows a pattern located too close to the gear's inner diameter.
6. Disassemble the gearcase and change the shims as directed in **Table 11**. Refer to **Figure 116** for shim location and function. Make gear pattern corrections in 0.10 mm (.004 in.) increments. Reassemble the gearcase and reset the rolling torque first, then verify gear lash and finally recheck gear pattern. Do not proceed until rolling torque, gear lash and gear pattern are within specifications.

CAUTION
*If the contact pattern must be corrected, rolling torque and gear backlash must again be verified after the pattern correction, before continuing with **Final assembly**.*

7. Remove the outer propshaft and propshaft bearing carrier. Do not remove any pressed bearings from the housings or shafts. Clean all of the marking compound from the tube gear teeth and lubricate all internal components with clean gear oil. Proceed with the *Final Assembly* after all parts are clean and lubricated.

Final Assembly (DP-S Models)

1. Install 2 new propshaft seals into the outer propeller shaft (tube gear) using seal installer

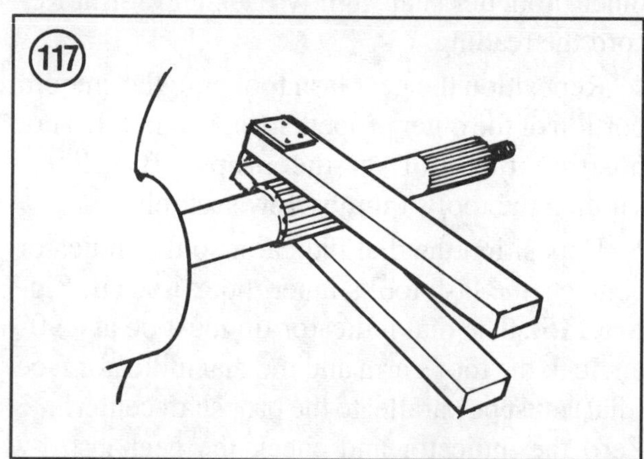

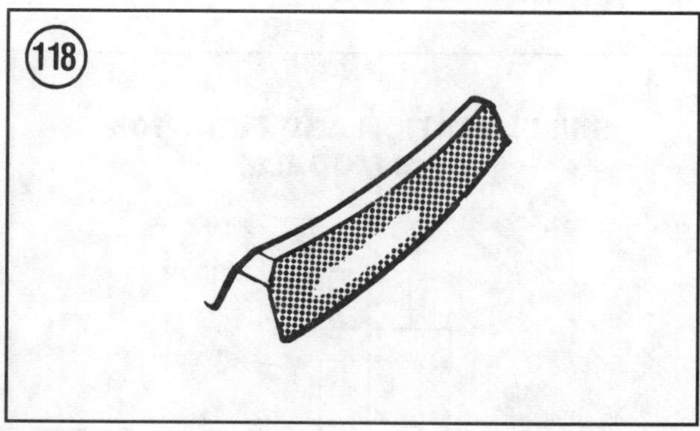

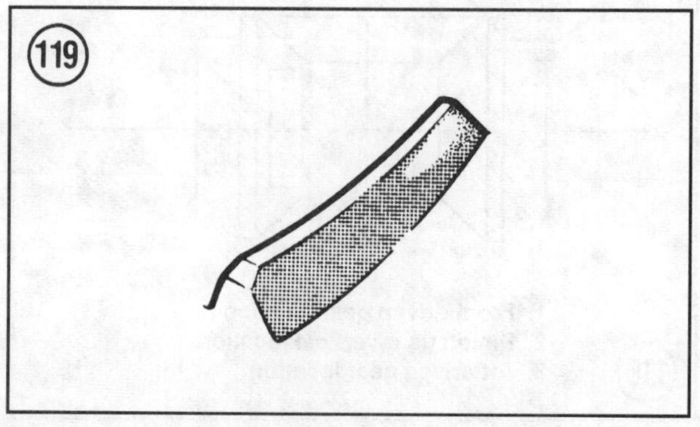

part No. 884975-9. Refer to **Figure 121** and proceed as follows:

a. Position the double lip, single case seal (36, **Figure 101**) onto the deep (wide) shouldered edge of the seal installer with the steel edge facing away from the tool shoulder and into the gearcase.

b. Press the inner (double lip, single case) seal into the propshaft until the tool seats on the propshaft.

c. Position the outer (single lip) (37, **Figure 101**) seal onto the shallow (narrow) shouldered edge of the seal installer with the spring side of the seal facing the tool shoulder and away from the gearcase.

d. Press the outer seal into the propshaft until the tool seats on the propshaft. The outer seal should be 1 mm (0.039 in.) from the end of the shaft as shown in **Figure 121**.

e. Lubricate the seals and pack the area between the seals with OMC Triple Guard Grease or equivalent (**Table 5**).

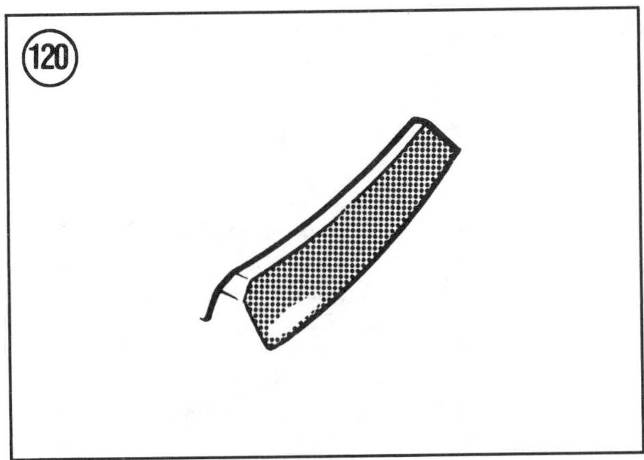

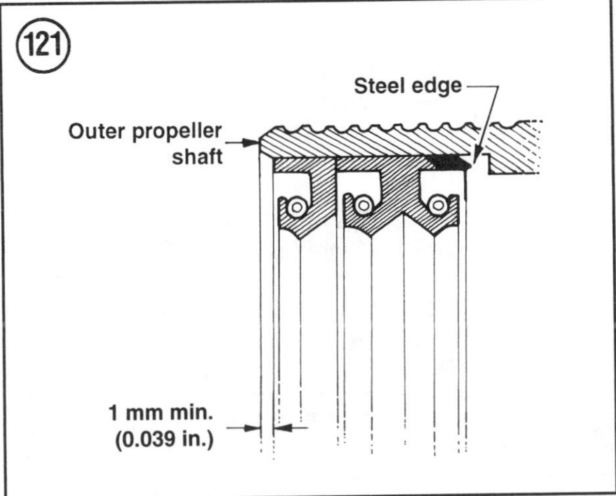

2. Install seal protector part No. 884976-2 into the tube gear seals. Carefully slide the tube gear over the inner propshaft and seat it against the small roller bearing. Remove the seal protector.

3. Install 2 new propshaft seals into the propshaft bearing carrier. Install the seals *back-to-back* with the spring side of each seal facing away from each other. Coat the outer diameter of the seals with Volvo White Sealing Compound or equivalent (**Table 5**). Install the seals as follows:

a. Position both seals onto the short end of installer part No. 3855925-8. Make sure the seals are oriented *back-to-back* and the outer diameters are coated with sealing compound. Press the seals into the propshaft bearing carrier until the tool seats against the carrier.

b. Remove the installation tool.

c. Lubricate the seals and pack the area between the seals with OMC Triple Guard Grease or equivalent (**Table 5**).

4. Coat 2 new O-rings with Volvo White Sealing Compound or equivalent (**Table 5**). Install the O-rings into the propshaft bearing carrier grooves. Coat both propshaft bearing carrier flanges with sealing compound.

5. Install seal protector part No. 884807-9 into the propshaft carrier seals. Carefully slide the propshaft bearing carrier over the outer propshaft and seat it into the gear housing. Make sure the lubricant drain hole is pointing straight down. Remove the seal protector.

6. Coat a new O-ring with Volvo White Sealing Compound or equivalent (**Table 5**). Install the O-ring into the thin groove on the propshaft bearing carrier rear flange.

7. Install the tab washer over the O-ring and engage the tab to the hole in the top of the propshaft bore.

8. Coat 2 new O-rings with Volvo White Sealing Compound or equivalent (**Table 5**). Install the large (thick) O-ring into the propshaft bearing carrier retaining ring outside diameter groove. Install the small (thin) O-ring into the propshaft bearing carrier retaining ring inner face groove.

9. Liberally coat the retaining ring with gear lubricant. Install the retaining ring to the gearcase and thread as far as possible by hand. Be careful not to displace the tab washer or O-rings. Refer to *Overall rolling torque verification* and reset the overall rolling torque to the exact setting recorded prior to gear lash and gear pattern verification.

10. Install the lubricant drain/fill plug (with a new O-ring). It may be necessary to turn the propshaft bearing carrier retaining ring *slightly* to allow the drain/fill plug to be installed. Tighten the drain plug to specification (**Table 4**).

11. Install the lower gearcase to the upper gearcase as described previously in this chapter. Do not fill the drive unit with lubricant until the drive unit has passed the pressure and vacuum tests as described under *Pressure and vacuum tests*, in this chapter.

Table 1 LOWER GEARCASE SPECIFICATIONS (DP-C1/D1 AND DPX MODELS)

Drive unit lubricant capacity	
DP-C1/D1	2.7 L (2.8 qt.)
DPX	2.0 L (2.1 qt.)
Fixed dimensions: pinion gear and driven gears	
Pinion gear overall - H prefix	
DP-C1/D1	276.00/277.00 mm (10.866/10.905 in.)[1]
Gear dimension (pinion gear)	60.00 mm (2.362 in.)
Shaft dimension (drive shaft)	217.75 mm (8.573 in.)
DPX	229.10 mm (9.020 in.)
Gear dimension (pinion gear)	60.00 mm (2.362 in.)
Shaft dimension (drive shaft)	169.85 mm (6.687 in.)
Front gear overall - G prefix	60.00/61.00 mm (2.362/2.402 in.)[1]
Gear dimension (front gear)	39.50 mm (1.555 in.)
Bearing dimension (front gear)	20.85 mm (0.821 in.)
DP-C1/D1 bearing carrier overall - F prefix	79.00/80.00 mm (3.110-3.150 in.)[1]
Bearing carrier only - C prefix	19.00 mm (0.748 in.)
Gear dimension (aft gear)	39.50 mm (1.555 in.)
Bearing dimension (aft gear)	20.75 mm (0.817 in.)
Inner propshaft dimension (small bearing)	120.00 mm (4.724 in.)
Gear lash	
Inner propshaft (front gear)	0.08-0.17 mm (0.003-0.007 in.)
Outer propshaft (aft [tube] gear)	
DP-C1/D1	0.15-0.27 mm (0.006-0.011 in.)
DPX	0.11-0.34 mm (0.004-0.013 in.)
Overall rolling torque (at 60 rpm)	
DP-C1/D1	1.2-2.3 N•m (10.6-20.4 in.-lb.)
DPX	3.0 N•m (26.6 in.-lb.)
Pressure test (3 minutes, no leakage)	48 kPa (7 psi)

1. If the correction number stamped on the gear housing is above 50, use the smaller nominal figure. If the correction number on the gear housing is below 50, use the larger nominal figure.

Table 2 LOWER GEARCASE SPECIFICATIONS (SX AND DP-S MODELS)

DP-S gearcase mounting stud height	28.95-29.05 mm (1.1450-1.144 in.)
Drive unit lubricant capacity	
SX	2.1 L (71 oz.)
DP-S	2.4 L (81 oz.)
Drive shaft (initial) rolling torque	0.23-0.45 N•m (2-4 in.-lb.)
Gear lash	
SX models	0.13-0.30 mm (0.005-0.012 in.)
DP-S models	
Inner propshaft (front gear)	0.15-0.30 mm (0.006-0.012 in.)
Outer propshaft (aft gear)	0.15-0.35 mm (0.006-0.014 in.)
Nominal (fixed) dimension	
Propeller shaft gear (SX models)	2.69 mm (0.106 in.)
Front gear (DP-S models)	1.40 mm (0.055 in.)
Overall rolling torque at 3 rpm	
SX models	
1.43:1, 1.51:1 and 1.60 gear ratio	1.58-2.60 N•m (14-23 in.-lb.)
1.66:1, 1.85:1, 1.97:1 and 2.18:1 gear ratio	1.24-2.03 N•m (11-18 in.-lb.)
DP-S models	
1.68:1 and 1.78:1 gear ratio	2.0-3.0 N•m (18-27 in.-lb.)
1.95:1 and 2.30:1 gear ratio	3.0-4.0 N•m (27-35 in.-lb.)
Pressure test specifications (3 minute minimum test)	
Low pressure	20.7-34.5 kPa (3-5 psi)
High pressure	110-124 kPa (16-18 psi)
Vacuum test specifications (3 minute minimum test)	
Low vacuum)	10-16.8 kPa (3-5 in.-Hg.)
High vacuum	47-54 kPa (14-16 in.-Hg)

Table 3 SPECIAL TORQUE VALUES (DP-C1/D1 AND DPX MODELS)

Fastener	N.m	in.-lb.	ft.-lb.
Lubricant dipstick	Securely	Securely	Securely
Lubricant drain plug (DP-C1/D1)	10	88	7.4
Lubricant drain plug (DPX)	17	150	12.5
Lubricant fill plug	35	–	25.8
Pinion nut	110	–	81
Propeller mounting hardware			
DP-C1/D1			
Front propeller nut	60-75	–	45-55
Rear propeller cone	100-120	–	74-89
Rear propeller cone, center screw	70-80	–	52-59
DPX			
Front propeller nut	60	–	45
Rear propeller outer nut	70	–	50
Rear propeller nut, inner bolt	70-80	–	52-59
Propeller shaft bearing carrier (DP-C1/D1)	40	–	30
Lower gearcase mounting hardware			
Small fasteners	15	132	11.2
Large fasteners	38	–	28.0

Table 4 SPECIAL TORQUE VALUES (SX AND DP-S MODELS)

Fastener	N.m	in.-lb.	ft.-lb.
Anode			
Upper anode	6.8-9.5	60-84	–
Propshaft anode (SX models)			
Anode through-bolt	6.8-9.5	60-84	–
Bracket screws	16-19	142-168	12-14
Exhaust plate (DP-S models)	19.5-22.5	–	14-17
Lubricant dipstick	5.4-8.1	48-72	–
Lubricant drain plug (SX)	6.8-9.5	60-84	–
Lubricant drain plug (DP-S)	14-20	124-180	10-15
Lubricant level plug	5.4-8.1	48-72	–
Lower gearcase mounting hardware			
3/8-16 thread	30-33	–	22-24
7/16-14 thread	43-54	–	32-40
Magnet (DP-S)	Securely		
Pinion nut			
SX models	203-217	–	150-160
DP-S models	98-118	–	72-87
Propeller mounting hardware			
SX propeller nut	95-108	–	70-80
DP-S front propeller nut	60	–	45
DP-S rear propeller nut	70	–	50
Propshaft bearing carrier (SX)	271-305	–	200-225
Bearing retainer block screw (SX)	27-34	–	20-25
Bearing retainer set screw (SX)	4.8-6.4	42-60	–
Trim tab (SX models so equipped)	19-22	–	14-16
Water tube guide (SX-S models)	14-16	124-142	10-12

Table 5 RECOMMENDED LUBRICANTS, SEALANTS AND ADHESIVES[1]

	Part Number
Lubricants	
Volvo DuraPlus GL5 Synthetic Gear Lube	(dealer stock item)
Volvo Penta Propeller Shaft Grease	1141644-3
or Quicksilver Special Lubricant 101	92-13872A-1
Volvo DuraPlus Power Trim/Steering Fluid	3851039-2
OMC EP/Wheel Bearing Grease	(dealer stock item)
OMC Moly Lube	175356
OMC Triple Guard Grease	(dealer stock item)
or Quicksilver 2-4-C Multi-Lube	(dealer stock item)
OMC Needle Bearing Assembly Grease	378642
or Quicksilver Needle Bearing Grease	92-825265A-1
Sealants	
Volvo Master Gasket Sealant	840879-1
Volvo Black Silicone Sealant	1161277-7
or OMC RTV Black Silicone Sealant	263753
Volvo White Sealing Compound	1141570-0
or OMC Gasket Sealing Compound	508235
or Quicksilver Perfect Seal	92-34227-11

(continued)

Table 5 RECOMMENDED LUBRICANTS, SEALANTS AND ADHESIVES[1] (continued)

	Part Number
Sealants (continued)	
OMC Black Neoprene Dip	909570
or Quicksilver Liquid Neoprene	92-25711-2
OMC Pipe Sealant with Teflon	9100048
or Quicksilver Loctite 567 PST pipe sealant	92-809822
3M Marine Sealant 101 (polysulfide [OMC or locally available])	506852
Adhesives	
OMC Type M Adhesive	318535
or Scotch Grip 1300 Adhesive (OMC or locally available)	982551
or Quicksilver Bellows Adhesive (contact cement)	92-86166-1
OMC Locquic Primer	772032
or Quicksilver Locquic Primer	92-809824
OMC Ultra Lock Threadlocking Adhesive (high strength)	500422
or Quicksilver Loctite 271 Threadlocking Adhesive	92-809819
OMC Nut Lock Threadlocking Adhesive (medium strength)	500418
or Quicksilver Loctite 242 Threadlocking Adhesive	92-809821
Miscellaneous	
Volvo DuraPlus Corrosion Shield	362002-8
Quicksilver Storage Seal Rust Inhibitor	92-86145A12
OMC Dielectric Grease	503243
or Quicksilver Dielectric Silicone Grease	92-823506-1

1. Obtain Volvo supplies from a Volvo-Penta Dealer, Quicksilver supplies from any Mercury Marine Dealer and OMC supplies from any OMC Stern Drive, Evinrude or Johnson Dealer.

Table 6 VOLVO SPECIAL TOOLS (DP-C1/D1 AND DPX MODELS)

Description	Application	Part No.
Front propeller nut (gear lash)	DP-C1/D1 and DPX	852196-5
Rear propeller nut (gear lash)	DP-C1/D1 and DPX	852201-3
Consumer propeller tool kit	DP-C1/D1	873058-2
Bearing remover	DP-C1/D1 and DPX	884140-5
Drive handle	DP-C1/D1 and DPX	884143-9
Slide hammer	DP-C1/D1 and DPX	884161-1
Bearing installer	DP-C1/D1 and DPX	884168-6
Threaded rod and plate	DP-C1/D1 and DPX	884241-1
Bearing remover/installer	DP-X	884265-0
Bearing installer	DP-C1/D1 and DPX	884266-8
Drive shaft remover	DP-C1/D1 and DPX	884267-6
Bearing plate	DP-C1/D1 and DPX	884348-4
Tube gear puller	DP-C1/D1 and DPX	884789-9
Pinion bearing remover	DP-C1/D1	884791-5
Pinion bearing installer	DP-C1/D1	884792-3
Sleeve installer	DP-C1/D1 and DPX	884793-1
Bearing remover	DP-C1/D1 and DPX	884794-9
Bearing installer	DP-C1/D1 and DPX	884795-6
Bearing remover	DP-C1/D1 and DPX	884796-4
Bearing remover/installer	DP-C1/D1 and DPX	884797-2
Bearing installer	DP-C1/D1 and DPX	884798-0
Bearing, sleeve and seal installer	DP-C1/D1 and DPX	884801-2

(continued)

Table 6 VOLVO SPECIAL TOOLS (DP-C1/D1 AND DPX MODELS) (continued)

Description	Application	Part No.
Sleeve	DP-C1/D1 and DPX	884802-0
Remover	DP-C1/D1 and DPX	884803-8
Bearing installer	DP-C1/D1 and DPX	884806-1
Seal protector	DP-C1/D1 and DPX	884807-9
Gearcase spline socket	DP-C1/D1 and DPX	884830-1
Sleeve remover	DP-C1/D1 and DPX	884831-9
Split bearing remover	DP-C1/D1 and DPX	884832-7
Seal protector	DP-C1/D1 and DPX	884976-2
Tilt suspension tool	DP-C1/D1 and DPX	885143-8
Gearcase holding fixture	DP-C1/D1 and DPX	885192-5
Consumer propeller tool kit	DPX	885195-8
Adaptor	DP-C1/D1 and DPX	885197-4
Spanner wrench	DPX	885221-2
Pinion bearing remover	DPX	885226-1
Spacer	DPX	885227-9
Spacer	DPX	885228-7
Pressure tester	DP-C1/D1 and DPX	3810152-3
Front propeller nut tool	DP-C1/D1 and DPX	3855876-3
Drive handle	DP-C1/D1 and DPX	9991801-3

Table 7 VOLVO SPECIAL TOOLS (SX AND DP-S MODELS)

Description	Application	Part No.
Drive handle	DP-S	884143-9
Puller	DP-S	884832-7
Puller	DP-S	884789-9
Dismantling tool	DP-S	884803-8
Seal protector	DP-S	884807-9
Fixture tool	DP-S	884831-9
Installation tool	DP-S	884975-9
Seal protector	DP-S	884976-2
Guide plate	SX-C	3850218-3
Spline socket	SX and DP-S	3850598-8
Pinion shim fixture	SX-S	3850599-6
Shim fixture	SX and DP-S	3850600-2
Spanner wrench	SX and DP-S	3850601-0
Gear lash extension tool	SX	3850602-8
Retainer block installation tool	SX	3850603-6
Drive handle	SX	3850609-3
Drive handle	SX	3850610-1
Puller bridge and threaded rod	SX	3850611-9
2 Jaw puller head	SX	3850612-7
Alignment plate	SX	3850613-5
Support tool	SX	3850614-3
Bearing installer	SX	3850616-8
Propshaft bearing installer	SX and DP-S	3850617-6
Spline socket	SX	3850618-4
Guide plate	SX and DP-S	3850619-2
Pinion bearing installer	SX	3850620-0
Bearing installer	SX and DP-S	3850621-8

(continued)

Table 7 VOLVO SPECIAL TOOLS (SX AND DP-S MODELS) (continued)

Description	Application	Part No.
Bearing remover	SX	3850622-6
Large bolt	SX and DP-S	3850623-4
Bearing installer	SX	3850624-2
Bearing remover	SX	3850625-9
Shim ring tool	SX	3850626-7
Seal installer	SX	3850627-5
Remover/installer	SX	3850707-5
Pinion nut holder	SX	3854864-0
Shim fixture	SX-C/C1	3855098-4
Consumer propeller tool kit	DP-S	3855516-5
Bearing remover	SX and DP-S	3855859-9
Threaded rod, nut and washer	SX and DP-S	3855860-7
Bearing installer	DP-S	3855861-5
Bearing remover	DP-S	3855862-3
Guide plate	DP-S	3855863-1
Bearing installer	DP-S	3855864-9
Bearing installer	DP-S	3855865-6
Bearing installer	DP-S	3855866-4
Spacer	DP-S	3855867-2
Sleeve installer	DP-S	3855869-8
Shim fixture	DP-S	3855870-6
Shim fixture	DP-S	3855871-4
Shim fixture	DP-S	3855872-2
Gear lash tool	DP-S	3855873-0
Front propeller nut tool	DP-S	3855876-3
Spanner wrench	DP-S	3855877-1
Bearing remover	DP-S	3855898-0
Propshaft adaptor	DP-S	3855919-1
Nut	DP-S	3855920-9
Pusher tip	DP-S	3855921-7
Tube	DP-S	3855922-5
Drive shaft puller	DP-S	3855923-3
Remover	DP-S	3855924-1
Bearing and seal installer	DP-S	3855925-8
Support base	DP-S	3855926-6
Bearing installer	DP-S	3855928-2
Pinion nut starting tool	DP-S	3855930-8
Drive handle	SX and DP-S	9991801-3

13

Table 8 STANDARD TORQUE VALUES (METRIC FASTENERS)

Screw or Nut Size	N·m	in.-lb.	ft.-lb.
M5	4.1	36	–
M6	8.1	70	6
M8	17.6	156	13
M10	35.3	312	26
M12	47.5	–	35
M14	81.3	–	60

Table 9 STANDARD TORQUE VALUES (U.S. FASTENERS)

Screw or Nut Size	N·m	in.-lb.	ft.-lb.
6-32	1.0	9	–
8-32	2.3	20	–
10-24	3.4	30	–
10-32	4.0	35	–
12-24	5.1	45	–
1/4-20	7.9	70	6
1/4-28	9.5	84	7
5/16-18	18.1	160	13
5/16-24	19.0	168	14
3/8-16	30.5	270	23
3/8-24	33.9	300	25
7/16-14	48.8	–	36
7/16-20	54.2	–	40
1/2-13	67.8	–	50
1/2-20	81.3	–	60

Table 10 GEAR LASH AND PATTERN CORRECTION GUIDE–DP-C1/D1 MODELS

Shim location	Pinion gear	Front gear	Carrier (rear gear)	Inner propshaft
DPC1/D1 Gear lash				
Both gears below specification				
Changes required[1]:	add	subtract	subtract	add[2]
Both gears above specification				
Changes required[1]:	subtract	add	add	subtract[2]
Front (inner propshaft) gear below specification				
Changes required[3]:	no change	subtract	no change	add
Front (inner propshaft) gear above specification				
Changes required[3]:	no change	add	no change	subtract
Aft (tube) gear below specification				
Changes required[3]:	no change	subtract	no change	add
Aft (tube) gear above specification				
Changes required[3]:	no change	add	no change	subtract
DP-C1/D1 Gear pattern				
Pattern too close to outer diameter of gear				
Changes required[3]:	add	add	add	subtract[2]
Pattern too close to inner diameter of gear				
Changes required[3]:	subtract	subtract	subtract	add[2]

1. Change one-half of the total desired change at the pinion gear. Change the other one-half by changing the same quantity (thickness) as the pinion gear at each driven gear.
2. Add or subtract the total quantity (thickness) of shims changed at the front and rear driven gears.
3. Change equal amounts (thickness) of shims at each location, except where noted.

Table 11 GEAR LASH AND PATTERN CORRECTION GUIDE–DPX AND DP-S MODELS

Shim location	Pinion gear	Front driven gear	Inner propshaft bearing (tube gear or rear gear for gear pattern adjustment)
DPX and DP-S gear lash			
Both gears below specification			
Changes required[1]:	add	subtract	add[2]
Both gears above specification			
Changes required[1]:	subtract	add	subtract[2]
Front (inner propshaft) gear below specification			
Changes required[3]:	no change	subtract	add
Front (inner propshaft) gear above specification			
Changes required[3]:	no change	add	subtract
Aft (tube) gear below specification			
Changes required:	no change	no change	add
Aft (tube) gear above specification			
Changes required:	no change	no change	subtract
DPX and DP-S gear pattern			
Pattern too close to outer diameter of gear			
Changes required[3]:	add	add	subtract[2]
Pattern too close to inner diameter of gear			
Changes required[3]:	subtract	subtract	add[2]

1. Change one-half of the total desired change at the pinion gear and the other one-half by changing the same quantity (thickness) as the pinion gear at each driven gear.
2. Since the position of this bearing is dependent on the front driven gear, any change to the front driven gear requires the exact opposite change at this bearing just to maintain position. Make any required shim changes in addition to the shims needed to maintain position.
3. Change equal amounts (thickness) of shims at each location, except where noted.

Chapter Fourteen

Intermediate Housing and Transom Shield (Bracket)

DP-C1/D1 and DPX drive units use an intermediate housing and suspension fork to allow the drive unit to tilt and trim. DP-C1/D1 models use a steering helmet and yoke shaft assembly to steer the drive unit. DPX models use externally mounted hydraulic cylinders to steer the drive unit. A transom shield assembly provides a water tight connection between the engine and drive unit. The drive unit consists of the lower gearcase, intermediate housing, suspension fork and upper gearcase assemblies. The transom shield consists of the outer transom plate, the steering helmet assembly (DP-C1/D1 models) and mounting collar. The mounting collar connects the flywheel housing to the transom shield.

SX and DP-S drive units use a transom bracket assembly to provide a water tight connection between the engine and drive unit. A gimbal ring and pivot housing in the transom bracket allow the drive unit to tilt, trim and steer. The drive unit consists of the upper and lower gearcase assemblies.

If you are not sure which drive unit (and transom assembly) you are working on, refer to Chapter Twelve for drive unit identification.

Table 1 and **Table 2** list special torque values. **Table 3** and **Table 4** list torque values for standard fasteners and **Table 5** lists recommended lubricants, sealants and adhesives. **Tables 6** and **Table 7** list manufacturer recommended tools. **Tables 1-7** are at the end of the chapter.

INTERMEDIATE HOUSING (DP-C1/D1 AND DPX MODELS)

The intermediate housing and suspension fork provides a means of connecting the upper and lower gearcases to each other and a means of connecting the upper gearcase to the transom shield assembly. **Figure 1** shows an exploded view of the intermediate housing and suspension fork.

The upper gearcase lower output gear bearing bore requires shimming to properly preload the lower output gear bearing to the upper gearcase. Refer to *Upper Gearcase to Intermediate Housing Shimming Procedure* in Chapter Twelve.

The lower gearcase upper drive shaft bearing race (pressed into the intermediate housing), requires shimming to properly preload the drive shaft tapered roller bearing. Refer to *Lower Gearcase to Intermediate Housing Shimming Procedure* in Chapter Thirteen.

The steering tube holding the suspension fork to the intermediate housing also transfers water from the lower gearcase to the water hose connector located at the top of the suspension fork. This water passage is under vacuum from the engine mounted water supply pump. Any leaks in these passages will cause air to be drawn into the cooling system, resulting in engine overheating. Always replace all seals and O-rings when servicing this area. The lower seal (21, **Figure 1**) will generally remain in the lower gearcase when it is removed. The retainer (22, **Figure 1**) will generally remain in the suspension fork and will be driven from the suspension fork when it is separated from the intermediate housing.

The only difference (in service procedures) between DP-C1/D1 and DPX model intermediate housings and suspension forks is that the DPX model suspension fork and intermediate housing have mounting bosses for the hydraulic steering rams that are standard equipment on DPX models.

Removal/Installation

1. Drain the drive lubricant as described in Chapter Twelve.
2. Remove the lower gearcase from the intermediate housing as described in Chapter Thirteen.
3. Remove the drive unit from the transom shield and separate the upper gearcase from the intermediate housing as described in Chapter Twelve.
4. Place the intermediate housing assembly onto a clean workbench.
5. When finished servicing the intermediate housing, install the upper gearcase to the intermediate housing and install the drive unit to the transom shield as described in Chapter Twelve.
6. Install the lower gearcase to the intermediate housing as described in Chapter Thirteen.
7. Pressure test the drive unit before filling with lubricant as described in Chapter Twelve.
8. Fill the drive unit with lubricant as described in Chapter Twelve.

Disassembly

Figure 1 is an exploded view of the DP-C1/D1 and DPX model intermediate housing and suspension fork assembly. Trim cylinder, hydraulic line and trim pump service procedures are covered in Chapter Fifteen.

1. Remove the 2 screws holding the water outlet fitting to the suspension fork with a hex wrench as shown in **Figure 2**. Remove the water outlet fitting and O-ring. Discard the O-ring.
2. Place the housing and fork assembly on the edge of a workbench. Place a suitable container underneath the steering tube or be ready to catch the tube and retainer once it is driven free.
3. Drive the steering tube from the suspension fork and intermediate housing with driver part No. 884311-2 and drive handle part No. 9991801-3 or equivalent. Press against the tube at the water outlet fitting end and drive the tube down and out. Catch the retainer (22, **Figure 1**) and steering tube (24, **Figure 1**) as they come free.
4. Separate the suspension fork from the intermediate housing. Remove the 2 thrust washers

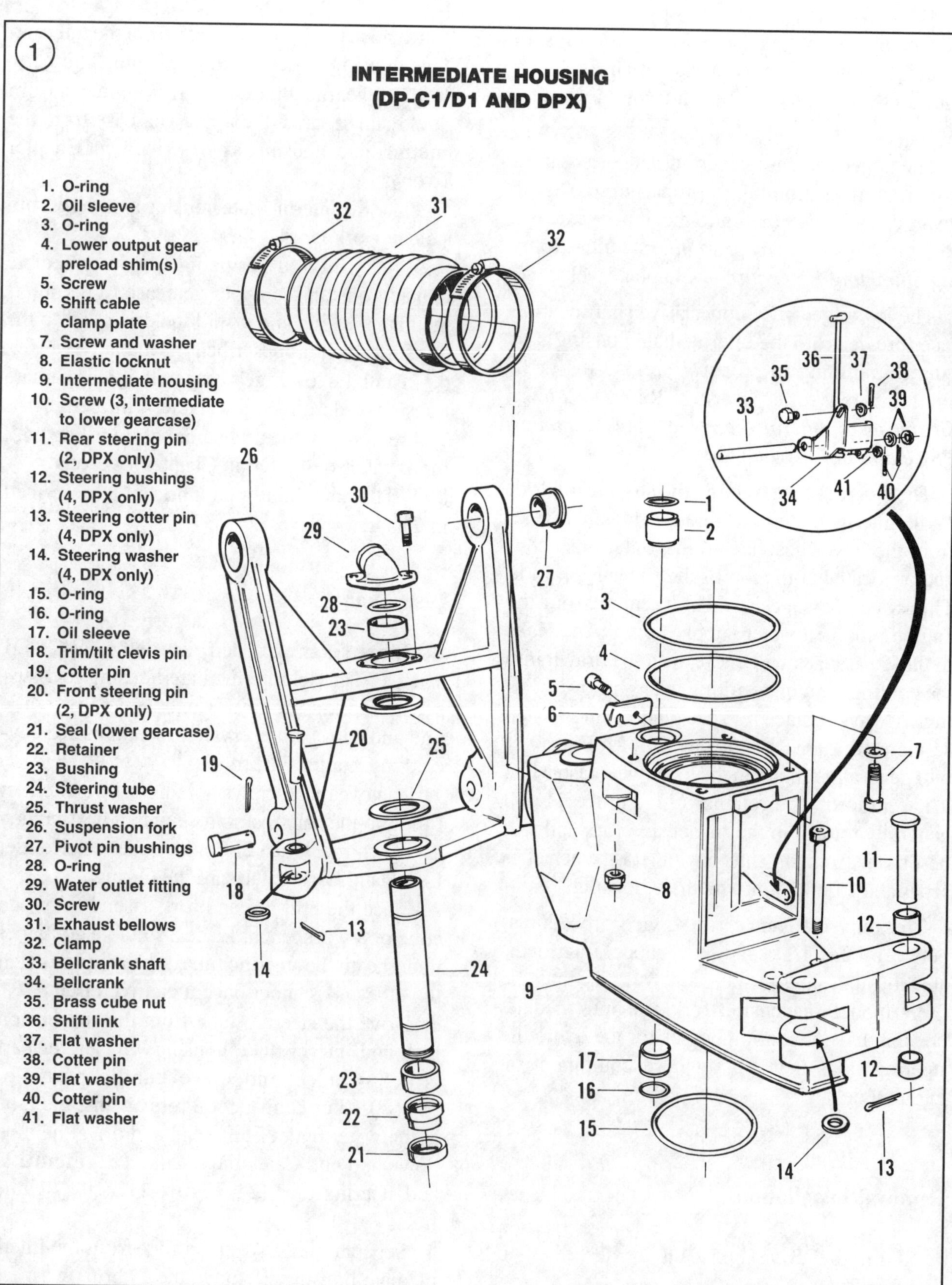
1
INTERMEDIATE HOUSING
(DP-C1/D1 AND DPX)
1. O-ring
2. Oil sleeve
3. O-ring
4. Lower output gear preload shim(s)
5. Screw
6. Shift cable clamp plate
7. Screw and washer
8. Elastic locknut
9. Intermediate housing
10. Screw (3, intermediate to lower gearcase)
11. Rear steering pin (2, DPX only)
12. Steering bushings (4, DPX only)
13. Steering cotter pin (4, DPX only)
14. Steering washer (4, DPX only)
15. O-ring
16. O-ring
17. Oil sleeve
18. Trim/tilt clevis pin
19. Cotter pin
20. Front steering pin (2, DPX only)
21. Seal (lower gearcase)
22. Retainer
23. Bushing
24. Steering tube
25. Thrust washer
26. Suspension fork
27. Pivot pin bushings
28. O-ring
29. Water outlet fitting
30. Screw
31. Exhaust bellows
32. Clamp
33. Bellcrank shaft
34. Bellcrank
35. Brass cube nut
36. Shift link
37. Flat washer
38. Cotter pin
39. Flat washer
40. Cotter pin
41. Flat washer

(25, **Figure 1**) from the intermediate housing or suspension fork.

5. Drive the upper and lower suspension fork bushings (23, **Figure 1**) from the suspension fork with remover/installer part No. 884259-3 and drive handle part No. 9991801-3 as shown in **Figure 3**, typical.

6. If the pivot pin bushings (27, **Figure 1**) on each side of the suspension yoke have not yet been removed and discarded, do so at this time.

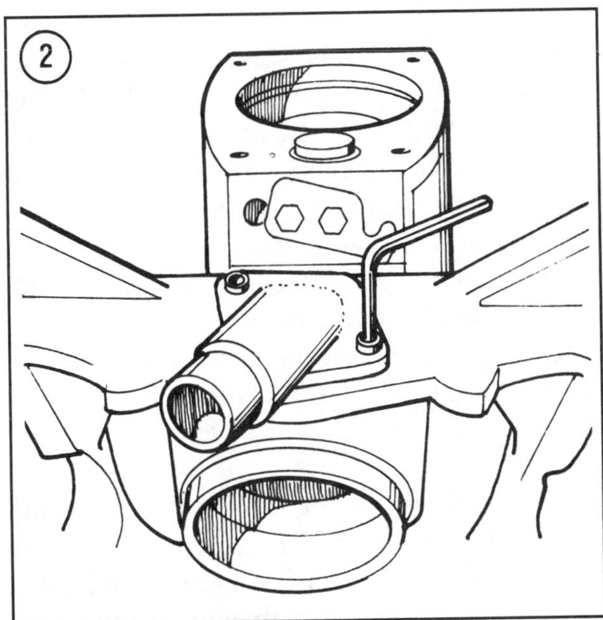

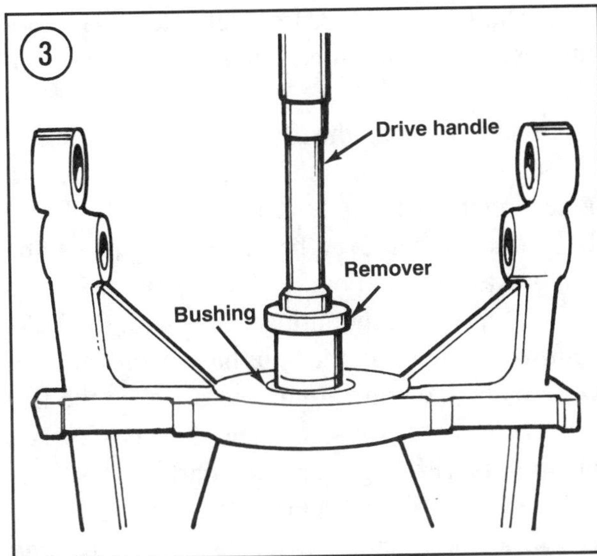

7. If the shift bellcrank requires service, remove and discard the cotter pins (40, **Figure 1**) and disconnect the shift link from the bellcrank (if not already disconnected). Withdraw the bellcrank shaft (33, **Figure 1**) and remove the bellcrank (34, **Figure 1**) and washers (39, **Figure 1**) from the intermediate housing.

8. *DPX models*—If the steering bushings (12, **Figure 1**) are worn or damaged, drive the bushings from the intermediate housing with a suitable drift. Discard the bushings.

Cleaning and Inspection

1. Clean all components in a suitable solvent and blow dry with compressed air.
2. Clean all corrosion and sealant residue from mating surfaces and bushing bores.
3. Check the seal and bushing surfaces on the steering tube for grooving and corrosion. Replace the steering tube if damaged.
4. Check the suspension fork and intermediate housing for excessive corrosion, cracks, excessive wear or mechanical damage. Replace components as necessary.
5. Inspect the water outlet fitting for excessive corrosion and cracks around the O-ring sealing area. Replace the water outlet fitting if necessary.

Assembly

1. Using installer/remover part No. 884259-2 and drive handle part No. 9991801-3, install new upper and lower suspension fork bushings. Wipe the outer diameter of the bushings with Volvo Penta Propeller Shaft Grease or equivalent (**Table 5**), before installation.
2. Grease new pivot pin bushings with propeller shaft grease. Install the bushings into each side of the suspension fork.
3. Grease the thrust washers (25, **Figure 1**) with propeller shaft grease. Place a thrust washer on each of the upper and lower surfaces of the intermediate housing steering tube bore.

4. Align the suspension fork with the intermediate housing. Adjust the position of the thrust washers to align with the steering tube bore.

5. Grease the steering tube with propeller shaft grease. Carefully install the tube from the bottom of the suspension fork bore and push it into position. Make sure that both thrust washers and the upper and lower suspension fork bushings are aligned and not damaged.

6. Install the retainer (22, **Figure 1**) into the suspension fork lower bushing bore. Position the large diameter of the retainer toward the suspension fork and the small diameter toward the lower gearcase.

7. Coat the mating surface of the water outlet cover with Volvo White Sealing Compound or equivalent (**Table 5**). Coat a new O-ring with Volvo Penta Propeller Shaft Grease or Equivalent (**Table 5**). Position the O-ring into the suspension fork groove, then install the water outlet cover. Coat the threads of the 2 cover screws with sealing compound. Install and tighten the screws securely.

8. If the shift bellcrank assembly was removed, begin reassembly by greasing the bellcrank pivot pin, bellcrank and shift link rod with Volvo Penta Propeller Shaft Grease or equivalent (**Table 5**).

9. Position the bellcrank in the intermediate housing and install the pin from the port side of the housing, making sure that the end of the shaft with the cotter pin hole is installed first.

10. Position the 2 flat washers (39, **Figure 1**) on the starboard side of the bellcrank and pilot the bellcrank shaft through them. Separate the washers and install a new stainless steel cotter pin through the shaft, between the 2 washers. Bend both prongs of the cotter pin for a secure attachment.

11. If removed, reattach the shift link (36, **Figure 1**) to the starboard side of the bellcrank and secure it with a flat washer and a new stainless steel cotter pin. Bend both prongs of the cotter pin for a secure attachment.

12. *DPX models*—If removed, install new steering pin bushings into the intermediate housing with a suitable drift.

TRANSOM SHIELD (DP-C1/D1 AND DPX MODELS)

The transom shield and mounting collar provides a waterproof passage between the engine and stern drive for the input drive shaft, remote control shift cable, cooling water, trim system hydraulic lines and the engine exhaust.

DP-C1/D1 models incorporate a steering yoke and helmet assembly (2, **Figure 4**) that is mounted at the top of the transom shield. If either the yoke or helmet requires service, they are replaced as an assembly. A steering arm is attached to the yoke and helmet assembly. The steering arm allows connection of the Volvo power steering cylinder to the drive unit. A trim sending unit is driven off of a gear rack on the steering helmet and is mounted in the center of the steering yoke shaft. Service procedures for the trim sending unit are covered in Chapter Fifteen.

DPX models do not incorporate a steering yoke or helmet as they are steered by externally mounted hydraulic rams. A hydraulic manifold (4, **Figure 5**) for the hydraulic steering lines occupies the space normally used by the steering yoke shaft on DP-C1/D1 models. Refer to Chapter Sixteen for steering system service information.

On all models, the flywheel cover extends through the transom shield mounting collar and is secured by 6 clamp bolts (19, **Figure 6**). These bolts must be removed before the engine can be removed from the boat. Refer to **Figure 7** for a view of a typical mounting collar with the bolts removed. Whenever the bolts have been removed or tightened, engine alignment between the flywheel cover and transom shield must be checked at 3 points with alignment tool part No. 884502-6. The tool is simply a tapered wedge. The tool is inserted between the cast bosses on the top and each side of the flywheel cover and the leading edge of the transom shield mounting collar (**Figure 8**). When the tool can be inserted the same distance at each of the cast bosses, the unit is correctly aligned. Once alignment is verified, fold over the locking tab washers under the clamp bolts to secure the bolts.

The output shaft in the flywheel housing is splined to fit the universal joint assembly yoke. The output shaft uses 2 ball bearings and seals. One ball bearing is mounted in the crankshaft or flywheel, the other ball bearing is mounted in the flywheel housing. Refer to **Figure 6** for an exploded view of the mounting collar and flywheel housing components for GM models. Ford models use a flywheel housing that consists of a separate flywheel cover and a dedicated bearing housing. If the output shaft requires service, refer to *Flywheel Cover* in Chapters 6-8 as appropriate.

Mounting collar design for DP-C1/D1 models differs only in that 4-cylinder and V-6 models use a spacer plate (15, **Figure 6**) between the mounting collar and transom plate.

Figure 4 shows a DP-C1/D1 model transom shield assembly. DPX models use a mechanical trim sender and external hydraulic steering. **Figure 5** shows a typical DPX transom shield assembly.

Steering Helmet Service (DP-C1/D1 Models)

To replace the steering helmet and yoke shaft assembly or replace the steering bushings or O-rings, refer to **Figure 4** and proceed as follows.

1. Remove the drive unit as described in Chapter Twelve.

NOTE
The trim sending unit cannot be removed until the steering helmet and yoke shaft have been lowered slightly or removed.

2. Remove the trim sending unit clamp screw (51, **Figure 4**) from the steering arm. Remove the retaining bracket and spacer sleeve.
3. Remove and discard the socket head screw (35, **Figure 4**) securing the steering arm to the yoke shaft.
4. Pull the steering helmet and yoke shaft (2, **Figure 4**) down and out of the transom shield.
5. Remove the trim sending unit from the steering arm and set it aside. Remove and discard the trim sender O-ring.
6. Remove the trim sending unit gear wheel and shaft. Remove and discard the shaft O-ring. Inspect the shaft bushing and washer. Replace the bushing and washer as needed.
7. Remove the steering arm (53, **Figure 4**) from the transom shield.
8. Remove the upper and lower steering bushings from the transom shield. See **Figure 9**. The bushings may be fixed to the transom shield with epoxy and difficult to remove. Do not damage the transom shield while removing the bushings.
9. Remove the steering shaft seal (3, **Figure 4**) from the transom shield.
10. Clean and insect all components:
    a. Remove all corrosion from all mating surfaces and bushing bores.
    b. Inspect the trim sender gear rack for secure attachment to the steering helmet. If the rack is damaged or loose, replace the rack or tighten the attachment hardware securely.
    c. Inspect the steering bushing at the rear of the steering helmet. Replace the bushing if worn.
    d. Inspect the yoke shaft-to-steering helmet pivot hardware and steering shaft. Check for wear in the steering shaft bushing and seal area. If any part of the steering helmet and yoke shaft assembly is cracked, worn excessively or mechanically damaged, replace the steering helmet and yoke shaft assembly.
11. Install new steering bushings as follows:

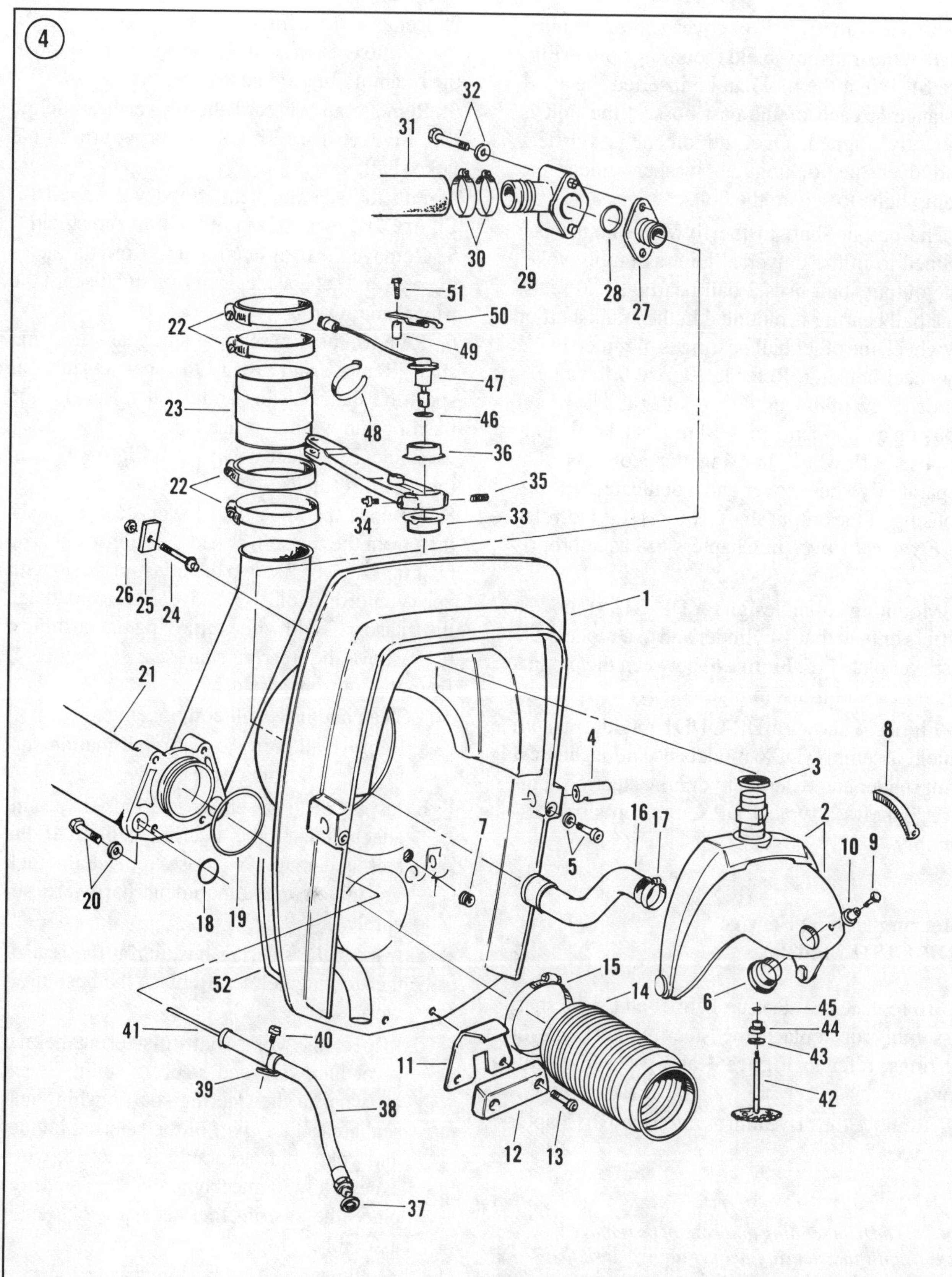
4
1
2
3
4
5
6
7
8
9
10
11
12
13
14
15
16
17
18
19
20
21
22
23
24
25
26
27
28
29
30
31
32
33
34
35
36
37
38
39
40
41
42
43
44
45
46
47
48
49
50
51
52

TRANSOM SHIELD ASSEMBLY (DP-C1/D1 MODELS)

1. Transom shield
2. Steering helmet and yoke shaft
3. Steering shaft seal
4. Pivot pin
5. Pivot pin retaining screw and washer
6. Steering helmet bushing
7. Plastic pipe plug
8. Trim sender gear rack
9. Screw
10. Nut
11. Support bracket
12. Anode
13. Screw
14. Exhaust bellows
15. Clamp
16. Water hose
17. Hose clamp
18. O-ring
19. O-ring
20. Screw and washer
21. Exhaust pipe
22. Hose clamp
23. Exhaust hose
24. Stud
25. Washer plate
26. Nut
27. Water nipple
28. O-ring
29. Water outlet fitting
30. Hose clamp
31. Water hose to engine
32. Screw and washer
33. Lower steering bushing
34. Grease fitting
35. Steering arm lock screw
36. Upper steering bushing
37. O-ring
38. Shift cable sleeve
39. Clamp
40. Screw
41. Remote control shift cable
42. Trim sender gear wheel
43. Washer
44. Bushing
45. O-ring
46. O-ring
47. Trim sending unit
48. Tie-strap
49. Spacer sleeve
50. Retaining bracket
51. Screw
52. Transom seal (175 cm [689 in.])
53. Steering arm

a. Affix each bushing into its respective transom shield bore using a marine grade epoxy.

b. Orient the bushings so the raised part on the bushing flange (7, **Figure 9**) fits into the relief (2, **Figure 9**) in the transom shield boss.

c. Allow the epoxy to cure for the full manufacturer recommended time span.

12. Install a new steering shaft seal into the transom shield.

13. Grease the steering bushings and seal with Volvo Penta Propeller Shaft Grease or equivalent (**Table 5**). Position the steering arm into the transom shield, between the steering bushings.

14. Align the marks on the trim sending unit as shown in **Figure 10**. Install the trim sending unit into the steering arm using a new O-ring. Install the spacer collar, retainer, ground strap and screw. Tighten the screw finger-tight at this time.

15. With the aid of an assistant, install the steering helmet and yoke shaft assembly into the transom shield being careful not to damage the shaft seal or bushings. Align the steering arm and seat the helmet and yoke shaft into the bushings.

16. Install a new steering arm socket head screw (35, **Figure 4**) and tighten it securely.

17. Install the washer, bushing and a new O-ring onto the trim sending unit gear wheel and shaft. Liberally coat all components with Volvo Penta Propeller Shaft Grease or equivalent (**Table 5**). Install the gear wheel and shaft into the steering helmet and yoke shaft. Be careful to engage the trim sending unit shaft, correctly. See **Figure 11**. Rotate the gear wheel as necessary to align the shafts. Seat the gear wheel into the yoke shaft when aligned.

18. Index the trim gear wheel to the steering helmet gear rack as follows:

a. Rotate the steering helmet to the full aft (down) position.

b. Rotate the gear wheel to position the marked gear tooth to starboard and slightly to the rear.

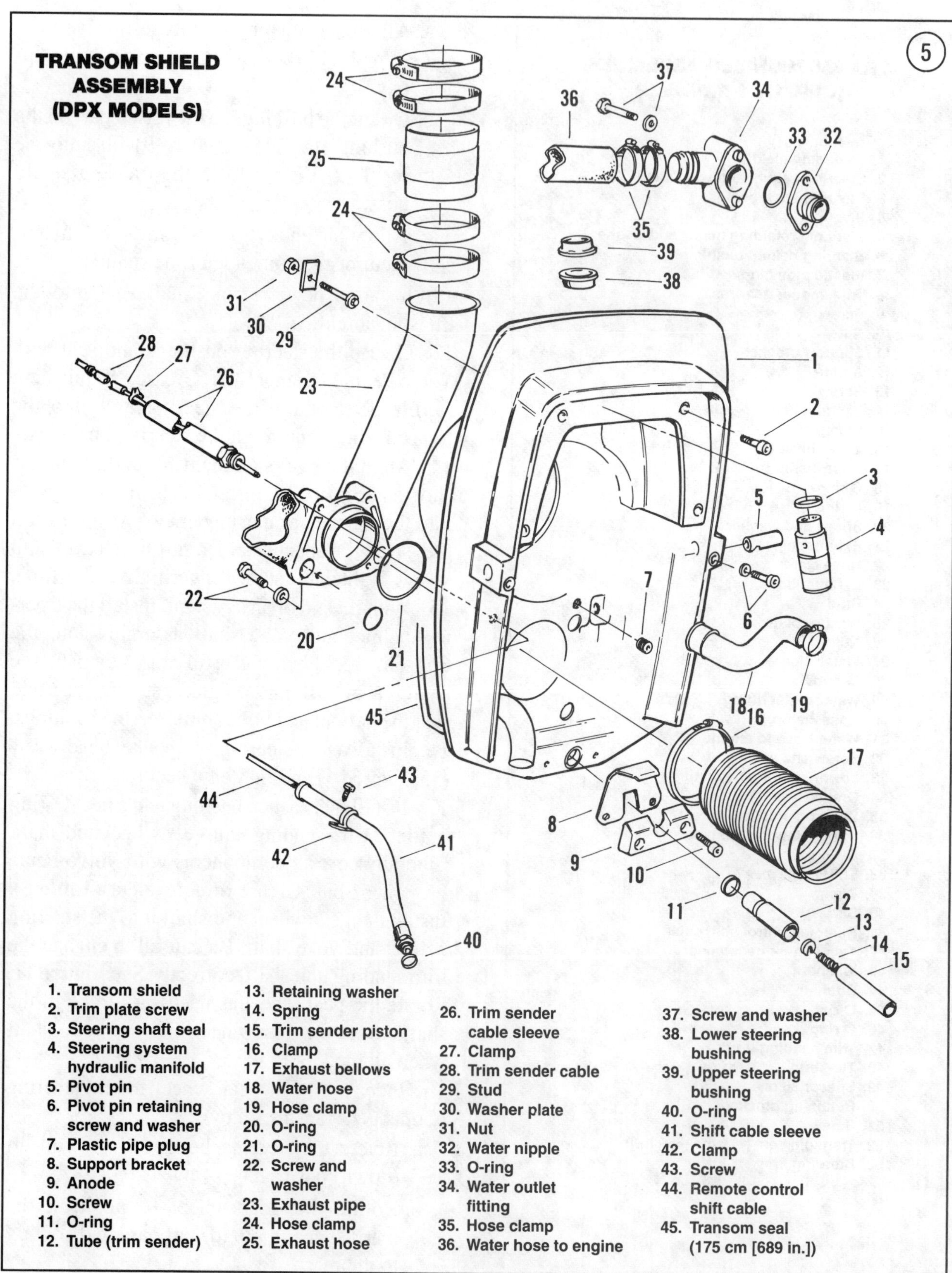

1. Transom shield
2. Trim plate screw
3. Steering shaft seal
4. Steering system hydraulic manifold
5. Pivot pin
6. Pivot pin retaining screw and washer
7. Plastic pipe plug
8. Support bracket
9. Anode
10. Screw
11. O-ring
12. Tube (trim sender)
13. Retaining washer
14. Spring
15. Trim sender piston
16. Clamp
17. Exhaust bellows
18. Water hose
19. Hose clamp
20. O-ring
21. O-ring
22. Screw and washer
23. Exhaust pipe
24. Hose clamp
25. Exhaust hose
26. Trim sender cable sleeve
27. Clamp
28. Trim sender cable
29. Stud
30. Washer plate
31. Nut
32. Water nipple
33. O-ring
34. Water outlet fitting
35. Hose clamp
36. Water hose to engine
37. Screw and washer
38. Lower steering bushing
39. Upper steering bushing
40. O-ring
41. Shift cable sleeve
42. Clamp
43. Screw
44. Remote control shift cable
45. Transom seal (175 cm [689 in.])

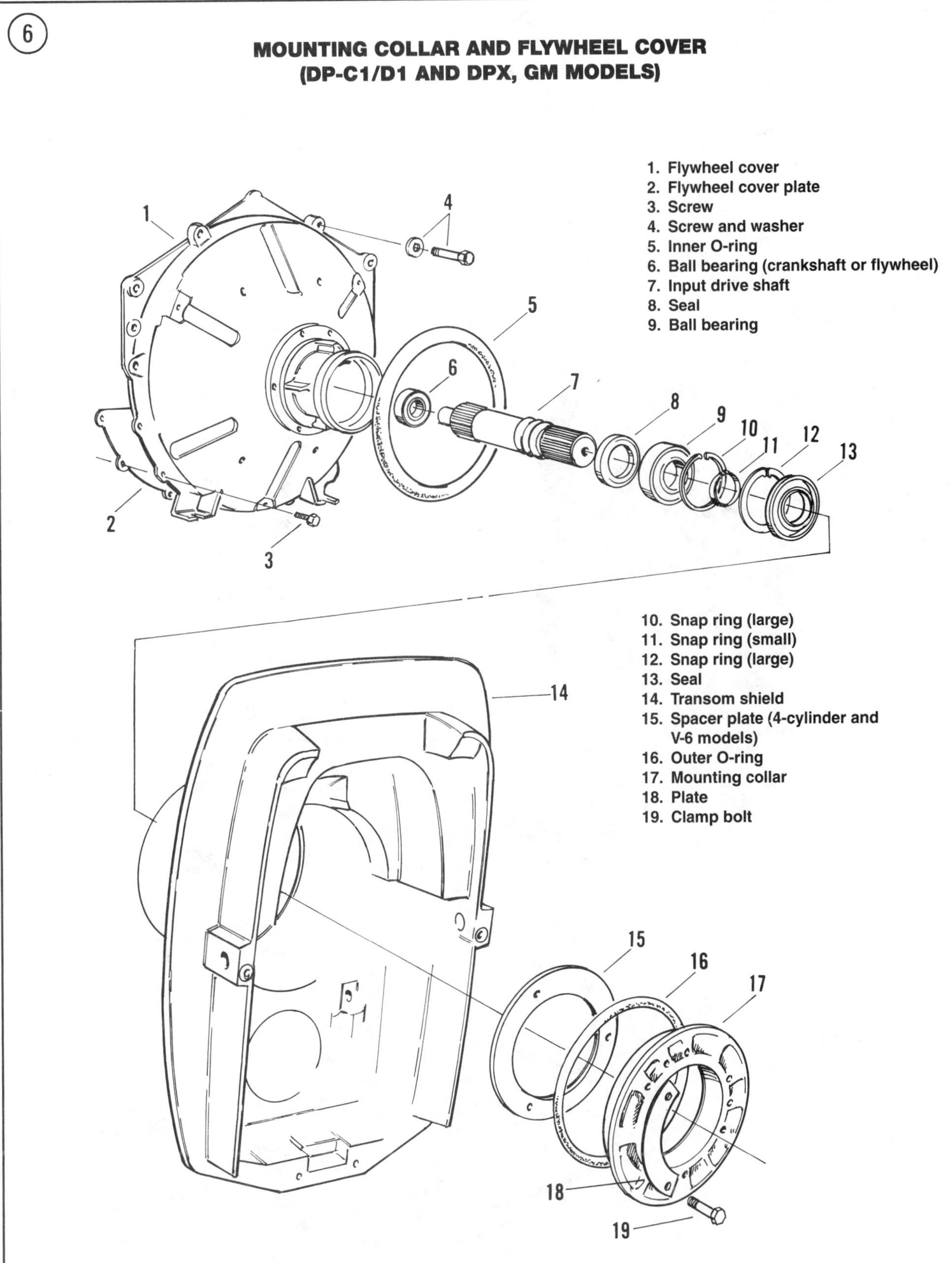
6
MOUNTING COLLAR AND FLYWHEEL COVER
(DP-C1/D1 AND DPX, GM MODELS)
1. Flywheel cover
2. Flywheel cover plate
3. Screw
4. Screw and washer
5. Inner O-ring
6. Ball bearing (crankshaft or flywheel)
7. Input drive shaft
8. Seal
9. Ball bearing
10. Snap ring (large)
11. Snap ring (small)
12. Snap ring (large)
13. Seal
14. Transom shield
15. Spacer plate (4-cylinder and V-6 models)
16. Outer O-ring
17. Mounting collar
18. Plate
19. Clamp bolt
1
2
3
4
5
6
7
8
9
10
11
12
13
14
15
16
17
18
19

c. Rotate the steering helmet forward (up) and engage the marked gear tooth on the wheel to the *first* tooth gap in the gear rack on the steering helmet. See **Figure 12**.

d. Rotate the steering helmet fully forward (up).

19. Install the drive unit as described in Chapter Twelve.

20. Adjust the trim sending unit as described in Chapter Fifteen. Make sure the ground strap is installed under the retaining screw.

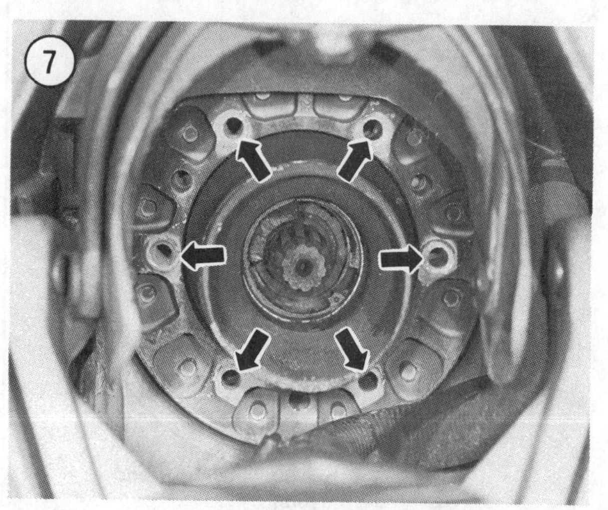

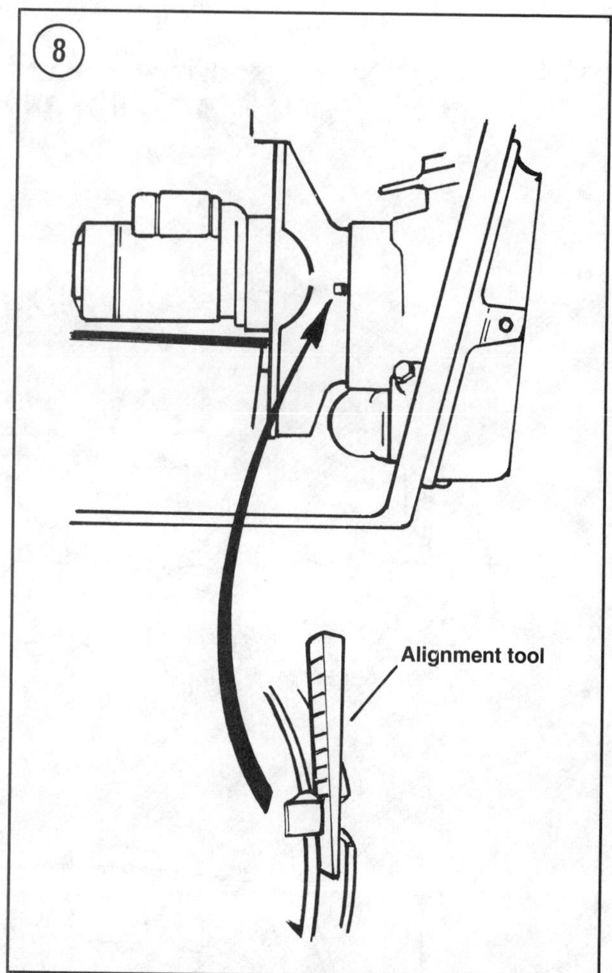

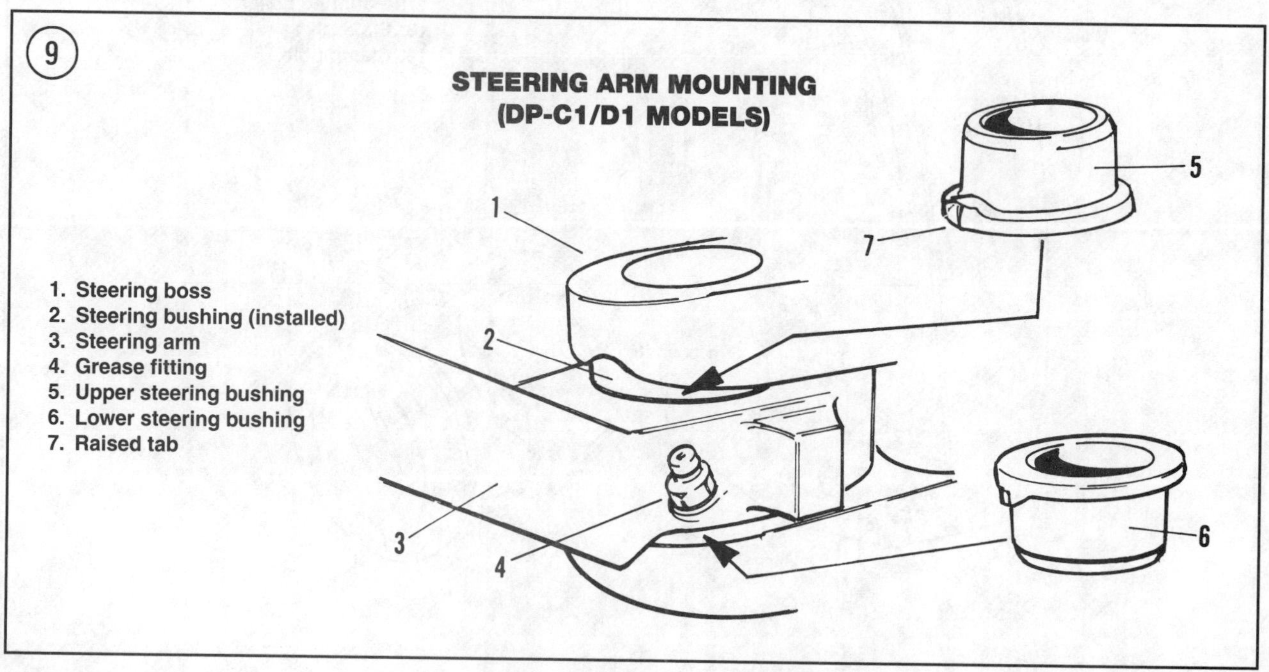

Transom Shield Service

Removal

Refer to **Figure 13** for DP-C1/D1 models and **Figure 14** for DPX models.

1. Remove the drive unit as described in Chapter Twelve.
2. Remove the engine as described in the appropriate engine service chapter. Make sure the 6 mounting collar screws (19, **Figure 6**) are completely removed before attempting engine removal.
3. Remove the hose clamp securing the exhaust bellows to the transom shield. Remove the exhaust bellows from the transom shield.
4. Measure the distance from the exhaust pipe tip to the transom shield mounting stud as shown in **Figure 15**. Record the dimension for reassembly.
5. Remove the 4 screws and washers securing the exhaust pipe to the transom shield. Remove the exhaust pipe. Discard the 2 small O-rings and 1 large O-ring.
6. Note the position of the grounding strap, then remove the 2 screws and washers securing the water outlet fitting to the transom shield. Remove the water outlet fitting. Discard the O-ring.
7. Remove the screw and clamp securing the shift cable sleeve to the transom. Remove the remote control shift cable from the shift cable sleeve.

8A. *DP-C1/D1 power steering models*—Disconnect the steering system from the transom shield as follows:

   a. Remove and discard the cotter pin securing the clevis pin to the steering arm. Remove the steering arm clevis pin.

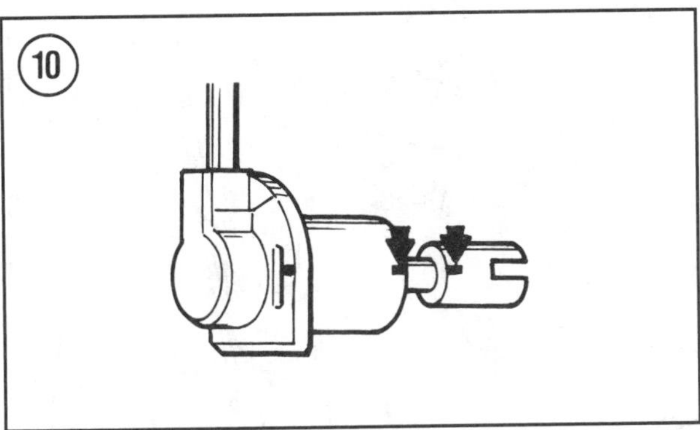

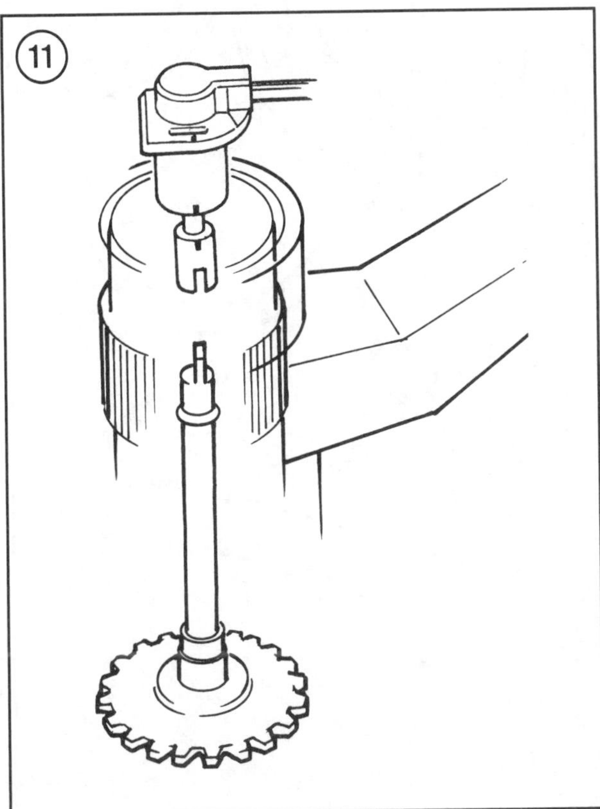

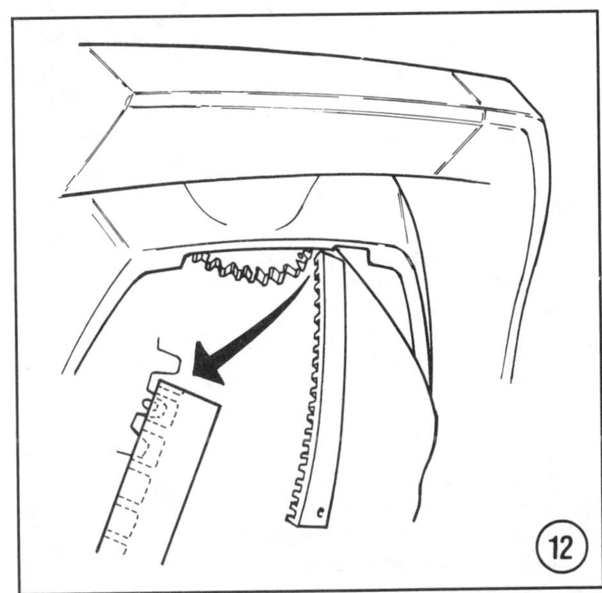

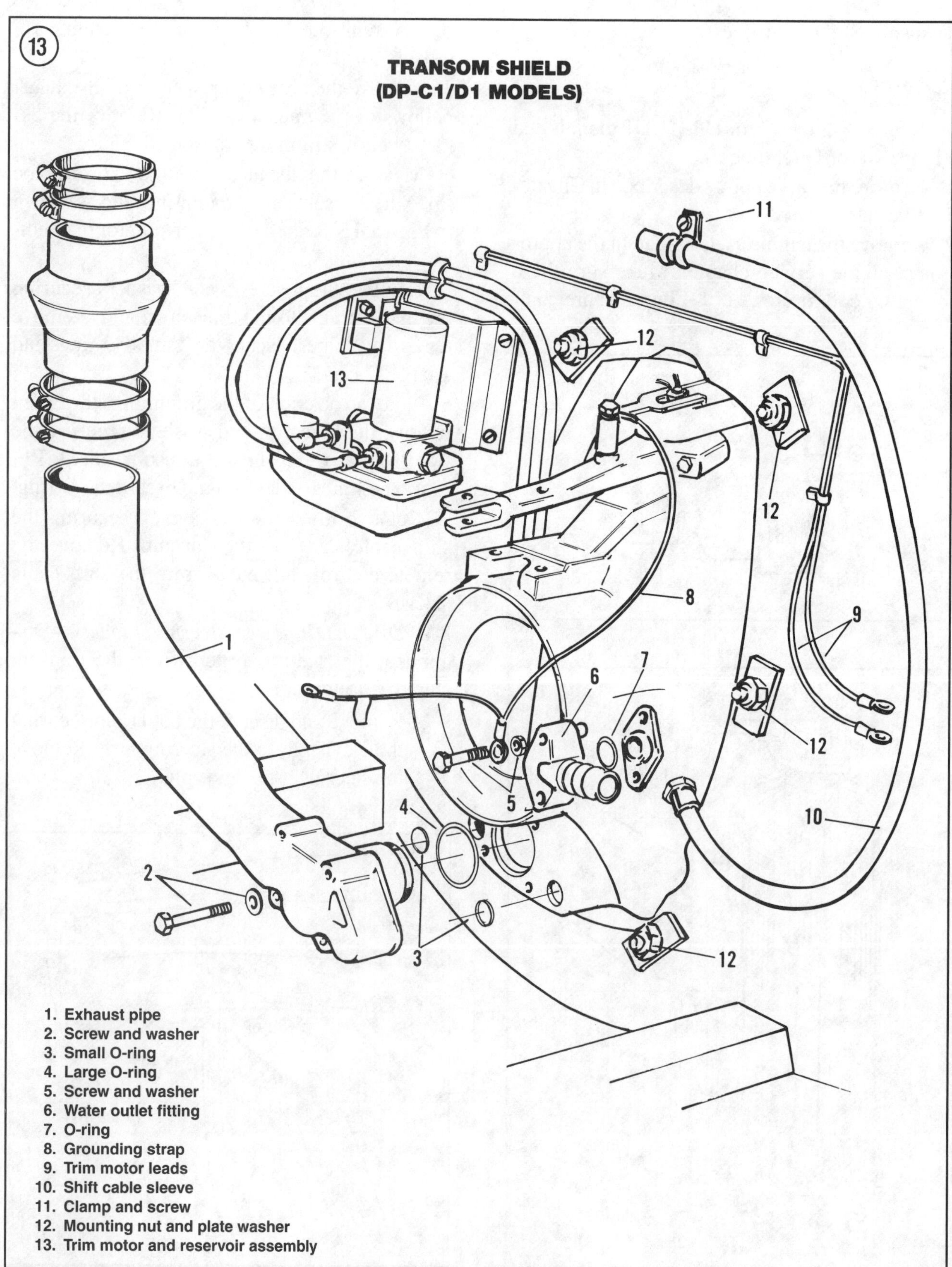
13
TRANSOM SHIELD
(DP-C1/D1 MODELS)
11
12
13
12
8
1
9
7
6
12
5
4
10
2
3
12
1. Exhaust pipe
2. Screw and washer
3. Small O-ring
4. Large O-ring
5. Screw and washer
6. Water outlet fitting
7. O-ring
8. Grounding strap
9. Trim motor leads
10. Shift cable sleeve
11. Clamp and screw
12. Mounting nut and plate washer
13. Trim motor and reservoir assembly

(14)

TRANSOM SHIELD (DPX MODELS)

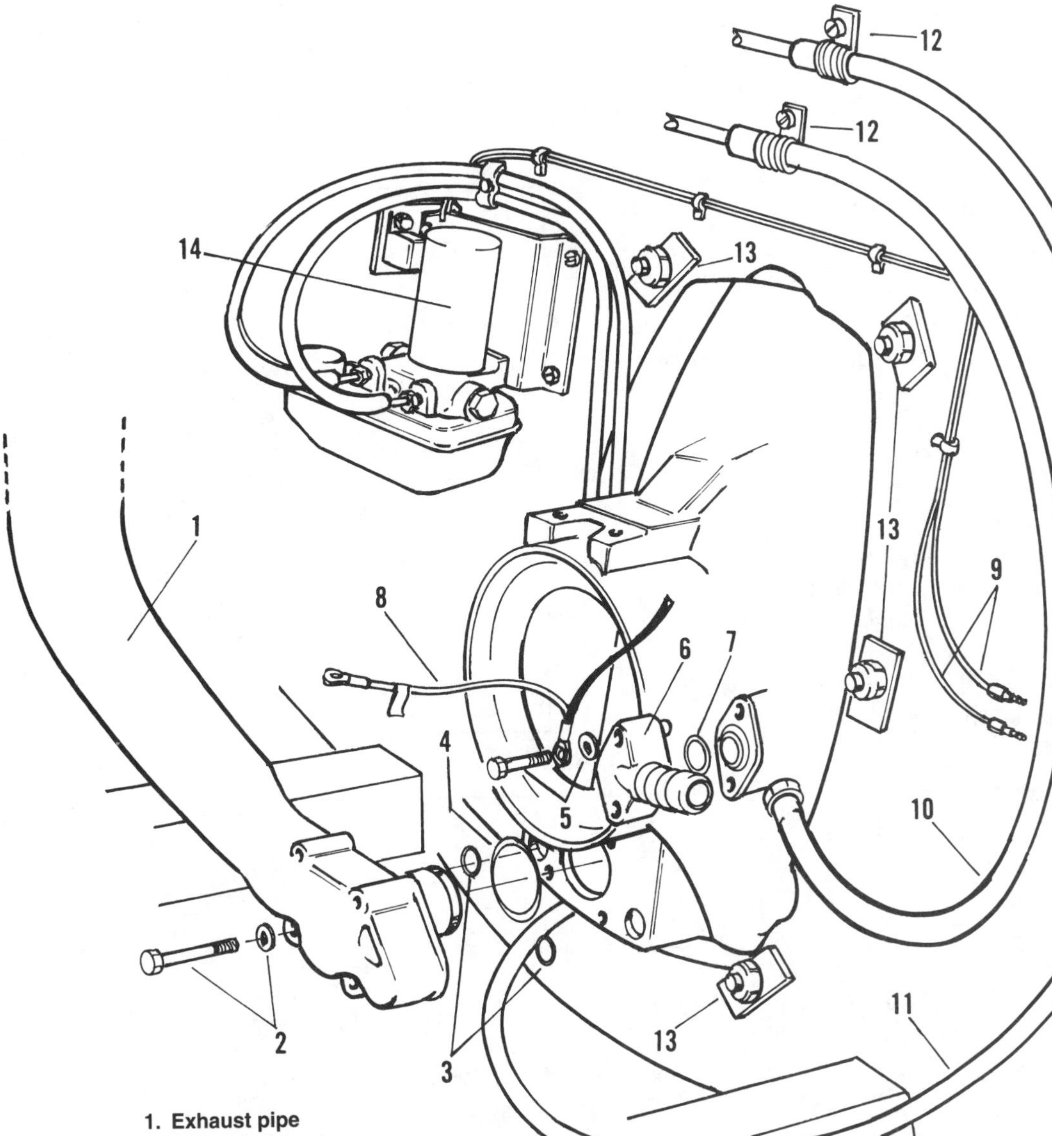

1. Exhaust pipe
2. Screw and washer
3. Small O-ring
4. Large O-ring
5. Screw and washer
6. Water outlet fitting
7. O-ring
8. Grounding strap
9. Trim motor leads
10. Shift cable sleeve
11. Trim sender cable sleeve
12. Clamp and screw
13. Mounting nut and plate washer
14. Trim motor and reservoir assembly

b. Bend the retaining tabs away from the 4 screws (A and B, **Figure 16**) on the steering cable mounting bracket. Remove the 4 screws securing the steering cable bracket to the transom shield.

c. Position the steering cable, cylinder and bracket to one side. Discard the 2 retaining tab plates (C, **Figure 16**).

8B. *DPX models*—Remove the 2 hydraulic lines from the top and side of the steering manifold (4, **Figure 5**). Remove the lines from the manifold's fittings. *Do not* remove the fittings from the manifold. Cap both lines on both ends. Refer to Chapter Sixteen if additional information is needed.

NOTE

Remove the trim pump assembly along with the transom shield ***without*** *disconnecting any hydraulic lines. It is necessary, however, to disconnect all electrical leads from the trim pump assembly.*

9. Disconnect the trim pump assembly power and ground leads, the 3-pin trim sender connector and all switching leads from the trim switch harness.

10. Remove the screws securing the trim reservoir and pump assembly to the transom. Set the trim pump assembly temporarily to one side.

11. *DPX models*—Refer to **Figure 5** and **Figures 17-19** and disconnect the mechanical trim

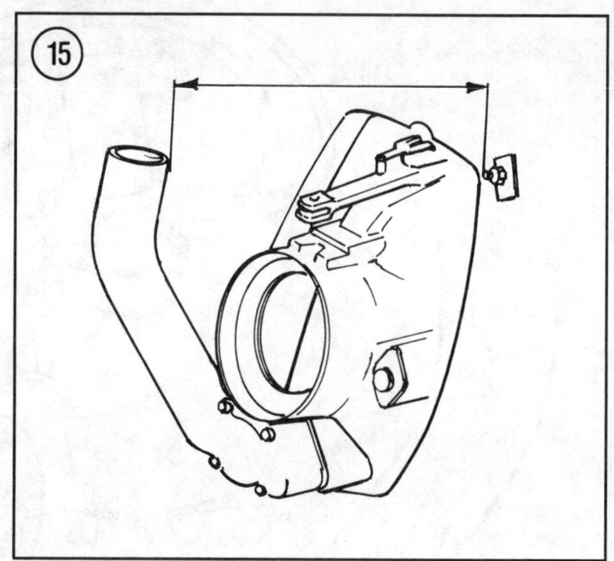

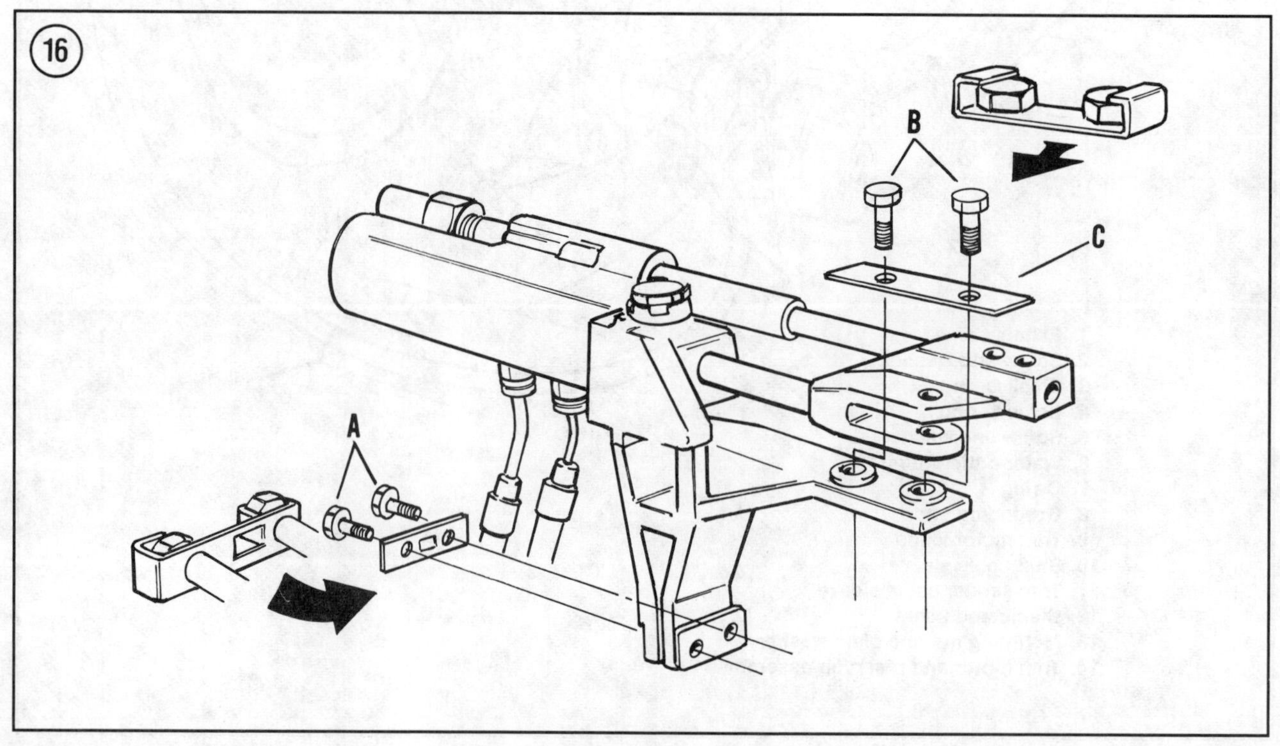

sender cable and sleeve from the bottom of the transom shield as follows:

a. Remove the 2 anode screws (A, **Figure 17**). Remove the anode (B, **Figure 17**) and support bracket (C, **Figure 17**). Pull the trim sender cable and sleeve out of the transom shield.
b. Remove the jam nut (A, **Figure 18**) inside the piston open end and unthread the piston (B, **Figure 18**) from the cable. Remove the piston and spring (C, **Figure 18**) from the cable.
c. Unthread the tube (D, **Figure 19**) from the cable sleeve. Remove the retaining washer (C, **Figure 19**) from the cable groove. Discard the cable sleeve and tube O-rings (A and B, **Figure 19**).
d. From inside the boat, pull the trim sender sleeve and cable assembly out of the transom shield and into the bilge area.

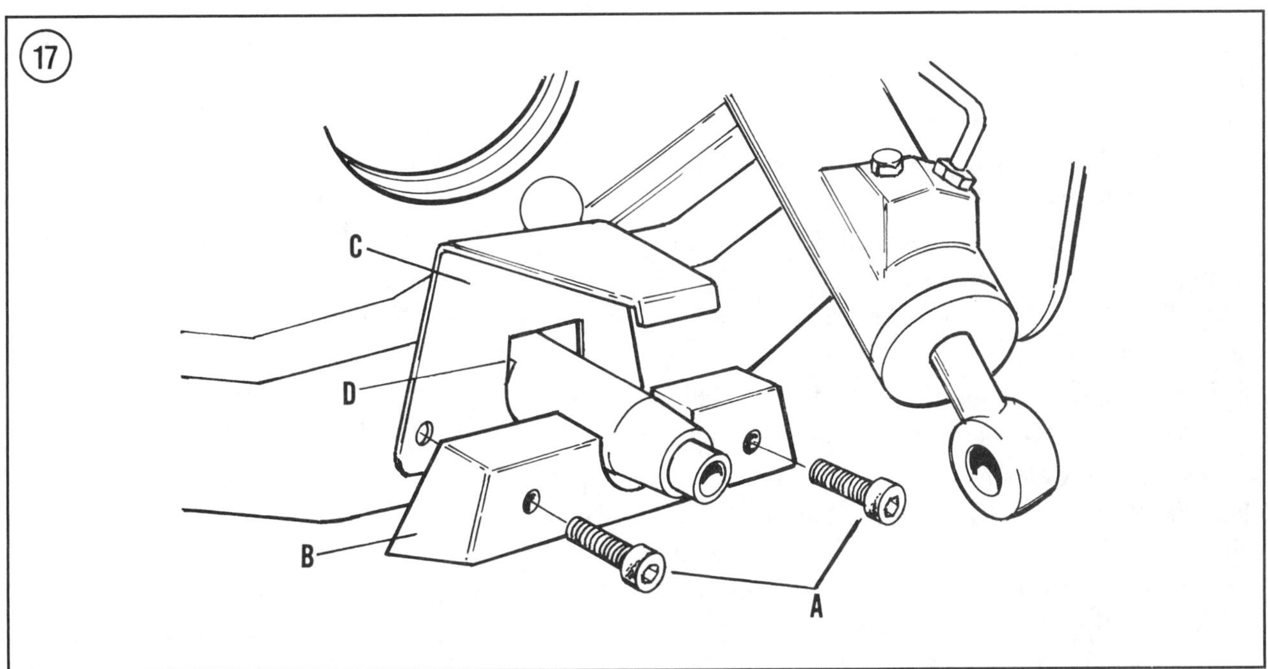

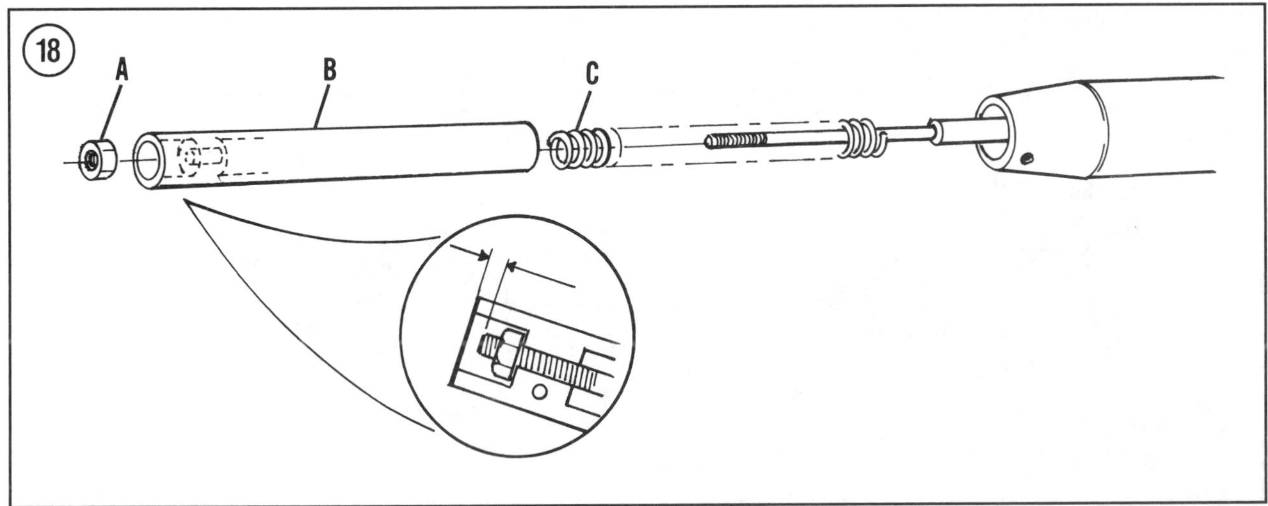

12. Remove any remaining ground straps or electrical leads.

13. While an assistant supports the transom shield outside the boat, remove the 6 nuts and washer plates from the 6 transom shield mounting studs.

14. With the aid of an assistant, remove the transom shield from the boat. Feed the trim pump assembly through the transom cutout as the shield is removed.

Cleaning and inspection

1. Remove the transom seal (52, **Figure 4** or 45, **Figure 5**). Clean the seal groove thoroughly with a suitable solvent.

2. Inspect the universal joint bellows removed during engine removal. Replace the bellows every 2 years or whenever deterioration or damage is noted.

3. Inspect the exhaust bellows. Replace the bellows whenever deterioration or damage is noted.

4. Inspect the water hose. If the water hose is damaged or deteriorated, replace it at this time. Make sure the new water hose is fully seated onto the nipple (27 **Figure 4** or 32, **Figure 5**) before seating the nipple into the transom shield.

5. Replace any of the transom shield mounting studs if their threads are damaged or corroded. Coat the mounting stud threads with Volvo White Sealing Compound or equivalent (**Table 5**) before installing the studs into the transom shield.

6. Inspect the shift cable sleeve. Replace the sleeve if it is damaged or deteriorated. Install a new sleeve with a new O-ring. Coat the threads of the sleeve with Volvo White Sealing Compound or equivalent (**Table 5**). Tighten the sleeve securely to the transom shield.

7. *DPX models*—Inspect the trim sender cable sleeve. Replace the sleeve if it is damaged or deteriorated.

8. Inspect the anode for deterioration. Replace the anode if has deteriorated to 2/3 its original size.

9. Thoroughly clean all old sealer from the transom. Inspect the transom. If the wood in the transom is rotted, it must to be replaced. Transom repairs are best performed by a competent marine fiberglass repair shop. If the wood is wet, but not rotted, allow the wood to dry, completely. Seal any bare wood or exposed areas with marine epoxy or several coats of marine varnish. Allow the epoxy or varnish to cure (dry) completely.

Installation

Coat the threads of all fasteners that are installed into the transom with 3M Marine Sealant 101 or equivalent (**Table 5**). This will prevent water entry and subsequent wood rot of the transom.

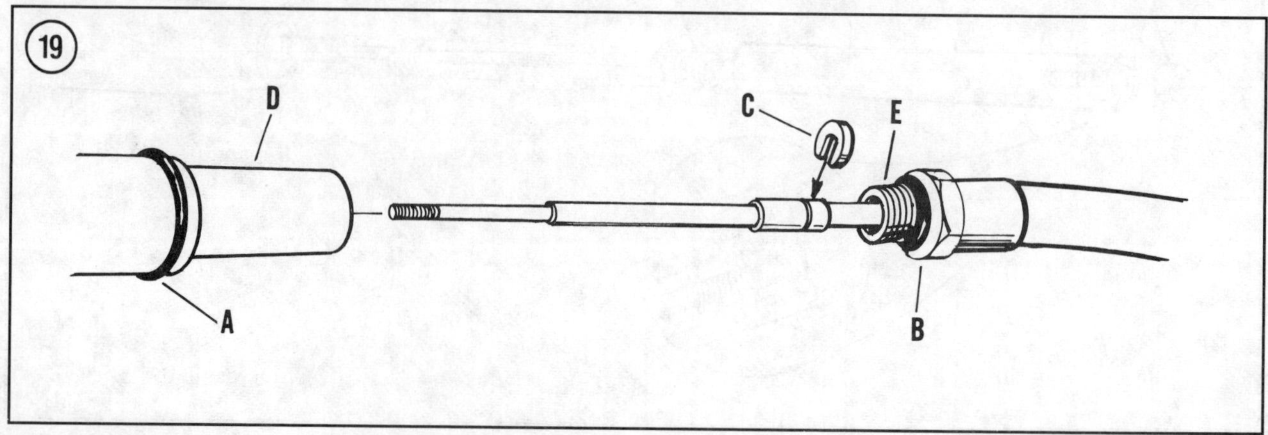

1. Glue a new transom seal into the transom shield groove with OMC Type M adhesive or equivalent (**Table 5**). The transom seal overall length before installation is 175 cm (68.9 in.). The ends of the seal must butt tightly together. Position the butt connection at the top of the transom shield groove.
2. Coat the 6 mounting studs with 3M Marine Sealant 101 or equivalent (**Table 5**).
3. With the aid of an assistant, feed the trim pump assembly into the transom cutout. Align the mounting studs with the transom holes and seat the transom shield against the transom.
4. Install the 6 washer plates and 6 nuts to the mounting studs. Tighten the nuts evenly to 40 N•m (29.5 ft.-lb.) initially, then to a final torque of 80 N•m (59.0 ft.-lb.).
5. Position the trim pump assembly to the transom and secure it in the original mounting holes. Coat the fasteners with 3M Marine Sealant 101 or equivalent (**Table 5**). Tighten the fasteners securely.
6. Reconnect all electrical leads to the trim pump assembly.
7. *DPX models*—Reconnect the trim sender cable and sleeve to the bottom of the transom shield as follows:
   a. From inside the bilge, push the cable sleeve (and trim sender cable) fully through the transom plate opening.
   b. Grease the trim cable end with Volvo Penta Propeller Shaft Grease or equivalent (**Table 5**). Install the retaining washer (C, **Figure 19**) into the cable groove.
   c. Install new O-rings (A, **Figure 19**) onto the tube and cable sleeve (B, **Figure 19**). Coat the threads of the cable sleeve (E, **Figure 19**) with Volvo White Sealing Compound or equivalent (**Table 5**).
   d. Securely tighten the tube (D, **Figure 19**) to the cable sleeve (E, **Figure 19**). Make sure the retaining washer (C, **Figure 19**) is not displaced.
   e. Install the spring (C, **Figure 18**) over the cable. Thread the piston (B, **Figure 18**) onto the cable until the cable is recessed 1 mm (0.040 in.) into the piston bore as shown in **Figure 18**. Install and tighten the jam nut (A, **Figure 18**) securely.
   f. Push the cable sleeve and tube assembly into the transom shield opening. Seat the tube into the opening.
   g. Rotate the tube as necessary to allow engagement of the support plate (D, **Figure 17**). Position the support plate and anode to the transom shield. Secure the plate and anode with 2 screws. Tighten the screws securely.
8. Slide the remote control shift cable into the shift cable sleeve. Secure the shift cable sleeve to the transom with the original clamp and screw. Seal the clamp screw threads with 3M Marine Sealant 101 or equivalent (**Table 5**).

9A. *DP-C1/D1 models*—Reconnect the steering system to the transom shield as follows:
   a. Position the steering cylinder, cable and bracket to the transom shield mounting holes.
   b. Secure the assembly to the transom shield with 4 screws and 2 new retaining tab washers. Tighten the 4 screws securely, then bend the tabs of the retaining washers securely up against the screw heads.
   c. Align the steering arm to the cylinder clevis end. Insert the clevis pin through the steering arm and steering cylinder clevis end. Install a new stainless steel cotter pin into the clevis pin. Bend both prongs of the cotter pin for a secure attachment.

9B. *DPX models*—Reconnect the 2 hydraulic lines to the top and side of the steering manifold (4, **Figure 5**). Tighten the line fittings securely.

10. Reconnect the water outlet fitting to the transom shield using a new O-ring. Coat the 2 screws with Volvo White Sealing Compound or equivalent (**Table 5**). Install the 2 screws and washers. Tighten the screws securely.

11. Install a new large O-ring and 2 small O-rings to the exhaust pipe. Position the exhaust pipe to the transom shield. Coat the 4 screws with Volvo White Sealing Compound or equivalent (**Table 5**). Install the 4 screws and washers hand-tight.

NOTE
*If the dimension shown in **Figure 15** was not recorded during disassembly, set the dimension to 465 mm (18.3 in.) for V-6 and V-8 engines up to 5.8 L (351 cid). Set the dimension to 508 mm (20 in.) for the 7.4 L (454 cid) and 8.2 L (502 cid) engines.*

12. Adjust the distance from the exhaust pipe tip to the transom shield mounting stud (**Figure 15**) to the dimension recorded during disassembly. Tighten the 4 screws evenly to 40 N•m (29.5 ft.-lb.). Recheck the dimension. If necessary, loosen the 4 screws, readjust and retighten.
13. Install the exhaust bellows to the transom shield. Position the clamp as shown in **Figure 20**. Tighten the clamp securely.
14. Reinstall the engine as described in the appropriate engine service chapter. Make sure alignment is verified as described previously.
15. Reinstall the drive unit as described in Chapter Twelve.

TRANSOM BRACKET (SX AND DP-S MODELS)

The transom brackets used on 1994-1996 SX and DP-S models are almost identical with the exception of the trim sending unit and its mounting location. On 1994 SX models, the trim sending unit is mounted to the starboard side of the gimbal ring on 2 cast bosses (**Figure 21**). The sending unit has an arm that contacts the pivot housing and rotates the sender as the pivot housing moves toward or away from the sender. Starting in 1995, the trim sending unit mounting location was moved to an integral location on the gimbal ring (**Figure 22**). The sender is connected to the starboard pivot housing pivot screw and detects the rotation of the screw as the pivot housing is raised or lowered. The 2 systems are not interchangeable. Adjustment of both types of trim sending units is covered in Chapter Fifteen.

Two small changes were made for 1996 models. The first was the addition of another hole at the top of the gimbal housing, right next to the hole for the trim sending unit leads. This extra

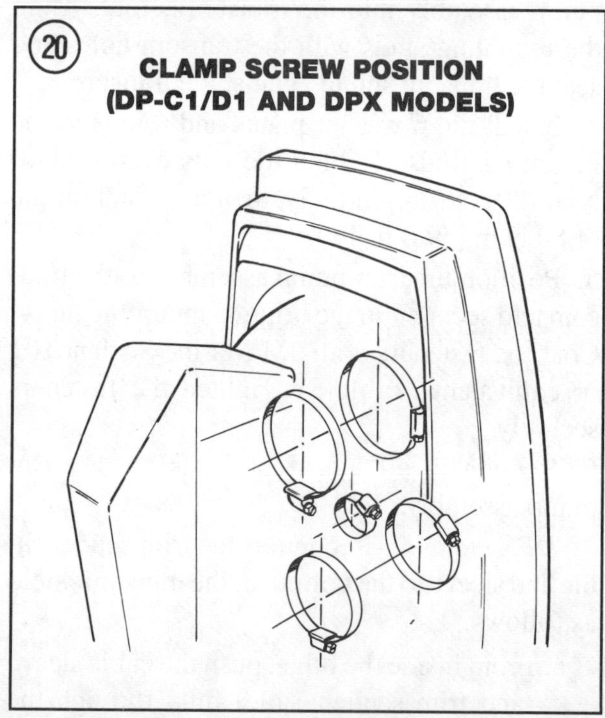
(20) CLAMP SCREW POSITION (DP-C1/D1 AND DPX MODELS)

(21)

hole is for the optionalVolvo Penta Active Corrosion Protection (ACP) System. A plug is installed in this hole at the factory. If the ACP system is added, the plug is removed and the ACP system wiring harness is routed through the hole.

The second change was an internal change to the trim sending unit. A third wire was added to allow the trim sender to operate the trim limit box required on all DP-S model drive units. The trim limit box allows programming limits to the maximum trim IN, trim OUT and tilt UP positions. Operation and programming of the trim limit box is covered in Chapter Fifteen.

A change was made only to the 7.4 and 8.2 L models in 1998. A sensor housing and two anodes were installed on the bottom of the steering support bracket. This chapter covers it in the gimbal ring removal section.

Gimbal bearing, gimbal bearing seal, universal joint and exhaust bellows and water hose service are covered under *Pivot Housing Service* in this chapter. Steering and tilt bushing service is covered under *Gimbal Ring Service* in this chapter. Complete removal of the transom bracket assembly is covered under *Transom Bracket Removal/Installation* in this chapter.

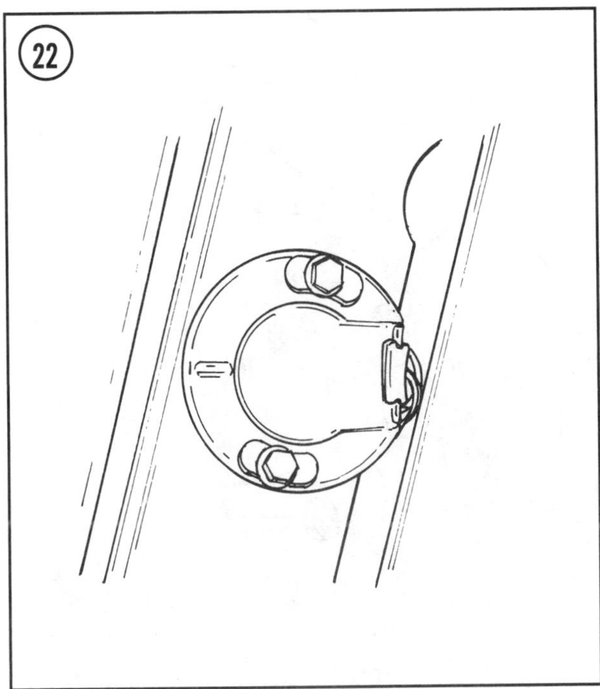

All hydraulic line service and complete trim cylinder removal and installation is covered in Chapter Fifteen.

Figure 23 shows an exploded view of a SX and DP-S transom bracket assembly.

Pivot Housing Service

The pivot housing can be quickly removed to allow easy access to the water hose, bellows, trim manifold, trim cylinder hydraulic lines and the gimbal bearing grease tube and fitting. The gimbal bearing and seal can be changed without removing the pivot housing, if so desired. Refer to **Figure 23** for the following procedure.

Pivot housing removal

1. Remove the drive unit as described in Chapter Twelve.
2. Remove the shift cable from the pivot housing, if not already removed.
3. Carefully lift the lip of the universal joint bellows from the pivot housing bore and push the bellows through the bore and free from the pivot housing.
4. Remove the snap ring securing the exhaust bellows to the pivot housing. Push the exhaust bellows through the bore and free from the pivot housing.
5. Remove the large plastic nut from the water tube nipple. Push the nipple through the bore and free from the pivot housing.
6. Remove the ground strap from the upper boss on the port side of the gimbal ring (A, **Figure 24**).
7. *1995-on models*—Remove the 2 screws and washers securing the trim sender to the starboard side of the gimbal ring. Remove the trim sender from the gimbal ring. Do not disconnect the sender electrical leads. See **Figure 21**.
8. Remove both pivot pin screws with a 1/2 in. hex drive socket. Support the pivot housing while breaking the port pin free to keep the

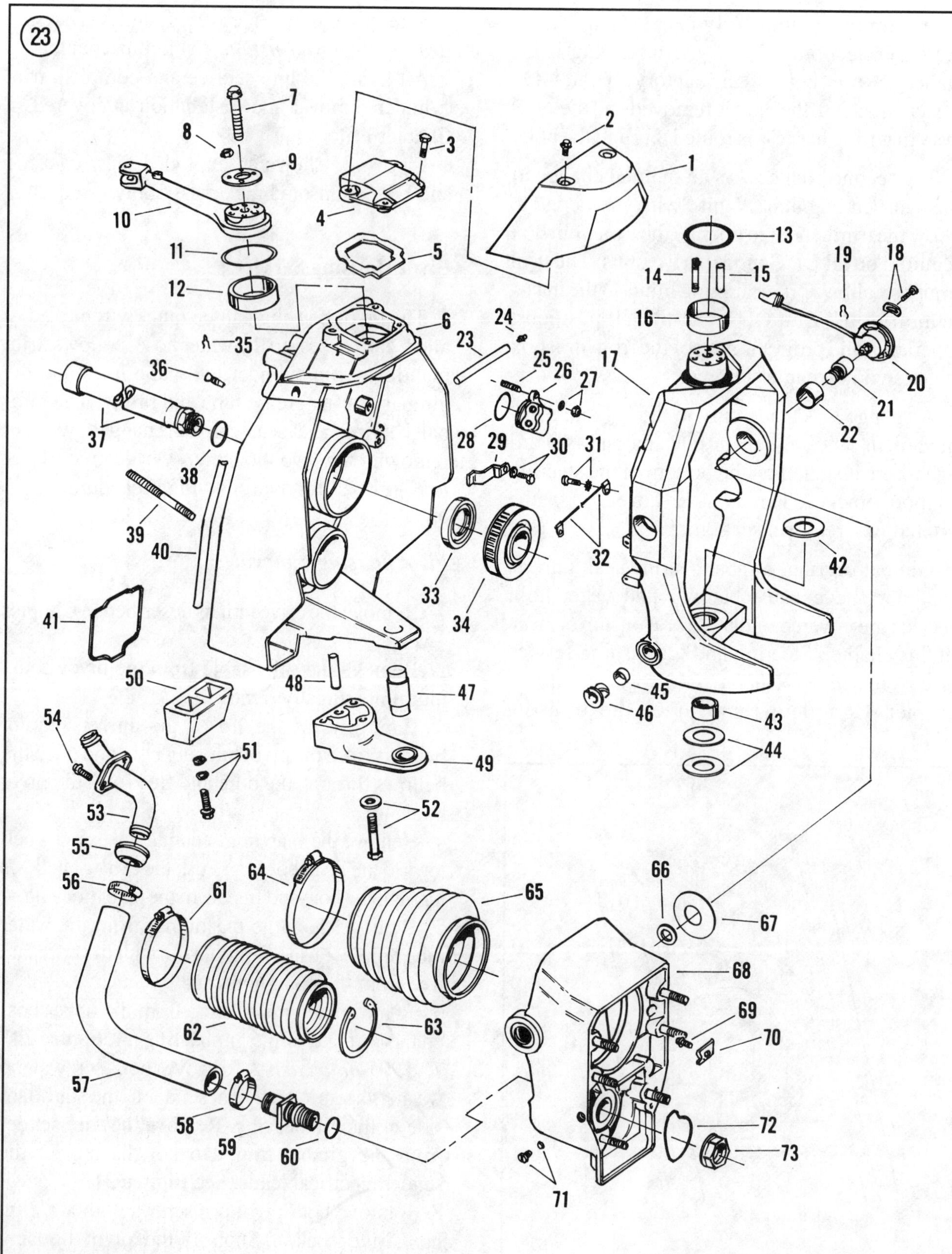
23
1
2
3
4
5
6
7
8
9
10
11
12
13
14
15
16
17
18
19
20
21
22
23
24
25
26
27
28
29
30
31
32
33
34
35
36
37
38
39
40
41
42
43
44
45
46
47
48
49
50
51
52
53
54
55
56
57
58
59
60
61
62
63
64
65
66
67
68
69
70
71
72
73

TRANSOM BRACKET (SX AND DP-S MODELS)

1. Plastic cover
2. Cover screw
3. Cover screw
4. Inner (metal) cover
5. Foam gasket
6. Gimbal housing
7. Steering arm bolt
8. Elastic locknut
9. Washer plate
10. Steering arm
11. Thrust washer
12. Upper steering bearing
13. O-ring
14. Stud
15. Dowel pin
16. Bearing sleeve
17. Gimbal ring
18. Screw and washer
19. Retaining clip (trim sender lead)
20. Trim sending unit
21. Pivot pin
22. Pivot pin bushing
23. Grease tube
24. Grease fitting
25. Stud (trim manifold)
26. Trim manifold
27. Elastic locknut and washer
28. O-ring
29. Retaining strap
30. Screw and washer
31. Screw and washer
32. Ground strap (pivot housing)
33. Seal
34. Gimbal bearing
35. Retaining clip (ACP system)
36. Plug (ACP passage)
37. Shift cable sleeve
38. O-ring
39. Gimbal housing stud
40. Transom seal
41. Exhaust pipe seal
42. Thrust washer
43. Steering bushing
44. Shim washers (as required)
45. Rubber grommet
46. Plastic bushing
47. Lower steering pin
48. Dowel pin
49. Lower support bracket
50. Anode
51. Screw, lock washer and flat washer
52. Screw and washer
53. Water tube and plate
54. Screw
55. Water tube grommet
56. Hose clamp
57. Water hose
58. Hose clamp
59. Water inlet nipple
60. O-ring
61. Clamp
62. Exhaust bellows
63. Snap ring
64. Clamp
65. Universal joint bellows
66. Thrust washer (metal)
67. Thrust washer (plastic)
68. Pivot housing
69. Screw
70. Retainer (shift cable)
71. Screw and O-ring
72. Seal
73. Plastic nut (water nipple)

housing from over-rotating upward. Refer to A, **Figure 25** for the location of the port pin.

9. Remove the pivot housing from the gimbal ring.

Pivot housing cleaning and inspection

1. Remove the water tube seal (72, **Figure 23**) from the pivot housing face.
2. Inspect the plastic, self-adhesive thrust washers that retain the metal thrust washer to the pivot pin bores. Remove the plastic washers (A, **Fig-**

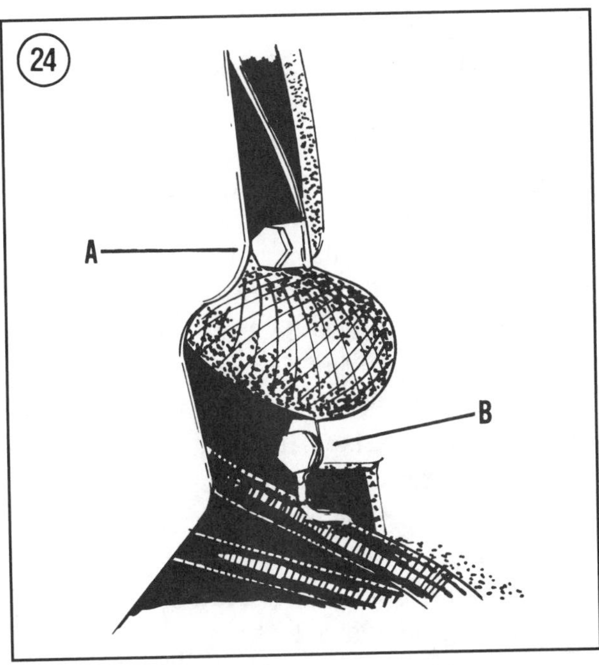

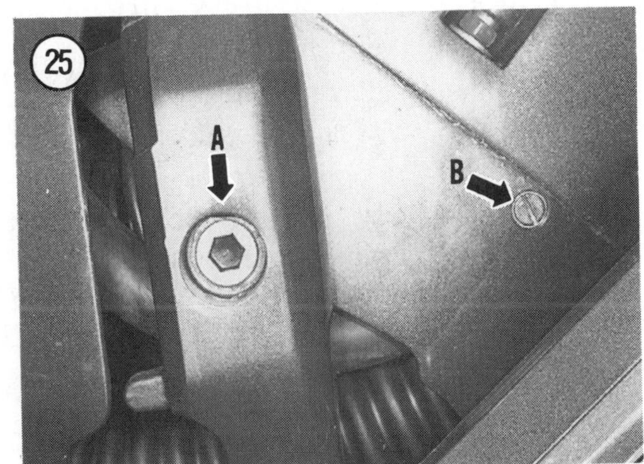

ure 26) if they are damaged or loose, or if the metal washers (B, **Figure 26**) are damaged and need replacement.

3. Clean the pivot housing in clean solvent. Remove all sealant and adhesive residue. Blow dry with compressed air.
4. Inspect the 6 drive unit mounting studs. Measure the installed height of the studs before replacing any damaged or loose studs. Apply Loctite 271 threadlocking adhesive to the threads during installation.
5. Remove the water drain plug on the starboard side of the pivot housing (B, **Figure 25**). Discard the O-ring. Install a new O-ring, lightly coated with OMC Gasket Sealing Compound or equivalent (**Table 5**). Install and tighten the drain plug to 5.7-6.8 N•m (50-60 in.-lb.).
6. Remove and discard the O-ring (60 **Figure 23**) on the water hose plastic nipple.
7. Inspect the ground straps. Replace any ground strap that is damaged.
8. Inspect the pivot pin threads in the pivot housing. The threads are Heli-coil inserts and may also be a threadlocking version of Heli-coil. If so, the middle threads will be slightly distorted in an octagonal fashion. If either type of Heli-coil is damaged, replace it as follows:
   a. Remove the old insert by grasping the outermost coil end with a good pair of needlenose pliers. Unthread the insert by turning it counterclockwise.
   b. Obtain a replacement insert from a Volvo or OMC Dealership. Installation kits are available from OMC dealerships.
   c. Run the installation kit thread tap through the bore to clean and recondition the threads.
   d. Position a new insert on the installation tool. Coat the new insert lightly with Loctite 271 threadlocking adhesive or equivalent (**Table 5**).
   e. Install the insert into the pivot housing following the instructions supplied with the installation kit.
   f. After installation, break the installation tab from the insert using needlenose pliers.

Bellows and water hose service

There is no orientation mark or specified installed position for the universal joint bellows. The exhaust bellows must be installed with the relief slots facing straight down. All clamps must

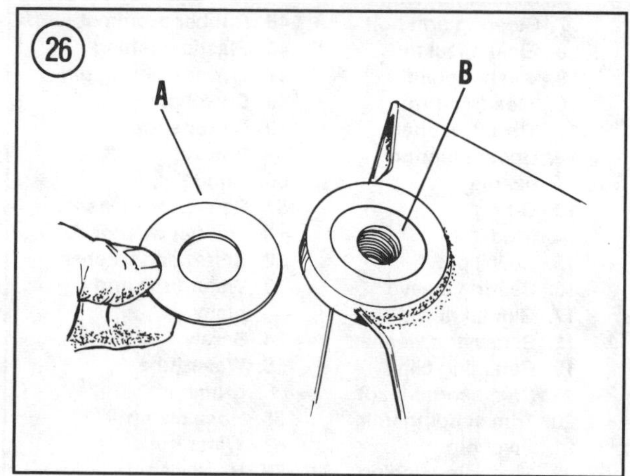

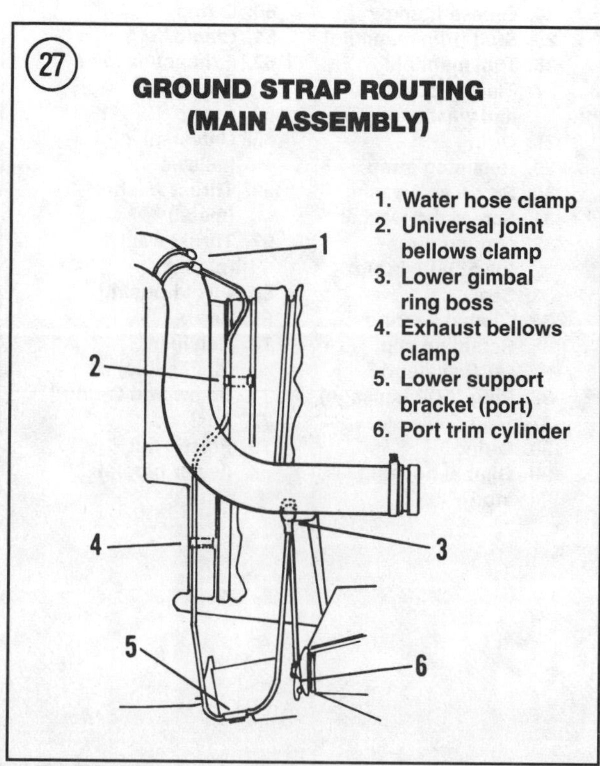

be installed as specified to prevent interference with other clamps, hoses and bellows. Refer to **Figure 27** for ground strap location and routing. Failure to install the ground straps will result in accelerated corrosion of the hose clamps.

1. Loosen the hose clamps around the universal joint and exhaust bellows. Remove the bellows. Discard the bellows if they are damaged or deteriorated.

CAUTION

Do not pry against the hydraulic lines when attempting to remove the water hose in Step 2. To ease removal, apply isopropyl (rubbing) alcohol to the hose connection.

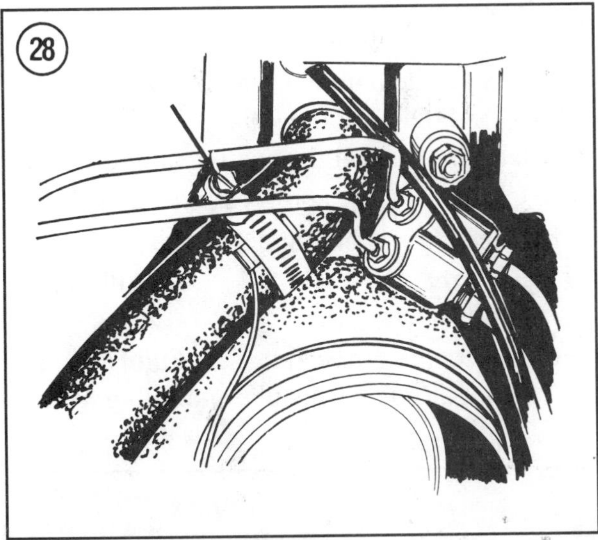

2. Loosen the hose clamp securing the water hose to the water tube at the top of the gimbal housing. See **Figure 28**. Carefully twist and remove the water hose. Discard the hose if it is damaged or deteriorated.
3. If the water hose is to be replaced, loosen the hose clamp securing the plastic water nipple (59, **Figure 23**) to the water hose. Remove the nipple from the hose.
4. If the water tube is to be removed, proceed as follows:
   a. Remove the 2 screws securing the water tube and plate (53, **Figure 23**) to the gimbal housing. Access these screws from the bilge.
   b. Pull the water tube and plate assembly from the gimbal housing. The water tube is curved and will require some manipulation to remove. If the water tube or grommet sticks in the gimbal housing, apply isopropyl (rubbing) alcohol to the area.
   c. Remove and discard the grommet.
   d. Clean the water tube and grommet bore in the gimbal housing.
5. Clean all sealer from the water tube and both bellows mounting bosses. Inspect the plastic nipple. Replace the nipple if it is damaged.
6. If removed, install the water tube as follows:
   a. Install a new grommet over the water tube with the large diameter facing the plate.
   b. Install the water tube and grommet into the gimbal housing.
   c. Coat the threads of the 2 screws with OMC Gasket Sealing Compound or equivalent (**Table 5**).
   d. Align the water tube plate to the gimbal housing. Install and tighten the 2 screws to 14-16 N•m (124-142 in.-lb.). See **Figure 29**, typical.
7. Coat the universal joint bellows mounting boss with a light coat of OMC Gasket Sealing Compound or equivalent (**Table 5**).
8. Install the hose clamp over the small end of the universal joint bellows. Install the universal

joint bellows over the mounting boss and engage the molded rib in the bellows to the cast groove in the mounting boss.
9. Position the hose clamp with the screw head pointing down (A, **Figure 30**), indexed at the 1 or 2 o'clock position. Install the ground strap tab under the hose clamp as shown in **Figure 27**. Tighten the clamp securely.
10. Install the hose clamp over the exhaust bellows. Install the exhaust bellows over the mounting boss (with the exhaust relief slots pointing down) and engage the molded rib of the bellows to the cast groove in the mounting boss.
11. Rotate the bellows as necessary to position the exhaust relief slots straight down. Position the hose clamp with the screw head facing up (B, **Figure 30**), indexed at the 3 o'clock position. Install the ground strap tab under the hose clamp as shown in **Figure 27**. Tighten the clamp securely.
12. Install a hose clamp over the gimbal housing end of the water hose. Install the water hose to the water tube. Position the hose clamp behind the trim lines as shown in **Figure 28**.
13. Install the ground strap tab under the hose clamp as shown in **Figure 27**. Rotate the hose as necessary to ensure that the nipple end of the hose is horizontal, then tighten the clamp securely.
14. If removed, install the plastic nipple to the water hose. Make sure the water drain hole in the nipple is pointing straight down. Secure the nipple to the water hose with a hose clamp. Position the screw clamp facing port, indexed at the 6 o'clock position. Tighten the clamp securely.

Gimbal bearing and seal service

The gimbal bearing is installed with OMC (Outboard Marine Corporation) part No. 3850038 installer. This tool is recessed deeper and has a longer pilot for the bearing than the Volvo part No. 3854357-5 installer. The use of the Volvo tool may result in contact between the tool and the bearing's inner race, resulting in bearing damage as the bearing is driven into the gimbal housing.

If the Volvo tool must be used, check for contact between the tool and the inner race. Check both sides of the bearing. Install the bearing with the side that has clearance (or the most clearance) against the tool.

The bearing can be installed in any direction as long as the tool does not contact the inner bearing race. However, the grease hole in the outer race must be aligned with the grease tube.
1. Remove the gimbal bearing with a suitable 3 jaw slide hammer, such as OTC part No. OEM-4184. Make sure the bearing is pulled straight from its bore and is not cocked. Discard the bearing.
2. Remove the gimbal bearing seal with a suitable 3 jaw slide hammer, such as OTC part No. OEM-4184. Discard the seal.
3. Clean and inspect the bearing and seal bores:
   a. Clean all sealer and grease from the bores.
   b. Check for nicks and burrs in the bores. Remove any nicks or burrs with emery cloth.
   c. Inspect the grease tube (23, **Figure 23**) and fitting. Replace the tube and fitting, if dam-

aged. Remove the grease tube with a pair of pliers.

d. Seal the grease tube to the gimbal housing with Loctite 271 threadlocking adhesive or equivalent (**Table 5**). Carefully drive the tube into the gimbal housing until it is seated.

e. Thread the grease fitting into the grease tube. Tighten the grease fitting securely.

4. Install a new seal into the gimbal housing as follows:

a. Thread installer, OMC part No. 3850038 or Volvo part No. 3854357-5 onto drive handle part No. 3850609-3 with the recessed side of the installer facing the drive handle.

b. Coat the metal case of the seal with OMC Gasket Sealing Compound or equivalent (**Table 5**).

c. Place the seal onto the installer with the spring side facing the tool.

d. Drive the seal into the gimbal housing until the tool seats against the gimbal housing.

5. Install a new gimbal bearing into the gimbal housing as follows:

a. Thread installer, OMC part No. 3850038 or Volvo part No. 3854357-5 onto drive handle part No. 3850609-3 with the recessed side of the tool facing away from the drive handle.

b. Rotate the corrugated band of the bearing race until the gap in the band aligns with the lubrication hole in the outer race.

c. Mark the outer race with a felt-tip marker to allow correct positioning of the grease hole to the grease tube.

d. Position the bearing into the gimbal housing bore. Align the outer race grease hole with the grease tube.

e. Position the installer against the bearing and drive the bearing into the gimbal housing until the bearing is seated in the bore. Drive only against the outer race.

f. Apply OMC EP/Wheel Bearing Grease or equivalent (**Table 5**) to the grease tube fitting until fresh grease is present at the bearing inner race.

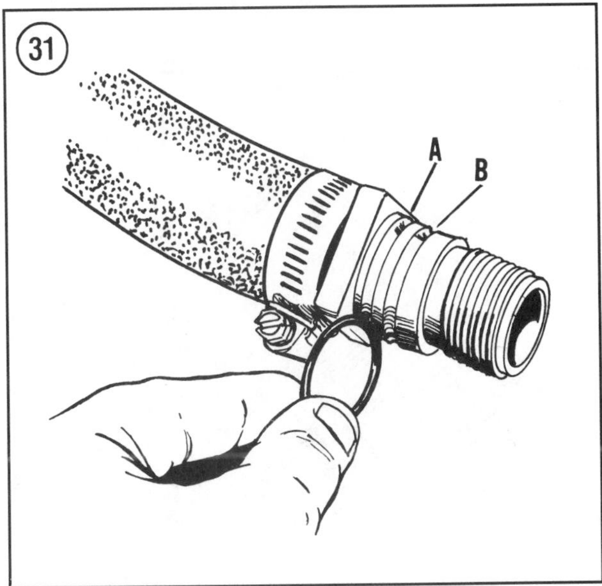

Pivot housing installation

1. Install a new O-ring in water nipple groove located directly against the nipple shoulder (A, **Figure 31**). Do not install an O-ring into the water drain groove (B, **Figure 31**).

2. If removed, install the metal thrust washers into the pivot housing bores and secure them in place with new plastic, self-adhesive thrust washers. See **Figure 26**.

3. Lightly glue a new water passage seal (72, **Figure 23**) into place with OMC Type M adhesive or equivalent (**Table 5**).

4. Lightly coat the lip in the inner diameter of the pivot housing, universal joint bellows bore with OMC Gasket Sealing Compound or equivalent (**Table 5**).

5. Position the pivot housing into the gimbal ring. Guide the water tube nipple into the pivot housing bore. Position the universal joint and exhaust bellows at the entrance to their bore.

6. Coat both pivot pin threads with antiseize compound (locally available).

7. Carefully align the pivot housing to the gimbal ring pivot pin bores. Install both pivot pins as far as possible by hand, making sure the threads are not crossed.
8. Verify that the pivot housing will pivot up and down without binding, then tighten both pivot pins to 142-163 N•m (105-120 ft.-lb.). Support the pivot housing when torquing the starboard pivot pin to prevent the housing from over-rotating upward.
9. Pull water tube nipple through the pivot housing. Make sure the nipple is seated into the pivot housing. Install the plastic nut and tighten to 11-14 N•m (97-124 in.-lb.). If the nipple is correctly seated in the pivot housing, several threads of the nipple will be visible through the nut.
10. Pull the universal joint bellows through the pivot housing bore. The bellows must be pulled over and seated against the housing lip. If necessary, tilt the housing and reach up from behind the housing to help feed the bellows through the opening. Make sure there are no flat spots on the bellows inner diameter (indicating that the bellows is fully engaged with the housing lip). The bellows must seat against the entire circular opening in order to seal.
11. Pull the exhaust bellows through the pivot housing bore. The groove in the bellows must be seated over the lip in the pivot housing bore. If the inner diameter is not perfectly round, the bellows is not correctly seated over the lip.
12. Secure the exhaust bellows with the snap ring. Position the opening formed by the ends of the snap ring at the 12 o'clock position.
13. Connect the pivot housing ground strap to the upper boss (A, **Figure 24**) on the port side of the gimbal ring. Tighten the screw securel y.
14. *1995-on models*—Install and adjust the trim sending unit as described in Chapter Fifteen.

Gimbal Ring Service

The gimbal ring must be removed to service the upper and lower steering bearings (bushings), the upper bearing sleeve and the upper bearing O-ring that prevents water entry into the boat. The vertical movement of the gimbal ring must be eliminated through a shimming procedure, performed during installation.

Removal

1. Remove the pivot housing, universal joint bellows and exhaust bellows as described previously in this chapter.
2. Remove the 2 screws securing the cover (1, **Figure 23**) to the gimbal housing. Remove the cover.
3. Remove the 2 screws securing the cover (4, **Figure 23**) to the gimbal housing. Remove the cover and discard the cover seal.
4. On 1998-on 7.4 & 8.2L models, remove four screws and two anodes from the steering support bracket.
5. Note the position of the ground straps, then remove 3 screws and washers. For models 7.4 and 8.2L (1998-on), remove 5 screws and washers securing the lower support bracket (49, Fig. 23) to the gimbal housing.
6. Remove the lower support bracket from the gimbal housing. If necessary, gently tap the bracket downward, alternating side to side with a rubber or plastic mallet to break it free. If the lower support pin (47, **Figure 23**) comes free, do not reinstall it at this time. Remove all thrust

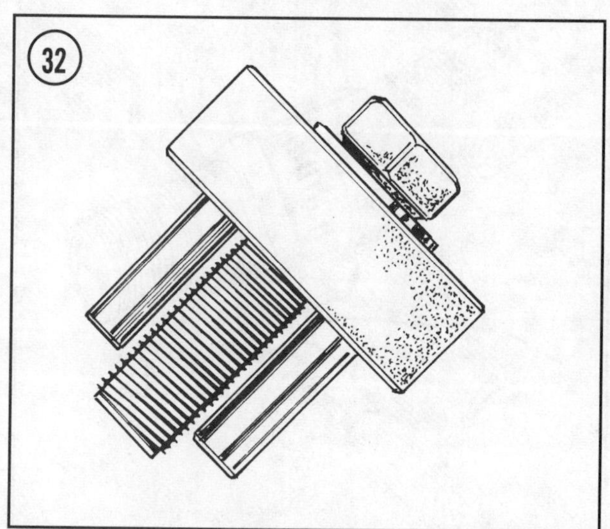

washers (44, **Figure 23**) from the lower edge of the support arm or lower bracket.

7. Remove the ground strap from the lower boss (B, **Figure 24**) on the port side of the gimbal ring.

8. Remove the 2 screws and washers securing the trim sender to the starboard side of the gimbal ring. See **Figure 21** or **Figure 22**. Do not disconnect the trim sender electrical leads. Allow the trim sender to hang by its electrical leads.

9. Remove the 2 plastic caps from the gimbal ring trim cylinder rod. Remove the 2 elastic stop nuts securing the trim cylinders to the gimbal ring (trim rod).

10. Slide each trim cylinder off of each side of the trim rod. Allow each cylinder to hang by its hydraulic lines temporarily. Pull the trim rod from the gimbal ring. Remove the plastic bushing (46, **Figure 23**) and rubber grommet (45, **Figure 23**) from each side of the gimbal ring.

11. Remove the 4 elastic locknuts and the center bolt from the steering arm. Access these fasteners from outside the boat. Remove the washer plate from the steering arm.

12. From outside the boat, attach steering arm puller part No. 3854361-7 (**Figure 32**) to the top of the steering arm. The puller should thread into the steering arm and press against the 2 dowels (15, **Figure 23**). Tighten the puller bolt to push the gimbal ring out of the steering arm. Guide and support the gimbal ring as it comes free and passes through the upper steering bearing.

13. Remove the puller from the steering arm.

14. Remove the thrust washer (11, **Figure 23**) from around the upper steering bearing and the thrust washer (42, **Figure 23**) from between the lower support arm and the gimbal ring.

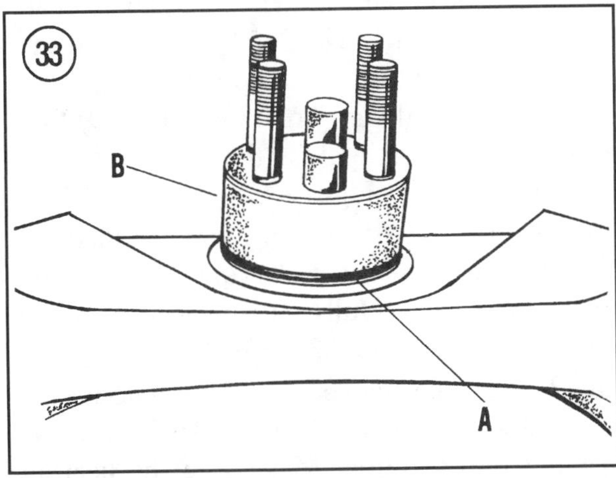

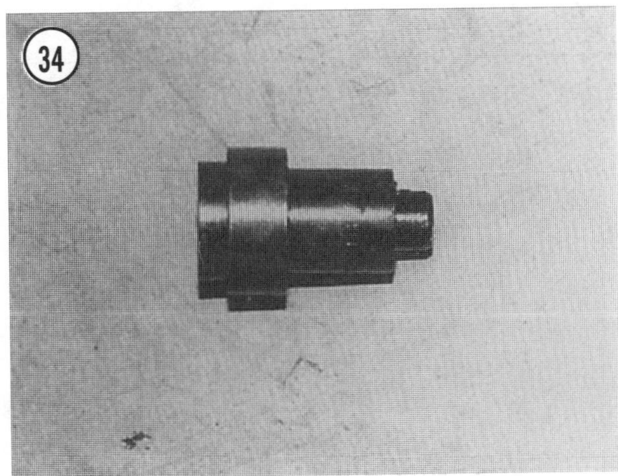

Bushing service

1. Remove and discard the O-ring (A, **Figure 33**) from the top of the gimbal ring.

2. Remove and inspect the lower steering pin from the lower support arm. Replace the pin if it is damaged or worn. Do not install the new steering pin at this time.

3. Remove and discard the pivot pin bushings as follows:

   a. Insert the large diameter end of remover tool part No. 3854358-3 (**Figure 34**) into a bushing.

   b. Drive the bushing free from the gimbal ring with a mallet.

   c. Repeat the procedure for the remaining bushing.

4. Remove and discard the lower steering bushing from the gimbal ring as follows:

   a. Insert the small end of remover tool part No. 3854355-9 into the inner (upper) surface of the bushing.

   b. Drive the bushing from the inside of the gimbal ring to the outside with a mallet.

5. Remove the upper steering bearing from the gimbal housing as follows:
   a. Assemble remover part No. 3854360-9 onto drive handle part No. 3854356-7 with the small diameter of the remover facing away from the drive handle.
   b. Position the assembly under the bearing and pilot the remover into the bearing.
   c. Drive the bearing up and out of the gimbal housing with a mallet. Discard the bearing.

CAUTION
The process in the next step can easily damage the gimbal ring if incorrectly performed. The bearing sleeve must be split without damaging the gimbal ring underneath. Proceed with caution.

6. If the gimbal ring upper bearing sleeve (B, **Figure 33**) is damaged, replace it as follows:
   a. Locate a suitable chisel that is the same width as the vertical height of the bearing sleeve.
   b. Position the chisel against the bearing sleeve and *carefully* split the sleeve from top to bottom with controlled strikes from a mallet.
   c. Remove and discard the sleeve from the gimbal ring.
   d. Clean the gimbal ring steering post and remove any corrosion, nicks or burrs.
7. If the gimbal ring upper bearing sleeve was removed, install a new sleeve as follows:
   a. Grease the steering post and inner diameter of the new sleeve with Volvo Penta Propeller Shaft Grease or equivalent (**Table 5**).
   b. Position the sleeve over the steering post.
   c. Install the steering arm over the 4 steering post studs and against the sleeve.
   d. Grease the steering arm center bolt and install it into the gimbal ring.
   e. Tighten the steering arm center bolt to pull the steering arm and steering bushing onto the gimbal ring. Tighten the bolt until the arm is seated on the ring.
   f. Remove the center bolt. Attach steering arm puller part No. 3854361-7 (**Figure 32**) to the steering arm as described previously and remove the steering arm from the gimbal ring.
   g. Inspect the bearing sleeve for damage. Make sure the sleeve is flush with the top of the steering post.
8. Install a new upper steering bearing into the gimbal housing as follows:
   a. Place installer part No. 3854359-1 (A, **Figure 35**) into the steering arm cavity (from the bilge area) with the recessed side facing down. The tool will act as a bearing stop, correctly locating the steering bearing just above flush in the gimbal housing bore.
   b. Lubricate the outer diameter of new steering bearing with gear lubricant (**Table 5**). Place the bearing (B, **Figure 35**) onto bearing installer part No. 3854360-9 (C, **Figure 35**). Slide the tool and bearing over threaded rod part No. 3854351-8 (D, **Figure 35**) and against the threaded rod's flange nut (E, **Figure 35**).
   c. Position the tool, bearing and threaded rod assembly under the steering bearing bore. Thread the rod fully into the pre-positioned installer part No. 3854359-1.
   d. Tighten the flange nut (while holding the rod with a backup wrench) to pull the bearing into position. Make sure the bearing starts squarely into the bore and pilots into

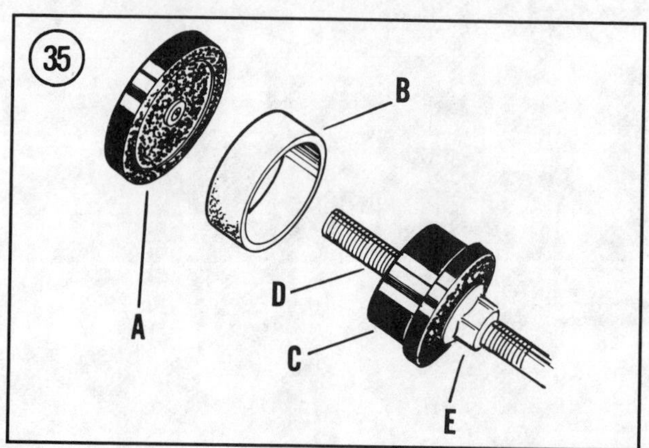

the recess of the installer located in the steering arm cavity.

e. Remove the tools and inspect the bearing. The bearing must be undamaged and just enough above flush to hold the thrust washer (11, **Figure 23**) centered.

9. Install a new lower steering bushing into the gimbal ring as follows:

a. Lubricate the outer diameter of a new bushing with gear lubricant (**Table 5**).

b. Insert the bushing onto the large diameter (short) end of installer part No. 3854358-3 (**Figure 34**).

c. Using a mallet, drive the bushing into the gimbal ring from the outside (bottom) until the bushing bottoms on the shoulder in the gimbal ring.

d. Remove the tool and inspect the bushing for damage.

10. Install new gimbal ring pivot pin bushings as follows:

a. Lubricate the outer diameter of the new bushings with gear lubricant (**Table 5**).

b. Pilot a bushing onto the large diameter (short) end of installer part No. 3854358-3 (**Figure 34**).

c. Using a mallet, drive the bushing into the gimbal ring from the outside until it is flush to 0.25 mm (0.010 in.) below the inner surface of the gimbal ring.

d. Remove the tool and inspect the bushing for damage.

e. Repeat the procedure for the remaining bushing.

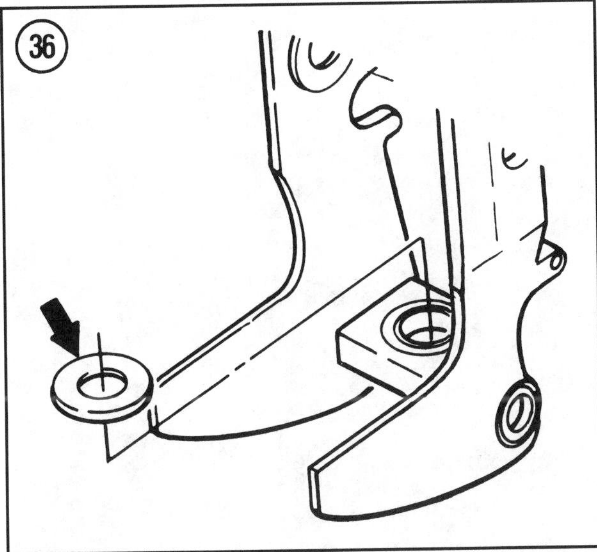

Installation

The pivot pin bushings and upper and lower steering bearings (bushings) are designed to run dry. Do not lubricate the bearing surfaces of these bushings. The grease will only attract dust and dirt, resulting in binding.

1. Install a new O-ring around the base of the steering post at the top of the gimbal ring (A, **Figure 33**). Lubricate the O-ring with Volvo Penta Propeller Shaft Grease or equivalent (**Table 5**).
2. Install the thrust washer around the upper steering bearing. Use a small amount of grease to hold the washer in position.
3. Position the steering arm into the steering arm cavity and center it over the steering bearing bore. Do not displace the thrust washer.
4. Carefully install the gimbal ring, guiding the upper steering post studs through the bearing and into the steering arm. Again, be careful not to displace the thrust washer (11, **Figure 23**).
5. Once the steering arm is piloted onto the studs, install the center bolt and hand-tighten. Install the washer plate and 4 new elastic locknuts. Hand-tighten the locknuts.
6. Install the thrust washer onto the gimbal ring (**Figure 36**), just below the lower support arm. Install the lower steering pin through the gimbal ring, thrust washer and into the lower support arm. If the pin will not remain in position, have an assistant hold it in place for Step 7.
7. While holding the gimbal ring in position, tighten the center bolt to pull the steering arm onto the gimbal ring dowel pins. Tighten the center screw to 88-98 N•m (65-72 ft.-lb.), then

tighten each of the 4 locknuts to 18-20 N•m (13-15 ft.-lb.).

8. Steer the gimbal ring back and forth, checking for freedom of movement. If binding is detected, the upper steering bearing or sleeve was damaged during installation and the gimbal ring will have to be removed and the damaged parts replaced. Do not proceed until the gimbal ring steers freely.

9. To shim the vertical movement of the gimbal ring and install the lower support bracket, proceed as follows:

a. Verify that 1 thrust washer (**Figure 36**) is present between lower support arm and the gimbal ring and that the lower steering pin is still in position.

b. Temporarily install the lower support bracket without any thrust washers. Install 1 bolt to hold the bracket against the gimbal housing.

c. Hold the gimbal ring upward, pinching the 1 thrust washer between the lower support arm and gimbal ring.

d. Measure the distance between the lower support bracket raised rib (around the steering pin) and the lower edge of the gimbal ring using thrust washers as gauges. Determine how many thrust washers can be installed in the gap between the bracket and gimbal ring while the gimbal ring is held upward. Record your results.

e. Remove the lower support bracket. Add one more thrust washer to the total determined in the previous step.

f. Install the predetermined amount of thrust washers over the lower steering pin, then install the lower support bracket and secure it with 3 screws and washers. Make sure the ground straps are installed on the port and starboard screws as noted during disassembly. Evenly tighten the screws to 24-27 N•m (18-20 ft.-lb.).

g. If the gimbal ring is correctly shimmed, it will be slightly preloaded, with no measurable vertical movement. The steering will also have a slight preload.

10. Grease the trim rod with Volvo Penta Propeller Shaft Grease or equivalent (**Table 5**). Install the rod into the gimbal ring. Position a plastic bushing and rubber grommet over the rod and into the recess on each side of the gimbal ring.

11. Make sure that each trim cylinder's bushings and grommets are installed, then slide each trim cylinder onto the trim rod. Install a flat washer and elastic locknut to each end of the rod. Evenly tighten the locknuts to 14-16 N•m (124-142 in.-lb.). Install the plastic cap over the ends of the trim rod and tighten the caps securely. If the ground straps were removed from the cylinders, reinstall them at this time.

12. Connect the ground strap to the lower boss (B, **Figure 24**) on the port side of the gimbal ring. Tighten the screw to 6.8-9.5 N•m (60-84 in.-lb.).

13. Install the trim sender to the starboard side of the gimbal ring. See **Figure 21** or **Figure 22**. Refer to Chapter Fifteen for adjustment procedures.

14. Install a new seal onto the steering arm metal access cover (**Figure 37**). Install the cover and secure with 2 screws. Tighten the screws to 6.8-9.5 N•m (60-84 in.-lb.).

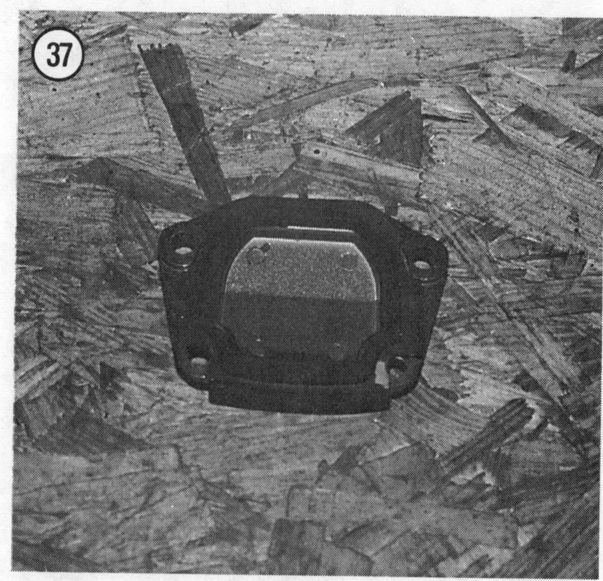

15. Install the plastic cover and secure with 2 screws. Tighten the screws to 6.8-9.5 N•m (60-84 in.-lb.).
16. If the ground strap was removed from the steering arm, reinstall the strap and tighten the screw and washer to 6.8-9.5 N•m (60-84 in.-lb.).
17. Reinstall the pivot housing as described in this chapter.

Transom Plate Removal/Installation

This procedure is for removing and installing the transom bracket as an assembly. If the bracket has already been partially disassembled, this procedure can still be used.

Removal

1. Remove the drive unit as described in Chapter Twelve.
2. Remove the engine as described in the appropriate engine chapter.
3. Pull the remote cable shift from the shift cable sleeve (inside the bilge).
4. Remove the 4 screws securing the exhaust pipe to the transom bracket. Remove the exhaust pipe. Remove and discard the exhaust pipe seal.
5A. *Mechanical steering models*—Disconnect the steering system from the transom bracket as follows:
   a. Remove the cotter pin securing the clevis pin to the steering arm. Be ready to catch the lower adaptor bushing as it falls free. Remove the clevis pin and the upper adaptor bushing from the steering arm.
   b. Remove the cotter pins (12, **Figure 38**) securing the upper and lower pivot bolts to the inner transom plate.
   c. Remove the upper and lower pivot bolts (11, **Figure 38**) securing the steering tube and anchor block assembly to the inner transom plate. Position the tube and cable assembly off to one side.

5B. *Power steering models*—The steering cylinder hydraulic lines should have been disconnected and plugged during engine removal. Disconnect the steering system from the transom bracket as follows:
   a. Remove the cotter pin securing the large clevis pin to the steering arm. Remove the large clevis pin from the steering cylinder and steering arm. See **Figure 39**.
   b. Remove the cotter pins (12, **Figure 38**) securing the upper and lower pivot bolts to the inner transom plate.
   c. Remove the upper and lower pivot bolts (11, **Figure 38**) securing the steering cylinder assembly to the inner transom plate. Position the steering cylinder and steering cable off to one side.

6. Disconnect the 2-pin main power lead and 3-pin switching harness leads from the trim pump assembly. These are quick-disconnect connectors. Remove any tie-straps securing the trim pump harnesses to the transom or other components.
7. Remove the 2 screws securing the trim motor assembly to the transom. Set the trim motor temporarily to one side.
8. Verify that the trim sending unit 2- or 3-wire connector is not connected to any boat or engine wiring harness or trim limit box.
9. Remove the screw and washer securing the ground strap (2, **Figure 38**) to the steering arm.
10. Remove the 2 washer-faced alignment bolts from the top of the inner transom plate (A, **Figure 40**).
11. Remove the 2 elastic locknuts (B, **Figure 40**) and washer plate from the 2 lower studs.
12. While an assistant supports the transom bracket outside the boat, remove the 4 elastic locknuts (C, **Figure 40**) and washers from the remaining studs. Remove the inner transom plate. It may be necessary to tap the plate with a rubber or plastic mallet to break it free from the transom.

14

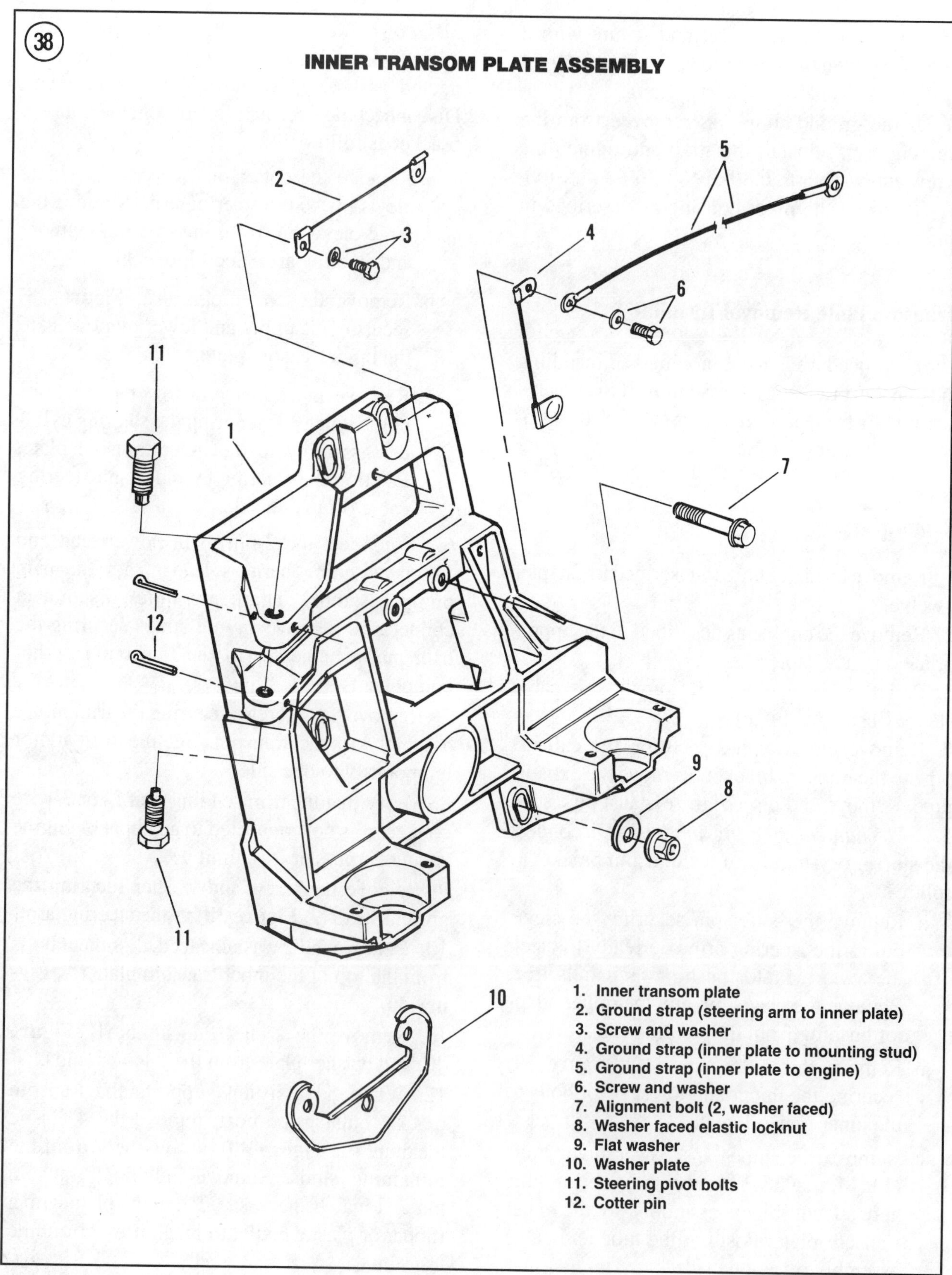
38
INNER TRANSOM PLATE ASSEMBLY
1
2
3
4
5
6
7
8
9
10
11
12
11
1. Inner transom plate
2. Ground strap (steering arm to inner plate)
3. Screw and washer
4. Ground strap (inner plate to mounting stud)
5. Ground strap (inner plate to engine)
6. Screw and washer
7. Alignment bolt (2, washer faced)
8. Washer faced elastic locknut
9. Flat washer
10. Washer plate
11. Steering pivot bolts
12. Cotter pin

13. With the aid of an assistant, remove the transom bracket from the boat. Feed the trim pump assembly through the transom cutout as the shield is removed.

Cleaning and inspection

1. Remove the transom seal (40, **Figure 23**). Clean the seal groove thoroughly with a suitable solvent.
2. Replace any of the transom shield mounting studs if their threads are damaged or corroded. Measure the installed height of the stud before removal. Coat the mounting stud threads with Loctite 271 threadlocking adhesive or equivalent (**Table 5**) before installing the studs into the transom shield. Reinstall all studs to their original mounting height.
3. Inspect the shift cable sleeve. Replace the sleeve if it is damaged or deteriorated. Install a new sleeve with a new O-ring. Coat the threads of the sleeve with Volvo White Sealing Compound or equivalent (**Table 5**). Tighten the sleeve to 62-71 N•m (46-52 ft.-lb.).
4. Inspect the anode (50, **Figure 23**) for deterioration. Replace the anode if has deteriorated to 2/3rds its original size. Tighten the anode screws to 16-19 N•m (12-14 ft.-lb.).
5. Thoroughly clean all old sealer from the transom. Inspect the transom. If the wood in the transom is rotted, it must be replaced. Generally, the best transom repairs are accomplished at a competent marine fiberglass repair shop. If the wood is wet, but not rotted, allow the wood to dry, completely. Seal any bare wood or exposed areas with marine epoxy or several coats of marine varnish. Allow the epoxy or varnish to cure (dry) completely.

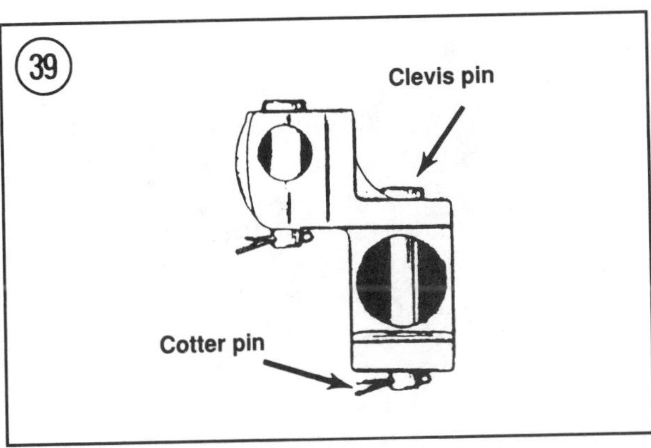

Installation

Coat the threads of all fasteners that are installed into the transom with 3M Marine Sealant 101 or equivalent (**Table 5**). This will prevent water entry and subsequent wood rot of the transom.

1. Glue a new transom seal into the gimbal housing groove with OMC Type M adhesive or equivalent (**Table 5**). The transom seal ends must butt tightly together. Position the butt joint at the top of the gimbal housing groove.
2. Glue a new exhaust pipe seal into the gimbal housing groove with OMC Type M adhesive or equivalent (**Table 5**).
3. Coat the 6 mounting studs with 3M Marine Sealant 101 or equivalent (**Table 5**).
4. With the aid of an assistant, feed the trim pump assembly into the transom cutout. Align the mounting studs with the transom holes and seat the transom shield against the transom.
5. Grease the bore of the inner transom plate (1, **Figure 38**) with Volvo Penta Propeller Shaft Grease or equivalent (**Table 5**). Position the inner plate over the studs and gimbal housing alignment tube. Make sure the trim lines are routed over the top port stud and into the relief located in the top port corner of the inner transom plate.
6. Coat the threads of the alignment bolts (7, **Figure 38**) with Volvo Penta Propeller Shaft Grease or equivalent (**Table 5**). Install the 2 washer faced alignment bolts through the inner transom plate and into the gimbal housing. It may be necessary to rotate the inner plate on the gimbal housing alignment tube to align and install the bolts. Tighten the bolts hand-tight at this time.

7. Install the 4 flat washers and 4 new elastic locknuts (C, **Figure 40**) over the studs protruding through the inner transom plate. Make sure the ground strap (4, **Figure 38**) is installed over the upper port stud. Tighten the nuts hand-tight at this time.
8. Install the washer plate and 2 new elastic locknuts over the 2 lower studs (B, **Figure 40**). Tighten the nuts hand-tight at this time.
9. Tighten the 6 elastic locknuts (B and C, **Figure 40**) to 27-34 N.m (20-25 ft.-lb.) in a crossing pattern, starting in the middle and working outward. Repeat the torque pattern at least twice to make sure the transom bracket is pulled evenly to the transom.
10. Tighten the 2 alignment bolts (A, **Figure 40**) to 16-19 N.m (12-14 ft.-lb.).
11. Position the trim pump assembly to the transom and secure it in the original mounting holes. Coat the fasteners with 3M Marine Sealant 101 or equivalent (**Table 5**). Tighten the fasteners securely.
12. Reconnect all electrical leads to the trim pump assembly.
13. Slide the remote control shift cable into the shift cable sleeve.

CAUTION
Failure to pilot the steering pivot bolts into the bushings of the anchor block or steering cylinder will result in a broken inner transom plate. Tighten the bolts slowly and carefully while holding the cylinder or anchor block in position. The cylinder or anchor block must pivot freely after the bolts are torqued.

14A. *Mechanical steering models*—Connect the steering system from the transom bracket as follows:

a. Position the steering cable, tube and anchor block assembly between the inner transom plate mounting bosses.
b. Install the upper and lower pivot bolts (11, **Figure 38**). Be careful to pilot the bolts into the anchor block bushings as they are tightened. Tighten both bolts to 54-61 N.m (40-45 ft.-lb.). Verify that the anchor block pivots freely on the bolts after torquing.
c. Secure both pivot bolts with new cotter pins (12, **Figure 38**).
d. Align the steering cable with the steering arm. Install an adaptor bushing into the top bore of the steering arm. Install the clevis pin through the adaptor and steering arm.
e. Grease the bottom adaptor bushing and position over the bottom of the clevis pin and into the steering arm. Secure the adaptor and clevis pin with a new stainless steel cotter pin. Bend both prongs of the cotter pin for a secure attachment.

14B. *Power steering models*—The steering cylinder hydraulic lines will be reconnected during engine installation. Connect the steering system from the transom bracket as follows:

a. Position the steering cable and cylinder assembly between the inner transom plate mounting bosses.
b. Install the upper and lower pivot bolts (11, **Figure 38**). Be careful to pilot the bolts into the cylinder bushings as they are tightened. Tighten both bolts to 54-61 N.m (40-45 ft.-lb.). Verify that the steering cylinder pivots freely on the bolts after torquing.

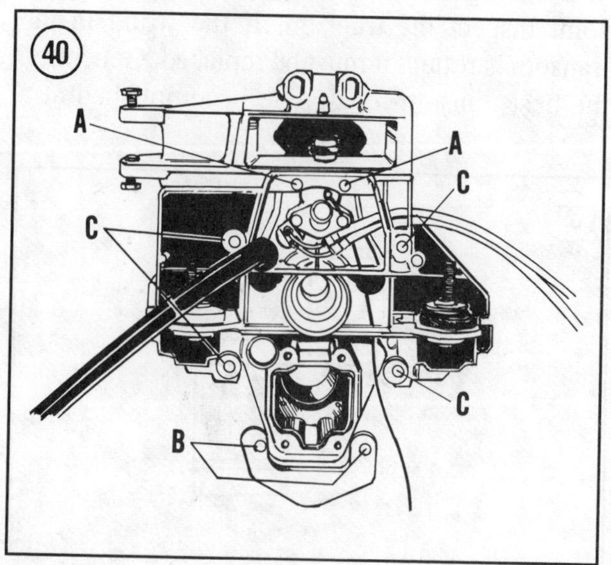

c. Secure both pivot bolts with new cotter pins (12, **Figure 38**).

d. Align the steering cylinder with the steering arm. Install the clevis pin through the cylinder end and the steering arm. See **Figure 39**.

e. Secure the clevis pin with a new stainless steel cotter pin. Bend both prongs of the cotter pin for a secure attachment.

15. Position the exhaust pipe to the transom bracket. Coat the threads of the 4 mounting screws with OMC Gasket Sealing Compound or equivalent (**Table 5**). Install the 4 screws and tighten to 27-34 N.m (20-25 ft.-lb.).

16. Reconnect the ground strap (2, **Figure 38**) to the steering arm. Tighten the screw and washer to 6.8-9.5 N.m (60-84 in.-lb.).

17. Reinstall the engine as described in the appropriate engine service chapter.

18. Reinstall the drive unit as described in Chapter Twelve. Make sure engine to coupler alignment is adjusted as described in Chapter Twelve.

Table 1 SPECIAL TORQUE VALUES (DP-C1/D1 AND DPX MODELS)

Fastener	N.m	in.-lb.	ft.-lb.
Exhaust pipe	40	–	29.5
Lubricant dipstick	Securely	Securely	Securely
Lubricant drain plug (DP-C1/D1)	10	88	7.4
Lubricant drain plug (DPX)	17	150	12.5
Lubricant fill plug	35	–	25.8
Lower gearcase mounting hardware			
Small fasteners	15	132	11.2
Large fasteners	38	–	28.0
Transom shield to boat (6 studs)	80	–	59.0
Upper gearcase mounting screws and nuts	38	–	28.0

Table 2 SPECIAL TORQUE VALUES (SX AND DP-S MODELS)

Fastener	N.m	in.-lb.	ft.-lb.
Anode	16-19	–	12-14
Exhaust pipe	27-34	–	20-25
Ground straps (dedicated fasteners)	6.8-9.5	60-84	–
Inner transom plate			
Alignment bolts (2)	16-19	–	12-14
Elastic locknuts (6)	27-34	–	20-25
Lower support bracket (gimbal ring)	24-27	–	18-20
Pivot housing pivot pins	142-163	–	105-120
Shift cable sleeve			
1994-1996	62-71	–	46-52
1997-on	54-61	–	40-45

(continued)

Table 2 SPECIAL TORQUE VALUES (SX AND DP-S MODELS) (continued)

Fastener	N·m	in.-lb.	ft.-lb.
Steering arm			
Center bolt	88-98	–	65-72
Elastic locknuts	18-20	–	13-15
Access cover (metal and plastic)	6.8-9.5	60-84	–
Steering system pivot bolts	54-61	–	40-45
Trim sending unit	2.0-2.7	18-24	–
Trim cylinder rod elastic locknut	14-16	124-142	10-12
Trim line fittings	9.5-12	84-108	–
Trim manifold mounting nut	12-15	108-132	–
Water drain plug (pivot housing)	5.7-6.8	50-60	–
Water tube outlet fitting (inside bilge)	14-16	124-142	10-12
Water inlet nipple (plastic nut)	11-14	97-124	–

Table 3 STANDARD TORQUE VALUES–METRIC FASTENERS

Screw or Nut Size	N·m	in.-lb.	ft.-lb.
M5	4.1	36	–
M6	8.1	70	6
M8	17.6	156	13
M10	35.3	312	26
M12	47.5	–	35
M14	81.3	–	60

Table 4 STANDARD TORQUE VALUES–AMERICAN FASTENERS

Screw or Nut Size	N·m	in.-lb.	ft.-lb.
6-32	1.0	9	–
8-32	2.3	20	–
10-24	3.4	30	–
10-32	4.0	35	–
12-24	5.1	45	–
1/4-20	7.9	70	6
1/4-28	9.5	84	7
5/16-18	18.1	160	13
5/16-24	19.0	168	14
3/8-16	30.5	270	23
3/8-24	33.9	300	25
7/16-14	48.8	–	36
7/16-20	54.2	–	40
1/2-13	67.8	–	50
1/2-20	81.3	–	60

Table 5 RECOMMENDED LUBRICANTS, SEALANTS AND ADHESIVES[1]

	Part Number
Lubricants	
Volvo DuraPlus GL5 Synthetic Gear Lube	(dealer stock item)
Volvo Penta Propeller Shaft Grease	1141644-3
or Quicksilver Special Lubricant 101	92-13872A-1
Volvo DuraPlus Power Trim/Steering Fluid	3851039-2
OMC EP/Wheel Bearing Grease	(dealer stock item)
OMC Moly Lube	175356
OMC Triple Guard Grease	(dealer stock item)
or Quicksilver 2-4-C Multi-Lube	(dealer stock item)
OMC Needle Bearing Assembly Grease	378642
or Quicksilver Needle Bearing Grease	92-825265A-1
Sealants	
Volvo Master Gasket Sealant	840879-1
Volvo Black Silicone Sealant	1161277-7
or OMC RTV Black Silicone Sealant	263753
Volvo White Sealing Compound	1141570-0
or OMC Gasket Sealing Compound	508235
or Quicksilver Perfect Seal	92-34227-11
OMC Black Neoprene Dip	909570
or Quicksilver Liquid Neoprene	92-25711-2
OMC Pipe Sealant with Teflon	9100048
or Quicksilver Loctite 567 PST pipe sealant	92-809822
3M Marine Sealant 101 (polysulfide [OMC or locally available])	506852
Adhesives	
OMC Type M Adhesive	318535
or Scotch Grip 1300 Adhesive (OMC or locally available)	982551
or Quicksilver Bellows Adhesive (contact cement)	92-86166-1
OMC Locquic Primer	772032
or Quicksilver Locquic Primer	92-809824
OMC Ultra Lock Threadlocking Adhesive (high strength)	500422
or Quicksilver Loctite 271 Threadlocking Adhesive	92-809819
OMC Nut Lock Threadlocking Adhesive (medium strength)	500418
or Quicksilver Loctite 242 Threadlocking Adhesive	92-809821
Miscellaneous	
Volvo DuraPlus Corrosion Shield	362002-8
Quicksilver Storage Seal Rust Inhibitor	92-86145A12
OMC Dielectric Grease	503243
or Quicksilver Dielectric Silicone Grease	92-823506-1

1. Obtain Volvo supplies from a Volvo-Penta Dealer, Quicksilver supplies from any Mercury Marine Dealer and OMC supplies from any OMC Stern Drive, Evinrude or Johnson Dealer.

14

Table 6 VOLVO SPECIAL TOOLS (DP-C1/D1 AND DPX MODELS)

Description	Application	Part No.
Bearing remover	DP-C1/D1 and DPX	884140-5
Drive handle	DP-C1/D1 and DPX	884143-9
Bearing installer	DP-C1/D1 and DPX	884168-6
Remover/installer	DP-C1/D1 and DPX	884259-3

(continued)

Table 6 VOLVO SPECIAL TOOLS (DP-C1/D1 AND DPX MODELS) (continued)

Description	Application	Part No.
Remover	DP-C1/D1 and DPX	884311-2
Alignment tool	DP-C1/D1 and DPX	884502-6
Hose clamp tool	DP-C1/D1 and DPX	884573-7
Remover	DP-C1/D1 and DPX	884831-9
Drive handle	DP-C1/D1 and DPX	9991801-3

Table 7 VOLVO SPECIAL TOOLS (SX AND DP-S MODELS)

Description	Application	Part No.
Gimbal seal and bearing installer	SX and DP-S	3850038[1]
Snap ring pliers	SX and DP-S	3850608-5
Drive handle	SX and DP-S	3850609-3
Insert tool	SX and DP-S	3854349-2
Socket removal tool	SX and DP-S	3854350-0
Threaded rod, nut and flange nut	SX and DP-S	3854351-8
Remover	SX and DP-S	3854355-9
Drive handle	SX and DP-S	3854356-7
Bushing remover/installer	SX and DP-S	3854358-3
Bearing installer	SX and DP-S	3854359-1
Bearing remover/installer	SX and DP-S	3854360-9
Steering arm puller	SX and DP-S	3854361-7

1. See text. Obtain this tool from an OMC Drive Systems Dealership.

Chapter Fifteen

Power Trim and Tilt System

Trimming refers to the process of changing the angle of the drive unit (propeller shaft) relative to the bottom of the boat. Trimming the drive unit up (out or away from the transom) raises the bow while underway, while trimming the drive unit down (in or toward the transom) lowers the bow.

While the trim system can be operated at any time, it is not recommended to change trim angle while operating in reverse gear. Trim changes are normally performed before accelerating onto plane, after obtaining the desired engine rpm or boat speed, when there is a weight distribution change in the boat or water conditions require it. Correct adjustment of the drive unit trim angle ensures maximum performance and efficiency under any given load and speed condition.

Trim the drive out as necessary to achieve a bow-up position for cruising, running *with* choppy waves or to achieve maximum performance when running at wide-open throttle. Excessive trim UP will cause propeller ventilation, causing a reduction in performance (propeller slippage) and possible propeller damage from cavitation burns (especially on DuoProp models).

Trim the drive in as necessary to hold the bow down when accelerating onto plane, operating at slow speeds or running *against* choppy waves. Excessive trim IN at high power settings and high speeds will cause the bow to plow or *dive* into the water, making handling difficult and some hulls unstable.

Trimming the drive unit cannot correct operational problems resulting from overloading or incorrectly loading the hull. Trimming also will not overcome an incorrect engine and drive unit installation, poor hull design or hull flaws, such as hook or rocker (**Figure 1**).

Trimming the drive unit to the extreme up position is considered *tilting*. The tilt function is normally used to reduce the draft of the boat for shallow water operation, beaching or launching, loading or transporting the boat.

Do not operate the engine above 1000 rpm if the drive unit is in the tilt range, and in no case can the drive unit be operated if the cooling water intakes are above the water. On SX and DP-S models, the tilt range is considered any trim angle above the point at which the upper gearcase thrust plates are no longer supported by the gimbal ring.

DP-C1/D1 models use an electronic *trim control unit* to limit the positive trim to a maximum of 5°. A tilt switch is used to over-ride the trim limit and allow tilting of the drive unit above the trim range. Negative trim limit is a function of the transom angle of the boat. DP-C1/D1 models are designed to be mounted on boats with transom angles of 10 - 15°. Negative trim is limited to 5° when the unit is installed in a boat with a standard 13° transom.

DP-S models also use an electronic control box, referred to as the *trim limit control box*. The manufacturer mandates that the DP-S drive unit be limited to 5° positive and 2° negative trim, controlled by the trim limit control box reading signals from the trim sending unit. If the boat is equipped with a standard 13° transom, these limits are factory programmed into the trim limit control box. The box can be reprogrammed if the drive unit is mounted in hull with a transom angle of 10-15° (other than 13°). The trim limit control box can also be programmed to control the maximum tilt angle of the drive unit to prevent contact with swim platforms. An override switch is used to over-ride the trim limit and allow operation of the drive unit above and below the limited trim range.

DPX models use a DP-C1/D1 trim system without the electronic control unit. It is the responsibility of the operator not to trim the drive unit excessively.

All of these systems are considered electrohydraulic systems. A reversible electric motor operates a hydraulic pump to provide the pressure required for raising or lowering the drive unit via the hydraulic cylinders. A trim switch on the dash or remote control box operates relays on the trim pump assembly. The relays control the polarity of the voltage going to the 2 wire permanent magnet trim motor. When the trim motor blue lead is positive and the green lead is negative, the motor operates in the UP direction. When the trim motor green lead is positive and the blue lead is negative, the motor operates in the DOWN direction. There is no dedicated ground lead.

The trim cylinders and pump assembly also provide protection against impact when operating in a forward direction. Valves in the trim cylinders will open during impact to dissipate the force of the impact, minimizing damage to the drive unit and transom assembly. This functional theory of this system is very similar to that of a shock absorber on a typical automobile.

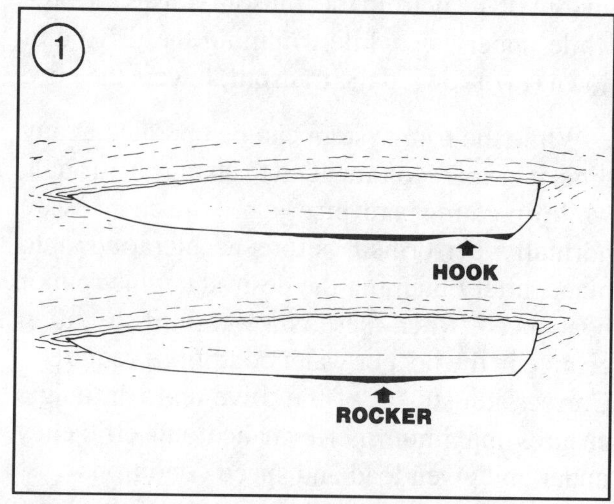

A malfunction of the trim system can result in the loss of the reverse lock function. This can cause the drive unit to *kick up* when operating in reverse gear or *trail out* when decelerating. Both of these conditions will cause a loss of control. Any defect noted in the trim system should be repaired immediately, before returning the boat to service.

This chapter covers removal, installation, adjustment and troubleshooting of the power trim system and related components. **Table 1** and **Table 2** list trim system specifications. **Table 3** and **Table 4** list common trim system problems and solutions. **Table 5** lists special torque values for SX and DP-S models and **Table 6** lists recommended lubricants, sealants and adhesives. **Table 7** and **Table 8** list recommended tools and equipment and **Table 9** and **Table 10** list trim limit control unit specifications. **Tables 1-10** are at the end of the chapter.

POWER TRIM AND TILT SYSTEM (DP-C1/D1 AND DPX MODELS)

Operation

The hydraulic trim system consists of an electric motor and hydraulic pump assembly, 2 hydraulic cylinders located outside the boat, the necessary hydraulic lines and electrical harnesses, a control switch and on DP-C1/D1 models, a trim indicator/trim limit control unit assembly or an analog trim indicator and separate trim limit control box. The fluid reservoir is an integral part of the motor and pump assembly. The trim cylinders are interconnected with stainless steel lines, allowing both cylinders to provide the same amount of lifting effort.

On DP-C1/D1 models a total of 4 relays are used; 2 on the trim pump assembly to reverse battery polarity as described previously and 2 relays mounted either at the dash or transom. One relay is normally closed and opens the blue lead (when activated by the digital trim gauge/analog control unit) to stop the trim motor when the 5° positive trim limit has been reached. The other relay is normally open and closes the blue lead (when the operator activates the tilt switch), allowing the drive unit to be tilted past the trim limit, up to the full tilt position. See **Figure 2** for a typical DP-C1/D1 trim system wiring diagram.

On DPX models a total of 2 relays are used, only the 2 on the trim pump assembly used to reverse battery polarity as described previously. See **Figure 3** for a typical DPX trim system wiring diagram.

All relays (1, **Figure 4**) used in this system use standard electrical connector positioning. Each relay has 5 terminals; labeled 30, 85, 86, 87 and 87A.

Terminal No. 30 (2, **Figure 4**) is always POWER IN to the relay from the battery, fuse or circuit breaker. This is often called LOAD IN.

Terminals No. 85 and No. 86 (3, **Figure 4**) are the control circuits of the relay. Whenever one of these terminals is grounded and the other terminal is connected to battery voltage, the relay is energized. The polarity of terminals No. 85 and No. 86 is not important, as long as one is positive and one is negative.

Terminals No. 87 (4, **Figure 4**) and No. 87A (5, **Figure 4**) are the load circuits of the relay, usually referred to as LOAD OUT. Terminal No. 87 is normally open to terminal No. 30. When the relay is energized, terminal No. 87 has continuity to terminal No. 30. Terminal No. 87A is normally closed to terminal No. 30. When the relay is energized, terminal No. 87A has no continuity to terminal No. 30. It is important to understand the function of each relay terminal before attempting to troubleshoot the system.

The DP-C1/D1 system is designed to be operated in 1 of 3 operating modes —Trim IN, Trim OUT and Trailer (tilt). The DPX system operates in only 2 modes —Trim IN and Trim OUT. In the trim IN mode, the trim motor green/white wire becomes positive as the trim IN relay (2,

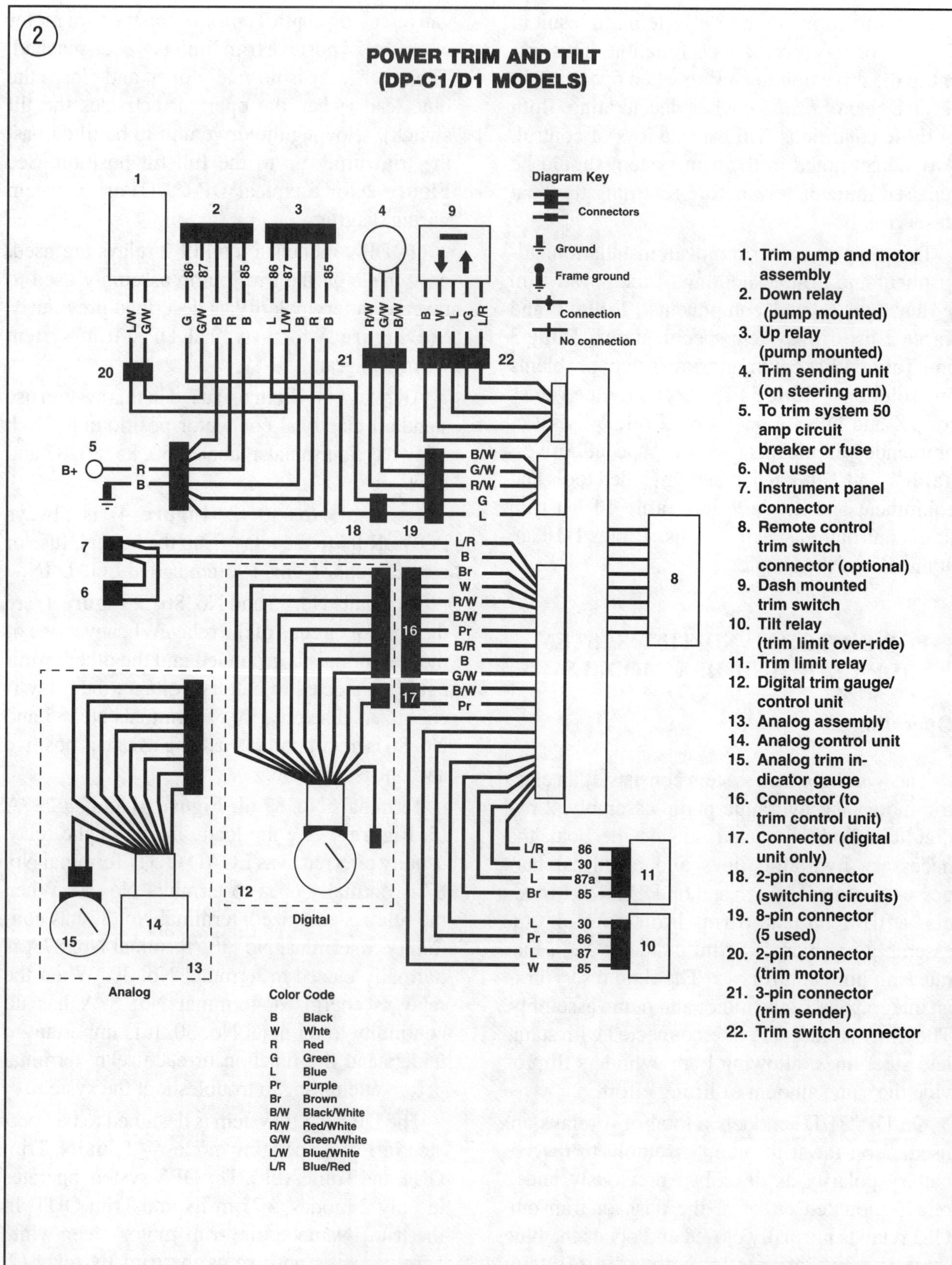
2
POWER TRIM AND TILT
(DP-C1/D1 MODELS)
Diagram Key
Connectors
Ground
Frame ground
Connection
No connection
1. Trim pump and motor assembly
2. Down relay (pump mounted)
3. Up relay (pump mounted)
4. Trim sending unit (on steering arm)
5. To trim system 50 amp circuit breaker or fuse
6. Not used
7. Instrument panel connector
8. Remote control trim switch connector (optional)
9. Dash mounted trim switch
10. Tilt relay (trim limit over-ride)
11. Trim limit relay
12. Digital trim gauge/ control unit
13. Analog assembly
14. Analog control unit
15. Analog trim indicator gauge
16. Connector (to trim control unit)
17. Connector (digital unit only)
18. 2-pin connector (switching circuits)
19. 8-pin connector (5 used)
20. 2-pin connector (trim motor)
21. 3-pin connector (trim sender)
22. Trim switch connector
Analog
Digital
Color Code
B Black
W White
R Red
G Green
L Blue
Pr Purple
Br Brown
B/W Black/White
R/W Red/White
G/W Green/White
L/W Blue/White
L/R Blue/Red

Figure 2 or **Figure 3**) is energized. The trim UP relay is not energized and holds the trim motor blue/white lead to ground through terminal No. 87A.

In the trim OUT mode, the trim motor blue/white wire becomes positive as the trim OUT relay (3, **Figure 2** or **Figure 3**) is energized. The trim IN relay is not energized and holds the trim motor green/white lead to ground through terminal No. 87A. On DP-C1/D1 models, the digital gauge/control unit or analog control unit will shut off the trim OUT relay when the 5° trim limit is reached, by activating the trim limit relay (11, **Figure 2**), opening the blue lead from the trim switch that activated the trim OUT relay.

In the trailer or tilt mode (DP-C1/D1 models), the operator presses a switch that activates the tilt relay (10, **Figure 2**). The tilt relay closes the blue lead to the trim OUT relay, allowing the operator to trim OUT the drive unit to the extension limit of the trim cylinders. The tilt and trim OUT switches must be pressed simultaneously. The tilt

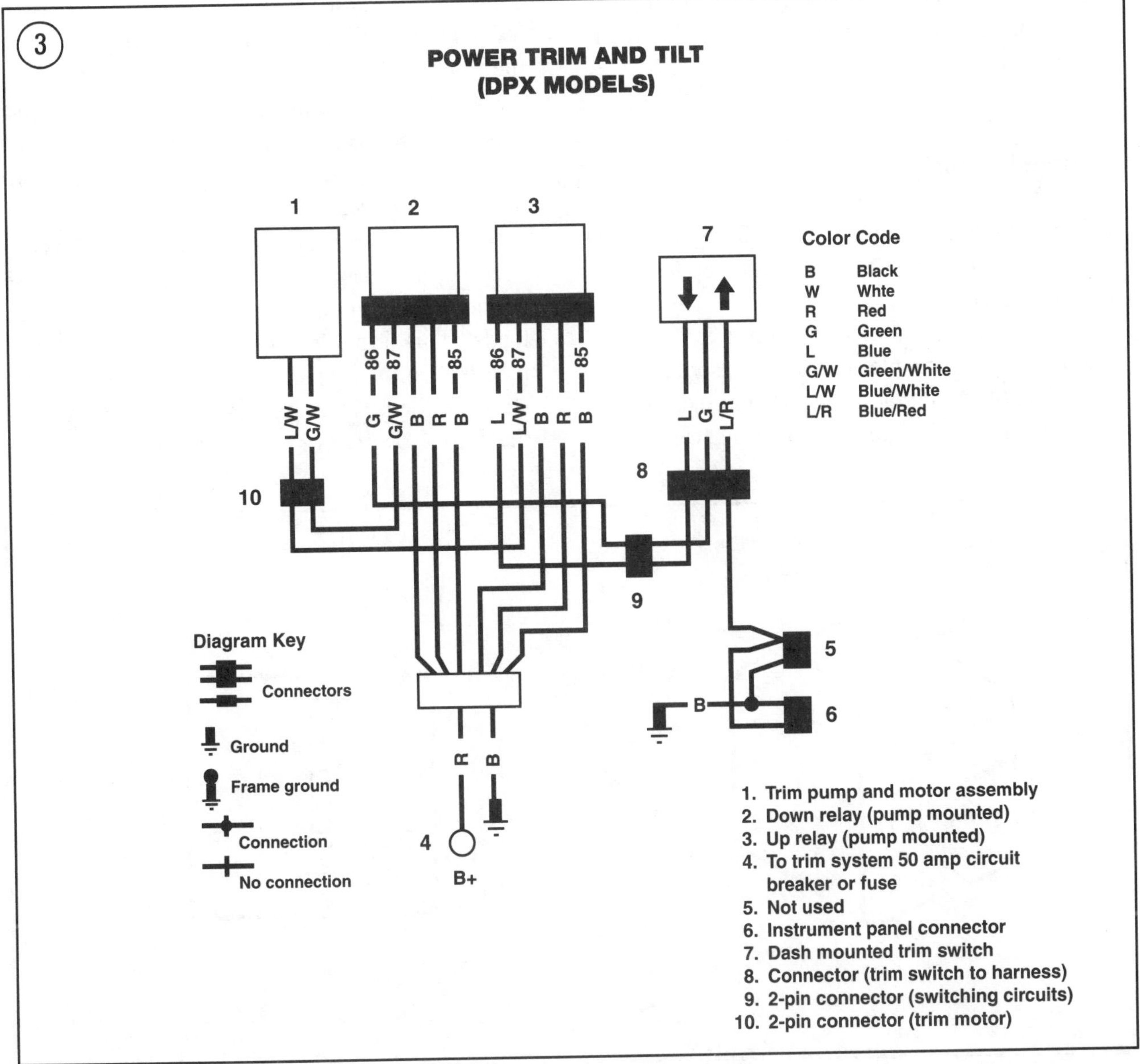

15

mode should only be used at engine speeds below 1000 rpm and the water intakes in the drive unit must be submerged at all times.

DPX models use a mechanical trim sending unit and are not equipped with an electronic trim control unit, trim limit relay or tilt relay. The operator is responsible for not over-trimming the drive unit while under way. The DOWN circuit is electrically the same as described for the DP-C1/D1, while the UP circuit is simplified to connect the blue lead from the switch directly to the trim motor UP relay. A trailer (tilt) switch is not required on DPX models. Refer to **Figure 3** for a wiring diagram of a typical DPX trim system.

Troubleshooting

Very few components on this trim system are serviceable. The trim cylinders are replaced as assemblies, as is the electric motor. The drive coupler between the electric motor and pump assembly is replaceable. The pump assembly has 2 serviceable filters and the thermal expansion valve, trim IN relief valve and trim OUT relief valve are replaceable. All other pump components are replaced with the valve body assembly. There is no manual release valve.

Before attempting to diagnose any malfunction with the power trim system, make the following preliminary checks.

1. Check the fluid level in the hydraulic reservoir (tank). Check the fluid with the drive unit in the full trim IN or DOWN position. The fluid level should be no higher than the MAX line and no lower than the MIN line cast into the side of the reservoir. If the fluid level is low, add sufficient fluid (**Table 1**) to bring it to the correct level. Do not fill the unit above the bottom lip of the filler neck.
2. Check all hydraulic lines and connections for signs of leakage or deterioration. Replace any damaged or deteriorated lines and tighten connections as necessary.
3. Check the trim system electrical leads, connectors and connections for corrosion, loose connections, damaged connectors and damaged leads. This includes the battery negative and positive connections, the engine main ground stud and the positive battery cable connection to the engine. Repair or replace as necessary.

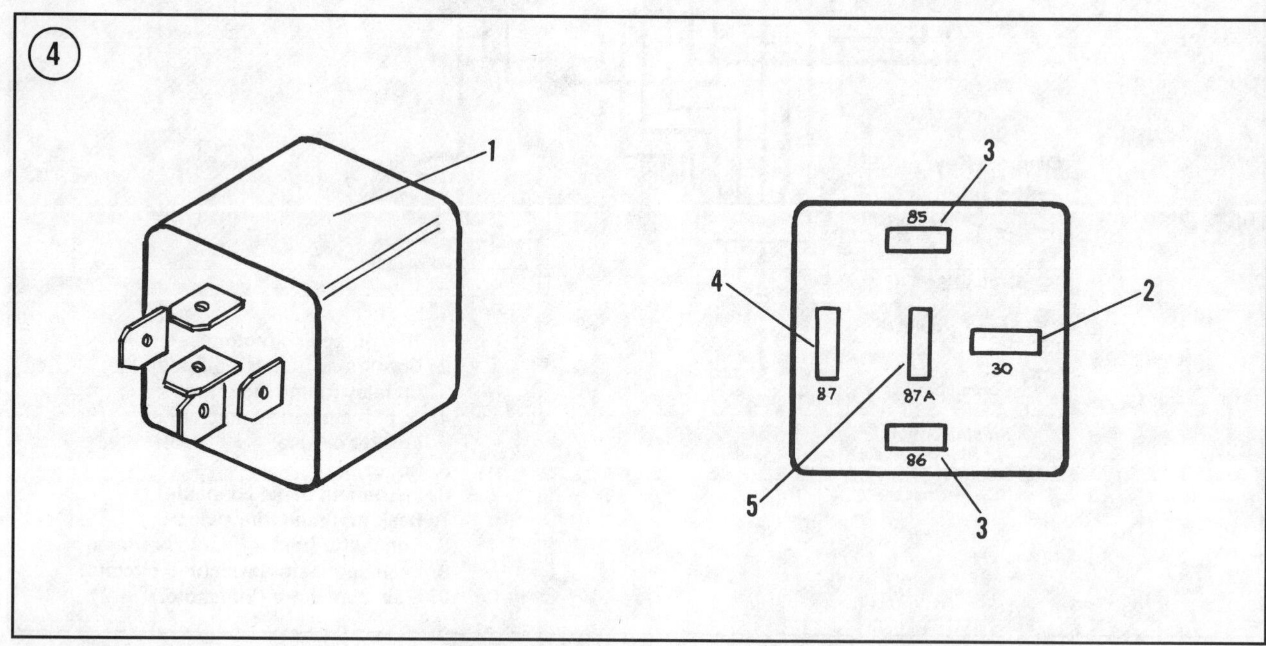

4. Check the trim system 50 amp fuse or circuit breaker for an open circuit. Replace the fuse, or reset or replace the circuit breaker as necessary.

Electrical troubleshooting

The trim motor is reversed by switching the polarity of the trim motor blue/white and green/white leads. There are 2 relays mounted on the trim pump assembly, one for each trim motor wire. Both relays hold their respective trim motor lead (blue/white or green/white) to ground when they are not activated. When the UP relay is activated it takes the blue/white trim motor lead off of ground and connects it to positive. The DOWN relay is inactive and holds the green/white lead to ground. Current can then flow from the positive terminal to the UP relay to the trim motor and back to ground through the DOWN relay causing the motor to run in the UP direction. When the DOWN relay is activated it takes the green/white trim motor lead off of ground and connects it to positive. The UP relay is inactive and holds the blue/white lead to ground. Current can then flow from the positive terminal to the DOWN relay to the trim motor and back to ground through the UP relay causing the motor to run in the DOWN direction. If the motor will run in one direction, but not the other, the problem cannot be the trim motor.

The ignition switch must be in the ON or RUN position for the trim system to function. The trim system receives power to operate the switching circuits through the 2-pin connector (7, **Figure 2** or 6, **Figure 3**) at the instrument panel. Refer to **Figure 2** for a standard DP-C1/D1 trim system wiring diagram and **Figure 3** for a standard DPX trim system wiring diagram.

To troubleshoot the electric motor and switching circuits, proceed as follows.

NOTE

On DP-C1/D1 models, if the drive unit will not trim above the trim limit position when the trailer (tilt) ***and*** *trim OUT switches are depressed simultaneously. Go to the end of this section and follow the procedure listed for that particular symptom, if that is the only problem.*

1. Connect the test lamp lead to the *positive* terminal of the battery and touch the test lamp probe to metal anywhere on the engine block. The test lamp should light. If the lamp does not light or is dim, the battery ground cable connections are loose or corroded, or there is an open circuit in the battery ground cable. Check connections on both ends of the ground cable.
2. Connect test lamp lead to a good engine ground.
3. Connect the test lamp probe to the circuit breaker or fuse terminal (5, **Figure 2** or 4, **Figure 3**). The test lamp should light. If the lamp does not light or is very dim, the fuse or circuit breaker is open, the battery cable connections are loose or corroded, or there is an open in the cable between the battery and the tested terminal. Reset the circuit breaker or replace the fuse, clean and tighten connections or replace the battery cable as required.
4. Disconnect the trim/tilt relays (2 and 3, **Figure 2** or **Figure 3**) from their connector bodies.
5. Connect the test lamp probe to the input side of each relay (red lead, terminal No. 30 position). The test lamp should light at each point. If not, repair or replace the red lead from the circuit breaker or fuse to each relay.
6. Connect the test lamp lead to the *positive* terminal of the battery and touch the test lamp probe to both black leads at each relay connector (terminal No. 85 and No. 87 positions). The test lamp should light at each point. If not, repair or replace each black lead (from the relay connector body to ground) that failed to light the test lamp. Reinstall both relays when finished.
7. *DP-C1/D1 models*—Disconnect the control unit connector (16, **Figure 2**) and the trim switch connector (22, **Figure 2**). Touch the test lamp probe to the black lead at each connector on the main wiring harness side of each connector (not

the switch or control unit side). The test lamp should light at each point. If not, repair or replace each black lead (from the appropriate connector body to ground) that failed to light the test lamp. Do not reconnect the connectors at this time.

8. Connect the test lamp lead to a good engine ground.

9A. *DP-C1/D1 models*—Disconnect the trim limit relay (11, **Figure 2**). Turn the ignition switch to the ON or RUN position. Connect the test lamp probe to the blue/red lead on the main harness side of each of the following 3 connectors: trim limit relay (11, **Figure 2**), trim switch (22, **Figure 2**) and control unit (16, **Figure 2**). The test lamp should light at each point. If not, repair or replace the blue/red lead from the defective test point back to the instrument panel connector.

9B. *DPX models*—Disconnect the trim switch connector (8, **Figure 3**). Connect the test lamp probe to the blue/red lead on the main harness side of the connector. The test lamp should light. If not, repair or replace the blue/red lead from the connector back to the instrument panel connector.

10. Reconnect all connections.

11. Remove both relays (2 and 3, **Figure 2** or **Figure 3**) from their connector bodies. Connect the test lamp probe to the green lead (terminal 86) of the DOWN relay connector (2, **Figure 3**). Turn the ignition switch to the ON or RUN position. Depress the trim IN button on the trim switch. The test lamp should light. If not, repair or replace the green lead circuit back to and including the trim switch.

NOTE

*On DP-C1/D1 models, the trim limit relay (11, **Figure 2**) must be de-energized and maintain continuity between terminals 30 and 87A in order for the blue lead circuit to function. If the trim control unit malfunctions or the trim angle is above positive 5°, the relay will be energized by the grounding of the brown lead at the control unit. When the relay is energized, terminals 30 and 87A will have no continuity. A jumper lead can be inserted across the relay connector (11, **Figure 2**) blue leads (terminals 30 and 87A) to bypass the trim limit relay and trim control unit for isolation purposes.*

12. Connect the test lamp probe to the blue lead (terminal 86) of the UP relay connector (3, **Figure 3**). Turn the ignition switch to the ON or RUN position. Depress the trim OUT button on the trim switch. The test lamp should light. If not, repair or replace the blue lead circuit back to the trim switch (including the trim limit relay and control unit on DP-C1/D1 models).

13. If Steps 11 and 12 have been satisfactorily performed, install the relays (2 and 3, **Figure 2** or **Figure 3**) and disconnect the 2-pin connector from the trim motor (20, **Figure 2** or 9, **Figure 3**).

14. Touch the test lamp probe to the green/white lead of the main harness side of the connector (not the trim motor side). Turn the ignition switch to the ON or RUN position. Depress the trim IN button on the trim switch. The test lamp should light. If not, replace the trim DOWN relay (2, **Figure 2** or **Figure 3**) and retest.

15. Connect the test lamp probe to the blue/white lead of the main harness side of the connector (not the trim motor side). Turn the ignition switch to the ON or RUN position. Depress the trim OUT button of the trim switch. The test lamp should light. If not, replace the trim UP relay (3, **Figure 2** or **Figure 3**) and retest.

16. If all previous tests are satisfactory and the electric motor still does not operate correctly, replace the electric motor.

17. *DP-C1/D1 models*—If the unit will not trim above the trim limit position when the trailer (tilt) switch and the trim OUT switch are depressed simultaneously, yet the unit will trim normally below the trim limit, refer to **Figure 2** and proceed as follows:

NOTE
If troubleshooting any other electric motor malfunction, go back to the beginning of this section and start there.

a. Remove the tilt relay (10, **Figure 2**) from its connector body.
b. Connect the test lamp lead to a good engine ground.
c. Turn the ignition switch to the ON or RUN position.
d. Touch the test lamp probe to the purple lead at the relay connector body. The test lamp should light, if not, check the purple lead for continuity back to the trim control unit. If the purple lead has continuity, replace the trim control unit.
e. Connect the test lamp lead to the *positive* terminal of the battery and touch the test lamp probe to the white lead at the relay connector body. Depress the trailer or tilt switch. The test lamp should light. If not, repair or replace the white lead from the relay connector body to the trim switch (including the trim switch), and on to ground through the trim switch assembly black lead.
f. If all tests have been satisfactory to this point, replace the tilt relay and retest.

Hydraulic troubleshooting

Refer to **Table 2** for common trim system problems and their solutions. All problems in **Table 2** assume the trim motor runs properly. Refer to *Electrical troubleshooting* in this chapter, if the trim motor does not run or does not run properly. Refer to **Figure 5** for a schematic of the hydraulic pump assembly (operating in the trim OUT mode, for reference).

This procedure is for troubleshooting internal leakage and assumes that all visible leaks have been isolated and corrected. External leaks, no matter how small, cannot be tolerated on a trim system.

If the drive unit leaks in both directions (UP and DOWN), the problem is most likely in one or both of the trim cylinders. If one trim cylinder fails, the other is usually soon to follow. Consider flushing the lines and replacing both cylinders at the same time.

To isolate the cylinders from the valve body and determine if the leakage is in the valve body or cylinders, refer to **Figure 6** and proceed as follows.

1. Trim the drive unit to the full UP position.
2. Block the drive unit securely, then cover the line fittings at the valve body with a shop towel.
3. Remove both lines (13 and 14, **Figure 6**) from the valve body and plug both lines with appropriate fittings. Tighten the fittings securely.
4. Remove the block from the drive unit. Let the drive sit for at least 1 hour.

NOTE
When the block is removed, the drive will settle slightly from the lines being opened and plugged. You are looking for movement beyond the initial settling.

5. If the drive unit still leaks down, the problem is in one or both trim cylinders. If the drive unit does not leak down, the problem is in the valve body.

To isolate the cylinders from each other and determine which cylinder, or if both cylinders are leaking, refer to **Figure 6** and **Figure 7** and proceed as follows.

1. Trim the drive unit to the full UP position and block the drive unit securely.
2. Cover the line fittings at the valve body with a shop towel.
3. Remove both lines (13 and 14, **Figure 6**) from the valve body and plug both lines with appropriate fittings. Tighten the fittings securely.
4. Cover the cylinder fittings with a shop towel, then remove the stainless steel interconnection line (9, **Figure 7**) from the transom end of both cylinders.

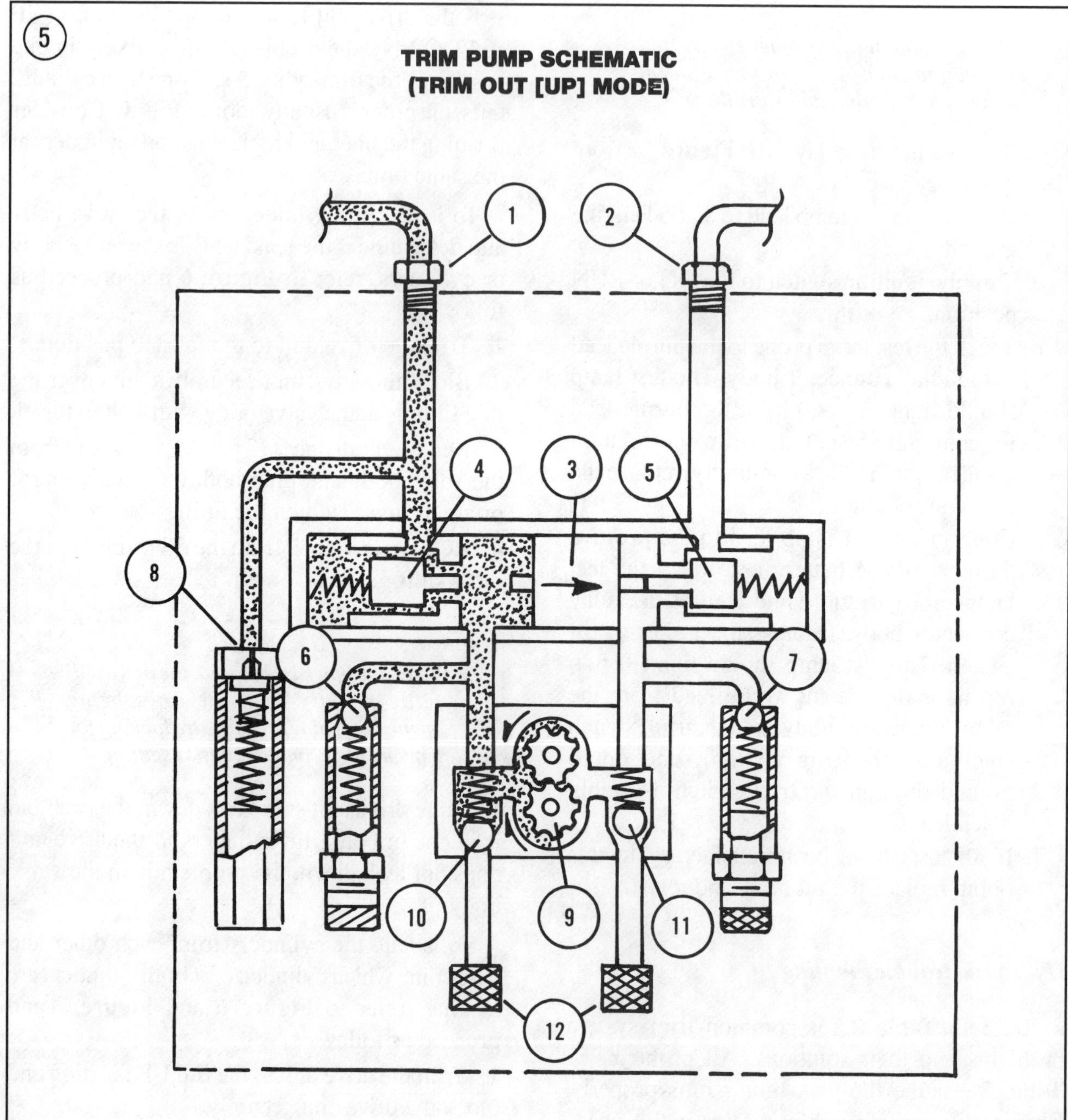

1. UP line connection
2. DOWN line connection
3. Pump control piston
4. Trim OUT check valve
5. Trim IN check valve
6. Trim OUT relief valve
7. Trim IN relief valve
8. Thermal expansion valve
9. Pump gear set
10. Inlet check ball (trim out)
11. Inlet check ball (trim in)
12. Inlet filter screen

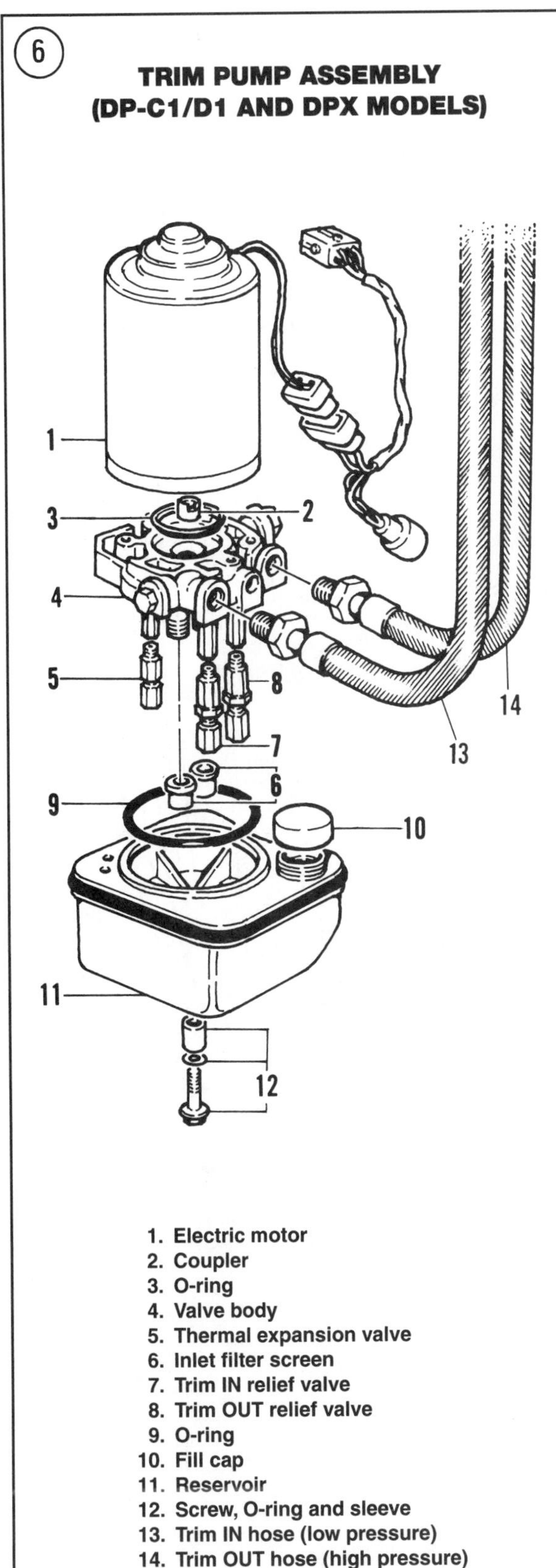

5. Plug the cylinders with part No. 852879-1 plugs (same as 11, **Figure 7**). Tighten the plugs securely.

6. Remove the cotter pin and tilt pin (3 and 4, **Figure 7**) from the starboard cylinder (2, **Figure 7**) at the suspension fork. Rotate the cylinder down and away from the suspension fork.

7. Remove the block from the drive unit. Let the drive sit for at least 1 hour.

NOTE
When the block is removed, the drive will settle slightly from the lines being opened and plugged. You are looking for movement beyond the initial settling.

8. If the drive unit still leaks down, the port trim cylinder is defective. Repeat the test using the starboard cylinder to support the drive unit and the port cylinder unpinned and rotated away from the suspension fork. Both cylinders must be tested for leaks.

9. If the drive unit does not leak down, repeat the test using the starboard cylinder to support the drive unit and the port cylinder unpinned and rotated away from the suspension fork. If the drive unit leaks down while supported by the starboard cylinder, the starboard cylinder is defective.

Trim Pump Removal and Disassembly

1. Trim the drive unit to the full DOWN position.

2. Disconnect the 2-pin trim motor connector (20, **Figure 2** or 10, **Figure 3**).

3. Note the orientation of the trim lines, if necessary mark the lines for reassembly. Wrap a shop towel around the line fittings (13 and 14, **Figure 6**). Remove the lines from the valve body. Cap the lines with suitable fittings.

4. Remove the 4 screws securing the trim pump assembly to the transom. Remove the trim pump from the transom.

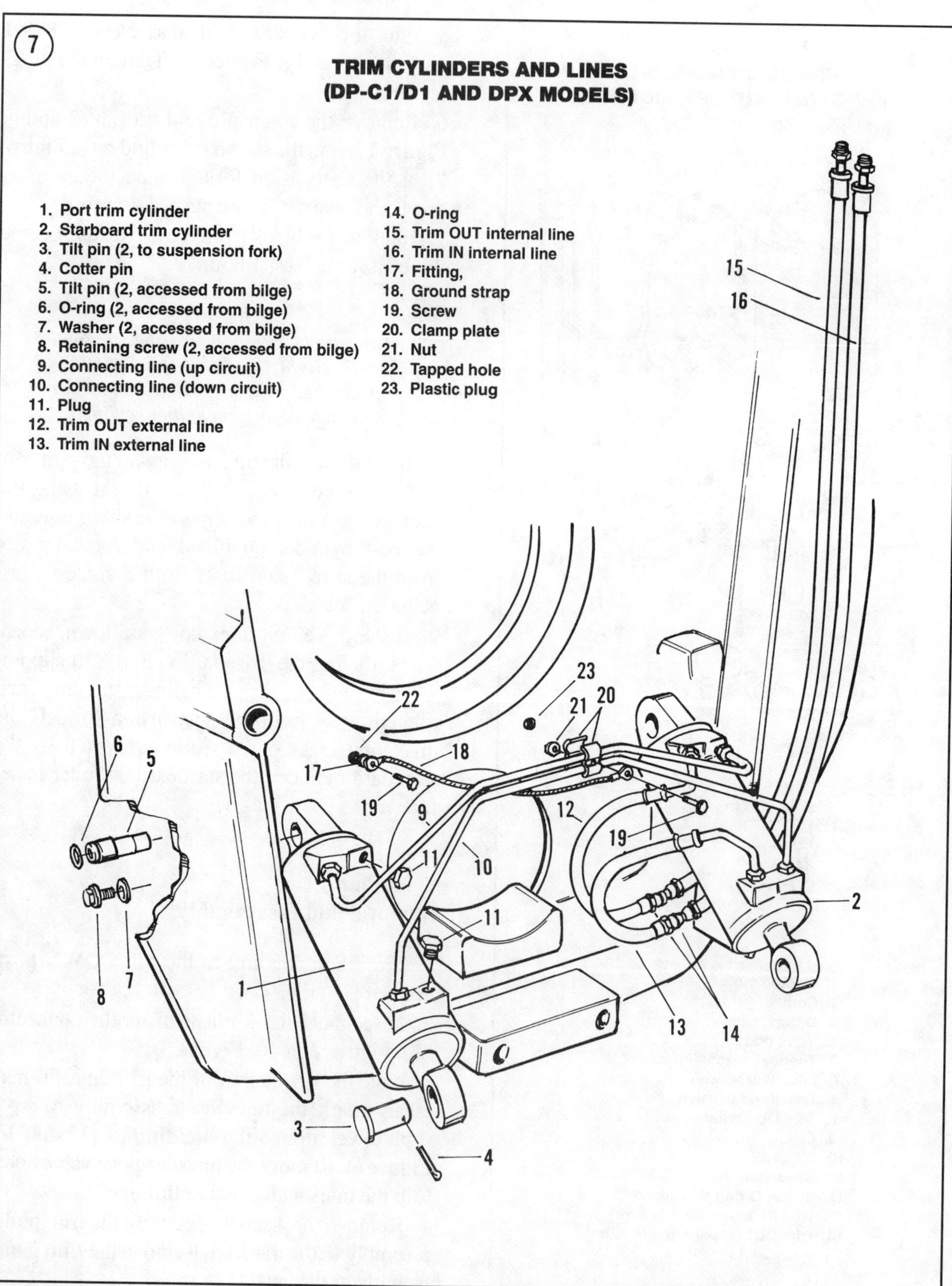
7
TRIM CYLINDERS AND LINES
(DP-C1/D1 AND DPX MODELS)
1. Port trim cylinder
2. Starboard trim cylinder
3. Tilt pin (2, to suspension fork)
4. Cotter pin
5. Tilt pin (2, accessed from bilge)
6. O-ring (2, accessed from bilge)
7. Washer (2, accessed from bilge)
8. Retaining screw (2, accessed from bilge)
9. Connecting line (up circuit)
10. Connecting line (down circuit)
11. Plug
12. Trim OUT external line
13. Trim IN external line
14. O-ring
15. Trim OUT internal line
16. Trim IN internal line
17. Fitting,
18. Ground strap
19. Screw
20. Clamp plate
21. Nut
22. Tapped hole
23. Plastic plug
15
16
23
22
21
20
6
5
17
18
19
9
12
19
11
10
2
11
8
7
1
13
14
3
4

5. Remove the 2 screws securing the trim pump to the bracket. Remove the trim pump from the mounting bracket.

6. Remove the fill cap and empty the reservoir into a suitable container.

7. Remove the 2 screws securing the electric motor to the valve body. Remove the electric motor. Discard the O-ring. Locate and secure the pump coupler (2, **Figure 6**).

8. Remove the screw (12, **Figure 6**) securing the reservoir to the valve body. Remove the sleeve and O-ring from the screw.

9. Remove the reservoir from the valve body. Discard the O-ring.

10. With a suitable pair of pliers, carefully remove the filters (6, **Figure 6**) from the valve body. Discard the filters.

CAUTION
Do not remove any of the following valves unless they are to be replaced. If removed, they must be discarded.

11. If the thermal expansion valve (5, **Figure 6**) is to be replaced, remove it with a 7/16 in. wrench. Discard the valve.

12. If the trim IN or trim OUT relief valves (7 and 8, **Figure 6**) are to be replaced, remove the appropriate valve with a 7/16 in. wrench. Discard the valve(s).

Cleaning and Inspection

1. Wash the reservoir, valve body and all loose parts (except the electric motor) in a clean, mild solvent, such as mineral spirits. Blow all parts dry with compressed air.

2. Immediately upon drying, liberally lubricate the valve body with Volvo DuraPlus Power Trim/Steering Fluid (**Table 6**).

3. Inspect all parts for dirt or debris that could block passages. Inspect all O-ring grooves and bores for nicks or burrs that could cause leakage.

4. Inspect the pump coupler for wear or distortion. Replace the coupler if it shows any wear, distortion or damage.

Assembly and Installation

Lubricate all components with Volvo DuraPlus Power Trim/Steering Fluid (**Table 6**) during assembly. Do not make any DRY assemblies. Refer to **Figure 6** for this procedure.

CAUTION
Replacement thermal expansion, trim IN and trim OUT valves are preset at the factory. These valves look different from original valves due to the self-contained cartridge design of the replacement valve. These valves' factory setting must not be disturbed during assembly. Tighten the replacement valve from the lowest portion of the valve to prevent disturbing the factory setting.

1. If the thermal expansion valve (5, **Figure 6**) was removed, install a new valve into the valve body. Tighten the lower portion of the valve securely to the valve body.

2. If the trim IN or trim OUT relief valves (7 and 8, **Figure 6**) were removed, install new valves into the valve body. Tighten the lower portion of each valve securely to the valve body.

3. Install a new filter (6, **Figure 6**) to each of the check ball towers. Use a 5/8 in. socket to press the filter into position, gently.

4. Install the coupler into the valve body and over the driven gear. Submerge the valve body in a clean container of Volvo DuraPlus Power Trim/Steering Fluid (**Table 6**) and rotate the pump coupler in both directions until all air has been purged from the valve body.

5. Install a new O-ring into the valve body electric motor mounting bore. Install the motor to the valve body being careful to align the drive shaft of the motor with the slot in the pump coupler and not to displace the O-ring.

6. Install and tighten the 2 motor mounting screws securely.
7. Install a new reservoir O-ring over the valve body. Position the Reservoir over the valve body.
8. Install a new O-ring over the reservoir screw, then install the sleeve over the screw. Install the screw assembly through the reservoir and into the valve body. Tighten the screw securely.
9. Position the trim pump assembly to the mounting plate. Secure the pump to the plate with 2 screws and lock washers. Tighten the 2 screws securely.
10. Secure the trim pump assembly to the transom with 4 screws. Tighten the 4 screws securely.
11. Reconnect the 2-pin trim motor connector (20, **Figure 2** or 10, **Figure 3**).
12. Reconnect the trim lines (13 and 14, **Figure 6**) to the valve body. Tighten the fittings securely.
13. Fill the reservoir with Volvo DuraPlus Power Trim/Steering Fluid (**Table 6**). Cycle the drive unit up and down several times to purge any air from the system. Maintain fluid level as necessary. Inspect all fittings for leaks. Correct any problems found.

Trim Cylinder Replacement

Refer to **Figure 7** for this procedure.

1. Remove the drive unit as described in Chapter Twelve.
2. Loosen or remove the clamps, then remove the exhaust and universal joint bellows from the transom shield. Refer to Chapter Fourteen if additional information is needed.
3. Place a suitable container under the trim cylinders.
4. Use a flare nut wrench to disconnect the 2 hoses (12 and 13, **Figure 7**) and connecting lines (9 and 10, **Figure 7**) from the starboard trim cylinder. If the port cylinder is to be removed, detach the line connections (9 and 10, **Figure 7**).

NOTE

If you do not have an extra grease fitting for use in Step 5, you can remove one from the drive unit for this procedure. Be sure to return the grease fitting to the drive unit and reinstall the fitting or plastic plug into the transom shield, when finished.

5. To remove the starboard cylinder, remove the plastic plug (23, **Figure 7**) from the transom shield and install a suitable grease fitting in place of the plug. See **Figure 8**.

6. Remove the 10 mm lock screw and washer that holds the trim cylinder attachment dowel in place. This screw is accessed from the bilge. **Figure 9** shows a typical retaining screw location.

7. Attach a hand grease gun to the grease fitting. Inject grease until hydraulic pressure forces the tilt pin (5, **Figure 7**) from the transom shield. The lock screw may be threaded into the tilt pin to allow pliers to be used to help pull the pin from the transom shield.

8. Remove and discard the O-ring from the tilt pin. If the tilt pin is corroded or damaged, discard the tilt pin.

9. Remove the trim cylinder from the mounting collar.

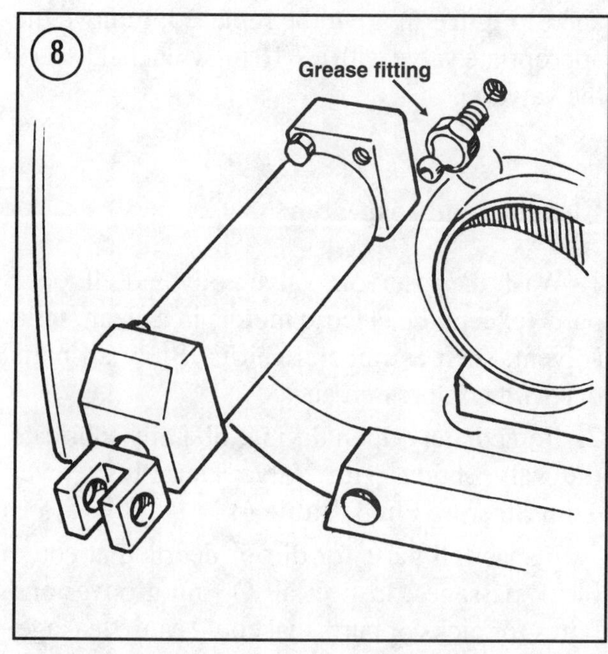

10. Thread the lock screw and washer into the tilt pin for safekeeping.
11. Remove the grease fitting and reinstall the plastic plug.
12. To remove the port cylinder, remove the screw (19, **Figure 7**) securing the ground strap to the transom shield.
13. Remove the fitting (17, **Figure 7**) from the tapped hole in the transom shield (22, **Figure 7**). Install a suitable grease fitting in place of the threaded fitting.
14. Remove the 10 mm lock screw and washer that holds the trim cylinder attachment dowel in place. Access this screw from the bilge. **Figure 9** shows a typical retaining screw location.
15. Attach a hand grease gun to the grease fitting. Inject grease until hydraulic pressure forces the tilt pin (5, **Figure 7**) from the transom shield. The lock screw may be threaded into the tilt pin to allow pliers to be used to help pull the pin from the transom shield.
16. Remove and discard the O-ring from the tilt pin. If the tilt pin is corroded or damaged, discard the tilt pin.
17. Thread the lock screw and washer into the tilt pin for safekeeping.

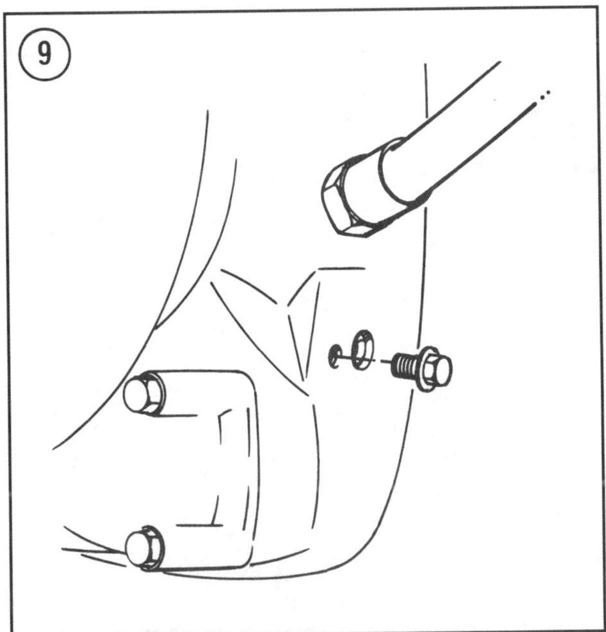

18. Remove the grease fitting and reinstall the threaded fitting into the port side tapped hole in the transom shield (22, **Figure 7**).
19. To install the trim cylinders, begin by greasing the tilt pins and O-rings with Volvo Penta Propeller Shaft Grease or equivalent (**Table 6**). Install the O-rings into the tilt pin grooves.
20. Position the trim cylinder(s) into the transom shield and align the tilt pin bores. Install the tilt pin(s) into the transom shield and through the trim cylinder(s). The pin(s) should be flush with the transom shield when seated.
21. Coat the threads of the lock screw(s) with propeller shaft grease. Install the screw(s) and washer(s) into the transom shield to secure the tilt pin(s). Tighten the screw(s) securely. See **Figure 9**.
22. Coat the thread of all hoses and connecting lines with Loctite PST pipe sealant or equivalent (**Table 6**). Install the lines as shown in **Figure 6**. Tighten all fittings securely.
23. Reconnect the ground strap to the transom shield fitting (17, **Figure 7**). Coat the screw threads with Volvo White Sealing Compound or equivalent (**Table 6**). Tighten the screw securely.
24. Reinstall the exhaust and universal joint bellows and the drive unit as described in Chapter Fourteen and Chapter Twelve, respectively.
25. Fill the reservoir with Volvo DuraPlus Power Trim/Steering Fluid (**Table 6**). Cycle the drive unit up and down several times to purge any air from the system. Maintain fluid level as necessary. Inspect all fittings for leaks. Correct any problems found.

Trim Sending Unit Service (DP-C1/D1 Models)

For additional service information on the transom shield, such as trim sender gear wheel and gear rack replacement, and gear wheel to gear rack indexing procedures, refer to Chapter Fourteen.

DPX models use a mechanical trim sending unit. Service procedures for cable replacement and adjustment at the transom shield are also covered in Chapter Fourteen.

Removal

To replace the trim sending unit on DP-C1/D1 models, proceed as follows.

1. Remove the steering bushing from the steering helmet as described in Step 3 of *Drive Unit Removal* in Chapter Twelve.
2. Rotate the steering helm as far forward (up) as possible without disengaging the trim gear wheel from the trim gear rack.
3. Disconnect the 3-pin trim sending unit connector (21, **Figure 2**).
4. Remove the screw securing the trim sender and bracket to the steering arm (**Figure 10**, typical). Remove the bracket and sleeve.
5. Remove and discard the socket head screw (**Figure 11**, typical) securing the steering arm to the steering helmet and yoke shaft assembly.
6. Pull the steering yoke shaft downward until the first grease groove is visible (**Figure 12**). Do not disengage the yoke shaft splines from the steering arm.
7. Remove the sending unit from the steering arm.

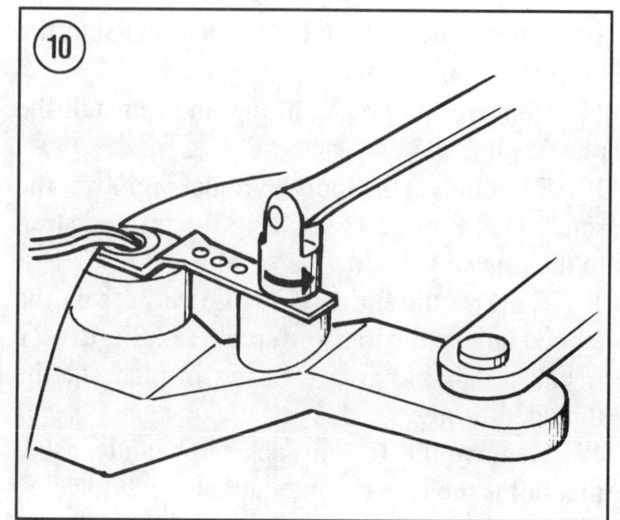

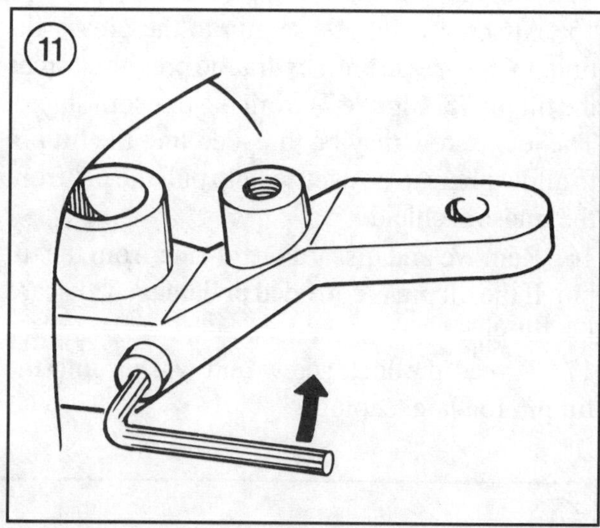

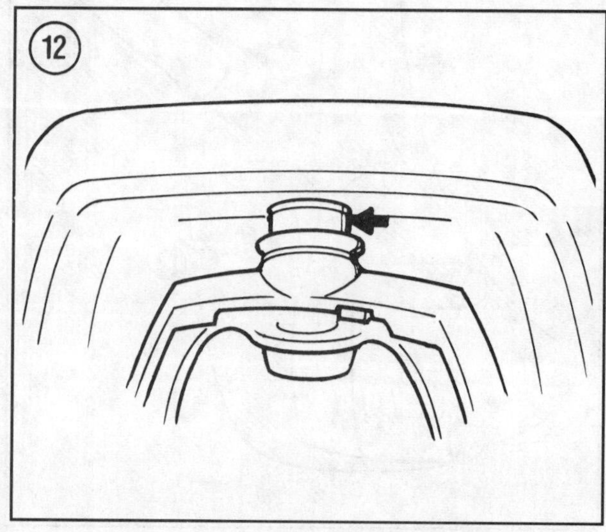

Trim sending unit troubleshooting

If the trim gauge is reading erratically or does not read at all, it may be the result of a faulty trim sending unit. Test the trim sending unit as follows.

1. Remove the trim sending unit as described in this chapter.
2. To measure the trim sending unit fixed resistance, calibrate an ohmmeter on the appropriate scale to read 800-1100 ohms. Connect one ohmmeter lead to the trim sender red/white lead and the other ohmmeter lead to the black/white lead. Note the reading, then rotate the sending unit

while continually noting the meter reading. The ohmmeter should indicate a constant reading of approximately 800-1100 ohms. Replace the sending unit if any other reading is noted.

3. To measure the variable resistance, move the ohmmeter lead from the red/white lead to the green/white lead. Turn the sending unit to align the marks on the shaft (**Figure 13**) and note the meter reading. The meter should read less than 100 ohms. Replace the sending unit if the reading is above 100 ohms.

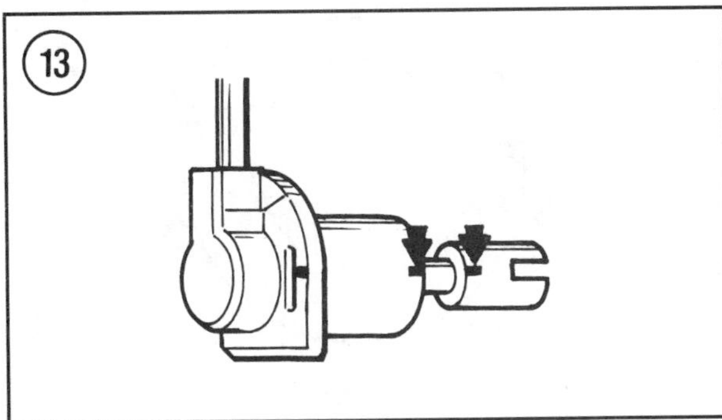

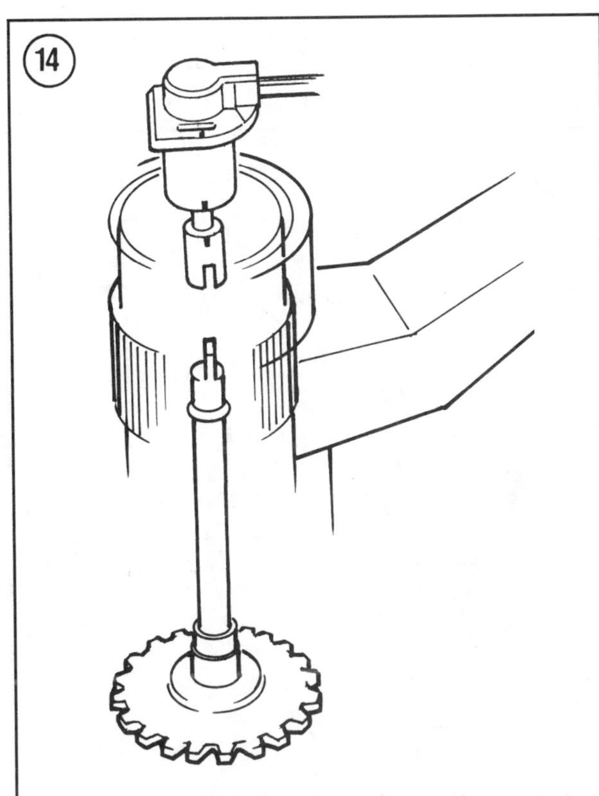

4. Continue to turn the sending unit shaft clockwise while noting the meter reading. The meter should smoothly increase to 800-1100 ohms within one revolution. If the meter jumps, reads erratically, or does not smoothly increase to 800-1100 ohms, replace the trim sending unit.

Installation

1. To install the sending unit, rotate the lower portion to align the marks as shown in **Figure 13**.

2. Install a new O-ring on the sending unit and insert it in the steering yoke with the marks pointing directly to starboard. It may be necessary to lift and turn the sending unit slightly to engage its slot with the tang on the trim gear wheel shaft as shown in **Figure 14**, before the unit will fully seat in the steering arm. Then rotate the sender to position the mark directly to starboard.

3. When you are sure you have indexed the trim sender to the trim gear wheel, push the steering yoke shaft up and seat it into the transom shield and steering arm.

4. Install a new socket head screw to the steering arm. Tighten the screw securely.

5. Install the screw through the ground strap and sending unit bracket, then install the sleeve over the screw.

6. Install the screw, ground strap and bracket assembly over the trim sender and tighten the screw securely.

7. Connect the trim sender 3-pin connector to the main wiring harness.

8. Rotate the steering helmet downward and install the steering bushing as described in Step 14 of *Drive Unit Installation* in Chapter Thirteen.

9. Calibrate the control unit as described in the next section.

Trim Control Unit Calibration (DP-C1/D1 Models)

The DP-C1/D1 drive unit is equipped with either a digital trim gauge/control unit or an analog trim gauge and separate control unit. The control unit is designed to limit positive trim to 5°. The control unit will only function correctly if the trim sending unit is correctly set and the control unit has been calibrated to the boat. Refer to **Table 9** for specifications.

Preliminary Steps

1. Verify that the drive unit is fully trimmed DOWN and the trim cylinders are fully retracted.
2. If the transom angle is unknown, measure the transom angle with a protractor, making sure to establish the level (angle) of the hull first. The transom angle must be within 10 - 15°, with 12-13° being the most common. Record the measured transom angle.
3. If there is any doubt that the trim gear wheel is properly indexed to the steering helmet gear rack, refer to Chapter Fourteen and index the gear wheel to the gear rack.
4. Verify that the trim sending unit mark (**Figure 15**) is positioned facing directly to starboard. Adjust the position of the sender as necessary by loosening the retaining screw and rotating it as shown in **Figure 16**. Tighten the trim sender retaining bracket securely when finished.
5. Apply a constant downward load of *approximately* 15 kg. (33 lb.) to the antiventilation plate as shown in **Figure 17** to make sure the drive unit is in its absolute lowest position. This load should be applied during all adjustments and checks to be made in the *Analog control unit and gauge* or *Digital gauge/control unit* sections.
6. Continue with the appropriate analog or digital procedure in one of the two following sections.

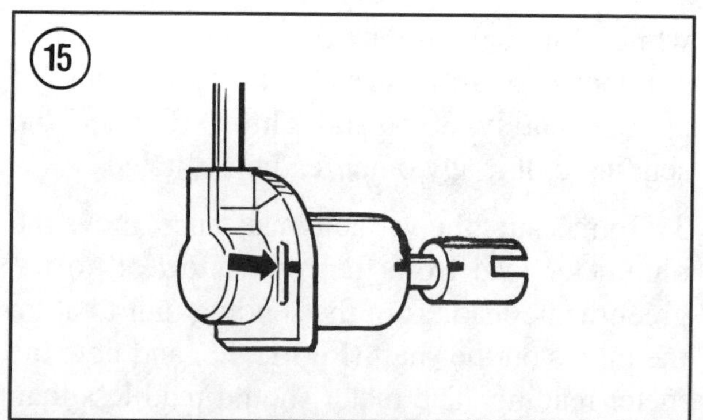

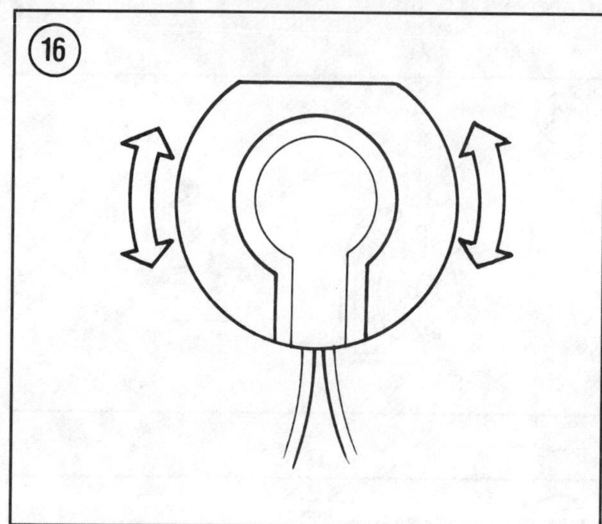

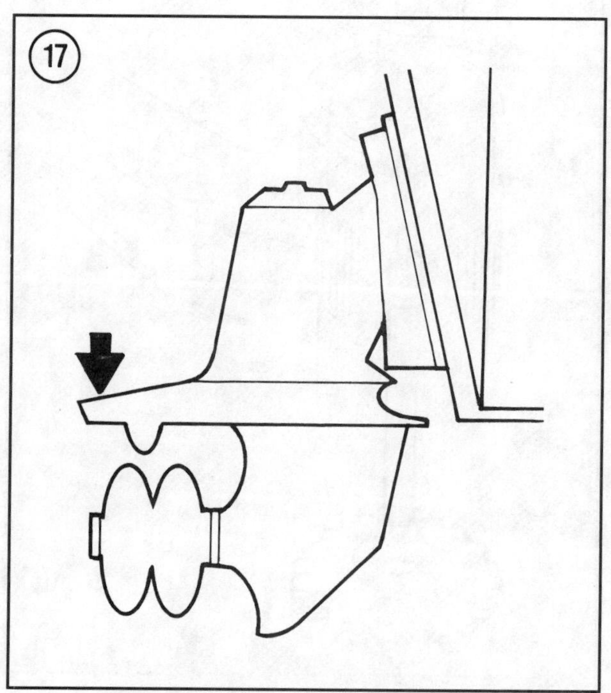

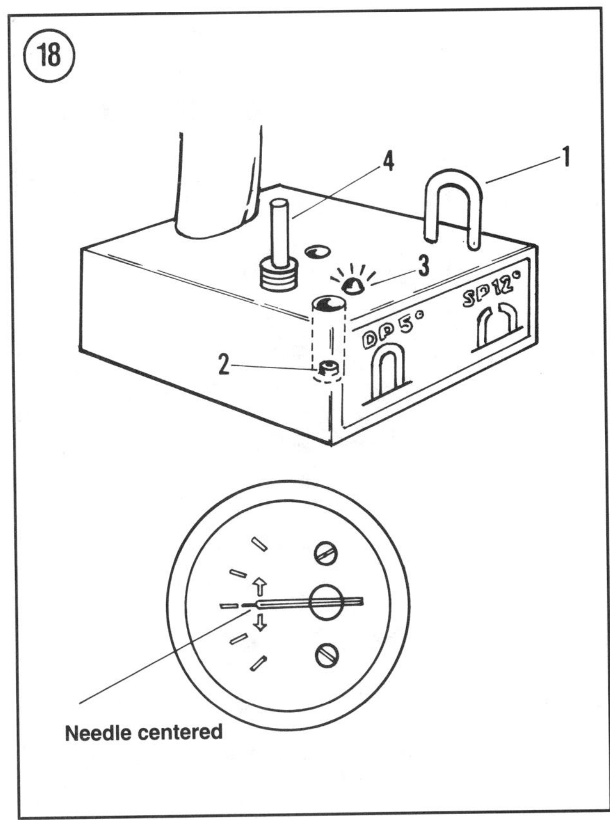

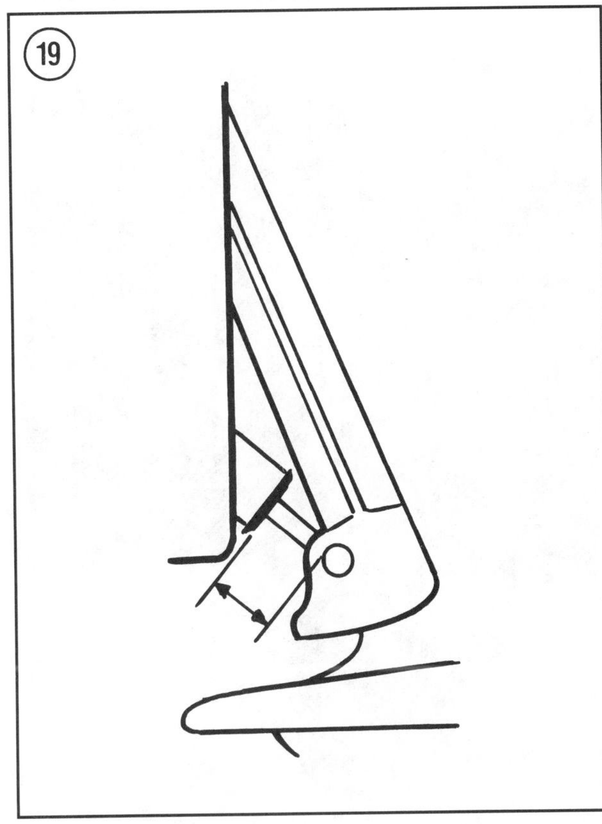

Analog control unit and gauge

The loop of wire protruding on the analog control unit (1, **Figure 18**) must NOT be cut. Cutting the wire will result in excessive positive trim, propeller ventilation and possible abnormal handling characteristics. Make sure that the *Preliminary steps* listed in this chapter, have been performed and that the constant downward load is being applied, before attempting this procedure.

1. Trim the drive unit out until the trim cylinders are extended to the specified dimension as shown in **Figure 19**, based on the transom angle for your boat. The specifications are as follows: 37 mm (1.46 in.) for 10° transoms, 40 mm (1.58 in.) for 11° transoms, 42 mm (1.65 in.) for 12° transoms, 45 mm (1.77 in.) for 13° transoms, 48 mm (1.89 in.) for 14° transoms and 51 mm (2.00 in.) for 15° transoms.
2. Turn the ignition switch to the ON or RUN position, then turn the recessed potentiometer screw at the bottom of the control unit bore (2, **Figure 18**) until the control unit light (3, **Figure 18**) just comes on. If in doubt, turn the potentiometer back and forth (turning the light off and on) until you are sure of the adjustment point.
3. Adjust the protruding potentiometer (4, **Figure 18**) to center the analog trim gauge in the middle of its travel as shown in **Figure 18**.

Digital gauge/control unit

The digital gauge has a switch on the back of the gauge (1, **Figure 20**) that must be set to the A position (lowest position). Make sure the switch is properly set before continuing. Incorrectly setting the switch will result in excessive positive trim, propeller cavitation damage and possible abnormal handling characteristics. Also make sure that the *Preliminary steps* listed in this chapter, have been performed and that the constant downward load is being applied, before attempting this procedure.

1. Turn the ignition switch to the ON or RUN position. Note the reading of the trim gauge.
2. Depending on the transom angle of the drive unit, the gauge should read -2 (10° transom), -3 (11° transom), -4 (12° transom), -5 (13° transom), -6 (14° transom) or -7 (15° transom). If the gauge reading does not match the specified angle based on your boat's transom angle, turn the potentiometer (2, **Figure 20**) on the back of the gauge until the correct reading is displayed.

POWER TRIM AND TILT SYSTEM (SX AND DP-S MODELS)

Operation

The power trim system used on these models consists of a valve body and hydraulic pump assembly, fluid reservoir and an electric motor contained in a single unit (**Figure 21**). The pump assembly is connected to a hydraulic cylinder on each side of the drive unit by hydraulic lines run through a manifold mounted in the transom bracket.

The electric motor is controlled by a pump mounted circuit board assembly that consists of 2 integral relay assemblies and an integral 10 amp circuit breaker (on 1994-1995 models) to protect the switching circuits. The circuit board on 1996 models may or may not contain the 10 amp circuit breaker, if not, a 10 amp in-line fuse will be installed across 2 of the circuit board terminals.

The circuit board receives power from an engine mounted 50 amp circuit breaker. The circuit breaker is typically located on the exhaust elbow or electrical bracket on the starboard side of the engine. The circuit board then sends power to the dash or remote control mounted trim switch through the integral 10 amp circuit breaker or external 10 amp fuse. The integral relays are used to reverse battery polarity in the same manner as the external relays described, at the beginning of this chapter.

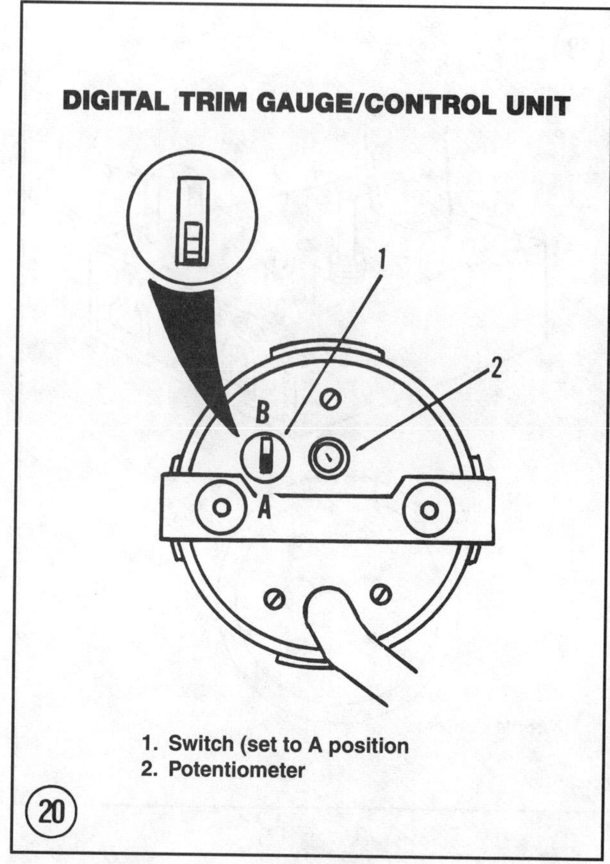

DIGITAL TRIM GAUGE/CONTROL UNIT

1. Switch (set to A position
2. Potentiometer

20

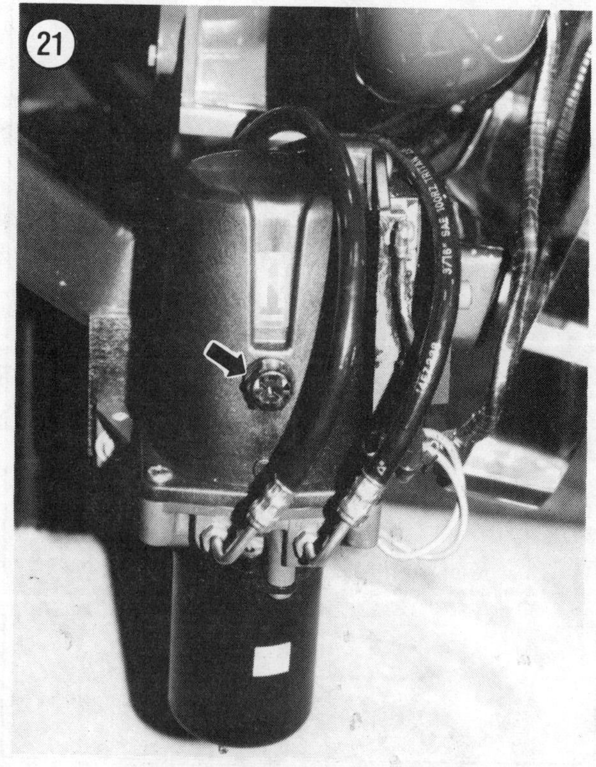
21

The DP-S system is designed to be operated in 1 of 3 operating modes—Trim IN, Trim OUT and override. The SX system operates in only 2 modes—Trim IN and Trim OUT. In the trim IN mode, the trim motor green wire becomes positive as the integral trim IN relay is energized. The integral trim OUT relay is not energized and holds the trim motor blue lead to ground. On DP-S models, the trim limit control box will shut off the trim IN relay when the 2° negative trim limit is reached, by opening the trim IN relay green/white activation lead.

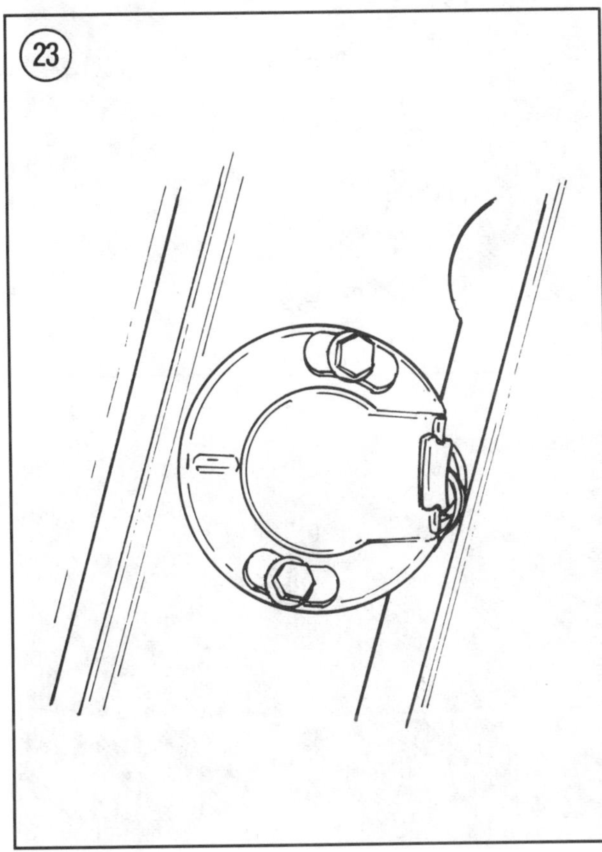

In the trim OUT mode, the trim motor blue wire becomes positive as the integral trim OUT relay is energized. The integral trim IN relay is not energized and holds the trim motor green lead to ground. On DP-S models, the trim limit control box will shut off the trim OUT relay when the 5° positive trim limit is reached, by opening the trim OUT relay blue/white activation lead.

In the override mode (DP-S models), the operator presses a switch that activates the override circuit inside of the trim limit control box. This allows the operator to trim the drive unit out or in, to the mechanical limit of the trim cylinders. The override and appropriate trim OUT or trim IN switches must be pressed simultaneously. The overriding the trim OUT limit should only be used at engine speeds below 1000 rpm, while making sure that the cooling water intakes in the drive unit are submerged at all times.

An electrical sending unit is installed on the starboard side of the gimbal ring. The sending unit is connected to a trim gauge on the instrument panel or dash. The trim gauge shows the bow position according to the trim angle of the drive unit. Three versions of the trim sending unit have been used. The trim sender used on 1994 SX models (**Figure 22**) has an arm that contacts the pivot housing and rotates the sender as the pivot housing moves toward or away from the sender. For 1995 SX models, the trim sending unit mounting location was moved to an integral location on the gimbal ring (**Figure 23**). The sender is connected to the starboard pivot housing pivot screw and detects the rotation of the screw as the pivot housing is raised or lowered. The 2 systems are NOT interchangeable. Adjustment of both types of trim sending units is covered in this chapter. On the final version of the trim sender, used on 1996 SX and DP-S models, a third wire was added to allow the trim sender to operate the trim limit control box required on all DP-S model drive units. The trim limit control box allows programming limits to the maximum trim IN, trim OUT and tilt UP positions. Operation and programming of the trim limit control box is covered in this chapter.

All 1994, 1995 and early production 1996 model trim pump assemblies are equipped with a manual release valve (**Figure 24**) that can be used to raise or lower the drive unit if an electrical malfunction occurs. When the valve is opened (turned counterclockwise), the drive unit can be manually moved to the desired position and the valve closed to secure the drive unit in that position. The manual release valve on these models features an integral thermal expansion valve in the manual release valve tip. If either the manual release valve or thermal expansion function fails, replace the valve as an assembly.

WARNING
Never operate the drive unit with the manual release valve open, as there will be no reverse lock and the drive unit will kick up in reverse or trail out on deceleration, causing a loss of control.

Late production 1996 models may be equipped with a redesigned valve body that does not include a manual release valve. The thermal expansion valve is relocated to be mounted on the valve body underneath the reservoir. The manual release check ball was also eliminated.

A failure of the late production system in the DOWN mode requires that the aft trim rod (**Figure 25**) be removed and the drive unit blocked or securely tied in the UP position in order to load the boat on a trailer. Do not attempt to operate the boat with the aft trim rod removed. There is no approved procedure for lowering the drive unit if the system fails in the UP mode.

WARNING
Never operate the drive unit with the aft trim rod removed, as there will be no reverse lock and the drive unit will kick up in reverse or trail out on deceleration, causing a loss of control.

Troubleshooting (General)

Very few components on this trim system are not serviceable. The trim cylinders can be re-

sealed or replaced as assemblies. The piston and cylinders are not available separately. A brush and seal kit is available for the electric motor or it can be purchased as an assembly. The valve body casting and gear housing casting are not individually serviceable. If either one is damaged, replace the valve body as an assembly, complete with all valves and the gear housing. All other components are individually available.

Before attempting to diagnose any malfunction with the power trim system, make the following preliminary checks.

1. Check the fluid level in the pump reservoir. Check the fluid with the drive unit in the full trim OUT or UP position. The fluid level should be level with the bottom of the fill plug hole on the reservoir (**Figure 26**). If the fluid level is low, add sufficient fluid (**Table 1**) to bring it to the correct level.
2. Check all hydraulic lines and connections for signs of leakage or deterioration. Replace any damaged or deteriorated lines and tighten connections as necessary.

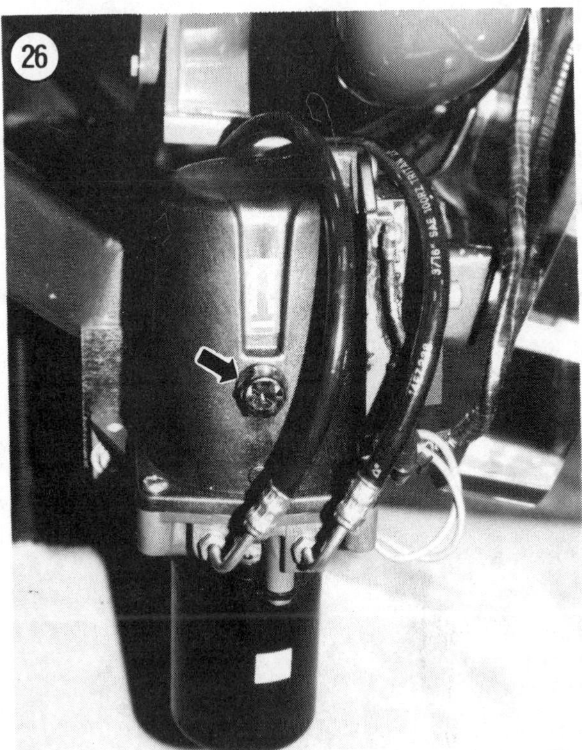

3. Check the trim system electrical leads, connectors and connections for corrosion, loose connections, damaged connectors and damaged leads. This would include the battery negative and positive connections, the engine main ground stud and the positive battery cable connection to the engine. Repair or replace as necessary.

Troubleshooting (Electrical)

The trim motor is reversed by switching the polarity of the trim motor blue and green leads. There are 2 relays mounted inside the trim pump circuit board assembly, one for each trim motor lead. Both relays hold their respective trim motor lead (blue or green) to ground when they are not activated. When the integral UP relay is activated it takes the blue trim motor lead off of ground and connects it to positive. The DOWN relay is inactive and holds the green lead to ground. Current can then flow from the positive terminal to the UP relay to the trim motor and back to ground through the DOWN relay causing the motor to run in the UP direction. When the DOWN relay is activated it takes the green trim motor lead off of ground and connects it to positive. The UP relay is inactive and holds the blue lead to ground. Current can then flow from the positive terminal to the DOWN relay to the trim motor and back to ground through the UP relay causing the motor to run in the DOWN direction. If the motor will run in one direction, but not the other, the problem cannot be the trim motor.

If the trim system is wired using standard Volvo harnesses, the trim system switching circuits are wired independently of the ignition switch. The unit will trim IN and out, regardless of ignition switch position. However, the ignition switch must be in the ON or RUN position for the trim indicator gauge to operate. The trim system receives power to operate the switching circuits through the 10 amp fuse or circuit breaker mounted on the trim pump. The 10 amp fuse or circuit breaker receives power directly from the trim system 50 amp circuit breaker.

NOTE

The trim motor is equipped with an internal thermal cutout switch. If the trim motor is operated for extended periods of time and develops sufficient heat, the cutout will open, stopping the motor. Allow the motor to cool and the cutout switch will automatically reset.

Refer to **Figure 27** for an internal schematic of the circuit board assembly, **Figure 28** for a typical SX trim system wiring diagram and **Figure 29** for a typical DP-S trim system wiring diagram.

The DP-S trim system requires the use of the trim limit control box (9, **Figure 29**). The trim limit control box will limit the total amount of

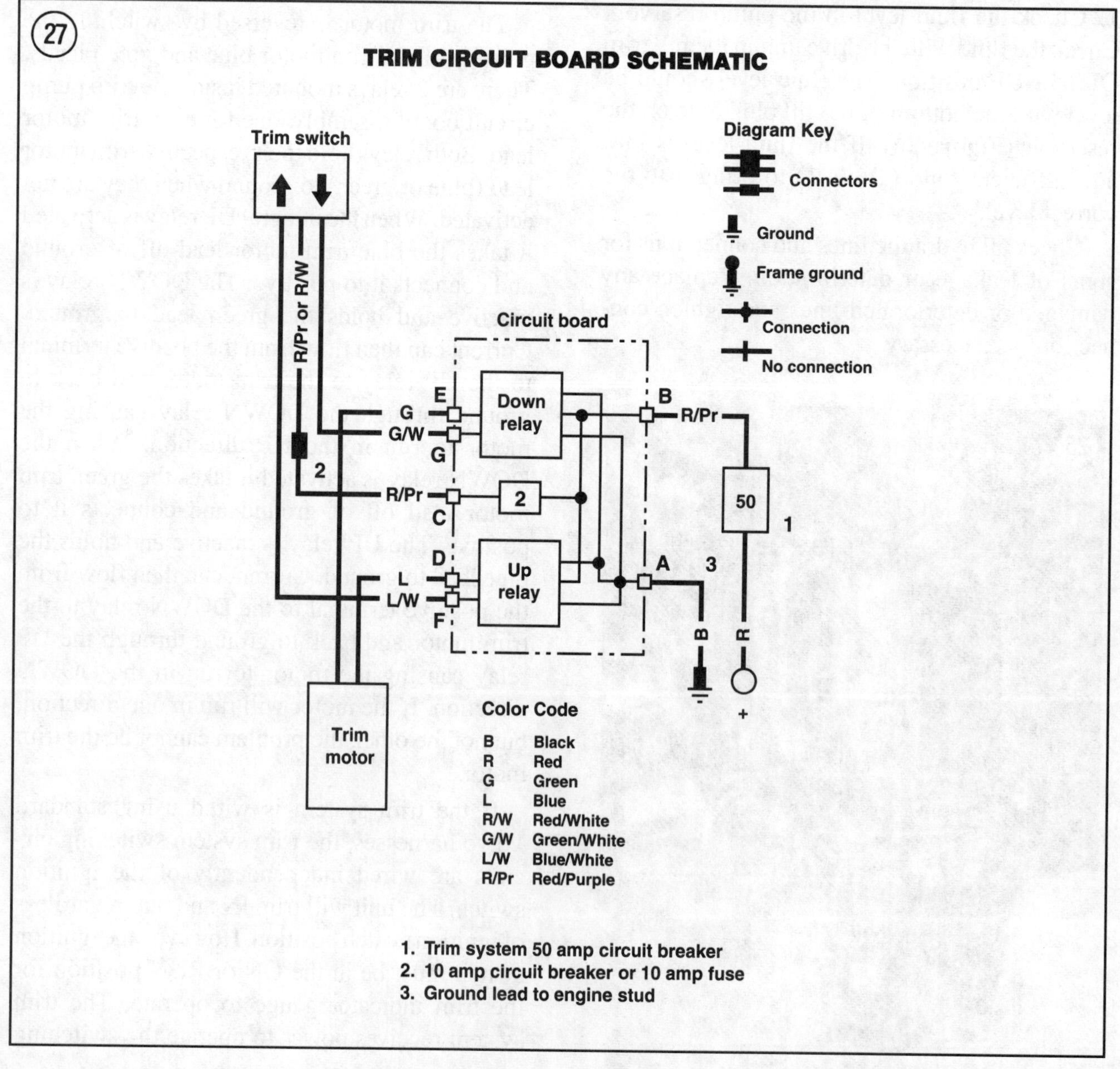

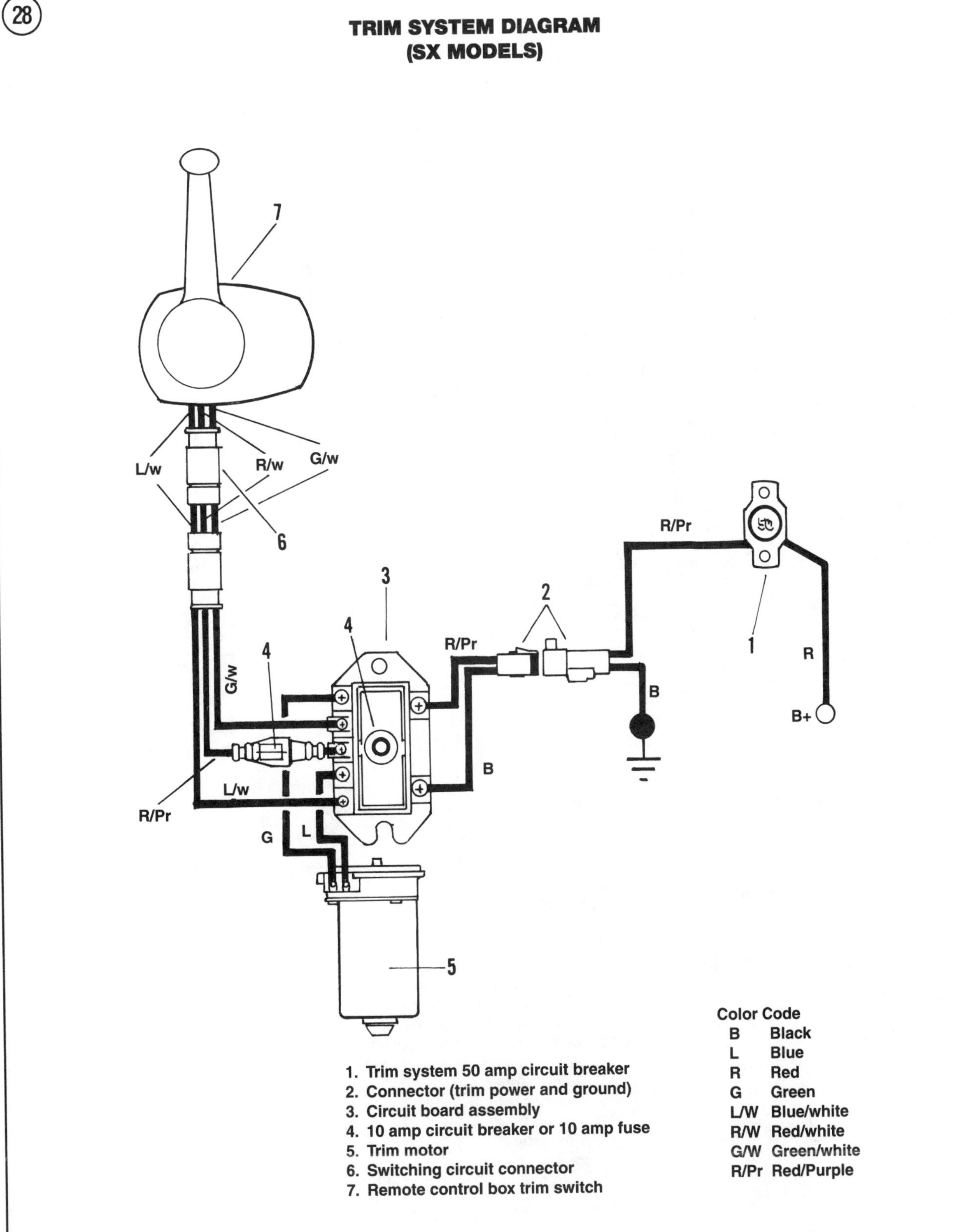
28
TRIM SYSTEM DIAGRAM
(SX MODELS)
7
L/w
R/w
G/w
6
R/Pr
3
2
4
R/Pr
4
G/w
1
R
B
B+
B
L/w
R/Pr
G
L
5
Color Code
B Black
L Blue
R Red
G Green
L/W Blue/white
R/W Red/white
G/W Green/white
R/Pr Red/Purple
1. Trim system 50 amp circuit breaker
2. Connector (trim power and ground)
3. Circuit board assembly
4. 10 amp circuit breaker or 10 amp fuse
5. Trim motor
6. Switching circuit connector
7. Remote control box trim switch

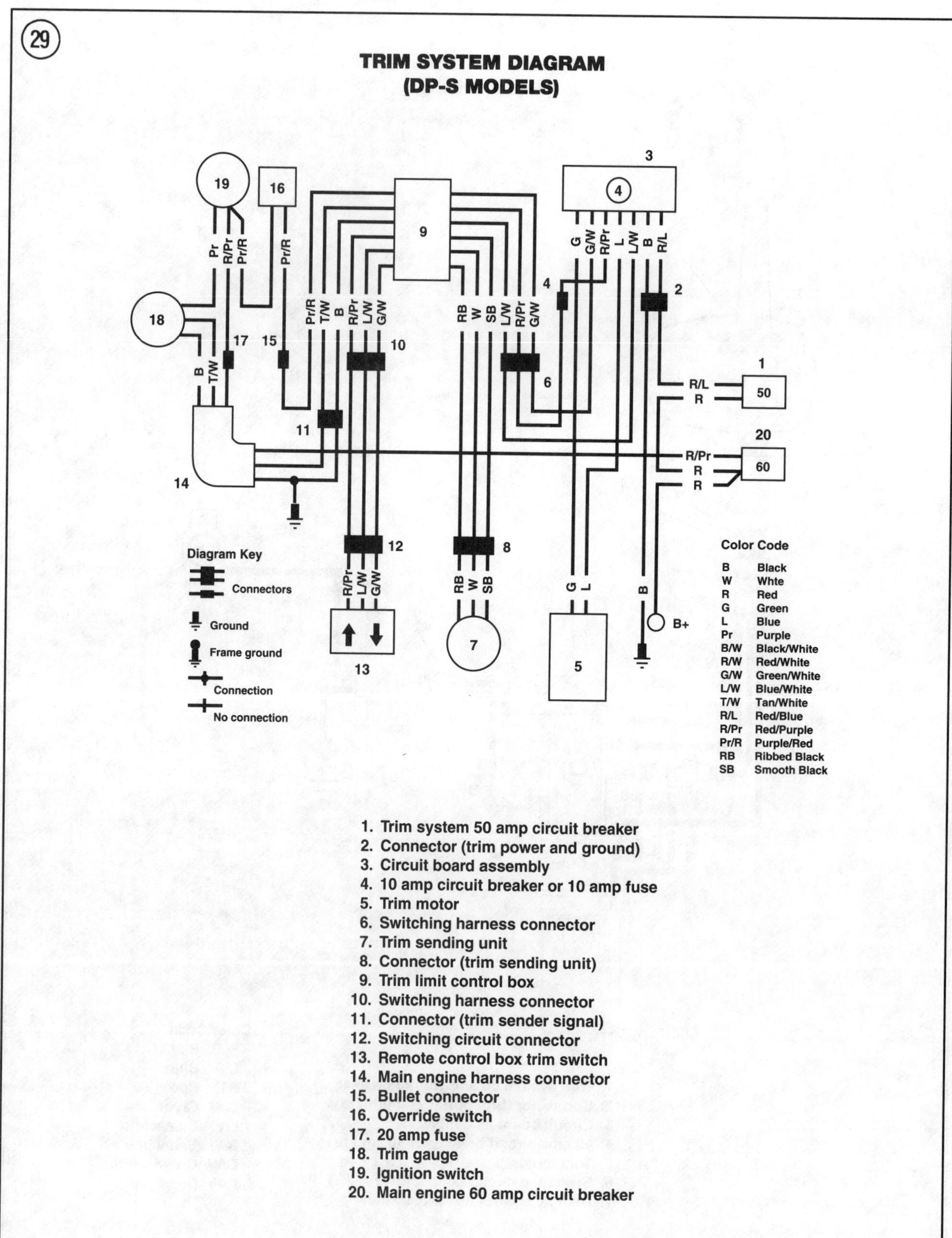
29
TRIM SYSTEM DIAGRAM
(DP-S MODELS)
Pr
R/Pr
Pr/R
Pr/R
Pr/R
T/W
B
R/Pr
L/W
G/W
RB
W
SB
L/W
R/Pr
G/W
G
G/W
R/Pr
L
L/W
B
R/L
B
T/W
R/L
R
R/Pr
R
R
R/Pr
L/W
G/W
RB
W
SB
G
L
B
B+
50
60
Diagram Key
Connectors
Ground
Frame ground
Connection
No connection
Color Code
B Black
W Whte
R Red
G Green
L Blue
Pr Purple
B/W Black/White
R/W Red/White
G/W Green/White
L/W Blue/White
T/W Tan/White
R/L Red/Blue
R/Pr Red/Purple
Pr/R Purple/Red
RB Ribbed Black
SB Smooth Black
1. Trim system 50 amp circuit breaker
2. Connector (trim power and ground)
3. Circuit board assembly
4. 10 amp circuit breaker or 10 amp fuse
5. Trim motor
6. Switching harness connector
7. Trim sending unit
8. Connector (trim sending unit)
9. Trim limit control box
10. Switching harness connector
11. Connector (trim sender signal)
12. Switching circuit connector
13. Remote control box trim switch
14. Main engine harness connector
15. Bullet connector
16. Override switch
17. 20 amp fuse
18. Trim gauge
19. Ignition switch
20. Main engine 60 amp circuit breaker

trim IN, trim OUT and tilt UP. Programming instructions for setting the limits is covered in *Trim Limit Control Box (DP-S Models)* section in this chapter. The trim limit control box depends on the trim sending unit signal to determine drive unit position. If there is any doubt that the trim sending unit is correctly adjusted, proceed to *Trim sender adjustment* in this chapter.

To eliminate the trim limit control box as a possible problem, disconnect connectors 6 and 10, **Figure 29**. Connect the trim pump harness directly to the trim switch harness, bypassing the trim limit control box. If the trim system will now run satisfactorily in both directions, the problem is in the trim limit control box, trim sending unit or control box programming.

To troubleshoot the trim electrical system on SX and DP-S models, refer to **Figure 27** and **Figure 28** or **Figure 29** for this procedure.

1. Connect the test lamp lead to the *positive* terminal of the battery and touch the test lamp probe to metal anywhere on the engine block. The test lamp should light. If the lamp does not light or is dim, the battery ground cable connections are loose or corroded, or there is an open circuit in the battery ground cable. Check connections on both ends of the ground cable.
2. Connect the test lamp probe to test point A, **Figure 27**. The test lamp should light. If the test lamp does not light or is dim, repair or replace the black lead from the circuit board to engine ground as necessary.
3. Connect the test lamp probe to test points D and E, **Figure 27**. The test lamp should light at each test point. If the test lamp does not light or is dim, replace the circuit board assembly.
4. Connect test lamp lead to a good engine ground.
5. Connect the test lamp probe to test point B, **Figure 27**. The test lamp should light. If the lamp does not light or is very dim, the circuit breaker is open or there is an open in the red/purple lead from the circuit board to the battery. Reset or replace the circuit breaker, or repair or replace the red/purple lead from the circuit board to the battery as required.
6. Connect the test lamp probe to test point C, **Figure 27**. The test lamp should light. If the lamp does not light, reset the circuit breaker (2, **Figure 27**), if so equipped. If the test lamp still does not light, replace the circuit board assembly. If the circuit board is not equipped with a circuit breaker, check the in-line fuse (2, **Figure 27**). Replace the fuse if its condition is questionable.

NOTE

If troubleshooting a DP-S drive unit, eliminate the trim limit control box as a possible problem by disconnecting connectors 6 and 10, ***Figure 29*** *and connecting the trim pump harness directly to the trim switch harness, bypassing the trim limit control box. If the trim system will now run satisfactorily in both directions, the problem is in the trim limit control box, trim sending unit or control box programming. Leave the trim limit control box bypassed for the rest of this procedure.*

7. Disconnect the switching circuit connector (6, **Figure 28** or 12, **Figure 29**) from the control box or disconnect the red/purple or red/white lead from the dash mounted trim switch. Connect the test lamp probe to the red/purple or red/white terminal of the harness. The test lamp should light. If the test lamp does not light or is dim, repair or replace the red/purple or red/white lead from the circuit board to the tested connector or terminal. Reconnect all leads when finished.
8. Connect the test lamp probe to test point F, **Figure 27**. Activate the trim switch in the trim OUT (UP) mode. The test lamp should light. If the test lamp does not light, test the trim switch as described in *Trim switch ohmmeter tests* in this chapter. If the switch tests good, repair or replace the blue/white lead from the circuit board assembly to the trim switch.
9. Connect the test lamp probe to test point G, **Figure 27**. Activate the trim switch in the trim IN (DOWN) mode. The test lamp should light.

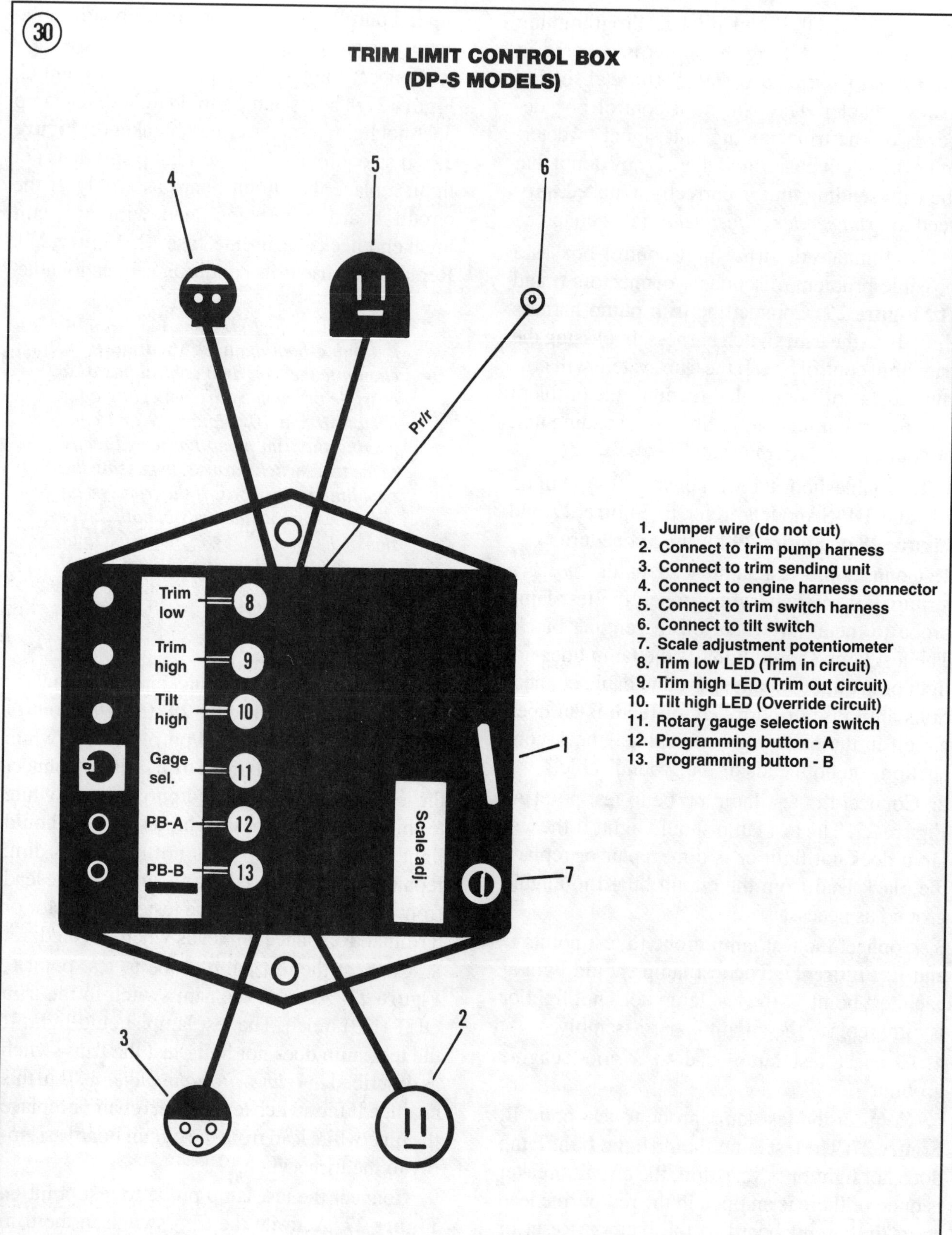
30
TRIM LIMIT CONTROL BOX
(DP-S MODELS)
Pr/r
Trim low
Trim high
Tilt high
Gage sel.
PB-A
PB-B
Scale adj.
1. Jumper wire (do not cut)
2. Connect to trim pump harness
3. Connect to trim sending unit
4. Connect to engine harness connector
5. Connect to trim switch harness
6. Connect to tilt switch
7. Scale adjustment potentiometer
8. Trim low LED (Trim in circuit)
9. Trim high LED (Trim out circuit)
10. Tilt high LED (Override circuit)
11. Rotary gauge selection switch
12. Programming button - A
13. Programming button - B

If the test lamp does not light, test the trim switch as described in *Trim switch ohmmeter tests* in this chapter. If the switch tests good, repair or replace the green/white lead from the circuit board assembly to the trim switch.

10. Connect the test lamp probe to test point D, **Figure 27**. Activate the trim switch in the trim OUT (UP) mode. The test lamp should light. If the test lamp does not light, replace the circuit board assembly.

11. Connect the test lamp probe to test point E, **Figure 27**. Activate the trim switch in the trim IN (DOWN) mode. The test lamp should light. If the test lamp does not light, replace the circuit board assembly.

12. If all previous tests are satisfactory and the electric motor still does not operate correctly, remove the electric motor as described in this chapter. Disassemble and inspect the electric motor to determine if a seal and brush kit will correct the problem. If not, replace the electric motor.

13. Reconnect the trim limit control box as shown in **Figure 29**. If the trim system malfunctions with the control box connected, first adjust the trim sending unit. If needed, proceed to *DP-S trim limit control box troubleshooting* in the next section.

DP-S trim limit control box troubleshooting

The trim control unit is equipped with 3 light emitting diodes (LED). Each LED indicates which mode the trim control unit is in. Whenever the trim IN switch is depressed, the Trim LOW LED (8, **Figure 30**) should illuminate. Whenever the trim OUT switch is depressed, the Trim HIGH LED (9, **Figure 30**) should illuminate and finally, whenever the tilt switch is activated, the tilt HIGH LED (10, **Figure 30**) should illuminate.

These lights are valuable troubleshooting tools. If the appropriate light illuminates when the selected switch is depressed, the trim switching circuits are working correctly.

The gauge selector switch (11, **Figure 30**) is a rotary switch with multiple positions. Position O is the programming position. Refer to **Table 10** for the correct operating position for your boat, based on the trim gauge being used.

To troubleshoot the DP-S trim limit control box, refer to **Figure 29** and **Figure 30** and proceed as follows.

1. If the trim limit control unit will not allow the trim pump to operate, check the battery voltage and the voltage to the trim limit control module (red/purple lead at 6, **Figure 29**). The module cannot operate below 9.5 volts.

2. If the trim needle bounces from full UP to full DOWN or the trim needle pegs in the up position, check the trim sending unit for correct adjustment and perform the ohmmeter tests listed under *Trim sending unit, troubleshooting* in this chapter. Also check to see that the trim sending unit connector has the ribbed black lead in position A, the white lead in position B and the smooth black lead in position C. Correct any problems found.

NOTE

To use the override function, the override switch and the desired trim IN or trim OUT switch must be simultaneously depressed.

3. If the override switch will not allow trimming above the positive 5° limit, proceed as follows:

   a. With the aid of an assistant, activate the override switch (16, **Figure 29**) on the dash or remote control box. Observe the tilt HIGH LED (10, **Figure 30**). If the tilt high LED illuminates, the override switch and leads are functioning correctly. If the LED does not illuminate, continue to substep b.

   b. Refer to **Figure 29** and disconnect the bullet connector (15, **Figure 29**). Connect a test lamp lead to a good engine ground and insert the test lamp probe into the key switch side bullet connector.

c. Activate the override switch. The test lamp should light. If not, check the purple/red lead for an open circuit back to the ignition switch and check for a defective override switch.

d. Turn the gauge selector switch (11, **Figure 30**) to position O. Check for trim system operation above the trim limit range. If the drive unit will now trim at will, the trim limit control box is incorrectly programmed or malfunctioning. Refer to programming section of *Trim limit control box (DP-S models)* at the end of this chapter, and reprogram the correct trim IN, trim OUT and tilt UP limits.

Trim switch ohmmeter tests

To perform this test, all leads must be disconnected from the trim switch. The test can be performed at the remote control harness plug-in (6, **Figure 28** or 12, **Figure 29**) for remote control models or directly at the switch terminals for dash mounted models.

1. Calibrate an ohmmeter on the R × 1 scale.
2. Connect 1 ohmmeter lead to the switch center terminal on dash mounted switches or to the red/white or red/purple lead of the remote control trim switch harness.
3. Connect the other ohmmeter lead to the green/white lead or green/white terminal. Activate the switch in the trim IN (DOWN) mode. The meter should read continuity (very low reading). Replace the trim switch if any other reading is obtained.
4. Move the ohmmeter lead from the green/white lead or terminal to the blue/white lead or blue/white terminal. Activate the switch in the trim OUT (UP) mode. The meter should read continuity (very low reading). Replace the trim switch if any other reading is obtained.
5. Reconnect all leads when finished.

Trim motor bench test

If the motor seems to run too slowly, does not cycle the drive unit in the specified time (**Table 2**), perform the following bench test on the trim motor. The bench test measures the stall torque and amperage draw of the motor in a controlled environment. The test must be performed in each direction (UP and DOWN) to see if the motor delivers at least the minimum specified torque and does not consume excessive current. Refer to **Figure 31** for this procedure.

1. Remove the trim pump assembly from the boat and separate the trim motor from the pump assembly as described in this chapter.
2. Clamp the motor in a vise with protective jaws. Do not crush the housing and damage the magnets.
3. Connect a fully charged 12-volt battery and an ammeter (with a 0-200 amp scale) in series with the motor. See A, **Figure 31**.

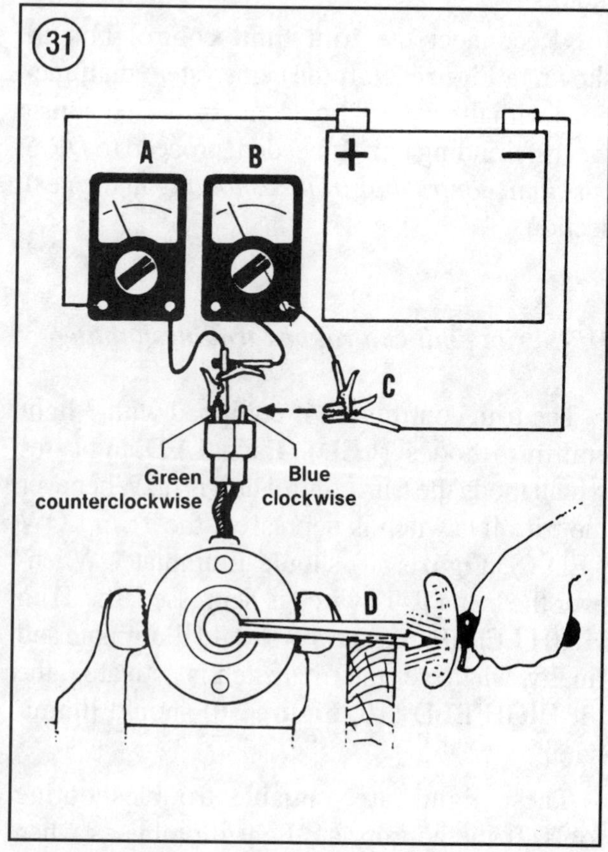

4. Connect a voltmeter (B, **Figure 31**) between the same motor terminal and the battery negative terminal.
5. Connect a jumper (C, **Figure 31**) to the negative battery terminal.
6. Connect an in.-lb. torque wrench to the motor armature shaft with a suitable socket (D, **Figure 31**).
7. Hold the torque wrench and complete the electrical circuit momentarily by attaching the jumper (C, **Figure 31**) momentarily to the other tilt motor lead.
8. Observe the torque indicated by the torque wrench and the reading indicated by the ammeter.
9. Reverse the connections to the motor leads and check the motor output and amperage draw in the opposite direction.
10. Replace the motor if the following conditions are not met with both polarity connections:
   a. The ammeter must indicate no more than a maximum of 185 amps.
   b. The stall torque should be at least a minimum of 20.6 in.-lb. (2.3 N•m).

Troubleshooting (Hydraulic)

Refer to **Table 4** for common trim system problems and their solutions. All problems in **Table 4** assume the trim motor runs properly. Refer to *Troubleshooting (Electric)* in this chapter, if the trim motor does not run or does not run properly. Refer to **Figure 32** for a schematic of the 1994-early 1996 hydraulic pump assembly and to **Figure 33** for a schematic of the late 1996 hydraulic pump assembly. Both of these schematics show the pump operating in the trim OUT mode (for reference). The late model pump can be easily identified by the absence of the manual release valve. **Figure 24** shows the early model pump and its manual release valve location.

This procedure is for troubleshooting internal leakage and assumes that all visible leaks have been isolated and corrected. External leaks, no matter how small, can not be tolerated on a trim system.

If the drive unit leaks in both directions (up and down), the problem is most likely in one or both of the trim cylinders. If 1 trim cylinder fails, the other is usually soon to follow. Consider flushing the lines and resealing or replacing both cylinders at the same time.

Volvo Pressure Tester (part No. 3854368-2) can be used to pressure test the trim pump assembly and allows direct reading of the pressures required to tilt the drive unit, the maximum (stall) pressure available in the trim IN and trim OUT modes and test the complete system or just the trim pump assembly for internal leakage (leak-down test).

Safety Precautions

The trim system internal hydraulic pressure must be relieved before any lines are disconnected from the trim pump, manifold or trim cylinders. Anytime a line is disconnected, plug both ends of the connection to prevent excessive leakage and contamination of the fluid.

WARNING
Eye protection must be worn during this procedure and any procedure involving disconnecting of any trim line from the trim pump, trim manifold and trim cylinders.

CAUTION
Install new line O-rings each time a line is removed from the pump, manifold, cylinders or tester.

1. To relieve the internal pressure on an early model system equipped with a manual release valve, proceed as follows:
   a. Trim the drive unit to the full UP position.
   b. Securely block or lock the drive unit in the full UP position. OMC Trailer Lock kit part No. 174448 can be used (and is recom-

mended) if a small amount of material is removed from one end of each trailer lock.

c. Open the manual release valve (6, **Figure 32**) until it contacts the snap ring retainer. Allow the drive unit to settle onto the trailer locks or blocks.

d. Cover the reservoir fill plug (17, **Figure 32**) with a shop towel and carefully and slowly remove the fill plug, allowing any internal pressure to vent before fully removing the plug.

e. Reinstall the fill plug and close the manual release valve to minimize fluid loss.

2. To relieve the internal pressure on late model systems not equipped with a manual release valve, proceed as follows:

a. Trim the drive unit to the full UP position.

b. Securely block or lock the drive unit in the full UP position. OMC Trailer Lock kit part No. 174448 can be used (and is recommended) if a small amount of material is removed from one end of each trailer lock.

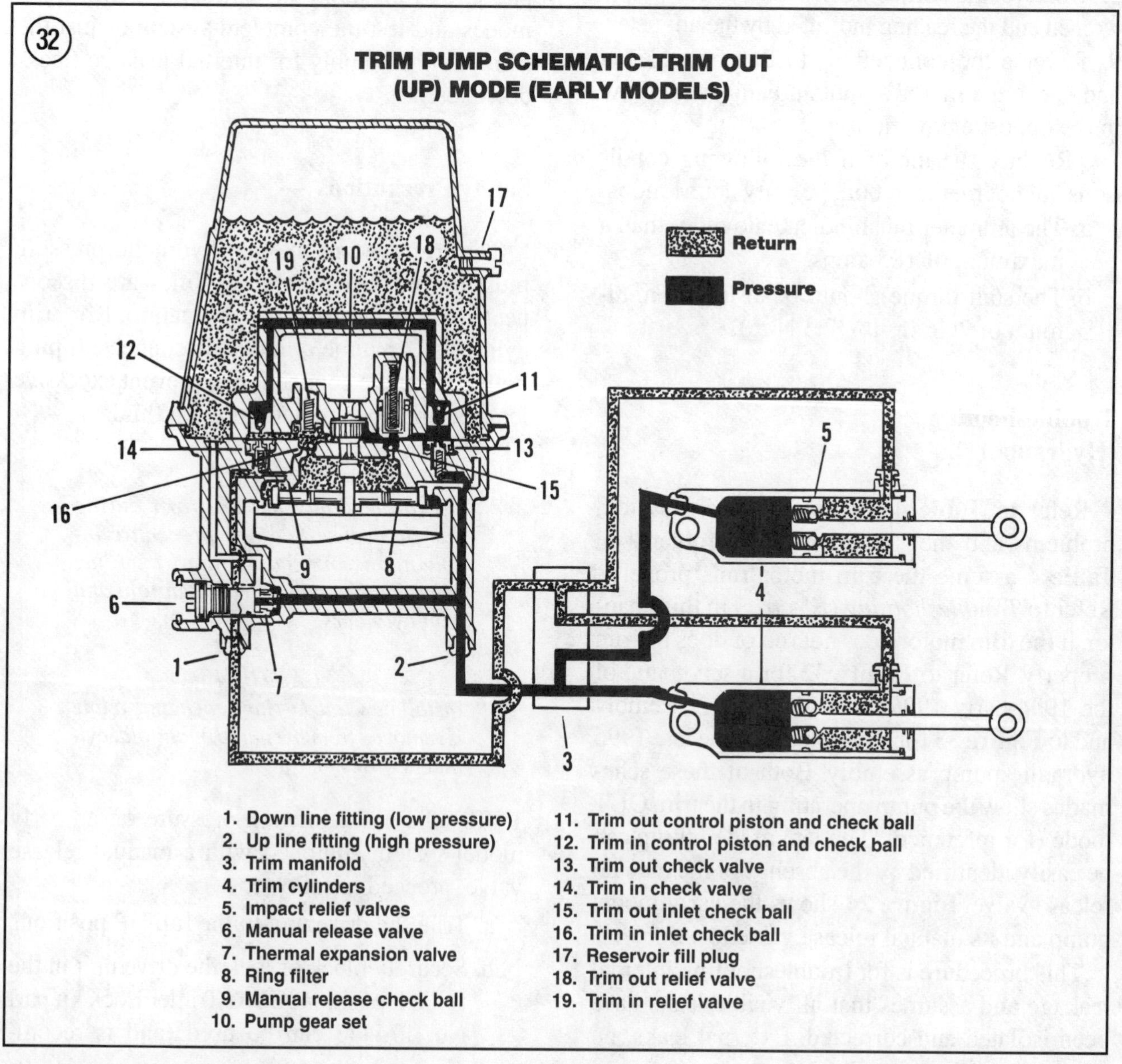

c. Cover the reservoir fill plug (15, **Figure 33**) with a shop towel and carefully and slowly remove the fill plug, allowing any internal pressure to vent before fully removing the plug.

d. Place a small container, such as a coffee can, underneath the trim pump.

e. Cover the UP line fitting at the trim pump (2, **Figure 33**) with several shop towels. Carefully and slowly loosen the line fittings, allowing internal pressure and fluid to vent as the drive settles onto the trailer locks or blocks.

f. After the pressure has been relieved, reinstall the fill plug to minimize fluid loss. If

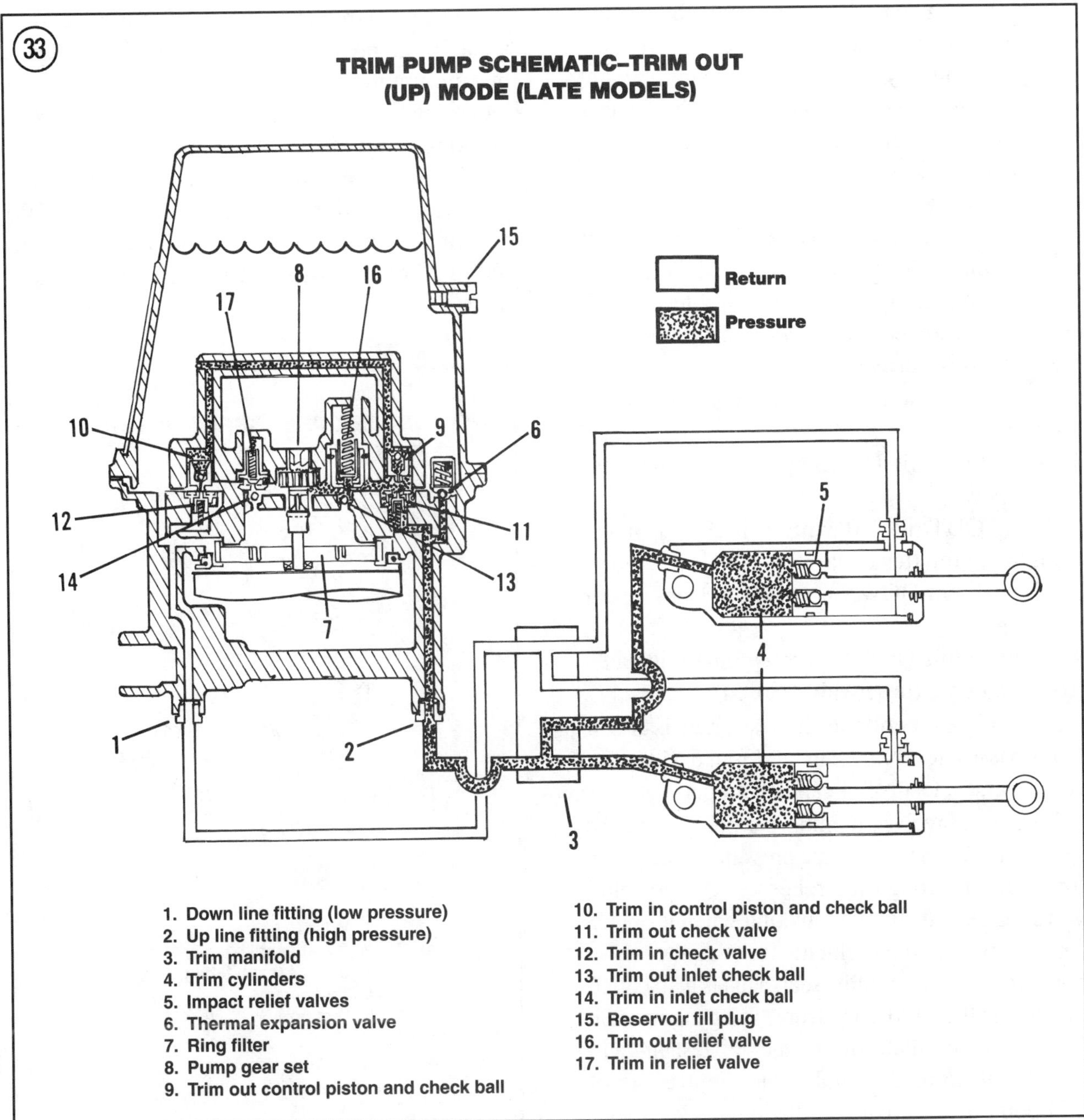

1. Down line fitting (low pressure)
2. Up line fitting (high pressure)
3. Trim manifold
4. Trim cylinders
5. Impact relief valves
6. Thermal expansion valve
7. Ring filter
8. Pump gear set
9. Trim out control piston and check ball
10. Trim in control piston and check ball
11. Trim out check valve
12. Trim in check valve
13. Trim out inlet check ball
14. Trim in inlet check ball
15. Reservoir fill plug
16. Trim out relief valve
17. Trim in relief valve

the UP line is not going to be removed, tighten the line fitting to specification (**Table 5**).

Test Connections and Test Procedures

The Volvo Pressure Tester (part No. 3854368-2) has 2 hydraulic ports marked A and B. The A port is always connected to the gauge, while the B port can be isolated from the gauge by closing the valve in the tester body. The A port must always be directly connected to the component (circuit) that is to be tested. When the tester's valve is closed, fluid cannot flow through the tester and the B port is isolated from the A port. See **Figure 34**.

A total of 4 separate tests, requiring 2 different tester connections, may be required to test the system completely. A minimum of 2 tests and 2 connections are required to verify that the system is functioning correctly.

The tests must be performed in the following order.

1. Trim OUT/tilt UP complete system (tester valve open).
2. Trim OUT/tilt UP with cylinders isolated from the pump (tester valve closed).
3. Trim IN/tilt DOWN complete system (tester valve open).
4. Trim IN/tilt DOWN with cylinders isolated from the pump (tester valve closed).

The only exception to the test order is if test No. 1 passes, test No. 2 can be skipped and if test No. 3 passes, test No. 4 can be skipped.

Each test involves running the pump until the relief valve opens, noting the pressure as the pump forces fluid through the relief valve. The relief valve makes a distinct squawking when it opens, caused by the rapid fluctuations of the valve bouncing on and off of its seat. This is also called measuring the STALL pressure. The gauge needle will vibrate (oscillate) during the stall test and will be difficult to read. Simply note the average or mid-point of the needle oscillations.

Once the stall pressure has been noted, stop the electric motor and begin the leak-down test. Leak-down is measured from the first point of needle stabilization as the electric motor is shut off and the relief valve closes. The needle may jump up slightly or drop slightly as this occurs. It is only important to note where the needle stabilizes at, immediately after the trim motor is stopped.

The acceptable leak-down rate for all tests is a maximum pressure drop of 1379 kPa (200 psi) in a minimum time span of 5 minutes. For example, if the trim OUT stall pressure was 9998 kPa (1450 psi) and the needle stabilized at 9653 kPa (1400 psi) when the trim motor stopped, the gauge cannot indicate lower than 8274 kPa (1200 psi) after a minimum of 5 minutes. Refer to **Table 2** for pressure and leak-down specifications.

34

IN-LINE PRESSURE TESTER

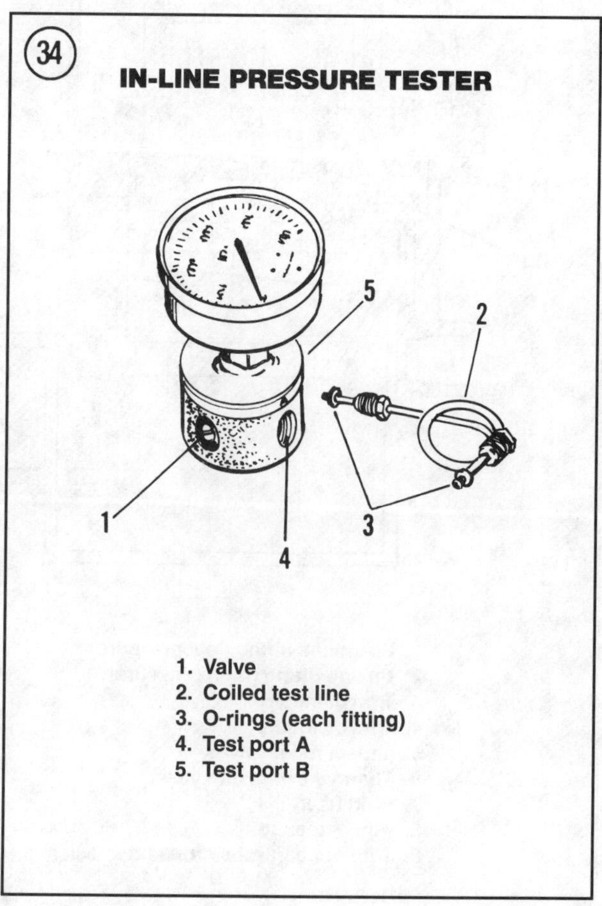

1. Valve
2. Coiled test line
3. O-rings (each fitting)
4. Test port A
5. Test port B

Test No. 1 (trim OUT/tilt UP, complete system)

To test the complete system (pump and cylinders) UP (OUT) circuits, proceed as follows.

CAUTION
Wear eye protection for this complete procedure. Wrap shop towels around each line fitting as it is loosened and removed to eliminate any dangerous fluid spray.

1. Relieve system pressure as described under *Safety precautions* in this chapter.

2. Remove the UP hydraulic line from the valve body (port fitting).

3. Using new O-rings, connect the tester coiled line assembly (2, **Figure 34**) between the valve body (UP) port and the port marked A (4, **Figure 34**) on the tester body. Tighten the fittings to specification (**Table 5**).

4. Using a new O-ring, connect the UP hydraulic line to the port marked B on the tester body. Tighten the fittings to specification (**Table 5**).

5. Verify that the tester valve (1, **Figure 34**) is opened at least one full turn.

6. Remove the trailer locks or block and trim the drive unit through several cycles to purge any air from the lines. Check the fluid level (with the drive unit full UP) and add fluid as necessary.

7. Trim the drive unit to the full DOWN position, then trim the drive unit to the full UP position. Observe the stall pressure when the drive unit reaches the full UP position, then observe the leak-down rate for a minimum of 5 minutes.

8. Compare your results to the specifications listed in **Table 2**. If the results are within specification, proceed to Test No. 3. If the results are not within specification, proceed to test No. 2.

Test No. 2 (trim OUT/tilt UP, pump only)

To isolate the cylinders from the pump and determine if the pump assembly trim UP (OUT) circuits are malfunctioning, proceed as follows.

1. Securely block or lock the drive unit in the full UP position. OMC Trailer Lock kit part No. 174448 can be used (and is recommended) if a small amount of material is removed from one end of each trailer lock.

2. Briefly operate the trim pump in the DOWN (IN) direction to settle the drive unit onto the blocks or trailer locks.

3. Close the tester valve (1, **Figure 34**) fully.

4. Operate the trim pump in the UP (OUT) direction. Observe the stall pressure as the pump operates, then turn off the pump and observe the leak-down rate for a minimum of 5 minutes.

5. Compare your results to the specifications listed in **Table 2**. If the results are within specifications, the cylinders are internally leaking and are the cause of the failure of Test No. 1. Remove both cylinders and reseal them. Replace the cylinders if the cylinder bores or pistons are scored.

6. If the results are not within specifications, the trim pump UP circuits are defective. Disassemble the pump and locate the defective valve or component. If the leak-down rate is excessive, pay particular attention to the thermal expansion valve, manual release valve (early models) and trim OUT/tilt UP check valve. If the stall pressure is too low, pay particular attention to the trim OUT check ball, the trim OUT/tilt UP relief valve and spring and the gear housing to valve body mating surface.

7. Once this test has been passed, proceed to Test No. 3 in the next section.

Test No. 3 (trim IN/tilt DOWN, complete system)

To test the complete system (pump and cylinders) DOWN (IN) circuits, proceed as follows.

CAUTION
Wear eye protection for this complete procedure. Wrap shop towels around each line fitting as it is loosened and removed to eliminate any dangerous fluid spray.

1. Open the tester valve (1, **Figure 34**) at least 1 complete turn and relieve system pressure as described under *Safety precautions* in this chapter.
2. Remove the pressure tester from the valve body UP port and UP hydraulic line, then reattach the UP hydraulic line to the valve body UP port (port fitting) with a new O-ring. Tighten the fitting to specification (**Table 5**).
3. Remove the DOWN hydraulic line from the valve body (starboard fitting).
4. Using new O-rings, connect the tester coiled line assembly (2, **Figure 34**) between the valve body (DOWN) port and the port marked A (4, **Figure 34**) on the tester body. Tighten the fittings to specification (**Table 5**).
5. Using a new O-ring, connect the DOWN hydraulic line to the port marked B on the tester body. Tighten the fittings to specification (**Table 5**).
6. Verify that the tester valve (1, **Figure 34**) is opened at least 1 full turn.
7. Remove the trailer locks or block and trim the drive unit through several cycles to purge any air from the lines. Check the fluid level (with the drive unit full UP) and add fluid as necessary.
8. Trim the drive unit to the full UP position, then trim the drive unit to the full DOWN position. Observe the stall pressure when the drive unit reaches the full DOWN position, then observe the leak-down rate for a minimum of 5 minutes.
9. Compare your results to the specifications listed in **Table 2**. If the results are within specification, system testing is complete. If the results are not within specification, proceed to test No. 4.
10. If testing is complete, relieve system pressure as described under *Safety precautions* in this chapter.
11. Remove the pressure tester from the valve body DOWN port and DOWN hydraulic line, then reattach the DOWN hydraulic line to the valve body DOWN port (starboard fitting) with a new O-ring. Tighten the fitting to specification (**Table 5**).
12. Remove the blocks or trailer locks and cycle the drive unit several times to bleed the air from the lines. Recheck the fluid level only when the drive unit is in the full UP position. Add fluid as necessary.

Test No. 4
(trim IN/tilt DOWN, pump only)

To isolate the cylinders from the pump and determine if the pump assembly trim DOWN (IN) circuits are malfunctioning, proceed as follows.

1. Trim the drive unit to the full DOWN position, then briefly operate the trim pump in the UP (OUT) direction to minimize internal pressure.
2. Close the tester valve (1, **Figure 34**) fully.
3. Operate the trim pump in the DOWN (IN) direction. Observe the stall pressure as the pump operates, then turn off the pump and observe the leak-down rate for a minimum of 5 minutes.
4. Compare your results to the specifications listed in **Table 2**. If the results are within specifications, the cylinders are internally leaking and are the cause of the failure of Test No. 3. Remove both cylinders and reseal them. If the cylinder bores or pistons are scored, replace the cylinder(s).
5. If the results are not within specification, the trim pump DOWN circuits are defective. Disassemble the pump and locate the defective valve or component. If the leak-down rate is excessive, pay particular attention to the manual release valve and manual release check ball (early models) and trim IN/tilt DOWN check valve. If the

stall pressure is too low, pay particular attention to the trim IN check ball, the trim IN/tilt DOWN relief valve and spring and the gear housing to valve body mating surface.

6. Once this test has been passed, system testing is complete.

7. Open the tester valve (1, **Figure 34**) at least one complete turn and relieve system pressure as described under *Safety precautions* in this chapter.

8. Remove the pressure tester from the valve body DOWN port and DOWN hydraulic line, then reattach the DOWN hydraulic line to the valve body DOWN port (starboard fitting) with a new O-ring. Tighten the fitting to specification (**Table 5**).

9. Remove the blocks or trailer locks and cycle the drive unit several times to bleed the air from the lines. Recheck the fluid level only when the drive unit is in the full UP position. Add fluid as necessary.

Trim Pump Service

The trim/tilt pump is installed by the boat manufacturer. For this reason, its location varies according to the design of the boat manufacturer.

Keeping all components, lines and assemblies clean cannot be over-emphasized. Cleanliness is critical when you are working on any hydraulic system. Plug or cap all lines or ports immediately after opening them to the atmosphere.

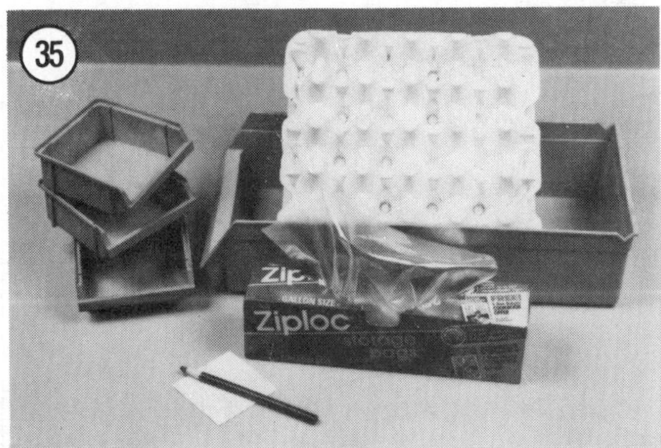

To prevent any possible confusion, use a cupcake tin, plastic zipper bags or several small containers (**Figure 35**) to store and properly label the numerous screws, springs, valves and other small components.

Refer to **Figure 36** for an exploded view of the 1994-early 1996 model trim pump and **Figure 37** for the late 1996-on models trim pump.

Safety Precautions

The trim system internal hydraulic pressure must be relieved before any lines are disconnected from the trim pump, manifold or trim cylinders. Anytime a line is disconnected, plug both ends of the connection to prevent excessive leakage and contamination of the fluid.

WARNING
Eye protection must be worn during this procedure and any procedure involving disconnecting of any trim line from the trim pump, trim manifold and trim cylinders.

CAUTION
Install new line O-rings each time a line is removed from the pump, manifold, cylinders or tester.

1. To relieve the internal pressure on early model systems equipped with a manual release valve, proceed as follows:
   a. Trim the drive unit to the full UP position.
   b. Securely block or lock the drive unit in the full UP position. OMC Trailer Lock kit part No. 174448 can be used (and is recommended) if a small amount of material is removed from one end of each trailer lock.
   c. Open the manual release valve (32, **Figure 36**) until it contacts the snap ring retainer. Allow the drive unit to settle onto the trailer locks or blocks.

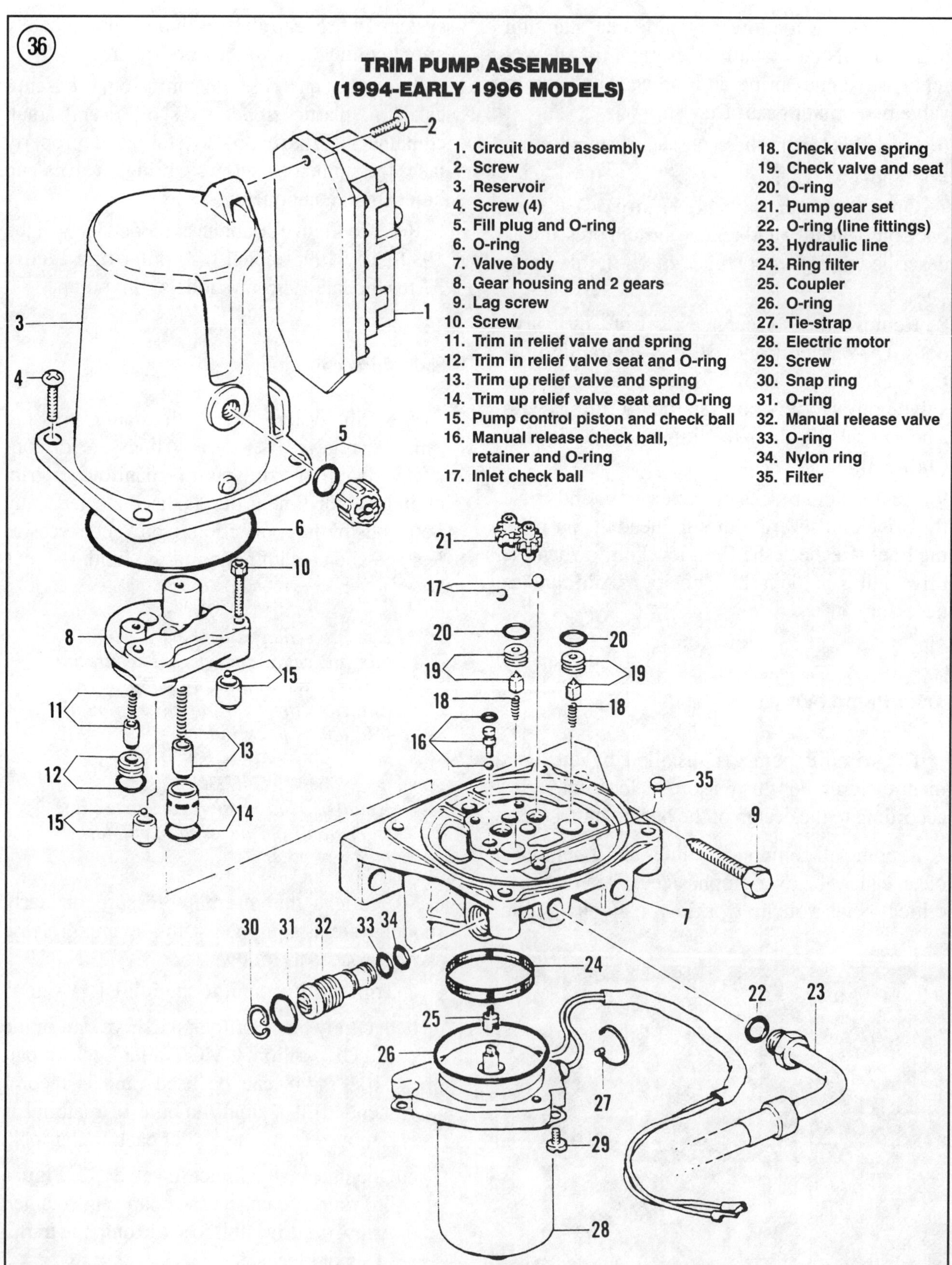
36
TRIM PUMP ASSEMBLY
(1994-EARLY 1996 MODELS)
1. Circuit board assembly
2. Screw
3. Reservoir
4. Screw (4)
5. Fill plug and O-ring
6. O-ring
7. Valve body
8. Gear housing and 2 gears
9. Lag screw
10. Screw
11. Trim in relief valve and spring
12. Trim in relief valve seat and O-ring
13. Trim up relief valve and spring
14. Trim up relief valve seat and O-ring
15. Pump control piston and check ball
16. Manual release check ball, retainer and O-ring
17. Inlet check ball
18. Check valve spring
19. Check valve and seat
20. O-ring
21. Pump gear set
22. O-ring (line fittings)
23. Hydraulic line
24. Ring filter
25. Coupler
26. O-ring
27. Tie-strap
28. Electric motor
29. Screw
30. Snap ring
31. O-ring
32. Manual release valve
33. O-ring
34. Nylon ring
35. Filter

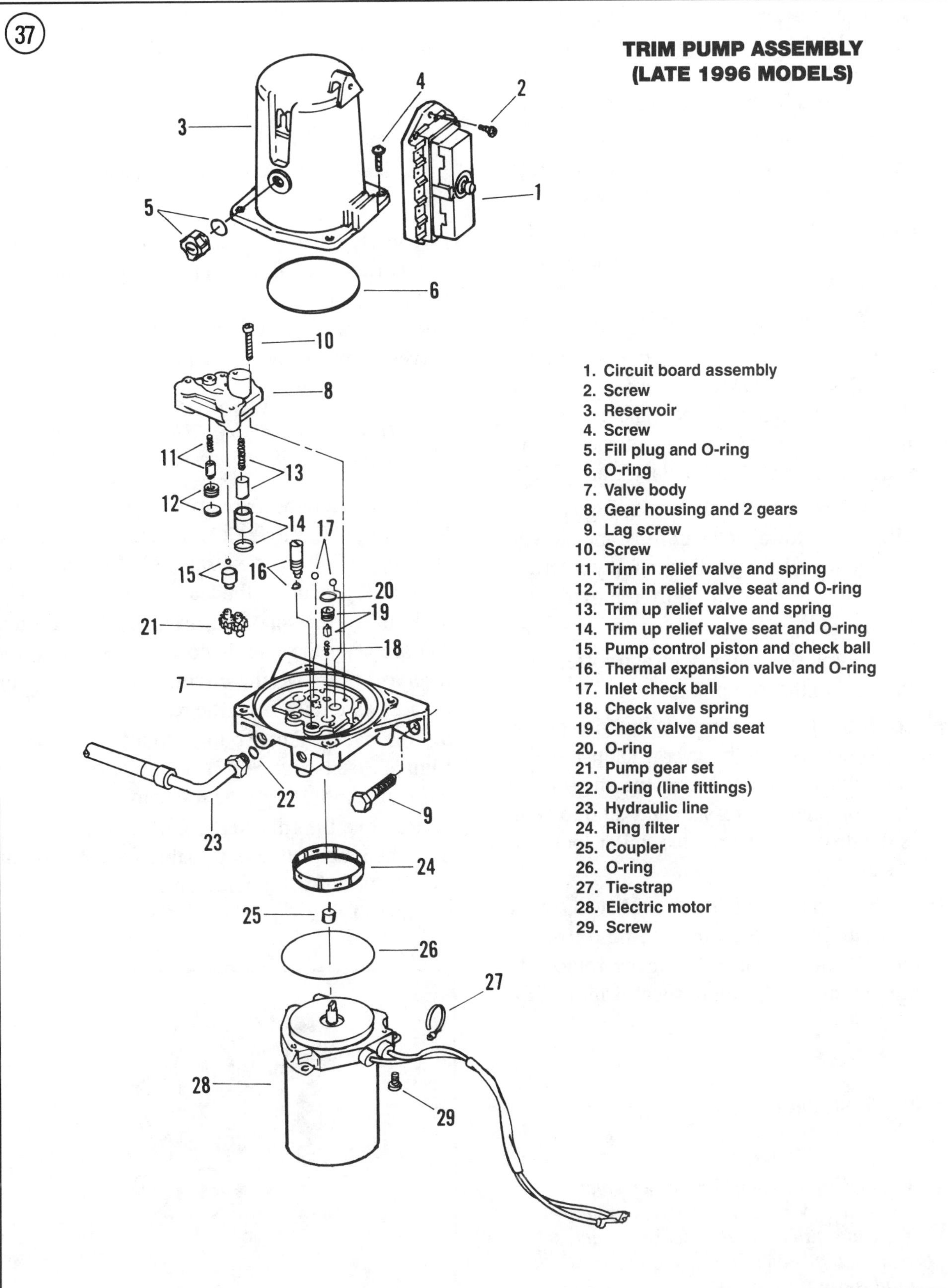

TRIM PUMP ASSEMBLY (LATE 1996 MODELS)

1. Circuit board assembly
2. Screw
3. Reservoir
4. Screw
5. Fill plug and O-ring
6. O-ring
7. Valve body
8. Gear housing and 2 gears
9. Lag screw
10. Screw
11. Trim in relief valve and spring
12. Trim in relief valve seat and O-ring
13. Trim up relief valve and spring
14. Trim up relief valve seat and O-ring
15. Pump control piston and check ball
16. Thermal expansion valve and O-ring
17. Inlet check ball
18. Check valve spring
19. Check valve and seat
20. O-ring
21. Pump gear set
22. O-ring (line fittings)
23. Hydraulic line
24. Ring filter
25. Coupler
26. O-ring
27. Tie-strap
28. Electric motor
29. Screw

d. Cover the reservoir fill plug (5, **Figure 36**) with a shop towel and carefully and slowly remove the fill plug, allowing any internal pressure to vent before fully removing the plug.

e. Reinstall the fill plug and close the manual release valve to minimize fluid loss.

2. To relieve the internal pressure on late model systems not equipped with a manual release valve, proceed as follows:

a. Trim the drive unit to the full UP position.

b. Securely block or lock the drive unit in the full UP position. OMC Trailer Lock kit part No. 174448 can be used (and is recommended) if a small amount of material is removed from one end of each trailer lock.

c. Cover the reservoir fill plug (5, **Figure 37**) with a shop towel and carefully and slowly remove the fill plug, allowing any internal pressure to vent before fully removing the plug.

d. Place a small container, such as a coffee can, underneath the trim pump.

e. Cover the UP line fitting at the trim pump (2, **Figure 33**) with several shop towels. Carefully and slowly loosen the line fitting, allowing internal pressure and fluid to vent as the drive settles onto the trailer locks or blocks.

f. After the pressure has been relieved, reinstall the fill plug to minimize fluid loss. If the UP line is not going to be removed, tighten the line fitting to specification (**Table 5**).

Removal/Installation

CAUTION

Wear eye protection for this complete procedure. Wrap shop towels around each line fitting as it is loosened and removed to eliminate any dangerous fluid spray.

1. Relieve system pressure as described under *Safety precautions* in this chapter.

NOTE

If the lines are reversed on reassembly, the drive unit will not trim OUT under load, and in some circumstances, may trim IN under load.

2. Clearly label the hydraulic lines for reassembly purposes. Disconnect the hydraulic lines from the pump. Discard the line O-rings. Cap the lines and valve body ports as soon as possible to prevent leakage and contamination.

WARNING

Disconnect the negative battery cable to prevent possible injury in Step 3.

3. Disconnect the trim motor green and blue leads (D and E, **Figure 27**) from the circuit board assembly. Cut the tie-strap (27, **Figure 36** or **Figure 37**) securing the leads to the valve body.
4. Remove the screw (2, **Figure 36** or **Figure 37**) securing the circuit board assembly to the reservoir. Remove the circuit board and wiring harness assembly from the reservoir.
5. Remove the 2 trim pump mounting screws (9, **Figure 36** or **Figure 37**). Remove the trim/tilt pump assembly from the transom.
6. Remove the fill plug from the reservoir and drain as much fluid as possible from the pump assembly into a suitable container. Discard the fill plug O-ring.

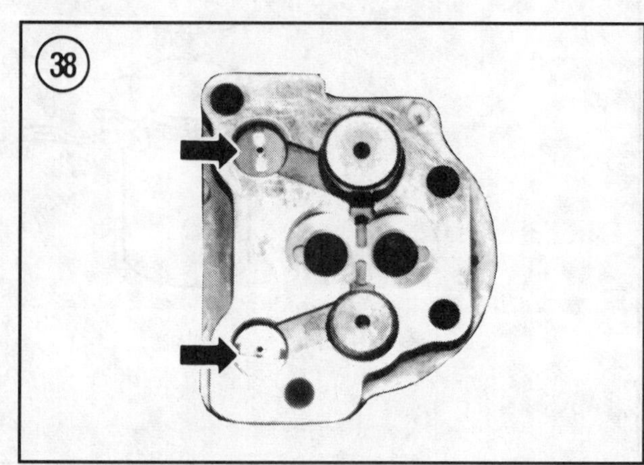

7. To install the trim pump assembly, position the pump to the transom and install the 2 lag screws. Tighten the screws securely.
8. Position the circuit board and wiring harness to the reservoir and install the retaining screw. Tighten the screw securely.
9. Connect the blue and green trim motor leads to the circuit board assembly and tighten the screws securely. Refer to **Figure 27** for a wiring diagram.
10. Secure the trim motor leads to the valve body with a new tie-strap.
11. Using new O-rings, reconnect the hydraulic lines to the trim pump. Tighten the fittings to specification (**Table 5**).
12. Fill the reservoir with Volvo DuraPlus Power Trim/Steering Fluid (**Table 6**). Install the fill plug using a new O-ring.
13. Remove the blocks or trailer locks and cycle the drive unit several times to bleed the air from the lines. Recheck the fluid level only when the drive unit is in the full UP position. Add fluid as necessary.

Disassembly

Refer to **Figure 36** (1994-early 1996 models) or **Figure 37** (late 1996 models) for this procedure.

1. Wipe the outside of the pump unit with a cloth moistened in a mild solvent, such as mineral spirits. Wipe the solvent off with a clean lint-free shop towel or lint-free paper towel.
2. Remove the 3 Phillips-head screws holding the pump motor to the valve body. Separate the motor from the valve body. Remove and discard the O-ring seal from the valve body. Locate and secure the pump coupler (25, **Figure 36** or **Figure 37**).
3. Remove the ring filter (24, **Figure 36** or **Figure 37**).
4. Remove the 4 Phillips screws holding the pump reservoir to the valve body. Separate the reservoir from the valve body. Remove and discard the O-ring.

NOTE

Use extreme care when working with the gear housing or manifold. Any damage inflicted to either component will require replacement of the valve body and gear housing as an assembly.

5. Remove the 4 socket head screws (10, **Figure 36** or **Figure 37**) holding the gear housing to the valve body. To prevent valve body or gear housing damage, remove the screws in 1 turn increments.
6. Remove the gear housing from the manifold. Be prepared to catch the 2 pump control pistons and check balls (15, **Figure 36** or **Figure 37**) if they fall from the gear housing.
7. If they do not fall out, remove the 2 pump control pistons (**Figure 38**) and check balls (**Figure 39**) from the gear housing. Be careful not to scratch the piston bores or lose the check balls.

CAUTION

*Do not attempt to pull the relief valves from the gear housing. They must be pushed out with a small drift. If the gear housing has not been previously disassembled, it will be necessary to drill a 3 mm (1/8 in.) hole in the exact center of each tower (**Figure 40**). This will allow a small pin punch to be inserted through the hole and press the relief valves, springs and seats (**Figure 41**) from the gear housing.*

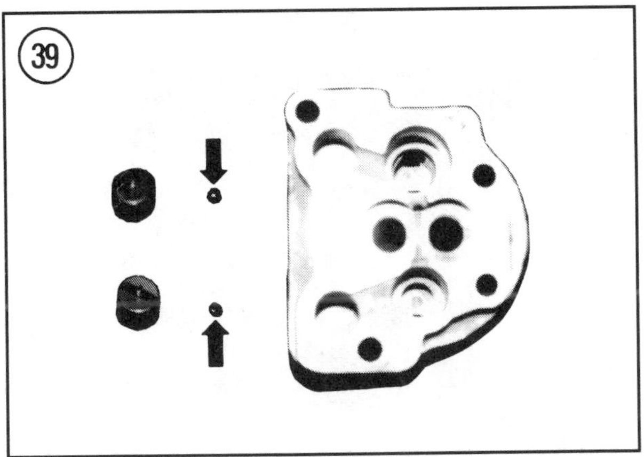

8. If necessary drill a 3 mm (1/8 in.) hole through the center of each relief valve tower in the top of the gear housing. Insert a small punch through the hole and press both valve assemblies from the gear housing. Discard both valve seat O-rings.
9. Mark the gears for assembly purposes, then remove the 2 pump gears and 2 inlet check balls (**Figure 42**) from the valve body. On early models, also remove the filter (35, **Figure 36**) from the valve body.

CAUTION
Hydraulic pressure must be used to remove the trim OUT/tilt-UP check valve and the trim IN/tilt-DOWN check valve. Do not try to pry the valve seats from the valve body as the valve body will be damaged.

10. Fill both valve body hydraulic line ports with OMC Needle Bearing Assembly grease (**Table 6**).

NOTE
*On early models, it is necessary to cover the manual release check ball port (on the electric motor side), when removing the trim IN/tilt DOWN check valve. See **Figure 43**.*

11. Thread a 7/16 in. fine thread bolt into each valve body hydraulic line port. Withdraw the bolt and add more grease as needed until each check valve seat is pushed free of the valve body. Withdraw the valve and spring (**Figure 36** or **Figure 37**). Remove and discard the O-ring from each seat.
12. *Early models*—Insert a suitable tool through the opening (**Figure 43**) on the electric motor side of the manual release check ball, then push the check ball and retainer (**Figure 44**) from the manifold. Remove and discard the O-ring from the retainer.

NOTE
On early models, the thermal expansion valve is an integral part of the manual release valve tip. If either the thermal expansion valve or the manual release valve are damaged or malfunctioning, they are replaced as an assembly.

13. *Early models*—Use snap ring pliers to remove the snap ring from the manual release valve bore. Remove the manual release valve. Remove

40

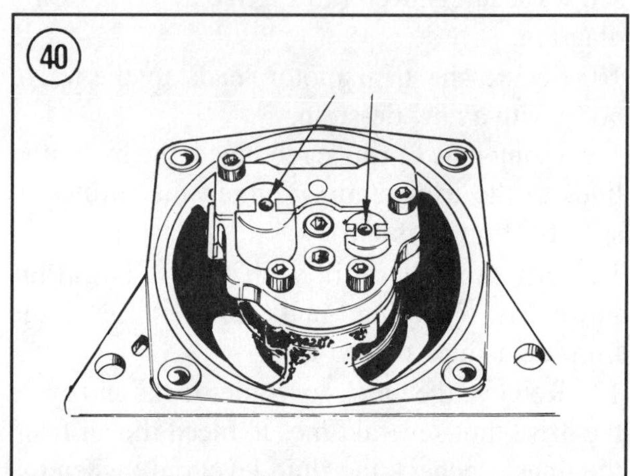

41

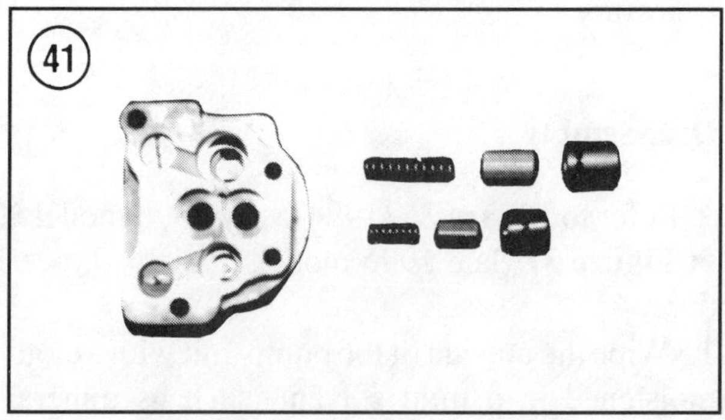

42

and discard the valve's 2 O-rings (A, **Figure 45**) and nylon seal ring (B, **Figure 45**).

14. *Late models*—Remove the thermal expansion valve assembly (16, **Figure 37**) from the valve body. Discard the O-ring.

43

44

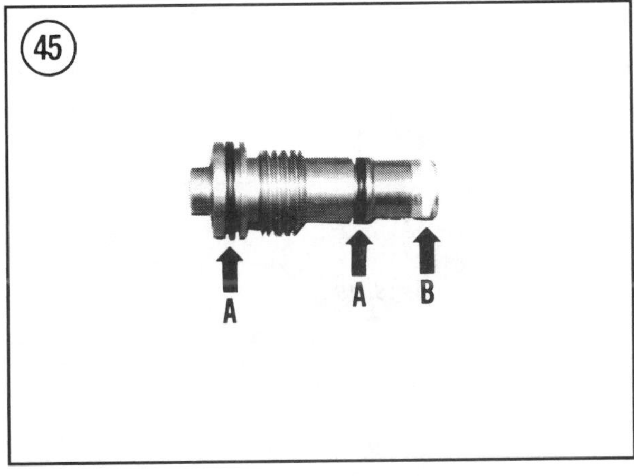

45

Cleaning and Inspection

1. Clean the gear housing and valve body with a mild solvent and blow dry with low-pressure compressed air.
2. Inspect the gear housing to valve body mating surfaces. If either one is excessively scored, the pump will not be able to develop its specified stall pressure. Replace the valve body as an assembly if it is damaged.
3. Inspect the gear housing control piston and relief valve bores for scoring or wear. Replace the gear housing and valve body as an assembly if the bores are damaged.
4. Inspect the valve body inlet check ball seats and check valve bores. On early models, inspect the manual release valve and manual release check ball seats and bores.
5. Check all removed components (springs, valve seats, valve tips and check balls) for damage or wear. Replace all suspect components.
6. Inspect the electric motor pump coupler for wear, damage or distortion. Replace the coupler, if necessary.
7. Clean and inspect the ring filter and on early models, the second filter (35, **Figure 36**). Replace any filter that is damaged or cannot be satisfactorily cleaned.

Assembly

Lubricate all components with Volvo DuraPlus Power Trim/Steering Fluid (**Table 6**) during assembly. Do not make any DRY assemblies. Refer to **Figure 36** (early models) or **Figure 37** (late models) for this procedure.

1. *Early models*—Install 2 new O-rings and a new nylon seal ring onto the manual release valve (**Figure 45**). Lubricate the valve, then screw the valve assembly into the valve body bore. Tighten the valve to 45-55 in.-lb. (5.1-6.2 N•m).

2. *Early models*—Use snap ring pliers to install the snap ring in the groove in the valve body bore. Be sure the snap ring is fully seated.
3. *Early models*—Install the manual release check ball and retainer with a new O-ring (**Figure 44**). Lubricate the check ball and O-ring liberally, then press the retainer into the valve body until it is flush with the body surface. Do not press it below the body surface.
4. *Early models*—Install the filter (35, **Figure 36**) into its bore.
5. *Late models*—Using a new O-ring, install the thermal expansion valve (16, **Figure 37**) into its valve body bore. Tighten the thermal expansion valve to 5.1-6.4 N•m (45-57 in.-lb.).
6. Install new O-rings, then install each check valve spring, valve and seat into the valve body check valve bores (**Figure 46** and **Figure 47**). Seat the check valve seats flush with the valve body surface.
7. Pressure test the up and down circuits (and check valves) of the valve body as follows:
   a. Secure each check valve to the valve body with a 10-32 × 1/2 in. machine screw and a 5/32 in. flat washer. Install each screw and washer into the threaded hole next to each trim-out/tilt-UP check valve seat. Tighten the screws snugly. Make sure the washer does not contact the valve tip in the center of each seat.
   b. Screw pressure adapter part No. 3854366-6 (**Figure 48**) into the UP hydraulic line port (port side) and tighten it securely.
   c. Attach a suitable gearcase pressure tester (**Table 8**) to the pressure adapter. Pump the gearcase pressure tester until a reading of 207 kPa (30 psi) is observed on the gauge.
   d. The valve body must hold pressure without leakage. If leakage is noted on the pressure tester, squirt trim fluid around all areas of the UP circuit until the source of leakage is found. Perform repairs as necessary until there is no leakage.
   e. Repeat the test procedure for the DOWN hydraulic line port (starboard fitting). Note that the manual release check ball hole (**Figure 43**) CANNOT leak during this test. If leakage is detected at this hole, remove the manual release check ball and retainer and thoroughly clean the check ball and check ball seat. Using a suitable punch, lightly seat the check ball into the seat and

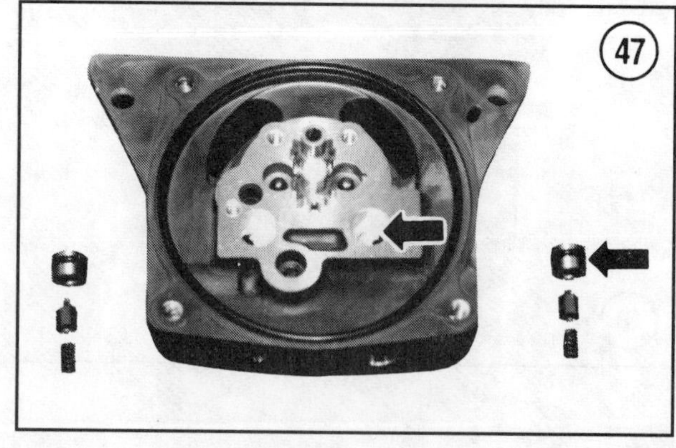

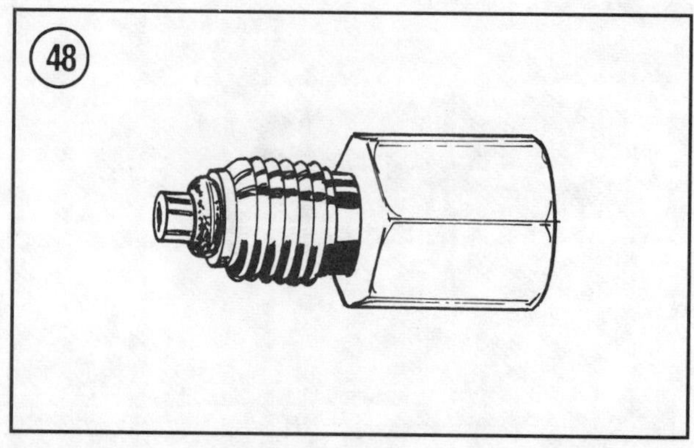

recheck leakage. If necessary replace the check ball and increase the force used to seat the ball until leakage is eliminated or reduced to extremely minimal amounts. The check ball must be lubricated in order to seal. Do not attempt to pressure test the circuit if the check ball is dry.

NOTE
The pump gears can only be installed in one direction. To determine the correct orientation, insert the pump coupler into each end of each gear. The pump coupler will fit fully into only one side of each gear. Install the gears with the deep recess facing the electric motor and the shallow recess facing the reservoir.

8. Lubricate the 2 inlet check balls and the 2 pump gears (**Figure 42**). Install the check balls and gears into the valve body. Oriente the gears in their original position, making sure that the shallow recess of the gears is facing up (towards the reservoir).

9. Install a new O-ring on the trim-UP relief valve seat (**Figure 49**) and lubricate the valve, O-ring and bore. Install the trim-UP relief valve in the gear housing.

10. Install a new O-ring on the trim-DOWN relief valve seat (**Figure 50**) and lubricate the valve, O-ring and bore. Install the trim-DOWN relief valve in the gear housing.

11. Lubricate and install the 2 check balls (**Figure 39**) and pump control pistons (**Figure 38**) into the gear housing.

12. Position the gear housing onto the manifold and over the gears, being careful not to let the pistons and check balls fall from the gear housing. Make sure the filter (35, **Figure 36**) is in place on early models.

13. Install the 4 socket head retaining screws (10, **Figure 36** or **Figure 37**) and tighten evenly in 1 turn increments to pull the gear housing evenly to the valve body and compress the relief valves. Once seated, tighten the screws evenly to a final torque of 4.0 N•m (35 in.-lb.).

14. Insert a small screwdriver into one of the pump gear recesses. Rotate the pump gears and check for ANY binding, rough or tight spots. The pump must turn freely, without binding. If binding is noted, loosen the 4 screws 1/2 turn and reposition the gear housing to the valve body. Retighten the screws per Step 13 and recheck binding. Do not proceed until the pump gears turn freely, without binding.

15. Install the pump coupler (25, **Figure 36** or **Figure 37**), then install the ring filter with the foam gasket side facing away from the valve body and towards the electric motor.

NOTE
The pump must be primed before installing the electric motor. When the pump is primed, a noticeable increase in the effort required to turn the gears will be noted.

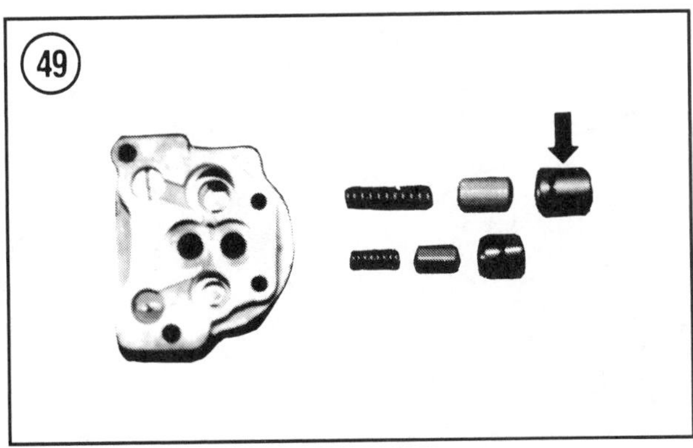

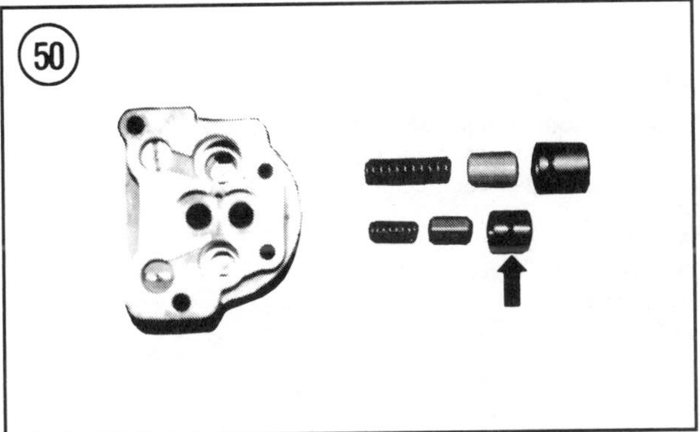

16. Prime the pump as follows to purge air and ensure proper operation.
   a. Fill the cavity within the ring filter to the top of the ring filter with Volvo DuraPlus Power Trim/Steering Fluid.
   b. Use a small screwdriver to rotate the pump coupler in both directions until all air bubbles stop coming from the inlet check ball openings.

17. Using a new O-ring, install the electric motor as follows:
   a. Position the pump against the valve body and align the pump coupler to the electric motor shaft.
   b. Seat the motor against the valve body and rotate the pump to align the screw holes. The holes will only align in one position. Do not install the screws if the motor is not seated against the valve body.
   c. When the screw holes are aligned and the motor can be seated to the valve body with hand pressure, install the 3 motor mounting screws. Tighten the screws evenly to 4.0-5.9 N•m (35-52 in.-lb.).

18. Install the reservoir using a new O-ring. Install and evenly tighten the 4 screws to 4.0-5.9 N•m (35-52 in.-lb.). Install the fill plug with a new O-ring. Tighten the fill plug hand-tight.

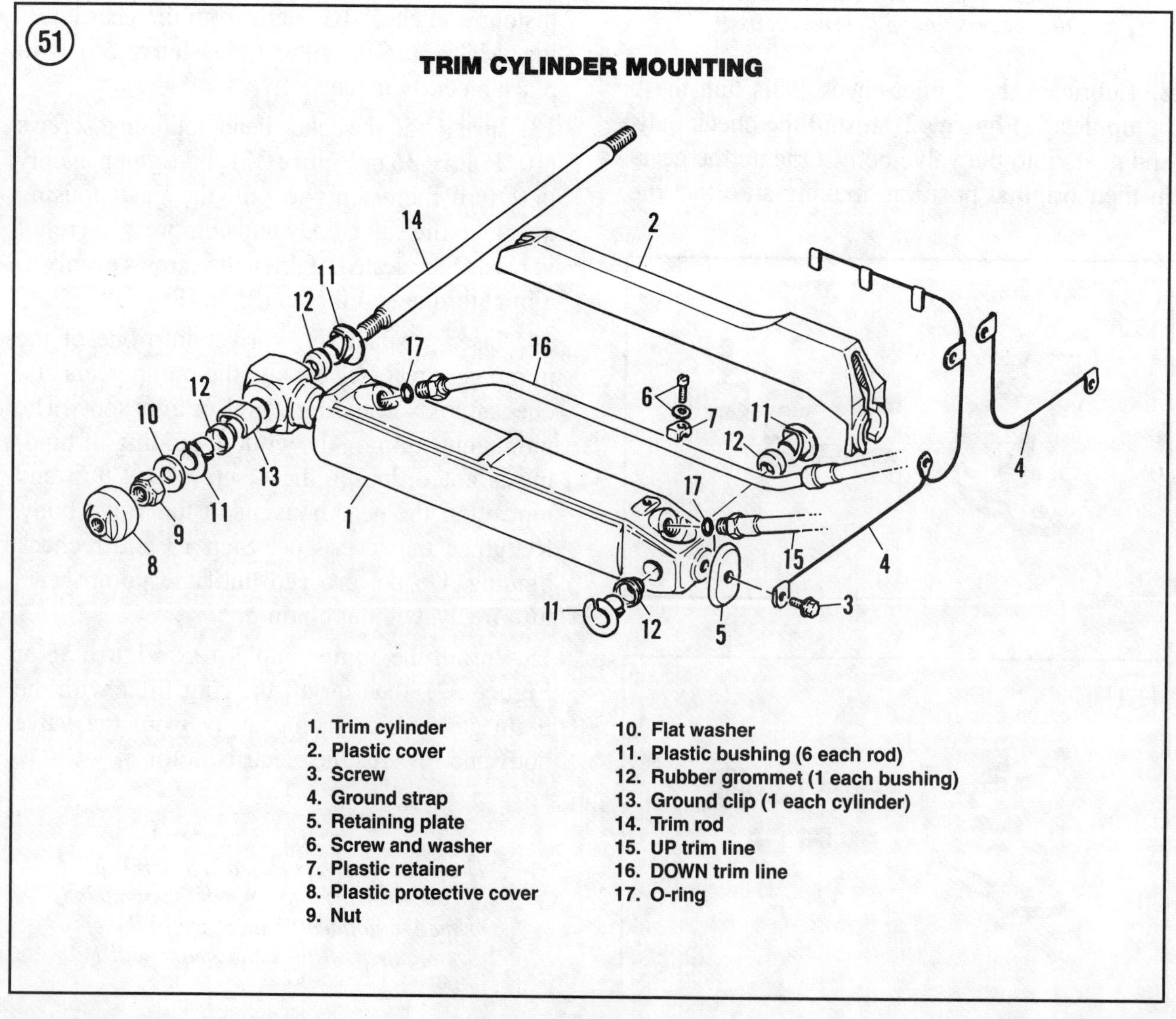

19. Install the pump as described previously in this chapter.

Trim Cylinder Removal/Installation

If a hydraulic cylinder is determined to be leaking internally it may be resealed. However, none of the metal components are available separately. If the cylinder, piston, rod, end cap or eyelet are damaged, replace the cylinder as an assembly. If 1 cylinder is leaking, the other cylinder will be soon to follow. It is recommended to reseal or replace both cylinders at the same time, if either requires service.

Refer to **Figure 51** for this procedure.

1. Remove the drive unit as described in Chapter Twelve.

CAUTION
Wear eye protection for this complete procedure. Wrap shop towels around each line fitting as it is loosened and removed to eliminate any dangerous fluid spray.

2. Relieve trim system pressure as described under *Safety precautions* in this chapter. Install the recommended trailer locks over the trim rams to prevent accidental discharge of oil caused by erroneous trim ram movement.
3. Remove the screw (3, **Figure 51**), grounding strap (4, **Figure 51**) and retainer plate (5, **Figure 51**) from the front of the cylinder, then remove the trim cylinder plastic top cover.
4. Position a suitable drain pan under the trim cylinder being removed.
5. Remove the screw and washer (6, **Figure 51**) and line retainer (7, **Figure 51**) securing the DOWN trim line to the trim cylinder.
6. Cover each trim cylinder line fitting with a shop towel, then loosen each fitting with a flare nut wrench to avoid rounding the fitting. Remove both lines from each cylinder and cap the lines as soon as possible to prevent leakage and contamination. Discard the line fitting O-rings. If the cylinders are not to be disassembled and resealed, and are going to be reused, plug the cylinder fittings as soon as possible to prevent contamination.
7. Remove both plastic protective covers (8, **Figure 51**) from the gimbal ring trim cylinder rod. Remove an elastic locknut and flat washer from one end of the trim rod (**Figure 51**). Pull the trim rod out of the cylinder, gimbal ring and opposing trim cylinder. Be prepared to support each cylinder as it comes free from the trim rod. If necessary, use an aluminum or brass drift to drive the trim rod from the trim cylinders and gimbal ring, supporting each cylinder as it comes free. Set each trim cylinder removed onto a clean workbench.
8. Inspect the plastic trim bushings (11, **Figure 51**) and tapered rubber grommets (12, **Figure 51**) for damage. Replace any damaged bushing and grommets. A total of 6 bushings are used on the trim rod, 1 on each side of the gimbal ring and 2 in each trim cylinder.
9. To install the trim cylinders, begin by greasing the gimbal ring trim rod with Volvo Penta Propeller Shaft Grease or equivalent (**Table 6**). Slide the rod into the gimbal ring until it is centered. Install a bushing assembly over each end of the trim rod and into the gimbal ring bore. The bushing assemblies should be nearly flush with the gimbal ring when correctly installed.
10. Slide another bushing assembly over each end of the gimbal ring trim rod with the rubber grommet facing out.
11. Position each trim cylinder over the trim rod and inner bushing, then install each outer bushing assembly over the trim rod and into each trim cylinder.
12. Install a flat washer and elastic locknut to the trim/tilt rod. Tighten both elastic locknuts until they are seated, then tighten the nuts to 14-16 N•m (124-142 in.-lb.). Install the plastic protective covers over the elastic locknuts and tighten them securely.

13. Install the trim lines using new O-rings. Tighten each line fitting to 84-108 in.-lb. (9.5-12.2 N•m).
14. Install each cylinder's DOWN line retainer (7, **Figure 51**) and secure it with a screw and washer. Tighten each cylinder's screw securely.
15. Hook the plastic cover over the rear of each cylinder and rotate it down over the front of each cylinder. Secure each cover with a retaining plate, ground strap and screw. Tighten each cylinder's screw securely.
16. Fill the reservoir with Volvo DuraPlus Power Trim/Steering Fluid (**Table 6**). Install the fill plug using a new O-ring.
17 Remove the blocks or trailer locks and cycle the trim system several times to bleed the air from the lines. Recheck the fluid level only when the trim cylinder rams are fully extended. Add fluid as necessary.
18. Install the drive unit as described in Chapter Twelve.

Disassembly

CAUTION
Wear eye protection for this complete procedure.

1. Hold the trim cylinder over a suitable container with both trim line ports facing down and into the suitable container.
2. Expel all remaining fluid in the cylinder by manually cycling the trim ram through its full range of travel. Cycle the ram several times to ensure all fluid is removed.
3. If present, remove both trim rod bushing assemblies from the trim cylinder. Clamp the trim cylinder into a soft-jawed vise. To prevent damage and possible crushing of the cylinder, clamp only across the gimbal ring trim rod mounting bore.
4. Unscrew the cylinder end cap with a spanner wrench such as OMC part No. 326485 or Volvo part No. 3854365-8 and a breaker bar. The end cap is best removed by tapping the breaker bar with a mallet. Unscrew the end cap until there is approximately one thread left.
5. Pull the trim ram out of the cylinder until it contacts the end cap, then unthread the end completely and remove the trim ram and end cap assembly from the cylinder bore.

NOTE
If the trim rod eyelet is difficult to remove in the next step, insert a piece of paper between the holding blocks and trim rod. Also apply mild heat to the eyelet to

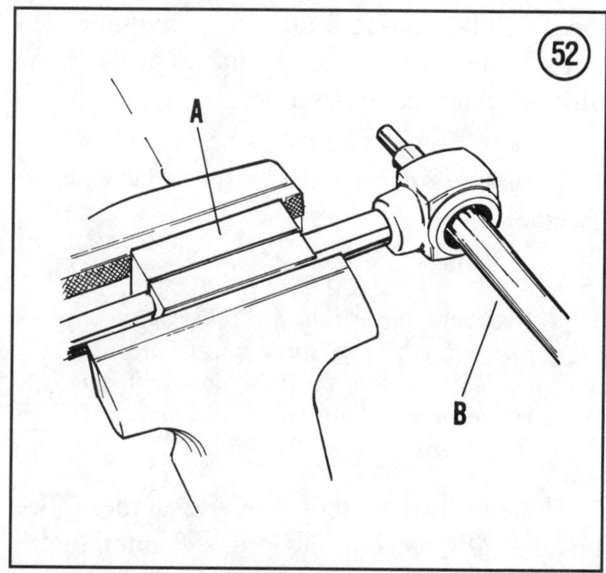

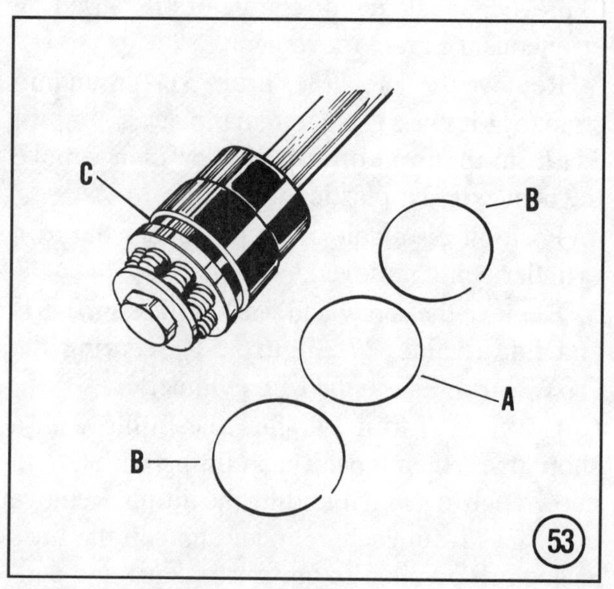

loosen the threadlocking adhesive. A heat lamp, heat gun or propane torch may be used.

6. Thoroughly clean all oil and grease from the trim cylinder rod surface. Clamp the trim rod in a vise using clamp blocks part No. 3854367-4 (A, **Figure 52**). Unscrew the trim rod eyelet using a breaker bar or trim pivot rod inserted through the eyelet (B, **Figure 52**).
7. Slide the end cap off of the trim rod. Remove and discard the O-ring (A, **Figure 53**) and 2 back up rings (B, **Figure 53**) from the piston groove (C, **Figure 53**).
8. Remove and discard the internal and external O-rings from the end cap with a dental probe or suitable instrument. Carefully pry the trim rod scraper ring from the end cap (**Figure 54**). Do not damage the end cap in the process. Discard the scraper ring.

Cleaning and Inspection

1. Wash all components in clean solvent and blow dry.
2. Inspect the cylinder internal walls and threads, and the piston and trim rod external surfaces for scoring, excessive wear or other damage. Replace the trim cylinder as an assembly if any of the components are damaged.
3. Inspect the cylinder end cap for mechanical damage and excessive corrosion on the threaded area, the O-ring grooves and the scraper ring bore. Replace the trim cylinder as an assembly if the end cap is damaged and not reusable.
4. Remove all threadlocking sealant from the piston and eyelet threads.
5. Inspect the trim rod eyelet for mechanical damage and excessive corrosion. Replace the trim cylinder as an assembly if the end cap is damaged and not reusable.
6. Inspect the piston's impact relief valves for broken or damaged springs. With a suitable drift, press against each check ball, each check ball should be held firmly to its seat. Replace the trim cylinder as an assembly if any of the impact relief valves are damaged or leaking.

NOTE
If the impact relief valves are believed to be leaking due to debris caught in the check ball seats, clamp the trim rod in the holding blocks (part No. 3854367-4) and loosen the large bolt head securing the impact relief valve spring retaining washer just enough to allow opening of each valve with a suitable drift. Flush each check ball and seat with clean solvent while the valve is held open. When finished flushing the valves, retighten the large bolt head securely. If the valves still leak, replace the trim cylinder as an assembly.

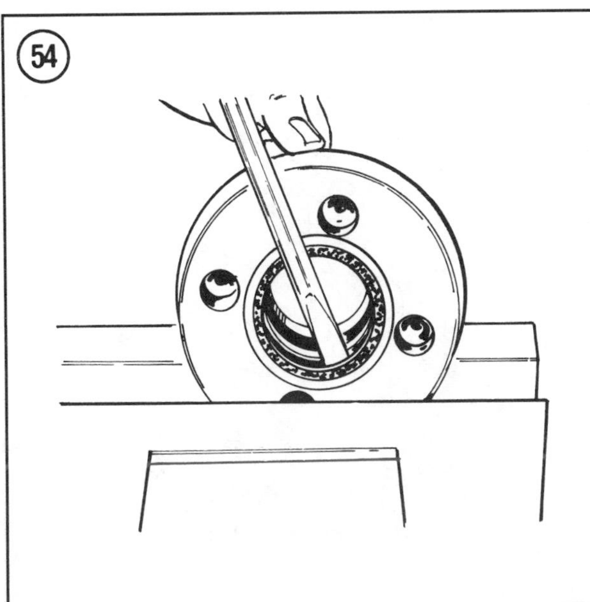

Assembly

Lubricate all components with Volvo DuraPlus Power Trim/Steering Fluid (**Table 6**) during assembly. Do not make any DRY assemblies.

1. Install a new scraper ring into the end cap with seal installer part No. 3854364-1. Position the scraper lip against the tool. Press the scraper into the end cap until the tool seats against the end

cap. The scraper should be flush with the end cap surface.

2. Install new internal and external O-rings into their respective end cap grooves.

3. Place seal protector part No. 3854363-3 over the trim rod and slide the end cap over the tool and into position on the trim rod. Remove the seal protector.

4. Clean the trim rod threads and apply a light coat of Loctite 242 threadlocking adhesive (**Table 6**) to the threads.

5. Clamp the trim rod into a vise using clamp blocks part No. 3854367-4 (A, **Figure 52**). Install the trim rod eyelet and tighten it securely using a breaker bar or trim pivot rod inserted through the eyelet (B, **Figure 52**).

6. Install a new piston O-ring and position a new backup ring on each side of the O-ring.

NOTE

If the backup rings do not fit tightly against the bottom of the piston groove, hold the ring(s) in your hand and overlap the ends of the ring, temporarily reducing the effective diameter of the ring. Reduce diameter until the ring is approximately 75 percent of the piston diameter. Hold the ring in this position for a few minutes and allow it to take a set. Then carefully install the ring into the piston groove being careful not to expand it further than necessary.

7. Clamp the trim cylinder into a soft-jawed vise. To prevent damage and possible crushing of the cylinder, clamp only across the gimbal ring trim rod mounting bore. Position the cylinder bore straight up.

8. Lubricate the cylinder bore and piston liberally. Carefully insert the piston and trim rod assembly into the bore. Be careful not to catch either of the backup rings between the piston and cylinder bore. Once the cylinder tapered wall is reached, apply a steady downward pressure to the eyelet, while wiggling the eyelet in a circular motion. Be patient and allow the O-ring and backup rings to work past the taper and into the cylinder bore.

9. Once past the tapered wall, push the piston as far as possible into the bore while still allowing enough space between the end cap and cylinder to fill the cylinder with fluid.

10. Fill the cylinder with as much fluid as possible to reduce the bleed time and effort. When filled, thread the end cap into the cylinder and tighten to 34-41 N•m (25-30 ft.-lb.) with a spanner wrench such as OMC part No. 326485 or Volvo part No. 3854365-8 and a suitable torque wrench. Attach the spanner wrench at a 90° angle to the torque wrench.

CAUTION

Do not move the trim rod or hydraulic fluid will be expelled from the trim cylinder line ports. Cap the ports or install the cylinder immediately to prevent leakage and possible injury.

11. Install the cylinders as described previously in this chapter.

Trim Manifold Replacement

Depending on the installation (boat), it may be necessary to remove the engine and inner transom plate from the boat to gain adequate access.

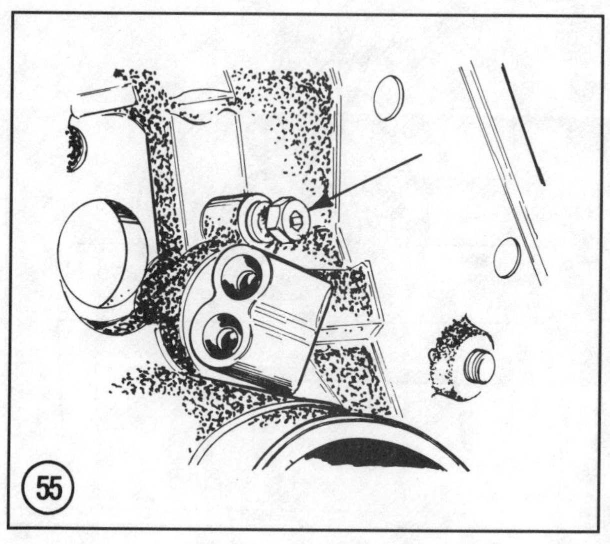

If so, refer to the appropriate engine service chapter and Chapter Fourteen, as necessary.

1. Remove the drive unit as described in Chapter Twelve.

2. Remove the pivot housing as described in Chapter Fourteen.

CAUTION
Wear eye protection for this procedure. Wrap shop towels around each line fitting as it is loosened and removed to eliminate any dangerous fluid spray.

3. Relieve trim system pressure as described under *Safety precautions* in this chapter. Install the recommended trailer locks over the trim rams to prevent accidental discharge of oil caused by erroneous trim ram movement.

NOTE
If the lines are reversed on reassembly, the drive unit will not trim OUT under load, and in some circumstances, may trim IN under load.

4. Clearly label the hydraulic lines and note all line routing and positioning for reassembly purposes. Disconnect the 2 internal hydraulic lines from the bilge side of the trim manifold. A flare crowfoot adapter will make the task easier. Discard the line O-rings. Cap the lines as soon as possible to prevent leakage and contamination. If the fittings cannot be accessed at this time, they can be removed later, during Step 8.

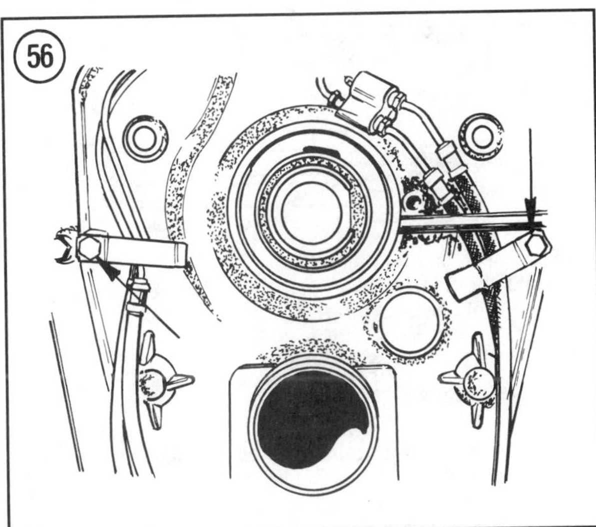

5. Disconnect the 4 external trim cylinder lines from the trim manifold.

6. Remove the elastic locknut and flat washer from the trim manifold mounting stud. Discard the locknut. See **Figure 55**.

7. Using a suitable drift, drive the manifold from the bilge area and out of the transom plate. Remove and discard the manifold O-ring. Remove all sealer and corrosion from the manifold bore.

8. If it was impossible to remove the 2 internal trim lines in Step 4, pull the trim lines through the transom plate along with the manifold in Step 7, then remove the lines from the manifold.

9. If internal line replacement is desired, remove the lines from the trim pump and remove any clamps securing the lines to the transom or other components. Remove the trim lines one at a time and install the new lines in the same manner, making sure each line is correctly identified. Connect each new line to the trim pump using a new O-ring and tighten each line fitting to specification (**Table 5**).

10. If external line replacement is desired, remove the line fittings from each trim cylinder as described under *Trim Cylinder Service, Removal/installation* in this chapter. Discard the O-ring(s). Remove the clamp plate and screw (**Figure 56**) securing each pair of trim lines to the transom plate. Install the new line(s) using new O-rings and the original line routing. Secure each pair of lines with the clamp plate and screw. Tighten the clamp plate screw(s) securely. Connect the new trim line(s) to the cylinder(s), using new O-ring(s). Tighten the line fittings to specification (**Table 5**).

11. To install the manifold, first install a new O-ring in the manifold groove. Coat the O-ring and outer diameter of the manifold with OMC Gasket Sealing Compound or equivalent (**Table 6**). If necessary, reattach the internal trim lines

using new O-rings, being careful to reposition the lines in exact same position as removed.

12. Install the manifold over the mounting stud and seat it into the transom bracket bore. If the internal trim lines are attached, be sure to see that the lines are routed correctly on the bilge side of the transom plate. Install the flat washer and a new elastic locknut. Tighten the locknut to specification (**Table 5**). See **Figure 55**.

13. Connect 4 external trim lines to the manifold using new O-rings. Tighten each line fitting to specification (**Table 5**).

14. If not performed previously, install the internal trim lines to the manifold using new O-rings. Tighten each line fitting to specification (**Table 5**).

15. Install the pivot housing as described in Chapter Fourteen.

16. Install the drive unit as described in Chapter Twelve.

17. Fill the reservoir with Volvo DuraPlus Power Trim/Steering Fluid (**Table 6**). Install the fill plug using a new O-ring.

18. Remove the blocks or trailer locks and cycle the drive unit several times to bleed the air from the lines. Recheck the fluid level only when the drive unit is in the full UP position. Add fluid as necessary.

Trim Sending Unit Removal/Installation

Do not remove the trim sending unit unless it is to be replaced. The removal process usually breaks the sender leads while pulling them out of the transom bracket. It may be easier to perform this procedure if the pivot housing is removed first. If so desired, remove the pivot housing as described in Chapter Fourteen.

1. Disconnect the sending unit wiring harness from the engine harness 2-pin connector (SX models) or the trim limit control box 3-pin connector (DP-S models).

2. Note the position of the leads in the connector body. Then remove the connector body by pushing the pins out of the connector body with

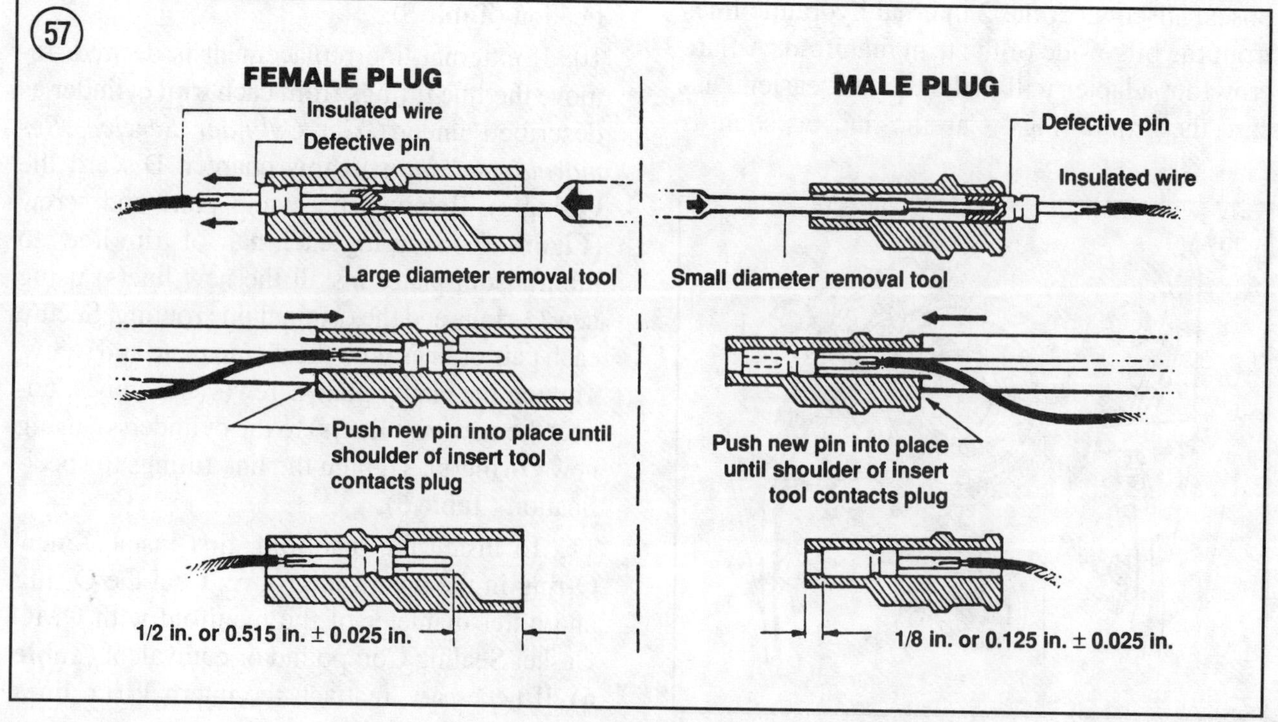

remover part No. 3854350-0. Lubricate the connector body with Isopropyl (rubbing) alcohol to ease pin removal. See **Figure 57**.

3. Remove the spring locking clip securing the trim sender lead to the transom plate. The clip is removed from the bilge side and is located just below the steering arm and just above the inlet water tube.

4. Remove the 2 screws and washers securing the trim sending unit to the gimbal ring.

5. Steer the drive unit to a full port turn. Reach behind the gimbal ring and cut the tie strap securing the trim sender leads to the trim system starboard cylinder hydraulic lines.

6. Pull the trim sender leads out of the transom bracket.

7. To install the trim sending unit, coat the molded sealing plug on the sender leads with OMC Gasket Sealing Compound or equivalent (**Table 6**).

8. Feed the trim lines through the transom bracket bore.

9. With the aid of an assistant, seat the sealing plug into the transom bracket bore by pulling gently from the bilge, while pushing firmly from the outside.

10. Install the spring locking clip over the sealing plug groove.

11. Install the connector body onto the leads with installer part No. 3854349-2. Lubricate the body with isopropyl (rubbing) alcohol to ease installation. Make sure the pins are seated into the connector body as shown in **Figure 57**. If the trim sending unit has 2 wires, pin location is not important. However, if the trim sending unit has 3 wires, install the ribbed black lead in position A, the white lead in position B and the smooth black lead in position C.

12. Install a tie-strap loosely over the trim lines and trim sender leads at the gimbal bearing grease extension tube.

NOTE

If the pivot housing was removed for easier access, install the pivot housing at this time. Refer to Chapter Fourteen for installation procedures.

13A. *1994 models*—Install the trim sending unit onto the gimbal ring bosses and secure the sender with 2 screws and washers. Tighten the screws hand-tight. Proceed to *Adjustment (1994 models)*, in this chapter.

13B. *1995-1996 models*—Refer to *Adjustment (1995-1996 models)* in this chapter, before installing the sender unit to the gimbal ring.

Troubleshooting

If the trim gauge is reading erratically or does not read at all, it may be the result of a faulty trim sending unit. The 1994 model trim sender uses a moveable arm. The 1995 trim sender uses a rotary shaft and 2 leads. The 1996 trim sender uses a rotary shaft and 3 leads. The trim sending unit can be tested as follows.

1. Remove the 2 screws and washers securing the trim sending unit to the gimbal ring. Remove the trim sending unit from the gimbal ring and let it hang by its leads.

2. Disconnect the trim sending unit connector from the engine harness or trim limit control box.

3. *1994 models*—Connect an ohmmeter, calibrated to read 190-210 ohms to the trim sending unit leads. Rotate the sending unit arm through its full travel while observing the meter. The meter should read 190-210 ohms relaxed and approximately 0 ohms when fully rotated against the spring. The readings should increase and decrease smoothly in direct proportion to the arm movement. Replace the sending unit if it does not test as specified.

3. *1995 models*—Connect an ohmmeter, calibrated to read 190-210 ohms to the trim sending unit leads. Rotate the trim sending unit shaft while observing the meter. The meter should cycle smoothly from a low reading of approximately 0 ohms up to a maximum of 190-210 ohms, repeating as the shaft travels through each

rotation. Replace the sending unit if it does not test as specified or if the readings are erratic.

4. *1996 models*—To measure the trim sending unit fixed resistance, calibrate an ohmmeter on an appropriate scale to read 620-630 ohms. Connect 1 ohmmeter lead to the trim sender ribbed black lead and the other ohmmeter lead to the white lead. Note the reading, then rotate the sending unit while continually noting the meter reading. The ohmmeter should indicate a constant reading of approximately 620-630 ohms. Replace the sending unit if any other reading is noted.

5. *1996 models*—To measure the first variable resistance, move the ohmmeter lead from the white lead to the smooth black lead. Slowly rotate the sending unit shaft counterclockwise until the ohmmeter reads INFINITY. Continue to (slowly) rotate the shaft counterclockwise and watch for the ohmmeter to jump to a full continuity reading (0 ohms). Continue rotation while watching for a smooth increase in resistance to 620-630 ohms, followed by the jump to infinity as the complete cycle begins again.

6. *1996 models*—To check the second variable resistance, move the ohmmeter lead from the ribbed black lead to the white lead. Slowly rotate the sending unit shaft counterclockwise until the ohmmeter reads INFINITY. Continue to (slowly) rotate the shaft counterclockwise and watch for the ohmmeter to jump to a reading of 620-630 ohms. Continue rotation while watching for a smooth decrease in resistance to full continuity (0 ohms), followed by the jump to infinity as the complete cycle begins again. Replace the trim sending unit if it does not perform as specified.

Adjustment (1994 Models)

If the trim indicating gauge does not show a full DOWN reading when the drive unit is trimmed fully DOWN, proceed as follows.

1. Trim the drive unit to the full trim IN (DOWN) position.
2. Loosen the sending unit mounting screws.
3. Turn the ignition switch to the ON or RUN position and with the aid of an observer, rotate the sending unit (**Figure 58**) as required to provide a full DOWN reading on the trim gauge.
4. Tighten the mounting screws to specification (**Table 5**) and recheck the adjustment.

Adjustment (1995-On Models)

1A. *1995 models*—Attach an ohmmeter, calibrated on an appropriate scale to read 10-12 ohms, across the trim sending unit leads.

1B. *1996 models*—Attach an ohmmeter, calibrated on an appropriate scale to read 10-12 ohms, to pin A and pin C of the trim sending unit connector. This will be the ribbed black and smooth black leads.

2. Rotate the sending unit shaft until the ohmmeter reads 10-12 ohms.

3. Hold the pivot housing in the full DOWN (IN) position or if the drive unit is installed, trim the drive unit to the full DOWN (IN) position.

4. Install the sending unit into the gimbal ring and engage the sending unit shaft to the pivot pin. Try not to disturb the preset shaft position. Index the sender shaft in a position that will still allow

some adjustment after the retaining screws and washers have been installed.

5. Install the retaining screws and washers (**Figure 59**) and tighten them hand tight.

6. Rotate the sending unit as necessary to obtain an ohmmeter reading of 10-12 ohms with the pivot housing held in the full DOWN (IN) position or the drive unit trimmed to the full DOWN (IN) position. Hold the sending unit in position and tighten the mounting screws to 2.0-2.7 N•m (18-24 in.-lb.)

7. Verify that the ohmmeter reading did not shift during the tightening of the screws. Readjust as necessary.

Trim Limit Control Box (DP-S Models)

The trim limit control box will not function correctly if the trim sending unit is incorrectly wired, incorrectly adjusted or malfunctioning. Make sure the trim sender connector has a ribbed black lead in position A, a white lead in position B and a smooth black lead in position C.

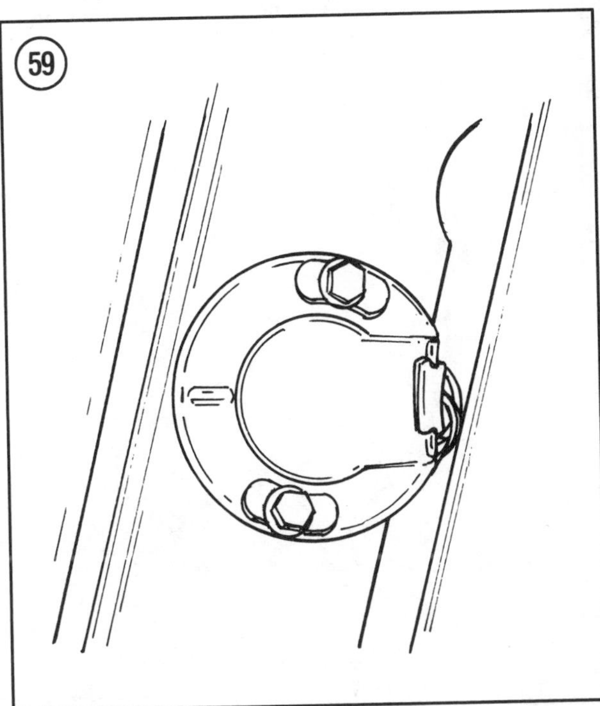

If there is any doubt that the trim sending unit is correctly adjusted, refer to *Adjustment* in this chapter and verify correct adjustment.

The jumper wire (1, **Figure 60**) must not be cut. Cutting the jumper automatically increases the factory programmed trim limits to -6° and +12°. These are the recommended trim limits for the SX single propeller drive unit. The lead should only be cut if the trim limit control box is being used on a SX drive unit. Operating a drive DP-S unit at these increased trim angles will cause propeller cavitation damage and possible abnormal handling characteristics.

Programming Trim and Tilt Limits

Refer to **Table 10** and **Figure 60** for this procedure. If the transom angle is unknown, measure the transom angle with a protractor, making sure to establish the level (angle) of the hull first. The transom angle must be within 10 - 15°, with 12-13° being the most common. Record the measured transom angle.

1. Turn the gauge selector switch (11, **Figure 60**) to the 0 position. All three LED should blink simultaneously.

2. Adjust the drive unit to a trim angle of -2°. This is done by trimming the drive unit UP or DOWN until the trim ram extends the specified amount, based on your boat's transom angle as shown in **Figure 61** and specified in **Table 10**.

3. When the -2° trim angle has been verified, press the PB-A button (12, **Figure 60**) for at least 4 seconds. The green trim low LED (8, **Figure 60**) should illuminate, then extinguish as the program is accepted by the trim limit box. All LED's will again blink when the button is released.

4. Adjust the drive unit to a trim angle of +5°. This is done by trimming the drive unit UP or DOWN until the trim ram extends the specified amount, based on your boat's transom angle as shown in **Figure 61** and specified in **Table 10**.

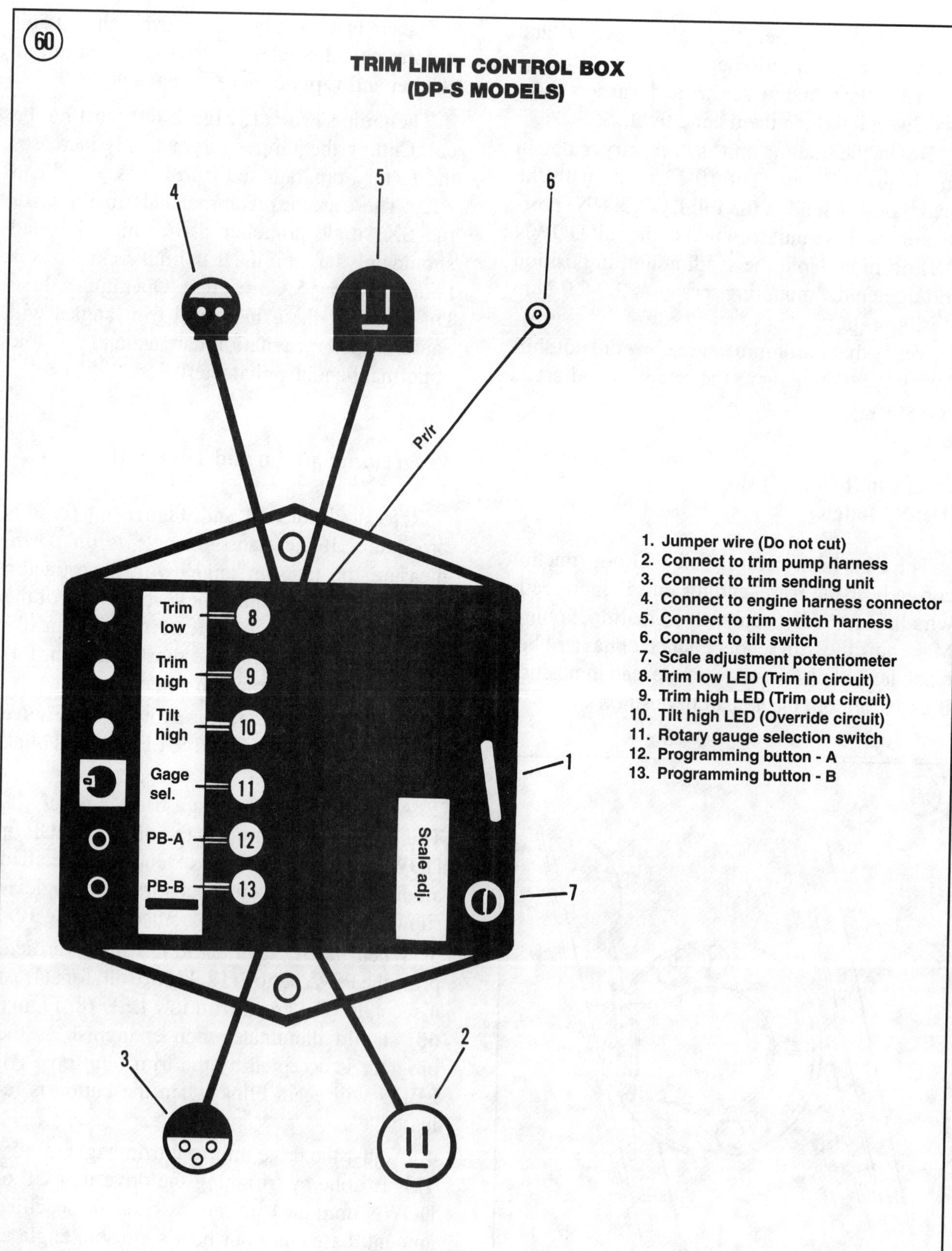
60
TRIM LIMIT CONTROL BOX
(DP-S MODELS)
4
5
6
Pr/r
Trim low
8
Trim high
9
Tilt high
10
Gage sel.
11
PB-A
12
PB-B
13
Scale adj.
1
7
3
2
1. Jumper wire (Do not cut)
2. Connect to trim pump harness
3. Connect to trim sending unit
4. Connect to engine harness connector
5. Connect to trim switch harness
6. Connect to tilt switch
7. Scale adjustment potentiometer
8. Trim low LED (Trim in circuit)
9. Trim high LED (Trim out circuit)
10. Tilt high LED (Override circuit)
11. Rotary gauge selection switch
12. Programming button - A
13. Programming button - B

5. When the +5° trim angle has been verified, press the PB-B button (13, **Figure 60**) for at least 4 seconds. The yellow trim high LED (9, **Figure 60**) should illuminate, then extinguish as the program is accepted by the trim limit box. All LED's will again blink when the button is released.

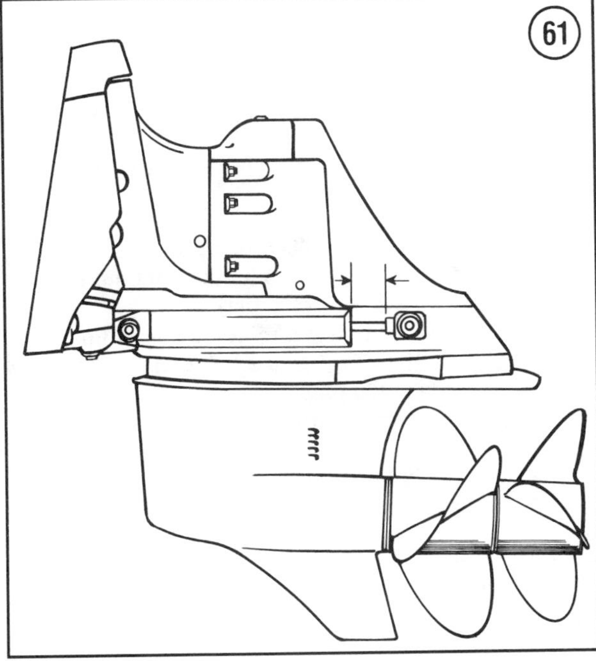

6. Trim the drive unit UP to desired maximum tilt position. Allow at least 13 mm (1/2 in.) clearance between the drive unit and any obstruction, such as a swim platform.

7. When the desired maximum tilt angle has been verified, press the PB-A AND PB-B buttons (12 and 13, **Figure 60**) simultaneously for at least 4 seconds. The red tilt high LED (10, **Figure 60**) should illuminate, then extinguish as the program is accepted by the trim limit box. All LED's will again blink when the button is released.

8. Rotate the gauge selector switch (11, **Figure 60**) to the correct position as specified in **Table 10**, based on the trim indicator used in your boat. All LED's should extinguish at this point.

9. Trim the drive unit to the full DOWN position by depressing the override and trim IN buttons simultaneously.

10. Turn the ignition switch to the ON or RUN position and adjust the Scale adjustment potentiometer (7, **Figure 60**) until the trim indicator gauge reads full DOWN.

11. Turn the ignition switch off. Programming is complete.

Tables 1-10 are on the following pages.

Table 1 POWER TRIM/TILT SPECIFICATIONS (DP-C1/D1 AND DPX MODELS)

Recommended fluid	Volvo DuraPlus Power Trim/Steering Fluid
Approximate fluid capacity	1.0 L (1.1 qt.)
Maximum allowable trim out (up)	5° positive
Maximum allowable trim in (down)	Determined by transom angle
Trim sending unit resistance values, measured through a full rotation	
Red/white to black/white	800-1100 ohms, constant reading
Green/white to black/white	100 ohms (or less) to 800-1100 ohms

Table 2 POWER TRIM/TILT SPECIFICATIONS 1994-1997 (SX AND DP-S MODELS)

Recommended fluid	Volvo DuraPlus Power Trim/Steering Fluid
Approximate fluid capacity	1.6 L (54 fl.-oz.)
Hydraulic pressure values	
Trim up relief valve	8,274-11,032 kPa (1200-1600 psi)
Maximum leak-down specification	1,379 kPa (200 psi) in 5 minutes minimum
Trim in relief valve	2,758-5,516 kPa (400-800 psi)
Maximum leak-down specification	1,379 kPa (200 psi) in 5 minutes minimum
Thermal expansion valve	15,514-18,962 kPa (2,250-2,750 psi)
Impact relief valve's opening pressure	12,411 kPa (1800 psi)
Outdrive cycle time (one complete cycle)	40 seconds maximum
Trim motor stall test	
Minimum torque reading (both directions)	2.33 N•m (20.6 in.-lb.)
Maximum amperage draw (both directions)	185 amps
Trim sending unit resistance values	
Adjustment value (drive unit full down)	10-12 ohms*
1994-1995 models (full travel specifications)	0-190 to 0-210 ohms
1996 models (3-wire sender), measured through full counter clockwise rotations	
Pin A (ribbed black) to Pin C (smooth black)	Infinity to 0 ohms to 620-630 ohms
Pin A (ribbed black) to Pin B (white)	620-630 ohms, constant reading
Pin B (white) to Pin C (smooth black)	Infinity to 620-630 ohms to 0 ohms
Valve body (check valve) test pressure	207 kPa (30 psi), no leakage

*1996 models–measured across Pin A (ribbed black) and Pin C (smooth black).

Table 3 POWER TRIM/TILT SPECIFICATIONS (1998-ON SX AND DP-S MODELS)

Recommended fluid	Volvo DuraPlus Power Trim/Steering Fluid
Hydraulic pressure values	
Trim out/tilt up	2000-2137 kPa (290-310 psi)
Trim in/tilt down	4068-4206 kPa (590-610 psi)
Trim motor stall test	
Trim-in stall	5171-5861 kPa (750-850 psi)
Tilt-up stall	9308-9998 kPa (1350-1450 psi)
Trim-in stall/leak down	690 kPa (100 psi) 5 minutes min.)
Tilt-up stall/leak down	690 kPa (100 psi) 5 minutes min.)
Impact relief valve opening pressure	12411kPa (1800 psi)

Table 4 POWER TRIM/TILT TROUBLESHOOTING (DP-C1/D1 AND DPX MODELS)

Condition	Probable cause	Solution
No trim up or down (motor runs fast)	Sheared pump coupler	Replace pump coupler
Drive unit leaks down (reverse lock still holds)	Thermal expansion valve Defective valve body	Replace valve Replace valve body
Drive unit leaks down and reverse lock fails	Defective cylinder Defective valve body	Isolate and replace cylinder Isolate cylinders from valve body and check leak down
No reverse lock (but holds in forward)	Defective valve body	Replace valve body
Drive unit will not trim out under load	Trim UP relief valve Defective valve body	Replace relief valve Replace valve body
Drive unit tilts erratically or with a jumpy motion	Air in system	Check fluid level and cycle unit to remove air
	Incompatible fluids flush, add correct fluid	Drain reservoir and cylinders,
Drive unit will not trim in from full tilt position	Thermal expansion valve is blocked or stuck shut Defective valve body	Replace valve Replace valve body

Table 5 POWER TRIM/TILT TROUBLESHOOTING (SX AND DP-S MODELS)

Condition	Probable cause	Solution
No trim up or down (motor runs fast)	Sheared pump coupler	Replace pump coupler
Drive unit leaks down (reverse lock still holds)	Is or valve Manual release valve (if equipped) Thermal expansion valve Trim OUT check valve Sticking pump control piston	Replace valve seals or valve Replace valve Test and replace valve Clean and inspect piston
Drive unit leaks down and reverse lock fails	Defective cylinder Defective valve body component(s)	Isolate and repair cylinder Isolate cylinders from valve body and check leak down
No reverse lock (but holds in forward)	Trim IN check valve Manual release valve (if equipped) Manual release check ball (if equipped) Possible defective cylinder body and check leak down	Test and replace valve Replace valve seals or valve Pressure test for leakage Isolate cylinders from valve
Drive unit will not trim out under load	Trim OUT relief valve Trim OUT inlet check ball	Inspect/replace relief valve Inspect/replace check ball

(continued)

Table 5 POWER TRIM/TILT TROUBLESHOOTING (SX AND DP-S MODELS) (continued)

Condition	Probable cause	Solution
Drive unit will not trim out under load (continued)	Trim IN pump control piston	Clean and inspect piston
	Thermal expansion valve	Replace valve
	Manual release valve (if equipped)	Replace valve seals or valve
	Worn or leaky gear housing	Test trim OUT stall pressure
	Reversed lines	Check line routing
Drive unit will not trim in, or trims in slowly	Trim IN relief valve	Inspect/replace relief valve
	Trim IN inlet check ball	Inspect/replace check ball
	Trim OUT pump control piston	Clean and inspect piston
	Manual release check ball (if so equipped)	Pressure test for leakage
	Manual release valve (if equipped)	Replace valve seals or valve
	Worn or leaky gear housing	Test trim IN stall pressure
Drive unit tilts erratically or with a jumpy motion	Air in system	Check fluid level and cycle unit to remove air
	Incompatible fluids	Drain reservoir and cylinders, flush, add correct fluid

Table 6 TORQUE VALUES (SX AND DP-S MODELS)

Fastener	N.m	In.-lb.	ft.-lb.
Electric motor to valve body	4.0-5.9	35-52	–
Gear housing to valve body	4.0	35	–
Manual release valve (early models)	5.1-6.2	45-55	–
Reservoir to valve body	4.0-5.9	35-52	–
Thermal expansion valve (internal)	5.1-6.4	45-57	–
Trim cylinder end caps	34-41	–	25-30
Trim sending unit	2.0-2.7	18-24	–
Trim cylinder rod elastic locknut (4)	14-16	124-142	10-12
Trim line fittings	9.5-12	84-108	–
Trim manifold mounting nut	12-15	108-132	–

Table 7 RECOMMENDED LUBRICANTS, SEALANTS AND ADHESIVES*

	Part No.
Lubricants	
Volvo DuraPlus GL5 Synthetic Gear Lube	(dealer stock item)
Volvo Penta Propeller Shaft Grease	1141644-3
or Quicksilver Special Lubricant 101	92-13872A-1
Volvo DuraPlus Power Trim/Steering Fluid	3851039-2
OMC EP/Wheel Bearing Grease	(dealer stock item)
OMC Moly Lube	175356

(continued)

Table 7 RECOMMENDED LUBRICANTS, SEALANTS AND ADHESIVES*

	Part No.
Lubricants (continued)	
OMC Triple Guard Grease	(dealer stock item)
or Quicksilver 2-4-C Multi-Lube	(dealer stock item)
OMC Needle Bearing Assembly Grease	378642
or Quicksilver Needle Bearing Grease	92-825265A-1
Sealants	
Volvo Master Gasket Sealant	840879-1
Volvo Black silicone sealant	1161277-7
or OMC RTV black silicone sealant	263753
Volvo White Sealing Compound	1141570-0
or OMC Gasket Sealing Compound	508235
or Quicksilver Perfect Seal	92-34227-11
OMC Black Neoprene Dip	909570
or Quicksilver Liquid Neoprene	92-25711-2
OMC Pipe Sealant with Teflon	9100048
or Quicksilver Loctite 567 PST pipe sealant	92-809822
3M Marine Sealant 101 (polysulfide [OMC or locally available])	506852
Adhesives	
OMC Type M adhesive	318535
or Scotch grip 1300 adhesive (OMC or locally available)	982551
or Quicksilver Bellows Adhesive (contact cement)	92-86166-1
OMC Locquic Primer	772032
or Quicksilver Locquic Primer	92-809824
OMC Ultra Lock threadlocking adhesive (high strength)	500422
or Quicksilver Loctite 271 threadlocking adhesive	92-809819
OMC Nut Lock threadlocking adhesive (medium strength)	500418
or Quicksilver Loctite 242 threadlocking adhesive	92-809821
Miscellaneous	
Volvo DuraPlus Corrosion Shield	362002-8
Quicksilver Storage Seal Rust Inhibitor	92-86145A12
OMC Dielectric grease	503243
or Quicksilver Dielectric silicone grease	92-823506-1

*Obtain Volvo supplies from a Volvo-Penta Dealer, Quicksilver supplies from any Mercury Marine Dealer and OMC supplies from any OMC Stern Drive, Evinrude or Johnson Dealer.

Table 8 VOLVO SPECIAL TOOLS (SX AND DP-S MODELS)

Application	Description	Part No.
Pin installation tool (Amphenol)	Trim sending unit	3854249-2
Pin removal tool (Amphenol)	Trim sending unit	3854350-0
Snap ring pliers (No. 1)	Valve body	3854362-5
Seal protector (end cap)	Trim cylinder	3854363-3
Seal installer (end cap)	Trim cylinder	3854364-1
Spanner wrench (end cap)	Trim cylinder	3854365-8
Spanner wrench (end cap)	Trim cylinder	326485 (OMC)
Pressure adaptor	Valve body	3854366-6
Holding block, 2 required	Trim cylinder rod	3854367-4
In-line pressure tester	Complete system	3854368-2

Table 9 TOOL AND EQUIPMENT MANUFACTURERS

Stevens Instruments 111 Greenwood Avenue Waukegan, Illinois 60079-9375 Phone: 847-336-9375 Fax: 847-662-6808 Manufacturers of marine service products S-34 gearcase pressure tester

Table 10 TRIM LIMIT CONTROL UNIT SPECIFICATIONS (DP-C1/D1)

DP-C1/D1 analog control unit adjustment point	
Boat transom angle	Trim ram extension
10°	37 mm (1.46 in.)
11°	40 mm (1.58 in.)
12°	42 mm (1.65 in.)
13°	45 mm (1.77 in.)
14°	48 mm (1.89 in.)
15°	51 mm (2.00 in.)
DP-C1/D1 digital control unit adjustment point	
Boat transom angle	Trim gauge reading*
10°	-2
11°	-3
12°	-4
13°	-5
14°	-6
15°	-7

*Drive fully trimmed IN (down).

Table 11 TRIM LIMIT CONTROL UNIT SPECIFICATIONS (DP-S)

DP-S trim limit control box specifications		
Boat transom angle	Trim ram extension for negative 2° setting	Trim ram extension for positive 5° setting
10°	46 mm (1.81 in.)	72.9 mm (2.87 in.)
11°	49.8 mm (1.96 in.)	76.2 mm (3.00 in.)
12°	54.1 mm (2.13 in.)	80.8 mm (3.18 in.)
13°	57.9 mm (2.28 in.)	84.8 mm (3.34 in.)
14°	61.7 mm (2.43 in.)	88.6 mm (3.49 in.)
15°	65.3 mm (2.57 in.)	92.5 mm (3.64 in.)

(continued)

Table 11 TRIM LIMIT CONTROL UNIT SPECIFICATIONS (DP-S) (continued)

DP-S trim limit box gauge selection setting	
Gauge used	Selector switch position*
Volvo part No. 3851788	1
VDO part No. 01-210-415	1
Volvo part No. 857449	2
VDO part No. X-19-270-3123	2
VDO Vanguard part No. 1-275-810-136A	2
OMC (all compatible part numbers)	3
Faria part No. GP9318B	3
Teleflex part No. 20742 and 58031	4
Medallion part No. SIK-140-30W, Rev. A	4
Medallion part No. SIK-112-30W, Rev. A	4
Faria part No. GP9374D	5

* Positions 6 and 7 are not used.

Chapter Sixteen

Steering Systems

Volvo Penta stern drives may be equipped with a manual (not power assisted) or power steering system. Proper operation of the stern drive steering system is essential for safe boating. The steering system should be rigged *only* by an experienced marine technician and serviced by one equally qualified. The boater should perform routine checks and maintenance to ensure there are no problems and should constantly monitor the operation of the steering system. If a problem is suspected, it is important to have it inspected by trained personnel as soon as possible. This chapter covers steering safety precautions, steering system troubleshooting and maintenance.

Table 1 provides troubleshooting for power steering systems, **Table 2** lists power steering specifications, Volvo special tools are listed in **Table 3**, and **Table 4** provides stock numbers for common lubricants, sealant and adhesives. **Tables 1-4** are found at the end of this chapter.

SAFETY PRECAUTIONS

The steering system connects the stern drive with the steering wheel (**Figure 1**). When properly installed and maintained, the steering system gives control of the vessel to the operator. A steering system that hesitates or jams will prevent you from avoiding obstacles, such as other boats on the water. If the steering system is loose, the boat will weave regardless of your attempts to maintain a straight course. A steering system failure can cause the complete loss of control, that can result in a serious accident and possible loss of life.

The most important safety precaution you can observe is proper lubrication and maintenance of the steering system. This is especially important whenever the stern drive unit receives a severe blow, such as hitting any object in the water or when trailering the boat. Damaged or weak components may fail at a later time while on the water. Know what to look for and have any problems corrected as soon as possible.

If you must make required adjustments yourself, make them very carefully and use only the fasteners supplied with steering attachment kits or equivalent fasteners sold as replacement items at marine dealerships. It is also a good idea to have your work rechecked by an experienced marine technician to make sure that no safety hazards exist.

If the engine is removed or if any other service that affects the steering system is performed, make sure that:

a. Cable movement is not restricted. See **Figure 2**. Cable restrictions can result in possible jamming of the system. On power steering models, a cable restriction can cause the drive unit to go into a full turn without anyone ever turning the steering wheel.

b. The stringer (mount) does not interfere with the power steering pump and pulley. (**Figure 3**, typical).

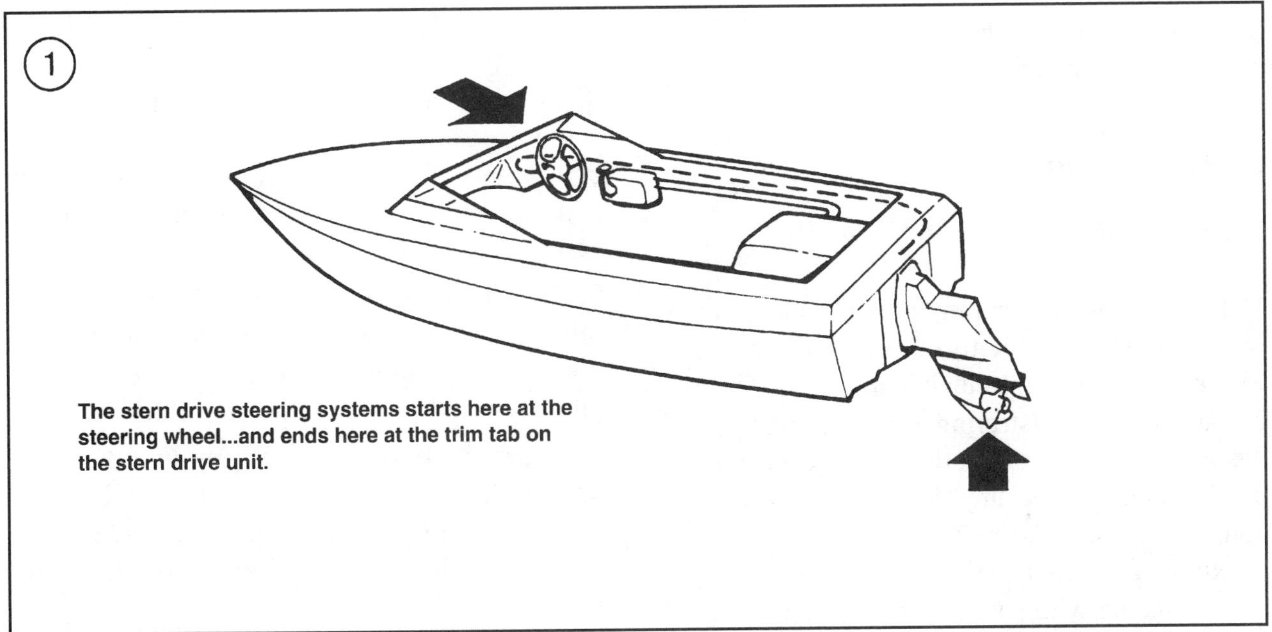

1
The stern drive steering systems starts here at the steering wheel...and ends here at the trim tab on the stern drive unit.

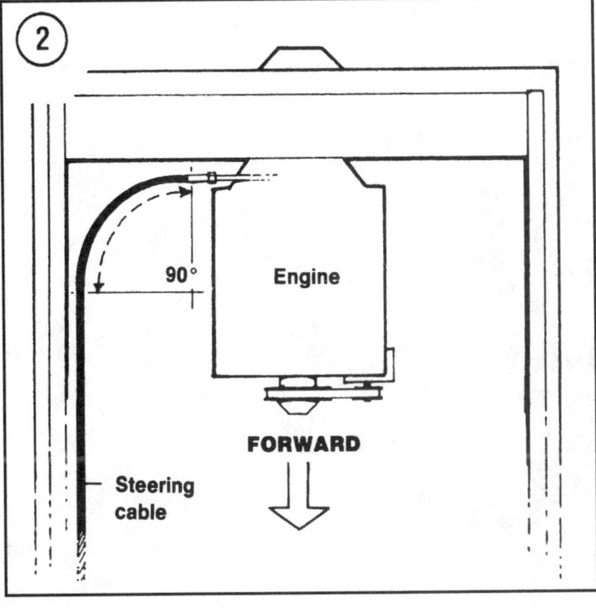

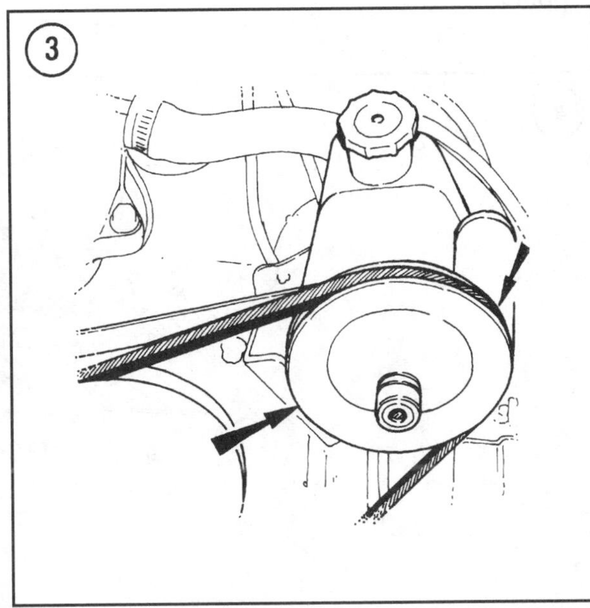

c. The power steering components and the push/pull cable moves freely and will operate the power steering valve only when you turn the steering wheel (**Figure 4**).

MECHANICAL STEERING SYSTEM

A mechanical steering system (**Figure 5**) consists of the helm or steering wheel assembly (A), the connecting cable (B) and hardware (C) that attaches the steering wheel to the steering arm on the inner transom bracket.

Cable Removal/Installation

The steering cable must be serviced as an assembly.

1. Remove the cotter pin from the clevis pin which holds the cable to the steering arm See **Figure 6**. Remove the clevis pin.
2. Turn the helm (steering wheel assembly) to the port full lock position, then remove the cotter pin holding the locking sleeve over the cable coupler nut. See **Figure 7**.
3. Remove the cable. Prior to installation, lubricate the cable with special steering cable lubricant available from your marine lubricant supplier.
4. Insert the steering cable through the steering tube.
5. Move the stern drive steering arm to its center position.
6. Center the steering cable arm. Connect the cable to the steering arm. Install the clevis pin, then install a new cotter pin and spread the ends.
7. Thread the coupler nut on the tube. Hold the tube adjusting sleeve or tube nut with a wrench and tighten the coupler nut to 35 ft.-lb. (48 N•m) torque.
8. Position the locking sleeve on the steering cable and slide it over the coupler nut until the cotter pin hole in the sleeve is between the nut and cable grease fitting. Install a new cotter pin and spread the ends. See **Figure 7**.
9. Turn the steering wheel lock to lock. The drive unit should move fully in each direction. If not, loosen the adjusting nuts and move the cable guide tube as required to obtain full travel.
10. Turn the steering wheel unit until the drive unit is centered. If the steering wheel is not centered at this point, readjust the cable guide slightly as described in Step 9 to center the wheel.
11. Repeat Step 8 to make certain that both adjustments are correct.

4

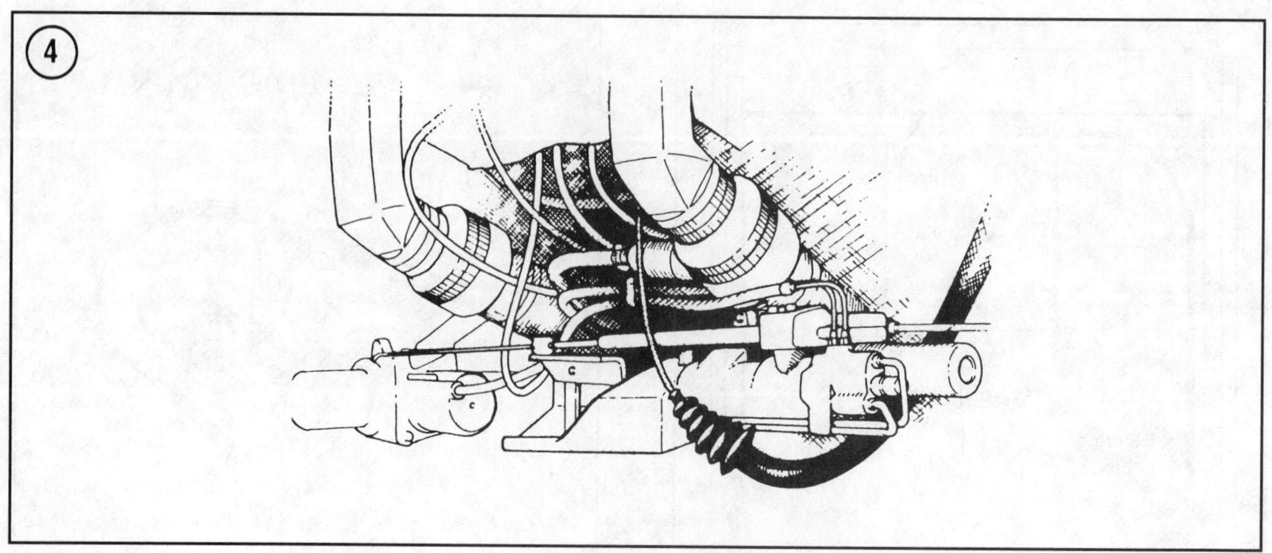

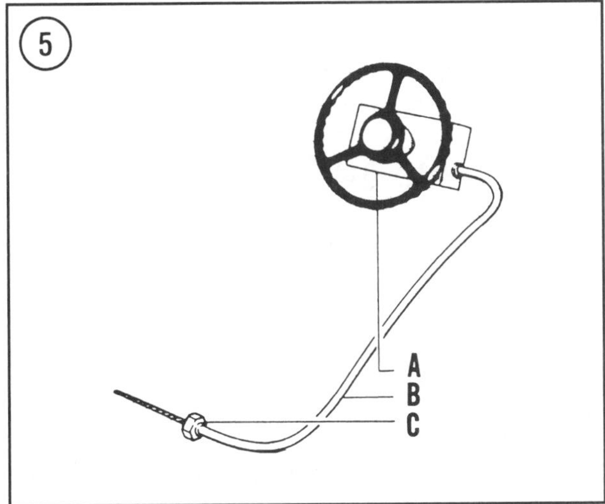

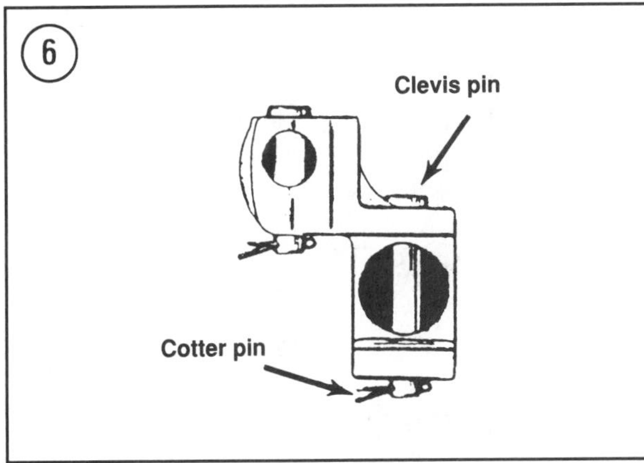

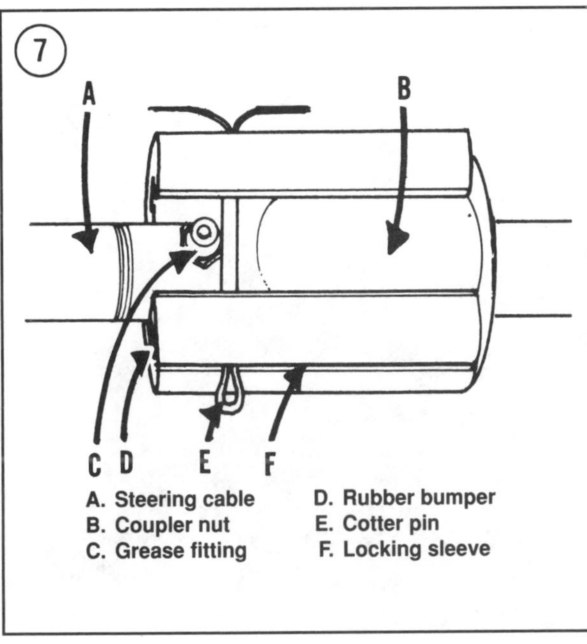

A. Steering cable
B. Coupler nut
C. Grease fitting
D. Rubber bumper
E. Cotter pin
F. Locking sleeve

Steering System Lubrication

See Chapter Four.

Trim Tab Adjustment

Proper adjustment of the trim tab will provide equal steering effort in both directions. If the boat seems to steer more easily in one direction than the other, operate it in a straight line with a balanced load on a stretch of water where wind or current will not be a factor in steering. If steering effort is not equal under these conditions, adjust the trim tab as follows.

1. Determine in which direction the steering is easier.
2. Loosen the trim tab bolt.
   a. If steering is easier to the port, turn the trim tab slightly to the port.
   b. If steering effort is easier to the starboard, turn the trim tab slightly to the starboard.
3. Tighten the trim tab bolt and recheck the steering effort by running the boat.
4. If the steering effort is not equal, repeat Steps 1-2, then recheck the steering effort again by running the boat.
5. When steering effort is satisfactory when turning in either direction, tighten the trim tab bolt.

POWER STEERING SYSTEM

Steering Cable Routing (All Models Except DPX)

In addition to the components used in the manual steering system, the power steering system uses a power steering pump, oil cooler and a combination steering valve/piston assembly. Hydraulic hoses and lines connect these components.

The power steering pump is mounted on the front of the engine and is belt-driven from the crankshaft pulley (**Figure 8**). On models with a combination control valve/piston, the assembly is mounted on the inner transom bracket (**Figure 9**) and connects to the steering arm and steering cable ram. **Figure 10** shows the relationship of the system components.

The valve spool in the control valve assembly moves about 1/8 in. (3.2 mm) (total) in response to the movement of the steering cable housing. Although the amount of spool movement is small, it is enough to open a valve and direct hydraulic pressure to one side or the other of the piston. If the cable housing is held by its housing, it will affect the movement of the valve spool and result in hard steering in one or both directions. Make sure the area around the steering cable housing is clear and the cable housing is not forced to take sharp bends, so that nothing restricts cable movement inside the housing. See **Figure 2**, typical. Wiring harnesses and other control cables should not be tied to the steering cable housing.

Fluid Level Check

Although the dipstick is marked with both HOT and COLD lines, perform this procedure with the engine at normal operating temperature and OFF. The drive unit position, should be straight ahead.

1. Remove the engine compartment cover or hatch.
2. Unscrew the power steering pump reservoir cap and remove the cap/dipstick.
3. Wipe the dipstick with a clean shop cloth or paper towel. Reinstall the cap/dipstick, wait a few moments, then remove the cap again and check the fluid level on the dipstick.
4. If the fluid level is below the recommended level on the dipstick shown in **Figure 11**, add sufficient power steering fluid to bring the level to the FULL HOT mark on the dipstick.
5. Reinstall the cap/dipstick in the power steering pump reservoir.
6. Turn the steering wheel from lock to lock several times, then repeat Steps 2-5 as required.

Bleeding the Hydraulic System

A low fluid level and/or air in the fluid are the most frequently encountered causes of pump noise. The power steering system must be bled to correct the problem. It must also be bled if a hydraulic line has been disconnected while servicing the system.

1. With the engine stopped (OFF), check the fluid level as described in this chapter.

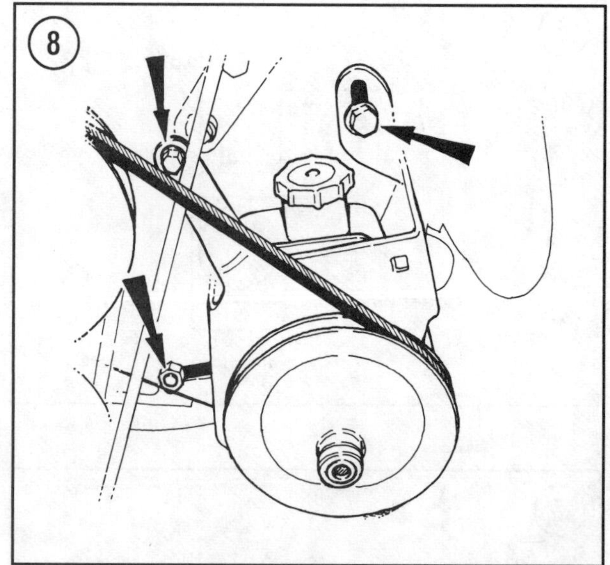

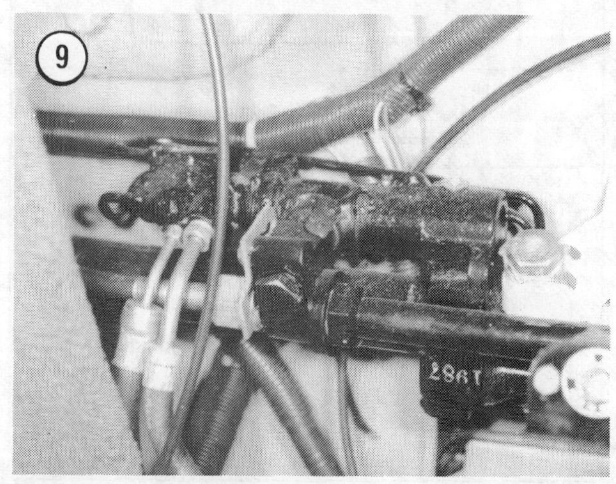

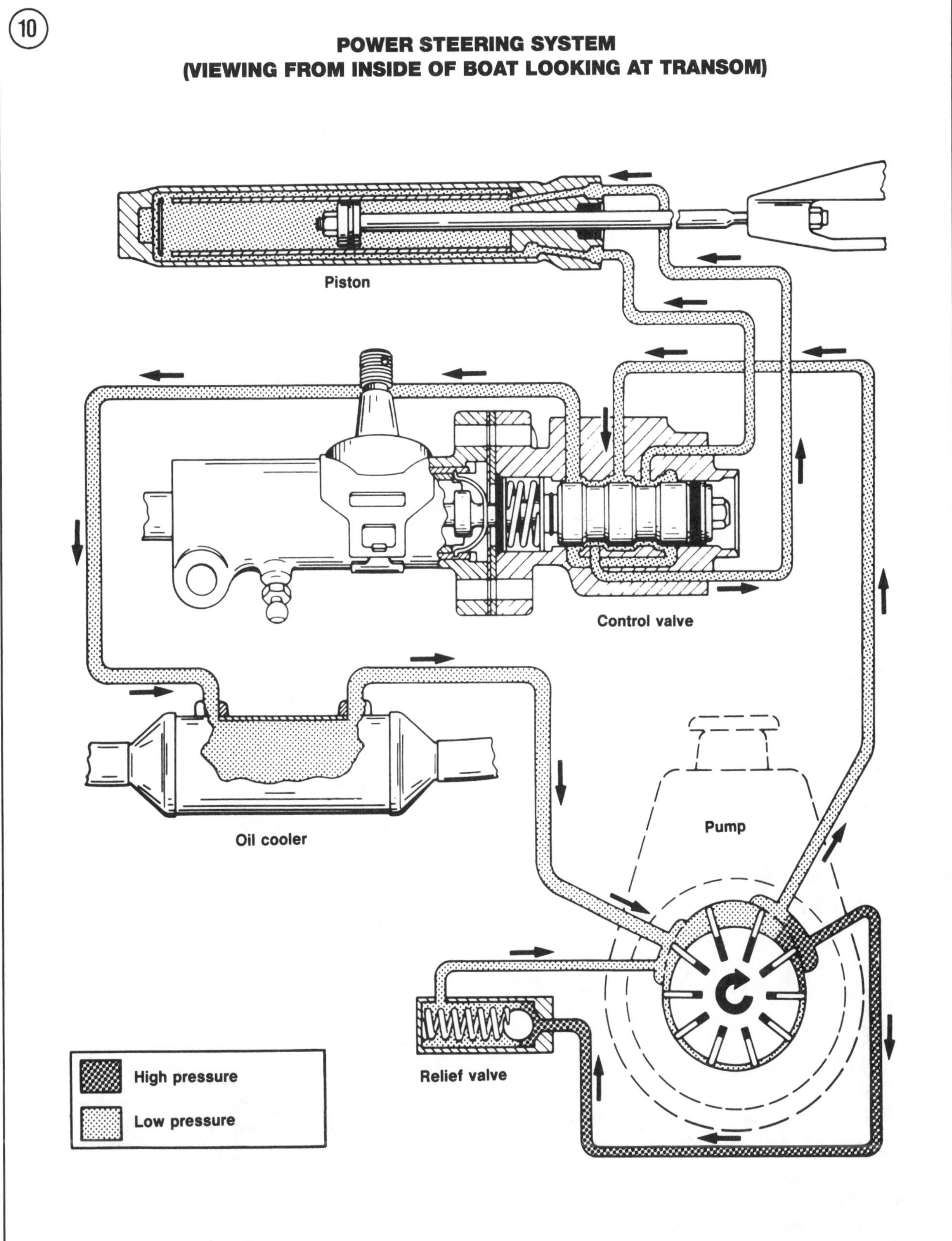
10
POWER STEERING SYSTEM
(VIEWING FROM INSIDE OF BOAT LOOKING AT TRANSOM)
Piston
Control valve
Oil cooler
Pump
Relief valve
High pressure
Low pressure

2. Start the engine and run at 1,000-1,500 rpm until it reaches normal operating temperature.
3. Turn the steering wheel from lock to lock several times, then center the steering wheel and shut off the engine.
4. Remove the power steering pump cap/dipstick and recheck the fluid level. Fill the reservoir as necessary.
5. Turn the steering wheel from side to side without hitting the stops. Keep the fluid level in the pump reservoir just above the integral pump casting. If there is air in the fluid, it will appear light tan in color or foamy in appearance.
6. Turn the steering wheel to the center position. Start and run the engine for 2-3 minutes, then shut it off. Recheck the fluid in the reservoir. If it still contains air, repeat Step 5 and Step 6 until the fluid does not foam and the level remains constant.
7. When all air has been bled from the system, run the boat on the water to make sure that the steering operates properly and is not noisy.
8. Recheck the fluid level (engine at normal operating temperature) to make sure it is at the FULL HOT mark on the dipstick.

Power Steering Pump Removal/Installation

The power steering system, including the pump is equipped with metric fittings. Replacement high pressure hoses must also have metric fittings. Metric flare nut wrenches must be used to loosen or tighten the fitting nut to prevent rounding the corners of the nut. When a return line is removed, a new clamp should be installed.

All except DPX models

Refer to **Figure 12** for this procedure. The actual mounting brackets may be different from shown.

1. Locate the high-pressure hose and return hose at the rear of the power steering pump. The lower hose (13, **Figure 12**) is the high-pressure hose. The return hose (12, **Figure 12**) is clamped onto the fitting.
2. Place shop cloths under the fittings to catch fluid that will escape when the hoses are detached.
3. Loosen or remove the clamp from the return hose, then pull the return hose from the fitting. Catch the fluid in the shop cloths, then exchange the fluid-soaked cloths with dry ones. Secure the hose in an upright position to prevent further drainage. Try to keep the area as clean as possible.
4. Use a metric flare nut wrench to loosen the high-pressure hose at the rear of the pump. Detach the high-pressure hose and secure it in an upright position.
5. Loosen the pump mounting fasteners and slip the drive belt from the pulley. If the belt must be replaced, it may be necessary to remove other belts before the power steering drive belt can be removed completely.
6. Unbolt the pump and bracket from the engine.
7. If the pump will be replaced, remove the bracket from the old pump and attach it to the new unit.
8. Position the pump assembly on the engine and install the mounting fasteners finger-tight.
9. Attach the high pressure hose and the return hose to the pump but tighten only finger-tight.
10. Make sure the belt is in good condition and the pulley is dry, then install the drive belt.

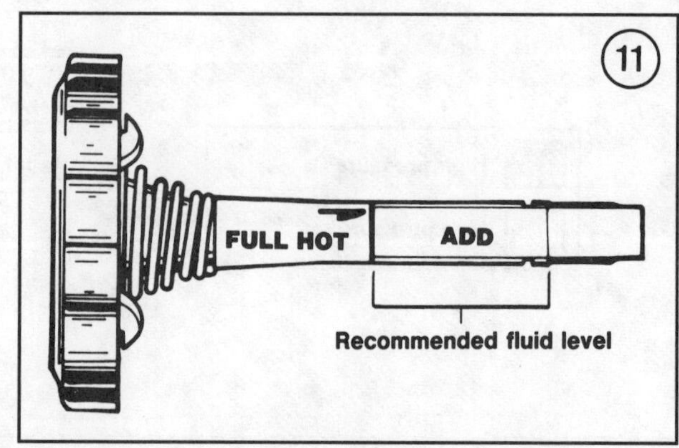

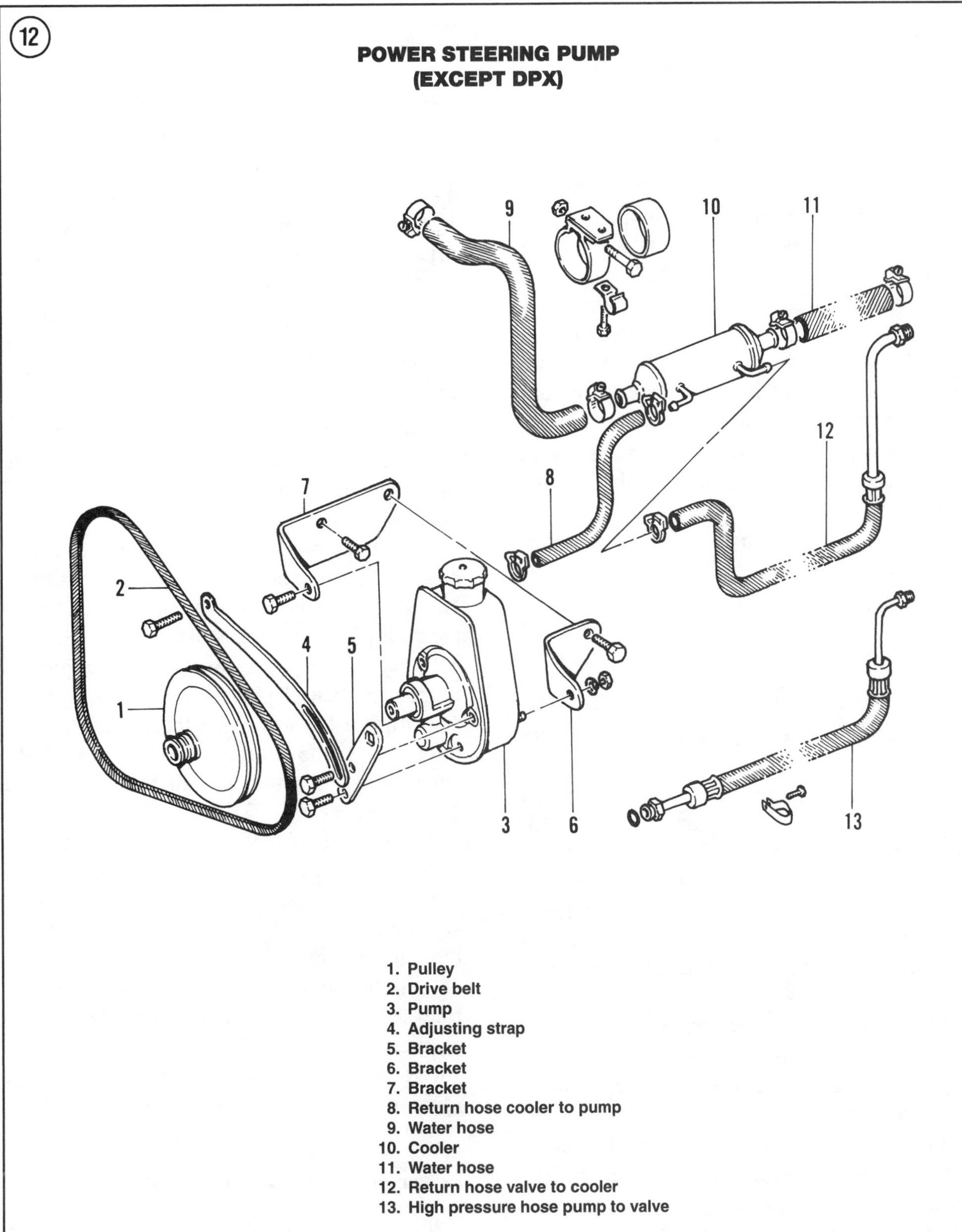

1. Pulley
2. Drive belt
3. Pump
4. Adjusting strap
5. Bracket
6. Bracket
7. Bracket
8. Return hose cooler to pump
9. Water hose
10. Cooler
11. Water hose
12. Return hose valve to cooler
13. High pressure hose pump to valve

NOTE
*Do not pry against the pump reservoir to adjust belt tension. The bracket (5, **Figure 12**) has a square opening that will accept a square drive for a 1/2 in. drive socket for moving the pump.*

11. Pivot the pump away from the engine to tighten the belt, then tighten the pump mounting fasteners. The proper tension should allow the belt to deflect 1/4-1/2 in. (6.3-12.7 mm) with finger pressure midway between the pulleys.
12. Tighten the fittings on the high pressure and return lines on the rear of the pump. Make sure the hoses are correctly routed and are away from everything that might cause abrasion.
13. Fill the pump reservoir with power steering fluid and bleed the system as described in this chapter.
14. Recheck the belt tension of a new belt after running the engine for about 5 minutes.

DPX models

Refer to **Figure 13** for this procedure. The actual mounting brackets may be different from shown.

1. Locate the high-pressure hose and return hoses at the power steering pump. The hose (13, **Figure 13**) at the side is the high-pressure hose. The high-pressure hose is attached to the steering control valve. The return hose (8, **Figure 13**) is clamped onto the fitting near the bottom of the pump and the other end is attached to the reservoir.
2. Place shop cloths under the fittings to catch fluid that will escape when the hoses are detached. A container can be used to catch some of the oil from the reservoir.
3. Loosen or remove the clamp from the return hose, then pull the return hose from the fitting. Catch as much fluid as possible in a container, but some oil will spill into the shop cloths. Exchange the fluid-soaked cloths with dry ones. Secure the hose in an upright position to prevent further drainage. Try to keep the area as clean as possible.
4. Use a metric flare nut wrench to loosen the high-pressure hose at the pump. Detach the high-pressure hose and secure it in an upright position.
5. Loosen the pump mounting fasteners and slip the drive belt from the pulley. If the belt must be replaced, it may be necessary to remove other belts before the power steering drive belt can be removed completely.
6. Unbolt the pump and bracket from the engine.
7. If the pump will be replaced, remove the bracket from the old pump and attach it to the new unit.
8. Position the pump assembly on the engine and install the mounting fasteners finger-tight. Make sure the pulley aligns properly and that all brackets are installed correctly.
9. Attach the high-pressure hose and the return hose to the pump but tighten only finger-tight.
10. Make sure the belt is in good condition and the pulley is dry, then install the drive belt.
11. Pivot the pump away from the engine to tighten the belt. Tighten the adjustment screw (17, **Figure 13**) to tighten the drive belt, then tighten the pump mounting fasteners to lock the adjustment. The proper tension should allow the belt to deflect 1/4-1/2 in. (6.3-12.7 mm) with finger pressure midway between the pulleys.
12. Tighten the fittings on the high-pressure and return lines on the pump. Make sure the hoses are correctly routed and are away from everything that might cause abrasion.
13. Fill the pump reservoir with power steering fluid and bleed the system as described in this chapter.
14. Recheck the belt tension of a new belt after running the engine for about 5 minutes.

Power Steering Pump Leakage

The power steering pump may develop problems such as growling noises or loss of power when the engine is running slowly. It may also

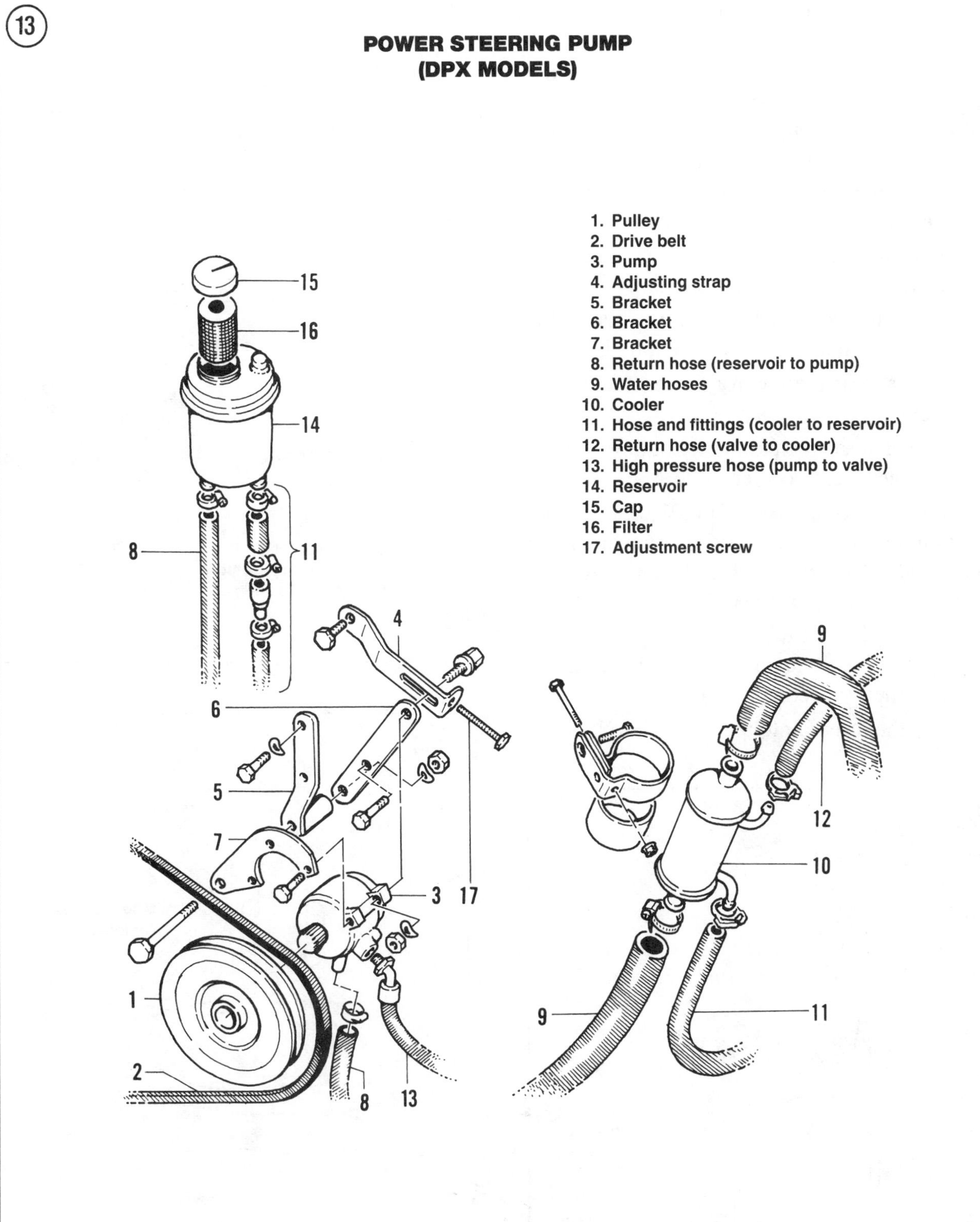
13
POWER STEERING PUMP
(DPX MODELS)
1. Pulley
2. Drive belt
3. Pump
4. Adjusting strap
5. Bracket
6. Bracket
7. Bracket
8. Return hose (reservoir to pump)
9. Water hoses
10. Cooler
11. Hose and fittings (cooler to reservoir)
12. Return hose (valve to cooler)
13. High pressure hose (pump to valve)
14. Reservoir
15. Cap
16. Filter
17. Adjustment screw
15
16
14
8
11
4
9
6
17
5
12
7
10
3 17
1
9
11
2
8
13

require the frequent addition of fluid. If any of these conditions occur, check for leaks.

Figure 14 shows some common points that may leak. If a leak is found at any of the points shown, the pump should be replaced. Service replacements for the sealing rings shown at F, **Figure 15** may be difficult to find. In addition to these leakage points, check the following:

a. Return hose and/or clamp. The hose and/or clamp should be replaced if damaged.
b. Cross-threaded or loose high-pressure fitting. Tighten or replace as required.
c. Leakage at the control valve or cylinder. Replace as necessary.
d. Power steering fluid in the cooling system. Replace the oil cooler.

Seepage leaks are the most difficult to locate. If the engine is kept clean as suggested, it will be much easier to locate such leaks. A suggested procedure for locating small leaks is as follows:

a. Clean the entire power steering system (pump, hoses, control valve, power cylinder and the connecting lines).
b. Fill the reservoir to the correct level.
c. Start the engine and turn the steering wheel from stop to stop several times, then shut off the engine.
d. Recheck the areas mentioned for dampness. Correct any problems as necessary.

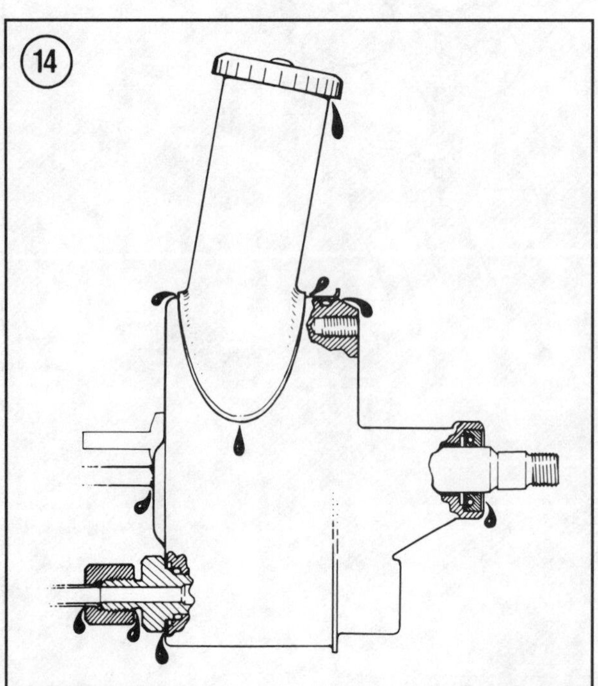

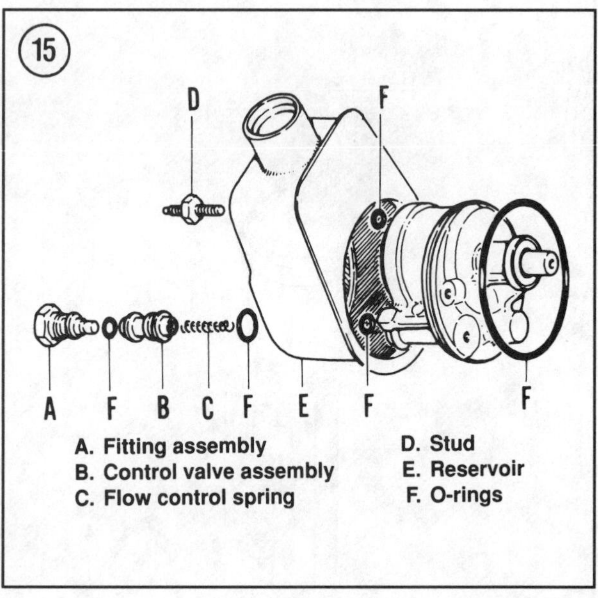

A. Fitting assembly
B. Control valve assembly
C. Flow control spring
D. Stud
E. Reservoir
F. O-rings

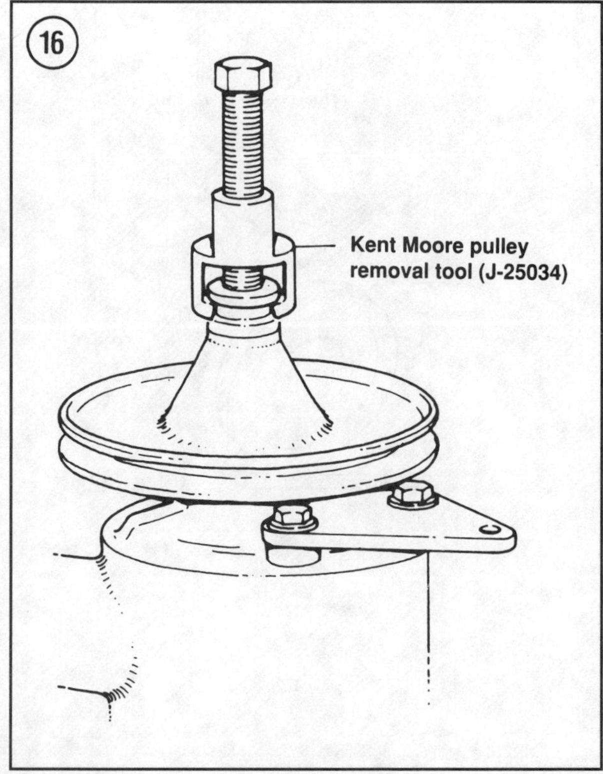

Power Steering Pump Overhaul

Individual parts for the pump is not available from Volvo Penta and if trouble is encountered, it is recommended that the complete pump be replaced. It may be necessary to install the pulley from the original pump on the replacement pump. See **Figure 16**. Do not damage the pulley by using the incorrect puller.

Control Valve and Piston Unit (All Models Except DPX)

A combination control valve/cylinder is used on all models except DPX models. See **Figure 17** or **Figure 18**. Individual parts for the combination control valve/cylinder assembly are not available from Volvo Penta and if trouble is encountered, replace the complete assembly.

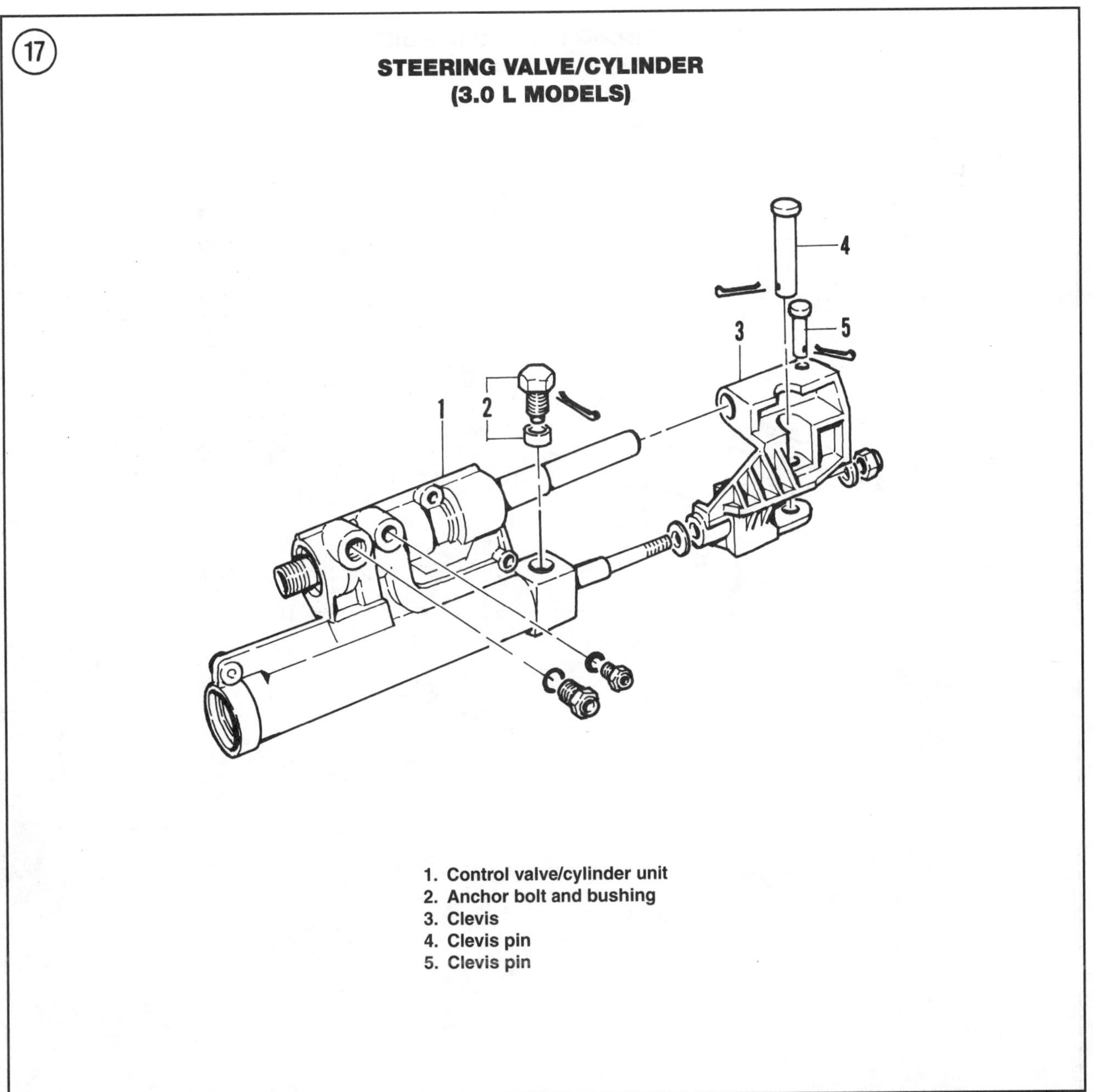

1. Control valve/cylinder unit
2. Anchor bolt and bushing
3. Clevis
4. Clevis pin
5. Clevis pin

DPX models are equipped with hydrostatic steering which has no mechanical connection between the steering wheel and the stern drive steering cylinder. In normal use, the engine mounted power steering pump supplies oil pressure to the control unit (3, **Figure 19**) which directs the pressurized oil to the steering cylinder (8, **Figure 19**) to turn the stern drive unit. If the engine is not running or for some other reason the power steering pump is not supplying the necessary pressure, steering can be accomplished manually through the use of an emergency pump located in the control unit. Individual parts of the control unit and the steering cylinder are not readily available. The faulty unit should be replaced.

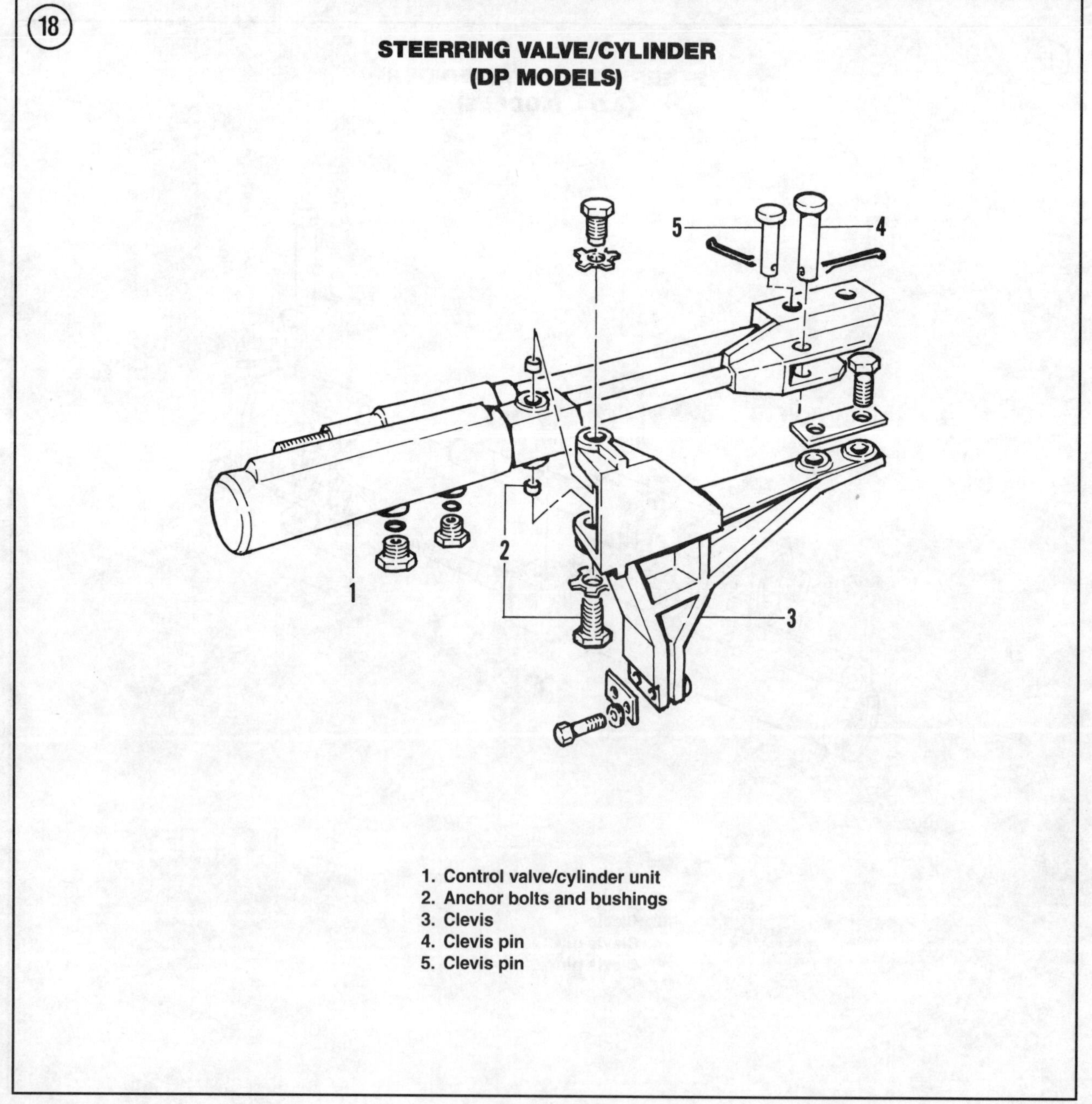

1. Control valve/cylinder unit
2. Anchor bolts and bushings
3. Clevis
4. Clevis pin
5. Clevis pin

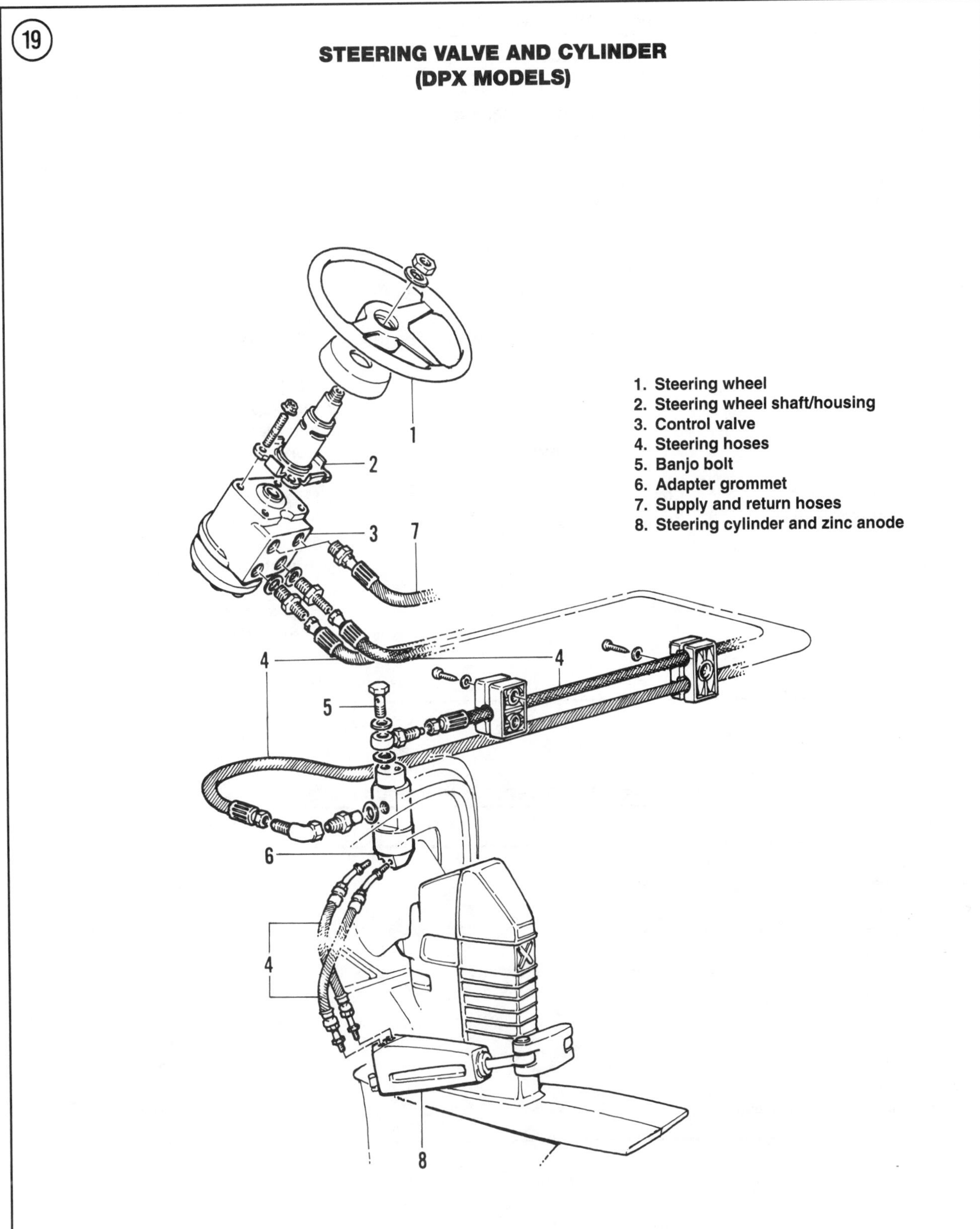
19
STEERING VALVE AND CYLINDER
(DPX MODELS)
1
2
3
7
4
4
5
4
6
4
8
1. Steering wheel
2. Steering wheel shaft/housing
3. Control valve
4. Steering hoses
5. Banjo bolt
6. Adapter grommet
7. Supply and return hoses
8. Steering cylinder and zinc anode

Table 1 POWER STEERING DIAGNOSIS

Trouble	Possible cause	Correction
Whining noise	Pump shaft bearing failing (scored)	Flush system, replace pump.
Rattling noise	components loose	check cable nut, bushings, & pressure hose rubbing other parts.
Chirp or squealing noise	Loose belt	Adjust tensioner to specifications
Groaning noise	Low fluid level or air in system.	Locate and correct leak, fill and bleed system.
Growling noise Pump	Restricted hose causing back pressure	Locate & correct restricted part.
	Steering cable in a bind.	Check correct length and routing.
Steers hard to right (starboard)	Restriction of cable movement by the bulkhead, cable to long.	Eliminate restriction. Replace cable.
Steers hard to left (port)	Restriction of cable movement by the bulkhead, cable to short.	Eliminate restriction. Replace cable.
Steering wheel surges or jerks while in full turn, either direction, with engine running.	Low pressure.	Replace pump if defective.
	Air in system.	Locate and repair leak, fill reservoir and bleed system.
	Pump belt slipping.	Correct tension to specifications.
Turning wheel fast to the right or left increases steering effort, momentary.	Low fluid level.	Fill reservoir and bleed system.
	Internal leakage	If defective replace pump.
	Pump belt slipping.	Adjust tension, or replace belt.
Power steering fluid Milky, foamy.	Air in system.	Find and correct leak. Fill reservoir Bleed system. Keep fluid level up when cold. Pump still foams with correct fluid level, replace pump.

Table 2 POWER STEERING SPECIFICATIONS

Torque specifications	N•m	in.-lb.	ft.-lb.
Power steering mounting bolts	34	–	25
Power steering pump fitting	50 - 102	–	37 - 75
Cylinder to transom plate	54 - 61	–	40 - 45
Hose clamp to pump & oil cooler	1.4 - 2.0	12 - 17	–
Inlet control valve hose fitting	14 - 16	–	10 - 12
Power steering pump hose fitting	20 - 35	–	15 - 26
Control valve hose fitting	20 - 23	–	15 - 17
Steering cable anchor nut	14	120	–
Piston rod to clevis locknut	31 - 38	–	23 - 28
Anchor block jam nut	47 - 54	–	34 - 40
Trim tab bolt	19 - 22	–	14 - 16
Pump relief value pressure	–	–	6895-7584 kPa

Index

E

F

G

H

I

3.0 GL/GS

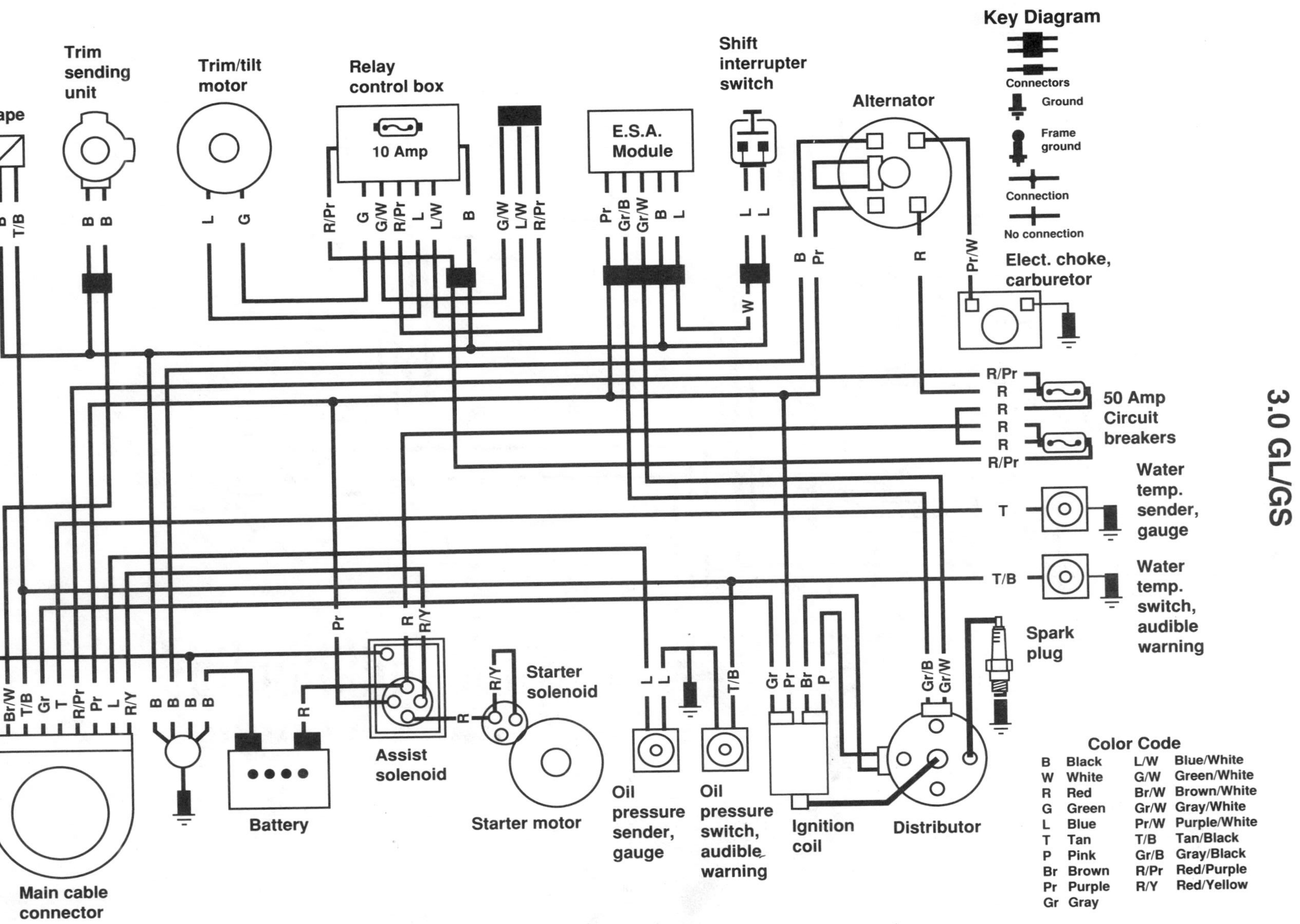
Tape
Trim sending unit
Trim/tilt motor
Relay control box
10 Amp
E.S.A. Module
Shift interrupter switch
Alternator
Key Diagram
Connectors
Ground
Frame ground
Connection
No connection
Elect. choke, carburetor
50 Amp Circuit breakers
Water temp. sender, gauge
Water temp. switch, audible warning
Spark plug
Main cable connector
Battery
Assist solenoid
Starter solenoid
Starter motor
Oil pressure sender, gauge
Oil pressure switch, audible warning
Ignition coil
Distributor
Color Code
B Black
W White
R Red
G Green
L Blue
T Tan
P Pink
Br Brown
Pr Purple
Gr Gray
L/W Blue/White
G/W Green/White
Br/W Brown/White
Gr/W Gray/White
Pr/W Purple/White
T/B Tan/Black
Gr/B Gray/Black
R/Pr Red/Purple
R/Y Red/Yellow

4.3 GL AND GS MODELS

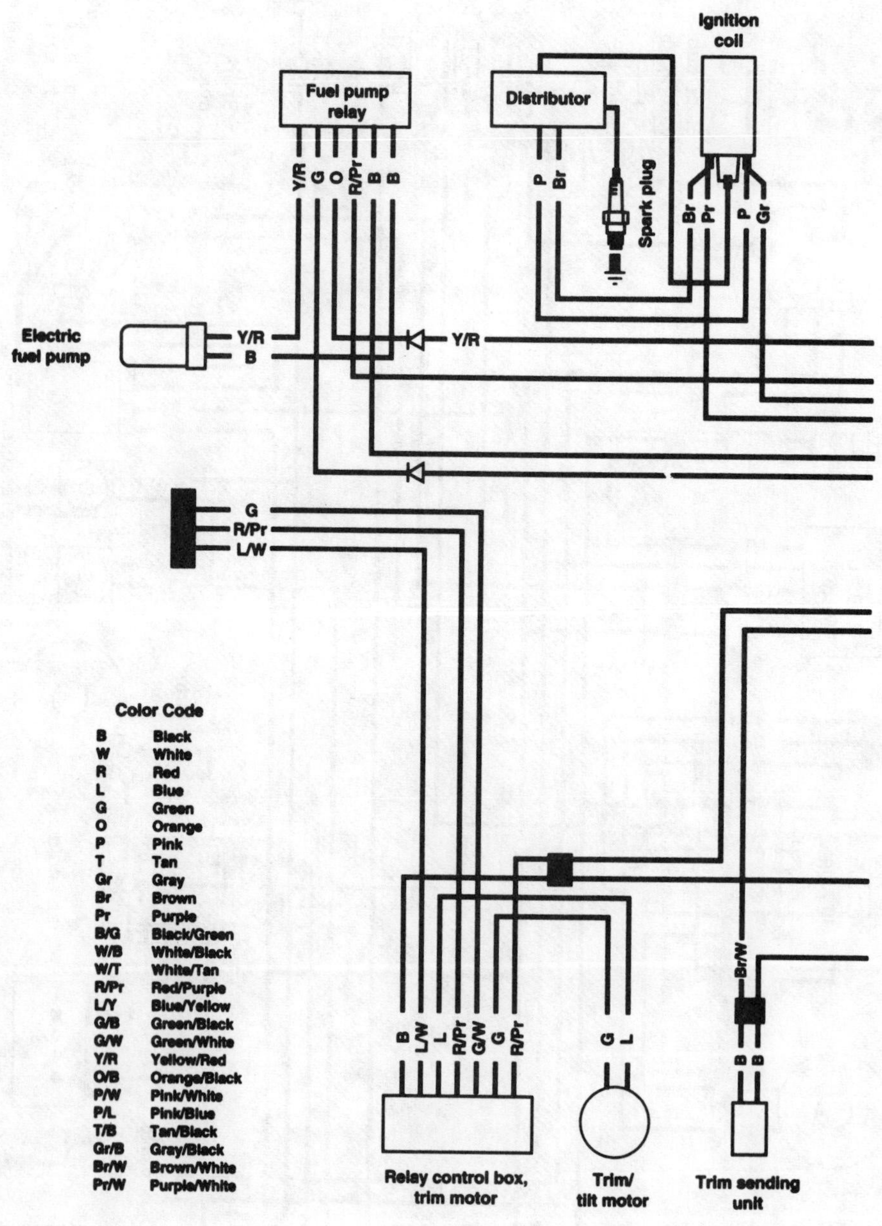

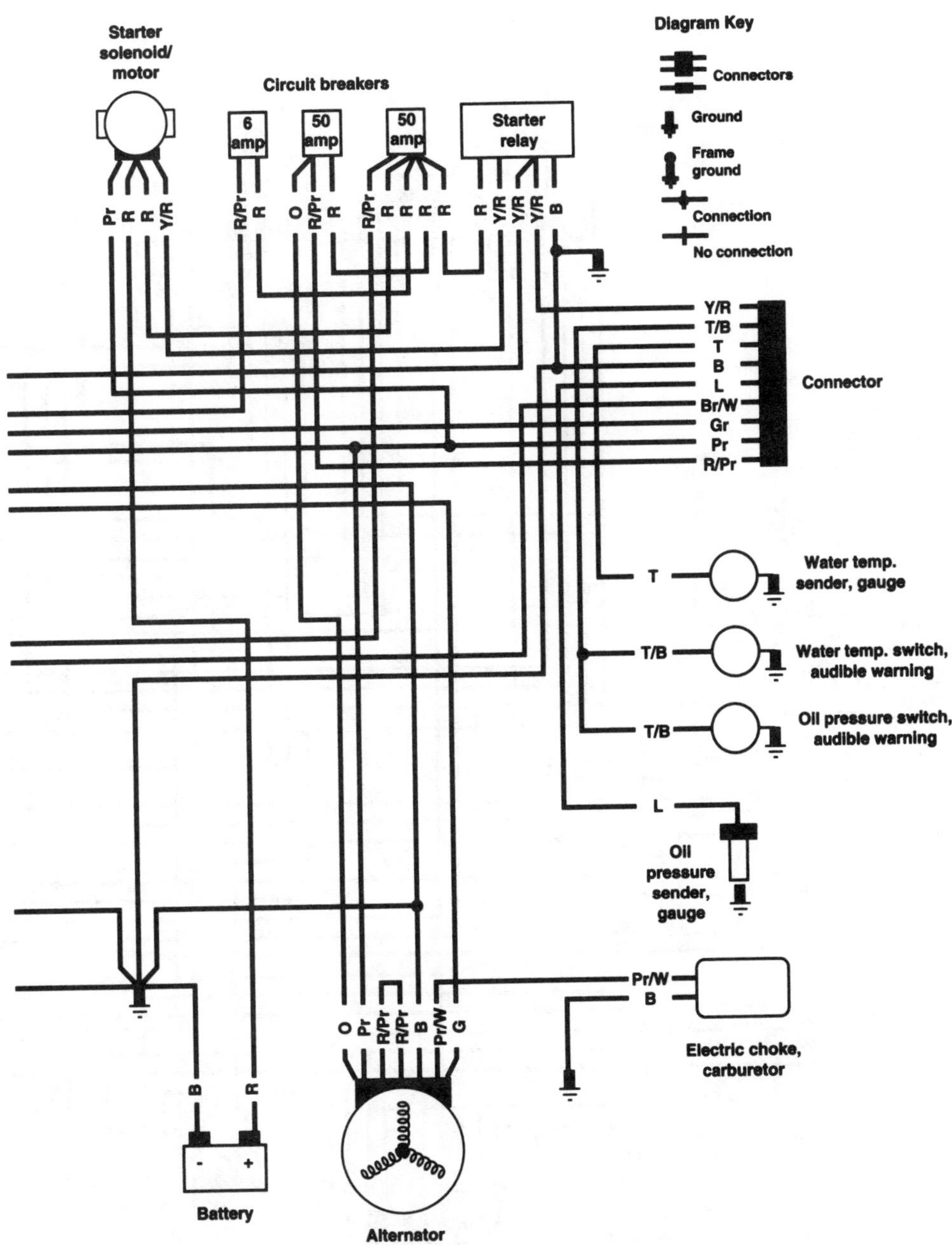
Starter solenoid/ motor
Circuit breakers
6 amp
50 amp
50 amp
Starter relay
Pr R R Y/R
R/Pr R
O R/Pr R
R/Pr R R R R
R Y/R Y/R Y/R B
Diagram Key
Connectors
Ground
Frame ground
Connection
No connection
Y/R
T/B
T
B
L
Br/W
Gr
Pr
R/Pr
Connector
T
Water temp. sender, gauge
T/B
Water temp. switch, audible warning
T/B
Oil pressure switch, audible warning
L
Oil pressure sender, gauge
Pr/W
B
Electric choke, carburetor
O Pr R/Pr R/Pr B Pr/W G
B R
Battery
Alternator

4.3 AND 5.7 Gi MODELS

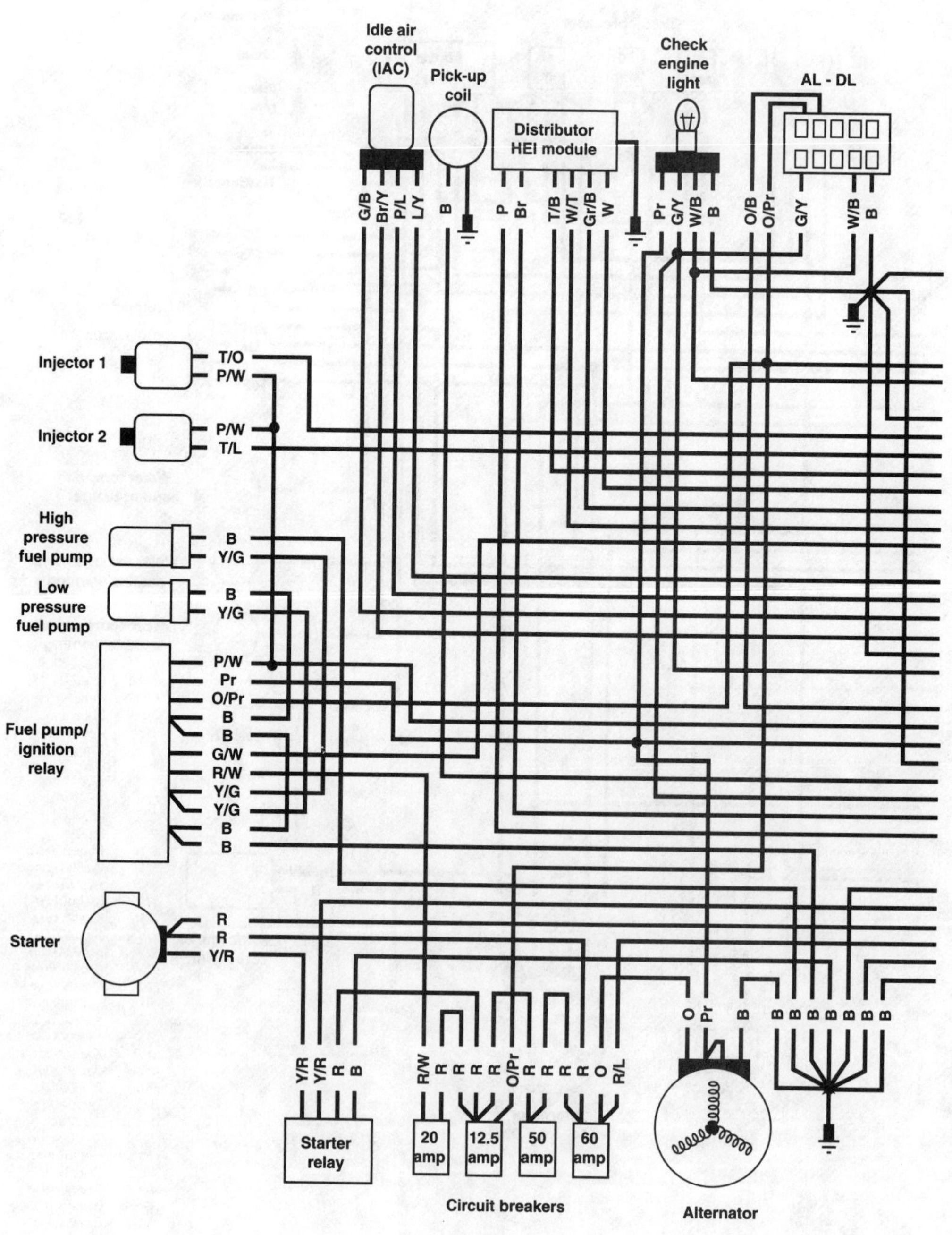

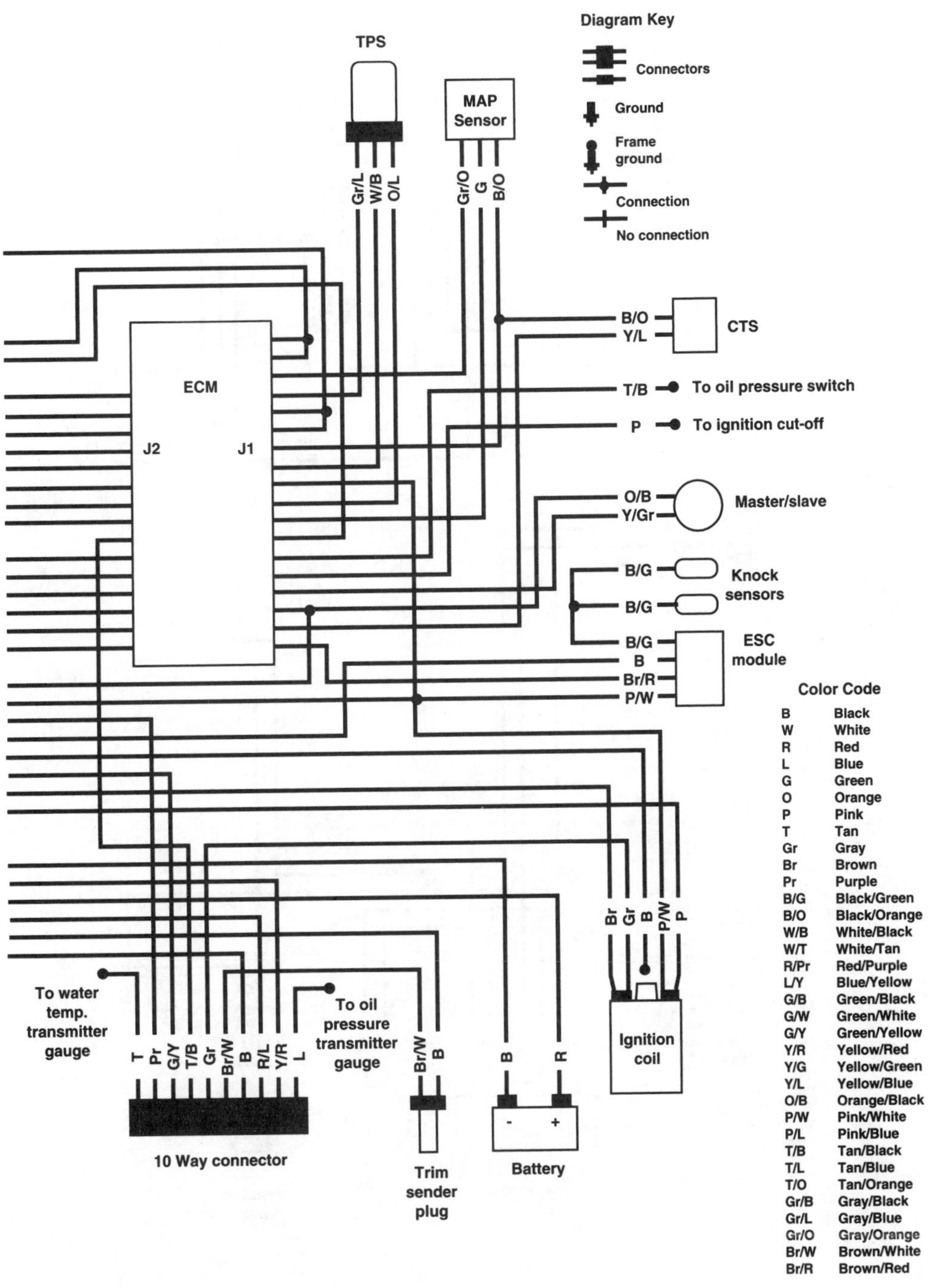
Diagram Key
Connectors
Ground
Frame ground
Connection
No connection
TPS
Gr/L
W/B
O/L
MAP Sensor
Gr/O
G
B/O
ECM
J2
J1
B/O
Y/L
CTS
T/B
To oil pressure switch
P
To ignition cut-off
O/B
Y/Gr
Master/slave
B/G
B/G
Knock sensors
B/G
B
Br/R
P/W
ESC module
Br
Gr
B
P/W
P
Ignition coil
To water temp. transmitter gauge
T
Pr
G/Y
T/B
Gr
Br/W
B
R/L
Y/R
L
To oil pressure transmitter gauge
10 Way connector
Br/W
B
Trim sender plug
B
R
-
+
Battery
Color Code
B Black
W White
R Red
L Blue
G Green
O Orange
P Pink
T Tan
Gr Gray
Br Brown
Pr Purple
B/G Black/Green
B/O Black/Orange
W/B White/Black
W/T White/Tan
R/Pr Red/Purple
L/Y Blue/Yellow
G/B Green/Black
G/W Green/White
G/Y Green/Yellow
Y/R Yellow/Red
Y/G Yellow/Green
Y/L Yellow/Blue
O/B Orange/Black
P/W Pink/White
P/L Pink/Blue
T/B Tan/Black
T/L Tan/Blue
T/O Tan/Orange
Gr/B Gray/Black
Gr/L Gray/Blue
Gr/O Gray/Orange
Br/W Brown/White
Br/R Brown/Red

5.0 AND 5.8 FL MODELS

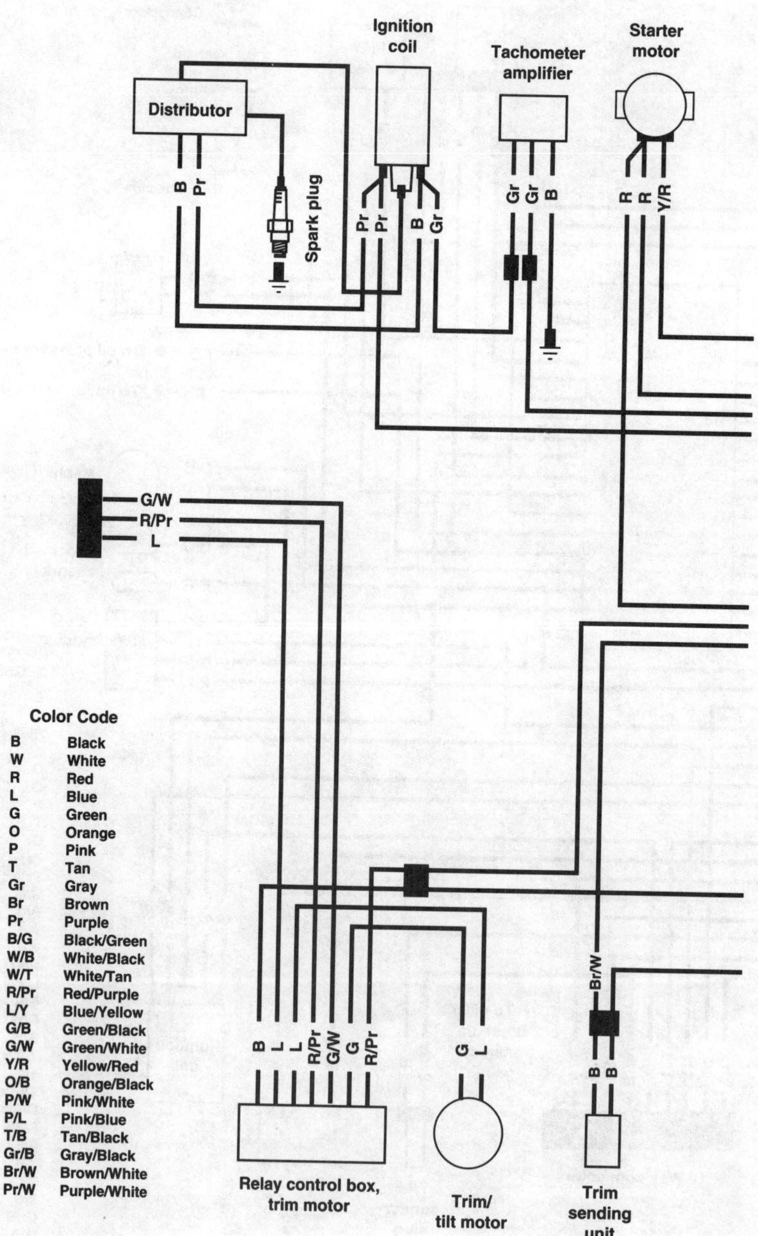

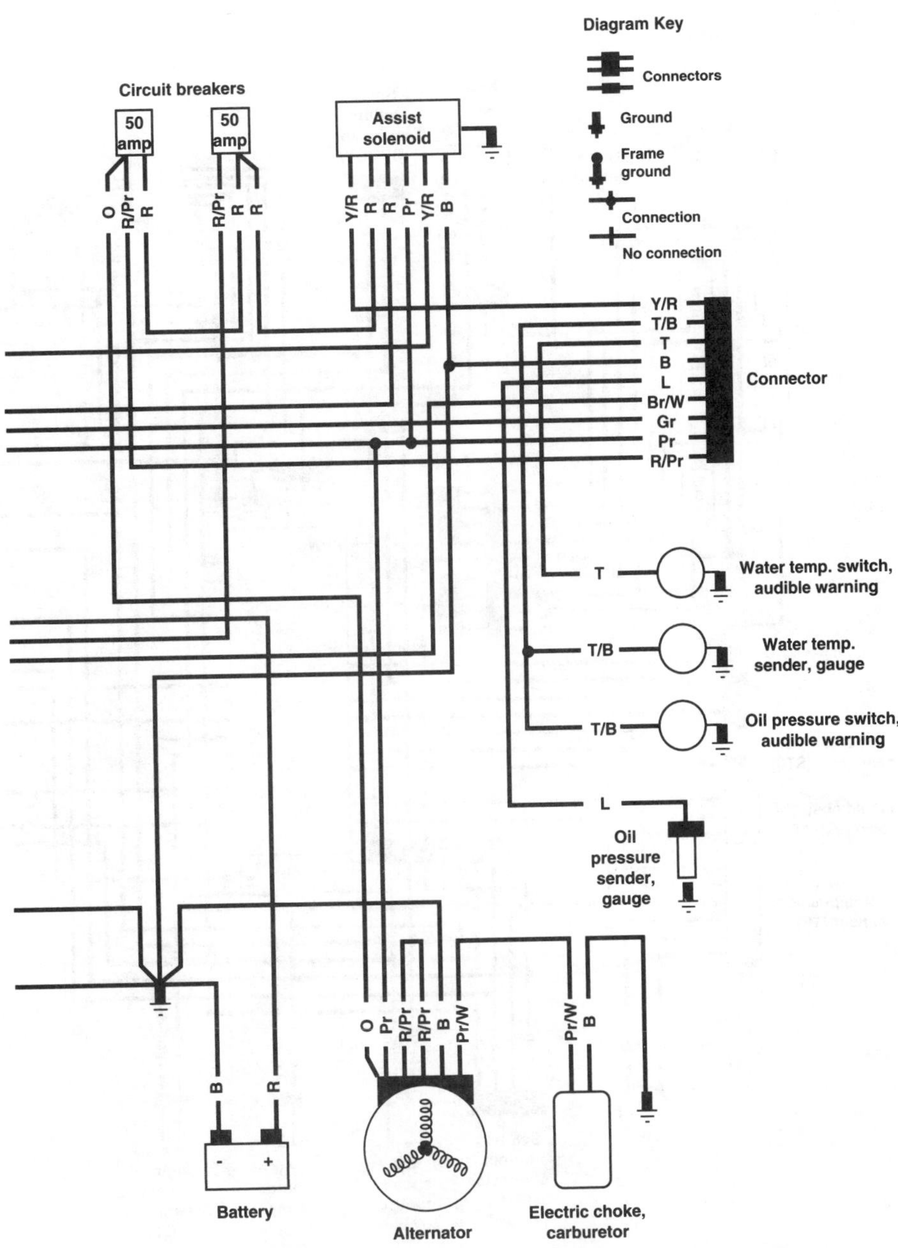
Diagram Key
Connectors
Ground
Frame ground
Connection
No connection
Circuit breakers
50 amp
50 amp
Assist solenoid
O
R/Pr
R
R/Pr
R
R
Y/R
R
R
Pr
Y/R
B
Y/R
T/B
T
B
L
Br/W
Gr
Pr
R/Pr
Connector
T
Water temp. switch, audible warning
T/B
Water temp. sender, gauge
T/B
Oil pressure switch, audible warning
L
Oil pressure sender, gauge
O
Pr
R/Pr
R/Pr
B
Pr/W
Pr/W
B
B
R
Battery
Alternator
Electric choke, carburetor

5.0 AND 5.8 Fi MODELS

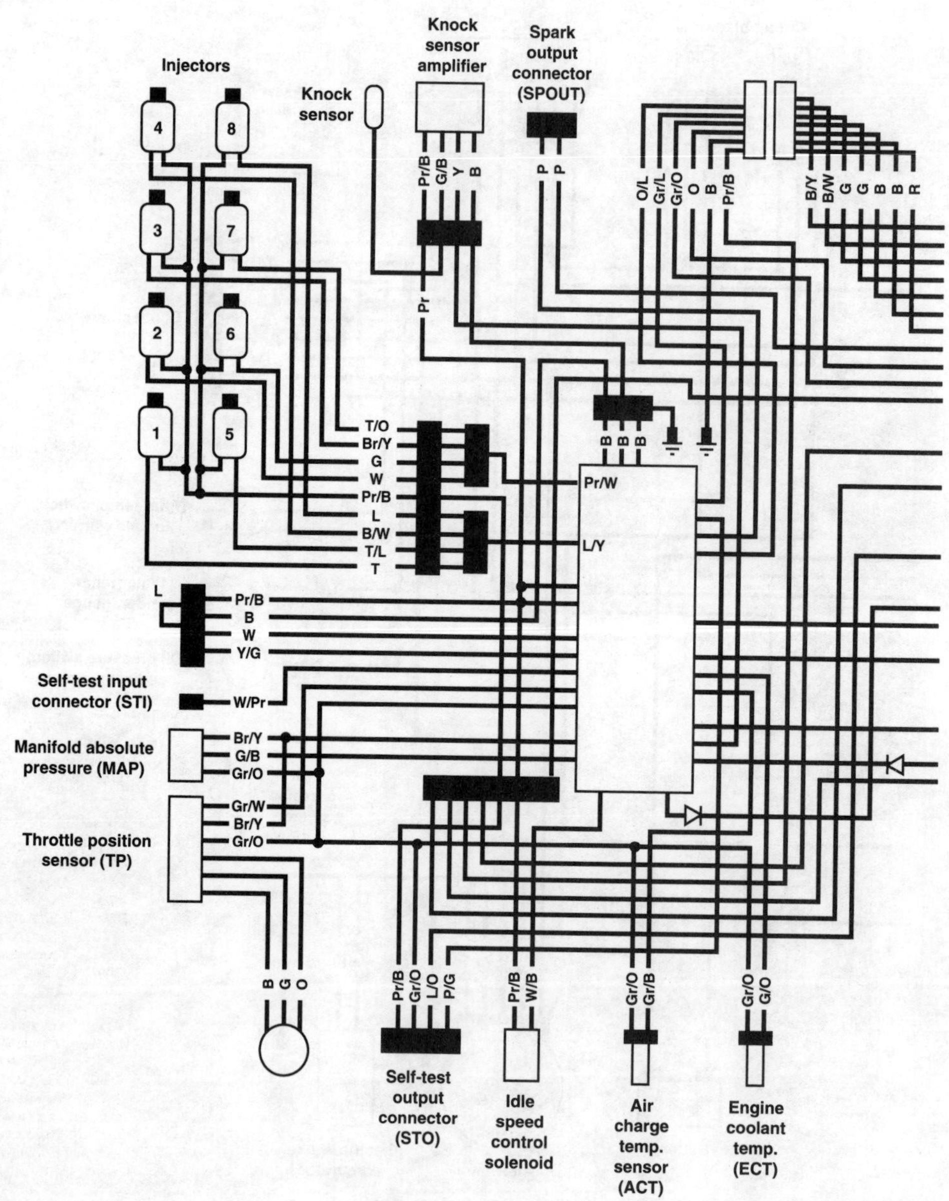

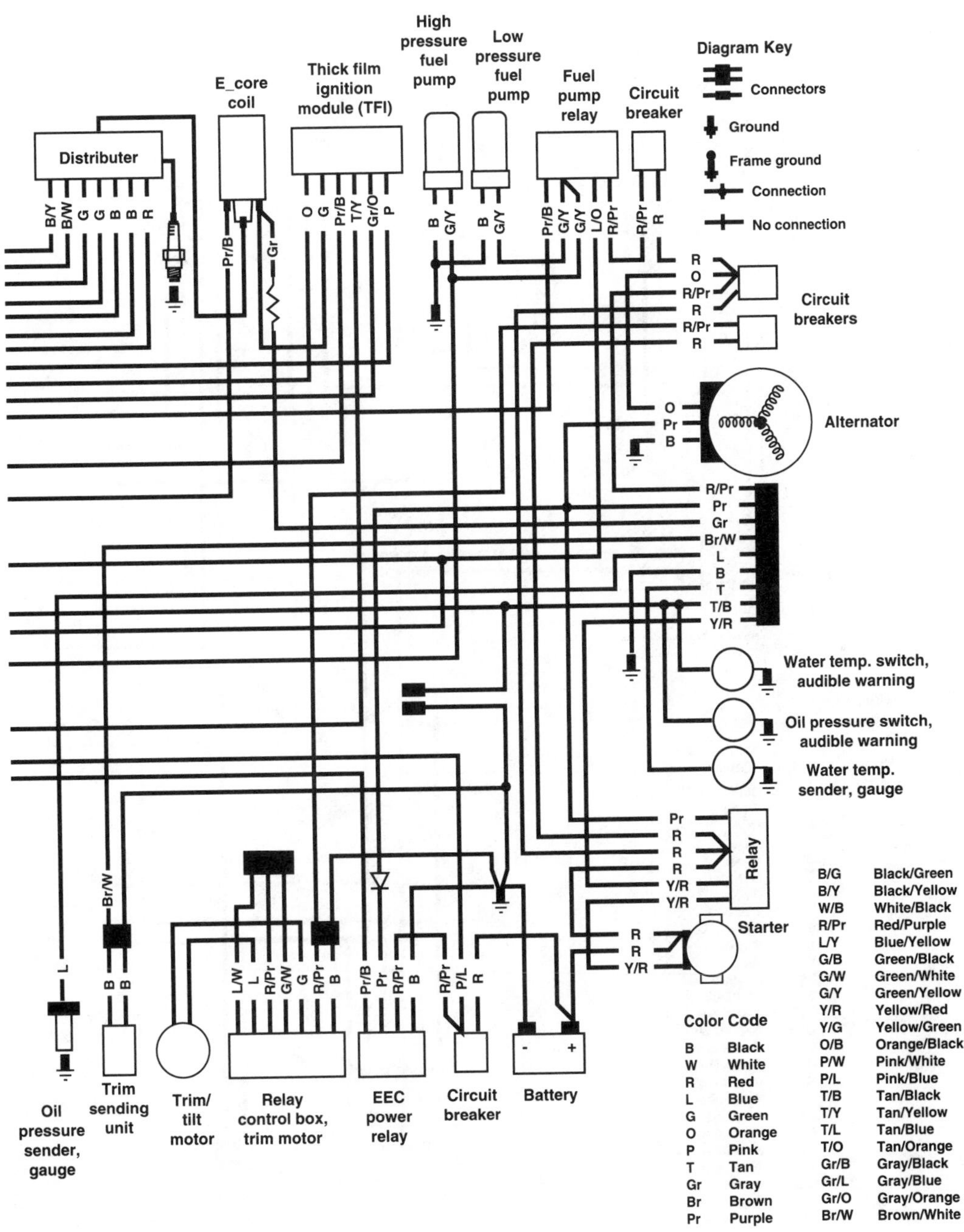
High pressure fuel pump
Low pressure fuel pump
E_core coil
Thick film ignition module (TFI)
Fuel pump relay
Circuit breaker
Diagram Key
Connectors
Ground
Frame ground
Connection
No connection
Distributer
Circuit breakers
Alternator
Water temp. switch, audible warning
Oil pressure switch, audible warning
Water temp. sender, gauge
Relay
Starter
Oil pressure sender, gauge
Trim sending unit
Trim/ tilt motor
Relay control box, trim motor
EEC power relay
Circuit breaker
Battery
Color Code
B Black
W White
R Red
L Blue
G Green
O Orange
P Pink
T Tan
Gr Gray
Br Brown
Pr Purple
B/G Black/Green
B/Y Black/Yellow
W/B White/Black
R/Pr Red/Purple
L/Y Blue/Yellow
G/B Green/Black
G/W Green/White
G/Y Green/Yellow
Y/R Yellow/Red
Y/G Yellow/Green
O/B Orange/Black
P/W Pink/White
P/L Pink/Blue
T/B Tan/Black
T/Y Tan/Yellow
T/L Tan/Blue
T/O Tan/Orange
Gr/B Gray/Black
Gr/L Gray/Blue
Gr/O Gray/Orange
Br/W Brown/White

7.4 AND 8.2 GL MODELS

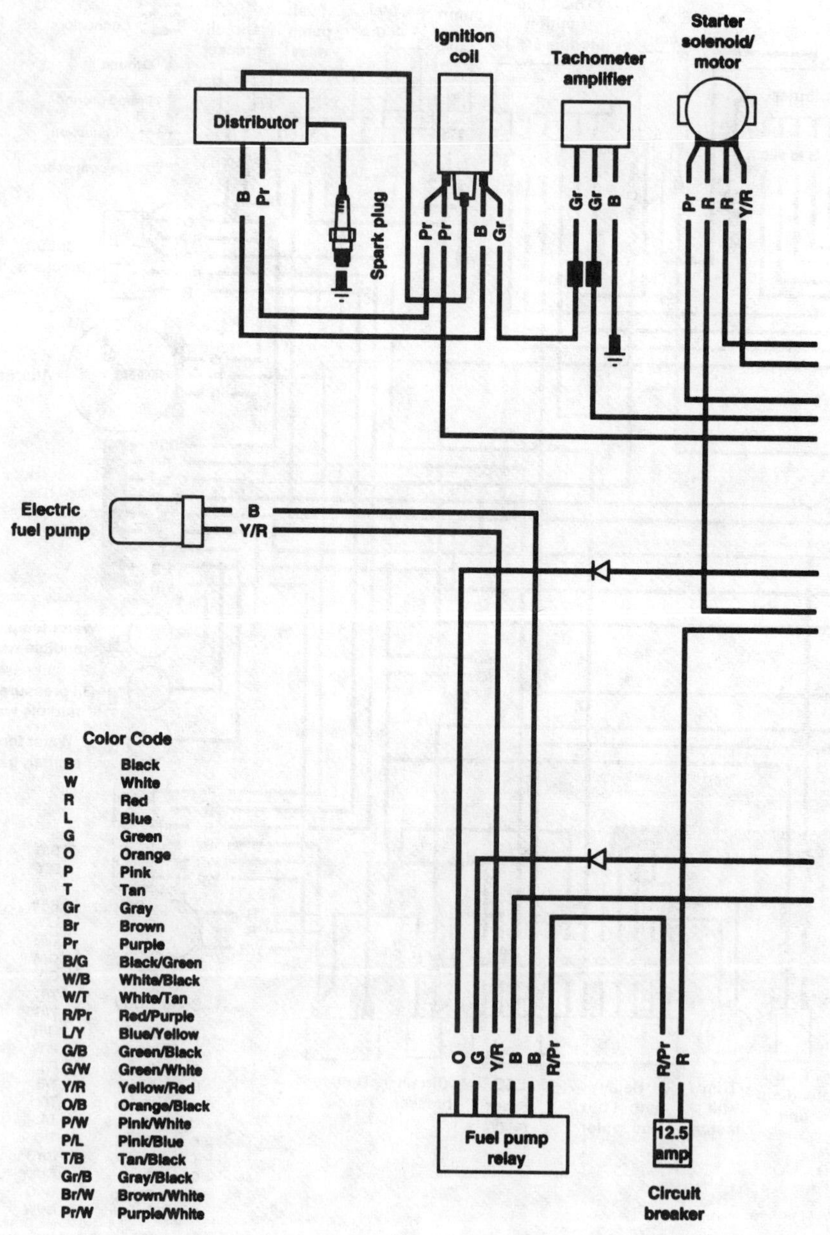

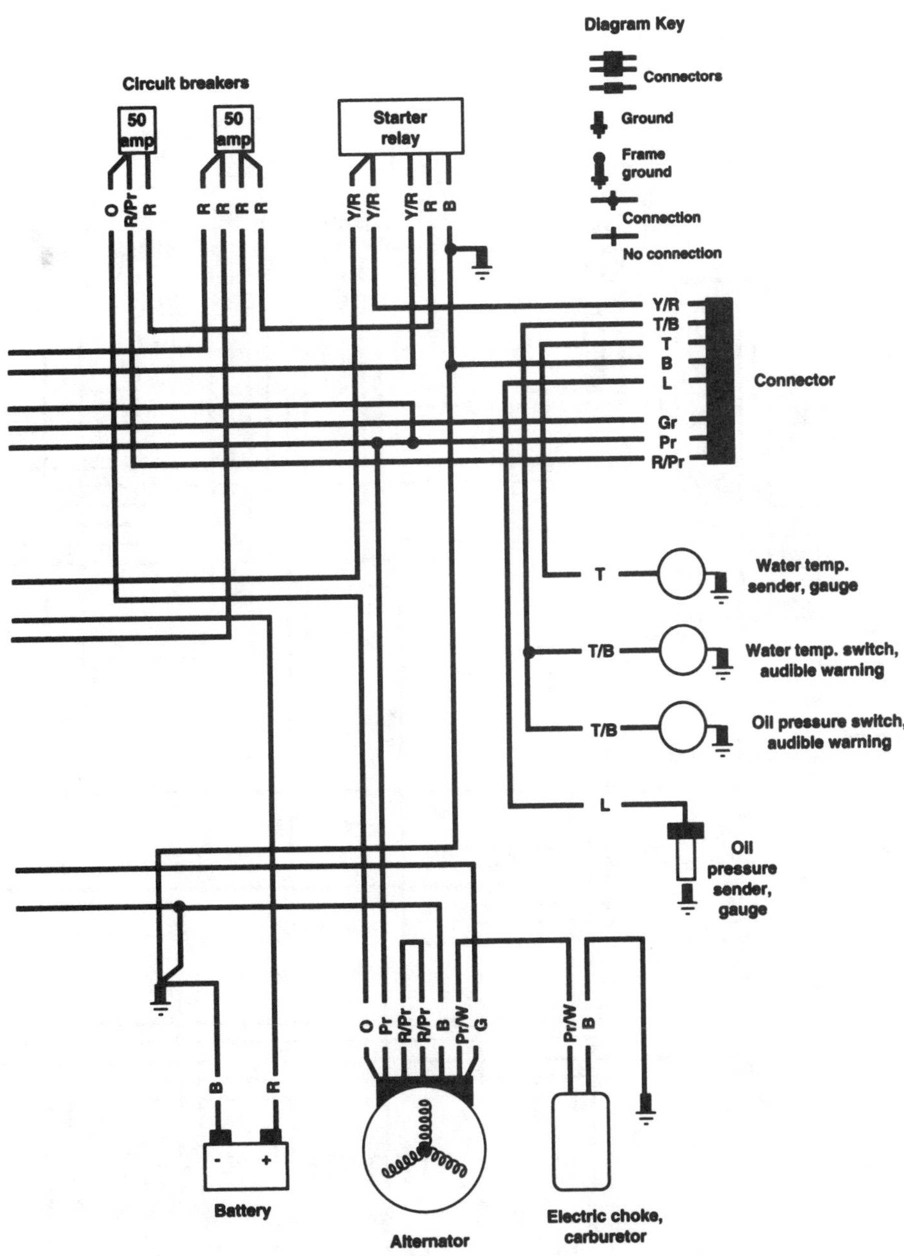
Diagram Key
Connectors
Ground
Frame ground
Connection
No connection
Circuit breakers
50 amp
50 amp
Starter relay
O
R/Pr
R
Y/R
B
Y/R
T/B
T
L
Gr
Pr
Connector
Water temp. sender, gauge
Water temp. switch, audible warning
Oil pressure switch, audible warning
Oil pressure sender, gauge
G
Pr/W
Battery
Alternator
Electric choke, carburetor

7.4 Gi AND GSi MODELS

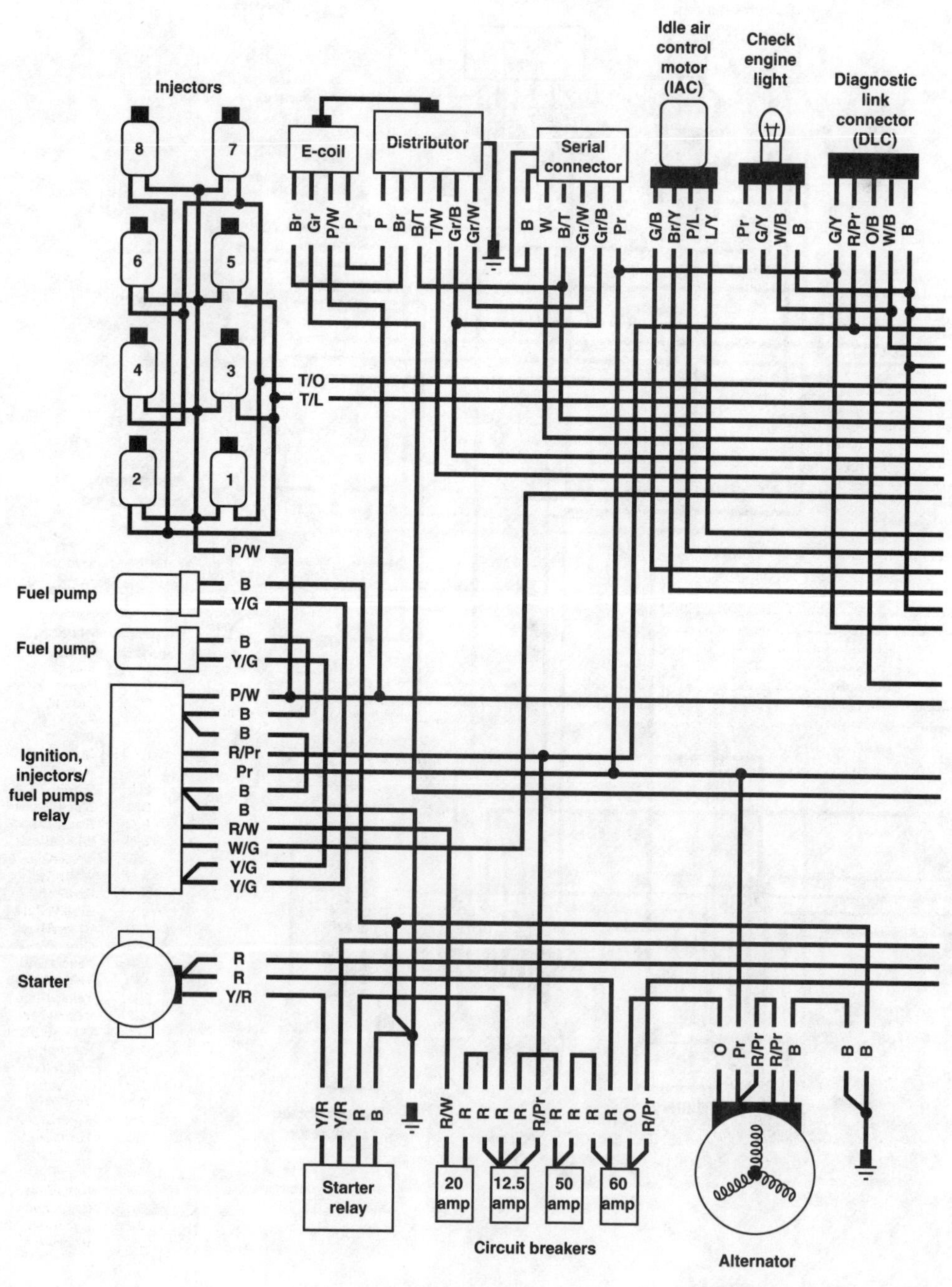

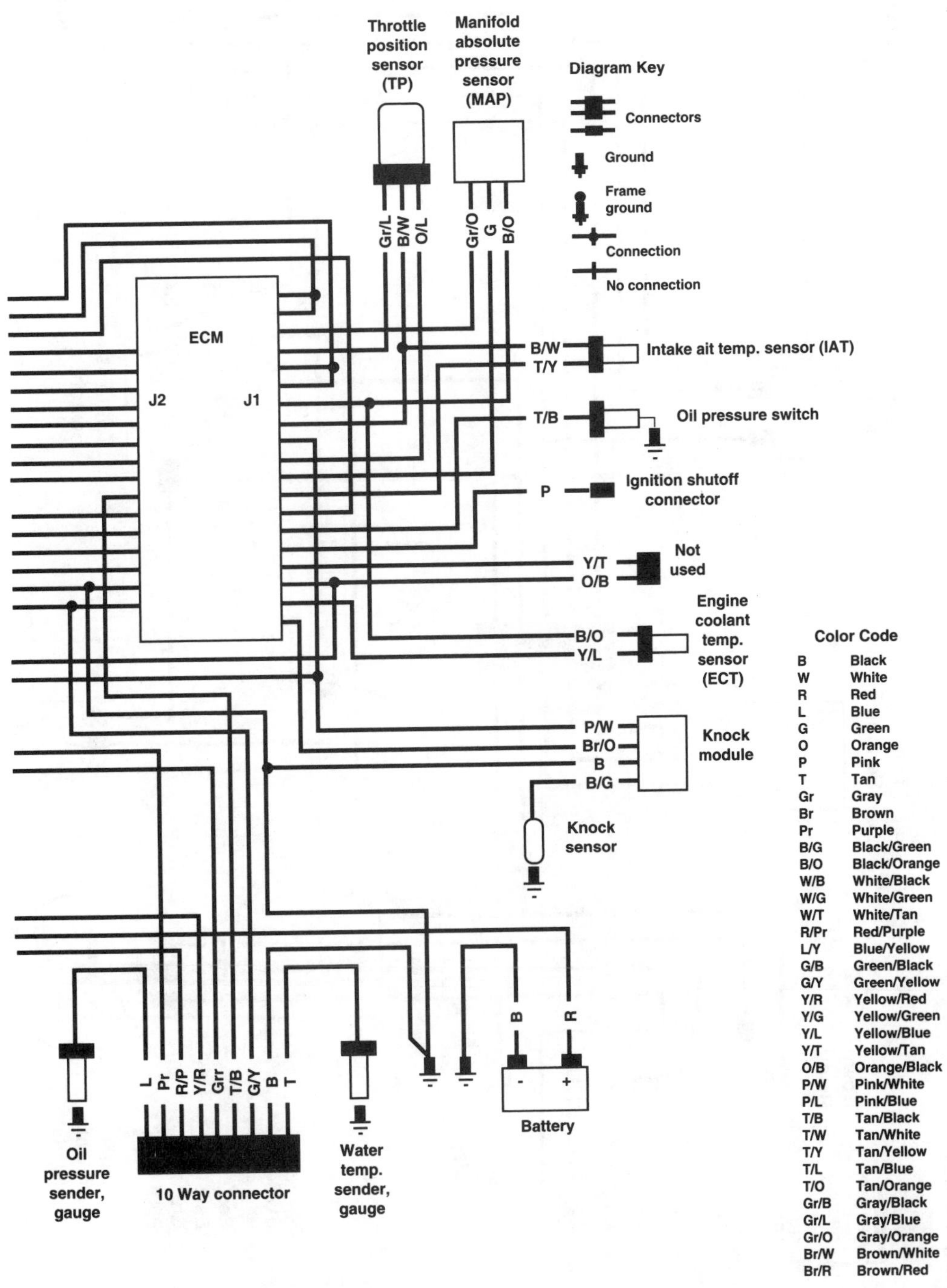
Throttle position sensor (TP)
Manifold absolute pressure sensor (MAP)
Diagram Key
Connectors
Ground
Frame ground
Connection
No connection
Gr/L
B/W
O/L
Gr/O
G
B/O
ECM
J2
J1
B/W
T/Y
Intake ait temp. sensor (IAT)
T/B
Oil pressure switch
P
Ignition shutoff connector
Y/T
O/B
Not used
B/O
Y/L
Engine coolant temp. sensor (ECT)
P/W
Br/O
B
B/G
Knock module
Knock sensor
B
R
Battery
L
Pr
R/P
Y/R
Grr
T/B
G/Y
B
T
Oil pressure sender, gauge
10 Way connector
Water temp. sender, gauge
Color Code
B Black
W White
R Red
L Blue
G Green
O Orange
P Pink
T Tan
Gr Gray
Br Brown
Pr Purple
B/G Black/Green
B/O Black/Orange
W/B White/Black
W/G White/Green
W/T White/Tan
R/Pr Red/Purple
L/Y Blue/Yellow
G/B Green/Black
G/Y Green/Yellow
Y/R Yellow/Red
Y/G Yellow/Green
Y/L Yellow/Blue
Y/T Yellow/Tan
O/B Orange/Black
P/W Pink/White
P/L Pink/Blue
T/B Tan/Black
T/W Tan/White
T/Y Tan/Yellow
T/L Tan/Blue
T/O Tan/Orange
Gr/B Gray/Black
Gr/L Gray/Blue
Gr/O Gray/Orange
Br/W Brown/White
Br/R Brown/Red

POWER TRIM/TILT (EARLY MODELS)

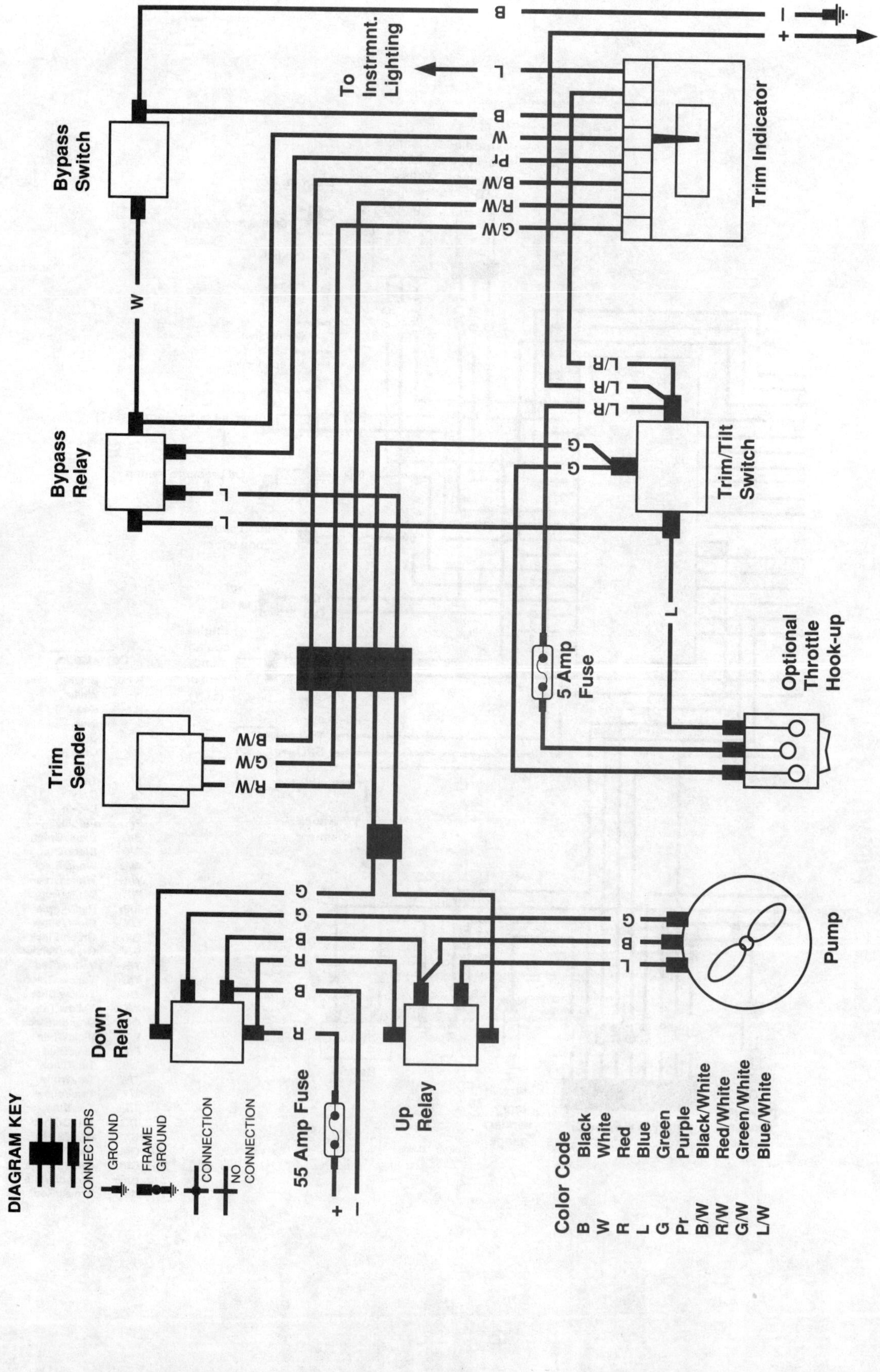

DIAGRAM KEY
CONNECTORS
GROUND
FRAME GROUND
CONNECTION
NO CONNECTION

Down Relay
Trim Sender
Bypass Relay
Bypass Switch
55 Amp Fuse
\+
\-
R B R B G G
R/W G/W B/W
L L
W
Up Relay
To Instrmnt. Lighting
G/W R/W B/W Pr W B L B
5 Amp Fuse
G G
L/R L/R L/R
L B G
L
Trim/Tilt Switch
Trim Indicator
Pump
Optional Throttle Hook-up
\+ \-

Color Code

B	Black
W	White
R	Red
L	Blue
G	Green
Pr	Purple
B/W	Black/White
R/W	Red/White
G/W	Green/White
L/W	Blue/White

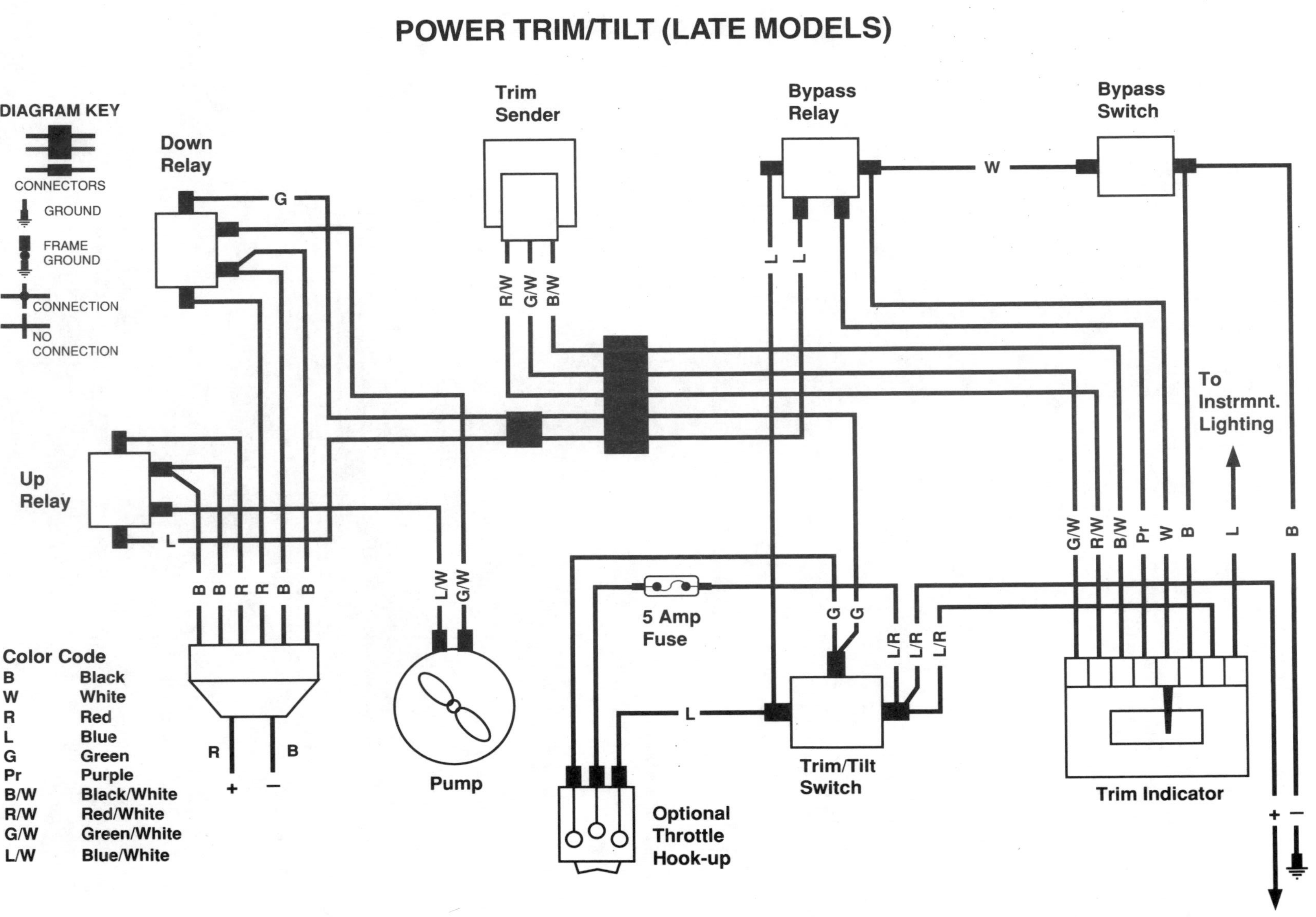
POWER TRIM/TILT (LATE MODELS)
DIAGRAM KEY
CONNECTORS
GROUND
FRAME GROUND
CONNECTION
NO CONNECTION
Down Relay
Up Relay
Trim Sender
Bypass Relay
Bypass Switch
To Instrmnt. Lighting
5 Amp Fuse
Pump
Optional Throttle Hook-up
Trim/Tilt Switch
Trim Indicator
Color Code
B Black
W White
R Red
L Blue
G Green
Pr Purple
B/W Black/White
R/W Red/White
G/W Green/White
L/W Blue/White

NOTES

NOTES

NOTES

NOTES

NOTES

NOTES

MAINTENANCE LOG

Date	Maintenance Performed	Engine Hours